2000 4th International Conference on

Algorithms and Architectures for Parallel Processing

Published Volume

1997 3rd International Conference on
Algorithms and Architectures for Parallel Processing (ICA^3PP-97)
Eds. Andrzej Goscinski, Michael Hobbs and Wanlei Zhou
ISBN: 0-7803-4229-1

2000 4th International Conference on

Algorithms and Architectures for Parallel Processing

ICA³PP
2000

Hong Kong *December 11–13 2000*

Editors

Andrzej Goscinski
Deakin University, Australia

Horace H S IP
City University of Hong Kong, Hong Kong

Weiji Jia
City University of Hong Kong, Hong Kong

Wanlei Zhou
Deakin University, Australia

Sponsors

Deakin University, Australia
City University of Hong Kong, Hong Kong
The Croucher Foundation
IEEE Hong Kong Section

World Scientific
Singapore • New Jersey • London • Hong Kong

Published by

World Scientific Publishing Co. Pte. Ltd.

P O Box 128, Farrer Road, Singapore 912805

USA office: Suite 1B, 1060 Main Street, River Edge, NJ 07661

UK office: 57 Shelton Street, Covent Garden, London WC2H 9HE

British Library Cataloguing-in-Publication Data
A catalogue record for this book is available from the British Library.

Cover designed by John Wedlick, modified by Roy Walshe and Danika Taylor, Media and Publishing Services, Deakin University.

The papers in this book comprise the proceedings of the meeting mentioned on the cover and title page. They reflect the authors' opinions and, in the interest of timely disseminaiton, are published as presented and without change. Their inclusion in this publication does not necessarily constitute endorsement by the editors, the World Scientific Press, The Institute of Electrical and Electronic Engineers, Inc., or the sponsors of the conference.

ISBN 981-02-4481-9 (pbk)

Printed in Singapore by Uto-Print

Preface

Welcome to The fourth IEEE International Conference on Algorithms and Architecture for Parallel Processing (ICA3PP2000).

Cluster and scalable parallel computing have proved their abilities in attaining very high performance at very low cost for information processing. With the rapid enhancement of the bandwidth of interconnection networks and performance of PCs and workstations, as well as the improvement of operating systems and software, parallel processing and distributed computing are becoming more cost-effective. The objective of ICA3PP2000 is to bring together researchers all over the world to advance the theories and technologies in parallel and distributed computing. The main focus of ICA3PP2000 is on two broad areas of parallel and distributed computing, i.e., *architectures, algorithms and networks*, and *systems and applications*.

The conference committee received 127 full manuscripts from researchers and practitioners of 15 countries. Each paper is sent to at least three international reviewers. Papers were reviewed and selected based on their originality, significance, correctness, relevance, and clarity of presentation. From the high quality submissions, 34 long papers and 26 short papers were accepted for presentation at the conference. That represents the acceptance rates of 26.8% and 47.2% for long and short papers, respectively. All the accepted papers are included in the proceedings. The proceedings editors will recommend some high quality papers from the conference to the publication in a special issue of an international journal. This book also includes 4 papers of the special session on High-Performance Data Management and 9 poster papers.

We are delighted to be able to invite Professor Benjamin Wah, University of Illinois at Urbana-Champaign, USA, Professor Amnon Barak, Hebrew University of Jerusalem, Israel, and Professor Wei Zhao, Texas A&M University, USA, as guest speakers. The conference also invited four well-known international scholars for offering two interesting tutorials.

The editors of the conference proceedings would like to take this opportunity to thank all the authors who have submitted their valuable works to this conference for consideration. We thank all the presenters and participants, many of them travel a great distance, for participating in the conference. The editors also thank the PC members and additional technical reviewers for their efforts in reviewing the large number of papers and upholding the high quality of the conference. We greatly appreciate the efforts of the organizers of the special session. Thanks also go to the members of the organization committee for their consistent supports and many other colleagues who have made this conference possible.

Last but not least we would like to express our gratitude to all of the organizations who support our efforts to bring the conference to fruition. We are grateful to IEEE, Hong Kong Chapter for the cooperation; to The Croucher Foundation for their sponsorship, and to Deakin University and City University of Hong Kong for the sponsorships and organizations.

Welcome to Hong Kong in the best seasons!

Weijia Jia and Wanlei Zhou
Program Committee Co-Chairs
September 1, 2000

CONTENTS

Appendices

Chapter 1
Cluster Computing

Efficient deployment of shared memory models on clusters of PCs using the SMiLEing HAMSTER approach

http://hamster.in.tum.de/

Martin Schulz
Lehrstuhl für Rechnertechnik und Rechnerorganisation, LRR–TUM
Technische Universität München
D-80290 München, Germany
E-mail: schulzm@in.tum.de

Despite the long and extensive history of work in the DSM area and the well accepted fact that the shared memory paradigm provides the user with an easy–to–use environment, DSM systems for cluster architectures are still mainly research based. The reasons for this can for a good part be seen in two major obstacles: first, the inherent performance problems of software DSM systems prohibiting the users from gaining optimal performance for their applications compared to hand–coded message passing codes; and second, the abundance of available programming models and the absence of one single clear standardization approach for cluster environments with their special challenges. The HAMSTER project presented in this work aims at overcoming both of these problems by providing a comprehensive infrastructure for the implementation of arbitrary shared memory models built on top of an efficient hybrid hardware/software DSM system. The implementation of HAMSTER based shared memory models requires only very little effort. This allows to provide a large number of different programming models on top of a single architecture resulting in an extremely flexible and versatile programming environment.

1 Motivation

Despite its well known advantages with respect to ease-of-use, the shared memory paradigm is significantly underrepresented on cluster architectures. Only on tightly coupled machines like SMPs or custom–built CC-NUMA architectures, this paradigm is widely accepted as it is natively supported by the hardware and the corresponding operating systems. On clusters, this support is generally missing and therefore the use of shared memory is currently mostly restricted to software Distributed Shared Memory (DSM) systems [1] with their well–known problems like false sharing and high overheads due to complex update protocols.

A second problem with the deployment of shared memory systems comes from the fact, that each system, software DSM systems as well as those found on tightly coupled machines, generally only supports one single, mostly different, programming model and API. This leads, unlike in the message passing world, which has converged to more or less two standard APIs, MPI [2] and PVM [3], to an abundance of different memory and task models each with their own API. The result is a drastic reduction of portability and potential reuse and also a steep increase in the learning curve. There have been some recent approaches for a standardization in the area of shared memory, most notably OpenMP [4] and the POSIX thread standard [5], but their implementations are currently restricted to tightly coupled machines. Only a few projects aim at providing these standard models on cluster architectures, like TreadMarks for OpenMP [6] and the SISCI project for the POSIX threads [7].

In order to successfully tackle these problems, a general shared memory infrastructure with an efficient cluster-wide global memory abstraction is needed that allows the quick and easy implementation of arbitrary programming models and hence a fast retargetability. This infrastructure has to efficiently provide all services needed to create shared memory models, including memory management, synchronization, and consistency control in a highly flexible way.

The HAMSTER (Hybrid-dsm based Adaptive and Modular Shared memory archiTEctuRe) approach targets the implementation of such an infrastructure for clusters of PCs interconnected by the Scalable Coherent Interface (SCI) [8]. It is part of the efforts in the SMiLE (Shared Memory in a LAN-like Environment) project [9] that investigates the utilization of SCI for message passing and shared memory programming through both hardware and software developments. SCI, as a standardized [10] cutting edge interconnection technology with a link speed of up to 400 MB/s and latencies of under 2 μs, offers remote memory access capabilities in the form of hardware distributed shared memory (HW-DSM). Combined with traditional software DSM mechanisms for memory management and access control, this feature is used to build a hybrid DSM system, the SCI Virtual Memory or SCI-VM [11,12], which forms the core for the HAMSTER framework.

Even though the current system is restricted to SCI based clusters, the general concept in this work is applicable to any loosely coupled NUMA architecture and could be ported without major problems. This work therefore presents a general efficient approach to utilize the advantages NUMA architectures for the implementation of DSM systems and hence the basis for any kind of shared memory programming model on such systems.

On top of this hybrid DSM core, HAMSTER provides independent modules for memory management, synchronization, consistency control, task management, and cluster configuration. Each module is designed in a flexible way avoiding any restrictions or bias towards a special programming model. Combined they form a single interface allowing the implementation of arbitrary shared memory programming models. Such programming models can take full advantage of the comprehensive services and good performance of the HAMSTER framework, while being able to exhibit any arbitrary API to the

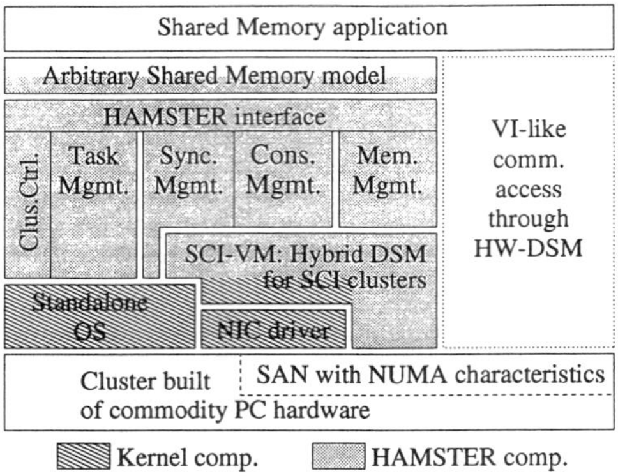

Figure 1: The HAMSTER framework for SCI based clusters of PCs.

application. This allows both the port of existing shared memory programming models with large existing code bases to the cluster environment, as well as the implementation of application area specific models with special capabilities and optimizations.

The remainder of this paper is organized as follows. Section 2 introduces the complete HAMSTER framework including a description of the main building blocks. Section 3 gives an overview of the realization of higher level programming models using HAMSTER and discusses the complexity of such implementations. Section 4 provides performance results obtained in various experiments. The paper is wrapped up with an overview of related work in Section 5 and a brief outlook and some concluding remarks in Section 6.

2 HAMSTER: Hybrid-dsm based Adaptive and Modular Shared memory archiTEctuRe

The HAMSTER project provides a general framework for shared memory programming on cluster architectures with minimal hardware DSM support. It is designed in a flexible way to allow easy retargetability to various programming paradigms and executions models. This is achieved by modularizing the individual services required for the implementation of shared memory programming models. In addition, each module is in itself designed in a way that allows an easy adaption through a wide range of parameters and/or mechanisms.

Figure 2 gives an overview over the complete system. It is built on top of a cluster of commodity–off–the–shelf PC hardware running both Linux and Windows NT in combination with a high–speed system area network (SAN).

For the SMiLEing HAMSTER project SCI [8,10] is deployed due to its high performance and its remote memory access capabilities, which are exhibited in the form of hardware DSM. This hardware capability, in combination with an additional software component responsible for the memory setup and control, can be used to create an efficient hybrid hardware/software global memory abstraction with NUMA characteristics, the SCI Virtual Memory or SCI-VM [11,12]. This technique is very similar to the VI approach [13] proposed for the message passing world, as all communication can be handled in hardware without any OS or protocol overhead.

With this DSM system as the basis, HAMSTER provides several independent modules for the core services needed by shared memory programming models. Most significant are the modules for memory, synchronization, and consistency management. The first one provides mechanisims for a controlled memory allocation and includes both the option to transparently distribute the memory and to control the memory placement at allocation time. This flexibility can be used to initially migrate SMP applications to a HAMSTER based system using the transparent memory allocation followed by an incremental memory layout optimization using distribution hints.

The modules for coherency and synchronization management [14] provide all services required to implement a coherent and race–free application. This includes mechanisms to control the relaxed memory consistency of the SCI-VM and typical shared memory synchronization constructs like locks and barriers. In order to allow the greatest possible flexibility, these two modules are kept orthogonal to each other, i.e. synchronization does not include a consistency guarantee or vice versa. The decision on how to combine these two modules is left to the programming model implementation and can be tailord to its specific needs.

In addition to these pure shared memory service modules, a separate module is responsible for the task management, i.e. the distributed creation of activities and their accounting. This also includes maintaining a global activity counter as well as the controlled termination of an application. The latter is especially important for the implementation of dynamic task models like they are present in multithreading environments.

Due to the inherent connection between the concepts of virtual memory and processes, the creation of programming models with a global virtual memory also requires some form of global process abstraction. In the HAMSTER system, this is realized with the help of a cluster control component that provides a global execution environment. It's tasks include the cluster configuration (i.e. the identification of participating nodes) and the creation and management of a global node name space. In addition, the cluster control com-

Programming Model	#Lines	#API calls	Lines/call	Platform
SPMD model	360	19	18.9	NT & Lin.
ANL macros	125	21	5.6	NT & Lin.
TreadMarks API	326	13	25.1	NT & Lin.
Dist. POSIX threads	597	39	15.3	Linux
WIN32 threads (subset)	562	13	43.2	NT

Table 1: Implementation complexity of programming models using HAMSTER.

ponent also provides a simple message passing mechanism for control messages, as such an instrument is used by almost any implementation of a programming model.

The services exported by all of these modules are combined in one single interface, depicted in Figure 2 as the "HAMSTER interface", providing all mechanisms needed for the implementation of arbitrary shared memory models in structured and flexible way. This allows the implementation of such models with minimal amount of effort and code. The final applications, however, have no direct contact to the HAMSTER environment. They run fully transparent on top of the respective programming model and its API, using the benefits of the HAMSTER infrastructure without having to use yet another shared memory API.

3 Flexibility in implementing the target programming model

The HAMSTER interface is designed in a way that allows the implementation of programming models with minimal effort. Often the functionality required by the target programming model can be achieved by specializing a similar service of HAMSTER. Normally only a few specialized API calls have to be implemented separately. An indication of the complexity of programming models implemented using the HAMSTER framework is given in Table 1. The information is based on lines of code necessary to implement a certain programming model in relation to the complexity of the programming model expressed through the number of available API calls. While such a measure is by nature highly inaccurate, it anyway gives a first impression of the amount of work required for such an implementation.

The table lists some of programming models currently available on top of the HAMSTER framework. This includes distributed thread environments for both Windows NT and Linux each based on their respective native thread API, an implementation of the TreadMarks[15] API allowing TreadMarks applications to run unmodified, a simple SPMD programming model, and a direct implementation of the ANL macros used by the SPLASH-II benchmark suite [16]. Each of these programming models differs greatly in terms of execution model, memory management, transparency, and consistency model.

Despite the clear functional differences, Table 1 shows that neither of the programming models required extreme effort to be implemented on top of HAMSTER; on average not more than 25 lines of code had to be written per API call for most of the programming models. These codes often only map the API call to routines exported by the HAMSTER interface specializing the HAMSTER services through the wide range of possible parameters. The only noticeable exception is the implementation of the distributed Win32 thread API for Windows NT. The (in comparison to the other models) rather large number of lines per API call can be explained by the fact that Win32 calls often have many parameters which adds extra complexity for their handling. In addition, only a subset of the Win32 API is implemented, but the code already contains the complete forwarding and remote execution environment needed for a distributed thread implementation. Hence it can be expected that the ratio will be smaller once the full Win32 thread API is completed.

Keeping the effort necessary to create a HAMSTER based shared memory model at such a low level, opens the possibility to easily add a large variety of models to the HAMSTER framework. Only the specifics of the individual model have to implemented or deduced from the general mechanisms of HAMSTER through specialization; the actual core with all its complexity of typical DSM systems stays the same for any programming model. This approach therefore has the potential to unify the large number of existing shared memory models on top of a single system with a single core.

4 Experimental evaluation and results

Providing meaningful performance results for the evaluation of a framework like HAMSTER is a difficult task as many of the features and benefits can not be quantified using performance metrics. An example for this is the effort necessary to retarget the system to new programming models, which has already been discussed in Section 3. In addition, the HAMSTER system exhibits a great flexibility prohibiting the presentation its performance impact using only a single experiment. Each programming model can address different performance characteristics and will use different subsets of the overall capabilities and features of the system. This section, therefore, provides the results from several experiments using various programming models on top of HAMSTER each showing different performance aspects of the overall framework.

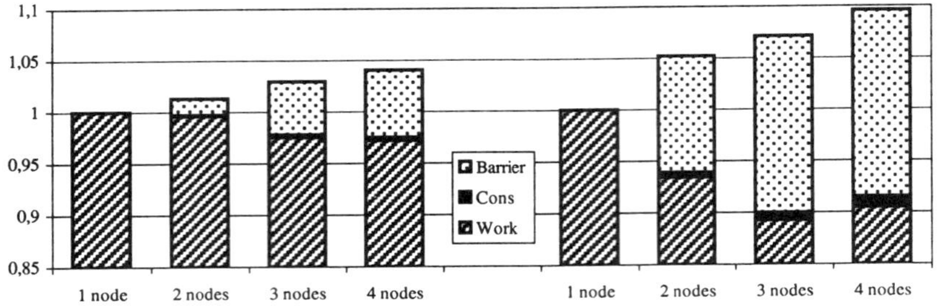

Figure 2: Performance details for SOR (left) and Gaussian (right).

All experiments were conducted on the SMiLE cluster platform using either Linux (kernel version 2.2.5) or Windows NT 4.0 (SP 5) as the base operating system. The compute nodes are Dual Intel Xeon (tm) 450 MHz based machines with 512 MB of main memory each. The cluster is interconnected with switched fast Ethernet for control and with an SCI ring for communication traffic. For the SCI host adapters, the PCI–SCI bridge D310 from Dolphin Interconnect Solutions AS is deployed.

4.1 Raw performance and consistency management overhead

The first set of experiments shows the raw performance of the global virtual memory abstraction achieved by the hybrid DSM system, as this describes the base performance for any HAMSTER based programming model. Two codes are used for this purpose: Successive Over Relaxation and Gaussian Elimination both on 1024x1024 matrixes. Both codes have been implemented using the SPMD programming model and executed under Windows NT and with locality optimizations in place [a].

The speed-up of both codes is rather good achieving 3.8 for the SOR and 3.5 for the Gaussian code on 4 nodes. More interesting, however, are the detailed measurements shown in Figure 2. The graph shows the normalized total summed execution times of both codes on up to 4 nodes. The time is split into three categories: actual work, consistency overhead, and barrier wait. The numbers for work and barrier waits are directly measured using Windows NT's high performance counters, while the consistency overhead was computed as a difference of the work timing for a run with and one without consistency enforcing mechanisms enabled.

[a] Only one processor per node has been used in these experiments in order to avoid any side effects from intra-node contention.

The results show that in the SOR code the consistency overhead caused by the actual consistency enforcing mechanisms (and the cache invalidations they infer) is negligible and also the barrier time is rather low. In addition, the time needed for the actual work is reduced with increasing number of nodes due to the increased total cache size resulting in the high speedup.

This effect is even larger on the Gauss code, but here also the barrier overhead is significantly larger. This comes from the fact, that the Gaussian algorithm requires many more barriers (one per matrix line in contrast to one per iteration in the SOR case). This also explains the higher overhead of consistency control as together with every barrier the complete and global memory coherence is enforced. In summary, however, the overheads involved are still rather low allowing for a good overall performance.

4.2 Numerical kernel performance

The second set of experiments was conducted using an LU decomposition kernel based on the LU kernel from the SPLASH-2 suite [16] It was implemented using the distributed WIN32 thread API on top of Windows NT mentioned above. The code was ported without major code changes; just the locality hints already present in the SPLASH-2 codes have been used to optimize the memory layout only requiring simple annotations for the SCI-VM at memory allocation points.

The LU code was executed on up to four nodes with two CPUs each and with two different matrix sizes of 1024x1024 and 2048x2048. Figure 3 presents the summed execution time for both matrix sizes over all nodes with various cluster configurations. The left bars in each graph show the results with two threads per node using the SMP configuration, the right bars the single processor case with only one CPU per node utilized.

In this representation, the simplifying assumption is used that the amount of work necessary for the computation is equal to the sequential work measured, as it can be expected that superlinear cache effects play a significantly lower role compared to the raw memory benchmarks discussed above. Using this assumption an overhead estimation for the cross cluster access times can be made by computing the difference between the time measured for the work and the assumed real work time. It should be noted that in the SMP case this overhead does also include increased access times due to intra–node bus contention (especially in the 2 thread, one node version).

The figures show that this overhead is almost negligible in most cases, especially when applying the LU code to the a larger matrix. Also the barrier times are kept within reasonable bounds allowing for good scalability. Only

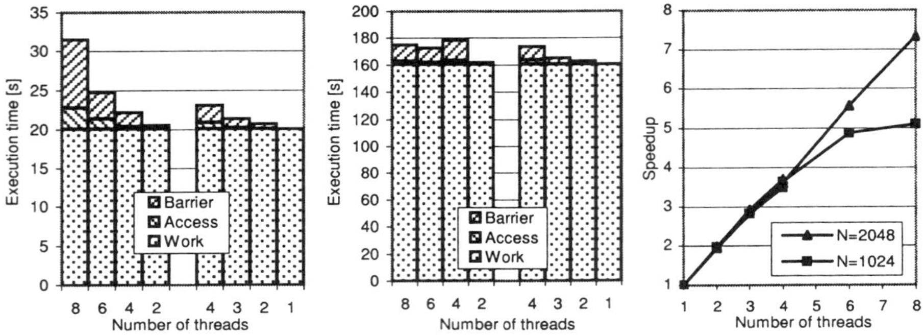

Figure 3: Work distribution of the LU code with up to 8 threads (4 nodes/8 CPUs) — 1024x1024 matrix (left) and 2048x2048 matrix (middle), Speedup (right).

with larger number of CPUs and with small data sets the barrier time increases significantly most likely due to load imbalances.

These results can also be seen in the right graph of Figure 3, which shows the same results translated into application speed-ups, again separated into the SMP and the single CPU case. Overall the LU application executed as a multithreaded application on top of HAMSTER provides good scalability properties allowing a speedup of up to 7.3 on 8 CPUs. Only when used with small data sets and larger number of CPUs the speed up is limited caused by the increased barrier times shown above.

4.3 Full application performance

Besides these smaller experiments based on numerical kernels, it is also worth looking at the overall performance of large applications. For this purpose a spectral analysis code [17,18] from the area of nuclear medical imaging, or more precisely of Positron–Emission–Tomography is used. The application is used in clinical routine to allow a better and more precise evaluation of PET scans. It gives doctors a functional overview over evolving processes in the human body and can e.g. help in detecting tumors or regional brain malfunctions.

The task model of this application is a simple master/slave model in which the master has the duty to organize both the distribution of the raw data and the collection of the results. The application was originally implemented using TreadMarks [15]. For the experiments here, the code was just re-linked with the

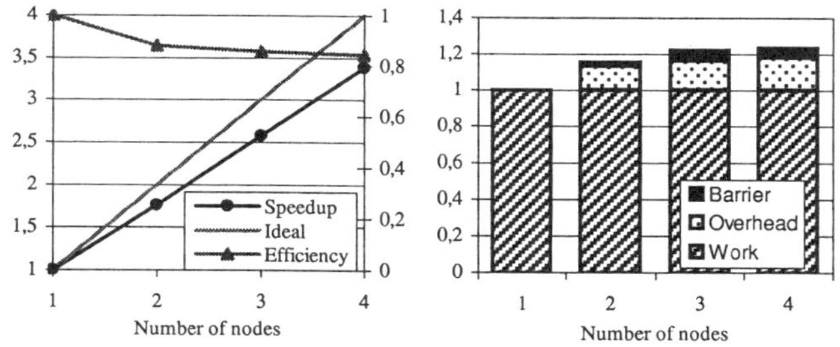

Figure 4: Performance of the spectral analysis code on up to four nodes — speed-up and efficiency values (left), parallelization overhead (right).

TreadMarks programming model on top of HAMSTER running under Linux; there was no need for any code modifications or optimizations.

The summary of the performance of this code is given in Figure 4 for up to 4 nodes. The left diagram shows speed-up (left axis) and efficiency values (right axis). It indicates that the application scales very well and that this also seems to continue beyond four nodes. Also the right diagram showing the total execution time on all nodes supports this observation. The separation into actual work, i.e. the work that also has to be done by the sequential program, the parallelization overhead, and the time spent in synchronization constructs shows a rather stable overhead.

5 Related work

As mentioned earlier, work on shared memory models for clusters of PCs is mostly done with the help of pure software DSM systems. Typical representatives of this group are TreadMarks[15] and Shasta[19]. However, each system only delivers one single system specific API together with a very restrictive static task model, unlike in the HAMSTER approach, where arbitrary programming APIs with arbitrary task and execution models are possible. Only some systems, like CVM[20], allow the adaptation of single system parameters like e.g. the coherency protocol.

As in HAMSTER, the DSM projects SHRIMP[21] and Cashmere[22] both deploy hardware mechanisms to create a hybrid software/hardware solution for DSM. In SHRIMP a custom–designed network adapter with an automatic global update functionality[23] is used, while Cashmere utilizes DEC's memory channel[24], a high-performance SAN with remote write capabilities. Neither of the two hardware components provides real hardware DSM like it can be used in SCI based systems; especially the capability to perform remote reads is missing in those systems. Therefore, in both much more emphasis has to be given to the software component of the DSM system reducing the impact of the underlying high-performance network.

Only a few projects utilize similar techniques than the SCI Virtual Memory and try to deploy real hardware DSM directly. Most prominently is the SciOS project[25], which provides a global memory abstraction using SCI's DSM capabilities in a fashion similar to the system V shared memory concept.

6 Conclusions and Outlook

Shared memory programming for clusters still suffers from major obstacles preventing it to move into mainstream. The two most severe ones are the inherent overhead of software DSM solutions and the abundance of different APIs and models available which reduces portability and increases the learning curve. The HAMSTER project presented in this work aims at overcoming these two problems by providing a comprehensive infrastructure which allows the easy implementation of arbitrary shared memory models on top of a single high–performance hybrid DSM core. It is built on top of commodity–off–the–shelf components connected with a high–speed networking technology with minimal hardware DSM support.

This work has shown that the HAMSTER approach is flexible enough to provide all mechanisms necessary to implement any model ranging from strict SPMD like models all the way to distributed thread packages while maintaining good performance. HAMSTER in addition offers the options of a clean migration and optimization path by offering both transparent and explicit data placement. This allows applications to be ported using the transparency and afterwards to be optimized incrementally through simple locality hints.

Acknowledgments

This work is partly supported by the European Commission in the Fourth Framework Programme under ESPRIT HPCN Project EP23174 (Standard Software Infrastructure for SCI based parallel systems – SISCI). The SCI device driver is kindly provided in source by Dolphin ICS. The spectral analysis code for PET images was developed by Martin Völk, Klinikum Rechts der Isar, TU München.

1. B. Nitzberg and V. LO. Distributed Shared Memory: A Survey of Issues and Algorithms. *IEEE Computer*, pages 52–59, August 1991.
2. Message Passing Interface Forum (MPIF). MPI: A Message-Passing Interface Standard. Technical Report, University of Tennessee, Knoxville,

June 1995. http://www.mpi-forum.org.
3. A. Bengelin, J. Dongarra, A. Geist, R. Manchek, and V. Sunderam. *A User' s Guide to PVM Parallel Virtual Machine.* Oak Ridge National Laboratory, Oak Ridge, TN 37831-8083, July 1991.
4. WWW:. OpenMP: Simple, Portable, Scalable SMP Programming . http://www.openmp.org, December 1999.
5. Technical Committee on Operating Systems and Application Environments of the IEEE. *Portable Operating Systems Interface (POSIX) — Part 1: System Application Interface (API).* IEEE, 1995 edition, 1996. ANSI/IEEE Std. 1003.1.
6. C. Hu, H. Lu, A. Cox, and W. Zwaenepoel. OpenMP for Networks of SMPs. In *Proceedings of IPPS/SPDP*, pages 302–310, April 1999.
7. M. Schulz. SISCI-Pthreads, SMP–like programming on an SCI–cluster. In P. Sloot, M. Bubak, and B. Hertzberger, editors, *Proceedings of HPCN–Europe 98*, volume 1401 of *Lecture Notes in Computer Science*, pages 566–575, Berlin, April 1998. Springer.
8. H. Hellwagner and A. Reinefeld, editors. *SCI: Scalable Coherent Interface. Architecture and Software for High-Performance Compute Clusters*, volume 1734 of *LNCS State-of-the-Art Survey.* Springer Verlag, October 1999. ISBN 3-540-66696-6.
9. W. Karl, M. Leberecht, and M. Schulz. Supporting Shared Memory and Message Passing on Clusters of PCs with a SMiLE. In A. Sivasubramaniam and M. Lauria, editors, *Proceedings of CANPC'99*, volume 1602 of *Lecture Notes in Computer Science*, Berlin, 1999. Springer Verlag.
10. IEEE Computer Society. *IEEE Std 1596–1992: IEEE Standard for Scalable Coherent Interface.* New York, NY 10017, USA, August 1993.
11. M. Schulz. *SCI: Scalable Coherent Interface. Architecture and Software for High-Performance Compute Clusters*, volume 1734 of *LNCS State-of-the-Art Survey*, chapter 17, True shared memory programming on SCI-based clusters. Springer Verlag, October 1999. ISBN 3-540-66696-6.
12. M. Schulz. SCI-VM: A flexible base for transparent shared memory programming models on clusters of PCs Martin Schulz. In J. Rolim, F. Müller, and et. al., editors, *Parallel and Distributed Computing / Proceedings of HIPS '99*, volume 1586 of *Lecture Notes in Computer Science*, pages 19–33, Berlin, 1999. Springer Verlag.
13. Compaq Computer Corp., Intel Corporation, and Microsoft Corporation. *Virtual Interface Architecture Specification*, December 1997. Available with NDA via www.viarch.org.
14. M. Schulz. Efficient Coherency and Synchronization Management in SCI based DSM systems. In Geir Horn and Wolfgang Karl, edi-

tors, *Proceedings of SCI-Europe 2000, The 3rd international conference on SCI–based technology and research*, August 2000. Available at http://wwwbode.in.tum.de/events/.

15. C. Amza, A. Cox, S. Dwarkadas, P. Keleher, H. Lu, R. Rajamony, W. Yu, and W. Zwaenepoel. TreadMarks: Shared Memory Computing on Networks of Workstations. *IEEE Computer*, 29(2):18–28, February 1995.
16. S. Woo, M. Ohara, E. Torrie, J. Singh, and A. Gupta. The SPLASH–2 Programs: Characterization and Methodological Considerations. In *Proceedings of the 22nd International Symposium on Computer Architecture*, pages 24–36, June 1995.
17. V.J. Cunningham and T. Jones. Spectral analysis of dynamic PET studies. *Journal of Cerebral Blood Flow and Metabolism*, 13(1):15–23, January 1993.
18. Martin Völk. Parallelisierung eines Spektralanalysealgorithmus mittels TreadMarks. Diplomarbeit, TU München, February 1999.
19. D. Scales, K. Gharachorloo, and C. Thekkath. Shasta: A Low Overhead, Software–Only Approach for Supporting Fine–Grain Shared Memory. Technical Report WRL Research Report 96/2, Digital Western Research Laboratory, November 1996.
20. P. Keleher. *CVM: The Coherent Virtual Machine*. University of Maryland, cvm version 1.0 edition, November 1996.
21. M. Blumrich, R. Alpert, Y. Chen, D. Clark, S. Damianakis, C. Dubnicki, E. Felten, L. Iftode, K. Li, M. Martonosi, and R. Shillner. Design Choices in the SHRIMP System: An Empirical Study. In *Proceedings of the 25th ISCA*, May 1998.
22. R. Stets, S. Dwarkadas, N. Hardavellas, G. Hunt, L. Kontothanassis, S. Parthasarathy, and M. Scott. CASHMERE-2L: Software Coherent Shared Memory on a Clustered Remote-Write Network. In *Proceedings of SOSP'97*, October 1997.
23. A. Belias, L. Iftode, and J. Singh. Evaluation of Hardware: Write Propagation Support for Next–Generation Shared Virtual Memory Clusters. In *Proceedings of the ICS*, 1998.
24. R. Gillett. Memory Channel: An Optimized Cluster Interconnect. *IEEE Micro*, 16(2):12–18, February 1996.
25. P. Koch, J. Hansen, E Cecchet, and X. Ronsset de Pina. SciOS: An SCI-based Software Distributed Shared Memory. In *Proceedings of SWDSM '99*, June 1999.

PARALLEL PROGRAMMING WITH DISTRIBUTED OBJECT GROUPS — THE TACO APPROACH

JÖRG NOLTE, MITSUHISA SATO, YUTAKA ISHIKAWA
Real World Computing Partnership
Tsukuba Mitsui Bldg. 16F, 1-6-1 Takezono
Tsukuba 305-0032, Ibaraki, Japan
{jon,msato,ishikawa}@trc.rwcp.or.jp

Distributed object groups are a powerful means to initiate and coordinate parallel activities. TACO (*Topologies and Collections*) is a pure template library that introduces the flavour of distributed data parallel processing by means of reusable topology classes and C++ templates. This paper introduces TACO's basic abstractions and provides a performance analysis for basic collective operations as well as a Laplace simulation to demonstrate the combination of global and local synchronization often found in iterative numerical simulations.

1 Introduction

Collective operations on distributed object groups are a powerful means to coordinate parallel computations and control distributed or replicated resources. While efficient fine-grained data-parallel computing is hard to achieve without proper compiler support and appropriate optimization techniques, efficient coarse-grained as well as medium-grained data-parallel computing is well possible on a library basis only. Thus we can introduce the flavour of data-parallel programming without language extensions and data-parallel programming can be conveniently combined with common parallel programming techniques where appropriate.

The genericity and inheritance mechanisms of state of the art object oriented languages allow us to base our collections on a small set of well defined classes thus giving programmers an effective means to control, extend and adapt the behaviour of distributed collections in a well structured manner.

2 Collections and Topologies

In most data-parallel languages as well as commonly used communication libraries like MPI the notion of a group is usually an abstract concept and the programmer has to rely on an efficient implementation of this concept without any reasonable means of control. Since it is notoriously hard to find suitable implementations of collections that perform well on all use cases and all network architectures, TACO gives the programmer a powerful means of control over collections through reusable *topology* classes, that reveal the internal structure of a collection. Like the STL which offers multiple container types for different usage patterns, programmers can choose or adapt different TACO topology classes for different application patterns without sacrificing the group concept as such.

TACO's collections are based on distributed graphs and therefore a collection can have any user defined topology such as n-dimensional grids, lists or trees (fig. 1).

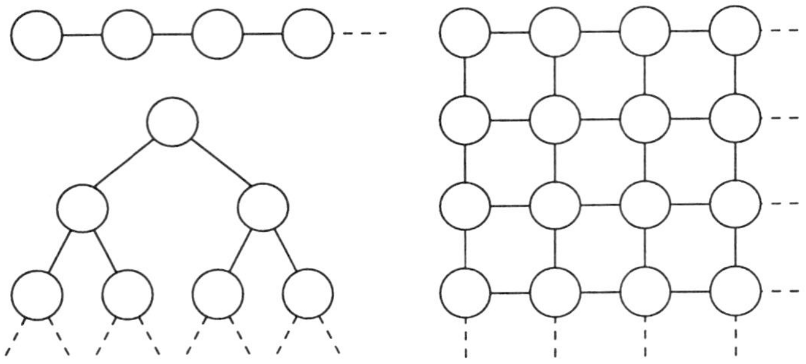

Figure 1. Topologies

Topologies are implemented as distributed linked object sets by means of global pointers to objects. These sets can be collectively addressed by issuing a collective method to a *leader object* that represents the entire collection. All objects that are reachable from this leader object participate in collective operations. Reachability is defined through an STL style iterator [1] that (recursively) iterates all members of a collection. Thus topology classes offer the unique opportunity to control the order of execution and degree of parallelism of collective operations.

All TACO topology classes provide `join()` methods to add new members to the collection or to join existing collections. Thus all collections are inherently created dynamically. However, for convenience reasons we provide several template classes that create and join entire collections (fig. 2). The `CollectionOf` class creates arbitrary collections and the members do not need to be aware, that they are part of a collection. The `GroupOf` template is similar but requires its member types to be derived from a topology class and thus to be group-aware (fig. 2). Both classes allow the passing of arbitrary arguments to the constructor of the members.

The size of collections is not limited by the number of available nodes. The

GroupOf<Member> group(*args..., size, dist*);
CollectionOf <Any, **BinTree** > coll(*args..., size, dist*);

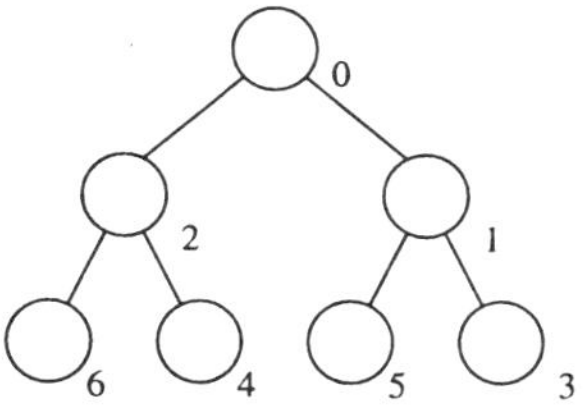

Figure 2. Collections

mapping of members to nodes is controlled by a polymorphic *dist* parameter (fig. 2) that refers to an array of node numbers or to an instance of a mapping class providing a subscript operator that delivers a node number for a given member rank.

TACO provides various convenience functions named `m2f()` and `vm2f()` for methods returning void to convert ordinary methods with arbitrary arguments into functors on the fly. Notably the resulting functors can also be used in conjunction with the STL and standard STL functors can be used with TACO as well.

The implementation of TACO's collective operations is a very thin layer based on the Multiple Threads Template Library (MTTL) [2], a very efficient communication and threading library on top of either the PM [3] or MPI communication layer. Amongst several other features the MTTL provides a concept for *global pointers*, multi threaded remote function invocation and global synchronization variables. A synchronization variable is a kind of future [4], that blocks any reading access until the variable is (remotely) initialized. These few prerequisites were already sufficient to implement distributed collections and efficient higher-order operations.

2.1 Basic Collective Operations

TACO's collective operations are based on the parallel traversal of distributed graphs. An asynchronous global `map()` operation is provided to initiate data parallel computations and apply a *void-functor* to all members of the collection. The asynchronous `map()` operation is complemented with a synchronous reduce() operation that first applies the specified *functor* to all members of the collection in parallel and then applies an associative and commutative binary *reduce-functor* to combine all results. Furthermore, for convenience reasons we added a step() operation, that resembles a synchronously executed map() operation. Internally step() is currently implemented as a global reduction.

Figure 3 shows the execution of reduce() operation on a binary tree. The numbers indicate logical time steps.

result = group. **reduce** (*functor, reduce-functor*);

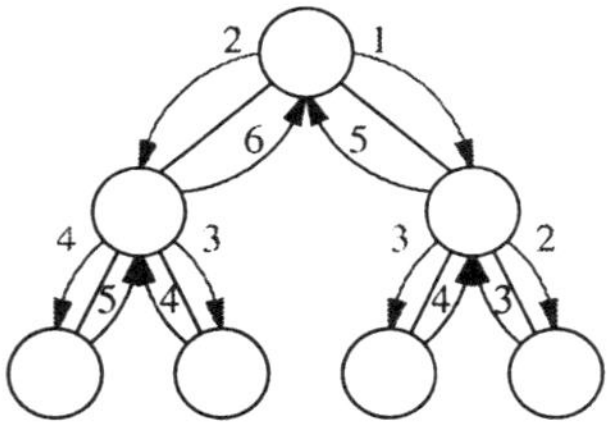

Figure 3. Reduce

All collective methods assume that the members of a collection define an STL style iterator [1] that (recursively) iterates all members of a collection. The iterator determines the order in which the specified *functor* is passed to the members of the collection. Each functor is first propagated asynchronously to the other members of the collection in the order defined by the iterator before it is applied to the local object instance. In case of reductions we use the asynchronous apply() method in conjunction with lazy synchronization to synchronize on the availability of results. All results are collected in exactly the same order in which the functor has been spread (fig. 3). Thus, the behaviour remains deterministic and application programmers can get control over collective operations either through the iterator method of the topology class or by means of custom iterators defined by application classes.

2.2 Masked Operations and Selections

Dynamic sub-setting of collections is achieved through masked operations that are executed conditionally depending on the current state of the individual members of the collection. Conditions are expressed by means of boolean predicate functors. The masked collective `map()` and `reduce()` operations apply the specified functor only to those members for whom the specified *predicate* evaluates to `true`. In case of masked reductions the identity element of the reduction functor is filled in for all members that fail to match the specified predicate.

Since the masked operations require visiting all members of the collection they should only be applied if either the majority of members can be expected to match the predicate or the state of the members changes rapidly and unpredictably. Otherwise *selections* should be applied to specify subsets of a collection.

CollectionOf <Any, **BinTree** > coll(...);
SelectionOf <Any, **List**> sel(*predicate,* coll);

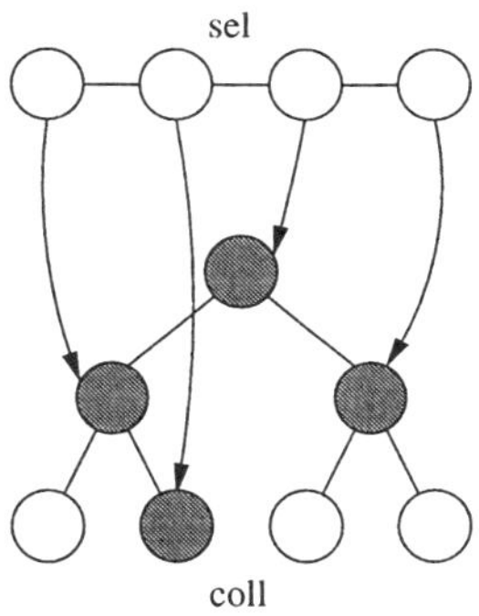

Figure 4. Selections

Selections are indirect collections that refer to specific members of other collections. Unlike masked operations, selections allow dynamic sub-setting of collections with minimal communication overhead. When a selection is created, the membership is determined by a boolean *predicate* functor. Collective operations applied to the selection are in fact applied to the original collection defined in the order of the selection's topology class.

Note, that the topology of the selection and the original group may differ as shown in figure 4. This allows us to create multiple selections with different topologies and we can choose those topologies that are most appropriate for the collective operations we are going to apply. When an application initially has a topology that does not support collective operations very well, we can easily create a complete selection with a tree topology that refers to all members of the original collection and apply collective operations on the selection instead.

3 Case Study: Laplace Simulation

We have chosen a two dimensional Laplace heat distribution simulation as a case study for typical iterative numerical algorithms, where a parallel iteration step is followed by a global convergence test that might be followed by a data exchange step between neighbours.

We implemented two versions of the algorithm on top of TACO, both based on a striped distribution of the heat matrix. Since a striped implementation has only two neighbours we have chosen a distributed doubly linked list as application topology.

```
class HeatStripe: public HeatMatrix, public DblList<HeatStripe> {
public:
  ...
  void exchange() { ...  }; // exchange data with neighbours
};
```

The `HeatStripe` class implements a distributed, striped heat matrix where each stripe has one overlapping row with each of its neighbours. `HeatStripe` is derived from both a `HeatMatrix` class that provides a common sequential implementation for the Laplace problem and TACO's `DblList` topology class that implements a distributed linked list.

The parallel algorithm is straightforward. First we declare a group of an arbitrary number of `HeatStripe` instances that are mapped according to a cyclic strategy to an arbitrary number of nodes. Since the doubly linked list is a very bad topology for collective operations, we simply create an unconditional selection of our stripe group thus giving our group effectively two topologies: the doubly linked list for the data exchange between neighbours and a 4-ary tree for collective operations.

```
Cyclic cyclic(8); // cyclic distribution strategy
GroupOf<HeatStripe> stripes (..., 128, cyclic);
SelectionOf<HeatStripe,QuadTree> sel(stripes);
...
double diff;
do {
   diff = sel.reduce(m2f(&HeatMatrix::next_step), Max<double>());
   sel.step(m2f(&HeatStripe::exchange));
} while (diff > epsilon);
```

A global reduction is applied to perform an iteration step on all members of the group simultaneously and to perfom the convergence test against a predefined epsilon. Since the reduction is synchronous we can be sure that all members of the group have completed the iteration step before we issue the collective `step()` operation to exchange the newly computed overlapping rows with its neighbours. The data transfer is performed using remote memory write operations (single sided communication) provided by the MTTL. We also used a synchronous collective `step()` operation here to ensure that the exchange phase is completed before the next iteration step begins.

3.1 Global vs. Local Synchronization

Although our first approach is very compact TACO's collective operations are strongly over-specified with regard to the synchronization requirements of the exchange step. We do not need to wait until *all* members of the group have completed their iteration step.

Fortunately, TACO allows us to mix global and local synchronization mechanisms as appropriate. Therefore we can synchronize the exchange phase locally with neighbouring objects by means of a barrier implementation which is directly based on the MTTL's synchronization variables.

```
class HeatStripe: public HeatMatrix, public Barrier,
     public DblList<HeatStripe> {
public: ...
  double next_step()
  {
      double result;
      result =  HeatMatrix::next_step();
      Barrier::sync(); // wait for neighbours
      exchange();
      return result;
  }
};
```

The synchronization with the neighbours and the exchange phase are now part of the `next_step()` method and thus we can omit the collective `exchange()` from the main program.

```
...
do {
   diff = sel.reduce(m2f(&HeatStripe::next_step), Max<double>());
} while (diff > epsilon);
```

This optimization requires only a little additional programming overhead but has a strong impact on the overall performance.

4 Performance

We measured the performance of the Laplace simulation on the RWC PC Cluster II consisting of 128 Pentium Pro nodes (200MHz CPU) interconnected by a 160MByte/sec Myrinet network running the Score [3] system software on top of a Linux System. The label *taco-heat* refers to our first approach which is "naively" based on TACO's collections. The refined version which uses local synchronization for the exchange phase is referred to as *taco-lsync*.

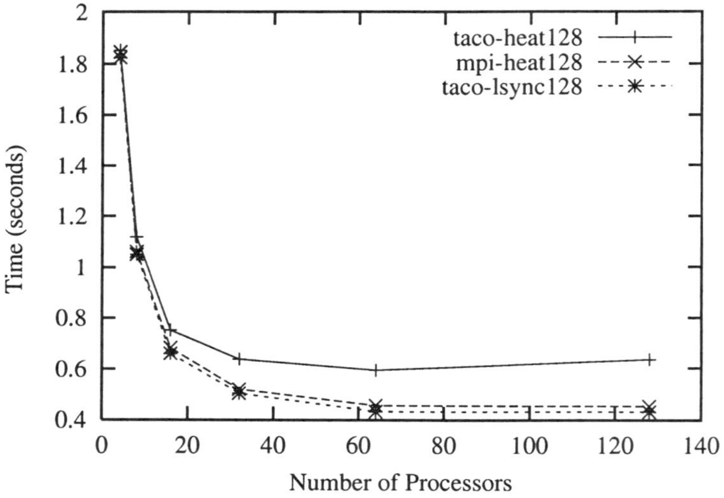

Figure 5. Laplace 128x128

For comparison with standard message passing libraries we also implemented a third version *mpi-heat* on top of MPICH-PM/CLUMP [5], which is a very efficient port of MPICH for Myrinet networks. The MPI implementation is built around a collective `MPI_AllReduce()` for global convergence tests and using `MPI_Send()` and `MPI_Recv()` for data exchange as well as synchronization.

We performed two sets of measurements, one for a small heat matrix (128 by 128, fig. 5) and one for a significantly larger matrix (1024 by 1024, fig. 6). In case of the small problem it is no surprise that the naive version *taco-heat* does not perform very well for large numbers of processors. The unnecessary global synchronization during the exchange phase dominates the result. Here

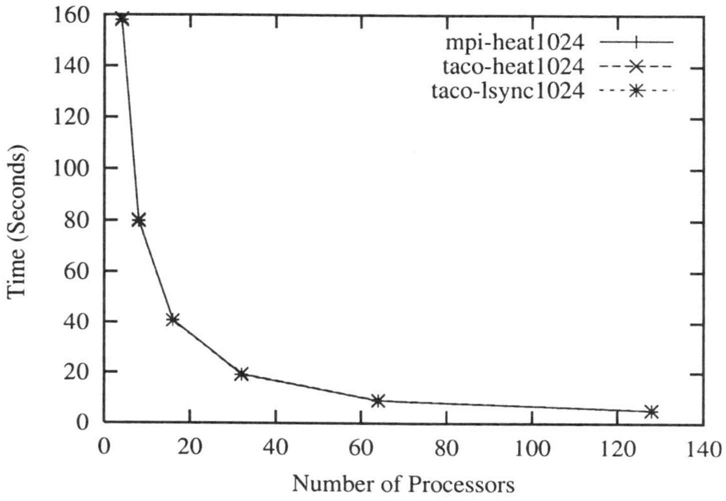

Figure 6. Laplace 1024x1024

we can see clearly the reason for the old criticism on the often over-specified lock-step semantics in data parallel processing. The refined version *taco-lsync* already outperforms the MPI version. This clearly indicates how important it is not to rely on data-parallelism alone in a pure library implementation like ours.

However, in case of the large problem size (fig. 6), the differences between the three versions have completely vanished. The previously dominating global synchronization costs are only proportional to the number of nodes and therefore we do not have to care about these costs once the problem size is large enough.

To assess more accurately, what "large enough" in practice means we measured the basic costs for the collective operations we used (fig. 7). For the TACO `reduce()` operation we used a 4-ary balanced tree topology, which performs well on our network but is not supposed to be optimal. TACO's reduction has a similar semantics as a `MPI_Bcast` directly followed by a `MPI_Reduce`, therefore we also measured this combination for comparison. TACO does not only outperform this combination, but surprisingly even the much simpler `MPI_Reduce` for larger number of nodes.

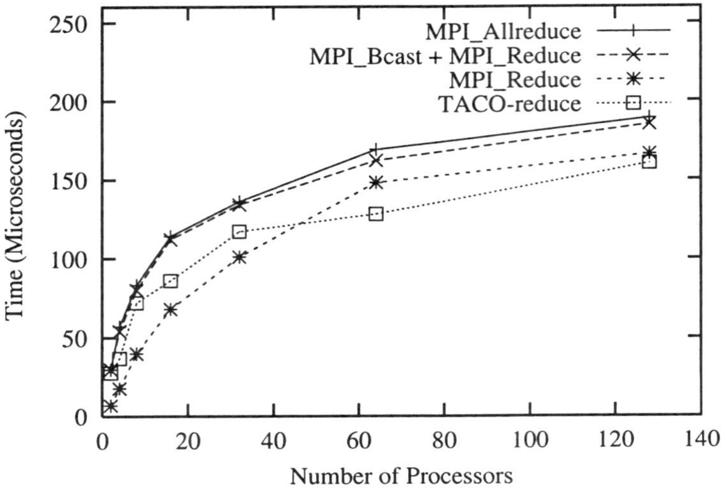

Figure 7. Basic reduction operations

5 Conclusion

Collections and collective operations are neither new nor did we invent the notion of topologies as such. In fact our work has been strongly inspired by the collection concept of pC++ [6] and ICC++ [7], the *communities* in Ocore [8], *groups* in HPC++ [9] and – last but not least – the topology concept of Promoter [10].

However, while most data-parallel approaches traditionally concentrate strongly on regular array structures, we deliberately based our collections on flexible graphs similar to ARTS [11]. Therefore existing collections can easily be changed dynamically at run time and collections might choose any user defined addressing scheme to access individual member objects. Furthermore, and most importantly since TACO exposes its group concept in a structured way it offers programmers a unique means of control over collective operations without sacrificing the group concept as such. This is of utmost importance with regard to performance tuning.

TACO does not try to provide a rich set of collective operation mechanisms and algorithms for many application cases like the Amelia Vector Template Library [12]. TACO focuses on simple, yet powerful and fairly easy to understand mechanisms instead that allow programmers to construct more complex application specific libraries with modest effort.

Although fine grained parallel computing is also possible with TACO, we do not expect satisfactory performance results since we cannot apply compiler level optimizations like the language-based approaches. However, the performance for fine grained structures can be significantly improved when the members of TACO's collections are themselves containers holding entire sets of small objects. Therefore TACO can serve well as a basis for libraries or runtime systems for fine-grained data-parallel processing.

References

1. A. Stepanov and M. Lee. The Standard Template Library. Technical Report HPL-94-34, Hewlett Packard Laboratories, 1994 revised 1995.
2. Y. Ishikawa. Multiple threads template library. Technical Report TR-96-012, Real World Computing Partnership, 1996.
3. Yutaka Ishikawa, Hiroshi Tezuka, Atsuhi Hori, Shinji Sumimoto, Toshiyuki Takahashi, Francis O'Carroll, and Hiroshi Harada. RWC PC Cluster II and SCore Cluster System Software – High Performance Linux Cluster. In *Proceedings of the 5th Annual Linux Expo*, pages 55 – 62, 1999.
4. R. H. Jr. Halstead. Multilisp: A Language for Concurrent Symbolic Computation. *ACM Transactions on Programming Languages and Systems*, 7(4), 1985.
5. Toshiyuki Takahashi, Francis O'Carroll, Hiroshi Tezuka, Atsushi Hori, Shinji Sumimoto, Hiroshi Harada, Yutaka Ishikawa, and Peter H. Beckman. Implementation and Evaluation of MPI on an SMP Cluster. In *Parallel and Distributed Processing – IPPS/SPDP'99 Workshops*, volume 1586 of *Lecture Notes in Computer Science*. Springer-Verlag, April 1999.
6. Francois Bordin, Peter Beckman, Dennis Gannon, Srinivas Narayana, and Shelby X. Yang. Distributed pC++: Basic Ideas for an Object Parallel Language. *Scientific Programming*, 2(3), Fall 1993.
7. A. Chien, U.S. Reddy, J.Plevyak, and J. Dolby. ICC++ – A C++ Dialect for High Performance Parallel Computing. In *Proceedings of the 2nd JSSST International Symposium on Object Technologies for Advanced Software, ISOTAS'96*, Kanazawa, Japan, March 1996. Springer.
8. H. Konaka, M. Maeda, Y. Ishikawa, T. Tomokiyo, and A. Hori. Community in Massively Parallel Object-based Language Ocore. In *Proc. Intl. EUROSIM Conf. Massively Parallel Processing Applications and Devel-*

opment, pages 305–312. Elsevier Science B.V., 1994.

9. Peter Beckman, Dennis Gannon, and Elizabeth Johnson. Portable Parallel Programming in HPC++. Technical report, Department of Computer Science, Indiana University , Bloomington, IN 47401.
10. M. Besch, H. Bi, P. Enskonatus, G. Heber, and M. Wilhelmi. High-Level Data Parallel Programming in PROMOTER. In *Proc. Second International Workschop on High-level Parallel Programming Models and Supportive Environments HIPS'97*, Geneva, Switzerland, April 1997. IEEE-CS Press.
11. Lars Büttner, Jörg Nolte, and Wolfgang Schröder-Preikschat. ARTS of PEACE – A High-Performance Middleware Layer for Parallel and Distributed Computing. *Journal of Parallel and Distributed Computing*, 59(2):155–179, Nov 1999.
12. Thomas J. Sheffler. The Amelia Vector Template Library. In *Parallel Programming using C++*, pages 43–90. MIT Press, 1996.

A STUDY OF I/O PERFORMANCE FOR CLUSTER SYSTEMS*

WEN LI[1] ZHIYONG LIU[2] AND XIANGZHEN QIAO[1]

1(National Research Center for Intelligent Computing System, Institute of Computing Technology, Chinese Academy of Sciences, Beijing 100080, {wenli,qiao}@ncic.ac.cn)

2(National Natural Science Foundation of China, Beijing 100083,

zliu@rose.nsfc.gov.cn)

Cluster computing systems are increasingly used to solve I/O intensive applications in many different fields. For such applications, I/O requirements quite often present a significant obstacle on the way of achieving good performance. I/O access strategies in parallel applications are one of the most important factors, which influence I/O performance greatly. However, the research work on different strategies on cluster systems is lack. In this paper we first describe the I/O subsystem of cluster computing systems, then analyze the file storage styles and different I/O access strategies. An analytical model for the analysis of different file storage schemes and I/O strategies is developed. To compare the performance of different I/O access strategies, some experimental results on Dawning 2000 cluster system are shown. The results show that the performance of parallel I/O read strategy is distinct better than read strategy based on message passing.

1 Introduction

Cluster computing systems are increasingly being used to solve I/O intensive applications in many different fields. For such applications, the I/O requirements quite often present a significant obstacle in the way of achieving good performance.

* This work is supported by National "863" Project and National Natural Science Foundation (Grant. 69933020).

Moreover, commodity storage technology trends show that the disparity between peak processor speeds and disk transfer rates will continue to increase. I/O performance depends on three factors: hardware, software, and I/O strategies exhibited by many parallel applications. At present, many I/O hardware subsystems do provide good performance. Software and I/O patterns are the main factors for low I/O performance.

So far, to improve I/O performance, many research work on parallel file systems [1,2,5] have been done. Standard I/O interfaces and Collective I/O technique [3,4] are another way to improve I/O performance. Research work on I/O patterns of parallel application [6] focus on request size distribution and temporal request structure, and what parallel file system should do according to these patterns. And most of these work are for massively parallel computer systems such as the Intel Paragon and the IBM SP.

I/O access strategies of parallel applications have great influence on I/O performance [8]. However, the research work on different access strategies on cluster systems is lack. In this paper, we first describe the I/O subsystem of cluster computing systems, then analyze file storage styles and different I/O access strategies. To compare the performance of different I/O strategies, some experimental results on Dawning 2000 cluster are shown. The results show that the performance of parallel I/O read strategy is distinctly higher than read strategy based on message passing.

The rest of this paper is organized as follows. In sec. 2, we discuss the I/O subsystem of cluster system. In sec. 3 we propose an analytical model for file storage and I/O access strategies. In sec. 4 we present the different experimental I/O performance results on Dawning 2000-1 cluster system. At last, we draw a conclusion.

2 I/O Subsystem of Cluster Systems

Cluster is constituted of multiple independent computers through high though-put LAN. Generally, a computer with large capability for storage is used as a control node, which is served as an interface between user and cluster. Most files are stored on the control node. The other computers are used as computing nodes, which have a small hard disk to store local data or files. Distributed file systems such as NFS are used in cluster systems. Distributed file systems can provide distributed access to files from multiple client machines, and their consistency semantics and caching behavior are designed accordingly for such access.

From the view of physical reading and writing, NFS can not provide parallel reading or writing. All reading and writing requirements are served in FIFO I/O queue. From the view of logical reading and writing, i.e., from the application development view, parallel reading can be achieved and the correctness can be guaranteed by system, while the correctness of parallel writing needs developers themselves to guarantee. In the following, we study the features of storage, I/O styles of cluster systems, and the I/O performance from application development view.

3 Analytical Model for File storage and I/O Access Strategies

For the case that multiple computing nodes write results to a file, program should collect all the data to a computing node through message passing, then write the result data to the local disk or control node.

For the case that all computing nodes read different sub-domain data from a same file, there are three styles, which programmers can adopt. A master is a processor, which an executable parallel program is submitted to. Other processors in the same program are called slaves. (1) When a file is stored on the control node, processors get the sub-domain data of the file from the control node. (2) When each processor has a file copy on its local hard disk, each processor gets the sub-domain data from its local hard disk. (3) When the file is stored on a local hard disk of computing node, the sub-domain data is got from the local harddisk of the computing processor. In general, a file locates only on one node, on a processor or on a control node. These two cases have the similar result of reading operation. Here we only discuss the case one. For the case one, there are still two strategies of data distribution. (a) Each processor opens the same file and reads subdomain data of the file in parallel. The distributing time of a file is Tpr. We call this strategy

PRC, which means parallel reading from control node. (b) The master processor opens a file and reads the whole data, then distribute the subdomain data to each processor. The distributing time is Tmr. We call this strategy MRD, which means master reading then distributing a file.

Tpr = Max (Trs(i)+Tsdc(i)) (i=0,...,n);

Tmr = Trwh +Tsdcwh +Tsdm;

Where n represents the number of processors; Trs(i) represents the time of reading

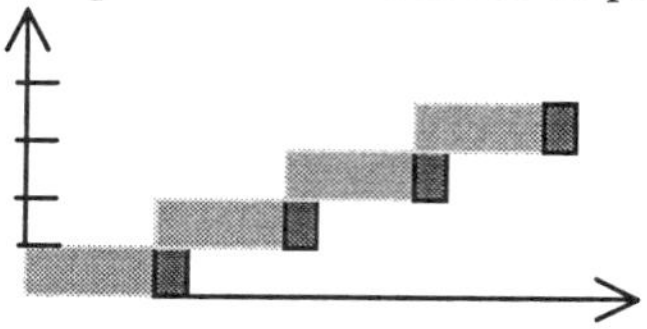

Fig. 1

Fig. 2

subdomain data from the hard disk of the control node to the send buffer of it. Tsdc represents the time of message transmission from the send buffer of the control node to the receive buffer of each processor node. Trwh represents the time of reading whole file from the hard disk of the control node to the send buffer of it. Tsdcwh is the time of transferring whole file from the sending buffer of the control node to the receiving buffer of the master. Tsdm represents message transmission time from the master to each processor.

Fig.1 shows the reading procedure by 4 nodes in strategy (a). The light parts mean the reading procedure and the dark parts mean the transmission. Because all initial reading operations are at the beginning of program, they are all in the I/O request queue. Then they are served in a FIFO fashion. However, when j is not equal to i, there is some overlap between Tio(i) and Tsdc(j). So reading operations by all processors can form the approximate pipeline. Because the bandwidth of transmission is far higher than the bandwidth of reading, the time-cost difference between stage Tio and Tsdc is big. Based on the formula of average disk access [7], Tio(i) can be represented as following:

Tio= Tas(average seek time) + Tar(average rotational delay) +
 Trd(reading data block) + Tco(controller overhead).

Where Tas, Tar, and Tco are fixed value. For a same file, when the number of processors increases, the size of sub-domain data will decrease. Therefore the Trd and Tio will come down. And on the whole the overlap between I/O procedure and transmission will go up. This trend keeps on when the size of sub-domain data is large enough and Trd is still the main cost of Tio.

Fig.2 shows the reading procedure by 4 nodes in strategy (b). The main cost of this strategy is the reading time from the harddisk to the send buffer of control node. There is no overlap between reading and transmission in the logical view. But there is some overlap between I/O operations for file operation system.

In a word, strategy (a) can achieve remarkable higher I/O performance than strategy (b).

4 Experiments of I/O Strategies on Dawning 2000-□

Dawning 2000-I system consists of 32 computing processors and a control processor. The processors use 300MHz PowerPC 604e and each has 256Mbytes of memory each. RAID is attached to the control node. These nodes are connected through a 100Mbps switched Ethernet.

For the above mentioned reading strategies: (a) and (b), we test the performance of average reading operation by 1 to 24 computing nodes for different file sizes, which are 256KB, 1MB, 4MB. For example, when 4 computing nodes read a file with 256KB in average reading operation, each computing node reads 64KB subdomain data. Figure 3 and Figure 4 shows the I/O performance of two reading strategies. Let Pio represent the I/O performance. Then the I/O performance is defined as:

Pio=Fsize/Tread;

Where Fsize is the size of a file, and Tread is the time used for reading.

When the number of computing nodes is ranging from 1 to 24 in strategy b, the I/O performance ranges from 4MB/s to 6MB/s in Fig.4. This means that the time spending on transferring data from harddisk to sending buffer, Trwh, is the major contributor to the time cost. It takes about 0.05 (s) when one computing node reads a file with 256KB. And I/O performance is 4.48MB/s. When 24 computing nodes read a file with 256KB, the I/O performance is 5.40MB/s. Fig.4 also shows there is some improvement of the I/O performance as increasing the number of computing nodes for reading a same volume file. This indicates that there is some overlap on Trwh□Tsdcwh and Tsdm. On the whole, the I/O performance does not vary much for different size files by different number of processors involved in reading.

Fig.3 shows the I/O performance of the strategy (a) is obviously higher than the strategy (b)'s. The performance is 21.4MB/s by one computing node reading a

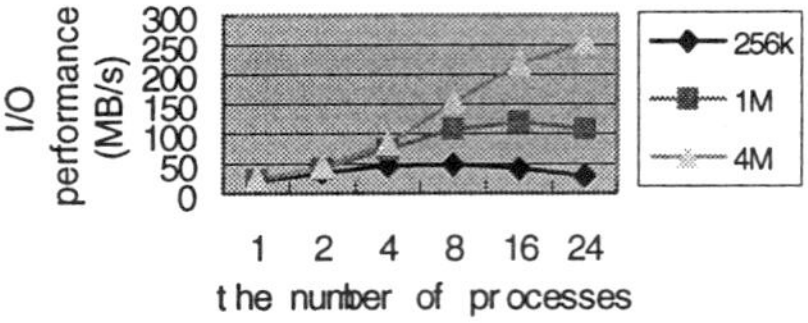

Fig. 3. performance of strategy (a)

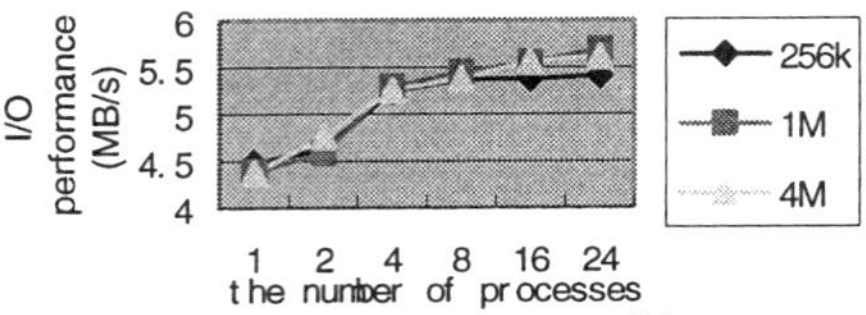

Fig. 4 Performace of strategy(b)

256KB file, 48.6MB/s by 24 computing nodes. It is 24.06MB/s by one processor reading a 4Mbytes file, 254.4MB/s by 24 processors. Fig.3 also shows that I/O performance improves obviously with the number of processor reading a same volume file increasing when the size of subdomain data is above a certain value (64KB). This indicates there is a big overlap between Trs and Tsdc. Furthermore, it can achieve the highest I/O performance when the size of subdomain data is 64KB, which is the same as the size of a logical block of the file system. Therefore, when the size of subdomain data block size is the same as the size of a logical block of a file system, the highest I/O performance can be reached. So when we know the size of a logical block of a file system, we can choose the best number of the processors.

5 Conclusions

I/O systems have emerged as a major performance bottleneck in parallel systems. Program developments are important factors to the I/O performance. In this paper we analyze and validate the I/O performance by different I/O strategies on cluster systems. A theoretical analytical model is presented for the analysis of file storage and I/O strategies in cluster systems. From theoretical analysis and experimental results, it shows the strategy (a): parallel reading from control node has remarkably higher I/O performance than the strategy (b): master reading then distributing the file. And when the size of subdomain data block size is the same as the size of a logical block of the file system, the highest I/O performance can be reached.

References

1. Evgenia Smirni, C.E.Elford, A.J.Lavery,and A.A.Chien, "Algorithmic Influences on I/O Patterns and Parallel File System Performance", Proc. Of the 1997 International Conference on Parallel and Distributed Systems,1997.
2. P.J.Varman and R.M.Verma,"Tight Bounds for Prefetching and Buffer Management Algorithms for Parallel I/O Systems", IEEE Transactions on parallel and Distributed Systems,Vol.10, No.12,December,1999.
3. B.Nitzberg and V.Lo, "Collective Buffering:Improving Parallel I/O performance", the 6th International Symposium on High Performance Distributed Computering ,1997,Portland.
4. Phillip M. Dickens and Rajeev Thakur, "Improving Collective I/O Performance Using Threads", Proc. of the 13th International Parallel Processing Symposium and 10th symposium on parallel and distributed Proc, April, 1999, San Juan.
5. P. E. Crandall, R. A. Aydt, A.A.Chien and D.A.Reed," Input / Output Characteristics of Scalable Parallel Applications", Proc. of Supercomputer 95. Dec. 95.
6. Huseyin Simitci and Daniel A.Reed, "Comparison of Logical and Physical Parallel I/O Patterns", the International Journal of High Performance Computing Applications, (12) 3:364-380.
7. David A. Patterson and John L. Hennessy,"Computer Architecture: A Quantitative Approach", China Machine Press. 1998,9.
8. KeShen and Edward J.Delp,"A Spatial-Temporal Parallel Approach for Real-Time MPEG-VIDEO Compression", Proc. of the 25th International Conference on Parallel Processing August 13-15,1996,Bloomingdule, ppII100-II107.

A REDUCED COMMUNICATION PROTOCOL FOR NETWORKS OF WORKSTATIONS

WEIMIN ZHENG , XINMING OU, JUN SHEN,

Dept. of Computer. Tsinghua Univ.Beijing 100084, P.R.China

zwm-dcs@mail..tsinghua.edu.cn

To fully exploit the high performance potential provided by the rapidly developing communication hardware, new communication protocols specifically designed for parallel computation in networks of workstations are needed. We designed such a protocol, FMP(Fast Message Passing protocol) and used this protocol to implement MPI and PVM, which run over a network of workstations interconnected by Myrinet. We also design a simple method to deal with deadlocks.

Keywords: parallel computing, message passing, communication protocol, Myrinet

I Introduction

With the fast development of the communication equipment, network of workstations has become a more and more popular environment for parallel computing because of its high performance-price rate[1]. Recently, most message passing functions used in network of workstations take TCP/IP as underlying communication protocol. For the unreliability in long-distance communication and the heterogeneity of the hosts and networks, it incorporates a great deal of concerns over error-detecting, error- correcting and flow control[2]. But in networks of workstations, hosts are often homogeneous and near to each other. The reliability of underlying hardware is so high that it is even impossible for an error to occur during the execution of a parallel program. Moreover, TCP/IP is embedded in the kernel of Unix operating system. This also affects the performance of message passing functions based on TCP/IP. With the rapid growth of the bandwidth in physical layer, the bottleneck of speed has migrated from hardware to software, as illustrated in figure1.

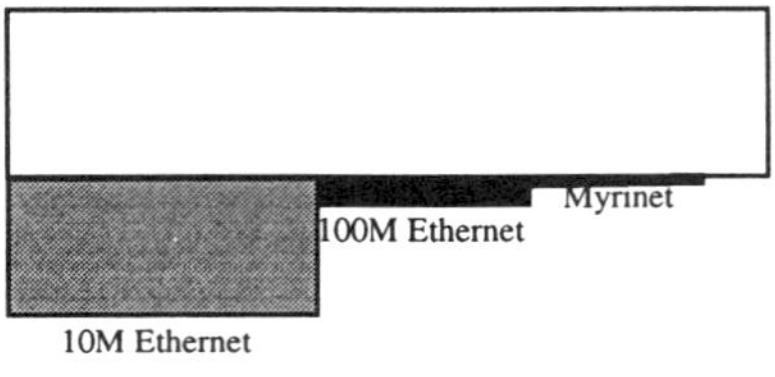

Figure 1 Analysis of communication overhead

Our goal is to design a reduced communication protocol, which exploits the maximum communication potentials of the fast hardware, thus greatly reduce the execution time of parallel programs on networks of workstations.

II System overview

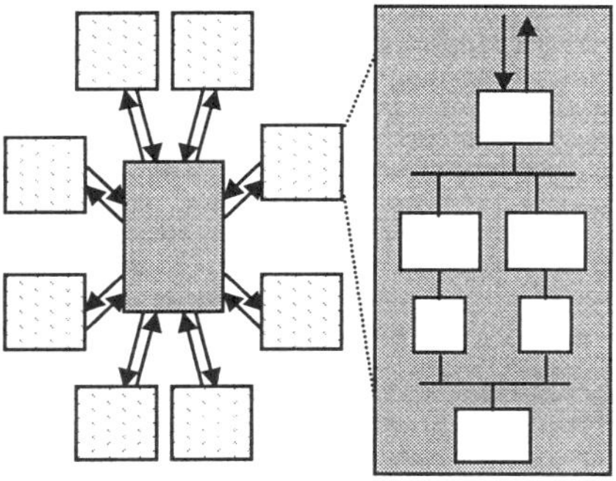

Figure 2 Hardware architecture

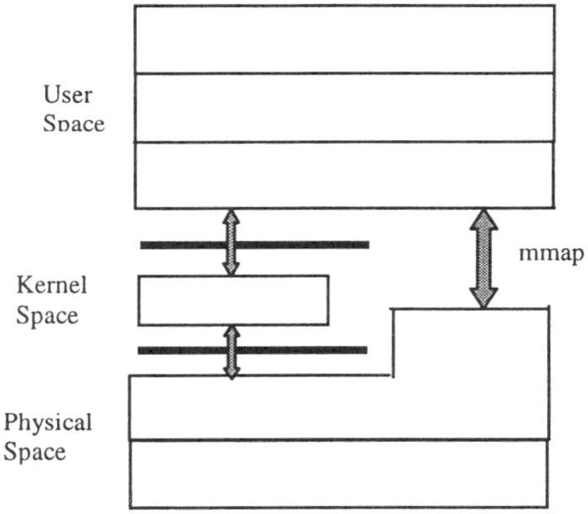

Figure 3 Software architecture

The system architecture of FMP is illustrated in figure 2. Eight SUN Ultra2 workstations are interconnected with a Myrinet Switch. Each node is a SMP with two 200MHz UltraSPARC-I CPU, 256MB memory and a Myrinet[4] network adapter card on Sbus. The software architecture of FMP protocol is illustrated in figure 3. NC_FMP and LM_FMP are network part and local part respectively.

III Crucial Techniques

Buffer Management

FMP is an asynchronous protocol in that connection need not be set up before sending and receiving. Buffer management in such kinds of communication protocols is a very important issue. If we let all processes on a host share a single send buffer and a single receive buffer, different processes in that host must be synchronized when accessing the buffers. This will make sending and receiving extremely inefficient. In FMP we use another policy. Each process has its own receive buffer but share a single send buffer, as illustrated in figure4.

Buffers in FMP are all queues. When a process wants to send a message, it puts the message on the tail of the send queue. The Myrinet control program MCP will find that there are a message in the send queue, removes it from the head and transmits it. When a message arrives on a host, the MCP will put it at the tail of the appropriate queue. When the process associated with that queue is ready to receive the message, it checks the queue and removes it. There is no need to synchronize different receiving processes, since each process has its own receive queue. However, we must synchronize different sending processes because only one send queue exists.

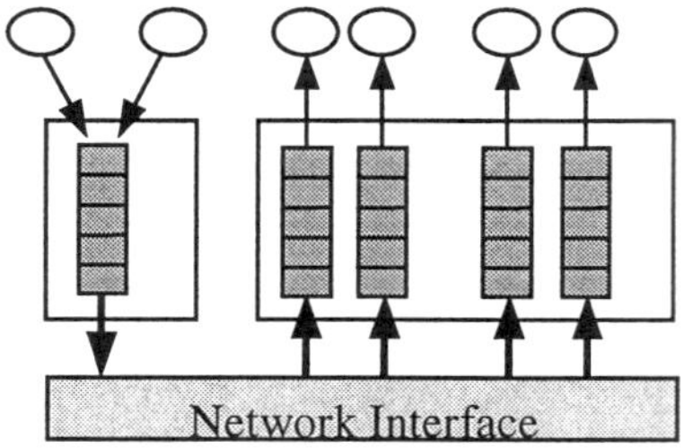

Figure 4 Buffers in FMP

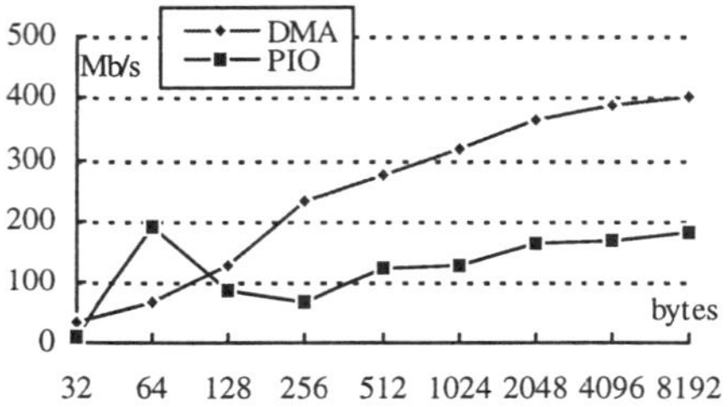

Figure 5 Transmit properties of PIO **and DMA**

DMA or PIO

For a message to be sent, it must be copied to the buffer on the network adapter card. We choose different methods according to the size of messages. PIO for short ones and DMA for large ones. If DMA is chosen, the sending process must first write the message into an area acquired from kernel, since kernel space cannot be swapped out. Then the CPU on the Myrinet Card will start a DMA operation and transmit the message. To make the DMA operation and the network transmission become parallel, we employ a pipeline technology.

Avoiding Deadlock

Since FMP is an asynchronous, connectionless communication protocol, it is possible that one process send a message to another process before the destination process is ready to receive it. If too many unexpected messages arrives and the buffer is exhausted, other processes will not be able to send data to it. To avoid such kind of deadlock, we let the sending or receiving process move some messages from its receiving buffer into a temporary area in the process's address space when sending or receiving is blocked. Thus we can prevent the buffer from being exhausted.

Local Communication

In a network of SMP workstations, communicating processes may happen to reside on the same host. In such conditions, message passing between two processes is carried out using the local communicating part of FMP protocol, LM_FMP. Sending and receiving of messages are implemented as various memory copy functions. Each process on a host has a channel number assigned to it. And each channel is associated with a message-header queue. The header of a local message destined to a channel is put into the tail of the corresponding header-queue. If the message is small enough, the body of the message is embedded into the header. Otherwise a pointer in the header indicates the place where the body of the message is stored. (Figure 6)
How the body of large messages should be stored is a question worth discussing.
A straight-forward solution is to allocate a continuous memory block from the shared memory. This makes it easy to copy data into or from the buffer. But the

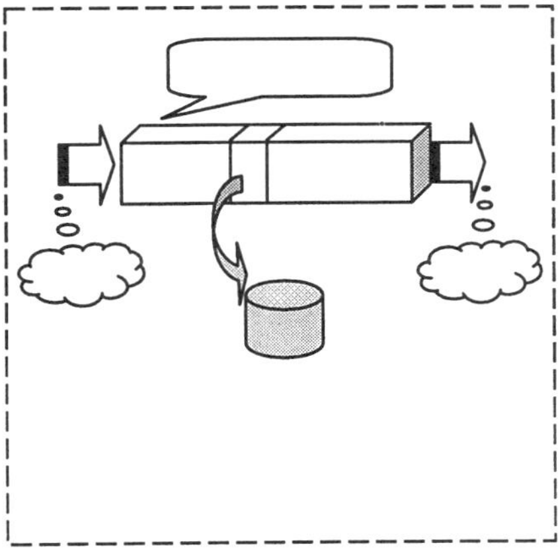

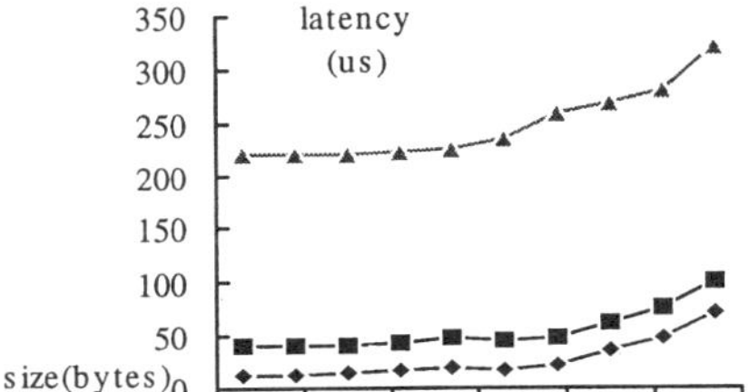

	1	8	16	64	256	512
—◆— NC_FMP(p£ ©	12.4	14	15.7	17.5	35.4	49.1
—■— NC_FMP(i)	40.2	40.6	42	44.5	62.5	76.5
—▲— TCP/IP	220	220	222	235	268	281

memory allocation algorithm in this policy is difficult to devise and tends to create lots of small fragments of free spaces which are hard to utilize.

IV Performance of FMP

We test the performance of FMP protocol and compare it with TCP/IP. First, we measure the point-to-point communication latency and bandwidth of FMP by calling FMP sending and receiving functions directly in user's program. Then, we test the overall performance of MPI based on FMP by a series of benchmarks.

Point-to-point Performance of FMP

Latency

From the latency graph we can see that the latency of FMP is one magnitude-level smaller than TCP/IP. That is because the reduced communication protocol eliminates most of the overhead in preparing to send a message and confirming its arrival, which on a large scale determines the latency. We can also notice that the latency of polling mode is only one-thirds of that of interrupting mode. This testifies that context switch plays an important role in communication overhead.

Bandwidth

The bandwidth in FMP is approaching the rate of DMA. This explains why although the bandwidth in FMP is much higher than TCP/IP, it is still lower than the 1.28Gbps provided by the Myrinet. In transmission of long messages, DMA becomes the bottleneck. And if we adopt other bus architectures, for instance, if we use PCI bus instead of SBUS, we can achieve even better bandwidth.

Benchmark Test of MPI based on FMP

NAS Benchmark Test Result

Prog	MPI/FMP	MPI/P4	Improve
bt.A.9	525.84	567.85	7%
bt.A.16	273.70	329.75	17%
sp.A.9	291.92	387.61	25%
sp.A.16	151.90	296.26	49%
ft.A.8	31.30	38.39	18%
ft.A.16	17.70	23.26	24%

To illustrate the overall performance of FMP protocol, we use NAS Benchmark to compare the execution time of MPI/FMP and MPI/P4. Above are parts of the results. The program name of NAS Benchmark is as 'prog.CLASS.nproc', where prog represents the problem to be solved by the parallel program, CLASS indicates the scale of the problem and nproc is the number of processors used in the program. The execution time is in seconds. All results show improvements in MPI/FMP.

V Conclusion

In this article, we present FMP--a communication protocol specifically designed for network of workstations to eliminate the unnecessary software overhead of TCP/IP. FMP is a complete protocol in that functions in all levels are implemented, from the physical layer (Myrinet control program, network driver) to application layer (MPI and PVM). Our goal is to extensively exploit the performance potential of advanced communication equipment. The philosophy of FMP is to make the protocol as simple as possible, assuming the reliability of the underlying hardware. From our performance test, this approach is feasible and successful in improving both the point-to-point features and the overall execution speed of parallel applications.

References

1. C.L. Dong, W.M. Zheng, et al., A scalable parallel workstation cluster system, *Proc. of APDC'97,* Shang Hai, China, 1997, 307-313.
2. J. Kay and J. Pasquale. The importance of non-data-touching overheads in TCP/IP, *Proceedings of the 1993 SIGCOMM*, September 1993, 259-260.
3. Gordon Bell. 1995 Observations on Supercomputing Alternatives: Did the MPP Bandwagon Lead to Cul-de-Sac? *Communications of the ACM*, March 1996, 39(3): 11-15.
4. Nanette J. Boden, Danny Cohen, Robert E. Felderman, Alan E. Kulawik, Charles L. Seitz, Jakov N. Seizovic, and Wen-King Su, Myrinet: a gigabit-per-second local area network. *IEEE Micro*, February 1995, 15(1): 29-36.
5. T. von Eicken, D. E. Culler, S. C. Goldstein, and K. E. Schauser, Active Messages: A Mechanism for Integrated Communication and Computation, *Proc. of the 19th ISCA*, May 1992, 256-266.

A SOFTWARE DEVELOPMENT METHODOLOGY TO SUPPORT DISTRIBUTED COMPUTING CLUSTERS

DAVID LEVINE, KANNAN BHOOPATHY, JEFF MARQUIS, BEHROOZ SHIRAZI

Department of Computer Science and Engineering, University of Texas at Arlington, 300 Nedderman Hall, Arlington, Texas 76019-0015
E-mail:levine@cse.uta.edu

With the growing popularity of distributed computing clusters, where nodes can be single processors or symmetric multiprocessors (SMPs), there is a significant need for programming tools that aid in the creation of software that exploits both shared memory and distributed memory programming paradigms. The software must be capable of exploiting a shared memory programming paradigm at the intra node level and a distributed memory paradigm at inter node level. Developing software for these hybrid systems is difficult and time consuming. The current version of the PARSA Software Development Environment [1] supports only the shared memory paradigm. This paper presents enhancements to the PARSA methodology to support both shared and distributed memory paradigms in an integrated manner. Current shared memory capabilities are used to support the shared memory paradigm and the message passing facilities of MPI (Message Passing Interface) [2] are employed to support the distributed memory paradigm between nodes.

1 Introduction and History

Distributed computing clusters are gaining in popularity because of increasing processor performance, network speed, as well as decreasing processor cost and communication latency. One key advantage of applications running on distributed computing clusters is that they are economically scalable. That is, the performance of the application increases when the system is expanded by adding inexpensive SMP nodes or single processor nodes. However, developing software that can effectively utilize these systems is difficult, time consuming and requires much expertise.

Partially, this is due to a lack of robust programming tools. Contemporary parallel and distributed programming tools i.) are architecture specific (shared memory or distributed memory) or ii.) support non-standard programming languages or iii.) support extensions to standard languages making applications non-portable.

In this paper we present enhancements to the PARSA™ Software Development Environment that make it suitable for developing distributed computing cluster software using standard programming languages and libraries. Before presenting PARSA and our proposed enhancements we present other development systems and methodologies and their deficiencies for developing distributed computing cluster software.

CILK[3] is an algorithmic multithreaded parallel programming language based on ANSI C. It is designed for general purpose parallel programming but it is especially effective for exploiting dynamic, highly asynchronous parallelism. The philosophy behind CILK is that programmers should concentrate on structuring applications to expose parallelism and exploit locality and leave the runtime system to efficiently schedule the computations. OpenMP[4] is an application programming interface (API) for parallel programming on multi-platform shared-memory computers. It supports the shared memory parallel programming model only. OpenMP also provides an incremental path for parallelization of existing serial programs. TreadMarks[5] is a distributed shared memory (DSM) system for standard UNIX systems. DSM systems enables processes executing on different machines to share memory, even though the machines physically do not share memory. CODE[6] is a graphical programming environment for parallel application development on shared memory and distributed memory architectures. CODE allows programmers to express programs using an abstract computational model. The application is expressed as a graph with nodes and arcs with declarative annotation. Comparison Summary: The disadvantages of the tools mentioned above are (1) they are bound to a specific architecture, (2) they use a non-conventional programming language for application specification, and/or (3) they provide non-standardized routines or libraries which makes it difficult to port applications between different platforms.

2 PARSA

PARSA is unique among the programming tools presented in this paper in that it is extremely easy to use, architecture independent, based on standard programming languages, and exploits multiple processors by efficient management of scheduling threads. In the next section we briefly describe how applications are developed in PARSA and how those applications utilize shared memory systems. We then present extensions that make it suitable for developing distributed computing cluster software.

The PARSA Programming Methodology: is a comprehensive software development environment that allows programmers to utilize systems that have multiple processors. Applications developed consist of Graphical Objects (or GOs) and arcs. Graphical Objects represent computational tasks within applications and arcs represent the relationship between graphical objects. Graphical Objects consist of an interface section and a functionality section. The functionality section of a graphical object defines the task to be performed, and is programmed in a standard programming language (currently C or FORTRAN). Arcs are the PARSA graphical mechanism used to specify the dependencies that exist between graphical objects within an application.

PARSA supports various types of parallelism: forall and while graphical objects to support regular (or data) parallelism and repeat parallelism. When application development is complete the code generation process converts the graphical representation of applications to multi-threaded source code which is then linked with a thread management library to control the execution at run-time.

In this paper the multi-threaded, shared memory version of PARSA is extended to allow MPI communications between graphical objects executing on different nodes of a distributed computing cluster.

3 Combining Shared Memory and Distributed Memory Paradigms

We define distributed computing clusters as a collection of autonomous symmetric multiprocessors (for the purposes of this paper single processor systems are categorized as SMPs) linked by a computer network and equipped with distributed system software such that the whole system is perceived as a single integrated computing facility by the user of the system.

At each SMP node threading is used to exploit multiprocessor performance within the node. Between nodes distributed memory message passing is used to exploit multinode performance.

MPI[2] (Message Passing Interface) is used as the middleware for process and communication management to exploit multinode performance. MPI is preferred over raw sockets, as provided by the operating system, because MPI transparently handles creation and termination of processes, provides a higher level abstraction for process synchronization, and has automatic marshalling and unmarshalling of data at the sending and receiving processes.

Extending PARSA to support distributed computing cluster programming: graphical objects represent distributed processes and arcs represent data being physically passed from the system executing the source graphical object to the system executing the destination graphical object. The mapping of processes to SMP nodes is based on a simple round robin scheme that assigns a process to one of the nodes available for the application. The PARSA execution model is maintained by placing an MPI send call at the end of graphical object A and placing an MPI receive at the beginning of GO B.

4 Distributed Computing Cluster Issues

When an application is developed for a distributed computing cluster environment there are many issues that must be considered including: process creation and termination and the cost of inter-process communication.

Communication Cost: in general, when developing message passing based applications, it is beneficial to reduce the number of messages sent and received. In the PARSA-based distributed environment an arc connecting graphical object A and graphical object B becomes a message. Hence, the number of messages passed is equal to the number of arcs between objects. However, more than one arc can be specified between two graphical objects, so to reduce the number of messages the arcs are combined such that only one message is sent between any two objects. To make a single message between any two graphical objects a complex data type is created for each pair of objects.

Process Management: the number of processes to be spawned is automatically determined from the application specification. Creation and termination of the processes without requiring user intervention is done by MPI process management features as well as mapping processes to nodes. The available SMP nodes are specified in a file given when the application is invoked.

5 Performance

In this section we present the performance of PARSA-generated code for a sample application, matrix multiplication. The performance of the distributed code generated by PARSA is compared with a custom designed MPI version and a sequential version. We have run each of the versions with varying size matrices on a single SMP and a distributed computing cluster of SMPs. We use a four 266 MHz Pentium processor machine and a 266 MHz Pentium processor machine with Linux installed and MPICH[10], was used as the MPI library.

Performance on SMP: Figure one shows the run-time statistics. The graph shows that when the problem size increases, the PARSA-generated distributed version significantly outperforms both the sequential and manually developed distributed MPI code. Figure two shows the speedup (defined as the ratio of the run-time of the serial code to the run-time of the parallel code.) Figure three represents the speedup of the PARSA-generated distributed version over the manually coded distributed code. We can see from Figures two and three that as the problem size grows the PARSA-generated distributed version runs faster than the manually coded distributed MPI code.

Performance on a Distributed Cluster: we compare the performance of the three versions on a distributed system. Figure four show the statistics. It shows the running time of the sequential, distributed MPI custom designed and the PARSA-generated distributed version. The graph shows again that when the problem size increases, the PARSA-generated version significantly outperforms both the sequential and manually developed distributed MPI code. Figures five shows the speedup achieved by the manually developed distributed MPI code and the PARSA-generated distributed version. Figure six is a graph that compares the speedup of the PARSA-generated version over the manually developed code.

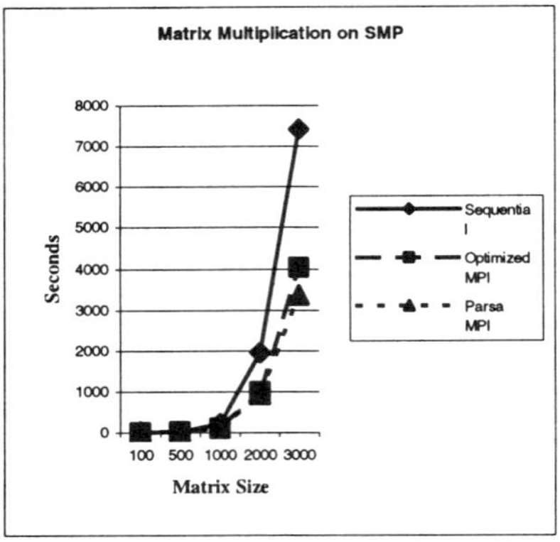

Figure 1

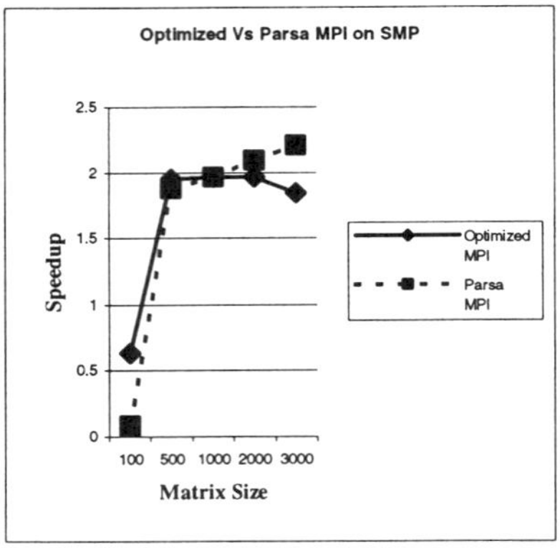

Figure 2

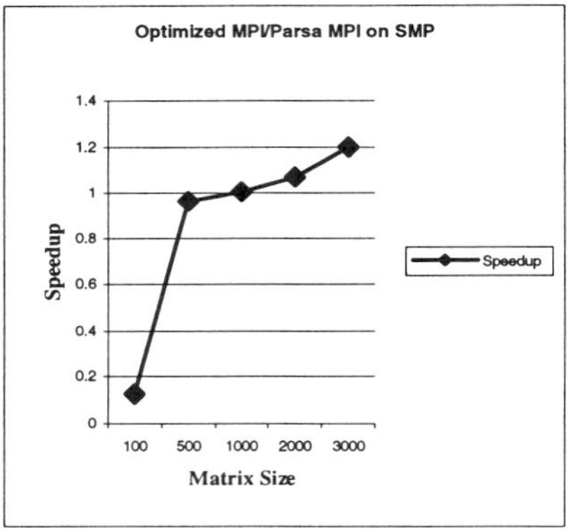

Figure 3

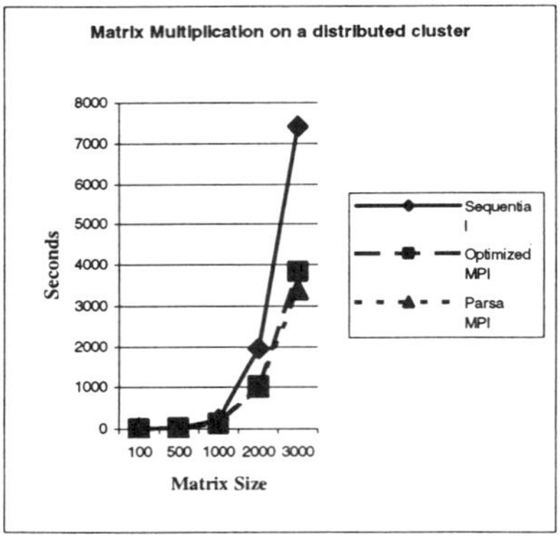

Figure 4

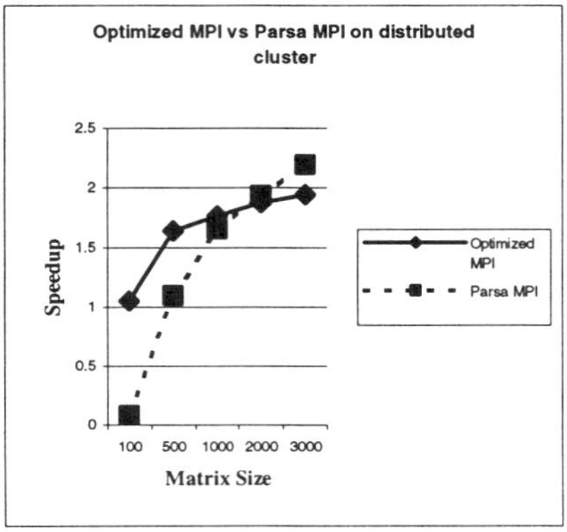

Figure 5

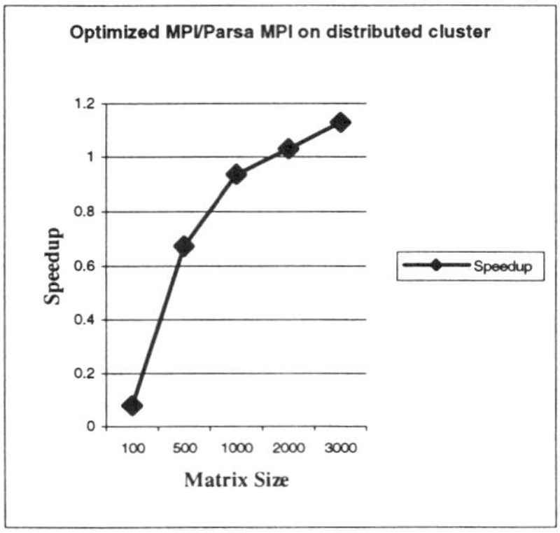

Figure 6

6 Conclusions and Future Work

In this paper we presented a uniform methodology for developing software for distributed computer clusters. We also proposed enhancements to an existing tool, PARSA, which employs threads for concurrent tasks on shared memory multiprocessors (SMPs) and MPI for communicating between concurrent tasks executing on a distributed cluster of SMPs. We proposed and validated that the PARSA programming methodology and execution model would not need to change to support distributed computing cluster software development. We also showed the run-time performance of the PARSA-generated distributed computing cluster version using the proposed methodology outperforms the custom designed distributed MPI code and the sequential code for matrix multiplication.

Important issues were ignored including load balancing and heterogeneity that need to be addressed in future work. The proposed methodology can also use CORBA, the industry standard middleware for integrating enterprise applications. Research on deploying CORBA to develop distributed multithreaded applications on distributed computing clusters is currently being conducted.

References

1. Prism Parallel Technologies, Inc, "The PARSA Software Development Environment Programming and Reference Manual".
2. Mark Snir, William Gropp et al, "MPI: The Complete Reference", MIT Press 1998.
3. Supercomputing Technologies Group, MIT Laboratory for Computer Science, "Cilk 5.2 Reference Manual", 1998.
4. OpenMP Architecture Review Board, "OpenMP C and C++ Application Programming Interface, Version 1.0", 1998.
5. Amza et al, "TreadMarks: Shared Memory Computing on Networks of Workstations", IEEE Computer, Vol. 29, No. 2, pp. 18-28, February 1996.
6. Parallel Programming Group, Department of Computer Science at University of Texas at Austin, "CODE 2.0 Reference Manual", March 1993.
7. Al Geist, Adam Beguelin et al, "PVM: Parallel Virtual Machine", MIT Press 1994.
8. Dave Butenhoff, "Programming with POSIX threads", Addison Wesley, 1996.
9. Couloris, Dollimore et al, "Distributed Systems: Concepts and Design", Addison Wesley, 1994.
10. William Gropp and Ewing Lusk, "User's guide for mpich, a portable implementation of MPI Version 1.2.0", Mathematics and Computer Science Division, Argonne National Laboratory and University of Chicago, 1999

Chapter 2
Interconnection Networks and Routing

TRIPWIRE: A SYNCHRONISATION PRIMITIVE FOR VIRTUAL MEMORY MAPPED COMMUNICATION

DAVID RIDDOCH[1], STEVE POPE, DEREK ROBERTS, GLENFORD MAPP
DAVID CLARKE, DAVID INGRAM, KIERAN MANSLEY, ANDY HOPPER[1]
{djr, slp, der, gem, djc, dmi, kjm, ah}@uk.research.att.com

AT&T Laboratories Cambridge, 24a Trumpington Street, Cambridge, England

[1]*Laboratory for Communications Engineering, Department of Engineering, University of Cambridge, England*

Existing user-level network interfaces deliver high bandwidth, low latency performance to applications, but are typically unable to support diverse styles of communication and are unsuitable for use in multiprogrammed environments. Often this is because the network abstraction is presented at too high a level, and support for synchronisation is inflexible. In this paper we present a new primitive for in-band synchronisation: the *Tripwire*. Tripwires provide a flexible, efficient and scalable means for synchronisation that is orthogonal to data transfer. We describe the implementation of a non-coherent distributed shared memory network interface, with Tripwires for synchronisation. This interface provides a low-level communications model with gigabit class bandwidth and very low overhead and latency. We show how it supports a variety of communication styles, including remote procedure call, message passing and streaming.

1 Introduction

It is well known that traditional network architectures, such as ethernet and ATM, deliver relatively poor performance to real applications, despite impressive increases in raw bandwidth. This has been shown to be largely due to high software overhead. To address this problem a variety of user-level network interfaces have been proposed.[1,2,3,4,5,6] These have achieved dramatically reduced overhead and latency, and deliver substantial performance benefits to applications.

However, these new interfaces are typically unsuitable for use in general purpose local area networks. The interface is often designed to support a particular class of problem, and is thus a poor solution for others. In some cases the interface does not scale well with the number of applications and endpoints on a single system. What is needed is a network interface that will deliver high performance for a wide variety of communication styles, and do so in a multiprogrammed environment.

For data transfer, non-coherent distributed shared memory offers very low overhead and latency, and high bandwidth. Small messages can be transferred with a few processor reads or writes, and larger messages using DMA. Messages are delivered directly into the address space of the receiving application with no CPU involvement, and because the interface presented is low-level, it is also very flexible.

A key problem for distributed shared memory based communications, however, is that of *synchronisation*. For example, the DEC Memory Channel has a communication latency of only $2.9\mu s$, yet acquiring an uncontended spin-lock takes $120\mu s$.[7] In order to realise high performance for applications in a multiprogrammed environment it is critical that applications be able to synchronise in a timely, efficient and scalable manner.

Mechanisms used for synchronisation in existing solutions include polling known locations in memory corresponding to endpoints, raising an interrupt when certain pages are accessed, or sending out-of-band synchronisation messages. These solutions are inflexible, and typically give high performance only for restricted styles of communication and classes of problem.

The main contribution of this paper is a novel in-band synchronisation primitive for distributed shared memory systems: the *Tripwire* . Tripwires provide a means to synchronise with reads and writes across the network to arbitrary memory locations. This enables very flexible, efficient and fine-grained synchronisation. Using Tripwires, synchronisation becomes orthogonal to data transfer, decoupled from the transmitter, and a number of optimisations which reduce latency become possible.

In the rest of this paper we present a new gigabit class network interface which provides non-coherent distributed shared memory with Tripwires for synchronisation. We describe the low-level software interface to the network, support for efficient and scalable synchronisation, and go on to give some performance results. We also show how the network interface can be used to implement a variety of higher-level protocols, including remote procedure call, message passing and streaming data. Initial results suggest that excellent performance and scalability is delivered to a wide variety of applications.

This project derives from earlier work remoting peripherals[8] in order to support the Collapsed LAN.[9]

2 The Interconnect Hardware

We have implemented a user-level Network Interface Controller (NIC) based on a non-coherent shared memory model. The current implementation of the NIC is a 33 MHz, 32 bit PCI card, built from off the shelf components including a V3 PCI bus bridge, an Altera FPGA, and HP's G-Link chip set and optical transceivers. The latter serialise the data stream at 1.5 Gbit/s, and were chosen to map neatly onto the speed of the target PCI bus.

This platform has enabled us to perform synchronisation experiments at gigabit speeds whilst retaining the flexibility of FPGA timescales. Figure 1 shows a schematic for the NIC.

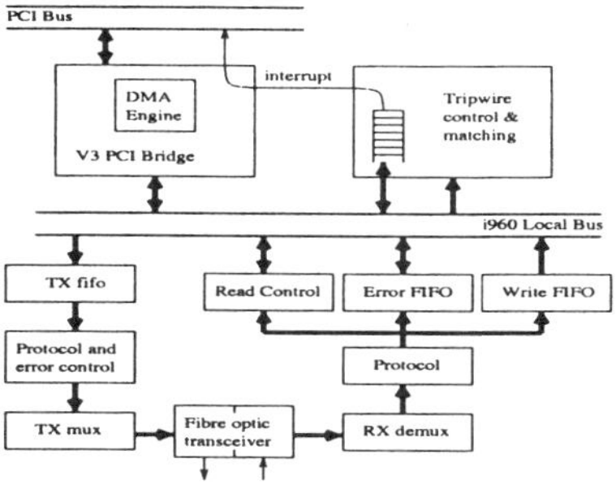

Figure 1. Logical structure of the CLAN NIC

2.1 Non-coherent shared memory

The basic communications model supported by the NIC is that of non-coherent shared memory. Using this model, a portion of the virtual address space of one application is mapped over the network onto physical memory in another node, which is also mapped into the address space of an application on that node. Data transfer is achieved by an application issuing processor read or write instructions to the mapped addresses — known as Programmed I/O or PIO. The NIC also has a programmable DMA[a] engine, which enables concurrent processing and communication.

Read and write requests arriving at the NIC are processed in FIFO order, and likewise at the receiving NIC; thus PRAM[10] consistency is preserved. Applications must use memory barrier instructions at appropriate places to ensure that writes are not re-ordered by the processor or memory management hardware when order is significant.

It should be noted that this interface is not intended to provide an SMP-like shared memory programming model. Although some algorithms designed to run on an SMP might work correctly on a non-coherent memory system, the performance is likely to be very poor due to the non-uniform memory access times. Rather it is intended that higher-level communications abstractions be implemented on top of this interface, hiding the details of the hardware and peculiarities of the platform, including:

- The latency for network reads is nearly twice that for writes.
- On some platforms there may be size and alignment restrictions when accessing remote memory.

---

[a] Direct Memory Access

2.2 *Wire protocol*

Write requests for remote memory arrive at the NIC over the PCI bus, and are serialised immediately into packets, each of which represents a write burst. A write packet header simply contains a destination address, and is followed by the burst data. The length of the burst is not encoded in the header, and so a packet can start to be emitted as soon as the first word of data arrives at the NIC, and finishes when no more data within the burst is available. Thus the minimum packet size is just a header and a single word of data, and the maximum is bounded only by the largest write burst that is generated. This burst based protocol is similar to that used in the Cray T3D supercomputer network.[11]

The address of any data word within a packet can be calculated from the address in the packet header and the offset of the data word within the packet. A consequence of this is that packets may be split at any point, as a new header for the second part of the packet can be calculated trivially. Similarly consecutive packets that happen to represent a single burst can easily be identified, and coalesced. This technique is well known within the memory system of single systems, but here is being extended into the LAN.

The utility of this can be seen when implementing a switch, an important function of which is to schedule the network resource between endpoints. It is important that a large packet does not hog an output port of the switch unfairly, and so it should be possible to split packets. Using the protocol presented it is possible to do this in a worm-hole switch with no buffering, whilst preserving the efficiency of large packets when there is no contention. Even if a packet is split, it may potentially be coalesced at another switch further on its route.

Hardware flow control is based on the Xon/Xoff scheme, but we expect to move to a new scheme combining Xon/Xoff with credits in the next implementation of the NIC. Error detection is performed using parity.

It should be noted that other physical layers and link layer protocols are possible and desirable, and could make use of existing commodity high performance switches.

2.3 *True zero copy*

The network interface and on-the-wire protocol described above are able to support true zero copy through the whole network. Read and write requests (whether from programmed I/O or DMA) are serialised by the NIC immediately, without buffering. This is shown in Figure 2(a).

At the receiving NIC incoming data is transfered directly into host memory, again without buffering. The delivery of the data does not involve any processing

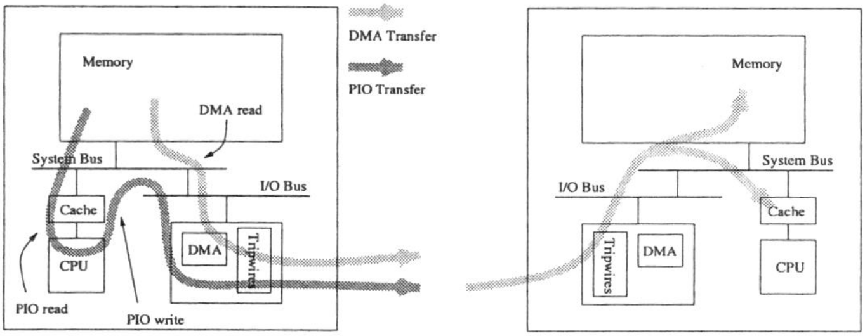

(a) PIO and DMA network writes

(b) The receiving node

Figure 2. Path of data through the system

on the CPU in the receiving node, and so has very low overhead. As shown in Figure 2(b), the cache on the receiving node snoops the system bus, and if data in the cache is written by a remote node, it will be updated or invalidated.

2.4 *Synchronisation*

In traditional network architectures all messages pass through the operating system kernel, which implicitly provides a handle to provide synchronisation with message transmition and arrival. Shared memory interfaces, however, do not of themselves offer any means for efficient synchronisation between communicating processes.

Within a single system, shared memory systems typically use some lock primitive such as the mutex and condition variable of pthreads, or semaphores. Mechanisms used in existing distributed shared memory systems include:

- Polling memory locations, otherwise known as *spinning*. This technique provides the best latency when servicing a single endpoint, but does not scale well with the number of endpoints and the processor resource is wasted whilst polling.

- Generate an interrupt on page access. This has been used on a number of systems, and allows the receiving process to synchronise with remote accesses to it's pages. However, the granularity is at the level of the page, so it is not possible to selectively synchronise with specific events within a data transfer.

- Explicit out-of-band synchronisation messages (as used by the Scalable Coherent Interface[12]). This solution complicates the network interface and is inflexible.

If the performance advantages of memory mapped networking are to be fully realised, then an efficient and flexible user-level synchronisation mechanism must be provided.

2.5 Tripwires for synchronisation

Here we present a novel primitive for in-band synchronisation: the *Tripwire* . Tripwires provide a means to synchronise with cross network accesses to arbitrary memory locations. Each Tripwire is associated with some memory location (which may be local or remote), and *fires* when that memory location is read or written via the network.

For example, an application can setup a Tripwire to detect writes to a particular memory location in its address space, and will be notified when that location is written to by a remote node. It is also possible to setup Tripwires to detect reads, or to specify a range of memory locations.

This is achieved by snooping the addresses in the stream of memory traffic passing through the NIC, and comparing each of them with the addresses of the memory locations associated with each of the Tripwires,[b] without hindrance to the passing stream. The comparison is performed by a content-addressable memory, and a synchronising action is performed when a match is detected.

The synchronising action performed is to place an integer identifier for the Tripwire into a FIFO on the NIC and raise an interrupt. The device driver's interrupt service routine retrieves these identifiers, and does whatever is necessary to synchronise with the application owning the Tripwire. This is not the only possible type of action — others include setting a bit in a bitmap in host memory (in the address space of the application) or incrementing an event counter.

We believe that the combination of non-coherent shared memory with Tripwires for synchronisation provides a flexible and efficient platform for communications:

- The choice of *non-coherent* shared memory allows a relatively simple and highly efficient implementation with very low latency. For example, although the SCI specification includes hardware based coherency, to date very few implementations have included it.

- Communications overhead is very low; small transfers can be implemented using just a few processor writes, and larger transfers using DMA.

---

[b]The current incarnation of the NIC supports 4096 Tripwires.

- Multicast can be implemented efficiently with suitable support in the switch.
- Tripwires allow highly flexible, efficient and fine-grained synchronisation; it is possible to detect reads or writes to arbitrary DWORDS in memory.
- Synchronisation is completely orthogonal to data transfer. It is possible to synchronise with the arrival of a message, an arbitrary position in a data stream, or on control signals such as flags or counters.
- Synchronisation is decoupled from the transmitter. The recipient of a message decides where in the data stream to synchronise, and can optionally tune this for optimal performance.
- It is possible to reduce latency by overlapping scheduling and message processing with data transfer. See section 4.3.
- As well as synchronising with accesses to local memory by remote nodes, Tripwires can be used to synchronise with accesses to remote memory by the local node. This can be used to detect completion of an outgoing asynchronous DMA transfer for example.

Together these points mean that it is possible to implement a wide variety of higher level protocols efficiently, including remote procedure call (RPC), streaming, message passing and shared memory based distribution of state.

The current incarnation of the NIC requires that applications interact with the device driver to setup Tripwires and synchronise when a Tripwire fires. A new version, under active development, will enable applications to program Tripwires at user-level through a virtual memory mapping onto the NIC. When a Tripwire fires, notification will be delivered directly into the application's host memory, and so synchronisation may also take place at user-level. Only when the application blocks waiting for a Tripwire or other event need the driver request that the NIC generate an interrupt as the synchronising action.

3 Low Level Software

The device driver for the NIC targets the Linux 2.2 kernel on x86 and Alpha platforms, and WinDriver portable driver software (Linux and Windows NT), and requires no modifications to the operating system core. The NIC can thus be used in the vast majority of recent commodity workstations.

The interface presented by the device driver and hardware is wrapped in a thin library. The main purpose of this layer is to insulate higher levels of code from changes to the division of functionality between user-level, device driver and hardware implementation. For example, a future incarnation of the hardware may provide facilities to perform connection setup entirely at user-level.

This layer also makes it easy to write code which can be used both at user-level and for in-kernel services,[c] since it abstracts above the device driver and hardware interface.

3.1 Endpoints

An *endpoint* is identified by host address and a port number. Fixed size[d] out-of-band messages are demultiplexed by the device driver into a per-endpoint queue, and are used for connection setup, tear down and exceptional conditions. The message queue resides in a segment of memory shared by the application and device driver, and so messages can be dequeued without a system call. This technique is used throughout the device driver interface to reduce the overhead of passing data between the device driver and application. This technique is described in detail elsewhere.[13]

The out-of-band message transfer is itself implemented in the device driver using the NIC's shared memory interface and Tripwires, using a technique similar to that shown in Section 4.1.

An API is provided to create and destroy endpoints, and manage connections. To amortise the relatively high cost of creating endpoints and their associated resources, they may be cached and reused across connection sessions.

3.2 Apertures

An *aperture* represents a region of shared memory, either in the local host memory or mapped across the network. An aperture is identified by an opaque descriptor, which may be passed across the network and used by an application to map a region of its virtual address space onto the remote memory region, or used as the target of a DMA transfer.[e]

The NIC uses a very simple direct mapping between PCI bus addresses and network addresses, and provides no explicit protection. As such the physical pages of memory in an aperture must be contiguous, and must be locked down to prevent them from being swapped out by the operating system. Basic protection is provided by the virtual memory system at the granularity of the page — a process may only create mappings to remote apertures for which it holds a descriptor. However, a

---

[c] Such as IP and NFS, see Section 6.
[d] 40 byte payload.
[e] In this context the descriptor is known as an RDMA cookie.

faulty or malicious node could circumvent this protection. We will be addressing these problems in future revisions of the NIC.

It should be noted that although facilities are provided for managing connections, this is not the only model supported. Any number of apertures may be associated with an endpoint, and mappings can be made to any aperture in any other host, provided the application has a descriptor for that aperture.

3.3 Tripwires

An API is provided to allocate Tripwires, and to setup and enable Tripwires to detect local and remote reads and writes. The application may test the state of a Tripwire, or block until a Tripwire fires.

When a Tripwire fires the NIC places an integer identifier for the Tripwire into a FIFO and raises an interrupt. The interrupt service routine wakes any process(es) waiting for that Tripwire, and sets a bit in a bitmap. This bitmap resides in memory shared by the application and device driver, and so it is possible to test whether a Tripwire has fired at user-level. Thus polling Tripwires is very efficient.

A Tripwire may be marked *once only*, so that it is disabled when it fires. This improves efficiency for some applications, by saving a system call to disable the Tripwire, but is unlikely to be necessary when Tripwire programming is available at user-level.

A *Tripset* groups a number of Tripwires from a single endpoint together so that the application can wait for any of a number of events to occur.

3.4 DMA

The NIC has a single DMA engine, which reduces communications overhead by allowing concurrent data transfer and processing on the CPU. There is currently no direct user-level interface to DMA hardware, so DMA requests must be multiplexed by the device driver.

All DMA interfaces that we are aware of require that the application invoke the device driver or access the hardware directly for each DMA request. We have implemented a novel interface which reduces the number of system calls required and schedules the DMA engine fairly among endpoints. The application maintains a queue of DMA requests in a region of memory shared with the device driver, and the device driver reads requests from that queue.

When the first request is placed in the queue, the application must invoke the device driver. After that the device driver will dequeue entries asynchronously, driven by the DMA completion interrupt, until the queue is empty. The application may continue to add entries to the queue, and only need invoke the device driver if the queue empties completely. The device driver maintains a circularly linked list of DMA request queues which are not yet empty, and services them in a round-robin fashion. Note that this asynchronous interface would work just as well if the DMA engine were managed on the NIC.

3.5 Multiple endpoints

The primitives discussed above are sufficient to manage communication through a single end-point efficiently. There is also a need for non-blocking management of multiple endpoints to support common event driven programming models typically used in server applications. Traditionally some variant on the BSD *select* system call is used. However, the deficiencies of these are well known, and even with sophisticated optimisations[14] do not scale well with the number of endpoints.

We have developed a solution to this problem in the form of an *asynchronous event queue*. Tripwire, DMA completion and out-of-band message events are delivered by the device driver into a circular queue. The API allows the application to register and unregister interest in individual events, poll for events and block until the queue is non-empty.

As with out-of-band messages above, this queue is maintained in memory shared by the device driver and application. The cost of event delivery is $O(1)$ and events are dequeued without a system call — so this interface is very efficient. Indeed event delivery becomes more efficient when a server is heavily loaded with network traffic, since the server is less likely to have to make a system call to block before retrieving an event. More information is given elsewhere.[13]

Ideally such a mechanism should be a standard part of an operating system, but while that is not the case it is important to be able to block waiting for I/O activity on other devices in the system as well as the network. To support this the asynchronous event queue itself is integrated with the system's choice of 'select' variant, and becomes 'readable' when the queue is not empty.

A number of other solutions to this problem with $O(1)$ cost have been proposed, including POSIX realtime signals, the `/dev/poll` interface in the Solaris operating system and others.[15] The main contribution of our approach is the delivery of events directly to the application without a system call.

4 Programming the NIC

4.1 Simple message transfer

Figure 3 shows how a simple, one-way, point-to-point message transfer protocol is implemented.

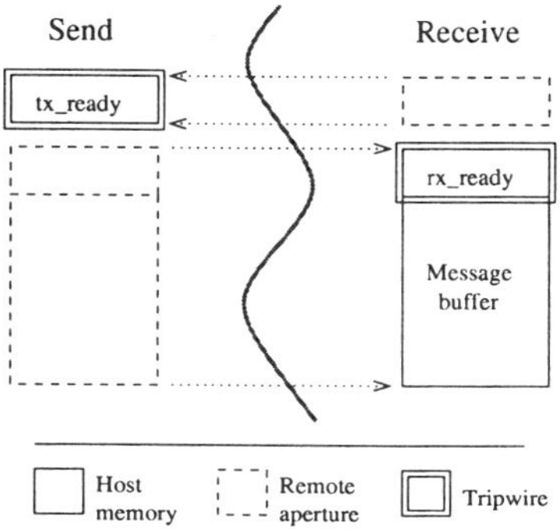

Figure 3. Message transfer using semaphores

On the transmitting side `tx_ready` is a boolean flag which is *true* when the buffer is free for sending. On the receive side `rx_ready` is true when a valid message is ready in the buffer. Initially `tx_ready` is set to true and `rx_ready` is set to false.

To send a message the sender must wait until `tx_ready` is true, set it to false (to indicate that the buffer is busy), copy the message into the remote buffer and set `rx_ready` to true. The receiver waits for `rx_ready` to become true, clears it, copies the message out of the buffer and resets `tx_ready` to true, so that the buffer can be used again.

```
void send_msg(const void* msg)
{
    while( !tx_ready )
        tripwire_wait(tx_ready_trip);
    tx_ready = 0;
    memcpy(remote->buffer, msg, msg_length);
    remote->rx_ready = 1;
}

void recv_msg(void* msg)
{
    while( !rx_ready )
        tripwire_wait(rx_ready_trip);
    rx_ready = 0;
    memcpy(msg, buffer, msg_length);
    remote->tx_ready = 1;
}
```

Example 1: Simple message transfer.

This protocol will work as described on any PRAM-consistent shared memory system — the difficulty being synchronising with updates to the `tx/rx_ready` flags. This is achieved using Tripwires.

A C program implementing this protocol is shown in Example 1. For simplicity the example shows that the message data is copied twice — into and out of the message buffer — but this is not necessary. The sender could write the message data directly into the remote buffer, and on the receiving side the application could read the message contents directly from the message buffer, giving true zero copy.

We have used this simple protocol to support a remote procedure call (RPC) style of interaction. The client writes a request into the server's message buffer, and when the RPC completes the result is written back into the client's message buffer. This arrangement only requires two control flags and two Tripwires (one in the client and one in the server), since the order in which messages can be sent is restricted.

4.2 A distributed queue

A disadvantage of the above protocol is that the sender and receiver are tightly coupled — they must synchronise at each message transfer. This prevents streaming and hence decreases bandwidth. This can be alleviated by using a queue as shown in Figure 4. The corresponding C program is shown in Example 2.

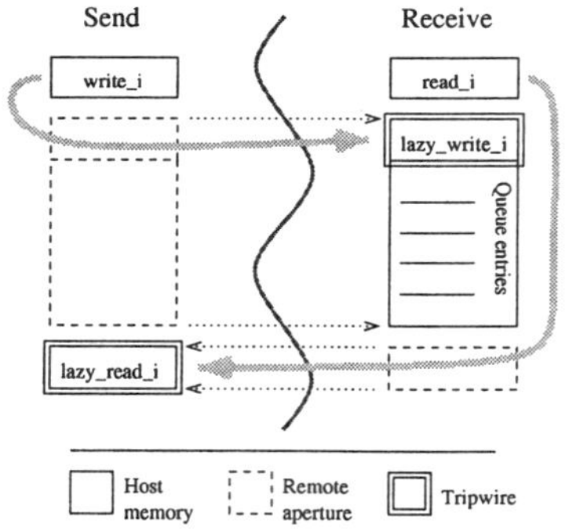

Figure 4. A distributed queue

This implementation works similarly to a type of queue commonly used within applications. Fixed size messages are stored in a circular buffer. Two counters, `read_i` and `write_i`, give the positions in the buffer at which the next message should be dequeued and enqueued respectively.

The traditional implementation uses an additional flag to distinguish between the full and empty cases when the counters are equal. However, this requires a lock to ensure atomic update, which would significantly degrade performance in a distributed implementation. For this reason we do not use the additional flag; the queue is considered to be empty when the counters are equal, and full when there is only one empty slot in the receive buffer. This effectively reduces the size of the queue by one.

```
void q_put(const q_elm* elm)
{
    while( (write_i + 1) % q_size == lazy_read_i )
        tripwire_wait(lazy_read_i_trip);
    remote->q[write_i] = *elm;
    write_i = (write_i + 1) % q_size;
    remote->lazy_write_i = write_i;
}

void q_get(q_elm* elm)
{
    while( read_i == lazy_write_i )
        tripwire_wait(lazy_write_i_trip);
    *elm = q[read_i];
    read_i = (read_i + 1) % q_size;
    remote->lazy_read_i = read_i;
}
```

Example 2: A distributed queue.

The distribution of the control state between the sender and receiver is motivated by the desire to avoid cross-network reads. The sender 'owns' the `write_i` counter, which it updates each time a message is written into the remote buffer. A copy of this counter, `lazy_write_i`, is held in the receiver, the sender copying the value of `write_i` to `lazy_write_i` each time the former is updated. The `read_i` counter is maintained similarly, with the receiver owning the definitive value.

Thus the sender's and receiver's lazy copies of `read_i` and `write_i` respectively may briefly be out-of-date. This is *safe* though, since the effect is that the receiver may see fewer messages in the buffer than there really are, and the sender may believe that the buffer contains more messages than it does. The inconsistency is quickly resolved.

4.3 Discussion

When designing the two protocols given above, care was taken to ensure that all cross-network access were writes. This is important because reads have a relatively high latency, and generate more network traffic. In each case the control variables that must be read by an endpoint are stored in local memory. This memory is cacheable, so polling the endpoints is very efficient.

It is interesting to note that both of the protocols given above will work correctly without Tripwires, by polling the values of the control variables, and this choice can be made independently in the transmitter and receiver. Tripwires merely provide a flexible way to synchronise efficiently, and a number of enhancements are possible:

- If a message is expected soon, the application may choose to poll the control variables for a few microseconds before blocking. This reduces latency and overhead by avoiding a system call.[16]
- It is possible to overlap data transfer with scheduling of the receiving application. This is done by setting a Tripwire in the receiving application for some memory location that will be written early in the message transfer, and going to sleep. The application will be rescheduled as the rest of the message is being transfered, thus reducing latency.
- It is even possible to begin processing the header of a message in parallel with receiving the body, by setting separate Tripwires for the header and body of the message.
- DMA or PIO can be used for the data transfer. The choice will depend on the characteristics of the application and the size of the messages.
- The distributed queue can be adapted in a number of ways, including support for streaming unstructured data, sending multi-part messages, and passing meta-data.

5 Raw Performance

In this section we present a number of micro-benchmarks which demonstrate the raw performance of the hardware, and how this translates into high performance for practical applications. All tests are performed at user-level.

5.1 System characterisation

The test nodes are 530 MHz Alpha systems running the Linux 2.2 operating system. Fine grain timing was performed using the free running 32-bit cycle counter. A number of system parameters were first measured:

- The system call overhead (measured using an *ioctl*) is about $.75\mu s$. The true overhead of system calls is made significantly worse, however, by the effect they have on the cache.
- The scheduler overhead when a single process is un-blocked is $8\mu s$.
- The interrupt latency is $3\mu s$.

5.2 Shared memory

These benchmarks exercise the distributed shared memory interface, and use 'spinning' for synchronisation.

1. The round-trip time for a single DWORD was measured by repeatedly writing a word to a known location in a remote application, which then copied that word into a known location in the sending application. The round-trip time is $3.7\mu s$. This gives an application to application one-way latency of $1.4\mu s$.

2. The raw bandwidth was found by measuring the interval between the arrival of the first DWORD of a message at the processor, and arrival of the last DWORD. Figure 5 shows the results for DMA and PIO. Peak bandwidth is 910 Mbit/s, and is limited by a stall for one cycle on the receiving V3 PCI bridge at the start of each burst.

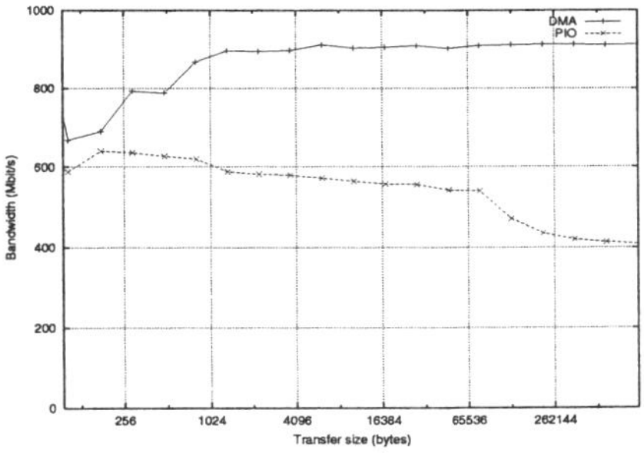

Figure 5. Raw bandwidth vs. size

The plots given in Figure 5 need some further explanation. Firstly, it is not possible to meaningfully measure the bandwidth for messages smaller than about 256 bytes, since blocking effects of the cache and various bus bridges dominate. The latency across the NIC hardware (measured using a logic analyser) is about $.5\mu s$, so $.9\mu s$ are spent traversing buses and bridges — which are likely holding data back in order to generate large bursts — and cache loading.

The surprising results for programmed I/O are due to a bug in the V3. Under some circumstances, the V3's internal FIFOs lock, causing the V3 to emit single word bursts until the FIFOs drain. A workaround in our FPGA logic detects this condition, and backs off for a time to allow the V3 to recover. This effect causes the negative gradient seen in the figure.

The receiving V3 generates 16 DWORD bursts on the PCI bus for PIO traffic, and 256 DWORDS for DMA traffic. Together with the additional V3 stall at the start of each burst, this severely limits the PIO bandwidth. To address this we have some initial work implementing coalescing of bursts on the receiving NIC. Initial tests suggest that with this logic in place the performance of PIO will be very similar to that of DMA.

5.3 An event-based server

The benchmarks presented in this section are designed to exercise the Tripwire synchronisation primitive, and show how this interface scales and performs under load.

The server is built using a single-threaded event processing model, the main event loop being based on the standard BSD *select* system call. The file descriptor corresponding to an asynchronous event queue (section 3.5) is a member of the *select set*, and becomes readable when there are entries in the queue. In this case a handler extracts events from the queue and dispatches them to call-back functions associated with each endpoint. This event queue is serviced until it is empty, and then polled for up to $15\mu s$ before returning to the main select loop.

When a connection is established a Tripwire is initialised to detect client requests. This Tripwire is registered with the asynchronous event queue, and the request management code receives a call-back whenever a request arrives.

The test client makes a connection to the server, and issues requests to perform the various benchmarks. When waiting for an acknowledgement or reply the client spins, which is reasonable since the reply will usually arrive in less time that it takes for a process to go to sleep and be rescheduled.

5.4 Round-trip time

In the first set of tests we measure the round-trip time for a small message under differing conditions of server load. Each test is repeated a large number of times, and the result reported is the mean:

- When a large ($> 15\mu s$) gap is left between each request the server goes to sleep between requests, and the round-trip time consists of the transmit overhead, the hardware latency, the interrupt overhead, the rescheduling overhead, the message processing overhead and the reply. The total is $16.8\mu s$.

- As explained in Section 3.5, a server using the asynchronous event queue becomes more efficient when kept busy, since it avoids going to sleep. In this benchmark messages are sent as quickly as possible, one after another, but with only one message in flight at a time. In this case the round-trip time consists of the same steps as above, but without the reschedule, and improved cache performance. The round-trip time is reduced to just $7.9\mu s$.

- Figure 6(a) shows how the server performs as the number of connections increases. The two traces correspond to the server being busy and idle, as above. The client chooses a connection at random for each request. As expected, the *response time is independent of the number of connections.*

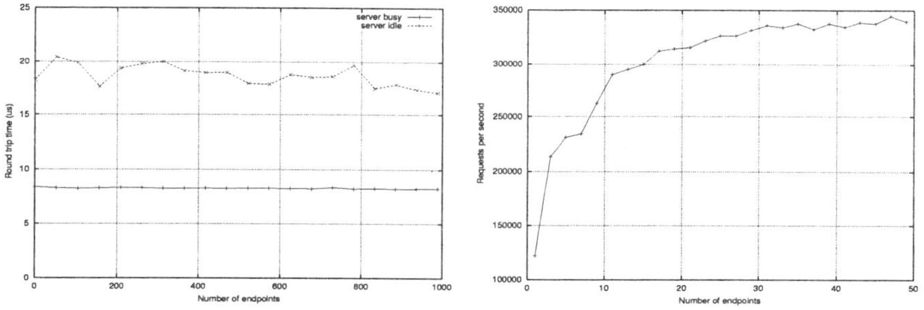

(a) Round-trip time

(b) Request throughput

Figure 6. Scalability with number of endpoints

- In the final test multiple requests are sent by the client on different connections before collecting each of the replies. This simulates the effect of multiple clients in the network, and is shown in Figure 6(b). Note that even when the server is overloaded the performance of the network interface is not degraded.

  The curve is tending towards 340000 requests per second, and given that the server is effectively performing a no-op, we can assume that all the processor time is spent processing messages. Thus the total per-message overhead on the server when fully loaded is $1/340000s$, or $2.9\mu s$.

5.5 Bandwidth

Figure 7 shows the bandwidth achieved sending various sizes of message one way to the server, the server acknowledging each message.

- For curve (a) each message is sent as a single DMA, and acknowledged by

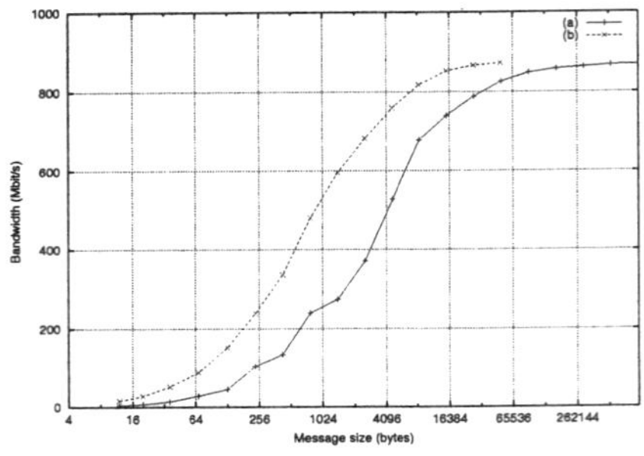

Figure 7. Unidirectional bandwidth vs message size for (a) single messages in flight and (b) streaming

the server. The client waits for the acknowledgement before sending the next message.

- Curve (b) shows the bandwidth when streaming messages. Each message is sent using DMA, and the next is started without waiting for acknowledgement of the first.

Curve (b) corresponds closely to the theoretical throughput for a link with a bandwidth of 900 Mbps and a setup time of $6\mu s$. This consists of the $3\mu s$ interrupt latency and the time taken to setup the next transfer. The interrupt overhead will be eliminated when user-level programmable DMA and chaining are supported in the hardware. Note that half the maximum available bandwidth is achieved with messages of about 750 bytes in size.

Another study[17] has compared the performance of a number of user-level communication interfaces implemented on the Myrinet interconnect, which has raw performance comparable with the CLAN NIC. Their 'Unidirectional Bandwidth' experiment is equivalent to this one, and out of AM, BIP, FM, PM and VMMC-2, only PM gives better performance than the CLAN NIC. PM[18] is a specialised network interface not suitable for general purpose networking.

6 Supporting Applications

It is important that innovations in network interface design translate into real performance improvements at the application level, for existing as well as new applications. Support for existing applications can be provided at a number of levels:

- Implement an in-kernel device driver.

- Recompile applications against a source-compatible API.
- Replace dynamically loaded libraries.

Of these 2 is likely to give the best performance, but is at best inconvenient, and often not possible. An in kernel solution will provide binary compatibility with existing applications, but performance is likely to be relatively poor due to the high overheads associated with interrupts, the protocol stack, cache thrashing and context switches. The last solution works well when the network abstraction is provided at a high level, as is the case with middleware such as CORBA.

We are actively porting a number of representative protocols and applications to our network interface, and this section presents some initial results.

6.1 IP

The Internet Protocol is the transport of choice for the majority of communication applications, and has been implemented over almost all network technologies. Because the protocol is presented to applications at a very low level, and must be fully integrated with the other I/O subsystems,[f] it is difficult to provide a fully functional implementation at user-level. We have thus chosen initially to provide support by presenting the network interface to the kernel using a standard network device driver.[19]

The implementation is illustrated in Figure 8. A single connection is made on demand between pairs of nodes which need to communicate using IP. The receiving node pre-allocates a small number of buffers, and passes RDMA cookies for these buffers to the sending node through a distributed queue (as described in Section 4.2). Completion messages are passed through another queue in the opposite direction.

Data transfer consists of the following steps:

1. The Linux networking subsystem passes in a buffer (`struct sk_buff`) containing the packet data to send.
2. The packet data is transfered across the network by DMA, using an RDMA cookie from the distributed queue as the target.
3. A completion message is written into the completion queue.
4. On the receive side, a Tripwire is used to synchronise with writes into the completion queue. The buffer containing the packet data is passed on to the networking subsystem.

---

[f] Using *select* or *poll* on UNIX systems

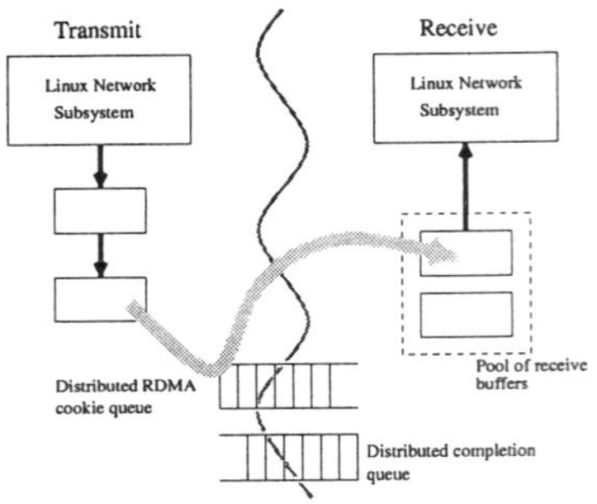

Figure 8. The implementation of CLAN IP

5. New buffers are allocated if necessary, and their RDMA cookies are passed back to the transmitting node. The distributed RDMA cookie queue effectively provides flow control, so we aim to prevent it from emptying, since this would cause the sender to stall.

Although the development of this implementation is still work in progress, we have some preliminary results from an early version. In Table 1 we compare the round trip time and small message bandwidth for CLAN IP with fast- and gigabit ethernet technology. The test uses TCP/IP, repeatedly sending and returning a message.

Table 1. Round trip time and bandwidth for CLAN and ethernet.

	RTT	B/W at 1KByte
CLAN IP	$100\mu s$	225 Mbit/s
100 Mbit ethernet	$160\mu s$	23 Mbit/s
Gigabit ethernet	$260\mu s$	23-28 Mbit/s

Figure 9 shows the bandwidth achieved against message size for the same test. The gigabit ethernet was configured to use jumbo frames and large socket buffers (256 kilobytes) to improve its performance, whereas CLAN IP is using just 32 kilobytes per socket buffer.

Due to a bug in the CLAN NIC which caused deadlocks[9] at the time of this experiment, the bandwidth is limited to 250 Mbit/s, so no conclusions can be drawn

[9] The deadlocks are due to our implementation using a shared bus for transmit, receive and Tripwire traffic. The shared bus architecture is a consequence of using off-the-shelf components.

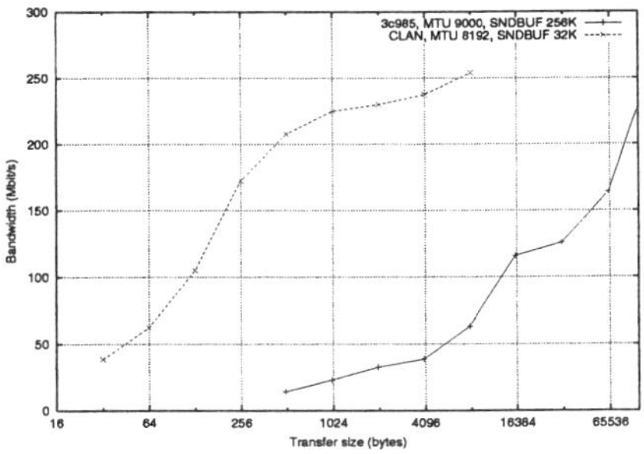

Figure 9. TCP/IP bandwidth for CLAN and gigabit ethernet, as a function of message size

as to the maximum bandwidth that can be achieved over CLAN IP. Further, this implementation was only able to support a single packet in flight at any one time. We expect the small message bandwidth to be significantly improved with the new implementation, which allows streaming. Despite these problems CLAN IP is able to deliver nearly 10 times the performance of gigabit ethernet for 1 kilobyte messages.

6.2 NFS

Another service which we have implemented in the Linux kernel is the Sun Network File System Protocol[20] (NFS). The implementation consists of two sets of modifications:

- The SunRPC layer runs over a custom socket implementation over the CLAN NIC.
- A number of DMA optimisations are added at higher levels in the NFS subsystem to increase performance for file data transfer.

A CLAN connection is setup when a filesystem is mounted. NFS messages are passed through the socket layer via the SunRPC layer, whilst file data is transfered using DMA directly from the Linux buffer cache into the receiving node. As a further optimisation it is possible to transfer file data directly from the disk to the receiving node, bypassing local host memory altogether. Whether this results in a performance gain depends on the pattern of file access, and the performance of the disk controller cache.

We have not been able to perform any standard NFS benchmarks, since these mandate the use of the UDP protocol, and often implement the client side NFS. It would be necessary to implement an ethernet UDP to CLAN bridge to make use of these tests.

As an initial empirical guide we have timed the task of compiling the Linux kernel on a local file system, and one imported over NFS. In both cases the *ext2* file system is used. For the local filesystem the compile time is 6 minutes 42 seconds, and over NFS it is 6 minutes 45 seconds. Although compilation is typically a CPU bound process, it was not parallelised in this test, so file system overhead makes a significant contribution to the compile time. This result suggests that importing a file system over CLAN NFS has very low overhead.

6.3 MPI

In order to test the performance of existing applications designed to use clusters of workstations, we have ported the Message Passing Interface standard to the CLAN network. The LAM[21] implementation was chosen for its efficient interface to the transport layer, requiring the implementation of only 9 functions. The entire MPI standard is fully supported.

Synchronisation is achieved by spinning, so this implementation is most suitable for use in a system dedicated to a single problem. The round-trip time is $16\mu s$, which compares favourably with other systems, such as MPI-BIP,[22] which has a round-trip time of $19\mu s$. It is interesting to note that MPI-BIP is implemented at a higher level than our version, so reducing the library overheads.

We are developing a second version using Tripwires for synchronisation, which will be suitable for use in a general purpose workstation, and coexist well with other applications. This implementation will spin for a few micro-seconds before going to sleep if no events occur — so we expect the performance to be comparable with the first version when heavily loaded.

We have tested our first implementation using the *N-body* problem, and will present these results and a detailed discussion of the implementation at a later date.

7 Related Work

Although designed as a multiprocessor system, rather than an interconnect for heterogeneous networks, the FLASH[2] project shares many of our goals. These include efficient support for a wide range of protocols in a general purpose multiprogrammed environment. The FLASH multicomputer provides cache-coherent distributed shared memory and message passing. Protocol specific message handlers run on a dedicated protocol processor in each node, and can be used to provide flexible and efficient synchronisation.

The Myrinet network interface has been used to implement a large number of user-level networks. Like the CLAN NIC, it is implemented as a PCI card, and provides gigabit class raw performance. A programmable RISC processor is used to implement a particular communications model, making this platform ideal for research purposes. A disadvantage of this approach is that at any one time, the network is programmed to support just one model, and so it is difficult to provide simultaneous support for diverse protocols. Another problem is that data is staged in memory on the NIC, which leads to a latency/bandwidth tradeoff, as explored in the Trapeze[23] project.

Other important distributed shared memory based systems include DEC Memory Channel,[3] the Scalable Coherent Interface,[12] SHRIMP[6] and BIP.[22] All of these have addressed the requirements for high bandwidth, low latency data transfer, providing excellent performance for a particular class of problem, but support for synchronisation is often inflexible.

The U-Net[1] project was the first to present a user-level interface to local area networks, using off-the-shelf communications hardware. U-Net heavily influenced the Virtual Interface Architecture,[24] which provides a communication model based on asynchronous message passing through work queues. Completion queues multiplex transmit and receive events, so performance scales well with the number of endpoints. Disadvantages include relatively high overhead, which leads to poor performance for small messages, and high per-endpoint resource requirements.[25] End to end flow control must be explicitly handled by the application, as buffer overrun on the receive side leads to the connection being closed.

8 Conclusions

The CLAN project has addressed the problem of synchronisation in distributed shared memory systems. Our solution, the *Tripwire*, provides an efficient means for flexible and scalable synchronisation.

Tripwires have a number of advantages over existing solutions to the synchronisation problem. Synchronisation is orthogonal to data transfer, since applications may synchronise with arbitrary in-band data. A consequence of this is that synchronisation is decoupled from the transmitter, allowing great flexibility in the receiver.

In this paper we have presented a high performance network interconnect based on distributed shared memory with Tripwires for synchronisation, and shown that it delivers gigabit class bandwidth and very low overhead and latency for data transfer. The low-level software interface provides a flexible means for synchronisation that is highly scalable. These characteristics translate to high throughput and short response times for high-level protocols and practical applications.

For applications such as parallel number-crunching and multicomputer servers the performance is comparable with, and often exceeds that achieved by other specialised network interfaces. At the same time superior performance is delivered to multiprogrammed systems, making the CLAN NIC suitable for general purpose local area networks, and expanding the space of problems that can be tackled on them.

We believe that significant benefits are drawn from tailoring the network abstraction to the application, and by presenting the network interface at a low level it is possible to implement a wide range of abstractions efficiently.

9 Future Work

The authors are currently working on a number of enhancements to the CLAN network. We have just built the first prototype of a high performance, worm-hole routed switch, and will soon begin testing. Like the NIC, the switch is based on FPGA technology, and will allow us to experiment with wire protocols and routing.

In the next revision of the NIC we will implement user-level programmable Tripwires. This should further the reduce the overhead of synchronisation, and will be achieved by providing *Virtual Memory Mapped Commands* as used in the SHRIMP multicomputer[6]. We also intend to provide DMA chaining, which should significantly reduce message passing overhead and increase small message bandwidth. Another enhancement is hardware delivery of Tripwire notification to user-level. This will reduce the number of interrupts taken and reduce Tripwire notification latency.

At a higher-level, we are investigating how this network interface can be used to improve the performance of middleware. We are developing a software implementation of the Virtual Interface Architecture, and intend to implement a high-performance transport for a CORBA ORB.

Other areas for future research include:

- User-level reprogramming of aperture mappings. A number of other projects have enhanced existing network interfaces with flexible memory management[26][27]. It should be possible to extend this with re-mapping of local and remote apertures at user-level, using a pool of virtual memory mappings onto the NIC.

- Hardware delivery of out-of-band messages directly into an user-level queue. Together with reprogramming of aperture mappings, this would make it possible to perform connection setup entirely at user-level.

Acknowledgements

The authors would like to thank all of the members of AT&T Laboratories Cambridge and the Laboratory for Communications Engineering. David Riddoch is also funded by the Royal Commission for the Exhibition of 1851.

The work on coalescing write bursts to improve PIO bandwidth was performed by Chris Richardson whilst on an internship at AT&T.

References

1. Thorsten von Eicken, Anindya Basu, Vineet Buch, and Werner Vogels. U-Net: A User-Level Network Interface for Parallel and Distributed Computing. In *15th ACM Symposium on Operating Systems Principles*, December 1995.
2. Jeffrey Kuskin, David Ofelt, Mark Heinrich, John Heinlein, Richard Simoni, Kourosh Gharachorloo, John Chapin, David Nakahira, Joel Baxter, Mark Horowitz, Anoop Gupta, Mendel Rosenblum, and John Hennessy. The Stanford FLASH Multiprocessor. In *21st International Symposium on Computer Architecture*, pages 302–313, April 1994.
3. R. Gillett and R. Kaufmann. Using the Memory Channel Network. *IEEE Micro*, 17(1), 1997.
4. Maximilian Ibel, Klaus Schauser, Chris Scheiman, and Manfred Weis. High Performance Cluster Computing using SCI. In *Hot Interconnects V*, August 1997.
5. Nanette Boden, Danny Cohen, Robert Felderman, Alan Kulawik, Charles Seitz, Javoc Seizovic, and Wen-King Su. Myrinet — A Gigabit-per-Second Local-Area Network. *IEEE Micro*, 15(1), 1995.
6. Matthias Blumrich, Kai Li, Richard Alpert, Cezary Dubnicki, Edward Felten, and Jonathan Sandberg. Virtual Memory Mapped Network Interface for the SHRIMP Multicomputer. In *21st Annual Symposium on Computer Architecture*, pages 142–153, April 1994.
7. David Culler and Jaswinder Pal Singh. *Parallel Computer Architecture, A Hardware/Software Approach*, chapter 7, page 520. Morgan Kaufmann.
8. Steve Hodges, Steve Pope, Derek Roberts, Glenford Mapp, and Andy Hopper. Remoting Peripherals using Memory-Mapped Networks. Technical Report 98.7, AT&T Laboratories Cambridge, 1998.
9. Maurice Wilkes and Andrew Hopper. The Collapsed LAN: a Solution to a Bandwidth Problem? *Computer Architecture News*, 25(3), July 1997.
10. Richard Lipton and Jonathan Sandberg. PRAM: A Scalable Shared Memory. Technical report, Princeton University, 1988.
11. David Culler and Jaswinder Pal Singh. *Parallel Computer Architecture, A Hardware/Software Approach*, chapter 10, page 818. Morgan Kaufmann.
12. IEEE. Standard for Scalable Coherent Interface, March 1992. IEEE Std 1596-1992.
13. David Riddoch and Steve Pope. A Low Overhead Application-Device Driver Interface for User-Level Networking. Paper in preparation.

14. Gaurav Banga and Jeffrey Mogul. Scalable kernel performance for Internet servers under realistic loads. In *USENIX Technical Conference*, June 1998.
15. Gaurav Banga, Jeffrey Mogul, and Peter Druschel. A scalable and explicit event delivery mechanism for UNIX. In *USENIX Technical Conference*, June 1999.
16. Stefanos Damianakis, Yuqun Chen, and Edward Felten. Reducing Waiting Costs in User-Level Communication. In *11th International Parallel Processing Symposium*, April 1997.
17. Soichiro Araki, Angelos Bilas, Cezary Dubnicki, Jan Edler, Koichi Konishi, and James Philbin. User-Space Communications: A Quantitative Study. In *SuperComputing*, November 1998.
18. Hiroshi Tezuka, Atsushi Hori, and Yutaka Ishikawa. PM: A High-Performance Communication Library for Multi-user Environments. Technical Report TR-96015, Tsukuba Research Center RWCP, 1996.
19. Alessandro Rubini. *Linux Device Drivers*, chapter 14 Network Drivers. O'Reilly, 1998.
20. Sun Microsystems. NFS: Network File System Protocol Specification, 1989. RFC 1050.
21. LAM / MPI Parallel Computing. `http://www.mpi.nd.edu/lam/`.
22. Loic Prylli, Bernard Tourancheau, and Roland Westrelin. The design for a high performance MPI implementation on the Myrinet network. In *EuroPVM/MPI*, pages 223–230, 1999.
23. Kenneth Yocum, Darrell Anderson, Jeffrey Chase, Syam Gadde, Andrew Gallatin, and Alvin Lebeck. Balancing DMA Latency and Bandwidth in a High-Speed Network Adapter. Technical Report TR-1997-20, Duke University, 1997.
24. *The Virtual Interface Architecture*. `http://www.viarch.org/`.
25. Philip Buonadonna, Andrew Geweke, and David Culler. An implementation and analysis of the virtual interface architecture. In *Supercomputing*, Nov 1998.
26. Cezary Dubnicki, Angelos Bilas, Yuqun Chen, Stefanos Damianakis, and Kai Li. VMMC-2: Efficient Support for Reliable, Connection-Oriented Communication. In *Hot Interconnects V*, August 1997.
27. Matt Welsh, Anindya Basu, and Thorsten von Eicken. Incorporating Memory Management into User-Level Network Interfaces. In *Hot Interconnects V*, August 1997.

SIMULATION OF SELF-SIMILAR TRAFFIC AND A TCP TRAFFIC SIMULATOR

MING LI, WEIJIA JIA
Dept. of Computer Science, City University of Hong Kong, Kowloon, Hong Kong
E-mail: {mingli, wjia}@cs.cityu.edu.hk

WEI ZHAO
Dept. of Computer Science, Texas A&M University, College Station, USA
E-mail: wzhao@cs.tamu.edu

This paper presents a simulation method of self-similar traffic and a type of TCP traffic simulators based on autocorrelation sequences. The impulse function of a simulator is carried out. The parameter estimations for modeling the impulse function of the simulator are determined by multidimensional nonlinear least squares fitting. The existence and the uniqueness of solutions for the multidimensional nonlinear least squares are proved based on convex analysis.

Keywords: traffic simulation, self-similarity, linear systems, curve fitting

1 Introduction

Simulations of short-range dependent processes have been paid attention to in many fields of engineering for years and successful applications have been achieved [1-10]. One of the popular methods for simulating short-range dependent processes is based on the power spectra of the processes to be simulated. A remarkable event in traffic engineering as well as in random processes is the discovery that package-switched traffic is of long-range dependence or self-similar [11-15]. Self-similar (long-range dependent) processes are different from short-range dependent ones substantially. For instance, the autocorrelation functions of self-similar processes are nonsummable while the autocorrelation functions of Poisson processes are summable. Because the autocorrelation functions are nonsummable, the power spectra of self-similar processes contain the components of Dirac-δ functions. Thus, conventional simulation methods based on power spectra are difficult to use since the explanations of the power spectra of self-similar processes are in the field of distribution theory and this would take us too far from realistic applications [16-20]. Therefore, we study the simulation based on autocorrelation functions.

In the aspect of traffic simulation, efforts have been made on the parametrically estimated autocorrelation functions [21-22], variance-time plot model [23-24] and ARMA model [25]. As mentioned in Section 2, there may be a variety of autocorrelation functions for the same type of traffic. Therefore, it is essential to find a simulation method without a priori information of the parametric estimations of autocorrelation functions.

Traffic simulation may be performed as follows. Let $w(n)$ be a white noise sequence, $h(n)$ be an impulse function of a simulator (linear system), $y(n)$ be the output to the simulator and $x(n)$ the traffic to be simulated. Then, the simulation depends on designing a filter h such that $y = w*h$ under the condition of $r_y = r_x$ where r_y and r_x are the autocorrelation sequences of y and x respectively. As discussed in Section 3, an analytical expression of h may not be achieved even if the analytical expression of r_x is known. Therefore, we study analytical expression of impulse functions by least squares fitting without a priori information of the parametric estimations of autocorrelation functions. However, because of the nonlinearity of impulse functions, the least square fitting concerned is nonlinear. Mathematically, multidimensional nonlinear least squares fitting may result in a nonlinear set of equations. Consequently, it is essential to give the proof of the existence and the uniqueness of solutions.

The paper is structured as follows. Section 2 gives the related contents of the self-similar processes and puts forward the problems. Section 3 discusses the design of simulators. Section 4 proves the existence and the uniqueness of solutions for the multidimensional nonlinear least squares fitting related to the design of simulators. Section 5 gives an application of our method to designing a type of simulators for wide-area TCP traffic. Finally, Section 6 concludes the paper.

2 Problems Put Forward

A traffic data sequence in communication networks is called traffic trace $x(t)$. For wide-area TCP traffic, $x(t)$ indicates the number of bytes in the packet at t. The self-similar processes can be defined by autocorrelation functions and they are classified into two models. One is exactly self-similar model and the other asymptotically self-similar model [26-27].

Let $X = (X_t\colon t = 1, 2, \cdots)$ be a covariance stationary second-order stochastic process with mean $\mu = E(X_t)$ and variance $\sigma^2 = Var(X_t)$. A process X is called exactly second-order self-similar with parameter $H \in (0.5, 1)$, if its autocorrelation function is

$$r(k) = \frac{1}{2}\,[(k+1)^{2H} - 2k^{2H} + (k-1)^{2H}],\ k \in I, \tag{2-1}$$

where I is the set of integers. A process X is called asymptotically second-order self-similar with parameter $H \in (0.5, 1)$, if its autocorrelation function is with the form

$$r(k) \sim ck^{2H-2}\ (k \to \infty), \tag{2-2}$$

where $c > 0$ is a constant and $\sim$ stands for asymptotically equivalent.

The main properties and constraint of self-similar processes are summarized below.

P1: $r(k)$ is an even function.
P2: $r(0) \geq |r(k)|$.
C1: $\sum_k r(k) = \infty$.

It was concluded that the exactly second-order self-similar model is too narrow to model real traffic [27, pp. 713] while the asymptotically self-similar model with fixed finite lag has not been specified exactly [26, pp. 101-102]. This is a problem for simulating a self-similar traffic trace desired based on the exact knowledge of its closed form of autocorrelation function. For instance, [21] proposed the following correlation structure

$$r(k) = e^{-\beta k} \ (\beta > 0) \tag{2-3}$$

for *compressed-video* sequences but the function $e^{-\beta k}$ is not of long-range dependence because $e^{-\beta k}$ is summable. [22] presented the following model also for *compressed-video* sequences

$$r(k) = L k_i^{-\beta} U(k \geq k_i) + \sum_{i=1}^{J} w_i \exp(-\lambda_i k) U(k < k_i),\ k = 1, 2, \cdots, 0 < \beta < 1. \tag{2-4}$$

where $\sum_{i=1}^{J} w_i = 1$ and $L k_i^{-\beta} = \sum_{i=1}^{J} w_i \ exp(-\lambda_i k_i)$, L is a constant, k_i is the lag value corresponding to the "knee" of the curve of an autocorrelation function approximated, λ_i is the rate of exp(.) and $U(.)$ is the indicator function. Eq. (2-3) is obviously different from (2-4) but they are for the same type of traffic. In addition, for the same traffic traces provided in [32], [24] used variance-time plot to obtain $H \approx 0.81$~0.82, [25] utilized ARMA model to get $H \approx 0.582$~0.591 and other more [28-31]. Hence, the variety of the Hurst parameter estimations for the same traffic is obvious. Consequently, it is meaningful to simulate traffic without a priori information of the parametric estimations of autocorrelation functions.

When the impulse functions are modeled by multidimensional nonlinear least squares fitting, a nonlinear set of equations appears. Thus, for the proposed method of traffic simulation, the existence and the uniqueness of solutions for the multidimensional nonlinear least squares fitting are issues that should be discussed.

3 Scheme of Simulation

Let $w(n)$ be the white noise sequence with mean μ and standard deviation σ, $h(n)$ be the impulse response of a linear time-invariant system (simulator) and $y(n)$ the output sequence to the system. The relationship between them is

$$y(n) = w(n) * h(n), \tag{3-1}$$

where $*$ stands for the operation of convolution. Suppose that simulation of a sequence $x(n)$ is required and its measured autocorrelation function is r_x. Then, to simulate x can be achieved by designing a filter h such that

$$r_x = r_y, \tag{3-2}$$

where r_y is the autocorrelation function of y. In this case, y is statistically identical to x in the sense of $r_x = r_y$. In frequency domain, Eq. (3-1) is expressed as

$$Y(\omega) = W(\omega)H(\omega), \tag{3-3}$$

where $Y(\omega)$, $W(\omega)$ and $H(\omega)$ are Fourier transforms of y, w and h respectively. Let

$$H(\omega) = \sigma^{-2}[S_x(\omega)]^{0.5}, \tag{3-4}$$

where $S_x(\omega)$ is the power spectrum of x. Then,

$$Y(\omega) = \sigma^{-2}W(\omega)[S_x(\omega)]^{0.5}. \tag{3-5}$$

In time domain, there is

$$y(n) = \sigma^{-2}w(n) * \mathcal{F}^{-1}\{[\mathcal{F}(r_x)]^{0.5}\}, \tag{3-6}$$

where $\mathcal{F}$ and $\mathcal{F}^{-1}$ are operators of Fourier transform and its inverse respectively. Clearly, in this case,

$$S_y(\omega) = S_x(\omega) \text{ and } r_x = r_y. \tag{3-7}$$

where $S_y(\omega)$ is the power spectrum of y. Thus, we obtain a simulator

$$h(n) = \sigma^{-2}\, \mathcal{F}^{-1}\{[\mathcal{F}(r_x)]^{0.5}\}. \tag{3-8}$$

Eq. (3-4) is the representation of simulator in frequency domain while (3-8) in time domain. Both are suitable for simulating self-similar processes as well as short-range dependent processes. Eq. (3-6) means that the simulation of x is a white noise colored by $\sigma^{-2}\mathcal{F}^{-1}\{[\mathcal{F}(r_x)]^{0.5}\}$.

It is noted that the analytic expression of h is difficult to obtain even if the analytic expression of r_x is known if x is of long-range dependence. For instance, if a nonsummable autocorrelation function is

$$r_x = \exp(-10t) + 0.2u(t-10),\ t \ge 0, \tag{3-9}$$

then

$$\mathcal{F}(r_x) = \frac{1}{10 + j\omega} + 0.2\pi\delta(\omega) + \frac{0.2}{j\omega}\exp(-j10\omega), \tag{3-10}$$

where $u(t)$ is Heaviside's unit function and $\delta(\omega)$ is Dirac-δ function. The difficulty to perform the operation of $\mathcal{F}^{-1}\{[\mathcal{F}(r_x)]^{0.5}\}$ over (3-10) is clear. Therefore, we focus on the design of filters based on the parameter estimations of impulse functions.

4 Parameter Estimations of Impulse Functions

In fact, a real-traffic trace concerned is a sequence with finite length. Besides, the length is finite when practical numerical computation is performed. Without losing the generality, the maximum possible length of x is assumed as $p \in I_0$ (= 0, 1, 2, $\cdots$). Let $N \in I_0$ and $N \gg p$. Then, N may be regarded as an "infinite" in the engineering sense. Thus, the following set

$$\mathcal{H} = \left\{ h; \|h\| = \sum_{n=0}^{N} |h|^2 < \infty \right\} \tag{4-1}$$

is a Hilbert space. Define a set of impulse functions with m parameters

$$h_1(n) = h_1(n; a_1, a_2, \cdots, a_m) \tag{4-2}$$

and the set

$$\mathcal{H}_1 = \{h_1(n); h_1(n) = h_1(n; a_1, a_2, \cdots, a_m)\}. \tag{4-3}$$

The set $\mathcal{H}_1$ is constructed such that

$$\mathcal{H}_1 \subset \mathcal{H}. \tag{4-4}$$

In the expressions above, $h(n)$ is the model to be fitted while $h_1(n)$ is the modeling of $h(n)$. Let $M^2(h_1) = E[(h_1 - h)^2]$ be the mean square error. The value of $M^2(h_1)$ is used to evaluate the quality of curve fitting. In our scheme, $M^2(h_1) < 10^{-3}$ is required. Hence, one of the methods to construct an impulse function based on the measured autocorrelation sequences of traffic is to find a function h_1 that fits h under the condition of $M^2(h_1) < 10^{-3}$.

Let the error

$$e(n) = h_1(n) - h(n) \tag{4-5}$$

and the cost function

$$f(e) = \sum_n [h_1(n) - h(n)]^2 = J(a_1, a_2, \cdots, a_m). \tag{4-6}$$

It is clear that the estimation of $(a_1, a_2, \cdots, a_m)$ is the approximated vector root of $J(a_1, a_2, \cdots, a_m) \triangleq J(\boldsymbol{a}) = 0$. Thus, the partial derivative of J with respect to the parameters $\boldsymbol{a}$, which will be zero at the J minimum, has components

$$\frac{\partial J}{\partial a_i} = 2\sum_n (h_1 - h)\frac{\partial h_1}{\partial a_i}, \; i = 1, 2, \cdots, m. \tag{4-7}$$

Basically, h is nonlinear. Thus, Eq. (4-7) yields a nonlinear set of equations in m dimensions. Because a nonlinear set of equations may have no (real) solutions or may have more than one solution [33] [35], it is needed to study both the existence and the uniqueness of solution of $J = 0$ for the purpose of modeling h.

Statement 1. Let $h \in \mathcal{H}$ be an impulse obtained by (3-8). There exists a unique element $h_1 \in \mathcal{H}_1$ such that

$$\|h-h_1\| = \inf_{s\in\mathcal{L}_1}\|h-s\| \tag{4-8}$$

where $\|h - h_1\| = \|e\| = \sum_k [h_1(k) - h(k)]^2 = f(e)$.

Proof. $\mathcal{L}$ is an obvious convex set and $f(e) = \|e\|$ is a convex functional defined on $\mathcal{L}$ because $f[\lambda e_1 + (1-\lambda)e_2] \le \lambda f(e_1) + (1-\lambda)f(e_2)$ $\forall e_1, e_2 \in \mathcal{L}$ and $\lambda \in [0, 1]$. Therefore, the extremum of $f(e)$ exists.

Suppose that $\tilde{e} \in \mathcal{L}$ is a local minimum point of $f(e)$. That is,

$$f(\tilde{e}) \le f(e),\ e \in P, \tag{4-9}$$

where P is a neighbor of $\tilde{e}$:

$$P = \{e \in \mathcal{L} \,\|e - \tilde{e}\| \le \varepsilon\}. \tag{4-10}$$

Now, suppose that Statement 1 is not true. That is, there is another point $\bar{e} \in \mathcal{L}$ such that $f(\bar{e}) < f(\tilde{e})$. Obviously, $\bar{e} \notin P$. Thus, $\|\bar{e} - \tilde{e}\| > \varepsilon$. Consequently, the number

$\lambda_1 = \dfrac{\varepsilon}{\|\bar{e} - \tilde{e}\|} \in (0, 1)$. Let

$$\lambda_2 = 1 - \lambda_1. \tag{4-11}$$

As f is convex,

$$f(\lambda_2\tilde{e} + \lambda_1\bar{e}) \le \lambda_2 f(\tilde{e}) + \lambda_1 f(\bar{e}) < \lambda_2 f(\tilde{e}) + \lambda_1 f(\tilde{e}) = f(\tilde{e}).$$

However, the above expression does not hold because $\|\lambda_2\tilde{e} + \lambda_1\bar{e} - \tilde{e}\| = \lambda_1\|\bar{e} - \tilde{e}\| = \varepsilon$, i.e., $\lambda_2\tilde{e} + \lambda_1\bar{e} \in P$. This is in contradiction to Eq. (4-9). Thus, Statement 1 follows. □

According to Statement 1, for a given $r \in \mathcal{L}$, if $h_1 = h_1(n; a_{10}, a_{20}, \cdots, a_{m0})$ is such that $\|h-h_1\| = \inf_{s\in\mathcal{L}_1}\|h-s\|$, the vector $(a_{10}, a_{20}, \cdots, a_{m0})$ is called the approximated root of $J(\boldsymbol{a}) = 0$ and expressed as

$$(a_{10}, a_{20}, \cdots, a_{m0}) = argmin\ J(a_1, a_2, \cdots, a_m). \tag{4-12}$$

The extent of approximation is evaluated by $M^2(h_1)$. Thus, if $(a_{10}, a_{20}, \cdots, a_{m0})$ is such that $M^2(h_1) < 10^{-3}$, the fitted model $h_1(n)$ is acceptable in our scheme. In the paper, the vector $(a_{10}, a_{20}, \cdots, a_{m0})$ is obtained by Levenberg-Marquardt method, which has become the standard of nonlinear least squares [33].

5 A Type of Impulse Functions for Simulation of TCP Traces

In this section, we first illustrate a simulation result. Then, a type of impulse functions for the simulation of wide-area TCP traffic is discussed.

5.1 Simulation of TCP Trace

By the Box-Muller method [34-35], the following is called second-order stationary white random sequence with mean μ and standard deviation σ.

$$w(n) = C\{\mu + \sigma\,[-2ln(\alpha(n))]^{0.5}cos(2\pi\alpha(n))\}, \tag{5.1}$$

where $\alpha(n)$ is a random number uniformly distributed between 0 and 1 and $C > 0$ is a constant. The raw data named dec-pkt1 is provided in [32], containing an hour's worth of all wide-area traffic between Digital Equipment Corporation and the rest of the world.

Generally, both of the magnitude and timestamp of a traffic trace $dec\text{-}pkt1(t_n)$ ($n \in I_0$) are random sequences. Therefore, the simulation of $dec\text{-}pkt1(t_n)$ is in two aspects. One is the simulation of the magnitude $dec\text{-}pkt1$ and the other t_n. Since the simulation procedures of both sequences are the same, we only demonstrate the simulation of $dec\text{-}pkt1(n)$ for the sake of simplicity and this would not affect the generality of the simulation principle discussed. Fig. 1 (a) indicates $dec\text{-}pkt1(n)$ and r_{pkt1} in Fig.1 (b) is the measured autocorrelation function in the normalized case. By (3-6), the simulation is shown in Fig.1 (c). Statistically, dec-pkt1(n) and $y(n)$ in Fig. 1 are identical in the sense of $r_y = r_{pkt1}$.

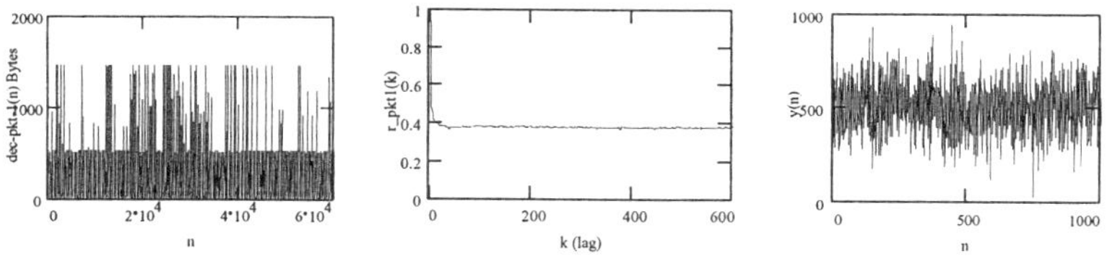

(a) (b) (c)

(a): TCP trace of dec-pkt-1 (b): Measured autocorrelation sequence (c): Simulated sequence

Figure 1. Illustrations of simulation

5.2 Filters Design based on Nonlinear Least Squares Fitting

With Eq. (3-8), the measured impulse function $h(n)$ in the normalized case can be obtained as Fig. 2 shows. It is known that the "insights" for choosing a suitable type of trial models and a set of good first guesses are crucial for the method for nonlinear least squares fitting. Hence, empirical models from experiments are particularly important. Based on the experimental analysis, we propose the following:

$$h_1(n) = h_1(n; a_1, a_2, \cdots, a_6) = \cos(n/a_1)\exp(-n/a_2) + a_5\sin(n/a_3)\exp(-n/a_4)u(n - a_6), \quad (5\text{-}2)$$

where $a_1, a_2, a_3, a_4 \in (0, \infty)$, $a_5 \in (-\infty, \infty)$, $a_6 \in I_0$. Obviously, the set

$$\eta_1 = \{h_1(n); h_1(n) = h_1(n; a_1, a_2, \cdots, a_6)\} \quad (5\text{-}3)$$

is a subset of $\mathcal{k}$:

$$\eta_1 \subset \mathcal{k}. \quad (5\text{-}4)$$

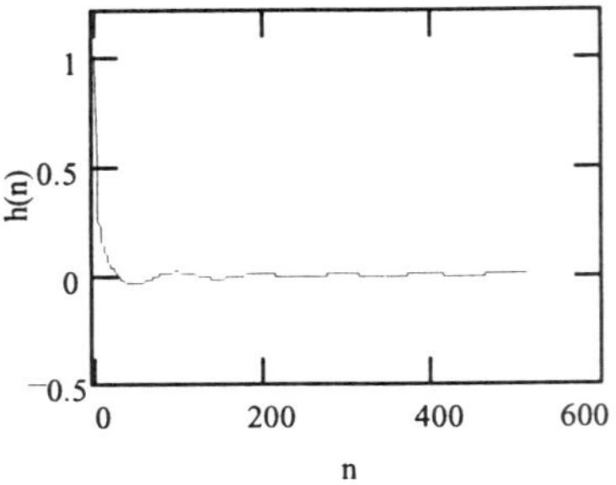

Figure 2. Measured impulse function $h(n)$

Thus, there exists a unique approximated vector root of the following cost function (Statement 1):

$$J(a_1, a_2, \cdots, a_6) = \sum_k (h_1 - h)^2. \quad (5\text{-}5)$$

By Levenberg-Marquardt method, the approximated vector root is obtained

$$(a_{10}, a_{20}, \cdots, a_{60}) = (172.788, 3.14, 17.279, 500, -0.01, 30). \quad (5\text{-}6)$$

The mean square error at this point is

$$M^2(h) = 1.886\times10^{-4}. \quad (5\text{-}7)$$

Therefore, $h(n)$ is modeled by the following function:

$$h_1(n) = \cos(n/172.788)\exp(-n/3.14) - 0.01\sin(n/17.279)\exp(-n/500)u(n - 30). \quad (5\text{-}8)$$

Figs.3 (a) ~ (f) indicate each element of $(a_{10}, a_{20}, \cdots, a_{60})$. Fig.4 shows the function $h_1(h)$ and the comparison. Thus, Eq. (5-2) stands for a type of simulators for TCP traffic. The simulators in Z domain are expressed as

$$H_1(z) = H_{11}(z) + H_{12}(z) + H_{13}(z), \quad (5\text{-}9)$$

where

$$H_{11}(z) = \frac{z[z - \exp(-1/a_2)\cos(1/a_1)]}{z^2 - 2\exp(-1/a_2)z\cos(1/a_1) + \exp(-2/a_2)}, \quad (5\text{-}10)$$

$$H_{12}(z) = a_5\exp(-a_6/a_4)\cos(a_6/a_3)z^{-a_6}\frac{z\exp(-1/a_4)\sin(1/a_3)}{z^2-2\exp(-1/a_4)z\cos(1/a_3)+\exp(-2/a_4)}, \tag{5-11}$$

and

$$H_{13}(z) = a_5\exp(-a_6/a_4)\sin(a_6/a_3)z^{-a_6}\frac{z[z-\exp(-1/a_4)\cos(1/a_3)]}{z^2-2\exp(-1/a_4)z\cos(1/a_3)+\exp(-2/a_4)}. \tag{5-12}$$

In frequency domain, the simulators are

$$H_1(\omega) = H_{11}(\omega) + H_{12}(\omega) + H_{13}(\omega), \tag{5-13}$$

where

$$H_{11}(\omega) = \frac{(1/a_2)+j\omega}{[(1/a_2)+j\omega]^2+(1/a_1)^2}, \tag{5-14}$$

$$H_{12}(\omega) = a_5\exp(-a_6/a_4)\exp(-j\omega a_6)\cos(a_6/a_3)\frac{1/a_3}{[(1/a_4)+j\omega]^2+(1/a_3)^2}, \tag{5-15}$$

$$H_{13}(\omega) = a_5\exp(-a_6/a_4)\exp(-j\omega a_6)\sin(a_6/a_3)\frac{(1/a_4)+j\omega}{[(1/a_4)+j\omega]^2+(1/a_3)^2}. \tag{5-16}$$

6 Conclusions

We present a traffic simulator (3-8) to simulate traffic with white noise input. To model $h(n)$ by multidimensional nonlinear least squares fitting, the existence and the uniqueness of solutions are proved. A type of impulse functions (5-2) for simulating wide-area TCP traffic is proposed.

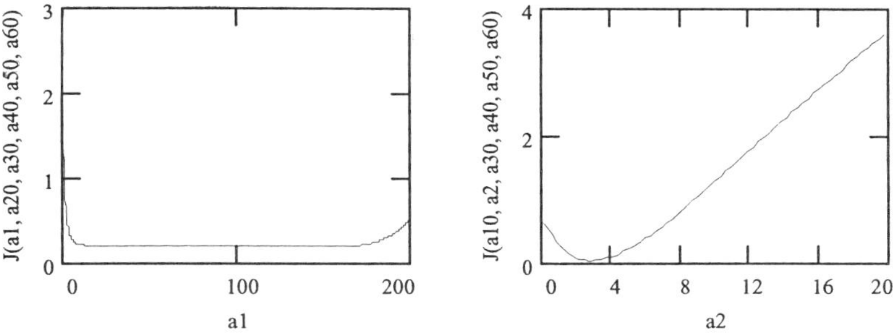

(a) (b)

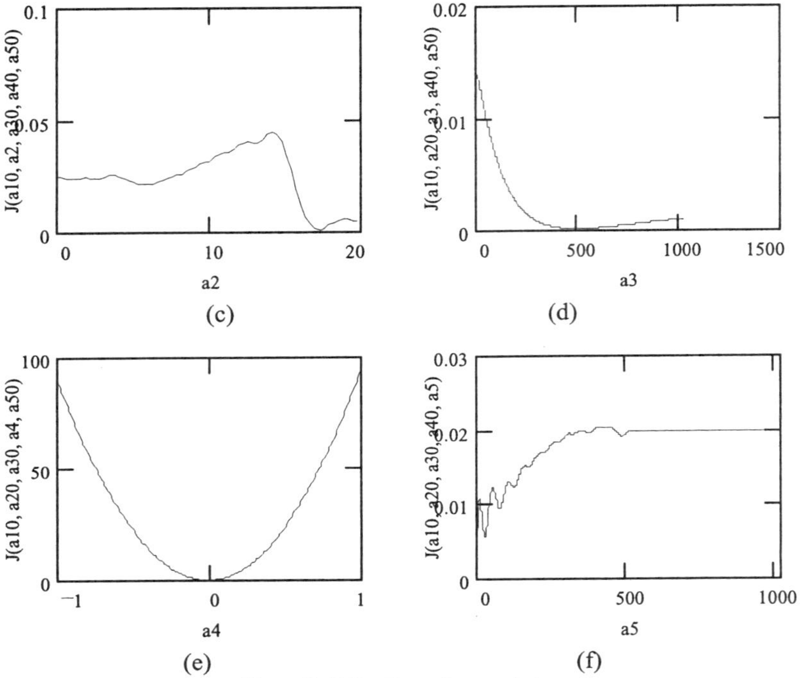

Figure 3. Estimations of parameters

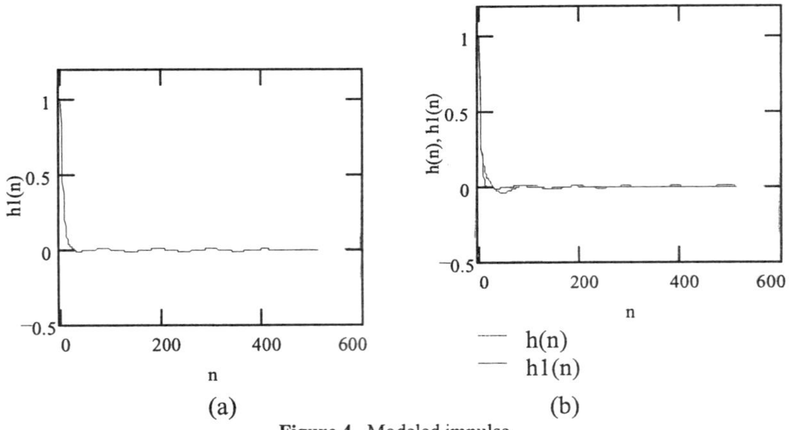

Figure 4. Modeled impulse

7 Acknowledgements

Authors are grateful to Dr. Vern Paxson for his timely responses to our inquires about traffic data and Jeff Mogul of Digital's Western Research Lab for his work on traces. This work was partially sponsored by City University of Hong Kong under grants.

References

1. Yang, J. N., Simulation of random envelope processes, *J. of Sound and Vibration*, 21 (1), pp. 73-85, 1972.
2. M. Li, B. H. Xu, and Y. S. Wu, "An H_2-Optimal Control of Random Loading for a Laboratory Fatigue Test", *J. of Testing and Evaluation*, JTEVA, Vol. 26, No. 6, Nov., 1998, pp. 619-625
3. M. Li, W. J. Jia, W. Zhao, and et al, "An On-Line Correction Technique of Random Loading with a Real-Time Signal Processor for a Laboratory Fatigue Test", *J. of Testing and Evaluation*, JTEVA, Vol. 28, No. 5, September 2000, pp. 409-414
4. M. Li, Y. S. Wu, and B. H. Xu, System Analysis of Instron 2165 Testing System before Doing a Fatigue Test in Random Loading, *J. of Experimental Mechanics*, vol. 12 , No. 3, Sept. 1997, pp. 481-486, China
5. M. Li, A Method for the Analog of Response Load Spectrum in Random Fatigue Tests, *J. of Experimental Mechanics*, Vol.6, No.1, 1991, pp. 73-76, China
6. M. Li, B. H. Xu, and et al, The principle and its experiments of the method of optimal pre-filters for the analog of load spectrum in random fatigue tests, *J. of Science & Technology of China Naval Ship*, No.6, 1991
7. Q. S. Li, A New Exact Approach for Analyzing Free Vibration of SDOF Systems with Non-Periodically Time Varying Parameters, ASME, *Int. J. of Vibration & Acoustics*, Vol. 122, pp.175-179, 2000.
8. Q. S. Li, J. Q. Fang, D.K. Liu, Evaluation of Wind-Induced Vibrations of Structures By Stochastic Finite Element Method, Vol.8, No.5, pp.477-490, *Structural Engineering and Mechanics*, 1999
9. Q. S. Li, J. Q. Fang, D.K. Liu, Exact Solutions for Free Vibration of Single-Degree-Of - Freedom Systems with Non-Periodically Varying Parameters, *J. of Vibration & Control*, Vol.6, No.3, pp.449-462, 2000.
10. J. Q. Fang, A. P. Jeary, Q. S. Li, C. K. Wong, Random Damping in Buildings and Its AR Model, *J. of Wind Engineering and Industrial Aerodynamics*, Vol.79, pp.159-167, 1999
11. V. Paxson, S,. Floyd, Wide Area Traffic: The Failure of Poisson Modeling, *IEEE Trans. on Networking*, vol. 3, no. 3, June 1995, pp. 226-244
12. M. E. Crovella, A. Bestavros, Self-Similarity in World Wide Web Traffic: Evidence and Possible Causes, *IEEE/ACM Trans. on Networking*, vol. 5 (6), Dec., 1997, pp. 835-846
13. W. E. Leland, M. S. Taqqu, W. Willinger, and D. V. Wilson, On the Self-Similar Nature of Ethernet Traffic (Extended Version), *IEEE Trans on Networking*, vol. 2, no. 1, Feb., 1994, pp. 1-15
14. A. Erramilli, O. Narayan, and W. Willinger, Experimental Queueing Analysis with Long-Range Dependent Packet Traffic, *IEEE/ACM Trans. on Networking*, vol. 4, no. 5, April, 1996, 200-223

15. H. Michiel and K. Laevens, Teletraffic Engineering in a Broad-Band Era, *Proc. of IEEE*, vol. 85 (12), Dec., 1997, pp. 2007-2033
16. R. Carmona, W. L. Hwang, and B. Torresani, Practical Time-Frequency Analysis: Gabor and Wavelet Transforms with an Implementation in S, Academic Press, 1999, pp. 244-247
17. J. Lighthill, An Introduction to Fourier Analysis and Generalised Functions, Cambridge University Press, 1958
18. A. Papoulis, The Fourier Integral and Its Applications, McGraw-Hill, Inc. 1962, Appendix
19. P. A. M. Dirac, The Principles of Quantum Mechanics, Fourth Edition (Revised), Clarendon Press, Oxford, 1984
20. R. P. Kanwal, Generalized Functions, Theory and Technique, Second Edition, Birkhauser, 1997
21. M. M. Krunz, A. M. Makowski, Modeling Video Traffic Using M/G/∞ Input Processes: A Compromise Between Markovian and LRD Models, *IEEE J. on Selected Areas in Communications*, vol. 16., no. 5, June 1998, pp. 733-748
22. C. C. Huang, M. Devetsikiotis, I. Lambadaris, and A. R. Kaye, Modeling and Simulation of Self-Similar Variable Bit Rate Compressed Video: A Unified Approach, *Proc., ACM SIGCOMM'95*, 1995, pp. 114-125
23. V. Paxon, Fast Approximate Synthesis of Fractional Gaussian Noise for Generating Self-Similar Network Traffic, *ACM SIGCOMM, Computer Comm. Review*, 1999, pp. 5-18
24. H. F. Zhang, Y. T. Shu, and Oliver Yang, Estimation of Hurst Parameter by Variance-Time Plots, *IEEE Pacific Rim Conf. On Communications, Computers and Signal Processing, vol. 2*, Oct., 1997, pp. 883-886
25. S. Bates, S. McLaughlin, Testing the Gaussian Assumption for Self-Similar Teletraffic Models, *Proc. of IEEE Sig. Proc. Workshop on Higher Order Statistics*, 1997, pp. 444-447
26. J. Beran, Statistics for Long-Memory Processes, Chapman & Hall, 1994
27. B. Tsybakov, N. D. Georganas, Self-Similar Processes in Communications Networks, *IEEE Trans on Information Theory*, vol. 44, no. 5, Sep., 1998, pp. 1713-1725
28. M. Li, W. J. Jia, and W. Zhao, Modeling Autocorrelation Functions of Asymptotically Self-Similar Traffic and Verification of Long-Range Dependence, to appear on the *Conf. Proc., ICCT'2000*, Aug. 21-25, 2000, Beijing
29. M. Li, W. J. Jia, and W. Zhao, Modeling Autocorrelation Functions of Self-Similar Teletraffic in Communication Networks based on Optimal Approximation in Hilbert Space, Submitted to *J. of Applied Mathematical Modelling*
30. M. Li, W. J. Jia, and W. Zhao, A Whole Correlation Structure of Asymptotically Self-Similar Traffic in Communication Networks, *Conf. Proc., IEEE WISE'2000*, June 19-20, 2000, Hong Kong, pp. 461-466
31. M. Li, W. J. Jia, and W. Zhao, A Form for Modeling Autocorrelation Functions of Self-Similar Traffic on Ethernet and Its Analysis, Submitted to *European Transaction on Telecommunications*
32. Data traces can be obtained via anonymous ftp from bellcore.com under /pub/wel/lan_traffic
33. W. H. Press, S. A. Teukolsky, W. T. Vetterling, B. P. Flannery, Numerical Recipes in C: The Art of Scientific Computing, Second Edition, Cambridge University Press, 1992, Chap. 7, , Chap. 9, pp. 289
34. R. O. Harger, An Introduction to Digital Signal Processing with MATHCAD, PWS Publishing Company, 1999, Chap. 24
35. J. E. Dennis, Jr., R. B. Schnabel, Numerical Methods for Unconstrained Optimization and Nonlinear Equations, Prentice-Hall, 1983

ON THE REARRANGEABILITY OF SHUFFLE-EXCHANGE NETWORKS

HUNG Q. NGO AND DING-ZHU DU

Computer Science Department, University of Minnesota, Minneapolis, MN 55455, USA.

E-mail: {hngo,dzd}@cs.umn.edu.

Let $m(n)$ be the minimum positive integer k so that the Shuffle-Exchange network with k stages, $N = 2^n$ inputs and N outputs is rearrangeable. Beneš conjectured that $m(n) = 2n - 1$. The best bounds known so far are $2n - 1 \le m(n) \le 3n - 4$. In this paper, we verify Beneš conjecture for $n = 4$, and use this result to show that $m(n) \le 3n - 5$.

1 Introduction

Shuffle-Exchange networks (SE networks for short) were initially proposed by Stone [1] (1971) to be an efficient interconnecting architecture for parallel processors. Various applications benefit from this interconnecting pattern such as FFT, matrix transposition, polynomial evaluation, ... A k-stage SE network with parameter n, denoted by $(SE_n)^k$, is a network with $N = 2^n$ inputs and N outputs, consisting of k SE stages, where each SE stage includes a *perfect shuffle* pattern [1] followed by an array of $\frac{N}{2}$ 2×2 crossbars. A typical drawing of a 7-stage SE network with $n = 4$ (i.e. $(SE_4)^7$) is shown in Figure 1.

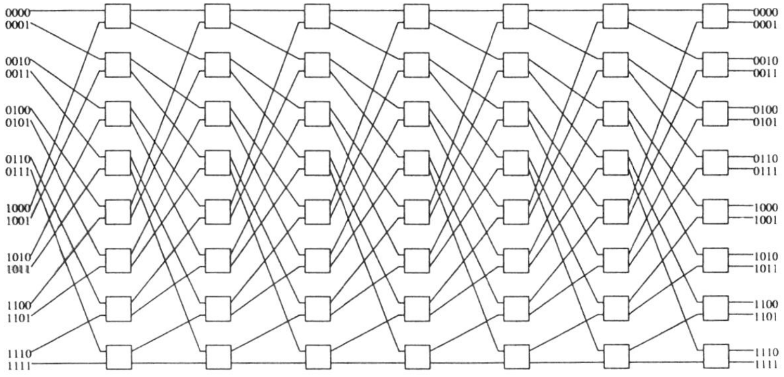

Figure 1. The 7-stage SE network for $N = 16$, i.e. $(SE_4)^7$

A standard question to be addressed on any multistage interconnection network (MIN) is that if the network is *rearrangeable.* An N-input N-output MIN is rearrangeable if and only if any one to one mapping from the inputs to the outputs is routable by the network. *Universality* is another term that is often used synonymously with *rearrangeability.* In the context of SE networks, a long standing question was that how many SE stages are sufficient for a SE network to be rearrangeable. In fact, it is not entirely clear that increasing the number of stages would increase the rearrangeability of a SE network. There has been a very slow progress toward answering this question. For convenience, let us use $m(n)$ to denote the minimum positive integer so that $(SE_n)^{m(n)}$ is rearrangeable. The algorithm discussed by Stone [1] showed that $m(n) \leq n^2$, thus $m(n)$ is well defined. Beneš conjectured in 1975 [2] that $2n-1$ SE stages is necessary and sufficient to route all $N!$ perfect matchings from the inputs to the outputs, i.e. $m(n) = 2n-1$. Parker [3] (1980) showed that $n+1 \leq m(n) \leq 3n$, where the lower bound was obtained by a counting argument, and the upper bound by group calculations plus the rearrangeability of the Beneš network. [4] Wu and Feng [5] (1981) gave an explicit algorithm to route all matchings, proving $m(n) \leq 3n-1$. Huang and Tripathi [6] (1986) improved the bound to $m(n) \leq 3n-3$. Raghavendra and Varma [7] (1987) verified the conjecture for $N = 8$. They used that result to show $m(n) \leq 3n-4$. [8] They also specified a permutation which $(SE_n)^k$ can not route if $k \leq 2n-2$, in effect showing $2n-1 \leq m(n)$. With a different formulation, Linial and Tarsi [9] (1989) also verified the conjecture for $N = 8$ and showed $m(n) \leq 3n-4$. From their formulation it is easy to see that at least $2n-1$ stages are needed to route all permutations. Feng and Seo [10] (1994) gave a proof of the conjecture, which was incomplete as pointed out by Kim, Yoon, and Maeng [11] (1997).

In this paper, we give a proof that $m(4) = 7$ using a new method, and then adapting Linial and Tarsi's results to show that $m(n) \leq 3n-5$.

2 Preliminaries

This section presents related concepts and previous results on the problem. Throughout the paper, we shall assume that $n \in \mathbb{N}$ and $N = 2^n$. The following definitions and lemmas are from Linial and Tarsi. [9]

Definition 2.1. For $k \in \mathbb{N}$, a $N \times k$ 01-matrix A, denoted by $A_{N\times k}$ is said to be *balanced* if

(i) Either $k \leq n$ and every row vector $v \in \mathbb{F}_2^k$ occurs exactly 2^{n-k} times as rows of A.

(ii) or $k > n$ and every n consecutive column vectors of A form a balanced matrix.

Definition 2.2. Given a balanced matrix $A_{N\times(n-1)}$, a column vector $x \in \mathbb{F}_2^N$ is said to *agree* with A if appending x into A yields an $N \times n$ balanced matrix (the matrix $[A, x]$).

Lemma 2.3. *If A and B are two $N \times (n-1)$ balanced matrices, then there exists a vector $x \in \mathbb{F}_2^N$ that agrees with both A and B.*

Lemma 2.4. *Let $A_{N\times n}$ be a 01-matrix such that deleting any column of A yields a balanced $N \times (n-1)$ matrix. Then, either (i) A is balanced, or (ii) each row of A has an even number of 1's, or (iii) each row of A has an odd number of 1's.*

Lemma 2.5. *Let $A_{N\times k}$ be a balanced matrix with $k \leq n$, and let T be a non-singular $k \times k$ 01-matrix, then AT is also balanced, where all the arithmetic is done modulo 2.*

Notice that when x agrees with A, we can insert x into any position between the columns of A to get a balanced matrix. It is also easy to see that $(SE_n)^m$ $(m > n)$ is rearrangeable if and only if for every two given balanced matrices $A_{N\times n}$ and $B_{N\times n}$ there exists an $N \times (m-n)$ balanced matrix M such that the matrix $[A, M, B]$ is balanced. Here the rows of A are binary representations of the inputs and the corresponding rows of B are binary representations of the matched outputs.

3 Main Results

To illustrate the idea and introduce notations needed for the main theorem, we first reproduce a known result [9,7] using the new method.

Lemma 3.1. *$m(3) = 5$, namely the network $(SE_3)^5$ is rearrangeable.*

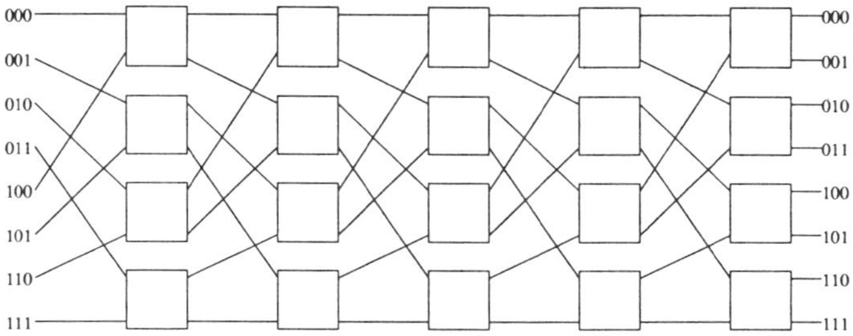

Figure 2. The 5-stage SE network for $N = 8$, i.e. $(SE_3)^5$

Proof. We use the same approach as that of Raghavendra and Varma, [7] namely from first principles. However, the method is different and more intuitive. Figure 2 shows a typical drawing of a 5-stage SE network for $N = 8$. For convenience, the network can be redrawn and the switches can be labeled as shown in Figure 3. In the figure, the inputs and outputs have been numbered

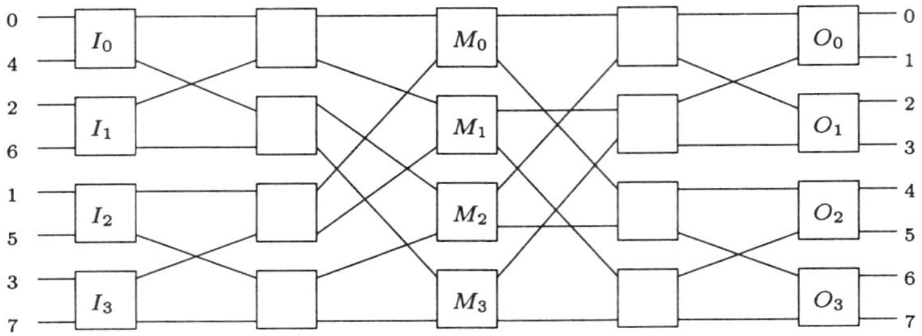

Figure 3. A redrawing of the $(SE_3)^5$ network

in decimals for convenience. We write $x \in I_i$ ($y \in O_j$) if input x (output y) is connected to input switch I_i (output switch O_j). Given a perfect matching π (or permutation) from the inputs $\{0,4,2,6,1,5,3,7\}$ to the outputs $\{0,1,2,3,4,5,6,7\}$, we first construct a 4×4, 2-regular multi-bipartite graph $G(\pi) = (I, O, E)$ whose bipartitions are $I = O = \{0,1,2,3\}$. I and O correspond to the input and output switches respectively. We shall refer to $G(\pi)$ as G if π is clear from the context. $(i,j) \in E$ iff $\pi(x) = y$ for some $x \in I_i$ and $y \in O_j$, introducing multiple edges if necessary. We now need some notations. Suppose we have colored the edges of G with colors in $C = \{0,1,2,3\}$. For each $c \in C$, let $L(c)$ ($R(c)$) be the multi-set of the vertices in I (O) which are incident to an edge colored c. For each subset $S \subseteq C$, let $L(S) = \bigcup_{c \in S} L(c)$ and $R(S) = \bigcup_{c \in S} R(c)$, where the union is multi-set union. For each $e \in E$, let $l(e)$ ($r(e)$) denote the vertex in I (O) incident to e. Similarly, for any subset $A \subseteq E$, let $L(A) = \{l(e) \mid e \in A\}$ and $R(A) = \{r(e) \mid e \in A\}$.

To this end, we observe from Figure 3 that the realizability of the matching is equivalent to the existence of a coloring of G with colors in C such that

(P_0) Each color appears exactly twice.

(P_1) For each $c \in C$, $L(c)$ has a representative from each of $\{0,1\}$ and $\{2,3\}$.

(P_2) $L(\{0,1\}) = L(\{2,3\}) = \{0,1,2,3\}$. In other words, $L(\{0,1\})$ and $L(\{2,3\})$ have distinct elements.

(P_1') For each $c \in C$, $R(c)$ has a representative from each of $\{0,1\}$ and $\{2,3\}$.

(P_2') $R(\{0,2\}) = R(\{1,3\}) = \{0,1,2,3\}$. In other words, $R(\{0,2\})$ and $R(\{1,3\})$ have distinct elements.

The conditions are chosen so that the two edges colored $c \in \{0,1,2,3\}$ will be routed through middle switch M_c. We will not state and prove the correctness of any routing algorithm based on the coloring here, as it is straightforward.

We now describe a procedure to properly color all such G as follows. Along the way, we shall also prove that our procedure works.

Phase 1. As G is 2 regular and bipartite, it is the union of even cycles. G thus can be decomposed into two 4×4 perfect matchings by taking alternate edges on each cycle. Let the matchings be M_1 and M_2 (whose vertex sets are the same as G.)

Phase 2. From each M_i ($i = 1,2$), construct a 2×2 2-regular bipartite graph G_i by combining within each bipartition of M_i the pairs of vertices $\{0,1\}$ and $\{2,3\}$. Figure 4 illustrates the results of our first two phases. Obviously, $L(E(G_i)) = R(E(G_i)) = \{0,1,2,3\}$, for $i = 1,2$. Here and henceforth the L and R functions are applied in the context of the original graph G.

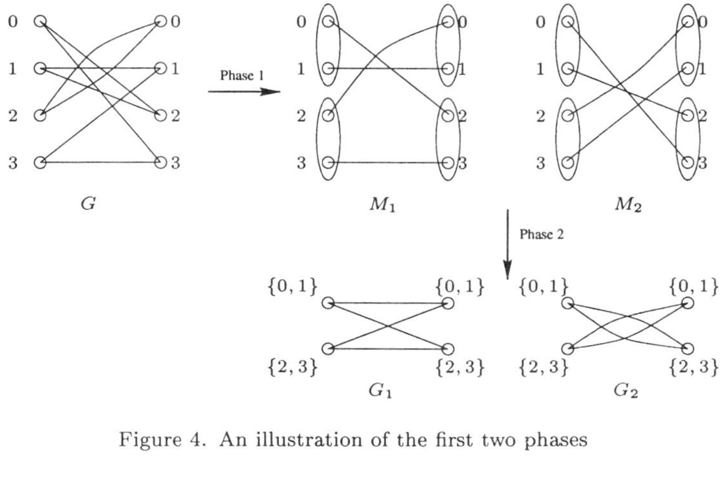

Figure 4. An illustration of the first two phases

We call the graphs G_1 and G_2 the *basic components* of G. Since the basic components are 2×2 2-regular bipartite graphs, they can only be either a 4-cycle or a union of two 2-cycles. A basic component is said to be of *type 1* if it is a 4-cycle and of *type 2* otherwise. In Figure 4, G_1 is of type 1 and G_2

is of type 2.

Phase 3. As each coloring of G_1 and G_2 induces uniquely a coloring of G, we are to color G_1 and G_2 so that the coloring satisfy conditions P_0, P_i and P'_i, $1 \leq i \leq 2$. We call an edge whose color is $c \in C$ a *c-edge.* Consider two cases:

Case 1. Both G_1 and G_2 are of type 1. In this case we color the graphs as shown in Figure 5a. It is easy to see that the coloring satisfies all prescribed conditions. The basic idea is that as we have used each color exactly twice, to enforce P_1 and P'_1 we need to make sure that if there is a c-edge going from $\{0,1\}$ to $\{0,1\}$, then the other c-edge must go from $\{2,3\}$ to $\{2,3\}$ in either basic components, and similarly if a c-edge going from $\{0,1\}$ to $\{2,3\}$ then the other c-edge must go from $\{2,3\}$ to $\{0,1\}$. To enforce P_2 and P'_2, on the left side (the I side) we *separate* each color pair $\{0,1\}$ and $\{2,3\}$, while on the right (the O side) we separate the pairs $\{0,2\}$ and $\{1,3\}$.

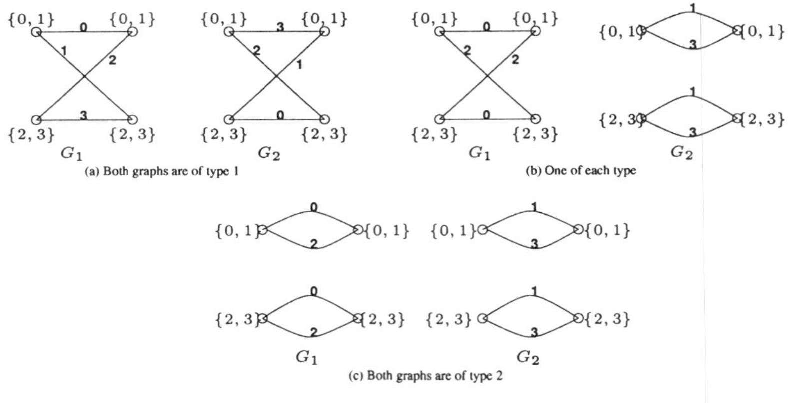

Figure 5. Illustration of the colorings when $n = 3$

Case 2. There is one graph of type 2. Without loss of generality, assume G_2 is of type 2 as illustrated in Figures 5b and 5c. In this case we color G_1 with $\{0,2\}$ and G_2 with $\{1,3\}$. Notice that P_0, P_1, P'_1, and P'_2 are satisfied even if we switch colors in one (or both) 2-cycles of G_2. To ensure P_2, we do this switching if necessary at each 2 cycle of G_2.

□

Secondly, we use the idea to derive a more elaborate proof for the case where $N = 16$. Firstly, we redraw the network as shown in Figure 6, so that it is easier to derive the conditions similar to the P_i and P'_i. From the figure, the

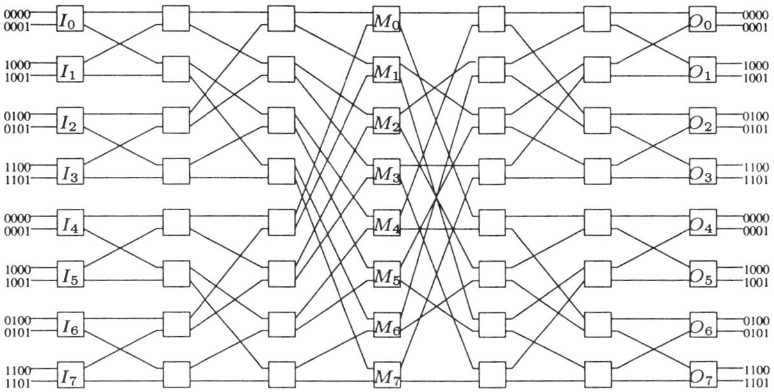

Figure 6. A redrawing of the $(SE_4)^7$ network

following proposition is easy to see. We reuse all notations introduced in the proof of Lemma 3.1. Again, as a valid coloring induces a routing algorithm in a straightforward way, we shall not describe the algorithm here.

Proposition 3.2. *The fact that $(SE_4)^7$ is rearrangeable is equivalent to the fact that for any 8×8 2-regular multi-bipartite graph $G = (I, O)$ with bipartitions $I = O = \{0, \ldots, 7\}$, there exists an edge coloring of G using colors in $C = \{0, \ldots, 7\}$ satisfying the following conditions:*

(P_0) Each $c \in C$ appears exactly twice.

(P_1) For each $c \in C$, $L(c)$ has a representative from each of $\{0,1,2,3\}$ and $\{4,5,6,7\}$.

(P_2) For each pair $\{c_1, c_2\} \in \{\{0,1\},\{2,3\},\{4,5\},\{6,7\}\}$, $L(\{c_1,c_2\})$ has a representative from each of $\{0,1\}$, $\{2,3\}$, $\{4,5\}$, and $\{6,7\}$.

(P_3) $L(\{0,1,2,3\}) = L(\{4,5,6,7\}) = \{0,1,\ldots,7\}$. In other words, the elements of $L(\{0,1,2,3\})$ and $L(\{4,5,6,7\})$ are all distinct.

(P_1') For each $c \in C$, $R(c)$ has a representative from each of $\{0,1,2,3\}$ and $\{4,5,6,7\}$.

(P_2') For each pair $\{c_1, c_2\} \in \{\{0,4\},\{2,6\},\{1,5\},\{3,7\}\}$, $R(\{c_1,c_2\})$ has a representative from each of $\{0,1\}$, $\{2,3\}$, $\{4,5\}$, and $\{6,7\}$.

(P_3') $R(\{0,4,2,6\}) = R(\{1,5,3,7\}) = \{0,1,\ldots,7\}$. In other words, the elements of $R(\{0,4,2,6\})$ and $R(\{1,5,3,7\})$ are all distinct.

Note that the conditions were specifically chosen so that each pair of edges with the same color $c \in C$ shall be routed through middle switch M_c without causing any conflict. From now on, we shall refer to a *valid* coloring of G as the coloring satisfying the prescribed conditions in Proposition 3.2.

Theorem 3.3. *$m(4) = 7$, namely the network $(SE_4)^7$ is rearrangeable.*

Proof. Given any perfect matching π from the inputs to the outputs, we first construct the 8×8 2-regular multi-bipartite graph G in a similar way as the G in Lemma 3.1. The bipartitions of G are $I = O = \{0, \ldots, 7\}$, and $(i, j) \in E(G)$ if for some $x \in \{0, \ldots, 15\}$ we have $x \in I_i$ and $\pi(x) \in O_j$. To color G properly, i.e. the coloring satisfies the conditions of Proposition 3.2, we decompose G into 4 basic components. The decomposition is formally described below. Figure 7 illustrates the decomposition procedure.

Phase 1 Decompose G into two edge disjoint 8×8 perfect matchings M_1 and M_2.

Phase 2 For each $i = 1, 2$, construct the graph G_i by collapsing the pairs of vertices $\{0, 1\}$, $\{2, 3\}$, $\{4, 5\}$, and $\{6, 7\}$ on each bipartition of M_i. It is clear that the graphs G_i are 4×4 2-regular bipartite graphs.

Phase 3 For each $i = 1, 2$, decompose G_i into two edge disjoint 4×4 perfect matchings M_{i1} and M_{i2}.

Phase 4 For each $i = 1, 2$ and $j = 1, 2$, construct the graph G_{ij} by collapsing the pairs of vertices $\{01, 23\}$ and $\{45, 67\}$ on each bipartition of M_{ij}. As before, the G_{ij} are called *basic components* of G, and can only be one of two types: (a) type 1 corresponds to a 4-cycle and (b) type 2 corresponds to two 2 cycles. We are now ready to color the basic components so that the (uniquely) induced coloring on G is valid.

As we have seen in the proof of Lemma 3.1, the number of type-2 basic components can roughly be thought of as the degree of flexibility in finding a valid coloring for G. Our basic idea is to give different colorings of G based on the number of basic components of type-2. Although the idea is simple, the cases are quite tricky and long. Due to limited space, the reader is referred to Ngo and Du [12] (2000) for the full proof. □

To this end, we use the formulation of Linial and Tarsi to show an auxiliary lemma and then combine the lemma with Theorem 3.3 to improve the upper bound of $m(n)$. The following lemma has been shown by Varma and Raghavendra [8], however the proof was rather long. We straightforwardly extend Theorem 3.1 in Linial and Tarsi work [9] to obtain a much shorter proof.

Lemma 3.4. *If $m(k) = 2k - 1$ for a fixed $k \in \mathbb{N}$, then $(SE_n)^{3n-k-1}$ is rearrangeable whenever $n \geq k$.*

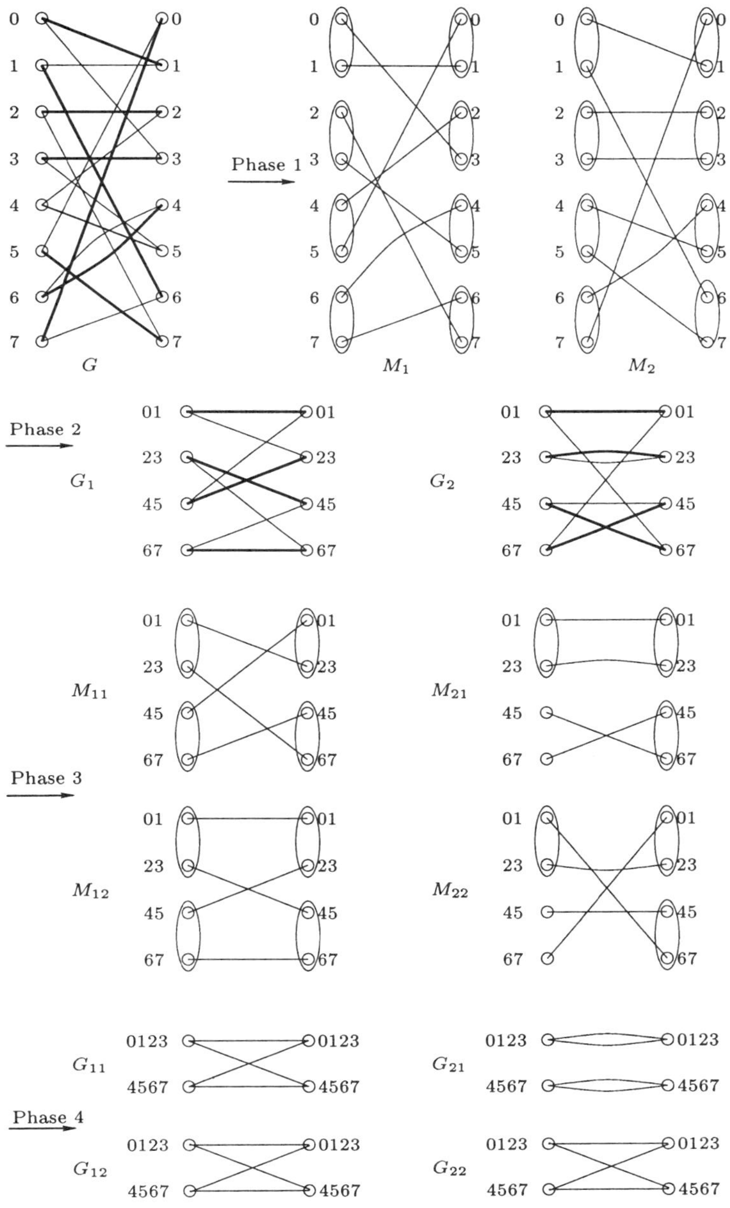

Figure 7. An illustration of the basic component decomposition

Proof. The assertion in the lemma is equivalent to the fact that if we know $m(k) = 2k - 1$, then for every two $N \times n$ balanced matrices $A = [a_1, \dots, a_n]$ and $B = [b_1, \dots, b_n]$, there exists an $N \times (2n - k - 1)$ balanced matrix M such that the matrix $[A, M, B]$ is balanced. Here a_i and b_i are the ith columns of A and B respectively. We shall construct the $(2n - k - 1)$ column vectors which form M. The construction takes several steps as follows.
Step 1. Repeatedly apply Lemma 2.3 to constructs vectors $\{u_1, \dots, u_{n-k}\}$ such that for $i = 1, \dots, n - k$, u_i agrees with $[a_{i+1}, \dots, a_n, u_1, \dots, u_{i-1}]$ and $[u_{i-1}, \dots, u_1, b_n, \dots, b_{i+1}]$. Let $U = [u_1, \dots, u_{n-k}]$ and $U^R = [u_{n-k}, \dots, u_1]$, then after this step both $[A, U]$ and $[U^R, B]$ are balanced.
Step 2. We want to construct vectors $x_1, \dots, x_{k-1}$ such that if we let $X = [x_1, \dots, x_{k-1}]$, then $[A, U, X]$ and $[X, U^R, B]$ are both balanced. Notice that as U is an $N \times (n-k)$ balanced matrix, each row of U occurs exactly 2^k times, and so do the rows of U^R in the same positions. Hence, the rows of U and U^R can be partitioned into 2^{n-k} classes of 2^k identical row vectors in each partition. For v be any column of U or U^R, let $v^{(i)}$ be the subvector of v with entries in the ith partition, where $0 \leq i \leq 2^{n-k} - 1$. Notice that $v^{(i)} \in \mathbb{F}_2^k$ for each i. Also, for each $i = 0, \dots, 2^{n-k} - 1$, let

$$A^{(i)} = [a_{n-k+1}^{(i)}, \dots, a_n^{(i)}]$$

and

$$A^{(i)} = [b_n^{(i)}, \dots, b_{n-k+1}^{(i)}]$$

Then, since Beneš conjecture is true for k (i.e. $m(k) = 2k - 1$), there exist vectors $x_1^{(i)}, \dots, x_{k-1}^{(i)}$ such that $[A^{(i)}, X^{(i)}, B^{(i)}]$ is balanced. The vectors $x_1, \dots, x_{k-1}$ are obtained by pasting together the $x_j^{(i)}$ preserving the positions of the partitions.

After this step, $[A, U, X]$ is balanced because at the positions where the rows of U are identical we have $[A^{(i)}, X^{(i)}]$ being a $2^k \times k$ balanced matrix. The fact that $[X, U^R, B]$ is balanced can be shown similarly.
Step 3. Now we define an $N \times (n - k)$ matrix W from U such that $[A, W, X, U^R, B]$ is balanced. Define W as follows (all arithmetics are done over $\mathbb{F}_2$).

$$w_i = \begin{cases} u_i & 1 \leq i \leq \frac{n-k}{2} \\ u_i + u_{n-k-i} & \frac{n-k}{2} + 1 \leq i \leq n - k - 1 \\ u_{n-k} + a_n & i = n - k \end{cases}$$

We are left to show that $[A, W, X, U^R, B]$ is balanced. The balancedness of $[X, U^R, B]$ has already been established, so we only need to show that

$[A, W, X, U^R]$ is balanced. We do this by considering the following types of submatrices:

(a) Submatrices of the form $[a_i, \ldots, a_n, w_1, \ldots, w_{i-1}]$ where $2 \leq i \leq n - k + 1$. We apply Lemma 2.5 and use the fact that $[a_i, \ldots, a_n, u_1, \ldots, u_{i-1}]$ is balanced. $[a_i, \ldots, a_n, w_1, \ldots, w_{i-1}]$ can be obtained from $[a_i, \ldots, a_n, u_1, \ldots, u_{i-1}]$ by an invertible linear transformation with the invert map preserves the a_j $(i \leq j \leq n)$ and

$$u_j = \begin{cases} w_j & 1 \leq j \leq \frac{n-k}{2} \\ w_j + w_{n-i-k} & \frac{n-k}{2} + 1 \leq j \leq n - k - 1 \\ w_{n-k} + a_n & j = n - k \end{cases}$$

(b) Submatrices of the form $[a_i, \ldots, a_n, w_1, \ldots, w_{n-k}, x_1, \ldots, x_{k+i-n-1}]$ where $n-k+2 \leq i \leq n$. Similarly, in this case we use Lemma 2.5 and the balancedness of the matrix $[a_i, \ldots, a_n, u_1, \ldots, u_{n-k}, x_1, \ldots, x_{k+i-n-1}]$

(c) Submatrices of the form $[w_i, \ldots, w_{n-k}, x_1, \ldots, x_{k-1}, u_{n-k}, \ldots, u_{n-k-i+1}]$ where $1 \leq i \leq n - k$. Here we use the fact that $[a_n, u_1, \ldots, u_{n-k}, x_1, \ldots, x_{k-1}]$ is balanced.

□

Theorem 3.5. *For $n \in \mathbb{N}$ and $n \geq 4$, a SE network with $3n - 5$ stages is rearrangeable.*

Proof. This is immediate from Theorem 3.3 and Lemma 3.4. □

4 Discussions

In this paper, we have verified that the 7-stage SE network for $n = 4$ is rearrangeable. This result and an extension of another formulation were used to show that $3n - 5$ SE stages are sufficient for the rearrangeability of the SE network with 2^n inputs and 2^n outputs.

It was conjectured that $2n-1$ SE stages are necessary and sufficient for the SE network to be rearrangeable. However, there has been very slow progress on proving the conjecture. We hope that our work, besides improving the bound, contribute to the effort of attacking this difficult problem.

Acknowledgments

This work was supported in part by the National Science Foundation under grant CCR-9530306.

References

1. H.S. Stone. Parallel processing with perfect shuffle. *IEEE Trans. Comput.*, 20:153–161, 1971.
2. V. E. Beneš. Proving the rearrangeability of connecting networks by group calculations. *Bell System Tech. J.*, 54:421–434, 1975.
3. D. Stott Parker, Jr. Notes on shuffle/exchange-type switching networks. *IEEE Trans. Comput.*, 29(3):213–222, 1980.
4. V. E. Beneš. *Mathematical theory of connecting networks and telephone traffic*. Academic Press, New York, 1965. Mathematics in Science and Engineering, Vol. 17.
5. Chuan Lin Wu and Tse Yun Feng. The universality of the shuffle-exchange network. *IEEE Trans. Comput.*, 30(5):324–332, 1981.
6. Shing Tsaan Huang and Satish K. Tripathi. Finite state model and compatibility theory: New analysis tools for permutation networks. *IEEE Trans. Comput.*, 35(7):509–601, 1986.
7. C. S. Raghavendra and Anujan Varma. Rearrangeability of the five-stage shuffle/exchange network for $N = 8$. *IEEE Trans. Comm.*, 35(8):808–812, 1987.
8. A. Varma and C. Raghavendra. Rearrangeability of multistage shuffle/exchange networks. *IEEE Trans. Comm.*, COM-36, 10:1138–1147, 1988.
9. Nathan Linial and Michael Tarsi. Interpolation between bases and the shuffle exchange network. *European J. Combin.*, 10(1):29–39, 1989.
10. Tse-yun Feng and Seung-Woo Seo. A new routing algorithm for a class of rearrangeable networks. *IEEE Trans. Comput.*, 43(11):1270–1280, 1994.
11. M.K. Kim, H. Yoon, and S.R. Maeng. On the correctness of inside-out routing algorithm. *IEEE Trans. Comput.*, 46(7):820–823, 1997.
12. Hung Q. Ngo and Ding-Zhu Du. On the rearrangeability of shuffle-exchange networks. Technical Report TR00-045, Dept of Computer Science, University of Minnesota, 2000.

PREDICTABILITY OF MESSAGE TRANSFER IN CSMA-NETWORKS

J. KAISER
University of Ulm, Department of Computer Structures, Germany
E-mail: kaiser@informatik.uni-ulm.de

M.A. LIVANI
Siemens AG, Information and Communication Mobile, Germany
E-mail: Mohammad.Livani@icn.siemens.de

W. JIA
City University of Hong Kong, Department of Computer Science, China
E-mail: weijia@cs.cityu.edu.hk

The paper describes a novel approach to establish predictable message transfer between a set of co-operating nodes controlling a physical process. The protocol allows the coexistence of different classes of criticality in a real-time communication network. The approach exploits a priority scheme to guarantee static preplanned message slots for hard real-time communication and enforces a dynamic earliest deadline first scheduling scheme for SRTMs. Soft real-time or SRTMs can be sent at any time without interfering with the hard real-time traffic. The mechanism is embedded in the media access control (MAC) layer of the communication system and realised by a new variant of the virtual time CSMA (VTCSMA) scheme. One of the benefits of our approach is that it can be applied to all kinds of CSMA-networks including Ethernet and wireless LAN.

1 Introduction

Distributed Real-Time Systems comprising a large number of intelligent processing nodes which co-operatively control real world processes like industrial plants or traffic systems become the popular architecture for such applications. All processing nodes are autonomous and work concurrently. To avoid a single point of failure, these nodes are not co-ordinated by a single central control entity but exchange messages to disseminate critical information and co-ordinate joint actions. Therefore, these systems need a predictable communication subsystem. Usually there are highly time-critical messages which require bounded transmission times otherwise the system may fail unpredictably causing serious effects or damage to the environment. These messages are called hard real-time messages (HRTM) and the transfer of each individual HRTM must be certain. Besides time critical message transfer there may be also less critical information which should be accommodated by the communication system. This information can be visual data from camera supervising a plant, statistical data gathered by a smart sensor or navigational information in a robot which is used to create a map for long term route planning rather than for short term steering. Although the transmission of the data may have timing constraints e.g. in the example of transferring frames from the camera, these constraints are soft in the sense that a temporary violation of the timing constraints leading to a quality reduction can be tolerated. Messages of this class are refered to as soft real-time messages (SRTM).

To accomodate hard real-time traffic, conflicting timing requirements between HRTMs resulting in a temporary overload situation have to be omitted. This can only be achieved by proper off-line scheduling of the communication resources. If HRTMs and SRTMs share the same communication medium, it has to be guaranteed that the SRTMs by no means interfere with the hard part. Some static hard scheduling schemes take the approach to consider every message as a periodic HRTM [1, 2]. This method is safe but it does not only consume more resources than actually needed, but also may end up with an infeasible system. Combining static pre-planned message scheduling and a dynamic message scheduling would be beneficial. Protocols like the IEEE 802.11 [3] for wireless LAN communication, the shared channel concept [4] and recently, the TTP/A protocol [5] implement this approach. However, they use a centralised approach with a single master [3] or an ubiquitous global time [2] [4] to guarantee exclusive communication of messages. We did not consider a central master because it constitutes a single point of failure and consumes additional bandwidth. The other approaches require global time in all nodes which has to be provided by a respective protocol. Simple nodes like the camera sensor, the sensor distributing navigational information or actuators which may not transmit critical messages at all, have to participate in the clock synchronisation protocol. If a node does not obey the global time discipline, it will inevitably corrupt the communication. This paper proposes an approach to realise a bus arbitration scheme which supports the coexistence of messages with different real-time requirements. It provides pre-planned time slots for HRTMs. For SRTMs, dynamic EDF-scheduling is applied. SRTMs and even non real-time messages (NRTM) can be sent any time and the scheme guarantees that they will not interfere with HRTMs. To enforce the reservations and the scheduling decisions, we devised a dynamic priority scheme presented in this paper.

2 Controlling the access to the network

The media access control layer responsible for arbitration and collision control in a network plays a key role for the predictable message transfer. We can distinguish between mechanims which statically avoid collisions [2, 4, 6, 7] and collision resolution mechanisms. It has to be noted that static collision avoidance schemes need complete off-line resolution of conflicting temporal requirements.

The most popular protocol based on collision resolution is the CSMA/CD (Carrier Sense Multiple Access/ Collision Detection) protocol of Ethernet. This protocol inherently suffers from unpredictable delays when collisions occur. Therefore, it is less suited for critical real-time applications. However, there are CSMA protocols which try to avoid collisions dynamically. Whenever the medium is free, the nodes do not immediately start transmitting messages but delay sending for a predefined amount of time. This technique is e.g. used in the IEEE 802.11 wireless communication standard [3]. A more general solution which realises a priority based network arbitration is provided by the virtual time CSMA protocol (VTCSMA) [8]. The basic idea is that different priorities can be realized on a CSMA bus by waiting times. The higher the priority of a message, the shorter its waiting time. The VTCSMA algorithm is a general approach, which maps different message parameters (e.g. deadline or arrival time) onto waiting periods, hence prioritizing messages and scheduling them according to different strategies (e.g. earliest deadline-first or first-come-first-serve)[9].

3 Scheduling of messages

Our protocol exploits VTCSMA as a basic mechanim to prioritize messages and thus enforce proper message scheduling. Additionally, we take account of the fact that HRTM traffic needs preplanning. For HRTM a time slot (Fig. 1) is statically reserved.

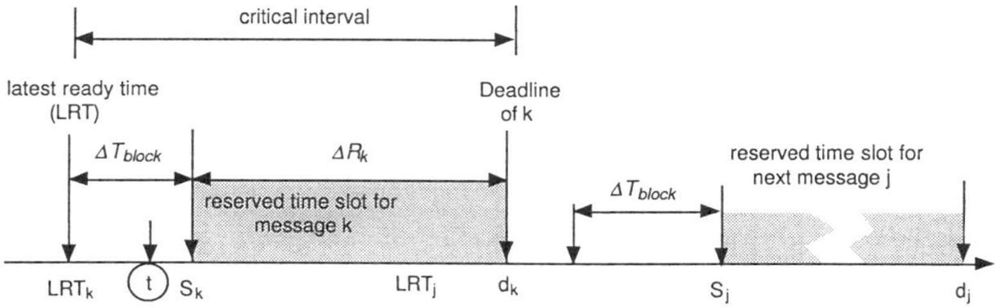

Fig. 1 Reserved time slots and critical interval for HRTMs

The reserved time slots are maintained in a data structure called calendar. The calendar is available at all nodes of the system which transmit HRTM. In contrast to the TDMA approach, however, the enforcement of the schedule is not dictated by global time but by the priority scheme. The benefit is that nodes which do not send HRTM do not need access to a global time base and can send their messages any time. Our scheme uses three priority classes. A HRTM gains the highest possible priority at the beginning of its reserved time slot. When a HRTM is in the sending queue and the reserved time-slot arrives, a HRTM is sent without any waiting time. Because no other HRTM is scheduled during this interval and all other messages always have a non-zero waiting period, no collision will corrupt the transfer.

However, due to the non-preemptive nature of message transmission on CSMA buses, every message in the worst case may be delayed by one message, which just has been started before the ready time of the respective HRTM. We define ΔT_{block} as the longest possible message transmission time. A HRTM k (with a reserved time-slot beginning at S_k) must be ready before S_k - ΔT_{block} (Fig. 1). Between S_k - ΔT_{block} and S_k, k is transmitted with a waiting time of $\Delta Cmin$, which is the minimum waiting time that can be distinguished from zero. This assures that a HRTM k gains the bus after S_k - ΔT_{block}. Consider the situation illustrated in Fig. 1. If at time t the bus becomes idle, and HRTMs k and a SRTM l compete for the bus, then k is transmitted with no contention, and finishes before d_k. If k has already been transmitted, then l is transmitted with a waiting time $2*\Delta C_{min} \leq C_l \leq K*\Delta C_{min}$ (K is a system constant with $K > 2$. (see below)). Before its latest ready time, the waiting time for a HRTM is a random period between $(p+1)*\Delta C_{min}$ and $\Delta C_{max} = 2*p*\Delta C_{min}$. This assures that outside the reserved lot, a HRTM has a lower priority than a SRTM.

The proposed scheduling approach for hard real-time communication requires access to a global time reference with bounded inaccuracy. To guarantee that messages k and j do not collide, their senders must agree that t is inside of the reserved time-slot of k, and outside of the reserved time-slot of j. This agreement is guaranteed by leaving a gap between different reserved time-slots. A more detailed discussion of the temporal properties is ound in [10, 11].

For the soft real-time distributed activities the approach guarantees optimal scheduling by applying VTCSMA-D on the bus which complies to EDF scheduling. The waiting period $\Delta C_l(t)$ of a SRTM l at the time t is determined as function of the deadline in the interval: $2 \bullet \Delta C_{min} \leq \Delta C_l(t) \leq K \bullet \Delta C_{min}$. K is a system constant selected to assure that the waiting time for a SRTM is always shorter than for a non real-time message or an early HRTM. Thus, SRTMs have always priority except in the reserved slots for HRTMs.

Non real-time messages (NRTM) do not change their importance by the passage of time. Therefore, a fixed waiting time is assigned to NRTMs. In order to fulfil the requirement that a NRTM only use the bus in absence of real-time messages, the waiting time for a NRTM is $\Delta C_{NRT} > \Delta C_{min} + \Delta C_{max}$.

4 Simulation

To evaluate our scheme, we selected the SAE benchmark for electric vehicles [12]. It is defined for a couple of distributed sensors and actuators communicating via a network. The benchmark comprises 42 messages classes exchanged by 7 computing nodes. We distinguish respective sets of periodic and sporadic hard and SRTMs. The total data load caused by the messages, including headers, CRC, inter-frame spacing, etc. is about 0.466 Mbit/s. Because we wanted to use the SAE benchmark which reflects a realistic load instead of using a synthetic load generator, we could not increase the bus load by simply increasing the number or length of messages. Instead, we varied the bus bandwidth. This is equivalent to varying the load at constant bus speed. In order to simulate the worst case situation for scheduling, the message arrival times have been adjusted such that deadlines of SRTMs are equal, hence resulting in the maximum number of collisions. Although very pessimistic, this case must be taken into account to show whether message loss for HRTMs is possible or not. We simulated the bus scheduling for a period of 1000 seconds[1]. The simulation (cf. Fig. 2) shows that our scheduling mechanism is superior to the pure EDF scheduling based on VTCSMA-D, because in the worst case of equal deadlines, VTCSMA-D results in timing failure even under an average bus load of about 25%.

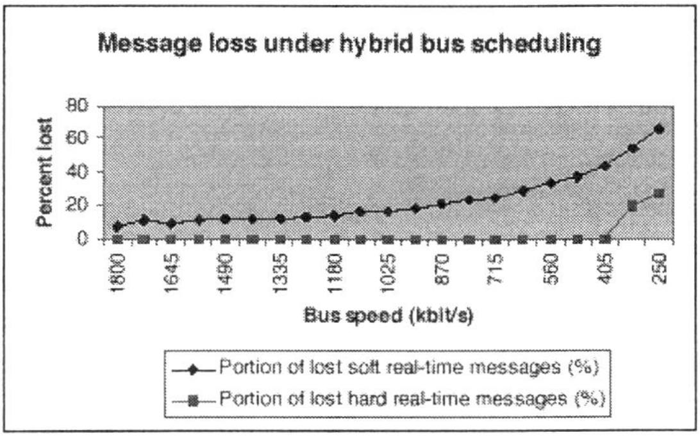

Fig. 2. Simulation of the hybrid bus scheduling algorithm

In contrast, the hybrid scheduling mechanism guarantees timely message delivery of HRTMs even under loads above 100%. In this case, of course, a great portion of SRTMs will miss their deadlines. The point at which HRTMs were lost was at the bus speed of 0.405 Mbit/s (about 115% average bus load). Although only 0.07% of HRTMs were lost, this would not be acceptable in a safety critical system as a electric vehicle. In our scheme, however, HRTMs are not really lost because of the unpredictable bus arbitration. Rather, at higher bus loads some HRTMs could not reserve any time-slot. Because the calendar for HRTMs is assumed to be constructed off-line, this violation would be recognized before the system actually is in operation. It has to be emphasized that this extreme bus utilization usually makes no sense in a real system. Here, it served as a worst case scenario to prove the guarantees preserved by the priority-based arbitration mechanism.

5 Conclusion

The paper describes a hybrid bus scheduling mechanism, which combines reservations for hard real-time traffic with the EDF scheduling used for soft real-

---

[1] The rate "η"of the virtual clock of the VTCSMA algorithm was set to η=8, i.e. the virtual clock runs eight times faster than real-time. η is a critical value in the VTCSMA protocol which roughly trades shorter waiting periods against the number of collisions. Because of space restrictions a detailed descussion of VTCSMA is not possibel here. The interested reader is refered to [9].

time activities. The contribution of the paper is how to enforce these scheduling decisions in a decentralized way on a general CSMA network like Ethernet or wireless LAN. We adapted the VTCSMA-D [9] algorithm to a specific priority-based arbitration scheme which guarantees transmission of HRTMs under all load conditions and schedules SRTMs according to EDF in a best effort manner. The approach has been validated by simulations which proved that in worst-case settings, HRTMs are transmitted as long as respective reservations can be provided.

References

1. K. Tindell and A. Burns: „Guaranteed Message Latencies for Distributed Safety-Critical Hard Real-Time Control Networks", *Report YCS-94-229, Department of Computer Science, University of York, May 1994*
2. H. Kopetz and G. Grünsteidl, "TTP - A Time-Triggered Protocol for Fault-Tolerant Real-Time Systems", *Research Report No. 12/92, Inst. für Techn. Informatik, Techn. University of Vienna, 1992*
3. Brian.P. Crow, Indra Widjaja, Jeung G. Kim, Prescott T. Sakai: "IEEE 802.11 Wireless Local Area Networks", *IEEE Communication Magazine, September 1997*
4. M. Mock, e. Nett: "Real-Time Communication in Autonomous Robot Systems", in: *Proc. of the 4th Int. Symp. on Autonomous Decentralized Systems, Tokyo, Japan, 1999*
5. H. Kopetz, M. Holzmann, W. Elmenreich: " A Universal Smart Transducer Interface: TTP/A", in: *Proc. of the 3rd Int. Symp. on Object-Oriented Real-Time Distributed Computing", Newport Beach, California, March 20006.*
6. R.M. Grow: " A timed token protocol for local area networks", in: *Proc. of Electro/82, Token Access Protocols, 1982*
7. S.T. Levi, S.K. Tripathi, S.D. Carson, A.K. Agrawala, "The MARUTI Hard Real-Time Operating System", *ACM Operating Systems Review 23(3):90-105, July 1989*
8. M.L. Molle and L. Kleinrock, "Virtual Time CSMA: Why two clocks are better than one", *IEEE Transactions on Communications 33(9), Sep. 1985.*
9. W. Zhao and K. Ramamritham, "Virtual Time CSMA Protocols for Hard Real Time Communcations", *IEEE Tr. Software Eng. 13(8), 1987*
10. M.A. Livani, J. Kaiser, W. Jia, "Scheduling Hard and Soft Real-Time Communication in the Controller Area Network (CAN)", *Control Engineering Practice, Vol. 7 Number 12 pp. 1515-1523, Dec. 1999.*
11. M.A. Livani and J. Kaiser, "Evaluation of a Hybrid Real-time Bus Scheduling Mechanism for CAN", *Lecture Notes in Computer Science 1586 (Jose Rolim et al. Eds.), pp. 425-429, Springer Verlag Berlin, 1999*
12. SAE, "Class C Application Requirement Considerations", *SAE Technical Report J2056/1, June 1993.*

Optimal Core Selection for Multicast Tree Routing in Hypercube Networks

Yong He[a] Weijia Jia[b] and Pui-On Au[b]

[a]*Dept of Mathematics, Zhejiang University, Hangzhou, China Department*

[b]*Dept. of Computer Science, City University of Hong Kong, SRC, China*

This paper proposes a set of novel efficient fault-tolerant multicast routing algorithms on hypercube networks using shared tree routing approach. The algorithms can select an optimal core (root) for constructing the shared tree so as to minimize the average delay for multicast messages. Simulation results indicate that our algorithms are efficient as compared with the existing multicast algorithms for balancing both objectives of short average delay and less resource utilizations over hypercube networks.

Introduction

Interconnection networks are used in parallel computer systems with a variety of different architectures. Particular usage of Interconnection networks and parallel computers are not only in the scientific computations but also in information processing such as knowledge search, mining and parallel service for today's e-commerce applications. Massively parallel computers (MPCs) with hypercube topologies are used in information dissemination-based applications for performance, reliability, and availability, such as in large-scale scientific computations, distributed databases, and media-on-demand servers etc. On those applications, efficient routing for the dissemination messages have been the important issues to the success of the applications. Hypercube possesses many attractive properties, such as strong connectivity (which admits a good fault-tolerance capability), low diameter, regularity, symmetry and ability to embed many other topologies. Some researchers have studied the multicast problems for hypercube topologies [Choi, Lan Wu et al]. Most of them focus on the construction of a source-based tree. This paper presents a novel optimal core selection algorithm and shared-tree generation algorithms for efficient multicast communications on hypercube networks. The issues discussed in this paper include:

Optimal Core Selection Algorithm that can minimize the average distance (delay) from the selected core to each receiver in a destination group.

Tree Generation Algorithm that can minimize the number of links used and at the same time to achieve the shortest end-to-end average delay.

Efficient Multicast Routing Algorithm that will reduce the end-to-end (average) delay even there exist some faulty nodes along the routing path.

Network Topology and Delay Metrics

Denote a hypercube network as a graph $G = (V, E, d)$, where V is the set of nodes, representing routers or switches in V; E is the set of edges (links), representing the logical connectivity; $d(u,v)$ is the function mapping edges to the distances (minimum delay) for each link $(u, v) \in E$. Formally, a ***m*-dimensional hypercube** H_m is a graph on the node set $\{0,1\}^m$, each node v is identified by m coordinates, $(x_0, x_1, \ldots, x_{m-1})$, where $x_i=0$ or 1 for $0 \le i \le m-1$. Two nodes $u \in H_m$ and $v \in H_m$ are neighbors if and only if u and v differ exactly in one coordinate. Thus H_m has 2^m nodes and every node has m neighbors. The delay (denote as static distance) of all links is defined as uniform, i.e., **one** unit. Therefore for two nodes $v_j = (x_{j0}, x_{j1}, \ldots, x_{j,m-1})$, $j = 1, 2$, the static delay between the two nodes is defined as the Hamming distance shown below:

$$d(v_1, v_2) = \sum_{i=0}^{m-1} |x_{1i} - x_{2i}| = \text{cardinality of the set } \{i \mid x_{1i} \neq x_{2i}\} \quad (2\text{-}1)$$

Assume that $g=\{v_1, \ldots, v_n\}$ is a group of members that subscribe multicast service from some sources. We define cost metrics as:

Tree Routing Cost: Based on the distance definition (2-1), for a given group of destinations g ={v_1, ..., v_n} and its root r, tree routing cost function f is defined as

$$f(r)=\sum_{j=1}^{n} d(r,v_j) \qquad (2\text{-}2)$$

where $v_j \in$ g and r $\in$ G is the root for a multicast tree. For the individual sources s, we may like to minimize f(s). Considering a set of sources S={s_1, ..., s_k}, the global routing cost for group g can be derived as:

$$F(S)=\sum_{i=1}^{k}\sum_{j=1}^{n} d(s_i,v_j)=\sum_{j=1}^{n}\sum_{i=1}^{k} d(s_i,v_j) \qquad (2\text{-}3)$$

Multicast delay for

(1) Source tree for a source node s is defined as

$$D_S(s) = max_{1\leq j\leq n}\{d(s, v_j)\} \qquad (2\text{-}4)$$

where $v_j \in$ g and s$\in$G is the source, which is the maximum propagation delay.

(2) Shared tree routing is to route the message from the source node s to the root of the shared tree and then the message is routed from the root to all the destinations in the group.

$$D_{ST}(s) = d(s, r) + max_{1\leq j\leq n}\{d(r, v_j)\} \qquad (2\text{-}5)$$

where $v_j \in g$; $s, r \in G$ and s is the source and r is the root of the tree.

Optimal Core Selection Algorithm

This section considers the core selection problem on a m-dimensional hypercube H_m. Denote the multicast group $g = \{v_1, v_2, ..., v_n\}$ where $v_j = (x_{j0}, x_{j2},..., x_{j,m-1})$, $1 \leq j \leq n$. We search for a node such that the objective function $f(v)$ (2-2) is minimized. We call such node that achieves the objective as the optimal core. The following algorithm will enable us to select such a core.

Alg-1: The core selection algorithm for H_m

Input: A group = $\{v_1, v_2, ..., v_n\}$ on H_m ; $v_j = (x_{j0}, x_{j2},..., x_{j,m-1})$ $j=1,2,..., n$;

Output: The Core $v^*=(x_0, x_1,..., x_{m-1})$;

Begin

For i=0 to m−1 do

  $|D_i|$ = *Cardinality of the set* $\{x_{ji}=0 \mid j=1, 2,..., n\}$;

  $|\overline{D_i}|$ = *Cardinality of the set* $\{x_{ji}=1 \mid j=1, 2,..., n\} = n-|D_i|$;

For i=0 to m−1 do

If $|D_i| > |\overline{D_i}|$ *then* $x_i=0$;

Else if $|D_i| < |\overline{D_i}|$ *then* $x_i=1$;

Else if $|D_i| = |\overline{D_i}|$ *then* $x_i=1$ *or 0 arbitrarily.*

Output $v^*=(x_0, x_1,\dots, x_{m-1})$ *as the core.*
end

The following theorem gives a sufficient and necessary condition whether a node is the optimal core (root).

Theorem 1: Alg-1 can find out the optimal core in time complexity $O(mn)$.
Proof: For any node $v = (u_0, u_2, \dots, u_{m-1})$, if it is selected as the core, by (2-2) the objective function can be evaluated as

$$f(v)=\sum_{j=1}^{n} d(v,v_j)=\sum_{j=1}^{n}\sum_{i=0}^{m-1}|u_i - x_{ji}|=\sum_{i=0}^{m-1}\sum_{j=1}^{n}|u_i - x_{ji}| \overset{\Delta}{=} \sum_{i=0}^{m-1} d_i \quad (3\text{-}1)$$

Since m sum factors in the most right item of the above equation are independent from each other, we can treat them separately. Recall that each coordinate is either 0 or 1, hence d_i is equal to either $|D_i|$ or $|\overline{D_i}|$. For the selected core $v^* =(x_0, x_1,\dots, x_{m-1})$ in Alg-1, the objective function can be calculated as

$$f(v^*)=\sum_{i=0}^{m-1}\sum_{j=1}^{n}|x_i - x_{ji}| \overset{\Delta}{=} \sum_{i=0}^{m-1} d_i^* \quad (3\text{-}2)$$

First, consider $|D_i|>|\overline{D_i}|$, $i=0,1,\dots, m-1$, we have $d_i^* = |\overline{D_i}|$ as $x_i=1$ in the algorithm, otherwise $x_i=0$. Thus *Alg*-1 fulfills the optimal condition for choosing the ith coordinate of the core. The same arguments can apply for the cases of $|D_i|<|\overline{D_i}|$ and $|D_i|= |\overline{D_i}|$. For the complexity, it is clear that Step 1 only needs $O(n)$ basic operations for each $i=0,1,\dots, m-1$, hence the time complexity of the algorithm is $O(mn)$. Q.E.D.

With Alg-1, it is clear that if the number of members in group g is odd, then the optimal core must be unique since it is impossible that $|D_i|= |\overline{D_i}|$ for any $i=0, 1,\dots, m-1$. Example 1: Consider a 4-dimentional hypercube H_4 and multicast group g consists of seven members: (0, 0, 0, 1), (1, 0, 0, 0), (0, 0, 1, 1), (1, 0, 1, 1), (0, 0, 1, 1), (1, 1, 0, 0) and (1, 1, 0, 1). It can be seen that

$|D_1|=5$, $|D_2|=2$, $|D_3|=2$, $|D_4|=4$, $|\overline{D_1}|=2$, $|\overline{D_2}|=5$, $|\overline{D_3}|=5$, and $|\overline{D_4}|=3$ respectively. Hence $x_1=1$, $x_2=0$, $x_3=0$, $x_4=1$. The optimal core is $v=(1, 0, 0, 1)$ and the objective function $f(v)=|\overline{D_1}|+|D_2|+|D_3|+|\overline{D_4}|=9$. Reader can easily check this is indeed the minimal value of $f()$. Shared Tree Generation Algorithm can relatively easy constructed as the optimal core has been selected. One can use Dijkstra algorithm to build it. We have improved the shared tree and the details are omitted for saving the space.

Performance Evaluation

This section reports performance results of our algorithms in fault-free case. To obtain the performance data, we use a discrete event simulation model to simulate multicast routings. The simulation program is written in C and runs in a SUN SPARC-20 workstation. The network simulated is devised with a 6-dimensional hypercube. The bandwidth of each link is uniformly measured as 10Mbps. For each simulation, 2 millions of multicast packets are randomly generated as a Poisson process and the average size of each packet is about several tens of Kbytes (20-30 Kb). Simulation starts when the first multicast packet is generated and ends when all the packets have reached their destinations. We collected the statistics data when the systems were stable. In our simulation, we take into consideration of number of members in the group from 3 to 15 and the distribution of the members is randomized in the network. Fig. 1 demonstrates that the average delay of various group sizes in the multicast group. From this diagram, we have the observations that our multicast algorithm is scalable with the randomly generated member distributions. In Fig. 2, our optimal core multicast algorithm is compared with the random core generation under the same distribution of group members. It can be seen that our algorithm incurs much less delay, particularly in the cases of heavy loading of multicast traffic in which every node is a multicast message source.

Conclusions

The algorithms presented can be extended to *m*-dimensional hypercube networks with faulty nodes as long as the faulty nodes do not affect the connectivity. In multiple faulty nodes case, heuristic algorithms can be applied to partition the hypercube networks with faults into several sub-hypercubes, each contains one fault. For each sub-hypercube, one may find its optimal core and construct the shared subtree. The subtrees may be further connected into a shared tree to cover the whole network.

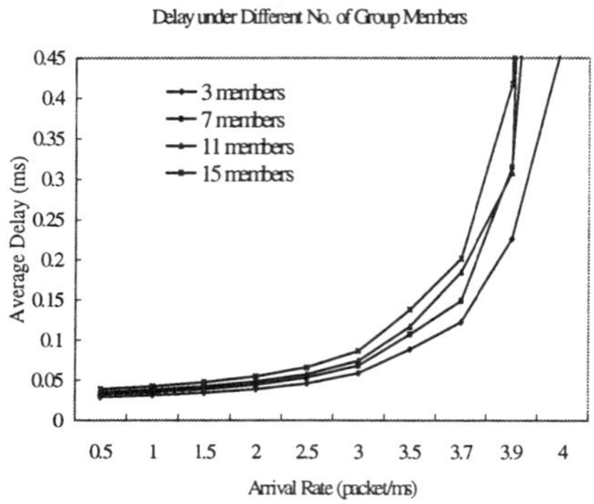

Fig. 1

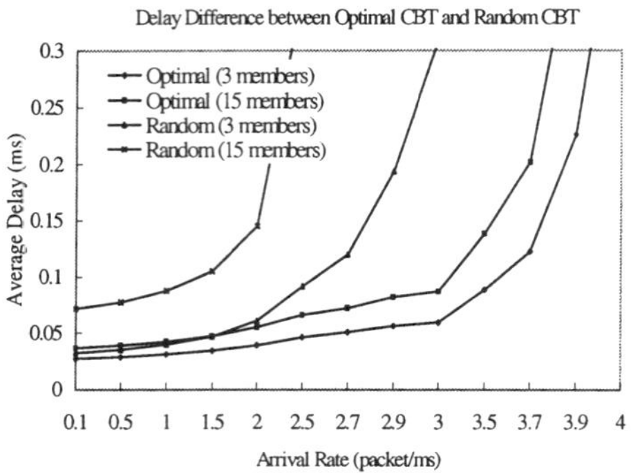

Fig. 2

Acknowledgments: This work was partially sponsored by City University of Hong Kong under research grants No. 7000130, 7001060. Yong He did this work while he is visiting City University of Hong Kong. His research was also partially supported by NSF of China under grants 19701028 and National 973 Fundamental Project of China.

References

Choi. Y, Esfahanian, A.H., Ni, L.M. "One-to-*k* Communication in Distributed-Memory Multiprocessors," *Proc. 25th Annual Allerton Conf. on Communication, Control, and Computing,* Sept. (1987), pp.268-270.

Lan, Y. R. Esfahanian, A.H. and Ni. L.M., "Multicast in Hypercube Multiprocessors," *J. of Parallel Distributed Computing,* Vol. 8, 1990, pp. 30-41.

Wu. J., "Unicasting in faulty Hypercubes Using Safety Levels", *IEEE Trans. Computers,* Vol. 46, pp. 241-247, 1997.

Wu J, Yao K. J, "A Limited-Global-Information-Based Multicasting Scheme for Faulty Hypercubes," *IEEE Trans. On Computers,* Vol. 44, 1995, pp. 1162-1167.

Chapter 3
Parallel Architecture & Parallel I/O Systems

Cache Performance of Scheduled Dataflow Architecture

Joseph M. Arul
Krishna M. Kavi
and
Shuaib Hanief

{arulj, kavi, haniefs}@ece.uah.edu
Department of Electrical and Computer Engineering
The University of Alabama in Huntsville
309, Sparkman Drive
Huntsville, AL 35899
USA

Abstract

In this paper we present our evaluation of the execution performance and cache behavior of a new multithreaded architecture being investigated by the authors. Our architecture uses non-blocking multithreaded model based on dataflow paradigm. In addition, all memory accesses are decoupled from the thread execution. Data is *pre-loaded* into the thread context (registers), and all results are *post-stored* after the completion of the thread execution. The non-blocking nature of threads reduces the number of context switches, thus reducing the overhead in scheduling threads. Our functional execution paradigm eliminates complex hardware required for dynamic scheduling of instructions used in modern superscalar architectures. We compare the execution and cache performance of our architecture with that of MIPS architecture as facilitated by DLX simulator. For the cache performance, we used the Dinero IV trace driven cache simulator.

Key Words. Multithreaded Architectures, Scheduled Dataflow Architectures, Superscalars, Decoupled Architectures, Memory Latency

1. Introduction

Multithreading[1] has been touted as the solution to minimize the loss of CPU cycles due to the disparity in memory and processor speeds, by executing several instruction streams simultaneously. While there are several different approaches to multithreading, there is a consensus that multithreading, in general, achieves higher instruction issue rates in processors that contain multiple functional units (e.g., Superscalars and VLIW) or multiple processing elements (i.e., Chip Multiprocessors) ([Butler 91], [Kavi 98a], [Krishnan 99], [Lam 92], [Tsai 99], [Wall 91]).

Our architecture differs from other multithreaded architectures in two ways: i) our programming paradigm is based on dataflow, which eliminates the need for complex runtime scheduling, thus reducing the hardware complexity significantly, and ii) complete decoupling of all memory accesses from execution pipeline. The underlying dataflow and non-blocking models of execution permit a clean separation of memory access (which is very difficult to coordinate in other programming models). Data is pre-loaded into an enabled thread's register context prior to its scheduling on the execution pipeline. After a thread completes execution, the results are post-stored from its registers into memory. The instruction set implements dataflow computational model, while the execution engine relies on control-flow like scheduling of instructions. We have completed the definition of the instruction set and developed an instruction level simulator. Using this simulator, we have performed initial evaluations of the architecture. We compared the execution performance of our architecture with that of conventional scalar RISC processors using DLX simulator [Hennessy 96]. For comparing cache behaviors we generated address traces for both DLX and our architecture, and used Dinero-IV [Edler99] cache simulator.

2. Related Research and Background

2.1 Dataflow Model and Architectures

The dataflow model and architecture have been studied for more than two decades and held the promise of an elegant execution paradigm with the ability to exploit inherent parallelism in applications. However, the actual implementations of the model have failed to deliver the promised performance. Nevertheless, several features of the dataflow computational model have found their place in modern processor architectures and compiler technology (e.g., Static Single Assignment, register renaming, dynamic scheduling and out-of-order instructions execution, I-structure like synchronization, non-blocking

---

[1] We acknowledge that there are alternative techniques for overcoming memory latency (e.g., RAMBUS [Rambus 96], [Cuppu 99], IRAM [Saulsbury 96]).

threads). Most modern processors utilize complex hardware techniques to detect data and control hazards, and dynamic parallelism -- to bring the execution engine closer to an idealized dataflow engine. It is our contention that such complexities can be eliminated if a more suitable implementation of the dataflow model can be discovered. Some of the limitations of the pure dataflow model that prevented its practical implementations include the following:

a) Too fine-grained (instruction level) multithreading,
b) Difficulty in exploiting memory hierarchies and registers, and
c) Asynchronous triggering of instructions

Many researchers have addressed the first two limitations of dataflow architectures ([Kavi 95, 98b] [Papadopoulos 90, 91], [Takesue 87], [Thoreson 87], [Tokoro 83]). Here we present a new architecture that addresses the third limitation. Some researchers have proposed designs in which the dataflow scheduling is applied only at thread level (i.e., macro-dataflow), while each thread is comprised of conventional control-flow instructions [Govindarajan 95], [Hum 95], [Sakai 93]. In such systems, the instructions within a thread do not retain functional properties, and hence, introduce Write-After-Write (WAW) and Write-After-Read (WAR) dependencies. This in turn requires complex hardware to perform dynamic instruction scheduling. In our system, the instructions within a thread still retain functional properties of dataflow model, and thus eliminate the need for complex hardware. The results (or data) flow from instruction to instruction, where each instruction specifies a location for the data to be stored. Our deviation in the proposed decoupled Scheduled Dataflow (SDF) system from pure dataflow is a deviation from *data driven execution* (or token driven execution) that is traditionally used for the implementation of "pure" dataflow processors.

3. Decoupled Scheduled Dataflow Architecture

Our architecture consists of two processing units: Synchronization Pipeline (SP) and Execution Pipeline (EP). SP is responsible for scheduling enabled threads on EP, pre-loading thread context (i.e., registers) with data from the thread's Frame memory, and post-storing results from a completed thread's registers in Frame memories of destination threads. A thread is enabled when all its inputs are received: the number of inputs is designated by its synchronization count, and the input data is stored in its Frame memory. The EP performs thread computations including integer and floating point arithmetic operations. In this section we will describe the two processing units in more detail.

3.1 Execution Pipeline

Figure 2 shows the block diagram of the Execution Pipeline (EP).

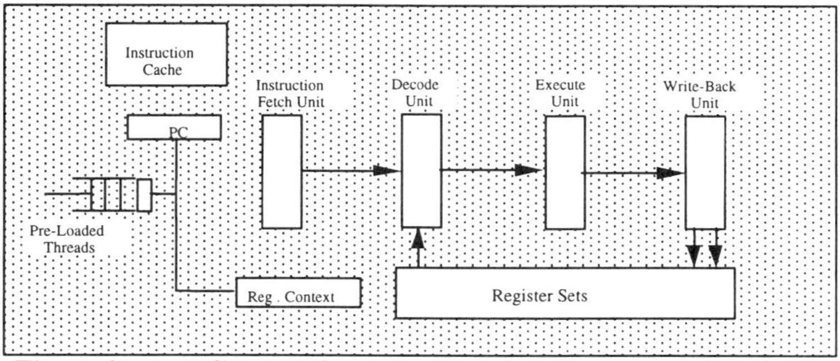

Figure 2. General Organization of Execution Pipeline (EP).

Instruction fetch unit behaves like a traditional fetch unit, relying on a program counter to fetch the next instruction[2]. The information in the Register context can be viewed as a part of the thread continuation: <ip, fp>, where fp refers to a register set assigned to the thread during its execution.

Decode (and register fetch) unit obtains a pair of registers that contains the two source operands for the instruction. *Execute unit* executes the instruction and sends the results to write-back unit along with the destination register numbers. *Write-back unit* writes two values to the register file.

In our architecture we view registers in pairs where a pair of registers contain the operands for an instruction; data is stored in either the left or right half of a register pair by a predecessor instruction. In the previous dataflow architectures such as ETS, instruction is not scheduled for execution immediately when the operands are matched. Instead, operands are saved in the register-pair associated with the instruction. The enabled instruction is scheduled for execution at a later time. Figure 3 shows the organization of the operand registers. Note that our register files require two write ports since the write-back unit may store results in (up to) two destination registers.

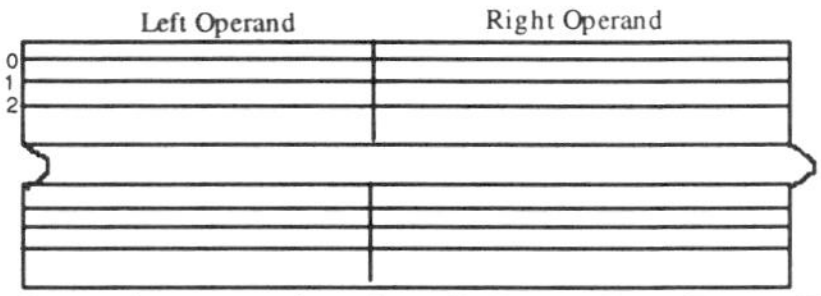

Figure 3. Operand register pairs for Scheduled Dataflow Architecture.

As can be seen, the Execution Pipeline (EP) behaves more like a conventional pipeline while retaining the primary dataflow properties; data flows from instruction to instruction. This eliminates the need for complex hardware for detecting Write-After-Read (WAR) and Write-After-Write (WAW)

[2] Since both EP and SP need to execute instructions, our instruction cache is assumed to be dual ported.

dependencies and register renaming. The EP does not access data cache memory, and hence require no pipeline stalls (or context switches) due to cache misses.

3.2. Synchronization Pipeline

Figure 4 shows the organization of the Synchronization pipeline (SP). The primary pipeline consists of the following stages: *Instruction Fetch unit* fetches an instruction belonging to the current thread using PC. *Decode unit* decodes the instruction and fetches register operands (using Register Context). *Effective Address unit* computes effective address for memory access instructions. LOAD and STORE instructions only reference the Frame memories of threads, using a frame-pointer (FP) and an offset into the frame — both the frame-pointer and the offset are contained in registers. *Memory Access unit* completes LOAD and STORE instructions. Pursuant to a post-store, the synchronization count of a thread is decremented. *Execute unit* decrements synchronization counts. When the count becomes zero, the thread is moved to enabled list for pre-load and subsequent execution on EP. I-Structure accesses (IFETCH and ISTORE) are also handled in the Execute unit. Finally, *Write-Back unit* completes LOAD (pre-load) and IFETCH instructions.

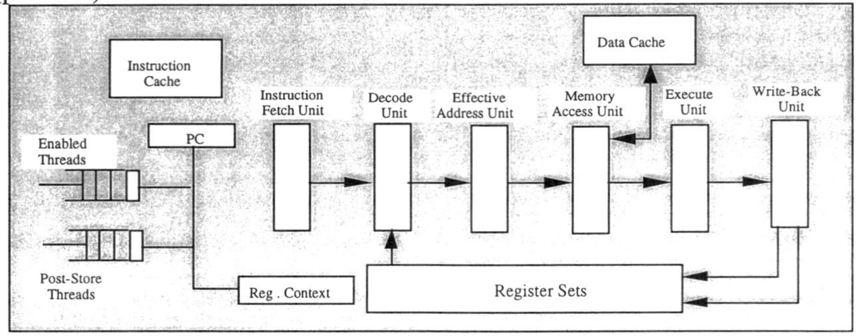

Figure 4. The Synchronization Pipeline.

In addition to accessing memory (for pre-load and post-store), Synchronization Pipeline (SP) holds thread continuations awaiting inputs and allocates register contexts for enabled threads. In our architecture a thread is created using a FALLOC[3] instruction. FALLOC instruction creates a frame and stores instruction pointer (IP) of the thread and its synchronization count (Synch Count) indicating the number of inputs needed to enable the thread. When a thread completes its execution and "post-stores" results (performed by SP), the synchronization counts of awaiting threads are modified.

---

[3] FALLOC and FFREE take 2 cycles in our architecture. FORKEP and FORKSP take 4 cycles to complete. This number is based on the observations made in Sparcle [Agarwal 93] that a 4-cycle context switch can be implemented in hardware.

An enabled thread is scheduled by allocating a register context to it, and "pre-loading" the registers from its Frame memory. In order to speed up frame allocation, SP pre-allocates fixed sized frames for threads and maintains a stack of indexes pointing to the available frames. The Execution processor (EP) pops an index from the stack and uses it as the address of the frame (i.e., FP) in response to a FALLOC instruction. SP pushes de-allocated frames when executing FFREE instruction subsequent to post-stores of completed threads. The register sets (Reg. Context) are viewed as circular buffers for assigning (and de-allocating) to enabled threads. These policies permit for fast context switch and creation of threads. A thread moves from "pre-load" status (at SP), to "execute" status (at EP) and finishes in "post-store" status (at SP). We use FORKSP to move a thread from EP to SP and FORKEP to move a thread from SP to EP. Figure 5 shows a more complete view of the SP.

The scheduler unit is responsible for determining when a thread becomes enabled and allocating a register context to the enabled thread. Although not implemented in our current environment, the scheduler may change the priorities between pre-load and post-store threads based on the number and availability of register contexts. Giving Enabled threads higher priority (if register contexts are available) would produce more threads for Execution Pipeline (and more overlap between EP and SP). However, if register contexts are unavailable, executing post-store threads will release register sets.

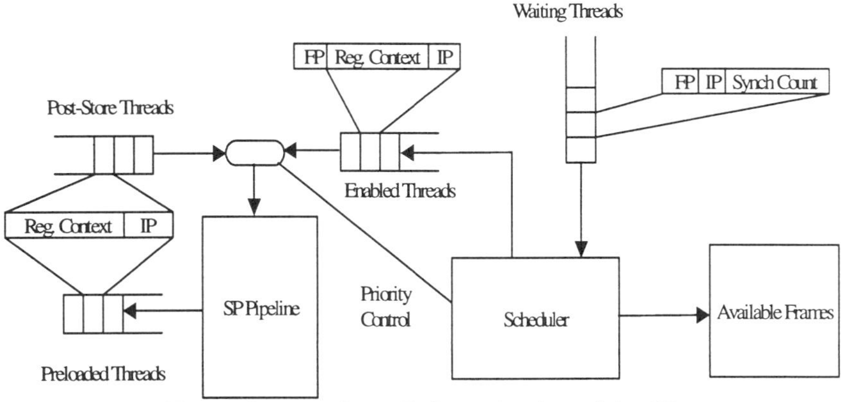

Figure 5. Overall Organization of the SP.

Notice how a thread is identified differently during its life cycle. Initially, when a thread is created, a frame is allocated. Such a thread (called Waiting) will be identified by a Frame Pointer (FP), an Instruction Pointer (IP) that points to the first instruction of the thread, usually a pre-load instruction, and a synchronization count (Synch Count) indicating the number of inputs needed before the thread is enabled for execution. When the synchronization count becomes zero, the thread is moved to the Enabled list, following the allocation of a Register Context. At this time, a FP, a Reg. Context, and IP identify the thread. Once a thread completes the "pre-load" phase, it is moved to the Pre-Loaded list and handed off to the Execution Processor (EP). At this time, Register Context and the Instruction Pointer identify threads. Note that the IP will now point to the first instruction beyond the pre-load (referring to the first executable instruction). After EP completes the execution of a thread, the thread is then moved to the Post-Store list and handed off to the SP for post-storing (by executing FORKSP instruction). At this time a Register Context and an IP identify the thread. Now the IP points to the first post-store instruction.

4. Evaluation of the Decoupled Scheduled Dataflow Architecture

Initially, we relied on analytical models and Monte Carlo simulations to compare the proposed architecture with Rhamma, ETS and conventional RISC processors [Kavi 99a-b]. More recently we developed an instruction level simulator for Scheduled Dataflow architecture (SDF). At present the simulator assumes a perfect cache. However, we will show the cache behavior of our architecture by using address traces from our simulator and show the expected cache behavior for our architecture.

4.1 Execution Performance Of Scheduled Dataflow

In this section we compare the execution cycles required for Scheduled Dataflow with those for a conventional RISC system using DLX simulator [Hennessy 96]. The programs used for this comparison include a recursive Fibonacci program, Matrix Multiply, Livermore Kernel 5 as well as the code segment for picture zooming [Terada 99]. We used dlxcc to generate DLX code in our comparisons. We equate a thread in SDF with a function in DLX – if a SDF thread executes 5(unrolled) loop iterations, so does the equivalent DLX function. The results are shown in Table 1 below. For the above examples we used a degree of 5 unrolling for Matrix Multiply, Livermore Loop 5 and Zoom program. We also used 5 (concurrent) threads for these 3 programs in SDF. In both platforms, we assumed one cycle per arithmetic and memory access instructions.

As can be seen from Table 1, SDF system outperforms MIPS architecture when the program exhibits greater parallelism (e.g: Matrix Multiply, Zoom and Livermore Loop 5), Livermore Loop exhibits less parallelism than Matrix Multiply even though both programs have three nested loops and it is due to a loop carried dependency in Livermore loop.

Zoom exhibits moderate parallelism; however, a significant serial fraction (in the outer loop) exists, limiting the speed-up (Amdhal's law). SDF under performs when the program exhibits little parallelism (e.g: Fibonacci). This is in line with general acceptance that multithreaded architectures are not very effective for sequential (or single threaded) applications. The speed achieved for Matrix Multiply really surprised us. Part of the speed up is because of the multithreading, partly due to the decoupling of memory accesses and partly due to lack of any pipeline stalls (due to the non-blocking dataflow model). Data dependencies encountered by DLX (from Load to ALU ops) led to more cycles being wasted in DLX. In addition, since SDF threads are equated to function in DLX, DLX has used stack for exchanging data, which may have caused some unnecessary memory accesses. It is satisfying to note that it is possible to design non-blocking multithreaded architectures with completely decoupled memory accesses, and achieve scalable performance. Our architecture incurs unavoidable overheads for creating threads (allocation of frames, allocation of register contexts) and transferring threads between SP and EP such as FORKEP and FORKSP instructions. At present, data can only be exchanged between threads by storing them in threads' frames (memory). These memory accesses can be avoided by storing the results of a thread directly into another thread's register context. One could have eliminated storing (and loading) thread data in memory by allocating all frames directly in register sets (by providing sufficient register sets in hardware).

Table 1. Execution Performance of Scheduled Dataflow compared to DLX

	Matrix Multply				Livermore 5		
N	DLX Cycles	SDF Cycles	Speed UP	Loop=N	DLX Cycles	SDF Cycles	Speed Up
25*25	966090	306702	3.150	50	87359	56859	1.536
50*50	7273390	2159780	3.368	100	354659	215579	1.645
75*75	24464440	6976908	3.506	150	801959	476299	1.684
100*100	57891740	16175586	3.579	200	1429259	839019	1.703
				250	2236559	1303739	1.715
				300	3223859	1870459	1.724
				350	4391159	2911789	1.508
				400	5738459	3309899	1.734
				450	7265759	4182619	1.737
	Fibonacci				Zoom		
N	DLX Cycles	SDF Cycles	Speed UP	N	DLX Cycles	SDF Cycles	Speed UP
5	615	842	0.7304	5,5,4	10175	9661	1.0532
10	7014	10035	0.699	10,10,4	40510	37421	1.0825
15	77956	111909	0.6966	15,15,4	97945	83331	1.1754
20	864717	1241716	0.6964	20,20,4	161580	147391	1.0963
25	9590030	13771467	0.6964	25,25,4	271175	229601	1.1811
30	1.06E+08	1.53E+08	0.6964	30,30,4	391150	329961	1.1854
				35,35,4	532285	448471	1.1869
				40,40,4	645520	585131	1.1032

We have also compared the SDF with recent RISC superscalar processor with dynamic instruction scheduling (i.e: out of order instruction issue and completion, predicated instructions). The result is not shown in this paper due to the limited space. However, SDF system eliminates the need for complex hardware required for dynamic instruction scheduling. The hardware savings can be used to include additional register-sets, which can help in an increased degree of thread parallelism and thread granularities.

4.2 Effect of thread level parallelism On Execution Behaviour

In this section we present the performance benefits of increasing the thread level parallelism (i.e., number of ready threads). Figure 6 shows the impact of increasing the number of threads for Matrix Multiply. Similar behavior was observed with other benchmarks. Likewise, when the thread granularity was increased (achieved with a greater degree of loop unrolling), the performance increases with coarser grained threads, albeit non-linearly.

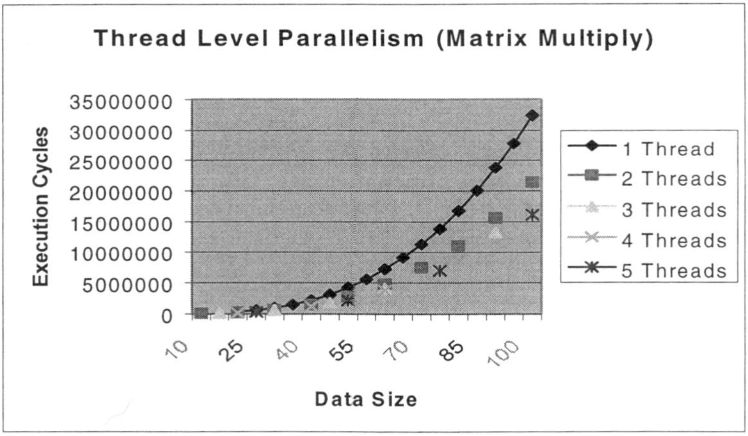

Figure 6 Effect of Thread Level Parallelism On SDF Execution (Matrix Multiply)

4.2 Cache Behavior of Scheduled Dataflow Architecture (SDF)

Currently the instruction set simulator does not include cache memories. In this section, we compare the cache behavior of SDF programs with that of DLX collecting the address traces on both systems and using Dinero IV[Edler99] to generate cache behaviors. Table 2 presents the cache behavior for Matrix Multiply, Livermore Loop using 5 threads and a single thread for Fibonacci program using 256K bytes and a block size of 64 bytes. Even though different cache and the cache behavior are not shown in this paper, SDF cache behavior is similar to cache memories in conventional systems when the cache parameters (like associativity, block size, and cache size) are different.

Table 2. Cache behavior of SDF compared to DLX architecture

Matrix Multiply						
N*N	DLX Refs	DLX Misses	DLX Rate	SDF Refs	SDF Misses	SDF Rate
25	286714	61	0.02	156470	382	0.24
50	1627928	237	0.01	1094360	614	0.06
75	5462503	530	0.01	3526250	1010	0.03
100	12910828	940	0.01	8164640	1558	0.02

Livermore						
Loop=N	DLX Refs	DLX Misses	DLX Rate	SDF Refs	SDF Misses	SDF Rate
50	22429	8	0.000356681	24177	22	0.00090996
100	88829	13	0.000146349	91913	31	0.00033728
150	199229	17	8.53289E-05	203249	40	0.0001968
200	353629	22	6.22121E-05	358185	49	0.0001368
250	1104058	27	2.44552E-05	556721	58	0.00010418
300	794429	32	4.02805E-05	798857	67	8.387E-05
350	1080829	36	3.33078E-05	1084593	76	7.0072E-05
400	1411229	41	2.90527E-05	1413929	88	6.2238E-05
450	1785629	46	2.57612E-05	1786865	97	5.4285E-05

Fibonacci						
N	DLX Refs	DLX Misses	DLX Rate	SDF Refs	SDF Misses	SDF Rate
5	260	5	0.01923	134	8	0.0597
10	3014	10	0.00332	1702	13	0.0076
15	33546	14	0.00042	19076	18	0.0009
20	372152	18	4.8E-05	211758	23	0.0001
25	4127350	23	5.6E-06	2348634	28	1E-05
30	40975448	27	6.6E-07	26046952	33	1E-06

The best cache behavior can be achieved when the block size is equal to frame size. Since the input data from a thread's frame is pre-loaded into the thread's context, the frame can be pre-fetched and so, the pre-fetching would be more effective in this architecture. Once it is preloaded, the frame is freed and can be allocated for the next thread to be created.

In SDF, the I-structure and the frames are mapped to different areas of memory. So, the Matrix Multiply and the Livermore Loop 5 of SDF cache behavior as compared to DLX do not perform any better. The Fibonacci program in SDF presents a very similar result as of DLX.

4.4 Effect of separate Data and I-structure Caches on SDF.

Table 3 presents the cache behavior for the unified cache as well as the effect of having a separate cache for data and I-structure.

Table 3. Effect of separate I-Structure Cache

Matrix Multiply						
N	SDF Refs	Unified Misses	Unified Miss Rate	I-Struct Misses	I-Struc Miss Rate	Frame Misses
25	156470	382	0.002441363	81	0.00051767	11
50	1094360	614	0.000561059	319	0.00029149	11
75	3526250	1010	0.000286423	3132	0.0008882	11
100	8164640	1558	0.000190823	6215	0.00076121	11

Livermore Looop 5						
Loop=N	SDF Refs	Unified Misses	Unified Miss Rate	I-Struct Misses	I-Struc Miss Rate	Frame Misses
50	24177	22	0.000909956	12	0.00049634	10
100	91913	31	0.000337275	21	0.00022848	10
150	203249	40	0.000196803	30	0.0001476	10
200	358185	49	0.000136801	39	0.00010888	10
250	556721	58	0.000104181	48	8.6219E-05	10
300	798857	67	8.38698E-05	57	7.1352E-05	10
350	1084593	76	7.00724E-05	66	6.0852E-05	10
400	1413929	88	6.22379E-05	78	5.5165E-05	10
450	1786865	97	5.4285E-05	87	4.8689E-05	10

One must note that using a single cache for both the frame data (data cache) and the I-structures (arrays) cause more conflict misses. For unified case, single 256K cache (64byte blocks) and for split case 128K I-structure cache and 128K frame cache were used. The Livermore loop program using separate I-structure cache, the cache misses are very similar to DLX cache misses. However, in the

Matrix Multiply program the cache misses show different behavior due to the fact that the program accesses rows of one matrix and columns of another matrix, and the strides have caused more conflict misses for larger data sizes.

From the tables below it should be noted that data cache (used for thread frames) encounters no conflict misses. This can be attributed to our "stack" of frames allocated and the reuse of frames. The misses also indicate the maximum number of frames needed by the program during its execution. So Matrix Multiply requires a maximum of 11 frames, whereas Livermore Loop requires 10 frames, and these frames could be eliminated by allocating register sets to threads on creation.

5. Conclusions

In this paper we presented a dataflow multithreaded architecture that utilizes control-flow like scheduling of instructions which separates memory accesses from instruction execution to tolerate long latency operations. The primary goal is to show that it is possible to design efficient multithreaded dataflow systems. Using an instruction set level simulator for our architectures, we compared the execution performance and cache behavior of SDF with that of a single pipelined MIPS processing system. Our results are very encouraging. When the degree of parallelism is high, SDF substantially outperforms MIPS. We also investigated the impact of increasing thread granularity and thread level parallelism. As with any multithreaded system, SDF shows performance improvements with coarser grained threads and increased thread level parallelism.

While decoupled access/execute implementations are possible within the scope of conventional architectures, multithreading model presents greater opportunities for exploiting the separation of memory accesses from execution pipeline. In our model, threads exchange data only through the frame memories of threads. The use of frame memories for thread data permits for a clean decoupling of memory accesses into pre-loads and post-stores. This also leads to greater data localities and very low cache-miss rates. Using a separate I-structure cache can further reduce the data cache misses.

At this time we do not know if our approach performs better than modern superscalar systems that use dynamic instruction scheduling (e.g., out of order instruction issue and completions). However, we strongly believe that the use of dataflow instructions reduces the complexity of the processor by eliminating the need for complex logic (e.g., scoreboard) needed for resolving data dependencies, register renaming, out-of-order instruction scheduling and branch predictions. The silicon area saved may be used to include more register-sets and registers per set to improve thread level parallelism and thread granularities. Moreover, our current instruction set and the compiler are not optimized. We will soon develop quantitative comparisons of our architecture with conventional scalar and superscalar architectures for a wider range of benchmark programs (including SPEC-95 programs).

6. References

[Agarwal 93] A. Agarwal, et. Al. "Sparcle: An evolutionary processor design for multiprocessors", *IEEE Micro,* pp 48-61, June 1993.

[Bohm 91] A. D. W. Bohm, D. C. Cann, J. T. Feo, and R. R. Oldehoeft, "SISAL Reference Manual: language version 2.0", Tech, Report CS91-118, Computer Science Dept., Colorado State University.

[Butler 91] M. Butler, et. Al. "Single instruction stream parallelism is greater than two", *Proc. of 18th Intl. Symposium on Computer Architecture (ISCA-18)*, pp 276-286, May 1991.

[Cuppu 99]V. Cuppu, B. Jacob, B. Davis and T. Mudge. "A performance comparison of contemporary DRAM architectures", *Proc of the Intl. Symposium on Computer Architecture (ISCA-26),* pp 222-233, May 1999.

[Edler 99] J.Edler and Mark D. Hill, "DineroIV Trace-Driven Uniprocessor Cache Simulator", http://www.cs.wisc.edu/ ~markhill/ DineroIV

[Giorgi 99] R. Giorgi, K. M. Kavi and H.Y. Kim. "Scheduled Dataflow Instruction Manual", Dept. of Electrical and Computer Engineering, UAH. http://crash1.eb.uah.edu/~kavi /Research/sda.pdf

[Govindarajan 95] R. Govindarajan, S.S. Nemawarkar and P; LeNir. "Design and performance evaluation of a multithreaded architecture", *Proceeding of the first High Performance Computer Architecture (HPCA-1)*, Jan. 1995, pp 298-307.

[Grunwald 97] W. Grunewald, T. Ungerer, "A Multithreaded Processor Design for Distributed Shared Memory System," *Proc. Int'l Conf. on Advances in Parallel and Distributed Computing*, 1997.

[Hennessy 96] J.L. Hennessy, and D.A. Patterson. *Computer Architecture: A Quantitative Approach*, Morgan Kaufmann Publisher, 1996.

[Hum 95] H.H.-J. Hum, ET. al., "A Design Study of the EARTH Multiprocessor," *Proceedings of the Conference on Parallel Architectures and Compilation Techniques (PACT),* Limassol, Cyprus, June 1995, pp. 59-68.

[Kavi 00] K. M. Kavi, J. Arul, R. Giorgi and A.R. Hurson. "A decoupled scheduled dataflow multithreaded architecture", Submitted to the 2000 International Symposium on Computer Architecture (ISCA-27). Also: http://crash1.eb.uah.edu/~kavi/Research/ ISCASDF.pdf

[Kavi 99a] K.M. Kavi. H.S. Kim and A.R. Hurson. "Scheduled dataflow architecture: A synchronous execution paradigm for dataflow", *IASTED Journal of Computers and Applications.* Vol. 21, No. 3 (Oct. 1999), pp 114-124.

[Kavi 99b] K.M. Kavi, H.-S. Kim, J. Arul and A.R. Hurson "A decoupled scheduled dataflow multithreaded architecture", *Proceedings of the 1999 International Symposium on Parallel Architectures, Algorithms and Networks (I-SPAN-99),* Fremantle, Western Australia, June 23-25, 1999, pp 138-143.

[Kavi 98a] K.M. Kavi, B. Lee and A.R. Hurson. "Multithreaded systems: A survey", *Advances in Computers,* Academic Press, 1998, pp 287-327.

[Kavi 98b] K.M. Kavi and A.R. Hurson. "Design of cache memories in dataflow architectures", *Euromicro Journal on Systems Architecture.* Vol. 44, No. 9-10, June 1998, pp 657-674.

[Kavi 95] K.M. Kavi, et. al. "Design of cache memories for multi-threaded dataflow architecture", *Proceedings of the 22nd Intl. Symp. on Computer Architecture* (ISCA-22), June 1995, St. Margherita Ligure, Italy, pp. 253-264.

[Krishnan 99] V. Krishnan and J. Torrellas. "A chip-multiprocessor architecture with speculative multithreading", IEEE Trans. on Computers, Sept. 1999, pp.866-880.

[Lam 92] M. Lam and R.P. Wilson. "Limits of control flow on parallelism", *Proc. of the 19th Intl. Symposium on Computer Architecture (ISCA-19)*, pp 46-57, May 1992.

[Papadopoulos 91] G.M. Papadopoulos and K.R. Traub. (1991). "Multithreading: A Revisionist View of Dataflow Architectures," *Proceedings of the 18th International Symposium on Computer Architecture (ISCA-18)*, pp. 342-351.

[Papadopoulos 90] G.M. Papadopoulos and D.E. Culler. "Monsoon: An explicit token-store architecture", *Proc. of 17th Intl. Symposium on Computer Architecture (ISCA-17)*, pp 82-91, May 1990.

[Rambus 96] Rambus. "Memory latency comparison", Tech. Rept. Rambus, Inc. (http://www.rambus.com/).

[Sakai 93] S. Sakai, et. al, "Super-threading: Architectural and Software Mechanisms for Optimizing Parallel Computations," *Proc. of 1993 Int'l Conference on Supercomputing*, July 1993, pp. 251-260.

[Saulsbury 96] A. Saulsbury, F. Pong, and A. Nowatzyk. "Missing the memory wall: A case for processor/memory integration," *Proceedings of the 23rd International Symposium on Computer Architecture,* May 1996, pp 90-101.

[Smith 82] Smith, J.E. "Decoupled Access/Execute Computer Architectures", *Proc of the 9th Annual Symp on Computer Architecture*, May 1982, pp 112-119.

[Takesue 87] M. Takesue. "A unified resource management and execution control mechanism for Dataflow Machines". *Proc. 14th Annl. Intl. Symp. on Computer Architecture(ISCA-14)*, June 1987, pp. 90-97.

[Thekkath 94] R. Thekkath and S.J. Eggers, ''The effectiveness of multiple hardware contexts," *Proceedings of the 6th International Conference on Architectural Support for Programming Languages and Operating Systems*, pp.328--337, October 1994.

[Thoreson 87] S.A. Thoreson and A.N. Long. "A Feasibility study of a Memory Hierarchy in Data Flow Environment". *Proc. Intl. Conference on Parallel Conference*, June 1987, pp. 356-360.

[Tokoro 83] M. Tokoro, J.R. Jagannathan and H. Sunahara. "On the working set concept for data-flow machines", *Proc. 10th Annul. Intl. Symp. on Computer Architecture (ISCA-10)*, July 1983, pp. 90-97.

[Tsai 99] J. Y. Tsai, J. Huang, C. Amlo, D. Lilja, and P. C. Yew. "The Superthreaded processor architecture", IEEE Trans. on Computers, Sept. 1999, pp. 881-902.

[Wall 91] D.W. Wall. "Limits on instruction-level parallelism", *Proc of 4th Intl. Conference on Architectural support for Programming Languages and Operating Systems (ASPLOS-4),* pp 176-188, April 1991.

AN INTEGRATION OF PIPELINED SYSTEM AND DISTRIBUTED SYSTEM FOR REAL-TIME CLASSIFICATION OF REMOTELY SENSED IMAGES

J. YOU[1,2], D. ZHANG[1] and J. CAO[1]

[1] *Department of Computing, The Hong Kong Polytechnic University*
Kowloon, Hong Kong
E-mail: {csyjia, csdzhang, csjcao}@comp.polyu.edu.hk
[2] *School of Compiting and Information Technology*
Griffith University, Nathan Campus, Brisbane, QLD, Australia 4111
E-mail: you@cit.gu.edu.au

This paper describes a system integration approach to achieve real-time classification of satellite images by parallelism. In contrast to the traditional systems which deal with data acquisition, compression, transmission and analysis separately, our smart remote sensing system integrated a pipelined architecture on-board a satellite and a network of workstation clusters at the ground station. The pipelined system is responsible for the enhancement and compression of the image data captured from the camera on-board a satellite. A network of workstation clusters at the ground station is dedicated to the comprehensive analysis of such pre-processed remote data transmitted from the satellite in a parallel virtual machine environment, which includes the decoding of the compressed image data and image classification by textures. Both the system design and implementation strategies are briefly described. In addition, a parallel search algorithm is introduced to speed up the classification tasks based on the accelerated cascading technique and the dynamic processor allocation scheme. The time complexity analysis and experimental results show the effectiveness and efficiency of the proposed techniques.

1 Introduction

With the advances of remote sensing techniques, the fast and accurate analysis of satellite imagery has played an important role in both military and civilian applications. There have been increasing needs for the classification of satellite images by generating discrete classes of known identity for land cover types [13]. Multi-spectral techniques have been extensively investigated and several approaches for classification have been proposed[14]. However, the gray value assigned to a particular pixel of a remotely sensed image is the average reflectance of different types of ground covers present in the corresponding pixel area. Thus, a pixel may represent different possible classes with various degrees of similarities. Consequently, the use of such intensity values for individual pixels would lead to a high rate of misclassification error if the number of classes is large. Although the approaches based on fuzzy set theory have been reported effective in analyzing remote sensing images [10], some spatial knowledge about target regions and their inter-relationships are required.

The classification of ground-cover types of satellite images by textures can be considered as allocating an unknown input satellite image sample to one of possible ground-cover types in the training remotely sensed image collections. Briefly stated, there is a finite number of classes C_i, $i = 1, ..., m$. A training ground-cover collection comprising a number of so-called training images belonging to each class is available. Based on the feature extracted from these sets, a classifier is designed to recognize a given test image of unknown class to one of the m classes. The key step in any classification problem is the image feature extraction policy which reduces the dimension of data to a computationally reasonable amount while preserving much of the discriminant information present in the actual data. It is very important to develop a general classification scheme invariant of scale and orientation changes. This paper focuses on the classification strategy which is not affected by the zooming and/or rotation of the camera on-board the satellite.

There has been considerable interest in the development and application of smart sensing techniques to achieve real-time imaging [16]. The underlying challenge is how to reduce the redundancy information existed in remote sensing data and match the image transmission rate between the satellite and the computation power on ground. This paper presents an effective approach by developing a parallel system which integrates a pipelined smart sensor onboard satellite and a network of workstation clusters at the ground station. In other words, with such a real-time remote sensing system, the scanning images obtained from satellite are pre-processed on-board in real-time, and only the useful image data are compressed and transmitted to the ground station simultaneously. A pipeline architecture is designed for the fast image enhancement and compression. The classification of ground-cover types of the satellite image data is further performed by parallel texture classification on a network workstation clusters in a parallel virtual machine (PVM) environment at the ground station. A parallel searching algorithm is introduced to facilitate the fast processing.

The purposes of this paper are: (1) to develop an adaptive texture feature classifier invariant of rotation and scale changes; (2) to integrate a pipeline system on board a satellite and a distributed system at the ground station to achieve real-time remote sensing; (3) to simplify and speed up a texture classification procedure for classification of satellite images by parallel searching through a 2D matrix; (4) to run experimentation on remotely sensed data to demonstrate the potential of the proposed method; (5) to provide some theoretic analysis for the performance evaluation. The work is organized as follows: Section 2 introduces a dynamic method to extract texture features; Section 3 discusses the multi-scale and multi-resolution texture class database for classification of satellite images by textures; Section 4 summarizes the basic parallel searching strategies for fast classification and the corresponding time complexity analysis; Section 5 describes the general strategy of system integration for smart sensing and real-time computing; Section 6 and Section 7 presents our experimental results and conclusion respectively.

2 Dynamic Texture Feature Extraction

The statistical approach to texture classification pioneered by Laws[8] is notable for its computational simplicity. He introduced the notion of a single parameter, the local "texture energy"(TE) evaluated at each pixel location (i, j) in the convolved image over a large window size $15 * 15$ as the measure of texture features in the spatial domain. Although individually Laws' masks can be used in isolation as a texture classifier, they are subject to a number of limitations due to the lack of robustness with respect to the fixed masks. One feasible approach to improve the performance is to replace the fixed masks with adaptive masks "tuned" to be invariant to changes in rotation and scale. This process involves the determination of texture class 'tuned' mask which when applied to a textured image smooth out regions of common texture so that the variance of the convolved image, typically over a 15×15 local window, is (a) reasonably constant over all locations within a region of uniform texture, so that such a region is essentially converted into a region of uniform gray scale, (b) markedly different in value between regions of different texture. The approach reported here is an extension of the work of Benke *et al*'s. Although Benke-Skinner introduced and applied the adaptive mask concept [2], we have further revised this methodology which lead to satisfactory segmentation of as 15 distinct textures using a single mask [17].

The problem of texture class classification is to find a way of assigning a new texture sample on the basis of a set of measurements to one of a number of possible classes. The group method requires in the hierarchical approach a single mask to be tuned so that within each texture class, dispersion of the texture energy (TE) is minimal, while the dispersion between classes is maximized. At the same time, it is useful to attempt to restrain the TE to be linear in the numeric rank of the textures. We use figures of merit for mask tuning of the form $D = XY/Z$, where X is the well-known expression for the regression of the least-squares line of best fit line $(x, f(x))$ through the points $(x, TE(x))$

$$X = \frac{\sum_{x=1}^{N} (TE(x) f(x))^2}{\sum_{x=1}^{N} f^2(x) \sum_{x=1}^{N} TE^2(x)}$$

while Y and Z are measure of inter and intra dispersion respectively:

$$Y = \min\{\frac{ABS(TE(x,sx,rx) - TE(y,sy,ry))}{TE(x,sx,rx) + TE(y,sy,ry)}\}$$

$$Z = \max\{\frac{ABS(TE(x,sx,rx) - TE(x,sy,ry))}{TE(x,sx,sx) + TE(x,sy,ry)}\}$$

where sx, sy refer to different scales, rx, ry refer to different rotations while x, y refer to different textures in the given texture set, and $TE(x, sx, rx), TE(y, sy, ry$ represent the texture energy with certain scale and orientation.

3 Texture Class Database

In texture classification, the success of the classifier is judged by the number of similar textures which have been dispersed. Moreover, such a classifier should be rotation and scale invariant. In a word, the more the textures can be separated with less rotation and scale effect, the more powerful the classifier is. Thus a dynamic and large texture class database is required for our mask tuning scheme. By introducing a 2D linked list, we create a dynamic texture class database of large size, in which the low labels are texture class, while the columns are labeled by orientation and scale. Fig. 1 shows the structure, in which each texture sample is a node of the list.

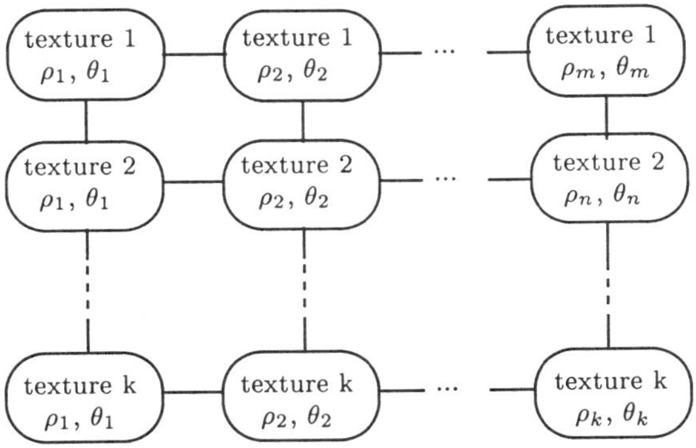

Fig. 1. Two dimensional linked list
($\rho_1, \rho_2, \ldots \rho_k$ refers to the scale factor;
$\theta_1, \theta_2, \ldots \theta_k$ refers to the rotation angle)

With such a structure, the user can easily add, delete and sort a certain texture sample by adding, deleting or sorting the node in the list, respectively. Meanwhile the size of the list depends on the number of textures to be involved in classification, which is determined by the user dynamically. The textures used in our initial test were selected from Brodatz's well-known compilation[3]. We chose the following 15 textures, including eight Brodatz textures used by other researchers augmented by seven visually similar textures: calfd24, canvd20, canv21, corkd4, grassd9, paperd57, pebblesd54, pigskind92, raffiad84, sandd28, sandd29, strawd15, wired6, wired14 and woold19. To show the feasibility of such a tuning scheme for the classification of remotely sensed image data, 8 different types of grand cover images, i.e. forest, rocks, mountain, desert, cloud, sea, beach and residential area, were included in the texture album. Fig. 2 illustrates 8 ground cover types of the remotely sensed image data.

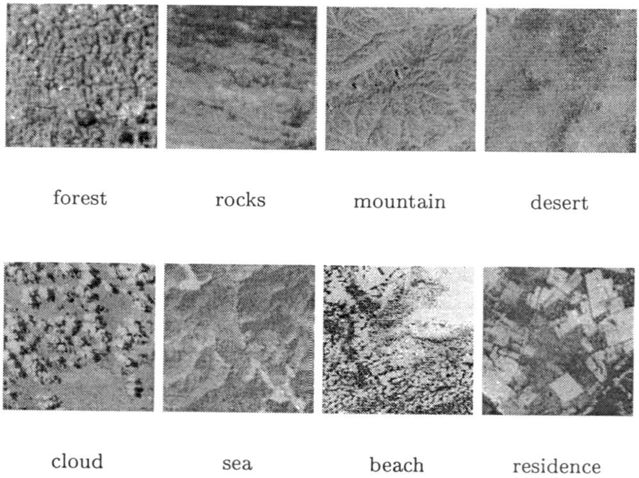

Fig. 2. Samples of the ground cover types of the satellite images

4 Parallel Texture Classification – A System Integration Approach

Fast searching and indexing is a key issue for efficient image classification. Indexing tabular data for exact matching or range searches in traditional databases is a well-understood problem, and structures like B-trees provide efficient access mechanisms. However, in the context of similarity matching for visual images, traditional indexing methods may not be appropriate. Consequently, data structures for fast access of high-dimensional features for spatial relationships have to be developed. As detailed in Section II, we introduce "texture energy" TE via 'tuned' mask as texture feature measurement for classification. Corresponding to the texture class database, a 2D matrix is used to represent the texture energy entities in the database, which is row ordered in terms of the TE measurement. The classification task is to identify candidates in the matrix which has the minimum difference with the input sample measurement. This section describes a system integration approach to achieve real-time classification of satellite images by textures. The pipeline architecture is proposed for an on-board real-time smart sensor system to preprocess the sensed image data, compress the meaningful regions and transmit the compressed data to the ground station for further analysis. The techniques for distributed computing is adopted for the parallel implementation of texture classification on a cluster of workstation clusters at the ground station.

4.1 A Pipeline System for Smart Sensing

The essential computation in our smart sensor system is the mask-based convolution for texture classification and wavelet transform for image compression. Such a computation task which involves product-sum arithmetic within local windows can be implemented in parallel in an SIMD style, where an input image from the sensor is entered into the system in a line-scanned format and passed through the pipeline with different programmable processing elements (PEs) at the same scanning rate. Each PE performs the local product-sum over the entire image simultaneously and forwards the result to the controller for the final output. Fig. 3 illustrates the general structure of PE for 5×5 neighborhood size, where shift registers within each PE store four contiguous scan lines and window registers hold the 5×5 neighborhood processing matrices. Both the local neighborhood processing and image data transfer are completed within a single clock period controlled by the system controller. In each discrete clock period, a new pixel is clocked into the PE and all shift registers are shifted by one element simultaneously. The input/output of each PEs can operate at the same rate. Therefore, PEs can be cascaded together for parallelism.

4.2 Parallel Virtual Machine (PVM)

Parallel Virtual Machine (PVM) is viewed as a general and flexible parallel computing environment which enables concurrent executions on loosely coupled networks of processing elements and supports a message-passing model of synchronization [4]. Thus it provides a low-cost homogeneous multi-computing

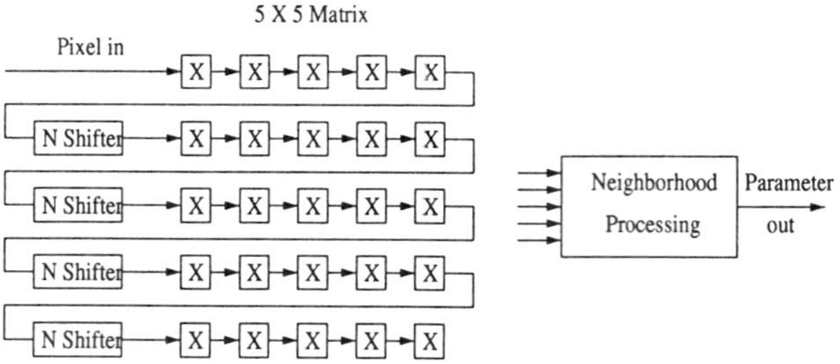

Fig. 3. The connection of registers for a 5 × 5 neighborhood in pipeline

environment by using existing workstation resources for parallelism. PVM can be implemented on different architectures such as single CPU systems, vector machines and multiprocessors, where the connection between these elements may be through different networks. The initiation and termination of processes across the network for a particular application are made via a library of standard interface routines.

The utilization of workstation clusters for parallel computing has drawn increasing interests because of its potential benefits such as performance and reliability. Some researchers even predict that workstation clusters in practice can replace supercomputers in the future. Although we are not sure about this argument, we believe that workstation cluster can take over some tasks which were done by supercomputers, especially those computation intensive tasks such as vision-related tasks. Another obvious advantage that workstation clusters are superiors to supercomputers is the availability. Currently, there are a variety of systems which provide message-passing services for parallelism such as PVM, Express, Linda and P4. In the work reported here, we use PVM to implement the relevant algorithms for image transform and matching on a network of workstation clusters. The software developed includes a master program and slave programs. The master program controls the data processed by a number of slave programs. It can run on one machine and spawn copies of the slave programs to any number of nodes in the network. The following presents a brief description of the master and slave control programs:

The Master Program:

- *Initialize the system*
- *Allocate a memory array for the image data*
- *Read an image into the memory array*

- *Segment the image into a number of sub-images*
- *Register in the PVM process by obtaining its Task Identifier (TID)*
- *Spawn copies of the slave programs on the slave machines*
- *Send control messages to slave machines*
- *Send sub-image data to slave machines*
- *Wait for the slave machines to report back*
- *Collect data from slave machines for final output*

The Slave Program:

- *The slave programs are spawned by the master program at run-time*
- *Initialize the data structure for the processed image segments*
- *Registers in the PVM process and obtains its Task Identifier (TID)*
- *Wait for data to be sent from the master*
- *Receive the data and perform the specified operation*
- *Inform the master machine when the result data is ready*
- *Send the data to the master*
- *Exit from PVM process*

5 Experimental Results

The potential of the proposed classification scheme is demonstrated by labeling different regions of grand-cover types of satellite images. Fig. 4 is an example of our smart sensor system for flood prediction and control. Fig. 4(a) is the original satellite image taken in the area of Yangtze River, and Fig. 4(b) is the segmented image at the ground station based on the compressed image data transmitted from the on-board smart sensor system, where the segmented image delineated by the boundaries of two regions – water and land will be used to guide the flood control.

A series of experiments have been conducted to demonstrate the advantages and potentials of PVM for parallel image processing in a distributed computing environment. The program codes were written in Ansii standard C and executed on a network of SUN SPARC workstations under the UNIX operating system. The parallel performance improvement is measured by the following ratio:

$$\gamma = \frac{T_s - T_p}{T_s}$$

where T_s refers to the sequential execution time and T_p refers to the parallel execution time. In addition, the impact of communication overheads in relation to message size is also investigated.

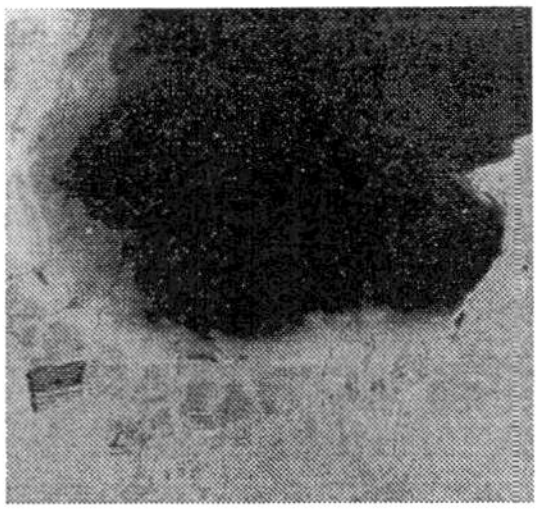

(a)

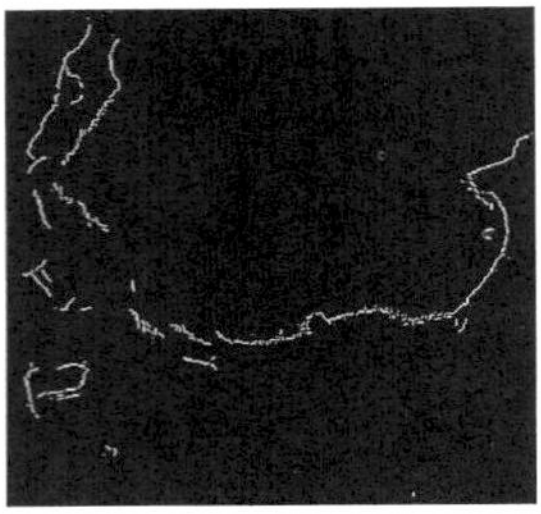

(b)

Fig. 4. An example of image segmentation for flood control in remote sensing

The performance of both sequential and parallel detection of interesting points using Moravec operator is compared. Table 1 lists the performance evaluation in terms of the average execution time on different images with various sizes ranging from 128*128 to 512*512. The sequential processing is performed on a single SUN SPARC workstation while the parallel implementation is on 4 SUN SPARK work stations. It is clear that the speed-up will be more effective when the image size is larger, the algorithm is more complicated and more processes are involved for the parallel implementation.

Table 1: The comparison of execution time in parallel and sequential

image size	execution time (in sequential)	execution time (in parallel)
128*128	3.3 sec.	1.79 sec.
256*256	15.7 sec.	7.07 sec.
512*512	140.7 sec.	46.62 sec.

It is noted that the inter-process communication overheads will have negative impacts on system efficiency. Our concern is how to maximize the the gain from parallel processing in terms of the data size, the bandwidth of the communication channel, and the complexity of algorithms. The time for the PVM process to pack, transmit and unpack data from the master to any slave is referred to as the PVM overheads, which is determined by the PVM process and various communication factors such as node link length, composition, topology and so on. It is desirable to determine the optimal data size with minimum overheads effects. of different sizes during the discrete wavelet transforms DWT of 512×512. Fig. 5 depicts the average time to pack and send a message versus the message size and Fig. 6 depicts the average number of message bytes packed and sent per microsecond with respect to different message size for DWT on PVM clusters.

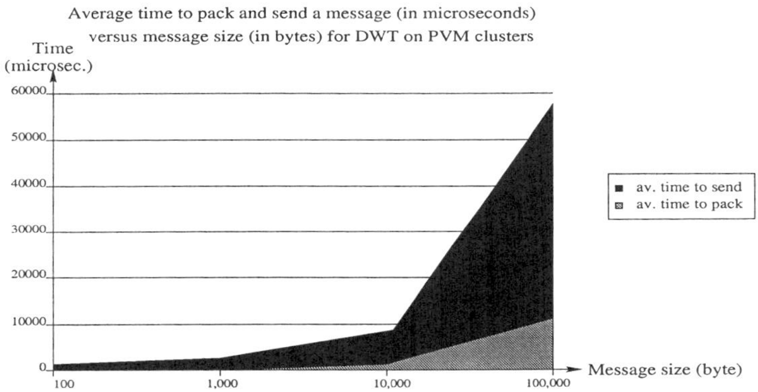

Fig. 5. The average time to pack and send a message vs message size for DWT on PVM clusters

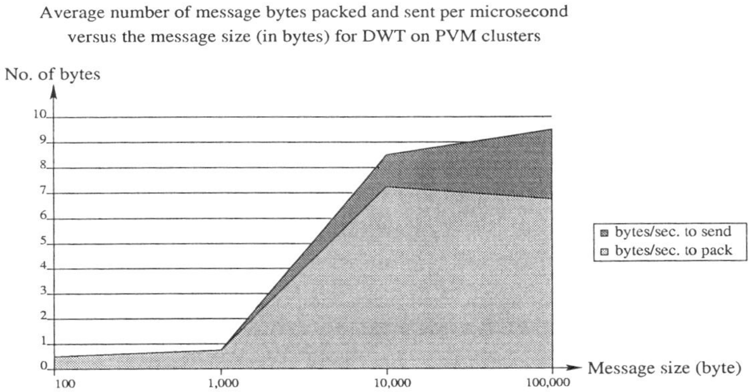

Fig. 6. The average speed for message packing and sending for DWT on PVM clusters

In our PVM based implementation with a master/slave model, the tasks for the master node include reading and segmenting image data, sending subimage data to each slaves, coordinating the transform results produced by slaves, collecting the result from slaves for the final output. In the case of discrete wavelet transform, Table 3 shows different execution time with different number of slaves for the wavelet transform on 512 × 512 image based on pyramid algorithm.

Table 2: Wavelet Transform: the execution time vs. the number of slaves

No. of Slaves	Execution Time (Sec.)
1	36.76
2	24.94
4	17.94
8	12.45

6 Conclusion

In this paper the rotation and scale invariant texture feature extraction is introduced for effective classification of images involving textures of unknown rotation and scale changes. It was found that the tuning process, although computationally intensive, converged efficiently; and that the classifier values of mean of the texture energy TE for a particular texture at different orientations and different scales were tightly clustered. As a result, this dynamic global texture classifier associated with the 'tuned' mask will recognize an unknown input texture samples as belonging to a particular class in the texture database irrespective of scale and rotation. In addition, the execution time can be further reduced by using parallel search algorithms for classification. The proposed parallel algorithms for classification of both single image and multiple images employ efficient parallel algorithms for row-search and minimum-find and are robust in terms of the classification tasks and the number of processors. In addition, the integration of on-board smart sensor system and the the parallel virtual machine (PVM) environment at the ground station provides a general approach to real-time remote sensing. The experimental results demonstrate the potentials of the proposed method.

References

1. A. Astron, *Smart Image Sensors.* Sweden: Linkoping University Press, 1993.
2. K.K. Benke, D.R. Skinner and C.J. Woodruff, "Convolution operators as a basis for objective correlates for texture perception," *IEEE Trans. Syst., Man, Cybern.*, vol. 18, pp. 158-163, 1988.
3. P. Brodatz, *Textures: A Photographic Album for Artists and Designers*, Dover Publications, New York, 1966.

4. Al Geist, A. Beguelin, J. Dongarra, W. Jiang, R. Manchek and V. Sunderam, *PVM: Parallel Virtual Machine, A User's Guide and Tutorial forNetwork Computing*, MIT Press, Cambridge, MA, 1994.
5. D. Gerogiannis, "Load balancing requirements in parallel implementations of image feature extraction tasks," *IEEE Trans. Parallel and Distributed Systems*, vol. 4, pp. 994-1013, 1996.
6. D.G. Goodenough, M. Goldberg, G. Plunkell and J. Zelek, "An expert system for remote sensing," *IEEE Trans. Geosci. Remote Sensing*, vol. GRS-25, pp. 349-359, 1987.
7. K. Huang, *Advanced Computer Architecture*, McGraw-Hill, 1993.
8. K.I. Laws, *Textured Image Segmentation*, Ph.D Thesis, University of Southern California, January 1980.
9. P.M. Mather, *Computer Processing of Remotely Sensed Images: An Introduction.* New York: Wiley, 1987.
10. D.P. Mandal, C.A. Murthy and S.K. Pal, "Analysis of IRS imagery for detecting man-made objects with a multivalued recognition system," *IEEE. Trans. Systems, Man and Cybernetics – Part A: Systems and Humans*, vol. 26, pp. 241-247, 1996.
11. M. Pietikäinen, A. Rosenfeld, and L.S. Davis, "Experiments with texture classification using averages of local pattern matches," *IEEE Trans. Systems, Man and Cybernetics*, vol. 13, pp. 421-425, 1983.
12. T.R. Reed and J.M.H. du Buf, "A review of recent texture segmentation and feature extraction techniques," *CVGIP: Image Understanding*, vol. 57, pp. 359-372, 1993.
13. A.H.S. Solberg, A. Jain and T. Taxt, "Multisource classification of remotely sensed data: Fusion of Landsat TM and SAR images," *IEEE Trans. Geosci. Remote Sensing*, vol. 32, pp. 768-778, 1994.
14. A.H.S. Solberg, T. Taxt and A. Jain, "A Markov random field for classification of multisource satellite imagery, " *IEEE Trans. Geosc. Remote Sensing*, vol. 34, pp. 100-113, 1996.
15. M. Unser, Local linear transforms for texture measurements. Signal Processing 11, 1986, 61-79.
16. D.J. Verbyla, *Satellite Remote Sensing of Natural Resources.* Lewis Publisher, 1995.
17. J. You and H.A. Cohen, "Classification and segmentation of rotated and scaled textured images using texture 'tuned' masks," *Pattern Recognition*, vol. 26, pp. 245 - 258, 1993.
18. D. Zhang and Z. Li, "Design of a smart sensor system for real-time remote sensing image processing on-board satellite," *Proc. of SPIE*, vol. 657, pp. 164-170, 1986.

Parallel Algorithm for Computing Shape's Moments on Arrays with Reconfigurable Optical Buses

Chin-Hsiung Wu
Department of Information Management, Chinese Naval Academy Kaohsiung, Taiwan, R. O. C.

Shi-Jinn Horng, Yuh-Rau Wang
Department of Electrical Engineering, National Taiwan University of Science and Technology, Taipei, Taiwan, R. O. C.
E-mail: horng@mouse.ee.ntust.edu.tw

Abstract

The major contribution of this paper is in designing an efficient parallel algorithm for computing two-dimensional moments via rectangular decomposition. We decompose the $N \times N$ image into n non-overlapped rectangles, since the moment computation of rectangles is easier than that of the whole image. By integrating the advantages of both optical transmission and electronic computation, the proposed parallel algorithm is time and/or cost optimal.

Key Words– rectangular decomposition, shape's moments, moment invariants, reconfigurable optical bus.

1 Introduction

Moments are by far widely used in image analysis, pattern recognition and low-level computer vision [8]. Hu [8] first proposed a set of moment invariants based on the 10 low order moments. These moment invariants are simple functions of moments and independent of scaling, translation and rotation.

For a 2-D digital image $f(x,y)$, its (p,q)th order moment is defined as:

$$m_{pq} = \sum_{x=1}^{N}\sum_{y=1}^{N} x^p y^q f(x,y), \tag{1}$$

where $f(x,y)$ is an integer representing the intensity function (gray level or binary value) at pixel (x,y). For a binary image, $f(x,y)$ is defined as follows:

$$f(x,y) = \begin{cases} 1 \text{ if } (x,y) \in R \\ 0 \ \text{ otherwise,} \end{cases} \tag{2}$$

[a] This work was supported by the National Science Council under the contract no. NSC-89-2213-E011-007.

where R is the object region. From Eq. (2), Eq. (1) is simplified into another form:

$$m_{pq} = \sum_{(x,y)\in R} x^p y^q. \tag{3}$$

It means that m_{pq} is a shape model based on the area of the object region R.

The main difficulty concerning the use of moments is the computational burden. To compute the moments of a two-dimensional (2-D) image directly by using Eqs. (1) or (3), it involves a significant amount of multiplications and additions. Previously, some fast algorithms for computing shape's moments had been proposed using various computational methods [7,9,16,17,20,21]. In many applications, such as military and industrial applications, the speed of computations is very important. Thus, designing parallel algorithms for computing shape's moments is therefore both of theoretical interest and practical importance. For an $N \times N$ binary image, Chung [5] proposed a constant time algorithm for computing the horizontal/vertical convex shape's moments of order up to 3 on an $N \times N$ reconfigurable mesh. Chung's algorithm holds only when each row/column in the object has no holes; that is, it is only suitable for convex objects. In this paper, we will develop a more efficient algorithm to overcome the disadvantage of Chung's algorithm. Our research mainly concerns about the lower order moments up to order 3 since these lower order moments can provide sufficient information for pattern recognition [3,5,8].

The array with a reconfigurable optical bus system is defined as an array of processors connected to a reconfigurable optical bus system whose configuration can be dynamically changed by setting up the local switches of each processor. Due to unidirectional signal propagation and predictable delay of the signal per unit length, the optical buses enable synchronized concurrent access in a pipelined fashion. Recently, two related models have been proposed, namely the array with reconfigurable optical buses (AROB) [14] and linear array with a reconfigurable pipelined bus system (LARPBS) [13]. A major difference between them lies in that the counting is allowed in the AROB model during a bus cycle but it is not permitted in the LARPBS model. Many algorithms have been proposed for these two relative models [10,15]. These indicate that arrays with a reconfigurable optical bus system are very efficient for the parallel computation.

The main contribution of this paper is in designing an efficient parallel algorithm for computing the shape's moments. The idea of our algorithm is based on the rectangular decomposition. We first partition the object into a number of non-overlapped rectangles. Then, compute the contributions to moments of each extracted rectangle. Finally, the shape's moments can be obtained from the summations of the corresponding contributions to moments of all non-overlapped rectangles. By integrating the advantages of both optical transmission and electronic computation, an $O(1)$ time parallel algorithm for computing shape's moments is derived. The performance of our algorithm is dependent on the complexity of the input image. Let the $N \times N$ image can be partitioned into n non-overlapped rectangles. If n is bounded by $O(N)$, then our algorithm requires $N \times N$ processors; $N \times N^{1+1/c}$ processor for c is a constant and $c \geq 1$, otherwise. Compared to the Chung's algorithm [5], our algorithm can achieve the same performance, but without the limitation for the object shape. In the sense of the product of time and the number of processors used, the proposed algorithm is time and/or cost optimal.

The remainder of this paper is organized as follows. We give a brief introduction to the AROB computational model in Section 2. Section 3 describes the parallel rectangular decomposition algorithm. In Section 4, we discuss the relationships between shape's moments and rectangular decomposition. Based on these relationships, an efficient algorithm for computing shape's moments is derived. Finally, some concluding remarks are included in the last section.

2 The Computational Model

A linear array with pipelined optical buses (1-D APPB) [6] of size N contains N processors connected to the optical bus with two couplers. One is used to write data on the upper (transmitting) segment of the bus and the other is used to read the data from the lower (receiving) segment of the bus.

The AROB model is essentially a mesh using the basic structure of a classical reconfigurable network (RN) [2] and optical buses. The linear AROB (LAROB or 1-D AROB) extends the capabilities of the 1-D APPB by permitting each processor to connect to the bus through a pair of switches. Each processor with a local memory is identified by a unique index denoted as P_i, $0 \leq i < N$, and each switch can be set to either cross or straight by the local processor. The optical switches are used for reconfiguration. If the switches of processor P_i, $1 \leq i < N-1$, are set to cross, then the LAROB will be partitioned into two independent sub-buses, each of them forms an LAROB. Each processor uses a set of control registers to store information needed to control the transmission and reception of messages by that processor. An example for an LAROB of size 5 is shown in Figure 1(a). Two interesting switch configurations derivable from a processor of an LAROB are also shown in Figure 1(b).

A 2-D AROB of size $M \times N$, denoted as 2-D $M \times N$ AROB, contains $M \times N$ processors arranged in a 2-D grid. Each processor is identified by

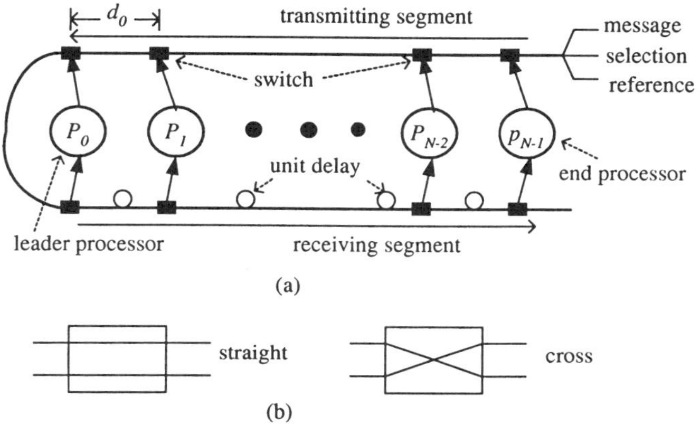

Figure 1: (a) An LAROB of size 5. (b) The switch states.

a unique 2-tuple index (i, j), $0 \leq i < M$, $0 \leq j < N$. The processor with index (i, j) is denoted by $P_{i,\ j}$. Each processor has four I/O ports, denoted by E, W, S and N to be connected with a reconfigurable optical bus system. The interconnection among the four ports of a processor can be reconfigured during the execution of algorithms. Thus, multiple arbitrary linear arrays like LAROB can be specified in a 2-D AROB. The two *terminal* processors which are located in the end points of the constructed LAROB may serve as the *leader* processors (similar to P_0 in Figure 1(a)). The related position of any processor on a bus to which it is connected is its distance from the *leader* processor. For more details on the AROB, see [14]. An example of a 2-D 4×4 AROB and the ten allowed switch configurations are shown in Figure 2.

3 Rectangular Decomposition

The rectangular decomposition of an $N \times N$ binary image is defined to partition it into a number of non-overlapped rectangular regions with black pixels (i.e. 1's), instead of representing it by a 2-D array. These rectangles have their edges parallel to the image axes and contain a number of black pixels. Let R_i, $0 \leq i < n$, denote the rectangles, where n is the number of extracted rectangles. Only the two locations of any two opposite corners of each rectangle would be sufficient to represent the whole rectangle. That is, $R_i = (x_i, x'_i, y_i, y'_i)$, where (x_i, y_i) and (x'_i, y'_i) are the coordinates of the top-left corner and the bottom-right corner of rectangle R_i, respectively. For example, the image

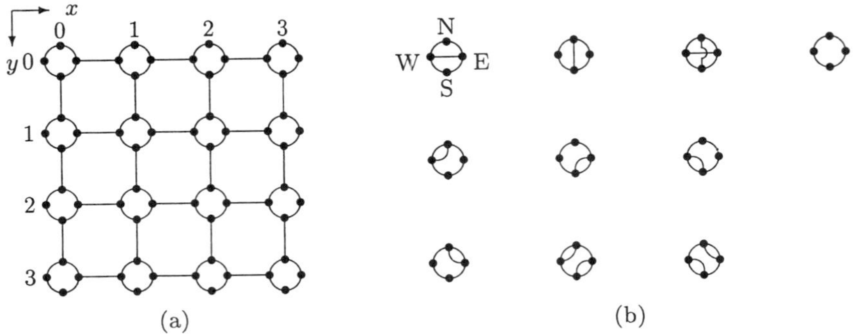

Figure 2: (a) A 4 × 4 AROB model. (b) The allowed switch connection patterns.

shown in Figure 3(a) can be partitioned into non-overlapped rectangles as shown in Figure 3(d), and rectangle R_i, $0 \leq i < n$, can be represented by either (x_i, x_i', y_i, y_i') or (x_i, y_i, l_i, h_i), where l_i and h_i represent the length and height of rectangle R_i, respectively.

The most important characteristic of the rectangular decomposition is that a perception of image parts greater than that of a pixel and all the image operations on the pixels belonging to a rectangle may be substituted by a simple operation on the rectangle. Therefore, the space and time complexities of applications fully depend on the cardinality of the set of rectangular regions. In the worst case, each rectangular region consists of only one black pixel. Like the chessboard image, the number of rectangular regions would be $N^2/2$. In the most cases, however, the rectangular decomposition is superior to quadtree decomposition, because the number of non-overlapped regions resulted by rectangular decomposition is significantly less than that of quadtree decomposition.

There were several approaches proposed to partition the input image into a set of non-overlapped rectangles. Theoretically, an optimal partition algorithm must decompose the original image into the minimum number of non-overlapped rectangles [12]. Unfortunately, the computational complexity of optimal rectangular decomposition algorithm is significant and it is hard to implement it. Therefore, in practice, a simple and suboptimal algorithm is more valuable than an optimal one which is complex and hard to be implemented. Especially, it is important to design a fast suboptimal algorithm in the real time applications. This problem can be overcome by using parallel processing systems. The sequential algorithms proposed previously scanned the input image in a raster format and extracted the rectangles recurrently [1,11]. If we parallelize these algorithms straightforwardly, it requires $\Omega(\log N)$ time. Based on the reconfigurability and the power of the AROB model, a constant time and cost optimal algorithm for rectangular decomposition on a binary image can be derived in the following.

Given an $N \times N$ binary image B, assume each pixel of it can be either a black pixel or a white pixel. Without loss of generality, it is assumed that initially the index and label of pixel (i, j), $1 \leq i, j \leq N$, are identical and equal to $(i-1) \times N + j$. Let the data structure of a rectangle consist of four fields x, y, l and h, respectively. That is, the coordinates of the top-left corner of the rectangle are represented by x and y, the length and height of the rectangle are represented by l and h, respectively. Initially, image B is stored in the local variable $b(i, j)$ of processor $P_{i,j}$, $1 \leq i, j \leq N$. The final result (the top-left corner, length and height of the extracted rectangle) is stored in the local variable $rect(i, j)$ of processor $P_{i,j}$, $1 \leq i, j \leq N$. The parallel rectangular decomposition algorithm (PRDA) is listed below; an illustration of it is shown in Figure 3.

Algorithm PRDA;

1: For each row, connect the bus of the processor which contains black pixel relative to its previous processor (according to the column index order) having black pixel; disconnect it, otherwise. In this way, two processors with the black pixels will be connected together. As a result, several sub-buses can be constructed which represent the corresponding rectangles with one unit of height on each row. Then, label each rectangle with the minimum index of the pixel to which it belongs. From the definition of index, the index of the top-left corner is the minimum among the pixels within the rectangle. The length (or interval) of the newly extracted rectangle can be calculated using the largest column index and the smallest column index of each sub-bus.

2: The extracted rectangles then can be extended by merging the adjacent rectangles along the y-axis according to the following criterion: the adjacent rectangles have the same intervals, i.e., their corresponding sub-buses have the same x-coordinates. Then, relabel each newly extracted rectangle. The pixels with the same label will form a new rectangle.

3: For each newly extracted rectangle, the pixel whose index is equal to its label is located at the top-left corner. Calculating the height of the newly extracted rectangle, the bottom-right corner of each extracted rectangle can be found.

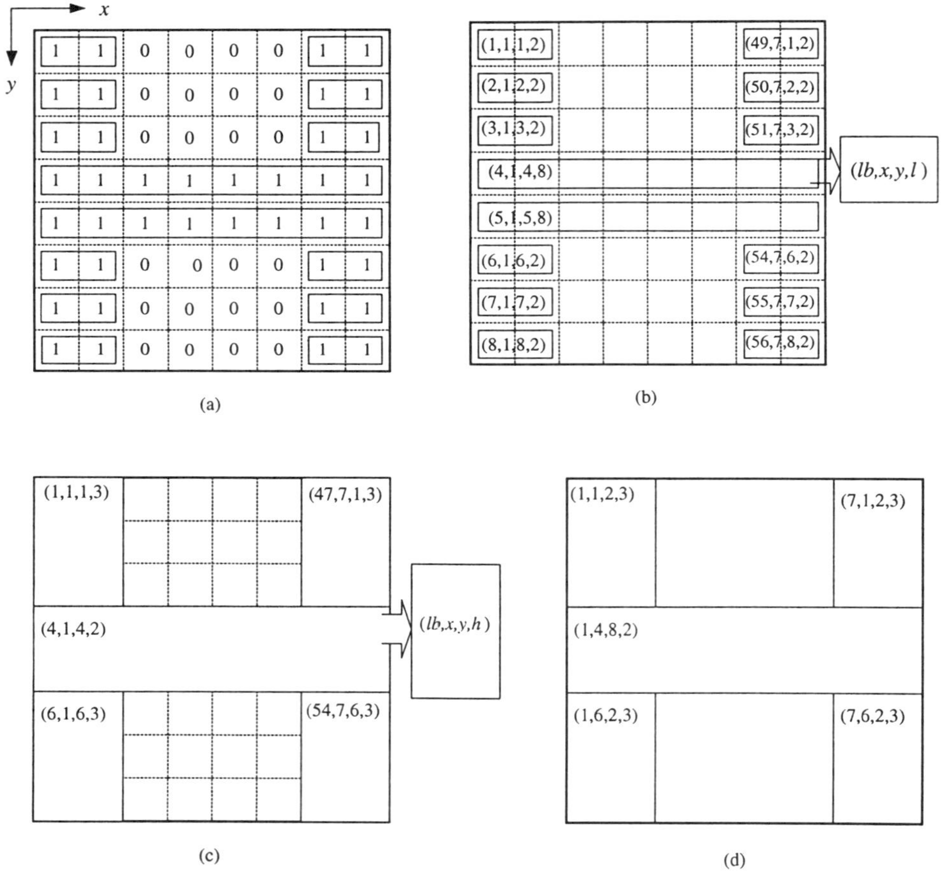

Figure 3: An illustration of algorithm PRDA. (a) The row bus decomposition, after Step 1. (b) The value of (lb, x, y, l) of each sub-bus after Step 1, where lb, x, y and l represent the label, coordinates and length of a rectangle. (c) The value of (lb, x, y, h) of each sub-bus after Step 2. (d) Each extracted rectangle is described by (x, y, l, h) and stored in *rect* on the top left-corner of the extracted rectangle, the final result.

Lemma 1 *Given an $N \times N$ binary image, the rectangular decomposition can be done in $O(1)$ time on an $N \times N$ AROB.*

Proof: Step 1 identifies each piece of the continuous black pixels. Step 2 finds the possible block size of a rectangle for the continuous black pixels. In Step 2, continuous rectangles with one unit of height and the same interval are merged into a new rectangle of larger size along the y-axis. The newly extracted rectangle consists of continuous black pixels (i.e., no white pixels within them), since the intervals of the merged rectangles each with one unit of height are identical. After Step 1, the labels of continuous black pixels are updated except the leftmost corner of each piece of continuous black pixels. After Step 2, the labels of black pixels of the newly extracted rectangle are updated except for the topmost piece of continuous black pixels of it. Therefore, the label of the newly extracted rectangle is equal to the label of the topmost piece of continuous black pixels of it, and this is equal to the index of the leftmost corner of the topmost piece of continuous black pixels. Hence, the top-left corner of the extracted rectangle is located at processor $P(i, j)$ whose label is never updated. *Q.E.D.*

4 Computing Shape's Moments

We first derive the relationships between moments and rectangular decomposition. For a digital object B represented by n non-overlapped rectangles, R_1, $R_2, \cdots, R_n$, computing the 2-D shape's moments of B can be reduced to computing the moments of these n rectangles. From the definition of moments, computing the double summations in Eq. (1) of a rectangle is easier than that of the original object. Thus, compared to a direct method, the computational complexity can be reduced significantly.

We now compute the moments of these non-overlapped rectangles. Since the summations in Eq. (1) are linear operations, the moments of the whole object can be derived from the summations of the contributions to moments of these rectangles. The (p, q)th order moments of theses rectangles can be computed as follows. From the data structure of rectangles defined in Section 3, we can easily find the location of the four corners of each extracted rectangles. For a rectangle R_i, $1 \leq i \leq n$. assume the coordinates of its top-left corner are (x_i, y_i), and its length and height are l_i and h_i, respectively. Then the coordinates of the other three corners of R_i are $(x_i + l_i - 1, y_i)$, $(x_i, y_i + h_i - 1)$ and $(x_i + l_i - 1, y_i + h_i - 1)$, respectively.

For a binary digital image, thus the (p, q)th moment of a rectangle R_i

becomes:

$$m_{pq,i} = \sum_{x=x_i}^{x_i+l_i-1} \sum_{y=y_i}^{y_i+h_i-1} x^p y^q. \tag{4}$$

Let

$$r_{p,i} = \sum_{x=x_i}^{x_i+l_i-1} x^p = \sum_{k=0}^{l_i-1} (x_i+k)^p, \text{ and} \tag{5}$$

$$s_{q,i} = \sum_{y=y_i}^{y_i+h_i-1} y^q = \sum_{k=0}^{h_i-1} (y_i+k)^q \tag{6}$$

be the contributions to the p-order and q-order moments for dimension x and dimension y, respectively. As a further refinement of the 2-D moment computation, the double summation in Eq. (4) can be split into two separate summations:

$$m_{pq,i} = r_{p,i} \cdot s_{q,i}. \tag{7}$$

Then the contributions to lower order moments up to order 3 for dimension x can be derived from Eq. (5) as follows:

$$\begin{aligned}
r_{0,i} &= \sum_{k=0}^{l_i-1} (x_i+k)^0 = l_i \\
r_{1,i} &= \sum_{k=0}^{l_i-1} (x_i+k)^1 = x_i l_i + \sum_{j=0}^{l_i-1} j \\
r_{2,i} &= \sum_{k=0}^{l_i-1} (x_i+k)^2 = x_i^2 l_i + 2x_i \sum_{j=0}^{l_i-1} j + \sum_{j=0}^{l_i-1} j^2 \\
r_{3,i} &= \sum_{k=0}^{l_i-1} (x_i+k)^3 = x_i^3 l_i + 3x_i^2 \sum_{j=0}^{l_i-1} j + 3x_i^3 \sum_{j=0}^{l_i-1} j^2 + \sum_{j=0}^{l_i-1} j^3.
\end{aligned} \tag{8}$$

The sums of j, j^2 and j^3 in Eq. (8)can be derived as follows:

$$\sum_{j=0}^{l_i-1} j = \frac{l_i(l_i-1)}{2}$$

$$\sum_{j=0}^{l_i-1} j^2 = \frac{l_i^3}{3} - \frac{l_i^2}{2} + \frac{l_i}{6}$$

$$\sum_{j=0}^{l_i-1} j^3 = \frac{l_i^4}{4} - \frac{l_i^3}{2} + \frac{l_i^2}{4}. \tag{9}$$

The contributions to the corresponding moments for dimension y (i.e., $s_{q,i}$) can be obtained from Eqs. (8)-(9) by replacing x_i with y_i and l_i with h_i.

Similarly, the corresponding moments of other rectangles can be obtained from Eqs. (4)-(9) by replacing x_i, y_i, l_i and h_i with their corresponding values. Thus, the 2-D shape's moments of order (p,q) can be obtained by summing up the contributions to the corresponding moments of all n non-overlapped rectangles:

$$m_{pq} = \sum_{i=1}^{n} m_{pq,i}. \tag{10}$$

Initially, assume that the given image B is stored in the local variable $b(i,\ j)$ of processor $P_{i,\ j}$, $1 \leq i,\ j \leq N$. Finally, the results are stored in the local variable $m_{pq}(1,1)$ of processor $P_{1,1}$. Following the definitions of moments, rectangular decomposition, and the relationship between them, the detailed moments algorithm (PSMA) is listed as follows.

Algorithm PSMA;

1: Perform the rectangular decomposition for the given image applying Lemma 1. After that, the results R_i, $1 \leq i \leq n$, are stored in the local variable $rect(x,y)$ in processor $P_{x,\ y}$.

2: //For each rectangle R_i, compute its moments $m_{pq,i}$, $1 \leq i \leq n$, according to Eqs. (7)-(9). //

2.1: For rectangle R_i, $1 \leq i \leq n$, compute its 1-D moments $r_p(x,y)$ (i.e., $r_{p,i}$ in Eqs. (5) and (8)) and $s_q(x,y)$ (i.e., $s_{q,i}$ in Eq. (6)) of dimension x and dimension y according to Eqs. (5)-(9), respectively.

2.2: For rectangle R_i, $1 \leq i \leq n$, compute its 2-D moments by computing Eq. (7) (i.e., $m_{pq}(x,y) = r_p(x,y) \times s_q(x,y)$).

3: Compute the shape's moments m_{pq} by summing up $m_{pq,i}$, $1 \leq i \leq n$, according to Eq. (10). As a result, the 2-D moments m_{pq} are stored in the local variable $m_{pq}(1,1)$ of processor $P_{1,\ 1}$.

Theorem 1 *Given an $N \times N$ binary image B, the shape's moments up to order 3 can be computed in $O(1)$ time either on an $N \times N$ AROB if n is bounded by $O(N)$ (i.e., image B is simple), or on an $N \times N^{1+\frac{1}{c}}$ AROB for a constant c and $c \geq 1$ if n is bounded by $O(N^2)$ (i.e., image B is complicated).*

Initially, image B is stored in the local variable $b(x, y)$ *of processor* $P_{x, y}$, $1 \leq x, y \leq N$.

Proof : The correctness of this algorithm directly follows from Eqs. (4)-(10). The time complexity is analyzed as follows. Step 1 takes $O(1)$ time using $N \times N$ processors by Lemma 1. Step 2 takes $O(1)$ time. The time complexity of Step 3 is dependent on the complexity of image B. If n is bounded by $O(N)$ (i.e., image B is partitioned into $O(N)$ non-overlapped rectangles after Step 1), then these $O(N)$ contributions to moments can be added in constant time using $N \times N$ processors. In the worst case, there are $O(N^2)$ non-overlapped rectangles (i.e., n is bounded by $O(N^2)$) after Step 1; then we will apply the block sum algorithm proposed by Wu *et al.* [19] to sum up these $O(N^2)$ contributions in Step 3. In this case, Step 3 takes $O(1)$ time using $N \times N^{1+\frac{1}{c}}$ processors for a constant c and $c \geq 1$. Hence, the time complexity is $O(1)$. □

5 Concluding Remarks

In this paper, we design an efficient parallel algorithm for computing shape's moments based on rectangular decomposition. The rectangular decomposition partitions the image into a number of non-overlapped rectangles, where the number of rectangles is dependent on the image complexity. Compared to the result derived in [5], our algorithm is more flexible and suitable for any shape.

References

1. M. Aoki, Rectangular region coding for binary image data compression, *Pattern Recognition*, **11** (1979), 297-312.
2. Y. Ben-Asher, D. Peleg, R. Ramaswami and A. Schuster, The power of reconfiguration, *Journal of Parallel and Distributed Computing*, **13** (1991), 139–153.
3. K. Chen, Efficient parallel algorithms for computation of two-dimensional image moments, *Pattern Recognition,* **23** (1990), 109-119.
4. H. D. Cheng, C. Y. Wu and D. L. Hung, VLSI for moment computation and its application to breast cancer detection, *Pattern Recognition,* **31** (1998), 1391-1406.
5. K. L. Chung, Computing horizontal/vertical convex shape's moments on reconfigurable meshes, *Pattern Recognition,* **29** (1996), 1713-1717.
6. Z. Guo, R. G. Melhem, R. W. Hall, D. M. Chiarulli, and S. P. Levitan, Pipelined communications in optically interconnected arrays, *Journal of Parallel and Distributed Computing,* **12** (1991), 269–282.
7. M. Hatamian, A real time two-dimensional moment generation algorithm

and its single chip implementation, *IEEE Trans. ASPP,* **34** (1986), 546-553.
8. M. K. Hu, Visual pattern recognition by moment invariants, *IRE Trans. Inform. Theory,* **IT-8** (1962), 179-187.
9. X. Y. Jiang and H. Bunke, Simple and fast computation of moments, *Pattern Recognition,* **24** (1991), 351-354.
10. K. Li, Y. Pan and S. Q. Zheng, Fast and processor efficient parallel matrix multiplication algorithms on a linear array with a reconfigurable pipelined bus system, *IEEE Trans. Parallel and Distributed systems,* **9** (1998), 705-720.
11. S. A. Mohamed and M. M. Fahmy, Binary image compression using efficient partitioning into rectangular regions, *IEEE Transactions on Communications,* **43** (1995), 1888-1893.
12. T. Ohtsuki, Minimum dissection of rectilinear regions, in *Proc. IEEE Int. Conf. Circuits and Systems,* (1982), 1210-1213.
13. Y. Pan and K. Li, Linear array with a reconfigurable pipelined bus system— concepts and applications, *Information Sciences – An International Journal,* **106** (1998), 237-258.
14. S. Pavel and S. G. Akl, On the power of arrays with reconfigurable optical bus, in *Proc. Int. Conf. Parallel and Distributed Processing Techniques and Applications*, (1996), 1443-1454.
15. S. Pavel and S. G. Akl, Matrix operations using arrays with reconfigurable optical buses, *Parallel Algorithms and Applications,* **8** (1996), 223-242.
16. W. Philips, A new fast algorithm for moment computation," *Pattern Recognition,* **26** (1993), 1619-1621.
17. M. H. Singer, A general approach to moment calculation for polygons and line segments, *Pattern Recognition,* **26** (1993), 1019-1028.
18. P. Thangavel and V. P. Muthuswamy, Parallel algorithms for addition and multiplication on processor arrays with reconfigurable bus systems, *Information Processing Letters,* **46** (1993), 89-94.
19. C. H. Wu, S. J. Horng and H. R. Tsai, Template matching on arrays with reconfigurable optical buses, in *Proc. the Int. Symp. Operations Research and its Applications*, (1998), 127-141.
20. L. Yang and F. Albregtsen, Fast and exact computation of Cartesian geometric moments using discrete Green's theorem, *Pattern Recognition,* **29** (1996), 1061-1073.
21. M. F. Zakaria, P. J. A. Zsombor-Murray and J. M. H. H. Kessel, Fast algorithm for the computation of moment invariants, *Pattern Recognition,* **20** (1987), 639-643.

A PARALLEL PREFETCHING ARCHITECTURE

S. MANOHARAN AND S-M KIM
Department of Computer Science, University of Auckland, New Zealand

This paper proposes a hardware prefetching scheme which uses a second processor for prefetching data for the primary processor. The second processor costs about 20% but speeds up tested benchmarks by about 45%.

1 Introduction

Prefetching brings data into the cache before it is expected by the processor, thereby eliminating potential misses. There are two major prefetching schemes. In a hardware scheme, the hardware predicts memory access patterns and brings data into the cache before required by the processor [1,2,3]. In a software scheme, the compiler predicts memory access patterns and places prefetch instructions in the code [4,5]. Software prefetching, however, requires some hardware support, such as the provision and implementation of a prefetch instruction, and its effectiveness is mainly determined by compiler algorithms used for prefetching.

Hardware prefetching schemes make use of the regularity of data accesses. Chen proposed one of the most sophisticated hardware schemes [1]. This scheme predicts future data accesses by keeping track of past access patterns. Chen proposes three strategies of increasing complexity. The simplest strategy prefetches data required for iteration i of a loop during iteration $i-1$. For small loops, this strategy cannot hide the entire memory latency. The second strategy aims to fix this problem by using a lookahead program counter. This lookahead PC runs ahead of the normal PC, and is responsible for issuing prefetches. For small loops, this will enable prefetches to be issued multiple iterations in advance. The third strategy extends the second one by detecting access patterns across loop levels. A major drawback of Chen's scheme is that it does not improve the performance of applications with indirect memory accesses. Besides, it requires modifications to the processor architecture, which is usually expensive.

This paper proposes an alternative hardware scheme for prefetching, where a second processor is used solely for the purpose of prefetching data for the primary processor. The scheme does not *predict* memory access patterns, but rather uses the second processor to run ahead of the primary processor so as to *detect* future memory accesses and prefetch these references. It can handle indirect memory references unlike Chen's scheme. Provided the processor can support prefetch instructions, our scheme requires no modifications to the processor architecture.

At first glance, the use of a second processor solely for the purpose of prefetching may look like an overkill. With current hardware prices, one should note that a dual processor commodity computer is only about 20% more expensive than an otherwise comparable single processor computer. To justify the use of a second processor for prefetching, it is desirable to achieve about 20% speedup through prefetching. As our experimental results will show, the speedups achieved on benchmarks are up to 96% and average 45%.

It may be possible to achieve similar speedups by simply parallelizing an application. However, in this case the application developer is left with the task of parallelizing. Besides, not all applications lend themselves to parallelization. The goal of this paper is to identify a form of parallelization which separates out some of the memory fetches and issues them using the second processor as a separate thread of execution. As with classical parallelization, there are applications which do not lend themselves to prefetching: an application in which the difference between the total computation time and total memory access time is large, will not be able to benefit much through prefetching.

The rest of this paper is organized as follows. Section 2 describes the architectural details of our prefetching scheme, with section 2.1 briefly outlining the binary code splitter that generates program images for the two processors. Section 3 presents some experimental results comparing the performance of some benchmark applications with and without prefetching. The final section concludes with a summary.

2 A Two Processor Architecture for Prefetching

Our architecture for prefetching consists of two identical processors. One processor, the *execution engine*, executes the program as normal. The other processor, the *prefetch engine*, executes a variant of the program where the memory access instructions are replaced by prefetch instructions and all other instructions, except address computation instructions and control-flow instructions, are deleted. The two engines start from the same entry point of the program, but the prefetch engine will eventually run ahead of the execution engine. This is because it does not execute any data-oriented instructions.

The architecture somewhat resembles a decoupled-architecture which distributes address generation and execution to two separate processors [6]. There is a major difference, however. The address generation engine is an integral part of a decoupled-architecture, and cannot be dispensed of. The prefetch engine in our architecture, however, is only there to boost the performance of the execution engine, so it can be safely turned off, without stalling the execution engine.

Given that the prefetch engine issues prefetch instructions, we need to use microprocessors that support a prefetch instruction. Most of the modern processors, such as the Pentium, MIPS R10K, and the Alpha, fall under this category. We choose to use the Alpha microprocessor [7] since we had a cycle-level simulator available for the Alpha.

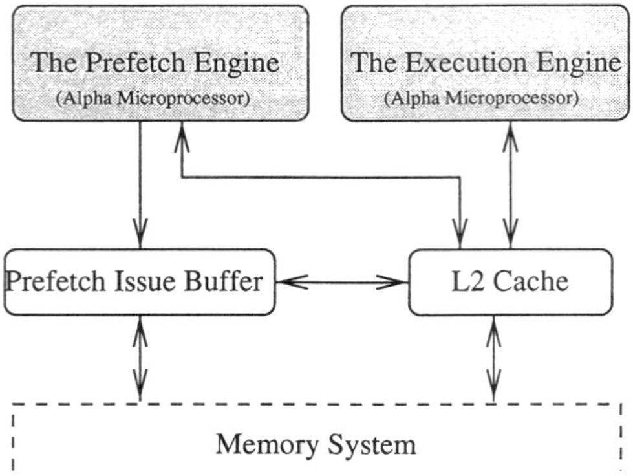

Figure 1. Prefetching with dual processors

The organization of the execution and prefetch engines with respect to the prefetch issue buffer [8], L2 cache, and the memory system is shown in Figure 1.

The prefetch issue buffer keeps a number of prefetches and the information associated with them until the data corresponding to the prefetches are obtained from the memory and placed into the L2 cache. A prefetch is placed in the prefetch issue buffer only if the line specified by the prefetch address is not in the L2 cache; otherwise the prefetch request is simply dropped.

The prefetch engine does not do any data-oriented computations. However, results of these computations are required for the control flow at the end of each basic block. To ensure correct control flow of the prefetch engine, synchronization instructions are inserted into the executables of both execution and prefetch engines. At a synchronization point, the contents of the registers of the execution engine are copied into the registers of the prefetch engine via a pre-defined area in the memory. This makes the results of data-oriented computations available to the prefetch engine, thus ensuring correct control flow. The memory locations used by synchronization instructions will usually be cached in the L2 cache, so that the best-case synchronization cost is proportional to the L2 cache latency rather the full memory latency.

2.1 The Code Splitter

The code splitter takes as its input a compiled binary executable, and outputs two binary images executable by the prefetch and execution engines. The binary image for the execution engine is identical to that of the original binary executable except that some synchronization instructions have been inserted. The binary image for the prefetch engine will have corresponding synchronization instructions, and will have the memory access instructions replaced by prefetch instructions, and all other instructions except address computation and control flow instructions deleted. The sole reason for using a code splitter is to save time having to write a compiler that generates separate binary images for the execution and prefetch engines. New compilers can directly create separate binary images for the execution and prefetch engines.

The code splitter considers for prefetching only array memory accesses, including indirect memory addresses. Scalar memory accesses are not prefetched. In addition, the code splitter places synchronization instructions at the appropriate places in the program (loops and conditional branches are the candidates for synchronization).

3 Experimental Results and Evaluation

To test our architecture and the prefetching mechanism, we use a cycle-level simulator for the Alpha architecture. The simulator simulates the EV4 architecture with the exception that it does not simulate out of order execution and super-scalar instruction issue. Neither does it simulate the instruction cache. It nevertheless simulates the primary and secondary data caches, the write buffer, a prefetch issue buffer, and a memory subsystem. System calls are also simulated, so that any statically-linked binary executable can run on the simulator.

We report results from running seven benchmark applications: MXM, CHOLSKY, MXT, VARIANCE, INRPROD, VPENTA, and BTRIX. MXM multiples two matrices of sizes 128KB and 32KB, storing the result in a matrix of size 64KB. It uses a four-way unrolled, outer product matrix multiply algorithm. CHOLSKY performs a Cholesky decomposition on a three-dimensional array of size 160KB. MXT transposes a two-dimensional matrix of size 256KB. VARIANCE computes the variance of all elements in a one-dimensional array of size 2MB. INRPROD computes the inner product of two vectors of size 250KB. VPENTA is from the NAS kernels, and inverts three pentadiagonals simultaneously. It uses seven 2D arrays, each of size 40KB, and two 3D arrays, each of size 120KB; one of the 3D arrays is the output. BTRIX is also from the NAS kernels, and performs a block tridiagonal matrix solution along one dimension of a 4D array. It uses four 4D arrays, one of which is 540KB in size, and the rest three are 90KB.

3.1 Effect of Memory Latency

The speed-up one can get through prefetching depends on the relative contributions of computation time and memory access time to the total execution time. If the memory access time is relatively small, then there is nothing to gain from prefetching. Similarly, if the relative memory access time is large, then there is not enough computation to overlap with the memory accesses, and thus prefetching cannot be effective. Prefetching is most effective when both computation and memory access equally contribute to the total execution time. In this case, a speed-up close to 100% is achievable.

This experiment shows the result of varying the memory latency. Figure 2 shows how speed-up varies with memory latency for the benchmarks studied. A speed-up close to 100% is achievable when both computation and memory access equally contribute to the total execution time. The maximum speed-up is often less, when the applications are either computation-intensive, or memory-intensive.

3.2 Indirect Memory Access

The previous experiments considered only direct memory accesses. The prefetch engine, in these cases, did not require any memory access. However, when there are indirect memory accesses in the application, the prefetch engine will need to be able to load from the memory. For instance, consider the following code fragment.

```
for ( int i = 0; i < MAX; ++i )
    sum += a[b[i]];
```

Inserting a synchronization point in the loop instead of loading $b[i]$ will be a poor choice, for it will slow down the loop rather than speeding it up. In order to prefetch $a[b[i]]$ efficiently, the prefetch engine will need to load $b[i]$.

Table 1 reports results from five applications that use indirect memory accesses. The memory latency used for the experiment is 50 cycles. CFF2D and IS are from the NAS kernels; CFF2D performs a complex radix fast Fourier

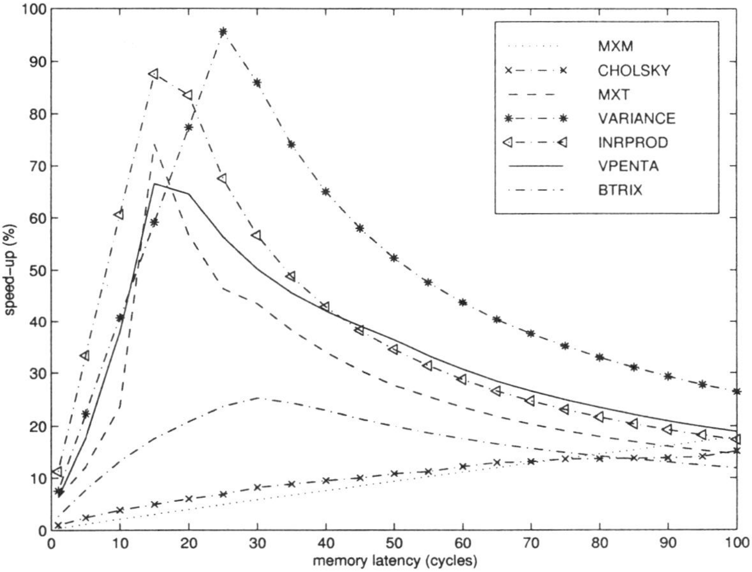

Figure 2. Speed-up vs. memory latency

Table 1. Prefetching effectiveness and indirect memory accesses

Application	Total execution time without prefetching	Total execution time with prefetching	Speed-up
CFF2D	3,324,305	2,925,093	14%
IS	28,753,396	21,623,544	33%
VARIANCE/LL	35,733,775	31,543,052	13%
INRPROD/LL	6,587,186	7,467,407	13%
PIC-1D	5,109,242	4,348,065	18%

transform on a 2D input array, while IS performs a bucket sort on 200,000 integers. VARIANCE/LL and INRPROD/LL are linked-list versions of the VARIANCE and INRPROD benchmarks. PIC-1D is one of the Livermore Loop kernels.

All five applications show reasonable speed-ups resulting from prefetching. The linked-list versions of VARIANCE and INRPROD do not gain as much speed-up as their non-linked-list versions (see Figure 2). This is because there is more stress on the memory system due to additional (indirect) memory accesses.

4 Summary and Conclusions

This paper proposed a hardware scheme for data prefetching, where a second processor is used solely for the purpose of prefetching data for the primary processor. The main advantage of the scheme is that prefetching is effected without having to change an existing processor design (provided that the processor supports a prefetch instruction). Unlike other hardware schemes which *predict* memory access patterns to prefetch, our scheme *detects* future memory access locations and prefetches them. Therefore chances of not being able to use the prefetched data is smaller in our scheme. We evaluated and validated the scheme using some benchmark applications. The results indicate that hardware prefetching is a promising technique that offers worthwhile speed-ups.

References

1. Tien-Fu Chen. *Data Prefetching for High-Performance Processors.* PhD thesis, University of Washington, July 1993.
2. Nathalie Drach. Hardware implementation issues of data prefetching. In *Proc. ICS*, pages 245–254. 1995.
3. Fredrik Dahlgren, Michel Dubois, and Per Stenstrom. Sequential hardware prefetching in shared-memory multiprocessors. *IEEE Transactions on Parallel and Distributed Systems*, 6(7), July 1995.
4. Allan Porterfield. *Software Methods for Improvement of Cache Performance on Supercomputer Applications.* PhD thesis, Rice University, May 1989.
5. Todd Mowry. *Tolerating Latency through Software-Controlled Data Prefetching.* PhD thesis, Stanford University, March 1994.
6. J Smith. Decoupled access/execute architectures. *ACM Transactions on Computer Systems*, 2(4):289–308, November 1984.
7. Richard Sites, editor. *Alpha Architecture Reference Manual.* Digital Press, 1992.
8. S Manoharan and S R Bathula. Hardware support for software prefetching. In *Proc. 4th ACAC*, pages 97–108. 1999.

EFFECTIVELY EXPLOITING A PARALLEL ALGORITHM FOR VIRTUAL REALITY SCENE GENERATION

RONALD POSE
School of Computer Science and Software Engineering,
Monash University,
Clayton, Victoria 3168, AUSTRALIA
E-mail: rdp@cs.monash.edu.au

Abstract. Virtual reality and other immersive interactive computer graphics systems are often considered as high performance computer graphics systems without regard to the application itself. Virtual reality systems apply highly parallel graphics rendering engines in an attempt to achieve desired performance. Sadly, even state-of-the-art parallel graphics techniques provide inadequate performance. Exploiting parallel graphics technology is sound but with virtual reality much of the computation performed is valid for a very short time, and then has to be recomputed. The *Priority Rendering* algorithm avoids this problem and allows the effective exploitation of parallel graphics rendering engines.

1 Introduction

Virtual reality and other immersive computer graphics applications use high performance computer graphics rendering engines, often employing parallelism in both hardware and software. Even so, their performance is inadequate for low-latency virtual reality systems. Either motion fluidity or image quality usually has to be sacrificed to maintain real-time interactive performance.

The problem is that to meet desired performance parameters, one has to generate over 60 photo-realistic frames per second, each of over 1,000,000 pixels, and display them on a head-mounted display worn by the user. The system tracks the user s head in real-time to determine the view of the virtual world to show the user. Only then can the graphics rendering be performed. Delays in generating the images are perceived as a lag in response. i.e. the user moves his head and has to wait for the viewed world to catch up. This latency can lead to serious consequences such as motion sickness and disorientation.

Using multiple high performance graphics pipelines is difficult since the large graphics pipeline delays themselves may be noticeable. Parallelism has to be applied effectively to solve the problem; a brute force graphics approach is insufficient. The problem is such that it is possible to overload the available graphics performance, so the aim must be to provide the best possible user experience, given limited computational resources.

We first outline the conventional approach. Then show how this does not perform so well in virtual reality applications. A new way of thinking about the original problem leads to a different approach. The key is to consider the system as a whole rather than treat it as just another high performance computer graphics system. Our new conceptual approach is called *Delayed Viewport Mapping* and its realization in the form of an *Address Recalculation Pipeline* (ARP) involves a great deal of parallelism in its implementation [1]. A technique of exploiting the new architecture has also been developed [2] that can also have a parallel implementation involving both hardware and software. This technique, *Priority Rendering*, effectively exploits parallel rendering in the virtual reality domain, and is described here with an emphasis on parallelism in its implementation.

2 Conventional approach to high performance computer graphics

Computer graphics involves much computation. With so many steps involved there is an obvious case for some kind of pipelining. Both software and hardware pipelining is exploited in high performance graphics systems.

One approach is to subdivide the job based on objects in the virtual environment. i.e. use separate graphics rendering engines in parallel for each graphical object or groups of objects. Such a technique has been used successfully in animation. Various objects and background scenes are drawn separately on transparencies and can then be overlaid to give the desired composite scene. Apart from the possibilities for parallel creation of the images with this technique, it is also possible to move and animate objects within a scene without redrawing the whole scene. This is called image composition. In its simplest form the images not only have X and Y screen coordinates, but also depth, Z coordinates associated with each pixel. When combining images the system will choose the pixel at a particular screen coordinate with the lowest Z value, i.e. the one closest to the viewer. Apart from having parallelism within the graphics renderer, we can also run many renderers in parallel using image composition to form the final viewable image, and reduce the amount of graphics actually rendered by re-using previously rendered background scenes etc.

This appears to be attractive for virtual reality. The background scene is often fairly static; changes are restricted to a few objects which are the current focus of attention. However this assumes that the effective camera angle is fixed, or in the virtual reality case, that the viewer s viewpoint is fixed. That is not the case.

If the user moves his head, the virtual environment has not changed in itself, but what the viewer expects to see is now different. Even a slight change of head orientation invalidates every pixel in the display. So virtual reality systems using conventional, albeit parallel graphics techniques, end up having to regenerate all the graphics. Note even the background appearance has changed and is recalculated.

Figure 1 depicts a conventional computer graphics system as might be employed for virtual reality. It comprises two distinct processes communicating via the display buffer. On the left is the computer graphics software and hardware. The output of which is an image composed of pixels that are placed in the display buffer. On the right is a conventional raster display that reads pixel values from the display buffer and sends them to the display device. The raster display section runs at a constant speed, typically between 60 and 100 Hz. display refresh rate. On the other hand, the computer graphics section typically runs slower with its performance dependent on the complexity of the graphics it is rendering. It is not unusual to find high performance virtual reality systems which struggle to get beyond 10 frames per second from their graphics renderers.

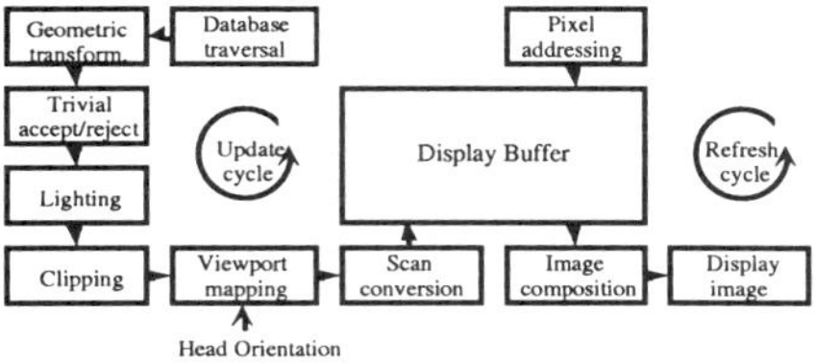

Figure 1. Conventional Virtual Reality Display Architecture

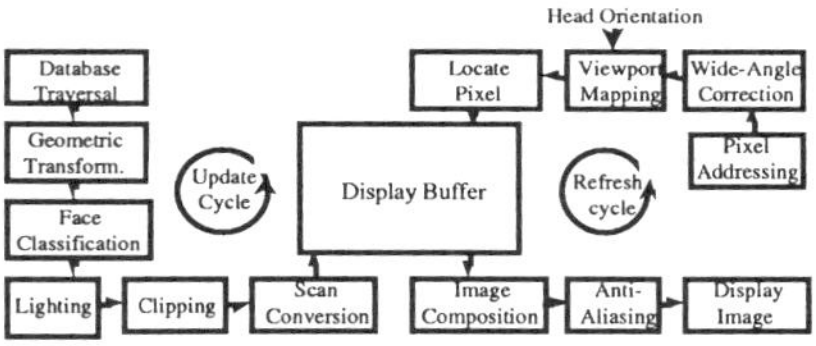

Figure 2. Delayed Viewport Mapping using an Address Recalculation Pipeline

Image composition can also be used, albeit not effectively, allowing an obvious form of parallelism. Multiple graphics renderers (the left side of figure 1) combine their outputs before feeding the resulting image into the display buffer.

3 Re-examining the virtual reality problem

Our difficulties with virtual reality applications have a cause clearly indicated in figure 1. The user s head orientation is input to the graphics update cycle. Thus every change in user head orientation, no matter how slight, causes all the graphics in all graphics rendering engines, to be recalculated. This negates the advantages of image composition where only those images that have changed will be re-rendered.

The virtual world may be completely static, yet all the graphics are being re-rendered. What is required is a representation in which a static virtual world has a static computer graphics analogue that doesn t need continual re-rendering.

Imagine the world is a room with four walls, floor and ceiling made of glass through which you see the world beyond. A static virtual world is indistinguishable from one painted onto the walls, floor and ceiling.

Here is a model for a graphics system that meets our requirements. Instead of a screen in front of the user s eyes, we place the viewer in a room with graphics displays completely surrounding him. That approach is taken in virtual reality *CAVEs*. We adapt that to head-mounted displays by selecting the parts of the image surrounding the user that should be displayed in front of his eyes. We call this technique *Delayed Viewport Mapping*, since we have delayed selecting the viewer s viewpoint until after graphics has already been rendered. We have also devised a highly parallel hardware implementation called an *Address Recalculation Pipeline* (ARP)[3]. The parallelism in the ARP has also been investigated [1].

4 The Address Recalculation Pipeline

The advantages obtained through the use of *Delayed Viewport Mapping* are not free. The easiest way to picture the ARP s operation is to begin with the viewer s eyes and trace a path through to the encapsulating display memory that mimics the glass room we imagined earlier.

Between the viewer and the head-mounted display is a viewing lens with some distorting characteristics that spread the image so as to cover the user s full field of view. We draw a vector from the eye through a pixel of the display device, have it bent to mimic the lens distortion, and finally have it intersect the encapsulating cubic display memory surface. That point of intersection identifies the pixel in the display memory that really should be on the display device at that point. Given the viewing lens is fixed, the bending of the vectors can be described by a lookup-table. The information from the head tracker takes the form of a rotation matrix by which we can multiply the vector, thus rotating it to the viewer s current orientation.

The ARP is implemented as a pipeline with the first stage being the lens distortion correction lookup-table. The second stage doing matrix multiplication to re-orient the vector so it is aligned with the user s current viewpoint. The third stage determines the intersection with the encapsulating display surface, locating the required pixel. Note the output of the third stage is an address in the display memory, hence the name *Address Recalculation Pipeline.*

With a display device with over a million pixels and a refresh rate around 100 Hz, the ARP second stage is doing over 100,000,000 matrix multiplications per second. The third stage involves divisions that are expensive computationally.

The new system using an ARP is depicted in figure 2. The ARP is in the top right of the figure. Note the head orientation feeds into the ARP section, not into the graphics rendering section on the left of the figure. The graphics is now independent of the viewing orientation of the user. With viewport independence we now re-introduce image composition. If parts of the virtual world appear to change, only those graphics renderers handling the changing objects are invoked. Image composition hardware merges these objects with the existing static scenery.

In our implementation the parallel rendering engines each have their own display memory. i.e. the left hand side of figure 2 is replicated. A single ARP drives all the display buffers. The display buffer outputs go through image composition hardware pipeline stages, and an image smoothing stage, before the final image is displayed. The real picture is somewhat more complex [3,4].

The ARP is easily implemented with cheap, parallel hardware. Such computation is easier than complex graphics calculations. It does require hardware since the volume of computation would severely tax a software implementation.

5 The problem of translational movement

Translational movement of the user within the virtual environment results in relative movement between the user and the objects in the virtual world that is observable to the user. The user's own movement has the most dramatic effect, since it affects the display of even static parts of the virtual world.

When translating, objects in the world appear to move relative to you. Close objects appear to move more than distant ones. Very distant objects may not appear to move at all. Thus we have to concentrate especially on close objects.

Actually what is important is not the distance of the object from the user, but rather how long its graphics image will be valid. In the static situation this corresponds closely to the distance of the object from the user and its relative speed.

6 Priority Rendering

A scheme has been devised which bases the allocation of objects to display memories and hence to graphics rendering engines based on the expected validity times of their images. We call this *Priority Rendering*, since it in effect produces a prioritized list of objects in the order in which they should have their graphics images recomputed in order to maintain the illusion of virtual reality without the serious problems we set out to solve [2,5]. It not only produces a prioritized list, but indicates the rate at which the various objects should have their images updated.

Because the allocation to display memories is no longer based on depth within the scene, the hardware must maintain Z-values for each pixel and do image composition based on individual pixels depths.

This method requires that some approximation of the validity time of objects images be obtained. It need not and cannot be exact since it is impossible to predict if the user will move within the virtual world or whether some object in the virtual world will change or move, but it should be reasonably close. If one gets it wrong and under-estimates the validity time of an object s image, then it will end up being recomputed more frequently than required, wasting some of our processing capacity, but not visible by the user. On the other hand if one over-estimates the object s validity time, it will not be updated as often as it needs and will appear slightly out of date. However unlike traditional approaches to virtual reality, the virtual world as a whole is kept up to date, with perhaps a few objects not quite keeping up.

There is not space in this paper to provide the detailed analysis of *Priority Rendering* and its performance in various situations. We have found that we do an order of magnitude less graphics computing than a conventional system in dealing with translational movements, while still presenting identical images to the user. Human factors can also be considered [6]. Humans cannot translate or rotate at infinite speed. Applying human parameters we can reduce the rendering load by more than another factor of two. With that incorporated we are well over an order of magnitude better than a conventional system in handling translation in the virtual world. With our system we also get rotations for free in terms of graphics re-calculations, whereas in a conventional system rotations are the biggest computational load. So in effect we get identical images with several orders of magnitude less graphics computation, but requiring an ARP and its computation.

7 Conclusion

Using conventional graphics for virtual reality, parallelism can be employed, but not effectively. With *Priority Rendering*, and its *Address Recalculation Pipeline*, we have shown how to exploit effectively, parallel graphics rendering hardware.

The results are dramatic, with overall performance orders of magnitude better than the traditional approach. *Delayed Viewport Mapping* has enabled image composition to be used with effectively superlinear speedup.

The performance is due not to parallel graphics itself, but due to a radical new approach to the problem which transforms it into one requiring less computer graphics. Its new form employs parallel hardware in the form of an ARP and a new method of organizing the graphics computation, *Priority Rendering*, ideally suited to efficient parallel implementation

Acknowledgements

Matthew Regan was responsible for much of this system. The prototype was funded by an Australian Research Council small research grant. Patenting of this technology was supported by a Monash Research Fund grant

References

1. Pose, Ronald (2000) Parallelism in a Computer Architecture to Support Orientation Changes in Virtual Reality and Other Immersive Interactive Graphics Systems. In Proc. PART-2000, Sydney, Australia, November 2000.
2. Regan, Matthew and Pose, Ronald (1994) Priority Rendering with a Virtual Reality Address Recalculation Pipeline. Proceedings of SIGGRAPH 94. In Computer Graphics, Annual Conference Series 1994. pp. 155-162.
3. Regan, Matthew and Pose, Ronald (1993) An Interactive Graphics Display Architecture. Proceedings of IEEE Virtual Reality Annual International Symposium. (18-22 September 1993, Seattle USA), pp. 293-299.
4. Regan, Matthew and Pose, Ronald (1994) Display Memory Access Issues and Anti-Aliasing with a Virtual Reality Address Recalculation Pipeline. Proceedings of the 9th Eurographics Workshop on Graphics Hardware, SINTEF, Oslo, Norway, Sept. 12-13, 1994, pp. 23-27.
5. Pose, Ronald and Regan, Matthew (1998) Updating Graphical Objects Based on Object Validity Periods, US Patent Application No. 847,567, Replaces US Patent Application No. 307,330, Filed 24 April 1997, US Patent Number 5,841,439, Granted 24 November 1998.
6. Pose, Ronald and Regan, Matthew (1994) Techniques for Reducing Virtual Reality Latency with Architectural Support and Consideration of Human Factors. In Multimedia, Hypermedia & Virtual Reality, LNCS 1077 Springer-Verlag, 1996.

Chapter 4
Parallel and Distributed Databases

THREE DIMENSIONAL GRID STRUCTURE FOR EFFICIENT ACCESS OF REPLICATED DATA

M. MAT DERIS

College University Terengganu,Faculty of Science and Technology , 21030,MengabangTelipot,Kuala Terengganu,Malaysia.

E-mail: mustafa@uct.edu.my

A.MAMAT, P. C. SENG, H. IBRAHIM

University Putra Malaysia,Faculty of Computer Science and Information Technology, 43400, UPM Serdang, Malaysia.

E-mail: {ali,pua,hamidah}@fsktm.upm.edu.my

In this paper, a new protocol called Three Dimensional Grid Structure (TDGS) protocol, is being proposed to manage data replication in a distributed database system. The protocol provides high availability for read and write operations with limited fault-tolerance at low communication cost. It can be viewed as analogues to a quorum-based protocol in the context of logical structure. With TDGS protocol, a read operation is limited to two data copies, while a write operation is required with minimal number of copies. In comparison to other protocols, TDGS requires lower communication cost for an operation, while providing higher data availability.

1 Introduction

Distributed database (DDB) system technology is one of the major recent developments in the database area, where it moves from centralization which resulted in monolithic gigantic databases towards more decentralization and autonomy of processing [11]. With advances in distributed processing and distributed computing that occurred in the operating systems arena, the database research community did considerable work to address the issues of data distribution, distributed query processing, distributed transactions management, and etc [10]. One of the major issue in data distribution is replicated data management. Typical replicated data management parameters are data availability and communication costs: the higher the data availability with lower communication costs the better the system is.

Replication is a useful technique for distributed database systems where a data item will be accessed (i.e., read and written) from multiple locations that may be geographically distributed world wide or in local area network environment. For example Financial instruments' prices will be read and updated from all over the world [18] . Student's results, will be read and updated/modified from lecturers throughout departments.

By storing multiple copies of data at several sites in the system, there is an increased data availability and accessibility to users despite site and communication failures. It is an important mechanism because it enables organizations to provide users with access to current data where and when they need it. However, expensive synchronization mechanisms are needed to maintain the consistency and integrity of data [1]. One of the simplest protocols for managing replicated data is one where read operations on the data items are allowed to read any copy, and write operations are required to write all copies of the data item which is called read-one write-all (ROWA) protocol. The ROWA protocol provides read operations with high degree of availability at low cost and severely restricts the availability of write operations since they cannot be executed at the failure of any copy. This protocol results in the imbalance of availability as well as the communication cost of read and write operations: read operations have a higher availability and low communication cost whereas write operations have a lower availability with higher communication cost. Voting protocols [9,10] become popular because they are flexible and easily implemented. A weakness of these protocols is that writing a data item is fairly expensive: A write quorum of copies must be larger than the majority of votes. To optimize the communication cost and the availability of both read and write operations, the quorum protocol generalize the ROWA protocol by imposing the intersection requirement between read and write operations. Write operations can be made fault-tolerant since they do not need to access all copies of data items. Dynamic quorum protocols have also been proposed to further increase availability in replicated databases [4,17]. However, these approaches do not address the issue of low-cost read operations . Tree quorum algorithm [2,3] uses quorums that are obtained from a logical tree structure imposed on data copies. However, this protocol has some drawbacks. If more than a majority of the copies in any level of the tree become unavailable, write execution cannot be executed.

Recently, several researchers have proposed imposing logical structure on the set of copies in the database by using logical information to create intersecting quorums. Protocol that use logical structure such as grid protocol, executes operation with low communication costs while providing fault-tolerance for both read and write operations [1]. However, this protocol still require a bigger number of copies that are available to construct a quorum [14]. The focus of this paper is on modeling a technique to optimize the communication costs and the availability of both read and write operations of replicated data in the distributed database systems by means of synchronous replication.

In this paper, we describe Three Dimensional Grid Structure (TDGS) protocol to improve the read and write operations with respect to the logical structure. As with the original grid quorum approach, the improved performance for read operations has resulted into degraded write availability. Nevertheless, TDGS protocol provides the minimum communication cost and higher availability of executing read and write operations in replicated database due to the minimum number of quorum size required. This approach is particularly useful if failures are infrequent, and hence represents an alternative design philosophy to the quorum approach. Thus our protocol supports the analogues of quorum protocol for efficient execution and fault-tolerance.

This paper is organized as follows: In Section 2, we review two replica control protocols; Tree Quorum and Grid Configuration protocols. In Section 3, the model and the protocol of the TDGS is presented. In Section 4, the performance of the proposed protocol is analyzed in terms of communication/message cost and availability, and a comparison with other protocols is given.

2 Review of Replica Control Protocol

In this section, we review some of the replica control protocols namely: Tree Quorum (TQ) protocol, and Grid Configuration protocol, which are then compared to the proposed TDGS protocol.

2.1 Tree Quorum Protocol

Agrawal and El-Abbadi [2] proposed a logical tree structure over a network of sites to achieve fault-tolerant distributed mutual exclusion. One advantage of this protocol is that a read operation may access only one copy and the number of copies to be accessed by a write operation is always less than a majority of quorum, i.e., the size of quorum may increase to maximum of n/2 +1 sites when failures occur. Write operations in the tree protocol must access a write quorum which is formed from the root, a majority of its children, and a majority of their children, and so forth until the leaves of the tree are reached. In Figure 1, an example of a ternary tree with thirteen copies is illustrated. For read operations, a read quorum can be formed by the root or the majority of the children of the root. If any node in the majority of the children of the root fails, it can be replaced by the majority of its children, and so on recursively. In the best case, a read quorum consists of only root, {1}. As the root fails, a quorum is formed by the majority of the copies at level 1, e.g., {2,3},{3,4}, or {2,4}.Nodes 2 and 3 are replaced by the majority of their children, respectively, if no majority at level 1 is accessible and only site 4 is accessible. Such quorums are {4,5,6} or {4,9,10}. If copies at level 0 and level 1 fail, a quorum is formed by the majorities of the children of the selected majority at level 1, e.g., { 5,7,8,10} or {9,10,11,12}. For write operations, the size of a write quorum for a given tree is fixed, but the members can be different. Such quorums are {1,2,3,5,6,8,10},{1,3,4,9,10,11,13}, etc.

The desirable aspects of this protocol are that the cost of executing read operations is comparable to the ROWA protocol while the availability of write operations is significantly better [1]. There are some drawbacks from this protocol, as an example, if more than a majority of the copies at any level of the tree become unavailable, write operations cannot be executed.

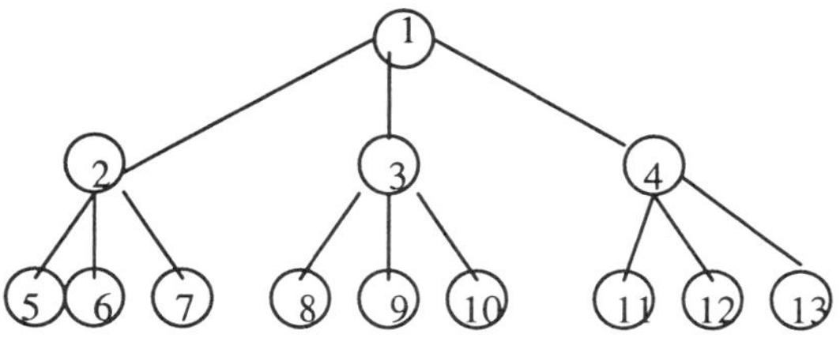

Figure 1: A tree organization of 13 copies of data items

2.2 The Grid Configuration Protocol

Maekawa [12] proposed using the notion of finite projective planes to obtain a distributed mutual exclusion algorithm where all quorums are of equal size. Cheung et al. [8], extended Maekawa's grid protocol for replicated data that support read and write operations. In this protocol, n copies of data items are logically organized in the form of a $\sqrt{n}$ x $\sqrt{n}$ grid as shown in Figure 2.

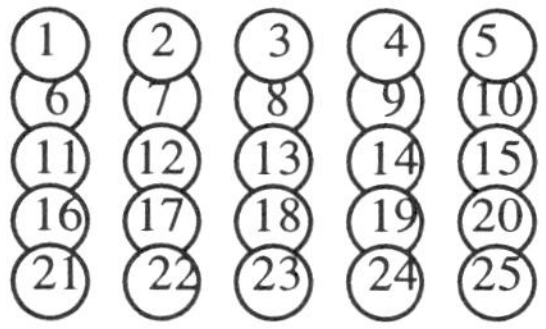

Figure 2. A grid organization with 25 copies of a data item

Read operations on the data item are executed by acquiring a read quorum that consists of a copy from each column in the grid. Write operations on the other hand, are executed by acquiring a write quorum that consists of all copies in one column and a copy from each of the remaining columns. The read and write operations of this protocol is of the size $O(\sqrt{n})$, and we will refer to this protocol as the *sqrt(R/W)* protocol. In Figure 2, copies {1,2,3,4,5} are sufficient to execute a read operation whereas copies {1,6,11,16,21,7,13,19,25} will be required to execute a write operation. However, it still has a bigger number of copies for read and write quorums, thereby degrading the communication cost and data availability . It is also vulnerable to the failure of entire column or row in the grid [1].

The notion of quorums has been generalized by Agrawal and Abbadi [1] in the context of the grid structure. In general, a grid quorum has a length *l* and a width *w*, and is represented as a pair <*l*,*w*>. A read operation is executed by accessing a read grid quorum <*l*,*w*>, which is formed from *l* copies in each of *w* different columns. A write operation is executed by writing a write grid quorum, <*l*,*w*>, which is formed from a) l copies in each of w columns as well as b) any $\sqrt{n} - l + 1$ copies in each of $\sqrt{n} - w+1$ columns. (The second component of the write quorum is to ensure the intersection between two write quorums). In order to ensure the quorum intersection property between read and write quorums, if the read grid quorum is of size $<l, w>$ then the write grid quorum must be $<\sqrt{n}-l+1, \sqrt{n}-w+1>$. The reconfiguration grid protocol based on majority grid quorum has been proposed by [1] to further increase the fault-tolerance of write operations. Both read and write quorums have dimensions $<\sqrt{n}/2+1,\ \sqrt{n}/2+1>$, i.e., both operations are executed by accessing a majority of copies in a majority of the columns. This will increase the fault-tolerance when compared with the *sqrt(R/W)* protocol. However this protocol has the availability that is not in the closed form (definition 4.2.3)

3 Model

A distributed system consists of a set of distinct sites that communicate with each other by sending messages over a communication network. A site may become inaccessible due to site or partitioning failure. No assumptions are made regarding the speed or reliability of the network.

A distributed database consists of a set of data items stored at different sites in a computer network. Users interact with the database by invoking transactions, which are partially ordered sequences of atomic read and write operations. The execution of a transaction must appear atomic: a transaction either commits or aborts[5,7].

In a replicated database, copies of a data item may be stored at several sites in the network. Multiple copies of a data item must appear as a single logical data item to the transactions. This is termed as one-copy equivalence and is enforced by the replica control protocol. The correctness criteria for replicated database is one-copy serializability [6], which ensures both one-copy equivalence and the serializable execution of transactions. In order to ensure one-copy serializability, a replicated data item may be read by reading a quorum of copies, and it may be written by writing a quorum of copies. The selection of a quorum is restricted by the quorum intersection property to ensure one-copy equivalence: For any two operations o[x] and o'[x] on a replicated data x, where at least one of them is a write, the quorum must have a nonempty intersection. The quorum for an operation is defined as a set of copies whose number is sufficient to execute that operation.

Briefly, a site S initiates a TDGS transaction to update its replicated data. For all accessible replicated data, a TDGS transaction attempts to access a TDGS quorum. If a TDGS transaction gets a TDGS write quorum without nonempty intersection, it is accepted for execution and completion, otherwise it is rejected. We do not need to worry about the read quorum if two transactions attempt to read a common data item, because read operations do not change the values of the replicated data. Since read and write quorums must intersect and any two TDGS quorums must also intersect, then all transaction executions are one-copy serializable (theorem 3.2.1).

3.1 *The TDGS Protocol*

In this section, we proposed using a TDGS protocol to define quorums for both read and write operations. We then apply grid paradigm that was proposed by Cheung et al.[8] to TDGS quorum, and thus reduce the cost of executing read operations, while maintaining a high degree of data availability.

With TDGS protocol, copies are logically organized into a box-shape structure with four planes. Figure 3, is an example of the box-shape structure that consists of four planes with the black circle represents a copy at location A,B,C,…,and X. In this paper, we shall restrict our attention to the case where the number of copies in each plane are equal (perfect square), i.e., if l denotes the length (column) of the plane, and w is the width (row) of the plane, then $l = w$. For example, as shown in Figure 1, each plane consists of 9 copies where $l = w = 3$. The number of copies, n, in the TDGS protocol can be calculated using property 3.1.

Property 3.1: We assume that the minimum number of copies in a box-shape structure is 8. Let $n \geq 8$ be a number of copies in the TDGS protocol. The organization of n copies is in the form of box-shape with four equal planes. Each plane has a length l and a width w. Since $l = w$, then n equals to $4l(l-1)$.
***Proof*:** Let a box-shape structure consists of four planes $\alpha_1,\alpha_2,\alpha_3$, and α_4 as depicted in Figure 4. Let $m(\alpha_i)$ be a number of copies of α_i. Suppose that α_1 is opposite with α_2 , then $m(\alpha_1) = m(\alpha_2) = l * w$. Subsequently $m(\alpha_3) = m(\alpha_4) = (l-2)*w$.Then the number of copies in a box-shape structure, n, is:

$$= 2(l*w) + 2(l-2)*w$$
$$= 2l^2 + 2(l-2)*l, \text{ since } l = w.$$
$$= 4l(l-1)$$

Therefore, from property 3.1, l can be calculated as: $l = [1+ \sqrt{(1+n)}]/2$. … (1)

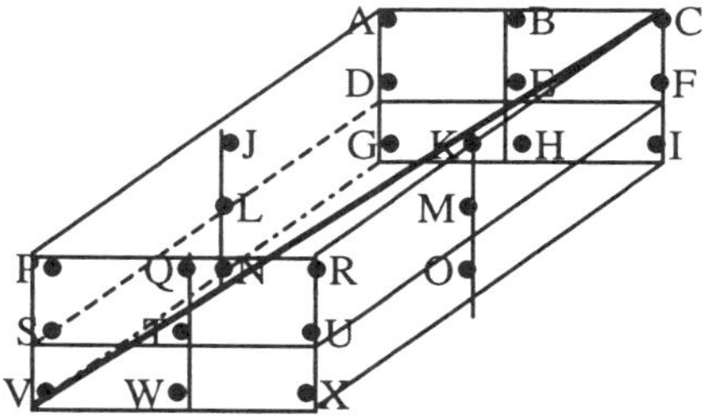

Figure 3: A TDGS organization with 24 copies of a data item

Definition 3.1. A pair of copies that can be constructed from a hypotenuse edge in a box-shape structure (organization) is called hypotenuse copies.

For TDGS quorum, read operations on a replicated data item are executed by acquiring a read quorum that consists of any hypotenuse copies. In Figure 3, copies {V,C},{I,P}, {X,A}, or {G,R} are hypotenuse copies from which is sufficient to execute a read operation. Since each pair of them is hypotenuse copies, it is clear that, read operation can be executed if one of them is accessible, thus increased the fault-tolerance.

Write operations on the other hand, are executed by acquiring a write quorum from any plane that consists of hypotenuse copies, and all copies which are vertices that one of which is hypotenuse copy. For example, if the hypotenuse copies, say {V,C} are required to execute a read operation, then copies {V,C,I,A,G } are sufficient to execute a write operation, since one possible set of copies of vertices that correspond to {V,C} is {C,I,A,G}. Other possible write quorums are {V,C,I,R,X }, { C ,V ,P,R,X}, {C,V,P,A,G}, etc. It can be easily shown that a write quorum intersect with both read and write quorums in this protocol (Section 3.2).

3.2 The Correctness

In this section, we will show TDGS protocol is one-copy serializable. We start by defining sets of groups (*coterie*)[9] and to avoid confusion we are referring to sets of copies as *groups*. Thus, sets of *groups* are sets of sets of copies.

***Definition* 3.2.1**. *Coterie*. Let **U** be a set of *groups* that compose the system. A set of *groups* **T** is a coterie under **U** iff

i) $G \in \mathbf{T}$ implies that $G \neq \varnothing$ and $G \subseteq \mathbf{U}$.
ii) If $G, H \in \mathbf{T}$ then $G \cap H \neq \varnothing$ (intersection property)
iii) There are no $G, H \in \mathbf{T}$ such that $G \subset H$ (minimality).

***Definition* 3.2.2**. Let **R** be a set of read quorums which consists of *groups* of hypotenuse copies, that is sufficient to execute read operations, and **W** be a set of write quorums which consists of *groups* that are sufficient to execute write operations under TDGS protocol, then from Figure 3.,

R = { {V,C}, {I,P}, {X,A}, {G,R} },

and **W**={{V,C,I,A,G},{V,C,I,R,X},{C,V,P,A,G},{C,V,P,R,X},
{I,P,V,R,X},{I,P,V,A,G},{P,I,C,A,G},{P,I,C,R,X},
{A,X,R,C,I},{A,X,R,P,V},{X,A,G,C,I},{X,A,G,P,V},
{G,R,X,C,I},{G,R,X,P,V},{R,G,A,C,I},{R,G,A,P,V} }

By definition of coterie, then **W** is a coterie, because it satisfies all coterie's properties.

The correct criterion for replicated database is one-copy serializable. The next theorem gives us a way to check TDGS is correct.

Theorem 3.2.1. The TDGS protocol is one-copy serializable.
Proof: The theorem holds on condition that TDGS protocol satisfies the quorum intersection properties, i.e., write-write and read-write intersections. For the case of write-write intersection, since **W** is a coterie then it satisfies write-write intersection. However, for the case of read-write intersection, it can be easily shown that $\forall G \in \mathbf{R}$ and $\forall H \in \mathbf{W}$, then $G \cap H \neq \varnothing$.

In addition, TDGS allows us to construct a write quorum even though three out of four planes are unavailable as long as the hypotenuse copies are accessible. In other words, this protocol tolerates the failure of more than three quarter of the copies in the TDGS protocol. Consider the case when only one plane which consists of four copies of vertices and hypotenuse copies are available, e.g., the set {C,V,P,R,X} is available as shown in Figure 3. A TDGS transaction can be executed successfully by accessing those copies in a TDGS quorum. Hence the write quorum is formed by accessing those available copies. Read operations, on the other hand, need to access the available hypotenuse copies. Thus the proposed protocol enhances the fault-tolerance in write operations compared to the grid configuration protocol.

Therefore, this protocol ensures that read operations have a significantly low cost, i.e., two copies, and have a high degree of availability, since they are not vulnerable to the failure of more than three quarter of the copies. Write operations, on the other hand, are more available than the grid configuration protocol since only five copies (as derived in Section 4.1.3) are needed to execute write operations.

4 Performance Analysis and Comparison

In this section, we analyze and compare the performance of the TDGS quorum protocol and other protocols: tree quorum and grid configuration on the communication cost and the data availability. However, for the grid configuration, we only discuss the *sqrt(R/W)* protocol, since the reconfiguration protocol has the availability that is not in the closed form.

4.1 Communication Costs Analysis

The communication cost of an operation is directly proportional to the size of the quorum required to execute the operation. Therefore, we represent the communication cost in terms of the quorum size. C_{XY} denotes the communication cost with X protocol for Y operation, which is R (read) or W(write).

4.1.1 Grid Configuration (GC) Protocol

Let n be the number of copies which are organized as a grid of dimension $\sqrt{n} \times \sqrt{n}$. Read operations on the replicated data are executed by acquiring a read quorum that consists of a copy from each column in the grid and write operations are executed by acquiring a write quorum that consists of all copies in one column and a copy from each of the remaining columns, as discussed in Section 2.1. Thus, the communication cost ,C_{GCR} ,can be represented as:

$$C_{GCR} = \sqrt{n},$$

and the communication cost, C_{GRW} , can be represented as:

$$C_{GCW} = \sqrt{n} + (\sqrt{n} - 1) = 2\sqrt{n} - 1.$$

4.1.2 Tree Quorum (TQ) Protocol

Let h denotes the height of the tree, D is the degree of the copies in the tree, and $M = \lceil (D+1)/2 \rceil$ is the majority of the degree of copies. When the root is accessible, the read quorum size is 1. As the root fails, the majority of its children replace it, thus the quorum size increases to M. Therefore, for a tree of height h, the maximum quorum size is M^h. Hence, the cost of read operation, C_{TQR} , ranges from 1 to M^h [2,9] i.e., $1 \leq C_{TQR} \leq M^h$. The cost of a write operation, C_{TQW} , can be represented as: $C_{TQW} = \sum M^i$, i = 1...h

4.1.3 TDGS Protocol

The size of a read quorum in TDGS is hypotenuse copies, i.e., 2. Thus, the cost of a read operation ,C_{TDGSR} ,can be represented as:

$$C_{TDGSR} = 2,$$

and the cost of a write operation , C_{TDGSW} , can be represented as:

hypotenuse copies +
(all copies of vertices in a plane - hypotenuse copy in the same plane).
= 2 + (4-1) = 5.

For example, if hypotenuse copies is {V,C}, then all copies of vertices in plane α_1 that correspond to {V,C} is {C,I,A,G}. The hypotenuse copy in plane α_1 is {C}. Therefore, $C_{TDGSW} = |\{V,C\}|+|\{C,I,A,G\}|-|\{C\}| = 2+(4-1) = 5$.

4.1.4 Comparison of Costs

Table 1. shows the read and write costs of the three protocols between TDGS, TQ, and GC, for different total number of copies. For simplicity, we choose TQ with complete tree quorum structure, GC with perfect square configuration structure, and TDGS with four equal planes.

Table 1. Comparison of the read and write cost between TQ, GC and TDGS under the different set of copies

	Number of copies in the system								
	13	16	24	25	40	48	49	80	81
TQ(R)	4				8				
TQ(W)	7				15				
GC (R)		4		5			7		9
GC(W)		7		9			13		17
TDGS(R)			2			2		2	
TDGS(W)			5			5		5	

From Table 1, it is apparent that TDGS has the lowest costs for both read and write operations in spite of having a bigger number of data copies when compared with TQ and GC quorums. It can be seen that, TDGS needs only 2 copies for the read quorum for all instances. On the contrary for TQ with a tree of height 2 on 13 copies, the maximum cost is 4, meanwhile for GC with 16 copies, the cost is 4. So as for write operations, TDGS needs only 5 copies for the write quorum for all instances. Conversely, the cost is 13 for GC with 48 copies, and 15 for TQ with a tree of height 3 on 40 copies.

4.2 *Availability Analysis*

In this section, three replica control protocols are analyzed and compared in terms of the operation availability. In estimating the availability of operations, all copies are assumed to have the same availability *p*, and A_{xy} will represent the availability of Y operation with X protocol.

4.2.1 Grid Configuration (GC) Protocol

In the case of the quorum protocol, read quorums can be constructed as long as a copy from each column is available. Then, the read availability in the GC protocol, A_{GCR} is:

$$= \left(\sum_{i=1}^{\sqrt{n}} \binom{\sqrt{n}}{i} p^{i} (1-p)^{\sqrt{n}-i} \right)^{\sqrt{n}}$$

$$= [1-(1-p)^{\sqrt{n}}]^{\sqrt{n}}$$

On the other hand, write quorums can be constructed as all copies from a column and one copy from each of the remaining columns are available. Then the write availability in the GC protocol, A_{GCW} is:

$$= \sqrt{n}\left(1-(1-p)^{\sqrt{n}}\right)^{\sqrt{n}-1} p^{\sqrt{n}} + \binom{\sqrt{n}}{2}\left(1-(1-p)^{\sqrt{n}}\right)^{\sqrt{n}-2}\left(p^{\sqrt{n}}\right)^{2} + \ldots \left(p^{\sqrt{n}}\right)^{n}$$

$$= [1-(1-p)^{\sqrt{n}}]^{\sqrt{n}} - [(1-(1-p)^{\sqrt{n}}-p^{\sqrt{n}}]^{\sqrt{n}}.$$

4.2.2 Tree Quorum (TQ) Protocol

The availability of the read and write operations in the TQ can be estimated by using recurrence equations based on the tree height h. Let AR_{h+1} and AW_{h+1} be the availability of the read and the write operations with a tree of height h, respectively. D denotes the degree of sites in the tree and M is the majority of D. Then the availability of a read operation for a tree of height h+1 can be represented as:

$$AR_{h+1} = p + (1-p) \sum_{i=M}^{D} \binom{D}{i} AR_h^i \left(1 - AR_h\right)^{D-i}$$

and the availability of a write operation for a tree of height h+1 is given as:

$$AW_{h+1} = p \sum_{i=M}^{D} \binom{D}{i} AW_h^i \left(1 - AW_h\right)^{D-i}$$

where p is the probability that a copy is available, and $R_0 = W_0 = p$.

4.2.3 TDGS protocol

In the TDGS protocol, a read quorum can be constructed from any hypotenuse copies. The read availability, A_{TDGSR} is:

= 1- probability { all the hypotenuse copies are not available}

Since it has 4 hypotenuse copies, thus

$$A_{TDGSR} = 1-(1-p^2)^4. \qquad \ldots (2)$$

On the contrary, a write quorum can be constructed as follows: Let $\{\alpha_1,\alpha_2,\alpha_3,\alpha_4\}$ be a set of planes in the TDGS protocol as shown in Figure 4 below. Each of which consists of l x l copies. Let {V,C} be the hypotenuse copies, then write availability

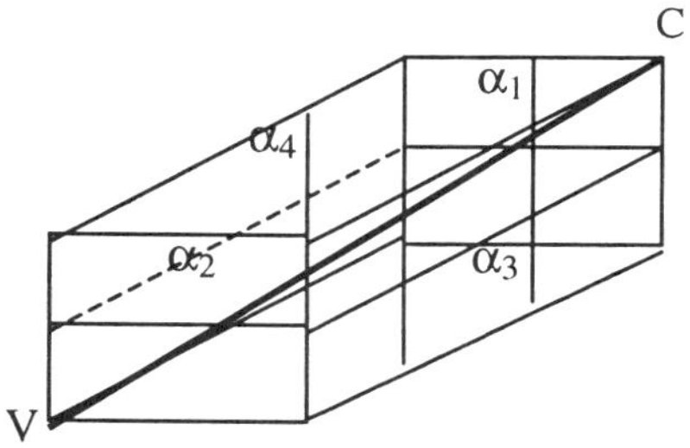

Figure 4 . Represents four planes in the TDGS structure

that consists of hypotenuse copies {V,C}, W_{VC} ,can be represented as:

Probability{ V is available}* [φ available]
+ Probability{ C is available}* [ϕ available]
- Probability{C and Vare available}*[(φ and ϕ)are available] ... (3)

where, $\varphi = \Omega_1 + \{\Omega_3 - (\Omega_3 \cap \Omega_1) - (\Omega_3 \cap \Omega_2) + (\Omega_3 \cap \Omega_1) \cap (\Omega_3 \cap \Omega_2)\}$,
$\phi = \Omega_2 + \{\Omega_4 - (\Omega_4 \cap \Omega_2) - (\Omega_4 \cap \Omega_1) + (\Omega_4 \cap \Omega_2) \cap (\Omega_4 \cap \Omega_1)\}$,
and Ω_i = Probability of plane α_i available.

The probability of α_i available, Ω_i , can be represented as:

Probability{ all copies of vertices from α_i are available}
+ Probability{ (all copies of vertices + 1 copy) from α_i are available}
+ ...+ Probability { all copies from α_i are available}

$$= p^4 \sum_{j=0}^{m-4} \binom{m-4}{j} p^j (1-p)^{m-4-j} \quad ,$$

$$= p^4, \text{ since } \sum_{j=0}^{m-4} \binom{m-4}{j} p^j (1-p)^{m-4-j} = 1$$

where m is a number of copies in each plane.

Thus, $\Omega_i = p^4$, for i = 1,2,3,4. ... (4)

To calculate $\Omega_3 \cap \Omega_1$,we shall need the following proposition.

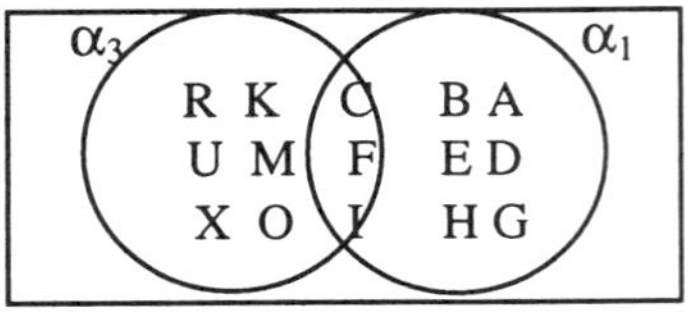

Figure 5. Two planes α_1 and α_3 consists of 3 x 3 copies of each plane

Proposition 4.2.3. Let α_1 and α_2 be two planes, each of which consists of l x l copies. The availability of each plane,Ω_i ,i=1,2 is the availability of all copies of vertices in each plane. Intersection copies between α_1 and α_2 consists of a copies of two vertices and other l-2 copies, then $\Omega_1 \cap \Omega_2 = p^{4+l}$. ... (5)

Proof (by example): Let α_1 and α_2 are planes each of which consists of 3 x 3 copies as depicted in Figure 5. Each copy has the same availability with probability, say p. Consider a *group* G= {C,F,I} consists of intersection copies between plane α_1 and α_2 where two of them are copies of vertices i.e., {C,I}. The probability of G, P(G) is the probability of copies of vertices and the probability of other (l-2) copies in G. Thus, $P(G) = p^2.p^{l-2}= p^l$. {R,X} is a *group* of vertices of plane α_3 available but not in α_1, and {A,G} is a *group* of vertices of α_1 available but not in α_3. If $\Omega_i \setminus \Omega_j$, i≠j = 1, 3 is the probability of copies of vertices of plane α_i available but not in α_j, then $\Omega_3 \setminus \Omega_1 = \Omega_3(\{R,X\}) = p^2$, and $\Omega_1 \setminus \Omega_3 = \Omega_1(\{A,G\}) = p^2$. Thinking as a Venn diagram, then

$$\Omega_3 \cap \Omega_1 = (\Omega_3 \setminus \Omega_1) *P(G) *(\Omega_1 \setminus \Omega_3)$$

$$= p^2 * p^l * p^2 = p^{4+l} = p^7, \text{ since } l = 3.$$

Substitute (4)-(5) into φ and ϕ , then

$$\varphi = \phi = p^4+p^4 (1-2p^l+p^{2l}) \qquad \text{... (6)}$$

where, from equation (1), $l = [1+\sqrt{(1+n)}]/2$.

Since, the probability {V is available } = probability {C is available}= p, then , by substituting equation (6) into equation (3), W_{VC} is:

$$= [p^4+p^4 (1-2p^l+p^{2l})] [2p - p^2\{p^4+p^4 (1-2p^l+p^{2l})\}] \qquad \text{... (7)}$$

Similarly, with the write availability that consists of other hypotenuse copies, thus $W_{IP}=W_{AX}=W_{RG}=W_{VC}$. To compute the write availability, A_{TDGSW} , it is analogues to the read availability. Let $W_i = \beta$, $i \in \mathbf{R}$,then A_{TDGSW} is:

$$= \binom{4}{1} \text{x } W_i - \binom{4}{2} \text{x } (W_i \cap W_j) + \binom{4}{3} x\,(W_i \cap W_j \cap W_k)$$

$$- W_i \cap W_j \cap W_k \cap W_l, \qquad \text{for } i,j,k,l \in \mathbf{R}$$

$$= 1-(1-\beta)^4. \qquad \ldots \quad (8)$$

***Definition* 4.2.3.** Let A(x) be the availability function with respect to x. A(x) is in the closed form if $0 \le x \le 1$ then $0 \le A(x) \le 1$.

Theorem 4.2.3. The read and write availabilities under TDGS protocol are in the closed form.
***Proof*:** For the case of read availability, from equation (2) and by definition 4.2.3, as $0 \le p \le 1$ then $0 \le A_{TDGSR} \le 1$. Similarly, for the case of write availability where $0 \le A_{TDGSw} \le 1$ as $0 \le \beta \le 1$.

4.2.4 Comparison of Availabilities

The read and the write availabilities of the three protocols, TQ , GC, and TDGS are compared in Figure 6. We assume that all data copies have the same availability, and n =48.

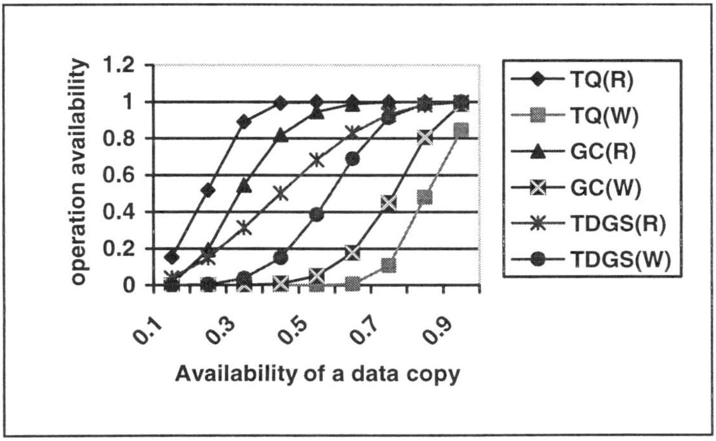

Figure 6. Comparison of the read and write availability between TQ,GC, and TDGS

Figure 6, shows the imbalance between read and write availability when the TQ protocol is used. For example, when an individual copy has availability 70%, read availability is 100% whereas write availability is approximately 10%. However, the GC and TDGS protocols show better performance by reducing the imbalance between read and write availability. Nevertheless, TDGS has higher write availability than GC because the number of data copies to be written in TDGS is smaller than that of GC. For example, when an individual copy has availability 70%, the write availability in the TDGS is more than 90%, whereas write availability in the GC is approximately 45%.

5 Conclusion

In this paper, a new protocol, called Three Dimensional Grid Structure (TDGS) protocol is being proposed to manage the data replication in distributed database systems .This protocol provides a convenient approach to high availability for read and write operations by imposing a box-shape logical structure on data copies. With TDGS protocol, a read operation is allowed as long as when one of the hypotenuse copies is available, and a write operation is allowed when the hypotenuse copies and all copies which are vertices that one of which is hypotenuse copy are available, thereby tolerates the failure of more than quarter of the copies. Compared to other protocols, TDGS requires significantly lower communication cost for an operation, while providing higher availability. If the distance between sites is to be considered, an area where the proposed TDGS protocol can be utilized is the local area network environment, otherwise it will particularly useful for designing large scalable distributed systems.

6 References

1. D Agrawal and A.El Abbadi, "Using Reconfiguration For Efficient Management of Replicated Data,"*IEEE Trans. On Knowledge and Data Engineering*,vol.8,no. **5** (1996). Pp 786-801.
2. D Agrawal and A.El Abbadi, "The Tree Quorum protocol: AN Efficient Approach for Managing Replicated Data,"*Proc.16th Int'l Conf. On Very Large Data Bases*, pp 243-254,Aug. 1990
3. D Agrawal and A.El Abbadi, "The generalized Tree Quorum Protocol: An Efficient Approach for Managing Replicated Data,"*ACM Trans. Database Systems*,vol.17,no. **4**(1992). pp 689-717.
4. D.Bell & J. Grimson, "*Distributed Database Systems*," (Addison Wesley Publishing Co, 1992).
5. B. Bhargava,"Concurrency Control in Database Systems," *IEEE Trans. Knowledge and Data Engineering*,vol 11,no. **1**(1999), pp.3-16.

6. P.A. Bernstein and N.Goodman, "An Algorithm for Concurrency Control and Recovery in Replicated Distributed Databases,"*ACM Trans. Database Systems*,vol 9,no. **4**(1994),pp596-615.
7. P.A. Bernstein, V. Hadzilacos, and N.Goodman, " *Concurrency Control and Recovery in Database Syatems*,"(Addison Wesley Publishing Co., 1987).
8. S.Y. Cheung, M.H. Ammar, and M. Ahmad,"The Grid Protocol: A High Performance Schema for Maintaining Replicated Data," *IEEE Trans. Knowledge and Data Engineering*,vol. 4, no. **6**(1992), pp 582-592.
9. S.M. Chung, "Enhanced Tree Quorum Algorithm For Replicated Distributed Databases," *Int'l Conference on Database* , Tokyo, 1990, pp 83-89.
10. T.M. Connolly, and C.E. Begg, "Database Syatems : A practical Approach to Design, Implementation, and Management", (2nd ed. Addison-Wesley, 1999).
11. R.Elmasri and S.B. Navathe,"Fundamentals of Database Systems",(3rd Ed., Addison-Wesley, 2000).
12. H. Garcia-Molina and D. Barbara,"How to Assign Votes in a Distributed System,"*J.ACM*,vol.32,no. **4**(1985), pp841-860.
13. S.Jajodia and D. Mutchles,"Dynamic Voting Algorithms for Maintaining the Consistency of a Replicated Database,"*ACM Trans. Database Systems*,vol 15,no. **2**(1990), pp. 230-280.
14. M. Maekawa," A $\sqrt{n}$ Algorithm for Mutual Exclusion in Decentralized Systems,"*ACM Trans. Computer Systems*,vol. 3,no. **2**(1992), pp 145-159.
15. M.Mat Deris, A.Mamat, and M.P.Hamzah, " Replicated Data Management for Transaction Sharing in Distributed Database", *IEEE 4th Int'l Conf. High Performance Computing*, Beijing, May 2000 ,pp 836-841.
16. M.T. Ozsu and P. Valduriez,"*Principles of Distributed Database Systems*", (2nd Ed., Prentice Hall, 1999).
17. J.F Paris and D.E Long, "Efficient Dynamic Voting Algorithms," *Proc. Fourth IEEE Int'l Conf. Data Eng*, pp. 268-275,Feb.1988.
18. O. Wolfson, S. Jajodia, and Y. Huang,"An Adaptive Data Replication Algorithm,"*ACM Transactions on Database Systems*, vol. 22, no **2** (1997),pp 255-314.

THE DESIGN OF A MOBILE DECISION SUPPORT SYSTEM

WU YEU[1], TIAN YONGHONG[1], AND WANLEI ZHOU[2]

[1]*College of Computer Science and Engineering, The University of Electronic Science and Technology, Chengdu, China, 610054. Email: ywu@uestc.edu.cn*

[2]*School of Computing and Mathematics, Deakin University, Melbourne, VIC 3168 Australia. Email: wanlei@deakin.edu.au*

The emergence of mobile computing environments brings out various changes in the requirements and applications involving distributed data and has made the traditional Intelligent Decision Support System (IDSS) architectures based on the client/server model ineffective in mobile computing environments. This paper discusses the deficiencies of the current IDSS architectures based on data warehouse, on-line analysis processing (OLAP), model base (MB) and knowledge based (KB) technologies. By adopting the agent technology, the paper extends the IDSS system architecture to the Mobile Decision Support System (MDSS) architecture. The logical structure and the application architecture of the MDSS and the mechanisms and implementation strategies of the User Access Agent System, a major component of the MDSS, are described in this paper.

Keywords: IDSS, mobile agent, MDSS.

1 Introduction

The development of Data Warehouse (DW) and On-Line Analysis Processing (OLAP) technologies has opened a new dimension for building Decision Support Systems (DSS) [6]. The Intelligent Decision Support System (IDSS) that combines the technologies of DW, OLAP, Model Base (MB), knowledge base (KB), and data mining is a higher-level decision support system [13]. The architecture of an IDSS can be depicted in Figure 1.

In the Client layer, clients interact with the User Interface of the IDSS, which in turn interacts with the middle layer of the application servers, such as OLAP and data mining. These middle layer servers will interact with the lower layer data servers, such as the data warehouse, the knowledge base and the model base.

Although IDSS can improve the speed and flexibility of decision-making by integrating large amount of decision-making data and information in the data warehouse, it has the following deficiencies:

1. Data in the data warehouse are synthesized and stored according to the decision-making subjects and they are relatively stable. So the IDSS cannot provide a real-time integration of decision-making data for distributed decision-making.
2. IDSS cannot provide transparent accesses required by the personalized decision-making information. In an IDSS, the contents and formats of the user

sharable (or accessible) decision-making information are determined by the OLAP or the data mining servers. Users have to understand the abilities and access methods of these analysis applications.

3. IDSS does not support the mobile computing mode. The emergence of the mobile computing environments has changed the ways we process and utilize distributed data [2,3,5]. Compared to traditional distributed computing environments in fixed networks, mobile computing environments have properties such as mobility (including mobility of computing platforms, mobility of accessed resources, and personal mobility), and network adaptability (including frequent network disconnections, low reliability, asymmetrical network communications). The IDSS based on the traditional client/server model can no longer satisfy the requirements of mobile computing environments. Therefore it is necessary to introduce a new and flexible architecture.

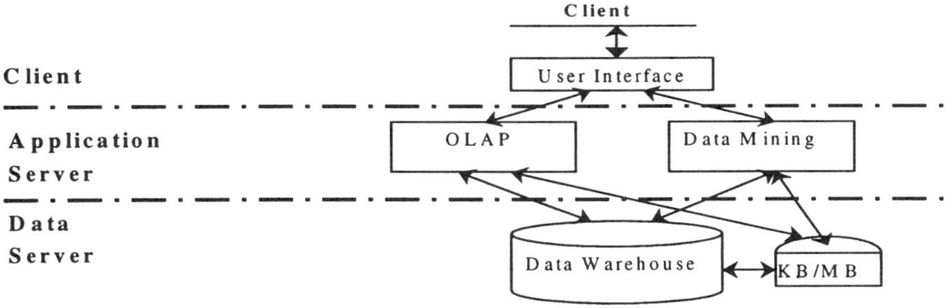

Figure 1. IDSS application architecture

In recent years, the agent technology has attracted attentions from many researchers [7,14]. The agent technology, in particular the mobile agent technology, provides a new approach for the analysis and design of distributed and open systems in mobile computing environments [11]. In this paper we adopt the mobile agent technology in distributed decision support systems and extend the IDSS to a mobile decision support system (MDSS).

2 Mobile Agent Technology

The concept of agents first appeared in the research of distributed artificial intelligence [10], in which they are defined as programs or computing entities used to model the behaviors of human beings and to provide related services, whereas mobile agents are those agents who are dynamic and distributed. That is, mobile agents are autonomous software entities with some intelligence. They can autonomously represent the user or other software entities to move among network nodes in order to search for some resources or to complete some specific functions. Because of the introduction of distributed mobile computing concepts, the mobile agent technology can successfully deal with tasks that cannot be performed well by the traditional client/server model. Agent technology has the following advantages and characteristics:

- Dynamic execution.
- Asynchronous computing.
- Parallel computation.
- Intelligent routing.

The characteristics and advantages of the mobile agent technology enable mobile agent systems to work smoothly in an environment of low bandwidth and unstable network connections, and therefore are suitable to mobile users. Introducing the mobile agent technique into the mobile computing environment, especially the mobile decision support systems, will bring a number of advantages [12], for example, it can support mobile users to carry out decision analysis in an unstable network connection situation, and can reduce the information transmission dramatically. Mobile agents can provide mobile users with personalized services, and can autonomously perform the induction according to the knowledge of network capacity and task models, relieving mobile users from knowing the capacities and access methods of individual decision support systems.

3 The MDSS Model Based on the Agent Technology

3.1 The Logical Structure of the MDSS

We can abstract the IDSS logical structures based on the traditional client/server model into a two-layered structure consisting of a *Source Schema* and a *Client Schema* [8]. The source schema is also called the server schema, and in a client/server system using the "lean client machine" and the application server structure the server schema can be further categorized into two sub-schemas: an Application Schema and a Data Schema. The data schema describes the logical structure of the global data in the IDSS data warehouse; it is the global conceptual view of the IDSS. The application schema describes the logical structure of the analysis data of DSS applications (such as OLAP and DM applications) within the IDSS; it is the complete set of the decision support information schemas provided by the IDSS for users. The client schema is the sub-set (can be the complete set in special cases) of the application schema; it is actually the decision support information schemas presented to users.

Our MDSS structure adds a new layer, the *agent layer*, between the client and server of the IDSS. That is, it has a three-layered structure consisting of the source schema, the agent schema, and the client schema. In the MDSS, the source schema describes the global data, including data sources from the data warehouse, the OLTP database, and the external data, and the logical structure of the analysis data of DSS applications on top of the global data. The data warehouse is the main data source for the MDSS to perform its decision analysis and processing. The OLAP and data mining based on the data warehouse carry out the main tasks of information analysis. In order to be logically symmetric, we use the term of *information sources* to represent the data warehouse, the OLTP database, and the external data. Figure 2 compares the logical structures of the IDSS and the MDSS.

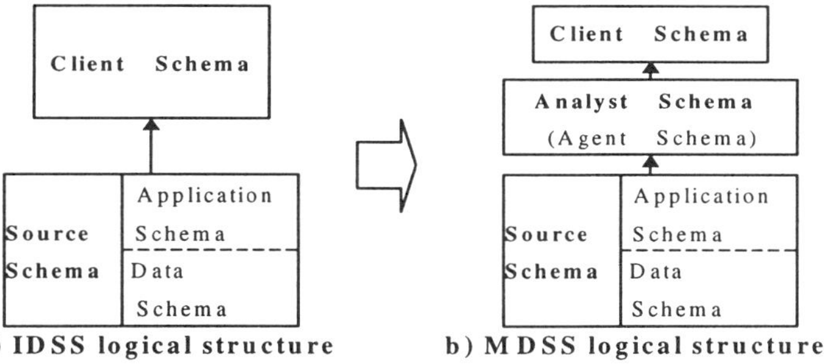

Figure 2. Comparison of logical structures

In the MDSS, the function of the agent is to access various data sources and DSS applications on behalf of the user. That is, it acts like an analyst. Therefore we represent the agent layer as the agent schema in Figure 2. The agent schema is the bridge between the application schema and the client schema; it describes a special client schema, and is the conceptual view of the application schema.

3.2 The Application Structure of the MDSS

Figure 3 depicts the four-layered system application structure of the MDSS based on the agent technology. The application structure of the MDSS consists of the following components:

1. Data platform of the MDSS: Data platform is the DSS data sources used for the organization of analysis data. MDSS data platform includes data warehouse, the OLPT database, the external database, and other data sources, such as file system, electronic forms, E-Mails, etc. The fundamental data platform of the MDSS is data warehouse. The data warehouse integrates the original operational data decentralized in an enterprise and data received externally, and carries out most of the decision analysis.
2. Data analysis and application of the MDSS: In the application structure of the MDSS, all DSS applications are provided to the User Access Agent System

(UAAS) in terms of DSS service methods. DSS service methods are relatively stable in comparison with other DSS application programs. That is, in certain time interval, the interface of a DSS service method remains unchanged. The basic data analysis of the MDSS is OLAP. Based on multi-dimensional analysis, the OLTP describes the requirements for the multi-layered, multi-angled analysis and processing of data during the management and decision-making processes. In the mean time, data mining and traditional DSS analysis are also used as the means for complementary analysis.

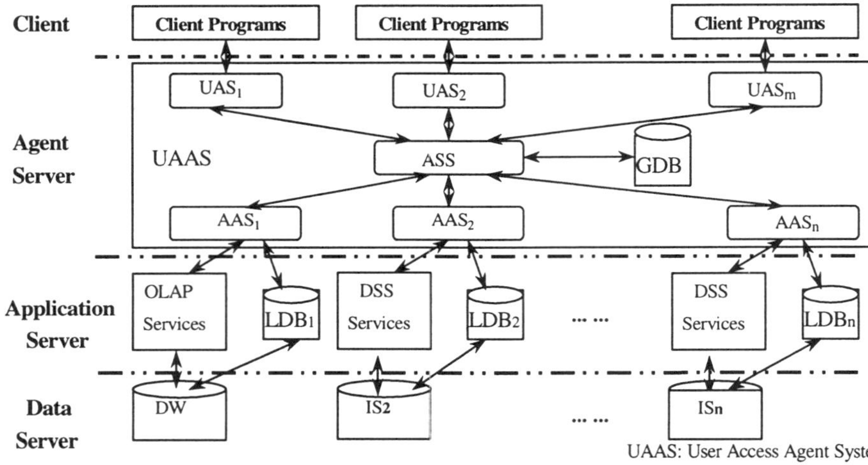

UAAS: User Access Agent System
UAS: User Agent Sub-System
ASS: Agent Server Sub-System
AAS: Application Agent Sub-System
IS: Information Source

Figure 3. Application structure of the MDSS

3. Knowledge base and model base of the MDSS: The domain base plays a crucial role in the MDSS. When an agent carries out the process of decision analysis based on multiple information sources, it needs to use knowledge from the domain knowledge base during every step of the process. Domain base is an extended model base and method base; its contents include the global information search schema, the logical structure of the information source and stored information, the semantics of decision search and security authentication information, interfaces of the application methods for various DSS decision information applications, decision analysis rules for various information soures, etc.
4. Middleware of the MDSS: The middleware of the MDSS is the User Access Agent System. It accepts decision analysis requests from mobile users through friendly interfaces; migrates among various DSS application systems according

to certain strategies; and invoking various DSS application methods to carry out decision analysis in order to obtain the information required by the user.

Compared to the IDSS in Figure 1, the MDSS has the following characteristics:

- Distribution and cooperation: MDSS is an extension of the distributed decision support system. It also requires various decision support applications to cooperate via the agent to accomplish the decision analysis.
- Mobility: The UAAS allows mobile users to access the decision support systems in the situations where the network connections are unstable and access positions are mobile.
- Autonomy: Through the UAAS, the decision support applications of the OLTP system based on data warehouse and other data sources can be independently designed, constructed, and managed.
- Adaptability and scalability: Various decision support application systems, no matter it is the OLTP based on data warehouse, the data mining, or the DSS applications based on the OLTP data sources, can be smoothly integrated with users through UAAS.

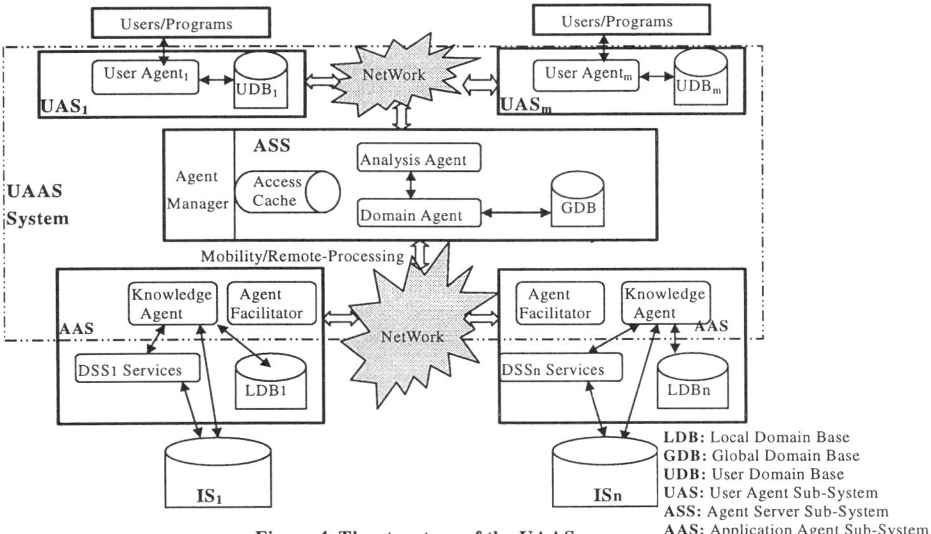

Figure 4. The structure of the UAAS

4 The User Access Agent System

The kernel of the MDSS application structure is the User Access Agent System (UAAS), depicted in Figure 4. The UAAS includes a User Agent Subsystem (UAS), an Agent Server Subsystem (ASS), and an Application Agent Subsystem (AAS).

- The UAS provides users with personalized interfaces and interacts with the user. It accepts the decision analysis requests from users and passes the requests to the ASS. The UAS consists of a User Agent (UA) and a User-access Domain Base (UDB).
- The ASS decomposes and maps the decision analysis requests from users, coordinates the decision analysis in the system on behalf of the users, and returns the results in appropriate format back to the user agent. The ASS includes the Analysis Agent (AA), Domain Agent (DA), Agent Manager (AM), Access Cache (AC) and Global Domain Base (GDB).
- The AAS is consisted of the Knowledge Agent (KA) based on the DSS data sources, the Agent Facilitator (AF), and the Local Domain Base (LDB). It is responsible for the interaction between the local DSS applications and data sources. It also provides decision analysis and processing functions for certain (e.g. local) decision supporting information.

Note that all agents in the UAAS are static agents except for the analysis agent (AA). According to the decision analysis requests from users, the AA migrates within the system and coordinates various DSS applications to perform a coordinated decision analysis to obtain the information required by users.

4.1 Description of the UAAS Components

4.1.1 Description of the Agents

An Agent in the UAAS is an active object [12] of (D, M, SD, P), in which D is a set of local data, M is a set of methods, SD is a set of structural dependency relationship among the methods (including trigger dependency, order dependency, real-time dependency, etc.), and P is a set of interruption and re-synchronization points.

The functions of each Agent in the UAAS can be described as follows:

- The User Agent (UA) is the interface between the UAAS and the user. It includes the following functions: (1) user login and authentication; (2) deciding the user accessible decision information resources and access interfaces, and creating personalized access interfaces according to the user requests; (3) accepting and formalizing user requests for decision analysis, and presenting these requests to the analysis agent (AA); (4) receiving the analyzing results from the AA and returning them to the user; (5) copying the knowledge required by the users from the global knowledge base when the user agent subsystem is started.
- The Analysis Agent (AA) is used to process the user requests for decision analysis. It needs to inquire from the domain agent (DA) about the processing methods for the user decision analysis requests and the corresponding domain schemas. It then uses the divide-and-conquer strategy to solve the global

analysis requests from the users, and creates sub-analysis agents to execute the tasks of decision analysis. The sub-analysis agents can use remote processing or migration to interact with the knowledge agent of the service agent sub-system.

- The Domain Agent (DA) dictates the domain schemas that satisfy the user analysis requests through the access to the global domain base (GDB). It also collaborates with the knowledge agent to maintain the data consistency between the local domain base and the global domain base, and collaborates with the UA to maintain the data consistency between the user access domain base and the global domain base.
- The Knowledge Agent (KA) has the following three functions: (1) invoking the DSS application services to carry out the decision analysis on the local information sources through the original database methods and application methods; (2) learning of the local domain knowledge; and (3) maintaining the data consistency between the local domain base and the global domain base through write-through or write-back strategies.
- The Agent Facilitator (AF) is used to organize and manage the receiving, servicing, and starting of the AA when it migrates to the DSS application server, and to interacting among AAs.
- The Agent Manager (AM) is the manager of the UAAS and has the following functions: (1) the management of the security and authentication of the UAAS; (2) the service for the life cycle of agents in the UAAS, which includes the tasks for agent creation, execution, suspension, recovery, and termination; (3) the resource distribution of UAAS, including the distribution of memory and file resources; (4) position service for mobile agents, and following the positions of the frequently migrating agents in the UAAS; and (5) the management of an access cache to preserve the analysis results during network disconnections.

4.1.2 Management of the Access Cache

In order to support the access of decision support systems by mobile user machines in the case of unstable network connections, the MDSS adapts the access cache technique. That is, a data cache, managed by the AM, is attached to the agent server to temporarily store the decision analysis results of mobile users. By using this mechanism, a mobile user machine can have an unstable connection with the MDSS during the period when the UAAS is processing its decision analysis request. When the UAAS completes the user's analysis request, it automatically stores the analysis results into the access cache. The AM will automatically return the results to the mobile user machine according to its present position when the mobile user machine logs into the MDSS again.

4.1.3 The Organization of the Domain Base for Supporting Mobile Computing

In order to support mobile computing, the MDSS organizes its domain bases in a layered architecture. A layered architecture can improve the security of the system and balance the load to the domain bases, therefore reduce the information traffic during the decision analysis and support the decision analysis search effectively in an unstable network connection situation. The organization of the MDSS domain bases is depicted in Figure 5. It has the following characteristics:

- The domain base of the MDSS is divided into three layers: the *local conceptual layer*, the *global conceptual layer* and the *user view layer*. These layers correspond to the local domain bases, the global domain base, and the user-access domain bases (UDB). The domain bases in these three layers form a unified distributed domain base system. In this system, all local domain bases distributed on DSS application servers in various information sources form the local conceptual layer. They store the local information for local DSS information sources. The global domain base is stored in the agent server, forming the global conceptual layer. The user-access domain base is the decision support schema that a current user can access and is a sub-set of the global domain base. The UDB also stores the information of the personalized decision access schema for the user.
- Strategies for data consistency: The data consistency in the domain bases has two aspects: the first is the knowledge consistency between the global domain base and the local domain bases, and the second is the knowledge consistency between the global domain base and the user-access domain bases.

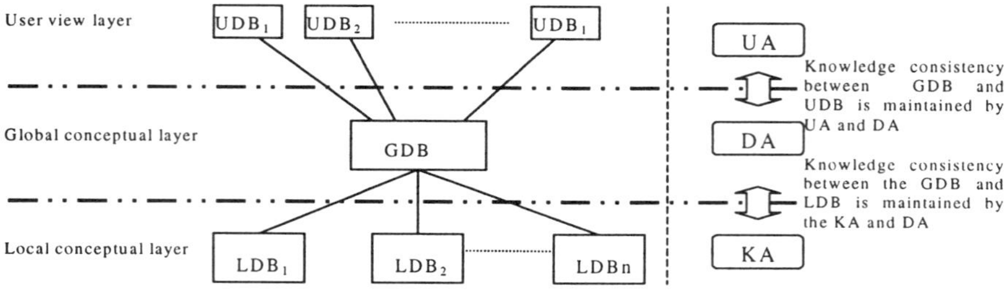

Figure 5. Organization of the MDSS domain bases

The sources that cause the inconsistency between the GDB and the LDBs include: updating the data of the local data source causes the change of the data analysis schema; changing of the local DSS application methods; stopping the use of a local DSS application system because of certain reasons, etc. A monitoring protocol can be used to maintain the knowledge consistency between the GDB and LDBs. The concept of the monitoring protocol was originally used in the consistency maintenance for caches of multiple processors in parallel processing systems [4]. In the design of the MDSS, knowledge agents can monitor the changes of the analysis schema in local DSS. When these changes cause a change of the system analysis schema, the KA notifies the DA to invalidate the changed analyzing subject, or to carry out an updated processing. This method is the monitoring protocol. There are two strategies for maintaining the knowledge consistency between the GDB and the LDBs: via write-through or via write-back. Because the amount of data used in maintaining the knowledge consistency between the GDB and the LDBs is relatively small, using the write-back strategy will not form a processing bottleneck when the system runs smoothly. So we adopt the write-back method in our MDSS.

The sources that cause the inconsistency between the GDB and the UDBs include: the change of the analysis schema in the GDB causes the invalidation of the existing analysis schemas of the UDB; the user uses an unregistered user machine to access the MDSS, etc. The maintenance of knowledge consistency between the GDB and the UDBs is relatively straightforward. When an analysis schema of the GDB changes, the UAAS records the contents of the change. When a user logs into the system and the UAAS discovers that there exists changed analysis schema, the changed information will be passed to the mobile user machine to update the UDB. When a user accesses the MDSS using an unregistered user machine, after passed through the authentication procedure, a new UDB is created for the user machine and the information of the user accessible analysis schema is copied to the user machine.

4.2 The Workflow of the UAAS

The workflow of the UAAS can be described in the following:

1. A user registers and invokes the local user agent subsystem (UAS). If the user is the first time to register or the access information is to be changed, the UAS copies the accessible knowledge of the user from the GDB.
2. The user agent (UA) accesses the GDB; authentication of the user and the privileges of the user; the user inputs the decision analysis request via an access interface; the UA passes the request to the analysis agent (AA).
3. The AA inquires the domain schema for the decision analysis request from the doman agent (DA)
4. The DA returns the matched information to the AA; the AA decomposes the user's global request and decides the following processing methods according to the result of the decomposition.
   - If the global request only involves one DSS application, then the AA uses the remote processing method to access the knowledge agent (KA) of the DSS application server.

- If the global request involves multiple DSS applications, then the AA spans a number of sub-analysis agents (SAA). These SAAs use the migration method to access the KAs on the related DSS application servers. The AA then becomes an agent coordinator to coordinate the communication and collaborated analysis of the SAAs to complete the user's global analysis request.

5. The SAA that has migrated to the local DSS server asks the local KA to process the local analysis request; the KA first carries out the mapping of the local analysis request, producing the execution sequence of local DSS analysis methods, then the KA invokes the DSS service methods to carry out the decision analysis on the information sources in the local DSS to obtain the data or decision information required to satisfy the user decision analysis. During the process of analysis, the SAA constantly carries out collaborated operations according to the commands of the AA and communicates with other SAAs. After the completion of local analysis, according to the analysis control workflow, the SAA migrates to a next DSS server or returns to the AA.
6. The AA integrates all analysis data or decision information and stores the results in the access cache of the agent server; the agent manager (AM) returns the analysis results to the proper user agent (UA) according to the position information of the mobile user found from the position service of the AM.
7. The UA returns the analysis results to the user and continues to process user requests or goes into sleep.

5 Remarks

The widely spread use of mobile computers requires us to provide effective means for mobile users to access enterprise information systems and the technology of decision support has become a crucial factor of information strategies of modern enterprises. However, how to construct a flexible and effective decision support system on the distributed information systems of enterprise, in order to support mobile users to access the decision support system in any time and from anywhere is still unclear. The model for constructing mobile decision support systems based on the agent technology presented in this paper provides a way to solve this problem.

We are currently building a prototype based on our model and are carrying out further researches on the model, including the learning issues of styles and interests of the user-access system, the security issues of the MDSS in a mobile computing environment, the performance issues, and so on.

In the MDSS, a user request of decision analysis (called the global analysis request) involves multiple data sources and DSS analysis applications. How to quickly and effectively decompose the global analysis requests into sub-analysis requests for various analysis sources is crucial to the performance of the whole system. It is therefore necessary to find an effective strategy to decompose a global analysis request into sub-analysis requests for individual analysis sources. We discuss the decision analysis techniques based on multiple analysis sources for the MDSS in another paper.

References

1. J. Dale, A mobile agent architecture for distributed information management, Ph.D. Thesis, University of Southampton, 1997.
2. M.H. Dunham and Helal A., Mobile computing and database: anything new? *ACM SIGMOD Record*,1995,24(4), 5-9.
3. G.H.Forman and Zahorjan J., The challenges of Mobile Computing. *IEEE Computer*,1994,17(4):38-47.
4. K. Hwang, *Advanced computer architecture: parallelism, Scalability, programmability* [Second Edition], Tsinghua University Press, China,1999, 153-154.
5. T. Imielinski and Korth H.(editors), *Mobile Computing* , Kluwer Academic Publishers,1996.
6. Inmon, W. H. *Building the Data Warehouse Second Edition*, Addison-Wesley, 1996.
7. K. Lee and H. V. Leong, Agent-based mobile computing, *Proceedings of the 2nd Asia-Pacific Web Conference (APWeb'99)*, CSREA Press, 267-271, Hong Kong, Sept. 1999.
8. J. Matthias, etc, Architecture and Quality in Data Warehouse: An Extended Repository Approach, *Information Systems*, Vol.24, No.3, 1999.
9. Z. Maamar, SAMDW-Software Agent Meet Data Warehouse, New Generation Data Warehouse Technologies, *IEICE Transaction on Information and Systems*, Vol-E82-D, No.1, Jan. 1999.
10. H.S..Nwana, Software agents: An overview, *Knowledge Engineering Review*, Vol. 11, No.3, Sep,1996,205-244.
11. A. Pham and A. Karmouch, Mobile Software Agents: An Overview, IEEE Communications, 36(7):26-37, Jul. 1998.
12. E. Pitoura and Bhargave B., A framework for providing consistent and recoverable agent-based access to heterogeneous mobile databases. *ACM SIGMOD Record*, 1995, 24(3):44-49.
13. E. Turban, and J. E.Aronson. *Decision Support Systems and Intelligent Systems* [Fifth Edition], Tsinghua University Press, China, 2000, 108-135, 215-217.
14. W. Zhou and J. Zhong, Managing Mobile Transactions, *Proceedings of the 16th IASTED International Conference on Applied Informatics*, 317-320, Garmisch-Partenkirchen, Germany, Feb. 1998.

EFFICIENT PARALLEL PROCESSING METHODS FOR ROAD MAP QUERIES

SUNGWON JUNG
Department of Computer Science
Sogang University
1, Shinsoo-Dong, Mapo-Gu
Seoul, Korea, 121-742
Email: *jungsung@ccs.sogang.ac.kr*
Voice: +82-2-705-8930 Fax: +82-2-704-8273

Computing SPSP(Single Pair Shortest Path) is an important component of processing road map queries. SPSP problem has been traditionally studied as a special case of single source and all pair shortest path problems in the context of recursive query processing, transitive closure computation, and database query language. However, the above methods are not suitable for this domain due to the considerably large search space of road maps. In our previous paper [4], we proposed a very efficient and powerful data organization scheme named HiTi graph for computing SPSP on massive graphs such as road maps. In this paper, we study the parallel processing for both intra and inter (i.e. multiple) SPSP problems. Based on HiTi graph structure, we propose two parallel shortest path algorithms named PASPAH and ISPAH for intra and inter query SPSP problems respectively. We empirically analyze the performance of *PASPAH* and *ISPAH* algorithms on two-dimensional grid graphs by implementing them on BBN GP1000 shared memory multiprocessor system. The analysis of *PASPAH* and *ISPAH* shows that *inter* query shortest path problem has more potential for the parallel processing than *intra* query shortest path problem.

1 Introduction

A Single Pair Shortest Path (SPSP) computation is fundamental to topographical road map queries. In order to reduce the large search space of topographical road maps, a graph traversal approach is usually used [2,3]. Although the graph traversal approach reduces the search space significantly, its search space is still large for most real world road maps [1,6]. To cope with this limitation, two new approaches are proposed [1,4]. Agrawal and Jagadish studied SPSP computation in the context of problem of performing efficient search over disk-resident massive graphs [1]. We proposed a new graph model, named *HiTi* graph model for this problem [4]. These two methods narrow down the search space very significantly at the cost of storing the partially precomputed path information. However, their performance improvement is still limited to a single processor case. For interactive applications, further reduction in response time is beneficial. Thus, efficient parallel SPSP algorithms have been developed to improve the performance further.

Little research has been done on parallel SPSP algorithms. Mohr and Pasche [7] presented a new parallel shortest path algorithm named *OTOpar* which is a parallel implementation of *OTO* algorithm. *OTOpar* uses two processors where each processor uses A* algorithm with Manhattan distance estimation to build its corresponding tree, one rooted at the source node and the other rooted at the destination node. Their empirical analysis shows that the average execution time of *OTOpar* is roughly half of *OTO*. However, *OTOpar* algorithm is not scalable at all. That is, their performance improvement is limited by only two processors. Thus, we need more scalable parallel SPSP algorithms than *OTOpar*.

In this paper, we study the parallel processing for *intra* as well as *inter* query shortest path problems. *Intra* query SPSP problem deals with parallelizing a single transaction of SPSP problem. The parallel SPSP algorithm proposed by Mohr and Pasche [7] belongs to this category. *Inter* query SPSP problem deals with parallelizing *multiple* single-pair shortest-path computations. *Inter* query SPSP problem arises in the domain of automobile navigation systems where many vehicles send their shortest route computation requests to a central server. Then the server must be able to handle these multiple SPSP computation requests satisfying a real time constraint.

We have developed two parallel SPSP algorithms. One is for *intra* query SPSP problem and the other for *inter* query SPSP problem. Both algorithms are based on *HiTi* graph introduced in [4]. *HiTi* graph structure provides the opportunity for fine-grained parallel processing for *intra* query SPSP problem. This is because multiple parallel shortest-path computations can be initiated based on the nodes at a higher level of abstraction of a topographical road map. Note that *HiTi* graph structure can capture a hierarchical abstraction of the topographical road map and it is easy to identify the appropriate nodes at the higher level.

The rest of the paper is organized as follows. A formal framework and description of *HiTi* graph is discussed in section 2. In section 3, we give the detailed description of *intra* query parallel shortest path algorithm and empirically compare its performance with those of the previous works. Section 4 discusses two *inter* query parallel shortest path algorithms. We give empirical performance analysis of these two *inter* query parallel algorithms in this section. Finally, section 5 gives the concluding remarks.

2 Formal Framework and Description of HiTi Graph

A topographical road map can be viewed as a directed graph $G(V, E)$ where each node in V represent map objects (i.e., the intersecting points of the roads) in a road map. Edges (x, y, c) in E correspond to the connections between the nodes x and y with the cost (e.g. distance) c in V. Suppose that $G(V, E)$ is partitioned into a set of subgraphs (i.e. SG_1^1 (V_1^1, E_1^1), SG_2^1 (V_2^1, E_2^1), ..., $SG_{n_1}^1$ $(V_{n_1}^1, E_{n_1}^1)$) such that:

$$V_1^1 \cup V_2^1 \cup \cdots \cup V_{n_1}^1 \;=\; V, \quad E_1^1 \cup E_2^1 \cup \cdots \cup E_{n_1}^1 \;\subset\; E$$

$$V_i^1 \cap V_j^1 \;=\; \emptyset \;\; and \;\; E_i^1 \cap E_j^1 \;=\; \emptyset \;\; where \;\; 1 \leq i,j \leq n_1 \;\; and \;\; i \neq j$$

We name SG_i^1 (V_i^1, E_i^1) a level 1 *subgraph* i and the connections between all level 1 *subgraphs* are captured in $PE^1 = E - (E_1^1 \cup E_2^1 \cup \cdots \cup E_{n_1}^1)$. Then, each $(x,y,c) \in PE^1$ has the property that $x \in V_i^1$ and $y \in V_j^1$ where $i \neq j$.

Definition 2.1 *Let N_i^1 denotes a set of nodes in SG_i^1 (V_i^1, E_i^1) connected to/from nodes in other subgraphs SG_j^1 (V_j^1, E_j^1) where $i \neq j$ and $1 \leq i,j \leq n_1$. Specifically, $N_i^1 = \{x \mid (x,y,c) \in PE^1 \;\wedge\; x \in V_i^1\} \cup \{y \mid (x,y,c) \in PE^1 \;\wedge\; y \in V_i^1\}$. Set N_i^1 is called level 1* boundary nodes *of SG_i^1.*

Set N_i^1, level 1 boundary nodes of SG_i^1 in definition 2.1, consists of those nodes in V_i^1 that are directly connected to/from the nodes outside of V_i^1. For example, consider Figure 2.1 where a digraph G and its subgraphs SG_1^1, SG_2^1 and SG_3^1 are shown. Set N_2^1 of subgraph SG_2^1 is { G, H, M, O }. Each level 1 subgraph is described and identified by its boundary nodes, since they exclusively belong to one level 1 subgraph. Based on boundary nodes of SG_i^1, definition 2.2 gives formal definitions of level 1 *between* and *within* edge sets B_i^1 and W_i^1 of SG_i^1.

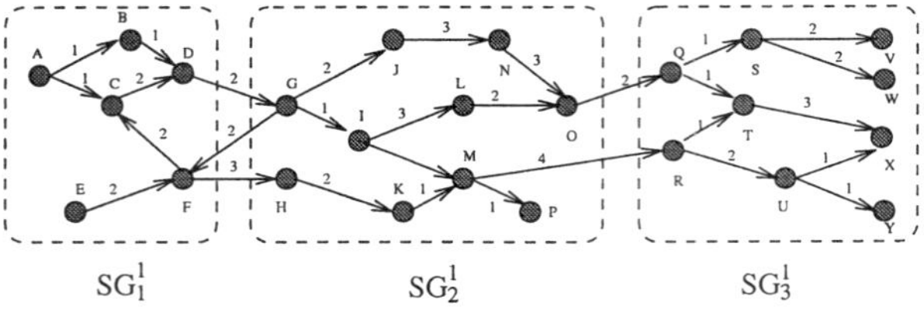

Figure 2.1. A digraph G and its level 1 subgraph SG_1^1, SG_2^1 and SG_3^1

Definition 2.2 *Let* $\{ SG_j^1 (V_j^1, E_j^1) \mid j = 1, n_1 \}$ *be a set of level 1 subgraphs of graph* $G(V, E)$ *with the corresponding* N_j^1. *Then, for each* SG_i^1 *where* $1 \le i \le n_1$, $B_i^1 = \{ (x, y, c) \mid (x, y, c) \in PE^1 \wedge x \in V_i^1 \}$ *and* $W_i^1 = \{ (x, y, f_c(x, y)) \mid (x, y) \in (N_i^1 \times N_i^1) \wedge (x \overset{f_c(x,y)}{\longrightarrow} y$ *in* $SG_i^1) \wedge x \neq y \}$. *Function* $f_c(x, y)$ *gives the shortest path cost (i.e. from node* x *to* y*) computed only within* SG_i^1.

Each *between* edge set B_i^1 of SG_i^1 consists of an edge (x, y, c) where x is in SG_i^1 and y is in a different level 1 subgraph. In other words, set B_i^1 contains connectivity information between level 1 subgraph SG_i^1 and other level 1 subgraphs of $G(V, E)$. Each set W_i^1 contains an edge $(x, y, f_c(x, y))$ if there exists a directed path from the boundary nodes x to y of SG_i^1. Function $f_c(x, y)$ gives the shortest path cost (i.e. from node x to y) computed only within SG_i^1. In other words, the shortest path cost computed by $f_c(x, y)$ may not be a global shortest path computed on $G(V, E)$. From the above definition of B_i^1 and W_i^1, we can observe the following three properties:

1. $PE^1 = \cup_{j=1}^{n_1} B_j^1$.
2. The edges in PE^1 exclusively partition graph $G(V, E)$ into a set of subgraphs SG_1^1 (V_1^1, E_1^1), SG_2^1 (V_2^1, E_2^1), ..., $SG_{n_1}^1$ $(V_{n_1}^1, E_{n_1}^1)$.
3. $E = (\cup_{j=1}^{n_1} E_j^1 \cup PE^1)$

As an example of definition 2.2, Table 2.1 shows the corresponding values of N_i^k, B_i^k and W_i^k of the three subgraphs shown in Figure 2.1. In the following example, $f_c(x, y)$ in W_i^1 gives the shortest path cost from node x to y. So far, we have introduced level 1 subgraphs

i	N_i^1	B_i^1	W_i^1
1	{D,F}	{(D,G,2),(F,H,3)}	{(F,D,4)}
2	{G,H,M,O}	{(O,Q,2),(M,R,4),(G,F,2)}	{(G,O,6),(G,M,3),(H,M,3)}
3	{Q,R}	∅	∅

Table 2.1. N_i^1, B_i^1, and W_i^1 of SG_i^1 in Figure 2.1

and their associated information such as level 1 *boundary* node sets, and *between* and *within* edge sets. In general, based on these level 1 subgraphs and their associated information, we can recursively define level k subgraphs SG_i^k and their corresponding N_i^k, B_i^k, and W_i^k for any $k \geq 2$. Their details are discussed in the following definitions.

Definition 2.3 *Let $\Psi^{k-1} = \{ SG_i^{k-1}(V_i^{k-1}, E_i^{k-1}) \mid i = 1, n_{k-1} \}$ be the set of all level k-1 subgraphs of graph $G(V,E)$ where $k \geq 2$. Then, a level k subgraph SG_i^k (V_i^k, E_i^k) is defined as a subgraph induced by all nodes of level k-1 subgraphs in $\Phi \subseteq \Psi^{k-1}$ where $|\Phi| \geq 2$.*

After all level k subgraphs in Ψ^k are defined, the following three requirements must be satisfied:

1. Each level *k-1* subgraph in Ψ^{k-1} is a subgraph of some level k subgraph in Ψ^k.
2. All level k subgraphs in Ψ^k do not overlap among themselves. That is,
$$V_1^k \cup V_2^k \cup \cdots \cup V_{n_k}^k = V, \quad E_1^k \cup E_2^k \cup \cdots \cup E_{n_k}^k \subset E$$
$$V_i^k \cap V_j^k = \emptyset \ and \ E_i^k \cap E_j^k = \emptyset \ where \ 1 \leq i,j \leq n_k \ and \ i \neq j$$
3. All edges belonging to level k *between* edge sets are removed from level *k-1 between* edges sets. As a result, $(\cup_{j=1}^{n_{k-1}} B_j^{k-1} \cap \cup_{j=1}^{n_k} B_j^k) = \emptyset$.

By satisfying the preceding first two requirements, all subgraphs in $\cup_{j=1}^{k+1} \Psi^j$ are related to each other in a complete balanced tree structure where Ψ^{k+1} contains only the root node of the tree symbolizing $G(V,E)$. This complete balanced tree is named a *subgraph tree* (ST). The root node of ST is considered as a level *k+1* subgraph and it has all level k subgraphs as child nodes. Recursively, each node symbolizing a level k subgraph has a set of level *k-1* subgraphs as child nodes. All leaf nodes of ST symbolizes level 1 subgraphs. This subgraph tree is named level *k+1* ST if the root of ST symbolizes level *k+1* subgraph (i.e. $G(V,E)$). The following Figure 2.2 shows an example of level 3 subgraph tree. This tree structure shows a level 3 subgraph $SG_1^3 = G$ induced by the nodes in three level 2 subgraphs (i.e. SG_1^2, SG_2^2 and SG_3^2). It also shows three level 2 subgraph SG_1^2, SG_2^2, SG_3^2, induced by the nodes in the six level 1 subgraphs SG_1^1, SG_2^1, SG_3^1, SG_4^1, SG_5^1, and SG_6^1.

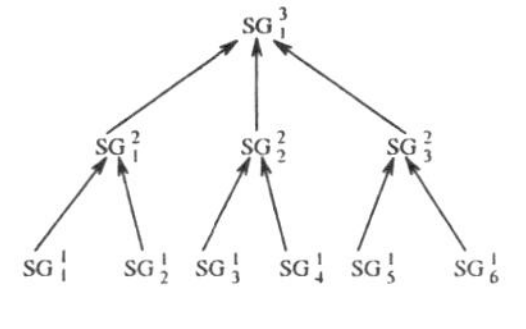

Figure 2.2. An example of level 3 subgraph tree ST

For each level k subgraph SG_i^k of ST where $1 \leq i \leq n_k$, there exists corresponding level k *boundary* nodes (i.e. N_i^k) and level k *between* and *within* edge sets (i.e. B_i^k and W_i^k). The semantics of the level k *boundary* nodes, level k *between* and *within* edge sets are same as that of level 1 *boundary* nodes, level 1 *between* and *within* edge sets. They are formally defined in definition 2.4.

Definition 2.4 *Let $PE^k = E - (E_1^k \cup E_2^k \cup \cdots \cup E_{n_k}^k)$. Then, $N_i^k = \{ x \mid (x,y,c) \in PE^k \wedge x \in V_i^k \} \cup \{ y \mid (x,y,c) \in PE^k \wedge y \in V_i^k \}$, $B_i^k = \{ (x,y,c) \mid (x,y,c) \in PE^k \wedge x \in V_i^k \}$ and $W_i^k = \{ (x,y,f_z(x,y)) \mid (x,y) \in (N_i^k \times N_i^k) \wedge (x \overset{f_c(x,y)}{\longrightarrow} y \ in \ SG_i^k) \wedge x \neq y \}$. Function $f_c(x,y)$ gives the shortest path (i.e. from node x to y) cost computed only within SG_i^k.*

By taking advantages of the above three definitions, we can efficiently obtain values of different levels of boundary node, *within*, and *between* edge sets. Based on *within* and *between* edge sets, the formal definition of *HiTi* graph is given as below:

Definition 2.5 *A HiTi graph is a directed labeled graph defined in terms of between and within edges associated with all nodes of a subgraph tree ST. A level $k+1$ subgraph tree ST defines a level k HiTi graph. It is represented by $H^k(P^k, A^k)$ where $P^k = \cup_{i=1}^{k} \cup_{j=1}^{n_i} N_j^i$ and $A^k = \cup_{i=1}^{k} \cup_{j=1}^{n_i} \{B_j^i \cup W_j^i\}$*

Definition 2.6 *Assume set X consist of a set of subgraphs (i.e. nodes) of a level $k+1$ subgraph tree ST. Then, $S_A^t(X) = \{ y \mid y$ is a level t ancestor subgraph of a subgraph in $X \}$, $S_A(X) = \cup_{t=1}^{k+1} S_A^t(X)$, and $S_C(X) = \{ Y \mid Y$ is a direct child node of a subgraph in $X \}$. Note that $S_C(\{SG_i^1\}) = \{SG_i^1\}$ for all the level 1 subgraphs SG_i^1 (i.e. leaf nodes) of ST.*

Definition 2.7 *Assume set X consist of a set of subgraphs. Then, $S_B(X)$ and $S_W(X)$ consist of* between *and* within *edge sets associated with all the subgraphs in X respectively. $S_{BW}(X) = S_B(X) \cup S_W(X)$, and $S_N(X)$ consists of* boundary *node sets associated with all subgraphs in X.*

Definition 2.8 *Let SG_i^1 and SG_j^1 be two distinct level 1 subgraphs defined in a level k subgraph tree ST. Then, $LUB_{ST}(SG_i^1, SG_j^1)$ is the least leveled common ancestor subgraph of SG_i^1 and SG_j^1.*

The examples of the definition 2.6, 2.7 and 2.8 are illustrated through the level 4 subgraph tree shown in Figure 2.3. Assume that $X = \{ SG_8^1, SG_{11}^1 \}$. Then, $S_A^1(X) = \{ SG_8^1, SG_{11}^1 \}$, $S_A^2(X) = \{ SG_4^2, SG_5^2 \}$, $S_A(X) = \{ SG_8^1, SG_4^2, SG_2^3, SG_1^4, SG_{11}^1, SG_5^2\}$, $S_C(X) = \{ SG_8^1, SG_{11}^1 \}$, $S_C(S_A^2(X)) = \{ SG_8^1, SG_9^1, SG_{10}^1, SG_{11}^1, SG_{12}^1 \}$, $S_B(X) = \{ B_8^1, B_{11}^1 \}$, $S_W(X) = \{ W_8^1, W_{11}^1 \}$, $S_N(X) = \{ N_8^1, N_{11}^1 \}$, and $LUB_{ST}(SG_8^1, SG_{11}^1)$ is SG_2^3.

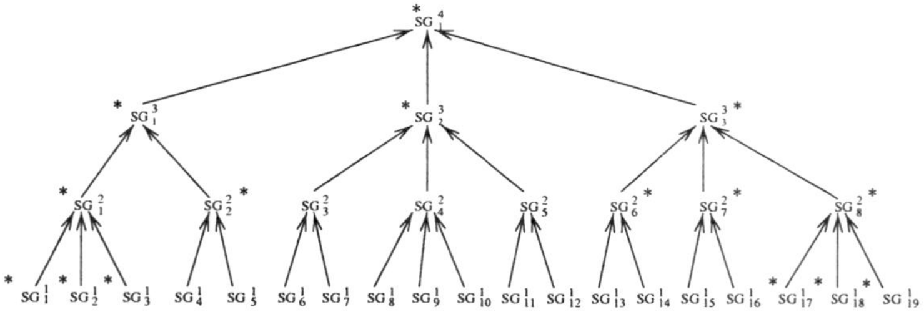

Figure 2.3. An example of level 4 subgraph tree ST

3 Intra Query Parallel Shortest Path Computation

Intra query SPSP problem deals with parallelizing a single transaction of SPSP problem. We describe a PArallel Shortest PAth algorithm based on *HiTi* graph (PASPAH) for intra query SPSP problem in this problem. To show the basic idea behind *PASPAH*, we first describe A* and *OTOpar* algorithms.

A* algorithm uses the function $f(u, DEST)$ to estimate the cost of the shortest path from node u to $DEST$. In the domain of road maps, the function $f(u, DEST)$ computes the

Euclidean distance between the node u and $DEST$. This is possible because the coordinates (i.e. longitude and latitude) of all nodes on a road map are assumed to be available. Assuming $(u.x, u.y)$ and $(DEST.x, DEST.y)$ are the corresponding coordinates of the nodes u and $DEST$, $f(u, DEST)$ computes $\sqrt{(DEST.x - u.x)^2 + (DEST.y - u.y)^2}$. Since Euclidean distance is not an over-estimated cost between node u and $DEST$, our algorithm finds the optimal shortest path. The detailed proof for the optimality of A* algorithm is found in ?. The following Figure 3.1 shows A* algorithm which finds the shortest path from the nodes $START$ to $DEST$ on $G(V, E)$. Note that $l(x, y)$ represents the cost associated with each edge $(x, y) \in E$.

```
begin
  For each node u ∈ V, λ(u) = ∞;
  Let λ(START) = 0, FSet = {START}, and ESet = ∅;
  while (FSet ≠ ∅) {
    Select a node u in FSet for which λ(u) + f(u, DEST) is minimum;
    FSet = FSet − {u} and ESet = ESet ∪ {u};
    If (u = DEST), then λ(u) is the shortest path cost and Stop;
    else {
      For every edge (u, v) in E, if λ(v) > λ(u) + l(u, v) {
        Let λ(v) = λ(u) + l(u, v);
        Let FSet = FSet ∪ {v} if v ∉ (FSet ∪ ESet); } } }
end
```

Figure 3.1. A* Algorithm: Finding the Shortest Path Cost from $START$ to $DEST$

The above A* algorithm is a variation of Dijkstra's algorithmic approach in that it finds the shortest path by building one tree rooted at the source node of the graph. Unlike A* algorithm, OTO finds the shortest path by alternatively building two trees, one rooted at the source node and the other rooted at the destination node. By running A* algorithm starting at the both end nodes, OTO keeps constructing these two trees until they are intersected at some node(s). When they are intersected, OTO check if it finds the shortest path by using an efficient stopping condition. If the stopping condition is met, the shortest path is obtained. Otherwise, OTO keep checking the stopping condition while buidling two trees. Figure 3.2. graphically show the explored search space of the algorithms A* and OTO. Note that in the figure, the rectangle and eclipse represent the entire and the

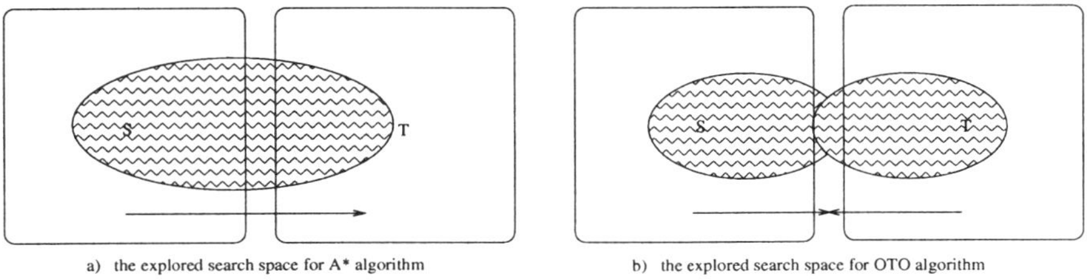

Figure 3.2. Relative size of explored search space for A* and OTO

explored search space respectively. Arrows indicate the direction of exploring the search space. It is intuitively obvious that A* algorithm explores the search space in an elliptical shape, which is shown in Figure 3.2 a. Since *OTOpar* explores the search space by applying A* algorithm from both the source (i.e. S) and destination (i.e. T) nodes, the size of its explored search space becomes smaller than that of A*. This is clearly illustrated in Figure 3.2 b. Based on this observation, we can infer that, if a middle node M lying on the shortest path is known, we can further narrow down the search space by applying A* algorithm from the middle node to both source and destination, simultaneously. Figure 3.3 illustrated the explored search space of $PASPAH$.

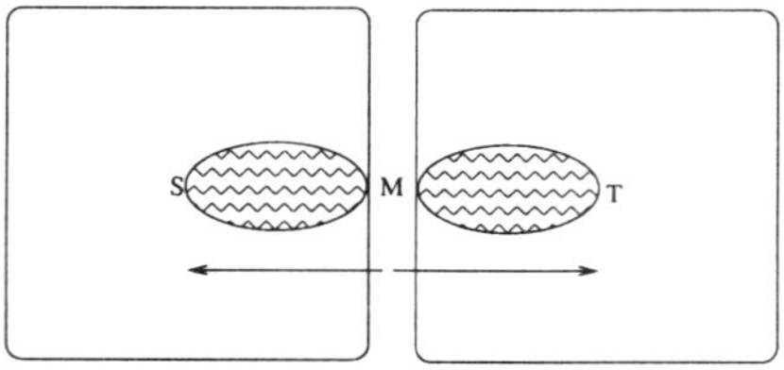

Figure 3.3. Explored search space of $PASPAH$

3.1 Use of HiTi Graph for Identifying Middle Nodes

The problem that remains is how to identify the middle node without computing the shortest path. This problem can be partially resolved by taking advantage of HiTi graph structure, which we explain through Figure 3.4. In Figure 3.4, the rectangles symbolize the level 1

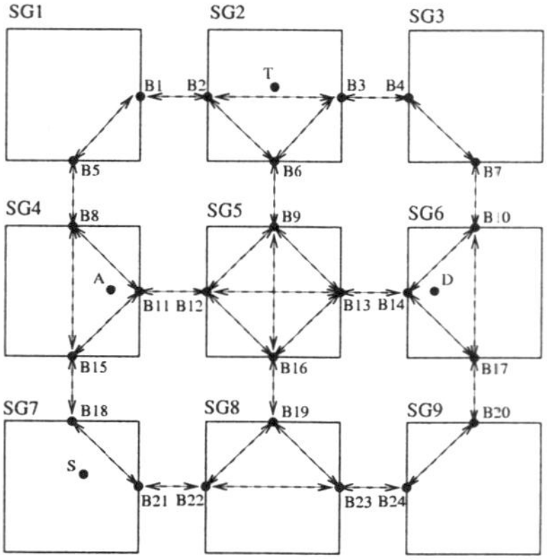

Figure 3.4. Level 1 HiTi graph created from level 1 subgraphs

subgraphs $SG1$ to $SG9$ and their boundary nodes are represented by $B1$ through $B24$. Level 1 HiTi graph defined on these level 1 subgraphs is then easily represented by all the boundary nodes interconnected by the arrows. Assume that we want to compute the shortest path from node S in SG_7 to node T in SG_2. It is clear from the figure that the shortest path from the nodes S to T must pass through at least one boundary node of SG_7 and one boundary node of SG_2. From this observation, we can approximate the two possible sets of middle node candidates for the shortest path. They are $M_1 = \{B18, B21\}$ and $M_2 = \{B2, B3, B6\}$ where set M_1 is chosen in this example.

Then, the shortest path cost from the nodes S to T can be computed by exploring the search space from each node in M_1 to S and T simultaneously. Let $SP\_COST(X, Y)$ represent the shortest path cost from the nodes X and Y. To obtain $SP\_COST(S, T)$, we first compute $SP\_COST(B18, S)$, $SP\_COST(B18, T)$, $SP\_COST(B21, S)$, and $SP\_COST(B21, T)$ in parallel. Note that each processor use A* algorithm to compute $SP\_COST(X, S)$ and $SP\_COST(X, D)$ where $X \in M_1$. $SP\_COST(S, T)$ is then obtained by selecting the minimum of $\{ SP\_COST(B18, S) + SP\_COST(B18, T), SP\_COST(B21, S) + SP\_COST(B21, T) \}$. Note that we choose M_1 over M_2 since the size of set M_1 is smaller than that of M_2. This way, we can minimize the number of processors involved for the computation.

As it might be noticed from the above example, there is a possible performance bottleneck problem in this approach. We re-take Figure 3.4 to explain the bottleneck in the following example. Assume the shortest path computation from the nodes A in $SG4$ to D in $SG6$. Since the number of the boundary nodes of $SG4$ and $SG6$ are equal, we will randomly choose one of them. In this example, set $\{B8, B11, B15\}$ is selected. Then, in order to compute $SP\_COST(A, D)$, our method will compute $SP\_COST(B8, A)$, $SP\_COST(B8, D)$, $SP\_COST(B11, A)$, $SP\_COST(B11, D)$, $SP\_COST(B15, A)$, and $SP\_COST(B15, D)$ in parallel. As we can see from Figure 3.4, since node A is located a lot closer to node $B11$ than the nodes $B8$ and $B15$, the actual shortest path from A to D is likely to pass through the boundary node $B11$. In such case, $SP\_COST(B11, A)$ and $SP\_COST(B11, D)$ computations will be done a lot faster than the others.

However, we have to wait until the rest of computations end, although we already got $SP\_COST(B11, A)$ and $SP\_COST(B11, D)$. This waiting time is required to guarantee the optimality of $SP\_COST(B11, A) + SP\_COST(B11, D)$ among the rest of results, which becomes the performance bottleneck of $PASPAH$. To cope with the performance bottleneck, it is necessary to minimize the waiting time. The minimization of the waiting time can be realized if we have a correct and efficient *stopping condition*. The *stopping condition* allows us to decide the optimality of $SP\_COST(B11, A) + SP\_COST(B11, D)$ before completing all the computation of $SP\_COST(B8, A)$, $SP\_COST(B8, D)$, $SP\_COST(B15, A)$, and $SP\_COST(B15, D)$.

3.2 Efficient Stopping Criteria

Before we explain *stopping condition*, we first examine how $SP\_COST(B8, A)$ in the above example is computed in A* algorithm. In A*, the search space is explored by permanently labeling a node x *the shortest path cost from* $B8$ *to* x until the next selected node x becomes the node A. The next unlabeled node x is selected from the search space such that $SP\_COST(B8, x) + EuDist(x, A)$ is minimum. Note that $EuDist(x, A)$ is the Euclidean distance estimation from the nodes x to A. Based on this observation, we now formally describe an *efficient stopping condition* in the following proposition.

Proposition 3.1 *Given a directed graph $G(V, E)$, assume that the shortest path from the nodes S to T must pass through at least one node from set $B = \{ B_1, B_2, \ldots, B_n \}$. Let set $C \subseteq B$ where $SP\_COST(X, S)$ and $SP\_COST(X, T)$ are already computed for each node $X \in C$ at time t_0. For each $X \in B - C$, let $N(X, S, t_0)$ and $N(X, T, t_0)$ be the next node at time t_0 selected by A* algorithm for the computation of $SP\_COST(X, S)$*

and $SP\_COST(X,T)$ respectively. Then, the shortest path cost $SP\_COST(S,T)$ is $Cost_0 = \min_{X \in C}$ { $SP\_COST(X,S) + SP\_COST(X,T)$ } if $Cost_0 \leq \min_{Y \in B-C}$ { $SP\_COST(Y, N(Y,S,t_0)) + EuDist(N(Y,S,t_0),S) + SP\_COST(Y, N(Y,T,t_0)) + EuDist(N(Y,T,t_0),T)$ }.

Proof: The proof is given in [5]. □

To exemplify how proposition 3.1 works, we show the *stopping condition* for the computation of $SP\_COST(A,D)$ in Figure 3.4. Assume that $SP\_COST(B11,A)$ and $SP\_COST(B11,D)$ are obtained at time t_0. Then, $PSP\_COST(A,D)$ is $Cost_0 = SP\_COST(B11,A) + SP\_COST(B11,D)$ if $Cost_0 \leq \min$ { $SP\_COST(B8, N(B8,A,t_0)) + EuDist(N(B8,A,t_0),A)$, $SP\_COST(B15, N(B15,D,t_0)) + EuDist(N(B15,D,t_0),D)$ }.

3.3 Formal Description of PASPAH

In the previous section, we described the basic idea as well as a theoretical foundation of $PASPAH$ when level 1 HiTi graph is given. We now formally present $PASPAH$ in Figure 3.5. Our $PASPAH$ is developed for shared memory multiprocessor systems with the following architecture assumptions:

- All processors have their own local memory.
- All Processors communicate with each others through globally shared memory.
- All processors share disk.

Based on the preceding assumptions, $PASPAH$ accesses a level $k+1$ subgraph tree, level k HiTi graph $H^k(P^k, A^k)$, and level 1 subgraphs $\cup_{i=1}^{n_1} SG_i^1(V_i^1, E_i^1)$, which are stored in the globally shared memory.

$PASPAH$ consists of five steps. At step 1, the boundary nodes of HiTi graph is marked with edge level numbers. This marking step is necessary to avoid traversing the unnecessary low level edges incident on the marked nodes. We take a level 4 subgraph tree in Figure 2.3 to exemplify this marking phase of boundary nodes of HiTi graph. Assume that we want to find a shortest path from a source node in SG_1^1 to a destination node $DEST$ in SG_{18}^1. Then, the necessary search space is at most $E_1^1 \cup E_{18}^1$ together with the corresponding *between* and *within* edge sets of the subgraphs marked with * in Figure 2.3. From this example, it is easy to see how *HiTi* graph can significantly reduce the search space necessary for a shortest path computation. That is, without using *HiTi* graph, the search space would be $G(V,E)$.

When a marked node is visited, the corresponding marked level (i.e. *low_level*) specifies the lowest level of the edges to be traversed from the marked node. Since the highest level (i.e. *high_level*) of the edges incident on the marked node can be easily identifiable, the nodes expanded directly from the marked node are only those reachable through the edges with the levels ranging from *low_level* to *high_level*. This marking step guarantees that the explored the search space of $PASPAH$ is at most $E_s^1 \cup E_t^1 \cup S_{BW}(S_C(\cup_{j=1}^{k+1} S_A^j(SG_i^1, SG_j^1)))$.

At step 2, we determine the level l subgraph SG_m^{l-1} whose boundary nodes will be used as the middle nodes as explained in the previous section 3.1. The step 3 is self explanatory. In step 4 and 5, the shortest path computation $SP(x,y)$ for each pairs of nodes (x,y) in the queue BQ is performed by step 5 in parallel by the available processors. Step 5 computes the shortest path from the nodes x to y by using $A*$ algorithm. Note that $A*$ algorithm in step 5 explores the neighbor nodes of the currently expanding node u by

```
begin
/* Assume we have a level k HiTi graph defined on a level k + 1 ST; */
/* {SG_1^1, SG_2^1, ..., SG_{n_1}^1} and H^k(P^k, A^k) are maintained as adjacency lists; */
/* All the edges in SG_t^1 for 1 <= t <= n_1 are assumed to be level 0 edges; */
Step 1:
  For 1 <= i, j <= n_1, find SG_i^1 and SG_j^1 where START ∈ SG_i^1 and DEST ∈ SG_j^1;
  Let l be the level number of LUB_ST(SG_i^1, SG_j^1);
  for (p = k + 1; p > l; p − −)    /* S_A^p(SG_i^1) == S_A^p(SG_j^1) */
    Mark all nodes in S_N(S_C(S_A^p(SG_i^1))) with level p − 1;
  if (l = 1) Mark all nodes in SG_i^1 with 0; /* SG_i^1 == SG_j^1 */
  else {
    for (p = l; p > 1; p − −) {
      Mark all nodes in S_N(S_C(S_A^p(SG_i^1))) with level p − 1;
      Mark all nodes in S_N(S_C(S_A^p(SG_j^1))) with level p − 1; }
    Mark all nodes in SG_i^1 and SG_j^1 with 0; }
Step 2:
  If (|S_N(S_A^{l-1}(SG_i^1))| <= |S_N(S_A^{l-1}(SG_j^1))|) SG_m^{l-1} = S_A^{l-1}(SG_i^1);
  else SG_m^{l-1} = S_A^{l-1}(SG_j^1);
Step 3:
  for each boundary node x in S_N(SG_m^{l-1})
    Enqueue (x, START) and (x, DEST) to a queue BQ;
Step 4:
  while (|BQ| > 0) {
    Dequeue (x, y) from BQ;
    A next available processor performs Step 5 for the shortest path computation (x, y) in parallel;}
  Cond = False;
  while (Cond = False) {
    Let S be the set of the shortest path cost(s) returned from the processors;
    Pair (x, START, c_1) and (x, DEST, c_2) for all (x, y, c) ∈ S where y = STARTorDEST;
    Find the minimum S_0 = c_1 + c_2 among (x, START, c_1) and (x, DEST, c_2) for all x;
    By using S_0, check the Stopping condition given in proposition 3.1;
    If (the stopping condition is met) {
      Abort all the computations being performed by other processors;
      Cond = True;
      The shortest path cost is S_0; } }
  Stop;
Step 5:
  Let λ(w) = ∞ for all the marked nodes w and λ(x) = 0;
  FSet = { x }; ESet = ∅;
  while (FSet ≠ ∅) {
    Select u from FSet with minimum λ(u) + f(u, y);
    /* the function f(u, y) estimates the cost of
       the shortest path from node u to y */
    FSet = FSet - { u }; ESet = ESet ∪ { u };
    if (u = y) return the shortest path cost (x, y, λ(y));
    Let τ be the highest level number of the edges incident on node u;
    if (u is marked) {
      Let β be the marked level number on node u;
      for each edge u --c--> v with the levels from β to τ having the edge cost c   {
        if ((v ∉ FSet) and (v ∉ ESet)) {
          λ(v) = λ(u) + c;
          FSet = FSet ∪ { v }; }
        else {
          if (λ(v) > λ(u) + c) λ(v) = λ(u) + c; } } } }
end
```

Figure 3.5. PASPAH: Find the shortest path cost from $START$ in SG_i^1 to $DEST$ in SG_j^1

following only those edges whose level number is not less than the marked level number of the node u. Whenever each processor finish its computation, it returns its result to the main (or coordinator) processor. The main processor exclusively checks the stopping condition described in the previous section 3.2. If the condition is satisfied, then it aborts all the computations being performed by other processors. Otherwise, it simply keeps checking the stopping condition until the condition is satisfied.

3.4 Performance Evaluation

We empirically compare $PASPAH$ with OTO, $OTOpar$ [7] and $SPAH$ [4] algorithms. $SPAH$ is an improved A* algorithm which takes advantage of HiTi graph structure. It only consists of Step 1 and Step 5 in $PASPAH$ where x and y in Step 5 is the same as $START$ and $DEST$ respectively. $OTOpar$ is a parallel implementation of OTO algorithm. It uses two processors where each processor uses A* algorithm with Manhattan distance estimation to build its corresponding tree, one rooted at the source node and the other rooted at the destination node. For fair comparisons, we modified OTO and $OTOpar$ so that they also utilize HiTi graph structure. In other words, in the modified OTO and $OTOpar$ named $MOTO$ and $MOTOpar$ respectively, we use $SPAH$ algorithm for building two trees from both source and destination nodes. Note that we use Euclidean distance for the lower bound estimation in $SPAH$ rather than Manhattan distance of $OTOpar$. This is because Manhattan distance estimation does not guarantee the optimal shortest path generation.

We implemented $SPAH$, $MOTO$, $MOTOpar$ and $PASPAH$ on a BBN GP1000 shared memory multiprocessor system, which has a nonuniform memory architecture. The BBN GP1000 multiprocessor currently consists of 85 nodes, each one with 4MBytes of local memory, linked together by a high speed butterfly switch. In this system, the globally shared memory is the sum of the memories local to all processors. Thus, the size of available main memory increases with increasing number of nodes in the system. The BBN GP1000 system can have up to 250 processing nodes.

For our empirical analysis, we create two dimensional grid graphs $G(V, E)$ with 4 adjacent nodes. In grid graph G, $|V|$ and $|E|$ are equal to 400×400 nodes and $4 \times 400 \times 399$ directed edges. From $G(V, E)$, we create a level 4 subgraph tree ST where each level 1 subgraph $SG_i^1(V_i^1, E_i^1)$ has $|V_i^1| = 50 \times 50$, $|E_i^1| = 4 \times 50 \times 49$. The level 2 subgraph tree ST consists of 64 level 1, 16 level 2, 4 level 3, and 1 level 4 subgraphs, which are shown in Figure 3.6.

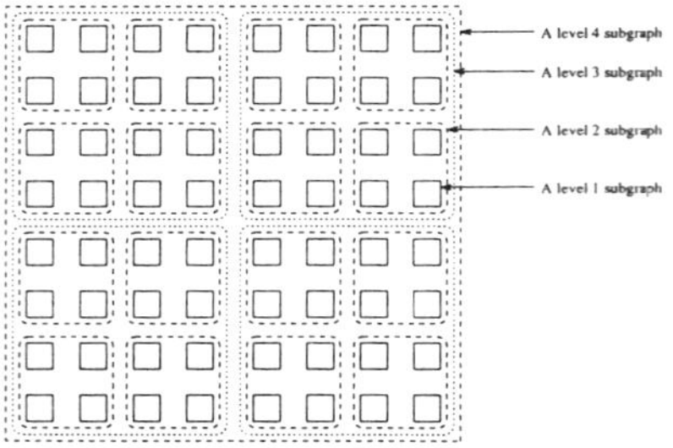

Figure 3.6. A 400×400 grid graph partitioned according to the level 4 Subgraph Tree

Based on the above level 4 subgraph tree, we create level 1 HiTi graph which will be used throughout this section. To show performance comparison between $PASPAH$, $MOTOpar$, $MOTO$, and $SPAH$, we create 5 level 3 HiTi graphs where $3 \leq |N_i^1| \leq 8$ and where the edge cost is generated based on a uniform distribution [100,120] with 5 different seeds. Note that $|N_i^1|$ is the total number of boundary nodes defined on level 1 subgraph SG_i^1. For each level 1 *HiTi* graph, we compute two different sets SET I and SET II of 20 shortest paths randomly prefixed pairs of source and destination nodes. SET I consists of the pairs whose source node location within the corresponding level 1 subgraph is not far apart from the destination nodes. A simplified example of these two sets is shown in Figure 3.7. We then compare the above 4 algorithms by observing their average execution times of

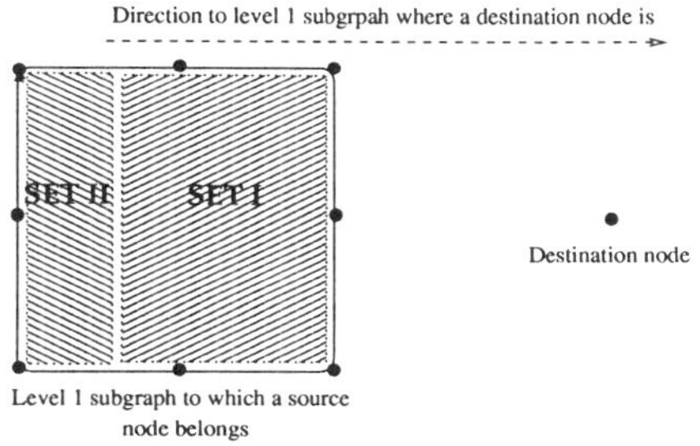

Figure 3.7. An example of sets I and II

two sets SET I and SET II over 5 different level 1 HiTi graphs. The performance of the four algorithms are given in Figure 3.8 a and b. As it is shown in Figure 3.8, $PASPAH$ requires 42 processors to achieve the maximum parallelism in this empirical analysis. Figure 3.8 a shows that $PASPAH$ outperforms the rest of the algorithms. However, Figure 3.8 b shows that $PASPAH$ does not perform significantly better than $SPAH$ and $MOTOpar$[a]. This is because, when source nodes comes from SET II, the explored search space of $PASPAH$ becomes almost same as those of $SPAH$ and $MOTOpar$. Thus, the average execution time of $PASPAH$ is not significantly better than $SPAH$ and $MOTOpar$. From this observation, we conjecture that the parallel processing for *intra* query SPSP problem is not very promising.

We have observed that $SPAH$ performs better than $MOTO$ and $MOTOpar$, which is a different result from the one given in [7]. Our empirical observation can be explained by the following two reasons. The first reason is that *HiTi* graph structure significantly reduces the advantage of using the two tree expansion approach given in [7]. In other words, the most of the nodes in the two level 1 subgraphs (i.e. where source and destination nodes are in) are already explored when two trees start to include the nodes in *HiTi* graph. The second reason is that the lower bound estimation of $MOTOpar$ is Euclidean distance which provides a lot tighter bound than Manhattan distance of $OTOpar$ in [7]. As a result, compared with $OTOpar$, $MOTOpar$ takes much longer time to stop building the two trees before it finds the shortest path.

[a]In Figure 3.8 b, the minimum execution time of $PASPAH$, $SPAH$, $MOTOpar$, and $MOTO$ are 8.36, 8.46, 9.92, and 15.56 seconds respectively.

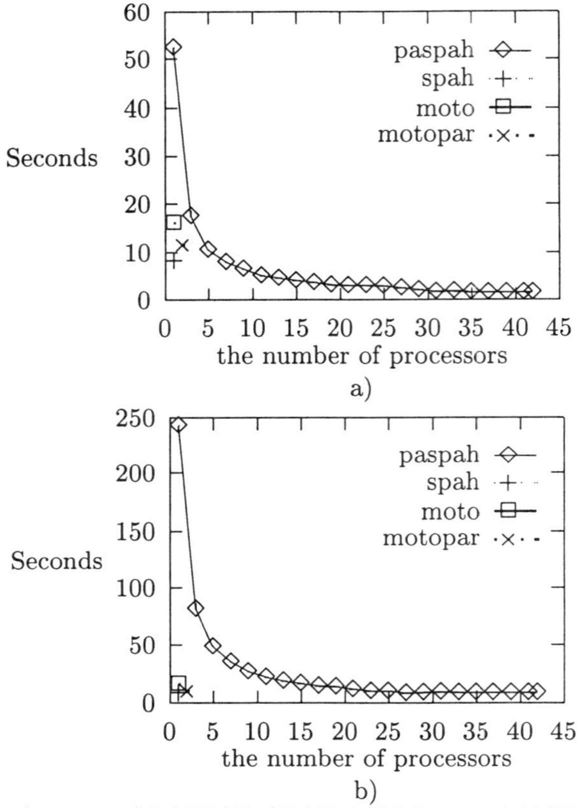

Figure 3.8. Performance of $PASPAH$, $SPAH$, $MOTOpar$, and $MOTO$ over: a) SET I b) SET II

4 Inter Query Parallel Shortest Paths Computation

In this section, we study the parallel processing for computing *inter* query shortest path based on *HiTi* graph. Efficient and fast computation of multiple SPSP shortest paths are very critical for those automobile navigation systems where all route computations are performed on a single server. For this purpose, we propose a new *inter* query parallel shortest path algorithm in the following subsection.

4.1 Formal Description of ISPAH Algorithm

As it was already shown in section 3.4, $SPAH$ outperforms $MOTO$ and $MOTOpar$. Due to the number of processors $PASPAH$ requires, $PASPAH$ is not appropriate for *inter* query parallel shortest paths computation. We therefore use $SPAH$ as the unit operation for parallelizing *inter* query shortest paths computation. In other words, $SPAH$ is performed in parallel for each shortest path computation request. The detail description of the *inter* query parallel shortest path algorithm, named Inter SPAH (*ISPAH*), is shown in Figure 4.1. Algorithm *ISPAH* executes $SPAH$ in parallel on a shared memory multiprocessor system.

```
begin
/* Assume we have a level k HiTi graph defined on a level k + 1 ST; */
/* {SG^1_1, SG^1_2, ..., SG^1_{n_1}} and H^k(P^k, A^k) are stored as adjacency lists
in the globally shared memory; */
/* All the edges in SG^1_t for 1 ≤ t ≤ n_1 are assumed to be level 0 edges; */
  Let R contain a set of source and destination nodes pairs (START, DEST);
  for each (START, DEST) ∈ R do in parallel {
    Perform SPAH for (START, DEST); }
    /* Note that SPAH consists of the Steps 1 and 5 in PASPAH given in Figure 3.5 */
    /* We maintain separate marking places for each (START, DEST)
    computation in the Step 1 */
end
```

Figure 4.1. ISPAH algorithm

For *SPAH* running on each processor, it accesses both local memory and globally shared memory for the computation. Algorithm *SPAH* accesses the globally shared memory only when it needs to accesses $G(V, E)$ or level k $HiTi$ graph $H^k(P^k, A^k)$. Other than that, *SPAH* accesses the local memory. Note that there is no memory access contention for reading or writing a local memory. In the following section, we empirically analyze the performance of $ISPAH$.

4.2 Performance Evaluation

We implemented $ISPAH$ on a BBN GP1000 shared memory multiprocessor system. For our empirical analysis, we used the same grid graph as described in section 3.4. Based on these data sets, we computed 43 randomly prefixed shortest paths. The performance is then measured in terms of the average *speedup* T_n, where T_n represents the total time taken by n processors to compute M shortest paths. We express the *speedup* S_n of n processors as T_1/T_n.

Figure 4.2 shows S_n as n is increased from 1 to 43. As we can see from Figure 4.2, the speedup of $ISPAH$ increases almost linearly up to 10 processors, after 10 it is beginning to level off, and after 25 processors, the performance is ever deteriorating. This occurs because of the globally shared memory access contentions. In $ISPAH$, all processors have to access a single $HiTi$ graph in a globally shared memory, which causes a severe memory access contention when more than 25 processors are used. In order to verify our conjecture of this memory access contention, we modified ISPAH so that an entire level k $HiTi$ graph $H^k(P^k, A^k)$ is replicated on the local memory of each processor. This revised $ISPAH$ is named a Modified ISPAH (MISPAH). We empirically analyzed $MISPAH$ the same way as we did for $ISPAH$.

Figure 4.3 shows the *speedup* of $MISPAH$ up to 43 processors showing the advantage of replicating a level k $HiTi$ graph on each processor. Although $MISPAH$ performs better than $ISPAH$, it is scalable up to 41 processors. From this analysis, we conjecture that

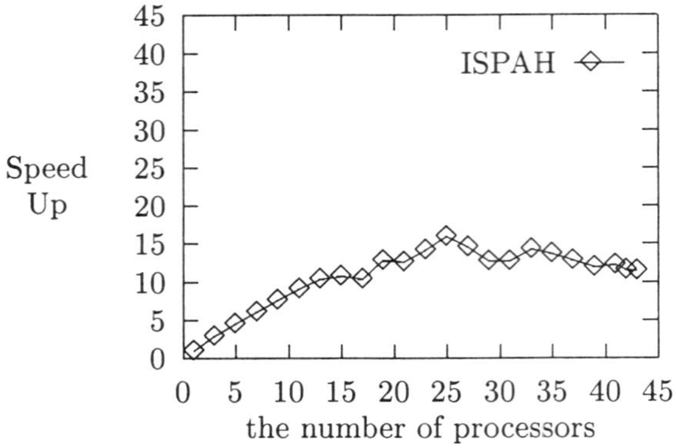

Figure 4.2. Performance of ISPAH

the parallel processing for *inter* query SPSP problems are much more promising than *intra* query SPSP problems.

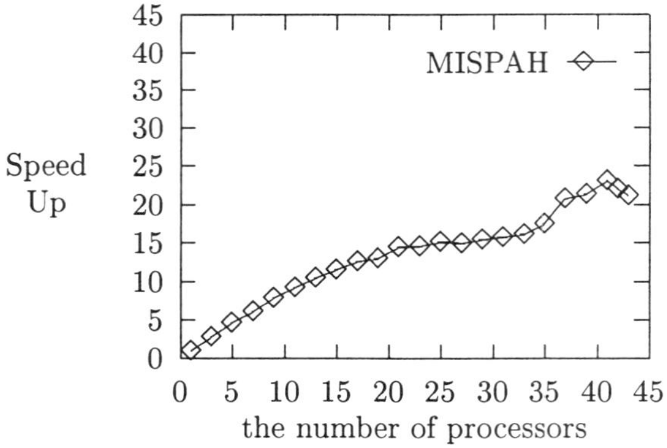

Figure 4.3. Performance of MISPAH

5 Conclusion

In this paper, we studied the parallel processing for *intra* as well as *inter* query shortest path problems on topographical road maps. Based on *HiTi* graph structure, we first developed a parallel shortest path algorithm named *PASPAH* for *intra* query shortest path problem. *HiTi* graph structure provides an opportunity for developing more scalable parallel shortest path algorithms than two tree building approach used in *MOTOpar* algorithm.

We empirically analyzed the performance of *PASPAH* by comparing its execution time on grid graphs with those of *MOTOpar* and *SPAH*. We used a BBN GP1000 shared memory multiprocessor system to implement *PASPAH*, *MOTOpar*, and *SPAH*. Our empirical analysis shows that, although *PASPAH* is more scalable than *MOTOpar*, the average execution time of *PASPAH* is not significantly better than those of *MOTOpar* and *SPAH*. From this analysis, we conjecture that the parallel processing for *intra* query shortest path problem is not very promising.

For *inter* query shortest path problem, we proposed a *HiTi* graph-based parallel algorithm named *ISPAH*. We empirically analyzed the performance of *ISPAH*. Our analysis shows that the speedup of *ISPAH* increases almost linearly for up to 10 processors. However, *ISPAH* is scalable up to 25 processors. This performance degradation occurs due to the severe memory access conflicts of processors. We then presented an improved version of *ISPAH* named *MISPAH* which reduces the memory access conflicts through partial data replication. The peformance analysis of *MISPAH* shows that it is scalable up to 41 processors. From this empirical analysis, we conjecture that *inter* query shortest path problem has more potential for the parallel processing than *intra* query shortest path problem.

References

1. R. Agrawal, and H. Jagadish, "Algorithms for Searching Massive Graphs", In *IEEE Transactions on Knowledge and Data Engineering*, Vol. 6, No.2, pp. 225-238, April 1994.
2. K. Hua, J. Su, and C. Hua, "Efficient Evaluation of Traversal Recursive Queries Using Connectivity Index", In *Proc. IEEE 9th Int'l Conf. Data Engineering*, pp. 549-558, 1993.
3. Y. Ioannidis, R. Ramakirishnan, and L. Winger "Transitive Closure Algorithms Based on Graph Traversal", In *ACM Transactions on Database Systems*, Vol. 18, No.3, pp. 513-576, September 1993.
4. S. Jung and S. Pramanik, "HiTi Graph Model of Topographical Road Maps in Navigation Systems", In *Proc. IEEE 12th Int'l Conf. on Data Engineering*, 1996.
5. S. Jung, "Efficient Parallel Processing Methods for Road Map Queries", In *SGU-CS Technical Report 2000-7*, Computer Science Dept., Sogang University, 2000.
6. R. Kung, E. Hanson, Y. Ioannnidis, T. Sellis, L. Shapiro, and M. Stonebraker, "Heuristic Search in Data Base System", In *Proc. 1st Int. Workshop Expert Database Systems*, pp. 96-107, Oct. 1984.
7. T. Mohr and C. Pasche, "A Parallel Shortest Path Algorithm", *Computing*, Vol 40, pp. 281-292, 1988.
8. S. Shekhar, A. Kohli, and M. Coyle, "Path Computation Algorithms for Advanced Traveler Information System (ATIS)", In *Proc. IEEE 9th Int'l Conf. Data engineering*, pp. 31-39, 1993.

CONCURRENCY CONTROL FOR SYSTEM WITH DATA BROADCAST[1]

MEI-WAI AU, EDWARD CHAN AND KAM-YIU LAM

Department of Computer Science
City University of Hong Kong
83 Tat Chee Avenue, Kowloon
email: {csedchan|cskylam}@cityu.edu.hk

Although data broadcast has been shown to be an efficient method for disseminating data items in mobile computing systems with large number of clients, the issue on how to ensure data consistency observed by mobile transactions has been largely ignored by researchers in the area. While data items are being broadcast, update transactions may install new values for the data items. If the executions of update transactions and broadcast of data items are interleaved without any control, the mobile transactions, which are generated by mobile clients, may observe inconsistent data values. In this paper, we propose a serialization checking method (SCM) for concurrency control between read-only mobile transactions and update transactions. SCM is based on the framework of an earlier algorithm, Update First with Ordering (UFO), but improves on that algorithm by reducing re-broadcast overhead when the probability of data conflict between updates and data broadcast is high.

1 Introduction

Recent advances in mobile communication technology have greatly increased the functionality of mobile information services and have made many mobile computing applications a reality. Various innovative applications, such as real-time traffic information and navigation systems, and real-time stock monitoring systems, are emerging [XSGFR97]. However, a number of technical hurdles need to be surmounted before these scenarios can materialize [AFZ95, IB94]. One of the most important issues is efficient dissemination of consistent data items to transactions from mobile clients [AFZ97, IB94]. In recent years, many efficient data dissemination methods have been proposed [AFZ97, DCKV97, LS97, P98, PC99, SNSR98, XSGFR97]. Most of them are based on data broadcast in which the broadcast server continuously broadcasts data items to mobile clients.

In data broadcast, mobile transactions do not need to inform the broadcast server before accessing a data item. They can get the data item from the "air" while it is being broadcast. However, if the updates to the database are done concurrently, the mobile transactions may observe inconsistent data values, e.g., the resulting execution schedule of the mobile and update transactions may be non-serializable.

In this paper, we study the problem of disseminating consistent data items to read-only mobile transactions while allowing updates to be performed concurrently at the database server. We propose a *Serialization Checking Method (SCM)* to ensure the consistency of data items observed

---

[1] The work described in this paper was partially supported by a grant from the Research Grants Council of Hong Kong Special Administrative Region, China [Project No. CityU1097/99E] and partially supported by a grant from CityU (Project No. 7001069).

by the mobile transactions. Allowing concurrent execution of data broadcast and update transactions not only can improve the response time of mobile transactions, it can also maintain the freshness of the data items, since most of data items represent real-time information. The SCM is based on the conflict checking framework proposed in the *Update-First with Order (UFO)* algorithm, which has many important advantages for mobile computing systems [LAC99]. The organization of the remaining parts of the paper is as follows. Section 2 reviews the related work on concurrency control in data broadcast. Section 3 defines our transaction models for mobile computing systems with data broadcast. Section 4 discusses the problem of data inconsistency when update and data broadcast are performed concurrently. Section 5 reviews how UFO resolves the concurrency control problem. Section 6 introduces SCM and explains how it avoids a performance problem in UFO. Examples are provided to explain the mechanisms of the SCM. The paper concludes in Section 7.

2 Related Work

Mobile computing has been the subject of much research in recent years [AFZ95, DCKV97, LS97, P98]. Unfortunately the important issue of concurrency control in data broadcast has not received adequate attention. Traditional concurrency control protocols are not suitable to mobile computing systems due to their heavy overhead for detecting data conflicts in a mobile environment [P95, P98]. Owing to the relatively poor quality of services of mobile networks, it is not easy to ensure data consistency and to detect data conflicts in a mobile network. One suggested solution is to relax the consistency requirement. In [PB95], a two-level consistency model is proposed. Semantically related data are grouped together into a cluster, and the data inside a cluster are mutually consistent. However, a certain degree of inconsistency is allowed among data items at different clusters.

In [SNSR98], a control matrix is proposed for data conflict resolution. For a database of n data items, a matrix of size $n \times n$ is used. For each broadcast cycle, the control matrix is broadcast together with the data items. A mobile client performs consistency checking using the matrix before reading any data item from the "air". This method can handle read-only transactions well as update transactions. The write operations are performed on local copies of the data items at the client. At the end of a transaction, the whole transaction including all of the read and write operations and the cycle numbers in which they are performed will be sent to the server for commitment.

In [P98, PC99], multi-version data broadcast approaches are suggested to resolve the problem of reading inconsistent data values. In addition to the most updated version, all the previous versions within a time frame need to be broadcast as well. Another method to detect the non-serializability problem is to broadcast serialization graphs [P98, PC99]. Each client maintains its local serialization graph to ensure that the schedules of all the committed transactions are serializable. The first drawback of this method is also the heavy overhead in broadcasting the serialization graphs since every data conflict at the database server has to be broadcast. Secondly, each client must listen to the transmission channel to maintain and update its serialization graph. This leads to another serious problem, which can affect the correctness of this approach: the need to maintain the serialization graphs at the client mobile even when it is disconnected. The mobile network is unreliable and disconnection is frequent. When disconnection occurs, the mobile client cannot obtain new serialization information about its transaction, making it virtually impossible to ensure serializability of transaction execution.

3 System Model

The mobile computing system model used throughout this paper consists of a base station, a number of mobile clients and a mobile network such as the GSM cellular radio system, which provides limited bandwidth for data broadcast [H94]. The mobile clients, which represent users equipped with mobile machines, communicate with the base stations through low bandwidth wireless channels of the mobile network.

At the base station, a database server is maintained. The database contains various useful information about the external environment such as stock updates, current traffic information and news. Their values can be highly dynamic. To maintain the validity or "freshness" of the data items, update transactions are generated to refresh the data values whenever the status of the corresponding objects in the external environment has changed such as when there is a change in stock price. Each update transaction is time-stamped. The time-stamp is used to indicate at which snapshot the update is generated. It is recorded with the new value into the data item as its version number. It is assumed that stale data items will be much less useful.

In the model, it is assumed that update transactions are short transactions, consisting mainly of one to several operations. Some update transactions may also contain read operations. Furthermore, a well-formed concurrency control protocol, such as two phase locking [BHG87], is used for concurrency control among the update transactions at the database server.

The database server continuously broadcasts data items from the database one by one until the end of a broadcast cycle. The length of a broadcast cycle may be fixed or variable. Each broadcast cycle follows the preceding cycle immediately. The data items may require different time for broadcast due to different sizes. A broadcast algorithm is adopted for selecting data items to broadcast[2]. In the model, the broadcast process is modeled as a long read-only transaction called the *broadcast transaction (BT)*. The set of data items in a broadcast transaction consists of those data items, which are broadcast in the period from (current time – life span of a mobile transaction) to current time. The execution of the BT and the update transactions are interleaved to reduce the blocking delay due to the installation of update transactions. (Note that treating the broadcast process as a transaction is mainly to ease the discussion of the algorithm. It actually does not process any transaction features such as the ACID properties.)

The mobile clients issue transactions, called *mobile transactions (MT)*, to access data items at database server. It is assumed that each MT is a set of data requests (read operations). The requests

[2] In the last few years, various broadcast algorithms based on the deadlines of the transactions and the access frequencies of the data items have been proposed [LS97, XSGFR97]. As we shall see later, our protocol does not depend on the broadcast algorithm selected and can be applied to any of these broadcast algorithms.

can be performed in any order. When all the requests are satisfied, the transaction is completed. An example for this type of transactions is a request for the weather forecasts of a few cities at the same time or a request for several stock data. A single request is issued instead of several separate requests simply because batching the requests can reduce the system overhead. The arrival sequence of the data items is unimportant as long as all requested data items are received before the deadline.

Each MT is defined with a (soft) deadline. Although they are not real-time transactions, meeting their deadlines is an important performance objective. The requirement may be a statistical one such as 95% of the mobile transactions has to be completed within 5 seconds after the submissions. Transactions, which have missed their deadlines, might still be of some use, but beyond a certain time interval they would be considered totally useless. The period between the arrival time of a transaction and the time when it is considered to be useless is called *drop period.* The assumptions of the system model are summarized below:

1. All update transactions are at the database server (base station).
2. The arrival rate of the update transaction is high due to the dynamic nature of the external environment.
3. All mobile transactions are read-only.
4. Mobile transactions can be *unordered.*
5. Each mobile transaction has a drop period. A mobile transaction will be aborted if it cannot get all the required data items from the broadcast program within the drop period.

4 Sample Inconsistent Cases

In this section we briefly describe the data inconsistency problem in data broadcast and illustrate the nature of the problems with some representative examples.

Example 1: Data conflict between a MT and an update transaction
Suppose the update transaction, U, updates data item d_5 and then data item d_2, and a mobile transaction, MT, wants to read d_2 and d_5. If the schedule is:

i) Broadcast transaction (BT) broadcasts d_2
ii) MT reads d_2
iii) U updates d_5 & d_2
iv) Broadcast transaction (BT) broadcasts d_5
v) MT reads d_5

The mobile transaction MT may observe inconsistent data values. The serialization graph is cyclic such as MT $\rightarrow$ U$\rightarrow$ MT and is non-serializable. The reason is that MT reads a data item, d_2, which is in conflict with U before the update from U and it reads a conflicting data item, d_5, after the update from U.

Example 2: A MT conflicts with two (or more) update transactions

Even though the serialization order between an update transaction and a mobile transaction is not cyclic, the final serialization graph can still be cyclic due to transitive dependencies[3]. Suppose there are two updates U_1 and U_2 such that U_1 will update d_2 and then d_1, and U_2 will update d_1 and then d_5. If the schedule is:

i) Broadcast transaction (BT) broadcasts d_2
ii) MT reads d_2
iii) U_1 updates d_2 & d_1
iv) U_2 updates d_1 & d_5
v) Broadcast transaction (BT) broadcasts d_5
vi) MT reads d_5

The serialization graph is cyclic such as $U_2 \rightarrow MT \rightarrow U_1 \rightarrow U_2$.

Example 3: Non-serializability involving two or more broadcast transactions.
A MT may not be able to get all its required data items from a single broadcast cycle. Non-serializability of transaction execution may occur over more than one broadcast transaction:

i) BT_1 broadcasts d_2
ii) MT reads d_2
iii) End of BT_1
iv) U updates d_5 & d_2
v) BT_2 broadcasts d_5
vi) MT reads d_5

The serialization graph is cyclic such as $MT \rightarrow U \rightarrow MT$.

Note that in the determination of the serializability of a serialization graph, we ignore the broadcast transactions as they are considered as "intermediate transactions". They do not have any real effect on database consistency. Their only function is to provide data items for the mobile transactions. (The reason of treating it as a transaction is to facilitate the analysis. Since the mobile transactions read data items from broadcast transactions, their serialization order will always be $BT \rightarrow MT$.)

The data inconsistency problem in the first two examples can be solved by adopting a *serial* execution method. For example, each transaction, either a broadcast or an update transaction, is defined with a unique time-stamp based on its arrival time. The execution order of the transactions follows their time-stamps. In this way, the final schedule will be serial. However, this method has three serious problems. Firstly, the concurrency of the system will be lowered. Secondly, the waiting time of update transactions can be very long as the broadcast transactions are long transactions. Blocking update transactions for long time may affect the "freshness" of the data items and the objective of broadcasting the most updated data values to mobile transactions may not be achieved. Thirdly, even if the serial approach is used, the problem in the third example above is still unresolved.

[3] If a transaction T_j reads an uncommitted data item from another transaction T_i, T_j will be dependent on T_i.

5 Update-First with Order (UFO)

The biggest problem in designing a concurrency control protocol for a mobile computing system using data broadcast is that the mobile transactions may read a data item at any time while the data item is being broadcast and the database server in general does not notice this. Thus, instead of detecting data conflicts between mobile transactions and update transactions, the UFO algorithm checks data conflicts between broadcast and update transactions [LCA99]. Although the UFO algorithm has been shown to give a good performance, its performance is highly affected by the probability of data conflicts between mobile transactions and update transactions since it resolves the data conflicts by data re-broadcast.

The basic principle of the UFO algorithm is to ensure that if a data conflict occurs between a broadcast transaction and an update transaction, the serialization order between them will always be U $\rightarrow$ BT. BT $\rightarrow$ U will be allowed only if it is impossible for a mobile transaction, which reads from BT, to be dependent on U directly or transitively. Since mobile transactions read data items from broadcast transactions, the serialization order is always BT $\rightarrow$ MT. Thus, serialization order between the update transactions and the mobile transactions will always be U $\rightarrow$ MT and the final serialization graph will be serializable [BHG87].

Basically, the UFO protocol consists of two parts:

1. Execution of update transactions; and
2. Conflict resolution between update and broadcast transactions.

5.1 Execution of Update Transactions

The execution of an update transaction is divided into two phases: the *execution phase* and the *update phase*. During the execution phase, the operations of an update transaction are executed and data conflicts with other update transactions are resolved using a conventional concurrency control protocol such as 2PL. The new values from the write operations are written in a private workspace of the transaction instead of updating the database immediately. When all the operations of the update transaction have been completed, it enters the update phase in which permanent updates of the database will be performed by copying the new values from its private workspace into the database. The data conflict with broadcast transaction will be checked in the update phase after the completion of the updates. (So, we can see that the update transactions adopt 2PL for resolving data conflicts with other update transactions and use an optimistic approach to detect conflicts with broadcast transaction.)

There are two important advantages in dividing the execution of the update transactions into two phases. Firstly, it can significantly reduce the blocking probability of the broadcast transactions. If a broadcast transaction wants to read a data item, which is locked by an update transaction, the broadcast transaction will be blocked until the update transaction is committed based on the principles of 2PL. At the same time, the update transaction, which is holding the lock, may be blocked due to data conflicts with other update transactions. Due to transitive blocking, the blocking time of the broadcast transactions can be very long. Dividing the execution of an update transaction into two phases can greatly reduce the blocking probability and blocking time of broadcast transactions since data conflicts between update and broadcast transactions will occur only when the update transaction is in the update phase, which is much shorter. Secondly, the detection of data conflicts between the update and broadcast transactions will become much easier. At the update phase, the system will know which data items have been accessed by the update transaction. By comparing the write set of the update transaction with the read set of the broadcast transaction, the system can determine whether there is any data conflict between them.

5.2 Conflict Resolution between Update and Broadcast Transactions

Data conflict between an update transaction and a broadcast transaction is detected when the update transaction enters its update phase. Re-broadcast is used to resolve the conflict. The purpose is to reverse the serialization order from BT $\rightarrow$ U to our desirable order, U $\rightarrow$ BT. The following defines the algorithm at the broadcast server. It is performed when an update transaction enters the update phase.

```
if O_BT ∩ O_U = { }
   BT and U have no dependency
else for each data item d_i ∈ {O_BT ∩ O_U}
          re-broadcast data item d_i
where  O_BT = set of data items of broadcast transaction, BT
       O_U  = set of data items of update transaction, U
```

By re-broadcasting the conflicting data item, the serialization order between the broadcast transaction and the update transaction is reversed. Noted that as described in Section 3, the set of data items in a broadcast transaction consists of those data items, which are broadcast in the period from (current time – the life span of a mobile transaction) to current time. Thus, the set of data items in the broadcast transaction is not fixed. After the broadcast of a data item, the data item will be included and the last data item in the broadcast transaction will be removed.

6 The Serialization Checking Method (SCM)

A performance problem of the UFO algorithm is that its performance is sensitive to the probability of data conflicts between update and broadcast transactions. If the conflict probability is high, the re-broadcast overhead will be quite significant leading to serious degradation in overall system performance. In SCM, this problem is alleviated because the consistency of data values observed by a mobile transaction is ensured by performing a check on its local serialization graph instead of relying on a data re-broadcast.

As can seen from Section 4, the main data inconsistency problem in a broadcast environment is that a data item captured from the air may later be updated by an update transaction. If the update transaction has further data conflict with the broadcast transaction, then it may cause cyclic schedule in a mobile client. Another reason for cyclic schedule is due to transitive dependencies among update transactions. To deal with these problems, mobile clients can be provided with data conflict information of update transactions to construct their local serialization graph. In case a cyclic schedule is formed, the mobile client will dispose the data item that is read before the update transaction in order to maintain a serializable schedule. To solve the first case, the SCM algorithm broadcasts the identities of the data items that are updated by a transaction at the database server if any of the data items are broadcast in the last drop period. To handle the case of transitive dependencies, SCM simply broadcasts information of the update transactions that has transitive dependencies with the broadcast data items.

6.1 Algorithm for the Server

Similar to the UFO algorithm, the execution of the update transactions is divided into two phases and conflict between an update transaction and the broadcast transaction will be detected when the update transaction enters its update phase. In case of data conflict, the dependency between the update transaction and the broadcast transaction will be broadcast instead of re-broadcasting the conflicting items. At the same time, the dependencies between the update transaction and other update transactions in the last drop period will also be broadcast.

After finishing an update transaction U, the following algorithm is performed:

if $D_B \cap D_U \neq \{\}$
then broadcasts message: D_U is updated
else if $D_U \cap D_{Ui} \neq \{\}$ where $U_i \in T_B$
    then broadcasts message: D_U is updated
where D_B = set of data items that are broadcast in the last drop period
    D_U = set of data items of update transaction, U
    T_B = set of update transactions in the last drop period

6.2 Algorithm for Mobile Transaction

Mobile transactions listen to the broadcast transaction for their required data items. They also listen to the message on update and build their local serialization graphs. Once the serialization graph is updated, a searching on the graph will be performed. If a cyclic schedule is formed, the mobile transaction resolves it by disposing the data item that it captures before the update transaction that caused the conflict. The data items will be captured from the 'air' again when it is broadcast in the next time. The process continues until all the required data items are captured or the drop period expired.

loop until (read-set = D_{MT}) or (drop period of MT has expired)
  if a data item d_i is broadcast
  then if $d_i \in D_{MT}$
      then read-set = read-set $\cup \{d_i\}$
  else if an update transaction D_U is broadcast
      then if (read-set $\cap D_U \neq \{\}$) or ($\exists U_i \in T_S$ s.t. $D_U \cap D_{Ui} \neq \{\}$)
          then $T_S = T_S \cup \{D_U\}$
              if a cyclic schedule is formed

then disposes the data item get before the update transaction in conflict

where D_{MT} = set of data items requested by MT

T_S = set of update transactions in the local serialization graph

6.3 Examples

In the following, we use two examples to illustrate the mechanism of the SCM algorithm.

Example 1:

This example is on cycle schedule formed by transitive dependencies. There are two update transactions in this example, U_1 and U_2. U_1 will update d_2 and d_1 and U_2 will update d_1 and d_5. The mobile transaction, MT, reads d_2 and d_5.

Steps	**Serialization graph for MT**
i) Server broadcasts d_2	-
ii) MT reads d_2	MT
iii) U_1 updates d_2 & d_1	MT
iv) Server broadcasts message: d_2 and d_1 are updated	MT
v) MT reads message: d_2 and d_1 are updated	$MT \rightarrow U_1$
vi) U_2 updates d_1 & d_5	$MT \rightarrow U_1$
vii) Server broadcasts message: d_1 and d_5 are updated	$MT \rightarrow U_1$
viii) MT reads message: d_1 and d_5 are updated	$MT \rightarrow U_1 \rightarrow U_2$
ix) Server broadcasts d_5	$MT \rightarrow U_1 \rightarrow U_2$
x) MT reads d_5	$MT \rightarrow U_1 \rightarrow U_2 \rightarrow MT$
xi) MT detects a cyclic schedule and disposes d_2 to resolve	$U_1 \rightarrow U_2 \rightarrow MT$

In this example the server checks for transitive dependencies between the update transaction U_2 and the broadcast data items at step vii). Since the server detects the dependencies, it broadcasts a message on the update transaction. So MT can construct its local serialization graph at step viii). When MT reads d_5, it detects that a cyclic schedule is formed at step x). MT resolves this by disposing data item d_2 that it reads before U_1.

Example 2:

This example illustrates that different mobile transactions may observe update transactions in different serialization order. The mobile transaction MT_1 reads d_1, d_3 and d_4 while MT_2 reads $d_1$and d_2. The update transactions U_1 updates d_2 and d_3, U_2 updates d_1.

Steps	**Serialization graph for MT_1**	**Serialization graph for MT_2**
i) MT_1 begins transaction	MT_1	-
ii) Server broadcasts d_1	MT_1	-
iii) MT_1 read d_1	MT_1	-
iv) MT_2 begins transaction	MT_1	MT_2
v) Server broadcasts d_2	MT_1	MT_2
vi) MT_2 read d_2	MT_1	MT_2

vii) U_1 updates d_2 & d_3	MT_1	MT_2
viii) Server broadcasts message: d_2 and d_3 are updated	MT_1	MT_2
ix) MT_1 and MT_2 reads message: d_2 and d_3 are updated	MT_1	$MT_2 \rightarrow U_1$
x) Server broadcasts d_3	MT_1	$MT_2 \rightarrow U_1$
xi) MT_1 read d_3	$U_1 \rightarrow MT_1$	$MT_2 \rightarrow U_1$
xii) U_2 updates d_1	$U_1 \rightarrow MT_1$	$MT_2 \rightarrow U_1$
xiii) Server broadcasts message: d_1 is updated	$U_1 \rightarrow MT_1 \rightarrow U_2$	$MT_2 \rightarrow U_1$
xiv) MT_1 and MT_2 reads message: d_1 is updated	$U_1 \rightarrow MT_1 \rightarrow U_2$	$MT_2 \rightarrow U_1$
xv) Server broadcasts d_4	$U_1 \rightarrow MT_1 \rightarrow U_2$	$MT_2 \rightarrow U_1$
xvi) MT_1 read d_4	$U_1 \rightarrow MT_1 \rightarrow U_2$	$MT_2 \rightarrow U_1$
xvii) MT_1 commits	$U_1 \rightarrow MT_1 \rightarrow U_2$	$MT_2 \rightarrow U_1$
xviii) Server broadcasts d_1	-	$MT_2 \rightarrow U_1$
xix) MT_2 read d_1	-	$U_2 \rightarrow MT_2 \rightarrow U_1$
xx) MT_2 commit	-	$U_2 \rightarrow MT_2 \rightarrow U_1$

The order of update transaction U_1 and U_2 observed by MT_1 and MT_2 are different. However both of them are correct. Please note that in our algorithm, the local serialization graphs kept by MT_1 and MT_2 will be $MT_1 \rightarrow U_2$ and $MT_2 \rightarrow U_1$ respectively since a mobile transaction will only keep update information on data items it has already read. This is because if an update transaction is before a mobile transaction, it will never cause a cyclic schedule.

6.4 Disconnection

An important property of mobile network is frequent disconnection, which may be voluntary or involuntary. In voluntary disconnection, the mobile client initiates a disconnection in order to conserve power of the mobile machine. Voluntary disconnection of a mobile client will only occur after the completion of its transaction. Thus, it neither affects the mechanism of SCM nor creates any problem regarding to the correctness of the protocol. Involuntary disconnection results from instability in mobile network. For example, in a cellular radio network, the strength of signal received by a mobile client is affected by a number of factors such as the distance between the mobile clients and the base station, as well as the height of the surrounding buildings. Disconnection may occur once the signal received by the mobile client is lower than a threshold level. Although the disconnection is usually temporary, its impact on the consistency of transaction execution can be very serious.

The main effect of disconnection on SCM is that at the time of broadcasting conflicting update transaction identities, a mobile client may be disconnected from the network. For this case, the mobile client cannot get the new data conflict information. One simple method to solve the problem is to broadcast additional information in a special header at the beginning of a broadcast cycle. This information consists of the identities and the time-stamps of all the data items which have been involved in any conflict between the update and broadcast transactions within the length of the broadcast transaction. When a mobile client reconnects, it has to wait until the start of a broadcast cycle. Then, it checks the header to see whether any of its accessed data items conflict with any update transaction while it is disconnected from the network. All such items will be marked invalid and the transaction must retrieve the current version of these data items again.

6.5 Comparison between UFO and SCM

Since SCM is based on the execution framework of UFO, it also shares many desirable properties of the UFO. For example, it can be applied to different broadcast algorithm since it does not affect the broadcast algorithm; All the data items observed by the mobile transactions are the most updated versions. On the other hand, the overhead of SCM is much smaller than UFO in case of high data conflict probability. The UFO algorithm resolves data conflict by data re-broadcast. However, in SCM, only the identities of the transactions will be broadcast in case of data conflict. Of course, the additional overhead of the SCM is that the mobile transactions need to maintain their local serialization graph. Considering that the bandwidth is the often the bottleneck resource in a mobile computing system, the most important performance objective should aim to minimize the bandwidth overhead instead of other processing overheads at the server or client sides.

The cost for the lower broadcast overhead in SCM is that the mobile transactions may observe different serialization order since the checking is only performed on their local serialization graphs. For most cases, this is not a big problem since the transactions from different mobile clients are assumed to be independent.

7 Conclusions

Data broadcast has been shown to be an efficient method for disseminating data items to transactions generated by mobile clients. Although research in the design of broadcast algorithms has received a lot of attention in previous years, the concurrency control issue has been greatly ignored. If the broadcast of data items and the execution of update transactions, which are important to maintain the freshness of the data items at the database, are uncontrolled, the mobile transactions may observe inconsistent data values. In this paper, we study the concurrency control between update transactions and mobile transactions, which consist of read-only operations. Based on the framework proposed in the UFO algorithm, a serialization checking method has been proposed. Similar to the UFO algorithm, the protocol is simple and can effectively maintain the schedule update and mobile transactions to be serializable. Unlike the UFO algorithm, overhead for ensuring data consistency observed by the mobile transactions is much lower since no data items need to be re-broadcast. This is because conflict is detected by simply searching the local serialization graph of the mobile transactions instead by data re-broadcast.

References

[AFZ95] Acharya, S., Alonso, R., Franklin, M., Zdonik, S., "Broadcast Disks: Data Management for Asymmetric Communications Environments" in *Proceedings of ACM SIGMOD*, 1995.

[AFZ97] Acharya, S., Franklin, M., Zdonik, S., "Balancing Push and Pull for Data Broadcast", in *Proceedings of ACM SIGMOD*, Tucson, Arizona, May 1997.

[BHG87] Bernstein, P.A., Hadzilacos, V., Goodman, N., *Concurrency Control and Recovery in Database System*, Addison-Wesley Publishing Company, 1987.

[DCKV97] Datta, A., Celik, A., Kim, J. and VanderMeer, D.E., "Adaptive Broadcast Protocol to Support Power Conservant Retrieval by Mobile Users", in *Proceedings of 13th International Conference on Data Engineering*, 1997.

[H94] Haug, T., "Overview of GSM: Philosophy and Results", *International Journal of Wireless Information Networks*, vol. 1, no. 1, pp. 7-16, 1994.

[IB94] Imielinski, T. and Badrinath, B.R., "Mobile Wireless Computing: Challenges in Data Management," *Communications of the ACM*, vol. 37, no. 10, Oct. 1994.

[LCA99] Lam, K.Y., Chan, Edward and Au, Mei-Wai, "Broadcast of Consistent Data to Read-Only Transactions from Mobile Clients", in *Proceedings of 2nd IEEE Workshop on Mobile Computing Systems and Applications*, New Orleans, Louisiana, USA, 1999.

[LS97] Leong, H.V. and Si, A., "Database Caching over the Air-Storage", *The Computer Journal*, vol. 40, no. 7, pp. 401-415, 1997.

[PB95] Pitoura, E. and Bhargava, B. "Maintaining Consistency of Data in Mobile Distributed Environment," in *Proceedings of the 15th International Conference on Distributed Computing Systems*, pp. 404-413, 1995.

[P98] Pitoura, E. "Supporting Read-Only Transactions in Wireless Broadcasting", in *Proceedings of the DEXA'98 Workshop on Mobility in Databases and Distributed Systems,* August 1998.

[PC99] Pitoura, E. and Chrysanthis, P.K., "Scalable Processing of Read-Only Transactions in Broadcast Push", in *Proceedings of the 19th IEEE International Conference on Distributed Computing System,* pp. 432-441, 1999.

[SNSR98] Shnmugasundram, J., Nithrakashyap, A., Sivasankaran, R., Ramamritham, K., "Efficient Concurrency Control for Broadcast Environments," *Technical Report, 1997-062*, Department of Computer Science, University of Massachusetts, Amherst, 1998.

[XSGFR97] Xuan, P., O. Gonzalez, J. Fernandez and Ramamritham, K., "Broadcast on Demand: Efficient and Timely Dissemination of Data in Mobile Environments", in *Proceedings of 3rd IEEE Real-Time Technology Application Symposium*, 1997.

Clustering Data for Large Transaction Databases

Chen Ning, Chen An*, Zhou Longxiang, Liu Lu*
PhD 97, Academy of Mathematics and System Sciences, Chinese Academy of Sciences, Beijing, 100080, P. R. China, E-mail: nchen@math08.math.ac.cn
*Economics and Management School, Beijing University of Aeronautics and Astronautics, 100083, P. R. China, E-mail: anchen1@yahoo.com

Clustering has been recognized as a primary data mining method for knowledge discovery. Clustering items or transactions are two tasks in transaction database, which can find potential useful patterns to improve the product profit. Unfortunately, most traditional clustering algorithms are based on metric distance functions as the similarity measures which are not appropriate for transaction data. In this paper, we study the problem of clustering items and clustering transactions in transaction databases. For the first task, we present a definition of similarity measure between items based on frequent itemsets firstly, then discuss several similarity measures between item groups. We also develop a hierarchical clustering algorithm for transaction database. For the second task, we propose a two-step algorithm of clustering transactions.

1 Introduction

In a given transaction database, there are two different clustering which are potentially useful. One is to cluster items which are often sold together into item groups. These item clusters can be used to improve the shelf management and increase the market profit. The other is to cluster customers such that customers with similar buying patterns are in a single cluster. These customer clusters can be used to characterize the different customer groups, and these characterizations can be used in targeted marketing and advertising such that specific products are directed towards specific customers based on their profiles.

Most previous work in clustering focused on numerical data whose inherent geometric properties can be exploited to naturally define distance functions between points. But seldom was focused on transaction database in which the attributes are binary type. An approach is to transform the transaction database into a high-dimensional data space. Each item corresponds to one binary (0/1) attribute (dimension). Each transaction corresponds to a d-dimensional vector (d is the number of items in the transaction database) $(v_1, v_2, \ldots, v_d)$, where v_j equals to 1 if the jth item is contained in the transaction, otherwise v_j is 0. However, many algorithms used to cluster data in spatial database are not applicable for transaction databases. The drawbacks of this approach are (1) a transaction database always contain hundreds even thousands of items which lead to the dimensionality of the transformed database is very large. As we known, most clustering algorithms for low-dimensional database do not work for high-dimensional database due to the curse of dimensionality [WSB 98]. (2) Although each dimension has only two values, dividing the dimension into two halves, the sparsity of the transformed data space also exists. With d dimensions, there are 2^d cells each presenting a different transaction in the data space. Assuming d=100, there are around 10^{30} cells, while the number of transactions is usually much less than 10^{30}. So the majority of the cells are empty. Since most transactions only contain very limited items, most values of the transformed database are 0. (3) As the transformed data space is non-coordinate, some operations such as addition, subtraction of vectors, and mean of a cluster to form condensed representations of clusters and to reduce the time and space requirements of clustering problem lose their meaning. (4) The well-known metric distances are not suitable to describe the similarity between binary data.

Clustering has been studied in statistics, machine learning, and data mining areas with different emphases. Clustering algorithms can be categorized into four main groups: hierarchical algorithms [GRK 98], partition algorithms (k-mean algorithm, k-medoids algorithms [KR 90], CLARANS [NH 94]), density-based algorithms (DBSCAN [EKSX 96]) and grid-based algorithms.

In this paper, we focus on the two tasks - item clustering and transaction clustering for transaction database. Finding a suitable similarity measure depicting the relations between items is the first important problem. As we know, frequent itemsets in association rules depict the co-occurrence relation of items presented in the transaction database. We propose a hierarchical algorithm of item clustering based on frequent itemsets for transaction databases. Although the results can be used to transaction clustering, the time complexity is high and it is based on the results of the former. We present a two-step algorithm of clustering transactions.

The rest of the paper is organized as follows: In section 2, we present a new definition of similarity measure between items based on frequent itemsets and discuss several similarity measures between item groups. We develop a hierarchical clustering algorithm for transaction database in section 3. In section 4, we propose a two-step algorithm of clustering transactions. Section 5 concludes the paper.

2 Preliminary Definition

Our clustering algorithm is based on co-occurrence that tries to group together the frequently co-occurring items. Let x and y be two items in the transaction database. If x and y are always sold together, i.e., either both x and y are contained in a transaction, or neither of them is contained in a transaction database. Association rules [AMS 96] capture the relationship among items that are presented in a transaction. Although frequent itemsets depict the co-occurrence relationship of items presented in the transaction database, they can not produce a clustering of items in the accepted definition because the items are not partitioned into disjoint groups. Furthermore, it requires k scans to identify the frequent itemsets, where k is the maximum length of frequent itemsets. Next, frequent itemsets are itemsets with support no less than the minimum support, they only consider the co-occurrence of the items, but neglect the case that some items are contained in a transaction, while others are not contained. We first describe a definition of similarity between two items based on frequent itemsets, combining support and confidence.

2.1 similarity between two items

Almost all clustering techniques involve a process of measurement, either of the magnitude of the distance between two objects, or of the magnitude of their similarity to each other. These things are recognized as similar or dissimilar is fundamental to the process of clustering. Despite its apparent simplicity, the concept of similarity and the procedure used to measure similarity are far from simple.

The reason of this problem is that the Minkowski distance considers not only the co-occurrence but also the co-nonoccurrence of the two items. Using it as the similarity measure, any two items which appear respectively in only one different transaction has the very large similarity. From this above example, we know that the well-known metric distances are not suitable to describe the similarity between binary data. We must find a suitable similarity measure depicting the relations between items.

Jaccards coefficient, a kind of correlation coefficient, is used to establish similarity between objects described by binary attributes. Due to the very large number of transactions, the computation of Jaccards coefficient between all pairs of items is very expensive. We transform the computation of Jaccards coefficient into computing frequent itemsets.

Definition: If the support of two items x_i and x_j is less than a given minimum support, the similarity between x_i and x_j is 0, otherwise, is the Jaccard coefficient between the two items.

$$\mathrm{Sim}(x_i,x_j) = \begin{cases} 1 & i=j \\ 0 & i \neq j, and \sup(\{x_i,x_j\}) < \mathrm{minsup} \\ \sup(\{x_i,x_j\}) / \sup(x_i)+\sup(x_j)-\sup(\{x_i,x_j\}) & otherwise \end{cases}$$

Let the number of items be m, the space of similarity between two items is O (m^2). Because the number of items is usually at most thousands, the similarity matrix can be stored in memory. Furthermore, only those non-zero similarities need be calculated and stored in memory, which reduce the space capacity.

2.2 similarity between item clusters

In this section, we will discuss several similarity measures between item clusters. Differences between methods arise because of the different ways of defining similarity between item clusters. Several agglomerative hierarchical techniques are proposed based on different similarity measures such as single linkage clustering, complete linkage clustering, average linkage clustering, mean linkage clustering. Because the normal definition of the mean of a cluster is not applicable in transaction database, we adopt another way to get the mean. Let $C=\{x_1,x_2,\ldots,x_i\}$ be a set of items. The SumSim of an item x is defined as the sum of all similarity between x and any other item in C, i.e. $\mathrm{SumSim}(x) = \sum_{x_i \in C, x_i \neq x} \mathrm{Sim}(x,x_i)$. The mean of C is defined as the item $m_i \in C$ such that $\forall x \in C$: $\mathrm{SumSim}(m_i) \geq \mathrm{SumSim}(x)$. A new approach is associate linkage clustering: the similarity between two item clusters is defined as the Jaccard's cofficient between all individuals of the two clusters. Let $C_i=\{x_1,x_2,\ldots,x_i\}$, $C_j=\{x_{i+1},x_{i+2},\ldots,x_{i+j}\}$ be two disjoint item clusters.

$S_{asso}(C_i,C_j) = \sup(\{x_1,x_2,\ldots,x_i,x_{i+1},x_{i+2},\ldots,x_{i+j}\}) / |trans(x_1) \cup trans(x_2) \cup \ldots \cup trans(x_{i+j})| = \dfrac{\sup(\{x_1,x_2,\ldots,x_{i+j}\})}{\sum_{k=1}^{i+j}(-1)^{k+1}\sum_{1\le i_p\le i+j,1\le p\le k}\sup(\{x_{i_1},x_{i_2},\ldots,x_{i_k}\})}$

Because the computation of the support of all subset of $(C_i \cup C_j)$ is time-consuming, and the intra-similarities of C_i and C_j have been calculated in the form level of the hierarchical algorithm, we can simplify the measure as following:

$$S_{asso}(C_i,C_j) = \frac{\sup(C_i \cup C_j)}{\sup(C_i)+\sup(C_i)-\sup(C_i \cup C_j)}$$

3 CITD: Clustering items in transaction database

Problem Statement:

Input: a transaction database $D=\{T_1,T_2,\ldots,T_N\}$ and a set of items $I=\{i_1,i_2,\ldots,i_m\}$ presented in D.

Output: a clustering of $\{C_1,C_2,\ldots,C_k\}$, where C_i is a set of items, satisfying $C_1 \cup C_2 \cup \ldots \cup C_k = I$ and $\forall\, C_i, C_j \in C, C_i \cap C_j = \varnothing$

Step1 Pre-process: Computation all frequent 1-itemset L_1 and 2-itemset L_2 using APRIORI. For all pairs of items contained in L_2, we compute the similarity between them according to definition (1). The similarity of all other item pairs equals to 0. The similarities are stored in a data structure S. After the pre-process, the remaining steps are independent of the origin transaction database.

Step 2 Clustering process: CITD is an agglomerative hierarchical clustering algorithm which starts with the disjoin set of clusters, placing each item in an individual cluster. A heap Q is used to keep every cluster, its closest cluster and the maximum similarity between the cluster and its closest cluster in one entry, and the entries are arranged in the heap in the increasing order of the maximum similarities. Pairs of items or clusters are then successively merged until the similarity of all items cluster is less than a given threshold: minsim. The pair of clusters merged at each step is the ones between which the similarity is the maximum.

The essential step of CITD is to modify the closest cluster and the maximum similarity of every cluster after one merge. It is simple for the first 3 linkages. For S_{mean}, the mean of the new cluster is computed which need compute the SumSim of all items of the new cluster since every item may become the mean of the new merged cluster. If we use S_{asso} as the measure between clusters, the modification method is as following:

$$S_{asso}(A, B) = \frac{\sup(A \cup B)}{\sup(A) + \sup(B) - \sup(A \cup B)}.$$

Since the supports of i-itemsets (i>2) are not computed in the pre-process, and it is expensive to scan the origin transaction database. In CITD, we keep a sample of the origin transaction database which can be stored in memory. The value of the support of an itemset can be evaluated by scanning the sample. In this case, the support of every cluster at each level is also stored in memory.

4 CTTD: Clustering Transactions in Transaction Database

In this section, we propose a two-step clustering on transactions. In the local clustering, transactions are partial clustered into subclusters in each partition which can be stored in memory. The distance between transactions is defined as the Jaccard's coefficient. In the global clustering, each subcluster is represented as the frequent items in it. The distance between sunclusters is defined as the Jaccard's coefficient of the frequent items of the subclusters.

Step 1 Partition: divide the transaction database D into n partitions, each partition can be stored in memory, i.e., $D = \{D_1, D_2, \ldots, D_n\}$

Step 2 Local clustering: input each partition D_i,(i=1,...,n) in turn and process partial clustering it in memory. The distance between two transactions is defined as:

$$\mathrm{dist}(T_i, T_j) = 1 - \frac{|T_i \cap T_j|}{|T_i \cup T_j|}.$$

In this step, we can use hierarchical clustering algorithm or k-medioid clustering algorithm such as CLARANS. In the former, the maximum distance of the merged clusters is used as the termination condition and different number of suclusters can be obtained from different partition. In the later, a same subcluster number k is given for each partition. Assuming the number of subclusters in D_i is i_j, the result of local clustering in D_i is a set of subclusters $\{I_{i1}, I_{i2}, \ldots, I_{ii_j}\}$. After every partition is processed, the whole database D is transformed into a set of subclusters: $\{ I_{ij} \mid i=1,\ldots,n,\ j=1,\ldots,i_j\}$. We denoted them as $\{I_1, I_2, \ldots, I_n\}$ where $n = \sum_{i=1}^{n} i_j$. Since each partition is stored in memory, local clustering is processed very efficiently.

Step 3 Global clustering: calculate the frequent itemsets of each subclusters. Each subcluster is represented as the frequent itemsets in it. Assuming the frequent itemsets of subclusters I_i is L_i, the distance between two clusters is defined as:

$$dist(I_i, I_j) = 1 - \frac{|L_i \cap L_j|}{|L_i \cup L_j|}.$$

In order to compute the distance efficiently, we restrict the computation of frequent itemsets on only frequent 1-itemsets and 2-itemsets, i.e., $L_i = L^1{}_i \cup L^2{}_i$. The frequent itemsets of each subcluster are calculated when the subcluster exists in memory in the first step so that another scan of the database is saved. As the local clustering, we can also use hierarchical clustering algorithms or k-medioid clustering algorithms such as CLARANS. After local clustering, the number of subclusters taken part in global clustering is much less than that of the origin database. So the efficiency of global clustering on subclusters is much higher than direct clustering on the origin database D.

5 Conclusion and Future Work

Clustering items or transactions in transaction databases can find potential useful patterns to improve product profit. Most traditional clustering algorithms that use distance or vector product methods between points for clustering are not appreciate for transaction data. In this paper, we first study the problem of clustering items in transaction databases. Future work includes expanding the algorithm to incremental environment and catagorical attributes database. In addition, there often exist hierarchical concepts of the items in a transaction database. Discovery the clustering of items on multi-level concepts is a meaningful task.

Reference

[AMS 96] Agrawal R., Mannila H., Skrikant R.: Fast Discovery of Association Rules, in Advances in Knowledge Discovery and data Mining (editors: Fayyad U. M. et. al.,), chapter 12, pp307-328, AAAI/MIT Press,1996

[EKSX 96] Ester M., Kriegel H.-P, Sander J., Xu X.: A Density-Based Algorithm for Discovering Clusters in Large Spatial Databases with Noise, Proceedings of the 2nd International Conference on Knowledge Discovery and Data Mining, Portland, Oregon, AAAI Press, 1996

[GRK 98] Guha S., Rastogi R., Shim K., CURE: An Efficient Clustering Algorithm for Large database, ACM Multimedia 1995, pp361-362

[HKK 98] Han E., Karypis G., Kumar V.: Hypergraph Based Clustering in High-Dimensional Data Sets: A Summary of Results Bulletin of the IEEE Computer Society Technical Committee on Data Engineering, 1998, pp15-22

[KR 90] Kaufman K L., Rousseeuw P.J., Finding Groups in Data: An Introduction to Cluster Analysis, John Wiley & Sons, 1990

[NH 94] Ng R., Han J.: Efficient and Effective Clustering Methods for Spatial Data Mining, Proceedings of the 20th International Conference on Very Large Databases, Santiago, Chile, Morgan Kaufmann, 1994, pp144-155

[WSB 98] Weber R., Schek H.-J., Blott S.: A Quantitative analysis and Performance Study for Similarity-search Methods in High-Dimensional Spaces, Proceedings of the 24th International Conference on VLDB, New York, USA, 1998, pp194-205

Chapter 5
Parallel Algorithms I

PARALLEL PROCESSING TO ACCELERATE CONVERGENCE OF RELAXATION SOLUTIONS OF INTEGRAL-DIFFERENTIAL-ALGEBRAIC EQUATIONS

ZU-LAN HUANG, RICHARD M. M. CHEN AND YAO-LIN JIANG

School of Creative Media, City University of Hong Kong, Hong Kong

Email: *richard.chen@cityu.edu.hk*,

In this paper we study the convergence performance of relaxation-based algorithm for linear integral-differential-algebraic equations (IDAEs) by a parallel approach. A parallel decoupling technique to speed up the convergence of the relaxation-based algorithms is derived.. This novel technique is suitable for implementation of parallel processing for complicated systems of IDAEs. Factors taking effect on the performance of parallel processing are discussed in detail. Large numerical examples running on a network of IBM RS/6000 SP2 system are given to illustrate how judicious partitionings of matrices can help improve convergence in parallel processing.

1 Introduction

We consider the relaxation solution of the following system of linear integral-differential-algebraic equations (IDAEs), which often arises from circuit simulation or other engineering fields:

$$\begin{cases} D\int_0^t \mathbf{x}(\tau)d\tau + \begin{bmatrix} M & 0 \\ 0 & 0 \end{bmatrix} \frac{d\mathbf{x}}{dt}(t) + \begin{bmatrix} A & B \\ C & N \end{bmatrix} \mathbf{x}(t) = \mathbf{f}(t), \\ \mathbf{x}_1(0) = (\mathbf{x}_1)_0, \qquad t \in [0,T] \end{cases} \tag{1}$$

where $D \in \mathbf{R}^{n \times n}$, $M, A \in \mathbf{R}^{n_1 \times n_1}$, $B \in \mathbf{R}^{n_2 \times n_2}$, $C \in \mathbf{R}^{n_2 \times n_1}$ and $N \in \mathbf{R}^{n_2 \times n_2}$ such that M and N are nonsingular matrices in which $n = n_1 + n_2$, t is a time variable, $[0, T]$ is a given finite time interval, $\mathbf{f}(t) = [\mathbf{f}_1(t), \mathbf{f}_2(t)]^t \in \mathbf{R}^n$ is a known input function and $\mathbf{x}(t) = [\mathbf{x}_1(t), \mathbf{x}_2(t)]^t \in \mathbf{R}^n$ is to be computed, where $\mathbf{x}_1(t), \mathbf{f}_1(t) \in \mathbf{R}^{n_1}$ and $\mathbf{x}_2(t), \mathbf{f}_2(t) \in \mathbf{R}^{n_2}$ for any given $t \in [0,T]$, and $(\mathbf{x}_1)_0 \in \mathbf{R}^{n_1}$ is a consistent initial value. In this paper the symbol "t" on the upper right corner of a matrix stands for the transposition operation of the matrix.

Since System (1) consists of integral, differential, and algebraic parts, it is quite general. For example, if we let $D = 0$ then it becomes a system of linear differential-algebraic equations (DAEs). On the other hand, if the algebraic part of System (1) does not exist, that is, the matrices B, C, N and the function $f_2(t)$ are nil, then it is a system of linear integral-differential equations (IDEs). Furthermore, it is obvious that System (1) also includes linear algebraic equations (AEs) and linear ordinary differential equations (ODEs) as its special cases.

Waveform relaxation (WR) or dynamic iteration methods are presented to simulate MOS VLSI circuits [10]. They suite for parallel processing implementations. The convergence theories of the WR methods for ODEs and DAEs have been proposed [4, 5, 10]. Some acceleration techniques of the WR method for ODEs and DAEs, for example, the Krylov's subspace method and convolution-based Chebyshev method had also been reported recently [4, 7].

However, the WR solution of a system described by linear IDAEs has been rarely considered to the best of our knowledge. Currently, the general convergence condition of the WR method and a novel idea to improve the corresponding convergence performance for IDAEs are provided in [6]. In this paper a decoupling technique will be presented, incorporated with concrete large dimensional examples, to show the parallel effects of the relaxation-based algorithm. Further, some important and critical issues in parallel implementation of the technique will be discussed. Finally, a numerical example with dimensions $80{,}000\times 80{,}000$ on a 24-processor IBM RS/6000 system is given to illustrate how the judicious partitioning of matrices can enhance the acceleration properties of the iterative algorithm.

The paper is organized as follows. In Section 2, the convergence conditions of the continuous-time and discrete-time WR for System (1) are presented. In Section 3, a parallel decoupling technique to accelerate the convergence of the WR solution for System (1) is given. In Section 4, we concern with the common issues in parallel computation. Numerical experiments will be provided in Section 5. Conclusion is included in Section 6.

2 Waveform Relaxation

The general form of the WR method with initial guess $\mathbf{x}^{(0)}(\cdot)$ for System (1) is

$$\begin{cases} D_1\int_0^t \mathbf{x}^{(k)}(\tau)d\tau + \begin{bmatrix} M_1 & 0 \\ 0 & 0 \end{bmatrix}\dfrac{d\mathbf{x}^{(k)}}{dt}(t) + \begin{bmatrix} A_1 & B_1 \\ C_1 & N_1 \end{bmatrix}\mathbf{x}^{(k)}(t) = D_2\int_0^t \mathbf{x}^{(k-1)}(\tau)d\tau \\ \qquad + \begin{bmatrix} M_2 & 0 \\ 0 & 0 \end{bmatrix}\dfrac{d\mathbf{x}^{(k-1)}}{dt}(t) + \begin{bmatrix} A_2 & B_2 \\ C_2 & N_2 \end{bmatrix}\mathbf{x}^{(k-1)}(t) + \mathbf{f}(t), \\ \mathbf{x}_1^{(k)}(0) = (\mathbf{x}_1)_0, \qquad t\in[0,T], \qquad k = 1, 2, \ldots \end{cases} \tag{2}$$

where $D = D_1 - D_2$, $M = M_1 - M_2$, $A = A_1 - A_2$, $B = B_1 - B_2$, $C = C_1 - C_2$ and $N = N_1 - N_2$ in which M_1 and N_1 are nonsingular matrices and $\mathbf{x}^{(k)}(t) = [\mathbf{x}_1^{(k)}(t), \mathbf{x}_2^{(k)}(t)]^T$ in which $\mathbf{x}_1^{(k)}(t) \in \mathbf{R}^{n_1}$ and $\mathbf{x}_2^{(k)}(t) \in \mathbf{R}^{n_2}$ for any $t \in [0,T]$.

Usually one takes the Jacobi or Gauss-Seidel form to split the matrices in System (1) to set up the iterative process. These partitionings result in the iterative algorithm (2) in which the unknown k-th iteration can be more easily solved than the original system (1). In general, partitionings of matrices can be completely arbitrary. The question is whether or not there is a partitioning such that the iterative process will converge. The following theorem [6] states the convergent condition.

Theorem 1: The waveform relaxation solution of System (1) according to the partitioning of (2) will converge if both spectral radii of $M_1^{-1}M_2$ and $N_1^{-1}N_2$ are less than 1, which can be expressed as

$$\rho(M_1^{-1}M_2)<1 \text{ and } \rho\left(N_1^{-1}N_2\right)<1 \tag{3}$$

This result is analogues to discretized equations. For brevity, we discuss only the p-step constant stepsize BDF method approximating the WR method (2). The BDF method is sufficiently robust for the analysis of the continuous-time case, as long as the discretization errors are less than the iteration errors. It consists of replacing $\frac{d\mathbf{x}^{(l)}}{dt}(t)(l=k,k-1)$ by the derivative of a polynomial which interpolates the computed solution at p+1 time points $t_n, t_{n-1}, \dots, t_{n-p}$, i.e., $\frac{1}{h}\sum_{j=0}^{n-1} a_j \mathbf{x}_{n-j}^{(l)}$ $(l=k,k-1)$ where h is the time-step and a_j $(j=0,1,\dots,p)$ are the coefficients of a BDF method. We also replace $\int_0^t \mathbf{x}^{(l)}(\tau)d\tau$ by $h\sum_{j=0}^{n-1}\mathbf{x}_{n-j}^{(l)}$ at time point $t_n\left(l=k,k-1\right)$.

The discrete-time form of the WR method (2) is

$$\begin{cases} hD_1\sum_{j=0}^{n-1}\mathbf{x}_{n-j}^{(k)} + \frac{1}{h}\sum_{j=0}^{p} a_j \begin{bmatrix} M_1 & 0 \\ 0 & 0 \end{bmatrix}\mathbf{x}_{n-j}^{(k)} + \begin{bmatrix} A_1 & B_1 \\ C_1 & N_1 \end{bmatrix}\mathbf{x}_n^{(k)} = hD_2\sum_{j=0}^{n-1}\mathbf{x}_{n-j}^{(k-1)} + \\ \qquad \frac{1}{h}\sum_{j=0}^{p} a_j \begin{bmatrix} M_2 & 0 \\ 0 & 0 \end{bmatrix}\mathbf{x}_{n-j}^{(k-1)} + \begin{bmatrix} A_2 & B_2 \\ C_2 & D_2 \end{bmatrix}\mathbf{x}_n^{(k-1)} + \mathbf{f}_n, \\ n=p,p+1,\dots,p', \qquad k=1,2,\dots \end{cases} \tag{4}$$

where $\mathbf{f}_n = \left[\mathbf{f}_1(t_n), \mathbf{f}_2(t_n)\right]^T$ and for any $k \geq 1$ the values $\mathbf{x}_n^{(k)}$ are known for n=0, 1, …, p-1, and the values $\mathbf{x}_n^{(k)}$ are unknown for $n=p,p+1,\dots,p'$ where $t_{p'}=T$.

The convergence condition of System (4) is described in the following theorem (see also [5])

Theorem 2: For a small enough time-step h, the discrete-time waveform relaxation iterative process (4) always converges if Condition (3) is satisfied.

When one uses WR to numerically solve a large system on a time interval [0,T], the interval should be broken into smaller pieces, which are usually called "windows", in order to improve convergence [10].

3 A Technique to Accelerate Convergence

3.1 A Comparison Criterion of Convergence Rate

From Condition (3) we know that the convergence of the relaxation-based algorithm is mainly dependent on the partitioning of M and N. We may simplify the analysis by letting $A_1=0$, $B_1=0$, $C_1=0$, and $D_1=0$ in the WR method (2). Then, the iterative processes will purely consist of ODEs and AEs which are independent of each other at each iteration k.

Let us first state a comparison theorem on partitioning of matrices. Let H be a real $n \times n$ matrix. A partitioning $H = P - Q$ is called regular if $P^{-1} \geq 0$ and $Q \geq 0$, and called weak regular if $P^{-1} \geq 0$ and $P^{-1}Q \geq 0$. Here $R \geq 0\ (R > 0)$ for a matrix R means all its elements are nonnegative (positive). It is well known for a regular partitioning $H = P - Q$: " $H^{-1} \geq 0$ if and only if $\rho(P^{-1}Q) < 1$ " [9]. L. Elsner has established the following comparison theorem in [3]:

Theorem 3: Let $H^{-1} \geq 0$ and $H = P_1 - Q_1 = P_2 - Q_2$ be weak regular partitionings. Then, $\rho(P_1^{-1}Q_1) \leq \rho(P_2^{-1}Q_2)$ if one of the following cases occurs

a) $Q_1 \leq Q_2$;

b) $P_1^{-1} \geq P_2^{-1}, Q_1 \geq 0$;

c) $P_1^{-1} \geq P_2^{-1}, Q_2 \geq 0$.

Further, if $H^{-1} > 0$ and $H = P_1 - Q_1 = P_2 - Q_2$ are regular partitionings, then $\rho(P_1^{-1}Q_1) < \rho(P_2^{-1}Q_2)$ as long as $0 \leq Q_1 \leq Q_2$ where $Q_1 \neq 0$ and $Q_1 \neq Q_2$.

3.2 A Decoupling Technique

For general circuits, the point-wise Jacobi and point-wise Gauss-Seidel methods will converge if M and N are strictly or irreducibly diagonally dominant. Most circuit matrices are of this type. Unfortunately their convergence is often slow, because the spectral radii of their iteration matrices are frequently close to one. Block Jacobi and block Gauss-Seidel methods can tackle the problem. But for circuits which contain tightly coupled nodes and/or strong feedbacks they still converge slowly [2].

Now in the time domain we apply a partitioning algorithm, which was originally derived to solve large static linear AEs [1], to speed up the convergence of the WR method. This new approach attempts to make the spectral radii $\rho(M_1^{-1}M_2)$ and $\rho(N_1^{-1}N_2)$ in Condition (3) small. It is a parallel approach, which leads to savings in computer runtime. It also reduces computer memory requirement for transient analysis of a large system.

For every iteration k we consider the ODEs in the simplified WR method (2). For the sake of clarity, we may write the equations as

$$M_1 \frac{d\mathbf{x}_1^{(k)}}{dt}(t)=\mathbf{g}_1^{(k-1)}(t),\quad \mathbf{x}_1^{(k)}(0)=(\mathbf{x}_1)_0,\, t\in[0,T] \tag{5}$$

From the above comparison theorem, if one allows M_1 to contain large and remote off-diagonal elements which represent the corresponding tightly coupling nodes and/or strong feedbacks among subcircuits, the spectral radius of the iterative matrix may become small in some situations.

Let M be of the form

$$\begin{bmatrix} M_{11} & M_{12} & \dots & M_{1r} \\ M_{21} & M_{22} & \dots & M_{2r} \\ \dots & \dots & \dots & \dots \\ M_{r1} & M_{r2} & \dots & M_{rr} \end{bmatrix}$$

Consider a partitioning $M = M_1 - M_2$ in which M_1 contains all M_{ii} $(i = 1, \dots, r)$ and some of the off-diagonal elements, which may represent either tightly coupling nodes and/or strong feedbacks. Let $(M_1)_{ij}$ be the matrix in M_1 corresponding to M_{ij} in M. In practice, M is very sparse, so most of the off-diagonal matrices $(M_1)_{ij}$ $(i \neq j)$ in M_1 are null matrices of dimensions $k_i \times k_j$. The remaining elements of M are contained in M_2 at the similar positions as in M but with opposite sign.

Let $\mathbf{x}_1^{(k)}(t)=[x_1^1(t),\dots x_1^r(t)]^t$ and $\mathbf{g}_1^{(k-1)}(t)=[g_1^1(t),\dots,g_1^r(t)]^t$ where $x_1^i(t)$ and $g_1^i(t)$ are k_i vector functions for simplicity, because the partitioning is applied for every iteration k. Also let $[x_1^1(0),\dots,x_1^r(0)]^t = [(x_1^1)_0,\dots,(x_1^r)_0]^t = (\mathbf{x}_1)_0$. Thus, for $t\in[0,T]$, the i-th subcircuit equation of Eq.(5) can be written as

$$(M_1)_{ii}\frac{d\mathbf{x}_1^i}{dt}(t)+J^i\frac{d\mathbf{z}^i}{dt}(t)=\mathbf{g}_1^i(t),\quad \mathbf{x}_1^i(0)=(\mathbf{x}_1^i)_0,\quad t\in[0,T] \tag{6}$$

where J^i is a matrix of dimensions $k_i \times l_i$ obtained by deleting the zero columns of $[(M_1)_{i,1},\dots,(M_1)_{i,i-1},(M_1)_{i,i+1},\dots,(M_1)_{i,r}]$ and $\mathbf{z}^i(t)$ is and l_i vector function obtained from $\mathbf{x}_1^{(k)}(t)$ by retaining the elements corresponding to the columns of J^i.

The solution of Eq. (6) is

$$\mathbf{x}_1^i(t)=-(M_1)_{ii}^{-1}J^i\mathbf{z}^i(t)+\tilde{\mathbf{x}}^i(t),\qquad t\in[0,T] \tag{7}$$

where

$$\tilde{\mathbf{x}}^i(t)=\left[(\mathbf{x}_1{}^i)_0+(M_1)_{ii}^{-1}J^i\mathbf{z}^i(0)\right]+(M_1)_{ii}^{-1}\int_0^t\mathbf{g}_1^i(s)ds,\qquad t\in[0,T] \tag{8}$$

Further, $\tilde{\mathbf{x}}^i$ satisfies the following initial value problem:

$$\begin{cases}(M_1)_{ii}\dfrac{d\tilde{\mathbf{x}}^i}{dt}(t)=\mathbf{g}_1^i(t), \\ \tilde{\mathbf{x}}^i(0)=(\mathbf{x}_1^i)_0+(M_1)_{ii}^{-1}J^i\mathbf{z}^i(0), \qquad t\in[0,T]\end{cases} \tag{9}$$

where $\mathbf{z}^i(0)$ is a known l_i vector obtained from $(\mathbf{x}_1)_0$ by retaining the elements corresponding to J^i. Thus, all items on the right hand side of Eq. (8) are known except $\mathbf{z}^i(t)$.

Define a m_1-vector function $\mathbf{z}(t)$ whose elements consist of all elements of $\mathbf{z}^i(t)$ $(i=1,\dots,r)$, without any duplication in terms of the elements of $\mathbf{x}_1^{(k)}(t)$. Since Eq. (7) is actually a system of AEs, we take the approach in [1] to solve it.

For $t\in[0,T]$, let the μ-th element of $\mathbf{z}(t)\left(1\le u\le m_1\le \min\left\{\sum_{i=1}^r l_i, n_1\right\}\right)$ be the α-th element of $\mathbf{x}_1^q(t)$ where $1\le q\le r$ and $1\le\alpha\le l_q$ and also be the β-th element of $\mathbf{z}^p(t)$ where $1\le p\le r$ and $1\le\beta\le l_p$, namely

$$(\mathbf{z}(t))_\mu=(\mathbf{x}_1^q(t))_\alpha=(\mathbf{z}^p(t))_\beta,\qquad t\in[0,T] \tag{10}$$

Observing Eq. (7) and Eq. (10), we can establish a relationship between the elements of $\mathbf{z}(t)$. That is

$$\mathbf{z}(t)=H\mathbf{z}(t)+\mathbf{w}(t),\qquad t\in[0,T] \tag{11}$$

where H is a matrix of dimensions $m_1\times m_1$ and is an m_1-vector function. Both H and $\mathbf{w}(t)$ can be expressed explicitly as in the following form.

Let us denote $E^i=-(M_1)_{ii}^{-1}J^i\,(i=1,\dots,r)$ in Eq. (7). Let $(\mathbf{z}(t))_{\mu_1}$ and $(\mathbf{z}(t))_{\mu_2}$ be the two distinct elements of $\mathbf{z}(t)$ for $t\in[0,T]$. According to Eq. (7) and Eq. (10), we have

$$(\mathbf{z}(t))_{\mu_1}=(\mathbf{x}_1^q(t))_\alpha=\sum_{\beta=1}^{l_q}(E^q)_{\alpha\beta}(\mathbf{z}^q(t))_\beta+(\mathbf{x}^q(t))_\alpha,\qquad t\in[0,T] \tag{12}$$

and for some p and β

$$(\mathbf{z}(t))_{\mu_2}=(\mathbf{z}^p(t))_\beta,\qquad t\in[0,T] \tag{13}$$

Viewing that Eq. (12) contains the element $(H)_{\mu_1\mu_2}$ if there is a p such that $p{=}q$. Hence, we may write out two formulae as follows:

$$(H)_{\mu_1\mu_2}=\begin{cases}(E^q)_{\alpha\beta}, & \text{for } p=q \text{ and } \mu_1\ne\mu_2\\ 0, & \text{otherwise}\end{cases} \tag{14}$$

and

$$(\mathbf{w}(t))_{\mu_1}=(\mathbf{x}^q(t))_\alpha,\qquad t\in[0,T] \tag{15}$$

Solving $\mathbf{z}(t)$ from Eq. (10), we have

$$\mathbf{z}(t)=\left(I_{m_1\times m_1}-H\right)^{-1}\mathbf{w}(t),\qquad t\in[0,T] \tag{16}$$

where $I_{m_1\times m_1}$ is the identity matrix. The matrix $(I_{m_1\times m_1}-H)$ in Eq. (16) is nonsingular because M_1 is a nonsingular matrix. Once $\mathbf{z}(t)$ is calculated from Eq.

(16), all subcircuit solutions can be computed in parallel from Eq. (7) to form $\mathbf{x}_1^{(k)}(t)$ which is the solution of Eq. (6). The resulting matrix H is often sparse.

At each iteration k, the AEs of the relaxation-based algorithm, according to the partitionings given in this section, have the same form as in Eq. (7). The above partition approach can be similarly applied to the AEs in the time domain. Thus, the solution $\mathbf{x}^{(k)}(t)=\left[\mathbf{x}_1^{(k)}(t),\mathbf{x}_2^{(k)}(t)\right]^t$ will be used as known vector function in the WR method studied before to solve for the (k+1)-st iteration unknown $x^{(k+1)}(t)=\left[x_1^{(k+1)}(t),x_2^{(k+1)}(t)\right]^t$.

3.3 An illustrated Example

We give a simple example to illustrate how to concretely solve $\mathbf{z}(t)$ in Eq. (11). The following matrix was emerged from computation of solution of a small RC circuit example in [2].

$$M=\begin{bmatrix} 831 & -5 & & & -800 & \\ -5 & 15.8 & -0.8 & & & \\ & -0.8 & 35.8 & -25 & & \\ & & -25 & 35.8 & -0.8 & \\ -800 & & & -0.8 & 815.8 & -5 \\ & & & & -5 & 15.8 \end{bmatrix}$$

The corresponding unknown is $x_1(t)=\left[v_1(t),v_2(t),\ldots v_6(t)\right]^t$ in $[0,T]$. According to the decoupling technique, we have

$$M_{11}=\begin{bmatrix} 831 & -5 \\ -5 & 15.8 \end{bmatrix},\ M_{22}=\begin{bmatrix} 35.8 & -25 \\ -25 & 35.8 \end{bmatrix},\ M_{33}=\begin{bmatrix} 815.8 & -5 \\ -5 & 15.8 \end{bmatrix}$$

where $x_1^1(t)=\left[v_1(t),v_2(t)\right]^t$, $x_1^2(t)=\left[v_3(t),v_4(t)\right]^t$, $x_1^3(t)=\left[v_5(t),v_6(t)\right]^t$.

Correspondingly, we have

$$J^1=\begin{bmatrix} 0 & -800 \\ -0.8 & 0 \end{bmatrix},\ J^2=\begin{bmatrix} -0.8 & 0 \\ 0 & -0.8 \end{bmatrix},\ \text{and}\ J^3=\begin{bmatrix} -800 & -0.8 \\ 0 & 0 \end{bmatrix}$$

where $\underline{z}^1(t)=\left[v_3(t),v_5(t)\right]^t$, $\underline{z}^2(t)=\left[v_2(t),v_5(t)\right]^t$, and $\underline{z}^3(t)=\left[v_1(t),v_4(t)\right]^t$. Let us write out E^1, E^2, and E^3 in their approximated forms:

$$E^1=\begin{bmatrix} 0.0003 & 0.9645 \\ 0.0507 & 0.3052 \end{bmatrix},\ E^2=\begin{bmatrix} 0.0436 & 0.0305 \\ 0.0305 & 0.0436 \end{bmatrix}\ \text{and}\ E^3=\begin{bmatrix} 0.9825 & 0.0010 \\ 0.3109 & 0.0003 \end{bmatrix}$$

We may also form $\underline{z}(t)=\left[v_1(t),v_2(t),v_3(t),v_4(t),v_5(t)\right]^t$ by the above definition. The numbers of q and α for all μ_1's and p and β for all μ_2's are listed in Tables 1 and 2, respectively.

Table 1. The numbers of q and α for all μ_1's

μ_1	Q	α
1	1	1
2	1	2
3	2	1
4	2	2
5	3	1

Table 2. The numbers of p and β for all μ_2's

p	β	μ_2
1	1	3
1	2	5
2	1	2
2	2	5
3	1	1
3	2	4

Based on these two tables, we can easily determine the elements of the matrix H from the matrices E^1, E^2 and E^3 as follows

$$H = \begin{bmatrix} 0 & 0 & 0.0003 & 0 & 0.9645 \\ 0 & 0 & 0.0507 & 0 & 0.3052 \\ 0 & 0.0436 & 0 & 0 & 0.0305 \\ 0 & 0.0305 & 0 & 0 & 0.0436 \\ 0.9825 & 0 & 0 & 0.0010 & 0 \end{bmatrix}$$

To determine the vector function $\underline{w}(t)$ on $[0,T]$, if we denote that $\psi^2(t)=[\psi_1^2(t),\psi_2^2(t)]^T$ and $\psi^3(t)=[\psi_1^3(t),\psi_2^3(t)]^T$ we then have $\underline{w}(t)=[\psi_1^1(t),\psi_2^1(t),\psi_1^2(t),\psi_2^2(t),\psi_1^3(t)]^T$ based on Table 1. Thus, we can obtain the function $\underline{z}(t)$ for simple example after substituting the matrix H and the vector function $\underline{w}(t)$ into Eq. (11).

4 Parallel Implementation of the Decoupling Technique

4.1 Data Decomposition

Given a processor mesh $P=\{p\in Z^n \mid 0\le p\le w-1\}$, since the size of the original data set is n, it is natural to define the size of each tile by vector $s=n/w$. If the matrix contains diagonal blocks with different sizes, we will label the size of blocks in increased order, and determine the size of each tile by the condition $s-b_i<\sum b_{t_j}\le s$. Here, we denote b_{t_j} as the size of j-th block in tile t, and denote b_i as the size of arbitrary block in the matrix. Under such partitioning, the size of each tile can rest on the average level to ensure load balance among processors.

4.2 Data Communication

To allow the parallel processors to start their parallel computations at each iteration in parallel, they should use the values of the neighbor processors computed in the previous iteration. The unknown set $x(t) \in \mathbf{R}^n$ is a function in time domain. For discrete-time case, assuming the time-step is h in the given time interval $[0,T]$, then each processor needs to receive as many as $n \cdot \frac{T}{h}$ data from neighbor processor at each iteration. Thus, the communication overhead will increase linearly with the size of the system. Not all the results of last iteration are useful for the next computation because the coefficient matrix on right hand is often sparse. The right-hand matrix is also partitioned into some sub-matrices and distributed on the parallel processors. If all elements on a column i of a sub-matrix on right hand side are zero, then we don't care last iterative results of the corresponding unknown $x_i(t)$. We mark such columns in each processor so as to reduce the number of messages per iteration per processor transferred. By experiences, such pre-processing will lead to much saving in communication.

For $i = 1,2, \ldots, p$ Do:
  Compute M_{ii}^{-1}, J^i and determine the values of α and β in Table 1 and Table 2
EndDo
For $k = 1,2,\ldots$ until convergence Do:
    For $i = 1,2, \ldots, p$, Do:
      Solve $V^i(t) = M_{ii}^{-1} \cdot g(t) + M_2 \cdot x_k^i(t)$
      Solve $E^i(t) = -M_{ii}^{-1} \cdot J^i$
    EndDo
    Construct the matrix H and $\underline{\omega}(t)$,   Solve $\underline{z}(t) = (I - H)^{-1}\underline{\omega}(t)$
    For i $= 1,2, \ldots, p$, Do:
      Solve $\psi_i(t)$ according to Eq. (8)
   Solve $x_k^i(t)$ according to Eq. (7)
  EndDo
EndDo

Figure 1. Pseudocode of parallel algorithm for decoupling technique in WR

4.3 Memory and Storage Consideration

The decoupling technique combined with appropriate partitioning of matrix may provide good qualities in decreasing the memory consumption and improving the system performance. A good form suitable for decoupling is a sparse matrix with a few non-zero elements off diagonal. When the matrix is dense, the dimension of H according to Eq. (11) will be very close to that of the original problem. The storage of the matrix H will result in large memory consumption in one processor, and as a consequence, the parallel algorithm of WR method will not be memory-scalable. Thus, under the condition of satisfying the convergent condition, the partitioning of the original system should take into account of this point and ensure the decoupling technique be applied to a relatively sparse matrix. There should be some tradeoff between fast convergence and efficient parallelism.

4.4 *Parallel Algorithm of Decoupling Technique in the WR Method for IDAEs*

Considering the system described in Eq. (5), the parallel algorithm for processor $p \in P$ is shown in Figure 1. The processes written in bold are executed in parallel.

5 A Numerical Example

In this section, we present a numerical example to illustrate the effectiveness of the decoupling technique. The following example has the same form as Eq. (1) in which the matrices D, $\begin{bmatrix} A & B \\ C & N \end{bmatrix}$ and M are

$$D = \begin{bmatrix} 1 & -1 & & & & \\ & 1 & -1 & & & \\ & & 1 & \cdots & & \\ & & & \cdots & -1 & \\ & & & & 1 & -1 \\ & & & & & 1 \end{bmatrix} \in R^{(n_1+n_2)\times(n_1+n_2)} \quad \begin{bmatrix} A & B \\ C & N \end{bmatrix} = \begin{bmatrix} 1 & & & & & \\ \frac{1}{2} & 1 & & & & \\ & \frac{1}{2} & 1 & & & \\ & & \cdots & \cdots & & \\ & & & \frac{1}{2} & 1 & \\ & & & & \frac{1}{2} & 1 \end{bmatrix} \in R^{(n_1+n_2)\times(n_1+n_2)}$$

$$M = \begin{bmatrix} 3 & -1 & & & & & 2 \\ -1.5 & 3 & -1 & & & & \\ & -1.5 & 3 & -1 & & & \\ & & \cdots & \cdots & \cdots & & \\ & & & -1.5 & 3 & -1 & \\ & & & & -1.5 & 3 & -1 \\ -5 & & & & & -1.5 & 3 \end{bmatrix} \in R^{n_1 \times n_1}$$

We would like to mention here that the matrix M has the same form as that produced by boundary elements or the MEI method in the electromagnetic field [8]. The decoupling and parallel implementation reported here are also well suited for this kind of problem.

We let T=2, $x_1(0) = [0, \ldots, 0]^t \in \mathbf{R}^{n_1}$, $f_1(t) = [J(t), 0, \ldots, 0]^t \in \mathbf{R}^{n_1}$ and $f_2(t) = [J(t), 0, \ldots, 0] \in \mathbf{R}^{n_2}$ where $J(t) = 5t (0 \le t \le 0.2)$ and $J(t) = 1 (0.2 \le t \le 2)$. Also let the initial guess $x^{(0)}(\cdot)$ be the zero function on [0,2], the time-step be 0.05, and the error tolerance be 10^{-8}.

The dimensions of the matrices are extensible. Here, we set n_1=79800, n_2=200. Then, we apply four different partitioning methods to the matrix M respectively, to illustrate how judicious partitioning can provide faster convergence.

Method 1 is the point-wise Jacobi partitioning.

Method 2 is the block Jacobi partitioning.

Method 3: M_1 consists of the diagonal blocks, the remote off-diagonal elements 2 and –5 of the matrix M.

Method 4: M_1 consists of the diagonal blocks, the lower triangular elements and the remote off-diagonal element 2 of the matrix M.

In Methods 2, 3 and 4, the dimensions of each partitioned block are set to 200×200. We take the Jacobi partitioning for the matrix N during the computation of each iteration.

The spectral radii of various partitioning methods are given in Table 3. We apply the above partitioning methods to solve the IDAE problem by waveform relaxation. The numbers of iterations of WR corresponding to different partitioning methods are also shown in Table 3.

Table3. The convergence qualities versus various partitioning methods on the matrix M_1

Method	1	2	3	4
$\rho(M_1^{-1}M_2)$	0.9718	1.3142	0.5038	0.2538
Number of Iterations	208	∞	21	8

Compared with the Jacobi partitioning, we observe that if the preconditioner M_1 contains some remote off-diagonal elements of M, the spectral radius of $M_1^{-1}M_2$ will become smaller. And the smaller the value of $\rho(M_1^{-1}M_2)$ is, the better the convergence performance is. The phenomenon is consistent with Theorem 3 in Section 2. We can also learn from this example that judicious partitionings will conduce to great improvement in convergence rate of the system. However, the tightly-coupled elements contained in preconditioner may degrade parallelism of the system. As a solution, our decoupling technique is then introduced to parallelize the problem.

Our parallel algorithm has been implemented on the message passing multi-processors. The language is ANSI C and MPI software is applied for message passing between the processors. The program is run on the 24-processors IBM RS6000/SP2 system. We run the parallel program on different numbers of processors, and get the accurate speedup corresponding to the numbers of processors in use respectively. Here, we would like to mention that during each iteration k, we take Method 4 for partitioning the matrix M and the Jacobi method for partitioning the matrix N. Meanwhile, we also estimate the speedups of the parallel system without consideration of communication between the processors, the work is accomplished by recording the runtime of each episode during sequential processing. The curves of speedups with different numbers of processors are illustrated in Figure 2.

From Figure 2 we observe that speedup of the parallel system increases with the number of processors approximately in a linear trend. The parallel implementation shows good scalability on the size of the system. Moreover, by comparison of the accurate speedups and their corresponding estimated values, we come to the conclusion that the communication overhead of our method is rather low, and the load balancing is reasonable. Thus, the decoupling technique is suitable for parallel processing.

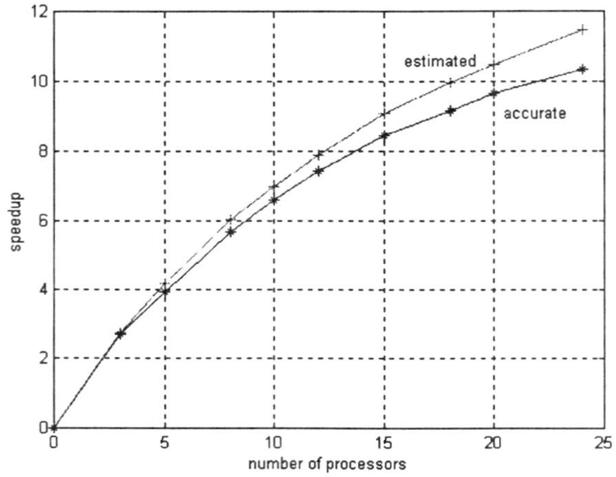

Figure 2. Speedups versus the numbers of participating processors

6 Conclusion

In this paper, we review the convergence condition of the WR method for linear integral-differential-algebraic equations, and put forward a parallel technique in the time domain to decouple the differential and algebraic terms for reducing the spectral radius of certain key matrices in systems. Results of the large numeral example have clearly demonstrated that our technique is not only effective to enhance the convergence rate of the original system, but also appropriate to be utilized on a parallel system.

Acknowledgement

This research was supported by the City University of Hong Kong and Hong Kong Research Grants Council Project 9040268.

References

1. R. M. M. Chen, "Solving a class of large sparse linear systems of equations by partitioning", Proc. 1973 IEEE International Symposium on Circuit Theory, Toronto, Canada (April 1973) pp. 223-226.
2. R. M. M. Chen and X. D. Jia, "A technique to improve the convergence speed of relaxation-based circuit simulations on tightly coupled circuits", Proc.1993 IEEE International Symposium on Circuit and System, Chicago, USA (May 1993) pp. 2133-2136.
3. L. Elsner, "Comparisons of weak regular splittings and multisplitting methods", Numer. Math., vol. 56 (1989) pp. 283-289.
4. Y. L. Jiang, W. S. Luk, and O. Wing, "Convergence-theoretics of classical and Krylov waveform relaxation methods for differential-algebraic equations", IEICE Transactions on Fundamentals of Electronics, Communications and Computer Sciences, vol. E80-A, no. 10 (October 1997) pp. 1961-1972.
5. Y. L. Jiang and O. Wing, "Monotone waveform relaxation for systems of nonlinear differential-algebraic equations", SIAM J. Numerical Analysis, vol. 38, no. 1 (2000) pp. 170-185.
6. Y. L. Jiang, R. M. M. Chen, and O. Wing, "Improving convergence performance of relaxation-based transient analysis by matrix splitting in Circuit Simulation", research paper to be published.
7. A. Lumsdaine, M. W. Reichelt, J. M. Ssquyres, and J. K. White, "Accelerated waveform methods for parallel transient simulation of semiconductor devices", IEEE Trans. on CAD of IC and Sys., vol. 15, no. 7 (July 1996) pp. 716-726.
8. K. K. Mei, R. Pous, Z. Chen, Y. W. Liu, and M. D. Prouty, "The measured equation of invariance: a new concept in field computations", IEEE Trans. On Antennas and Propagation, vol. 42, no. 3 (1994) pp. 322-328.
9. R. S. Varga, "Matrix iterative analysis", Academic Press, New York (1962).
10. J. K. White and A. Sangiovanni-Vincentelli, "Relaxation Techniques for the Simulation of VLSI Circuits", Kulwer Academic Publishers, Boston (1986).

Parallel Algorithms for Vector Median Filtering

Chin-Hsiung Wu
Department of Information Management, Chinese Naval Academy, Kaohsiung, Taiwan, R. O. C.

Shi-Jinn Horng , Yuh-Rau Wang
Department of Electrical Engineering, National Taiwan University of Science and Technology, Taipei, Taiwan, R. O. C.
E-mail: horng@mouse.ee.ntust.edu.tw

Lih-Gwo Jeng
Department of Information Management, Chinese Naval Academy, Kaohsiung, Taiwan, R. O. C.

Abstract

In this paper, we design three fast and flexible parallel algorithms for vector median filtering on the arrays with reconfigurable optical buses (AROB). In the sense of the product of time and the number of processors used, the proposed algorithms are cost or time optimal.

Key Words– parallel algorithm, vector median filter, reconfigurable optical bus system.

1 Introduction

The vector median filter (VMF) [2] is a well known technique in vector-valued image and signal processing, since it is invariant to scale and bias. It has been proved to be a highly effective tool for removing impulse noise from color images without degrading image contours [11]. Color images may be processed using vector median filter, where pixel values are treated as vector quantities rather than as separate components.

Given a two-dimensional (2-D) vector-valued image $A = a(i,j)$, $0 \leq i,j < N$, each pixel with d components $a_0(i,j), \cdots, a_{d-1}(i,j)$, $d \geq 1$, the vector median filtering operation is to replace the noisy pixel from image A by one of its neighbors within a neighborhood of that pixel. Usually, the neighborhood of a specified pixel is established using a $W \times W$ window centered at that pixel, where $W = 2w + 1$ is an odd number.

[a]This work was partially supported by the National Science Council under the contract no. NSC-89-2213-E011-007.

The vector median filter may be evaluated as follows. For each pixel $a(p,q)$, $0 \leq p,q < W$, within a specified window, the following sums of distances must be computed

$$S(p,q) = \sum_{k=0}^{W-1} \sum_{l=0}^{W-1} \|a(p,q) - a(k,l)\|, \tag{1}$$

where $\|a(p,q) - a(k,l)\|$ is the norm (or distance) between the two pixels. The norm may be measured on the basis of any L_α metric for $0 \leq \alpha < \infty$. Since the vector median filters based on Euclidean distance (L_2-norm) are rotation invariant, the distances are computed on the basis of L_2-norm in this paper. The pixel which yields the minimum value of S is selected as the vector median $vm(p,q)$ used at the corresponding pixel position in the filtered image. That is, the vector median of window $\mathcal{W} = \{a(p+k, q+l) \mid (-w \leq k, l \leq w)\}$ is the pixel $vm(p,q) \in \mathcal{W}$ such that

$$S_{vm} = \min\{S(p+k, q+l),\ -w \leq k, l \leq w\}. \tag{2}$$

The main drawback of vector median filters is their high computational complexity. Assume that each pixel contains constant components (i.e., d is a constant). A straightforward sequential algorithm for vector median filtering takes $O(N^2W^4)$ time. Previously, several fast algorithms for 1-norm vector median filtering were proposed [3,6]. Astola *et al.* [2] proposed an $O(WN)$ time algorithm for 1-D vector median filtering. They used $W-1$ distance computing elements (DCE) to calculate the pairwise distance. Angelopoulos and Pitas [1] proposed an $O(W^4)$ time mesh algorithm for vector median filtering using N^2 processors. They also examined the performance of the proposed algorithm on the MPP machine. In this paper, we will develop more efficient and fast algorithms for vector median filtering on the AROB model.

The array with a reconfigurable optical bus system is defined as an array of processors connected to a reconfigurable optical bus system whose configuration can be dynamically changed by setting up the local switches of each processor. More recently, two related models have been proposed, namely the array with reconfigurable optical buses (AROB) [9] and linear array with a reconfigurable pipelined bus system (LARPBS) [8]. A major difference between them lies in that the counting is allowed in the AROB model during a bus cycle but it is not permitted in the LARPBS model.

The main contribution of this paper is in designing fast and efficient algorithms for computing the vector median filtering on an AROB. We first develop two optimal basic operations for integer summation and shifting data matrix on an AROB model. Then using these operations, we design three efficient and scalable parallel algorithms for the vector median filtering problem on the AROB model. Our algorithms run in $O(W^4 \log W/p^4)$, $O(\frac{W^4N^2}{p^4q^2} \log W)$ and $O(1)$ times using $p^4N^2/\log W$, $p^4q^2/\log W$ and $W^4N^2 \log N$ processors, respectively. In the sense of the product of time and the number of processors used, the first two results are cost optimal and the last one is time optimal.

The rest of this paper is organized as follows. We give a brief introduction to the AROB model in Section 2. Section 3 describes some basic operations. We develop the efficient vector median filtering algorithms in Section 4. Finally, some concluding remarks are included in the last section.

2 The Computational Model

The AROB model is essentially a mesh using the basic structure of a classical reconfigurable network (RN) [4] and optical buses. The linear AROB (LAROB or 1-D AROB) extends the capabilities of the 1-D APPB by permitting each processor to connect to the bus through a pair of switches. Each processor with a local memory is identified by a unique index denoted as P_i, $0 \leq i < N$, and each switch can be set to either cross or straight by the local processor. The optical switches are used for reconfiguration. If the switches of one of the connected processors are set to cross, then the LAROB will be partitioned into two independent sub-buses, each of them forms an LAROB. Each processor uses a set of control registers to store information needed to control the transmission and reception of messages by that processor. An example for an LAROB of size 5 is shown in Figure 1(a). Two interesting switch configurations derivable from a processor of an LAROB are also shown in Figure 1(b).

A 2-D AROB of size $M \times N$, denoted as 2-D $M \times N$ AROB, contains $M \times N$ processors arranged in a 2-D grid. Each processor is identified by a unique 2-tuple index (i_1, i_0), $0 \leq i_1 < M$, $0 \leq i_0 < N$. The processor with index (i_1, i_0) is denoted by P_{i_1,i_0}. Let $P_{i_1,\,*}$ denote the i_1th row, where $*$ represents all indexes along the i_1th row. For example, $P_{1,\,*}$ is equivalent to $P_{1,\,i_0}$, $0 \leq i_0 < N$. Each processor has four I/O ports, denoted by E, W, S and N to be connected with a reconfigurable optical bus system. The interconnection among the four ports of a processor can be reconfigured during the execution of algorithms. Thus, multiple arbitrary linear arrays like LAROB can be specified in a 2-D AROB. The two *terminal* processors which are located in the end points of the constructed LAROB may serve as the *leader* processors (similar to P_0 in Figure 1(a)). The related position of any processor on a bus to which it is connected is its distance from the *leader* processor. For more details on the AROB, see [9].

A 2-D AROB model can be extended to a 3-D AROB model with two extra ports, U and D, for the communications of the neighboring processors in the

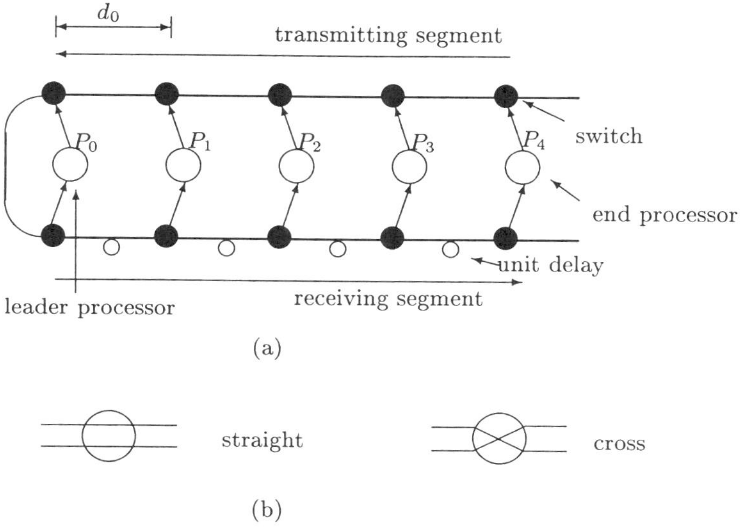

Figure 1: (a) An LAROB of size 5. (b) The switch states.

third dimension. For a 3-D AROB of size $M \times N \times L$, each processor is identified by a unique 3-tuple index $(i_2,\ i_1,\ i_0)$, $0 \leq i_0 < M,\ 0 \leq i_1 < N,\ 0 \leq i_2 < L$. The processor with index $(i_2,\ i_1,\ i_0)$ is denoted by $P_{i_2,\ i_1,\ i_0}$.

3 Basic Data Manipulation Operations

Conceptually, a 3-D $W^4 \times N \times N$ AROB may partition into W^2 AROBs, denoted $SA_{\alpha W+\beta}$, $0 \leq \alpha, \beta < W$, each of size $W^2 \times N \times N$; each $SA_{\alpha W+\beta}$ consists of W^2 layers, denoted by $\mathcal{M}_{\alpha W^3+\beta W^2+k}$, $0 \leq k < W^2$, each of size $N \times N$; each $\mathcal{M}_{\alpha W^3+\beta W^2+k}$ consists of $\frac{N^2}{W^2}$ blocks each of size $W \times W$, denoted by $B_{s,t}$, $0 \leq s, t < \frac{N}{W}$. Without loss of generality, assume that W is a factor of N and $W \ll N$. To make the algorithm presentation more comprehensible, the previous results which had been proposed on the AROB are summarized in the following.

Lemma 1 [7] *Given N integers or normalized real numbers each of size $O(\log N)$-bit, these N numbers can be added by the bus split technique in $O(\log N)$ time on an LAROB using N processors.*

Lemma 2 [8] *Given N numbers each of size $O(\log N)$-bit, the maximum (minimum) of these N numbers can be found either in $O(\log \log N)$ time on an*

LAROB using N processors, or in $O(1)$ time on an AROB using $N^2/2$ processors.

Lemma 3 [10] *Given N numbers each of size $O(\log N)$-bit, these N numbers can be added in $O(1)$ time on an $N \times \log N$ AROB.*

If the number of processors available in the system is p, $1 \leq p \leq N$, then each processor contains an array with $O(N/p)$ data items to be processed. Therefore, Lemmas 1 and 2 can be modified to run on an AROB using p processors. Assume that data item a_i, $0 \leq i < N$, is stored in the local variable $a(i \bmod p)[\lfloor i/p \rfloor]$ of processor $P_{i \bmod p}$, i.e., processor P_j holds data items a_j, $a_{j+p}, \cdots, a_{j+N-p}$. The summation operation can be performed as follows. Each processor first sums up the $O(N/p)$ numbers stored in its local memory sequentially. This takes $O(N/p)$ time. Then, apply Lemma 1 to sum up these p partial sums in $O(\log p)$ time. Thus, the summation operation can be done in $O(N/p + \log p)$ time on an LAROB using p processors. Especially, if $p = N/\log N$, then the time complexity is $O(\log N)$. The maximum (minimum) operation can also be done in $O(N/p)$ time on an LAROB with p processors by the similar method. Thus, we have the following lemmas.

Lemma 4 *Given N integers or normalized real numbers each of size $O(\log N)$-bit, these N numbers can be added in $O(N/p + \log p)$ time on an LAROB using p processors.*

Lemma 5 *Given N numbers each of size $O(\log N)$-bit, the maximum (minimum) of these N numbers can be found in $O(N/p)$ time on an AROB using p^2 processors.*

3.1 Shift

Let $A = a_{i,j}$, $0 \leq i,\ j < N$, be a data matrix of size $N \times N$ stored in the local variable $a(i,\ j)$ of a 2-D $N \times N$ AROB. Also let x and y be a pair of vertical and horizontal displacements. The 2-D shift is defined to circularly shift all data elements of A to up and left by x and y positions relatively to the original matrix A. That is, for a fixed pair of displacements x and y, $0 \leq x,\ y < N$, move $a(i,\ j)$, $0 \leq i,\ j < N$, to $a'((i - x) \bmod N,\ (j - y) \bmod N)$. For example, if $x = 2$ and $y = 3$, then $a(2,\ 3)$ is moved to $a'(0,\ 0)$. The detailed 2-D shift algorithm (2DSA) is shown in the following.

Procedure 2DSA$(a,\ x,\ y,\ a')$

1: // Rotate all data elements up by x positions. //

Processor $P_{i,\ j}$, $0 \leq i, j < N$, copies $a(i,\ j)$ to $ax((i - x) \bmod N, j)$, through the i_1-dimensional bus.

2: // Rotate all data elements to the left by y positions. //

Processor $P_{i,\ j}$, $0 \le i,j < N$, copies $ax(i,\ j)$ to $axy(i,\ (j-y) \bmod N)$, through the i_0-dimensional bus.

3: Processor $P_{i,\ j}$, $0 \le i,j < N$, copies $axy(i,\ j)$ to $a'(i,\ j)$.

Procedure 2DSA can be easily verified to run in $O(1)$ time for each step. We have the following lemma.

Lemma 6 *Procedure 2DSA can be computed in* $O(1)$ *time on a 2-D* $N \times N$ *AROB.*

Next, we will perform the 3-D shift. consider a 3-D $W^4 \times N \times N$ AROB with W^4 layers ($\mathcal{M}_0\tilde{}\mathcal{M}_{N^4-1}$), each layer of size $N \times N$. Let the data matrix A be stored in the local variable $a(0,i,j)$ of the first layer (i.e., $\mathcal{M}_0$). Also let x and y, $0 \le x,\ y < W$, be a pair of vertical and horizontal displacements relative to A, respectively. The 3-D shift is defined to circularly shift the data elements of A located on $\mathcal{M}_0$ up and left by x and y positions and then store them on SA_{xW+y} (i.e., $\mathcal{M}_{xW^3+yW^2+z}$, $0 \le z < W^2$). That is, for each pair of displacements x and y, $0 \le x,\ y < W$, move $a(i,\ j)$ located on $\mathcal{M}_0$, $0 \le i,\ j < N$, to $a'(xW^3 + yW^2 + z,\ (i-x) \bmod N,\ (j-y) \bmod N)$ located on $\mathcal{M}_{xW^3+yW^2+z}$, $0 \le x,\ y < W$ and $0 \le z < W^2$. Following the idea of procedure 2DSA, this operation can be also run in $O(1)$ time; the detailed 3-D shift algorithm (3DSA) is listed below.

Procedure 3DSA$(a,\ a')$

1: Processor $P_{i_2,\ i,\ j}$, $0 \le i,\ j < N$, broadcasts $a(0,\ i,\ j)$ to $a(k,\ i,\ j)$, $0 \le k < W^4$, through the i_2-dimensional buses.

2: For each SA_{xW+y}, $0 \le x,\ y < W$, call 2DSA$(a,\ x,\ y,\ a')$.

Lemma 7 *Procedure 3DSA can be computed in* $O(1)$ *time on a 3-D* $W^4 \times N \times N$ *AROB. Initially, the data matrix, A, is stored in the local variable* $a(0,\ i,\ j)$ *of* $\mathcal{M}_0$ *for all* $0 \le i,j < N$.

3.2 Inversion

Let D be a sparse data matrix of size $W^4 \times N \times N$, stored in the local variable $d(xW^3+yW^2, sW, tW)$ of the block $B_{s,t}$ of the $\mathcal{M}_{xW^3+yW^2}$ of a 3-D $W^4 \times N \times N$ AROB, $0 \le x,\ y < W$, $0 \le s,\ t < \frac{N}{W}$. The 3-D inversion is a reverse circular shift up and shift left operation. It is defined to move the data elements $d(xW^3 + yW^2,\ sW,\ tW)$, $0 \le s,\ t < \frac{N}{W}$, located at the block $B_{s,t}$ of the $\mathcal{M}_{xW^3+yW^2}$ back to $d'(0,\ (sW + x) \bmod N,\ (tW + y) \bmod N)$ located at the block $B_{s,t}$ of $\mathcal{M}_0$. Note that 3-D inversion is the inverse operation of procedure 3DSA, so that it can be done in $O(1)$ time as that of procedure 3DSA.

Lemma 8 *The 3-D inversion can be done in $O(1)$ time on a 3-D $W^4 \times N \times N$ AROB.*

4 Parallel Vector Median Filtering Algorithms

Given an $N \times N$ image $A = a(i,j)$, $0 \le i,\ j < N$, and a $W \times W$ window, the vector median filtering problem is to find the pixel, where the sum of distances between it and the others inside the filter window is the minimum, and the filter window moves over all pixels of the input image. Since the window is centered at each specified pixel, the image is shifted wraparoundly down and right by w positions. Then, the result $vm(i,j)$ of each window operation is stored in a location corresponding to the top-left corner of the window. That is, the result of median filtering $vm(i,j)$, $0 \le i,j < N$, is computed as follows. For each window whose top-left corner is $a(i,j)$, $0 \le i,j < N$, first compute the sum of distances for every pixel within the window from it to all the other pixels inside the window as:

$$\begin{aligned} & S(i+c, j+d) \\ &= \sum_{k=0}^{W-1} \sum_{l=0}^{W-1} \|a((i+c) \bmod N, (j+d) \bmod N) - a((i+k) \bmod N, (j+l) \bmod N)\|, \\ & 0 \le c, d < W. \end{aligned} \tag{3}$$

Then, find the minimum among these sums by setting

$$m(i,j) = \min\{S(i+c, j+d),\ 0 \le c, d < W\}. \tag{4}$$

Finally, the pixel whose sum is the minimum is the vector of this window. That is, set

$$vm(i,j) = a((i+c) \bmod N,\ (j+d) \bmod N),\ 0 \le c, d < W, \tag{5}$$

where $S(i+c, j+d)$ is the minimum (i.e., $S(i+c, j+d) = m(i,j)$).

Assume that the value of a pixel of the image is an $O(\log N)$-bit integer in the following. In the remainder of this section, we will develop several efficient parallel algorithms for vector median filtering on the AROB based on the number of processors available in the system. To implement Eqs. (3)-(5) on a 3-D AROB of size $W^4 \times N \times N$, we redefine the coordinates of the image in the following. Let the $N \times N$ image consist of $\frac{N}{W} \times \frac{N}{W}$ subimages each of size $W \times W$, denoted by $SI_{s,\ t}$, $0 \le s,\ t < \frac{N}{W}$. Without loss of generality, assume that W is a factor of N. Our algorithms can be easily extended for the general case when the shape of the image is not square. Then for each pair of the vertical and horizontal displacements x and y of each subimage $SI_{s,\ t}$, the sum of distances specified in Eq. (3) can be reformulated as

$$\begin{aligned} &S(sW+x+c,tW+y+d) \\ &= \sum_{k=0}^{W}\sum_{l=0}^{W}\left\| \begin{matrix} a((sW+x+c) \bmod N,(tW+y+d) \bmod N) \\ -a((sW+x+k) \bmod N,(tW+y+l) \bmod N) \end{matrix} \right\|, \end{aligned} \tag{6}$$

where $0 \le s,t < \frac{N}{W}$, and $0 \le c,d,x,y < W$.

As stated in Eqs. (3)-(5), there are N^2 vector medians to be computed. Considering a 3-D $W^4 \times N \times N$ AROB, it can be viewed as W^2 AROBs each of size $W^2 \times N \times N$, denoted by SA_{xW+y}, $0 \le x,y < W$; each SA_{xW+y} can be further viewed as $\frac{N}{W} \times \frac{N}{W}$ subAROB each of size $W^2 \times W \times W$, denoted by $SSA_{s,t}$, $0 \le s,t < \frac{N}{W}$. Each $SSA_{s,t}$ is responsible for a vector median computing. Thus, there are N^2 subAROBs to compute these N^2 vector medians. That is, $SA_{xW+\ y}$ is responsible for computing $vm(sW+x,tW+y)$ specified in Eq. (5), $0 \le s,t < \frac{N}{W}$, and $0 \le x,y < W$. In order to let these N^2 subAROBs compute Eq. (3) in parallel, we must shift the image pixel to their corresponding subAROBs (i.e., $a'(xW^3+yW^2+z,sW,tW) = a((sW+x) \bmod N,(tW+y) \bmod N)$. It means that for a specified subAROB $SSA_{x,\ y}$ with a fixed pair of displacements x and y, Eqs. (3)-(5) can be reformulated as

$$S(i_2,sW,tW) = \sum_{k=0}^{W-1}\sum_{l=0}^{W-1} \|a'(i_2,sW+\alpha,tW+\beta) - a'(i_2,sW+k,tW+l)\|, \tag{7}$$

where $i_2 = xW^3+yW^2+\alpha W+\beta$ and $0 \le \alpha,\beta < W$.

$$m(xW^3+yW^2,sW,tW) = \min\{S(xW^3+yW^2+\alpha W+\beta,sW,tW),\ 0 \le \alpha,\beta < W\}. \tag{8}$$

$$vm(xW^3+yW^2,sW,tW) = a'(xW^3+yW^2,sW+\alpha,tW+\beta), \tag{9}$$

where $S(xW^3+yW^2+\alpha W+\beta,sW,tW)$ is the minimum (i.e., $S(xW^3+yW^2+\alpha W+\beta,sW,tW) = m(xW^3+yW^2,sW,tW)$).

Based on Eqs. (7)-(9), the high level description of vector median filtering on a 3-D AROB is specified by the following three steps. First, shift the image pixels located at $\mathcal{M}_0$ to its corresponding AROBs according to the specified x and y displacements. Then, all subAROBs compute the vector medians simultaneously. Finally, the results of all subAROBs are moved back to their corresponding positions of $\mathcal{M}_0$. Assume that the image is initially stored in the local variables $a(0,i,j)$, $0 \leq i,\ j < N$, of a 3-D $W^4 \times N \times N$ AROB. Finally, the result is stored in the local variable $vm(0, sW+x,\ tW+y)$ of a 3-D $W^4 \times N \times N$ AROB, where x and y are a pair of displacements of each subimage $SI_{s,\ t}$. The detailed algorithm (VMFA) is listed in the following.

Algorithm VMFA $(a,\ vm)$

1: // Since the window is centered at each specified pixel, the image is shifted wraparoundly down and right by w positions. //

Call 2DSA$(a,\ -w,\ -w,\ a')$.

2: **Call** 3DSA$(a',\ a'')$.

3: Compute the vector median on each subAROB according to Eqs. (7)-(9).

3.1: For each block, compute Eq. (7) using Lemma 1.

3.2: For each subAROB, compute Eq. (8) using Lemma 2.

3.3: For each subAROB, find the vector median according to Eq. (9).

4: Move the vector medians located on each subAROB back to $\mathcal{M}_0$ using Lemma 8.

Theorem 1 *Algorithm VMFA can be computed in $O(\log W)$ time on a 3-D $W^4 \times N \times N$ AROB, where $W < N$.*

Proof: The correctness of this algorithm directly follows from Eqs. (7)-(9) and Lemmas 1-8. Steps 3.1-3.3 are used to implement Eqs. (7)-(9) for computing a subAROB. For computing Eq. (7), processor $P_{xW^3+yW^2+\alpha W+\beta,\ sW+\alpha,\ tW+}$ first copies $a'(xW^3+yW^2+\alpha W+\beta,\ sW+\alpha,\ tW+\beta)$ to all processors on its block (i.e., to another array variable named as $a''(xW^3+yW^2+\alpha W+\beta,\ sW+c,\ tW+d)$, $0 \leq c,d < W$ on processor $P_{xW^3+yW^2+\alpha W+\beta,\ sW+c,\ tW+d}$); then, processor $P_{xW^3+yW^2+\alpha W+\beta,\ sW+c,\ tW+d}$ computes the distance between $a''(xW^3+yW^2+\alpha W+\beta,\ sW+c,\ tW+d)$ and $a'(xW^3+yW^2+\alpha W+\beta,\ sW+c,\ tW+d)$; finally, each block sums up these W^2 distances. Since there are N^2 subAROBs, all N^2 vector medians can be correctly computed by the proposed algorithm. The time complexity is analyzed as follows. Steps 1, 2 and 4 each take $O(1)$ time by Lemmas 6, 7 and 8, respectively. Step 3.1 takes $O(\log W)$ time by Lemma 1. Step 3.2 takes $O(1)$ time by Lemma 2. Step 3.3 takes $O(1)$ time. Hence, the total time complexity is $O(\log W)$. *Q.E.D.*

Next, we will derive a scalable and cost optimal algorithm from Algorithm VMFA. If the number of processors available in the system is p^4N^2, then each processor holds an array with $O(\frac{W^4}{p^4})$ data to be processed. Without loss of generality, assume that p is a factor of W. Our algorithms can be easily extended for the general case while the shape of the image is not square. Thus, a 3-D AROB of size $p^4 \times N \times N$ consists of p^2 AROBs each of size $p^2 \times N \times N$, denoted by SA_{xp+y}, $0 \leq x, y < p$; each SA_{xp+y} can be further viewed as $\frac{N}{W} \times \frac{N}{W}$ subAROB each of size $p^2 \times W \times W$, denoted by $SSA'_{s,t}$, $0 \leq s, t, < \frac{N}{W}$. Each subimage $SI_{s,\ t}$, $0 \leq s,\ t < \frac{N}{W}$, also consists of $\frac{W}{p} \times \frac{W}{p}$ blocks, denoted by $B_{u,\ v}$, $0 \leq u, v < \frac{W}{p}$, each of size $p \times p$. In this case, we can use the SA_{xp+y} to compute the vector median for each pair of displacements x and y of each specified subimage $SI_{s,\ t}$. That is, we can compute one group of each subimage $SI_{s,\ t}$ at the $(u \cdot \frac{W}{p} + v)$th iteration. In order to let these p^2 AROBs compute the vector medians in parallel, we must shift the image pixels to its corresponding AROB, respectively. That is, shift the image pixels of each block $B_{u,\ v}$ to their corresponding SA_{xp+y} such that each processor of the SA_{xp+y} stores the image pixels up by x vertical displacement and left by y horizontal displacement corresponding to the original image pixels located on the $\mathcal{M}_0$ layer.

Based on Eqs. (7)-(9), each block $B_{u,\ v}$ of each subimage $SI_{s,\ t}$ can be computed at the $(u \cdot \frac{M}{p} + v)$th iteration by the following three steps. First, shift the image pixels located on the $\mathcal{M}_0$ to its corresponding SA_{xp+y} according to the specified x and y displacements. Then, each block computes the vector medians simultaneously. Finally, the results of each block$(vm(xp^3 + yp^2, sW, tW))$ are moved back to their corresponding positions of the $\mathcal{M}_0$. Repeating this process for each group of each subimage from left to right and then up to down, we can compute all vector medians. Assume that the image is initially stored in the local variables $a(0,\ sW + u,\ tW + v)$, $0 \leq s,\ t < \frac{N}{W}$, $0 \leq u,\ v < W$, of a 3-D $p^4 \times N \times N$ AROB. Finally, the result is stored in the local variable $vm(0,\ sW + up + x,\ tW + vp + y)$ of a 3-D $p^2 \times N \times N$ AROB.

Since each $SSA'_{s,t}$ is responsible for a vector median computing; totally, there are $\frac{N^2}{W^2}p^2$ vector medians to be computed at an iteration. Therefore, it requires $\frac{W^4}{p^4}$ iterations to compute the N^2 vector medians. Furthermore, if the number of processors available in the system is $p^4N^2/\log W$, then each processor holds an array with $O(\frac{W \log W}{p})$ data to be processed. Therefore, the summation operations used in Steps 3.1 of algorithm VMFA should be run in $O(\log W)$ using $p^4N^2/\log W$ processors applying Lemma 4; the minimum operation used in Step 3.2 of algorithm VMFA should be run in $O(\log\log W)$ time applying Lemma 2. This implies that the time complexity of algorithm VMFA becomes $O(\frac{W^4}{p^4} \log W)$, but the number of processors is reduced by a factor of $O(\log W)$ and the proposed algorithm is cost optimal.

Similarly, if the number of processors available in the system is p^4q^2, then each processor holds an array with $O(\frac{W^4N^2}{p^4q^2})$ data to be processed. Without loss of generality, assume that q is a factor of N and $W \leq q \leq N$. For this case, the 3-D shift operation can be done in $O(\frac{W^4N^2}{p^4q^2})$ using the pipelined optical buses. Since each SA contains only $p^2 \times q \times q$ processor, we can compute $\frac{p^2q^2}{W^4}$ vector medians at each iteration. By repeating Step 3 of algorithm VMFA for $\frac{N^2}{q^2}$ times, each SA can compute $\frac{p^2N^2}{W^4}$ vector medians. Since we have p^2 SAs, $\frac{p^4N^2}{W^4}$ vector medians can be computed. After repeating Step 3 of algorithm VMFA for $\frac{W^4}{p^4}$ times, all N^2 vector medians can be computed. Based on the divide-and-conquer technique as stated above, algorithm VMFA can be modified to run efficiently. This leads to the following result.

Theorem 2 *Algorithm VMFA can be computed in $O(\frac{W^4N^2}{p^4q^2}\log W)$ time on a 3-D $p^4 \times q \times q/\log W$ AROB, where $W \leq q \leq N$.*

On the other hand, a constant time algorithm for vector median filtering can be also derived. By increasing the number of processors a few used to the parallel algorithm, algorithm VMFA can be easily modified to run more efficiently. The time complexity of the proposed algorithm is dominated by computing the sum of distances and finding the minimum as shown in Steps 3.1 and 3.3 of algorithm VMFA, respectively. The summation of the $W \times W$ distances of each window can be computed in $O(1)$ time by Lemma 3, and the minimum of each window can be found by Lemma 2. Hence, the total time complexity of the modified algorithm can be reduced from $O(\log W)$ to $O(1)$ by increasing the number of processors from W^4N^2 to $W^4N^2\log N$.

5 Concluding Remarks

In this paper, fast and flexible algorithms for vector median filtering are proposed. To the best of our knowledge, this is the first constant time vector median filtering algorithm to be developed on any parallel computational models. Compared to other previous results as shown in Table 1.

References

1. G. Angelopoulos and I. Pitas, Two-dimensional vector median filters on mesh connected computers, in *Proc. Int. Conf. Image Processing*, pp. 650–653, 1994.
2. J. Astola, P. Haavisto and Y. Neuvo, Vector median filters, *Proceedings of the IEEE* **78**, No. 4(1990), 678-689.

Table 1: Summary of comparison results for parallel vector median filtering algorithms.

Algorithm	*Architecture*	*Processor*	*Time Complexity*
Astola *et al.* [2]	mesh	$W \times W$	$O(W^2N^2)$
Angelopoulos and Pitas [1]	mesh	$N \times N$	$O(W^4)$
This paper	AROB	$p^4 \times N \times N/\log W$	$O(W^4 \log W/p^4)$
		$p^4 \times q \times q/\log W$	$O(W^4N^2 \log W/p^4q^2)$
		$W^4 \times N \times N/\log W$	$O(\log W)$
		$W^4 \times N \times N \times \log N$	$O(1)$

3. M. Barni, A fast algorithm for 1-norm vector median filter, *IEEE Trans. Image Processing* **6**, No. 10(1997), 583-586.
4. Y. Ben-Asher, D. Peleg, R. Ramaswami, and A. Schuster, The power of reconfiguration, *Journal of Parallel and Distributed Computing* **13**, (1991), 139–153.
5. Z. Guo, R. G. Melhem, R. W. Hall, D. M. Chiarulli, and S. P. Levitan, Pipelined communications in optically interconnected arrays, *Journal of Parallel and Distributed Computing* **12**, No. 3 (1991), 269–282.
6. L. Lucat and P. Siohan, Vector-median type filters and fast-computation algorithms, in *Proc. Int. Symp. Circuits and Systems*, pp. 2469-2472, 1997.
7. R. Miller, V. K. P. Kumar, D. Reisis, and Q. F. Stout, Image computations on reconfigurable VLSI arrays, in *Proc. IEEE Computer Society Conf. Computer Vision and Pattern Recognition*, pp. 925-930, 1988.
8. Y. Pan and K. Li, Linear array with a reconfigurable pipelined bus system— concepts and applications, *Information Sciences – An International Journal* **106**, (1998), 237-258.
9. S. Pavel and S. G. Akl, On the power of arrays with reconfigurable optical bus. in *Proc. Int. Conf. Parallel and Distributed Processing Techniques and Applications*, pp. 1443-1454, 1996.
10. S. Pavel and S. G. Akl, Matrix operations using arrays with reconfigurable optical buses. *Parallel Algorithms and Applications* **8**, (1996), 223-242.
11. J. Zheng, K. P. Valavaris and J. M. Gaugh, Noise removal from color images, *Journal of Intelligent Robotic Systems* **7**, (1993), 257-285.

PARALLELIZING SYNCHRONOUS DATA-FLOW GRAPHS VIA RETIMING

TIMOTHY W. O'NEIL
Dept. of Comp. Sci. & Eng., University of Notre Dame, Notre Dame, IN 46556, USA
E-mail: toneil@cse.nd.edu

EDWIN H.-M. SHA
Dept. of Comp. Science, Erik Jonsson School of Eng. & C.S., Box 830688, MS EC 31, Univ. of Texas at Dallas, Richardson, TX 75083-0688, USA
E-mail: esha@cse.nd.edu

SISSADES TONGSIMA
High Perf. Comp. Lab., Nat'l Electronics & Comp. Tech. Center, 11th Floor Bangkok Thai Tower Bldg., 108 Rangnam Road, Phyathai, Rachathewee, Bangkok 10400, THAILAND
E-mail: stongsim@hpcc.nectec.or.th

Many common iterative or recursive DSP applications can be represented by synchronous data-flow graphs (SDFGs). A great deal of research has been done attempting to optimize such applications through retiming. However, despite its proven effectiveness in transforming single-rate data-flow graphs to equivalent DFGs with smaller clock periods, the use of retiming for attempting to reduce the execution time of synchronous DFGs has never been explored. In this paper, we do just this. We develop the basic definitions and results necessary for expressing and studying SDFGs. We review the problems faced when attempting to retime a SDFG in order to minimize clock period, then present an algorithm for doing this. Finally, we demonstrate the effectiveness of our method on several examples.

1 Introduction

Since the most time-critical parts of DSP applications are loops, we must explore the parallelism embedded in the repetitive pattern of a loop. One of the most useful models for representing DSP applications has proven to be the *multirate* or *synchronous data-flow graph* (*SDFG*) first proposed by Lee [1]. The nodes of a SDFG represent functional elements, while edges between nodes represent connections between them. Each node consumes and produces a predetermined fixed number of *delays* (i.e., data tokens) on each invocation. Additionally, each edge may contain some initial number of delays. This model has proven popular with designers of signal processing programming environments [2] with its use leading to numerous important results regarding the scheduling [3], hierarchization [4], vectorization [5] and multiprocessor allocation [1] of DSP programs.

A great deal of research has been done attempting to optimize various aspects of an application's execution by applying various graph transformation techniques to the application's SDFG. One of the more effective of these techniques is *retiming* [6, 7], where delays are redistributed among the edges so that hardware is optimized while the application's function remains unchanged. Retiming was initially applied to single-rate DFGs to optimize the application's schedule of tasks so that the *clock period* of the graph (i.e., the total computation time of the longest zero-delay path) was decreased in order for the application to be more efficiently scheduled for execution on multiprocessors [8]. It was later extended to the more general SDFG model in order to extend vectorization capabilities [9] or minimize the total delay count of a SDFG [10]. However, the problem of using retiming to minimize the clock period of a multirate DFG has remained unexplored. In this paper, we will discuss this problem and propose a method for accomplishing this task.

In addition to its ability to reduce clock period, scheduling alone typically yields a schedule requiring more resources than the schedule produced by retiming first. (Both of these ideas are elaborated upon in [11].) While the benefits are clear, reworking our retiming methods so that they may be applied to synchronous graphs is not easy. The difference between the single-rate and multi-rate models lies in the specification of production and consumption rates on each edge; in single-rate graphs all such rates are assumed to be the same, whereas different rates for different edges are typically specified when constructing SDFGs. Two pitfalls were noted in [12]. First of all, a retiming may be derived for a single-rate DFG by solving a linear programming problem [7]. The introduction of rates on the edges potentially changes this to a more complicated integer linear programming problem. Second, the introduction of rates invalidates the traditional results regarding the delay counts of paths and cycles, depriving us of many useful results derived for the single-rate case. Specifically, in the single-rate case, we seek to remove zero-delay path with excessive total computation times. It isn't clear what we want to avoid in the multi-rate case; a specific delay count on one path may or may not be adequate, depending on what rates have been specified.

Finally, the most popular method for retiming SDFGs has been to translate the SDFG to its single-rate equivalent, retime this new graph, then translate back [10,13]. There are two problems with this idea. First, as we will demonstrate, it may be impossible to translate a retimed single-rate graph back to a retimed SDFG. Second, even if this method works, the costs in performing the necessary translations and dramatically increasing our problem size may be prohibitive. It is clearly preferable to work with the original SDFG as much as possible.

In this paper, we will develop the basic definitions and results necessary for specifying and manipulating a SDFG and its single-rate equivalent. We will review retiming and point out the problems which arise when it is applied to SDFGs. We will propose a polynomial-time algorithm which retimes a given SDFG to have a specified clock period. Finally, we will demonstrate the effectiveness of our algorithm by applying it to several examples.

In the next section, we will formalize the fundamental concepts related to the study of synchronous data-flow graphs. We then discuss retiming and the problems we face as we apply it to SDFGs. Next is our retiming algorithm, followed by a detailed example. Finally, we summarize our work and point to future directions for study.

2 Synchronous Data-Flow Graphs

The concept of a synchronous data-flow graph was developed and used extensively by Lee and Messerschmitt [1], but was not rigorously defined until the work of Zivojnovic *et al* [10, 14]. In this section, we review their definitions and ideas in order to formalize these concepts.

2.1 Basic Definitions

A *synchronous data-flow graph* (*SDFG*) (sometimes called a *multirate* or *regular* data-flow graph) is a finite, directed, weighted graph $G = \langle V, E, d, t, p, c \rangle$ where: V is the vertex set of nodes or *actors*, which transform input data streams into output streams; $E \subseteq V \times V$ is the edge set, representing channels which carry data streams; $d : E \to \mathbf{N} \cup \{0\}$ is a function with $d(e)$ the number of initial tokens (*delays*) on edge e; $t : V \to \mathbf{N}$ is a function with $t(v)$ the execution time of node v; $p : E \to \mathbf{N}$ is a function with $p(e)$ the number of data tokens produced at e's source node to be carried by e; and $c : E \to \mathbf{N}$ is a function with $c(e)$ the number of data tokens consumed from e by e's sink node. (In this definition $\mathbf{N}$ is the set of natural numbers $\{1, 2, 3, ...\}$.) If $p(e) = c(e) = 1$ for all $e \in E$, we say that G is a *homogeneous data-flow graph* (*HDFG*). HDFGs are also sometimes referred to as *single-rate data-flow graphs* or simply *data-flow graphs*.

To illustrate, consider the SDFG given in Figure 1(a) below. The numbers above the nodes represent the execution times for the individual tasks, while the smaller numbers at either end of an edge denote tokens produced or consumed. As an example, $t(A) = 2$ while $t(B) = t(C) = 1$ in the figure. Furthermore, the numbers at either end of the edge connecting A and B indicate that node A produces one token on this edge when it executes, while node B consumes two tokens from this edge each time it fires.

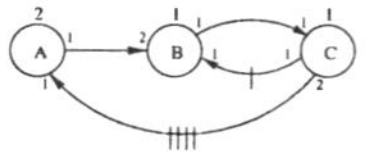

(a)

$$M = \begin{pmatrix} 1 & -2 & 0 \\ 0 & 1 & -1 \\ 0 & -1 & 1 \\ -1 & 0 & 2 \end{pmatrix}$$

(b)

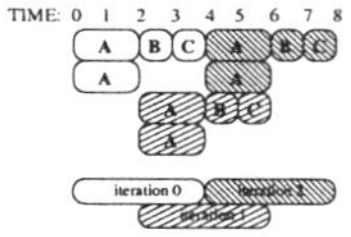

(c)

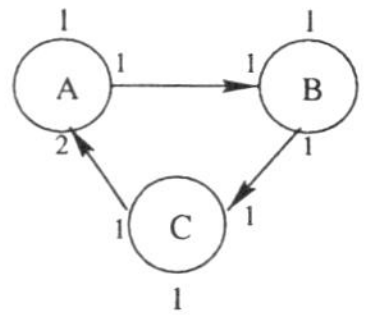

(d)

Figure 1: (a) A SDFG; (b) Its topology matrix; (c) Its repeating schedule; (d) An inconsistent SDFG

It is sometimes useful to characterize an SDFG by its *topology matrix*, an $|E| \times |V|$ matrix similar to an incidence matrix. Each row corresponds to one edge in the graph, while each column corresponds to a node. A positive $(i, j)^{th}$ entry in the topology matrix indicates the number of tokens produced by the jth node on the ith edge, while a negative entry here gives the number of tokens consumed by node j from edge i. All other entries are zero. As an example, the topology matrix of Figure 1(a) is given in Figure 1(b).

In [1] it was demonstrated that a repeating sequential schedule can be constructed for a SDFG G if the rank of the graph's topology matrix is one less than the number of nodes in the SDFG. (The reverse is not necessarily true, as we will see shortly.) If this condition holds there is a positive integer vector q in the nullspace of the topology matrix called a *repetition vector* for G. The repetition vector for G with the smallest norm is called the *basic repetition vector* (*BRV*) for G [15]. For example, the BRV for the SDFG in Figure 1(a) is $q = \begin{bmatrix} 2 & 1 & 1 \end{bmatrix}^T$. The elements of a BRV q indicate that q_j copies of node v_j must be executed during every iteration of the static schedule. In our example we must schedule two copies of A and one copy each of B and C each time; see Figure 1(c). Finally, a SDFG is *consistent* if it has a BRV. An example of an inconsistent SDFG with rank 3 topology matrix appears as Figure 1(d). It is clear that, if we attempt to execute this circuit, each node will fire once before node A deadlocks the system waiting for its second token.

2.2 *Constructing an Equivalent HDFG*

In order to study an SDFG, it is sometimes useful to create its *equivalent homogeneous data-flow graph (EHG)*. As the name implies, an EHG performs the same function as the original SDFG, but is constructed so that each edge carries at most one token. Since each node is expecting to either produce or consume more data than this, an EHG compensates by inserting multiple edges between nodes.

An algorithm for creating a graph's EHG appears in [11]. It is adapted from the method of [15] for constructing the EHG of *cyclostatic* DFGs, which not only permit multiple tokens to pass along edges but also specifies the pattern of their production or consumption. The algorithm first creates enough copies of each node to satisfy the specifications of the BRV. It then inserts edges. If nodes in a SDFG are connected by a zero-delay edge, then the first data token produced by the first copy of the source must be consumed by the first copy of the sink in the EHG. If there are delays on an edge, the data contained here is consumed first, so that the first new token produced is in fact needed by a later copy of the sink. The algorithm determines which copies of source and sink to map to one another based on how much data has been created and used. As an example of our algorithm in action, the EHG of Figure 1(a) appears in Figure 2(a).

There are two significant differences between our algorithm and that of [15]. First, the original algorithm was more concerned with making sure that the amount of data produced and consumed on an edge matched. This yields a simpler but more confusing graph. For purposes of clarity, we do not combine edges between nodes. If multiple tokens are to be sent between nodes in the EHG, each travels along its own edge. One benefit is that the delay counts between the original SDFG and the EHG match in our model. More significantly, the original algorithm also inserted control dependencies into the EHG, insuring that all copies of a node execute serially. Since we are concerned with maximizing parallelism, we concern ourselves only with the necessary data dependencies.

Finally, as derived in [15], we will say that a SDFG is *live* if its EHG has no zero-weight cycles. Otherwise the graph is *deadlocked*. An example of a consistent deadlocked graph appears as Figure 2(b), with its EHG in Figure 2(c). As we can see, the loop between nodes A and B_2 contains no delays, and so it is impossible to schedule them since each must precede the other. It should be clear that a SDFG must be both live and consistent in order for it to have a repeating static schedule.

3 Retiming

A great deal of research has been done attempting to optimize the schedule of an application's tasks after applying various graph transformation techniques to the application's HDFG. One of the more effective of these techniques is *retiming* [6, 7], where delays are redistributed among the edges so that the application's function remains the same while the execution time decreases.

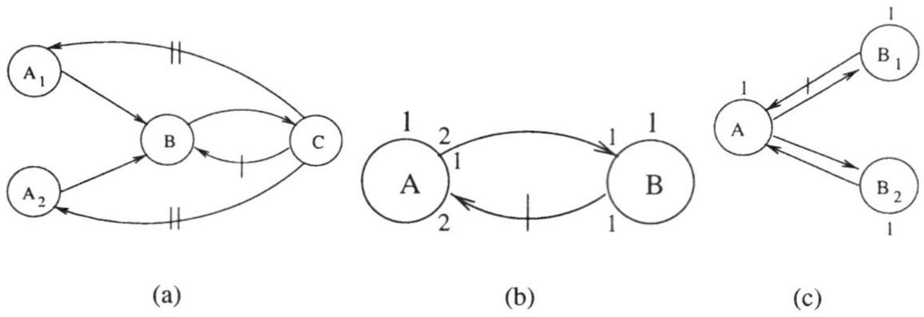

Figure 2: (a) Figure 1(a)'s EHG; (b) A deadlocked SDFG; (c) Its EHG

Despite its usefulness when applied to HDFGs, the application of retiming to SDFGs was explored only marginally prior to 1994 [13, 16] before being studied by Zivojnovic *et al* primarily as a way to minimize the delay count of a SDFG [10, 12]. In this section we intend to review the basics of retiming, explore some of the pitfalls which arise when studying retiming of SDFGs, demonstrate the effectiveness of retiming, and propose two algorithms for retiming SDFGs.

3.1 Basic Definitions

A *path* in either a SDFG or a HDFG is any sequence of nodes and edges. The *clock period* $cl(G)$ of a HDFG G is then defined to be the length of the longest zero-delay path [8]. This definition is problematic on two counts. First, it is not clear what the delay count of a path in a SDFG really is in light of the inconsistencies in the results from [10]. Second, suppose that we attempt to apply our definition directly to SDFGs, as demonstrated by Figure 2(b). We would conclude that the clock period equals 2, but in reality the graph must have an infinite clock period because of the problems scheduling nodes A and B_2. Thus, we are forced to define the clock period of a SDFG to be equal to the clock period of its EHG. As an example, the clock period of the SDFG in Figure 1(a) is 4 by our definition.

Similar problems arise when we attempt to minimize the clock period. We will say that an *iteration* of a SDFG is the execution of all nodes of its EHG once. The average computation time of one iteration is then called the *iteration period* of the SDFG and is equal to the iteration period of the EHG. (In Figure 1(a) the iteration period is also 4.) If a SDFG contains a loop, then the iteration period is bounded from below by the *iteration bound* [17], which is defined to be the maximum time-to-delay ratio of all cycles in the EHG. For example, the EHG in Figure 2(a) contains three loops: (A_1, B, C) and (A_2, B, C) each with total computation time of 4 and delay count 2; and (B, C) with computation time 2 and delay count 1. Thus the iteration period of the graph in Figure 1(a) is 2. This can be clearly seen from the schedule in Figure 1(c), where overlapped iterations create higher throughput. (The iteration period of an SDFG can be overestimated using the ideas from [14] without constructing the EHG, but our method yields a tighter bound, which is important as we attempt to minimize the iteration period of an SDFG next.)

A *retiming* $r : V \rightarrow \mathbf{N} \cup \{0\}$ is a function which specifies a transformation of a graph G. It

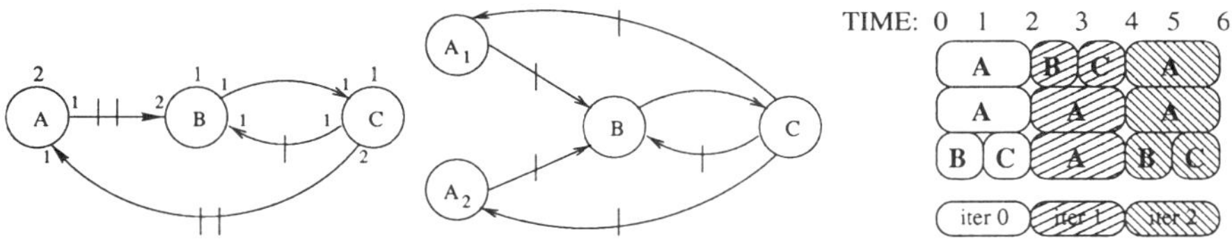

(a) (b) (c)

Figure 3: (a) Figure 1(a) retimed; (b) Its EHG; (c) Its repeating schedule

labels each vertex with a number of delays to be removed from each incoming edge and placed on each outgoing edge, changing G into the retimed graph $G_r = \langle V, E, d_r, t, p, c\rangle$ where $d_r(e) = d(e) + p(e)r(u) - c(e)r(v)$ for each edge $e = (u, v)$ in E [10, 12]. As an example, a retiming with $r(A) = 2$ and $r(B) = r(C) = 0$ transforms the SDFG of Figure 1(a) into that of Figure 3(a). Examining the EHG in Figure 3(b), we see that we have now achieved an optimal clock period of 2 which translates into the more compact schedule of Figure 3(c).

3.2 Problems Retiming EHGs

On first glance, it appears that we should just be able to retime the EHG via traditional methods and then map back to the original SDFG, as was done by Lee originally [13]. Unfortunately, the initial translation from SDFG to EHG is too complex to permit this. As an example, consider the unit-time SDFG given in Figure 4(a), with its EHG appearing in Figure 4(b). A retiming with $r(A) = r(B_1) = 1$ and $r(B_2) = r(C) = 0$ transforms the EHG into the graph shown in Figure 4(c) with clock period 2. We now wish to try and match this with some retimed version of the original SDFG, but have a problem with the delay count of the edge between A and B. If the new delay count is 1, the EHG should have no delay on the edge (A, B_2) and one delay on (A, B_1), exactly the opposite of what we actually have. On the other hand, if the retimed delay count is 2 or more, then both (A, B_1) and (A, B_2) should have non-zero delay counts, which also contradicts what we have. In any case, there can be no direct matching in this case. If we are to retime SDFGs, we must work directly on the original graph itself.

4 Retiming a SDFG

Since we cannot retime a SDFG by working with its EHG, we must develop methods for retiming the SDFG directly. In this section we refine the methods of [7] to deal with this situation.

4.1 Initial Problems

Unfortunately, the retiming algorithms we will propose will either be pessimistic or expensive. The reason for this is that the original methods we are using as a basis were themselves built on one result from [7]:

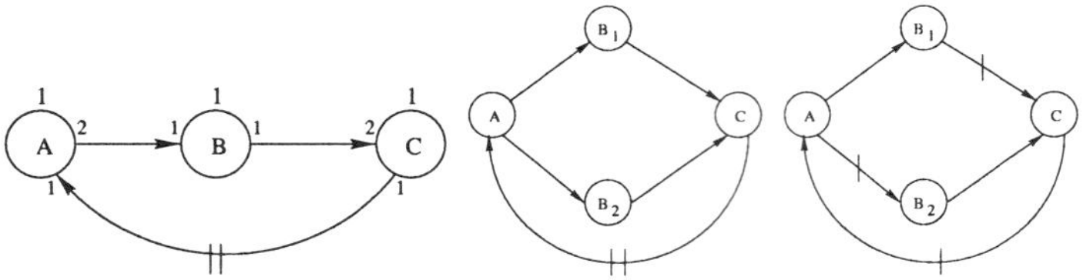

(a) (b) (c)

Figure 4: (a) A unit-time SDFG; (b) Its EHG; (c) Its retimed EHG

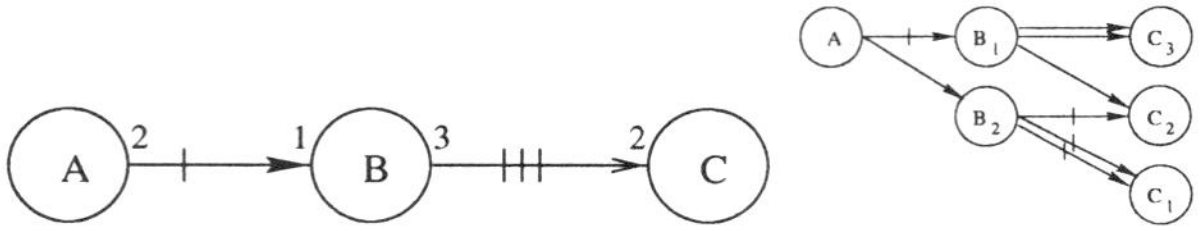

(a) (b)

Figure 5: (a) A path in a SDFG; (b) Its homogeneous equivalent

Thm 4.1 *Let G be a HDFG and c a potential clock period.* $cl(G) \leq c$ *iff every path in G with total computation time larger than c has delay count larger than* 1.

The problem now is that insufficient delays along a path in a SDFG do not necessarily translate into a zero-delay path in the EHG. As an example, consider the unit-time SDFG in Figure 5(a) below, with its EHG given in Figure 5(b). For $c = 2$, examining only the original SDFG would lead us to retime this path even though such an exercise is unnecessary. To avoid such false paths, we may need to construct intermediate EHGs for study, a very costly process.

In a similar vein, the nature of an EHG raises the question of what a path actually is. The traditional definition says that a path is a sequence of nodes and edges. Since we now have multiple edges between nodes, we must be very careful to consider all paths resulting from such multiple copies. To illustrate, the traditional definition would dictate that there is one path from A to C_3 in Figure 5(b). Because of the pair of edges between B_1 and C_3, we will abuse our definition slightly and say that there are in fact two paths between A and C_3 in the EHG when we do our calculations below. While this makes sense, it is somewhat different from what has always been done and so must be noted.

Another additional cost that the problem of insufficient delays forces us to pay comes in the form of additional checks for legality. In the original algorithms from [7], only one delay at a time was moved, a stipulation which did not cause the proposed retiming to become illegal at any intermediate step (as proven in [7]). Because we are now pulling groups of delays through nodes, this situation no longer exists, and so we will have to check for legality at every stage of an algorithm.

The question now is to determine exactly how many delays to view as sufficient. Let $e : u \to v$ be an edge in a SDFG. Each copy of u in the EHG creates $p(u)$ tokens. By our construction each of these is to travel along a separate edge. Since there are q_u copies of node u in the EHG, there must then be a total of $q_u \cdot p(e)$ edges to carry all of the data, each of which we expect to require a delay when we retime the graph. Similarly, q_v copies of v are each receiving $c(e)$ tokens, and so there must be $q_v \cdot c(e)$ edges for these data. We will use either of these figures as the number of tokens required by an edge in the SDFG during retiming.

4.2 Retiming Algorithm

We will seek our retiming via *relaxation* on the edges of our graph. We do this by sorting our vertices and then sweeping along the sorted list. When we get to a point where the current path is too long, we insert enough delays so as to break the path up into sufficiently small pieces. We then verify that we are allowed to do this. If we cannot then there is no retiming and we return with an error; otherwise we sweep further. Once our prospective retiming has been found, we test the retimed graph to make sure that the clock period is within our requirements. If it is we have found a way to retime the SDFG; otherwise there is no such retiming.

We begin our construction by considering Algorithm 1 below, the $O(|E|)$-time algorithm from [7] for finding the length of the longest zero-delay path into each vertex of a HDFG. This procedure first sorts the vertices so that those occurring early in the list are connected to vertices later in the list by zero-delay edges. It then traces through the list, associating each vertex with the length of its longest zero-delay path. If a vertex is not connected to a previous one, its path length must equal its own computation time; otherwise its path length equals its own time, plus the sum of the times of all the other vertices found along the path to this point. We require this algorithm not just for constructing our retiming, but also for verifying that our final retimed graph executes within the required time frame.

With this in hand we can now proceed to our primary method, given as Algorithm 2. We begin by retiming our SDFG with the result to date and constructing its EHG. The EHG is then handed to Algorithm 1 to find the lengths of the maximum paths to all vertices. At this point, if the longest path length is sufficiently small, we return our current retiming function as the final answer. Otherwise the vertices in our SDFG fall into one of two groups. If all copies of a vertex

Algorithm 1 Find computation time of most expensive zero-delay path to all vertices

Input: A HDFG $G = \langle V, E, d, t \rangle$
Output: The $|V|$-length vector τ
  Topologically sort the vertices of G, with u preceding v if there is a zero-delay edge from u to v in G
  for all v in order from the sorted list **do**
    if v has no zero-delay incoming edge in G **then**
      $\tau(v) \leftarrow t(v)$
    else
      $\tau(v) \leftarrow t(v) + \max\{\tau(u) | \exists e : u \to v \text{ in } G \text{ with } d(e) = 0\}$
    end if
  end for
  return τ

Algorithm 2 Retime a SDFG via Relaxation

Input: A SDFG $G = \langle V, E, d, t, p, c\rangle$, a potential clock period c
Output: A retiming r such that $cl(G_r) \leq c$ if one exists

```
for all v ∈ V do
  r(v) ← 0
end for
for i ← 1 to |V| do
  Construct the retimed graph G_r given the current r
  Construct the EHG H = ⟨V', E', d', t'⟩ for G_r
  τ ← MaxPath(H)                                   /* Apply Algorithm 1 */
  if max {τ(v)|v ∈ V'} ≤ c then
    return r                     /* All path lengths small enough; stop. */
  end if
  for all v in V do
    if no copy of v in H is incident on a zero-delay edge in H then
      Υ(v) ← ∞
    else
      Υ(v) ← max{τ(v_i)|v_i is a copy of v in H}
    end if
  end for
  for all v with Υ(v) ≤ c do
    r(v) ← r(v) + max { ⌈(q_v·p(e) − d_r(e)) / p(e)⌉ | e : v → u in G_r for some u }
  end for
  for all e : u → v in E do
    if d(e) + p(e)r(u) − c(e)r(v) < 0 then
      return FALSE               /* Retiming illegal; return with error */
    end if
  end for
end for
Construct the retimed graph G_r given the current r  /* Determine clock period */
Construct the EHG H for G_r
Υ ← MaxPath(H)                                /* Apply Algorithm 1 again */
if max{Υ(v)|v ∈ V'} > c then
  return FALSE                                  /* No feasible retiming */
else
  return r                               /* Otherwise r is the retiming */
end if
```

in the EHG are isolated (i.e., connected to the rest of the graph only by edges containing delays), we do not wish to retime the node and remove it from consideration. Otherwise the node lies along some zero-delay path and we may have to retime it. In this case we assign it a longest path length equal to the longest path length of any of its copies in the EHG.

We now consider nodes for further retiming. Since we want to push delays forward along our paths (rather than pulling them backward as was done in [7]), we retime those nodes which occur early in a path. This process is complicated by the different rates of production and consumption on each node. For example, for each delay drawn into node A in Figure 6(a), three delays are pushed onto the edge from A to B and two delays onto the edge from A to C. Therefore, for each outgoing edge from such a node, we calculate the number of delays needed to retime all copies of the edge in the EHG, subtract the number of delays currently on the edge, adjust for the different rates of production and consumption, and retime by the maximum of these needs. Once all nodes are retimed, we test the prospective retiming for legality, i.e. we check that retiming by our function doesn't result in some edge containing a negative number of delays. If we pass this test, we look further along our path for other nodes in need of retiming.

Once we have checked all nodes at least once and have derived a legal retiming function, it is time to test our answer. We repeat our earlier steps to find the lengths of the maximum zero-delay paths to each node one last time. Since the length of the largest zero-delay path in the EHG equals our clock period, this value is tested against our requested clock period. If it is still too large we cannot retime this SDFG to execute in the time we wish and must return with an error. Otherwise we have found our retiming.

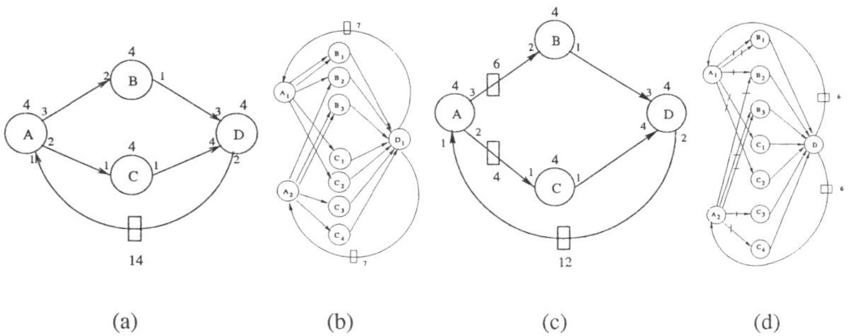

Figure 6: (a) An example SDFG; (b) Its EHG; (c) The retimed SDFG after first pass; (d) Its EHG

We now demonstrate our method by executing it on the SDFG of Figure 6(a) with $c = 4$. Sorting the vertices of Figure 6(b), computing longest path lengths and taking the maxima reveals that $\Upsilon(A) = 4$, $\Upsilon(B) = \Upsilon(C) = 8$ and $\Upsilon(D) = 12$ in this case. We thus only retime node A at this step. Since there are no delays on the edge (A, B), our initial retiming has $r(A) = q_A = 2$ and $r(v) = 0$ for any other node v. Pulling 2 delays through A pushes 6 delays onto (A, B) and 4 onto (A, C), as seen in the retimed graph in Figure 6(c), with its EHG appearing in Figure 6(d).

Looping back around, we see from Figure 6(d) that only node A is cut off; all other nodes lie along some zero-delay path. Thus $\Upsilon(A) = \infty$, $\Upsilon(B) = \Upsilon(C) = 4$ and $\Upsilon(D) = 8$ now, calling for us to retime nodes B and C. Since neither of the edges (B, D) nor (C, D) currently contains delays, our retiming now has $r(A) = 2$, $r(B) = q_B = 3$, $r(C) = q_C = 4$ and $r(D) = 0$. The new retimed graph is given below as Figure 7(a), with its EHG in Figure 7(b). Note that, due to node B's consumption rate of 2, a retiming of 3 applied to B requires us to pull $2 \times 3 = 6$ delays in so that the proper number of delays is pushed back out.

Studying the new EHG shows us that node D is now cut off, but node A requires further retiming. We have $\Upsilon(A) = 4$, $\Upsilon(B) = \Upsilon(C) = 8$ and $\Upsilon(D) = \infty$ now, so only node A must be retimed. Since both of the edges (A, B) and (A, C) are devoid of delays, we must add $q_A = 2$ onto the retiming for A, giving us the function $r(A) = 4$, $r(B) = 3$, $r(C) = 4$ and $r(D) = 0$.

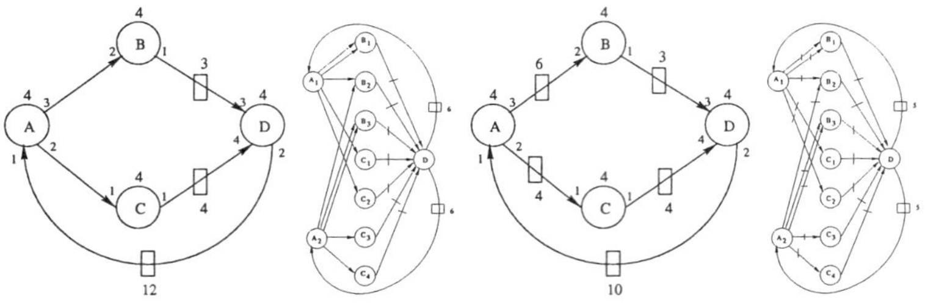

(a) (b) (c) (d)

Figure 7: (a) The retimed SDFG after two passes; (b) Its EHG; (c) Figure 6(a) retimed; (b) Its EHG

The application of this retiming to the original SDFG results in the graph of Figure 7(c) and we have found our answer.

However we have a final pass of the algorithm to perform. This time, all nodes in the SDFG have been isolated, so $\Upsilon(v) = \infty$ for all nodes v, insuring that no further retiming takes place. We now study the EHG of Figure 7(d), find that the maximum zero-delay path is an individual node with computation time 4 and conclude that we have found our retiming.

Let $G = \langle V, E, d, t, p, c\rangle$ be our SDFG with EHG $H = \langle V', E', d', t'\rangle$. Constructing the EHG and executing Algorithm 1 each execute in $O(|E'|)$ time; thus Algorithm 2 only requires $O\left(|V|^2 + |V||E'|\right)$ time. However, while we suspect that its success is both a necessary and sufficient condition for a SDFG to be retimable to a given clock period, it is unknown whether or not this is the case. In our defense, the algorithm from [7] upon which this method is based was also never proven both necessary and sufficient, but has been extremely useful in practice. We suspect that the algorithm we've described here will prove just as valuable despite this logical gap. Let $G = \langle V, E, d, t, p, c\rangle$ be our SDFG with EHG $H = \langle V', E', d', t'\rangle$. Since constructing the EHG and executing Algorithm 1 each require $O(|E'|)$ time, Algorithm 2 only requires $O(|V||V'| + |V||E'|)$ time to complete. However, while we suspect that its success is both a necessary and sufficient condition for a SDFG to be retimable to a given clock period, it is unknown whether or not this is the case. In our defense, the algorithm from [7] upon which this method is based was also never proven both necessary and sufficient, but has been extremely useful in practice. We suspect that the algorithm we have described here will prove just as valuable despite this logical gap.

5 Conclusion

In this paper, we have established a notation for expressing and studying synchronous data-flow graphs. We have presented the difficulties involved with retiming SDFGs, and then constructed a polynomial-time algorithm for retiming a synchronous graph so that it achieves a sufficiently small clock period. Finally, we have demonstrated the effectiveness of our algorithm on an example. (The interested reader may find further examples in [11].)

Regardless of how good our algorithm may be, it is still not proven to represent both a necessary and sufficient condition for retiming. This proof, or the construction of an alternate method which is necessary and sufficient, remain interesting open problems. Correcting the errors in [10] will definitely lead to greater understanding of our model and may open the door to removing this logical gap. It may also lead to a study of retiming applied to even more complicated models, such as cyclo-static or dynamic DFGs [15].

Acknowledgements

This work is partially supported by NSF grants MIP95-01006 and MIP97-04276, and by the A.J. Schmitt Foundation.

References

1. E.A. Lee and D.G. Messerschmitt. Static scheduling of synchronous data-flow programs for digital signal processing. *IEEE Trans. Comput.*, 36:24–35, 1987.
2. J.L Pino, S. Ha, E.A. Lee, and J.T. Buck. Software synthesis for DSP using Ptolemy. *J. VLSI Signal Process.*, 9:7–21, 1995.
3. G. Gao, R. Govindarajan, and P. Panangaden. Well-behaved dataflow programs for DSP computation. In *Proc. ICASSP-92*, volume 5, pages 561–564, 1992.
4. S. Ritz, M. Pankert, V. Zivojnovic, and H. Meyr. Optimum vectorization of scalable synchronous dataflow graphs. In *Proc. Int. Conf. Application-Specific Array Processors*, pages 285–296, 1993.
5. S. Ritz, M. Pankert, V. Zivojnovic, and H. Meyr. High-level software synthesis for the design of communication systems. *IEEE J. Selected Areas in Communications, Special Issue on Comput.-Aided Modeling, Analysis & Design of Communication Links*, 11:348–358, 1993.
6. C.E. Leiserson and J.B. Saxe. Optimizing synchronous systems. *J. VLSI & Comput. Syst.*, 1(1):41–67, 1983.
7. C.E. Leiserson and J.B. Saxe. Retiming synchronous circuitry. *Algorithmica*, 6:5–35, 1991.
8. L.-F. Chao. *Scheduling and Behavioral Transformations for Parallel Systems*. PhD thesis, Dept. of Comp. Science, Princeton University, 1993.
9. V. Zivojnovic, S. Ritz, and H. Meyr. Retiming of DSP programs for optimum vectorization. In *Proc. ICASSP-94*, volume 1, pages 465–468, 1994.
10. V. Zivojnovic, S. Ritz, and H. Meyr. Optimizing DSP programs under the multirate retiming transformation. In *Proc. 7th European Signal Process. Conf.*, volume 3, pages 1597–1600, 1994.
11. T.W. O'Neil and E. H.-M. Sha. Retiming synchronous data-flow graphs to minimize execution time. Technical Report 00-08, Univ. of Notre Dame, 2000. Available online at *www.cse.nd.edu/tech_reports/.*
12. V. Zivojnovic and R. Schoenen. On retiming of multirate DSP algorithms. In *Proc. ICASSP-96*, volume 6, pages 3310–3313, 1996.
13. E.A. Lee. *A Coupled Hardware and Software Architecture for Programmable Digital Signal Processors*. PhD thesis, Dept. of EECS, Univ. of California at Berkeley, 1986.
14. R. Schoenen, V. Zivojnovic, and H. Meyr. An upper bound of the throughput of multirate multiprocessor schedules. In *Proc. ICASSP-97*, volume 1, pages 655–658, 1997.
15. G. Bilsen, M. Engels, R. Lauwereins, and J. Peperstraete. Cyclo-static dataflow. *IEEE Trans. Signal Process.*, 44:397–408, 1996.
16. K.K. Parhi. Algorithm transformation techniques for concurrent processors. *Proc. IEEE*, 77:1879–1895, 1989.
17. M. Renfors and Y. Neuvo. The maximum sampling rate of digital filters under hardware speed. *Trans. Circuits & Sampling*, CAS-28:196–202, 1981.

TIME-MINIMAL AND PROCESSOR-TIME-MINIMAL LOOP TILING

Jingling Xue
School of Computer Science and Engineering
The University of New South Wales, Sydney 2052 Australia

This paper finds the best tile size and best processor count to minimise the execution time of a tiled double loop on a distributed memory machine. The scope of this work includes double loops with rectangular iteration spaces. The accuracy of our results is validated by experiments. The generality of our problem-solving techniques is demonstrated by a straightforward extension of our results when an alternative communication cost model is used.

1 Introduction

Loop tiling is a useful loop optimisation for improving parallelism, reducing communication overhead and enhancing cache locality [1,2,3,4,5,6,7,8,9]. This paper provides the optimal solutions to the two problems concerned with applying loop tiling to minimise the execution time of a tiled double loop on a distributed memory machine.

One problem, called the *time-minimal (tiling) problem*, is to find the best tile size to minimise the execution time of a double loop using exactly P processors. Given P processors, the other problem, called the *processor-time-minimal (tiling) problem*, is to find the best tile size and the best processor count p such that the execution time of a double loop on a p-processor machine is minimised, where $1 \leqslant p \leqslant P$.

Several researchers [10,11,12,13] have studied both problems under different assumptions and based on different communication cost models. The main results of this paper are summarised as follows. In solving the time-minimal problem, we prove formally that a tiling is not time-minimal if the processors are idle or if the processors are load imbalanced. We give the best tile size for minimising the execution time of a double loop. In solving the processor-time-minimal problem, we use an accurate execution time formula and derive the best tile size and the best processor count. By setting $P = +\infty$, the processor-time-minimal solution found also gives the best execution time achievable for a double loop on a given machine.

The rest of the paper is organised as follows. Section 2 defines time-minimal tiling and processor-time-minimal tiling problems. Section 3 derives time-minimal tilings. Section 4 derives processor-time-minimal tilings. Section 5 demonstrates that our results generalise easily when different communication cost models are used. Section 6 discusses the related work. Section 7 concludes the paper.

2 Problem Statement

The major part of the paper is restricted to double loops of the form:

$$\begin{array}{l} \text{do } i_1 = 1, N_1 \\ \quad \text{do } i_2 = 1, N_2 \\ \quad\quad S \end{array}$$

Table 1: SOR code.

PROGRAM	ITERATION SPACE
DO i = 1, N1 DO j = 1, N2 a(i,j) = $(1-\omega)$*a(i,j) + $\frac{\omega}{4}$(a(i+1,j) +a(i-1,j) + a(i,j+1) + a(i,j-1))	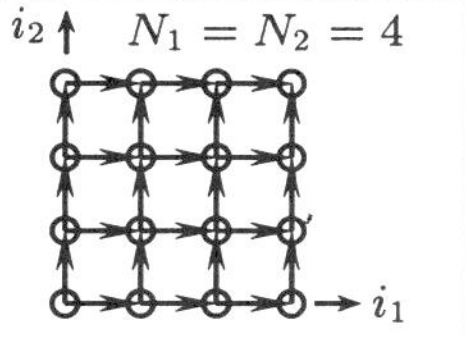

where S denotes a sequence of any statements, including possibly loops, provided that all iterations of the program take roughly the same amount of time to execute.

A *rectangular tiling* transforms the above double loop into:

do $t_1 = 1, N_1, n_1$
  do $t_2 = 1, N_2, n_2$
    do $i_1 = t_1, \max(t_1 + n_1 - 1, N_1)$
      do $i_2 = t_2, \max(t_2 + n_2 - 1, N_2)$
        S

where the size of tiles is defined by $n_1 \times n_2$, giving rise to $\lceil \frac{N_1}{n_1} \rceil$ tiles along the i_1 dimension and $\lceil \frac{N_2}{n_2} \rceil$ tiles along the i_2 dimension. To ensure that a rectangular tiling is legal, the two loops in the double loop must be usually permutable[2,14].

Table 1 gives the SOR example program used in our experiments.

The tiles are scheduled statically to processors at compile time and executed in the SPMD mode. As illustrated in Figure 1, the iteration space of a double loop is first tiled by rectangles of size $n_1 \times n_2$ and then the columns of tiles are distributed cyclically to a linear arrangement of P processors numbered from 1. The tiles in the same column are executed in the same processor. A processor is given at most $\lceil \lceil \frac{N_1}{n_1} \rceil / P \rceil$ columns. Precisely, the processors numbered from 1 to $(\lceil \frac{N_1}{n_1} \rceil - 1)\%P + 1$ are assigned $\lceil \lceil \frac{N_1}{n_1} \rceil / P \rceil$ columns and the remaining processors one column less.

The tiles are *block-distributed* if $P = \lceil \frac{N_1}{n_1} \rceil$ and *cyclically distributed* otherwise. A processor is said to be *idle* if it waits between executing two consecutive columns of tiles assigned to it. This can happen when $\lceil \frac{N_2}{n_2} \rceil < P < \lceil \frac{N_1}{n_1} \rceil$ or when communication overheads are expensive.

The following assumption about P is made:

$$P \leqslant \min(\lceil \frac{N_1}{n_1} \rceil, N_2) \tag{1}$$

Because the i_1 loop is distributed, some processors will have no work to do if $P > \lceil \frac{N_1}{n_1} \rceil$. Because the i_2 loop is collapsed, a processor will be *idle* between executing

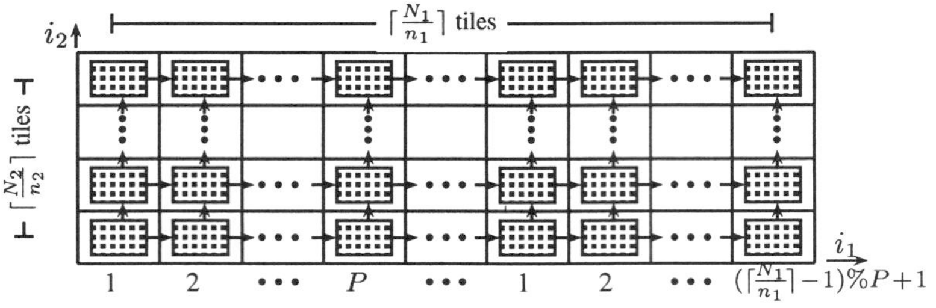

Figure 1: Cyclic distribution of tiles to P processors.

two consecutive columns of tiles assigned to it if $P > N_2$ (implying $P > \lceil \frac{N_2}{n_2} \rceil$). In the latter case, the same execution time can be achieved if fewer processors are used.

$P \leqslant \lceil \frac{N_1}{n_1} \rceil$ implies that $P \leqslant N_1$ and $n_1 \leqslant \frac{N_1-1}{P-1}$. In practice, $\frac{N_1}{P}$ and $\frac{N_1-1}{P-1}$ are very close. Therefore, the following simpler upper bound of n_1 will be assumed:

$$n_1 \leqslant \frac{N_1}{P}$$

The solution space for all tile sizes is $\{(n_1, n_2) \mid 1 \leqslant n_1 \leqslant \frac{N_1}{P}, 1 \leqslant n_2 \leqslant N_2\}$.

To generate message-passing code, the data dependences between tiles must be analysed. The dependences localised within a processor can be ignored. All cross-processor dependences must be satisfied by message passing. In order for tiling to be effective, most data dependences in the program should be constant or uniform. Therefore, the dependences between tiles will include the two dependence vectors:

$$\{\binom{1}{0}, \binom{1}{0}\}$$

which are represented by the arrows in Figure 1. The non-neighbouring communication due to non-constant cross-processor dependences can be implemented by systolic pipelining via the intervening processors. This scheme should not cause performance degradation due to the existence of dependence vectors $(1, 0)$ and $(0, 1)$.

Figure 2 gives the SPMD code executed at every processor[15].

```
do t1 = 1 + (p − 1)n1, N1, n1P
   do t2 = 1, N2, n2
      | Receive messages from neighbouring PEs |
      do i1 = t1, max(t1 + n1 − 1, N1)
         do i2 = t2, max(t2 + n2 − 1, N2)
            S
      | Send messages to neighbouring PEs |
```

Figure 2: SPMD Code for processor p in the SPMD mode.

The communication cost model used in this paper reflects the communication patterns in the SPMD code (Figure 2). Every processor receives a message from its left neighbour, executes a tile and sends a message to its right neighbour. The cost of this pair of send and receive for a message of L 4-byte elements is approximated as:

$$T_{\mathsf{msg}}(L) = a + c\,L \tag{2}$$

where a and c are obtained using the standard methods as described in[16].

Given a double loop whose iteration space is tiled and scheduled as illustrated in Figure 1 and executed using the SPMD mode given in Figure 2, this paper provides solutions to the following two problems:

Time-Minimal Tiling: Find a tile size (n_1, n_2) such that the execution time of the SPMD code given in Figure 2 on exactly P processors is minimised.

Processor-Time-Minimal Tiling: Find a tile size (n_1, n_2) and a processor count p such that the execution time of the SPMD code given in Figure 2 on p processors is minimised, where $1 \leqslant p \leqslant P$. By setting $P = +\infty$, the best execution time (or speedup) achievable for a program on a machine is also obtained.

It must be pointed out that like all previous researchers, we have developed our results in the continuous space by assuming that n_1, n_2 and p are positive real variables. The real solutions found are converted to the nearest integers where appropriate.

3 Time-Minimal Tile Size

This problem was initially studied in[13] and later in[10,11]. This problem is investigated here for three reasons. First, we prove formally that a tiling is not time-minimal if the processors are idle (Lemma 1) or load imbalanced (Lemma 2). In the previous work, these assumptions are used but not proved. Second, when a double loop contains loops, the execution time of a single iteration can be close to the per-byte transferring cost c. As a result, in the optimal solution found previously (Lemma 4), $n_2^* < 1$ is possible – simply approximating n_2^* as 1 is not always time-minimal. This issue was dealt with in[10] under their assumptions. Based on our communication cost model, we give the best tile size for the time-minimal problem. Finally, solving the time-minimal problem solves the half of the processor-time-minimal tiling problem.

The time-minimal tiling problem is solved as follows. First, the problem is divided into three cases leading to three execution time formulas. It is then shown that the optimal solution can always be found in one of the three cases. Finally, the optimal solution is derived by minimising the execution time formula in that case.

The execution time of a tile is the sum of computation and communication times:

$$T_{\mathsf{tile}} = n_1 n_2 t + a + b n_2$$

where t is the time for executing a single iteration, $n_1 n_2 t$ the time for executing a tile and $a + bn_2$ the time for transferring a message between two processors. In general,

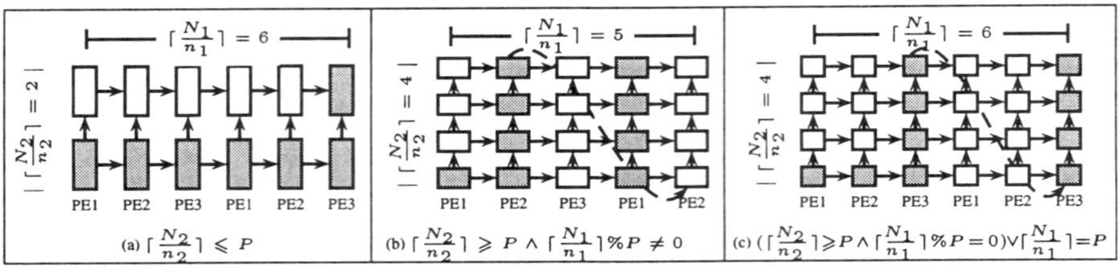

Figure 3: Three critical paths of the same iteration space tiled differently on a 3-processor machine.

$b = m \times c$, indicating that the message size per tile is proportional to the height n_2 of a tile[9]. In the case of the SOR code, $b = c$.

Figure 3 illustrates the derivation of execution time formulas. Case (a) overlaps with Cases (b) and (c). Cases (a) and (b) include the special case when $(\lceil \frac{N_2}{n_2} \rceil = P \wedge \lceil \frac{N_1}{n_1} \rceil \% P \neq 0)$. Cases (a) and (c) include the special case when $(\lceil \frac{N_2}{n_2} \rceil = P \wedge \lceil \frac{N_1}{n_1} \rceil \% P = 0) \vee \lceil \frac{N_1}{n_1} \rceil = P$. This overlapping between cases is exploited in our search for time-minimal tilings. Under some practical assumptions (to be stated), it is shown progressively that the best tile size can always be found in Case (c). Section 3.1 argues that Case (a) can be ignored because the time-minimal tile size can always be found in Case (b) or Case (c). Section 3.2 argues further that no tiling found in Case (b) can be time-minimal. Section 3.3 derives the time-minimal tile size for Case (c).

3.1 Execution Time Formula for Case (a)

Due to our earlier assumption $P \leqslant \lceil \frac{N_1}{n_1} \rceil$, we have $\lceil \frac{N_2}{n_2} \rceil \leqslant P \leqslant \lceil \frac{N_1}{n_1} \rceil$. Lemma 1 shows that the time-minimal solution cannot be attained if $\lceil \frac{N_2}{n_2} \rceil < P < \lceil \frac{N_1}{n_1} \rceil$, i.e., when processors can be idle. Because the two boundary cases $\lceil \frac{N_2}{n_2} \rceil = P$ or $\lceil \frac{N_1}{n_1} \rceil = P$ are included in Case (b) or Case (c), this case can thus be ignored.

The number of tiles along the critical path in this case is $\lceil \frac{N_1}{n_1} \rceil + \lceil \frac{N_2}{n_2} \rceil - 1$. Thus, the execution time formula can be expressed as follows:

$$T_{\rm a}(n_1, n_2) = (\lceil \frac{N_1}{n_1} \rceil + \lceil \frac{N_2}{n_2} \rceil - 1) T_{\rm tile} = (\lceil \frac{N_1}{n_1} \rceil + \lceil \frac{N_2}{n_2} \rceil - 1)(n_1 n_2 t + a + b n_2) \quad (3)$$

The execution time is approximated with all the ceilings removed:

$$T'_{\rm a}(n_1, n_2) = (\frac{N_1}{n_1} + \frac{N_2}{n_2} - 1)(n_1 n_2 t + a + b n_2) \quad (4)$$

By using the above simplified execution time formula, the following lemma establishes that a tiling is not time-minimal if the processors are idle.

Lemma 1 *$T'_a(n_1, n_2)$ is not minimised at (n_1, n_2) if $\lceil \frac{N_2}{n_2} \rceil < P < \lceil \frac{N_1}{n_1} \rceil$.*

Proof. Let (n_1, n_2) be a tile size such that $\lceil \frac{N_2}{n_2} \rceil < P < \lceil \frac{N_1}{n_1} \rceil$. Let $k \in \mathbb{Q}$ be such that $n_1 = \frac{N_1}{Pk}$. Since $P < \lceil \frac{N_1}{n_1} \rceil$, $k > 1$ holds. Construct a tile size $(n'_1, n'_2) = (n_1 k', n_2/k')$, where $1 \leqslant k' \leqslant k$, such that $\lceil \frac{N_1}{n'_1} \rceil = P$ or $\lceil \frac{N_2}{n'_2} \rceil = P$. Choose k' by considering two cases. Case (1) $n_2/k \geqslant 1$. Set $k' = k$. This implies that $\lceil \frac{N_1}{n'_1} \rceil = P$. Case (2) $n_2/k < 1$. Set $k' = n_2 P/N_2$. This implies that $\lceil \frac{N_2}{n'_2} \rceil = P$. To see that $1 \leqslant k' \leqslant k$, we use $\lceil \frac{N_2}{n_2} \rceil < P$ to infer that $1 \leqslant k'$ holds and the fact $n_2/k < 1$ and (1) to arrive at $k' < k$. In each of the two cases, (n'_1, n'_2) is a valid tile size.

The rest of the proof is to show $T'_a(n'_1, n'_2) < T'_a(n_1, n_2)$. Consider:

$$T'_a(n'_1, n'_2) = (\frac{N_1}{k' n_1} + \frac{k' N_2}{n_2} - 1)(n'_1 n'_2 t + a + b n_2/k')$$

Since $n'_1 n'_2 = n_1 n_2$ and $1 \leqslant k'$, it suffices to show that

$$\frac{N_1}{k' n_1} + \frac{k' N_2}{n_2} < \frac{N_1}{n_1} + \frac{N_2}{n_2}$$

which can be rewritten as follows:

$$\frac{N_2}{n_2}(k' - 1) = \frac{k' N_2}{n_2} - \frac{N_2}{n_2} < \frac{N_1}{n_1} - \frac{N_1}{k' n_1} = \frac{N_1}{k' n_1}(k' - 1)$$

This inequality indeed holds because $\frac{N_2}{n_2} \leqslant \lceil \frac{N_2}{n_2} \rceil < P = \frac{N_1}{k n_1} \leqslant \frac{N_1}{k' n_1}$. ■

3.2 Execution Times Formulas for Cases (b) and (c)

In both cases, $\lceil \frac{N_2}{n_2} \rceil \geqslant P$, implying that the processors are not idle. This section shows that Case (b) can also be ignored, leaving only Case (c) to be considered.

The execution time formulas in both cases can be derived in a similar manner. Let $q = (\lceil \frac{N_1}{n_1} \rceil - 1)\%P + 1$ be the last processor that completes execution. Due to the dependence vector $(1, 0)$, q cannot start executing its own tiles until after $q - 1$ leftmost tiles in the bottom row have been executed. Since q is assigned $\lceil \lceil \frac{N_1}{n_1} \rceil / P \rceil$ columns of tiles, the critical path consists of the $q - 1$ leftmost tiles in the bottom row plus all tiles allocated to q. The total number of the tiles along the critical path is thus $q - 1 + \lceil \frac{N_2}{n_2} \rceil \lceil \lceil \frac{N_1}{n_1} \rceil / P \rceil$. Hence, the execution time is given by:

$$T_{bc} = (q - 1 + \lceil \lceil \frac{N_1}{n_1} \rceil / P \rceil \lceil \frac{N_2}{n_2} \rceil)(n_1 n_2 t + a + b n_2)$$

Note that $q - 1 = (\lceil \frac{N_1}{n_1} \rceil - 1)\%P$ becomes $P - 1$ if $\lceil \frac{N_1}{n_1} \rceil \%P = 0$ and to $\lceil \frac{N_1}{n_1} \rceil \%P - 1$ otherwise. Thus, the execution time formula for Case (b) is.

$$T_b(n_1, n_2) = (\lceil \frac{N_1}{n_1} \rceil \%P - 1 + \lceil \lceil \frac{N_1}{n_1} \rceil / P \rceil \lceil \frac{N_2}{n_2} \rceil)(n_1 n_2 t + a + b n_2) \quad (5)$$

which is simplified with the ceiling on $\lceil \frac{N_2}{n_2} \rceil$ removed:

$$T'_b(n_1, n_2) = (\lceil \frac{N_1}{n_1} \rceil \% P - 1 + \lceil \lceil \frac{N_1}{n_1} \rceil / P \rceil \frac{N_2}{n_2})(n_1 n_2 t + a + b n_2) \tag{6}$$

The execution time formula for Case (c) is:

$$T_c(n_1, n_2) = (P - 1 + (\lceil \frac{N_1}{n_1} \rceil / P) \lceil \frac{N_2}{n_2} \rceil)(n_1 n_2 t + a + b n_2) \tag{7}$$

which is also approximated with the ceiling on $\lceil \frac{N_2}{n_2} \rceil$ removed:

$$T'_c(n_1, n_2) = (P - 1 + \lceil \lceil \frac{N_1}{n_1} \rceil / P \rceil \frac{N_2}{n_2})(n_1 n_2 t + a + b n_2) \tag{8}$$

By using the simplified formulas, we are able to establish that a tiling with results load imbalance among processors is not time-minimal. Thus, Case (b) can be ignored.

Lemma 2 *Let* $\frac{N_2}{n_2} \geqslant P$. *The combined function defined in terms of* $T'_b(n_1, n_2)$ *and* $T'_c(n_1, n_2)$ *is not minimised at* (n_1, n_2) *if* $\lceil \frac{N_1}{n_1} \rceil \% P \neq 0$.

Proof. Let (n_1, n_2) be a tile size such that $\lceil \frac{N_1}{n_1} \rceil \% P \neq 0$. By increasing n_1 and decreasing n_2 while maintaining $n'_1 \times n'_2 = n_1 \times n_2$, we can find a tile size (n'_1, n'_2) such that $\lceil \frac{N_1}{n'_1} \rceil \% P = 0$ and $\lceil \frac{N_1}{n'_1} \rceil / P = \lceil \lceil \frac{N_1}{n_1} \rceil / P \rceil - 1 = \lfloor \lceil \frac{N_1}{n_1} \rceil / P \rfloor$. Indeed, we can choose $n'_1 = \frac{N_1}{P \lfloor \lceil \frac{N_1}{n_1} \rceil / P \rfloor}$ and $n'_2 = \frac{n_1 n_2 P \lfloor \lceil \frac{N_1}{n_1} \rceil / P \rfloor}{N_1}$. Since $\lceil \frac{N_1}{n'_1} \rceil \% P = 0$, the execution time when the tile size (n'_1, n'_2) is used is given by:

$$T_c(n'_1, n'_2) = (P - 1 + \lceil \lceil \frac{N_1}{n'_1} \rceil / P \rceil \frac{N_2}{n'_2})(n'_1 n'_2 t + a + b n'_2)$$

By construction, $n'_1 n'_2 = n_1 n_2$, $n'_1 > n_1$, $n'_2 < n_2$ and $\lceil \lceil \frac{N_1}{n'_1} \rceil / P \rceil \frac{N_2}{n'_2} = \frac{N_1 N_2}{n_1 n_2 P}$. Hence, the above formula can be simplified to:

$$T_c(n'_1, n'_2) = (P - 1 + \frac{N_1 N_2}{n_1 n_2 P})(n_1 n_2 t + a + b n'_2) \tag{9}$$

The rest of the proof is to show that $T'_c(n'_1, n'_2) < T'_b(n_1, n_2)$. By comparing (6) and (9) and using the fact that $n'_2 < n_2$, it suffices to show that

$$P + \frac{N_1 N_2}{n_1 n_2 P} \leqslant \lceil \frac{N_1}{n_1} \rceil \% P + \lceil \lceil \frac{N_1}{n_1} \rceil / P \rceil \frac{N_2}{n_2}$$

i.e., that

$$P - \lceil \frac{N_1}{n_1} \rceil \% P \leqslant \lceil \lceil \frac{N_1}{n_1} \rceil / P \rceil \frac{N_2}{n_2} - \frac{N_1 N_2}{n_1 n_2 P} = \frac{P \lceil \lceil \frac{N_1}{n_1} \rceil / P \rceil - \frac{N_1}{n_1}}{P} \frac{N_2}{n_2}$$

By noting that

$$P - \lceil \frac{N_1}{n_1} \rceil \% P = P \lceil \frac{N_1}{n_1} / P \rceil - \lceil \frac{N_1}{n_1} \rceil \leqslant P \lceil \lceil \frac{N_1}{n_1} \rceil / P \rceil - \frac{N_1}{n_1}$$

and using the hypothesis $\frac{N_2}{n_2} \geqslant P$ given in the lemma, we obtain:

$$P - \lceil \frac{N_1}{n_1} \rceil \% P \leqslant \frac{P - \lceil \frac{N_1}{n_1} \rceil \% P}{P} \frac{N_2}{n_2} \leqslant \frac{P \lceil \lceil \frac{N_1}{n_1} \rceil / P \rceil - \frac{N_1}{n_1}}{P} \frac{N_2}{n_2}$$

■

3.3 *Time-Minimal Tile Size*

In the two preceding sections, we showed that a tiling is not time-minimal if the processors are idle (Lemma 1) or load imbalanced (Lemma 2). Hence, the time-minimal tile size can be found by solving Case (c). To avoid unnecessary complexity, we simplify, like previous researchers, the execution time formula in Case (c) to:

$$T(n_1, n_2) = (P + \frac{N_1 N_2}{n_1 n_2 P})(n_1 n_2 t + a + b n_2) \tag{10}$$

Lemma 3 shows that the best tile size (n_1, n_2) must be such that $n_1 = \frac{N_1}{P}$ or $n_2 = 1$. Lemmas 4 and 5 find the optimal other side of a tile in two cases, respectively. Lemma 6 gives a condition that allows both cases to be combined. Theorem 1 provides the best tile size for a double loop.

Lemma 3 *$T(n_1, n_2)$ is minimised when either $n_1 = \frac{N_1}{P}$ or $n_2 = 1$.*

Proof. By rearranging the terms in the function T given in (10), we get:

$$T(n_1, n_2) = (P + \frac{N_1 N_2}{n_1 n_2 P})(n_1 n_2 t + a + b \frac{n_1 n_2}{n_1})$$

T is strictly decreasing function of n_1 on every hyperbola $n_1 n_2 = c$ for some fixed c. Thus, T is minimised on such a hyperbola when n_1 is as large as possible while $n_2 \geqslant 1$ is maintained. The minimum is attained when either $n_1 = \frac{N_1}{P}$ or $n_2 = 1$. ■

The following result is due to Ohta, Saito, Kainaga and Ono[13].

Lemma 4 *$T(\frac{N_1}{P}, n_2)$ attains its minimum:*

$$T^* = (\sqrt{Pa} + \sqrt{N_2(b + \frac{N_1 t}{P}})^2 \tag{11}$$

when

$$n_2^* = \sqrt{\frac{N_2 a}{Pb + N_1 t}}$$

Proof. Solving $\frac{dT}{dn_2} = 0$ to get n_2^* and substituting n_2^* into $T(\frac{N_1}{P}, n_2)$ to obtain T^*. ■

Lemma 5 $T(n_1, 1)$ *attains its minimum:*

$$T^* = \begin{cases} \frac{N_1}{P}\sqrt{\frac{N_1 N_2(a+b)}{N_1 t}} \leqslant 1 & \rightarrow \quad (P + \frac{N_1 N_2}{P})(t + a + b) \\ 1 < \frac{N_1}{P}\sqrt{\frac{N_2(a+b)}{N_1 t}} < \frac{N_1}{P} & \rightarrow \quad (\sqrt{P(a+b)} + \sqrt{\frac{N_1 N_2 t}{P}})^2 \\ \frac{N_1}{P}\sqrt{\frac{N_2(a+b)}{N_1 t}} \geqslant \frac{N_1}{P} & \rightarrow \quad (P + N_2)(\frac{N_1}{P}t + a + b) \end{cases} \tag{12}$$

when

$$n_1^* = \max(1, \min(\frac{N_1}{P}, \frac{N_1}{P}\sqrt{\frac{N_2(a+b)}{N_1 t}})) \tag{13}$$

Proof. The unique positive solution to $\frac{dT}{dn_1} = 0$ is $n_1^0 = \frac{N_1}{P}\sqrt{\frac{N_2(a+b)}{N_1 t}}$. Being strictly convex function on $[1, \frac{N_1}{P}]$, $T(n_1, 1)$ must attain its minimum T^* at the point n_1^* as given. The three cases in T^* are distinguished depending on whether n_1^0 is to the left of, inside or to the right of the domain $[1, \frac{N_1}{P}]$ for $T(n_1, 1)$. ■

Lemma 6 $T(\frac{N_1}{P}, n_2)$ *is minimised at* $(\frac{N_1}{P}, \sqrt{\frac{N_2 a}{Pb+N_1 t}})$ *if* $\frac{N_2 a}{Pb+N_1 t}) \geqslant 1$.

Proof. If $\frac{N_2 a}{Pb+N_1 t}) \geqslant 1$, then $(\frac{N_1}{P}, \sqrt{\frac{N_2 a}{Pb+N_1 t}})$ is a valid tile size. Assume to the contrary that $T(\frac{N_1}{P}, n_2)$ is not minimised at $(\frac{N_1}{P}, \sqrt{\frac{N_2 a}{Pb+N_1 t}})$. By Lemma 3, the best tile size must have the form $(n_1^*, 1)$. By Lemma 5, $n_1^* = \max(1, \min(\frac{N_1}{P}, \frac{N_1}{P}\sqrt{\frac{N_2(a+b)}{N_1 t}}))$. Since $\frac{N_2 a}{Pb+N_1 t} \geqslant 1$, $N_2 a > Nt$ must hold. Thus, $n_2^* = \frac{N_1}{P}$. By Lemma 6, $T(\frac{N_2}{P}, n_2)$ is minimised at $(\frac{N_1}{P}, \sqrt{\frac{N_2 a}{Pb+N_1 t}})$ on $[\frac{N_1}{P}, 1]$. Thus, $T(n_1^*, 1) = T(\frac{N_1}{P}, 1) \leqslant T(\frac{N_1}{P}, \sqrt{\frac{N_2 a}{Pb+N_1 t}})$. Therefore, this lemma has been proved by contradiction. ■

A combination of Lemmas 3 – 6 leads to the following theorem.

Theorem 1 $T(n_1, n_2)$ *is minimised at* $(n_1^*, n_2^*) = (\frac{N_1}{P}, \sqrt{\frac{N_2 a}{Pb+N_1 t}})$ *if* $\frac{N_2 a}{Pb+N_1 t} \geqslant 1$ *and at* $(n_1^*, n_2^*) = \max(1, \min(\frac{N_1}{P}, \frac{N_1}{P}\sqrt{\frac{N_2(a+b)}{N_1 t}}))$ *otherwise.*

Table 2 lists three asymptotic time-minimal solutions derived from Theorem 1. In practice, $a \gg b$ and $a \gg t$. Thus, block tile distribution is almost always the best choice. However, if the double loop being tiled contains other loops in its loop body, t can be so close to a that cyclic title distribution may becomes the best choice.

Figure 4 gives some performance results of SOR on CM-5 and AP1000, respectively. According to both Theorem 1 and our experimental results, block tile distribution is the best on both machines for the particular iteration space size used. By fixing $n_1 = \frac{N_1}{P} = 40$ and varying n_2 over a range of values, both theoretical and

Table 2: Asymptotic time-minimal solutions.

	$a \to +\infty$	$b \to +\infty$	$t \to +\infty$
n_1^*	$\frac{N_1}{P}$	$\frac{N_1}{P}$	1
n_2^*	N_2	1	1

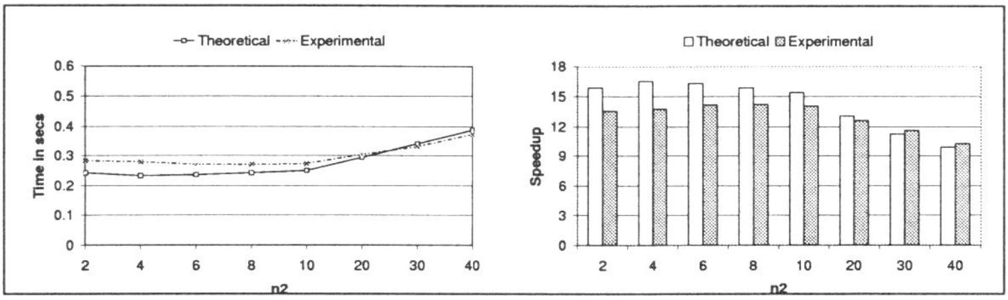

(a) CM-5: Theoretical: $n_1^* = 40, n_2^* = 4.0$; Experimental: $n_1^* = 40, n_2^* = 6.0$

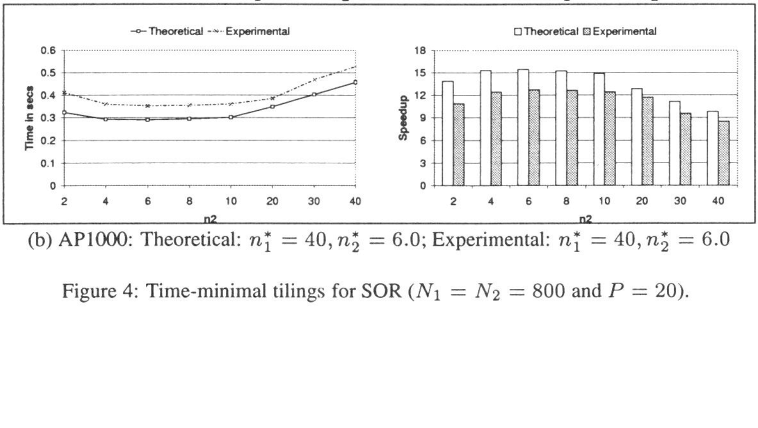

(b) AP1000: Theoretical: $n_1^* = 40, n_2^* = 6.0$; Experimental: $n_1^* = 40, n_2^* = 6.0$

Figure 4: Time-minimal tilings for SOR ($N_1 = N_2 = 800$ and $P = 20$).

experimental results are compared. In general, the execution times achieved using the theoretically predicted best tile sizes are close to the best observed in experiments. For double loops with rectangular iteration spaces, block tile distribution is almost always the best choice unless $N_1 \gg N_2$ or the double loop contains other loops in its loop body. Similar results and observations have also been reported previously in [10,17].

Table 3: The domains of the four functions defining $F(p)$.

Function	Domain
$B(p)$	$[2, \min(P_{\text{one}}, P]$
$C_1(p)$	$[\min(\max(2, \lfloor P_{\text{one}} \rfloor + 1), P_{\text{two}}), P]$
$C_2(p)$	$[\max(2, \lfloor P_{\text{one}} \rfloor + 1), \min(\lceil P_{\text{two}} \rceil - 1, P)]$ such that $N_2(a+b) < N_1 t$
$C_3(p)$	$[\max(2, \lfloor P_{\text{one}} \rfloor + 1), P]$ such that $N_2(a+b) \geqslant N_1 t$

4 Processor-Time Minimal Tiling

The problem becomes one of finding p to minimise the piece-wise objective function:

$$F(p) = \begin{cases} \frac{N_2 a}{pb+N_1 t} \geqslant 1 & \rightarrow \quad B(p) \\ \frac{N_2 a}{pb+N_1 t} < 1 & \rightarrow \quad \begin{cases} \frac{N_1}{p}\sqrt{\frac{N_1 N_2 (a+b)}{t}} \leqslant 1 & \rightarrow C_1(p) \\ 1 < \frac{N_1}{p}\sqrt{\frac{N_1 N_2 (a+b)}{t}} < \frac{N_1}{p} & \rightarrow C_2(p) \\ \frac{N_1}{p}\sqrt{\frac{N_1 N_2 (a+b)}{t}} \geqslant \frac{N_1}{p} & \rightarrow C_3(p) \end{cases} \end{cases} \tag{14}$$

where

$$B(p) = (\sqrt{pa} + \sqrt{N_2(b + \frac{N_1 t}{p})})^2$$

$$C_1(p) = (p + \frac{N_1 N_2}{p})(t + a + b)$$

$$C_2(p) = (\sqrt{p(a+b)} + \sqrt{\frac{N_1 N_2 t}{p}})^2$$

$$C_3(p) = (p + N_2)(\frac{N_1}{p}t + a + b)$$

such that

$$2 \leqslant p \leqslant P$$

The lower bound of p is not 1 because the formula (10) used in establishing Theorem 1 breaks down if the number of processors is 1. If required, the sequential execution time of the program can be checked to see if parallel execution is beneficial at all.

The objective function $F(p)$ gives the execution time on a p-processor machine using the best tile size found by Theorem 1. Once the best processor count p^* is found, the best tile size (n_1^*, n_2^*) on a p^*-processor machine is found by Theorem 1.

Based on the following two constants:

$$P_{\text{one}} = \frac{N_2 a - N_1 t}{b}$$

$$P_{\text{two}} = \sqrt{\frac{N_2 N_1 (a+b)}{t}}$$

Table 3 lists the domains of $B(p)$, $C_1(p)$, $C_2(p)$ and $C_3(p)$. To minimise $F(p)$, we minimise these four functions individually in their respective domains. Among the four optimal solutions found, the one that minimises $F(p)$ is the best processor count as desired. Sections 4.1 and 4.4 minimise the four individual functions. Section 4.5 gives the processor-time-minimal solution and presents some experimental results.

4.1 Minimising $B(p)$

The point at which $B(p)$ is minimised is related to the the *unique positive root* of:

$$\frac{dB}{dp} = \left(-\frac{a}{2\sqrt{ap}} - \frac{-\frac{N_1 N_2 t}{p^2}}{2\sqrt{b + \frac{N1 N_2 t}{p}}}\right)\left(\sqrt{ap} + \sqrt{b + \frac{N1 N_2 t}{p}}\right) = 0 \qquad (15)$$

All real roots of the above equation can be found from:

$$-\frac{a}{2\sqrt{ap}} - \frac{-\frac{N_1 N_2 t}{p^2}}{2\sqrt{b + \frac{N1 N_2 t}{p}}} = 0$$

Moving one term to the other side, squaring both sides and simplifying yields:

$$p^3 + \frac{N_1 t}{b} p^2 - \frac{N_1^2 N_2 t^2}{ab} = 0$$

By Descartes' rule[18] , this equation has exactly one positive real root, denoted P_{root}. By noting that $B(p)$ is strictly convex on $(0, +\infty)$, we have the following result.

Lemma 7 *$B(p)$ attains its minimum in its domain when*

$$p^* = \max(2, \min(P_{\text{one}}, P_{\text{root}}, P))$$

4.2 Minimising $C_1(p)$

Lemma 8 *$C_1(p)$ attains its minimum in its domain when $p^* = P$.*

Proof. The unique positive root to $\frac{dC_1}{dp} = (1 - \frac{N_1 N_2}{p^2})(t + a + b) = 0$ is $\sqrt{N_1 N_2}$. Due to our earlier assumption (1), $P \leqslant \sqrt{N_1 N_2}$ holds. It can be verified that $\frac{d^2 C_1}{dp^2} > 0$. This means that $C_1(p)$ is strictly convex in its domain. Hence, $p^* = P$. ■

4.3 *Minimising $C_2(p)$*

Lemma 9 *$C_2(p)$ attains is minimum in its domain when $p^* = \min(\lceil P_{\text{two}} \rceil - 1, P)$.*
Proof. The following equation

$$\frac{dC_2}{dp} = (-\frac{\sqrt{a+b}}{2\sqrt{p}} + \frac{\sqrt{N_1N_2t}\sqrt{p}}{2p^2})(\sqrt{P(a+b)} + \sqrt{\frac{N_1N_2t}{P}}) = 0$$

has two real roots: $-\sqrt{\frac{N_1N_2t}{a+b}}$ and $\sqrt{\frac{N_1N_2t}{a+b}}$. We find that $\frac{dC_2}{dp} < 0$ on $(0, \sqrt{\frac{N_1N_2t}{a+b}})$ and $\frac{dC2}{dp} > 0$ on $(\sqrt{\frac{N_1N_2t}{a+b}}, +\infty)$. Thus, $C_2(p)$ is strictly decreasing on $(0, \sqrt{\frac{N_1N_2t}{a+b}}]$ and strictly increasing on $[\sqrt{\frac{N_1N_2t}{a+b}}, +\infty)$. Because $\frac{N_1}{p}\sqrt{\frac{N_2(a+b)}{N_1t}} < \frac{N_1}{p}$ implies $N_1t > N_2(a+b)$, we have $\sqrt{\frac{N_1N_2t}{a+b}} > \sqrt{\frac{N_2N_2(a+b)}{a+b}} = N_2$. Due to our assumption (1), which implies $P \leqslant \min(N_1, N_2)$, $P < \sqrt{\frac{N_1N_2t}{a+b}}$ holds. This means that $C_2(p)$ is strictly deceasing in its entire domain. Hence, $p^* = \min(\lceil P_{\text{two}} \rceil - 1, P)$. ■

4.4 *Minimising $C_3(p)$*

Lemma 10 *$C_3(p)$ attains its minimum in its domain when*

$$p^* = \max(2, \lfloor P_{\text{one}} \rfloor + 1, \min(\sqrt{\frac{N_1N_2t}{a+b}}, P))$$

Proof. Follows from the fact that $C_3(p)$ is strictly convex in its domain and that $\sqrt{\frac{N_1N_2t}{a+b}}$ is the unique positive solution to $\frac{dC_3}{dp} = (a+b) - \frac{N_1N_2t}{p^2} = 0$. ■

4.5 *Processor-Time-Minimal Tile Size*

A combination of Theorem 1 and Lemmas 7 – 10 leads directly to the following result.
Theorem 2 *The processor-time-minimal tile size (n_1^*, n_2^*) is obtained from Theorem 1 by setting $P = p^*$, where p^* is from Lemma 7 – 10 such that $F(p^*)$ is minimised.* By setting $P = +\infty$ in this theorem, the best execution time achievable is obtained.

Table 4 lists three asymptotic solutions derived from Theorem 2.

Figure 5 compares some theoretical and experimental results of SOR on CM-5 and AP1000, respectively. The problem size 128×128 was used so that the best processor count does not exceed the limited number of processors available in our experiments. By Theorem 2, $p^* = 31.5$ for CM-5 and $p^* = 22$ for AP1000. By Theorem 1, block tile distribution is the best on both machines: $n_1^* = \frac{N_1}{P} \approx 4$ and $n_2^* \approx 4$ for CM-5 and $n_1^* = \frac{N_1}{P} \approx 6$ and $n_2^* \approx 6$ for AP1000. While theoretical and experimental best processor counts can differ quite widely due to the integral approximations of real optimal values, the speedups in both cases are very close.

Table 4: Asymptotic processor-time-minimal solutions.

	$a \to +\infty$	$b \to +\infty$	$t \to +\infty$
n_1^*	$\frac{N_1}{2}$	$\frac{N_1}{2}$	1
n_2^*	N_2	1	1
p^*	2	2	P

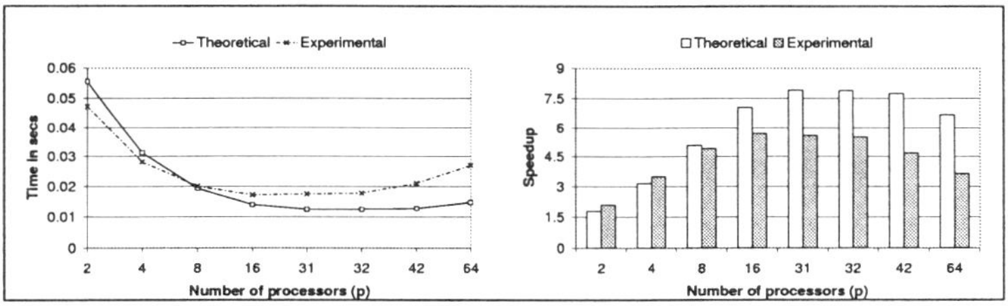

(a) CM-5: Theoretical: $p^* = 31.5$; Experimental: $p^* = 16$

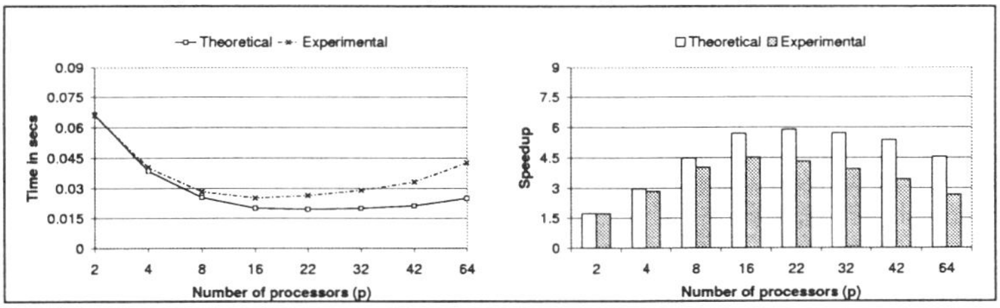

(b) AP1000: Theoretical: $p^* = 22$; Experimental: $p^* = 16$

Figure 5: Processor-time-minimal tiling for SOR ($N_1 = N_2 = 128$).

5 An Alternative Communication Cost Model

Our communication cost model $T_{\mathsf{msg}}(L) = a + c\,L$ includes $T_{\mathsf{msg}}(L) = a$ and $T_{\mathsf{msg}}(L) = c\,L$ as two special cases. The former is used in[12].

A factor that can have significant impact on communication performance is competition for bandwidth. In the following cost model given in[16]:

$$T_{\mathsf{msg}}(L) = a + c\,PL \tag{16}$$

The scaling factor P reflects the idea that the effective bandwidth available to each processor is $\frac{1}{P}$ of the true bandwidth. The problem-solving techniques used in this paper are quite general to accommodate a range of cost models.

If this new model is used, the execution time formula given in (8) will become:

$$S(n_1, n_2) = (P + \frac{N_1 N_2}{n_1 n_2 P})(n_1 n_2 t + a + b n_2 P) \tag{17}$$

All results for finding time-minimal tilings presented in Section 3.3 are the same if b is replaced with Pb. Specifically, these results are recast as follows.

1. Lemma 3 holds because S is still a strictly decreasing function of n_1 on every hyperbola $n_1 n_2 = c$ for some fixed c.

2. Lemma 4 is modified as follows. $S(\frac{N_1}{P}, 1)$ attains its minimum:

$$S^* = (\sqrt{Pa} + \sqrt{N_2(Pb + \frac{N_1 t}{P})})^2 \tag{18}$$

when

$$n_2^* = \sqrt{\frac{N_2 a}{P^2 b + N_1 t}}$$

3. Lemma 5 is modified as follows. $S(n_1, 1)$ attains its minimum:

$$S^* = \begin{cases} \frac{N_1}{P}\sqrt{\frac{N_1 N_2 (a+Pb)}{N_1 t}} \leqslant 1 & \rightarrow (P + \frac{N_1 N_2}{P})(t + a + Pb) \\ 1 < \frac{N_1}{P}\sqrt{\frac{N_2(a+Pb)}{N_1 t}} < \frac{N_1}{P} & \rightarrow (\sqrt{P(a+Pb)} + \sqrt{\frac{N_1 N_2 t}{P}})^2 \\ \frac{N_1}{P}\sqrt{\frac{N_2(a+Pb)}{N_1 t}} \geqslant \frac{N_1}{P} & \rightarrow (P + N_2)(\frac{N_1}{P}t + a + Pb) \end{cases} \tag{19}$$

when

$$n_1^* = \max(1, \min(\frac{N_1}{P}, \frac{N_1}{P}\sqrt{\frac{N_2(a+Pb)}{N_1 t}}))$$

4. Theorem 1 is modified as follows. The best tile size is $(\frac{N_1}{P}, \sqrt{\frac{N_2 a}{P^2 b + N_1 t}})$ if $\frac{N_2 a}{P^2 b + N_1 t} \geqslant 1$ and $\max(1, \min(\frac{N_1}{P}, \frac{N_1}{P}\sqrt{\frac{N_2(a+Pb)}{N_1 t}}))$ otherwise.

The derivation of processor-time-minimal tilings can be done similarly.

By comparing the best tile sizes obtained using the two cost models, we note that the results in the latter model can be derived from those in the former (simpler) model by replacing b with Pb. In practice, $b \ll P$. Unless P is sufficiently large, the best tile size found using the simpler cost model are accurate for practical purposes.

6 Related Work

The compiler community has explored the use of loop tiling to enhance the performance of loop-oriented programs on machines with multiple processors and/or memory hierarchies. In this section, only some previous research efforts directly related to the work of this paper are reviewed. The first attempt on finding the time-minimal tilings for double loops was made in [13], where the communication cost model same as ours is used. They assumed but did not prove that the best tile size can always be found in Case (c). Their optimal solution for Case (c) is repeated in Lemma 4. In addition to rectangular iteration spaces, they also considered non-rectangular iteration spaces. However, they did not address the processor-time-minimal tiling problem.

In [11], a different communication cost model is used. They assumed that computation and communication completely overlap with each other. They considered Cases (a) and (c) and found the best tile sizes in both cases to be (1,1). They suggested to obtain non-trivial tile sizes by making the execution time dependent on data locality.

In [10], a slightly more sophisticated communication cost model is used in an attempts to quantify separately various factors that impact the communication overheads between two participating processors. In solving the time-minimal tiling problem, their best tile size is similar in nature to that found by Theorem 1. In solving the processor-time-minimal tiling problem, they assumed that block tile distribution is always optimal. They found the best processor count using a quadratic objective function of the processor variable p while ours is cubic. These authors also studied during the last few years the problem of tiling higher-dimensional loop nests [17,19,20].

In [12], the authors exploited the DOALL parallelism at the level of tiles. They assumed that an unbounded number of processors is available so that all tiles in the same wavefront can be executed simultaneously. Based on the cost model $T_{\mathsf{msg}}(L) = a$, they derived the best tile sizes for some special class of programs.

7 Conclusion

In this paper, we have provided the optimal solutions to both the time-minimal tiling problem and the processor-time-minimal tiling problem. In particular, we have provided formal proofs that if the processors are idle or load imbalanced under a particular tiling scheme, then that tiling scheme is not the best possible. Our experimental results indicate that our theoretically predicted best tile sizes and processor counts can yield execution times close to the best observed during experiments. We have demonstrated that the problem-solving techniques used in the paper are general enough to accommodate other communication cost models. The results of this paper can be used for hand turning parallel codes and in optimising compilers.

Acknowledgements

This is work is supported by an Australian Research Council Grant A1007149.

References

1. P. Boulet, A. Darte, T. Risset, and Y. Robert. (Pen)-ultimate tiling. *Integration, the VLSI Journal*, 17:33–51, 1994.
2. F. Irigoin and R. Triolet. Supernode partitioning. In *15th Annual ACM Symposium on Principles of Programming Languages*, pages 319–329, San Diego, California., Jan. 1988.

3. Fabrice Rastello and Yves Robert. Loop partitioning versus tiling for cache-based multiprocessors. In *1998 International Conference on Parallel and distributed Computing and Systems*, pages 477–483. IASTED Press, 1998.
4. N. Mitchell, L. Carter, J. Ferrante, and K. Högstedt. Quantifying the multi-level nature of tiling interactions. *International Journal of Parallel Programming*, 26(26):641–670, 1998.
5. Y. Song and Z. Li. New tiling techniques to improve cache temporal locality. In *ACM SIGPLAN'99 Conf. on Programming Language Design and Implementation*, pages 215–228, 1999.
6. G. Rivera and C.-W. Tseng. A comparison of compiler tiling algorithms. In *The 8th International Conference on Compiler Construction*, Amsterdam, Mar. 1999.
7. M. E. Wolf and M. S. Lam. A loop transformation theory and an algorithm to maximize parallelism. *IEEE Transactions on Parallel and Distributed Systems*, 2(4):452–471, Oct. 1991.
8. M. J. Wolfe. More iteration space tiling. In *Supercomputing '88*, pages 655–664, Reno, Nev., Nov. 1989.
9. J. Xue. *Loop Tiling for Parallelism*. Kluwer Academic Publishers, Aug. 2000.
10. R. Andonov and S. Rajopadhye. Optimal orthogonal tiling of 2-D iterations. *Journal of Parallel and Distributed Computing*, 45(2):159–165, Sept. 1997.
11. P. Y. Calland, J. Dongarra, and Y. Robert. Tiling on systems with communication/computation overlap. *Concurrency: Practice and Experience*, 11(3):139–153, 1999.
12. E. Hodzic and W. Shang. On supernode transformation with minimized total running time. *IEEE Transactions on Parallel and Distributed Systems*, 9(5):417–428, May 1998.
13. H. Ohta, Y. Saito, M. Kainaga, and H. Ono. Optimal tile size adjustment in compiling for general DOACROSS loop nests. In *1995 ACM International Conference on Supercomputing*, pages 270–279. ACM Press, 1995.
14. J. Xue. On tiling as a loop transformation. *Parallel Processing Letters*, 7(4):409–424, 1997.
15. P. Tang and J. Xue. Generating efficient tiled code for distributed memory machines. *Parallel Computing*, 2000. To appear.
16. I. Foster. *Designing and Building Parallel Programs: Concepts and Tools for Parallel Software Engineering*. Addison-Wesley, 1994.
17. R. Andonov, S. Rajopadhye, and N. Yanev. Optimal orthogonal tiling. In David Pritchard and Jeff Reeve, editors, *1998 European Parallel Processing Conference*, Lecture Notes in Computer Science 1470, pages 480–490, Sept. 1998.
18. L. Griffiths. *Introduction to the Theory of Equations*. Jon Wiley & Sons, Inc., 1947.
19. R. Andonov and N. Yanev. n-dimensional orthogonal tiling. Technical Report LIMAV-RR-96-6, Universitè de Valenciennes, Sept. 1996.
20. R. Andonov, N. Yanev, and H. Bourzoufi. Three-dimensional orthogonal tile sizing problem: Mathematical programming approach. Technical Report LIMAV-RR-96-3, Universitè de Valenciennes, Mar. 1996.

MESH SIMPLIFICATION IN PARALLEL

FRANK DEHNE

School of Computer Science, Carleton University, Ottawa, Canada, frank@dehne.net

CHRISTIAN LANGIS AND GERHARD ROTH

National Research Council, Ottawa, Canada, {Christian.Langis,Gerhard.Roth}@nrc.ca

This paper presents a parallel method for progressive mesh simplification. A progressive mesh (PM) is a continuous mesh representation of a given 3D object which makes it possible to efficiently access all mesh representations between a low and a high level of resolution. The creation of a progressive mesh is a time consuming process and has a need for parallelization. Our parallel approach considers the original mesh as a graph and performs first a greedy graph partitioning. Then, each partition is sent to a processor of a coarse-grained parallel system. The individual mesh partitions are converted in parallel to the PM format using a serial algorithm on each processor. The results are then merged together to produce a single large PM file. This merging process also solves the border problem within the partition in a simple and efficient way. Our approach enables us to achieve close to optimal speedup. We demonstrate the results experimentally on a number of data sets.

1 Introduction

Mesh simplification is the process of approximating a high-resolution mesh by a coarser mesh with a lower triangle count. Traditional mesh simplification methods produce a coarser mesh but only at a single given resolution. By contrast, the Progressive Mesh (PM) representation [6] is a continuous resolution mesh. This category of representation stores in a compact fashion all resolutions between the lowest resolution (which is predefined) and the original high resolution mesh.

In a PM representation, an arbitrary mesh M is stored as a much coarser mesh M^0 together with a sequence of vertex splits that indicates how to incrementally convert M^0 back into the original mesh M = M^n. The PM representation of M thus defines a continuous sequence of meshes $M^0, M^1, ..., M^n$ of increasing accuracy. The inverse of the vertex split is the edge collapse. With these two operations it is possible to create a mesh at any given resolution between the original high resolution mesh (M) and the lowest resolution mesh M^0 (see Figure 1).

$$(\hat{M} = M^n) \xrightarrow{ecol_{n-1}} \ldots \xrightarrow{ecol_1} M^1 \xrightarrow{ecol_0} M^0$$

$$M^0 \xrightarrow{vsplit_0} M^1 \xrightarrow{vsplit_1} \ldots \xrightarrow{vsplit_{n-1}} (M^n = \hat{M})$$

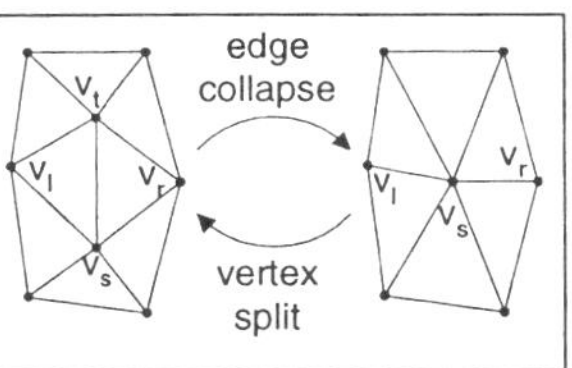

Figure 1: Simplification/refinement operation

Since the simplification and refinement operations are very efficient, they can be performed in real-time. The PM representation has many applications. The most obvious is to use the representation for real-time level of detail (LOD) control for graphical rendering [10, 3]. Another application is the incremental transmission of a mesh on a network. The coarse M^0 can be transmitted first, and the higher resolutions can be displayed incrementally as the vertex split operations are transmitted. Finally, the PM representation can be used to perform viewpoint dependent refinement [9].

While the display of the PM format is efficient, the creation of the PM sequence of edge collapses/vertex splits is more time consuming. At each step in the process it is necessary to choose which edge to collapse. This makes it necessary to compute the geometric error produced by each potential edge collapse and associate a cost with it. Once a cost is assigned to every edge, all potential edge collapses are sorted by cost. For large meshes this is a computationally intensive process.

Therefore, the creation of the PM sequence is a potential application for parallel processing. Our approach is to parallelize at the coarse-grained multiprocessor level by assigning different portions of the input mesh to different processes. We use a greedy graph partitioning algorithm to divide the mesh into disjoint subsets. Each mesh subset is sent to a "slave" processor where it is converted into the PM format using a serial algorithm. An important issue in such partition based parallel algorithms is the partition border problem. In this application, this problem manifests itself in the question of how to rejoin the PM representations at the border of the mesh partitions. We provide a solution to the partition border problem that is both simple and efficient. Our solution enables our parallelization approach to have a close to linear speedup, which is optimal. To our knowledge, no such parallel implementation of a continuous mesh creation algorithm exists in the literature.

The remainder of this paper is organised as follows. In Section 2, we give an overview of the parallel mesh simplification algorithm. In Section 3, we discuss the parallel implementation itself. Section 4 shows the results of our experimental performance analysis and we discuss the quality of our PM obtained in Section 5. Section 6 concludes the paper.

2 Parallel Mesh Simplification

Our parallel implementation of the mesh simplification makes use of a standard serial algorithm for mesh simplification [6]. The approach for our parallelization is to partition the original high resolution mesh on a master processor and then to send each mesh partition to a slave processor. Each slave processor simplifies its associated mesh subset into a PM. Once this task is complete, each slave returns its

PM to the master processor which now merges them together to create a single PM file for the entire mesh. The following is the basic outline of our parallel algorithm:

```
Parallel_Simplification(Mesh M, PartitionSize p)
    if (ProcID == 0)                              //Master
section
        (M1, ..., Mp) = Partition(M, p)
        for i=1..p
            send Mi to Proci
        for i=1..p
            receive PMi from Proci
        merge ∀PMi into PM
        return PM
    else                                          //Slave section
        receive MProcID from Proc0
        PMProcID = Simplify(MProcID)
        send PMProcID to Proc0
```

Figure 2: Global structure of our parallel algorithm

2.1 Greedy Partition Method

The first step is to partition the mesh. We use is a simple greedy method where the graph partitioning problem is solved by accumulating vertices (or faces) in subsets when travelling through the graph. A starting vertex v_s is chosen and marked. The accumulation process is performed by selecting the neighbours of v_s, then the neighbours of the neighbours and so on until the subset has reached the required number of vertices. Then, other subsets are created the same way until the p-way partition is complete (e.g. each vertex is part of one subset). In the general case, such a p-way partition is built from p partial Breadth-First-Search traversals of the graph. The algorithm terminates when all vertices have been visited [2].

This simple greedy heuristic will yield acceptable partitions in much less time than more complicated methods. Furthermore, the algorithm can be made probabilistic if necessary [1]. It suffices to initialize it with a random vertex seed to generate different partitions for a same input graph. Figure 3 shows one 8-way partition example of this algorithm on a 3D mesh representing a duck [13].

The subsets being built may get blocked in the process before they reach full size. Then, two versions of the algorithm are possible: allow subset size imbalance or subset multi-connectivity. The former produces uneven subset sizes (workload on processors) and the latter produces bigger edge-cuts (more communication between processors). We chose the latter for better load balancing [4].

Figure 3: An exploded view of a 8-way partition of the 4K faces NRC Duck

2.2 *Partition Border Problem*

The main algorithmic problem for parallel progressive mesh simplification is the border problem. That is, how do we handle the triangles intersecting the border between different parts of the mesh as each part is processed in parallel on a different processor. Recall that the vertex set V of the mesh is partitioned into p disjoint subsets V_i whose union is V. Therefore, there are edges (and faces) between partition subsets (part of the edge-cut). Ideally, those edge-cut edges need to be dealt with just like subset edges. That is, during the parallel execution, at synchronisation points, there is an exchange of information between slave processors (potentially through the master processor) regarding the state of the mesh. Then, either of the neighbouring slave processors processes the shared edges using the edge information from the neighbours. This interdependence management scheme is costly but most applications are border-sensitive and require it. The graphs considered here are meshes representing 3D objects. The human eye accuracy sets the required quality level of processing. Hence, *invisible* degradation of the optimal result is allowed. In fact, we chose to avoid the border problem as long as possible. By not collapsing the edge-cut, one might expect to see the mesh separator in full resolution when the PM mesh is displayed at a coarse resolution. Fortunately, this is not the case. The edge-cut will be indirectly simplified along with any other edge. This phenomenon is shown in Figure 4.

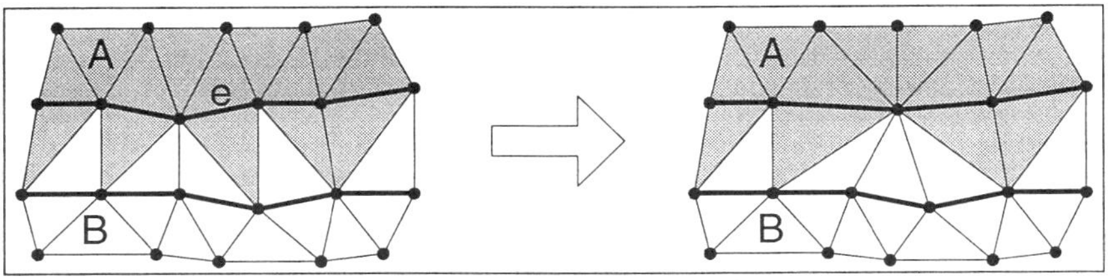

Figure 4: Edge-cut face deletion

The partition snapshot represents the border between two subsets at some point during simplification. The two bold lines represent the link of each subset (the edge borders of subsets). The darker triangles belong to subset A and those in white belong to B. In this situation, the edge e from subset A will be collapsed. Note that, this edge has part of its neighbourhood in subset B. More precisely, e has seven edges and six triangles joined to B by four vertices of B. However, if we simply force the collapse of e, the collapse affects only the structure (topology) of subset A. The neighbourhood part outside of A (vertices and edges and triangles of B) is left unchanged, topologically. It is only used to compute the best vertex position and the edge collapse cost for e. Following the collapse, two faces from A are deleted, including one from the edge-cut (between subsets). Therefore the parallel algorithm can simplify meshes as much as the sequential algorithm does, without the need for synchronisation steps or communications between processors.

3 Parallel Implementation

The code was written in C, using an MPI package for communication (more precisely, the free LAM-MPI [11]). The master processor partitions the mesh into p subsets. The partitioner will return a size |V| integer array. Each array cell corresponds to a mesh vertex and contains a subset ID $\in$ [1..p] indicating the processor to which the vertex is assigned. The next step is to send that partition array to the slave processors. Then, all processors read the same mesh file into a *Mesh* object exactly as in the sequential version. With the partition array at hand, the slave processors build a working mesh structure of edges and faces which are either part of their partition subset or adjacent to it (surrounding edge-cut). Those edge-cut elements are included to address the border problem. Next, the slave processors build their edge collapse priority queues. In the parallel version, they do so with one extra condition: each edge must have both end-points in the slave processor's vertex subset to allow a collapse. From that point on, the slave processor's task remains the same as in the sequential program: it has a priority queue of edges to collapse.

After simplification, the slave processors must transmit their sub-results to the master processor for merging. This caused a technical difficulty. The data is now in the form of vectors, stacks and hashbags of vertices, edges and faces. Previously, the master sent an array of integers to the slaves. Now, the slave processors respond with arrays of more general objects. Our version of MPI does not support data communication other than standard data types. Therefore, we had to manually convert our arrays of objects to streams of standard data types and then back to objects. Once the data has been correctly communicated to the master processor and reconverted, the master contains p sets of four items sent by the p slaves: p hashbags of not deleted faces, p stacks of deleted faces, p vectors of collapsed edges and p vectors of new vertices. Those edge collapses were created independently. The master processor's task is to synchronise them. For each collapse, an edge, a vertex and two faces are extracted from the data of one slave processor. The slaves collapse sets are visited in round-robin and their collapses are extracted one after another, from the best collapse performed to the most destructive one (See [4]). Another problem to be dealt with are duplicate faces. As mentioned, the subsets are sent to slave processors along with their surrounding edge-cut. Therefore, slave processors work independently on duplicate data. Consequently, all faces from the edge-cut will be replicated in the data returned by the slaves. For this reason, as the PM mesh is built, it must constantly be filtered for duplicate faces.

4 Performance Analysis

To evaluate the quality and performance of our implementation, we performed a series of tests on a network of Linux/Pentium 120Mhz/32Mb workstations (some were Pentium MMX 166Mhz). P_0 was the master processor. We tested our program with 2, 4, 8, and 16 processors connected to a 10Mbps Ethernet network. We ran these tests when most of the machines were idle. Unfortunately, there was no guarantee that the timings were not influenced by other users. This is clearly a very low cost and not state-of-the-art parallel processing platform. However, since we are mainly interested in measuring speedup, this platform was sufficient. Furthermore, if our method performs well on such a low cost platform, it will clearly be even better on more expensive and newer parallel machines.

Our tests were conducted on two basic input meshes: the NRC Duck [13] and the Stanford Dragon [14]. We used various size meshes as input and processed each using various numbers of processors. The performace results are shown in Tables 1 and 2 below. Besides the total running time (T), we also measured the time to transfer the partition array to slave processors and read the input mesh on each processor (PC) as well as the PM computation time on each slave processor (S). Of particular importance is the load balance between slave processors. Recall that the mesh partitioning was obtained by a greedy partitioning algorithm as outlined in Section 2.1. We measured the difference between the slowest and fastest slave processor with respect to S in order to see how the computational load is balanced between processors. For each input size and number of processors, we performed five test runs. The bold numbers are averaged values and the italicised numbers in square 1ckets are their standard deviations. The blank lines no. 16 and 17 in Table 2 are caused by memory overflow. For meshes of such size, we needed to partition them among at least four processors so that each partition can fit into a processor's memory.

|V|	number of vertices in the input mesh
p	number of processors
PC	time to transfer the partition array to slave processors and read the input mesh on each processor
S	progressive mesh computation time on each slave processor
ΔS	difference between slowest and fastes slave processor with respect to S
T	total execution time for the entire algorithm

	|V|	p	PC	S	ΔS	T
1	2031	1	-	-	-	618.0
2		2	**0.0** *[0.0]*	**283.2** *[42.6]*	**71.0** *[57.8]*	**295.6** *[41.1]*
3		4	**0.2** *[0.4]*	**133.0** *[4.1]*	**51.6** *[16.2]*	**150.4** *[4.2]*
4		8	**0.2** *[0.4]*	**66.8** *[8.6]*	**35.0** *[7.8]*	**84.2** *[8.2]*
5		16	**1.2** *[1.5]*	**30.4** *[1.3]*	**18.0** *[2.0]*	**49.2** *[2.4]*
6	12281	1	-	-	-	4774
7		2	**2.0** *[0.0]*	**2244** *[70.7]*	**640** *[117.5]*	**2350** *[72.1]*
8		4	**2.4** *[0.5]*	**1368** *[243.6]*	**539** *[304.9]*	**1473** *[242.6]*
9		8	**3.8** *[3.1]*	**642** *[79.1]*	**319** *[91.4]*	**747** *[80.8]*
10		16	**8.4** *[6.3]*	**322** *[30.8]*	**178** *[40.5]*	**445** *[36.4]*
11	50044	1	-	-	-	26345
12		2	**13.4** *[0.5]*	**11966** *[422]*	**2792** *[619]*	**12376** *[382]*
13		4	**12.8** *[5.1]*	**6920** *[136]*	**2686** *[181]*	**7321** *[145]*
14		8	**15.2** *[12.0]*	**3325** *[246]*	**1553** *[311]*	**3764** *[272]*
15		16	**67.3** *[17.6]*	**1813** *[119]*	**979** *[128]*	**2321** *[167]*

Table 1: Parallel simplification statistics: NRC Duck. (The bold numbers are averaged values and the italicised numbers in square 1ckets are their standard deviations.)

	|V|	p	PC	S	ΔS	T
1	5205	1	-	-	-	572
2		2	**0.8** *[0.4]*	**265.4** *[2.3]*	**79.2** *[2.9]*	**307.2** *[3.1]*
3		4	**1.0** *[0.0]*	**132.2** *[7.8]*	**42.2** *[15.0]*	**171.6** *[7.4]*
4		8	**1.4** *[0.8]*	**66.0** *[7.6]*	**31.0** *[11.1]*	**107.6** *[6.2]*
5		16	**2.6** *[2.7]*	**39.0** *[2.6]*	**25.4** *[2.5]*	**80.8** *[5.2]*
6	22998	1	-	-	-	3813
7		2	**5.4** *[1.2]*	**1878** *[310]*	**560** *[362]*	**2079** *[308]*
8		4	**6.0** *[2.4]*	**949** *[38]*	**328** *[71]*	**1141** *[39]*
9		8	**6.8** *[3.6]*	**462** *[22]*	**178** *[36]*	**657** *[28]*
10		16	**11.2** *[12.4]*	**233** *[13]*	**108** *[17]*	**425** *[12]*
11		1	-	-	-	34811

12		2	**52.8** [*28.4*]	**15617** [*452*]	**4057** [*161*]	**16577** [*429*]
13	100250	4	**68.5** [*56.5*]	**7158** [*70*]	**2086** [*126*]	**8211** [*174*]
14		8	**82.8** [*1.8*]	**3449** [*68*]	**1260** [*127*]	**4427** [*96*]
15		16	**162.8** [*3.1*]	**1776** [*75*]	**709** [*99*]	**2874** [*130*]
16		1	-	-	-	-
17		2	-	-	-	-
18	198318	4	**103** [*12*]	**29640** [*1367*]	**9483** [*2768*]	**32103** [*1638*]
19		8	**184** [*20*]	**11338** [*58*]	**3749** [*307*]	**13714** [*59*]
20		16	**369** [*73*]	**5620** [*13*]	**1873** [*131*]	**8315** [*353*]

Table 2: Parallel simplification statistics: Stanford Dragon. (The bold numbers are averaged values and the italicised numbers in square 1ckets are their standard deviations.)

We now discuss our performance results in Tables 1 and 2. The main observation is that, despite the low cost communication network, the total time (T) observed for our method shows close to linear speedup. As expected, speedups are slightly lower for smaller data sets (|V|) and improve for larger data sets. The time for partitioning the data set (PC) increases with growing number of processors, as expected. What is very interesting to observe is that S often shows a more than linear speedup. How is this possible? The parallel algorithm does not explicitly collapse the edges that span the boundaries of the partition. The number of such edges increases with growing p. This effect does actually decrease the total work performed and, therefore, we can observe more than linear speedup. The load balancing of our method is measured in the ΔS column. Here, we observe that the load imbalance can be as high as 50%. Note, however, that finding an optimal partitioning of a mesh while minimizing the number of edges crossing boundaries is an NP complete problem. In our solution, we are using a greedy heuristic and for such a simple heuristic to be within a factor two of optimal is actually quite good. We need to balance the time it takes to compute the partitioning (PC) versus the imbalance created (ΔS) and the close to linear speedup for the total time T seems to indicate that the greedy heuristic used is a good compromise solution. With respect to the variances measured, we observe that they are fairly large. Clearly, the heuristic itself creates fluctuations but another important factor here is that we were performing our experiments in a multi-user environment. Furthermore, we observe that the variances for the total time (T) observed are considerably smaller than those for the other times measured.

In summary, we conclude that the total time (T) observed for our method shows close to optimal linear speedup, even on a very low-cost, low-tech, communication network. We plan to test the method on other more advance machines, like a Cray T3E or IBM SP2, where we expect to obtain even better timing results.

5 Quality Analysis

Besides analyzing the runtime of our method, we also need to study the quality of the progressive mesh simplication obtained in comparison with the results of a purely sequential algorithm. Here, the main concern is about the edges that span the boundaries of the partition. Everything else is processed with a sequential algorithm and is therefore of the same quality. With respect to the edges that span the boundaries of the partition, anomalies could appear in the obtained progressive meshes, along those boundaries. For example, the boundaries could become visible because there are “breaks” or different triangle densities along those boundaries. In Figure 4, process A collapses edge e whose neighbourhood contains four vertices from B. Furthermore, B collapses edges connected to those four vertices, indeed widening the extent of e’s neighbourhood (vertices) on B’s side. An edge collapse can be considered as the merge of a pair of vertices. Merging those four vertices with other vertices of B extends the neighbourhood of e on B’s side. Therefore, any vertex in B merged to one of those four neighbourhood vertices becomes part of e‘s neighbourhood. However, as edge collapses are not communicated between slave processors, A will never be aware of it. Thus, the border edge neighbourhoods may include too few vertices from the adjacent vertex subsets. On the other hand, border edges remain as duplicates, and this may alleviate the problem. We examined progressive meshes obtained from using our algorithm on the NRC duck and other data and observed that, there are no visible breaks or inconsistency along the borders of our partitioning.

6 Conclusion

This paper presented a parallel algorithm for progressive mesh simplification. Our experiments show that the proposed method yields close to optimal speedup, even on a low-cost parallel platform. We presented a very simple solution for the problem of how to manage the border between different parts of the mesh partitioning. As mesh simplifications are becoming more important in 3D graphics, and parallel processing platforms are becoming more affordable (e.g. multi processor Pentium boards), parallel progressive mesh simplification methods will have an important role to play in such applications as parallel VR systems or the transmission of 3D models over networks.

7 Bibliography

1. Gilles 1ssard, Paul 1tley. *Fundamentals of Algorithms*. Prentice-Hall, Chapter 10, 1996.

2. P. Ciarlet, F. Lamour. *An Efficient Low Cost Greedy Graph Partitioning Heuristic*. CAM Report 94-1, UCLA, Department of Mathematics, 1994.
3. Andrea Ciampalini, Paolo Cignoni, Claudio Montani, Roberto Scopigno. *Multiresolution Decimation Based on Global Error*. The Visual Computer 13 pp. 228-246, Springer-Verlag, 1997.
4. Christian Langis, *Mesh Simplification in Parallel*, MCS thesis, Carleton University, 1999.
5. Brian Cort. *An Implementation of a Progressive Mesh Simplification Algorithm*. Visual Information Technology Group, Institute for Information Technology Group, NRC Canada, 1997.
6. Hugues Hoppe, Tony DeRose, Tom Duchamp, John McDonald, Werner Stuetzle. *Mesh Optimization*. Technical Report 93-01-01, Dept. Of Computer Science & Engineering, University of Washinton and SIGGRAPH 93 Proceedings, pp. 19-26. 1993.
7. M. Eck, TD. Rose, T. Duchamp, H. Hoppe, M. Lounsbery, W. Stuetzle. *Multiresolution analysis of arbitrary meshes*. Computer Graphics Proceedings Annual Conference Series, SIGGRAPH 95, ACM Press, pp.173-181, 1995.
8. Hugues Hoppe. *Progressive Meshes*, Microsoft Corporation and SIGGRAPH 96, 1996. http://www.research.microsoft.com/~hoppe/
9. Hugues Hoppe. *View-Dependent Refinement of Progressive Meshes*. Computer Graphics, SIGGRAPH 97 Proceedings, pp. 189-198, 1997.
10. Hugues Hoppe. *Efficient Implementation of Progressive Meshes*. Microsoft Corporation Report MSR-TR-98-02 and Computer & Graphics, 1998.
11. http://www.mpi.nd.edu/lam/
12. Patrick R. Morin. *Two Topics in Applied Algorithmics*. MCS thesis, Carleton University, 1998.
13. Dr. Gerhard Roth, Visual Information Technology Group, Institute for Information Technology, National Research Council of Canada, Gerhard.Roth@nrc.ca, http://www.vit.iit.nrc.ca/~roth
14. http://www-graphics.stanford.edu/data/3Dscanrep/

Chapter 6
Tools and Environments for Parallel and Distributed Software Development

A FULLY DECENTRALIZED AND OBLIVIOUS MULTI-NODE BROADCAST ALGORITHM IN HYPERCUBES

SATOSHI FUJITA
Faculty of Engineering, Hiroshima University
Kagamiyama 1-4-1, Higashi-Hiroshima 739-8527, Japan
E-mail: fujita@se.hiroshima-u.ac.jp

MASAFUMI YAMASHITA
Graduate School of Information Science and Electrical Engineering
Kyushu University, 6-10-1 Hakozaki, Higashi-ku, Fukuoka 812-8581, Japan
E-mail: mak@csce.kyushu-u.ac.jp

This paper proposes an algorithm for solving the multi-node broadcast problem in hypercubes. The proposed scheme is **decentralized** in the sense that no nodes play a special role such as a coordinator, and **oblivious** in the sense that the broadcast route for a token is determined independently of other tokens. A difficult problem we encounter during the design of such algorithms is how to balance the load of communication which may change dynamically. We overcome this problem by defining a class of broadcast routes and by carefully associating them to tokens. Our algorithm works efficiently in wide range of traffic load, and is asymptotically optimal when the traffic load of network is either heavy or low.

1 Introduction

In a parallel computer, the nodes (i.e., processing elements) communicate with each other by passing messages through the communication network. **Broadcast** means to distribute information to every node, and is used in many important applications; e.g., a popular synchronization mechanism known as *barrier synchronization* synchronizes execution among cooperating nodes by using broadcast, and in the *parallel branch-and-bound* paradigm for solving combinatorial optimization problems, broadcast is used to let all nodes know a better upper and lower bounds discovered by each node.

Quick completion of broadcast significantly improves the overall performance of those many applications. This is a main motivation that the problem of broadcasting has been investigated extensively in the past three decades[6]. Unfortunately however, most of those studies have been carried out under strong assumptions on the timing of broadcast initiation to reduce the difficulty of analyses of problem, although in most of applications, broadcasts are initiated asynchronously and repeatedly.

We challenge to solve this problem in general. Suppose that nodes asynchronously initiate broadcasts to distribute a piece of information called a *token* to every other node. We call the problem of designing an algorithm for quickly completing each of broadcasts the **multi-node broadcast problem**. It is neither the broadcast problem[7,11], which assumes that no nodes initiate another broadcast while a broadcast is in process, nor the gossiping problem[1,2,3,5,4,9,8], which assumes that nodes simultaneously initiate broadcast exactly once. We even allow that a node repeats initiating broadcasts.[a]

In this paper, we consider the multi-node broadcast problem in hypercubes. A binary hypercube is well known as one of the most popular network topologies for realizing parallel computers[13], and as a rich source of theoretical study of parallel computation[10]. A multi-node broadcast algorithm is said to be **decentralized**, if no nodes play a special role such as a coordinator, and said to be **oblivious**, if the broadcast initiator can calculate the broadcast route of the token from its current local information (i.e., without taking into account the status of other tokens). It is widely accepted that these two properties are necessary for algorithms to fully enjoy the advantage of distributed computation, in spite of the fact that such algorithms, in theory, cannot be optimal in some sense because of the lack of strong control and/or global information. We, therefore, confine ourselves to pursue a multi-node broadcast algorithm which is both decentralized and oblivious. Note that Stamoulis and Tsitsiklis proposed a *centralized* multi-node broadcast algorithm which achieves almost optimal load balancing by using edge-disjoint spanning trees of the given graph rooted at a coordinator node[12], and Hayakawa, Fujita, and Yamashita proposed an *adaptive* multi-node broadcast scheme which uses the distribution of the queue lengths, which is locally observable to each node, to balance the load over the given interconnection network[15].

The remainder of this paper is organized as follows. Section 2 defines the model and the multi-node broadcast problem formally. In Section 3, we propose our multi-node broadcast algorithm and analyze its performance. Section 4 concludes the paper with future problems.

2 Preliminaries

2.1 Model

Let $Q_n = (V, E)$ denote an undirected n-cube, where $V = \{0,1\}^n$ is the set of **nodes** representing processors and E is the set of **edges** representing

[a] We however introduce a weak assumption on the timing of broadcast initiation, in order to exclude unrealistic cases such that every node repeats broadcast initiation in a short period beyond the network communication capacity, since in such cases no algorithms work well.

communication links between neighboring processors, where for all $u, v \in V$, $\{u, v\} \in E$ iff u and v differ in exactly one bit. We number the bits in u ($\in V$) from left to right, i.e., the most significant bit is referred to as the first bit and the least significant bit is referred to as the nth bit. For each $\{u, v\} \in E$, if u and v differ in the ith bit, then we denote as $u = \oplus_i v$ and call $\{u, v\}$ the ith edge incident on u. Note that if $v = \oplus_i u$ then $u = \oplus_i v$. Let $E_i \subset E$ be the set of the ith edges of Q_n. Let $N = 2^n$ $(= |V|)$.

Nodes in V communicate to each other by passing **tokens** through the underlying communication network in the store-and-forward manner[10]. We further assume that every token is *atomic*, i.e., we cannot manipulate the information in token, and tokens must be transferred as they are. When a node initiates a (multi-node) broadcast scheme, it computes information called *routing information* which specifies the destinations and routes the token will flow, and attaches it to the token. Then the token is sent out to the first node of each route specified in the routing information. Upon receiving a token, a node looks up its routing information, and forwards the token to the successor on each path specified in the routing information.

Each edge is assumed to be full-duplex, and conflicts of tokens at each edge are resolved by a *conflict resolution rule* (CRR, for short) specified as a part of multi-node broadcast scheme. We further assume that, for simplicity, the local computation time at nodes is negligible. Nodes, therefore, can send at most one token to each of their adjacent nodes, and simultaneously, can receive at most one token from each of them in a unit time, called **step**. Note that tokens sent out to different adjacent nodes in a step can be different.

Finally, the **broadcast time** of a token is defined to be the maximum elapsed time necessary to distribute the token to every other node.

2.2 Multi-Node Broadcast Problem

The performance of multi-node broadcast schemes is severely affected by the traffic congestion of the underlying network. The network is said to be at **light load** if no broadcast is in process when a node initiates broadcast, and no broadcast will be initiated until this broadcast completes (the broadcast problem investigates this situation). It is said to be at **heavy load** (with respect to a given time period) if all nodes in V initiate broadcast exactly once during the period (the gossiping problem investigates a special case of this situation). Finally, it is said to be at **medium load** if it is neither at light load nor at heavy load. In the following, in order to exclude trivial situations in which no algorithms can work well, we assume that a node can initiate its (next) broadcast only after passing at least N steps since it initiates the last broadcast (if any). A lower bound on the broadcast time for the light and heavy load cases is given as follows[15].

Theorem 1 (Lower Bounds) *(1) Any broadcast takes at least n steps on Q_n, and (2) if K ($\le N$) nodes simultaneously broadcast, then it takes at least $\lceil \frac{K-1}{n} \rceil$ steps to complete all of the K broadcasts on Q_n.*

2.3 Broadcast Scheme

This subsection presents a scheme for broadcasting a *single* token to all nodes in V in n steps, which will be used as a basic scheme in later sections. Note that the broadcast algorithm, in nature, does not need to include a rule to determine which token should be sent next among those waiting for their turns at an edge, i.e., conflict resolution rule (CRR, for short). The CRR, however, plays an important role in a multi-node broadcast algorithm, as will be discussed later.

In the broadcast scheme, the routing information for a token is given in the form of a permutation over $\{1, 2, \ldots, n\}$. A **permutation** π over $\{1, 2, \ldots, n\}$ is described as $(i_1, i_2, \ldots, i_n)$, where $i_j \in \{1, 2, \ldots, n\}$ for $1 \le j \le n$, and $i_j \ne i_k$ if $j \ne k$. For $1 \le j \le n$, denote i_j by $\pi(j)$.

Suppose that a node u wishes to broadcast a token. The broadcast algorithm arbitrarily selects a permutation π, and attaches it to the token as the routing information. Then the token is broadcast according to the following broadcast scheme.

Scheme SIMPLE { Let π be the permutation given to the token. }

Rule 1: { Start broadcasting. }
Broadcast initiator u sends a copy of the token to every neighbor $\oplus_{\pi(1)}u, \oplus_{\pi(2)}u, \ldots, \oplus_{\pi(n)}u$ simultaneously, and terminates.

Rule 2: { Forward token. }
If a node v receives a token from node $\oplus_{\pi(i)}v$ for $1 \le i < n$, then v sends a copy of the token to each of neighbors $\oplus_{\pi(i+1)}v, \oplus_{\pi(i+2)}v, \ldots, \oplus_{\pi(n)}v$ simultaneously, and terminates.

The following lemma immediately holds.

Lemma 1 *For any permutation π, scheme* SIMPLE *completes a single broadcast in n steps, that is optimal.*

In this scheme, for any $1 \le i < j \le n$, no edge in $E_{\pi(j)}$ is followed by an edge in $E_{\pi(i)}$ on any delivery path. Since each delivery path contains at most one edge in E_i for each $1 \le i \le n$, permutation π determines the order those edges occur in delivery paths.

Example 1 Let $n = 4$ and $u = 0000$. Suppose that node u wishes to broadcast token $t(u)$ and that permutation $\pi = (2, 1, 4, 3)$ is given to the token as the routing information. The broadcast proceeds as follows: (1) By Rule 1, node u sends token $t(u)$ to nodes 0001, 0010, 0100, and 1000, and then terminates. (2) Upon receiving the token,

- node 0001, which receives the token from $\oplus_4 0001$, forwards it to node $0011 (= \oplus_3 0001)$ by Rule 2, and terminate;
- node 0010, which receives the token from $\oplus_3 0001$, immediately terminates because 3 is the last element in permutation $(2, 1, 4, 3)$;
- node 0100, which receives the token from $\oplus_2 0001$, forwards it to nodes $1100 (= \oplus_1 0100)$, $0101 (= \oplus_4 0100)$, and $0110 (= \oplus_3 0100)$ by Rule 2, and terminate;
- node 1000, which receives the token from $\oplus_1 0001$, forwards it to nodes $1001 (= \oplus_4 1000)$ and $1010 (= \oplus_3 1000)$ by Rule 2, and terminate.

The third and fourth steps are executed in a similar way.

3 Multi-Node Broadcasting Algorithm TWIST

This section describes our multi-node broadcasting algorithm TWIST, that is both decentralized and oblivious. The basic idea of the algorithm is to define a class of permutations and to associate each broadcast initiator to one of the permutations, in such a way that the worst case congestion of edges would be minimized.

3.1 Algorithm Description

Let $m = \lfloor \frac{n-1}{2} \rfloor$. Note that if n is odd, then $n = 2m+1$, otherwise $n = 2m+2$. In the following, we define a set of $2m$ permutations, each of which will be used as the routing information for tokens broadcast according to SIMPLE.

Let $U = \{x0 \mid x \in \{0,1\}^{n-1}\}$ $(\subset V)$ be the subset of nodes consisting of all nodes in V with suffix 0. First, we consider the set $\{0,1\}^m$ of nodes in an m-cube, where $m = \lfloor \frac{n-1}{2} \rfloor$, and partition it into m subsets as $X_1, X_2, \ldots, X_m$ such that $|X_i| \leq \lceil \frac{2^m}{m} \rceil$ for all $1 \leq i \leq m$. Then, by using the partition of $\{0,1\}^m$, we partition V into $2m$ subsets, $V_1, V_2, \ldots, V_{2m}$, as follows:

Partition of U: Set U is partitioned into m subsets $V_1, V_2, \ldots, V_m$. For each $1 \leq i \leq m$, subset V_i consists of nodes in U whose subsequence of length m starting at the $(m+1)$st bit is in X_i.

Partition of $V - U$: Set $V - U$ is partitioned into m subsets $V_{m+1}, V_{m+2}, \ldots, V_{2m}$. For each $m + 1 \leq i \leq 2m$, subset V_i consists of nodes in $V - U$ whose prefix of length m is in X_i.

Lemma 2 *Set $\{V_1, V_2, \ldots, V_{2m}\}$ is a partition of V, and for each $1 \leq i \leq 2m$, $|V_i| \leq \frac{N}{2m} + \alpha\sqrt{N}$ where $\alpha = 0.7071$ for odd n and $\alpha = 1$ for even n.*

Proof. The first claim is clear since $\{V_1, V_2, \ldots, V_m\}$ is a partition of U, and $\{V_{m+1}, V_{m+2}, \ldots, V_{2m}\}$ is a partition of $V - U$. Since $|X_i| \leq \lceil \frac{2^m}{m} \rceil$, by construction, the size of V_i is at most

$$|V_i| \leq \left\lceil \frac{2^m}{m} \right\rceil \times 2^{n-m-1} < \frac{2^{n-1}}{m} + 2^{n-m-1} = \frac{N}{2m} + 2^{n-m-1}.$$

For odd n, since $n - m - 1 = m = \frac{n-1}{2}$, $2^{n-m-1} = 2^{n/2-1/2} = \sqrt{N/2}$; and for even n, since $m = \frac{n}{2} - 1$, $2^{n-m-1} = 2^{n-n/2+1-1} = \sqrt{N}$. Finally, since $\frac{1}{\sqrt{2}} = 0.7071$, the lemma follows. Q.E.D.

Example 2 Let $n = 9$. Note that $m = \lfloor \frac{9-1}{2} \rfloor = 8/2 = 4$. First, consider the set $\{0,1\}^4$ of nodes in a $4(= m)$-cube, and partition it into $4\ (= m)$ subsets, as follows: $X_1 = \{0000, 0001, 0010, 0011\}$, $X_2 = \{0100, 0101, 0110, 0111\}$, $X_3 = \{1000, 1001, 1010, 1011\}$, and $X_4 = \{1100, 1101, 1110, 1111\}$. By using the partition of $\{0,1\}^4$, subset $U = \{x0 \mid x \in \{0,1\}^8\}$ of nodes in V with suffix 0 is partitioned into 4 subsets V_1, V_2, V_3 and V_4 as follows:

$$\begin{aligned}
V_1 &= \{x00000, x00010, x00100, x00110 \mid x \in \{0,1\}^4\} \\
V_2 &= \{x01000, x01010, x01100, x01110 \mid x \in \{0,1\}^4\} \\
V_3 &= \{x10000, x10010, x10100, x10110 \mid x \in \{0,1\}^4\} \qquad \text{and} \\
V_4 &= \{x11000, x11010, x11100, x11110 \mid x \in \{0,1\}^4\}.
\end{aligned}$$

Similarly, subset $V - U = \{x1 \mid x \in \{0,1\}^8\}$ of nodes with suffix 1 is partitioned into 4 subsets V_5, V_6, V_7 and V_8 as follows:

$$\begin{aligned}
V_5 &= \{0000x1, 0001x1, 0010x1, 0011x1 \mid x \in \{0,1\}^4\} \\
V_6 &= \{0100x1, 0101x1, 0110x1, 0111x1 \mid x \in \{0,1\}^4\} \\
V_7 &= \{1000x1, 1001x1, 1010x1, 1011x1 \mid x \in \{0,1\}^4\} \qquad \text{and} \\
V_8 &= \{1100x1, 1101x1, 1110x1, 1111x1 \mid x \in \{0,1\}^4\}.
\end{aligned}$$

Note that $|V_i| = 4 \times 2^4 = 64\ (= \frac{|V|}{2m})$ for each $1 \leq i \leq 8$. Note also that, for example, for any $u \in V_1$, the subsequence of u of length four starting at the fifth bit (i.e., 0000,0001,0010, or 0011) is in X_1, and for any $v \in V_7$, the prefix of v of length four (i.e., 1000,1001,1010, or 1011) is in X_3.

Next, we define a set of $2m$ permutations, each of which will be associated to the nodes in a subset defined above. Permutations $\pi_1, \pi_2, \ldots, \pi_{2m}$ are defined as follows:

First m Permutations: For each $1 \le i \le m$,

$$\pi_i = (*, \overbrace{m+1, m+2, \ldots, 2m}^{m}, \overbrace{i, i+1, \ldots, m, \underbrace{1, 2, \ldots, i-1}_{i-1}}^{m})$$

where $*$ is "n" if n is odd (since $n - 2m = 1$), and $*$ is "$n, n-1$" if n is even (since $n - 2m = 2$).

Second m Permutations: For each $m+1 \le i \le 2m$,

$$\pi_i = (*, \overbrace{1, 2, \ldots, m}^{m}, \overbrace{m+i, \ldots, 2m, \underbrace{m+1, \ldots, m+i-1}_{i-1}}^{m})$$

where $*$ is "n" if n is odd, and $*$ is "$n, n-1$" if n is even.

It should be worth noting that in the first m permutations, no element in $\{1, 2, \ldots, m\}$ appears before elements in $\{m+1, m+2, \ldots, 2m\}$; and in the last m permutations, no element in $\{m+1, m+2, \ldots, 2m\}$ appears before elements in $\{1, 2, \ldots, m\}$.

Example 3 Let $n = 9$. Since $m = 4$, eight $(= 2 \times 4)$ permutations are defined as follows:

$$\pi_1 = (9, 5, 6, 7, 8, 1, 2, 3, 4) \quad \pi_2 = (9, 5, 6, 7, 8, 2, 3, 4, 1)$$
$$\pi_3 = (9, 5, 6, 7, 8, 3, 4, 1, 2) \quad \pi_4 = (9, 5, 6, 7, 8, 4, 1, 2, 3)$$
$$\pi_5 = (9, 1, 2, 3, 4, 5, 6, 7, 8) \quad \pi_6 = (9, 1, 2, 3, 4, 6, 7, 8, 5)$$
$$\pi_7 = (9, 1, 2, 3, 4, 7, 8, 5, 6) \quad \pi_8 = (9, 1, 2, 3, 4, 8, 5, 6, 7)$$

Note that in every permutation, element 9 $(= n)$ appears as the first element. Note also that in the first four permutations, elements in $\{5, 6, 7, 8\}$ appear before any element in $\{1, 2, 3, 4\}$; and in the last four permutations, elements in $\{1, 2, 3, 4\}$ appear before any element in $\{5, 6, 7, 8\}$.

Now we introduce the notion of "rank" of a token at an edge, which plays an important role in describing the CRR for TWIST. Let $t(u)$ be a token waiting to pass through an edge $e \in E_i$, and let π be the permutation associated with token $t(u)$. The **rank** of $t(u)$ at edge e is an integer j such that $i = \pi(j)$. The **furthest-destination-first-serve** (FDFS, for short) rule selects a token with the smallest rank among all conflicting tokens, where a tie is broken by the first-come-first-serve (FCFS) rule. In scheme TWIST, we use the FDFS rule as the CRR.

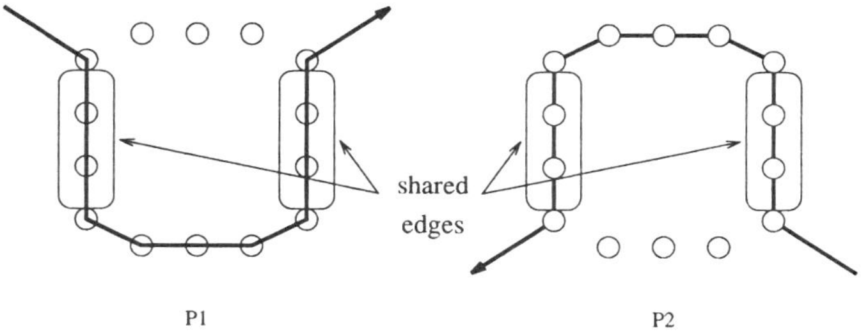

Figure 1. Edges shared by paths P_1 and P_2.

Example 4 Suppose that permutation $\pi = (9,5,6,7,8,1,2,3,4)$ is associated with token $t(u)$, and permutation $\pi' = (9,1,2,3,4,7,8,5,6)$ with token $t(v)$. Consider edge e in E_3. By definition, the rank of $t(u)$ at e is 8 (i.e., $3 = \pi(8)$) and the rank of $t(v)$ at e is 4 (i.e., $3 = \pi'(4)$). Hence whenever $t(u)$ and $t(v)$ conflict at edge e, $t(v)$ is selected earlier than $t(u)$.

Now, we are ready to describe TWIST.

Scheme TWIST

1) **Broadcast tokens:**
When a node u wants to broadcast token $t(u)$, it invokes SIMPLE with permutation π_i, where i is the index of the subset such that $u \in V_i$.

2) **Conflict resolution rule:**
Conflicts among tokens are resolved by the FDFS rule.

Property 1 *Scheme* TWIST *is both decentralized and oblivious.*

Let u and v be two nodes in V. Suppose that a delivery path of $t(u)$, denoted by P_1, shares an edge with a delivery path of $t(v)$, denoted by P_2. It is easy to see that if two edges e_1 and e_2 appear in paths P_1 and P_2 in the same direction and in the same order (e.g., e_1 appears before e_2 in each path), then every edge e on P_1 appeared between e_1 and e_2, must appear in P_2 as an edge between e_1 and e_2, and vice versa. Hence, the set of all edges shared by paths P_1 and P_2 in the same direction and in the same order must form a subpath of P_1 (and thus, of P_2). Figure 1 illustrates the set of edges shared by P_1 and P_2 (note that one shared path in the figure may be empty). By the description of TWIST, if two conflicting tokens are ordered at an edge e by being given a priority dependng on the length of their remaining paths, then the priority of those tokens is unchanged on the subsequent edges in the shared path. Further, if two conflicting tokens are ordered at an edge e' by a tie breaking, which determines the order of those tokens by the FCFS rule, then the order of those tokens of going through the next edge on the shortest path is unchanged until the first time at which the order of those tokens is determined by the length of the remaining delivery path. Finally, since any two tokens can conflict in at most one shared path even if they share two subpaths in common, we have the following claim.

Remark 1 *In* TWIST, *any token can delay the delivery of another token at most once by at most 1 step.*

3.2 Performance Analysis

Recall that we say that a machine Q_n is at "light load" if no broadcast is in process when a node initiates broadcast and no broadcast will be initiated until this broadcast completes; and at "heavy load" with respect to a given time period, if all nodes in V initiate broadcast exactly once during the period. Since TWIST performs each broadcast according to scheme SIMPLE, by Lemma 1, we immediately have the following theorem.

Theorem 2 (Light Load) *At light load,* TWIST *completes a broadcast in n steps, which is optimal.*

In what follows, we estimate the broadcast time at heavy load. The estimation is based on Remark 1 claimed at the end of the last subsection. To make the exposition simple, we first define a partition of set E as follows:

$$\mathcal{E}_1 = \bigcup_{i=1}^{m} E_i, \qquad \mathcal{E}_2 = \bigcup_{i=m+1}^{2m} E_i, \qquad \text{and} \qquad \mathcal{E}_3 = E_{2m+1} \cup E_n.$$

By using this notation, for any $u \in U$ and for any $w \in V$, the delivery path $P(u, w)$ of token $t(u)$ from u to w can be divided into the following three parts (some part can be empty): the first part $P_1(u, w)$ consists of edges in $\mathcal{E}_3$, the second part $P_2(u, w)$ consists of edges in $\mathcal{E}_2$, and the third part $P_3(u, w)$ consists of edges in $\mathcal{E}_1$. On the other hand, for any $v \in V - U$ and for any $w \in V$, the delivery path $P(v, w)$ of token $t(v)$ from v to w can be divided into the following three parts: the first part $P_1(v, w)$ consists of edges in $\mathcal{E}_3$, the second part $P_2(v, w)$ consists of edges in $\mathcal{E}_1$, and the third part $P_3(v, w)$ consists of edges in $\mathcal{E}_2$. Let $U = \{x0 \mid x \in \{0, 1\}^{n-1}\}$ be the set of nodes in V with suffix 0, as before.

The first part of a delivery path corresponds to the broadcast in 1-cube for odd n and that in 2-cube for even n. Since each edge is assumed to be full-duplex, by the FDFS rule, no tokens are delayed by other token in the first part for odd n. When n is even, on the other hand, a token $t(u')$ can delay the delivery of token $t(u)$ in the first part only if u' has the same prefix of length $n-1$ with u (in fact, a delay occurs only at an edge in E_{n-1}). Hence we have the following lemma.

Lemma 3 (First Part) *When n is odd, any delivery path of a token is not delayed by other token in the first part. When n is even, for any delivery path of a token, the delay in the first part of the path is at most 1 step.*

The following two lemmas evaluate the number of conflicting nodes, which can delay the delivery of $t(u)$ in the second or third part.

Lemma 4 (Second Part) *For any delivery path of a token, the delay in the second part of the path is at most 2^{n-m-1} steps.*

Proof. Let u be a broadcast initiator. Without loss of generality, assume $u \in U$. Recall that the second part of $P(u,w)$ (i.e., subpath $P_2(u,w)$) consists of edges in $\mathcal{E}_2$. Let e be an edge in $\mathcal{E}_2$, and suppose that a delivery path of $t(v)$ shares edge e with $P_2(u,w)$. If $v \in V-U$, $t(v)$ cannot delay $t(u)$ at edge e since $t(v)$ remains a shorter way to the destination than $t(u)$ at edge e. Hence if $t(v)$ delays the delivery of $t(u)$ in the second part, then v must be a node in U. Since $u \in U$ and $v \in U$, by definition, tokens $t(u)$ and $t(v)$ are given permutations such that any delivery paths of them do not use an edge in $E_1 \cup E_2 \cup \cdots \cup E_m$ $(= \mathcal{E}_1)$ before any edge in $\mathcal{E}_2$. Hence v must have the same prefix of length m with u. Since there are at most 2^{n-m-1} such nodes in U, the lemma follows. Q.E.D.

Corollary 1 *For any delivery path of a token $u \in U$ (resp. $u \in V-U$), the delay in the second part of the path by tokens originated by nodes in $V-U$ (resp. U) is at most 2^{n-m-1} steps.*

Lemma 5 (Third Part) *For any delivery path of a token, the delay in the third part of the path is at most $\frac{N}{m}+\beta\sqrt{N}$ steps, where $\beta = 2.1213$ for odd n and $\beta = 3$ for even n.*

Proof. Let u be a broadcast initiator and assume without loss of generality that $u \in V_1$ $(\subset U)$. Suppose that a delivery of token $t(u)$ is delayed by a token $t(v)$ in the third part, and let us count the number of such v's.

Nodes v in U: First, consider v's in subset U. Recall that U is partitioned into m subsets as $V_1, V_2, \ldots, V_m$. For any $v \in V_1$, token $t(v)$ can delay the delivery of token $t(u)$ in the third part. For any $v \in V_i$ $(2 \le i \le m)$, token $t(v)$ can delay the delivery of token $t(u)$ in the third part only at an edge in $E_i \cup E_{i+1} \cup \cdots \cup E_m$. Hence if $t(v) \in V_i$ delays the delivery of $t(u)$, then node v must have the same prefix of length $i-1$ with node u.

Since there are $\frac{|V_i|}{2^{i-1}}$ such nodes, in total, there are at most

$$|V_1| + \frac{|V_2|}{2} + \frac{|V_3|}{2^2} + \cdots + \frac{|V_m|}{2^{m-1}} < 2 \max_{1 \le i \le m} |V_i| \qquad (1)$$

such nodes in U. By Lemma 2, the above amount is bounded by $\frac{N}{m} + \gamma\sqrt{N}$ where $\gamma = \sqrt{2}$ for odd n and $\gamma = 2$ for even n.

Nodes in $V - U$: By Corollary 1, the number of nodes v in $V - U$ which can delay the delivery of $t(u)$ in the third part is at most 2^{n-m-1}, which is $\sqrt{N/2}$ for odd n and $\sqrt{N}$ for even n.

Hence the number of tokens which can delay the delivery of token $t(u)$ is at most $\frac{N}{m} + \beta\sqrt{N}$ where $\beta = \sqrt{2} + \frac{1}{\sqrt{2}} = (3/2)\sqrt{2} = 2.1213$ for odd n and $\beta = 2 + 1 = 3$ for even n, which completes the proof. Q.E.D.

Hence by Remark 1, and Lemmas 3, 4 and 5, we have the following theorem.

Theorem 3 (Heavy Load) *Under* TWIST, *even at the heavy load, any broadcast completes in at most* $\frac{N}{m} + \beta\sqrt{N} + 1$ *steps, where* $\beta = 2.1213$ *for odd* n *and* $\beta = 3$ *for even* n, *and* $m = \lceil \frac{n-1}{2} \rceil$.

4 Concluding Remarks

In this paper, we proposed a decentralized and oblivious multi-node broadcast algorithm TWIST for hypercubes, which asymptotically attains the lower bound on the broadcast time at both heavy and light loads. If all nodes in V simultaneously start broadcasting (i.e., if it is the "gossiping" case), then by a similar argument to Theorem 3, we have the following theorem.

Theorem 4 (Gossiping) *If all nodes simultaneously start broadcasting, then* TWIST *completes all of these broadcasts in* $\frac{N}{2m} + \sqrt{N} + 1$ *steps, which is asymptotically optimal.*

When Q_n is at "medium" load, a similar argument to the worst case analysis of TWIST could be applied to have an average case analysis. Another interesting idea to deal with the medium load case is to introduce a kind of randomization to the scheme; e.g., by coupling it with Valiant and Brebner's permutation routing algorithm[14], we would be able to obtain a randomized oblivious algorithm which asymptotically attains the lower bound with high probability. A formal discussion on the randomized algorithms will be given in another paper.

Acknowledgments: This research was partially supported by the Ministry of Education, Science and Culture of Japan, and Research for the Future Program from Japan Society for the Promotion of Science (JSPS): Software for Distributed and Parallel Supercomputing (JSPS-RFTF96P00505).

References

1. A. Bagchi, S. L. Hakimi, and E. Schmeichel. Gossiping in a distributed network. *IEEE Trans. Comput.*, 42(2):253–256, February 1993.
2. J.-C. Bermond and P. Fraigniaud. Broadcasting and gossiping in de Bruijn network. *SIAM J. Comput.*, 23(1):212–225, February 1994.
3. R. C. Entringer and P. J. Slater. Gossips and telegraphs. *J. Franklin Inst.*, 307:353–360, 1979.
4. S. Fujita and M. Yamashita. Optimal group gossiping in hypercubes under circuit switching model. *SIAM J. Comput.*, 25(5):1045–1060, May 1996.
5. S. Fujita and M. Yamashita. Fast gossiping on square mesh computers. *Inform. Process. Lett.*, 48:127–130, 1993.
6. S. M. Hedetniemi, S. T. Hedetniemi, and A. L. Liestman. A survey of gossiping and broadcasting in communication networks. *Networks*, 18:319–349, 1988.
7. S. Johnsson and C.-T. Ho. Optimum broadcasting and personalized communication in hypercubes. *IEEE Trans. Comput.*, 38(9):1249–1268, September 1989.
8. D. W. Krumme. Fast gossiping for the hypercube. *SIAM J. Comput.*, 21(2):365–380, April 1992.
9. D. W. Krumme, G. Cybenko, and K. N. Venkataraman. Gossiping in minimal time. *SIAM J. Comput.*, 21(1):111–139, February 1992.
10. F. T. Leighton. *Introduction to Parallel Algorithms and Architectures: Arrays, Trees, Hypercubes.* Morgan Kaufmann Publishers, Inc., 1992.
11. P. J. Slater, E. J. Cockayne, and S. T. Hedetniemi. Information dissemination in trees. *SIAM J. Comput.*, 10(4):692–701, November 1981.
12. G. D. Stamoulis and J. N. Tsitsiklis. An efficient algorithm for multiple simultaneous broadcasts in the hypercube. *Inform. Process. Lett.*, 46:219–224, July 1993.
13. A. Trew and G. Wilson, editors. *Past, Present, Parallel: A Survey of Available Parallel Computer Systems*, chapter 4, pages 125–147. Springer-Verlag, 1991.
14. L. G. Valiant. A scheme for fast parallel communication. *SIAM J. Comput.*, 11(2):350–361, May 1982.
15. Y. Hayakawa, S. Fujita, and M. Yamashita. A decentralized scheme for multi-node broadcasting on hypercubes. In *Proc. of the International Symposium on Parallel Architectures, Algorithms and Networks (I-SPAN'97)*, pages 487–493. IEEE, 1997.

COMPILER DRIVEN INITIALISATION AND EXECUTION OF PARALLEL APPLICATIONS ON CLUSTERS[1]

CHRISTOPHER MCAVANEY AND ANDRZEJ GOSCINSKI

School of Computing and Mathematics
Deakin University, Geelong
Victoria 3217, AUSTRALIA
{chrismc, ang}@deakin.edu.au

Parallel execution is a very efficient means of processing vast amounts of data in a small amount of time. Creating parallel applications has never been easy, and requires much knowledge of the task and execution environment needed to execute parallel processes. The parallelisation process can be made easy through using a parallelising compiler that parallelises a supplied application automatically. Executing the parallel application is also simplified when a well designed execution environment is used. Such an execution environment provides very powerful operations to the programmer transparently. Combining both a parallelising compiler and execution environment and providing a fully automated parallelisation and execution tool is the aim of this research. The advantage of using such a fully automated tool is that the user does not need to provide any additional input to gain the benefits of parallel execution. This report shows how the tool transparently supports the programmer creating parallel applications and their execution.

1 Introduction

The current trend to run parallel applications is to use clusters (of PC's or workstations). However there are two major obstacles that hinder making parallel computing part of the computing mainstream: finding and expressing parallelism in applications; and managing efficiently the available parallel processes and computational resources called parallelism management.

Finding and expressing parallelism can be performed manually, as has been done in the vast majority of applications; or automatically, using a parallelising compiler. The latter, despite huge research efforts has not achieved fully satisfactory results. More promising is using both methods. Currently designed and utilised parallelising compilers are only responsible for the identification of units of parallelism [7], including quite complex and time consuming data transformations for the programmer [1], which allow further and quicker parallelisation to be performed.

Parallelism management is also still in infancy. The problem is mainly addressed at the middleware level, by building software tools (e.g. PVM [12], MPI [3]) or extending existing operating systems (e.g. UNIX, Linux [10]). Current operating systems used in clusters only support communication among parallel

---

[1]This work was partly supported by the Deakin University Research Grant 0504003157

processes, help to coordinate them and provide some basic process management, e.g., single process creation and static allocation. The outcome of this approach is not satisfactory, performance is only acceptable and transparency has been completely neglected.

In general, despite some good results achieved in both areas, even if an application was fully parallelised automatically, programmers are still forced to deal with parallelism management problems such as the establishment of a virtual machine, mapping processes to computers of the virtual machine, instantiation of the processes on computers, load balancing and coordination of the execution of parallel applications on a cluster.

It was suggested that a parallelising compiler should not only parallelise an application but also it should generate information for and provide some services to a cluster operating system to benefit from them when controlling initialisation and execution of parallel processes. This approach relieves programmers from activities, which are irrelevant from the application point of view [4].

The aim of this research is to develop a new technology that would allow a parallelising compiler to automatically generate information for and provide some services to a cluster operating system that would be used to initialise and provide parallelism management. The automatic generation and execution of the parallelised program is to be carried out transparently without extra programmer input. The goal of this report is to show the first version of a tool, which is a product of the new technology, and forms the proof of concept. This tool, called parexec, supports the programmer by creating parallel programs; generating the necessary information for a cluster operating system; and automatically including operating system primitives that support parallelism management.

As this tool is treated as the proof of concept it only addresses, at this stage, loop parallelisation within the parallelising compiler. It uses the DOALL loop construct; it does not address many pure compilation issued, e.g. irregular loops, as they are not relevant to this research. This research addresses the relationship between parallelising compilers and operating systems for clusters.

This report is divided up into three major sections. The first shows the general approach presenting the three major components of the parexec tool that encompasses the parallelising compiler, linking of the parallelised code to the cluster operating system and the parallelism management of the cluster. The second shows the architecture of a relevant system (parallelising and executing tool - parexec tool) at the conceptual level. The third presents the results of the study of functionality of the tool including the performance results of the execution of a test program parallelised with the parexec tool. A summary follows these major sections.

2 The architecture and components of the parexec tool

Currently, application programmers must not only parallelise applications, but also establish a virtual machine, map parallel processes to the computers of this virtual machine, instantiate the parallel processes on the computers and coordinate the execution of the parallel processes. In order to automate these activities and relieve the programmers from the burden of these operating system oriented activities a parallelising compiler should be enhanced to form part of a parallelising and execution support tool (parexec), which provides information and carries out some activities that can be used by and support a cluster operating system. The information and activities include the definition of the number of parallel processes, insertion of process instantiation (execution and duplication) primitives and insertion of parallel process coordination primitives.

The proposed parexec tool is comprised of three components:

- a parallelising compiler that carries out parallelisation activities (component 1),
- parexec channel that links the parallel program and initialisation and execution information to the execution environment (component 2), and
- the execution environment that uses the information to manage parallelism and execute the parallelised program (component 3).

The conceptual architecture of the parexec tool is shown in Figure 1.

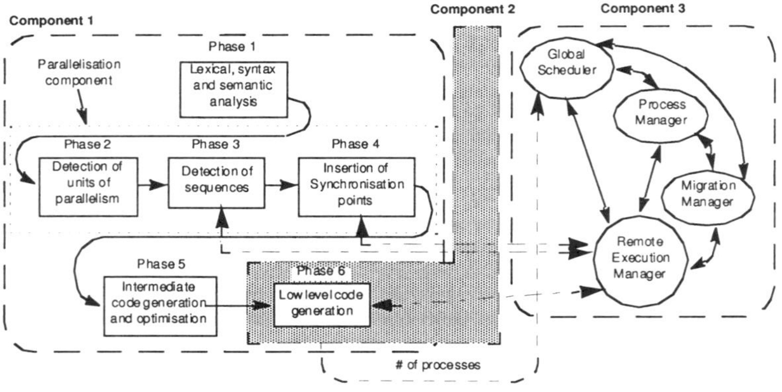

Figure 1. Architecture of the parexec tool

2.1 The parallelising compiler component

The parallelising compiler component is responsible for examining the original program and determining where it is suitable for parallelisation. It has been designed to parallelise programs without any decisions being required by the programmer, dealing with functional and data parallelism.

The language used by the parallelising compiler is Pascal; it was chosen because of its strict syntax and typing. This means that the ambiguities introduced by other procedural languages are not an issue and therefore the compilation process is simplified.

There are six Phases (Figure 1) used in the parallelising compiler, each Phase presenting information of the certain decisions made to the next. As we concentrate our research on supporting parallel processing on clusters of computers, where communication is a relatively slow operation in comparison to CPU processing, we address coarse grain parallelism. The Phases are as follows:

1. lexical, syntax and semantic analysis;
2. detection of units of parallelism;
3. detection of sequences;
4. insertion of synchronisation points;
5. intermediate code generation and optimisation; and
6. low level code generation.

Within the parallelising compiler a block construct is used [2]. These blocks group together consecutive statements from the source program and enable a clear logical construct to be used in the decisions of parallelisation. The blocks are classified further with the loop parallelisation capabilities of the compiler. The statements which are contained within the body of the loop can be classified as a block, determined by the dependencies between statements and the indices of the loop [11]. All the parallelism decisions performed within the parallelising compiler follow the block based parallelism model.

The loop parallelisation produces smaller blocks, which can be executed together in parallel. There can be one or many occurrences of these loop blocks, all of which do not have to communicate frequently. This is important when looking at the execution environment, as it is a cluster, it has a relatively slow communication medium between processors. It is therefore more efficient to have as small amount of communication between processes as possible to gain any benefits.

Phases 2, 3 and 4 are responsible for determining the parallel components of the original source program. The information passed between each Phase is vitally important to the whole parexec operation:

There are two constructs common to all Phases, a *syntax tree* and a *symbol table*. The syntax tree is created in Phase 1, but through these three Phases it is modified by the use of several different flags to signal blocks, synchronisation points, contain the number of iterations for a loop, and contain references to the symbol table. The symbol table is also created in Phase 1, but it is not modified past that point. It is purely used to specify the identity, type and scope of the identifiers used within the program. This is particularly important when looking at the scope of identifiers within blocks.

A parallel symbol table is created after Phase 2. This table contains information identifiers used within each parallel block. This information is used later on when inserting the primitives for the execution environment so that the correct information is passed to each parallel process once instantiated. The number of parallel processes to be created is known after Phase 3; this information is passed onto Phase 6 (part of the parexec channel component) when the insertion of the primitives occurs as each parallel processing primitive requires the number of processes to be created. After Phase 4, the synchronisation points are known and therefore the locations where parallel processes must wait are also known. This information is also passed onto Phase 6.

The types of loops that the parallelising compiler considers are those with a fixed or dynamic number of iterations. For example, a typical loop would be `for i := 1 to 20 do <loop body>`. Once a loop is parallelised it can be visualised as in Figure 2 where the parallel program is executing sequentially until the loop is reached. At this time the child processes, which are created using code of the loop block, are executed. In this example, there would be 20 child processes executing. The loop parallelisation method used within this parallelising compiler follows the SPMD model of parallelism (Figure 2). For dynamic loop iterations, the same rules apply, except the exact number of children is not known until run time.

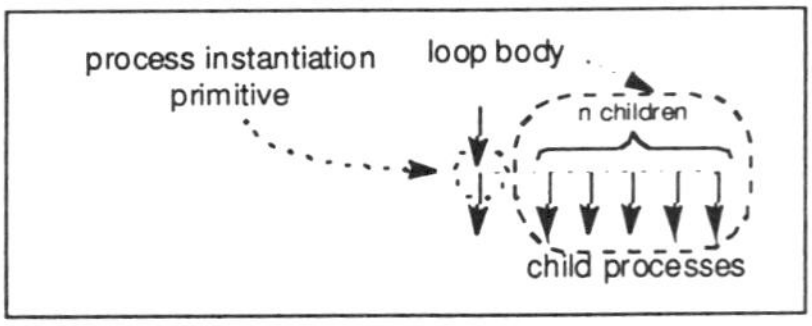

Figure 2. The approach to loop parallelisation

The decision to parallelise blocks is made after consideration of how the identifiers within the block are accessed. When the blocks are parallelised, it is the memory accesses that the identifiers make that ultimately determine how the original program can be parallelised. So for example, one statement assigns a value to an array identifier `grid_ref[i][j] := 5;` then the next block uses that value in `total_dist := total_dist + grid_ref[i][j];` then these two blocks could not be parallelised as one sets the value that the next wants to be able to read. If both blocks read that `grid_ref[i][j]` value then they can be parallelised. When it comes to loops a similar methodology is followed. Further parallelisation techniques through the use of distributed shared memory (DSM) are currently being examined as future work and is therefore not part of the discussion of this paper.

2.2 *Linking the parallelised program to the execution environment*

After parallelising a program into a set of units of parallelism there is a need to initialise the whole execution environment. The parexec channel component is responsible for providing a link between a parallelised program and the execution environment. This is performed by notifying the appropriate process management entities within the operating system, so that when the program is invoked, the physical parallelisation and parallelisation management of processes will occur automatically without any further input from the programmer. For instance, the

Global Scheduler (component 3) is notified of how many processes are to be created. This allows the process management system to coordinate the allocation of processes [9] so that the whole execution environment does not become overloaded and inefficient. It is during Phases 3, 4 and 6 (shown in Figure 1) that the parallel processing primitives that invoke the execution environment are identified.

The parexec channel is used to pass on each parallelisation decision made, in the parallelising compiler, to the execution environment to initialise and execute the parallelised program. The characteristics of the actual parallel processing primitive influence, what information is sent between the Phases. The actual process instantiation and termination primitives utilise this information provided and are inserted during Phase 6.

The linking to the execution environment is achieved by taking the instructions from the parallelising compiler and inserting the appropriate GENESIS library calls. There are two calls used, one that creates parallel processes and one that supports parallel process coordination. The latter is achieved by means of waiting for child processes to finish. Both calls are implemented as remote procedure calls (RPC's). They are placed into the parallelised program at the points the parallelising compiler specified during parallelisation, Phases 2, 3 and 4. It is these RPC's that specify the initialisation information and gather the results of the parallel processes.

The specific library calls used with our parallelising tool are `process_create(char *name, SNAME *child_psn, SNAME *child_uport)` and `process_wait(SNAME *child)`. These two primitives allow the parallelised program to create a requested number of child processes that execute in parallel and to synchronise either the parent process or any of the child processes, respectively. Both these primitives require only a few critical pieces of information to be able to perform their task. For the `process_create()` primitive the location of the file which contains the program to instantiate (the `char *name` parameter) as well as the number of occurrences of the process are required. The primitive returns the unique process identifier (`child_psn`) and communications port (`child_uport`) for all the parallel child processes instantiated. The location of the program to instantiate (the `name` argument) is specified by the parallelising compiler component of the parexec tool.

As there can be many parallel entities that are created throughout the execution of a parallel application unique names are therefore needed to specify each entity. It is proposed at this stage that the unique name consists of a slave name and a number. The number component is unique for the whole program and will not occur again when other programs are parallelised. The number is based on the process identification number of the parent process. The nature of the process identification is such that it is unlikely that the same slave identifier would be used. Using this naming style ensures that the correct child process is invoked. For the `process_wait()` primitive nothing is required upon calling but as with the create primitive, the unique process identifier is returned along with the status of all the parallel child processes instantiated.

Once the final low level code and associated parallel processing primitives have been generated, that code is translated into the executable byte code for the destination architecture. It is at this part of the Phase that the libraries from GENESIS are linked in.

The parallel management system of the execution environment acts upon both these primitives accordingly. When a process is created, under this scheme, the Global Scheduler is responsible for placing the processes. This means that the programmer does not have to provide any details about where part or all of the parallel program should be executed.

2.3 Execution environment

The third component of the parexec tool is responsible for the initialisation and execution of parallel processes on a cluster. The selection of the execution environment takes into account the level of granularity of the parallelising compiler. This is important so that the cluster's resources available are used both efficiently and to the fullest extent. Since our parallelising compiler focuses on coarse granularity, the latency between processors is less of an issue. Also the management of resources and parallel processes within the execution environment must be both efficient and transparent. These requirements can be satisfied by a cluster operating system called GENESIS [6].

After linking the parallelised program to the operating system, the program and processes it creates are coordinated by the parallel management system of GENESIS throughout its execution life. There are three essential services of the GENESIS execution environment: process mapping to computers of the cluster, process instantiation and process coordination. These services are performed by a parallel management system that is comprised of the following servers: Global Scheduler, Execution Manager, Migration Manager and Process Manager, which are shown in component 3 of Figure 1. It is these servers that are invoked through the library calls provided by the operating system and inserted within the parallelised programs during Phase 6 of component 1 of the parexec tool.

The primitives specified during the linking component of the parexec tool do not require specific information about the execution environment. All that is required is information, which is specific to the program being parallelised. This means that the processes created by GENESIS for the parallel program is performed transparently, the actual location of the executing process(es) is not provided by the programmer at all. The parallel management system takes care of where the actual processes execute through the three services listed above.

So for example, if 100 processes are requested to be created by the parallelised program that the parallelising compiler creates, then GENESIS would create them concurrently on computers of a cluster, selected by the Global Scheduler. The Global Scheduler of the parallel management system is responsible for keeping the load balanced throughout the cluster. Thus, the only directive from the parallelising compiler is to create *n* instances of the specified processes, the location is completely up to GENESIS.

The creation of these processes is performed through the process creation primitive within GENESIS [5]. This primitive allows the caller to specify how many occurrences of the one process to create. All the processes will be almost the same, the only difference being the identifier of the process. This powerful primitive performs these tasks totally transparently to the user.

Therefore as mentioned earlier in this section a cluster operating system provides many resources and services for the execution of parallel processes. All are provided with performance and transparency in mind.

3 Testing the parexec tool

The first part of the proof of concept was to develop a parallelising compiler, build the parexec channel and provide linking to the GENESIS cluster operating system. The second part was to show how the parexec tool works and how it performs. Thus, the aim of this section is to show and discuss the behaviour of the parexec tool. The first part addresses the parallelisation services provided by the tool. The second part presents the execution issues, including the performance results of running the parallelised and sequential programs.

3.1 The study of the parallelisation component

The Towers of Hanoi application was chosen to exploit specific loop parallelism capabilities within the parexec tool. After the parallelising compiler has performed its parallelisation, each child has the task of performing a recursive algorithm. The number of children depends on the number of iterations within the loop of the main body. If more loops were within the program more child processes would exist. As briefly described in Section 2, the number of processes that are actually executed at the one time is controlled by the parallelism management system, in particular the Global Scheduler of GENESIS. This ensures that the number of processes do not swamp the finite number of workstations within the cluster.

The sequential and parallelised versions of the program are shown in Block 1. On the left hand side the sequential program written in the Pascal language is presented. On the right hand side, the parallelised program in the C language with GENESIS parallelisation primitives automatically inserted by the parexec tool is given (lines 9 and 16 in `regular.c`)

The first section of Block 1 shows how the loop within the *main* part of the program has been detected and how there are no dependencies on the loop index which would make it complex. The block of code labelled `regular.c` is the resultant parallelised C/GENESIS code. Lines 7 through 9 are used to create the parameters required and call the GENESIS `process_create()` primitive. The first argument to this primitive is the location of the file containing code for the child to be instantiated, the name of the child is unique to the program. At line 16 synchronisation is performed using a `wait()` primitive.

a) Sequential Pascal

```
1  program regular;
2  var cnt : integer;
3
4  procedure tower( frompeg, topeg, auxpeg :
       char; n : integer );
5  begin
6      if( n = 1 ) then
7          break
8      else
9          begin
10             tower( frompeg, auxpeg,
                   topeg, n-1 );
11             tower( auxpeg, topeg,
                   frompeg, n-1 )
12         end
13 end;
14
15 begin
16     for cnt := 0 to 10 do
17     begin
18         writeln('Calling func now!');
19         tower('A', 'B', 'C', 15)
20     end
21 end.
```

regular.p

b) Parallelised C and GENESIS code

```
1  void main()
2  {
3      uint32_t *child_stats;
4      SNAME *returned_child_psns;
5      SNAME *child_psns, *child_uports;
6
7      child_psns = (SNAME *)malloc(sizeof(SNAME) * 11);
8      child_uports = (SNAME *)malloc(sizeof(SNAME) * 11);
9      if( proc_ncreate( "/home/chrismc/SLVS/slave-20024.exe",
           11, child_psns, child_uports ) < 0 )
10     {
11         NUCprintf("regular: ERROR - process create
               failed\n");
12         proc_terminate(0, (SNAME *)0);
13     }
14     child_stats = (uint32_t *)malloc(sizeof(uint32_t) * 11);
15     returned_child_psns = (SNAME *)malloc(sizeof(SNAME) *
           11);
16     proc_nwait( 11, child_stats, returned_child_psns );
17     proc_terminate(0, (SNAME *)0);
18 }
```

`cnt` variable is declared in another file and its prototype is located within an include file

11 iterations of the loop determined from the loop

parallelisation of the loop performed

synchronisation of the child processes

regular.c

Block 1..Test program showing both sequential and parallelised version of the main section.

a) Sequential Pascal (repeated)

```
1  program regular;
2  var cnt : integer;
3
4  procedure tower( frompeg, topeg, auxpeg :
       char; n : integer );
5  begin
6      if( n = 1 ) then
7          break
8      else
9          begin
10             tower( frompeg, auxpeg,
                   topeg, n-1 );
11             tower( auxpeg, topeg,
                   frompeg, n-1 )
12         end
13 end;
14
15 begin
16     for cnt := 0 to 10 do
17     begin
18         writeln('Calling func now!');
19         tower('A', 'B', 'C', 15)
20     end
21 end.
```

regular.p

b) Parallelised C and GENESIS code (continued)

```
1  void tower( char frompeg, char topeg, char auxpeg, int n )
2  {
3      if( n == 1 ) {
4          return;
5      } else {
6          tower(frompeg, auxpeg, topeg, n - 1);
7          tower(auxpeg, topeg, frompeg, n - 1);
8      }
9  }
```

recursive call to `tower()`

func.c

c)

```
1  void main(int argc, char **argv)
2  {
3      NUCprintf("%s\n", "'Calling func now!'");
4      tower('A', 'B', 'C', 15);
5      proc_terminate(0, (SNAME *)0);
6  }
```

slave code for `main()`

slave-20024.c

Block 2. Parallelised C version of the `tower()` routine and parallel slave.

The second section (Block 2) shows how the procedure `tower` was converted. As this procedure is a recursive one, no parallelisation was able to be performed. Therefore the right hand side contains the equivalent in C/GENESIS as the Pascal version on the left.

The third and final section (Block 2c) shows the child program, `slave-20024.c`, that is called from the parallelised *main* block of code. It contains the two statements (lines 3 and 4) that comprise the block of the loop from the original sequential program.

The actual primitives (lines 9, 12, 16 and 17 in `regular.c` and line 5 in `slave20024.c`, Block `2a and 2c`) are the links between the parallel program and the process management system of GENESIS. It is these links that allow the program to become parallel once it has begun executing.

3.2 Execution of the parallelised program

The objective of this section is to present the execution and performance results obtained when running a sequential and parallelised solution to the Towers of Hanoi problem, using the parexec tool. The process instantiation services of GENESIS are invoked by the primitives automatically inserted into the parallelised program. The setup of GENESIS for this experiment was 10 Sun 3/50 workstations interconnected by a shared 10 Mbps Ethernet network.

The amount of work to compute overall is very closely related to the overall execution time, since the child processes individually perform computations based on the work allocated. The application was run with 15 and 20 discs, each time calculating the result 10 times.

The experiments were performed in the execution environment, where load balancing was either activated or deactivated (in Figure 3, *loadbal* and *noloadbal*, respectively), and caching was used or unused (in Figure 3, *cache* and *nocache*, respectively). The load balancing mechanism, based on Global Scheduler decisions, migrates processes around the cluster when a load imbalance is detected [5]. This service of the parallelism management system of GENESIS also operates transparently and is invaluable. The *cache* curves represent the effect of the file caching service [8]. This service is the portal between GENESIS and the UNIX filesystem that holds the programs that are to be executed. Instead of each request for a program to be instantiated being made to the UNIX filesystem, a cached version allows a much smaller instantiation latency to be made. All the curves represent the speed-up gained as the number of workstations are increased.

The combination of automatic parallelisation and insertion of parallel primitives has provided positive performance results shown in Figures 3 and 4. Of the best effects provided by the parallelism management system is the load balancing. The test of 15 discs (Figure 3) is where the computation of each parallel process is relatively small and the different process management techniques do not have much effect. With the 20 disc test, the computation is a bit longer and as processes finish, the load balancing takes over and has more effect. As the individual parallel processes complete their work, the load balancing mechanism even out the processing load of each processor within the cluster and therefore the overall execution time decreases (i.e. speedup is greater). The maximum speed-up when the computation time is small reaches 3 times as fast and with the longer computation up to 7 times as fast.

The influence of the parexec tool on the overall performance is visible through the increasing speed-up as the number of workstations is increased. The more complex the program, the more potential there is for parallelism to be detected by the parallelising compiler and therefore the more speed-up created by the tool.

4 Conclusion and further work

This report demonstrates how a tool, encompassing a parallelising compiler, a cluster operating system with parallelism management and a channel between these two components, can provide a solution to the whole issue of improving execution performance and transparently support application programmers. The parallelising compiler component is a vital part of the solution. It is responsible for actually parallelising the original program. The parallelisation is carried out using analysis based on block parallelism. This enables efficient separation of the source program into parallel components for the parallelisation decisions that take place further within the parallelising compiler. Each block is examined during the parallelising compilation component for their dependencies upon each other and from that the decisions are made as to how a program is parallelised. The loop parallelisation techniques of this compiler are integral in enhancing the parallelism detection techniques within the programs presented. The linking of the output from the parallelising compiler is important for the initialisation and instantiation of processes throughout the execution life of the parallelised program. The chosen cluster operating system is very efficient in its use of the resources. The parallel management system is also invaluable because it removes the time consuming and error prone tasks required in setting up a virtual machine. Utilising such a system relieves this burden on parallel programming. The channel component links the parallelising compiler and the execution environment components so that the whole parallelisation process is transparent. One of the leading benefits of the parallelisation tool is that the programmer is not involved in the decision making process of parallelisation. Another benefit is that the parallel execution environment is able to make decisions about the placement of the parallel processes when the parallel primitives are invoked. This means that the most efficient parallel execution possible is exploited.

The benefits of the parexec tool's design is that the automation process of the parallelising compiler is completely transparent. This means that the programmer is not required to put any input into the decision making process of parallelisation and parallel process mapping, which also means that it is very easy to use such a parallelisation tool. The parexec tool was shown to improve the execution performance. The results show the parallelised program to be 3 to 7 times faster depending on the number of computers in the cluster. Whilst the results present definite improvements in processing times, there is scope for further improvement.

Current research concentrates on handling parallelisation of blocks with pointers and concurrency issues with sharing memory between blocks through Distributed Shared Memory. In particular knowing that memory sharing is available will also vary the decisions of the parallelising compiler component and increase the flexibility of the whole parexec tool.

References

1. D.F. Bacon, S.L. Graham and O.J. Sharp. "Compiler Transformations for High-Performance Computing", ACM Computing Surveys, 26(4), 1994.
2. D.J. Evans and A.M. Goscinski. "Automatic Identification of Parallel Units and Synchronisation Points in Programs for Parallel Execution on a Distributed System", Computer Systems: Science and Engineering, 1997.
3. A. Geist, W. Gropp, S. Huss-Lederman, A. Lumsdaine, E. Lusk, W. Saphir, T. Skjellum, and M. Snir. "MPI-2: Extending the Message-Passing Interface", In Euro-Par '96 Parallel Processing: Second International Euro-Par Conference, Lyon, France, Lecture Notes in Computer Science, vol. 1123-1124, Springer-Verlag, pp. 128-135, 1996.
4. A.M. Goscinski. "Parallel Processing on Clusters of Workstations", Networks: The Next Millennium, Proceedings of the IEEE Internations Conference on Networks '97 (SICON'97), Singapore, April 14-17, 1997.
5. A.M. Goscinski, M. J. Hobbs and J. Silcock. "GENESIS: The Operating System Managing Parallelism and Providing Single System Image on Clusters", Technical Report TR C00/03, School of Computing and Mathematics, Deakin University, 24 February 2000.
6. A.M. Goscinski. "Towards an Operating System Managing Parallelism of Computing on Clusters of Workstations", Future Generation Computer Systems, in press.
7. M.W. Hall, S.P. Amarasinghe, B.R. Murphy, S. Liao and M.S. Lam. "Detecting Coarse-Grain Parallelism Using an Interprocedural Parallelising Compiler", In Proceedings of Supercomputing, San Diego, December 1995.
8. M.J. Hobbs. "A Simple Open File Facility for RHODOS", Technical Report TR C95/05, School of Computing and Mathematics, Deakin University, January 1995.
9. M.J. Hobbs. "The Management of SPMD Based Parallel Processing on Clusters of Workstations", PhD Thesis, School of Computing and Mathematics, Deakin University, August 1998.
10. Linux Online, Inc. "The Linux Home Page at Linux Online", `http://www.linux.org/`
11. C.L. McAvaney and A.M. Goscinski. "Loop Parallelisation Using A Simple Parallelising Compiler With The RHODOS Distributed System", Technical Report TR C99/13, School of Computing and Mathematics, Deakin University, July 1999.
12. V.S. Sunderam, G.A. Geist, J. Dongarra and R. Manchek. "The PVM Concurrent Computing System: Evolution, Experiences and Trends", Parallel Computing, Vol. 20(4), pp. 531-546, April 1994.

REQUEST ASSIGNMENT USING PREDICTION FOR DISTRIBUTED WEB SERVERS

W. ZHU AND S. BALASUBRAMANIAM
Department of Computer Science and Electrical Engineering
University of Queensland
Australia
E-mail:{weiping, sasi}@csee.uq.edu.au

Clusters have been used in Web sites to support increase demands. Round Robin method is used as the default policy to assign requests to individual servers in a web site. To reduce possible contention incurred at the dispatcher, the current scheme allows client sites to cache the IP addresses of individual servers that were recently accessed by some users at the client site. With the cached IP addresses users can send their request directly to the servers which can lead to load imbalance. In this paper, a new concept of load balancing for web server is introduced, the dispatcher uses a prediction scheme to decide the target server for requests. Simulation results have shown the proposed method to perform better than the traditional Round-Robin scheduling.

1 Introduction

WWW is rapidly replacing other media to become the major resource for various information. Popular web sites, such as MSN, Yahoo, etc., receives millions requests everyday and the rate is increasing. To cope with the increasing demands, clusters consisting of a number of machines linked by a LAN have been widely used by popular web sites to provide better services. To fully exploit the available resource for better performance, incoming requests need to be evenly assigned to servers. Thus, a dispatcher is required in a web cluster that is based on a given policy to distribute incoming requests [7]. A typical cluster-based web server is shown in Fig. 1, in this example there are four servers plus a dispatcher (DNS). These servers are linked by fast Ethernet or Myrinet and can access all available documents, thus, an incoming request can be assigned to any of them. The most common policy used for distributing requests is the Round-Robin method because of its simplicity. Apart from its normal functions, the DNS (distributed name server) performs the dispatcher function and maps incoming URL addresses to the IP address of the servers.

To avoid being the bottleneck for handling incoming requests, after mapping a http request to a server, the server's IP address is returned to the client. This address is then cached at the client's system for a period specified by the

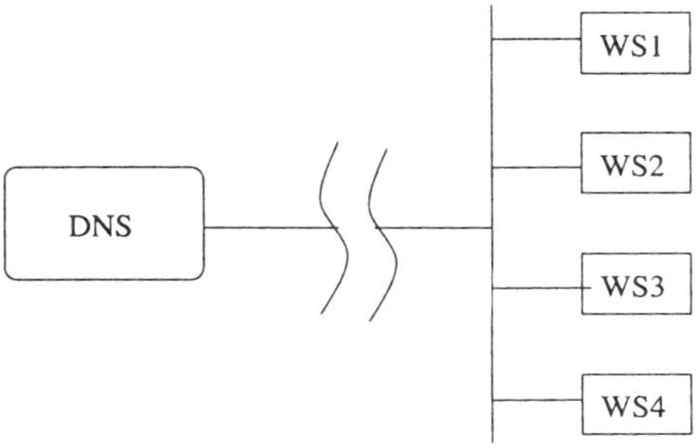

Figure 1. Distributed Web Server

DNS, referred to as the TTL (Time to live). Within the TTL period, the users at the client site can use the cached IP address to access the corresponding server directly and bypassing the DNS. Therefore, the workload at the DNS is reduced, especially when users are attracted on a web site for a period.

From a server's point of view, the requests arrived at the server can be classified into two classes; one is forwarded by the DNS, called normal requests; the other is from those client sites which cached the IP address of the server, we call them TTL requests in the rest of this paper. Although allowing TTL requests to be sent directly to servers reduces the workload at the DNS, this approach creates a problem — load imbalance between servers since not all normal requests trigger the same number of TTL requests. Those TTL requests cannot be ensured to be distributed evenly that threatens the weak load sharing established by the round robin method and can result in some servers are busy to cope with many TTL requests while some servers in the web site are idle at that time [5]. Various methods have been proposed to tackle this problem, most of them adopt ad hoc or heuristic approaches. Despite of this, the results obtained through simulation are encourage [1]. In this paper, we propose a different approach to tackle this problem. Apart from inheriting the advantages from other methods, the proposed approach uses forecasting methods to predict TTL requests, the prediction then guides the dispatcher to avoid assigning normal requests to the servers which would be overwhelmed by incoming TTL requests. Three methods are used to predict TTL requests in our simulations; the initial results show the systems with prediction perform better than the systems without it.

The rest of the paper is organized as follows. In Section 2, a number of prediction methods are presented, which include the methods to determine the appropriate models and parameters. Section 3 describes the simulation model, including dispatching policies used in simulations. Section 4 presents the results received from simulations. Section 5 discusses the future work and outlines the conclusion.

2 Prediction Methods

The number of requests sent to a server within a TTL period varies from a few to tens, depending on users and time. For instance, from 10:00 to 12:00am, the number of TTL requests following a normal request may be more than that from 5:00 to 6:00pm. TTL requests can be treated as a random process triggered by normal requests. To find the pattern and correlation between them, time series analysis is applied on an observed series of requests to extrapolate a pattern. We then can use the identified pattern for future values. So far, three basic methods, namely exponential smoothing, autoregressive process, and autoregressive moving average, have been tested.

2.1 Exponential Smoothing

Simple exponential smoothing has been used in many operating systems to estimate the next CPU burst from previous CPU bursts. Suppose the periodically collected workload can be viewed as a time series $y_1, ...y_n$ described by

$$y_t = \beta_0 + \epsilon_t \tag{1}$$

where β_0 is a constant representing the workload and ϵ_t denotes the error made in load measurement. β_0 may change slowly over time. The estimate workload made in time period i, yp_i, is given by the smoothing equation [2]

$$yp_i = \alpha * y_i + (1 - \alpha) * yp_{i-1} \tag{2}$$

where α is a smoothing constant between 0 and 1 and yp_{i-1} is the estimate of y_{i-1} in the time period $i - 1$. In effect, each smoothed value is the weighted average of the previous workload, where the weights decrease exponentially, depending on the value of α. If α is equal to 1, the previous workload is ignored altogether; if α is equal to 0, then current workload is ignored. α is chosen by using the least SSE (Sum of Squared Error), which is given by [2]:

$$SSE = min \sum_{i=1}^{n} (y_i - yp_i)^2 \tag{3}$$

which is the sum of differences between the predicted value and the real value.

Simple exponential smoothing is to compute a kind of moving average (MA) where the current and immediately preceding observations are assigned greater weight than the older observations. Therefore, it is useful for short-term prediction.

2.2 Autoregressive Process (AR(p))

If we periodically collect workload information from a server, the collected data form a time series. If the data are serially dependent in the sense that one can estimate a coefficient or a set of coefficients that describe consecutive data of the series from specific, time-lagged data, as follows:

$$y_t = \delta + \phi_1 y_{t-1} + \phi_2 y_{t-2} + .. + \phi_p y_{t-p} + \epsilon_t \tag{4}$$

we are able to use AR model to do the forecasting. The above formula is an AR model of order p that expresses the current time series value y_t as a function of past time series values $y_{t-1}, y_{t-2}, ...y_{t-p}$. While $\phi_i, 1 \leq i \leq p$, is the parameter for autoregression process. Similarly, ϵ_t is the error difference of the predicted value and the real value. The δ is the constant which is calculated by

$$\delta = \mu(1 - \phi_1 - ..., -\phi_p) \tag{5}$$

where μ is the mean of the time series, which is calculated by

$$\mu = \frac{\sum_{t=b}^{n} y_t}{n - b + 1} \tag{6}$$

where b is the starting value of the time series taken into consideration.

To consider the AR model, the Sample Autocorrelation samples (SAC) and the Sample Partial Autocorrelation values (SPAC) must be investigated. To correspond to an AR model, the SPAC and SAC must comply with the following rules.

1. The SAC dies down in a steady damped exponential fashion
2. The SPAC has nonzero partial autocorrelation at lags $1, 2, ...p$ and has zero partial autocorrelations at all lags after lag p (that is, cuts off after lag p).

2.3 Autoregressive Moving Average Process (ARMA(p,q))

If the workload variation of a server has the nature of autoregression and moving average, ARMA model can be used to describe its trend, as follows:

$$y_t = \delta + \phi_1 y_{t-1} + .. + \phi_p y_{t-p} + a_t - \theta_1 a_{t-1} - .., -\theta_q a_{t-q} \tag{7}$$

An ARMA model requires both the SAC and SPAC die down. Even if the values do not die down to zero, SAC and SPAC must die down in a damped exponential fashion. The constant δ is calculated exactly in the same manner as the AR process.

3 Simulation

To evaluate the performance of the proposed method, a series of simulations based on different models were carried out, the initial results are presented in this section.

3.1 Model Description

The model used in our simulation is shown in Fig. 2. There are three components in a DNS. The selector receives normal requests sent by clients and based on the predicted number of requests on servers to select a server for an arrived request. The predictor uses periodically collected workload from each server to predict the number of requests at each server, including TTL requests. The predict interval is 5 seconds, the predicted value is then passed to the selector to guide the selector in its selection.

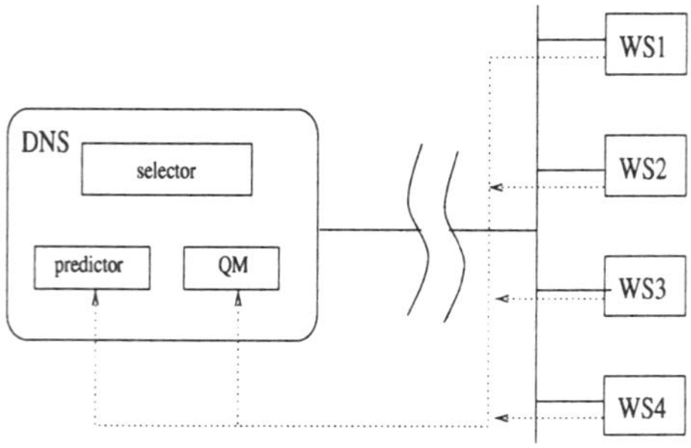

Figure 2. Components in our simulation

The third component in the DNS is called as Queue Manager (QM.) that is introduced to handle unexpected workload surge because prediction in general cannot guarantee absolute accuracy. In addition, since our prediction is based on previous collected data and lasts for 5 seconds, it is possible a decision made by the selector is not correct. Therefore, every time when the selector selects a server for a request, the selector asks the QM samples the queue of the server. If the returned value exceeds a specific threshold Qt, the selection is cancelled and the selector restarts its selection process. Thus, the QM works as an error compensator for the predictor [4].

The reason to have the predictor and QM in the DNS is to increase the accuracy in server selection [4]. Although the QM works as a dynamic selector, this may not be sufficient enough because the queue length at each server does not reflect on the future arrivals of TTL requests. Therefore, there is a need for a predictor to judge the load of a queue for near future. Due to the fact that all predictions are not accurate, the QM is used as a measure to correct the obvious errors.

Both normal and TTL requests in our simulations are modeled as Poisson process, but with different arrival rate. The service time for each request yields an exponential distribution. The TTL period is a constant that is set to 1 minute.

Three sets of simulations were carried out based on the three models previously discussed: one is based on exponential smoothing; one is based on a combination of AR and ARMA, called (AR(1+)), in which we use AR model for server 1-3 and ARMA for server 4; and another is based on ARMA. The reason of using AR(1+) instead of pure AR is because the samples we collected from server 4 show a decay SAC plot that is dominated by a damped exponential fashion, and the SPAC had a spike at lag 1 and was cutoff after lag 1. This behavior exhibits a strong AR(1) model. However, both the SAC and SPAC seem to decay but the values don't have the intention of approaching zero. Since this point must be taken into consideration, an ARMA(1,1) model is considered.

The exponential smoothing parameter was selected by using the SSE calculation mentioned earlier. Different values were tested and the one that produced the least SSE was chosen.

The method that was chosen to calculate the parameters for AR and ARMA processes was the simplest available method, which is the method of moments. For the AR(1) case, the parameter ϕ is simply dictated by the relationship [3]

$$\hat{\phi} = r_1 \tag{8}$$

where r_1 is the autocorrelation at lag 1.

Table 1. Parameters used in Simulations

model	WS1	WS2	WS3	WS4
δ	0.8556	1.2177	1.016	1.293
AR(1+) – ϕ	0.3800	0.3400	0.520	$\phi = 0.03, \theta = 0.35$
ARMA(1,1) (ϕ, θ)	0.421, 0.05	0.56, 0.25	0.56, 0.05	0.03, -0.35
Exp. smoothing	0.555	0.555	0.555	0.555

For the ARMA(1,1) case, the parameter ϕ, is estimated as [3]

$$\hat{\phi} = \frac{r_2}{r_1} \tag{9}$$

While the parameter θ is estimated as [3]

$$r_1 = \frac{(1 - \theta\hat{\phi})(\hat{\phi} - \theta)}{1 - 2\hat{\phi}\theta + \theta^2} \tag{10}$$

The parameters for each of the models are shown in Table 1.

Table 2. Maximum Queue length for simulation of 50 minutes

method	WS1	WS2	WS3	WS4
Round-Robin	15	11	11	10
Exp. smoothing	10	10	11	8
Exp. smoothing+QM	7	7	9	7
AR(1+)	17	11	11	11
AR(1+) + QM	9	10	11	9
ARMA(1,1)	16	10	11	15
ARMA(1,1) + QM	8	10	11	7

4 Results and Discussion

Instead of achieving load balancing, the objective used in our study is to avoid overloading a server while some servers are idle at the same time. The results obtained are reasonably satisfactory, compared to the Round-Robin method. For each of the three policies, three simulations were conducted, one for the Round-Robin, one for prediction only, and one for the predictor plus QM. The criteria used in the comparison are maximum queue length, average queue length and average waiting time of a request. The maximum queue length is an index for the capacity of a policy to avoid overloading a server. While the other two criteria statically show the quality of each policy. The

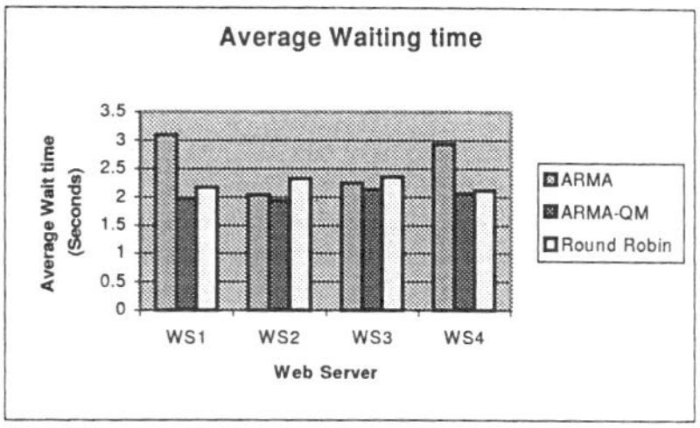

a) average que. leng. of exp. smooth

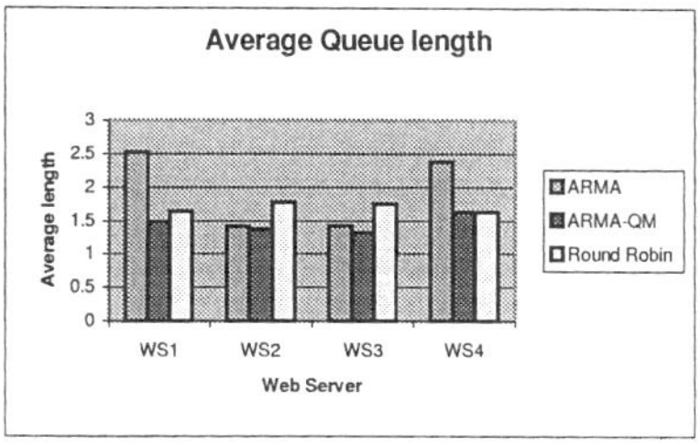

b) average wait time of exp. smooth

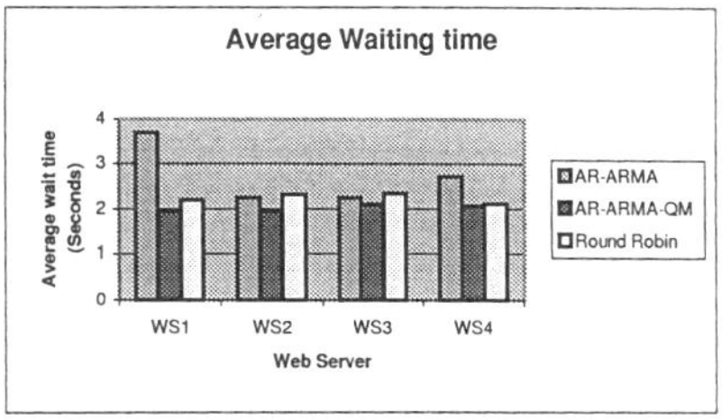

c) average que leng of AR(1+)

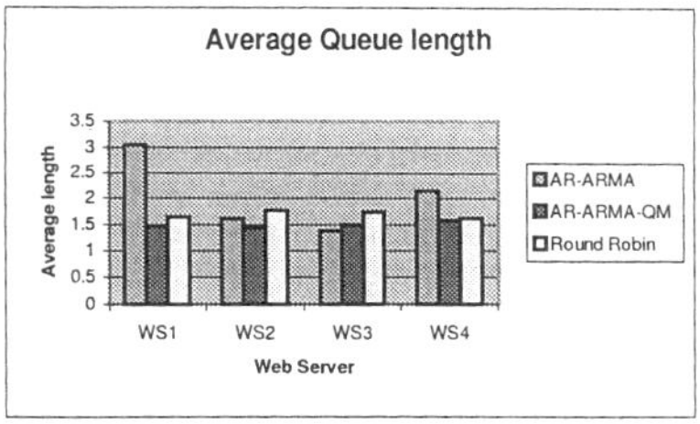

d) average wait time of AR(1+)

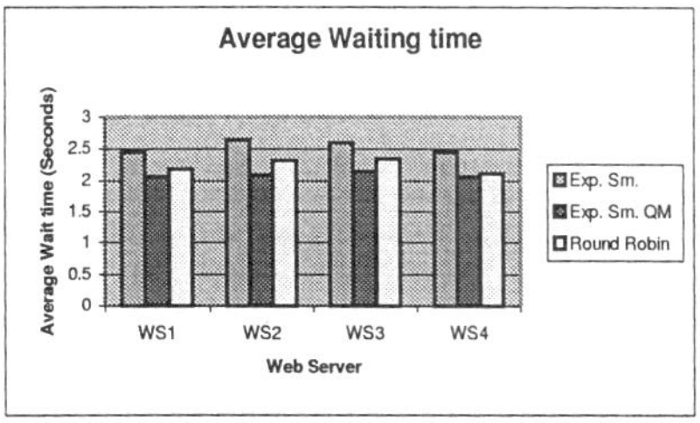

e) average que. Leng. of ARMA

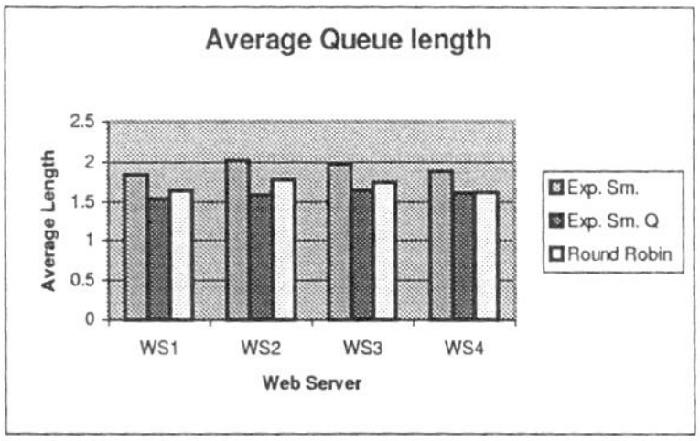

f) average wait time of ARMA

Figure 3. Average waiting time and queue length

parameters used in these simulations are presented in Table 1. Table 2 shows the maximum queue length obtained in our simulation.

The results show, except the exponential smoothing, the other two prediction only policies can only achieve a similar performance as the Round-Robin method. The exponential smoothing, as shown in the table, achieve much better performance, it reduces the maximum queue length from 15 to 10 on server 1 and achieve better or the same performance on the other three servers. The reason is because AR and ARMA models really suit stationary time series, the results that was modeled were a cross between stationary and non-stationary. This was because of the massive fluctuations that may occur from TTL requests. Once a big fluctuation occurs, the accuracy of AR and ARMA prediction deteriorates. The Exponential smoothing on the other hand follows closely to the previous value, which is dictated by recent events.

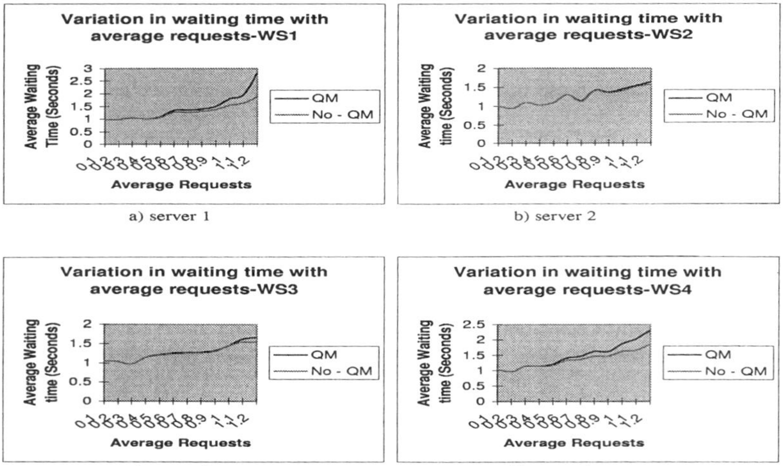

a) server 1 b) server 2 c) server 3 d) server 4

Figure 4. Average Waiting Time at Servers

All predictor plus QM policies perform better than the Round-Robin and predictor-only policies in terms of the maximum queue length, which drop dramatically. Among these three approaches, exponential smoothing plus QM performs the best due to the same reasons analyzed above. The QM dramatically improves the performance on all servers. The importance of QM can be seen from Fig. 4, which shows the difference between the predictor-only policy using the ARMA model and the predictor plus QM on the average waiting time under various workload on a particular server. The figure shows initially the two policies have a similar performance, but gradually as the workload increases the difference between them becomes obvious.

In terms of the average waiting time, the AR(1+)+QM and ARMA+QM policies perform slight better than the exponential smoothing-QM policy as shown in Fig 3 b), d) and f). This could have aroused from the reduction of high fluctuations. Since the AR(1+) and ARMA policies are most suited for stationary time series, the predicted values seem to hover over a specific mean. Therefore, the reduction in fluctuations may have increased the prediction accuracy, therefore, increasing the possibility of allocating incoming requests to the most appropriate web server. The difference between the AR(1+)+QM and the ARMA+QM policies is negligible in terms of the queue length, average waiting time, and average queue length.

All predictor plus QM policies outperform the Round-Robin method, because the Round-Robin method does not take into consideration the load differences between servers when it assigns a request to a server. Fig 3 show that the queue length has decreased by nearly 20%. The waiting time have decreased by about 5% to 16%. This also reflects on the maximum queue length, where lengths change from fifteen to eleven. The inefficiency of the Round-Robin method is mainly because the system allocates new task evenly to each server, if the TTL requests were not taken into consideration then the load on each server would be evenly distributed. Since the TTL request have the luxury of joining the queue and bypassing the DNS, there is no consideration of random load imbalance.

5 Conclusion

The results obtained are reasonably satisfactory, however, a more accurate prediction method for TTL request would enable the system to accurately allocate requests to servers. Methods to be considered include decision-making that combines information of both the client and the server. As shown by [1], load balancing could be achieved by combining the state information of the client and the server. Since majority of the load imbalance is due to the TTL request a certain amount of knowledge of the clients should be an advantage. This could be achieved by viewing access log files, and producing types of classes for clients who access servers the most and the least.

One future work that must be brought to attention is the fact that the TTL request could be dominated by the characteristics of the users and the servers. According to [6], there are workload characteristics for different server. Examples include web servers for research and educational purposes or servers for commercial ISPs.

The addition of such information with time series analysis could dramatically improve the prediction accuracy. A decision rule could be established from the additional information in order to improve the accuracy of prediction.

Results obtained from the simulations have shown that prediction methods are an effective policy for task assignment. The three time series-based policies, i.e., exponential smoothing-QM, AR(1+)+QM, and ARMA+QM, outperform the conventional Round-Robin method. This is because the Round-Robin method does not take into consideration the future impact of TTL requests. The system works better when combined with the Queue manager, which determines if the allocated web server is the most appropriate for the task in real time. The QM alone is not efficient enough because it relies mainly on number of clients in the queue. This information does not reflect on the potential impact of TTL requests. The prediction accuracy, however, could be improved by considering more information from the client side. This would enable more determination of TTL request that could be expected at the web servers.

References

1. M. Colajanni, P. S. Yu, D.M. Dias, *Analysis of Task Assignment Policies in Scalable Distributed Web-Server Systems*, IEEE transaction on parallel and Distributed Systems **9**, 6 (1998).
2. B. L. Bowerman, R.T. O'Connell, *Forecasting and Time Series*, 3rd edition, Duxbury Press, 1993.
3. J. D. Cryer, *Time Series*, PWS Publishers, 1986.
4. G. Chiruvolu, R. Sankar, N. Ranganathan, *VBR video traffic management using a predictor-based architecture*, Computer Communications **23**, 62-70 (2000)
5. N.G. Shivaratri, P. Krueger, M. Singhal, *Load Distributing for locally Distributed Systems*, Computer **25**, 12 (1992)
6. M.F. Arlitt, C.L. Williamson, *Internet Web Servers: Workload Characterization and Performance Implications*, IEEE/ACM Transactions on Networking **5**, 5 (October 1997).
7. T. Schroeder, S. Goddard, B. Ramamurthy, *Scalable Web Server Cluster Technologies*, IEEE Networks **5**, (2000).

MODELLING AND SIMULATION OF REACTIVE SYSTEMS

CHANGGUI CHEN AND WANLEI ZHOU
School of Computing & Mathematics, Deakin University
Clayton, VIC. 3168, AUSTRALIA
Email: changgui, wanlei@deakin.edu.au

Reactive systems concepts are an attractive paradigm for system design, development and maintenance because it separates policies from mechanisms. This paper presents the modelling and simulation of reactive systems for building distributed and fault-tolerant computing applications. The Actor concept is introduced to analyse and model the reactive components. The simulation of the Actors shows the usefulness of the reactive system approach in distributed environments.

1 Introduction

Reactive systems are ones that are supposed to maintain an ongoing interaction with their environment, rather than to produce some final result on termination [6]. An adequate description of reactive systems must refer to their ongoing behaviours, which are seen as reactions to external stimuli. Typical examples of reactive systems are flight reservation systems, industrial plant controllers, operating systems, most kinds of real-time computer embedded systems, and communication systems, etc. Such systems are often concurrent and distributed [1] [7].

Several systems, such as Meta, Disco and STATEMATE, and languages, such as Reactive C and Reactive Pascal that are based on reactive system concepts have been developed recently [12]. However, most of the research on reactive systems is concentrated on process control (such as controling a robot). In our research, we try to develop a platform based on the reactive systems concepts for building distributed and fault-tolerant computing applications. This paper attemps to model reactive systems using the *Actor* concept, which is a basic concept in Real-time Object-Oriented Modelling [10]. Actors are parallel autonomous agents, which are distributed in space and execute at their own rate and communicate asynchronously by sending messages. Their behaviors show that they have reactive characteristics, thus we can model reactive components as Actors. After that a simulation of these Actors written in Simjava is developed to evaluate the performance of our reactive system model. The entity concept from Simjava has similar semantics with the Actor so that Simjava provides a good simulation model for the reactive Actors.

The paper is organised as follows: In the next section, we describe the architecture of reactive systems. The Actor concept used to model the reactive components is introduced in Section 3. Section 4 addresses the reactive behaviours. The simulation of actors is presented in Section 5. Finally we conclude our work.

2 The architecture of reactive systems

A reactive system uses sensors and actuators to implement the mechanisms that interact with its environment or applications. Its decision making managers (DMMs) are used to implement the policies regarding to the control of the applications. Figure 1 depicts the architecture of the reactive system model. In this model, a DMM subscribes to sensors and receives reports from these sensors on the application's states. Then it uses actuators to change the states of the applications according to the policy it implemented. Sensors can be attached to applications to obtain their states (or events). These states or events are sent to the DMMs which react to them by using actuators to change the states of applications.

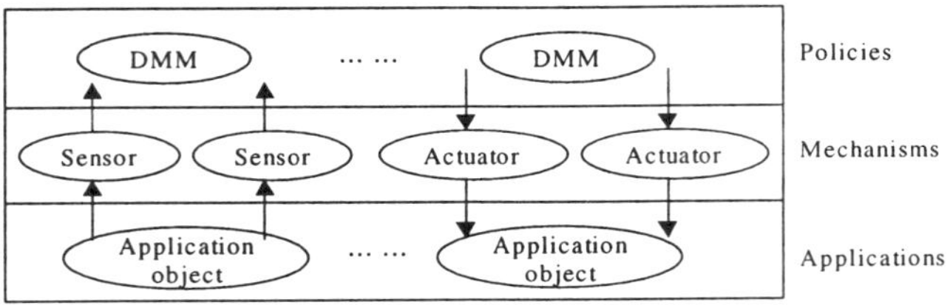

Figure 1: The reactive system architecture

With this architecture, we have a great advantage that it separates policies from mechanisms, i.e., if a policy is changed it may have no impact on related mechanisms and vice versa [12]. For example, if a decision making condition based on two sensors was "AND" and now is changed to "OR", the sensors can still be used without any changes required, i.e., the mechanism layer can remain unchanged. This advantage will lead to a better software architecture and have a great significance in developing distributed and fault-tolerant computing applications. In normal practice, most fault-tolerant computing policies are deeply embedded into application programs, therefore these applications can not cope with changes in environments, policies and mechanisms. To build better fault-tolerant computing systems that can cope with constant changes in environments and user requirements, it is essential to separate fault-tolerant computing policies from application programs. Hence, we can apply the reactive system model to develop better fault-tolerant computing applications [4] [11].

3 Actor model

A reactive system has three components: DMM, Sensor and Actuator. In this section we introduce the Actor concept to model them respectively.

An Actor represents an active object that has a clearly defined purpose. It may be used to model physical objects or abstract objects. Here, the term "active" means that an Actor may have its own execution thread and can, therefore, operate concurrently with other active objects in its domain. An Actor's behaviors illustrate that it has most of reactive characteristics. We can, therefore, model DMM, sensor and actuator as Actors respectively.

The key to identifying an Actor is its purpose. In fact, the purpose of an Actor is an abstraction, or distillation, of its various functional capabilities. This is both implied and enforced by the *encapsulation shell* of the Actor, which is an opaque both from without and from within the Actor.

To communicate with other entities in its environment, an Actor provides one or more interface components, which we call *ports*, in its encapsulation shell. The set of messages exchanged between two parties in a concurrent system typically conforms to a dynamic pattern or protocol.

We can implement three Actor classes in a reactive system: DMM actor, sensor actor and actuator actor. A DMM actor may have more than one sensor ports and actuator ports to connect to sensors and actuators, but we can define all the sensor ports using the same protocol, and so do all the actuator ports. A sensor actor has a port to connect to the DMM for reporting events and a port to connect to an application object for monitoring events. Similarly, an actuator actor has a port that connects to the DMM to receive decisions and another port that connects to an application object to change its state. The access protocols on these ports can be defined respectively.

4 Reactive behaviours

We refer to the internal operation of an Actor over time as its behaviour. At any point of time, an Actor has a state that determines how it will react when it receives a message through one of its ports. The set of such states, and the possible sequences in which the states can be visited, is described by the *statechart* [5], which constitutes an extensive generalisation of state-transition diagrams.

The behavioural description of the DMM actor includes following states and transitions. During its lifetime, the DMM progresses through three basic phases. On creation, it is initialised and enters "Listening" state, in which it listens to sensors connecting. Once there are sensors to connect to it (accompaning with a transition for connecting with the sensors), it enters the "Waiting" state. In this state, it waits to receive the sensor reports. If an event is received (a transition for receiving events occurs), it will enter "Operational" state, during which it makes decisions and then send them to actuators. Hence, two transitions: "decisionMaking" and "decisionSending" happen in the "Operational" state. After sending the decisions, the DMM enters the "Waiting" state again.

The sensor actor has two states and two transitions during its lifetime, and so does the actuator actor. Their behaviours can be described using the statechart, similar to the DMM's.

5 Simulation

We develop a simulation in this section to evaluate the effectiveness of the above reactive system model. The simulation tool we use is Simjava, which is a discrete event simulation package written in Java and conceptually based on the Simlibrary for C [8] [9]. The purpose of the simulation is to measure the execution time taken for communications among DMM, sensor and actuator actors. According to the time they take, we can evaluate their performance running in different environments.

5.1 Simulation model

A Simjava simulation contains a number of entities each of which runs in parallel in its own thread. These entities have the similar structure and illustrate the similar characteristics as the Actors we described above. Hence this simulation model is quite appropriate for our reactive Actors modelling.

An entity's behaviour is encoded in Java using its body() method. To simulate the Actors in a reactive system, we can create three entities to model the DMM, sensor and actuator actors. Without losing genericity, we assume that there are m DMMs and n sensors and actuators respectively in a reactive system. Each sensor can be subscribed by all DMMs and each DMM can subscribe to all sensors as well. Once a DMM makes a decision, the decision will be sent to the related actuators that change the application states.

5.2 Results and discussions

The simulation results confirm our intuition that as the numbers of DMMs and sensors/actuators increase, the execution time they used to communicate with each other increases as well.

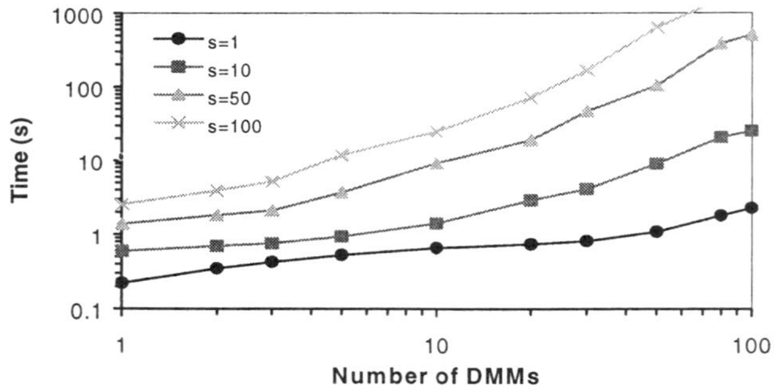

Figure 2: The execution times for Actors simulation

Figure 2 shows the simulation results, where s stands for the number of sensors. From Figure 2, we have two findings. The first is that, the simulation time with an increasing number of sensors increases more rapid than that with an increasing number of DMMs. In Figure 2, the values on vertical axis increase more quick than those on the corresponding horizontal axis. This is because, increasing the number of sensors, i.e., increasing applications, will increase the number of actuators so that the simulation has to take more time to receive more events and send more decisions to the actuators. This increase is by many times and is a non-linear increase, while the increase of simulation time with an increasing number of DMMs is simply by adding the times that each DMM takes together, which is a linear increase.

The second finding is that, among four time curves with different number of sensors, the bigger the number of sensors is, the steeper the curve is. That means, with the increasing number of DMMs, the simulation time with bigger number of sensors increases more rapid than that with smaller number of sensors. This can also be explained by the above reason.

5.3 Distributed simulation

To evaluate the reactive system model in a distributed environment, we have to build a distributed simulation. We can use the extension of the Simjava discrete event simulation package to utilise the Remote Method Invocation (RMI) [9] capabilities of the JDK1.2 to build the distributed simulation.

The distributed simulation shows a similar result to the local host simulation. Figure 3 shows the comparison of two groups of simulations, from where we have an observation. We can see that the time curves for the local simulation are steeper than those for the distributed simulation. That means, the increase of execution time for the distributed simulation is less than the increase for the local simulation! This is a good news for our reactive actors, because most of DMMs require reports from sensors located in different hosts. This result shows that DMMs and sensors running in a distributed environment is more effective than their running in a local host.

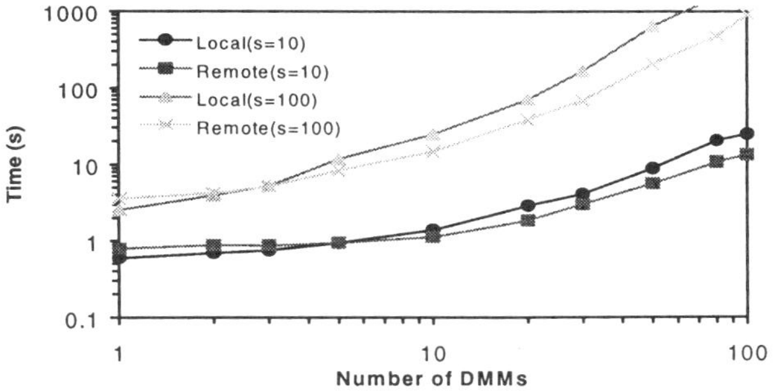

Figure 3: Two groups of simulations

6 Conclusion

The major advantage of the reactive system approach is the separation of policies and mechanisms. In the paper we introduced the Actor concept to model reactive systems. An Actor represents an active object and it exhibits some reactive characteristics. Hence the Actor is an appropriate tool for modelling reactive components. The simulation results show that DMMs, sensors and actuators can be used in a distributed environment effectively.

Two applications based on the reactive system concepts, one is the Teamwork support system and the other is the Network partitioning problem, can be refered to [2] [3]. They have showed the potential benefits of our reactive system approach. In both cases, the DMMs, sensors and actuators stay the same and perform the same functions no matter what changes others have. This leads to the easy design and maintanance of the applications.

References

1. P. Caspi, A. Girault and D. Pilaud. Distributing reactive systems. *The ISCA Int'l Conf. on Parallel and Distributed Computing Systems (PDCS'94).* Las Vegas, USA, 1994
2. C. Chen and W. Zhou. An Architecture for Resolving Network Partitioning. *The ISCA Int'l Conf. for Comp. And Their App. (CATA-2000),* 84-87, New Orleans, USA, 2000.
3. C. Chen, W. Zhou and Y. Yang Coordination Mechanism for Teamwork Support *The 1999 Asia Pacific Decision Sciences Institute Conf.*, 389-391, Shanghai, China, 1999.
4. C. Daniel, and P. Donna. *Distributed Computing Environments.* McGraw-Hill, Inc. New York, 1993.
5. D. Harel. "Statecharts: A Visual Formalism for Complex Systems." *Science of Computer Programming* 8, pp. 231-274, July, 1987.
6. D. Harel and A. Pnueli. On the development of reactive system. *Logics and Models of Concurrent Systems.* Spring-Verlag, Berlin, Heidelberg, New York, Tokyo. 1985.
7. D. Harel and M. Politi *Modeling Reactive Systems with Statecharts: The Statemate Approach.* McGraw-Hill Companies, January, 1998
8. F. Howell and R. McNab. "Simjava: a discrete event simulation package for Java with applications in computer systems modelling", *Proc. of 1st Int'l Conf. on Web-based Modelling and Simulation*, San Diego CA, Society for Computer Simulation, Jan 1998.
9. R. McNab and F.W. Howell "Using Java for Discrete Event Simulation" *Proc. 12th UK Comp. and Tele. Perf. Eng. Workshop (UKPEW)*, Univ. of Edinburgh, 219-228. 1996.
10. Bran Selic, Garth Gullekson and Paul T. Ward. *Real-Time Object-Oriented Modelling.* John Wiley & Sons, Inc. 1994
11. W. Zhou Detecting and tolerating failures in a loosely integrated heterogeneous database system. *Computer Communications*, 22, 1056-1067, 1999.
12. W. Zhou and E. Eide Java Sensors and Their Applications. *Pro. of the 21st Australian Computer Science Conf. (ACSC' 98)*, pp. 345-356, Perth, Australia, 4-6 Feb., 1998.

Chapter 7
Parallel Algorithms II

AMATEROUS: A PARALLEL WIRE ROUTER WITHOUT DETAILED/GLOBAL FEEDBACK

KOTARO TANAKA*, KAZUHIKO OHNO AND HIROSHI NAKASHIMA
Dept. Information and Computer Sciences, Toyohashi University of Technology, 1-1 Hibarigaoka, Tempaku Toyohashi, 441-8580 JAPAN
email: {kotaro,ohno,nakasima}@para.tutics.tut.ac.jp

This paper proposes a new parallel wire routing algorithm named *Amaterous*. As many successful parallel wire routers, Amaterous has global and detailed routers, but the feedback from the detailed to the global is removed so that both routers are parallelized efficiently and independently. For this feedback removal, Amaterous has an additional routing phase named *capacity path (c-path) router* that draws all the possible paths in each rectangular region of each routing layer prior to the global routing. Since the global router picks c-paths to form the global path of a net, it is assured that the global path is always converted successfully to its detailed counterpart which the detailed router generates from the c-paths. Therefore the global router does not need to know the result of the detailed routing and thus the feedback from detailed to global is removed.
We implemented Amaterous on a 16-node PC cluster and measured its performance with three MCM benchmarks. The result shows up to 12 fold speedup proving the efficiency of our algorithm. It is also shown that Amaterous is 1.2 to 3.6 times as fast as a state-of-art parallel router Amon2.

1 Introduction

Parallel processing plays an important role in the performance improvement of CAD applications, which is strongly required due to the rapid growth of the amount and complexity of digital circuits. The parallelization, however, is not always easy because of the sequentiality hidden in problems and well-tuned algorithms for them. Therefore straightforward approaches, such as do-all loop parallelization often used in scientific computation, are hardly applicable but sophisticated parallel algorithms are necessary for efficient parallel computation.

For example, in the wire routing problem that is the target of our research, multiple nets may be routed simultaneously exploiting *inter-net* parallelism. However the resulting paths for those nets can interfere each other revealing the hidden dependence, the source of sequentiality, among the routing of the nets. Thus most of successful parallel routers have two cooperative routers; *global* router that roughly determines a region for a net in which the path for

*Currently with Hitachi Microsoftware Systems, Inc.

the net should lie; and *detailed* router to draw the exact path of the net in the region. Since the regions, or *global paths*, for multiple nets may be overlapped, the global router is efficiently parallelized. The detailed routing of multiple nets is also performed in parallel if their global paths have no intersection.

This parallelization, however, still has a bottleneck due to the dependence between the global and detailed routing. When the global router draws the path for a net, it estimates the difficulty of the detailed routing, or *wireability*, of the path. The preciseness of the estimation depends on the detailed paths for other nets routed previously, and it greatly affects the real wireability. Thus the global router has to receive some feedback from the detailed router, which brings the dependence among the nets, in order to keep high wireability.

We observed this dependence is due to lack of confidence in global routing. That is, if it is assured that the detailed router always finds the path for a net lying in its global path, no feedback from detailed to global is necessary. In this paper, we propose a new parallel wire router named *Amaterous* based on this observation. Amaterous has an additional routing phase named *capacity path (c-path)* router to draw all the possible paths in each rectangular region of each routing layer prior to the global routing. Its global router picks c-paths to form the global path of a net ensuring that the detailed router successfully generates the exact path from the c-paths. Thus the feedback from the detailed to the global is removed so that both routers are parallelized efficiently and independently.

The rest of the paper describes Amaterous and its performance as follows. Section 2 overviews related works to make it clear why the feedback removal is essential. Section 3 gives the outline of Amaterous while its parallel implementation is discussed in Section 4 in detail. An experiment result with MCM benchmarks is shown in Section 5. Finally we conclude the paper summarizing future works in Section 6.

2 Related Works

2.1 Parallelism in Wire Routing

Wire routing problem has two types of parallelism; *intra-net* parallelism and *inter-net* parallelism. Parallel algorithms exploiting the former try to route one net or one subnet (branch) in a net by multiple processors. For example, parallelized maze routing[1,2,3] and line search[4] are regarded as a kind of parallel search to find optimal solution (path) in a large search space of possible solutions (paths). Another example is to divide a subnet into segments by bends and to assign a processor to a segment for parallel routing[5].

The latter is exploited in algorithms in which multiple nets or subnets are routed simultaneously. If a set of nets or subnets has no geometrical interference in its members, it is quite easy to route the (sub)nets in parallel[6,7,8,5]. Even if the (sub)nets potentially interfere each other, they may be routed in parallel expecting no or few real interference[9,10,4,5].

Note that an algorithm may exploit both types of parallelism. For example, multiple nets are routed in parallel and each (sub)net is routed also in parallel[9,7,4]. Another example is to switch the type of parallelism according to routing phases[8,5].

2.2 *Global and Detailed Routing*

Global routing is a well-known technique to bound a huge routing space so that routing of exact paths, or *detailed routing*, is performed in a reasonable time. The global routing for a net is to determine a region, or a *global path*, in which the exact path for the net should lie. Since the region is much narrower than the whole routing space, the detail routing to find the exact path works quickly.

Among various global routing techniques, such as weighted maze[5], hierarchical decomposition[11] and iterative improvement[9], it is common that the global router evaluates some cost function representing the difficulty of detailed routing, or *wireability*. One of most commonly used cost measure is *boundary capacity*[12] that represents how many paths can cross an edge of a coarse rectangular region. The *partition capacity*[5] is a similar concept but it indicates how many paths pass through a rectangular region.

The combination of global and detailed routing is also beneficial to parallel routing exploiting inter-net parallelism. For the global routing, it is good news that multiple global paths may have intersections because a boundary or a partition allows multiple detailed paths to pass through it. Thus multiple (sub)nets may be globally routed simultaneously without much care of the interference among them. For the detailed routing, it is easy to judge that a set of (sub)nets has no interference among its members if their global paths have no intersections. Therefore, many successful parallel wire routers have global and detailed routers[3,7,5].

2.3 *Feedback from Detailed to Global*

The capacity referred in the global routing is an estimation of the real wireability of the detailed routing. If the estimation is too optimistic, the detailed router will frequently fail to find the exact path for a global path. On the other hand, too pessimistic estimation will brings frequent failure of the global routing. Thus the preciseness of the estimation greatly affects the total wireability of the router.

The preciseness greatly depends on the results of the detailed routing as reported by Keshk[5]. For example, it was shown that 2.5 % of nets of MCC1-75 in MCM benchmark set[13] cannot be routed if the global router ignores the results of the detailed. Thus he claimed the necessity of the feedback from the detailed to the global and showed it makes MCC1-75 completely routed.

However, the feedback brings a bottleneck in parallel processing. If the global routing for a net has to know all the results of detailed routing of previously routed nets, we cannot exploit inter-net parallelism in the global routing. This sequentiality may be relaxed by grouping certain number of nets in order to reduce the frequency of the feedback as proposed by Keshk. This relaxation, however, not only degrades the estimation preciseness but also is insufficient to remove the bottleneck. In fact, his evaluation showed his Amon2 incurs about 50 % overhead caused by the feedback.

As stated in the introductory section, we observed this feedback may be removed if it is assured that the detailed router always finds the path for a net lying in its global path. This feedback removal also makes it possible to separate global and detailed routing into completely distinct phases to minimize the frequency of communication between them.

3 Overview of Amaterous

3.1 Terminology

Here we define a few terms to explain our new parallel wire router *Amaterous* (Fig. 1). The *routing space* is a 3-dimensional non-negative integer finite coordinate space, or grid space, $[0, X] \times [0, Y] \times [0, Z]$ in which *terminals* are located. A *net* is a set of terminals to be connected. A *subnet* of a net is a pair of its terminals, or a pair of a terminal and a subnet recursively. Thus the *routing* a net of terminals $\{t_1, \ldots, t_n\}$ is to find paths for subnets $\langle t_1, t_2\rangle$, $\langle\{t_1, t_2\}, t_3\rangle$, ..., $\langle\{t_1, \ldots, t_{n-1}\}, t_n\rangle$.

The *(detailed) path* for a subnet $\langle S, t\rangle$ is an ordered set of adjacent grid points $\{(x_1, y_1, z_1), \ldots, (x_m, y_m, z_m)\}$ where (x_1, y_1, z_1) is included in the path for the subnet S or the location of S if it is a terminal, (x_m, y_m, z_m) is the location of t, and one of the following holds for all $1 \leq i < m$.

$$\begin{cases} x_{i+1} = x_i \pm 1 \ \wedge \ y_{i+1} = y_i \ \wedge \ z_{i+1} = z_i \\ x_{i+1} = x_i \ \wedge \ y_{i+1} = y_i \pm 1 \ \wedge \ z_{i+1} = z_i \\ x_{i+1} = x_i \ \wedge \ y_{i+1} = y_i \ \wedge \ z_{i+1} = z_i \pm 1 \end{cases}$$

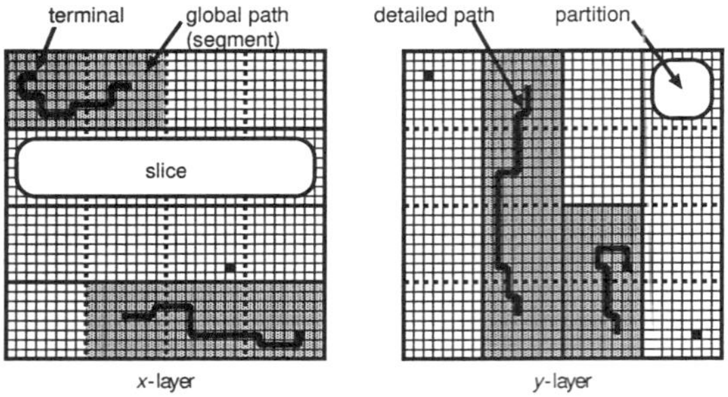

Figure 1. Routing Space

The union of the paths for a net N, denoted as $\pi_d(N)$, has no intersection with that of any other net $\pi_d(N')$, i.e. $\forall N \forall N'(N \neq N' \rightarrow \pi_d(N) \cap \pi_d(N') = \emptyset)$.

A xy-space of the routing space, or a *layer*, is subdivided into rectangular *partitions* by lines $\{x = X_1, \ldots, x = X_k\}$ and $\{y = Y_1, \ldots, y = Y_l\}$. A layer with even (odd) z-coordinate is referred to as x-layer (y-layer) because paths in the layer run in the direction of x-axis (y-axis) in a global view. A *partition segment* on an x-layer (y-layer) is a series of partitions in x (y) direction. The partition segment whose left and right (top and bottom) edges are on the routing space border is called *slice*. The partition where a terminal lies is referred to as the *home partition* of the terminal.

The *global path* for a subnet $\langle S, t\rangle$ is defined as an ordered set of adjacent partitions in a similar manner to the detailed path using coarse grid space $\{0, X_1, \ldots, X_k\} \times \{0, Y_1, \ldots, Y_l\} \times [0, Z]$. However, adjacent partitions (X_i, Y_i, z_i) and $(X_{i+1}, Y_{i+1}, z_{i+1})$ has to satisfy $Y_{i+1} = Y_i$ $(X_{i+1} = X_i)$ if they both lie in a x-layer (y-layer). That is, a layer has its own direction in which global paths have to run. Thus a global path consists of *global segments* each of which is a partition segment.

The union of global paths for a net N, denoted as $\pi_g(N)$, may have intersection with that of other net $\pi_g(N')$. Its detailed counterpart $\pi_d(N)$ has to included in it. The *capacity* of a partition on an x-layer (y-layer), or *partition capacity*, is the maximum number of paths simultaneously connecting the left and right (top and bottom) edges.

3.2 Capacity Path

For a given set of nets, Amaterous routes it by three distinct phases of routing; *c-path routing*, global routing and detailed routing.

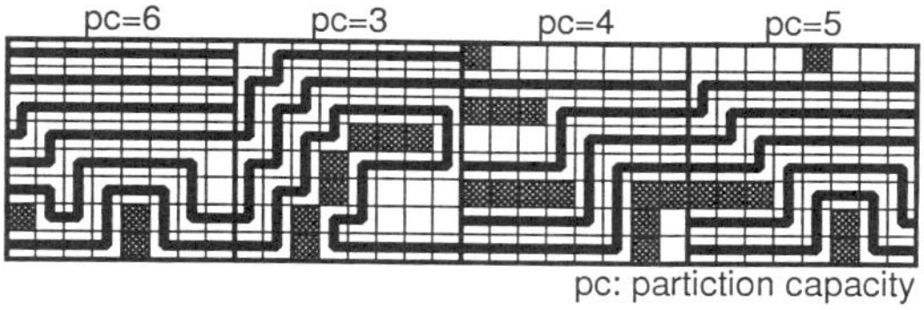

Figure 2. Capacity Path (c-path)

The first phase, c-path routing, is unique for Amaterous. For each slice in an x-layer, it finds out all the *capacity paths (c-paths)* that ideally satisfy the following conditions (Fig. 2).

1. A c-path has no intersection with initial obstacles including terminals nor any other c-paths.
2. The left end of a c-path is on the left edge of a partition and its right end is on the right edge of the same or another partition.
3. For each partition, the number of c-paths passing through it is equal to its partition capacity. That is, the number of c-paths passing through it is maximized.
4. For each partition segment, the number of c-paths passing through it is maximized on condition that those for partitions and partition segments included in it are maximized recursively.

The conditions for c-paths on y-layers are similarly given.

3.3 Global and Detailed Routing

After c-paths are routed as shown in Fig. 3(a), each terminal is connected to its *initial c-path* that passes through two or more partitions including its home partition as shown in Fig. 3(b). Thus a terminal has a partition adjacent to its home in which its initial c-path passes. This partition is called *initial partition* of the terminal.

The global routing of a two-terminal (sub)net is the process to find the cost optimal global path connecting initial partitions of both terminals. The cost of a global segment is the sum of the cost of each partitions in it if there is a c-path passing through it. The cost of a partition increases as its capacity decreases to avoid too much congestion. Moreover, the cost for a global segment through which no c-paths pass is infinite. Thus it is assured

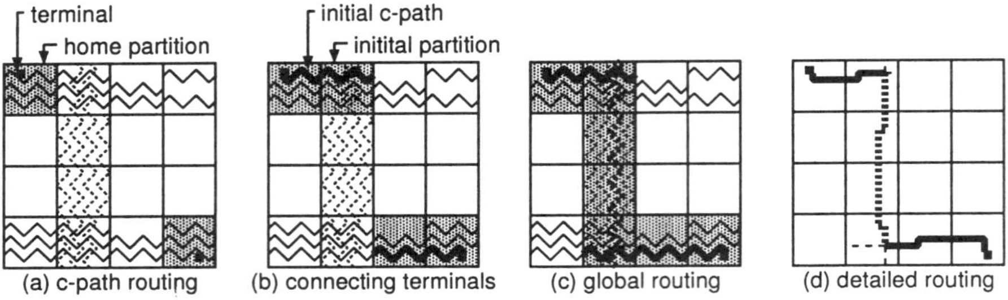

Figure 3. Routing Phases

that a global segment is always converted to its detailed counterpart using a c-path passing through it as the bottom-line. After a global path is settled, the capacity of each partition on the path is decreased and a c-path for each global segment is exclusively assigned to the path as shown in Fig. 3(c). The routing of a terminal and a subnet is a similar process connecting the initial partition of the terminal and the global path for the subnet.

When the global routing completes, each global segment has its own c-path. Thus at least we can form a detailed path by connecting c-paths for global segments by vias. The c-paths, however, have too many bends and are too lengthy as shown in Fig. 2. Thus the detailed router first tries to straighten each c-path keeping its connection of the both ends of a global segment. Finally, straightened paths are connected by vias and fragments are discarded as shown in Fig. 3(d).

4 Parallel Algorithm of Amaterous

4.1 Overview of Parallelization

Three routing phases of Amaterous, c-path, global and detailed routing, are parallelized following master-worker paradigm. For the c-path and detailed routing, slices in x-layers are cyclicly assigned to a half of worker processors while the other half are responsible for y-layers as shown in Fig. 4(a). One of processors, say P_0, also acts as the master.

In global routing, processors other than P_0 are workers to find global paths for subnets assigned to them as shown in Fig. 4(b). The processor P_0 has the master job only in this phase to distribute subnets to workers and to check the consistency of the results from them.

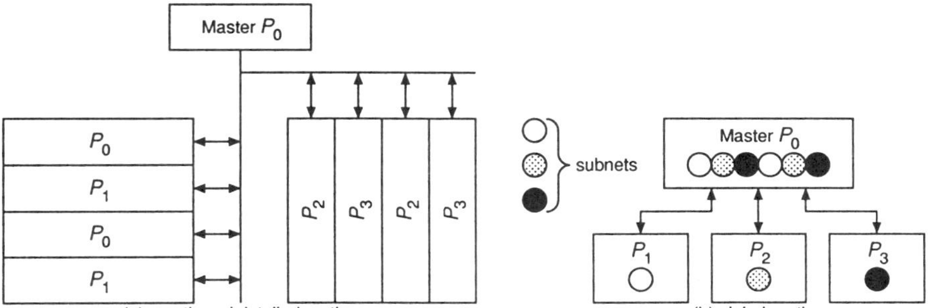

Figure 4. Parallelization of Routing Phases

4.2 C-path Routing

At first, the master distributes the locations of initial obstacles and terminals to workers. Then each worker for x-layers routes c-paths in the slices assigned to it independently by the following algorithm based on that for the partition capacity measurement proposed by Keshk[14].

for $p =$ leftmost partition **to** rightmost partition **begin**
  $e =$ left edge of p;
  for $g =$ bottom of e **to** top of e **begin**
    Draw a path from g touching right hand to the bottom edge of the slice, obstacles, terminals, or previously drawn paths, until reaching to one of the followings.
    1. the right edge of the slice.
    2. the top edge of the slice.
    3. the left edge of the partition currently visiting.

    In cases 2 and 3, erase the fraction of the path from the left edge of the partition currently visiting.
  end
end

The c-paths in slices on y-layers are similarly routed.

The c-paths shown in Fig. 2 are routed by this algorithm and satisfy the conditions discussed in Section 3.2. In general, this algorithm is sub-optimal becaues the fourth condition is not always satisfied. Although the resultant c-paths are practically acceptable and an optimal algorithm should require a impractically large computation time, we will further investigate the improvement of the algorithm to increase the number of c-paths passing through partition segments.

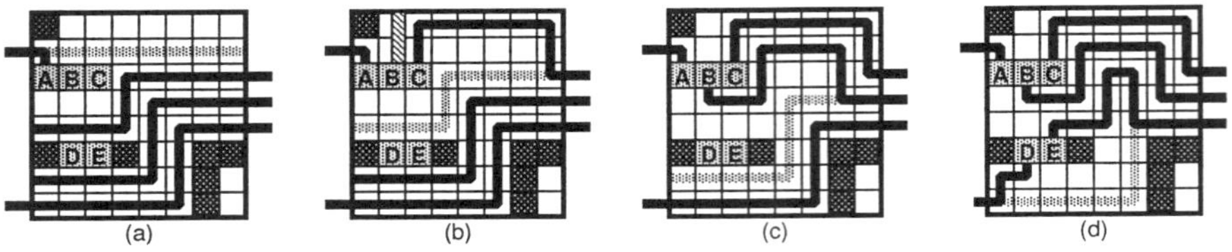

Figure 5. Connecting Terminals to C-paths

After the c-paths are settled, terminals are connected to them to determine their initial c-paths. Terminals in a partition are distributed to each layer as follows. If the height of the minimum rectangle including all the terminals is larger than its width, the terminals are equally distributed to x-layers. Otherwise, they are assigned to y-layers.

Fig. 5 illustrates the method to connect terminals to c-paths passing through a partition in an x-layer.

(a) From three terminals A, B and C that can be connected to the topmost c-path, A is chosen for the connection because it is leftmost and the c-path passes the left edge only. Thus the initial partition of A is the left neighbor. After the connection, the fraction of the c-path is erased.

(b) From remaining terminals B, C, D and E that can be connected to the second c-path, C is chosen for the connection because it is rightmost and above the c-path passing the right edge only. In order to reserve enough space for further connection, the path from C to the c-path is drawn touching left hand to obstacles and the barrier virtually constructed at its left.

(c) The terminal B is connected to the third c-path similarly.

(d) Both the terminals D and E are connected to the bottommost c-path that passes both left and right edges.

This process may fail to connect all the terminals to c-paths. If so, unconnected terminals are exchanged between workers for x- and y-layers. This is the only communication between workers in the c-path routing.

After all the terminals are connected to c-paths, abstracted information of c-paths and terminal/c-path connections are gathered by the master to construct *c-path map*. Note that exact geometrical data of c-paths are not included in the c-path map but kept in workers for the detailed routing.

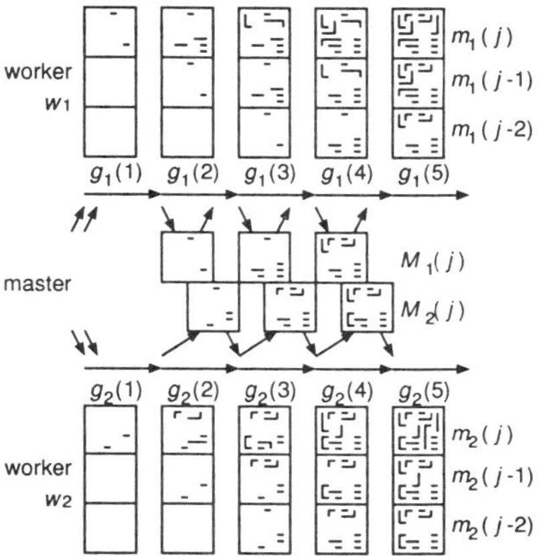

Figure 6. Master/Worker Communication in Global Routing

4.3 Global Routing

At the first step of the global routing, the master decomposes each net N of n terminals into subnet $S_1, \ldots, S_{n-1}$ as follows.

$$d(t,t') \equiv \text{Manhattan distance between terminals } t \text{ and } t'$$

$$d(t,S) \equiv \min_{t' \in S} d(t,t')$$

$$S_1 = \langle t_1, t_2 \rangle \text{ s.t. } d(t_1,t_2) = \min_{t,t' \in N} d(t,t')$$

$$S_i = \langle S_{i-1}, t_{i+1} \rangle \text{ s.t. } t_{i+1} \notin S_{i-1} \wedge d(t_{i+1}, S_{i-1}) = \min_{t \in N - S_{i-1}} d(t, S_{i-1})$$

After that, all the subnets of all the nets are sorted in ascending order of d defined above. Then, for k workers, the master picks $2 \times k \times l$ shortest two-terminal subnets to assign two groups of l subnets to each worker. The master also distributes the c-path map M to all the workers.

A worker w_i at first tries to find paths for the first (shorter) group of subnets $g_i(1)$ updating its own c-path map $m_i(0) = M$ to $m_i(1)$ keeping their difference $\Delta m_i(1)$ conceptually denoted as $m_i(1) - m_i(0)$. The routing result of $g_i(1)$ is sent to the master that checks the consistency of the result against those reported from other workers and updates its master map to make $M_i(1)$. Then the master picks the third group $g_i(3)$ for w_i that consists of shortest l remaining subnets of the pair of terminals or that of a terminal and a subnet whose global path has already been settled. The group $g_i(3)$ is sent to w_i

together with the difference of the master map $\Delta M_i(1) = M_i(1) - M_i(0)$ where $M_i(0) = M$ for all i.

During the master is in the work above, the worker w_i routes the subnets in the second group $g_i(2)$ updating its map to make $m_i(2) = m_i(1) + \Delta m_i(2)$ and send the result again. Then it receives $g_i(3)$ and $\Delta M_i(1)$ from which it reconstructs nearly up-to-date map by $m_i(2) \leftarrow m_i(0) + \Delta M_i(1) + \Delta m_i(2)$ for the routing of $g_i(3)$. It also reconstructs one period older but globally correct map by $m_i(1) \leftarrow m_i(0) + \Delta M_i(1) = M_i(1)$ discarding $m_i(0)$. In general, when w_i works on $g_i(j)$, it maintains three maps; globally correct $m_i(j-2) = M_i(j-2)$; nearly correct $m_i(j-1)$; and working version $m_i(j)$.

By this multiple version maintenance, the latency of the communication between the master and workers will be hidden as shown in Fig. 6. The effectiveness of the latency hiding depends on the number of subnets in a group, l. In general, a large l effectively hides the latency, but degrades the correctness of c-path maps referred by workers and thus consistency of routing results. Based on experiments, l is set to 10 in our implementation.

For the global routing of a subnet S_i that is the i-th longest in all the K subnets, we defined the cost of a global segment σ of the series of n partitions $p_1, \ldots, p_n$ as follows based on experiments.

$$
\begin{aligned}
C_k &\equiv \text{partition capacity of } p_k \\
cost(p_k) &= C_k^{-1.6+\lambda+\rho} \\
\lambda &= \begin{cases} 0.0 & \text{if } i \le K/3 \\ 0.1 & \text{if } K/3 < i \le 2K/3 \\ 0.2 & \text{if } 2K/3 < i \end{cases} \\
\rho &= \begin{cases} 0.0 & \text{if not ripped} \\ 0.1 & \text{if ripped once} \\ 0.2 & \text{if ripped twice or more} \end{cases} \\
cost(\sigma) &= \begin{cases} \displaystyle\sum_{k=1}^{n} cost(p_k) & \text{if there is a c-path passing through } \sigma \\ \infty & \text{otherwise} \end{cases}
\end{aligned}
$$

The parameter λ is to make short nets severely sensitive to the capacity so that enough c-paths are preserved for long nets. The parameter ρ is to relax the capacity sensitivity of subnets victimized for the rip-and-reroute discussed later.

After a global path is settled, the worker temporarily chooses c-paths for global segments of the path and marks them as consumed. The final choice of the c-path for each global segment is done by the master. If there are two or more c-paths passing thorough the global segment, the master chooses the best-fit one to minimize the length (number of partitions) of the fragments caused by the consumption. The fragments, if any, are not discarded but will be used for global segments of another paths.

Since the cost function is evaluated by looking up the c-path map maintained by each worker independently, a global path routed by a worker may be inconsistent with paths routed by other workers. That is, the path may have a global segment through which no c-paths pass because of the consumption by other workers. When the master finds such a path, it rejects the path and includes the correspondent subnet in the next group.

When a worker fails to find the global path for a subnet, the master tries to reroute it by ripping up paths that have already been settled. To make the algorithm terminating, the rerouted path cannot be ripped. The subnets for ripped paths are rerouted by workers relaxing the capacity sensitivity by the parameter ρ shown above.

4.4 Detailed Routing

When the global routing completes, the master decomposes its c-path map into submaps for slices and distributes each of them to the worker of detailed routing responsible for the slice. Each worker at first combines the submaps and geometrical data of c-paths in its slices generated in c-path routing to have the complete information of c-paths used for global paths.

Then each worker straightens c-paths in use in a slice of an x-layer by a modified version of *max-cap* algorithm proposed by KeshK[14], as follows (Fig. 7).

(a) Erase all the c-paths and fragments of c-paths that are not used for global paths.

(b) Give a total order to c-paths in use by the following relation $\gamma \prec \gamma'$ of the c-paths γ and γ'; if γ and γ' share a partition, $\gamma \prec \gamma'$ iff γ is above γ' in the partition; otherwise, $\gamma \prec \gamma'$ iff γ lies to the left of γ'. Thus we have an ordered set of c-paths $\{\gamma_1, \ldots, \gamma_n\}$ such that $\gamma_i \prec \gamma_j$ for all $i < j$.

(c) Redraw c-paths from γ_n to γ_1 by the algorithm shown in Section 4.2.

(d) Repeat the following for γ_1 to γ_n. If both ends of γ_i are on partition edges, draw a path from the left edge to the right by the maze routing algorithm assuming other c-paths and straightened paths are obstacles, giving higher priority to upper candidate paths. Otherwise, that is an end of γ_1 is a terminal, draw a path from the terminal to the edge which the other end is on.

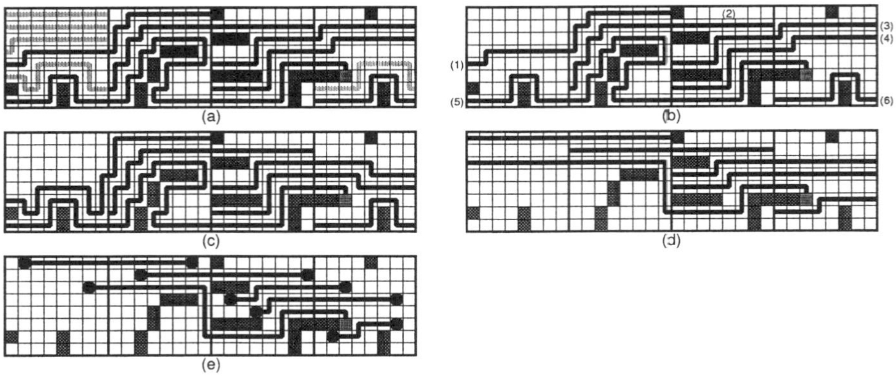

Figure 7. Detailed Routing

C-paths in y-layers are similarly straightened.

Then each worker of x-layers gives geometrical data of straightened paths in each partition to the worker of y-layers responsible for the slice intersecting at the partition. The worker of y-layer determines the location of each via at the crossing point of straightened x and y paths for adjacent global segments. Since the end of x and y paths to be connected by a via pass through partitions adjacent in z direction, the crossing point of the paths is always found. Finally, the worker erases fragments beyond vias to obtain the final result (Fig. 7(e)).

5 Experiments

5.1 Implementation

We implemented Amaterous on a PC cluster of 16 Pentium II (450 MHz) based PCs with 128 MB memory for each connected by 100Base-TX Ethernet. The parallelization package of PVM version 3.4.β7[15] is used. For the compilation, we used gcc version 2.7.2.3.

5.2 Workloads

The workloads for the performance evaluation of Amaterous are three MCM benchmarks[13] shown in Table 1. The number of layers used for each benchmark shown in the table is same as that for Amon2[5] and also for the state-of-art sequential router V4R[16]. The width of slice is also same as that for Amon2 for fair comparison of Amaterous and Amon2.

Table 1. MCM Benchmarks

benchmark	c	n	t	s	l	w
MCC1-75	6	802	2495	599×599	4	30
MCC2-75	37	7118	14695	2032×2032	6	80
MCC2-45	37	7118	14695	3386×3386	4	120

c: # of chips; n: # of nets; t: # of terminals;
s: size of routing space; l: # of layers; w: width of slice

5.3 Comparison of Amaterous and Amon2

Table 2 shows the performance data of the sequential version of Amaterous (S) and parallel one on the 16-node PC cluster (P) with respect to execution speed and routing quality, and also that of Amon2. Since Amon2 was implemented on the parallel computer AP1000 developed about a decade ago, it is hard to compare its 64-processor performance shown in rows (a) in the table[5] with that of Amaterous. Thus we ported Amon2 to our PC cluster to obtain the performance data shown in rows (b). This ported version, however, cannot route all the nets as shown in the table, probably because Amon2 is very sensitive to the communication performance relative to computation in which AP1000 outperforms our PC cluster by the order of magnitude. Since the execution time in rows (b) is obviously underestimated due to the unrouted nets, we estimated its real performance assuming that the execution time is proportional to the total wire length as shown in rows (c). This normalization should not cause overestimation because rip-and-reroute, which Amon2 does not have, is hardly parallelized.

The table shows that Amaterous is 3.4 and 1.6 times as fast as the raw performance of Amon2 on PC cluster for MCC1-75 and MCC2-45 respectively. As for the normalized performance, the speedup is 3.6 and 2.0. For MCC2-75, which both original and ported version of Amon2 cannot route completely, the execution time of Amaterous is almost equal to the normalized one of Amon2. However, if we may suppose that another one million or so grid points are added to the total wire length of Amon2 to route completely, Amaterous is 1.2 times as fast as Amon2. Thus we may conclude that Amaterous is faster, much faster in many cases, than Amon2.

On the other hand, our result of total wire length is 10 to 35 % worse than Amon2. The major reason of the degradation is that Amaterous requires every terminal to have its initial partition adjacent to its home. That is, even if both terminals of two-terminal (sub)net are in a partition, Amaterous draws paths from the terminals to the adjacent partitions and then connect them even in the best case. In the worst case in which their initial partitions are at

Table 2. Amaterous v.s. Amon2

benchmark	program	t	u	l	v
MCC1-75	Amaterous (S)	12.61	0	477	4990
	(P)	2.41	0	500	4824
	Amon2 (a)	(13)	0	382	2825
	(b)	8.25	1	366	2519
	(c)	8.61	—	—	—
MCC2-75	Amaterous (S)	459.99	0	7232	39141
	(P)	61.65	0	7439	40089
	Amon2 (a)	(173)	9	5498	22823
	(b)	50.31	17	4486	14885
	(c)	61.66	—	—	—
MCC2-45	Amaterous (S)	638.61	0	10105	31688
	(P)	52.19	0	10385	33482
	Amon2 (a)	(316)	0	9052	19554
	(b)	83.67	10	7310	13275
	(c)	103.61	—	—	—

t: execution time (sec); u: # of unrouted nets;
l: total wire length ($\times 10^3$ grid point); v: # of vias;

both sides of their home, the path should be much longer than the natural expectation. Although it is hard to devise a special method to route such short nets and, especially, short subnets keeping consistency with the concept of c-path, we will investigate this issue further. As for the number of vias, the difference from Amon2 is wider. Although our result is comparable to or better than V4R[16], the reduction of the number is also an important subject of our future study.

5.4 Parallel Speedup

Fig. 8 shows the parallel speedup relative to the sequential version of Amaterous. It shows that 5.0, 7.5 and 12.2 fold speedups are obtained with 16 PC nodes for MCC1-75, MCC2-75 and MCC2-45 respectively. The result of MCC2-45 shows that Amaterous is sufficiently scalable with a problem of large routing space.

The saturation observed in the case of MCC1-75 is mainly due to its small problem scale both in the number of nets and the size of routing space. In fact, the speedup of the global routing, which consumes about 60 % of the total execution time, is only 3.5. Since this benchmark is relatively easy to solve, we could enlarge the number of subnets in a group given to global routing worker, fixed to 10 so far, to hide master/worker communication latency more effectively.

The speedup of MCC2-75 is not very excellent too. It is also remarkable

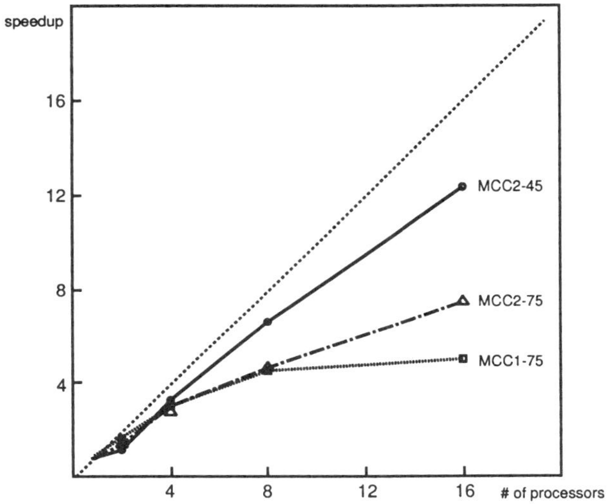

Figure 8. Parallel Speedup

that MCC2-75 is harder than MCC2-45 for the 16-node system contrary to the result of the sequential case as shown in Table 2. This is mainly due to that this problem is hard to route completely and thus the master has to perform rip-and-reroute repeatedly. Thus, when the master is in the work, workers become idle soon to degrade the parallel performance. An idea to make workers busy is to delegate the rip-and-reroute from the master to a worker so that other workers route other subnets speculatively assuming global paths for them are consistent to the rerouted path. The implementation and evaluation of this idea is left for our future work.

6 Conclusions

In this paper, we proposed a new parallel wire router named Amaterous. Its unique feature is the c-path router that draws candidate paths in each slice of the routing layer prior to the global and detailed routing. Since the global router picks c-paths to form the global path of a net, it is assured that the global path is always converted successfully to its detailed counterpart which the detailed router generates by straightening c-paths.

By the introduction of the c-path routing, the feedback from the detailed to global router is removed to make them efficiently parallelized. In fact, the experimental result shows up to 12 fold speedup for MCM benchmarks using a 16-node PC cluster. It is also shown that Amaterous is 1.2 to 3.6 times as fast as the parallel router Amon2.

Our future work is to improve the algorithm of Amaterous in the following points; increase the number of c-path passing through partition segments; reduce the wire length and vias for short subnets; delegate the rip-and-reroute from the global routing master to a worker; and tune the routing parameters such as the number of subnets in a group given to global routing worker.

Acknowledgments

We would like to express our thanks to Hesham Keshk and Tomita Laboratory of Kyoto University for their courtesy to give us the source code of Amon2.

References

1. T. Watanabe, H. Kitazawa, and Y. Sugiyama. A parallel adaptable routing algorithm and its implementation. *IEEE Trans. Computer-Aided Design*, CAD-6(2):241–250, March 1987.
2. Y. Won and S. Sahni. Maze routing on a hypercube multiprocessors. In *Proc. Intl. Conf. Parallel Processing*, pages 630–637, August 1987.
3. O. A. Olukotun and T. N. Mudge. A preliminary investigation into parallel routing on a hypercube computer. In *Proc. 24th Design Automation Conf.*, pages 814–820, June 1987.
4. H. Date and K. Taki. A parallel lookahead line search router with automatic ripup and reroute. In *Proc. European Conf. on Design Automation*, pages 117–121, 1993.
5. H. Keshk, S. Mori, H. Nakashima, and S. Tomita. A two phases, cooperative detailed/global parallel wire routing algorithm. *Trans. Information Processing Society of Japan*, 37(12):2376–2389, December 1996.
6. Y. Takahashi. Paralellel maze running and line search algorithms for LSI CAD on binary tree multiprocessors. In *World Conf. Information and Communication*, pages 128–136, 1989.
7. T. Yamauchi, T. Nakata, N. Koike, A. Ishizuka, and N. Nishiguchi. PROTON: A parallel detailed router on an MIMD parallel machine. In *Proc. IEEE Intl. Conf. Computer-Aided Design*, pages 340–343, November 1990.
8. H. Keshk, S. Mori, H. Nakashima, and S. Tomita. A new technique to improve parallel automated single layer wire routing. In *Proc. Performance Evaluation of Parallel Systems*, pages 134–141, November 1993.

9. J. Rose. LocusRoute: A parallel global router for standard cells. In *Proc. 25th Design Automation Conf.*, pages 189–195, June 1988.
10. Y. Takahashi. Parallel automated wire routing with a number of competing processors. In *Proc. Intl. Conf. Supercomputing*, pages 310–317, 1990.
11. R. J. Brouwer and P. Banerjee. PHIGURE: A parallel hierarchical global router. In *Proc. 27th Design Automation Conf.*, pages 360–364, 1990.
12. S. B. Akers. Routing. In M. A. Breuer, editor, *Design Automation of Digital Systems: Theory and Techniques*, volume 1, pages 283–333. Prentice Hall, 1972.
13. Collaborative Benchmarking Laboratory, Dept. of Computer Science, North Carolina State Univ. PDWorkshop'93 benchmark set. `http://www.cbl.ncsu.edu/CBL_Docs/pdw93.html`, March 1995.
14. H. Keshk, S. Mori, H. Nakashima, and S. Tomita. Amon: A parallel slice algorithm for wire routing. In *Proc. Intl. Conf. Supercomputing*, pages 200–209, July 1995.
15. Computer Science and Mathematics Division, Oak Ridge National Laboratory. PVM: Parallel virtual machine. `http://www.csm.ornl.gov/pvm/`, January 2000.
16. K. Y. Khoo and J Cong. An efficient multilayer MCM router based on four via routing. In *Proc. 30th Design Automation Conf.*, pages 590–595, 1993.

2D PROCESSOR ARRAY STRUCTURES FOR CONVOLUTION

NEIL DUNSTAN AND STEPHEN HODGSON
School of Mathematical and Computing Sciences
University of New England
email: neil or shodgson@cs.une.edu.au
fax: +61 0267733312

Two dimensional convolution is required by many image and signal processing procedures. Because convolution is computationally intensive many researchers have investigated specialized processor array designs for it. This paper investigates processor array designs for two–dimensional convolution focusing on two–dimensional structures both with and without rowwise communication paths. The designs are analysed with respect to the number of communication paths, processing cells and the execution time of processing cells as well as to throughput and latency. A hybrid configuration is developed with enhanced performance. It is shown that the configurations for any window row and column dimensions can be generated by a recursive algorithm.

1 Introduction

There has been extensive research into specialized hardware for computationally intensive tasks. Such tasks are commonly required in image and signal processing. The justification for specialized hardware is particularly apparent in the analysis of geophysical data from land, airborne and satellite surveys that generate enormous amounts of data to be processed by routine and repetitive algorithms. Geophysical surveys using electromagnetic sensing equipment, for such applications as the detection of unexploded ordnance and resource exploration, produce data sets of large volume which require many processor hours to analyse. Typical analysis includes identifying the position and classification of target objects or geological formations. Geophysical analysis commonly uses different sensor technologies to detect and classify subsurface objects. For example, the SAM (Sub-Audio Magnetics) system [3], developed by Geophysical Technology Limited (GTL), simultaneously measures magnetic, electromagnetic, electric and induced polarisation responses over areas of ground. By analysing and comparing the data sets, the presence of subsurface objects, such as bombs, shells and landmines, can be detected. The signal responses constitute a large volume of data which takes considerable time to process. Processing entails analysis to detect anomolies which could indicate the presence of subsurface objects.

Two–dimensional convolution is required by many image and signal processing procedures such as pattern matching and edge detection. The process involves convolving a two–dimensional input with a two–dimensional window. Processor Arrays have long been proposed for signal and image processing tasks. A typical architectural form is Systolic Arrays which are specialized networks of simple processing cells designed to solve specific problems [8]. The network features nearest neighbour connections between cells, data flows through the array at constant speed and the operation of the network is synchronous. The network is uniform with respect to timing, cell operations and cell interconnections. Recent derivative architectures, such are multirate arrays [9] are also suitable and have feasible hardware implementations as VLSI devices. Multirate arrays have different data streams travelling through the array at different rates.

It is now common for computer equipment to include dedicated chips to handle the processing of high volume data sets. Such chips are often referred to as Application Specific Integrated Circuits (ASICs) and are hardwired for some fixed operation. Though the development time and cost of VLSI implementation of processor arrays are prohibitive, recent advances in reconfigurable hardware have proven to be an enabling technology. Reconfigurable (or Custom) Computing is a maturing technology that allows hardware devices to be reconfigured for different operations, either between applications or dynamically during execution of some task. Reconfigurable hardware is available as off-the-shelf devices called Field Programmable Gate Arrays (FPGAs) such as those manufactured by Altera and Xilinx. FPGAs have traditionally been used for "glue logic" and for prototyping ASICs. Current generation FPGAs contain thousands of reconfigurable logic cells. The feasibility of using FPGAs for a range of image processing tasks has been shown by Athnas and Abbott [1] who developed a real-time image processing system using the Splash-2 Custom Computing Platform [2]. The Splash-2's reconfigurable hardware consists of many boards each having sixteen FPGA chips.

In this paper, a number of processor arrays based on mesh–connected, systolic and multirate architectures are considered for two–dimensional convolution. They include designs based on existing systolic arrays [7] and designs developed using multirate array synthesis techniques [4]. A hybrid design is developed which minimizes the number of processing elements, communication links and latency while retaining maximal throughput. A recursive algorithm is given that generates configurations for any given window row and column dimensions. The designs were tested by PVM emulation on a workstation cluster in the manner described in [5]. That is, configurations were implemented on the cluster using one node per processing element with point to point communication between neighbours.

2 Convolution

Consider the following generalised one–dimensional convolution filter where the input signal X^i is convolved with the window W^k. The output Y^i is

$$Y^i = \sum_{k=0}^{K-1} \psi(W^k, X^{i-k}), \; 0 \leq i < I \tag{1}$$

where K is called the window size.
Figure 1 is an illustration of one–dimensional convolution showing the window size placement for successive Y terms.

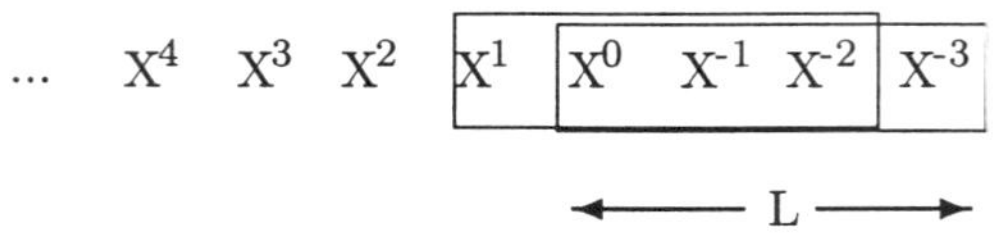

Figure 1. 1D convolution. $L = 4$

When the function ψ is multiplication, the output series for $K = 4$ is...

$$\begin{aligned} Y^0 &= W^0X^0 + W^1X^{-1} + W^2X^{-2} + W^3X^{-3} \\ Y^1 &= W^0X^1 + W^1X^0 \;\; + W^2X^{-1} + W^3X^{-2} \\ Y^2 &= W^0X^2 + W^1X^1 \;\; + W^2X^0 \;\; + W^3X^{-1} \\ &\cdots \end{aligned} \tag{2}$$

A generalized two dimensional filter is as follows: the two dimensional image $X^{i,j}$ is convolved with the window $W^{k,l}$. The output $Y^{i,j}$ is

$$Y^{i,j} = \sum_{k=0}^{K-1} \sum_{l=0}^{L-1} \psi(W^{k,l}, X^{i-k,j-l}), \; 0 \leq i < I, 0 \leq j < J$$

where the dimensions of the window are $K \times L$ and the dimensions of the problem, image or input matrix, is $I \times J$. The convolution product is $Y^{i,j}$. The function $\psi(W^{k,l}, X^{i-k,j-l})$ is typically multiplication, that is $\psi(W^{k,l}, X^{i-k,j-l}) = W^{k,l} \times X^{i-k,j-l}$ and is assumed to to be so in this paper. However, other functions might also be useful, for example $\psi(W^{k,l}, X^{i-k,j-l}) = |W^{k,l} - X^{i-k,j-l}|$ might be used to produce a sum of

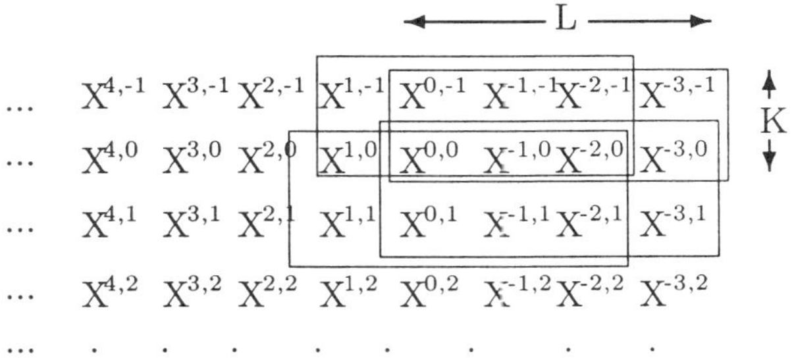

Figure 2. 2D convolution. $K = 2$, $L = 4$

absolute differences measure for object recognition applications. Figure 2 ilustrates two–dimensional convolution using a 2×4 window.

The output series for $K = 2$ and $L = 4$ is...

$$
\begin{aligned}
Z^{0,0} &= W^{0,0}X^{0,0} + W^{0,1}X^{0,-1} + W^{1,0}X^{-1,0} + W^{1,1}X^{-1,-1} \\
&\quad + W^{2,0}X^{-2,0} + W^{2,1}X^{-2,-1} + W^{3,0}X^{-3,0} + W^{3,1}X^{-3,-1} \\
Z^{0,1} &= W^{0,0}X^{0,1} + W^{0,1}X^{0,0} + W^{1,0}X^{-1,1} + W^{1,1}X^{-1,0} \\
&\quad + W^{2,0}X^{-2,1} + W^{2,1}X^{-2,0} + W^{3,0}X^{-3,1} + W^{3,1}X^{-3,0} \\
Z^{1,0} &= W^{0,0}X^{1,0} + W^{0,1}X^{1,-1} + W^{1,0}X^{0,0} + W^{1,1}X^{0,-1} \\
&\quad + W^{2,0}X^{-1,0} + W^{-1,1}X^{0,-1} + W^{3,0}X^{-2,0} + W^{3,1}X^{-2,-1}
\end{aligned}
$$

...

3 2D Processor Arrays for 2D Convolution

3.1 Mesh–connected processor arrays

An algorithm for mesh-connected processor arrays was proposed by Fang and Li [6]. The mesh architecture is a network of processing elements with North–South, East–West connections as illustrated in Figure 3.

The processing elements in the mesh correspond to coordinates of the input matrix (or image) and each processing element computes a convolution product. Processing elements are preloaded with corresponding $X^{i,j}$ values and successive column weights of the window. A series of North-South and East-West transfers of X values between neighbouring processing elements allow the correct positioning of values for computation. Latency is $2LK$ steps, where a step is taken to be a transfer operation. The throughput period (average time to produce an output) is $\frac{2KL}{I'J'}$ where I' and J' are the dimensions

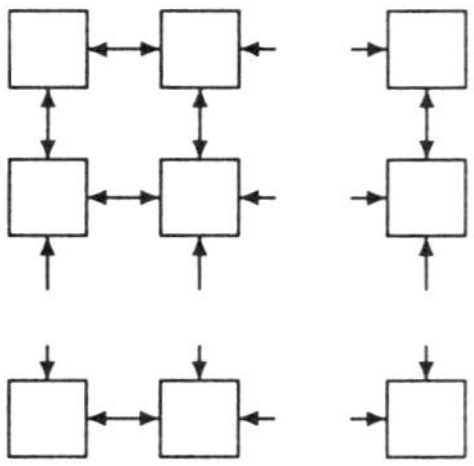

Figure 3. Mesh connected processor array

of network. These measures neglect the load time for the X array and for successive W columns. The processing elements require significant memory, control logic and communication paths.

3.2 *Systolic array*

A two dimensional systolic array proposed by Kung and Wong [7] uses Multiply Add (MAD) processing elements which simply multiply the incoming X value by the weight W and add the product to the incoming Y value. These simple processing elements are used for a wide variety of systolic array applications including matrix multiplication. The cell structure is show in Figure 4

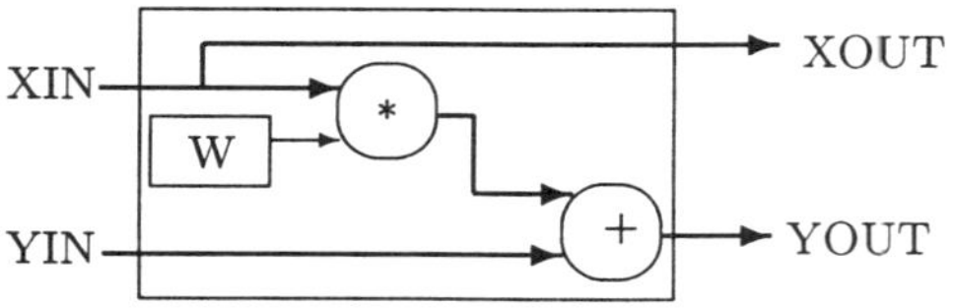

Figure 4. Multiply and Add Processing Cell Structure

The array is composed of K rows of L MAD processing elements. The processing elements are in the shape of the window and have corresponding window weights. A summation processing element adds the products of each row to produce convolution products. The array is illustrated in Figure 5. Note that the X links are half the speed of the other links.

The design has $K \times L + 1$ processing elements, counting the summation processing element at the end of the rows. Throughput period is one output

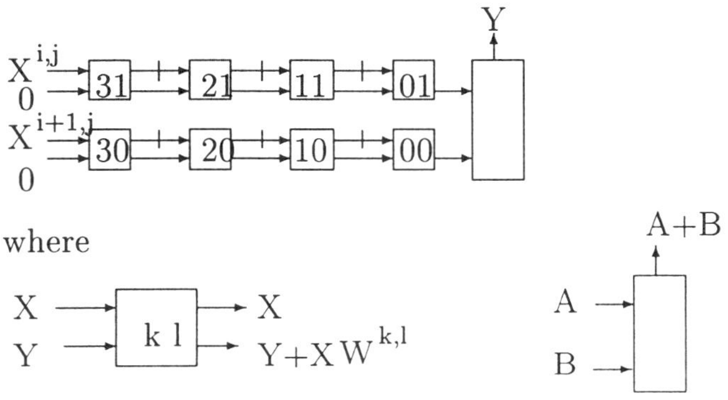

Figure 5. 2D systolic array for 2D convolution. $K = 2, L = 4$

produced every step, being the duration of the pipeline period. Latency is $L+1$ steps. In general, the summation processing element must add K values and for K large, the latency of this cell may exceed that of the MAD cells, thus increasing the pipeline period and step size. This situation can be avoided by implementing the summation as a series of two-value additions. There is at most log_2K levels in the series, giving an overall latency for the array of $L + log_2K$. The array with the adder series is illustrated in Figure 6.

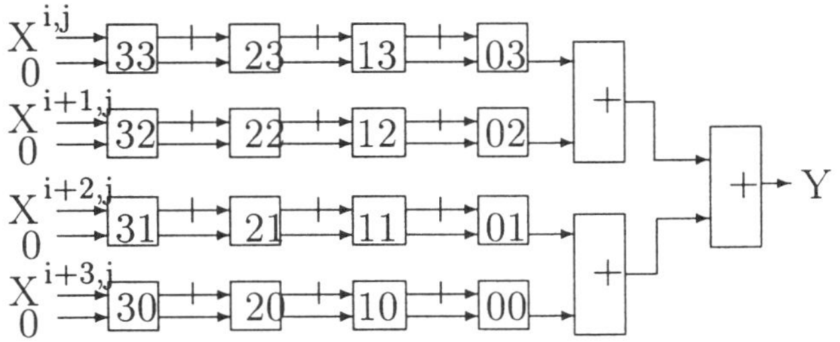

Figure 6. Systolic array with adder series. $K = 4$, $L = 4$

3.3 Row-connected multirate array for convolution

The multirate array of Figure 7 was presented in [4] as a decimation filter but may also be used for convolution. The multirate synthesis technique used to derive the array begins with an algorithm expressed as a System of Affine Recurrence Equations (SARE). The synthesis procedures involved are to apply a skewing transformation; eliminate the affine data dependencies so that the system has only uniform data dependencies; and to reduce the processor array to one of just two dimensions. The goal is to transform the system of equations into one where each value z is defined by an equation of the form

$$z(\begin{pmatrix} \pi \\ S \end{pmatrix} p) = \ldots$$

where π is a $1 \times n$ matrix representing the scheduling function for z (called $t_z()$); S is a $n-1 \times n$ matrix representing the allocation function for z (called $a_z()$) and p is a point in the domain of z. The processing elements are identical and their function is described below. Note the X links and the diagonal y links are half the rate of the horizontal and vertical y links.

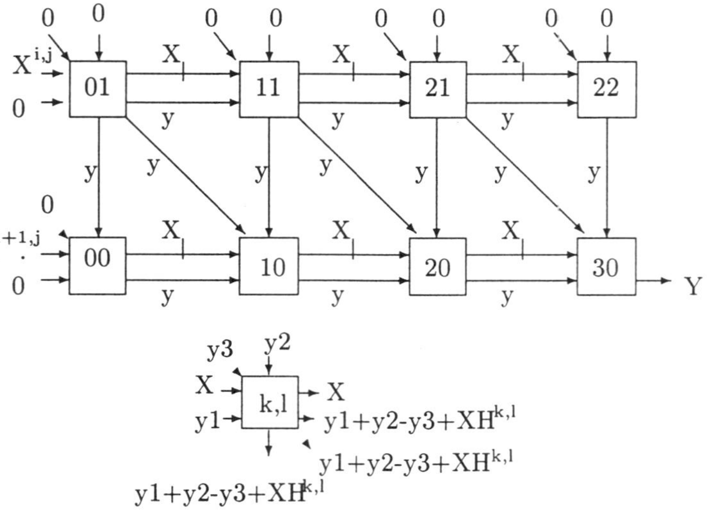

Figure 7. Row-connected multirate array for convolution. $K = 4$, $L = 2$

Data is entered into the array in the same fashion as for Kung and Wong's 2D design except that successive rows must be delayed in order to synchronize the arrival of row summations at the bottom-right processing element. The throughput period is an output produced every step, where a step is the duration of the processing element operation. Latency is $L + K - 1$ steps. L copies of the array could be arranged in a cascade as for the Kung et al.'s 2D array, giving it the same completion time.

The processing elements used in the row-connected design are Multiply Accumulate (MAC) cells which have three incoming Y values and one X value. These cells multiply the incoming X value by the weight W and add the product to an accumulation of the incoming Y values. Though more addition circuitry is required than for MAD cells, the time duration required needn't be any longer assuming that multiplication takes at least as long as two additions. That is, two additions can be performed concurrently with the multiplication. The cell structure is show in Figure 8.

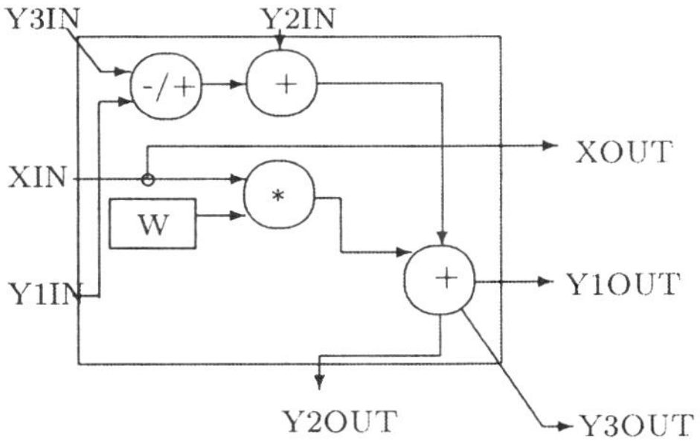

Figure 8. Multiply and Accumulate Processing Cell Structure

3.4 Hybrid Design

The synthesis technique used to derive the row-connected array design generates an homogeneous design, that is, all processing elements are identical. In order for the bottom-left processing cell to receive the partial sum results from the upper row of processing cells and thus produce the convolution result, all other processing elements must likewise receive an aggregate value from the upper row. The diagonal y stream acts to remove unwanted summations. This insight into the operation of the array leads to a modified version where the only communication between rows occurs at the end, with row-wise summations filtering down to the bottom-right processing element. The modified array therefore has less communication links and specialised processing elements at the ends of rows. The non-end-of-row processing elements are MAD cells and the end-of-row cells are MAC cells. The array clearly has less circuitry than the original row-connected multirate design, the same number of cells, the same throughput and latency. The array is illustrated in Figure 9.

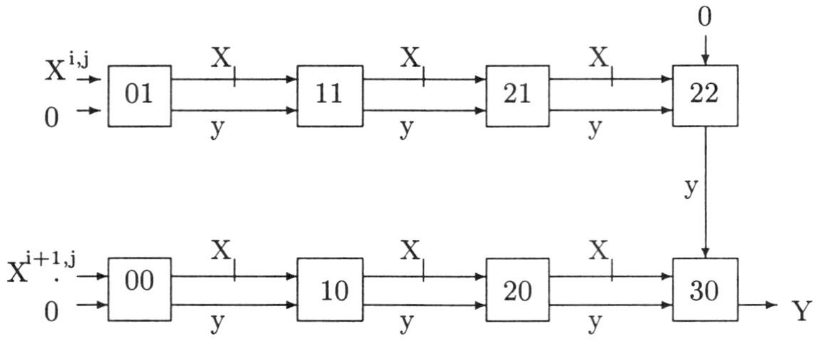

Figure 9. Modified Row-connected array

While the throughput period remains at one output per systolic step, the latency can be reduced to $L + log_2 K$ by arranging the rows as shown in Figure 10 where the array forms a kind of binary tree structure. Again, MAC cells are required at the ends of rows which gather summation data from neighbouring rows. The number of connections is limited to just three, being

- the neighbouring row to the left
- the rest of the row
- the neighbouring row to the right

The configuration for $K = 2$ (Figure 10b) has two rows of L MAD cells, except that the cell at the end of the second row is a MAC cell. The first row of the input matrix is feed into the first row of the processor array. Likewise the second row of the input matrix is feed into the second row of the processor array but it is delayed one step so that when the Lth input reaches the end of row cell, that cell also receives the summation from the first row as well. In the configuration for $K = 3$ (Figure 10c) the MAC cell at the end of the second row recieves summation data from both neighbouring rows.

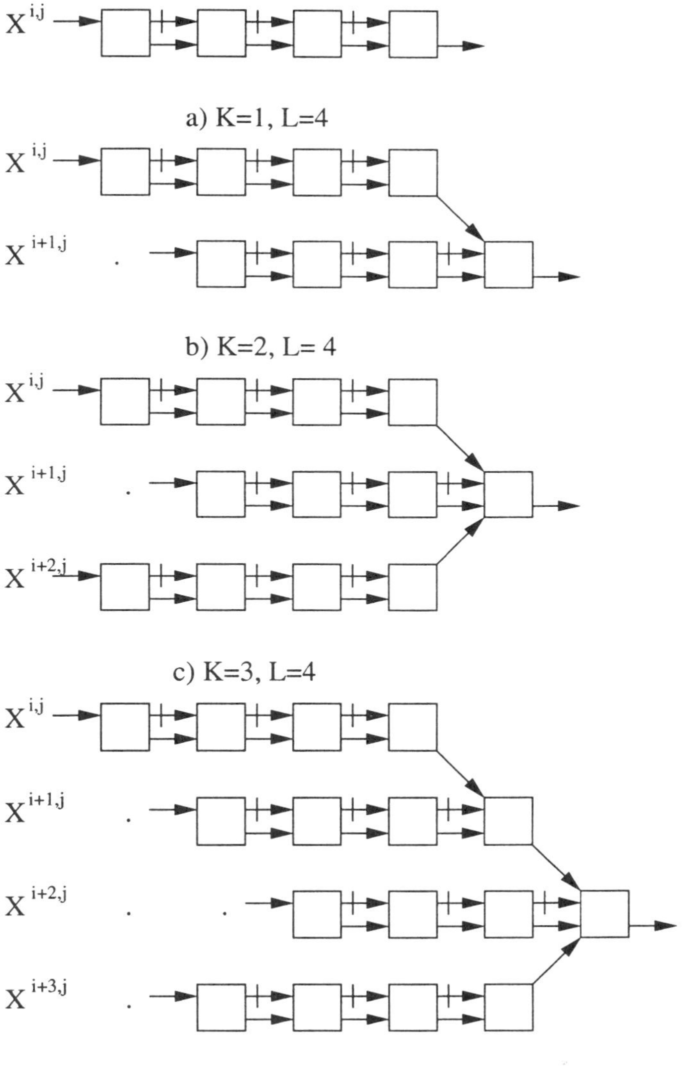

Figure 10. Binary Tree Row-connected arrays

The configurations of Figure 10 can be generated by the recursive algorithm

```
recdes( int line, int rows, int level, int K, enum direction arrow )
{
    if( rows < 1 )
        return;
    if( rows == 1 )
        draw_one( line, level, K, arrow );
    else if( rows%2 == 1 ) /* odd */
    {
        recdes( line, rows/2, level+1, K, left );
        draw_one( line, level, K, arrow );
        recdes( line, rows/2, level+1, K, right );
        }
    else if( rows%2 == 0 ) /* even */
    {
        recdes( line, rows/2, level+1, K, left );
        draw_one( line, level, K, arrow);
        recdes( line, rows/2-1, level+1, K, right );
        }
    }
```

In the case of *rows* being odd, $rows/2$ rows are drawn to the left, and $rows/2$ rows are drawn to the right of a middle row. The left and right group of rows feed summation data to the middle row, which is advanced by one level. For each level a delay is required for data entering that row. In the case of *rows* being even, $rows/2 - 1$ rows are drawn to the left and $rows/2$ rows are drawn to the right of an advanced middle row. In this way, each cell at the end of a row has at most three summation inputs and can therefore be implemented as a MAC cell.

4 Conclusion

A new, hybrid processor array design for two-dimensional convolution was developed that features two types of processing elements in a two-dimensional systolic structure. Both processing element types have the same operation duration since both are dominated by a multiplication function. Nevertheless, both processing element types have quite simple functions of the traditional multiply/accumulate variety. Their use permits configurations with only a small number (corresponding to the window size) of simple processing elements and a minimum of row-wise connections. The configurations can be automatically generated. The general design produces output with latency and throughput similar to that of Kung's two-dimensional systolic structure but with less processing elements.

Acknowledgement

This research is supported by the Australian Research Council and Geophysical Technology Limited.

References

1. P M Athnas and A L Abbott, Real-Time Image Processing on a Custom Computing Platform, *IEEE Computer*, February, 1995.
2. J M Arnold, D A Bell and E G Davis, Splash-2, *proc. Fourth Annual ACM Symposium on Parallel Algorithms and Architectures*, 1992.
3. M K Cattach, J M Stanley, S J Lee and G W Boyd, Sub-Adio Magnetics: A High resolution Technique for Simultaneously Mapping Electrical and Magnetic Properties, *Exploration Geophysics*, Vol. 24, 1993, pp 387-400
4. N Dunstan and P M Lenders, Systolic Arrays for 2D Decimation Filters, *proc. of the Second International Conference on Algorithms and Architectures for Parallel Processing*, Singapore, June, 1996
5. N Dunstan, Validation, Verification, Simulation and Emulation of Systolic Arrays, *proc. of the 4th Australasian Conference on Parallel and Real-Time Systems*, Newcastle, September, 1997, pp 412-421
6. Z Fang and X Li, Parallel Algorithms for 2–D Convolution, IEEE,1986. pp 262–269.
7. H T Kung and S W Song, A Systolic 2D Convolution Chip, *CMU Computer Science Department Technical Report*, CMU–CS–81–110, March, 1981
8. H T Kung, Why Systolic Architecture, *Computer*, January, 1982, pp. 37-46.
9. P M Lenders, N Dunstan and S Radjopadhye, Multirate and Sparse Systolic Architectures, *proc. Second Australasian Computer Architecture Workshop*, Melbourne, January, 1996.

QOS ROUTING ALGORITHMS FOR ANYCAST SERVICES *

JIANXIN WANG, JIANER CHEN, SONGQIAO CHEN, AND WEIPING WANG
Department of Computer Science, Central South University ,Changsha, Hunan, 410083 P.R.China,
E-mail: jxwang@mail.csut.edu.cn

WEIJIA JIA
Department of Computer Science, City University of Hong Kong, Kowloon, Hong Kong
E-mail: wjia@cs.cityu.edu.hk

In the Internet, a group of replicated servers is commonly used in order to improve the scalability of network service. Anycast service is a new network service that can improve network load distribution and simplify certain applications. In this paper, we propose two anycast QoS routing algorithms, RBH and RBHS, on networks with accurate and inaccurate link-state information, respectively. Both algorithms are randomized. The RBH algorithm uses the path length to determine the probability for choosing the next link, while the RBHS algorithm takes both the path length and the bandwidth safety into consideration. We measure the quality of QoS algorithms in terms of the accepting ratio on anycast QoS requests. Our simulation on a variety of network topologies and on various parameters shows that the RBH and RBHS algorithms perform much better than the static shortest-shortest algorithm.

1. Introduction

As more hosts are connected, network service demands eventually exceed capacity and network service degrades. Although it does not adversely affect typical Internet applications, such as email and file transfer, it does cause serious problems for applications with real-time requirements, such as video on demand and IP phone. To provide adequate service, some level of quantitative or qualitative determinism-IP services must be supplemented. QoS improves network services by managing network resource, and is used more effectively to meet the wide range of application requirements [1,2].

There are many aspects in the QoS study, including traffic shaping, packet scheduling, QoS routing, resource reservation, call admission control, and so on [2]. QoS routing has been recognized as an important piece in the evolution of QoS service offerings in the Internet. QoS routing is a dynamic routing protocol that has expanded its path-selection criteria to include QoS parameters, such as available bandwidth, link and end-to-end path utilization, node resources consumption, delay and latency, and induced jitter. Two QoS routing models have been proposed and studied extensively: the unicast QoS routing and the multicase QoS routing. Unicast

* This work was supported by China National Science Fund for Oversea Distinguished Young Scholars (No. 69928201), Foundation for University Key Teacher by the Ministry of Education and ChangJiang Scholar Reward Project.

routing determines a path from an IP source to a unique IP destination, while multicast routing finds paths from one IP source to many IP destinations.

In order to increase service availability and provide efficient load distribution in a network, it is common practice to replicate servers on the network. Examples of such services include World-Wide-Web "mirror" sites, video-on-demand, SOCKs servers, compute-servers, and proxy servers in the Internet [5]. A new network routing model, *anycast routing*, has been proposed [7], which is to find a path from an IP source to *any one* of a group of IP receivers. The anycast service has been defined as a standard service in Ipv6 [6].

There have been two different approaches to working on the problem: network-layer anycasting and application-layer anycasting. In [8], an application-layer anycasting communication paradigm was proposed to support server replication. Specifically, the authors developed and evaluated an implementation based on the use of anycast resolver to map anycast domain names into one or more IP addresses. In [9], the authors presented an optimal algorithm for mapping each anycasting query from clients into the one "best" video distribution server of replicas. Their algorithm was developed at application-layer of the network based on economic models and queuing theory. In [5], the authors investigated how the IP anycast service is exploited by hosts connected in the Internet without significantly impacting the routing and protocol processing infrastructure already in place. They designed and implemented a network-layer anycasting service for load distribution in the context of the IBM Olympic Web site on the Internet. In [10], the authors proposed and analyzed a routing protocol for anycast message. It is composed of two subprotocols: the routing table establishment subprotocol and the packet forwarding subprotocol. In the routing table establishment subprotocol, they proposed four methods (SSP, MIN-D, SBT and CBT) for enforcing an order among routers for the purpose of loop prevention. In the packet forwarding subprotocol, they proposed a weighted-random selection (WRS) approach for multiple path selection in order to balance network traffic.

In this paper, we concentrate on network-layer anycasting, especially on QoS routing for anycast services. Our main concern is on a anycast QoS request, to find a path from the given IP source to one of the given IP receivers, with the given QoS requirements satisfied. Our first anycast QoS routing algorithm, RBH, is developed based on networks with accurate link-state information, and our second anycast QoS routing algorithm, RBHS, is developed based on networks with inaccurate link-state information. Both algorithms are randomized. In the RBH algorithm, the probability for selecting the next link is determined by the path length, while in the RBHS algorithm, the probability for selecting the next link is determined by the path length and the bandwidth safety. We measure the quality of anycast QoS routing algorithms in terms of the network accepting ratio on a large number of anycast QoS requests. Our simulation on a variety of network topologies and on various parameters shows that our RBH and RBHS algorithms outperform the previousely proposed anycast routing algorithms.

The paper is organized as follows. We introduce the basic network model with accurate link-state information, and present the randomized QoS routing algorithm RBH for anycast QoS requests in section 2. In Section 3, we extend our network model by allowing inaccurate link-state information in the network model and develop an effective randomized anycast QoS routing algorithm, RBHS, on the model. In section 4, we describe the details of our simulation environment and evaluate the experimental results. Conclusion and further remarks are given in section 5.

2. Basic Network Model and An Anycast QoS Routing Algorithm

Considering the following basic model. Let $G = <V, E>$ be a network, where $V = \{v_1, v_2, \ldots., v_n\}$ is the set of nodes in G and $E = \{e_1, e_2, \ldots., e_m\}$ is the set of links in G. Each link e_j is associated with a bandwidth value B_j. A *anycast QoS request* $R = (S, A, B, N)$ consists of a source node S, an anycast address A, a bandwidth requirement B, and a delay requirement N that specifies the maximum number of hops the routing path may have. Note that we have somehow simplified the delay requirement and assume that all hops have the same delay and the total delay of a routing path is simply the additive sum of delays of the hops in the path. This will greatly simplify our discussion. On the other hand, our algorithm can be extended to include more complicated computation formulas for QoS path delay, such as the one suggested in [11].

For the anycast address A, we denote by $G(A)$ the group of designated recipient hosts: $G(A) = \{D^1, D^2, \ldots, D^w\}$, where $D^1, D^2, \ldots, D^w$□V. An *anycast QoS routing path* is a path in G from the source node S to any node in $G(A)$.

Problem A: *Given a network $G=<V, E>$ and an anycast QoS request $R = (S,A, B, N)$, find a path P form the source S to any node in $G(A)$ such that the bandwidth of every link in the path P is at least B , and the length of P (i.e., the number of hops in P) is bounded by N.*

The following is our RBH algorithm for the problem A.

Algorithm RBH (Random Based on Hops)
Input: a network $G = <V, E>$ and an anycast QoS request $R = (S, A, B, N)$.
Output: a routing path p that satisfies the anycast QoS request R.

1. **for** each link $l \in E$ in G **if** $B_l < B$ **then** delete l; Let G' be the resulting graph;
2. **for** each destination D in $G(A)$
   for each node v in G'
   find the length $H(v, D)$ and the next link $L(v, D)$ of the shortest path from v to D.
3. **for** each node v in G'

if $H(v, D) > N$ for all destination D in $G(A)$ **then** delete node v.
Let G'' be the resulting graph;

4. Search a path satisfying the anycast QoS request R:
   now = S; *nowdelay* = 0;
   repeat
   if there are links $e_1, e_2, \ldots, e_k$, where for each j, $e_j=[now, v_j]$
   then with probability p_j pick the link e_j; (*the probability p_j will be explained blow*)
   now = v_j; *nowdealy* = *nowdelay* + 1;
   until *now* is in $G(A)$;
   output the routing path;

==

We explain how the probability p_j is decided in the algorithm RBH. Suppose that in the **repeat** loop in step 4 of the algorithm, a partial path P from S to the node *now* has been constructed, such that the length $|P|$ (i.e., the delay) of the path P is *nowdelay*. We also assume that there are links $e_1, e_2, \ldots, e_k$, where for each j, $e_j = [now, v_j]$, and there exists at least a destination D in $G(A)$ such that

$nowdelay + 1 + H(now, D) \leq N$

Then the probability of selecting the destination D^i in the node *now* is given by

$$p_{D^i} = \frac{\sum_{t=1}^{w} \prod_{j \neq t} \left[H\left(now, D^t\right) + nowdelay\right]}{\prod_{t=1}^{w} \left[H\left(now, D^t\right) + nowdelay\right]} * \frac{1}{H\left(now, D^i\right)}$$

Note that, if $H(now, D^i) + 1 + nowdelay > \mathrm{N}$ then $P_D{}^i = 0$, and $H(now, D^i) + nowdelay$ is removed from the above expression.

Secondly, We decide the probability p_j with which we pick the link $e_j = [now, v_j]$.

$$p_j = \sum_{L(now, D^i) = e_j} p_{D^i}$$

According to the above formula for the probability p_j, we can see that the algorithm RBH dynamically justifies its routing strategy base in the routing algorithm. In general, a routing path with short delay has a high probability to be picked.

We analyze the complexity for the algorithm. It is clear that step 1 of the algorithm RBH takes time O(m). Step 2 of the algorithm can be done using a modified Dijkstra's algorithm, in which we find a shortest paths from each destination to all the nodes in the network. This takes time O(w*(m + n log n)), where w is the number of designated recipients in $G(A)$. Step3 takes time O(n) and step 4 takes time O(m). So the complexity of the algorithm RBHS is O(m + n log n).

Lemma 1. *If there exists a path from the source node to any node in G(A) that satisfies the given anycast QoS request R, then the randomized algorithm RBH finds a path for the anycast QoS request.*

Proof. Suppose there exists a path from the source S to $G(A)$ but the algorithm can not find one. Then the searching will reach a node which can not access any node in $G(A)$ or the length of any path passing this node does not satisfy the request .But in algorithm step 3, we have deleted all nodes that can not access any node in $G(A)$. In algorithm step 4, we will not choose the link that does not satisfy the length request .It also means in our algorithm, any node reachable from the searching process must be able to access at least one node in $G(A)$ and the length of the path satisfy the request. This derives a contradiction.

3. Anycast QoS Routing with Inaccurate Network Information

Network routings in general rely heavily on network's state information on resource availability at network nodes and links. In order to keep network state information accurate, many parameters associated with QoS requirements must update in time. Unfortunately, this is impractical when the network is highly dynamic and changes are frequent, because it brings out high computational cost and protocol overhead [11]. Thus, network routing algorithms must deal with the situations in which network state information is inaccurate. In this section, we primarily focus on anycast QoS routing with inaccurate network state information.

We focus on anycast QoS routing environment with inaccurate link state information. The uncertainty lies in the links. For each link l□E, we are given a probability S_l that the link l can guarantee the request bandwidth [17].

As we have seen, the accuracy of the link safety information has a direct impact on the performance of the routing algorithms, and update triggering policy directly impacts the accuracy of the link state information. Link state information will be more accurate when update is done more frequently, which will introduce much more overhead to the protocol. Generally, we can trade off between information accuracy and protocol overhead. There are several update triggering policies, such as The Threshold Triggering, The Equal Class Triggering, and The Exponential Class Triggering [6]. No matter which update triggering is used, the advertised information will be lag. So the safety of a link will remain the same value during the period of adjacent update times. Thus, in the time period between two consecutive update times, a deterministic routing algorithm, for example the safest-shortest algorithm, will keep on selecting the same path when requests on the same source and destination are given. This will most likely overload this path quickly with more traffic than it can handle, and resulting in poor QoS routing performance. On the other hand, randomized routing algorithms seem to be able to avoid this problem, and it also can balance network load.

Let $G = <V, E>$ be a network, where $V = \{v_1, \ldots, v_n\}$ is the set of nodes in G and $E = \{e_1, \ldots, e_m\}$ is the set of links in G. Each link e_j is associated with a function

f_j, such that $f_j\,(b)$ is the probability that the link e_j has bandwidth at least b. Consider an anycast QoS request R = (u_0, A, b, N_0, S_0), where u_0 is the source node and A is the anycast address that may contain many receivers, b is the bandwidth requirement, N_0 is the ``delay requirement'', i.e., the maximum number of hops allowed in the routing path, and $S_0$ is the ``safety rate requirement'', i.e., the minimum probability with which the routing path has bandwidth at least b.

Problem B: *Given a network G=<V, E> with inaccurate link-state information and an anycast QoS request R = (u_0, A, b, N_0, S_0), find a path P form the source u_0 to any node in G(A),where G(A)={D^1, D^2, ..., D^w}, D^1, D^2, ..., $D^w \in V$ and G(A)$\subset$V:*
1. The probability that the bandwidth of the path P is at least b is not smaller than the safety rate requirement S_0 :

$$\prod_{e_j \in P} f_j(b) \geq S_0$$

2. The number |P| of hops in the path P is not larger than the delay requirement N_0: $|P| \leq N_0$

Our goal is for each anycast QoS request R, to construct a QoS routing path satisfying the request when such a routing path exists, or report that no such a path exists. Our algorithm is presented as follows.

Algorithm RBHS (Random Based on Hops and Safety)
Input: the network $G = (V, E)$ with inaccurate link-state information and an anycast QoS request $R = (u_0, \mathrm{A}, b, N_0, S_0)$
Output: a routing path P that satisfies the anycast QoS request R
1. **for** each D^i in $G(A)$:
1.1 **for** each node v in G and $v \notin G(A)$, find the maximum safety rate from v to D^i :
  $maxsafe[D^i, v] = \max\{ \prod_{e_j \in P} f_j(b) \mid P \text{ is a path in } G \text{ from } v \text{ to } D^i \}$
1.2 **for** each node v in G and $v \notin G(A)$, find the length of the shortest path from v to D^i:
  $mindelay[D^i, v] = \min\{ |P| \mid P \text{ is a path in } G \text{ from } v \text{ to } D^i \}$
2. Search for a routing path satisfying the QoS request R:
  for H = 1 to *boundtimes* (**boundtimes* will be defined below*)
  $now = u_0$; $nowdelay = 0$; $nowsafe = 1$; $G'(A) = G(A)$;
  repeat
  for every D^i in $G'(A)$:
    for every node v_j adjacent to *now*:
     compute $P_j(D^i)$; (* the probability $P_j(D^i)$ will be explained below*)
    if there are links $e_1, e_2, \ldots, e_k$, where for each j, $e_j = [now, v_j]$
     then with probability p_j pick the link e_j; (* the probability p_j will be explained below *);
     if the link e_j has $p_j(D^i) = 0$ then remove D^i from $G'(A)$

$now = v_j$; $nowdelay = nowdelay + 1$; $nowsafe = nowsafe * f_j(b)$;
until either *now* is in $G'(A)$ or $G'(A)$ is empty;
if now is in $G'(A)$ then output the routing path and exit
else $H = H + 1$;

3. report ("QoS request cannot be satisfied").

Now, we explain how the probability $P_j(D^i)$ is decided. In step1 we can get the maximum safety and the minimum delay from each node v to all of the node in $G(A)$. Suppose that in the repeat loop in Step 2 of the algorithm, a partial path P from u_0 to the node *now* has been constructed, such that the length (i.e., the delay) of the path P is

$$nowdelay = |P|$$

and the safety rate of the path P is

$$nowsafe = \prod_{e_j \in P} f_j(b)$$

For each node v_j adjacent to the node *now* and not a previous node of *now* in the path P, we define

$$\text{if } \text{maxsafe}[D^i, v_j] * nowsafe * s_{e_j} \prec S_0 \text{ or } \text{mindelay}[D^i, v_j] + 1 + nowdelay > N_0$$

$$\text{then } P_j(D^i) = 0$$

$$\text{else}$$

$$P_j(D^i) = \alpha * \frac{\log(1 + \text{maxsafe}[D^i, v_j]}{\sum_{t=1}^{k} \log(1 + \text{maxsafe}[D^t, v_j]} + \beta * \frac{1/(1 + \text{mindelay}[D^i, v_j])}{\sum_{t=1}^{k} 1/(1 + \text{mindelay}[D^t, v_j])}$$

Where s_{ej} is the safety of link e_j; k is the number of nodes that are adjacent to the node *now* except the previous nodes in path P. if $P_j(D^i) = 0$, then $maxsafe[D^i, v_j]$ and $mindelay[D^i, v_j]$ will be removed from $\Sigma_{i=1}^{k} \log(1+maxsafe[D^i, v_i])$ and $\Sigma_{i=1}^{k}$ $(1/(1+ mindelay[D^i, v_i])$. The definition of α and β in the above equation is the same as that in our another paper[14].

In order to improve the probability of selecting the nearest destination and balance network load effectively, we compute the probability for each destination.

$$\text{If } \text{maxsaf } e[D^i, now] * nowsafe < S_0 \text{ or } \text{mindelay}[D^i, now] + nowdelay > N_0$$

$$\text{then } P(D^i) = 0$$

$$\text{else } P(D^i) = \frac{\dfrac{1}{\text{mindealy}[D^i, now)}}{\sum_{j=1}^{k} \dfrac{1}{\text{mindealy}[D^j, now)}}$$

After we compute $P_j(D^i)$ and $P(D^i)$, we will change the value of $P_j(D^i)$ according to $P(D^I)$ by $P_j(D^i) = P_j(D^i)*P(D^i)$. Then we can use them to get p_j which is the probability of picking the link $e_j = [now, v_j]$. We use a $w \times k$ matrix to describe $P_j(D^i)$:

$$P = \begin{bmatrix} P_1(D^1) & P_2(D^1) & \cdots & P_k(D^1) \\ P_1(D^2) & \cdots & \cdots & P_k(D^2) \\ \vdots & \vdots & \vdots & \vdots \\ P_1(D^w) & \cdots & \cdots & P_k(D^w) \end{bmatrix}$$

In this matrix, row i presents the probability for all nodes adjacent to *now* to receiver D^i, and column j presents the probability for picking the link e_j to all receivers.

In our algorithm, the probability p_j for selecting the link e_j is:

$$p_j = \frac{\sum_{i=1}^{w} e^{HP_j(D^i)}}{\sum_{i=1}^{w} \sum_{j=1}^{k} e^{HP_j(D^i)}}$$

Where H is a parameter to be decided. We will discuss its effect on algorithm performance in section 4.

We analyze the complexity for the algorithm. Step 1.1 of the algorithm can be done using a modified Dijkstra's algorithm, in which we find a maximum safety rate path from one destination Di to each of the nodes in the network. This takes time $O(m + n \log n)$. Step 1.2 can be similarly done in time $O(m)$ by a single Breadth First Search process from one destination Di. We will do step1.1 and step 1.2 for w times, where w is the number of receivers. So the time complexity of Steps 1 is $O(wn \log n + wm)$. In the main body of the algorithm, Step 2, the time complexity of the repeat loop is bounded by $O(m)$, and we will repeat at most *boundtimes* times. So, the time complexity of step 2 is bounded by O(*m*boundtimes*). Therefore, the time complexity if our algorithm is O(*w*nlogn+w*m+m*boundtimes*).

4. Analysis and Simulation Results

The focus of the section is on evaluating the performance of anycast QoS routing algorithms. We use simulation as the main tool for evaluating the quality of routing algorithms. We have developed a network simulator for testing routing performance.

4.1 Network Topologies

The topology of the simulated network was used in [15,16], and is loosely based on the Internet backbone in the U.S. The network has 28 nodes, 45 links and a diameter of 7. The average node degree is 3.2. Each link between two nodes in the graph represents a pair of unidirectional link transmitting in opposite directions. The mesh topology, although somewhat contrived, is of interest due to its regularity and large number of equal hop length multi-paths. We use 10*10 mesh topology for our simulation. We also test our algorithm on ISP topology (18 nodes and 29 links) [14], the ARPA network (21 nodes, 26 links)[16] and some other typical network topology.

4.2 Performance Measure

In our experiments, we measure the performance of the randomized anycast QoS routing algorithms RBH and RBHS compared with the shortest-shortest algorithms under Threshold triggering link state update policies and Holdtime 50[14]. We measure routing performance using *Acceptance Ratio* introduced in [14], defined as the percentage of the total requested bandwidth that was routed successfully. We also use another five metrics which are defined in [17] to test the algorithms.

4.3 Experimental Result

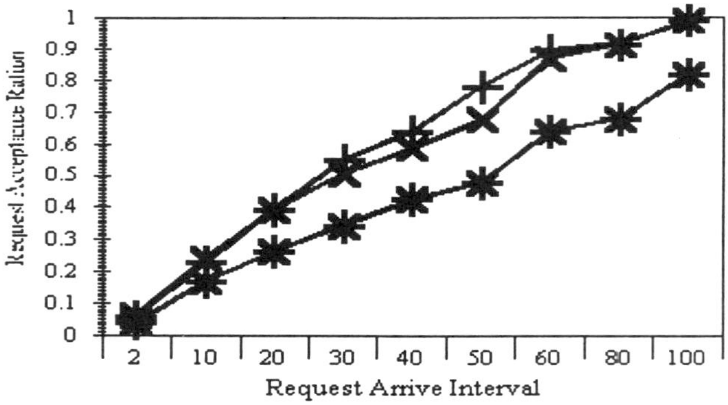

Figure 1. Simulation results for various network loads under accurate link-state information. *Static Shortest Path (SSP); +Random Based on Hops; ×Dynamic Shortest Path(DSP)

Figure 1 shows the simulation results of Request Acceptance Ratio (RAR) of RBH and both static and dynamic shortest path algorithms under accurate link-state information. From the figure, we can see RBH performs better than DSP under middle heavy network load and almost the same under light network load. But in very heavy network load environment, DSP performs a little better. It can be explained that when network load is very heavy, the congestion always happens in most nodes and links, the shortest path algorithm make less network resource cost. so under this condition, it is a better choice. The performance of RBH and DSP are better than SSP.

In Figure 2,we can see under inaccurate link-state information, the Request Acceptance Ratio of our randomized QoS anycast routing algorithm RBHS is higher than the dynamic shortest path algorithms with different Thresholds update policies. This result is under the environment with unbalanced network load. It can be explained that randomized QoS anycast routing algorithm RBHS is fit for balancing load.

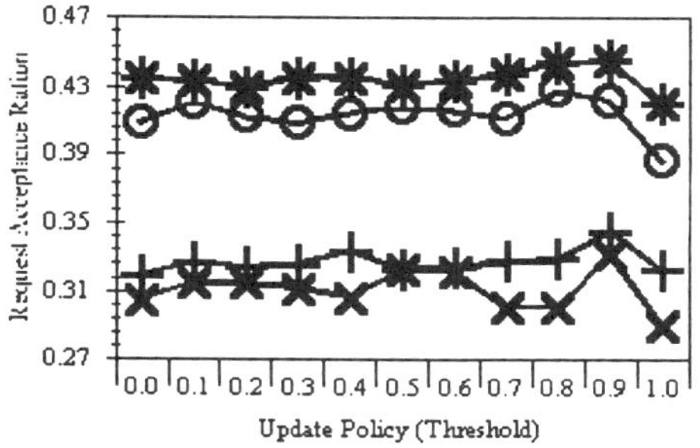

Figure 2. Simulation results for various TH under inaccurate network link-state information.
∗ RBHS algorithm in which the average inter-arrival time is equal to 30
+ RBHS algorithm in which the average inter-arrival time is equal to 20
O DSP algorithm in which the average inter-arrival time is equal to 30
× DSP algorithm in which the average inter-arrival time is equal to 20

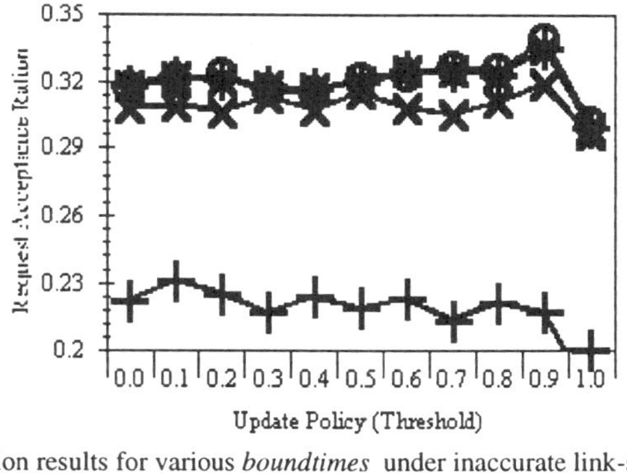

Figure 3. Simulation results for various *boundtimes* under inaccurate link-state information.
+ RBHS algorithm in which the *boundtimes* is equal to 1
× RBHS algorithm in which the *boundtimes* is equal to 5
∗ RBHS algorithm in which the *boundtimes* is equal to 10
ORBHS algorithm in which the *boundtimes* is equal to 100

In Figure 3, we give the simulation results for various *boundtimes* that is defined in our algorithm. To reduce the complexity for the algorithm, we may need choose small *boundtimes*, which, however, has direct impact on the performance of our algorithm. Form the figure 4., we can see that the *boundtimes* value should be set to 10.

In Figure 4, we test the effect of H on our algorithm RBHS. We can find out that the results vary a little with various H values, but we can get high average acceptance ration when H is equal to 12.

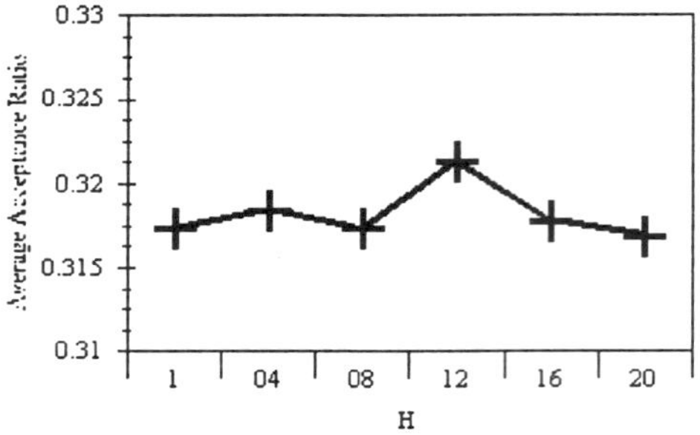

Figure 4. Simulation results for various *H* under inaccurate network link-state information.

5. Conclusions

We have developed two effective randomized anycast QoS routing algorithms (RBH and RBHS) on networks with accurate and inaccurate link-state information, respectively. Several new techniques are proposed in our algorithms. First, minimum hops for each node is used in both algorithms and the maximum safety rate is also used in the latter, which are used as metric for computing the probability of possible out-links. The two metrics are pre-computed for each node in the network, which can simplify the network complexity and provide the routing process with useful information. Randomness is used at the link level and depends dynamically on the routing configuration. This provides great flexibility for the routing process, prevents the routing process from overusing certain fixed routing paths, and adequately balances the safety rate and delay of the routing path. Meanwhile, we have established a network testing environment and introduced some parameters to measure the performance of anycast QoS routing algorithms compared with the typical shortest path algorithm. Experimental results show that our algorithms improve over shortest algorithms appearing in the literature.

REFERENCES

1. X. P. Xiao and L. M. Ni, "Internet QoS: A Big Picture," *IEEE Network*, vol. 2, pp. 6-18, Apr. 1999.
2. Z. L. Zhang, "End-To_End support for Statistical Quality-of-Service Guarantees in Multimedia Networks", *PhD thesis*, University of Massachusetts at Amherst, Amherst, MA, Feb. 1997.
3. B. Rajagppalan, R. Nair, H. Sandick and E. Crawley, "A Framework for QoS-based Routing in the internet," *RFC 2386, IETF*, Aug. 1998.
4. H. Newton, *Newron's Telecom Dictionary*, 12th Edition, Flatiron Publishing, 1997.

5. E. Basturk, R. Engel, R. Haas, V. Peris and D. Saha, "Using Network Layer Anycast for Load Distribution in the internet," *IBM Research Report*, RC 20938, July 1997.
6. R. Hinden and S. Deering, "IP Version 6 Addressing Architecture," *RFC 1884, IETF*, Dec. 1995.
7. C. Partridge, T. Mendez and W. Milliken, "Host Anycasting Service," *RFC 1546, IETF*, Nov. 1993.
8. S. Bhattacharjee, M. H. Ammar, E. W. Zegura, V. Shah and Z. Fei, "Application-layer Anycasting," *Proc. IEEE INFOCOM'97*, Apr. 1997.
9. Z. D. Wu, C. Noble and D. Huang, "Optimal Video Distribution Using Anycasting Srevice," in *Proc. of INET99*, June 1999
10. D. Xuan, W. J. Jia, W. Zhao and H. W. Zhu, "A Routing Protocol for Anycast Messages," *IEEE Trans. Parallel and Distributed Systems*, vol. 11, No. 6, June 2000.
11. D. H. Lorenz and A. Orda, "QoS Routing in Networks with Uncertain Parameters," *IEEE/ACM Trans. Networking*, vol. 6. pp. 768-778, Dec. 1998.
12. G. Apostolopoulos, R. Guérin S. Kamat and S.Tripathi, "Quality of Service Based Routing: A Performance Perspective," in *Proc. of ACM SIGCOMM'98*, pp. 17-28, Vancouver, Canada, Oct. 1998.
13. G. Apostolopoulos, R. Guérin S. Kamat and S.Tripathi, "Improving QoS Routing Performance Under Inaccurate Link State Information," in *Proc. ITC'16*, pp.1351-1362, June 1999.
14. J. X. Wang, W. P. Wang, J. E. Chen and S. Q. Chen, "A Randomized QoS Routing Algorithm On Networks with Inaccurate Link-State Information," in *Proc. WCC2000*, Aug. 2000.
15. S. Rampal, D. S. Reeves, "An Evaluation of Routing and Admission Control Algorithms for Multimedia Traffic," *Comput. Commun.* Vol 18, No. 10, pp: 755-768, Oct. 1995.
16. Q. Sun and H. Langendorfer, "Routing for Low Call Blocking in High-Speed General Topology Networks," *Computer Networks and ISDN Systems*, Vol 30, pp 795-804, July 1998.
17. J. X. Wang, W. P. Wang, J. E. Chen and S. Q. Chen, "An Effective Randomized QoS Routing Algorithm on Networks with Inaccurate Parameters," Univ. of Central South, Tech. Rep., 2000.

PARALLEL IMPLEMENTATION OF DYNAMIC EQUATIONS FOR SOLVING EIGENVALUE PROBLEMS OF COMPLEX MATRICES

ZU-LAN HUANG, YAO-LIN JIANG AND RICHARD M. M. CHEN

School of Creative Media, City University of Hong Kong, Hong Kong

Email: richard.chen@cityu.edu.hk

XIAO-LA LIN

Department of Electrical and Electronic Engineering, The University of Hong Kong, Hong Kong

Email: xlin@eee.hku.hk

In this paper we present a parallel implementation of dynamic equations for solving complex matrix eigenvalue problems. The principle of the approach is that the eigenvalue problems is first transformed into the associated problems of solving large systems of nonlinear dynamic equations by optimization techniques and then waveform relaxation is used to compute the resulting dynamic equations. The proposed algorithm can efficiently determine all eigenvalues and their eigenvectors for a general complex matrix. The convergence of transient solutions is pledged by a theorem. It is the first time that the waveform relaxation method is applied to compute the cubic dynamic equations. The algorithm is successfully implemented on a message passing multi-processor system, and the experimental results of general complex matrices are also given to confirm the effectiveness of our implementation.

1 Introduction

Numerical computation of eigenvalues and eigenvectors of large matrices is an important issue in many scientific and engineering applications. A promising approach based on nonlinear dynamic equations in the time domain [1, 2] has been proposed to solve the eigenvalue problems. This approach is different from most existing methods [3]. The resulting dynamic equations correspond to a neural network.

Cichocki and Unbehauen [1] discussed such a case where the matrix under consideration is real and has real eigenpairs. However, they gave no theoretical analysis to guarantee the convergence of the dynamic equations therein. Jiang, Chen, and Huang [2] have extended the work of [1] and given a theorem to pledge the convergence of transient solutions of the dynamic equations.

Often the dynamic equations solving eigenvalue problems were first mapped into a neural network, then the transient response of the neural network is obtained by hardware or software implementation of the neural network. We introduce the

WR method to compute their transient solutions in order to avoid the complicated neural network circuit design. Another benefit is that WR is a relaxation-based algorithm for transient responses of large systems and can be easily implemented by parallel processing [4 - 6].

This paper is organized as follows. The dynamic equations for determining all eigenpairs of a complex matrix are presented in Section 2. The WR method for computing the dynamic equations and the windowing technique to speed up the convergence of the algorithm is discussed in Section 3. The parallel WR and its implementation on a message passing multiprocessor are described in Section 4, and the experimental results are provided in Section 5. Finally, conclusions are drawn in Section 6.

2 Dynamic Equations for Solving Eigenvalue problems

For a complex matrix $\mathbf{A} \in \mathbf{C}^{n \times n}$, its eigenpairs { $\lambda_k, \mathbf{v}_k$ } (k = 1,2, ... ,n) satisfy the following linear algebraic equations

$$(\mathbf{A} - \lambda_k \mathbf{I}_{n \times n})\mathbf{v}_k = 0, \qquad (k = 1,2, \ldots ,n) \tag{1}$$

where $\mathbf{I}_{n \times n} \in \mathbf{R}^{n \times n}$ is the identity matrix. Let $\mathbf{A}_{\text{Re}}$ and $\mathbf{A}_{\text{Im}}$ denote the real and imaginary parts of the complex matrix **A**, respectively.

For each k, let $\lambda_{\text{Re},k}$ and $\lambda_{\text{Im},k}$ denote the real and imaginary parts of the complex number λ_k, respectively, and $\mathbf{v}_{\text{Re},k}$ and $\mathbf{v}_{\text{Im},k}$ denote the real and imaginary parts of the complex vector $\mathbf{v}_k$, respectively. Namely, $\mathbf{A} = \mathbf{A}_{\text{Re}} + j\mathbf{A}_{\text{Im}}$, $\lambda_k = \lambda_{\text{Re},k} + j\lambda_{\text{Im},k}$, and $\mathbf{v}_k = \mathbf{v}_{\text{Re},k} + j\mathbf{v}_{\text{Im},k}$, where the symbol "$j$" represents the imaginary component (namely, $j^2 = -1$). System (1) can be rewritten as the following 2n real value linear algebraic equations for k = 1,2, ... ,n

$$\begin{cases} (\mathbf{A}_{\text{Re}}\mathbf{v}_{\text{Re},k} - \mathbf{A}_{\text{Im}}\mathbf{v}_{\text{Im},k}) - \lambda_{\text{Re},k}\mathbf{v}_{\text{Re},k} + \lambda_{\text{Im},k}\mathbf{v}_{\text{Im},k} = 0 \\ (\mathbf{A}_{\text{Re}}\mathbf{v}_{\text{Im},k} - \mathbf{A}_{\text{Im}}\mathbf{v}_{\text{Re},k}) - \lambda_{\text{Re},k}\mathbf{v}_{\text{Im},k} - \lambda_{\text{Im},k}\mathbf{v}_{\text{Re},k} = 0 \end{cases} \tag{2}$$

We give a constraint for the eigenvectors $\mathbf{v}_k$ as

$$\mathbf{v}_k^H \mathbf{v}_k = \theta^2, \qquad (k = 1,2, \ldots ,n) \tag{3}$$

where 6 is a positive constant and the superscript "H" stands for conjugate transposition operation. That is

$$v_{\text{Re},k}^T v_{\text{Re},k} + v_{\text{Im},k}^T v_{\text{Im},k} = \theta^2, \qquad (k = 1,2, \ldots ,n) \tag{4}$$

where "T" stands for transposition operation.

Let $\mathbf{A}_{\text{Re}} = (a_{\text{Re},ij})$ and $\mathbf{A}_{\text{Im}} = (a_{\text{Im},ij})$. Further, for each k, let $\mathbf{v}_{\text{Re},k} = [v_{\text{Re},1k}, \ldots, v_{\text{Re},nk}]^T$ and $\mathbf{v}_{\text{Im},k} = [v_{\text{Im},1k}, \ldots, v_{\text{Im},nk}]^T$. By the penalty method in optimization, we can formulate an energy function of Eq. (1) and Eq. (3) for a given k as follows

$$E(t)=\frac{1}{2}\sum_{i=1}^{n}e_{1,ik}^{2}+\frac{1}{2}\sum_{i=1}^{n}e_{2,ik}^{2}+\frac{\delta}{4}\left(\sum_{i=1}^{n}v_{\mathrm{Re},ik}^{2}+\sum_{i=1}^{n}v_{\mathrm{Im},ik}^{2}-\theta^{2}\right)^{2} \quad (5)$$

where $e_{1,ik}=\left(\sum_{j=1}^{n}a_{\mathrm{Re},ij}v_{\mathrm{Re},jk}-\sum_{j=1}^{n}a_{\mathrm{Im},ij}v_{\mathrm{Im},jk}\right)-\lambda_{\mathrm{Re},k}v_{\mathrm{Re},ik}+\lambda_{\mathrm{Im},k}v_{\mathrm{Im},ik}$

and $e_{2,ik}=(\sum_{j=1}^{n}a_{\mathrm{Re},ij}v_{\mathrm{Im},jk}+\sum_{j=1}^{n}a_{\mathrm{Im},ij}v_{\mathrm{Re},jk})-\lambda_{\mathrm{Re},k}v_{\mathrm{Im},ik}-\lambda_{\mathrm{Im},k}v_{\mathrm{Re},ik}$.

The dynamic equations correspond to the search direction towards minimum $E(t)$ are

$$\begin{cases}\dfrac{d\lambda_{\mathrm{Re},k}(t)}{dt}=\mu\left(\sum_{i=1}^{n}e_{1,ik}v_{\mathrm{Re},ik}+\sum_{i=1}^{n}e_{2,ik}v_{\mathrm{Im},ik}\right)\\ \dfrac{d\lambda_{\mathrm{Im},k}(t)}{dt}=-\mu\left(\sum_{i=1}^{n}e_{1,ik}v_{\mathrm{Im},ik}+\sum_{i=1}^{n}e_{2,ik}v_{\mathrm{Re},ik}\right)\\ \dfrac{dv_{\mathrm{Re},lk}(t)}{dt}=-\mu\left[\sum_{i=1}^{n}e_{1,ik}a_{\mathrm{Re},il}+\sum_{i=1}^{n}e_{2,ik}a_{\mathrm{Im},il}-e_{1,lk}\lambda_{\mathrm{Re},k}-e_{2,lk}\lambda_{\mathrm{Im},k}+\delta v_{\mathrm{Re},lk}\left(\sum_{i=1}^{n}v_{\mathrm{Re},ik}^{2}+v_{\mathrm{Im},ik}^{2}-\theta^{2}\right)\right]\\ \dfrac{dv_{\mathrm{Im},lk}(t)}{dt}=-\mu\left[\sum_{i=1}^{n}e_{1,ik}a_{\mathrm{Im},il}+\sum_{i=1}^{n}e_{2,ik}a_{\mathrm{Re},il}-e_{1,lk}\lambda_{\mathrm{Im},k}-e_{2,lk}\lambda_{\mathrm{Re},k}+\delta v_{\mathrm{Im},lk}\left(\sum_{i=1}^{n}v_{\mathrm{Re},ik}^{2}+v_{\mathrm{Im},ik}^{2}-\theta^{2}\right)\right]\\ \lambda_{\mathrm{Re},k}(0)=(\lambda_{\mathrm{Re},k})_0,\quad \lambda_{\mathrm{Im},k}(0)=(\lambda_{\mathrm{Im},k})_0,\quad v_{\mathrm{Re},lk}(0)=(v_{\mathrm{Re},lk})_0,\quad v_{\mathrm{Im},lk}(0)=(v_{\mathrm{Im},lk})_0\end{cases} \quad (6)$$

where the initial value $\mathbf{v}_k(0)$ is not equal to zero vector, the positive number μ is a learning rate, and t is the time variable.

For simplicity, we denote that $\mathbf{x}(t)=[\lambda_{\mathrm{Re},k},\lambda_{\mathrm{Im},k},v_{\mathrm{Re},1k},\ldots,v_{\mathrm{Re},nk},v_{\mathrm{Im},1k},\ldots,v_{\mathrm{Im},nk}]^{T}$ for any given k. The dynamic equations correspond to the search direction towards minimum $E(t)$ can be written in brief as

$$\frac{d\mathbf{x}(t)}{dt}=f(x(t),w),\qquad \mathbf{x}(0)=\mathbf{x}_0 \quad (7)$$

where $w=[\mu,\delta,\theta]^{T}$. We call a constant vector $\mathbf{x}^{*}\in\mathbf{R}^{2n+2}$ as a stable solution of System (6) if it satisfies $f(\mathbf{x}^{*},\mathbf{w})=0$. Let the set N_s be composed of all stable solutions. The following theorem, which was proved in [2], implies that the stable solutions of System (6) correspond to the solutions of the eigenvalue problem Eq.(1) and Eq. (3).

Theorem For any given initial value $\mathbf{x}_0$, the solution $\mathbf{x}(t)$ of System (6) always converges to its stable solution set N_s.

3 Waveform Relaxation for Computing Dynamic Equations

The WR method has a dominant position in parallel processing for solving initial value problems of large circuits or systems [4, 5, 6]. The Jacobi, Gauss-Seidel, SOR or Newton splitting functions of System (6) are in line with the convergence condition of the WR method (see [2]).

For simplicity, in this paper we will adopt the point-Jacobi WR splitting for System (6) for our numerical examples. According to the general form (7) of the system, the expression of the point Jacobi WR during the (p+1)-st iteration can be described as

$$\begin{cases} \dfrac{d\lambda_{\mathrm{Re},k}^{(p+1)}(t)}{dt} = f_0\left(\lambda_{\mathrm{Re},k}{}^{(p+1)}, \lambda_{\mathrm{Im},k}{}^{(p)}, v_{\mathrm{Re},1k}{}^{(p)}, \ldots, v_{\mathrm{Re},nk}{}^{(p)}, v_{\mathrm{Im},1k}{}^{(p)}, \ldots, v_{\mathrm{Im},nk}{}^{(p)}\right) \\ \dfrac{d\lambda_{\mathrm{Im},k}^{(p+1)}(t)}{dt} = f_1\left(\lambda_{\mathrm{Re},k}{}^{(p)}, \lambda_{\mathrm{Im},k}{}^{(p+1)}, v_{\mathrm{Re},1k}{}^{(p)}, \ldots, v_{\mathrm{Re},nk}{}^{(p)}, v_{\mathrm{Im},1k}{}^{(p)}, \ldots, v_{\mathrm{Im},nk}{}^{(p)}\right) \\ \dfrac{dv_{\mathrm{Re},1k}^{(p+1)}(t)}{dt} = f_2\left(\lambda_{\mathrm{Re},k}{}^{(p)}, \lambda_{\mathrm{Im},k}{}^{(p)}, v_{\mathrm{Re},1k}{}^{(p+1)}, \ldots, v_{\mathrm{Re},nk}{}^{(p)}, v_{\mathrm{Im},1k}{}^{(p)}, \ldots, v_{\mathrm{Im},nk}{}^{(p)}\right) \\ \quad\vdots \\ \dfrac{dv_{\mathrm{Re},nk}^{(p+1)}(t)}{dt} = f_{1+n}\left(\lambda_{\mathrm{Re},k}{}^{(p)}, \lambda_{\mathrm{Im},k}{}^{(p)}, v_{\mathrm{Re},1k}{}^{(p)}, \ldots, v_{\mathrm{Re},nk}{}^{(p+1)}, v_{\mathrm{Im},1k}{}^{(p)}, \ldots, v_{\mathrm{Im},nk}{}^{(p)}\right) \\ \dfrac{dv_{\mathrm{Im},1k}^{(p+1)}(t)}{dt} = f_{2+n}\left(\lambda_{\mathrm{Re},k}{}^{(p)}, \lambda_{\mathrm{Im},k}{}^{(p)}, v_{\mathrm{Re},1k}{}^{(p)}, \ldots, v_{\mathrm{Re},nk}{}^{(p)}, v_{\mathrm{Im},1k}{}^{(p+1)}, \ldots, v_{\mathrm{Im},nk}{}^{(p)}\right) \\ \quad\vdots \\ \dfrac{dv_{\mathrm{Im},nk}^{(p+1)}(t)}{dt} = f_{2n+1}\left(\lambda_{\mathrm{Re},k}{}^{(p)}, \lambda_{\mathrm{Im},k}{}^{(p)}, v_{\mathrm{Re},1k}{}^{(p)}, \ldots, v_{\mathrm{Re},nk}{}^{(p)}, v_{\mathrm{Im},1k}{}^{(p)}, \ldots, v_{\mathrm{Im},nk}{}^{(p+1)}\right) \\ \lambda_{\mathrm{Re},k}(0) = (\lambda_{\mathrm{Re},k})_0, \quad \lambda_{\mathrm{Im},k}(0) = (\lambda_{\mathrm{Im},k})_0 \\ v_{\mathrm{Re},lk}(0) = (v_{\mathrm{Re},lk})_0, \quad v_{\mathrm{Im},lk}(0) = (v_{\mathrm{Im},lk})_0 \quad (l = 1,2\ldots n) \end{cases} \tag{8}$$

where $\mathbf{x}^{(p)} = \left(\lambda_{\mathrm{Re},k}{}^{(p)}, \lambda_{\mathrm{Im},k}{}^{(p)}, v_{\mathrm{Re},1k}{}^{(p)}, \ldots v_{\mathrm{Re},nk}{}^{(p)}, v_{\mathrm{Im},1k}{}^{(p)}, \ldots v_{\mathrm{Im},nk}{}^{(p)}\right)$ is the result of the p-th iteration. Since all the functions in the above decoupled system are independent, it is easy to parallelize the computation task. Furthermore, the Jacobi WR method can be accelerated by splitting the whole system into fewer coupling blocks according to both the size of system and the number of participating nodes.

Because the solutions of eigenvalue problems are effectively mapped to the stable solutions of their associated dynamic equations, the method depicted here can compute all the eigenvalues and eigenvectors for a given matrix by using a sufficient number of sets of random numbers as initial values.

In order to accelerate the convergence, the technique of windowing is recommended [7]. Substantial amount of computation can be saved using small subwindows for problems in which a large discrepancy exists between the speed of convergence on an interval and the ones on its subintervals.

4 Parallel WR Algorithm for Computing Complex Eigenvalues

During parallel processing, system decomposition is to split the given system into several subsystems, so that each subsystem can be computed individually. Assuming that the dimensions of the given matrix are $n \times n$, then the derived ODE system is composed of $2n$+2 ODE equations. If there are m processors available in the parallel system, to balance the workload of the system, about $\frac{2n+2}{m}$ ODE equations will be assigned on each processor for solutions. The dependencies of the equations on different processors are eliminated by Jacobi WR method. Furthermore, to accelerate the Jacobi WR, the unknowns being solved on one processor may be coupled, that is, the task for one processor can be treated as an individual ODE subsystem at each iteration.

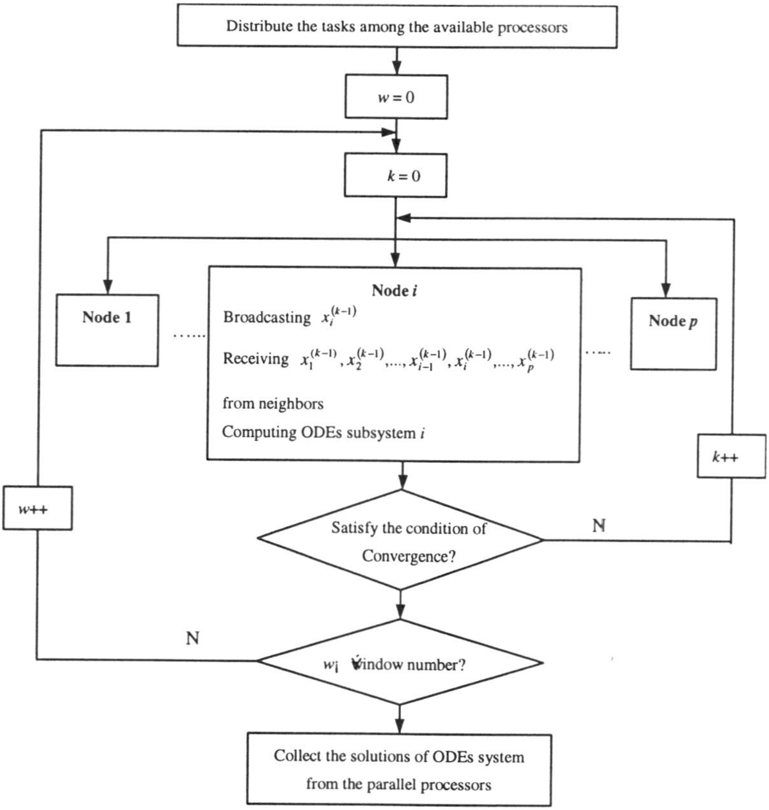

Figure 1. The flow chart of parallel WR algorithm for computing complex eigenvalues

For the ODE subsystems, we apply the algorithm of 4th order variable step Runge-Kutta to obtain the solutions.

To ensure the consistency between the solution of the ODE system and the eigenvalues of the given matrix, the time domain for ODE system should be long enough. To speed up the convergence of the waveform relaxation method, windowing technique is applied. The time interval will be split into a series of windows with equal length. The result of last window will be taken as the initial value for the computation of next window.

At the beginning of each iteration, the parallel processors will communicate with neighbor processors to receive the values computed in the previous iteration. With reference to the flow chart of our parallel algorithm (see Figure 1), the time complexity for data communication is expressed as $O(n_{kw} \cdot n_d \cdot p)$, in which we n_{kw} as the total iterative times through all windows, n_d as the dimension of the matrix, and p as the number of working nodes in the system.

5 Experimental Results

It is well known that the matrices produced by the modified nodal analysis for circuit simulation will have a form as

$$\mathbf{A} = \begin{bmatrix} 0 & 0 & \mathbf{P} \\ \left(-\mathbf{P}^T\right) & \mathbf{I} & 0 \\ 0 & \mathbf{M}_0 s + \mathbf{M}_1 & \mathbf{N}_0 s + \mathbf{N}_1 \end{bmatrix} \tag{10}$$

According to the basic form of the matrix produced by the modified nodal analysis for circuit simulation, we let $s = j$ and $m \times m$ (m is even) matrices **P**, $\mathbf{M}_1$, $\mathbf{M}_0$, $\mathbf{N}_0$ and $\mathbf{N}_1$ have the following forms:

$$\mathbf{P} = \begin{bmatrix} 4 & -1 & 0 & & & \\ -3 & 4 & -1 & 0 & & \\ 0 & -3 & 4 & -1 & & \\ & 0 & \cdots & \cdots & \cdots & 0 \\ & & & -3 & 4 & -1 \\ & & & 0 & -3 & 4 \end{bmatrix} \qquad \mathbf{M}_1 = \begin{bmatrix} 2 & -1 & & & \\ & 2 & -1 & & \\ & & \cdots & \cdots & \\ & & & 2 & -1 \\ & & & & 2 \end{bmatrix}$$

$$\mathbf{M}_0 = \begin{bmatrix} 1 & & & & & & \\ & 0 & & & & & \\ & & 1 & & & & \\ & & & 0 & & & \\ & & & & \cdots & & \\ & & & & & 1 & \\ & & & & & & 0 \end{bmatrix} \qquad \mathbf{N}_0 = \begin{bmatrix} 0 & & & & & & \\ & 1 & & & & & \\ & & 0 & & & & \\ & & & 1 & & & \\ & & & & \cdots & & \\ & & & & & 0 & \\ & & & & & & 1 \end{bmatrix} \qquad \mathbf{N}_1 = \begin{bmatrix} 2 & & & & \\ 1 & 2 & & & \\ & & \cdots & & \\ & & 1 & 2 & \\ & & & 1 & 2 \end{bmatrix}$$

For the matrix **A**, we set its dimension to be 3000 ($m = 1000$) and compute the corresponding eigenvalues and engenvectors. The integration of the time interval is 0.3 sec and the whole interval has been split into 30 windows. The error tolerance is set to be 10^{-8}, we give an initial vector $\mathbf{x}_0 = [1, 0, 1, 0, \ldots, 1, 0]^T$ and run our algorithm on a single processor to get one set of the complex eigenvalues and corresponding eigenvectors, CPU time consumed is t_s . Then we apply parallel WR algorithms on the multi-processors with the same sets of initial values for the solutions, the parallel CPU running time is t_p . We define speedup as the ratio of t_s to t_p , then the speedup curve of parallel computation over 2 processors, 4 processors, 6 processors and 8 processors are shown in Figure 2.

As illustrated in Figure2, our algorithm is highly parallelized. The speedup of our parallel algorithm shows a fabulous linear quality, the CPU time consumed in the serial part of the program is so small in comparison with the parallel parts such that it can almost be negligible. We also observe that the communication overhead of parallel processing for the example is rather low. When we run the program on eight processors, the speedup of the parallel system is 7.465, thus the percentage of communication time to the total computation time is less than 6%. In view of the linear speedup and low communication overhead, the parallel implementation is cost-effective for large applications.

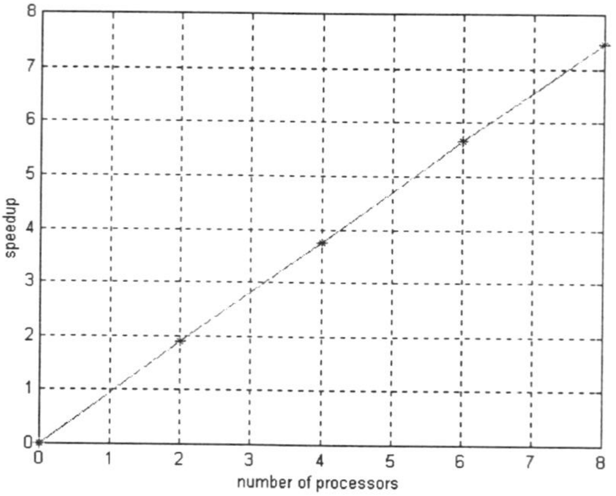

Figure 2. The speedup trend of our parallel WR algorithmover different numbers of processors

6 Conclusion

We have presented a complete form of nonlinear dynamic equations by optimization technique to determine all eigenvalues and eigenvectors of general complex matrices in engineering fields. The convergence of transient solutions is ensured by our theorem. We proposed a heuristic method that applying WR in circuit simulation to compute the cubic dynamic equations. The approach reported here, which differs from the most existing ones and has a potential application in solving general eigenvalue problems associated with large systems, has been successfully implemented for parallel processing. Results of the numerical example have illustrated that our Parallel WR algorithm is accurate and efficient for large size of complex matrices.

7 Acknowledgement

This research was supported by City University of Hong Kong and Hong Kong Research Grants Council Project No. 9040268.

References

1. A. Cichocki and R. Unbehauen, "Neural networks for computing eigenvalues and eigenvectors", Biological Cybernetics, vol. 68 (1992) pp. 155-164.
2. Y. L. Jiang, R. M. M. Chen, and Z. L. Huang, "A parallel approach for computing complex eigenvalue problems", accepted for publication in IEICE Transactions on Fundamentals of Electronics, Communications and Computer Science.
3. Y. Saad, "Numerical Methods for Large Eigenvalue Problems", Manchester University Press, New York (1992).
4. E. Lelarasmee, A. Ruehli, and A. L. Sangiovanni-Vincentelli, "The waveform relaxation method for time-domain analysis of large scale integrated circuits", IEEE Trans. on CAD of IC and Systems, vol. 1, no. 3 (July 1982) pp. 131-145.
5. G. D. Gristede, C. A. Zukowski, and A. E. Ruehli, "Measuring error propagation in waveform relaxation algorithms", IEEE Trans. on Circuits and Systems – Part I, vol. 46, no. 3 (March 1999) pp. 337-348.
6. Y. L. Jiang, W. S. Luk, and O. Wing, " Convergence-theoretics of classical and Krylov waveform relaxation methods for differential-algebraic equations", IEICE Transactions on Fundamentals of Electronics, Communications and Computer Sciences, vol. E80-A, no. 10 (October 1996) pp. 1961-1972.
7. H. Zhang, " A note on windowing for the waveform relaxation method", Applied Mathematics and Computation, vol.76, no.1 (1996) pp. 49 - 63.
8. " MPI: A Message-Passing Interface Standard", Message Passing Interface Forum, University of Tennessee (May 1994).

EFFECTIVELY EXPLOITING A PARALLEL ALGORITHM FOR VIRTUAL REALITY SCENE GENERATION

RONALD POSE
School of Computer Science and Software Engineering,
Monash University,
Clayton, Victoria 3168, AUSTRALIA
E-mail: rdp@cs.monash.edu.au

Abstract. Virtual reality and other immersive interactive computer graphics systems are often considered as high performance computer graphics systems without regard to the application itself. Virtual reality systems apply highly parallel graphics rendering engines in an attempt to achieve desired performance. Sadly, even state-of-the-art parallel graphics techniques provide inadequate performance. Exploiting parallel graphics technology is sound but with virtual reality much of the computation performed is valid for a very short time, and then has to be recomputed. The *Priority Rendering* algorithm avoids this problem and allows the effective exploitation of parallel graphics rendering engines.

1 Introduction

Virtual reality and other immersive computer graphics applications use high performance computer graphics rendering engines, often employing parallelism in both hardware and software. Even so, their performance is inadequate for low-latency virtual reality systems. Either motion fluidity or image quality usually has to be sacrificed to maintain real-time interactive performance.

The problem is that to meet desired performance parameters, one has to generate over 60 photo-realistic frames per second, each of over 1,000,000 pixels, and display them on a head-mounted display worn by the user. The system tracks the user s head in real-time to determine the view of the virtual world to show the user. Only then can the graphics rendering be performed. Delays in generating the images are perceived as a lag in response. i.e. the user moves his head and has to wait for the viewed world to catch up. This latency can lead to serious consequences such as motion sickness and disorientation.

Using multiple high performance graphics pipelines is difficult since the large graphics pipeline delays themselves may be noticeable. Parallelism has to be applied effectively to solve the problem; a brute force graphics approach is insufficient. The problem is such that it is possible to overload the available graphics performance, so the aim must be to provide the best possible user experience, given limited computational resources.

We first outline the conventional approach. Then show how this does not perform so well in virtual reality applications. A new way of thinking about the original problem leads to a different approach. The key is to consider the system as a whole rather than treat it as just another high performance computer graphics system. Our new conceptual approach is called *Delayed Viewport Mapping* and its realization in the form of an *Address Recalculation Pipeline* (ARP) involves a great deal of parallelism in its implementation [1]. A technique of exploiting the new architecture has also been developed [2] that can also have a parallel implementation involving both hardware and software. This technique, *Priority Rendering*, effectively exploits parallel rendering in the virtual reality domain, and is described here with an emphasis on parallelism in its implementation.

2 Conventional approach to high performance computer graphics

Computer graphics involves much computation. With so many steps involved there is an obvious case for some kind of pipelining. Both software and hardware pipelining is exploited in high performance graphics systems.

One approach is to subdivide the job based on objects in the virtual environment. i.e. use separate graphics rendering engines in parallel for each graphical object or groups of objects. Such a technique has been used successfully in animation. Various objects and background scenes are drawn separately on transparencies and can then be overlaid to give the desired composite scene. Apart from the possibilities for parallel creation of the images with this technique, it is also possible to move and animate objects within a scene without redrawing the whole scene. This is called image composition. In its simplest form the images not only have X and Y screen coordinates, but also depth, Z coordinates associated with each pixel. When combining images the system will choose the pixel at a particular screen coordinate with the lowest Z value, i.e. the one closest to the viewer. Apart from having parallelism within the graphics renderer, we can also run many renderers in parallel using image composition to form the final viewable image, and reduce the amount of graphics actually rendered by re-using previously rendered background scenes etc.

This appears to be attractive for virtual reality. The background scene is often fairly static; changes are restricted to a few objects which are the current focus of attention. However this assumes that the effective camera angle is fixed, or in the virtual reality case, that the viewer s viewpoint is fixed. That is not the case.

If the user moves his head, the virtual environment has not changed in itself, but what the viewer expects to see is now different. Even a slight change of head orientation invalidates every pixel in the display. So virtual reality systems using conventional, albeit parallel graphics techniques, end up having to regenerate all the graphics. Note even the background appearance has changed and is recalculated.

Figure 1 depicts a conventional computer graphics system as might be employed for virtual reality. It comprises two distinct processes communicating via the display buffer. On the left is the computer graphics software and hardware. The output of which is an image composed of pixels that are placed in the display buffer. On the right is a conventional raster display that reads pixel values from the display buffer and sends them to the display device. The raster display section runs at a constant speed, typically between 60 and 100 Hz. display refresh rate. On the other hand, the computer graphics section typically runs slower with its performance dependent on the complexity of the graphics it is rendering. It is not unusual to find high performance virtual reality systems which struggle to get beyond 10 frames per second from their graphics renderers.

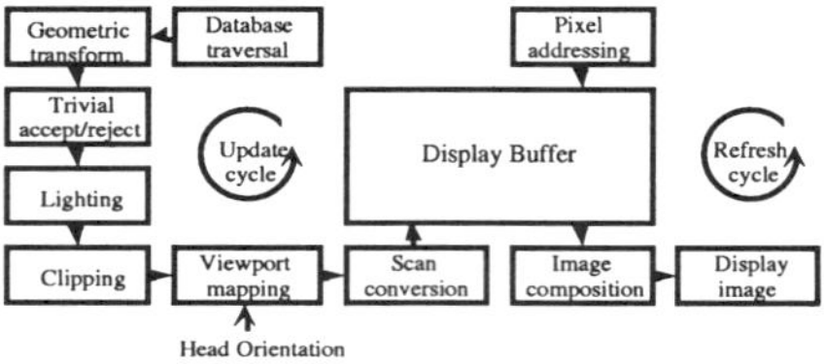

Figure 1. Conventional Virtual Reality Display Architecture

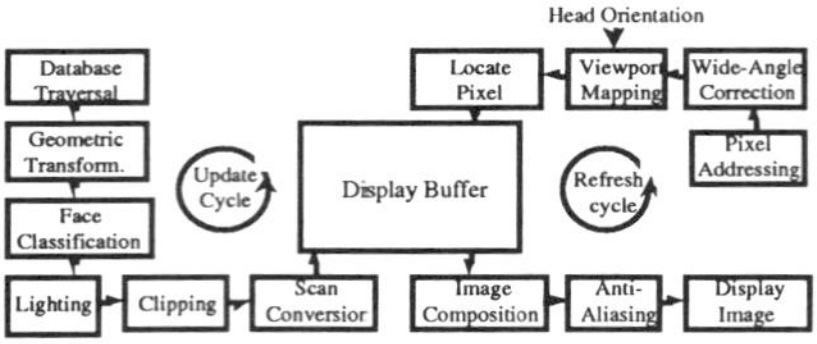

Figure 2. Delayed Viewport Mapping using an Address Recalculation Pipeline

Image composition can also be used, albeit not effectively, allowing an obvious form of parallelism. Multiple graphics renderers (the left side of figure 1) combine their outputs before feeding the resulting image into the display buffer.

3 Re-examining the virtual reality problem

Our difficulties with virtual reality applications have a cause clearly indicated in figure 1. The user s head orientation is input to the graphics update cycle. Thus every change in user head orientation, no matter how slight, causes all the graphics in all graphics rendering engines, to be recalculated. This negates the advantages of image composition where only those images that have changed will be re-rendered.

The virtual world may be completely static, yet all the graphics are being re-rendered. What is required is a representation in which a static virtual world has a static computer graphics analogue that doesn t need continual re-rendering.

Imagine the world is a room with four walls, floor and ceiling made of glass through which you see the world beyond. A static virtual world is indistinguishable from one painted onto the walls, floor and ceiling.

Here is a model for a graphics system that meets our requirements. Instead of a screen in front of the user s eyes, we place the viewer in a room with graphics displays completely surrounding him. That approach is taken in virtual reality *CAVEs*. We adapt that to head-mounted displays by selecting the parts of the image surrounding the user that should be displayed in front of his eyes. We call this technique *Delayed Viewport Mapping*, since we have delayed selecting the viewer s viewpoint until after graphics has already been rendered. We have also devised a highly parallel hardware implementation called an *Address Recalculation Pipeline* (ARP)[3]. The parallelism in the ARP has also been investigated [1].

4 The Address Recalculation Pipeline

The advantages obtained through the use of *Delayed Viewport Mapping* are not free. The easiest way to picture the ARP s operation is to begin with the viewer s eyes and trace a path through to the encapsulating display memory that mimics the glass room we imagined earlier.

Between the viewer and the head-mounted display is a viewing lens with some distorting characteristics that spread the image so as to cover the user s full field of view. We draw a vector from the eye through a pixel of the display device, have it bent to mimic the lens distortion, and finally have it intersect the encapsulating cubic display memory surface. That point of intersection identifies the pixel in the display memory that really should be on the display device at that point. Given the viewing lens is fixed, the bending of the vectors can be described by a lookup-table. The information from the head tracker takes the form of a rotation matrix by which we can multiply the vector, thus rotating it to the viewer s current orientation.

The ARP is implemented as a pipeline with the first stage being the lens distortion correction lookup-table. The second stage doing matrix multiplication to re-orient the vector so it is aligned with the user s current viewpoint. The third stage determines the intersection with the encapsulating display surface, locating the required pixel. Note the output of the third stage is an address in the display memory, hence the name *Address Recalculation Pipeline.*

With a display device with over a million pixels and a refresh rate around 100 Hz, the ARP second stage is doing over 100,000,000 matrix multiplications per second. The third stage involves divisions that are expensive computationally.

The new system using an ARP is depicted in figure 2. The ARP is in the top right of the figure. Note the head orientation feeds into the ARP section, not into the graphics rendering section on the left of the figure. The graphics is now independent of the viewing orientation of the user. With viewport independence we now re-introduce image composition. If parts of the virtual world appear to change, only those graphics renderers handling the changing objects are invoked. Image composition hardware merges these objects with the existing static scenery.

In our implementation the parallel rendering engines each have their own display memory. i.e. the left hand side of figure 2 is replicated. A single ARP drives all the display buffers. The display buffer outputs go through image composition hardware pipeline stages, and an image smoothing stage, before the final image is displayed. The real picture is somewhat more complex [3,4].

The ARP is easily implemented with cheap, parallel hardware. Such computation is easier than complex graphics calculations. It does require hardware since the volume of computation would severely tax a software implementation.

5 The problem of translational movement

Translational movement of the user within the virtual environment results in relative movement between the user and the objects in the virtual world that is observable to the user. The user's own movement has the most dramatic effect, since it affects the display of even static parts of the virtual world.

When translating, objects in the world appear to move relative to you. Close objects appear to move more than distant ones. Very distant objects may not appear to move at all. Thus we have to concentrate especially on close objects.

Actually what is important is not the distance of the object from the user, but rather how long its graphics image will be valid. In the static situation this corresponds closely to the distance of the object from the user and its relative speed.

6 Priority Rendering

A scheme has been devised which bases the allocation of objects to display memories and hence to graphics rendering engines based on the expected validity times of their images. We call this *Priority Rendering*, since it in effect produces a prioritized list of objects in the order in which they should have their graphics images recomputed in order to maintain the illusion of virtual reality without the serious problems we set out to solve [2,5]. It not only produces a prioritized list, but indicates the rate at which the various objects should have their images updated.

Because the allocation to display memories is no longer based on depth within the scene, the hardware must maintain Z-values for each pixel and do image composition based on individual pixels depths.

This method requires that some approximation of the validity time of objects images be obtained. It need not and cannot be exact since it is impossible to predict if the user will move within the virtual world or whether some object in the virtual world will change or move, but it should be reasonably close. If one gets it wrong and under-estimates the validity time of an object s image, then it will end up being recomputed more frequently than required, wasting some of our processing capacity, but not visible by the user. On the other hand if one over-estimates the object s validity time, it will not be updated as often as it needs and will appear slightly out of date. However unlike traditional approaches to virtual reality, the virtual world as a whole is kept up to date, with perhaps a few objects not quite keeping up.

There is not space in this paper to provide the detailed analysis of *Priority Rendering* and its performance in various situations. We have found that we do an order of magnitude less graphics computing than a conventional system in dealing with translational movements, while still presenting identical images to the user. Human factors can also be considered [6]. Humans cannot translate or rotate at infinite speed. Applying human parameters we can reduce the rendering load by more than another factor of two. With that incorporated we are well over an order of magnitude better than a conventional system in handling translation in the virtual world. With our system we also get rotations for free in terms of graphics re-calculations, whereas in a conventional system rotations are the biggest computational load. So in effect we get identical images with several orders of magnitude less graphics computation, but requiring an ARP and its computation.

7 Conclusion

Using conventional graphics for virtual reality, parallelism can be employed, but not effectively. With *Priority Rendering*, and its *Address Recalculation Pipeline*, we have shown how to exploit effectively, parallel graphics rendering hardware.

The results are dramatic, with overall performance orders of magnitude better than the traditional approach. *Delayed Viewport Mapping* has enabled image composition to be used with effectively superlinear speedup.

The performance is due not to parallel graphics itself, but due to a radical new approach to the problem which transforms it into one requiring less computer graphics. Its new form employs parallel hardware in the form of an ARP and a new method of organizing the graphics computation, *Priority Rendering*, ideally suited to efficient parallel implementation

Acknowledgements

Matthew Regan was responsible for much of this system. The prototype was funded by an Australian Research Council small research grant. Patenting of this technology was supported by a Monash Research Fund grant

References

1. Pose, Ronald (2000) Parallelism in a Computer Architecture to Support Orientation Changes in Virtual Reality and Other Immersive Interactive Graphics Systems. In Proc. PART-2000, Sydney, Australia, November 2000.
2. Regan, Matthew and Pose, Ronald (1994) Priority Rendering with a Virtual Reality Address Recalculation Pipeline. Proceedings of SIGGRAPH 94. In Computer Graphics, Annual Conference Series 1994. pp. 155-162.
3. Regan, Matthew and Pose, Ronald (1993) An Interactive Graphics Display Architecture. Proceedings of IEEE Virtual Reality Annual International Symposium. (18-22 September 1993, Seattle USA), pp. 293-299.
4. Regan, Matthew and Pose, Ronald (1994) Display Memory Access Issues and Anti-Aliasing with a Virtual Reality Address Recalculation Pipeline. Proceedings of the 9th Eurographics Workshop on Graphics Hardware, SINTEF, Oslo, Norway, Sept. 12-13, 1994, pp. 23-27.
5. Pose, Ronald and Regan, Matthew (1998) Updating Graphical Objects Based on Object Validity Periods, US Patent Application No. 847,567, Replaces US Patent Application No. 307,330, Filed 24 April 1997, US Patent Number 5,841,439, Granted 24 November 1998.
6. Pose, Ronald and Regan, Matthew (1994) Techniques for Reducing Virtual Reality Latency with Architectural Support and Consideration of Human Factors. In Multimedia, Hypermedia & Virtual Reality, LNCS 1077 Springer-Verlag, 1996.

PARALLEL BIOMETRICS COMPUTING IN A DISTRIBUTED ENVIRONMENT WITH APPLICATIONS TO PERSONAL IDENTIFICATION FOR NETWORK SECURITY

J. YOU[1,2], J. CAO[1] and D. ZHANG[1]
[1]*Department of Computing, The Hong Kong Polytechnic University Kowloon, Hong Kong*
E-mail: {csyjia, csjcao, csdzhang}@comp.polyu.edu.hk
[2]*School of Compiting and Information Technology Griffith University, Nathan Campus, Brisbane, QLD, Australia 4111*
E-mail: you@cit.gu.edu.au

This paper presents a new approach to provide efficient and effective personal identification and verification for the security of network access via parallel biometrics computing in a distributed environment. To overcome the limitations of the current existing password-based authentication services on the Internet, we apply biometrics computing technology to achieve high performance by integrating multiple personal features including signature, finger-prints, palm-prints and hand geometry in a hierarchical structure for fast and reliable identity verification and identification. To increase the speed and flexibility of the process, we use mobile agents as the steering tool for parallel processing in a distributed environment, which includes hierarchical biometric feature representation, multiple feature integration, dynamic biometric data indexing and flexible search. The experimental results demonstrate the feasibility and potential of the proposed method.

1 Introduction

Technology advances have led to the very rapid growth in Internet applications. E-commerce which is based on Internet and its related technologies and services has been showing its revolutionary impact on commercial transactions worldwide. The wide E-commerce applications require high security with reliable identification and verification of users who access to the services. The process of identifying and/or verifying a user's identity is known as authentication. However, the traditional security measures such as passwords, PIN (Personal Identification Number) and ID cards hardly satisfy the high security requirements because the use of passwords, PINs and ID cards are very insecure – they can be lost, stolen, forged or forgotten. More importantly, the password-based methods would become powerless on computer networks, especially the Internet, where attackers can monitor network traffic and intercept passwords or PINs. Therefore, there is an urgent need to authenticate individuals in various domains in today's automated, geographically mobile, increasingly electronically wired information society [2].

Biometric technology provides a totally new and yet effective solution to effective authentication, which would change the conventional security and access control systems by recognising individuals based on their unique, reliable and stable biological or behavioral characteristics, such as fingerprints, palmprints, iris patterns, facial features, speech patterns and handwriting styles. This new security technique overcomes many of the limitations of the traditional automatic personal identification technologies [3].

How to achieve high performance for personal identification from a large collection of biometric data remains a challenging task. In general, the design of such an automated biometric system involves biometric data acquisition, data representation, feature extraction, matching, classification and evaluation. Considering the reliability and convenience of biometric data collection from users, four biometric features, *i.e.*. signature, fingerprints, palm-prints and hand geometry are used in our proposed system.

This paper is organised in the following sections to present a platform-independent mobile agent as tool to support hierarchical biometric feature representation, dynamic biometric data indexing and flexible search for personal identification in a distributed environment . Section 2 highlights a hierarchical scheme for multiple biometrics feature representation and integration. The use of platform-independent mobile agent for parallel biometrics computing is briefly described in Section 3. Section 4 presents a case study of on-line identity verification by palmprint image matching. Finally, the conclusion is presented in Section 6.

2 Multiple Biometrics Feature Representation and Integration

How to represent an image by its biometric features is the first key issue in biometric-based identification and verification. It is unreasonable to expect that the image database retrieval should involve only a single attribute at a time. In the visual domain, many low-level attributes of the picture conspire to generate the rich image content. Thus many attributes need to be considered simultaneously for effective identification and verification. However, it is possible to demonstrate that the system performance does not always improve by using a larger number of features, and by adding features which lack discriminatory power and highly correlated. This section describes a hierarchical scheme for multiple feature representation and integration based on wavelet transforms.

2.1 Wavelet Based Multiple Feature Representation

In contrast to the existing approaches which extract each biometric feature individually, we introduce a hierarchical scheme for multiple biometrics feature representation and integration. Initially, we categorize biometric features into three classes based on their nature, i.e., texture feature, shape feature and frequency feature. For example, texture feature class will include fingerprints, palm-prints, tongue texture, iris patterns, *etc.* while the shape feature class will contain features such as facial feature, retina and hand geometry, and handwriting. Some features such as speech and texture will be also analyzed in frequency domain, which will belong to frequency feature class. Then we use a wavelet-based scheme to combine different feature classes based on their wavelet coefficients. In order to capture features at different scales and orientations, we use a wavelet filter bank to decompose an image into different de-correlated sub-bands for feature measures.

2.2 Multiple Feature Integration and Similarity Measures

The second key issue in biometrics identification and verification is the measure of feature similarities. Verification requires the person to be verified to be claim to an identity. Therefore, the system is expected to be able to directly match the person's characteristics against the characteristics related to the person's code. Identification requires further processing, where the system must match the characteristics of the individual to be identified against the whole set of characteristics stored in the database. We propose to combine image feature extraction and representation techniques in *Image Processing (IP)* with the term weighting and relevance feedback techniques in Information Retrieval (IR) for effective biometrics verification and identification.

3 Personal Identification by Hierarchical Biometric Feature Matching

The third key issue in biometrics-based verification and identification is feature matching which is concerned with verifying and identifying biometrics features which best match a query sample provided by a user. In contrast to the current approaches which often use fixed matching criteria to select candidates [5], we propose selective matching criteria associated with user's query for flexible searching. We propose a guided search procedure from coarse level to fine level for fast processing.

4 Parallel Implementation

Parallel computation has been used successfully in many areas of computer science to speed up the computation required to solve a problem. In the field of image processing and computer vision this is especially appropriate since it appears that the biological model for vision is a parallel model. In contrast to the conventional parallel implementation where either the dedicated hardware or the software are required, the parallel implementation of our parallel biometrics computing is carried out in a distributed computing environment. Three software tools are used for comparison – PVM (Parallel Virtual Machine), DSM (Distributed Shared Memory) and Mobile Agents.

PVM is viewed as a general and flexible parallel computing resource which enables the implementation of parallel processing on loosely coupled network. Such a network contains various computers as processing elements and supports a message passing model for communication between the processing elements. In our initial test, a four node PVM network, including 4 SPARC ELC stations, is used for the parallel implementation of our hierarchical matching scheme.

TreadMarks is a useful software which turns an existing network of workstations into a powerful shared-memory parallel computer for high performance.

Mobile agents are programs, typically written in a safe language, such as, TCL and Telescript, which may be dispatched from a client computer and transported to a remote server computer for execution. As an emerge paradigm for distributed computing, mobile agents can provide all functions supported by traditional client-server model.

5 Fast Palmprint Verification – A Case Study

Palmprint is referred to principal lines, wrinkles and ridges on the palm. Like fingerprints, palmprint has been used as a powerful means in law enforcement for criminal identification because of its stability and uniqueness. A key issue in palmprint identification involves the search for the best matching of the test sample from input and the templates in the palmprint database. Unlike the existing techniques, we propose a dynamic selection scheme to facilitate the coarse-to-fine palmprint pattern matching by combining global and local palmprint features in a hierarchical fashion. The global texture energy (GTE) is introduced to represent the global palmprint feature, which is characterized with high convergence of inner-palm similarities and good dispersion of inter-palm discrimination. Such a global feature is used to guide the dynamic selection of a small set of similar candidates from the database at coarse level for further matching. Interesting points are used as local feature points and the final identification at fine level is carried out by interesting point based image matching.

The parallel implementation for the hierarchical biometric feature extraction is carried out in two stages. At stage one, the global palmprint features are extracted at coarse level and candidate samples are selected for further processing. At stage 2, the regional palmprint features are detected and a hierarchical image matching is performed for the final retrieval output. Fig. 1 illustrates the multi-level extraction of palmprint features. Fig. 1(a) shows a sample of palmprint, Fig. 1(b) delineates the boundary of a palm as a global boundar feature, Fig. 1(c) detects global principal lines and Fig. 1(d) details the regional palmprint texture features for local feature representation at fine level.

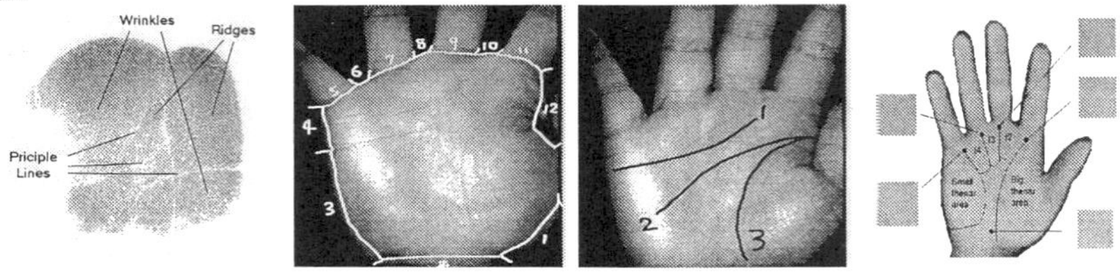

(a) (b) (c) (d)

Fig. 1. Hierarchical feature extraction

The advantages and potentials of a general distributed shared memory system for parallel image processing is demonstrated by the performance comparison listed in Table 1, where different numbers of processes were invoked by means of both PVM and DSM on the 512*512 size image. The parallel performance improvement is measured by the following ratio:

$$\gamma = \frac{T_p}{T_s}$$

where T_s refers to the sequential execution time and T_p refers to the parallel execution time. It is clear that DSM increase the speed better due to its less communication overheads. It is expected that the overall performance will be further improved by introducing dynamic task scheduling for parallelism.

Table 1: The performance comparison of DSM and PVM

number of processes	execution time (DSM)	execution time (PVM)
1	1.45 sec.	1.77 sec.
2	0.80 sec.	1.41 sec.
4	0.52 sec.	1.17 sec.
8	0.48 sec.	1.13 sec
16	0.22 sec.	0.27 sec
32	0.12 sec.	0.27 sec.

6 Conclusion

Biometric technology provides an alternative and yet effective solution to reliable authentication by recognising individuals based on their unique, reliable and stable biological or behavioural characteristics, which overcomes many of the limitations of the traditional automatic personal identification technologies. The use of wavelet transform provides a general scheme for the integration of multiple biometrics features to achieve high performance. The parallel implementation in a distributed computing environment reduce the execution time for real-time applications. Our preliminary experimental results demonstrate the effectiveness and efficiency of the proposed parallel biometrics computing approach to personal identification.

References

1. W.Li and D.G. Messerschmitt, " Mobile Agent-based Network Signaling for Resource Netotiations" Workshop on Resource Allocation Problem in Multimedia Systems, IEEE Real-time Systems Symposium, 1996, Washington DC..
2. A. Jain, R. Bolle and S. Pankanti, *Biometrics: Personal Identification in Networked Society*, Kluwer Academic Publishers, 1998.
3. W. Shen, M. Surette and R. Khanna, "Evaluation of automated biometrics-based identification and verification systems," *Proceedings of the IEEE*, vol. 85, no. 9, 1997, pp. 1464-1478.
4. S. Mallat, *A Wavelet Tour of Signal Processing*, Academic Press, San Diego, CA, 1998.
5. T.S. Huang, S. Mehrotra, and K. Ramchandran, "Multimedia analysis and retrieval system (MARS) project", *Proc. of 33rd Annual Clinic on Library Application of Data Processing - Digital Image Access and Retrieval*, 1996
6. G. Salton and M.J. McGill, *Introduction to Modern Information Retrieval*, McGraw-Hill Book Company, 1983.
7. P. Baltscheffsky and P. Anderson, The palmprint project: Automatic identity verification by hand geometry, *Proc. 1986 International Carnahan Conference on Security Technology*, Gothenburg, Sweden, 229-234 (1986).
   5*IEEE Trans. Patt. Anal. Machine Intell.* **10**, 849-865 (1988).
8. Al Geist, A. Beguelin, J. Dongarra, W. Jiang, R. Manchek and V. Sunderam, *PVM: Parallel Virtual Machine, A User's Guide and Tutorial forNetwork Computing*, MIT Press, Cambridge, MA, 1994.

Chapter 8
Parallel Processing on Web-Based Systems and Applications

GUCHA: INTERNET-BASED PARALLEL COMPUTING USING JAVA

L. F. LAU, A. L. ANANDA, G. TAN, W. F. WONG
School of Computing
National University of Singapore
3 Science Drive 2, Singapore 117543
{laulf, ananda, gtan, wongwf}@comp.nus.edu.sg

The +Gucha project is about harnessing the immense computational resource available in the Internet for parallel processing. In this paper, requirements and goals of an effective parallel computing system in the Internet environment are identified. These serve as the blueprint for the development of the Gucha system. Its infrastructure and features are discussed. Lastly, experimental results based on the running of several parallel applications in the Gucha environment are presented.

1. Introduction

The exponential growth of Internet in recent years has linked tens of millions of computers together. The combined computational power of even a small fraction of this pool of machines, which are idle most of the time, is many times more than what a central parallel supercomputer can offer. In fact, there have been many successful attempts to solve complicated mathematics and scientific problems by tapping this gigantic computational resource. A notable recent attempt would of course be the cracking of the 56-bit DES using "tens of thousands" of Internet-linked computers in 39 days [5]. Another commendable effort is the SETI project [19], which has made use of 1.3 million computers worldwide for intensive data processing in its search for extraterrestrial intelligence.

However, harnessing the resources of Internet-based computers for parallel computing, is by no means an easy task. It introduces new difficulties and problems that have never been addressed by parallel computing in LAN (local area network) environment.

Gucha is developed to provide Internet-based parallel computing with the objective of addressing the difficulties that such a computing environment might impose. In particular, the project aims to create an infrastructure to support parallel computations in an Internet-based environment and provide a programming interface that could enable programmers to develop parallel applications with ease.

2. Project Gucha: Design and Implementation

Gucha is a 100% pure Java implementation [6] and not based on native methods mechanism. Java is adopted in the implementation of Gucha for its cross-platform, secure, object-oriented and network-centric features. Detailed discussions of Java are beyond the scope of this paper but can be found in [9,10,17,25]. Gucha is a tool

+ Gucha in Sanskrit language means cluster.

for Internet-based parallel computing. To achieve this, the following factors have to be addressed:

2.1.1 Ease of Use

This involves two groups of users – the programmers who develop the parallel applications and the volunteers who contribute their machines for the computations. From a programmer's perspective, the programming interface must be flexible and simple. Developing parallel applications should be done with as much ease as sequential applications. In Gucha, this is achieved with the provision of features-rich networking APIs that will shield the programmer from the complexity of the underlying network communications. The collection of heterogeneous machines in the network would appear to him as a single high-performance parallel machine.

From a volunteer's perspective, contributing his machines to participate in computations should be simple and hassle-free. No technical knowledge of the program to be run should be required on his part. In Gucha, users are simply required to run a GUI-based program at their machines to join the pool of volunteers.

With Java's code mobility, Gucha also supports dynamic loading of applications from the network to be executed at the volunteers' machines. The loading and execution of applications are transparent to the volunteers. It is very much like the dynamic loading and execution of applets, but without the limitations that it imposed [9].

2.1.2 Heterogeneity and Portability

The Internet is a collection of machines of heterogeneous platforms and architectures. Thus, it will be an uphill task for the programmer to write codes for different systems and distribute the compiled binaries to the systems. By virtue of being a 100% pure Java implementation, Gucha is architectural neutral and portable to most platforms.

2.1.3 Security

This involves two aspects. Firstly, from a volunteer's perspective, by contributing his machine in a computation, he must have the assurance that it will be protected against malicious attacks (e.g. virus attack). In a COW setup, this is easily achievable by maintaining users access rights and accounts, so that the network is available only to trusted users. Using such an approach, security of volunteer's machine is enforced to a certain extent, but the setting up of such a computing environment would be tedious and introduces problems, such as scalability. In Gucha, no assumptions of access privileges of machines participating in computations and their underlying file system are made. Instead, protection of volunteers' machines can be enforced with Java's tight security model.

The second aspect involves computational security. Besides protecting volunteers, the environment must also ensure that the computation itself is secure from malicious attacks from volunteers. Preventing volunteers from *spying* on computations, which may be confidential, is also another concern. In Gucha, enforcing secure computations is a prime concern. To achieve this, cryptographic and authentication mechanisms for network communications among machines in the system are implemented. This is achievable through the use of APIs for cryptographic operations provided by Java Cryptography Architecture (JCA) [20,21,22,23].

2.1.4 Fault Tolerance

An Internet-based computing environment is governed by the following characteristics:

- Uncertain availability of machines. Machines join and leave a computation at the whim of volunteers. There is no direct control as to when a volunteer should join a computation and how long he should remain committed to it.
- Unpredictable network delay. The load of the Internet traffic and faulty network links are the major contributing factors.
- Unreliability of volunteers. Based on what we have discussed on security, the reliability of the computed results from volunteers' machines is questionable.

Gucha is designed to recover from unintentional faults caused by the first two characteristics. It polls machines in the system at regular interval to check whether they are still "alive". In the event that a volunteer leaves the system abruptly, Gucha is able to off-load the failed computation to another machine such that the overall computed results would not be affected.

Intentional faults caused by the third characteristic are harder to tackle. Known techniques, such as *replication* and *spot-checking* [15], to detect and recover from these faults are inefficient and unreliable. In Gucha, no solution is offered to counter this problem yet. Instead, through tight security enforcement, occurrences of such faults caused by rogue volunteers are minimized, if not avoided.

2.1.5 Network Load Balancing

Load balancing usually refers to the distribution of workload evenly among participating machines. However, in the Internet context, this is insufficient and the traffic load of network links should also be taken into account. A system with support for network load balancing should be able to detect congested network links and avoid assigning computations to machines reachable by those links, whenever possible. To achieve this, in Gucha, all the volunteers in the system are polled at regular intervals to measure the network transfer delays. We called this technique *bandwidth probing*. During task placement, information gathered from bandwidth probing is used to decide which volunteer a task should be allocated to.

2.1.6 Scalability

To tap the computational resources of tens of thousands of machine in the Internet for parallel computing effectively, the scalability of the system is an important issue. The communication architecture supported by the system, is a deciding factor in its scalability. In Gucha, for scalability reason, the architecture adopted is a hybrid between the centralized and decentralized one. The main benefits of this architecture are its abilities to reduce message traffic exchanges (as compared to a decentralized design) and improve fault-tolerance (as compared to a centralized design). An illustration of this communication architecture is given in Figure 2.1.

2.1.7 Accountability

In Gucha, an accounting system is put in place. Volunteers contributing their resources will be duly "rewarded" and clients consuming the resources, "billed" accordingly. The architecture of Gucha permits the implementation of this feature to be done easily. It involves the maintaining of databases at centralized locations to capture the contribution and usage of computing resources by entities in the Gucha system.

2.2 Network Communication Architecture

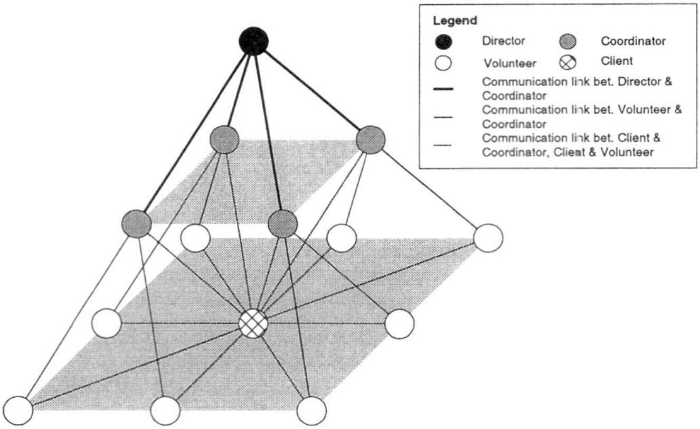

Figure 2.1. Network Communication Architecture of Gucha

The design of the network communication architecture of a computing system will directly, as well as indirectly, affect the implementation of the design goals listed. As shown in Figure 2.1, Gucha adopts hierarchical network communication architecture consisting of four entities: *director, coordinator*, *volunteer* and *client.* To prevent the diagram from getting too complicated, the direct communication links between volunteer and director, and that of client and director, are not shown.

The main function of the director is to provide lookup service for coordinators information in the Gucha system. As the name implies, coordinators serve as the middlemen between volunteers and clients during task distribution. Volunteers are machines that offer their resources for parallel computations. Clients are machines that tap these resources.

2.3 Scenario Walkthrough

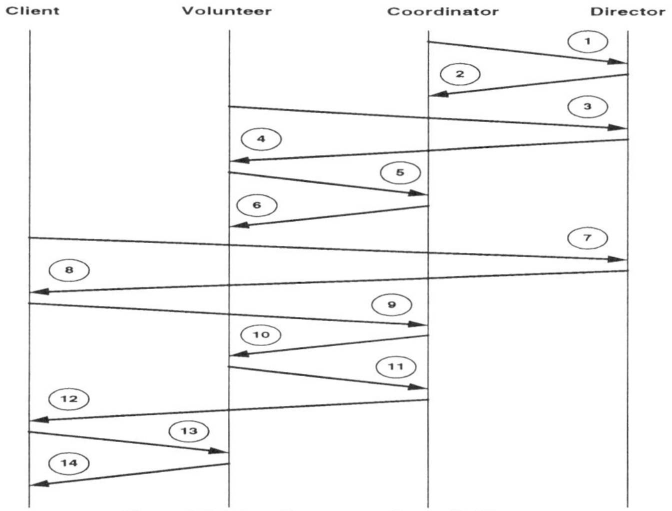

Figure 2.2. Interaction among Gucha Entities

A typical scenario, of how the entities might interact with each other, is shown in Figure 2.2. The sequence of the interactions is as follows:

(1) When a coordinator first started up, it will register with a specified director in the Gucha system. In its registration request to the director, it will supply a password for verification purpose.

(2) On receipt of the registration request, the director will check the information supplied by the coordinator against its database of legitimate coordinators. If it passes the check, it will be added to the director's list of active coordinators.

(3) When a volunteer first started up, it will contact the director for information of the active coordinators in the Gucha system.

(4) The director returns the list of active coordinators that have registered with it.

(5) From the list, the volunteer selects one coordinator, by random, for registration. In its request to the coordinator, the hardware information and lease time for volunteering is supplied.

(6) On successful registration, the coordinator will add the information supplied by the volunteer to its database of registered volunteers. A random number (called the volunteer-id) will be generated, and the volunteer, informed. This id will be used in subsequent communications between the volunteer and the coordinator for identity checking purpose.

(7) When a client first started up, it will contact the director for information of the active coordinators in the Gucha system.

(8) The director returns the list of active coordinators that have registered with it.

(9) The client will contact the first coordinator, in the returned list from director, for volunteers. In its request, it will supply a password for verification purpose and also the number of volunteers needed. If insufficient volunteers are returned, it will contact other coordinators in the network until all the volunteers required are found.

(10) On receipt of the request for volunteers, the coordinator will check the information supplied by the client against its database of legitimate clients. If the client passes the check, the coordinator will select a list of potential volunteers (based on the number of volunteers requested) for allocation to the client. For each of these volunteers, a random number (called the client-id) is generated. The coordinator will then inform every volunteer of its allocation and the client-id to be used during interactions with the client.

(11) The volunteer will acknowledge the receipt of the allocation notice by sending a confirmation reply to the coordinator.

(12) The coordinator will send the list of allocated volunteers and their corresponding client-ids to the client.

(13) With information received from the coordinator, the client will send task placement requests to the volunteers. Information, included in the requests, is the client-ids, arguments and bytecodes of the application to be run.

(14) The volunteer will check whether the client-id supplied by the client matches that given by the coordinator earlier. If they match, the volunteer will "class-load" the bytecodes supplied for task execution. Result of the execution is then sent back to the client.

2.4 Programming Model and Developer Interface

One of the Gucha's objectives is to provide programming interface that can help developers to program parallel applications with as much ease as sequential ones. Figure 2.3 gives an illustration of how simple developing parallel applications in Gucha could be. The APIs called by the developer hide all the implementation details of encryption and decryption of network communications fault tolerance and network load balancing. To the developer, the pool of volunteers in the Gucha system will appear as just one virtual supercomputer.

```
public static void main (String[] args) {
        ....
        // (1) Create the environment
        Gucha_Env env = new Gucha_Env(...);
        ....
        // (2) Generate tasks to TaskPool
        for (int i=0; i<numVolunteers; i++) {
          ....
          tidarray[I] = env.AddToTaskPool(...)
        }
        ....
        // (3) Distribute tasks to volunteers
        env.SendTasks();
        ....
        // (4) Collect computed results
        for (int i=0; i<numVolunteers, i++) {
          ....
          result[i] = env.getResult(tidarray(...);
        }
        ....
        // (5) Stop all unfinished tasks at volunteers
        env.StopTasks();
      }
```

Figure 2.3. Gucha Programming Model

The programming model in Figure 2.3 encompasses the following steps:

(1) **Create the environment.** In the background, the client contacts the director for the available coordinators in the Gucha system. An empty linked list (called the *TaskPool*) is also generated for the storage of tasks that will be generated.

(2) **Generate tasks to *TaskPool*.** The number of tasks generated depends on the number of volunteers specified by the developer for execution of the application. The tasks generated, in the form of arguments for the application, are stored in the *TaskPool*. For each task created, the developer will be issued a *task-id*, which is needed in the retrieval of result at stage (4).

(3) **Distribute tasks to volunteers.** In the background, the client contact the coordinators to get the volunteers needed. It will then transfer the bytecodes of the application and the respective argument to each of the volunteers found by invoking the *TaskPlacer* thread. The client might not be able to get all the volunteers it needs and the existing volunteers allocated might leave the system abruptly without finishing the task allocated. As such, the client will invoke the *VolunteerHunter* thread, which will hunt for new volunteers from the coordinators whenever there is a shortage. It will also invoke the *VolunteerAliveHandler* thread to check, at regular intervals, whether the volunteers allocated with tasks are still alive. Detection of failed volunteers will spin off the whole process of finding new volunteers and transferring of tasks, once allocated to those failed volunteers, to the new volunteers. This recovery mechanism is automatic and transparent to the developers. At this stage, for collecting results back from the volunteers, the client will also invoke the *ResultCollector* thread.

(4) **Collect computed results.** Results computed by the volunteers will be received by the *ResultCollector* thread and stored. The coordinator will also be informed to release allocations of the volunteers held by the client. To retrieve the computed results, the developer will have to supply the necessary *task-ids* issued earlier at stage (2).

(5) **Stop all unfinished tasks at volunteers.** This step is optional as it depends on the application's need. If the developer has acquired the necessary results, it can terminate existing execution of tasks at all volunteers by invoking the *StopTasks()* method. For applications that need to collect back all computed results, such invocation will not be necessary.

2.5 Constraints and Limitations

The design of Gucha can only achieve master-slave style of parallelism. This implies that volunteers participating in the execution a parallel application would not be able to communicate with each other during computation. Consequently, Gucha can only handle applications that can be broken down into non-communicating and independent functional tasks.

Communication between two entities in Gucha system involves encryption of data at the sending party and decryption by the receiving party. In addition, overheads caused by network transfer of data between the parties will also have a negative impact on the overall performance of the application. To offset this impact, the tasks sent to volunteers during task placement should be of large-grained size. This point is substantiated by experimental results in Section 3.

3 Experiments

For the sake of consistency in the measurement of the experimental results, a homogeneous collection of 64 Pentium PCs, running WinNT OS, is used to form the volunteers cluster. To show heterogeneity of the Gucha system, machines of different hardware configurations and OS (UltraSPARC, Solaris 2.7 OS) are chosen to form the director, coordinators and client. All the machines are connected to the network via 100Mbps links. The experiments are conducted when the load of all the machines and the network are low.

3.1 RC5 Cracking

RC5 [24] is fast block cipher that uses a parameterized algorithm with a variable block size, a variable key size and a variable number of rounds. The encryption routine of RC5 consists of three primitive operations: integer addition, bitwise exclusive-or, and variable rotation. The heavy use of data-dependent rotations and the mixture of different operations provide the security of RC5.

For the experiment, a sequential RC5 cracking program [16], for uncovering the 32-bits secret key used to encrypt a message, is ported over to Gucha. The program adopts a "brute force" search on all possible keys until it finds the one that decrypts the message. Time ($\mathbf{T_{seq}}$) needed to run the program on a machine (with same configuration as the volunteers) is measured.

The Gucha-ised version breaks up the key space to search into smaller ones (of equal size) and distribute them to the volunteers so that the search can be performed in parallel. For this experiment, the program is run with different number of volunteers in the network. Time ($\mathbf{T_{dis}}$) is measured from the moment the client creates the Gucha environment to the moment when the secret key is found by one of the volunteers and the result returned to the client. The speedup ($\mathbf{T_{seq}/T_{dis}}$) for each of above experiments is then computed. Result is as shown in Figure 3.1.

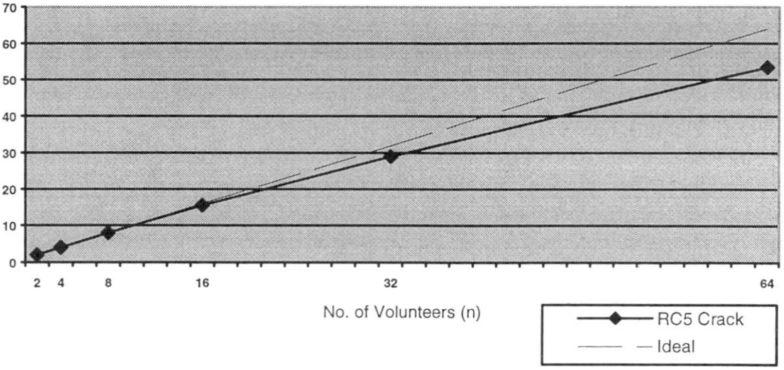

Figure 3.1. RC5 Cracking Experimental Results

3.1.1 Performance

The speedup curve (in Figure 3.1) obtained for Gucha-ised parallel cracking is very close to the ideal situation. Characteristics of this application are as follows:

- Highly computational intensive.
- Low bandwidth requirement. The bulk of the network communications among the entities in the system is only during task distribution and result collection stage. In these stages, the amount of data exchanged is usually not high.

3.2 Ray Tracing

Ray tracing is a method that creates photo-realistic synthetic images from a mathematical description of the scene to be generated. The computations involve millions of floating-point operations and consume large amount of processor time even with scenes of modest complexity. Fortunately, each ray in the algorithm is independent of each other, making ray tracing an ideal candidate for parallel processing.

For the experiment, a sequential Java Ray Tracing program [7] is ported to Gucha. The program is run on a standalone machine to generate a scene of 512x512 pixels.

The Gucha-ised version breaks up the scene to be generated into smaller sub-regions and distribute them to the volunteers so that the generation can be performed in parallel. Time is measured from the moment the client creates the Gucha environment to the moment the client collects back all the computed results from the volunteers. Speedup is then computed. Result is as shown in Figure 3.2

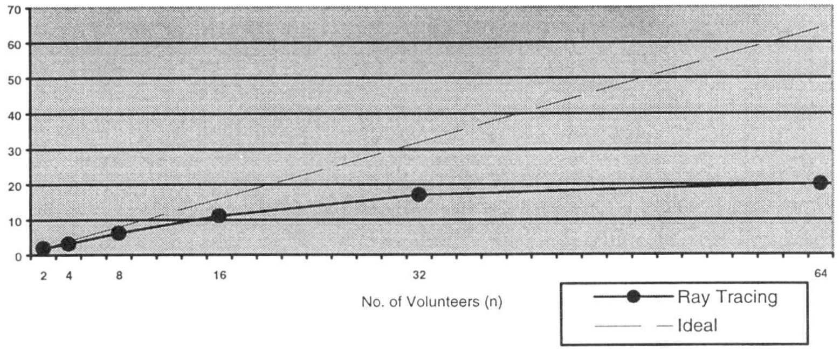

Figure 3.2. Ray Tracing Experimental Results

3.2.1 Performance

Unlike the previous case, from Figure 3.2, the speedup for Gucha-ised Ray Tracing starts to level off with 32 processors. The characteristics associated with this application are:

- Not as computationally intensive as RC5 cracking, basing on the time required for executing the program.
- Low bandwidth requirement. Data exchanges among entities are not too high.

3.3 Matrix Multiplication

The multiplication of two matrices is one of the most basic operations of linear algebra and scientific computing. The algorithm is fundamentally simple and involves a series of multiplications and additions.

For the experiment, the sequential version is run on a standalone machine to perform matrix multiplication on two square matrices of size 128x128.

In our experiment for performing parallel matrix multiplication on the Gucha system, efficiency is not the main objective. Instead, the impact of transferring large amount of data between entities (in particular, client and volunteers) on the Gucha performance is investigated. In the Gucha-ised parallel program, matrix A is broken up into groups of equal-sized rows, basing on the number of volunteers used. During computations, each sub-matrix A of certain rows and the entire matrix B are transferred to a volunteer to generate the results for the same rows in matrix C. Time is measured from the moment the client creates the Gucha environment to the moment the client collects back all the computed results from the volunteers to form matrix C. Speedup is then computed.

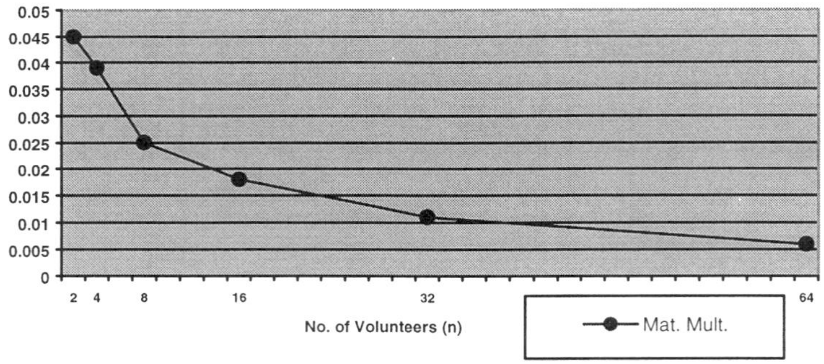

Figure 3.3. Matrix Multiplication Experimental Results

3.3.1 Performance

From Figure 3.3, the performance for Gucha-ised matrix multiplication is very poor. Not only there is no performance improvement, the speedup value decreases with the use of more volunteers. Characteristics of this application are:

- Low computation requirement. The size of the matrices used is not very large.
- High bandwidth requirement. The amount of data for a matrix of size 128x128 to be transferred from the client to a volunteer is already 1 Mbits. Hence, as more volunteers are involved in the computation, the network throughput at the client's end becomes a performance bottleneck.
- Long encryption and decryption time. Communication exchanges among the entities in the system are encrypted. As the amount of data involved is huge, time taken for data encryption and decryption would be significantly high.

From measurements, the overheads involved for transferring data from client to a volunteer and for the volunteer to perform the necessary decryption, during task allocation take up about 25% of the overall processing time.

3.4 Remarks

From the above experiments, the speedup of a Gucha-ised application depends largely on the computation to communication ratio involved. For good speedup results, computational performance gained for executing an application in parallel with a group of volunteers must be able to offset the loss incurred by communications overhead. In general, Gucha is well suited for executing coarse-grained applications with high computation to communication ratio.

4 Conclusions

Despite the dynamic and unpredictable nature of Internet as a computational resource, the potential of utilizing it for metacomputing is still great. Java, with all the features that it can provide as a programming language for network applications, is an attractive tool for developing systems that can harness this resource. Presently, there are a number of Java-based implementations for parallel computing [1,2,3,4,11,12,13,14,18]. However, most of these systems are not designed with Internet-based computing in mind, which makes their deployments in the Internet environment not feasible. Gucha aims to address deficiencies of the existing implementations for Internet-based parallel computations. Its implementation goals are *ease of use*, *heterogeneity*, *portability*, *security*, *fault tolerance*, *load balancing*, *scalability* and *accountability*. It is the only known Internet-based parallel computing system that supports dynamic code execution without the use of applets, network load scheduling and encryption of network communications. Preliminary testing based on the execution of parallel applications developed for the Gucha system has been promising. However, for good speedup results, Gucha should be used in executing coarse-grained applications with high computation to communication ratio.

References

1. A. Baratloo, M. Karaul, Z. Kedem, P. Wyckoff, "Charlotte: Metacomputing on the Web", 9th International Conference on Parallel and Distributed Computing Systems (PDCS), 1996. http://www.cs.ucsb.edu/research/superweb/
2. B. O. Christiansen, P. Cappello, M. F. Ionescu, M. O. Neary, K. E. Schauser, D. Wu, "Javelin: Internet-Based Parallel Computing using Java", http://www.cs.ucsb.edu/research/superweb/home.html
3. Luis F. G. Sarmenta, S. Hirano, S. A. Ward, "Towards Bayanihan: Building an Extensible Framework for Volunteer Computing using Java, http://www.cag.lcs.mit.edu/bayanihan
4. P. A. Gray, V. S. Sunderam, "The IceT Framework for Metacomputing", http://www.mathcs.emory.edu/~gray/abstract7.html
5. Data Security. RSA's Secret-Key Challenge Solved by Distributed Team in Record Time. http://www.rsasecurity.com/news/pr/980226.html

6. Sun Microsystems, "The 100% Pure Java Initiative White Paper", http://java.sun.com/100percent/wp.html
7. M. Armstrong, Y. Ma, "Java Ray Tracer", http://robotics.eecs.berkeley.edu/~mayi/CS184/
8. G. C. Fox, W. Furmanski, "Java for Parallel Computing and as a General Language for Scientific and Engineering Simulation and Modelling", http://www.npac.syr.edu/users/gcf/01/terri/SCCS_793
9. E. R. Harold, "Java Network Programming", O'Reilly & Associates, 1997.
10. M. O'Connell, "New benchmark results show Java ready for prime time of servers", http://www.sunworld.com/swol-07-javabenchmark.html?072098a
11. A. J. Ferrari, "JPVM: Network Parallel Computing in Java", Technical Report CS-97-29, Dept. of Comp. Sci, Unverisity of Virginia, Charlottesville, VA 22903, USA, http://www.cs.virginia.edu/~ajf2j/jpvm.html
12. David A. Thurman, "jPVM: The Java to PVM Interface, December 1996, http://www.isye.gatech.edu/chmsr/jPVM/
13. L. Vanhelsuwe, " Create your own supercomputer with Java", http://www.javaworld.com/jw-01-1997/jw-01-dampp.ibd.html
14. N. Yalamanchilli, W. Cohen, "Communication Performance of Java based Parallel Virtual Machines", ACM 1998 Workshop on Java for High Performance Network Computing, http://www.cs.ucsb.edu/conferences/java98/program.html
15. Luis F. G. Sarmenta, "An Adaptive, Fault-tolerant Implementation of BSP for Java-based Volunteer Computing Systems, http://www.cag.lcs.mit.edu/bayanihan
16. G. Hewgill, "RC5 and Java Toys", http://www.hewgill.com/rc5/index.html
17. P. Rao, "Using Java: Is Java Secure?", http://www.usenix.org/publications/java/usingjava12.htm
18. MPIJ 1.1, http://ccc.cs.byu.edu/OnlineDocs/docs/mpij/MPIJ.html
19. Search for Extraterrestrial Intelligence (SETI) Project, http://seti@home.ssl.berkeley.edu
20. Java Cryptography and Security: JCSI Public Release 3, http://security.dstc.edu.au/projects/java/release3.html
21. T. Sundsted, "In Java we trust", Java World January 1999, http://www.javaworld.com/javaworld/jw-01-1999/jw-01-howto_p.htm
22. "JCA/JCE and the DSTC Security Provider", http://security.dstc.edu.au/projects/java/misc/dstc_provider
23. J. Knudesen, "Java Cryptography", O'Reilly & Associates, 1998
24. R.L. Rivest, "The RC5 encryption algorithm", CryptoBytes, 1(1): 9-11, 1995
25. S.C. Chan, "An Overview of the Java Security", http://home.hkstar.com/~alanchan/papers/javaSecurity/index.html

JDM: BUILDING DISTRIBUTED SYNCHRONIZATION SUPPORT INTO JAVA

JIANNONG CAO[1,2], NICK K.C. CHEUNG[2], ALVIN CHAN[2]
[1]*National Key Lab for Novel Software Technology, Nanjing Univ. Nanjing, China*
[2]*Dept of Computing, Hong Kong Polytechnic Univ., Hung Hom, Kowloon, Hong Kong*

The monitor concept has been widely used in a concurrent programming environment for implicitly ensuring mutual exclusion and explicitly achieving process synchronization. It has also been extended to support high-level distributed programming. In this paper, we present the development and performance evaluation of a distributed monitor construct in Java, called JDM, for programming large-scale distributed systems. The distributed monitor construct is based on a well-know tree-based distributed mutual exclusion algorithm proposed by K. Raymond. To increase scalability of the construct, a two-level system architecture is developed, where the node level controls the access to the system-wide shared resources using Raymond's algorithm and the process level synchronizes local processes based on the local monitor concept. An object-oriented design of the system architecture is presented. Implementation and results of performance evaluation are reported and factors that influence the performance of the construct are discussed.

1 Introduction

The monitor construct [3] has been widely used for implicitly ensuring mutual exclusion and explicitly achieving process synchronization in a centralized multiprogramming environment [6]. Being a structured and flexible language-level programming construct, the monitor has also been extended to support high-level distributed programming. Distributed applications that require sharing resources in a distributed system, such as on-line network games and collaborative work, can be developed with the use of distributed monitors.

This paper presents the design and implementation of a high-performance distributed monitor construct. While relatively easier to implement in a concurrent system with shared memory, the monitor primitives are difficult to implement in a distributed system where processes communicate only through message-passing, First, a distributed mutual exclusion algorithm is needed to implement mutually exclusive access to operations in a distributed monitor. Furthermore, the structure of the distributed monitor mechanism needs to be carefully designed for implementing efficient and scalable monitor operations.

The distributed monitor construct presented in this paper is based on a well-known tree-based distributed mutual exclusion algorithm proposed by Kerry Raymond [8]. Raymond's algorithms is selected mainly because it is relatively

---

[1] The author is currently visiting Nanjing Univ. under the support by the National Key Lab Visitorship Fund from the Education Ministry of P. R. China.

easier to adapt to a large-scale distributed system such as the Internet, which is our target programming environment. According to Raymond's algorithm, a node and processes running on the node are treated as separate, individual entities. This system structure is inefficient in maintaining a scalable network topology as the joining and removing of processes or nodes require the entire spanning tree of the system to be re-structured. In order to increase scalability, a two level system architecture is developed for our distributed monitor construct: the *node level* which controls the access to the system-wide shared resources using Raymond's algorithm, and the *process level* which synchronizes local processes based on the local monitor concept. With this mutual exclusion hierarchy, processes and nodes are now distinguishable, thus possible redundant request messages induced by the original system structure will all be completely eliminated.

A prototype of the distributed monitor construct has been implemented using JAVA2^{TM}. A distributed application is developed with the use of the monitor construct in different settings as a study for evaluating the performance of the mechanism. Results of the property and performance study will be reported and factors that influence the system performance will be discussed.

The rest of this paper is organized as follows: Section 2 provides a review on monitor concept and the related work on distributed monitors. Distributed mutual exclusion algorithms, including Raymond's algorithm that is used to implement the distributed monitors, are also covered. The design and implementation issues of the distributed monitor construct are discussed in Sections 3 and 4 respectively. Section 4 also discusses results of experiments for performance evaluation of the construct. Finally, Section 5 concludes the paper with the description of our future work.

2 Related Work

The monitor construct is an encapsulation of local administrative data and procedures. The data represents the status of the shared resource being controlled by the monitor while the local procedures operate on these local data variables to change the status of the shared resources. At any time, one and only one process is allowed to be inside a monitor. Apart from guaranteeing mutual exclusion, a monitor can contain condition variables for the purpose of process synchronization [3].

In implementing the monitor construct, four primitives are required: the *enter* and *exit* mutual exclusion primitives and the *wait* and *signal* synchronization primitives. The *enter* primitive ensures mutually exclusive access to the requested monitor while the *exit* primitive releases the mutual exclusion of the monitor being accessed to other requesting processes. The *wait* primitive blocks the execution of the calling process and releases the mutual exclusion of the monitor that is on hold to other requesting processes. The *signal* primitive activates one of the processes waiting in either the entry queue or the condition queues of the specified monitor and releases the control of the signaling process to the awaken one.

The monitor construct has been implemented in several concurrent / parallel programming languages for shared-memory system environments [1, 2, 9]. To extend the concept to a distributed system, distributed mutual exclusion algorithms are needed. In the past, many algorithms have been proposed to solve the distributed mutual exclusion problem. These algorithms can be categorized into two main categories: centralized and distributed. In a *centralized algorithm*, one node in the network is designated as the control node that controls access to all shared objects. Centralized algorithms are simple and easy to implement. However, the control node may become the performance bottleneck in a distributed system. It can also be the single point of failure once the control node breaks down. In a *fully distributed algorithm*, all nodes have an equal amount of information and bear equal responsibility for decision making. As all nodes in the network participate in making the final decision, failed nodes in the distributed system will not affect other operational nodes and thus have no effect on the final decision.

Distributed mutual exclusion algorithms can be further classified into two major types: *quorum-based* and *token-based.* Quorum-based algorithms use a majority-voting mechanism for a requesting node to gain mutually exclusive access to a shared resource while token-based algorithms locate a token to a requesting node to achieve the same purpose. Quorum-based algorithms suffer from high communication overhead resulted from getting permissions from other sites to enter the critical section. They are also hard to scale, as they require the knowledge of the total number of nodes in the system. Token-based algorithms are considered more appropriate to be used to implement distributed monitors.

Two well known token-based distributed mutual exclusion algorithms are the one proposed by Suzuki and Kasami [7] and the tree-based algorithm proposed by Raymond [8]. Suzuki and Kasami's algorithm makes use of a passing token and is fully distributed. All nodes in the network are involved in making the decision of which node should hold the token. For a communication network containing N nodes, this algorithm requires at most N message exchanges for one distributed mutual exclusion invocation. The number of messages exchanged would increase if the sequence numbers contained in the messages were to be bounded. The algorithm is free of deadlock and starvation. However, it is not fault-tolerant. Raymond proposed a distributed mutual exclusion algorithm, which is based on logical tree topology of the processes. Using such a tree topology, message exchanges per distributed mutual exclusion invocation can be greatly reduced. The algorithm requires no priori knowledge on the number of processes in the distributed system. For a communication network containing N nodes, the average number of messages required per distributed mutual exclusion invocation is $O(\log N)$. Raymond's algorithm is free of deadlock and starvation and has limited support for fault-tolerance. More importantly, it is relatively easier to make the algorithm scalable to dynamic network topology changes.

Although many distributed mutual exclusion algorithms have been proposed, to our knowledge, not much work on implementing a distributed monitor construct has been reported. Based on Suzuki and Kasami's token-based distributed mutual exclusion algorithm [7], Mansfield proposed a decentralized monitor construct for resource sharing in distributed systems [10]. Despite being simple in concept, the mechanism was not implemented. In the design, a lot of information needs to be placed in the message for passing the token and it may cause a problem in implementation, because the size of the token message can become very large and may not fit within the packet size of the underlying communication system. Also, it is not scalable, as it requires a priori knowledge on the number of processes in the distributed system. The monitor construct is not designed to be fault tolerant of node and communication failures. Yuan and Hsu described the design and implementation of a distributed monitor facility, which is based on the client-server model [11]. The implementation made use of Sun's RPC mechanism. The distributed monitor facility is free of deadlock and starvation. To increase the reliability of the distributed monitor, it uses two servers, namely the primary and the backup monitor servers. The design of the distributed monitor facility is simple and easy to implement. However, since centralized servers are used, they may become the performance bottleneck in a large-scale distributed system such as the Internet.

3 Design of the Distributed Monitor Mechanism

3.1 A Two-Level System Structure of the Distributed Monitor Mechanism

In Raymond's algorithm [8], nodes in a distributed system are arranged in a logical tree structure. Each node communicates only with its immediate neighboring nodes in the spanning tree and therefore only needs to hold information about the neighbors. Two kinds of messages are used in the algorithm: *Privilege* and *Request* messages. When a node receives a Privilege message, if the node is the destined node, it is granted the right to enter its critical section. Each node has a variable `Holder` to indicate the relative position of the node that holds the privilege with respect to the current node. Once a non-privileged node wishes to enter its critical section, it sends a *Request* message to the node as indicated by `Holder`. On receiving a *Request* message at a non-privileged node, the node will forward the Request message to the node indicated by its `Holder`, so as to propagate the request to the privileged node. Once the privileged node has finished executing its critical section, if there are pending request messages from neighboring nodes, it will send a *Privilege* message to the node that has waited the longest time and set its `Holder` to point to that node.

Raymond's algorithm ensures mutual exclusion in a distributed manner: at any time, the privilege is either held by one and only one node or is in transit. No more than one node can obtain the privilege at the same time. Notice, however, that

Raymond's algorithm ensures mutual exclusion at the node level. It is assumed that each node contains only one process and therefore no distinction is made between a node and the processes running on the node. Therefore, with Raymond's algorithm, if there are more than one process running in a node which share resources, these processes are treated as separate, individual nodes in the network. This system structure is inefficient in maintaining a scalable network topology because the joining and removing of processes or nodes require the whole spanning tree of the system to be re-structured. Furthermore, nodes in the algorithm can be two processes running in the same physical network node and their accesses to the shared resources can be resolved by a local mechanism. In Raymond's algorithm, however, they will initiate two requests to the privileged node.

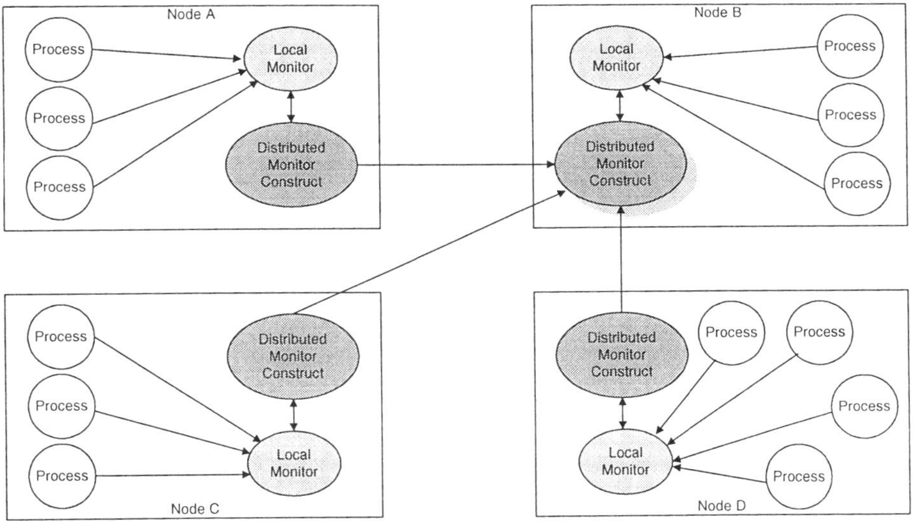

Figure 1 Two-level system structure

To address the above issues, we have developed a two-level system architecture for the distributed monitor mechanism. Figure 1 illustrates the proposed system structure, which consists of the original node level as used in Raymond's algorithm and an additional process level. The node level controls the access to the system-wide shared resources using Raymond's algorithm, and the process level synchronizes local processes running in a node based on the local monitor concept. The process that wins the local competition represents the node, as appeared in the original spanning tree, to request for accessing the system-wide shared resource. With this mutual exclusion hierarchy, processes and nodes are distinguishable. Redundant remote request messages can all be eliminated, resulting in a great reduction in the amount of inter-node communications.

3.2 The Runtime of the Distributed Monitor Mechanism

The runtime of the distributed monitor construct consists of mainly the replicated kernels resident at each node. There are two types of kernels: one for the local monitors at process level and one for all the monitors in the system at node level. As shown in Figure 2, each of the two monitor kernels maintains a monitor table, called Local Monitor Table (LMT) and System Monitor Table (SMT) respectively, to maintain the names of monitors that are existing in a node and in the system respectively. The system monitor table is consistent across all participating nodes in the system. User-specified monitors must register in both local and system monitor tables and be known to all participating nodes in the system through the updates of the system monitor tables.

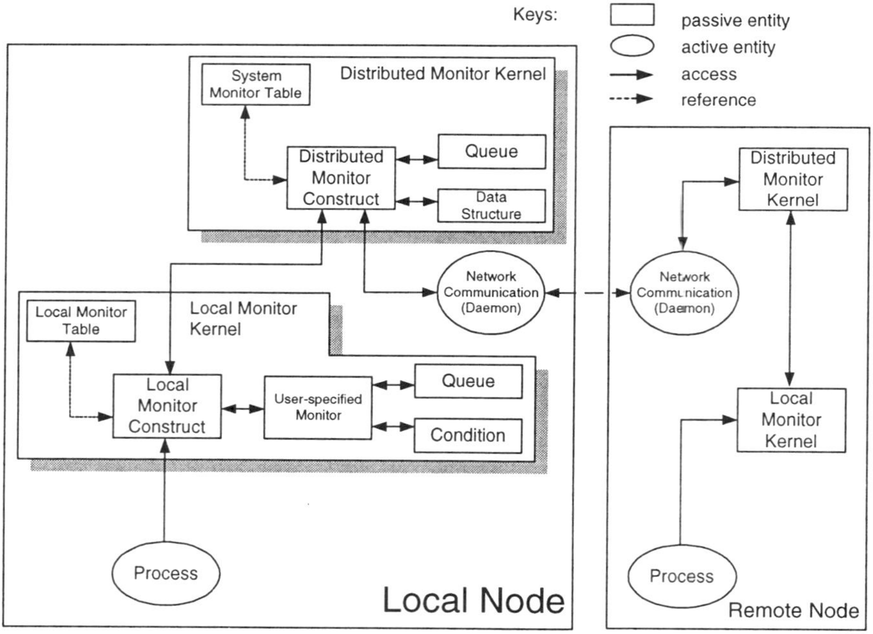

Figure 2 System Runtime - Interactions between entities of distributed monitors in distributed systems

The distributed monitor kernel is associated with a collection of data structures and functional procedures. The data structures represent the data set that each distributed monitor construct should maintain, which include entry queues, and the variables Privileged_Node, Request_Queue, In_Use, and Requested corresponding to the variables used in Raymond's algorithm. The functional procedures realize the monitor primitives for achieving distributed mutual exclusion and process synchronization. Each local monitor kernel is also associated with a collection of local administrative data and functional procedures. The data structure includes entry queues and condition variables of local monitors in the current node. The functional procedures realize the monitor primitives for achieving local mutual exclusion and process synchronization.

Our design of the runtime system architecture uses an object-oriented approach. As shown in Figure 2, the design consists of three main kinds of classes: the *local monitor class*, the *distributed monitor class*, and the *network communication daemon classes*.

The `Local Monitor` classes, including the `Local Monitor Kernel`, the `Monitor`, and the `Condition` classes, contain functions for ensuring distributed mutual exclusion at the process level. Together, they maintain two types of queues – the *entry queue* and the *condition queues*, and implement the four functional monitor primitives. The `Local Monitor Kernel` class implements the kernel for local monitors. The `Monitor` class is an abstract data type that can be used by a programmer as a super class to define new, specific monitors. The `Condition` class is another abstract data type that is used to define condition variables for specific monitors.

The `Distributed Monitor` classes, including the `Distributed Monitor Kernel` and the `DistMon-Data` classes, contain functions for guaranteeing the distributed mutual exclusion at the node level. The `Distributed Monitor Kernel` class implements the four monitor primitives at node level. The `DistMon-Data` class maintains the data structure of each monitor registered in the System Monitor Table.

The `Network Communication Daemon` classes are used to instantiate daemon processes running at the background for sending and receiving messages between nodes in the communication network. There are three classes: `message sender`, `message receiver`, and `message handler`. The `message sender` class is for sending Privilege and Request messages. The `message receiver` is for accepting messages from other nodes while the `message handler` is used to invoke the corresponding actions initiated by the received message.

The relationships among the various classes composing the distributed monitor construct are shown in Figure 3. A user-specified monitor is defined by inheriting the `Monitor` class and is then registered in both the Local and System Monitor Tables. Processes access the shared resource governed by the user-specified monitor with the statement `MonitorName.ProcedureName(parameter)`, which will be interpreted as the following statements:

```
enter(MonitorName)        // process level
enter(MonitorName)        // node level
ProcedureName(parameter)
exit(MonitorName)         // node level
exit(MonitorName)         // process level
```

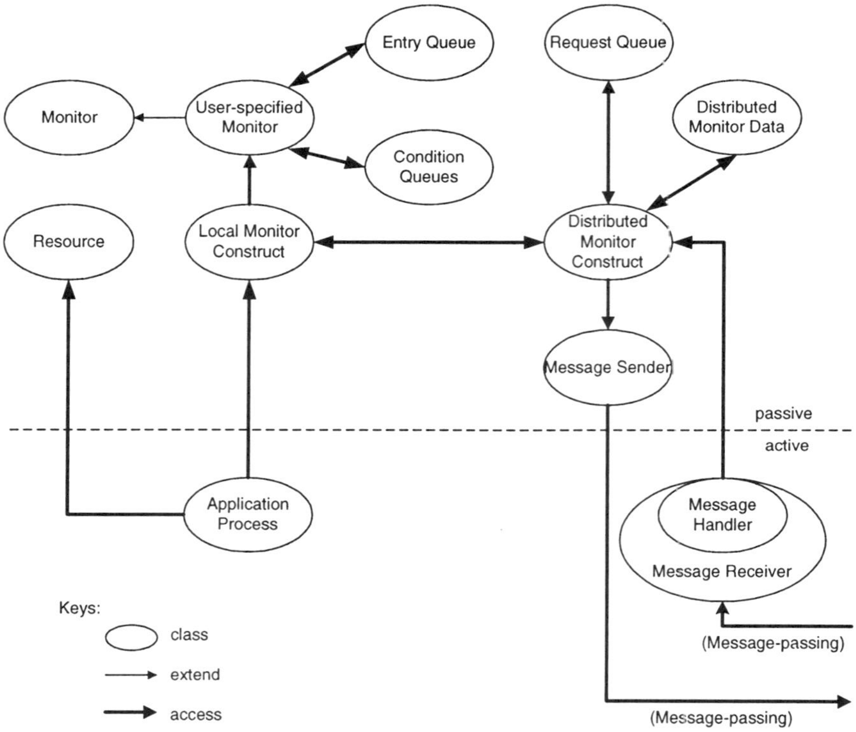

Figure 3 Class Relationships of the Distributed Monitor Construct

For a process accessing the shared resource governed by a distributed monitor construct, the enter primitives of the local and distributed monitor kernels will be invoked for acquiring the local and distributed mutual exclusion respectively. As shown in Figure 4, if the process is not being granted one of the permissions, it will either wait at the Entry_Queue of the process level or wait at the Request_Queue of the node level and send Request message to the Privileged_Node. Upon receipt of a Privilege message, the process will be dequeued from the Request_Queue and then can access the shared resource. When the process wants to release the shared resource, it invokes the exit primitives of the distributed and local monitor kernels. On releasing the distributed monitor, a Privilege message will be sent to the next Privilege_Node queuing at the head of the Request_Queue. The release of the local monitor then dequeues one of the waiting processes from either the Condition_Queue or Entry_Queue that is not empty.

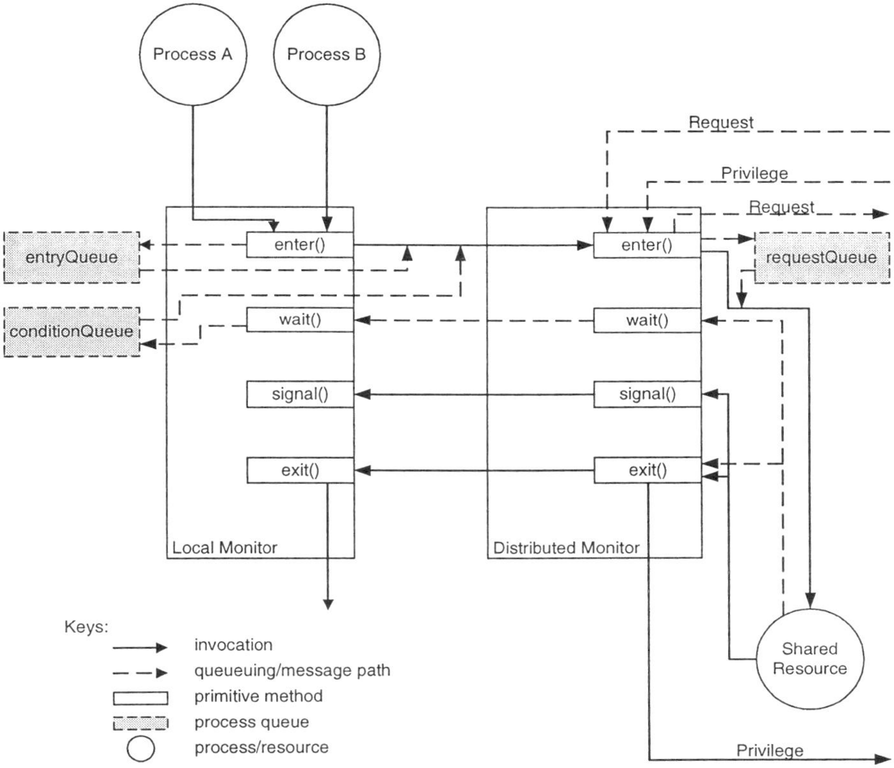

Figure 4 Method Invocations of the Distributed Monitor Construct

4 An Implementation in Java™

The proposed distributed monitor construct has been implemented in Java. Two important features of Java that have contributed to and have great influence in implementing the distributed monitor construct are (1) Java monitor - Java's facilities for controlling the concurrent accesses to shared resources, and (2) Java's thread-scheduling scheme. Three major implementation issues need to be addressed: (1) how to block a requesting process before it obtains the privilege to enter its critical section; (2) how to time-slice Java threads in `Network Communication Daemon` classes so as to respond to incoming messages; (3) the tradeoff between efficiency and fairness of the distributed monitor mechanism. Due to limit on space, details of how to address these issues will not be discussed here.

Making use of the distributed monitor construct, a Java application for solving the classic producer-consumer problem is developed with the use of JAVA2™ (formerly known as JDK - Java Development Kit - version 1.2) from Sun Javasoft.

The application program has been tested on nine Sun SPARC workstations. The properties and performance of the monitor construct are evaluated using the results obtained from the program runs.

To evaluate the performance of the distributed monitor construct, two measures are used: the average amount of time and the average number of messages used by a process to gain permission to enter its critical section. Using the same network topology with a total of 9 network nodes and a total of 9 processes, three different experiments were set up, each with a different number of processes running on the nodes. In the first scenario, each node has exactly one process running. This experiment is used to demonstrate the performance of the distributed monitor construct using Raymond's algorithm's: one process per node. In the second and the third scenarios, each node has zero to at most three processes. These two experiments are used to evaluate the performance of the distributed monitor construct making use of the two-level system architecture.

Three test runs for each of the experiments were carried out. The average amount of time and the number of messages for all the processes to gain the permission to enter the distributed monitor are shown in Figures 5 and 6 respectively.

From the results, it is easy to observe that with the same number of nodes and processes in the system, the performance of the distributed monitor construct increases as the level of the scattering pattern of the running processes decreases. This shows that the two-level system architecture adopted by the construct leads to reduction of redundant messages sent from processes running at the same node and thus increases the system performance. In addition to this general observation, several factors are found to have influence on the performance of the monitor construct to various extents. These factors include *logical tree topology of the system*, *process scattering pattern of the system*, *length of processes' critical sections*, and *delay of delivering messages over the communication network*. They are closely related and affect each other. From the results of our test runs, with various combinations of tuned parameters for the factors, it has been found that the distributed monitor construct gives the best performance over a distributed system with the following configuration:

- *the network has a star topology (node level),*
- *the number of processes running at a node that simultaneously request for privilege is at most two to three (process level),*
- *the lengths of the processes' critical sections are short and negligible in comparison with message delay in the underlying network, and*
- *the delay in message delivery is small.*

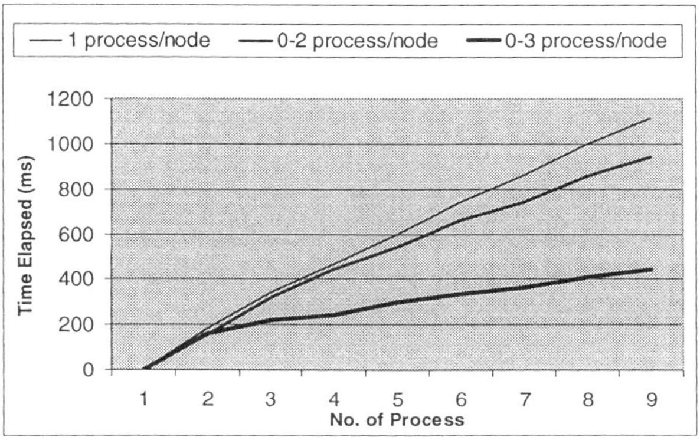

Figure 5 Average time per mutual exclusion entry

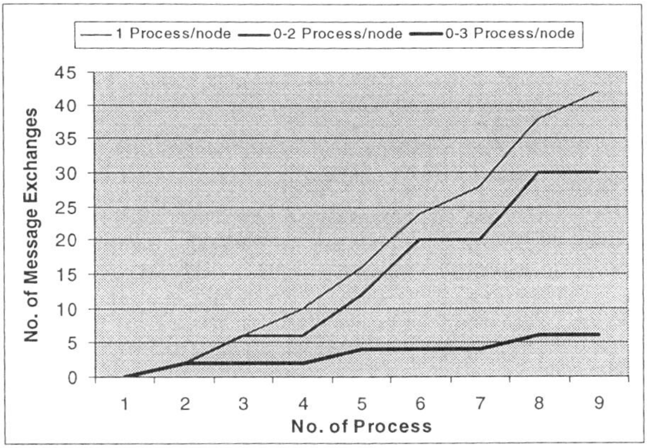

Figure 6 Message exchanges per process

5 Conclusions and Future Work

A distributed monitor construct in Java based on Raymond's tree-based distributed mutual exclusion algorithm has been developed. By improving Raymond's algorithm with a two-level system architecture, the construct is flexible and scalable to large number of processes in a wide area network. The construct ensures distributed mutual exclusion and is free of deadlock and starvation. It also achieves a good performance.

Our future works need to address several issues. First, since Raymond's algorithm assumes the existence of a spanning tree of the network nodes, an efficient distributed algorithm for creating a logical spanning tree over the nodes of the distributed system is to be developed. Second, Raymond's algorithm is limited in the provision of fault-tolerant – it is only tolerant to failed node that will eventually recover, provided that its neighboring nodes do not fail. Thus, in order to have a robust distributed monitor construct, the algorithm needs to be improved so as to make it tolerant to various kinds of failures, including link and node failures and network partitioning. Third, Raymond's algorithm is not scalable – addition and removal of nodes and processes cannot be handled. Tree management schemes for efficiently updating the tree structure without violating consistency of the on-going mutual exclusion session are therefore needed.

References

1. Bob Beck, *Shared-Memory Parallel Programming in C++*, IEEE Software, Volume 7, Number 4, July 1990, pp. 38-48
2. Butler W. Lampson and David D. Redell, *Experiences with Processes and Monitors in Mesa*, Communications of the ACM, Volume 23, Number 2, February 1980, pp. 105-117
3. C.A.R. Hoare, *Monitors: An Operating System Structuring Concept*, Department of Computer Science, The Queen's University of Belfast, Belfast BT7 INN, Northern Ireland. Communications of the ACM, October 1974 Volume 17 Number 10, pp. 549-557
4. Daniel J. Berg and J.Steven Fritzinger, *Advanced Techniques for Java™ Developers - Revised Ed.*, John Wiley & Sons, Inc., 1999
5. Glenn Vanderburg, , *Tricks of The Java™ Programming Gurus*, Sams.net Publishing, 1996
6. Gregory R. Andrews, *Concurrent Programming - Principles and Practice*, The Benjamin/Cummings Publishing Company, Inc., 1991
7. Ichiro Suzuki and Tadao Kasami, *A Distributed Mutual Exclusion Algorithm*, Osaka University, Japan. ACM Transactions on Computer Systems, Volume 3, Number 4, November 1985, pp. 344-349
8. Kerry Raymond, *A Tree-based Algorithm for Distributed Mutual Exclusion*, University of Queensland. ACM Transactions on Computer Systems, Volume 7, Number 1, February 1989, pp. 59-72
9. Thomas W. Doeppner Jr. and Alan J. Gebele, *C++ on a Parallel Machine*, Department of Computer Science, Brown University, Technical Report, CS-87-26, November 17, 1987
10. Tim Mansfield, *A Decentralized Implementation of Monitors*, Key Centre for Software Technology, Department of Computer Science, University of Queensland, St. Lucia, Queensland, 4067, Australia. Australian Computer Science Communications, Vol 12, No 1, Department of Computer Science, Monash University, 1990, pp. 266-274
11. Shyan-Ming Yuan and Yu-Kwen Hsu, *Design and Implementation of A Distributed Monitor Facility*, *Computer Systems – Science & Engineering*, Volume 12, Number 1, January 1997, pp. 43-51

SUPERBOUNDARY EXCHANGE: A TECHNIQUE FOR REDUCING COMMUNICATION IN DISTRIBUTED IMPLEMENTATIONS OF ITERATIVE COMPUTATIONS

HAIRONG KUANG, LUBOMIR F. BIC, MICHAEL B. DILLENCOURT

Information and Computer Science
University of California, Irvine, CA 92697-3425 USA
E-mail: {hkuang,bic,dillenco}@ics.uci.edu

We introduce a technique for lowering the communication cost in a certain type of distributed application, in which processors perform computation in each time step and must obtain boundary data from their neighbors before they can perform the next time step. A typical example of such an application is solving differential equations using the finite difference method. Our method, which we call *SuperBoundary Exchange*, consists of sending a larger boundary less often. This results in less frequent data exchange, trading off against larger messages and some redundant computation. We present experimental data showing that our method consistently results in significant speedup in communication-intensive applications, under varying assumption about the balance of computation load among the processors.

1 Introduction

As workstations become more powerful and less expensive, solving problems through distributed computation on a network of workstations, rather than on more specialized parallel processors, is becoming a much more popular and cost-effective approach. One obstacle to this approach is that communication across a network of workstation is more time-consuming than, for example, communication between processing units in a shared-memory parallel machine. For this reason, techniques for lowering communication costs play an important role in the development of distributed algorithms.

In this paper we introduce a technique for lowering the communication cost in a certain type of distributed application, typified by solving differential equations using the finite difference method [1]. In the finite difference method, we have a discrete d-dimensional grid of element locations, and we want to compute a value $u_{\mathbf{x},\mathbf{t}}$ at each grid location $\mathbf{x}$ and for each time step t. The value of $u_{\mathbf{x},\mathbf{t}}$ is a function of the values of $u_{\mathbf{r},\mathbf{t-1}}$, where $\mathbf{r}$ ranges over $\mathbf{x}$ and all neighbors of $\mathbf{x}$ in the element grid.

In a distributed implementation of the finite difference method, the element grid is partitioned, and each processor is assigned one of the partitions. In each time step t, each processor computes the values of $u_{\mathbf{x},\mathbf{t}}$ for all grid elements $\mathbf{x}$ assigned to it. If a grid element $\mathbf{x}$ is on the boundary of the partition (i.e., it is assigned to a processor P_1, but it has a neighboring grid element assigned to a different processor P_2), then the computation of $u_{\mathbf{x},\mathbf{t}}$ cannot be performed until P_1 has obtained from P_2 the values of $u_{\cdot,t-1}$ for all these neighboring elements. Thus at each time step there is data exchange (communication) with neighboring processors as well as computation. The data that must be obtained by a particular processor from neighboring processor to allow it to perform its computation is sometimes called the *ghost boundary* of the processor [1]. The technique introduced here, which we call *SuperBoundary Exchange*, reduces communication by sending a larger ghost boundary less often. In essence, the increased overhead of sending larger messages and performing some redundant computation is traded off against the reduced overhead of less frequent messages, and the net result is an overall increase in performance. The advantages of both these tradeoffs are well-known in other contexts. For example, the advantage of combining multiple small data transfers into a single larger one underlies block transfers between memory hierarchies, and combining small packets into larger ones is a well known technique for efficient message passing in networks [2]. The technique of replicating data to reduce message traffic is a classical technique in distributed data bases.

The organization of this paper is as follows. We describe the SuperBoundary Exchange technique in Section 2, and contrast it with another technique, send-ahead [3]. In Section 3, we describe the results of several experiments demonstrating that performance advantages of SuperBoundary Exchange. Some conclusions and final remarks are presented in Section 4.

2 The SuperBoundary Exchange Technique

We introduce the SuperBoundary Exchange Technique with the following simple example, illustrated in Figure 1. Suppose that we are solving a 1-dimensional finite difference equation

$$u_{x,t+1} = f(u_{x-1,t}, u_{x,t}, u_{x+1,t}), \tag{1}$$

on a network of processors. Suppose that the values of u associated with x in the range $1, \ldots, 100$ are computed on processor P_1, and that the values of u associated with x in the range $101, \ldots, 200$ are computed on processor P_2. In order to compute the value of $u_{100,t+1}$, P_1 must know the value of $u_{101,t}$; hence this data (the "ghost boundary") must be sent to P_1 by P_2 once it is known (and, symmetrically, P_1 must send $u_{100,t}$ to P_2 before P_2 can compute $u_{101,t+1}$). If each processor only stores the data for the x values directly associated with it, such an exchange of boundary data must occur at each time step in the computation. This is illustrated in Figure 1(a), which shows the computation from the end of time step 3 to the end of time step 6. The first row shows the computation at the end of time step 3. The next three double rows illustrate time steps 4, 5, and 6; each of these time steps is illustrated after the ghost boundary has been exchanged at the beginning of the time step (the dotted box indicates the ghost boundary), and then after the computation for the time step has been completed.

SuperBoundary Exchange is a technique for reducing the frequency of this boundary exchange. Suppose, at the beginning of time step $t+1$, P_1 sends the values $u_{98,t}$, $u_{99,t}$ and $u_{100,t}$ to P_2. Then at time $t+1$, P_2 has all data necessary to compute the values $u_{99,t+1}$, $u_{100,t+1}$, and $u_{101,t+1}$. At time $t+2$, P_2 has all data necessary to compute the values $u_{100,t+2}$, and $u_{101,t+2}$. It can then use this data to compute the value $u_{101,t+3}$. Hence no further boundary data must be exchanged until time $t+3$, and in general, data must only be exchanged every three iterations. This is illustrated for $t=3$ in Figure 1(b).

More generally, the ghost boundary is defined as all the elements that are needed by neighboring processors to compute all their values at the next time step. In a regular boundary exchange, first each pair of neighboring processors exchanges ghost boundaries, and then each of the processors computes the new values for all of its elements. This process is repeated for every time step.

A *SuperBoundary* of width k is defined inductively: a ghost boundary has width 1, and for $k>1$ a SuperBoundary of width k consists of the SuperBoundary of width $k-1$ together with all the elements whose neighbors are in the SuperBoundary of width $k-1$. In SuperBoundary Exchange with width k, an exchange of boundary data occurs once every k time steps. Thus, as the width is increased, the number of boundary exchange messages decreases, but the size of the messages and the amount of redundant computation increases.

The example of Figure 1 can be represented schematically as shown in Figure 2. Figure 2(a) represents the situation without SuperBoundary Exchange: before the computation at each time step, an exchange of data must occur. Figure 2(b) represents the situation with SuperBoundary Exchange using a boundary width of 3: an exchange of data occurs before the computation at time t. Each processor updates its own values and, to the extent possible, the received boundary values; after three time steps, the received data has become invalid, and a new SuperBoundary Exchange must occur.

Figure 3 schematically represents SuperBoundary Exchange in 2 dimensions, with a boundary width of 2. Here, the elements are connected as a grid, and the partition assigned to each processor is a square subgrid of the element grid. Each processor must communicate with 8 neighbors. We show the situation for one processor, processor 0, which we assume has 8 neigh-

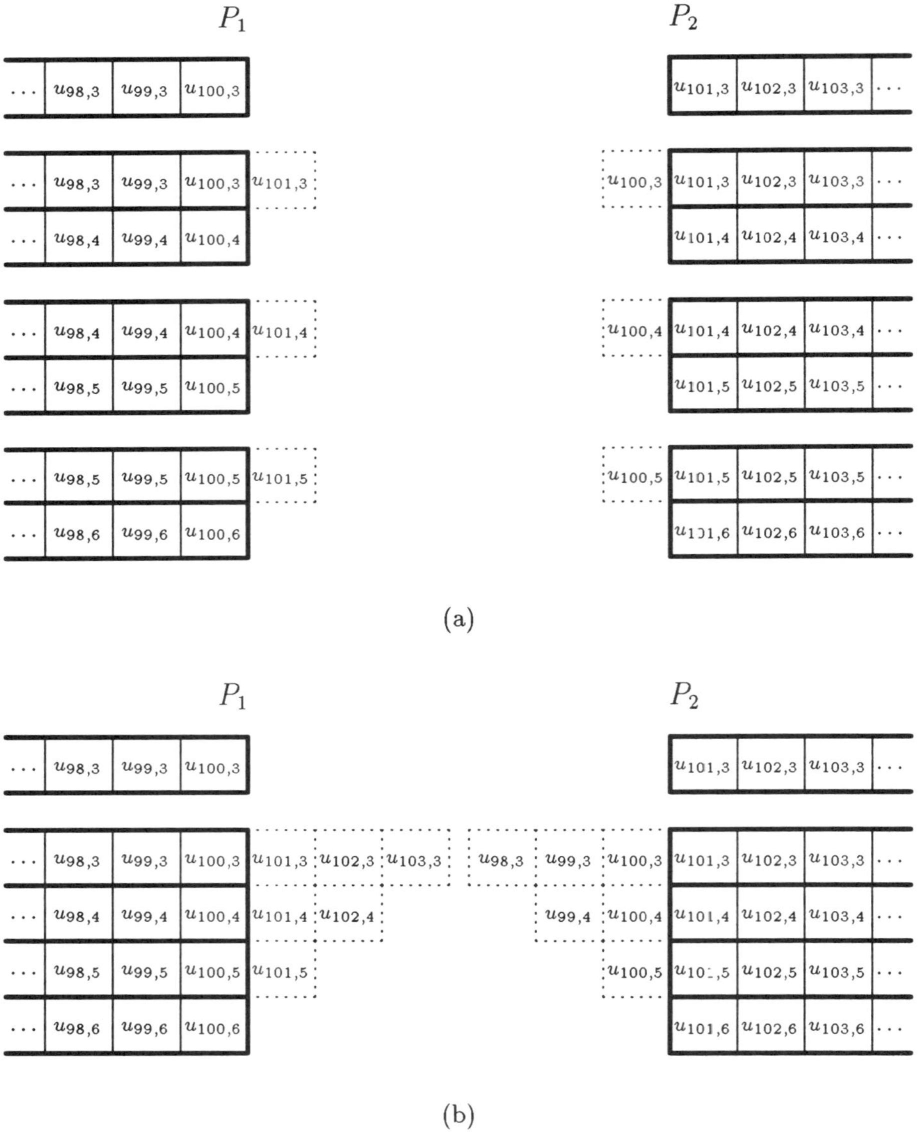

Figure 1. A simple example illustrating SuperBoundary Exchange. Both figures represent the interval from the end of time step 3 to the end of time step 6. (a) In the absence of SuperBoundary Exchange, the ghost boundary is exchanged at the start of each time step. (b) SuperBoundary Exchange: 2 additional boundary data items are exchanged at the start of time step 4, but no boundary information is exchanged at time 5 or at time 6.

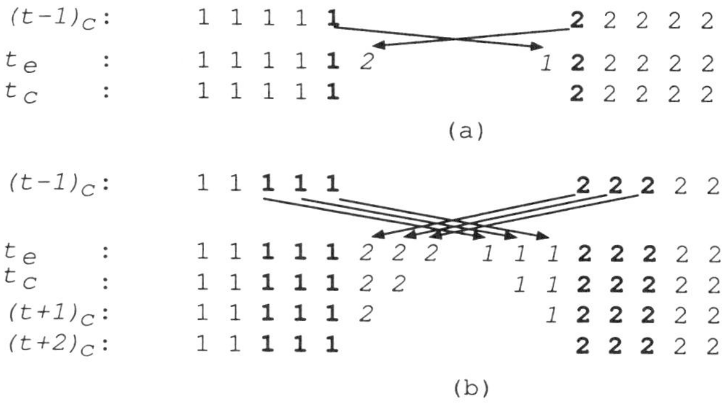

Figure 2. Schematic representation (a) with regular boundary exchange, and (b) with SuperBoundary Exchange, with a boundary width of 3.

bors numbered 1–8 clockwise from the upper-left neighbor, as shown in the upper-right portion of the figure. The upper-left portion of the figure, labeled $(t-1)_c$, shows the situation after the computation at time $t-1$; processor 0 has no boundary data from its neighbors. From left to right, the three diagrams at the bottom of the figure represent the situation after the data exchange at time t (t_e), after the computation at time t (t_c), and after the computation at time $t+1$ ($(t+1)_c$). At t_e, processor 0 has two "layers" of boundary data to work with. At t_c, the data for time t, including the data on the regular boundary has been computed. At $(t+1)_c$, the computation for time $t+1$ is complete, but there is no longer valid boundary data, so data must be exchanged again.

Notice that in the 2-dimensional case just described, if the subgrid assigned to each processor is an $n \times n$ grid, and the boundary width is k, then the number of grid element values that must be exchanged between neighbors once every k time steps is $O(k \cdot n)$. Hence the amount of additional memory required goes up linearly with the boundary width, but only with the square root of the amount of memory required to store the subgrid associated with the processor. Hence, SuperBoundary Exchange requires only a small amount of additional memory. The generalization of SuperBoundary Exchange to d dimensions is conceptually straightforward, and we omit the details here.

The SuperBoundary Exchange technique improves performance in two ways: by reducing communication overhead and by smoothing out random bursts. Communication overhead is reduced because the frequency of com-

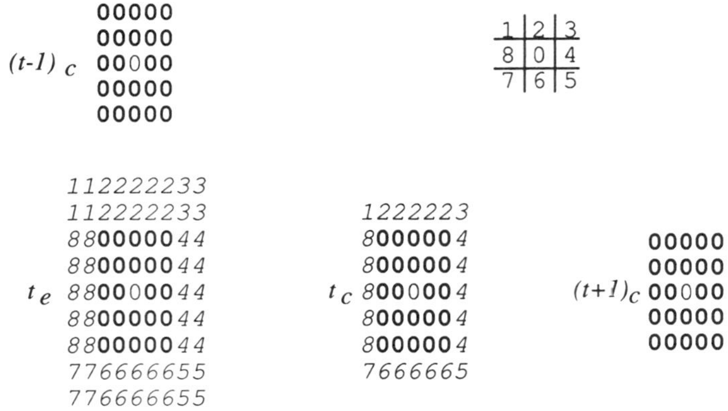

Figure 3. Schematic representation of 2-dimensional SuperBoundary Exchange, with a boundary width of 2.

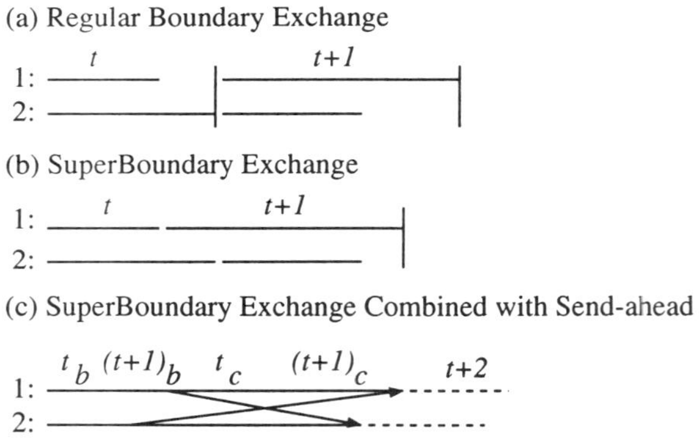

Figure 4. Smoothing out of random bursts using SuperBoundary Exchange and send-ahead.

munication (i.e., the number of messages) is reduced. Depending on the message size, the number of packets may be reduced as well, since several small messages are being combined into one larger one. wever, a ause uge.

The effect of smoothing out random bursts is illustrated in Figure 4(a) and (b). Suppose that Processor 1 takes less time than its neighbor, Processor 2, to perform the computation at time step t, but Processor 2 takes less time than Processor 1 to perform the computation at time step $t+1$. Under regular boundary exchange, the two processors must synchronize at every time step, and hence the time required for each time step is the time required by the slower processor. This is shown in Figure 4(a), where the horizontal lines represent the elapsed times for each time step and the vertical lines represent the synchronization points. Under SuperBoundary exchange with boundary width 2, the two time steps t and $t+1$ can be executed consecutively without synchronization as shown in Figure 4(b). As a result, the bursts are smoothed out and step $t+2$ can be started at an earlier time.

"Boundary precomputation" [4,3] is a different approach to reducing communication overhead. We now briefly discuss this method and its limitations, and then show how it can be combined with SuperBoundary Exchange.

The boundary precomputation method [3] actually consists of applying two separate observations. The first observation is that it is not necessary to compute all values at time t before sending the ghost boundary; instead, a processor can compute its boundary values at time t, then send them to its neighbors while it is computing its interior values at time t. We refer to this part of the boundary precomputation as "send-ahead." The second observation is that if a process finishes its computation for time t while it is waiting for the time-t ghost boundary to arrive from its neighbors; it can continue processing by computing the values at time $t+1$ at cells of distance 1 from its internal boundary, values at time $t+2$ at cells of distance 2 from its internal boundary, etc. We refer to this as "internal precomputation". It is pointed out that internal precomputation does not help overall performance. [3] One reason for this is that if communication is the dominant factor, each processor will reach a point of saturation, where it has done as much internal precomputation as it possible can; after this, it will only be able to advance the time at each grid element by one in each cycle, just as in the absence of internal precomputation. Because of this, we discuss send-ahead, but not internal precomputation, in the remainder of this paper.

SuperBoundary Exchange and send-ahead can be combined as follows. Suppose that the starting time is t and the boundary width is k. Immediately after a data exchange, each processor computes the value of the data along the superboundary that it needs to send at time $t+k$ and sends it to the appropriate neighbors; it then computes the rest of its data (the inner portion). Figure 5 schematically illustrates the combination of these two techniques, for a 1-dimensional problem with a boundary width of 3. The line labeled t_e shows the status at time t after data has been received: Processor 1 has received three boundary items from its neighbor, Processor 2. In the next three lines, it computes the values at time $t+3$ of the boundary values that it needs

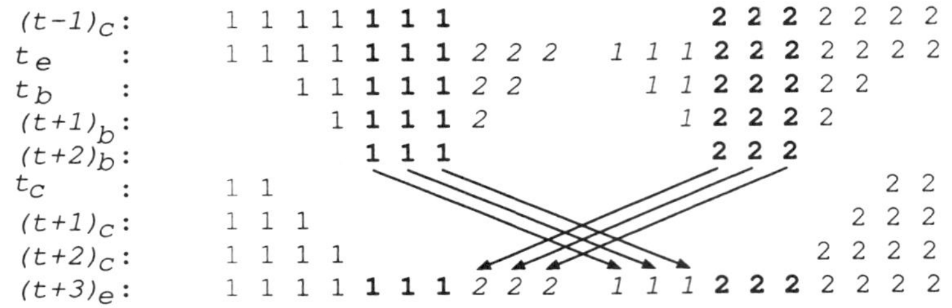

Figure 5. Schematic representation of the combination of SuperBoundary Exchange and send-ahead, for a 1-dimensional problem with a boundary width of 3. with a boundary width of 2.

to send to processor 2, and sends them to processor 2 when this computation is complete (after the line labeled $(t+2)_b$). It then computes its inner values for time $t+3$; this computation overlaps with waiting for the boundary values to arrive from Processor 2. If the boundary width is not too big, then the bulk of the computation (i.e., the computation of the inner values) is done while the processor is waiting for the boundary values from the neighboring processors, so the computation overlaps with the communication latency of the boundary messages from neighboring processors. This can represent a considerable advantage, because it means that the combination of SuperBoundary Exchange and send-ahead can smooth out the random fluctuations in load as illustrated in Figure 4(c).

3 Experimental results

We present experimental results in this section. All the experiments were performed using nine Sparcstation 5's connected by a 100Mbit/second switch. The nine workstations were arranged as a 3×3 toroidal grid. This arrangement eliminated boundary effects, so the configuration and experimental results can be viewed as a portion of a much larger collection of workstations. All implementations used the MESSENGERS system [5,6], and speedup was computed relative to a MESSENGERS implementation using the same 3×3 toroidal grid as a logical network but running on a single workstation. To decrease the variability of the presented data, all the experiments describe here were run three times, and in each case the number presented here is the average over the three runs.

A distributed computation may be dominated either by the communication cost or by the computation cost. Because SuperBoundary Exchange is intended to reduce the effect of communication overhead, it is primarily useful in situations where the communication costs dominate. For this reason, the parameters for our experiments were chosen to make the communication-to-computation ratio relatively high. We experimented with three different workload-balance scenarios: (1) *even workload balance*, in which the computation time required by each processor at each step is about the same; (2) *systematic workload imbalance*, in which there are certain processors that require more time in each time step to perform their computation; and (3) *fluctuating workload imbalance*, in which case there is imbalance in the computation time, but the specific processors requiring more time vary from time step to time step.

The application we used is a 2-dimensional finite difference problem, with an $n \times n$ element grid with n varying as discussed below. The 2D $n \times n$ elements were evenly distributed on 9 workstations, logically connected as a 3×3 grid, with each workstation performing the computation for a subgrid $(n/3) \times (n/3)$ elements. In each workstation, the communication overhead is approximately $4a(n/3)$, where a is a constant, while the computation cost is approximately $b(n/3)^2$, where b is a constant. The communication to computation ratio is c/n, where $c = 12a/b$. Therefore, when the problem size becomes smaller, the communication-to-computation ratio becomes bigger.

Our first experiment assesses the effect of the boundary width on the performance of a computationally balanced distributed application. Figure 6 shows the result of this experiment. The horizontal axis represents the boundary width, and the vertical axis represents the speedup. A boundary width of 1 means that we are using regular boundary exchange; larger values mean that we are using SuperBoundary Exchange. We experimented with three problem sizes: 540×540, 666×666, and 999×999. In all three cases, SuperBoundary Exchange increases the speedup significantly for low values of the boundary width, and as the boundary width is increased, the speedup reaches a maximum and then falls off. This is because for low values of the boundary width, the decrease in communication overhead far outweighs the additional cost due to redundant computation of boundary values. For high values of the boundary width, most of the communication savings has been realized, the program becomes computation-intensive, and the increased computation starts to cause a performance decrease. But this latter effect is gradual: even when the boundary width reaches 32, SuperBoundary Exchange still beats the regular boundary exchange for the two smaller problem sizes.

The remaining experiments compare the SuperBoundary Exchange technique, the send-ahead technique, and the combination of the two for the three

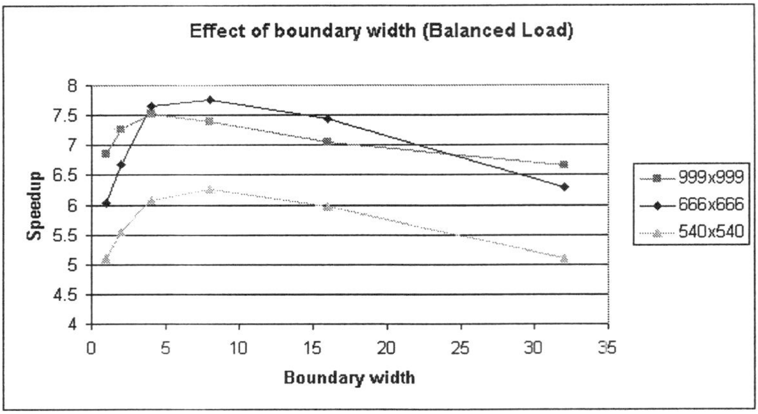

Figure 6. The effect of the boundary width on the performance of a computationally balanced application.

workload-balance scenarios discussed at the beginning of this section. Figure 7 shows the results for the balanced-workload case, fcr a problem of size 666 × 666. The gray line shows the performance when the send-ahead tech-

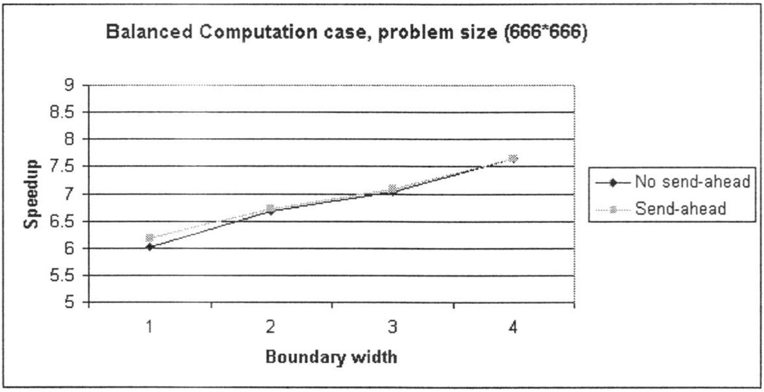

Figure 7. The effect of SuperBoundary Exchange, with and without send-ahead, on a balanced computation.

nique is used. From the figure, we can see that SuperBoundary Exchange

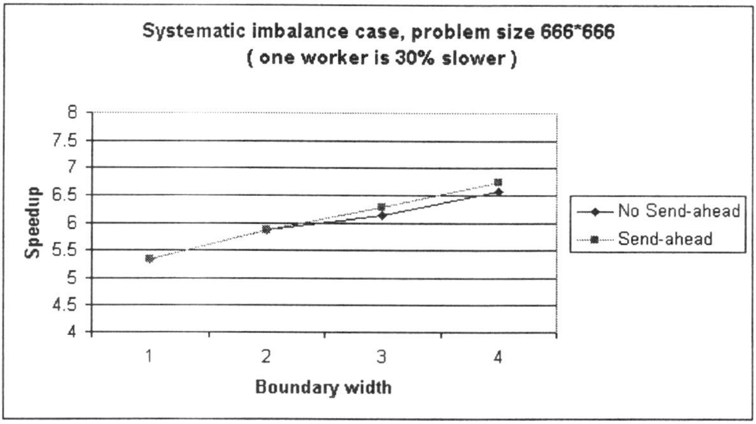

Figure 8. The effect of SuperBoundary Exchange, with and without send-ahead, on a systematically imbalanced computation.

improves the performance. Send-ahead helps slightly in the case of regular boundary exchange (i.e., for boundary width 1), but it does not help otherwise. Also, SuperBoundary Exchange speeds up the computation using regular boundary exchange much more than send-ahead does. There are several reasons explaining why send-ahead contributes so little in this case. First, the transmission time is negligible in our experiment network because workstations are connected by 100M/bit switch. Second, because the workload is evenly distributed, there is no idle waiting time to be eliminated by the send-ahead technique. In addition, send-ahead changes the computation order, and this may affect the hit rate on the memory cache.

Figure 8 shows the results for the case of systematic workload imbalance. In this experiment, we chose one processor and artificially increased its workload in each time step by 30%. As with the balanced case, SuperBoundary Exchange improves the performance, but the send-ahead technique doesn't help much. The explanation is the same as that of the balanced case: because the workload is systematically unbalanced, the idle waiting time can not be squeezed out.

Our final experiments address the case of fluctuating load imbalance. We ran the balanced experiment, but artificially increased the workload on each processor in each time step by a random amount. The random additional load was Gaussian, with a mean of 30% of the base load and a standard deviation

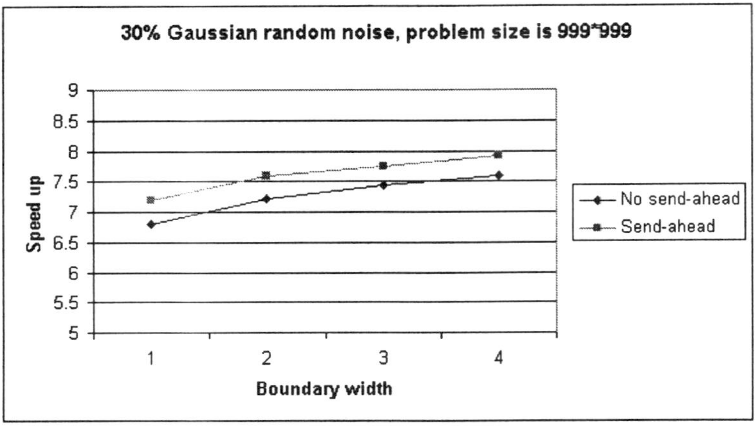

Figure 9. The effect of SuperBoundary Exchange, with and without send-ahead, on a computation of a 999×999 problem with fluctuating imbalance.

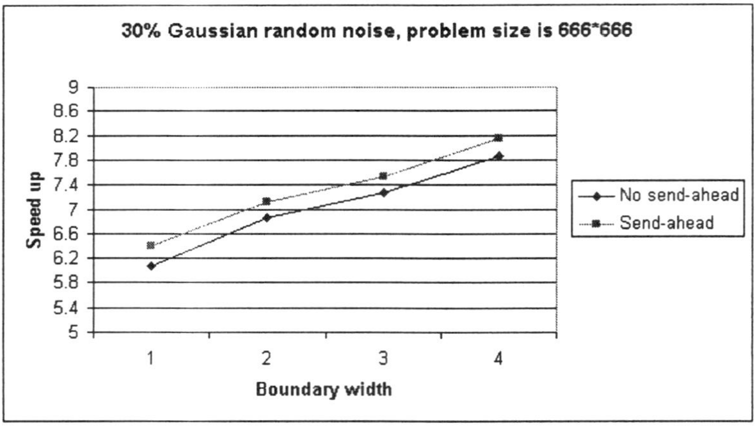

Figure 10. The effect of SuperBoundary Exchange, with and without send-ahead, on a computation of a 666×666 problem with fluctuating imbalance.

of 10% of the base load. Figures 10 and 9 show the results for problem sizes of 999×999 and 666×666, respectively.

If we compare the individual effects of send-ahead with the and Super-

Table 1. Summary of the results of our experiments. SuperBoundary Exchange provided significant speedup improvement for all communcation-intensive scenarios. Send-ahead provided additional improvement in the case of fluctuating load-imbalance, but provided no incremental benefit in the other two cases.

	Balanced Computation	Imbalance Computation	
		Systematic Imbalance	Fluctuating Imbalance
Computation Dominant	Better Hardware	Load Balancing	Load Balancing
Communication Dominant	SBX	SBX	SBX + Send-ahead

Boundary Exchange, we see that on the smaller problem SuperBoundary Exchange is better. On the larger problem, send-ahead is better than increasing the boundary width to 2, but for larger boundary widths SuperBoundary Exchange is better. The best results are obtained by combining the two methods: on the smaller problem, send-ahead together with SuperBoundary Exchange with a boundary width of 4 yields a 34% improvement in speedup. Send-ahead helps in this case because it helps smooth out the bursts due to the random fluctuations in computation time.

4 Conclusions and Final Remarks

In this paper we have introduced the SuperBoundary Exchange technique as a means of reducing communication overhead in distributed applications. The underlying tradeoff is fewer messages against potentially longer messages and some additional, redundant, computation. We have presented some experimental data comparing SuperBoundary Exchange with the send-ahead technique. The results of our experiments are summarized in Table 1. If the running time of the application is dominated by the computation time, then performance can be addressed by improving the hardware or by addressing load imbalance among processors. The technique introduced in this paper, SuperBoundary Exchange, reduces communication overhead, and hence is of use when the communication cost dominates. Our experiments indicate that this technique is useful whether or not there is load imbalance among the processors, and that it provides a significantly larger performance improvement than the send-ahead technique. In the case of fluctuating load imbalance, further improvement can be obtained by combining SuperBoundary Exchange with send-ahead. In the other two cases (balance, or systematic imbalance), send-ahead provides almost no incremental performance improvement beyond that provided by SuperBounday Exchange.

Although the SuperBoundary Exchange technique is of most use when the communication cost dominates, it can ultimately be applied even in a computation-dominated application. If computation dominates, appropriate ways to address performance concerns would include fine-tuning the computation at each grid element, adding more processors, and upgrading the hardware. As these enhancements are made, a point of diminishing returns will be reached, because the computation cost will decrease to the point where it is dominated by the communication cost. When this point is reached, and the application becomes communication-intensive, SuperBoundary Exchange can then be used to further enhance the performance of the application.

While the only application mentioned is finite difference equations, the SuperBoundary Exchange technique can be applied to a wider class of problems. The technique can be applied to any application in which there is an underlying space, a well-defined notion of neighbor, and an iterative computation where the computation at a particular location in one time step depends on the state of that location and its neighbors in the preceding time step. For example SuperBoundary Exchange could be applied in individual-based spatial simulations in which the behavior of entities is based solely on their interactions with nearby entities (e.g., models of the flocking of birds or the schooling of fish [7,8]). Here, the boundary data to be exchanged is the state of entities in nearby nodes, and SuperBoundary Exchange would require redundant computation of these behaviors after an exchange of data.

References

1. E. F. Van de Velde. *Concurrent Scientific Computing.* Springer-Verlag, 1994.
2. J. Nagle. Congestion control in TCP/IP internetworks. *Computer Commun. Review*, 14:11–17, October 1984.
3. J. Z. Lou and R. D. Ferraro. A parallel incompressible flow solver package with a parallel mutigrid elliptic kernel. In *Super Computing '95*, December 1995. `http://olympic.jpl.nasa.gov/Reports/flow_solver/pap.html`.
4. C.-C. Hui, G. K.-K. Chan, M. M.-S. Yuen, and I. Ahmad. Solving partial differential equations on a network of workstations. In *Proceedings of the Third IEEE Interational Symposium on High Performance Distributed*

Computing, pages 194–201, August 1994.

5. L. F. Bic, M. Fukuda, and M. B. Dillencourt. Distributed computing using autonomous objects. *IEEE Computer*, 29(8), Aug. 1996.
6. M. Fukuda, L. F. Bic, and M. B. Dillencourt. Messages versus MESSENGERS in distributed programming. *Journal of Parallel and Distributed Computing*, 57:188–211, 1999.
7. A. Huth and C. Wissel. The simulation of the movement of fish schools. *Journal of Theoretical Biology*, 156:365–385, 1992.
8. C.W. Reynolds. Flocks, herds, and schools: A distributed behavioral model. *Computer Graphics*, 21(4):25–34, July 1987.

The Design and Implementation of a Model for Database Publishing on the WWW

WanLei Zhou
School of Computing and Mathematics, Deakin University, Clayton, Victoria 3168, Australia
HaiYi Zhang
Department of Computer Science, Harbin Institute of Technology, HeilongJiang, 150001, China

Abstract

The paper studies database publishing technologies based on the WWW. The dramatic progress of the Internet, especially the WWW, makes it possible for people to share database information in a very large scale. Database publishing is an important application in this area and it involves the key technologies, such as the HTTP protocol, server technology, client browser technology, markup language HTML, etc. Typically, there are two means to publish databases on the web: CGI-based and Java-Based. This paper analyzes the advantages and disadvantages of the two methods. Then, it puts forward an approach to database publishing based on a new model: the extension of HTTP. The result of a preliminary evaluation shows that the new model is an efficient approach.

Keywords: WWW, Database Publishing, CGI, Java, Client/Server Computing, Database Connectivity.

1 Database publishing based on WWW

Database publishing means providing database information owned by an individual or an organization to other people to access [1, 4]. The publishing range can be local publishing or remote (distributed) publishing [17]. There are two kinds of interface for general databases: local interface and client/server interface [8], and database publishing must pass through database interfaces. In the environment of the World Wide Web, people are most interested in distributed (or client/server) database publishing [12].

The existing database publishing means can be classified into two types: CGI-based and Java (JDBC)-based. We analyze the advantages and disadvantages of the two methods here.

1.1 Common Gateway Interface (CGI)

CGI is one of the early and still most widely used techniques for integrating databases into the Web environment. It is the specification for transferring information between a Web server and a CGI program (script). Running a CGI script from a Web browser is mostly transparent to the user. However, several things must occur for a CGI script to execute successfully [3]:

Information can be passed from the browser to the CGI script in a variety of ways, including: passing parameters on the command line, passing environment variables to the CGI programs, passing data to CGI programs via standard input, and using extra path information. The script can return the results with embedded HTML tags, as plain text, or as an image. The browser then interprets the results like other document. This provides a very useful mechanism permitting access to any external databases that have a programming interface.

The main advantages of CGI are its simplicity and language independence, Web server independence, and its wide acceptance. Despite these advantages, the CGI-approach does have some problems. The first problem is that the communication between a client and the database server must always go through the Web server. This may possibly cause a bottleneck if there are a large number of users accessing the Web server simultaneously. For every request that is exchanged, the Web server has to convert data from or to an HTML document. This necessary conversion process adds significant overhead when processing a database query.

The second problem is the lack of efficiency and transaction support in a CGI-based approach. Every query that is submitted through CGI is treated as the first encounter. This, however, is due to the statelessness of HTTP. As a result, the database server has to perform the same logon and logout procedure, even if the same user submits multiple queries. The CGI script could attempt to overcome this problem by handling queries in a batch mode, but then transactions that required multiple interactive queries would be difficult.

Another important disadvantage is that the server has to generate a new process or thread for each CGI script. For a popular site that can easily acquire dozens of hits almost simultaneously, this can be a significant overhead, as the processes would compete for memory, disk, and processor time. The script developer may have to take into consideration that there may be more than one copy for the script executing at the same time, and consequently have to allow for concurrent access to data files used.

The final disadvantage of CGI is security. If appropriate measures are not taken, security can be a serious threat in CGI applications. Many of these security problems relate to the data that is input by the user at the browser end. If the user input is not checked and handled correctly by the script, dangerous security breaches could occur.

1.2 Java Database Connectivity (JDBC)

The JDBC approach [9]is another popular implementation for database publishing. The JDBC package is a set of Java classes that defines a database access API (application programming interface). It supports basic SQL functionality and it enables access to a wide range of relational DBMS products. In using JDBC, Java can be used as the host language for writing applications for database publishing.

The advantage of using JDBC drivers that make use of ODBC is that they are readily available for many of the most popular DBMSs for a very low price. The Java-based approach allows a connection between a client and a server to be set up during the cause of the communication, and therefore eliminates the need of multiple database connection operations when the user submits multiple queries. However, there are disadvantages with the Java-based approach:

- A JDBC driver that is not a pure Java implementation will not necessarily work with a Web browser.
- For security reasons, currently an applet that has been downloaded from the Internet can connect only to a database located on the host machine from which the applet originated. This is part of the sandbox concept designed into Java applets.
- Deployment costs increases with the need to install, administer, and maintain a set of drivers, or database software for each client system.

The major advantages of using JDBC are the cross-platform independence and the ability of delivering database functionality using Java applets through the Internet. The JDBC package specifies the interfaces between Java and databases (based on SQL2). JavaSoft (the group that defined JDBC) only specifies the interfaces. All implementation of JDBC drivers is done by third part companies with special expertise. A change of a driver will not change the program. However, since Java is an interpreting language, the efficiency of the program execution is rather low because the interpreting needs time.

After the consideration for the two publishing means, we propose a new database publishing method that is based on an extension of HTTP protocol.

2 The model of database publishing based on an extension of HTTP protocol

2.1 The model

As the progressing of the Internet, especially the WWW, the relationship between database publishing and Web server—HTTPD (HTTP Daemon) becomes more and more close [5, 6]. Therefore it seems to be a good strategy for the HTTPD to integrate the database functionality [2]. Here, we propose a model of database publishing based on an extension of HTTP protocol, as shown in Figure 1.
In the browser, we use the Netscape plug-in API to develop a database plug-in as the front end for data access. The plug-in is corresponding to the non-enroll MIME type which defines as database/x-SQL ([7, 11]). Its extended name is defined as db.

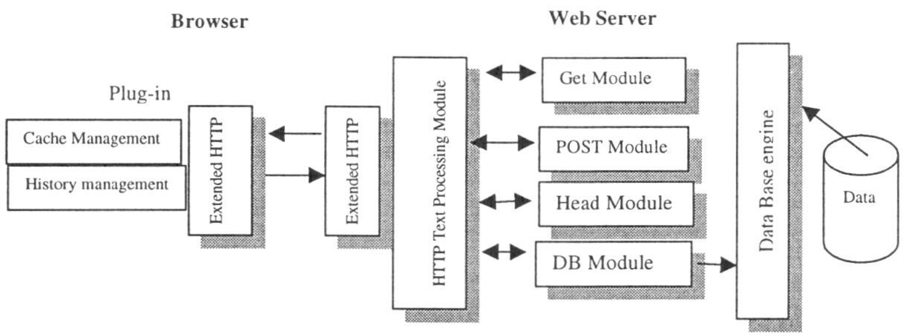

Figure 1 A publishing model based on the extended HTTP protocol

As soon as the browser meets MIME type that is data of database/x-SQL, it will call the database plug-in to deal with the data. Comparing to the publishing based on CGI, this publishing method is powerfully interactive. Its weakness is that when accessing the publishing database, it has to use the plug-in in the front end.

When the plug-in communicates with HTTP, it uses the extended HTTP protocol. In order to perform the search function, we extended a method called DATABASE for the method set of the HTTP/1.0 protocol [14] and defined request/response messages. But we still keep the statelessness property of the HTTP protocol. In the server end, we have several modules for different requests. After the HTTPD receives a request message, it can call a module related to the request method. Here, for the safety reasons, the database engine only provides searching function. It has no adding, deleting and modifying functions.

2.2 The management of the result set and history records

If the server sends the searching results to the front end every time and if the amount of data is huge, it will take a longer respond time, and the user will need to search some subset of the result set. Obviously, this approach will cost unnecessary time. So, we require that the database engine only return a fixed number of records for each searching. Since all the protocols in use are stateless, we create the buffer-

mechanism and history management in order to enhance the efficiency of the publishing.
The statelessness property of the extended protocol means that, if a buffer mechanism for searching result set is not created in the client end, in order to obtain the data the browser must interact with the server for every time in backward or forward browsing. That practice wastes time and therefore the efficiency is low. Here, we use the FIFO algorithm for result management at the client end. The data structure for the algorithm implementation is an FIFO queue of a fixed length. The searching respond message returned from the server end is sent to the queue. If necessary, the result item that is stored first is eliminated and it will be sent to the history stack (for the browser to use later).

We use the LRU algorithm for History record management. A result set is corresponding to a triple (*query statement, start record number, record number*). In fact, every entry of the history record stack is a triple corresponding to a result item.

3 Description of the extended protocol

We define a database message to describe the extended database access protocol based on the HTTP protocol. Refer to RFC1945 [14] for a more detailed description on the HTTP protocol. Here, the message pattern is in BNF and its general structure is defined by the Internet Mail formats [13].

(1) Meta-request message
Pattern: DATABASE database name HTTP-version CRLF
*(general-Header | Request-header | Entity-Header) CRLF
[Entity-Body]

When HTTPD receives the message, it can distinguish which database model that should be called to deal with the request from the DATABASE method. According to the request's database name, the database model interacts with the embedded database engine and receives meta-information of requested database, such as tables in database and attributes of individual area in the table. The database model packs the meta-information in the entity of meta-information response text, and sends to the browser end plug-in. The user can reference to those information for search operations.

(2) Meta-information message
Pattern: HTTP-version Status-code Reason-Phrase CRLF
* (General-Header | Response-Header | Entity-Header) CRLF [Entity-Body]

Here, the Status-Code points out that the request is successful or not. If successful, the Entity-Body gives the meta-information of requested database. Otherwise, the Reason-Phrase gives the reason of the failure, for instance, undiscovered database, illegal operation, etc, and the Entity-Body gives the detailed information about failure.

(3) Search request message

Pattern: DATABASE database name HTTP-version CRLF

* (General-Header | Request-Header | Entity- Header) CRLF [Entity-Body]

Here, Entity-Body has a pattern as follows:

[Start-Record: begin number of record CRLF]

Record-Number: record number of request CRLF

Query-statement

After the HTTPD receives the message, it can perform a searching operation. If this is a new searching, the head of the Start-Record might be omitted. The Record-Number stands for the record number for the current request. Following a request message, the database model can return the result. The Start-Record and Record-Number will divide the searching result of Query-Statement into several subsets and return a subset for each request. Here, a search request of the client must have a Query-Statement.

(4) Search respond message

Its pattern is the same as the search request message pattern. The only difference is the Entity-Body pattern. There are two kinds of Entity-Body patterns for a search respond message:

- *No Start-Record header* means for this time the searching statement of the request is different from that of the last time for the client end. The HTTPD can return the first Record-Number records of the result set. The pattern of the Entity-Body is:

  Total-RecordNumber : RecordNumber-In-This-Message : Meta-Information : Records

  Here, the Total-RecordNumber stands for the total record numbers of this searching. The RecordNumber-In-This-Message stands for the record numbers included in this message. The Meta-Information stands for the meta information that is included in the returning result set. The Records is the data of the result set.
- *With a Start-Record header.* HTTPD will return records from the result set starting from the Start-Record and returns the number of Record-Number records. The Entity-Body only includes the record set of the request.

4. The efficiency evaluation

In order to fairly evaluate the three database publishing methods: the CGI-Based, the Java-Based and the Extended HTTP protocol, we carried out some preliminary experiments using the mSQL database system [10] as the database engine. The result of our experiments indicated that in general, the database publishing method we proposed is the most efficient approach, the Java-based method is in the middle, and the CGI-Based method is the least efficient.

4.1 The environment and design for the experiments

The testing environment has the following components,

(1) Database system for testing: mSQL database, and the size is about 350 records.

(2) The configuration of computer for mSQL server execution: CPU-80586 100, operating system – Linux 1.2.3, memory—40 Mb.

(3) The browser for testing is Netscape Navigator3.0. The configuration of computer for running the client is: CPU—80586 100, operating system – NT4.0, memory – 32 Mb.

In order to guarantee accuracy, we set the following conditions during testing:

(1) Absolutely quiet for network, no network noise.

(2) Same client computer and server computer.

(3) Running on the same Netscape Navigator Browser at the client end and using the same mSQL engine.

Table 1 lists the testing front end for every method:

Publishing Means	*Testing front end*
Based on Java	Java Applet
Based on CGI	Java Applet
Extended HTTP Protocol	Netscape Plug-in

Table 1. Testing end of the publishing methods

Because the testing front end of the CGI-based method uses standard HTML pages, therefore it is impossible to test its respond time. Here we use Java Applet to test the front end. It simulates the browser to request CGI programs. We believe that using this method to test respond time should be the same as using a browser directly, because an applet running in a browser is an independent program, and the time for evaluating efficiency does not include processing time for the browser to process query results. In addition, we need to point out that the testing front end for the extended HTTP protocol simply is to (1) create the connection to HTTPD, (2) send query respond message, (3) receive query results and (4) close the connection. It does not process display of results (there is no GUI interface).

The testing procedures for the three testing front ends are listed in Table 2.

Publishing Means	*Testing procedure for Front End*
Based on Java	Connect to msqld; Select database; Query; Close the connection
Based on CGI	Connect to HTTPD; Send CGI request; Accept respond; Close HTTP connection
Expended HTTP Protocol	Connect to HTTPD; Send query request; Accept respond; Close HTTP connection

Table2. Tthe testing procedure for front ends

Here, wherever there is an interaction between the server end and the front end, the time spent in the interaction will be sampled. For example, the time sampling for the CGI-based method is:

Time sampling 1; create connection to HTTPD; **time sampling 2**;
send CGI request; **time sampling 3**;
accept respond, **time sampling 4**;
close connection; **time sampling 5**;
testing completed; obtaining time result for the operation.

4.2 The experiment process and analysis of results

Here, we use four query statements to test the respond time for all database publishing methods. The four query statements are: simple query, general query (conditional query), complex query and query with external connection. For every query statement of every database publishing method, we tested five groups of data and take an average number as the test result.

Table 3 presents the testing results. Where each query statement is listed below:

Statement 1: SELECT DISTINCT * FROM student

Statement 2: SELECT DISTINCT * FROM student WHERE age = 22

Statement 3: SELECT DISTINCT * FROM student WHERE age = 22 ORDER BY name

Statement 4: SELECT DISTINCT student.name, student.sex, student.age, student.phone, list.sdfhfg FROM student, list WHERE student.name = list.dshgfh ORDER BY student.name

Method / Interactive Time (ms) / Statement	Base on CGI	Based on Java	Extending HTTP	Number of records returned
Statement 1	1080	1073	987	75
Statement 2	1083	1040	1004	69
Statement 3	1130	897	1016	69
Statement 4	1670	1634	1533	69

Table 3. Testing Results

For each method, its efficiency can be defined as:

$$E = \frac{\text{The number of records returned for a single search}}{\text{Time of interaction for a single search (ms)}}$$

In order to compare the efficiency for different database publishing methods, we show the testing result in terms of E in Figure 2.

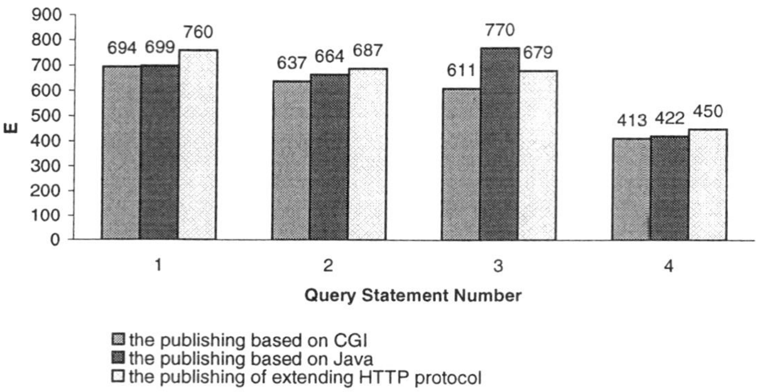

Figure 2. The comparison of efficiency for the three publishing methods

For every publishing method, its efficiency is the inverse ratio with respond time, but is a direct ratio with record numbers returned of a single interaction. Here, we need to pay attention to the fact that the testing result is a single interaction rather than repeated interactions. For database publishing based on Java, there is a connection between the client and the server and a following query does not repeat the starting procedure of the previous query. In such a case, its efficiency should be better than the method that based on the extended HTTP protocol.

From Figure 2, we can see that in general, the extended HTTP protocol is the best in terms of efficiency; the Java-based method is the second; then followed by the CGI-based method. The reasons why the Java-based method is better than the CGI-based method are that the Java-based method does not need to forward messages in the server end but directly interacts with the client; whereas the CGI-based method not only requires a starting time but also needs to forward messages for four times.

There are two reasons why the extended HTTP protocol method is better than the Java-based method. Firstly, Java execution is slow because of its interpretation. The extended HTTP protocol method also does not need a starting time and has no message forwarding. Secondly, when the Java front end interacts with the server, it includes four times of network interaction, and therefore there are eight times of network transmission in total. In general, network transmission time is much higher than the process time for the server end. This is the main reason.

5 Remarks

The World Wide Web and the Internet have revolutionized the information technologies. Services are now provided through the WWW in almost any application areas like business, commerce, education, etc [16, 18]. The popularity of WWW makes it possible for users everywhere to access and process information either in a local network or remotely. Web-based computing allows organizations to integrate disparate systems, especially database systems into a single, coherent environment [15] and to publish database information to service both internal and external customers effectively. However, as normally the services for database publishing are accessed by a huge number of users, the efficiency of the method used for database publishing is crucial. This paper analyzed the advantages and disadvantages of the two most popular methods in database publishing, and proposed a new method based on an extension to the existing HTTP protocol. The paper then evaluated the three methods through experiments and concluded that the new method is more efficient than the two existing methods.

References

1. M. Baentsch, G. Molter, and P. Sturm, "Introducing Application-level Replication and Naming into Today's Web", *Proceedings of the 5th International World Wide Web Conference*, http://www5conf.inria.fr/fich_html/papers/P3/overview.html, May 6-10 1996, Paris, France.
2. S. Chen, *Research on Database Publishing Technology Based on WWW and its Applications*, Harbin Institute of Technology, China, Master thesis, 1997.
3. T. Connolly and C.E. Begg, *Database Systems*, 2nd Ed., Addison-Wesley, 1999.
4. J. Davis and C. Lagoze, "'Drop-in' Publishing with the World Wide Web", *Proceedings of the 2nd International WWW Conference*, 1994.
5. M. Dieckmann, "When Worlds Collide: The Internet Meets the Corporate Database", *Database Programming and Design*, pp 48-54, Aug. 1995.
6. N. N. Duan, "Distributed Database Access in a Corporate Environment Using Java", *Proceedings of the 5th International World Wide Web Conference*, May 6-10, 1996, Paris, France, http://www5conf.inria.fr/fich_html/papers/P2/overview.html.
7. M. J. Garey, and D. Kossmann, "Reducing the Braking Distance of an SQL Query Engine", *VLDB* 1998, pp 158-169.

8. A. Goscinski and W. Zhou, "Client-Server Model", *The Encyclopedia of Electrical and Electronics Engineering*, J. Webster (Ed.), John Wiley & Sons Inc., New York, pp 431-451, 1999.
9. G. Hamilton, R. Cattell, and M. Fisher, *JDBC Database Access with Java*, Addison-Wesley, 1997.
10. D.J. Hughes, *Mini SQL: A Lightweight Database Engine*, Huges Technologies P/L, Australia, January 1996, http://Hughes.com.au.
11. T.M. Rajkumar and D.L. Dawley, "Designing and Managing Client/Server DBMSs", *Information Systems Management*, 1996:13(2):49-57.
12. B. Rasmussen, "Web Interface to SQL Dtabases", *Eurpoean Southem Observatory*, 1997.
13. RFC822: *Standard for the Format of ARPA Internet Text Messages*, Revised by David H. Crocker, August 13, 1982.
14. RFC1945: *Hypertext Transfer Protocol -- HTTP/1.0*, T. Berners-Lee, R. Fielding, and H. Frystyk, May 1996.
15. E. Sandewall, "Towards a World-Wide Data Base", *Proceedings of the 5th International World Wide Web Conference*, http://www5conf.inria.fr/fich_html/papers/P54/overview.html, May 6-10, 1996, Paris, France.
16. R. Vetter, "Web-Based Enterprise Computing," *IEEE Computer*, 32(5), pp. 112-116, May 1999.
17. S. Weibel, E. Miller, J. Godby, and R. LeVan, "An Architecture for Scholarly Publishing on the World Wide Web", *Proceedings of the 2nd International WWW Conference*, 1994, http://www.ncsa.uiuc.edu/SDG/IT94/Proceedings/Pub/Weibel/weibel_www_paper.html.
18. W. Zhou, "Surviving Network Partitioning in a Web-Based Application", *Proceedings of the 2nd Asia-Pacific Web Conference (APWeb'99)*, pp. 159-167, on-line publication URL: http://www.comp.polyu.edu.hk/APWEB99/, Hong Kong, September 27-30, 1999.

CONCURRENT FAIR QUEUEING: FAIR SERVICE FOR VIRTUAL WEB SITES

J. FRITZ BARNES
Vanderbilt University
Box 1679 STA B
Nashville, TN 37235
Email: J.Fritz.Barnes@vanderbilt.edu

When the demand for web pages exceeds the rate servers can generate replies, the excess demand delays web responses and can crash web servers. Requests for popular pages will delay all requests at the web server. Consequently, the popular pages use an unfair proportion of resources at the web server. As the use of virtual sites increases, this unfair service becomes an important problem. This paper presents a measure of fairness for web servers. We develop Concurrent Fair Queueing (CFQ) to control the scheduling of web responses and enforce fairness between classes of web requests.

1 Introduction

The web empowers individuals with the ability to publish information. However, the popularity of the web can overwhelm web sites resulting in download delays and inaccessible web pages. Poor performance results when rate of requests, or demand, for a web page exceeds the rate the server generates replies, or the supply. As the demand continues to exceed supply, browsers wait on pending requests, causing delays to increase[1]. Poor web performance will often limit repeat business from customers[2].

Internet Service Providers (ISPs) answer the problem of poor performance by adding virtual web hosting to their repertoire of services. The ISP maintains a set of web pages for customers, often called a virtual site, on a cluster of web servers. The ISP provides value-added services, such as providing high bandwidth to the web cluster, and maintaining the reliability of virtual web sites. Many small to mid-size companies use virtual web sites hosted at ISPs because annual expenses to maintain a virtual web server may exceed five times the cost an ISP will charge for hosting a virtual site[3].

ISPs must provide fair service to all virtual sites that share resources at the web server cluster. However, a single site can unfairly cause delays in generating responses for other virtual sites. Web servers generate responses using a first-come first-served scheduling policy. Therefore, unpopular requests incur unfair delays as they wait for the popular requests to be served. Web servers need mechanisms that provide fair service.

Diverse work exists in providing fair access to resources. Some of this work has looked at how routers allocate bandwidth to different flows, or categories of network traffic. Generalized Processor Sharing (GPS)[4,5] has been considered as a theoretical basis for handling fair allocation of bandwidth at routers. GPS provides a technique for the allocation of network bandwidth. However, it is an idealized solution. Weighted Fair Queueing (WFQ)[6], Packet Generalized Processor Sharing (PGPS)[5], and Worst-case Fair Weighted Fair Queueing (WF2Q)[7] have been proposed as packet-based representations of the GPS algorithm. These techniques schedule packets for a serial device. To handle web requests, these techniques need to be extended to handle concurrent scheduling.

We introduce Concurrent Fair Queueing (CFQ) to control how servers allocate resources to service web requests. CFQ controls the admission of requests to the web server.

In Section 2 we detail the attributes of the problem of providing fair services at web servers and provide a definition of fair web service. We analyze CFQ in Section 3, and conclude in Section 4.

2 Fair Service for Web Applications

This section presents a measurement of fair service for web applications. We first discuss the attributes of web servers that affect the definition of fair service.

2.1 Attributes of a Fair Service Solution

In this section, we discuss our design decisions. Specifically, we have decided that responses should use concurrency, request rates that exceeds supply should be trimmed, and that a solution cannot determine the running time of requests.

Web servers differ from network routers in the use of concurrency. Networks route a flow of packets to a single outgoing link and the work required does not vary significantly between packets. Yet, web servers benefit from generating multiple requests concurrently. While waiting for a read from disk to finish, the server can parse an incoming request. In previous work[8], we show that generating a single response at a time results in response throughput less than half the throughput when we concurrently service several requests at the same time. A mechanism for fair service must allow concurrent generation of responses.

If demand at web servers never exceeded the rate at which web servers could supply web pages, solutions enforcing fair service would be unnecessary. Unfortunately, high demand is commonplace. We propose that web servers should proactively react when the demand exceeds supply. Web servers should either reduce visual accuracy of pictures[9], switch to content with fewer embedded images and links[10], or selectively refuse service to some requests[8].

Network routers handle packets of data. The primary difference in handling a given packet is the size of the given packet. Larger packets require more time to transmit than smaller packets. A larger variety exists in workloads for web servers. Web workloads consist of a combination of network transfers, computation, and disk operations. Two requests may differ significantly in the amount of resources needed to service the request. Consequently, two different requests may involve very different overheads in generating a response. The web server should consider the differences of web pages.

2.2 *Definition of Fair Service*

Previous work has defined fair service for networks[6,5,7]. In this section, we adapt a definition for web service that considers the variability in work required to generate different requests. The primary difference in our definition is that we define fairness not by the amount of traffic served by a router, but by the amount of time required to generate a response. We characterize a system by weights $\phi_1, \phi_2, \ldots, \phi_n$. Let r_k^i be the amount of time required to generate the response for the kth request of class i. The set of requests $R^i = r_1^i, r_2^i, \ldots, r_m^i$ defines all responses created during the interval $(\tau, t]$. Than we define share of service S_i as:

$$S_i(\tau, t) = \frac{\sum_{k=1}^{m} r_k^i}{t - \tau} \tag{1}$$

A web server provides fair service if the following inequality holds for all request classes that have backlogged requests during the entire interval $(\tau, t]$:

$$\frac{S_i}{S_j} \geq \frac{\phi_i}{\phi_j}, j = 1, 2, \ldots, n \tag{2}$$

2.3 *Concurrent Fair Queueing*

In CFQ, we wish to allow the generation of multiple requests at the same time. Unlike GPS, we cannot infinitely work on requests because adding concurrency increases response times[8]. We therefore, divide the outgoing flow into pre-defined number of channels $\mathcal{N}$. Where a channel forms a connection between a web server and a single web client.

We refer to request classes that represent the flows allocated in the GPS and WFQ algorithms. We divide the channels between the service classes using the weights $\phi_1, \ldots, \phi_n$. The weights can be scaled to define a percentage of resources ($100\bar{\phi}_i$) that will be allocated to a class. We calculate $\bar{\phi}_i$:

$$\bar{\phi}_i = \frac{\phi_i}{\sum_{j=1}^{n} \phi_j} \quad (3)$$

The number of channels allocated to a given class of requests will equal:

$$N_i = \lfloor \bar{\phi}_i \mathcal{N} \rfloor \quad (4)$$

3 Analysis

We split the analysis into two parts. The first part determines whether CFQ meets our fairness definition. The second part experimentally evaluates the implementations ability to provide differentiated services.

3.1 Fairness and CFQ

In CFQ, the server generates multiple responses concurrently. As long as class i is continuously backlogged during an interval the following equation defines the class i's share of service:

$$S_i(\tau, t) = N_i(t - \tau) \quad (5)$$

For a class to be continuously backlogged there must be enough outstanding requests that the server generates N_i requests during the entire interval (τ, t).

The number of channels allocated to a class i (N_i) was defined in Equation 4. If we limit the selection of $\bar{\phi}_i$ such that $\bar{\phi}_i = \phi' / \mathcal{N}$, N_i will equal an integer. We can rewrite Equation 5: $S_i = \phi'(t - \tau)$.

The share of server resources allocated to a class will equal

$$\frac{S_i}{S_j} \geq \frac{\phi_i'(t-\tau)}{\phi_j'(t-\tau)}, j = 1, 2, \ldots, n \quad (6)$$

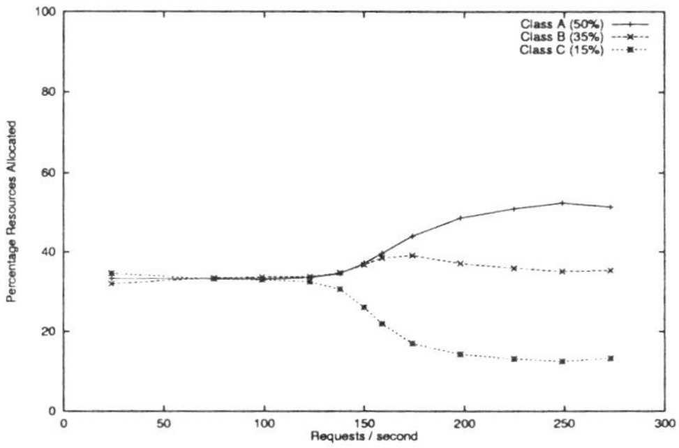

Figure 1. Server resources allocated to different request classes

As a result the definition holds. However, we have limited the class allocation weights, ϕ_i, such that they will generate an integer numbers of channels.

3.2 Allocation of Web Server Resources

This experiment measures the allocation of server resources to three request classes (A, B, C). Our test environment consists of four 500 MHz dual processor Pentium III computers. A 10 Mbps Ethernet connects the computers. All computers run the Linux operating system. These experiments use Apache version 1.3.6. We run a benchmark on three computers which make requests to a web server running on the fourth computer. The fourth computer uses the CFQ algorithm to perform admission control to the Apache web server. More information about the experimental setup and benchmark programs can be found in a previous paper[8].

The server allocates 50, 35, and 15 percent of the server's resources to classes A, B, and C respectively. We measure the resources allocated by the ratio of the number of responses of a particular class compared with the total number of responses generated.

Figure 1 graphs the percentage of the resources allocated to a specific class as the request rate increases. We calculate data points by counting the number of responses generated at a specific request rate. The percentage of responses for the three classes is equal (33%) initially because the demand for web pages does not exceed the rate that the server can service requests. When the requests rate exceeds 145 requests/second, the percentage of responses approaches the desired resource allocations.

4 Conclusions

Web servers need a notion of fair service that limits popular content from causing poor performance for other content contained on a web server. We present a notion for measuring fairness for web requests and a mechanism to enforce fairness. We have implemented an architecture supporting CFQ for web servers and presented results demonstrating that the allocation of resources meets specified percentages.

References

1. X. Chen and P. Mohapatra. Providing differentiated services from an internet server. In *Eigth International Conference on Computer Communications and Networks*, October 1999.
2. N. Bhatti, A. Bouch, and A. Kuchinsky. Integrating user-perceived quality into web server design. In *Proceedings of the Ninth International World Wide Web Conference*, May 2000.
3. J. Camp and S. Flynn. The internet data services report. Morgan Stanley Dean Witter White Paper. `http://www.msdw.com/techresearch/inetdata/info.html`, September 1999.
4. L. Kleinrock. *Queueing Systems Volume 2: Computer Applications.* Wiley, New York, 1976.
5. A. K. Parekh and R. G. Gallager. A generalized processor sharing approach to flow control in integrated services networks: The single-node case. *IEEE/ACM Transactions on Networking*, 1(3):344–57, June 1993.
6. A. Demers, S. Keshav, and S. Shenker. Analysis and simulation of a fair queueing algorithm. In *ACM SIGCOMM Conference. Applications, Technologies, Architectures, and Protocols for Computer Communications*, pages 1–12, September 1989.
7. J. C.R. Bennett and H. Zhang. WF^2Q: Worst-case fair weighted fair queueing. In *Proceedings of IEEE INFOCOM '96, the Conference on Computer Communications*, pages 120–8, March 1996.
8. J. F. Barnes, R. Pandey, and R. Olsson. Reducing interference in web hosting: A differentiated services approach. Technical report, University of California, Davis, 17 April 2000.
9. S. Chandra, C. Schlatter Ellis, and A. Vahdat. Differentiated multimedia web services using quality aware transcoding. In *INFOCOM 2000 - Nineteenth Annual Joint Conference of the IEEE Computer and Communications Societies*, March 2000.
10. T. F. Abdelzaher and N. Bhatti. Web content adaptation to improve server overload behavior. In *Proceedings of the Eigth International World Wide Web Conference*, pages 1563–77, May 1999.

Chapter 9
Distributed & Parallel Operating Systems and Middleware

UMM: UNIFIED META-OBJECT MODEL FOR OPEN DISTRIBUTED SYSTEMS

R. R. RAJE
Department of Computer and Information Science, Indiana University Purdue University Indianapolis, 723 W. Michigan Street, SL 280, Indianapolis, IN 46202, USA
E-mail: rraje@cs.iupui.edu

Abstract:- The success of organizations, in the era of interconnected world, will depend upon their ability to create robust and efficient software realizations for open distributed systems. Such systems, due to their nature, will require combining distributed objects (or components) adhering to different models. In this article, we present an overview of a meta-model, which allows a seamless integration of heterogeneous software components.

Key-Words:- Distributed, Objects, Meta-model, Aspects, Collaboration, Service

1 Introduction

In this new century, we will be much more dependent on the advances in the field of Information Technology. This observation is emphasized in the President's Information Technology Advisory Committee (PITAC) report. This report has identified five priorities for research, software being the first one [1]. It also recommends research in component-based software design, and the exploration of protocols, languages, data structures to promote interoperability of applications running current across wide-area networks. This paper addresses some of these challenges, especially as applied to the domain of open distributed systems.

Distributed systems (DS) assume the view that "the network is the computer" and are becoming ubiquitous in many critical domains. These systems are mainly characterized by a presence of heterogeneity, local autonomy over hardware and software resources, built-in openness and a probability of partial failure. Despite the achievements in software engineering, the development of software for large-scale de-centralized systems is still a challenge. As more organizations will be required to design open DS, it will be necessary, for these organizations, to create robust and effective software solutions for DS.

Out of the existing options, the software design of DS can efficiently be achieved by using the principles of distributed-object computing (distributed objects, by their definition, are components and hence, in this article we treat the terms objects and components as synonyms). Under this paradigm, DS are viewed as a collection of a large number of heterogeneous, interconnected, (possibly) mobile and "smart" components. These components constantly discover one another, offer/utilize services and negotiate the cost and the quality of these services. Such a view not only provides a scalable solution but also presents an uniform access to underlying resources, while hiding their heterogeneity.

Various distributed component models have been proposed by industry and academia. Each have their strengths and weaknesses. However, almost a majority of these have been designed and/or deployed for 'closed' systems, i.e., systems, although distributed in nature, running in a confined setup, such as a large corporation. In contrast, the software realization of open DS will require combining components that adhere to different models, thereby, increasing the complexity of software development. Hence, a comprehensive framework is required to tame this complexity and aid in the design of DS.

Many important issues need to be considered during the design of such a framework, specifically: a) a design of a meta-model for components, b) a multi-level approach for indicating the contracts and associated constraints of the components, c) guidelines for specifying and verifying the quality of components, d) a formal mechanism for precisely describing the computation achieved by each component, e) a set of rules for static and dynamic integration of components, f) mechanisms for evaluating the quality of the resulting component assemblages, g) a methodology for component-based software design, and h) validating this framework by creating proof-of-concept prototypes of distributed applications from different domains. Due to the space constraints, here we only describe the general architecture of the meta-model and briefly discuss related features.

2 Background

Many models have been suggested for distributed-component computing. For the sake of brevity, here, we briefly describe only the prominent ones.

Java-RMI and Jini: The computational model of Java is *write once and run anywhere.* The basic model of Java is incapable of initiating computations in a remote address space. To overcome this deficiency, Sun has released a mechanism, called RMI (Remote Method Invocation), which allows a programmer to invoke methods on specified remote-objects [2,3]. RMI is a language-centric model, where Java acts as the interface and implementational language. The Jini [4] architecture aims at replacing the notion of peripherals and applications with that of network-available services and clients that use those services. There are three components of the Jini architecture – a) infrastructure, b) programming model and c) services. Jini is built on Java and RMI.

Although, Jini is a correct step in the direction of providing a unified view to distributed computing, it does assume a homogeneous view, i.e., everything is Java, a view which may not be pragmatic in open systems.

CORBA: CORBA interfaces are specified in IDL (Interface Definition Language)[5,3]. The implementations of the objects can be written in any language, as long as there exists a proper mapping between IDL and the implementation language. A client object, residing on one machine, may request that an operation be performed on an object whose implementation resides on a different machine. This is accomplished by making use of the Object Request Broker (ORB), which is responsible for finding the object implementation, preparing the object implementation to receive the request, and communicating the data comprising the request. In addition, CORBA provides IIOP (Internet Inter-Object Protocol), which allows interoperability across the networks. CORBA supports many facilities and services and allows dynamic invocations via DII (Dynamic Invocation Interface). However, it does not allow complete object-to-object connectivity (due to a presence of the broker) and its introspection abilities are minimal (as offered by DII, without concrete notions of quality of service).

DCOM: DCOM[7,3] is Microsoft's answer to the distributed-object world. It is based upon their earlier model, COM. It is also a language independent model (interfaces are specified in MIDL). However, unlike CORBA, it is not a platform or operating system independent model. It does offer some level of introspection capabilities, as it allows a set of functions bound to a certain object that implements them, and which may be queried by a user employing the built-in QueryInterface function.

Web Object Model and DOM: The popularity of the WWW and its limitations have been well analyzed by many researchers[8]. They have argued that an attempt is necessary to amalgamate the web model and the distributed-object model[9]. Manola[8,9] has proposed a 'web object model', that allows the construction of object-like facilities that enable the development of powerful Web applications. The Document Object Model (DOM) proposed by W3C[9,10] provides a scripting interface to the document and defines how to manipulate the objects found in a HTML or XML document. Both these aim at integrating the principles of the Web and distributed-objects, but lack the richness of a meta-model.

Pragmatic Object Web: Pragmatic object web[11] is defined as the emerging synthesis of multiple object models. It is aimed at creating a hybrid object system. They describe different application projects which, in fact, reaffirm the motivation of our model. However, they do incorporate the traditional high-performance computing as the back-end, thereby constraining their approach. Also, they do not address factors such as precise specification of computation, user preferences, aggregations, market-based economic models, which are issues that form key components of our proposed model.

In addition to these models, there are many projects, such as Hadas [6], Infospheres [12], Legion [13], Globus [14], etc., which aim at developing infrastructures for open computing. A large percentage of them are created for traditional high-performance applications and are based on one of the existing (or a variation of an existing) distributed-object model. Hence, we have not described these projects here.

In recent past, there have been many projects, such as Agent TCL [15], Aglets [16], JATLite [17], etc., based on the principles of intelligent agents. Distributed (and mobile agents) are considered as one of the promising alternatives to develop open systems. Although agents are a powerful concept, we feel that they are at a higher level of abstraction (than objects). Also, many of the agent projects/frameworks use one or the other existing distributed-object model at the low-level and hence, we are not considering the agent model during the discussion of our proposed model. However, in our model, we have incorporated a few concepts from the domain of agents.

3 Meta Model for Objects

3.1 Why a Meta-model?

Components, by their definition, are independent of the language implementation, tools and the execution environment. However, as described earlier, many different models exist for the development and deployment of components in DS. Also, to a large extent these models were designed for geographically dispersed, but closely controlled systems. Hence, they will fall short when applied to future systems, which will be inherently open and distributed. Each model assumes only its own presence, which contradicts the local autonomy principle of DS. Even if any of the existing models becomes universally accepted, it will require the re-engineering of many systems, which may be technically sound, but not economically viable. Also, many of these models lack comprehensiveness as they do not consider concepts such as quality and economic frameworks. An open distributed system will, certainly, contain components adhering to different models. These components will have to interact with each other to facilitate the software realization of DS. In recent past, scripting languages such as Truce, Perl, Tcl, JavaScript, and Python have been used to 'glue' heterogeneous components. Such an approach is suitable for rapid prototyping; but, it does not contain the complete power of a rich meta-model. Hence, there is a need for a comprehensive meta-model, which will seamlessly encompass existing models. The design of any meta-model should extract useful features from existing approaches, but, reorient, integrate and enhance them, and incorporate innovative concepts to increase its comprehensiveness.

The first step in the creation of a meta-model is to investigate the existing models with an in-depth study of their architectures, and identifying strengths and weaknesses by developing prototype systems. Many of cur past and present projects, such as ARMI [18] and D-SIFTER [19], are aimed at exploring and experimenting with existing models. These experiments have provided us with a sufficient basis, from the perspectives of both architecture and application design, for the creation of the meta-model.

Below we describe a Unified Meta-object Model, which seamlessly encompasses existing and future models, thereby providing a solution for the software development of open distributed systems.

3.2 Unified Meta-object Model (UMM)

The three parts of the UMM are *object, service* and *collaboration*. The innovative aspects of the UMM are in the structure of these parts and their inter-relations.

Object

In UMM, objects are autonomous entities, whose implementations are non-uniform, i.e., each object adheres to some distributed-object model and there is no notion of either a centralized controller or a unified implementational framework. Each object has a state, an identity and a behavior. Thus, all objects have well-defined interfaces and private implementations. In addition, each object in UMM has three aspects: 1) *Computational Aspect*, 2) *Cooperative Aspect*, and 3) *Auxiliary Aspect.*

Computational Aspect: The computational aspect reflects the task(s) carried out by each object. It in-turn depends upon: a) the objective(s) of the task, b) the techniques used to achieve these objectives, and c) the precise specification of the functionality offered by the object. In DS, objects must be able to 'understand' the functionality of other objects. Thus, each object in UMM supports the concept of introspection, by which an object will precisely describe its service to other inquiring objects. There are various alternatives for an object to indicate its computation – ranging from simple text to formal descriptions. Both these extremes have advantages and drawbacks. The use of formal techniques will certainly alienate the ambiguity, but can add to an overhead (as formal methods are harder to understand and, thus, remain a forte of a smaller number of highly talented developers). The UMM takes a mixed approach to indicate the computational aspect of an object – a simple textual part, called *inherent attributes* and a formal precise part, called *functional attributes*. The inherent attributes are represented by a tuple of the form < *id, creator, object model, version, date*>. The name of each component of the tuple is self-explanatory of its significance. The inherent attributes will be specified by the developer of that object.

The functional part is formal and indicates the precise nature of the computation, its associated contracts and the level(s) of the quality of the service offered by the object. In [20] an argument is made in the favor of multi-level contracts for objects (components). They have classified the contracts into four levels – syntactic, behavioral, concurrency and quality of service. UMM integrates this multi-level contract concept into the functional part of the computational aspect. In an open system, each component will be offering a service (more about it is discussed later) and hence, the level related to the quality of service is especially critical in UMM. The level of the quality depends upon factors such as, the algorithm used, the execution model, resources required, time, precision and classes of the results obtained. UMM makes an attempt at quantifying the quality of service by creating an appropriate vocabulary and providing multiple levels of quality, which could be negotiated by the components involved in an interaction. The functional part is specified in a formal fashion by using the principles of denotational semantics. This part will also be specified by the creator of the component.

Cooperative Aspect: In UMM, objects do not exist in isolation. They are always in the process of cooperating with each other. This cooperation may be task-based (to achieve a certain task in DS, an object may associate with other objects, delegate sub-tasks to them and coordinate their activities) or greed-based (an object may offer its services only to accumulate compensation for its owner). The cooperative aspect depends on many factors: detection of other objects, cost of service, inter-object negotiations, images of collaborators, aggregations, duration, mode, and quality. More details about this aspect is mentioned in the collaboration part of the UMM.

Auxiliary Aspect: In addition to computation and communication, mobility, security, and fault tolerance are the necessary features of an open DS. The auxiliary aspect of an object will address these features. In UMM, each object can be potentially mobile. The developer of the object will decide whether it is mobile or not and for what duration it will stick to a specific role (stationary or mobile). The mobility of the object will be shown as a 'mobility attribute' (a notion similar to the inherent attribute). If an object is mobile, then the mobility attribute will contain the necessary information, such as its implementation details and required execution environment. Similarly, security in any global system is a critical issue. It is evident on many levels: i) intra-object ('how secure is each object?'), ii) inter-object ('how secure is an inter-object collaboration?'), and iii) resource ('how secure are the resources to which objects will have accesses?'). The security attribute of an object will contain the necessary information about its security features. As DS are prone to frequent failures, full and partial, fault tolerance is critical in these systems. Similar to mobility and security, each object, in UMM, contains fault-tolerant attributes in its auxiliary aspect.

As local autonomy is inherent in open DS, forcing every object developer to abide by certain rigid rules, although attractive, is doomed to fail. UMM tackles the issue of non-uniformity with two special categories of objects – *head-hunter* and *translator*. These objects are responsible for allowing the seamless integration of different object models and sustaining a cooperation among heterogeneous (adhering to different models) objects. Although, head-hunter and translator objects are special categories of objects, they also have all the three aspects in them.

`Head-hunter Objects:` The tasks of these objects are to detect the presence of new objects, offer memberships to them, register their functionalities, communicate and attempt match-making between service producers and consumers, while demanding their compensations (more about this is discussed later). A head-hunter object is analogous to a broker, or a binder or a Trader in other models, with one important difference – a broker is passive, i.e., the onus of registration is on the object and not on the broker. Thus, in a brokered model, an object (either a service provider or a seeker) initiates the registration process, as opposed to a head-hunter, which is active – it discovers other objects and makes an attempt to register them with itself. During the registration process, each object will inform the head hunter about its inherent, functional, mobility and security attributes. The head hunter object will use this information during the process of matching. An object may be registered with multiple head-hunters. Once a head-hunter creates a match between the supplier and seeker objects, it receives its compensation and no longer interferes in the communication between the matched pair. Head-hunters may cooperate with each other, (as these are also objects with cooperative aspects), in order to cater to a larger number of seeker/supplier objects. The functionality of the head hunter objects makes it necessary for them to communicate with objects belonging to any model, implying that the cooperative aspect of head hunter objects be universal, i.e. able to facilitate collaboration with any object. Once a head hunter object has created a seeker-supplier pair, the concerned objects, in this pair, must be able to establish a direct communication. Considering the heterogeneous nature of the objects, it is conceivable that the seeker and the provider be compliant to different models, thus, creating a need for a *translator* object.

`Translator Objects:` A translator object acts as a mediator between two objects adhering to different models. Thus, the cooperative aspect of a translator object has two parts - one each for the two models, to which the communicating objects adhere. The computational aspect of the translator object will indicate the two models it is proficient in. Like other objects, translator objects will register with the head hunters and while doing so, they will indicate their specialization (which models they can bridge efficiently). During a request from a seeker, the head hunter object will not only search for a provider, but it will also supply the necessary details of a translator, if deemed necessary.

Service

The concept of a service is the next part of the UMM. A service could be an intensive computational effort or an access to underlying resources. Irrespective of the nature of the service, objects offer them with an intention of accumulating compensation for their owners. The notion of service is a prerequisite for the concept of collaboration. In DS, it is natural to expect that each seeker have several choices for obtaining a specific service. Thus, each object, in addition to indicating its functionality, must be able to specify the cost and quality of the service offered. A seeker object will consider these factors while deciding on its collaborator.

The nature of the service offered by each object is dependent upon the computation performed by that object. In addition to the algorithm used, expected computational effort and resources required, the cost of each service will be decided by the motivation of the owner and the dynamics of demand and supply. In a dynamic environment costs must always be accompanied by the duration for which the costs are valid. As the system dynamics undergo constant changes, the methodologies used to fix the cost of a service will evolve as time progresses, thereby creating a need to indicate the time sensitiveness of the cost. The quality of service will be an indication given by an object, on behalf of its owner, about its confidence to carry out the required services in spite of the constantly changing execution environment and a possibility of partial failures. The techniques used to determine the cost, the time-validity and the quality of a service will depend upon the tasks carried out by the object and the objectives of its owner and will involve principles of distributed decision making.

The service offered by each object crosscuts its there aspects: a) the syntactic and quality features are reflected as a part of the computational aspect, b) the behavior ('what exactly is this service offering and what state changes will take place as a result of the execution of this service?') and the synchronization ('how would the service be affected in a concurrent scenario, i.e., will be the service affected if more than one clients access it concurrently and what kind of safe guards would be needed to ensure a specific-level of service?') are incorporated in the cooperative part, and c) any special features ('is this service fault-tolerant?') are indicated in the auxiliary aspect. Each object will publish these attributes and will export them to the concerned seekers.

Collaboration

The third and the final part of UMM is collaboration. Collaboration is a need for DS and a consequence of service. Collaboration is affected by many factors: detection, negotiations, images, aggregations, duration, mode and trust. The detection of collaborators, in UMM, is handled by the head hunter and translator objects (as described above). In an open environment there are many choices for a specific service and hence, each object must be able to negotiate with other objects. The notion of a large sea of objects meshes well with market-driven economic models. Objects demanding services must compensate the service providers (including head-hunter and translator objects). Once an inter-object communication is established, the associated objects will indulge in negotiations. This concept is similar to the one suggested (from the domain of intelligent agents) by Genesereth and Ketchpel [21]. Selecting a collaborator depends upon many factors ranging from trivial ones like the cost and quality of service to more sophisticated ones like maintaining images of different service providers. For example, depending upon the past experiences (how well and promptly was the task completed?), a seeker may choose to select a more expensive provider over a cheaper one. These images will be updated continuously, thereby, indicating the dynamic nature of the distributed applications.

Also, as indicated earlier, the costs of the services are time and market-dynamics dependent. Thus, each object should have an ability to negotiate with the others so as to adjust the costs and quality factors. Once an object has selected a collaborator, UMM then allows two modes of obtaining service: a) buying – a copy of the provider will be forever owned by the seeker, and b) leasing – a service is provided at an agreed cost for a certain amount of time and can be renewed (the idea is identical to the one used in Jini).

Just like the service component, the collaboration component of UMM is also spread over all three aspects: a) the inherent attributes ('who?') and the functional attributes ('what?') are a part of the computational attribute, b) the detection of other objects, inter-object negotiations, communication modes, images of the collaborators and selection are reflected in the cooperative aspect, and c) any special features of the object and/or of its collaborators are present in the auxiliary aspect of the object.

Thus, each object in UMM is formally represented as a 3-tuple: <CA, CoA, AA>, where CA = computational attribute, CoA = cooperative attribute and AA = auxiliary attribute. Each component of the tuple is further divided into sub-tuples, the size of each is variable. The interface of each object comprises of CA, CoA and AA. As each object in UMM must contain all the three aspects, preferably each class (objects are assumed to be instances of classes) in UMM will preferably implement Universal Interface (UI). An UI consists of: a) common features related to CA, b) common features related to CoA, c) common features related to AA and d) reflexive features (as an open environment will decree the use of dynamic detection of unknown objects). In addition, the UI will consists of the necessary mechanisms for low-level communication and collaboration, thus, relieving the communication burden from the application developer.

Anant – An Environment Based on UMM

At present, we are in the process of creating *Anant* (meaning *endless*), an environment based on UMM. Anant is being developed using Java, due to its inherent advantages. As that work is in the preliminary stages, here we describe only a few features of Anant.

For the benefits of a new environment to reach a large audience, it is necessary to provide an easy-to-use and effective interface to it. Thus, Anant will have a personalized interface, which will lessen the burden of the user. We are proposing a notion of a *personalized object (PO)* – another category of the general object in UMM. The tasks of a PO will be to accept queries from the user, contact the head hunters and translators (if needed), create an ensemble of objects necessary to achieve the task (as indicated in the query), coordinate the activities of all the constituent objects, collect the results, compose them and present them to the user. The user will specify the queries using the formal representations of all the aspects of the objects which they want PO to seek on their behalf. The results (which themselves may be objects with associated execution environments) will be 'personalized' by the PO based on the user preferences. The user will specify his/her preferences to the PO through a use of a standard layout language like XML. The notion of PO is similar to the personalized agents from the domain of AI, but more specialized due to the use of formal specification of the aspects as the 'communication language' between the user and the PO, rather than a natural language or an agent-language.

Testing and Validation

Any new environment must be evaluated and validated by developing prototype systems, experimenting with them, gathering feedback from them and incorporating the experiences gained into the environment to enhance its capabilities. In addition, these prototypes will provide the necessary means to compare and contrast with existing alternatives. Currently, we are involved in many inter-disciplinary projects, such as information filtering, which will ideal test-beds to validate UMM and Anant. As the development of Anant is in its preliminary stages, here we have not described any specific application scenario involving UMM. However, the applicability of UMM to many different domains, which involve distributed components scattered over open and interconnected system, is very obvious.

4 Significance and Conclusions

This paper addresses some of the key issues that will have to be resolved as the operations of society's enterprises expand ever more globally. Monolithic computing systems will no longer be capable of dealing with the geographical extension and computational complexity such operations will require. The response to this will be the creation of systems that automatically adjust with a minimum of human intervention to the changing requirements of the enterprise and the supporting open DS.

The meta-model, UMM, by its nature, does not decree the use of a specific implementational model. Also, it does allow a seamless integration of existing objects, with a minimum reorganization. The basic components of UMM, object, service and collaboration, themselves are not new. However, their internal structures, associated contracts, QoS, and explicit integration is innovative. These also provide an illusion of uniform and simplified access to underlying heterogeneous computational and network resources. An incorporation of a new model, in UMM, will only need the design and development of appropriate translator objects and modification of head hunter objects. Such an approach will not only tackle the model-heterogeneity but also address the scalability of the model and the environment.

References

1. President's Information Technology Advisory Committee. *Information*

Technology Research: Investing in Our Future, 1999.
2. Sun Microsystems, Inc. *Java^{TM} Remote Method Invocation Specification*, 1996.
3. Orfali R, and Harkey, D. *Client/Server Programming with JAVA and CORBA*. John Wiley & Sons, Inc., 1997.
4. Waldo, J. The Jini Architecture for Network-centric Computing. *Communications of ACM*, 42(7):76–82, July 1999.
5. Siegel, J. *CORBA Fundamentals and Programming*. John Wiley & Sons, Inc., 1996.
6. Israel, B. and Kaiser, G. Coordinating Distributed Components Over the Internet. *IEEE Internet Computing*, pages 83–86, 2(2), 1998.
7. Microsoft Corporation. *DCOM Specifications, www.microsoft.com/oledev/olecom*, 1998.
8. Manola, F. Towards a Object Model. *www.objs.com/OSA/wom.htm*, 1998.
9. Manola, F. Technologies for a Web Object Model. *IEEE Internet Computing*, 3(1):38–47, January-February 1999.
10. Wood, L. Programming the Web: The W3C DOM Specification. *IEEE Internet Computing*, 3(1):48–54, January-February 1999.
11. Fox, G. The Document Object Model Universal Access Other Objects CORBA XML Jini JavaScript etc. *www.npac.syr.edu/users/ gcf/msrcobjectsapril99*, 1999.
12. Infospheres Project. *www.infospheres.caltech.edu*, 1998.
13. Legion Project, www.cs.virginia.edu/~legion, 1999.
14. Globus Project. *www.globus.org*, 2000.
15. Kotz, D., Gray, R. *et al*,. Agent TCL: Targetting the Needs of Mobile Computers. *IEEE Internet Computing*, pages 58–67, 1(4), 1997.
16. Aglet Project. *www.trl.ibm.co.jp/aglets*, 2000.
17. JATLite Project. *java.stanford.edu*, 2000.
18. Raje, R. *et al*,. An Asynchronous Remote Method Invocation (ARMI) Mechanism for Java. *Concurrency: Practice and Experience*, 9(11), 1207-1211 (November 1997), 1997.
19. Raje, R. *et al*,. A Bidding Mechanism for Web-Based Agents Involved in Information Classification. *WWW Journal* , 1(1998):155–165, 1998.
20. Beugnard, A., Jezequel, J. *et al*,. Making Components Contract Aware. *IEEE Computer*, 32(7):38–45, July 1999.
21. Genesereth, M. and Ketchpel, S. Software Agents. *Communications of the ACM*, 37(7), 48-53, 1994.

A Framework for Distributed Virtual Sculpting

Frederick W.B. Li[†] Rynson W.H. Lau[†‡] Frederick Ng[†]

[†] Department of Computer Science, City University of Hong Kong, Hong Kong

[‡] Microsoft Research China, 5/F Beijing Sigma Center, Beijing 100080, China[a]

Although there has been a lot of work on collaborative distributed virtual environments, very few projects are on collaborative virtual sculpting, where the target objects are likely to be deforming continuously. A major problem is that the rendering of deforming objects is computation intensive. This leads to a large latency and decreases the interactivity of the system. To overcome this performance limitation, we recently developed an efficient technique for rendering deforming NURBS surfaces. In this paper, we propose a framework for collaborative virtual sculpting in a distributed virtual environment. To take advantage of the rendering method that we have developed, deformable objects in the environment are modeled using NURBS surfaces to accelerate their rendering in the client machines. We present a data structure for transmitting the deformable objects. We also introduce the idea of editing region and the corresponding locking mechanism for simultaneous virtual sculpting by multiple clients.

1 Introduction

With the introduction of distributed virtual environments [1], we may now interact with each other in a virtual environment via a local network or through the internet. This encourages multi-user virtual collaborations, where the participants may not need to be physically at the same location.

In [2,3], we proposed a framework for distributed virtual environments over the Internet, in which progressive multiresolution modeling [4], caching mechanisms and pre-fetching mechanisms were used to minimize the amount of date sent over the network. In this paper, we extend the work to collaborative virtual sculpting. The proposed method provides a multi-user collaborative environment for participants at different geographical locations to modify the shapes of 3D objects. This technique will be extremely useful in reducing the cost of the product design process in manufacturing and in sculpting art works.

In the new method, we model each deformable object with NURBS surfaces [5]. Although polygon meshes are widely used in object modeling, the vertex data is very often large in size and therefore time consuming for transmission. This reduces the interactivity of the collaborative sculpting, where the model deformation updates are needed to be sent across the network frequently. For NURBS surfaces, however, their representations are much more

---

[a]Part of this work was conducted while the author was a visiting researcher at Microsoft Research China, on leave from City University of Hong Kong.

compact and they can be deformed simply by changing the positions of the control points. Our distributed virtual sculpting method proposed here makes use of two methods that we have developed. First, we make use of the incremental property of NURBS surfaces to accelerate the rendering of the deforming objects in the client machines. Our approach in rendering deforming NURBS surfaces [6,7] was to incrementally update a pre-generated polygon model of each deforming surface and progressively refine the resolution of the polygon model according to the change in surface curvature. Second, we apply the virtual 3D sculpting method [8,9] that we have developed in here to allow direct object modification using the *CyberGlove*^{TM}. In this sculpting method, a parametric hand surface is created that interpolates all the key data points of the *CyberGlove*^{TM} and then mapped to the object to be deformed. By flexing the user's hand, the object can be deformed accordingly in an intuitive way.

The rest of paper is organized as follows. Section 2 gives a brief survey on related work. Section 3 reviews our deformable NURBS rendering method. Section 4 discusses the framework of our system. Section 5 presents a linear data structure to serialize the polygon model of the deforming surface. Section 6 introduces the idea of virtual sculpting, editing region and the corresponding locking mechanism. It also shows both the client-server and the client-client interactions. Section 7 presents some results and evaluates the new method. Finally, Section 8 briefly conclude the paper.

2 Related Work

Several frameworks and application systems for supporting distributed virtual environments have been proposed. They include **DIVE** [10], **SIMNET** [11], **NPSNET** [12], **MASSIVE** [13], **VLNET** [14] and **COVEN** [15]. These systems mainly address some system issues or focus on the interactions between the participants and the virtual objects in particular applications such as visualization, simulation, training and entertainment. Systems developed to support virtual sculpting are mainly for use in a single user environment. Galyean and Hughes developed a voxel based technique for virtual sculpting [16]. By using a 3D tracker, the user may edit a volumetric object by removing/clearing the voxels. The resultant voxel data is then converted to a polygon mesh using the marching-cube algorithm. Another system is THRED (Two Handed Refining Editor) [17,18] developed by Shaw et al. to incorporate both hands, each tracked by a 3D tracker, to sculpture polygonal surfaces. The dominant hand selects and manipulates vertices, while the less dominant hand sets the position and orientation of the scene and the level of subdivision of the surface. Kameyama [19] proposed a Virtual Clay Modeling System. The system uses a special input device with a 3D tracker and a tactile sensor. The tactile sensor is made of arrays of pressure sensors and is covered by a soft rubber pad. By pushing at the tactile sensor, the user may deform an object using his hands. However, the resulting object is in the form of grid surface data and must be converted to solid model data for use in design or manufacturing systems.

Distributed systems developed for collaborative virtual sculpting are rare. Nishino et al. [20] proposed a method for sharing interactive deformation in collaborative 3D modeling. In the method, the object for virtual sculpting is modeled by implicit surfaces. All clients have their own replicas of the object. Any client can edit the object only if it can obtain an update right from a central server. While a client is editing the object, it broadcasts the update parameters to all the participating clients, so that the clients can tessellate the updated object for rendering. After the client finishes the editing, it releases the update right by acknowledging the server.

3 Deformable NURBS Rendering Method

The idea of our deformable NURBS rendering method is that we maintain two data structures of each deforming surface, the surface model itself and a polygon model representing the surface model [6,7]. As the surface deforms, the polygon model is not regenerated but incrementally updated to represent the deforming surface. Two techniques are fundamental to our method: *incremental polygon model updating* and *resolution refinement*.

3.1 Incremental Polygon Model Updating

Incremental polygon model Updating is based on the incremental property of the polygonal representation of a surface obtained by evaluating the surface equation with some discrete parametric values. If a control point $P_{s,t}$ is moved to $\overline{P}_{s,t}$ with a displacement vector $\vec{V} = \overline{P}_{s,t} - P_{s,t}$, the incremental difference d between the two polygonal representations of the surface before and after the control point movement is as follows:

$$d = \overline{S} - S = \begin{bmatrix} \alpha_{1,1} & \cdots & \alpha_{1,n} \\ \vdots & \ddots & \vdots \\ \alpha_{m,1} & \cdots & \alpha_{m,n} \end{bmatrix} \vec{V} \tag{1}$$

where $1 \leq s \leq m$, $1 \leq t \leq n$, S and $\overline{S}$ are the polygon models of the surface before and after the control point movement, respectively. Each $\alpha_{s,t}$ is a *deformation coefficient*, a constant for each particular pair of (u, v) values. Hence, if the resolution of the polygon model representing the surface remains unchanged before and after the deformation, we may precompute the deformation coefficients and update the polygon model incrementally by the deformation coefficients and the displacement vector as shown in Equation(1). This technique is very efficient since we need to perform only one addition and one multiplication on each affected vertex of the polygon model to produce the updated polygon model. In addition, its performance is independent of the complexity of the deforming surface.

3.2 Resolution Refinement

The resolution refinement technique refines the resolution of the polygon model and to generate new deformation coefficients incrementally according to the change in local curvature of the surface. Consider the fact that a NURBS surface can be subdivided into a polygon model by applying the de Casteljau subdivision formula. We may subtract the surface equation in the form of de Casteljau subdivision formula before, $C(u)$, and after, $\overline{C}(u)$, the deformation, and substitute the resulting formula with the deformation coefficients α and the displacement vector $\overrightarrow{V}$ of the moving control point. We then have:

$$\overline{C}(u) - C(u) = C(\alpha) \tag{2}$$

Equation(2) shows the result by applying the de Casteljau subdivision formula to the Bernstein polynomials of the surface in the u parametric direction only. The other parametric direction is also in a similar form.

Hence, if the resolution of the polygon model needs to be increased, the new deformation coefficients can be calculated from adjacent deformation coefficients stored at existing vertices using the de Casteljau formula. If the resolution of the polygon model needs to be decreased, we may delete some quad-tree nodes from the polygon model.

4 System Overview

Instead of using a pure client-server model as we did in our earlier work [2,3], the new system is based on a hybrid model which merges the client-server and peer-to-peer architectures. Every participant can be a server or a client. An *object server* is the owner of a deforming object for sculpting.

The tasks of rendering the deformable objects are distributed between the object server and the clients. The object server generates an initial base model and the corresponding set of deformation coefficients of each deformable object that it possesses. These information are then sent to each participating client. A client equipped with a *CyberGlove*^{TM} may modify the shape of the

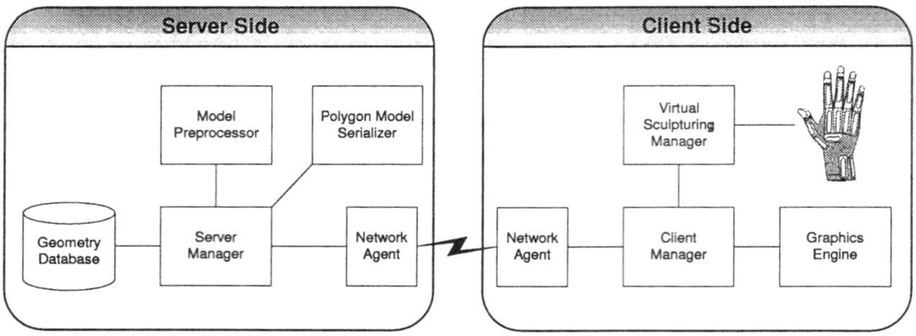

Figure 1: Main components of our system.

object and broadcasts the updated control points to all the other participants including the object server. The main components of our system is shown in Figure 1.

The client consists of 5 main components and the main functions of each component are as follows:

- *Client Manager*: It coordinates all other components at the client and handles all user inputs. For each object to be deformed, the client manager first requests the base model and the set of deformation coefficients from the server to construct the polygon model. It then passes the information to the graphics engine to be maintained there.
- *Virtual Sculpting Manager*: It generates a parametric hand surface for the *CyberGlove*^{TM} and performs virtual sculpting based on the user's hand gesture. The updated control points of the deforming object are then sent to the client manager.
- *Network Agent*: It handles all the network communications, including object requests and object updates.
- *Display Driver*: It accepts input from the viewer and generates output images to be displayed on the display screen. As the object is being deformed, the graphics engine receives the updated positions of the affected control points from the client manager, and updates the polygon model of the object.

The server consists of 4 main components, and the main functions of each component are as follows:

- *Server Manager*: It coordinates all other components at the server and handles all clients' requests and updates.
- *Model Preprocessor*: It generates a base model and a set of deformation coefficients of each deformable object needed. The data are then sent to the polygon model serializer.
- *Polygon Model Serializer*: It constructs a linear data packet from the base model and the set of deformation coefficients. The data packet is then sent to the clients upon requested.
- *Network Agent*: It handles all the network communications, including object requests and object updates.

5 Serialization of Polygon Model

In our incremental rendering method, the polygon model is maintained in a quadtree format. This pointer based structure is inefficient for both transmission and storage. Here, we adopt the linear quadtree structure [21] to facilitate efficient transmission. To traverse the quadtree nodes, we make use of the indexing scheme proposed by [22]. We also propose a new serialization structure to maintain the polygon model based on this indexing scheme.

A linear quadtree is a pointerless scheme to store a generic quadtree in the form of a one-dimensional array of nodes. Given a particular node $p > 0$, the node index in the array can be obtained by the following equations:

$$\text{Parent node index:} \quad \left\lfloor \tfrac{p-1}{4} \right\rfloor \tag{3}$$

$$\text{Child node indices:} \quad 4p+i,\ i = 1\ldots4 \tag{4}$$

In [22], Balmelli et al. suggested to store the quadtree in a linear array of nodes. Although it is simple, extra memory space is needed to hold the empty nodes if the quadtree is unbalanced. Unfortunately, most quadtrees are likely balanced in practice. To overcome this problem, we propose a new serialization structure to optimize the size of the data stream that holds the quadtree. The serialization structure is shown in Figure 2.

The serialized quadtree structure consists of three main sections. They are the *quadtree structure*, *packed vertices* and *packed deformation coefficients with control point ID's*. The quadtree structure is an array of boolean values encoding the presence of nodes in the linear quadtree using Balmelli's index scheme. The packed vertices are the list of (x, y, z) coordinates of the present quadtree nodes. The nodes are arranged in ascending order with respect to their node indices. The last section is a repeated sequence of records of packed

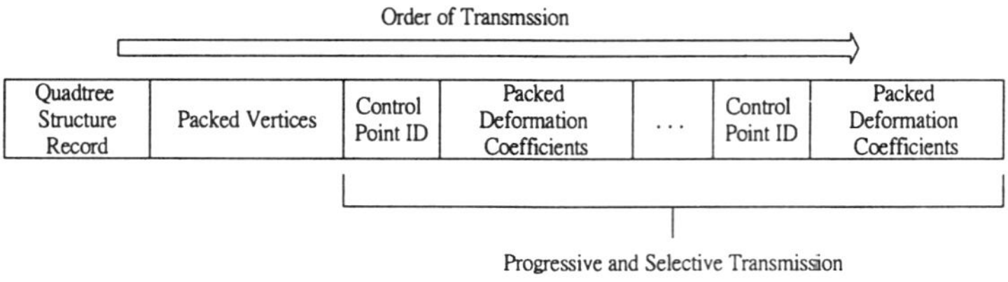

Figure 2: The data structure of the serialized quadtree.

deformation coefficients with its associated control point ID. This section is similar to the section of packed vertices, except that it is a linear array of scalar values of deformation coefficients. The control point ID indicates which control point that the set of the deformation coefficients belongs to.

6 Distributed Virtual Sculpting

6.1 Virtual Sculpting

We have recently developed an intuitive method for virtual sculpting[8,9], which is for object modification using the *CyberGlove*^{TM}. The idea is to create a bicubic B-spline Tensor product hand surface interpolating all key data points of the *CyberGlove*^{TM}. These data points indicate the finger joint positions of the user's hand. The object to be deformed is then mapped to the hand surface by *ray-projection*. In this technique, the user specifies a center of projection, P_c, and a set of rays are projected from P_c through individual object vertices onto the hand surface to establish the mapping. By changing the user's gesture, the object model can be deformed accordingly.

6.2 Defining and Locking of Editing Region

In a collaborative sculpting environment, multiple clients may sometimes want to edit the same object simultaneously. If we lock the entire object once a client requests to edit it, other clients would not be able to participate in the editing. To enhance the collaboration and the availability of objects for sculpting, we introduce the idea of *editing region*, which is a sub-region of a deforming object. When a client manipulates an editing region of a deforming object, the rest of the object will not be affected by this manipulation, and can be edited by other clients simultaneously. A client may modify one or more editing region(s) provided that the regions are not currently edited by other clients.

To define the editing region, we consider the local modification property [5] of NURBS surfaces. If the position of a control point $P_{i,j}$ is changed, only the shape of the surface within the parameter region $[u_i, u_{i+p+1}) \times [v_j, v_{j+q+1})$ is affected, where p and q are the degrees of the NURBS surface along u and v parameter directions, respectively. We refer to this region as the *deformation region*. An *editing region* is therefore the union of the deformation regions affected by the control points which are covered by the hand surface.

To implement the locking system for editing, we maintain at each client an *editing list*, an array of boolean flags each corresponding to a control point of the object for sculpting. A bit is set to TRUE if the corresponding control point is currently manipulated by one of the clients in the collaborative environment. When a client wants to modify the shape of an object, it first determines the editing region that the user is interested and compares the editing list with the set of control points covered the editing region. If all control points in the editing list are set to FALSE (i.e., they are all available), the client will be granted the right to edit that region and a *locking message* will be broadcasted to all participating clients to update their editing lists. When the client finishes the editing, it broadcasts a lock *release message* to all participating clients to clear the corresponding bits of the editing lists. However, if a client wants to modify the shape of an object and finds that part of or the whole editing region is locked, the client may need to wait until the region is released. We adopt a distributed locking scheme instead of a central server-based scheme to avoid the bottleneck caused by the large number of editing requests.

6.3 Client-Server Interactions

The distributed virtual sculpting process consists of two stages. The pre-processing and run-time stages. The client-server interactions occur in the pre-processing stage while the client-client interactions occur in the run-time stage. In the pre-processing stage, the server generates an initial polygon model (or the base model), hierarchical surfaces [7] and the set of deformation coefficients. This task executes only once for each deformable object. Upon a client's request, the server sends the surface definition, and the serialized quadtree structure consisting the *base model* and the set of deformation coefficients as described in section 5 to the client. After the client has received the base model, it refines the base model for rendering according to its own view parameters.

6.4 Client-Client Interactions

During run-time, if a client is editing an object, it is responsible for broadcasting *update messages* to all the participating clients. Each update message

Part Name	Size
Quadtree structure	68 bytes
Packed vertices	12.6 Kbytes
Each single control point ID	2 bytes
Each set of packed deformation coefficients	48 – 192 bytes

Table 1: Memory sizes of different parts of the serialized quadtree structure.

contains the ID's of the control points of the editing region and the updated (x, y, z) coordinates of those control points. After a participating client has received an update message, it performs the incremental polygon model updating and resolution refinement according to its current view parameters and renders the resulting polygon model for display.

7 Results and Discussions

We have implemented the new method using C++, OpenGL and Open Inventor. The server and the client modules communicate using TCP/IP. The test was executed on SGI Onyx2 and SGI Octane machines, each with one 195MHz R10000 CPU activated. Figure 3 shows a human head model used for sculpting. The human head model is a NURBS model with 400 control points. We apply knot insertion [5] to subdivide it into 400 Bézier surface patches and construct a hierarchical surface on these patches to form the base model for transmission. The record sizes of different parts of the serialized quadtree structure are shown in Table 1. In our test, the total size of all packed deformation coefficients is 58 Kbytes. The total size of the base model and the set of deformation coefficients is 71.6 Kbytes. This serialized quadtree structure can be transmitted in 0.056 seconds on a dedicated 10Mbit Ethernet LAN. If we assume that the bandwidth available to us in a non-dedicated LAN is 2Mbits and that the Internet bandwidth is one-tenth of this, i.e., 0.2Mbits, the time needed to transmit the serialized data structure will be roughly 0.28 seconds and 2.8 seconds. On the other hand, instead of sending the set of deformation coefficients together with the base model in the initial stage, they can be sent selectively and separately at run-time upon the clients' requests. This can reduce the network traffics and therefore the latency when many clients make object requests at the same time.

In our method, we use a distributed editing list instead of using a centralized server to control simultaneous editing. This can reduce both the workload of the server and the network latency when the clients raise their requests continuously. Whenever a client raises a request, it only needs to lookup its local

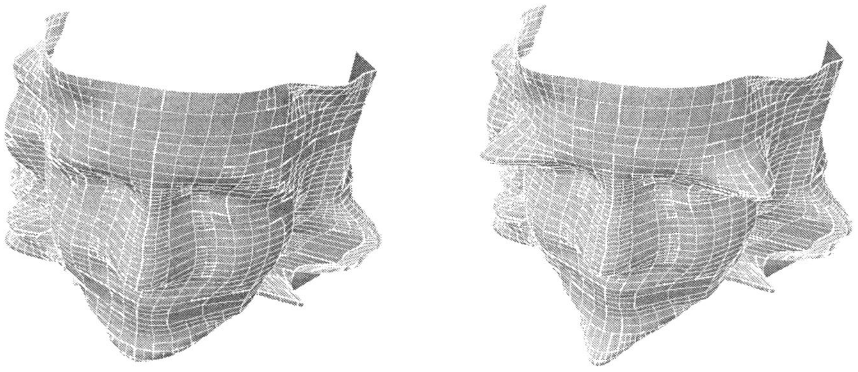

Figure 3: Human head model used in our experiments.

copy of the editing list, and a locking message is sent only if the requested editing region is available. Unlike Nishino's method [20], our method generates network traffics for successful requests only. For the tessellation process, both Nishino's method and our method delegate the tessellation task to the client. This can save sending polygon models from the server to clients. In addition, each client can have different polygon resolution for the deforming object according to its own view parameters, to enhance the rendering performance. However, we further accelerate the rendering process by incorporating our NURBS rendering algorithm. This can avoid the re-execution of the time consuming tessellation process in each frame time.

8 Conclusion

In this paper, we have presented a framework for collaborative virtual sculpting in a distributed virtual environment. We have introduced a serialized quadtree structure for transmitting deforming objects through the network for virtual sculpting. We have also presented the idea of editing region and the corresponding locking mechanism to allow simultaneous virtual sculpting by multiple users. Results show that our method can provide a reasonably fast response for clients to perform virtual sculpting even on the Internet environment.

Acknowledgments

The work described in this paper was partially supported by a CityU grant (Project Number 9030796).

References

1. M. R. Macedonia and M. J. Zyda, "A Taxonomy for Networked Virtual Environments," *IEEE Multimedia*, vol. 4, no. 1, pp. 48–56, 1997.
2. J. Chim, M. Green, R. Lau, H. Leong, and A. Si, "On Caching and Prefetching of Virtual Objects in Distributed Virtual Environments," *ACM Multimedia*, pp. 171–180, September 1998.
3. J. Chim, R. Lau, A. Si, H. Leong, D. To, M. Green, and M. Lam, "Multi-Resolution Model Transmission in Distributed Virtual Environments," *Proceedings of ACM Symposium on Virtual Reality Software and Technology*, pp. 25–34, November 1998.
4. R. Lau, M. Green, D. To, and J. Wong, "Real-Time Continuous Multi-Resolution Method for Models of Arbitrary Topology," *PRESENCE: Teleoperators and Virtual Environment*, vol. 7, no. 2, pp. 22–35, 1998.
5. L. Piegl and W. Tiller, *The NURBS Book*. Springer-Verlag, 1995.
6. F. Li, R. Lau, and M. Green, "Interactive Rendering of Deforming NURBS Surfaces," *Proceedings of Eurographics '97*, vol. 16, pp. 47–56, September 1997.
7. F. Li and R. Lau, "Real-Time Rendering of Deformable Parametric Free-Form Surfaces," *Proceedings of ACM Symposium on Virtual Reality Software and Technology*, pp. 131–138, December 1999.
8. J. Wong, R. Lau, and L. Ma, "Virtual 3D Hand Sculpturing with a Parameter Hand Surface," *Computer Graphics International*, pp. 178–186, June 1998.
9. J. Wong, R. Lau, and L. Ma, "Virtual 3D Sculpting," *To appear in Journal of Visualization and Computer Animation*, 2000.
10. C. Carlsson and O. Hagsand, "DIVE - a Multi-User Virtual Reality System," *Proceedings of IEEE Virtual Reality Annual International Symposium*, pp. 394–400, 1993.
11. J. Calvin, A. Dicken, B. Gaines, P. Metzger, D. Miller, and D. Owen, "The SIMNET Virtual World Architecture," *Proceedings of IEEE Virtual Reality Annual International Symposium*, pp. 450–455, 1993.
12. M. R. Macedonia, M. J. Zyda, D. R. Pratt, P. T. Barham, and S. Zeswitz, "NPSNET: A Network Software Archtecture for Large Scale Virtual Environements," *Presence*, vol. 3, no. 4, pp. 265–287, 1994.
13. S. Benford, J. Bowers, L. Fahlen, and C. Greenhalgh, "Managing Mutual Awareness in Collaborative Virtual Environments," *Proceedings of Virtual Reality Software and Technology*, pp. 223–236, 1994.
14. I. Pandzic, T. Capin, E. Lee, N. Thalmann, and D. Thalmann, "A Flexible Architecture for Virtual Humans in Networked Collaborative Virtual Environments," *Proceedings of Eurographics '97*, vol. 16, pp. 177–188, September

1997.
15. V. Normand and J. Tromp, "Collaborative Virtual Environments: the COVEN Project," *Proceedings of the Framework for Immersive Virtual Environments Conference (FIVE'96)*, 1996.
16. T. A. Galyean and J. F. Hughes, "Sculpting: An Interactive Volumetric Modelling Technique," *Proceedings of ACM SIGGRAPH '91*, vol. 25, no. 4, pp. 267–274, 1991.
17. C. D. Shaw and M. Green, "Two-Handed Polygonal Surface Design," *Proceedings of UIST 1994*, pp. 205–212, November 1994.
18. C. D. Shaw and M. Green, "THRED: A Two-Handed Design System," *Multimedia Systems Journal*, vol. 5, pp. 126–139, March 1997.
19. K. Kameyama, "Virtual Clay Modelling System," *Proceedings of ACM Symposium on Virtual Reality Software and Technology*, pp. 197–200, September 1997.
20. H. Nishino, K. Utsumiya, A. Sakamoto, K. Yoshida, and K. Korida, "A Method for Sharing Interactive Deformations in Collaborative 3D Modeling," *Proceedings of ACM Symposium on Virtual Reality Software and Technology*, pp. 116–123, December 1999.
21. I. Gargantini, "An Effective Way to Represent Quadtrees," *Communications of the ACM*, vol. 25, pp. 905–910, December 1982.
22. L. Balmelli, J. Kovačević, and M. Vetterli, "Quadtrees for Embedded Surface Visualization: Constraints and Efficient Data Structures," *Proceedings of IEEE International Conference on Image Processing (ICIP)*, vol. 2, pp. 487–491, October 1999.

An Intelligent Flight Data Recorder And Real-Time Monitoring System

Mohamed Aborizka and Krishna M. Kavi

{aborizka, kavi}@ece.uah.edu
Department of Electrical and Computer Engineering
The University of Alabama in Huntsville
Huntsville, AL 35899
USA

1. Introduction

In this paper we describe a new approach to the design of next-generation flight data recorders (FDRs or Black boxes) and real-time monitoring of airplanes using recent information, artificial intelligence, learning and network technologies. In this new system, ground-based *intelligent software agents* communicate with their on-board counterparts to continuously collect flight data. The data collected from numerous flights can be correlated and *data-mined* to construct scenarios that could lead to unsafe incidents. Such analyses can be utilized by the intelligent software agents to detect potentially unsafe conditions in real-time and provide early warning to the pilot.

Over 90 years ago, philosopher George Santayana said, "those who cannot remember the past are condemned to repeat it". Although modern aircraft designs rely on past failures to improve their safety, there exist no comprehensive data that can be used to correlate and track the complex set of events that may lead to an accident. According to NTSB annual review of aircraft accident data, a total of 1,935 U.S registered general aviation aircraft were involved in 1,907 accidents during the calendar year 1996. Of these, 360 accidents (involving 366 aircraft) resulted in fatalities. NTSB also concluded that pilots were either the sole cause or a contributing factor in 77 percent of all accidents and 83 percent of fatal accidents. It is our contention that the pilot is often unable to recognize potential problems early enough to take preventive measures, or the pilot is provided with insufficient time to explore alternate actions. This is partly because of the complex set of events leading to the problem and partly because the pilot is furnished with very limited information that is based only on the current flight (with no benefit of correlating the information to similar problems in other flights). Even the most experienced pilot, sometimes, may not be able make appropriate decisions under such time-critical conditions. Our intelligent agent based system will be able to track potential problems in real-time and provide early warning to the pilot. Data mining of previously collected data both from normal flights and accidents can form the basis for suggesting safe actions that can prevent accidents. Even in case of mechanical failures, our real-time data collection and monitoring can aid in the detection of failures or the identification of maintenance schedules.

2. Background and Related Research

Our project uses and extends the state-of-the-art research in the design of Flight Data Recorders, learning and artificial intelligence, software agent based programming paradigms, multi-agent based control systems, and real-time monitoring. In this section we describe briefly these related research areas.

2.1 Fight Data Recorders

Flight Data Recorders (FDR) were first introduced in the 1950s. The purpose of an airplane FDR system is to collect and record data from a variety of airplane sensors onto a medium designed to survive an accident. Depending on the age of an airplane, the FDR system may consists of an analog or a digital flight data acquisition unit and a digital recorder. FDR may have a tape or solid-state memory. The data collected in the FDR system can help investigators determine whether an accident was caused by a pilot error, an external events (such as weather), or an airplane system (such as mechanical or electrical failures). The first generation of FDRs recorded only five parameters including acceleration, air speed, compass heading, time and altitude. This data was embossed onto steal foil, and was capable of recording for 400 hours at which time the foil must be replaced. The second generation FDRs introduced in the 1970s aimed to collect more data but they were unable to process the incoming sensor data in a timely manner. This led to the development of a separate flight data acquisition unit (FDAU). The FDAU processes sensor data, digitizes and formats it for transmission to the FDR. The second generation of digital FDR (DFDR) used (magnetic) recording tape. Most DFDRs can record and store up to 18 operational parameters for a period 25 hours. Third generation FDRs (known as SSFDR) were introduced in 1990 and used solid-state technologies for recording data. These recorders can record up to 256 operational parameter for 25 hours [1] [2].

2.2 Knowledge Discovery and Data Mining

The amount of data being collected by FDRs exceeds the ability of human beings to analyze without the aid of automated analysis techniques. Data mining is an analysis process used to explore large data volumes to find consistent patterns and/or systematic relationships among variables. The knowledge discovery process takes the raw results from data mining and transforms them into useful and understandable information by applying various artificial intelligence techniques. Learning algorithms are an integral part of knowledge discovery [3]. Machine learning is one of the artificial intelligence techniques that has contributed to knowledge discovery [4]. There are several knowledge discovery techniques in use, including:

- Probabilistic and statistical techniques.
- Bayesian classification, inductive logic, data cleaning/pattern discovery, and decision tree analysis.
- Genetic algorithms.
- Neural networks.
- Hybrid approaches that integrate two or more of these techniques [5].

2.3 Software Agents

Intelligent agents are autonomous software entities that can navigate heterogeneous computing environments. They achieve their specified goals either alone or by working with other agents [6]. They often use intelligence and learning abilities to achieve their tasks and perform their assigned tasks autonomously. Agents may also interact with their environment (or other agents) and adapt dynamically to changing conditions. Intelligent agents are increasingly being used in a wide variety of applications, ranging from comparatively small systems such as email filters, to large, open, complex, mission critical systems such as air traffic control [7].

The programming paradigm that uses software agents differs drastically from other models used in distributed processing, including remote procedure calls and client-server models. The difference stems from the autonomy of software agents. For example, in classical client-server architecture, the server provides specific services to one or more clients (both servers and clients are computer systems). In agent systems, however, an agent can provide services at one time, adopting the role of server, while requesting services at other times, acting as a client. In addition, agents possess autonomy and thus differ from classical servers or clients. Even when donning the role of a server, an agent will be an active participant in a client-server system and adapts to changing requirements and resources. The advantages of the new programming paradigm are numerous. Including reduced network traffic (an agent need not maintain a continuous contact with its creator), tolerance of frequent network disconnection (agent can contact its creator when the connection is available), migration of tasks to data sources (this is achieved because of the autonomy), asynchronous processing, and decentralized structure [8].

2.4 Intelligent Multi-Agent Based Systems

Using a single agent to solve a complex problem may not always be feasible. In complex systems, an individual agent may be required to gather and analyze enormous amounts of knowledge. This may lead to situations where an agent may not be able to find any solutions to a given problem. Fortunately, most complex systems are distributed in nature and lend themselves to the use of multiple distributed agents. In multi-agent based systems, the knowledge needed to solve a problem is not available with a single agent, but distributed among the various agents. Each agent of a multi-agent system can either follow its own objectives and only contact other agents to obtain information, or contribute to a coordinated solution of the overall problem. Every individual agent is associated with a precisely defined task that is particularly suitable to the agent and whose solution is within the agent's capabilities. This task decomposition and distribution permits the processing of very complex problems. Existing single agent based systems can easily be integrated into a larger multi-agent based system, permitting incremental development of intelligent systems. Distributed problem solving with multi-agents systems is appropriate only when agents in the system are capable of communicating and cooperating with each other [8][9][10]. Due to the complexity of the systems invested by our research, multi-agent based approach will be utilized in our designs.

2.5 Multi-Agent Based Real-time Systems

Real-time systems present numerous challenges to a designer. They often have many stringent requirements on processing, timely response, power and size specifications. Certain real time systems may benefit from multi-agent based technologies, since multi-agent systems facilitate adaptability, reactivity and autonomy. Some of the multi-agent-based real-time systems include [11]:

- Surveillance systems.
- Network management systems.
- Manufacturing processing and monitoring systems.
- Multimodal interfaces.
- Remote cooperative work.
- Interactive television.

2.6 Real-time Monitoring

Real-time monitoring is utilized in many critical systems such as: nuclear reactors and air traffic control systems. In many cases, monitoring systems check for exceptional (or data outside of safe regions) conditions. In complex systems, the detection of exceptional conditions may not be sufficient to prevent potential accidents. It is necessary to correlate the conditions with complex interactions among the subsystems. The correlation may be in the form of defining a finite-state model for the system. The states of the model will track the system both in operational (good and safe) and problem (unsafe) conditions. Such models can then be utilized to define the set of state transitions that can lead to accidents. These models can be very detailed involving thousands of states. However, caution should be exercised to balance the number of states and the processing needed for real-time monitoring. While more states allow for more accurate monitoring, they also require more processing.

3. An intelligent flight data recorder and monitoring system (IFDR)

3.1 Multi-Agent Based FDR

We propose to design a multi-agent based FDR and monitoring system. In this section we outline a framework for such a system. Our goal is develop a system that can help a pilot make appropriate decisions using the knowledge base generated from data collected from other flights, the experience of pilots and other experts. In a full-fledged system, data from both normal flights and flights with problems will be collected and mined off-line for any patterns (or sequence of events) that identify unsafe situations. The real-time monitoring system can look for such patterns during a flight and provide the pilot with early warnings. Figure 1 shows our preliminary multi-agent based FDR architecture. It consists of three layers: the agent layer, the coordinator layer, and the knowledge base layer. The agent layer defines all the necessary agents including a data acquisition agent(s), agents to model the various subsystems of an aircraft, a decision agent and an agent to interface with the pilot.

Only the data acquisition agent(s) and the agent that interfaces with the pilot are resident on the aircraft itself, while the other agents are located at ground based computing systems. The coordinator layer manages the communication between different agents. The knowledge base layer stores common knowledge used by the different agents and the coordinator. The functions of the various agents are described below.

- The data acquisition agent(s) receives data from FDAU and also checks for any exceptional changes.
- The tracking agent continuously checks the communication between agents on the plane and agents on the ground station server. In the full-fledged implementation, the tracking agent may migrate from one ground-based system to another to maintain a constant contact with the agents onboard.
- The electrical, mechanical, …, agents are responsible for the detection of potential unsafe conditions in various aircraft subsystems.

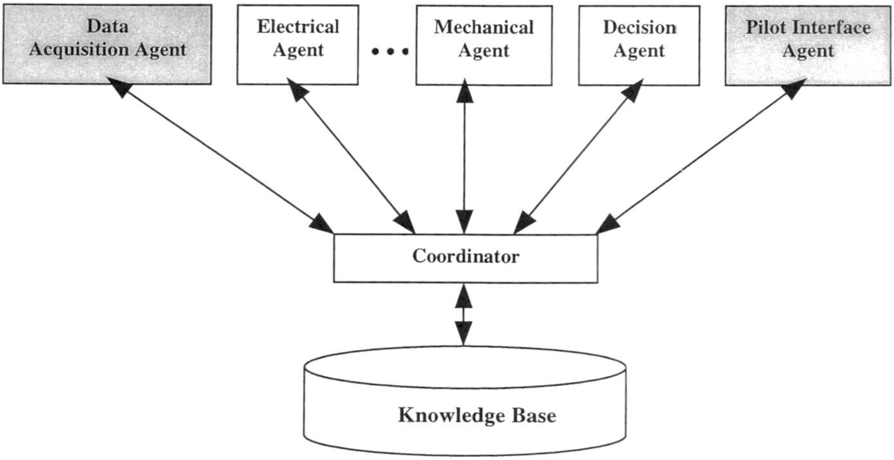

Figure 1. Architecture of IFDR

- The decision agent is responsible in arriving at a final decision based on the individual decisions of the various agents. All agents utilize the knowledge-base and finite state models for reaching their decisions.
- The pilot interface agent displays warning messages and suggest appropriate actions to the pilot [12].

3.2 IFDR in Action

Figure 2 shows a scenario for our multi-agent based FDR and monitoring system. As we mentioned above, only the data acquisition agent(s) and the agent that interfaces with the pilot are resident on the aircraft. All the other agents will be running on a ground-based computing server. This approach minimizes changes to current FDR designs and aircraft computer systems. All the major agents (data acquisition agent, interface agent, coordinating agent, decision agent, tracking agent) will be launched as an airplane starts its flight. As the data acquisition agent receives data from FDAU and detects any exceptional changes, the agent will transmit the changes to the coordinating agent. The coordinating agent may decide to launch specific subsystem agents (e.g., mechanical or electrical agent) to check the knowledge base for potentially problematic patterns. During this analysis, an agent may request for additional flight data. This request is communicated to the data acquisition agent onboard. *Note that such dynamic data collection is not feasible with current FDRs.* The results (or decisions) from these various agents are communicated to the decision agent, which takes a final decision and communicates the decision to the interface agent. The interface agent in turn provides necessary information to the pilot.

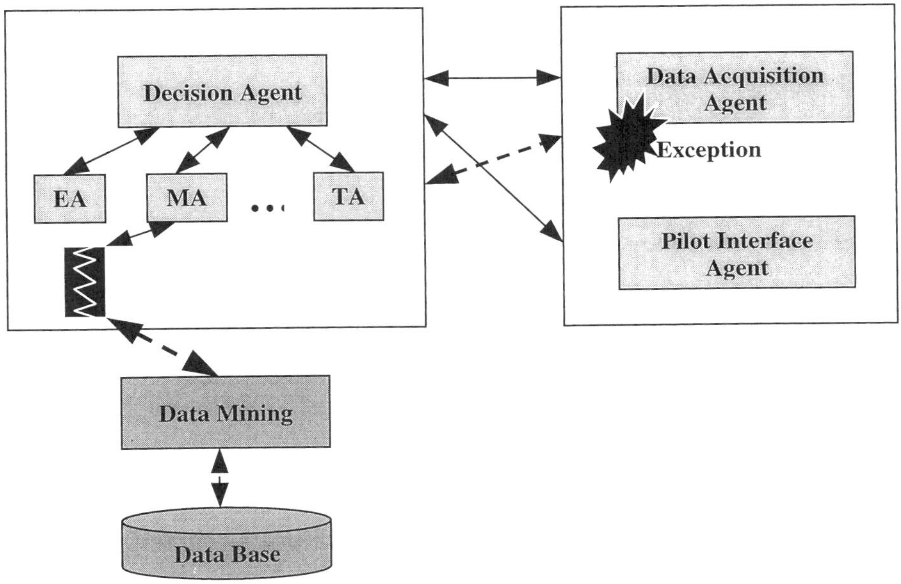

Figure 2. IFDR in Action

3.3 Feasibility of the Proposed Design

There are several requirements that must be met before our proposed intelligent FDRs and monitoring systems become reality. Since the aircraft resident agents must communicate with ground-based agents on (potentially) a continuous basis, a data communication network that spawns the globe is needed. However such a network is already being designed and will be operational in the near future. The ATN (Aeronautical Telecommunications Network) is a worldwide (digital) data network intended to provide a full and flexible support for seamless connectivity among mobile units, aircrafts, ground based computer systems and other service providers like the Aeronautical Operational Control (AOC), Aeronautical Administrative Communications (AAC), and Aeronautical Passenger Communications (APC), government authorities that provide Air Traffic Control (ATC) and flight information services (FIS). This network allows a collection of dissimilar transmission networks and interconnecting computers to operate as a single, cohesive, and virtual data network. Figure 3 shows the ATN infrastructure [13]. Our preliminary computations indicate that the data transmission requirements of the proposed intelligent FDR and monitoring systems are well within the capabilities of the ATN infrastructure.

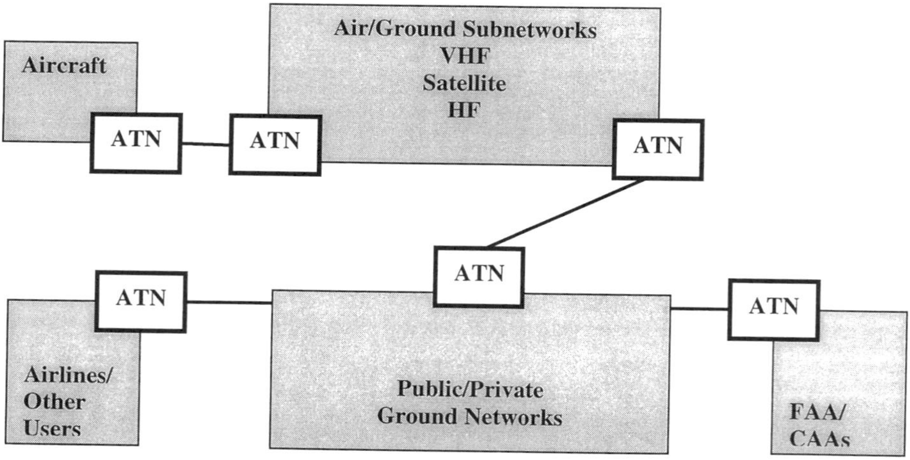

Figure 3. **Aeronautical Telecommunications Network**

As described in Section 2, the technologies for the development of intelligent and learning agents and data mining of large amounts of data already exist. Our initial analyses also indicate the modern computing systems are more than adequate to perform (off-line) data mining computations on the flight data collected.

4. Summary and Future Work

In this paper we described an approach for the design of intelligent FDRs and monitoring systems. Our approach uses a multiple agents to monitor the data collected by FDRs in real-time and use knowledge bases to detect potentially unsafe conditions. We feel that there are numerous advantages with our proposed design. We list a few of these advantages below.

- Currently, it is often difficult to locate FDRs after a crash, and located black boxes are often damaged. In the proposed system, there is no need to locate FDR after a crash since flight data is transmitted to ground-based computing systems in real-time. Real-time recording of data can also detect misreading or conflicting data due to failures of the FDR itself.

- Using flight data from several hundreds or even thousands of flights, it is possible to more accurately predict scenarios that may cause unsafe conditions. At present such analyses are not conducted.

- Using above analyses, it will be possible to develop intelligent agents to detect unsafe conditions in real-time to provide early warnings to the pilot. The information gathered from data mining can also be used to design safer aircrafts since it is now possible to identify sequences of events or combinations of factors that can cause unsafe situations. Traditional approaches to the design of control systems require precise mathematical models; however, such models may not be possible or difficult for describing complex interactions that may occur during a flight. Results from data-mining analyses can be used to develop fuzzy logic based control systems that can adjust to a variety of factors including weather-related, geographical data and individual pilot's judgments.

- Software agents can automatically log maintenance requirements using flight data.

We feel that the approach is feasible since all the necessary technology and network already exists. We are currently gathering flight accident data from the National Transportation Safety Board (NTSB) to build initial knowledge base. Using this knowledge base we will build an intelligent agent based system to aid in the accident investigations. A full-fledged intelligent FDR and real-time monitoring systems will be proposed based on the experience gained during this time.

5. References

[1]. Information on Flight data recorders can be obtained from the following web site. http://www.bath.ac.uk/~en8clf/desdev.htm.

[2]. Information on Flight data recorders can be obtained from the following web site. http://www.boeing.com/commercial/aeromagazine/aero_02/s/s01/story.html

[3] Brachman, R.J., and Anand, T. The Process Of Knowledge Discovery In Databases: A Human-Centered Approach. *In Advances In Knowledge Discovery and Data Mining*, eds. U.M. Fayyad, G. Piatesky-Shapiro, P. Smyth, and R. Uthurusamy, AAAI Press/MIT Press, Menlo Park, CA., 1996, PP 37-57.

[4] Fayyad, U.M., Piatesky-Shapiro, G., Smyth, P. From Data Mining To Knowledge Discovery: An Overview. *In Advances In Knowledge Discovery and Data Mining*, eds. U.M. Fayyad, G. Piatesky-Shapiro, P. Amyth, and R. Uthurusamy, AAAI Press/MIT Press, Menlo Park, CA., 1996, PP 1-31.

[5] Knowledge Discovery In Databases: Tools and Techniques. Web Site: http://www.acm.org/crossroads/xrds5-2/kdd.html

[6] Hedberg, S. *IEEE Expert,* v11, n6, 1996.

[7] Applications of Intelligent Agents. 1998. Web Site: http://www.springer.de/ comp/lncs/agent/jennings.pdf

[8] Walter Brenner, Rudiger Zarnekow, and Harmut Witting. *Intelligent Software Agents.* Springer Publishing Co. 1998.

[9] Gerhard Weiss. *Multi Agent Systems*. MIT Press. 1999.

[10] Gheorghe Tecuci. *Building Intelligent Agents*. Academic Press Publishing Co. 1998.

[11] Real-time Multi-Agent Systems. 1999. Web Site: http://www.fipa.org/cfp/cfp6.html

[12] Huaiqing Wang, and Chen Wang, Intelligent Agents in the Nuclear Industry, *IEEE Computer* , v30, n11, 1997.

[13] Aeronautical Telecommunications Network. Web Site: http://www.atnsi.com/

[14] Joseph Tardo and Luis Valente. Mobile Agent Security and Telescript. In *Proceeding of COMPCON Spring '96*, pages 58-63. IEEE, 1996.

[15] Dag Johanse, Robert van Renesse, and Fred B. Shneider. An Introduction to the TACOMA Distributed System. *Technical Report 95-23*, Department of Computer Science, University of Tromos∅, June 1995.

[16] Robert S. Gray. Agent Tcl: A flexible and secure mobile-agent system. In *Proceeding of the fourth annual Tcl/Tk Workshop (TCL 96),* July 1996.

[17] David Wong, Noemi Paciorek, and Dana Moore. Java-based Mobile Agents. *Communications of the ACM*, 42(3):92-102, March 1999.

[18] Danny Lange and Mitsuru Oshima. *Programming and Deploying Java Mobile Agents with Aglets*. Addison-Wesley Publishing Co.1998.

[19] David Wong, Noemi Paciorek, and Tom Walsh. Concordia: An Infrastructure for Collaborating Mobile Agents, *In Proceeding of Workshop on Mobile Agents* MA '97, Berlin, 1997.

[20] Anand R. Tripathi, Neeran M. Karnik, Ram D. Singh, and Tanvir Ahmed. Development of Mobile Agent Applications with Ajanta. *Technical Report*, Department of Computer Science, University of Minnesota, 1999.

PREFETCHING AND CACHING METADATA IN A DISTRIBUTED NFS SERVER

WEI LIU, XINMING OU, WEIMIN ZHENG, MIN WU, MEIMING SHEN
Department of Computer Science and Technology, Tsinghua University, Beijing, 100084, P.R.China
{lw, oxm, wumin}@est4.cs.tsinghua.edu.cn
{zwm-dcs, smm}@tsinghua.edu.cn

The paper describes a name and attribute cache(NACache) in a distributed NFS server. The distributed NFS server provides the identical NFS service as the common NFS server and no modification to NFS client software. The NACache stores the metadata information of the distributed server and employs the prefetching approach to optimize the performance of metadata operations. It retrieves all file attributes and names in a single request and stores them in the NACache. In the paper, the design and implementation of the NACache in the distributed NFS server is presented. And the performance of our system is evaluated via the Andrew Benchmark. According to the experimental results, we conclude that the NACache can improve the system performance substantially and the perfetching approach can increase the hit rate in the cold cache state significantly.

1 Introduction

As a simple and effective network file system, NFS has been widely used across variety of computer systems. NFS protocol is designed to support the various network types and operating systems. However, the stand-alone NFS server is difficult to keep up with the demand of the sharply increasing file services. To provide a scalable and high performance NFS server, we designed and implemented a distributed NFS server that consists of multiple independent servers connected by high speed network.

With the explosive development of Internet, the service providers have to continuously upgrade their hardware to follow the users' demands. We developed a prototype of a distributed NFS server on a cluster of workstations. The distributed NFS server manages the files and directories dispersedly and each machine in the system can provide identical NFS service to clients. When a client mounts one machine in the system, it can access the whole file space in the cluster. We introduce a distributed naming mechanism[1] to improve the system performance, scalability and availability. Many research results[2, 3] show that lookup is the most common NFS operation to reach an NFS server. A name and attribute cache, called NACache, with prefetching is presented in the paper. Due to the distributed metadata, NACache is quite effective to improve the server performance for metadata access. It is very important to an NFS server to reduce the response time for metadata operation.

Deceit[4] is a prototype of distributed NFS too. The main difference between Deceit and our distributed NFS server is the cache management. We introduce the NACache with prefetching into our distributed NFS server to improve the performance substantially. Mether-NFS[5] adopted another method to implement the distributed NFS service. It implements a DSM as part of the file system space and provides a shared memory space for a cluster of computers. However our distributed system is based on message passing mechanism. In addtion, we can construct a distributed NFS server based on the traditional distributed file systems, such as AFS[6], Coda[7] and xFS[8]. However, they do not optimize the performance of the file systems according to the characteristic of the NFS protocol.

In the paper we describe the organization and structure of the NACache in our distributed NFS server. The rest of the paper is organized as follows. Section 2 compares our system to related work. Section 3 minutely describes the design of the distributed NFS server. Section 4 presents the architecture of NACache with prefetching and Section 5 provides and analyses the experimental results of the NACache. Section 6 concludes this paper.

2 Distributed NFS Server

With the sharply increasing of network technology, the stand-alone server is hard to carry the burden of abundant requests. So the distributed NFS server is presented to augment the processing power and storage space. If the administrator finds that the system can not support so many users, he may add some new servers into the distributed server without any modification to clients' programs and configurations. In order to minimize the users' interference, we make the most of modifications in the server side.

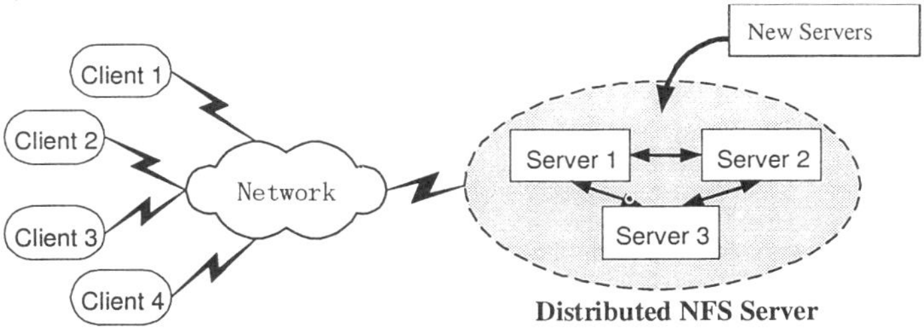

Figure 1. Distributed NFS server and clients

As show Figure 1, the clients can access the whole distributed NFS server via one node in the cluster. For example, when client 1 mounts server 1, it can access the entire file space exported by the distributed NFS server and these data are distributed across the nodes in the cluster system. Due to metadata and data are stored on different servers, caching is an effective way to reduce the internal traffic between cooperative servers. We find the metadata-related operations are major in NFS communication, such as *lookup*, *getattr* and *readdir*. When the NACache is introduced into the distributed system, most metadata requests from the clients can be satisfied by the NACache located in the mounted server.

3 Prefetching and Caching Metadata

In order to improve the distributed NFS server, we designed and implemented a name and attribute cache, NACache in our server. NACache stores the file attributes and handles on server-side and reduces the network hops when a request processed by the NFS server.

3.1 *NFS Operation*

Most of the NFS operations are related to metadata management, including 11 operations: lookup, readdir, getattr, setattr, readlink, link, symlink, unlink, mkdir, rmdir, and rename. In UNIX environment, NFS clients are implemented below the VFS layer. The system calls of file systems are decomposed to a collection of VFS operations. NFS clients implement its protocol under the VFS layer independent on the operating systems. NFS client program generally maintains a cache mapping the file or directory to file ID. In UNIX, the component-by-component lookup approach is used to resolve the file path. In NFS client, a cache entry is treated as validate in 30 seconds. When the entry is reused after 30 seconds, a time-stamp validation request will be sent to server to validate it via the getattr operation.

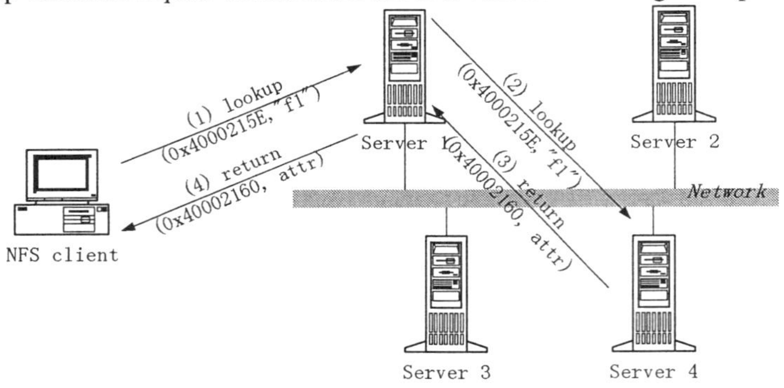

Figure 2. An example of NFS lookup operation on distributed server

When the metadata is manipulated in one node of the system, a name and attribute cache is necessary to reduce the amount of requests crossing the servers. As shown in Figure 2, a client request will be forwarded to the destination by the server which the client mounts. If there is a name and attribute cache is located in the server 1, the requests from clients may be satisfied in server 1 and are not needed to forward to other servers. The file ID represents to a file or directory. The operation lookup(0x4000215E, "f1") means to look up the file "f1" under the directory with ID 0x4000215E. The high 4 bits of the ID means the metadata location of the file or directory and the directory is located in server 4.

3.2 *NACache with Prefetching*

The name and attribute cache is one of most important structure in our distributed NFS server. Hash approach is employed to lookup in the NACache. If a hash conflict occurs, the subsequent entry will be linked to the same hash node to form a Hash Chain. There are five fields in each cache entry as shown in Figure 3, including Hash Chain, Free Chain, LRU Chain, Key and Inode. The Free Chain and LRU Chain consist of the free and used cache entry respectively. The Key field in a cache entry is a tuple of (handle of the directory, file name in the directory). And the Inode field contains all information about the file in the directory.

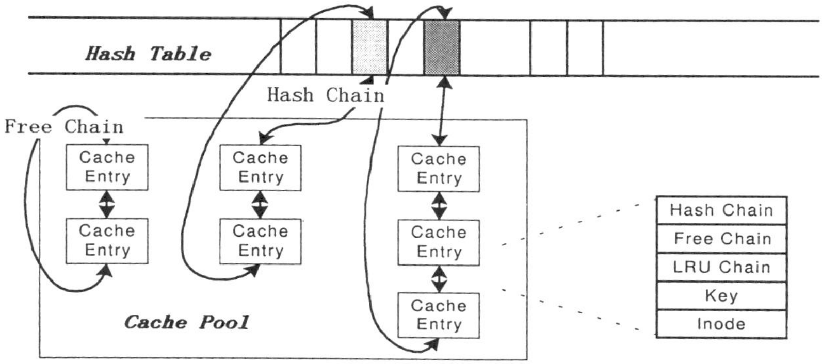

Figure 3. Structure of NACache

According to our test results, the rate of no hash conflict is about 70% and the rate of once hash conflict is about 23%. So the Hash Chain method will not degrade the rehash performance very much. When searching a key in the NACache, we firstly determine if it is in the Hash Chain. If the key is in Hash Chain, we retrieve the Inode field from the NACache and return it; if the key is not in Hash Chain, we have to retrieve the Inode field from the corresponding server, add the entry into the NACache and return the Inode field. We use the LRU algorithm to replace the cache entries.

In NFS version 2 protocol, readdir is used to fetch the directory information from NFS server. It returns the file name list of a given directory. And no file handles and attributes are returned. When a UNIX user type "ls -l directory" to browse a directory containing 30 entries, the ls command opens the directory and reads it, and then calls stat 30 times to retrieve the attributes of the 30 files and directories. In NFS version 2, a readdir request would be followed by 30 sequential lookup operations to retrieve the file attributes and file handles(including sub-directories). We prefetch the attributes and file handles in a single operation when a readdir request arrives at a server. So the following 30 lookup operations can be satisfied in the NACache, significantly reducing the internal network cost.

An Inode information may be cached on multiple machines. A directory-based consistency protocol is implemented in our NACache. When an Inode information is modified, the server storing the information will notify the servers which cache the Inode to invalidate the cache. The method is simple and easily implemented.

4 Experimental Results

We implemented our distributed NFS server on a Linux cluster which comprises 8 dual Pentium II 400 machines connected by 100Mbps Ethernet. We use the Andrew Benchmark[9] to test the system performance. Also we test the performance of command "*ls -l*" to evaluate the effect of the prefetching in the NACache. The Andrew Benchmark is composed of five phases: making the directories, copying the files, scanning the directory tree, searching a word in all files and compiling the programs in the directory. The benchmark covers the basic operations in file systems and the last phase is a practical application. We select the MPICH source tree as the dataset which consists of 138 directories, 2613 files and 241 symbolic links and the size is more than 16Mbytes.

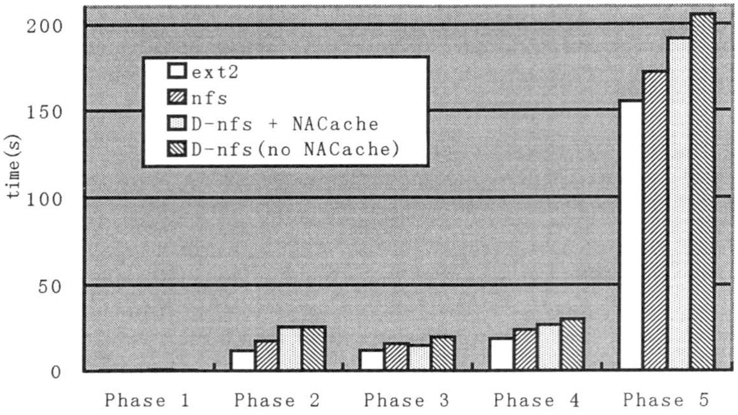

Figure 4. Comparison among EXT2, NFS, Distributed NFS with and without NACache

We test the execution time of each phase in Andrew Benchmark on three file systems. Ext2 is the native file system in Linux operating system. It is a local file system so it has the best performance among the three file systems. The common NFS server is implemented in the kernel level and our distributed NFS is implemented in the user level. Our experiment is on one client, so the processing capability of different systems is compared. The distributed NFS server has the comparable performance with the single NFS, especially in Phase 3. Phase 3 focuses on the performance of reading metadata. We can believe that the NACache with perfetching contributes to the improvement. From Figure 4, we observe that the distributed NFS server has worse performance on the data operations because the data cache is still absent in the system. Now we are developing a unique cache which integrates the memory and disk file cache into one cache space to improve the performance on data operations.

In addition, perfetching metadata improves the hit rates of the NACache. We use command "find . -print -exec ls -l { } \; >/dev/null" to recursively scan the Linux source tree. The execution time of above command is recorded in the following table.

		execution time(s)	total number of *lookup*	number of *lookup* served by NACache	NACache hit rate
with prefetching	cold cache	20.7	4500	3652	81.2%
	warm cache	18.8	4500	4500	100.0%
without prefetching	cold cache	22.5	4498	0	0.0%
	warm cache	18.8	4498	4498	100.0%

When the NACache is warm, the hit rate is 100% because all test metadata are filled in the

NACache. In the case of cold cache, when the prefetching function is not included in the NACache, the *lookup* operations always miss because the cache is empty and these metadata are accessed only once. However, when the prefetching function is included into the NACache, most of *lookup* operations can be served by the NACache because these cache entries are prefetched via *readdir* operations. The experiment shows the effect of the prefetching in the NACache. Although the test is not based on tracing data, the prefetching method optimizes the cache performance in fact when the cache is in the cold state. Prefetching metadata in a single *readdir* is an optimistic way to improve cache performance.

5 Summary

Our distributed NFS server provides a solution of constructing scalable NFS services. It can eliminate the possible bottleneck caused by the central server. Distributing the metadata and real data across multiple servers is the major contribution of the distributed NFS server. The NACache improves the performance of the distributed server significantly. It reduces the internal traffic and the response time for client requests. Moreover modification and reconfiguration to clients are not needed. The clients can access a transparent distributed NFS server as a single server.

6 Reference

1. Wei Liu, Xinming Ou, Min Wu, Weimin Zheng and Meiming Shen, A Distributed Naming Mechanism in Scalable Cluster File System, Proc. of the 4th Intl Conf on High Performance Computing in Asia-Pacific Region, Vol. I, Beijing, China, 2000, pp.37-41
2. Dan Duchamp, Optimistic Lookup of Whole NFS Paths in a Single Operation, Proc. of USENIX Summer 1994 Technical Conference, Boston, USA, 1994, pp161-169
3. Brian Pawlowski, Chet Juszczak, et al., NFS Version 3 Design and Implementation, In Proceedings of Summer 1994 USENIX Conference, pp137-151, 1994, Boston
4. A. Siegel, K. Birman, K. Marzullo, Deceit: a flexible distributed file system, Proceedings of the Workshop on Management of Replicated Data, 1990
5. R. G. Minnich, D. V. Pryor, Mether: supporting the shared memory model on computing clusters, Proceedings of the Compcon Spring '93, 1993
6. Mirjana Spasojevic and M. Satyanarayanan, An Empirical Study of a Wide-Area Distributed File System, In ACM Transactions on Computer Systems, 14(2), May. 1996
7. M. Satyanarayanan, Coda: A Highly Available File System for a Distributed Workstation Environment, Proc. of the 2nd IEEE Workshop on Workstation Operating Systems, Pacific Grove, CA, Sep. 1989
8. Thomas E. Anderson, Michael D. Dahlin, et al., Serverless Network File Systems, In Proceedings of the 15th ACM Symposium on Operating Systems Principles, Dec. 1995
9. John H. Howard, Michael L. Kazar, et al., Scale and Performance in a Distributed File System, ACM Transactions on Computer Systems, 6(1), 1988, pp. 51-81

Chapter 10
High-Performance Scientific Computing

NIMROD/O: A TOOL FOR AUTOMATIC DESIGN OPTIMISATION USING PARALLEL AND DISTRIBUTED SYSTEMS

DAVID ABRAMSON †, ANDREW LEWIS §, TOM PEACHEY †

† School of Computer Science and Software Engineering, Monash University, CLAYTON, VIC 3168, Australia
davida@csse.monash.edu.au

§ High Performance Computing Facility, Griffith University, Nathan, Qld, 4111, Australia

This paper describes a novel tool called Nimrod/O that allows a user to run an arbitrary computational model as the core of a non-linear optimization process. Nimrod/O allows a user to specify the domain and type of parameters to the model, and also a specification of which output variable is to be minimized or maximized. Accordingly, a user can formulate a question like: "what parameter settings will minimize the model output?". Nimrod/O currently employs a number of built-in optimization algorithms, namely BFGS, Simplex, Divide and Conquer and Simulated Annealing. Jobs can be executed on a variety of platforms, including distributed clusters and Computational Grid resources. The paper demonstrates the utility of the system with a number of case studies.

1 Introduction

Computational science and engineering (CS&E) has become the preferred method of design for a number of disciplines, including aircraft and automotive manufacture, electronics and RF design, environmental engineering, chemical engineering and rational drug design. The driving technologies common to these different areas are the availability of affordable super-computing hardware and robust computational models. The most significant advantage of CS&E is that it allows a designer to experiment with a number of different scenarios before committing to an actual implementation, so the design cycle is reduced and the product (or outcome) quality can be improved.

To date, there are very few generic computational frameworks that support the routine application of CS&E in the product design and development cycle. Thus, in many cases software developers must build an appropriate computational model using conventional programming languages, and then run the model as though it were just another executable program. Whilst this is sufficient, it can be error prone when a large number of alternatives are being considered, because the user must track the path taken as variables are changed and designs are evaluated. Further, if any form of *automatic* optimization is required (like minimizing or maximizing some objective function), then the optimization code has to be integrated into the computational model itself. The major disadvantage of this approach is that the optimization technology must be *re-engineered* each time a new model is applied.

For a number of years we have been experimenting with a generic tool, called Nimrod, that allows a user to execute a CS&E model over a range of design parameters using high performance computers. Nimrod makes it very easy for a user to specify a range of parameters over which a model must be executed. It then distributes each different execution across a range of computational resources, such as individual workstations, parallel machines and clusters. A version of Nimrod called Nimrod/G supports execution on a computational Grid, in particular, using the Globus toolkit [1][2][3]. A new version called Nimrod/L is currently being built using the Legion environment [4], and a commercial version called enFuzion is also available for workstation clusters [5][6]. A wide range of case studies has been developed [7][8][9][10].

Nimrod can be used to support CS&E based design because it allows a user to explore many different scenarios selecting the ones that minimize or maximize the objective function. However, its biggest disadvantage is that Nimrod explores *all of the search space exhaustively*. Whilst this is feasible for small experiments it rapidly becomes impractical for large, high dimensioned problems.

A number of projects have addressed parts of the design optimization problem over the years. The DAKOTA project at Sandia laboratories [11] investigated the combination of optimization with computational models. DAKOTA is a C++ based tool kit that allows a user to choose different optimization algorithms to guide the search for optimal parameter settings. DAKOTA has been successfully demonstrated on a number of structural mechanics applications. However, DAKOTA does not support rapid prototyping and still requires the construction of new programs for each different type of experiment which is performed. NEOS is a distributed web based optimization engine that allows a user to solve optimization problems using special remote optimization servers. However, NEOS relies on the objective function being specified in an algebraic form and does not support objective functions implemented by CS&E models. Likewise, NetSolve [12] provides a web based engine for solving linear algebra problems, but does not explicitly address optimization using CS&E objective functions. SciRun [13] is an interactive tool which allows a user to build a CS&E model very rapidly using a graphical programming interface. However, it does not support optimization.

In this paper we describe Nimrod/O, a tool which augments the distributed parameter sweep functionality of Nimrod with automatic optimization. We believe that Nimrod/O is the first system to combine rapid application development, parallel and distributed supercomputing and optimization in the one tool. Nimrod/O is modular, and incorporates a number of standard non-linear optimization methods. It uses a declarative style developed for Nimrod, which allows a user to specify the types of parameters and commands necessary for running the underlying CS&E model. The user can then specify which optimization algorithm (or combination of algorithms) to apply to the problem. Thus, if a user already has a robust CS&E model, it can be converted into a parallel optimizing design tool very quickly.

The paper describes the Nimrod system as background, and then shows the architecture of Nimrod/O. It then discusses the types of optimization algorithms that are supported, followed by a set of case studies. The case studies implement problems in environmental engineering, mechanical engineering and RF electronic design.

2 Nimrod and Nimrod/G

Nimrod is a tool that manages the execution of parametric studies across distributed computers. It takes responsibility for the overall management of an experiment, as well as the low-level issues of distributing files to remote systems, performing the remote computation and gathering the results. EnFuzion [5] is a commercial version of the research system Nimrod.

When a user describes an experiment to Nimrod, they develop a *declarative* "plan" file which describes the parameters, their default values, and the commands necessary for performing the work. The system then uses this information to transport the necessary files and schedule the work on the first available machine.

When the user invokes Nimrod on a workstation, the machine becomes known as the "root" machine because it controls the experiment. When the dispatcher executes code on remote platforms, each of these is known as a computational "node". Thus a given experiment can be conducted with one root and multiple nodes, each of a different architecture if required.

Nimrod/G is a "Grid aware" version of Nimrod built on the Globus toolkit [1]. It exploits an understanding of its problem domain as well as the nature of the computational Grid to provide a high level interface to the user. Specifically, it provides transparent access to the computational resources, and implements user level scheduling. Nimrod/G is described in more detail in [26] and [27].

Nimrod/O makes use of Nimrod to perform its remote execution, as discussed in the next section. This isolates the optimisation algorithms from the functions required to access high performance computers of varying architecture.

3 Nimrod/O architecture

The architecture of Nimrod/O is summarized in Figure 1. Nimrod/O accepts a declarative plan file as previously developed for Nimrod. This file indicates the name and domains of the various parameters and provides descriptions of how to run the CS&E model.

Nimrod/O is built to allow the integration of a number of different optimization engines. These are linked together into the one executable, and are chosen by command line arguments. The CS&E model is actually executed on a distributed supercomputer using Nimrod, so Nimrod/O is not concerned with the details of how jobs are run. Since Nimrod, Nimrod/G and enFuzion all share a common API, it is possible to substitute different back end engines depending on the type of supercomputing facilities that are available. For example, the Nimrod/G backend allows jobs to be run on a globally distributed computation grid like GUSTO [2][16], whereas the enFuzion backend supports department level clusters efficiently.

The system supports concurrency in a number of places. First, if the algorithm itself is parallel (like P-BFGS discussed in the next section) then the system supports concurrent execution within the algorithm. For example, in P-BFGS a number of points are evaluated concurrently, and Nimrod/O does this by requesting Nimrod to run the model multiple times with different parameters. Second, the system allows different searches (possible using different optimization algorithms) to be performed in parallel using different starting locations. Because many of the algorithms we have considered depend on the choice of an initial point, it is important to run the optimization more than once, starting it at different places. Nimrod/O supports this by multi-threading its internal control and using the Nimrod backend to run multiple jobs. When we evaluate the performance of the system later in the paper, we use this feature to demonstrate the variability in final objective function values that are obtained.

Currently, the value of the objective function is returned from the application via a special file. However, in future we expect to add other methods of extracting the function value such as using environment variables to convey the information. A special cache server (called NimCache) is placed between Nimrod/O and Nimrod. This process caches all function requests, and if it detects a request for a point that has already been calculated, it returns the previous result.

4 Optimization algorithms

The current implementation of Nimrod/O supports 4 non-linear search heuristics, namely P-BFGS, Simplex, Divide and Conquer and Simulated Annealing.

4.1 P-BFGS

In general, gradient descent methods like the BFGS method, use the derivative of the cost function, as well as its value, to select a search direction, essentially reducing the multivariate optimization problem to uni-variate minimization along a search vector; a line search. They thus consist of two main operations that are executed repeatedly, namely gradient calculations and line searching. The P-BFGS algorithm is based on the quasi-Newton BFGS (Broyden, Fletcher, Goldfarb, Shanno) method, widely regarded as one of the most efficient and robust gradient descent methods for use with continuous functions [17][18][19].

The BFGS method maintains an approximation to the Hessian, H, of f, where:
New approximations to the solution vector, x, are derived by:

1. Compute a search direction, $d = -H^{-1}\nabla f(x)$
2. Find a new x, using a line search, i.e. $x_{+} = x + \lambda d$
3. Update H using the current approximation to H, x and x_+ $H_{ij} = \partial^2 f / \partial x_i \partial x_j$

The P-BFGS algorithm performs step 1 by computing the finite difference approximations for the gradient in parallel. It also uses a modified parallel line search algorithm for step 2. There is insufficient space in this paper to discuss the algorithm in detail, however, more information can be found in [20].

4.2 Simplex

The Simplex algorithm used is based on the method of Nelder and Mead [21]. In common with other such methods, at each iteration it examines a simplex of points and then changes the simplex in response. A simplex is a geometrical figure consisting, in N dimensions, of N+1 points, or vertices, and all their interconnecting line segments. For example, in two dimensions, a simplex is a triangle.

The algorithm is started with N+1 points, defining a simplex, and their associated cost function evaluations. It then takes a series of steps, at each step moving the point of the simplex where the cost function is highest through the opposite face of the simplex to a lower point.

If the cost function value at a reflection trial point is found to be particularly advantageous, the simplex is expanded in the given direction; if it is less advantageous, the simplex is contracted. Should no progress be possible, the simplex is simultaneously contracted in all dimensions. These steps are repeated until the cost function values at all points fall within a desired tolerance of each other.

The basic method has been modified in the current study in two ways.

- Simple bounds have been applied to all trial points, so that the search is contained within a given space.
- The evaluation of trial points has been parallelised. At each step, in a high proportion of cases at least two function evaluations will be made: the initial reflection, and either an expansion of it, or a contraction. The modified algorithm evaluates all three of these possibilities concurrently, yielding a speedup observed to approach a factor of two, for the use of three processors.

4.3 Divide and Conquer

The Divide and Conquer (DC) method is a simple heuristic which performs a repeated subdivision of the search space. The domain for each of the N parameters is subdivided into three parts and the objective function is computed at the $(3+1)^N$ grid points that result. The grid point which produces the minimum objective and its neighbours give the domain for the next iteration. There are two variants of this procedure, depending depending on a parameter called "drift". If "drift" is allowed then the next search is centred on the end value, so the next search domain will be partly outside the previous space. Alternately with drift disabled the new domain will be a proper subset of the previous space. The search terminates when the absolute value of the difference in the objective values at the best and worst grid points, as a proportion of the mean of those values, is less than the tolerance.

4.4 Simulated Annealing

Simulated annealing (SA) is a *Monte Carlo* method, based on the analogy between the aggregation of many particles in a physical system as it is cooled and the optimization of large combinatorial problem. In the physical system, annealing is the process of heating a solid until it melts, followed by a cooling operation until the substance crystallizes. Fast cooling leads to a process called *quenching* in which the crystal that is formed has a metastable amorphous structure (or imperfect lattice), with a very large internal energy. Slow cooling allows the system to reach its equilibrium (lowest energy level) at each decremental temperature. Hence it is possible to reach the zero energy level or ground state. In the optimisation perspective, search space can be viewed as a physical system in which elements or variables correspond to particles. The atomic bonding force is equivalent to the set of constraints imposed on the problem. The energy of the system is modelled as the penalty cost, so that when the system reaches the ground state, the process arrives at the global optimum configuration. Simulated Annealing has been applied to a wide range of problems from continuous systems to combinatorial optimization. In this work, we have experimented with both a public domain package [22] and one that we have written ourselves.

5 Case Studies

In this section we examine the performance of Nimrod/O on 5 real world case studies, shown in Table 1. Table 2 shows which algorithms were applied to the case studies, since we were not able to apply all algorithms to all problems. The exact details of the case studies are not discussed here. All of them required the optimisation of a particular objective function value. The number of parameters is shown in Table 1, and varies from 1 to 7.

Problem	Number of Dimensions	Description
Smog	2	Photo Chemical Pollution Model [23]
S-Plate	1	Static Strength of a Biaxially Loaded Plate – Simple cutout
C-Plate	3	Static Strength in a Biaxially Loaded Plate – Complex cutout
Ceramic	3	Radio frequency properties of a ceramic bead [24]
Antenna	7	Multi frequency antenna

Table 1 – Problem definitions

Problem	Algorithm				
	Exhaust	P-BFGS	Simplex	DC	SA
Smog	X	X			
S-Plate	X	X			
C-Plate	X	X	X	X	
Ceramic	X	X	X		X
Antenna			X		

Table 2 – Problem-Algorithm assignment

5.1 Results

Table 3 shows the results obtained when an exhaustive search is performed on 4 of the case studies. In these cases, the domain of the parameters is either integer, or converted into a number of discrete values. We were only able to run an exhaustive search on 4 of the problems, because the search space for the Antenna problem is too large to enumerate, even for a coarse decomposition.

The "# Func. Evals" column indicates how many model executions were required. The "Optimal Cost" column shows the value of the best objective function value. The "Time for 1 Func. Eval" column shows the average time to run the model once. The "Number of CPUs" column shows how many processors were available on the cluster we used. The "Wall Clock Time" column shows how long it took to run the entire experiment with 64 CPUs.

From these results, it can be seen that for many of the problems, an exhaustive search is expensive even when a reasonably sized cluster is available. For example, the Smog case study required 60 days of continuous use of a 64 way cluster!

Table 4 shows the results of applying the various algorithms to the problems. The "#Starts" column indicates how many independent runs were performed for the problem-algorithm pair. The "Best Cost", "Worst Cost" and "Mean Cost" columns indicate the best, worst and mean costs across the independent starts. If only one start was performed then the worst and mean are omitted. If a '*' is present in the

"Opt" column, then the best cost was optimal. The "# Iterations" indicates how many iterations of the algorithm were required to achieve the best reported solution. For Simplex, DC and SA this involves sending out a number of function values for concurrent evaluation before computing a new position. In P-BFGS, each iteration involves both a gradient computation and a line search. The "#Func Evals" column reports the total number of times the model was run in order to find the best solution. The "Wall Clock Time" column indicates how long it took to find the best solution. The last column shows the ratio of the wall clock time for each problem with the time for an exhaustive search (from Table 3). The "Ave # of Processors Required" indicates how many processors were needed on average to achieve the best result in the time shown. This is calculated on the assumption that all independent starts are run concurrently and that each algorithm requires some number of processors to operate in the time that is reported.

One of the most striking features of the data in Table 4 is the variability of the results across different problems and search algorithms. P-BFGS performs well on all problems for which the optimal cost was known, achieving optimal in all cases. However, Simplex does not manage to achieve optimal on any of the problems attempted, although the comparison is a little unfair since the running times are quite different from P-BFGS. In addition, the cost achieved on C-Plate using Simplex, whilst not optimal, is also quite acceptable. DC performs well on the one problem on which it was attempted, and our particular version of SA does not perform well on Ceramic. However, this SA code is still under development and further enhancements may substantially improve its performance. Further, we obtained good results using the ASA package [22] on the Ceramic problem, but did not have all of the statistics to allow a fair comparison at this stage. Accordingly, we have not reported the ASA results in Table 4. Our results do indicate that one of the algorithms managed to achieve an optimal cost for each of the problems, validating the idea of making multiple algorithms available from the one optimization package.

The timing performance of the various algorithms indicates that whilst some of the searches might still take a large amount of time, in most cases the automatic optimization was faster than an enumerative search. For the Smog problem, P-BFGS achieves optimal 17.4 times faster than a 64 processor cluster performing exhaustive search. Moreover, it does this with only 5.1 processors on average. Similarly, P-BFGS achieves optimal on Ceramic 11.2 times faster than exhaustive search, using only 27.1 processors on average. At the other extreme, P-BFGS is about the same speed as an exhaustive search on C-Plate using 48 processors. However, DC solves this problem 5 times faster than exhaustive search with 53.8 processors. The variation in the number of processors used is a reflection of the parallelism available within the optimisation algorithm itself, and the number of parallel starts that were performed. For example, running Simplex on the Antenna problem did not use many processors because we only performed one start, and the algorithm has little internal parallelism. The DC algorithm on the C-Plate problem, on the other hand, achieves high parallelism using only one start because the algorithm itself is naturally parallel.

Problem	# Func Evals	Optimal Cost	Time for 1 Func. Eval. (Secs)	Number of CPUs	Wall Clock Time (Hrs:Mins:Secs)
Smog	10000	68	31680	64	1375: 0: 0
S-Plate	201	15.0	204	64	0: 10: 40
C-Plate	2541	14.7	326	64	3: 35: 35
Ceramic	12896	-39.8	3000	64	167: 55: 0
Antenna	-	-	7800	-	Not Possible

Table 3 – Exhaustive Search of case studies

It may be noted, since the exhaustive search data was available for 4 of the problems, it was not necessary for search algorithms to actually run the model again in order to provide the timing results in Table 4. In particular, for the Ceramic problem, we allowed the algorithms to perform a table lookup using the data from the exhaustive search, and then we predicted the total run time using the time required to execute the model once. Thus, when SA was performed on the Ceramic problem, we did not actually have to wait 370 hours for the result.

6 Conclusions

In this paper we have shown the design and implementation of a novel tool called Nimrod/O, which allows a user to produce an optimizing decision support system using existing computational models. The tool provides a range of optimization algorithms, and using a simple declarative specification technique, these algorithms can be applied to an arbitrary computational model even if source code for the model is not available. A range of backend tools means that we can target platforms ranging from department level clusters to a global computational grid.

The paper reports work which is in progress, so we do not regard Nimrod/O as a completed system. We plan to perform more work on the core optimization algorithms to improve their performance. We also plan to improve the engineering of Nimrod/O to allow arbitrary external optimization libraries to be integrated easily. In the coming months we plan to add a restart and recovery feature to allow long running experiments to be terminated and restarted at a later time. One of the most significant algorithmic enhancements is to improve the parallelism of the optimization methods themselves, with the hope of delivering shorter run times overall.

Acknowledgements

The Nimrod/O project has been supported by the Australian Research Council, as part of an ARC Collaborative Grant. We wish to acknowledge our partners in this grant, namely the Environment Protection Authorities of Queensland, Victoria and Western Australia. We wish to thank Turbo Linux Inc. for access to the enFuzion software, and the Distributed Systems Technology CRC, for access to Nimrod/G. We also acknowledge our research partners in the Globus group, in particular Ian Foster from Argonne National Laboratories.

The case studies discussed in this paper involved the work of a number of colleagues. We wish to acknowledge

- Dr Martin Cope, Dr Steven Spencer and Dr Maciej Skierski for their assistance with the Smog study;
- Professor Rhys Jones, Dr John Sawyer and Mr Paul Chaperon for their assistance with the Plate study;
- Mr Seppo Saario and Dr Jun Lu for their assistance with the Ceramic and Antenna studies.

References

1. Foster, I., Kesselman, C., *Globus: A Metacomputing Infrastructure Toolkit*, International Journal of Supercomputer Applications, 11(2):115-128, 1997.
2. http://www.globus.org/
3. Foster, I. and Kesselman, C. Globus: A Toolkit-Based Grid Architecture. In The Grid: Blueprint for a Future Computing Infrastructure, pages 259-278. Morgan Kaufmann Publishers, 1999.
4. Grimshaw, A. and Wulf, W., et al, "The Legion vision of a woroldwide virtual computer", Communication of the ACM, 40(1):39-45, 1997.
5. Turbo Linux Inc, www.turbolinux.com
6. Abramson, D. "Parametric Modelling: Killer Apps for Linux Clusters", Linux Journal, May 2000.
7. http://hathor.csse.monash.edu.au/RJK/
8. Abramson, D., Power, K., and Sosic, R., "Simulating Computer Networks using Clusters of PCs", HPC-TelePar'99 at the 1999 Advanced Simulation Technologies Conference (ASTC'99), April 11-15, San Diego, California,USA
9. D. Abramson, I. Foster, J. Giddy, A. Lewis, R. Sosic, R. Sutherst, N. White, "The Nimrod Computational Workbench: A Case Study in Desktop Metacomputing", Australian Computer Science Conference (ACSC 97), Macquarie University, Sydney, Feb 1997, pp 17 - 26.

10. Lewis, A., Abramson D., Sosic R., Giddy J., "Tool-based Parameterisation : An Application Perspective", Computational Techniques and Applications Conference, Melbourne, July 1995.
11. Eldred, M., Outka, D., Fulcher, C. and Bohnhoff, W. "Optimization of complex mechanics simulations with object-oriented software design.", Proceedings of the 36th AIAA/ASME/ASCE/AHS/ASC Structures, Structural Dynamics, and Materials Conference, pp 2406 - 2415, New Orleans, LA, April 1995.
12. Casanova, H. and Dongarra, J. "NetSolve: A Network Server for Solving Computational Science Problems", The International Journal of Supercomputing Applications and High Performance Computing, Vol 11, Number 3, pp 212-223, 1997.
13. Parker, S. and Johnson, C. "SCIRun: A Scientific Programming Environment for Computational Steering", Proceedings of IEEE Supercomputing 1995, San Diego, December 95.
14. Abramson D., Sosic R., Giddy J. and Hall B., "Nimrod: A Tool for Performing Parametised Simulations using Distributed Workstations", The 4th IEEE Symposium on High Performance Distributed Computing, Virginia, August 1995.
15. Foster, I., and Kesselman, C. (editors), *Computational Grids. The Grid: Blueprint for a Future Computing Infrastructure*, Morgan Kaufmann Publishers, USA, 1999.
16. http://www-fp.globus.org/overview/testbeds.html
17. Gill, P.E., Murray, W. and Wright. M, "Practical Optimization". Academic Press, London, 1981.
18. Fletcher. R. "Practical Methods of Optimization." 2nd ed., Wiley, New York, 1987.
19. Press. W. H. , "Numerical Recipes: the Art of Scientific Computing". Cambridge University Press, 1986.
20. Lewis, A and Abramson, D. "A Parallel BFGS algorithm and its application to Automatic Design Optimization", Griffith University High Performance Computing Facility Technical Report, 2000.
21. Nelder, J.A., and Mead, R.,"A simplex method for function minimization", Comput. J., 7, pp. 308-313, 1965.
22. Ingber, L, "Very fast simulated re-annealing", Journal of Mathematical Computer Modeling, Vol 12, #8, pp 967-973, 1989. See http://www.ingber.com.
23. McRae G.J., Russell A.G. and Harley R.A., 1992. CIT photochemical airshed model -users manuals, Carnegie Mellon University, Pittsburgh, PA and California Institute of Technology, Pasadena, CA.
24. Lewis, A., Saario, S., Abramson, D. and Lu, J., "An Application of Optimisation for Passive RF Component Design", to appear, Conference on Electromagnetic Field Computation, Milwaukee, June 4-7th, 2000.

25. Lewis, A, Abramson, D and Simpson, R., "Parallel non-linear optimization : Towards the design of a decision support system for air quality management", IEEE Supercomputing 97, San Jose, 1997.
26. Abramson, D., Giddy, J. and Kotler, L. "High Performance Parametric Modeling with Nimrod/G: Killer Application for the Global Grid?", International Parallel and Distributed Processing Symposium (IPDPS), pp 520-528, Cancun, Mexico, May 2000.
27. Buyya, R., Abramson, D. and Giddy, J. "Nimrod/G: An Architecture of a Resource Management and Scheduling System in a Global Computational Grid", HPC Asia 2000, May 14-17, 2000, pp 283 – 289, Beijing, China.

Problem	Alg'm	Starts	Best Cost	Opt	Worst Cost	Mean Cost	# Iter'ns for Best	# Func Evals for Best	Wall Clock for Best (Hrs:Mins:Secs)	W'll Clk Exh'st / W'll Clk Best	Ave # of Procs req'd
Smog	P-BFGS		68	*	-	-	2	46	79: 12: 0	17.4	5.1
S-Plate	P-BFGS		15	*	15	15	2	46	0: 34: 0	0.3	36.8
C-Plate	P-BFGS		14.7	*	15.7	15.1	7	240	3: 37: 11	1.0	48.0
C-Plate	Simplex		15		16.7	15.4	7	21	0: 38: 0	5.7	24.0
C-Plate	DC		14.7	*	-	-	8	430	0: 43: 26	5.0	53.8
Ceramic	P-BFGS		-39.8	*	26.3	-2.1	5	61	15: 0: 0	11.2	27.1
Ceramic	Simplex		-9.4		37.4	16.9	10	24	9: 10: 0	18.3	17.5
Ceramic	SA		-18.5		-14.2	-17.5	22	472	370: 0: 0	0.5	8.5
Antenna	Simplex		35.7	-	-	-	23	84	49: 50: 0	-	3.7

Table 4 – Results of Case Studies with Nimrod/O

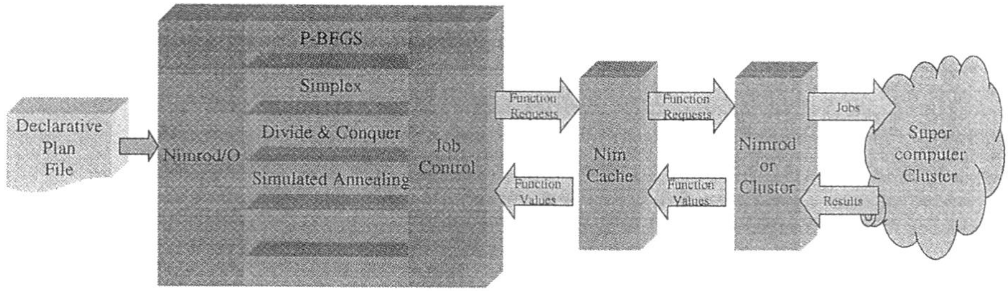

Figure 1 - Architecture of Nimrod/O

A NEW COMPUTATION EFFICIENT ADAPTIVE ALGORITHM FOR PARALLEL-CASCADE TRUNCATED VOLTERRA SYSTEM

SENG KAH PHOOI, MAN ZHIHONG, CHUI WAI YIP

School of Engineering, The University of Tasmania, Hobart 7001, Australia. Email: kp_seng@utas.edu.au , Zhihong.Man@utas.edu.au

H. R. WU

School of Computer Science & Software Engineering, Monash University, Australia

This paper proposes a new algorithm for adaptive truncated Volterra filters employed parallel-cascade structures. Parallel-cascade realizations implement higher order Volterra systems as a parallel connection of multiplicative combinations of lower order truncated Volterra systems. A Lyapunov theory-based adaptive parallel-cascade Volterra filter is developed. A Lyapunov function is first defined for the error between the parallel-cascade truncated Volterra system output and the desired response. Then the system coefficients are then adaptively adjusted based on Lyapunov theory so that the error converges to zero asymptotically. This scheme is independent of signals' stochastic properties. It has excellent convergence and high stability properties that are guaranteed by the Lyapunov stability theory. Furthermore, it does not suffer from severe ill-conditioning that often encounters in least squares Volterra filters. It also provides an alternative solution to unique solution estimation problem that exists in most of the stochastic gradient Volterra filters. Simulation examples of adaptive filtering are included to demonstrate the performance of this scheme.

1 Introduction

While linear filters are useful in a large number of applications and relatively simple from conceptual and implementation view points, there are many practical situations that requires involving nonlinear signal processing. A simple but highly pervasive type of nonlinearity where linear filters do not perform adequately includes the saturation-type nonlinearity. Therefore the development of filters using nonlinear model will be desired for many applications. Among those filters developed using nonlinear structure models [1]-[6], Volterra filters have received increasing attention in the signal literature. Several researchers have used Volterra series representation [7]-[8] of nonlinear systems to implement nonlinear channel equalizers [9],[10]. Other applications of nonlinear modeling and filtering in communication problems include echo cancellation [11]-[12] performance analysis of data transmission systems, noise cancellation, and detection of nonlinear functions of Gaussian processes [13]. Nonlinear filters have also been successfully employed in modeling biological phenomenon, image processing and other areas.

One of the realizations of nonlinear Volterra filter is *parallel-cascade* realization illustrated in Figure 1. Parallel-cascade realizations implement higher order Volterra systems as a parallel connection of multiplicative combinations of lower order truncated Volterra systems. Each branch in the Figure 1 consists of lower order Volterra systems combined in a multiplicative manner. This structure and its algorithm are attractive because of the modularity of the parallel-cascade realizations to approximate nonlinear systems efficiently using a reduced number of branches. This realization and its variations have several advantages over direct-form realizations. It is conceptually and computationally simpler to implement lower order Volterra system components than higher order Volterra systems. The realization results in modular interconnections of low-order Volterra systems enabling efficient implementation of higher order Volterra systems using VLSI circuits. The second advantage relates to efficiency of implementation obtained through approximations. The parallel-cascade realizations provide a systematic method of approximating nonlinear systems by discarding less relevant branches in the realization [19],[20].

Several researchers have employed parallel-cascade filter [19]-[22]. Adaptive parallel-cascade filters for quadratic systems models were presented in [21] and [22]. The structure of [21] is not constrained to result in a unique solution to the estimation problem and the filter exhibits relatively slow convergence behavior. The work in [22] constrains the filter structure to provide convergence to a unique solution but it requires appropriate training to select its initial settings. Recently, authors in [19],[20] have presented the parallel-cascade realizations and approximations of truncated Volterra systems and applied this concept to high order Volterra filter. They claimed that this filter is capable of converging to a unique solution and does not require the use of a training signal to initialize the algorithm. They have designed the LMS and NLMS adaptive parallel-cascade Volterra algorithms. In the LMS parallel-cascade structure, singular value, LU or LDL^T decompositions are employed. This results three different sets of weights update expressions for the time dependence components. However, the speed of convergence and the steady-state characteristics are controlled by the positive constant or step-size. Because of the nonlinearities in the system model, derivation of the stability bounds for the step-size is a very difficult problem. The step-size selection is a simpler task for the NLMS parallel-cascade algorithm. However it is assumed that the level of measurement noise in the desired response signal and the level of nonstationary in the operating environment are relatively low. Furthermore authors argued that the estimation error is bounded for certain choice of the step-size as long as the input signal and the desired response signal are bounded in some sense. There is no theoretical analysis on the step-size bound.

The objective of this paper is to present a Lyapunov theory-based adaptive parallel-cascade Volterra filter that employs parallel-cascade realizations of the system model. A Lyapunov function is first defined for the error between the parallel-cascade truncated Volterra system output and the desired response. Then the system coefficients in the parallel-cascade realization are then adaptively adjusted based on Lyapunov theory so that the error converges to zero asymptotically. This scheme is independent of signals' stochastic properties. Its computational complexity is less than that of the existing parallel-cascade truncated Volterra filters proposed in [19],[20]. It is robust to high level of noise and can operates in nonstationary environment. It does not suffer the aforementioned stability bound step-size problem in LMS or NLMS parallel-cascade algorithm. It has excellent convergence and high stability is guaranteed by the Lyapunov stability theory. Furthermore, it does not suffer from severe ill-conditioning that often encounters in least squares Volterra filters. It also provide a solution to unique solution in estimation problem. Simulation examples of adaptive filtering are included to demonstrate the performance of the proposed scheme.

The paper is organized as follow. The following section describes the parallel-cascade realization of truncated Volterra system. Section 3 presents the Lyapunov theory-based adaptive parallel-cascade Volterra filter. The design of the proposed filter is discussed in section 4. Section 5 contains simulation examples for the proposed scheme and validates the performance analysis. Finally, the concluding remarks are made in Section 6.

2 Parallel-Cascade Realization of Truncated Volterra Systems

An alternative to direct-form realizations of truncated Volterra system is the parallel-cascade realization shown in Figure 1. The output of a homogenous and casual pth order Volterra system with N -sample memory is related to its input as

$$y(k)=+\sum_{m_2=0}^{N-1}\sum_{m_2=m_1}^{N-1}\cdots\sum_{m_p=m_{p-1}}^{N-1}h_p(m_1,m_2...,m_p)\times x(k-m_1)x(k-m_2)...x(k-m_p) \quad (2.1)$$

where $h_p(m_1,m_2, \ldots, m_p)$ represents the pth order Volterra kernal of the system.

A pth-order Volterra system can be realized using l-th order and $(p-l)$-th order Volterra systems as illustrated in Figure 1. The input-output relationship in the expression (2.1) can be compactly written using matrix notation as

$$y(k) = X_{N,l}^{T}(k)H_{N,l,p-l}(k)X_{N,p-l}(k) \quad (2.2)$$

In the above expression, the column vector $X_{N,p(}n)$ has $\binom{N+p-1}{p}$ elements and contains all possible pth-order product signals of the form $x(k-m_1)x(k-m_2) \ldots x(k-m_p)$, where $0 \le m_1 \le m_2 \le \ldots \le m_p \le N-1$. Let $x(k-m_1)x(k-m_2) \ldots x(k-m_l)$ be the element of $X_{N,l}(k)$, and let $x(k-n_1)x(k-n_2) \ldots x(k-n_{p-1})$, where $0 \le n_1 \le n_2 \le \ldots \le n_{p-l} \le N-1$, be the jth element of $X_{N,p-l}(k)$. Then, $H_{N,l,p-l}$ is a coefficient matrix of dimension of $\binom{N+l-1}{l}\times\binom{N+(p-l)-1}{p-l}$ such the (i,j)-th element scales $x(k-m_1)x(k-m_2) \ldots x(k-m_l)$ $x(k-n_1)x(k-n_2) \ldots x(k-n_{p-1})$ in the expression (2.1).

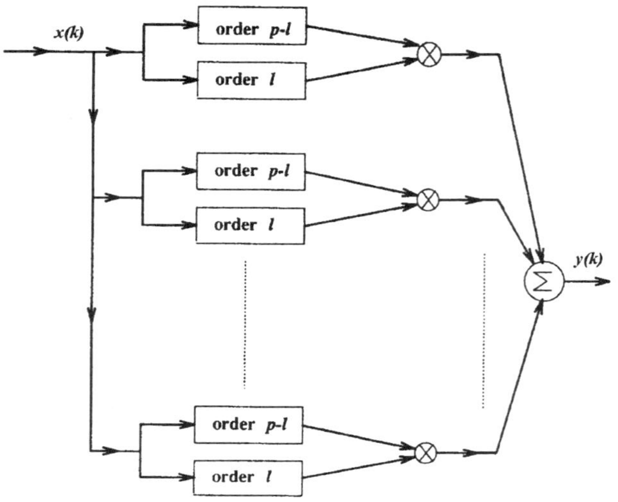

Figure 1: Parallel-cascade realization of a *p*th-order truncated Volterra system

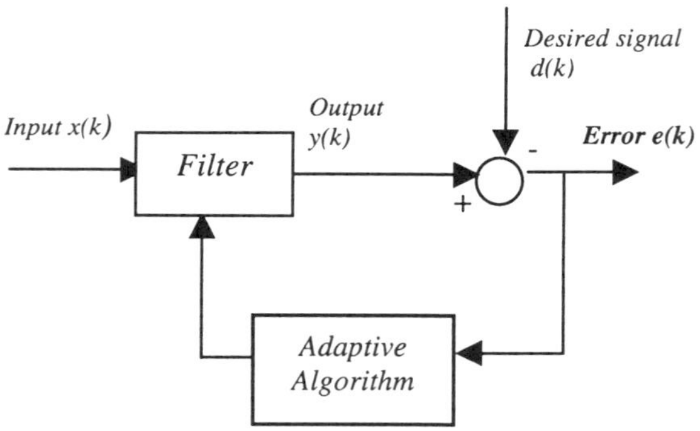

Figure 2: Adaptive Filtering Problem

3 Lyapunov Theory-Based Adaptive Parallel-Cascade Volterra Filter

Authors in [16]-[17] have proposed Lyapunov theory-based adaptive filtering for FIR filter and Lyapunov Adaptive RBF filtering respectively. Those algorithms used in [14]-[15] are the modification of RLS using Lyapunov stability theory. They are not gradient-based method and are independent of the stochastic properties of the signals. Based on the input observations and a collection of desired response, the filter parameters are updated in the Lyapunov sense so that the error between the desired response and the filter output can asymptotically converge to zero. These algorithms have provided a new approach in adaptive algorithm design. The idea can be extended to adaptive parallel-cascade realization Volterra filter and may give alternative solution to problems encountered in conventional parallel-cascade Volterra filters.

Figure 2 illustrates the adaptive filtering problem. Consider the problem of estimating a desired response signal $d(k)$ as the output of a pth-order adaptive Volterra system employing the parallel-cascade structure . The output of the adaptive filter may be written as the expression (2.1). In the Lyapunov approach, a Lyapunov function (3.1) is defined for the dynamic error between the desired response and the filter output.

$$V(k) = e^2(k) \tag{3.1}$$

The adaptive filter coefficients are iteratively updated so that the error converges to zero asymptotically instead of minimizing the cost function in conventional approach [1],[8],[11]. The error signal is defined as

$$e(k) = d(k) - y(k) \tag{3.2}$$

The coefficient update strategy for the Lyapunov theory-based adaptive parallel-cascade Volterra filter can be derived as

$$H_{N,l,p-l}(k) = H_{N,l,p-l}(k-1) + g(k)\alpha(k) \tag{3.3}$$

where $g(k)$ is the adaptation gain and $\alpha(k)$ is a priori estimation error defined as

$$\alpha(k) = d(k) - X_{N,l}^T(k)\, H_{N,l,p-l}^T(k-1) X_{N,p-l}(k) \tag{3.4}$$

The adaptation gain $g(k)$ in (3.3) is adaptively adjusted using Lyapunov stability theory as (3.5) so that the error $e(k)$ asymptotically converges to zero.

$$g(k) = \frac{X_{N,l}(k) X_{N,p-l}^T(k)}{\| X_{N,l}(k) \|^2 \| X_{N,p-l}(k) \|^2} \left(1 - \kappa \frac{| e(k-1) |}{| \alpha(k) |} \right) \tag{3.5}$$

where $0 \le \kappa < 1$. The design detail of the algorithm are presented in next section.

4 The Design of The Lyapunov Theory-Based Adaptive Parallel-Cascade Volterra Filter

The design of the adaptive filter using Lyapunov theory is described by the following theorem 4.1.

Theorem 4.1: For the given desired response $d(k)$, if the weight vector $H_{N,l,p-l}(k)$ of the filter $y(k) = X_{N,l}^T(k) H_{N,l,p-l}(k) X_{N,p-l}(k)$ is updated as follows

$$H_{N,l,p-l}(k) = H_{N,l,p-l}(k-1) + g(k)\alpha(k)$$

and
$$g(k) = \frac{X_{N,l}(k)X^T_{N,p-l}(k)}{\| X_{N,l}(k)\|^2 \| X_{N,p-l}(k)\|^2}\left(1-\kappa\frac{|e(k-1)|}{|\alpha(k)|}\right) \quad (4.1)$$

where $0 \le \kappa < 1$, then the error $e(k)= d(k) - y(k)$ asymptotically converges to zero.

Proof: Define a Lyapunov function

$$V(k) = e^2(k) \quad (4.2)$$

$$\begin{aligned}
\Delta V(k) &= V(k) - V(k-1)\\
&= e^2(k) - e^2(k-1)\\
&= \left(d(k) - X^T_{N,l}(k)H_{N,l,p-l}(k)X_{N,p-l}(k)\right)^2 - e^2(k-1)\\
&= (d(k) - X^T_{N,l}(k)\left(H_{N,l,p-l}{}^T(k-1) + g(k)\alpha(k)\right)X_{N,p-l}(k))^2 - e^2(k-1)\\
&= (d(k) - X^T_{N,l}(k)H_{N,l,p-l}(k-1)X_{N,p-l}(k) - X^T_{N,l}(k)g(k)\alpha(k)X(k))^2 - e^2(k-1)\\
&= (\alpha(k) - X^T_{N,l}(k)g(k)\alpha(k)X_{N,p-l}(k))^2 - e^2(k-1)\\
&= \alpha^2(k)\left(1 - X^T_{N,l}(k)g(k)X_{N,p-l}(k)\right)^2 - e^2(k-1) \quad (4.3)
\end{aligned}$$

Using the expression (4.1) in the expression (4.3), we have

$$\Delta V(k) = -(1-\kappa^2)e^2(k-1) < 0 \quad (4.4)$$

Remark 4.1: The deficiency of (4.1) that the values of $X_{N,l}{}^T(k)$, $X_{N,p-l}(k)$ or $\alpha(k)$ may be zero and rise singularities problem is also noticed. Therefore the adaptation gain may be modified as the expression (4.5) o avoid singularities.

$$g(k) = \frac{X_{N,l}(k)X^T_{N,p-l}(k)}{\| X_{N,l}(k)\|^2 \| X_{N,p-l}(k)\|^2 + \lambda_1}\left(1-\kappa\frac{|e(k-1)|}{|\alpha(k)|+\lambda_2}\right) \quad (4.5)$$

where λ_1, λ_2 are small positive numbers, $0 \le \kappa < 1$, then the error $e(k)$ asymptotically converges.

Remark 4.2: Design of the new parallel algorithm for the parallel-cascade Volterra filter based on Lyapunov theory is a new approach in adaptive algorithm. A Lyapunov function instead of a cost function of the error between the desired response and the filter output is first defined: $V(k) = e^2(k)$. Then the adaptation gain in the algorithm is designed based on Lyapunov stability theory. According to Lyapunov theory [18], if a positive define function, $V(k)=e^2$ is found such that its discrete time difference taken along a trajectory is always negative $\Delta V(k)<0$, then as time k increases, $V(k)$ will finally converge to zero and therefore the error will also converge to zero asymptotically. However, if $g(k)$ are adjusted using (4.5), then the $e(k)$ will converge. Hence the stability of the error dynamics between the desired response and the parallel-cascade Volterra system output is guaranteed even with the introduction of additive noise or large bounded input disturbances at the input. This statement is verified by the simulation examples. Unlike LMS or gradient-based algorithm, this technique is independent of signals' statistic properties by observing those expressions (3.1)-(4.5).

Remark 4.3: Adaptive parallel-cascade filters for quadratic systems models were presented in [21] and [22]. The structure of [21] is not constrained to result in a unique solution to the estimation problem and the filter exhibits relatively slow convergence behavior. The work in [22] constrains the filter structure to provide convergence to a unique solution but it requires appropriate training to select its initial settings. The design algorithm for the proposed parallel-cascade Volterra filter is not a gradient-based algorithm. It does not perform searching or global minimum in the error surface. The error convergence to zero asymptotically is desired to achieve. Hence, this leads to the unique solution. Therefore, this scheme is not sensitive to initial condition for converging to optimal solution.

Remark 4.4: Authors in [19],[20] have presented the parallel-cascade realizations of high order Volterra filter. However, the speed of convergence and the steady-state characteristics are controlled by the positive constant or step-size. Due to the nonlinearities in the system model, derivation of the stability bounds for the step-size is a very difficult problem. Furthermore, it is assumed that the level of measurement noise in the desired response signal and the level of nonstationary in the operating environment are relatively low. The proposed scheme is robust to high level of noise and can operate in nonstationary environment. It is highly stable and stability is guaranteed by the Lyapunov theory. It has excellent convergence and the convergence rate depends on the constant κ in (4.1). Hence the proposed algorithm can be made to converge fast by selecting the smaller constant κ.

Remark 4.5: Due to the fact the number of kernel increases exponentially as the filter order increases and this leads computation complexity also increases exponentially.

5 Simulation Examples

In this section, we present the results of the simulation that demonstrate the good properties of the Lyapunov theory-based adaptive parallel-cascade Volterra filter. The first part of the simulation example demonstrates the performance of the Lyapunov theory-based adaptive parallel-cascade Volterra filter when an additive noise is introduced at the filter input. The second part of the simulations illustrates the performance of the proposed scheme when the system is subjected to a large disturbance for a short duration.

5.1 Example 1 - Additive noise

In this example, *Fig. 3a* illustrates a speech signal is corrupted with the additive noise *n(k)*, uniform distributed random noise {0 1}. The adaptive gain is updated according to expression (4.5) and $\lambda_1 = \lambda_2 = 0.01$, $\kappa = 0.001$. The result illustrated in *Fig. 3b* shows the comparison of the reference signal *d(k)* and the filter output signal *y(k)*. It is seen that the output of the parallel-cascade Volterra filter can follow the desired reference signal closely and the effects of noise is well eliminated. *Fig. 3c* reveals the square output error, $e^2(k)$. It is noticed that the proposed scheme has fast error convergence speed and good tracking property

5.2 Example 2 - Large bounded disturbance

This example evaluates the performance of the proposed scheme when the system model has encountered a large input disturbance. The additive noise is also consider in this example except a sudden large disturbance is introduced within iterations 500-700. *Fig. 4a* shows the desired response, *d(k)* and the filter input signal, *x(k)*. *Fig. 4b*, *4c* reveal the output signal, *y(k)* and the square output error, $e^2(k)$ of the Lyapunov theory-based adaptive parallel-cascade Volterra filter respectively. Simulation result has revealed a good tracking and high stable properties of the proposed scheme.

6 Conclusion

This paper has presented a new algorithm for adaptive truncated Volterra filters employing parallel-cascade structures. Parallel-cascade realizations implement higher order Volterra systems as a parallel connection of multiplicative combinations of lower order truncated Volterra systems. The theoretical analysis and simulations have indicated that the proposed filter has fast convergence speed, highly stable compared to existing NLMS or LMS parallel-cascade realization filter [19],[20]. It is signals' statistic independent and its computational complexity is less compared to those in [19],[20]. Even under noisy conditions, the proposed filter remain stable and perform well. Furthermore, the proposed scheme has good tracking performance and can operate in stationary and nonstationary environments. The design and analysis of this scheme is extremely simplified and the stability concerns for the adaptive algorithm is guaranteed by the Lyapunov stability theory. In conclusion the new design is an attractive alternate to currently available stochastic gradient adaptive truncated Volterra high order filters in practical applications.

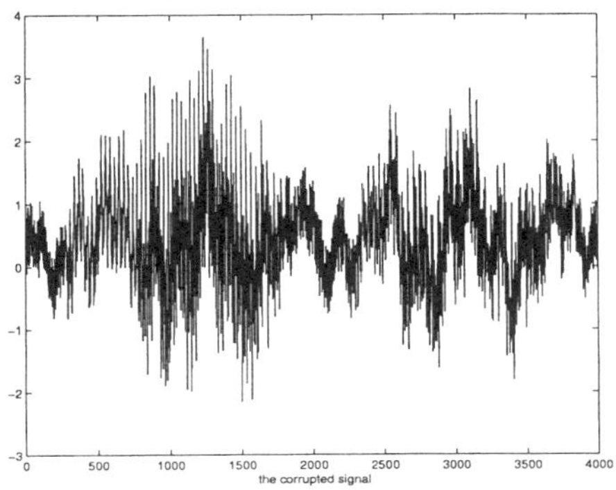

Fig. 3a: The corrupted input signal

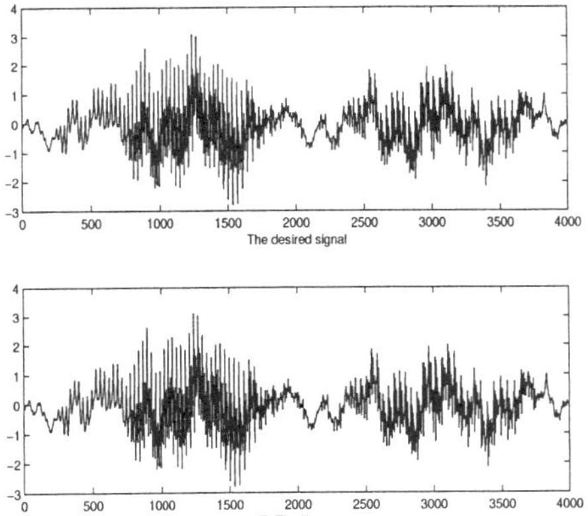

Fig. 3b: Desired output,*d(k)* & filter output,*y(k)*

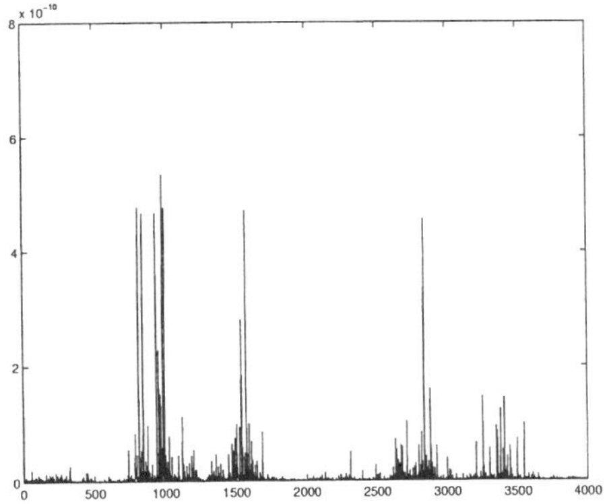

Fig. 3c: The square error, $e^2(k)$

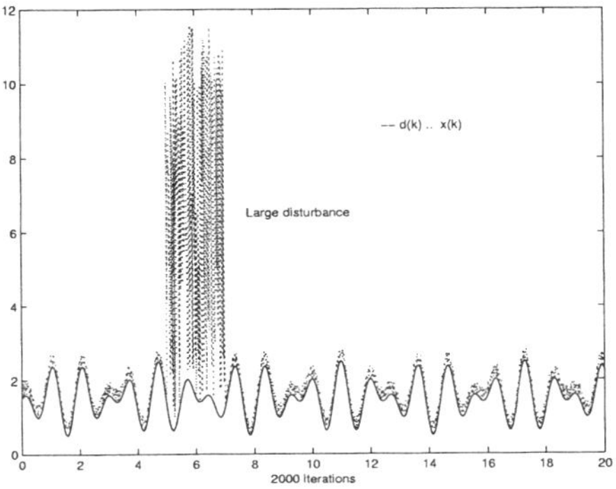

Fig. 4a: The desired response,*d(k)* & input signal,*x(k)*

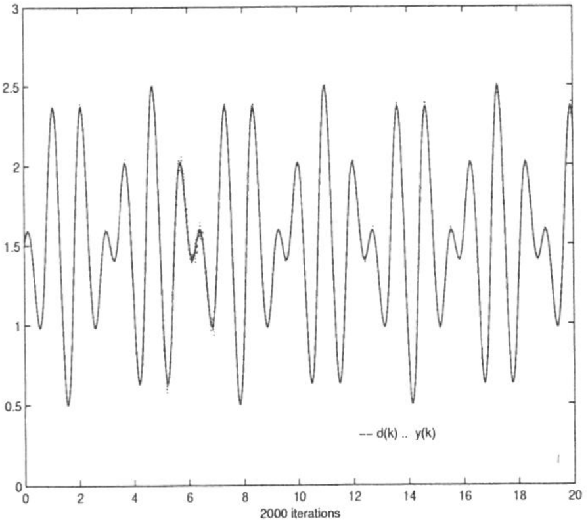

Fig. 4bThe desired response,*d(k)* & filter output,*y(k)*

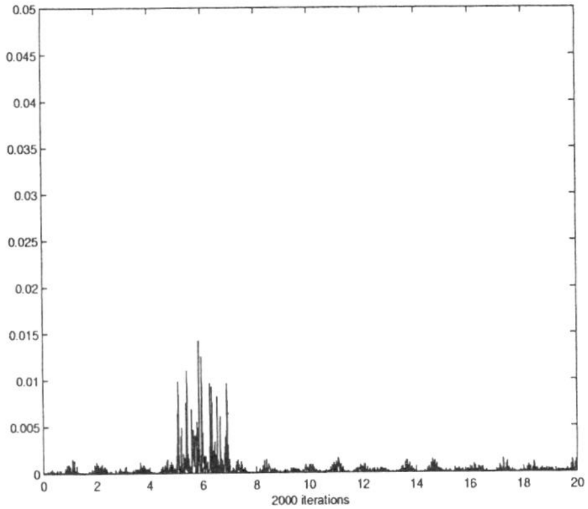

Fig. 4c: The square output error, $e^2(k)$

References

1. V. John Mathews, "Adaptive Polynomial Filters", IEEE SP Magazine, July (1991) pp. 10-26.
2. Lee Y. H, S. A. Kassam, "Generalized median filtering and related nonlinear filtering technique", IEEE Trans. Acoust., Speech, Signal Proc., vol. ASSP-33, **3** June (1985) pp. 672-683.
3. Maragos, P. and R. W Shafer, "Morphological filters, part I: Their set theoretic analysis and relations to linear shift invariant filters", IEEE Trans. Acoust., Speech, Signal Proc., **ASSP-35:8** August (1987) pp. 1153-1169.
4. Oppenheim, R. W. Schafer, T. G . Stockham, "Nonlinear filtering of multiplied and convolved signals", Proc of IEEE **56:8** August (1968) pp. 1264-1291.
5. T. Koh, E. J. Powers, "Second order Volterra filtering and its application to nonlinear system identification", IEEE Trans. Acoust., Speech, Signal Proc., **33:6** Dec (1995) pp. 61445-1455.
6. R. Nowark, B. Van Veen, "Volterra filter approximations", University of Wisconsin-Madison ECE Technical Report ECE-94-16.
7. W. J. Rugh, Nonlinear System Theory, The Volterra-Wiener Approach. Baltimore, MD: Johns Hopkins University Press, 1981.
8. M. Schetzen, The Volterra and Wiener Theory of the Nonlinear Systems. New York: Wiley (1980).
9. M. Bellafemina, S. Benedetto, "Identification and equalization of nonlinear channels for digital transmission", in Proc. of the 1985 IEEE Int. Symp. Circuits Syst., Kyoto, Japan, June (1985) pp. 1477-1480.
10. S. Benedetto, E. Biglieri, V. Castellini, Digital Transmission Theory. Englewood Cliffs, NJ: Prentice-Hall (1987).
11. G. L. Sicuranza, A. Bucconi, P. Mitri, "Adaptive echo cancellation with nonlinear digital filters", in Proc. 1984 IEEE Int. Conf. Acoust., Speech, Signal Processing, San Diego, CA, , Mar. (1984) pp. 3.10.1-4.
12. M. J. Smith, C.F.N. Cowan, P.F.Adams, "Nonlinear echo cancellers based on transpose distributed arithmetic", IEEE Trans. Circuits Syst., CAS-**35** **1** Jan. (1988) pp. 6-18.
13. R. J. Kenefic, D.D. Weiner, "Application of the Volterra functional expansion in the detection of nonlinear functions of Gaussian processes", IEEE Trans. Commun., COM-**33** **3**, Mar. (1985) pp. 276-279.
14. I. W. Sandberg, "On Volterra expansions for time-varying nonlinear systems", IEEE Trans. Circuits Syst., CAS-**30** **2** Feb. (1983) pp. 61-67.
15. V. Z. Marmarelis, "Practicable identification of nonstationary nonlinear systems", Proc. Inst. Elec. Eng., **128** Pt. D **5**, , Sept. (1981) pp. 211-214.
16. Man ZhiHong, H.R.Wu, W.Lai and Thong Nguyen, "Design of Adaptive Filters Using Lyapunov Stability Theory", The 6th IEEE International Workshop on Intelligent Signal Processing and Communication Systems, **1** (1998) pp. 304-308.

17. S. K. Phooi, Man Zhihong, H.R. Wu, "Nonlinear adaptive RBF neural filter with Lyapunov adaptation algorithm and its application to nonlinear channel equalization", Proc. of the Fifth Int. Symposium on Signal processing and its applications, Brisbane, **1** August (1999) pp. 151-154.
18. Slotine, J-J. E. and Li, W. Applied nonlinear control, Prentice-Hall, Englewood Cliffs, NJ (1991).
19. Thomas M. Panicker, V. John Mathews, "Parallel-Cascade Realizations and Approximations of Truncated Volterra Systems", IEEE Trans. Signal Processing, **46:10** Oct (1998) pp. 2829-2832.
20. Thomas M. Panicker, V. John Mathews, "Adaptive Parallel-Cascade Truncated Volterra Filters", IEEE Trans. Signal Processing, **46:10** Oct (1998) pp. 2664-2673.
21. Y. Lou, C. L. Nikias, A.N. Venetsanopoulos, "Efficient VLSI array processing structures for adaptive quadratic digital filters", Circuit Syst. Signal Process. **2** (1988) pp. 253-273.
22. S. Marsi, G.L. Sicuranza, "On reduced-complexity approximation of quadratic filters", Pro. 27th Asilomar Conf. Signals, Syst., Comput., Pacific Grove, CA, Nov (1993) pp. 1026-1030.

EFFICIENT AND SCALABLE PARALLELIZATION OF TIME-DEPENDENT MAXWELL EQUATIONS SOLVER USING HIGH PERFORMANCE FORTRAN

YI PAN

Department of Computer Science, Georgia State University, Atlanta, GA 30303, USA

E-mail: pan@cs.gsu.edu

JOSEPH J.S. SHANG

Air Force Research Laboratory, Building 146, 2210 Eighth Street, WPAFB, OH 45433-7521, USA

E-mail: shang@fim.wpafb.af.mil

An efficient and scalable parallelization of a sequential Fortran time-dependent Maxwell equations solver using High Performance Fortran (HPF) has been implemented. This paper describes the background of the project, the theory behind the efficiency being achieved, the parallelization methodologies employed, and the experimental results obtained on the Cray T3E massively parallel computing system. Experimental runs show that the execution time is reduced drastically through parallel computing. The code is scalable up to 98 processors on the Cray T3E. Based on the experimentation carried out in this research, we believe that a high level parallel programming language such as the High Performance Fortran is a fast, viable and economical approach to parallelize many existing sequential codes which exhibit a lot of parallelism.

1 Introduction

Computational electromagnetics (CEM) in the time domain is the most general numerical approach for describing dynamic or wide-band frequency electromagnetic phenomena. Computational simulations are derived from discretized approximations to the time-dependent Maxwell equations [1-10]. High numerical efficiency of CEM simulation procedures can be attained either by algorithmic improvements to solve the Maxwell equations or by using scalable parallel distributed memory computer systems. Since the massive volume of data processing are involved in solving the Maxwell equations, distributed memory computer systems are viable means to solve the memory shortage problem on workstations or vector computer systems. The other advantage is reduced time when parallel processing is employed to solve the Maxwell equations. Hence, parallelization of existing sequential Fortran code for solving Maxwell equations is an important effort towards developing efficient and accurate CEM code in analyzing refraction and diffraction phenomena for aircraft signature technology.

Previously, three versions of of the solver were available. One is the sequential Fortran version developed by the second author of this paper for vector machines such as the CRAY C90. The second is the MPI (Message Passing Interface) [15-16] version implemented by Dr. Marcus Wagner of IBM [11]. The third one is the Power Fortran version [14] developed by the first author during the summer of 1997 when he was an AFOSR Faculty Research Fellow at WPAFB. The description of the programs and their performance results are summarized in [11]. Using the message passing paradigm has several disadvantages: the cost of producing a message passing code may be between 5 and 10 times that of its serial counterpart, the length of the code grows significantly, and it is much less readable and less maintainable than the sequential version. For these reasons, it is widely agreed that a higher level programming paradigm is essential if parallel systems are to be widely adopted. The previous results obtained show that the performance of the parallel PFA code is even better than the MPI counterpart besides the advantages stated above [11]. This suggests that a higher level programming paradigm such as HPF is a viable and alternative way to parallelize CEM codes.

However, the results achieved so far is only a preliminary step in achieving a scalable version of the MAX3D code. The major problem with the PFA version is that it is not portable across different parallel computer systems since Power Fortran is only available on SGI Power Challenger and Origin 2000.

The primary research objectives of this research are to develop parallel code for the MAX3D using High Performance Fortran (HPF). HPF is more powerful than Power Fortran and is available in almost every major parallel computer systems. Our goals are to further improve the scalability of the Power Fortran version of the MAX3D code, investigate the possibility of using HPF to implement parallel CEM applications, make the parallel code portable across several parallel platforms. These objectives have been accomplished through implementation of the parallel code for the MAX3D via PGHPF (a HPF compiler developed by Portland Group). Experimental runs show that the execution time is reduced drastically through the usage of HPF. The time spent for the implementation is about two months. Compared with MPI implementation, it is much shorter. Since HPF is a general parallel language and not targeted to any particular machine, its performance is usually not as good as specialized parallel language such as Power Fortran on the SGI machines. Yet, the HPF code we produced is still scalable up to 98 processors on the Cray T3E. Based on the experimentation carried out in this research, we show that the High Performance Fortran is a viable and alternative way to parallelize many existing sequential codes which exhibit a lot of parallelism besides MPI. In many cases, using HPF to implement a sequential Fortran code is more economical than using MPI. HPF also solves the problem of limited memory size on a single processor and provide a fast way to port the code on parallel computer systems.

In the following sections, we will present the work performed, the methods used, and the results achieved during the research, and outline the impact of the achieved research results.

2 Methodologies

High Performance Fortran (HPF) is an informal standard for extensions to Fortran to assist its implementation on parallel architectures, particularly for data-parallel computation [18]. Among other things, it includes directives for expressing data distribution across multiple memories, extra facilities for expressing data parallel and concurrent execution, and a mechanism for interfacing HPF to other languages and programming models. HPF is available on almost any popular parallel computer systems, such as T3E, SP2, SGI Origin 2000, and is much easy to use and fast to port than MPI [15-16]. HPF allows you to add HPF directives in the sequential Fortran code and to apply the capabilities of a multiprocessor system to the execution of a single job. It splits the job into concurrently executing pieces, thereby decreasing the wall-clock run time of the job. Although HPF uses a lot of complicated analysis tools to analyze the user program and can produce a corresponding parallel version without user intervention, the quality of the parallel code produced in such a way is usually very poor. In my study, I found that using the PGHPF compiler's option `-Mautopar` to parallelize the MAX3D code automatically, the parallel results are not effective. The compiler is simply not intelligent enough to make a smart decision. Another problem with automatic parallelization is that it can create a large number of temporary arrays. Hence, automatic parallelization has to be combined with hand tuning to produce more efficient code. In my research, only hand parallelization is used to avoid memory waste and increase efficiency.

The HPF model can be seen as a collection of distinguishable, but complementary, programming styles. The models and methods we used in the implementation are data sharing and work sharing. In data sharing, data, such as an array, are spreaded over the memory of all of the available processors so that each processor operates primarily on its own part. In work sharing, the loop iterations are distributed within loops among the system's processors with the goal of executing them in parallel. For instance, you can use the INDEPENDENT directive to divide the iterations of a DO loop among processors, or you can let the compiler divide the work for you by choosing implicit array syntax. One natural and powerful strategy involves distributing an array, data sharing, and the iterations of a DO loop that operate on that array, work sharing, over your available processors. Processors executing a DO loop in parallel help you realize the power of the CRAY T3E and other parallel computing system. In the following sections, the details of data allocation and parallelization schemes are discussed.

2.1 Distributed Data Allocation

In a parallel program, data can be shared or private. Arrays can also be distributed to speedup the code. Arrays are distributed across all processors via the `!HPF$` DISTRIBUTE directive in HPF. The DISTRIBUTE directive names the variables that are to be shared data objects and specifies how they are to be distributed across the PEs. If the data is not specified as shared, it is private (the default). In a program that declares a private data item, each processor gets a copy of storage for that item. In many programming models, this data is called replicated. When an array is shared , its elements are distributed across the available PEs.

The DISTRIBUTE directive can specify array distribution within the directive by following the array name with distribution information contained in parentheses. The distribution information may include the keywords BLOCK or CYCLIC, which tell the compiler how to distribute array elements among the available PEs.

The DISTRIBUTE directive allows data to be distributed over processors in a variety of patterns. The ALIGN directive is used to s[ecify that certain data objects are to be mapped in the same way as certain other data objects. Operations between aligned data objects are likely to be more efficient than operations between data objects that are not known to be aligned. The BLOCK distribution distribute a block of consecutive memory locations to a processor. In our implementation, U0, U1, U2, F, and G are all aligned and have the same distribution, as shown below. Hence, we can parallelize the code across dimension K efficiently when working on these large arrays. The ONTO clause specifies the processor arrangement declared in a `PROCESSORS` directive. In our case, the arrangement is `PROCS` .

```
!HPF$ PROCESSORS PROCS(NUMBER_OF_PROCESSORS())

!HPF$ ALIGN U1(I,J,K,L) WITH U0(I,J,K,L)
!HPF$ ALIGN U2(I,J,K,L) WITH U0(I,J,K,L)
!HPF$ ALIGN F(I,J,K,L) WITH U0(I,J,K,L)
!HPF$ ALIGN G(I,J,K,L) WITH U0(I,J,K,L)
!HPF$ DISTRIBUTE U0(*,*,BLOCK,*) ONTO PROCS
```

Similarly, since we need to parallelize HZETA on dimension J, the H array is distributed on dimension J as follows:

```
!HPF$ DISTRIBUTE H(*,BLOCK,*,*) ONTO PROCS
```

Since different phases require different data distributions, it would be nice to dynamically distribute an array during execution. HPF provides such mechanism. They are `DYNAMIC` and `REDISTRIBUTE` directives. In our research, we also tried to use these two directives to distribute arrays dynamically. Since redistribution of large arrays such as U0 and H take a lot of time, the overhead incurred is lager than the saving in time. Hence, we did not use this redistribution scheme in our final implementation. Another distribution method is `CYCLIC`. This distribution distributes an array of elements cyclically to different processors. We found this method was not efficient for the MAX3D code.

2.2 Parallelization

The major part of the parallelization process for the MAX3D code is loop parallelization since the codes contain several big loops. The model of parallelism used focuses on the Fortran DO loop. The compiler executes different iterations of the DO loop in parallel on multiple processors.

The essential compiler directive for multiprocessing in HPF is `!HPF$ INDEPENDENT`. This directive directs the compiler to generate special code to run iterations of a DO loop in parallel. The loop is also called shared loop. In a shared loop, the iterations are divided among the available tasks. A shared loop can be specified by the INDEPENDENT directive. A private loop, by contrast, is executed only by the task that invokes it; no work is shared among tasks. Private loops are not preceded by an INDEPENDENT directive. For example, the following directive specifies that loop K in subroutine FXI should be parallelized and I, IM, etc, are private variables.

```
!HPF$ INDEPENDENT, NEW(I, IM, IP, J, SSXI, RSSXI, UI1, UI2, UI3,&
!HPF$&RX, RY, RZ,                                                &
!HPF$&UJX, UJY, UJZ, SUJ, RSUJ, UJ1, UJ2, UJ3, UK1, UK2, UK3,    &
!HPF$&UP1, UP2, UP3, UP4, UP5, UP6,                              &
!HPF$&UC2, UC3, UC5, UC6, FP2, FP3, FP5, FP6, FP, FM2, FM3, FM5,&
!HPF$&FM6, FM)
      DO 1 K=1,KLM
      DO 1 J=1,JLM
      DO 2 I=1,ILM
```

Shared loops specify the behavior of all tasks collectively, but they define the behavior of individual tasks only implicitly. Shared loops do not guarantee the order in which iterations will be executed. The lack of a defined order lets the system execute iterations concurrently.

Inside a shared loop, each task executes its assigned loop iterations as if each task were its own serial region. The assignment of loop iterations is accomplished by aligning the iterations according to the distribution of the array named in the ON clause of the INDEPENDENT directive.

There is an implicit barrier synchronization at the end of a shared loop, at which all tasks wait until the last one has completed. The shared loop ends after the DO loop that immediately follows the INDEPENDENT directive. After the shared loop has finished executing, the tasks continue to execute in parallel.

For multiprocessing to work correctly, the iterations of the loop must not depend on each other; each iteration must stand alone and produce the same answer regardless of when any other iteration of the loop is executed. Not all DO loops have this property, and loops without it cannot be correctly executed in parallel. However, many of the loops encountered in practice fit this model. Further, many loops that cannot be run in parallel in their original form can be rewritten to run wholly or partially.

Many loops that have data dependencies can be rewritten so that some or all of the loop can be run in parallel. The essential idea is to locate the statement(s) in the loop that cannot be made parallel and try to find another way to express it that does not depend on any other iteration of the loop. Through loop merge and loop switch, we eliminate a lot of data dependencies in the code. Some data dependencies can not be eliminated due to the nature of the computations involved in the code. Our strategy is to parallelize the loops which do not have any data dependencies. For example, loop K in subroutine HZETA has data dependencies. However, loop J does not. Hence, we parallelized loop J instead of loop K in subroutine HZETA. Similarly, we parallelized loop K in subroutines FXI and GETA. This is also reflected in their data distribution: array F, G, and H are distributed on different dimensions as shown previously.

No. of Processors	FXI	GETA	HZETA	SUM
4	0.59236	0.89535	0.8809	2.8894
8	0.31400	0.45646	0.44389	1.4939
16	0.16963	0.25290	0.22604	0.83692
32	0.099733	0.15042	0.11862	0.50716
48	0.074417	0.10890	0.11501	0.37680
64	0.053583	0.076501	0.064894	0.25680
90	0.053734	0.07640	0.064764	0.25511
98	0.02948	0.04119	0.06406	0.1443
128	0.02948	0.04108	0.06384	0.1430

Table 1. Execution Times in the Major Subroutines.

3 Performance Results

During this research, we used the CRAY T3E computer system at the Ohio Supercomputer Center, which is a powerful scalable parallel system with 128 processing elements. Its Peak performance can reach 76.8 GFLOPS. Each processor is a DECchip 64-bit super-scalar RISC processor. It has four-way instruction issue with two floating-point operations per clock. Each processor has on-chip 8 Kbyte direct-mapped L1 instruction cache and on-chip 8 Kbyte direct-mapped L1 data cache. It also has on-chip 96 Kbyte three-way-set-associative L2 unified cache. Each processor has a local memory of 16 Mwords (or 128 Mbytes). The clock speed is of the processor is 300 MHz and the peak performance of the processor is 600 MFLOPS. Although the speed is quite fast, compared with other parallel systems such as the SGI Origin 2000, the cache and local memory sizes of the T3E are much smaller (Each processor in the SGI Origin 2000 contains a 4 Mbytes secondary cache). This limits the power of the T3E for programs using a lot of memory space such as the MAX3D code. Actually, the effect of smaller cache size on the T3E is not only on parallel programs, but also on sequential programs. Although the processor speed in the T3E is higher than those in the SGI Origin 2000 or the IBM SP2, the system performce of the T3E is no better than the SGI Origin 2000 as shown below in our research.

Several experiments are carried out to tune our parallel code and to adjust our strategy as to how to distribute the various arrays and which loops and subroutines to parallelize. In this section, some experimental results are reported for the final parallel code produced. All the times are in seconds in the following presentation.

Table 1 lists the the timing information for the major subroutines in the code. The corresponding times are also presented in Figure 1. Since these subroutines are repeated many times, the time spent there contributes heavily to the total time of the code. As shown in Figure 1, all the subroutines are scalable up to 98 processors. When using 128 processors, no further reduction in time is achieved. It is also clear that the subroutine SUM spends the most time compared to other subroutines. Due to memory size, the program cannot be executed on the T3E with fewer than 4 processors.

Table 2 shows the execution times the code after loop transformations and hand parallelization. Because of the limited memory space available on

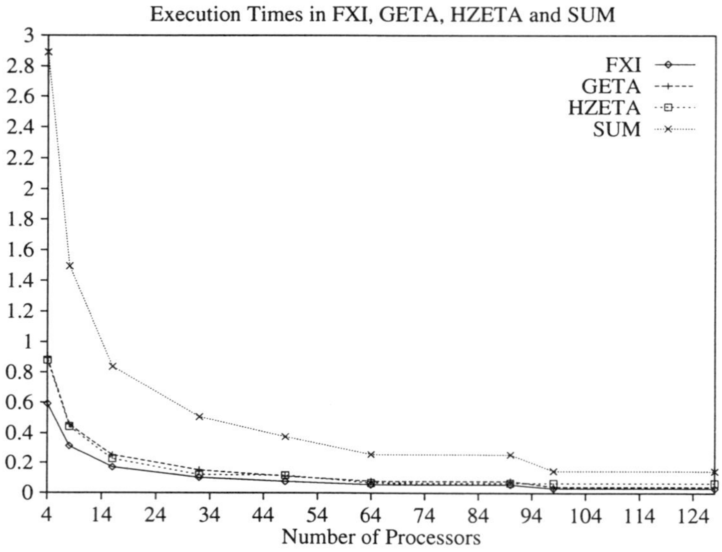

Figure 1. Execution Times of the Major Subroutines.

each processor in the T3E system, the parallel program could be run on the T3E with one or two processors. Hence, Table 2 only shows the execution times using at least four processors. Due to the requirement of the HPF compiler we used, many huge arrays have to be initialized before their usage, a lot of overhead is introduced. Hence, the execution time on the T3E with four processors is larger than the execution time on the Origin 2000 with four processors. However, the HPF code on the T3E is more scalable than the PFA code on the Origin 2000. From Figure 2, we can also see that the execution time reaches its minimum when 98 processors are used. Clearly, the parallel code not only reduces the total execution time drastically, but also is scalable up to 98 processors on the T3E system.

We can also see that the time is not reduced when we increase the number of processors from 64 to 71 or 90. This is natural since we parallelize the code on dimension K which has a size of 97. 71 or 90 processors are not enough to partition the array on dimension K. Due to array padding, the actual size on dimension K is 98 and hence has a perfect partition over 98 processors. Increasing the processor number is not effective unless we can use 196 processors. We predict that the execution time can be further reduced by using 196 processors. Unfortunately, the T3E system has only 128 processors.

Because the timing information is not available on the T3E when using only one processor, we cannot calculate the speedup exactly. In order to estimate the speedup, we assume that the program is executed optimally on the T3E with four processors. This assumption is quite reasonable since experiments indicate that the MAX3D code is run efficiently with a small number of processors. With this assumption, we can estimate the execution

No. of Processors	**Execution Time**
4	16331
8	8713
16	4853
32	2919
64	1659
71	1680
90	1688
98	1127
128	1148

Table 2. Total Parallel Execution Times for Problem Size (73 $\times$ 61 $\times$ 97).

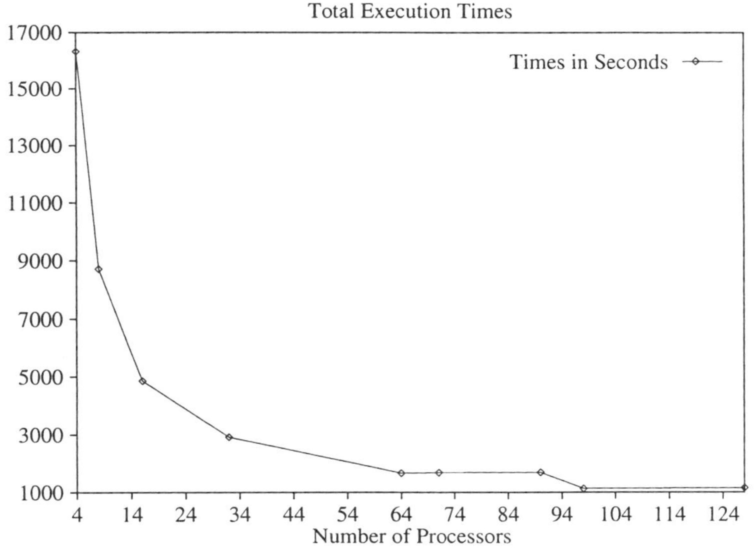

Figure 2. Execution Times of the HPF Code.

time on the T3E with one processor via multiplying the execution time on the T3E with four processors by four. Table 3 shows the speedups of the HPF code after loop transformations and hand parallelization using the above assumption. The corresponding data is also shown in From Figure 3. It is clear that the code is still quite scalable when the number of processors used is 98.

The experiments conducted in this research are limited to a fixed problem size (73 $\times$ 61 $\times$ 97). When the problem size changes, the scalability and efficiency may also change. Theoretically, when the problem size is bigger, the ratio of computation over communication is also getting bigger. This implies that the communication overhead becomes relatively smaller. It is our conjecture that the parallel code will be more scalable and efficient when

No. of Processors	**Speedup**
1	1
2	2
4	4
8	7.49
16	13.46
32	22.38
64	39.38
71	38.88
90	38.70
98	57.96
128	56.90

Table 3. Speedups for Problem Size (73 × 61 × 97).

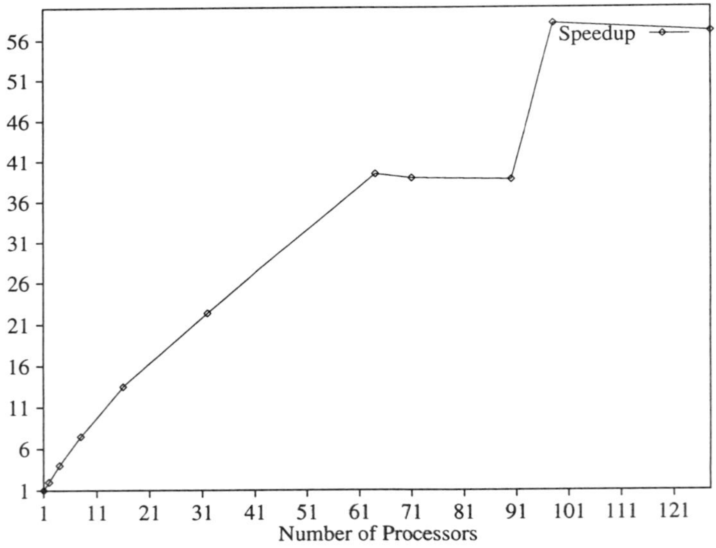

Figure 3. Speedups for Problem Size (73 × 61 × 97).

computing larger problems. However, more experiments are needed to confirm our conjecture.

4 Conclusions

As we all know, the message passing paradigm has several disadvantages: the cost of producing a message passing code may be between 5 and 10 times that of its serial counterpart, the length of the code grows significantly, and it is much less readable and less maintainable than the sequential version. Most importantly, the code produced using the message passing paradigm usually uses much more memory than the corresponding code produced using high level parallel languages since a lot of buffer space is needed in the message passing paradigm. For these reasons, it is widely agreed that a higher level programming paradigm is essential if parallel systems are to be widely adopted. The results obtained in my summer research show that the performance of the parallel PFA code is even better than the MPI counterpart besides the advantages stated above. However, the current version is implemented in Power Fortran, and can only be run on SGI Power Challenger and Origin 2000. The current PFA version also has the problem of not scalable when the the number of processors is larger than 16. On the other hand, HPF is more powerful than Power Fortran and is available in almost every major parallel computer systems.

HPF has reached a critical stage in its history. Having struggled while the compiler technology evolved into a usable state, the parallel computing community has now found it possible to write portable, high-performance implementations for selected applications in HPF. This research indicates that large scale data-parallel applications such as CEM simulations can use HPF to achieve reasonable performance. However, there are a number of pitfalls ahead. Notable among these are the general drift away from Fortran for advanced applications, remaining difficulties with HPF optimization technology, inadequacy of support for irregular problems in current implementations, the continuing need for advanced mathematical library support, and the emergence of competing paradigms such as MPI and PVM.

This research addresses the portability and scalability problems of the MAX3D code through using HPF. Our results achieved during the research have demonstrated that the sequential MAX3D code can be parallelized much more quickly using HPF than using MPI, and the doce produced this way can still be executed efficiently. Further, the code is still quite scalable. Although the HPF code is running more slowly than the corresponding MPI code and the PFA code on the SGI Origin 2000, the problem will be alleviated in the future or running on other machines. The problem is partially due to the HPF compiler called PGHPF we used during this research. The PGHPF High Performance Fortran compiler supports all HPF 1.1 extensions to Fortran 90 and a growing number of HPF 2.0 features [19]. The PGHPF compiler version we used is 2.3 and it requires that all arrays be initialized before their usage. It also has some other limitations and bugs which will be eliminated in the future. On the other hand, MPI or PFA do not have the initialization requirement. This could save a lot of time when a large number of big arrays are used in the code. Another possible reason is because processors on the T3E has small memory and cache space. Hence, the HPF code on one processor is slower than its counterparts. Nevertheless, the scalability of the HPF code is quite good and is better than that of the PFA code and close to that of the MPI code. As newer version comes out and HPF compilers become more mature, we expect that the performance of the HPF MAX3D code will be improved substantially in the near future with little change in the code.

5 Acknowledgements

This research was supported by the Air Force Office of Scientific Research under grant F49620-93-C-0063. We would also like to thank Mark Young of

Portland Group for his help in using PGI's gphpf. Computational resources for the work presented here were provided by the Ohio Supercomputing Center, Columbus, Ohio.

References

1. Joseph S. Shang and Datta Gaitonde and K. Wurtzler. Scattering Simulations of Computational Electromagnetics. 27th AIAA Plasmadynamics and Lasers Conference, AIAA-96-2337, AIAA, 1996.
2. Joseph S. Shang and Datta Gaitonde. High-Order Finite-Volume Schemes in Wave Propagation Phenomena. 27th AIAA Plasmadynamics and Lasers Conference, AIAA 96-2335, AIAA, 1996.
3. Joseph S. Shang and Datta Gaitonde. On High Resolution Schemes for Time-Dependent Maxwell Equations. 34th Aerospace Sciences Meeting and Exhibit, AIAA 96-0832, AIAA, 1996.
4. Joseph S. Shang and Robert M. Fithen. A Comparative Study of Characteristic-Based Algorithms for the Maxwell Equations Journal of Computational Physics, 125: 378 - 394, 1996.
5. Joseph S. Shang and S.J. Scherr. Time-Domain Electromagnetic Scattering Simulations on Multicomputers. 26th AIAA Plasmadynamics and Lasers Conference , AIAA 95-1966, AIAA, 1995.
6. Joseph S. Shang and D.A. Calahan and B Vikstrom. Performance of a Finite Volume CEM Code on Multicomputers. Computing Systems in Engineering, 6(3): 241 - 250, 1995.
7. Joseph S. Shang and Datta Gaitonde. Scattered Electromagnetic Field of a Re-Entry Vehicle. Journal of Spacecraft and Rockets, 32(2) : 294 - 301, 1995.
8. Joseph S. Shang and Datta Gaitonde. Characteristic-Based, Time-Dependent Maxwell Equation Solvers on a General Curvilinear Frame. AIAA Journal, 33(3): 491 - 498, 1995.
9. Joseph S. Shang. A Fractional-Step Method for Solving 3-D Time-Domain Maxwell Equations. 31th Aerospace Sciences Meeting and Exhibit, AIAA 93-0461, AIAA, 1993.
10. Joseph S. Shang. Characteristics Based Methods for the Time-Domain Maxwell Equations. 29th Aerospace Sciences Meeting, AIAA 91-0606, AIAA, 1991.
11. J.S. Shang, M. Wagner, Y. Pan, and D.C. Blake, "Strategies for adopting FVTD on multicomputers," IEEE Computing in Science & Engineering, (formerly known as IEEE Computational Science and Engineering), Vo. 2, No. 1, pp. 10-21, Jan./Feb. 200
12. Michael Wolfe. High Performance Compilers for Parallel Computing, Addison-Wesley Publishing Company, 1996.
13. James Laudon and Daniel Lenoski. The SGI Origin: A ccNUMA Highly Scalable Server, the 1997 International Symposium on Computer Architectures, Denver, Co, pp. 241-251.
14. Chris Hogue. MIPSpro (TM) Power Fortran 77 Programmer's Guide, Silicon Graphics, Inc. 1996.
15. Marc Snir, et al. MPI : the complete reference, MIT Press, Cambridge, Mass., 1996.
16. W. Gropp, E. Lusk, A. Skjellum. Using MPI : portable parallel program-

ming with the message- passing interface, MIT Press, Cambridge, Mass., 1994.
17. C. H. Koelbel. The High performance Fortran handbook, MIT Press, Cambridge, Mass., 1994.
18. K. Hwang and Z. Xu. Scalable Parallel Computing, McGraw-Hill Companies, Inc., 1998.
19. Douglas Miles, Vincent Schuster, and Mark Young. The PGHPF High Performance Fortran Compiler: Status and Future Directions, The 2nd Annual HPF User Group meeting, Porto, Portugal, 25 - 26 June 1998.

A NEW CONCURRENT ALGORITHM FOR ADAPTIVE FILTERING IN PARALLEL SIGNAL PROCESSING

SENG KAH PHOOI, MAN ZHIHONG, CHUI WAI YIP

School of Engineering, The University of Tasmania, Hobart 7001, Australia. Email: kp_seng@utas.edu.au , Zhihong.Man@utas.edu.au

H. R. WU

School of Computer Science & Software Engineering, Monash University, Australia

This paper introduces concurrency in LAF (Lyapunov theory-based adaptive filtering) algorithm for adaptive filtering. The proposed super filter consists of numbers of sub-filters. The sum of all sub-filter output forms the output of the super filter. This implementation will be particularly useful in the real-time implementation of large order filter when the computational time per iteration is critical and the LAF, RLS and LMS algorithms are not suitable. This scheme operates as follow: a Lyapunov function is first defined for the error between the super filter output and the desired response. Those sub-filters weight parameters are adaptively adjusted by the CLAF algorithm using the Lyapunov stability theory (LST) so that the error converges to zero asymptotically. This scheme is independent of signals' stochastic properties. It has excellent convergence and high stability properties that are guaranteed by the LST. Detail of design, convergence, robustness to input disturbances or additive noise, time saving in computation will be discussed. Simulation examples are included to demonstrate the performance of the proposed scheme.

1 Introduction

Recursive least squares (RLS) adaptive filtering has a wide variety of applications [1]-[3]. Various fast RLS algorithms have developed in [1],[4]-[11]. However, all these computational organizations suffer from serious numerical problems due to the finite precision with which calculations are made and in fact, they fail after a limited number of recursions [6],[9],[14]. Fast algorithms such as FRLS seek efficient ways of solving the normal equation [1] by exploiting various redundancies. However, it appears that this approach has almost reached a plateau, and we have to look in other directions for further developments in various aspects such as convergence, stability, computation complexity and robustness to noise.

The emergence of stable Lyapunov theory-based adaptive filtering (LAF) algorithm [13], has been a major development in the design of adaptive algorithm. The LAF has provided good performance for a computational cost that is of the same order as stochastic gradient (SG) or fast least square (FRLS) algorithms that lie in the range of few Ns approximately , where N is the filter length. Furthermore, LAF also provides better stability and convergence properties. Hence it is necessitated further progress in the LAF design. When the order of the filter is few hundreds or thousands, such as for echo cancellation in audio conferencing, implementation of FRLS may be infeasible in real-time applications especially for nonlinear filters. FRLS has higher computational complexity, while SG is not suited because of the slow convergence rate. LAF might provide a solution to the convergence and stability problems, but not the computational time saving when a very large filter order is implemented. Therefore the exploitation of concurrency in corresponding to the saving in the computational time required per iteration is necessary. Therefore these reasons lead to the proposed CLAF algorithm.

2 Concurrent Lyapunov Theory-Based Adaptive Filtering (CLAF)

Figure 1 illustrates the adaptive filter using CLAF algorithm. The filter is referred as a super filter and is decomposed into q sub-filters by partitioning $X(n)$ and $W(n)$ into q vectors each as

$$X^T(n)=[X_1(n), X_2(n), \ldots, X_i(n), \ldots, X_q(n)]^T \qquad (2.1)$$

$$W^T(n)=[W_1(n), W_2(n), \ldots, W_i(n), \ldots, W_q(n)]^T \qquad (2.2)$$

$X_i(n)$ and $W_i(n)$ are the data vector and weight vector of the ith sub-filter, respectively. The dimension of both $X_i(n)$ and is $W_i(n)$ $N_i \times 1$ such that $\sum_{i=1}^{q} N_i = N$.

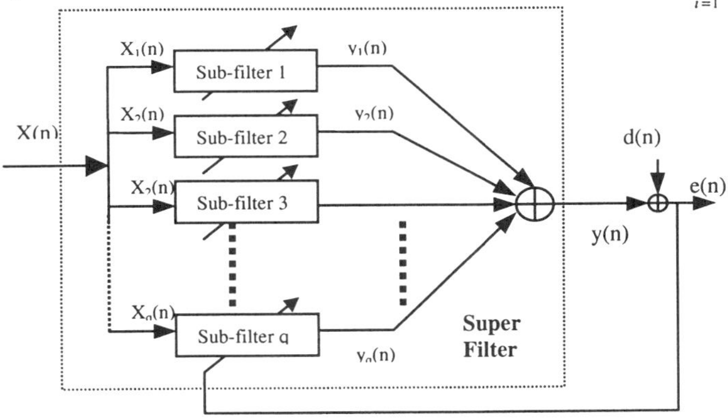

Figure 1: The proposed super filter with CLAF algorithm

$W_i(n)$ for the ith sub-filters, are computed independently and concurrently using their respective data vectors. The CLAF is applied to the filter to adaptively update the filter coefficients so that the error converges to zero asymptotically. The desired response can be expressed as follow:

$$d(n) = \sum_{i=1}^{q} d_i(n) \qquad (2.3)$$

where $d_i(n)$ represents the component of $d(n)$ that is contributed by the ith subsystem. In this case, $d_i(n) = d(n)$ for all $1 \leq i \leq q$ is assumed. If we know the

$d_i(n)$'s, we can easily implement the super filter as q sub-filters, each operating in parallel and independent of each other. The output $y(n)$ of the super filter is computed by summing the outputs of the sub-filters.

$$y(n) = \sum_{i=1}^{q} y_i(n) \tag{2.4}$$

The error, $e(n)$ is denoted as

$$e(n) = d(n) - y(n) \tag{2.5}$$

The sub-filters' parameters are adjusted based on this $e(n)$. In other words, we assume $e_i(n) = e(n)$ and $d_i(n) = d(n)$ for all $1 \le i \le q$. The sub-filters' coefficient vectors are updated using the following equation:

$$W_i(n) = W_i(n - 1) + K_i(n)\alpha(n) \tag{2.6}$$

where $K_i(n)$ is the adaptation gains for each sub-filters respectively and $\alpha(n)$ is the *a priori* estimation error defined as

$$\alpha(n) = d(n) - \sum_{i=1}^{q} W_i(n-1) X_i(n) \tag{2.7}$$

The $K_i(n)$ in (2.6) is adaptively adjusted using Lyapunov stability theory as (2.8) so that the error $e(n)$ asymptotically converges to zero.

$$K_i(n) = \frac{X_i(n)}{\| X_i(n) \|^2} \left(1 - \beta_i \frac{| e(n-1) |}{| \alpha(n) |} \right) \tag{2.8}$$

where the sum of $\beta_i(n)$ must be less 1 or $0 \le \sum_{i=1}^{q} \beta_i < 1$. We refer to this algorithm as CLAF algorithm because those sub-filters can be run in parallel.

3 Design of the CLAF Algorithm

The design of the CLAF using LST is described by the following theorem:

Theorem 3.1: For the given desired response $d(n)$, if the weight vectors $W_i(n)$ of the super-filter $y(n) = \sum_{i=1}^{q} W_i(n) X_i(n)$ is updated as follows

$$W_i(n) = W_i(n - 1) + K_i(n)\alpha(n)$$

and
$$K_i(n) = \frac{X_i(n)}{\| X_i(n) \|^2} \left(1 - \beta_i \frac{| e(n-1) |}{| \alpha(n) |} \right) \tag{3.1}$$

where $0 \le \sum_{i=1}^{q} \beta_i < 1$, then the error, $e(n)$ asymptotically converges to zero.

Proof: Define a Lyapunov function

$$V(n) = e^2(n) \tag{3.2}$$

Then, $\Delta V(n) = V(n) - V(n-1) = e^2(n) - e^2(n-1)$

$$= (d(n) - \sum_{i=1}^{q} W_i^T(n) X_i(n))^2 - e^2(n-1)$$

$$= (d(n) - \sum_{i=1}^{q} (W_i^T(n-1) + K_i(n)\alpha(n)) X_i(n))^2 - e^2(n-1)$$

$$= (d(n) - \sum_{i-1}^{q} W_i^T(n-1) X_i(n) - \sum_{i-1}^{q} K_i(n)\alpha(n) X_i(n))^2 - e^2(n-1)$$

$$= (\alpha(n) - \sum_{i-1}^{q} K_i(n)\alpha(n) X_i(n))^2 - e^2(n-1)$$

$$= \alpha^2(n)\left(1 - \sum_{i-1}^{q} K_i(n) X_i(n)\right)^2 - e^2(n-1) \qquad (3.3)$$

Using expression (3.1) in expression (3.3), we have

$$\Delta V(n) = -(1 - \sum_{i-1}^{q} \beta_i^2) e^2(n-1) < 0 \qquad (3.4)$$

Remark 3.1: The deficiency of expression (3.4) that the values of $X_i(n)$ and $\alpha(n)$ may be zero and rise singularities problem is also noticed. Therefore the adaptation gain may be modified as the adaptation law (3.5) to avoid singularities.

$$K_i(n) = \frac{X_i(n)}{\lambda_1 + \| X_i(n) \|^2}\left(1 - \beta_i \frac{| e(n-1) |}{\lambda_2 + | \alpha(n) |}\right) \qquad (3.8)$$

where λ_1, λ_2 are small positive numbers and $0 \le \sum_{i=1}^{q} \beta_i < 1$, then the error $e(n)$ asymptotically converges.

4 Comparison and Discussion

Saving In Computation Time: Before proceeding to the computational time required per iteration by CLAF, it is worthwhile to examine the same for LMS and RLS if their inherent concurrency is exploited. Authors in [14] have proposed a new family of concurrent algorithms for adaptive filter, these include PLMS and PRLS [14]. Here we define μ as the time required for one multiplication and neglect the time required for addition operations. For standard LMS, it requires $2N\mu$ time if we have just one processor. When the LMS algorithm is implemented concurrently, we have $N+1$ processor and allocate one processor for each coefficient and one (called EP) for computing $e(n)$. Thus we can observe from table 1 that the total time required is about 2μ + (*plus*) the time required by the processor for accessing $y_i(n)$ + the time required for global broadcast of $e(n)$ to N processor. Therefore the time required is very small and independent of N. This strategy may not be advantageous for small values of N, but for high order filter it will offer significant saving.

In the same way, authors in [14] allocate one processor for each sub-filter in PRLS and exploit its natural concurrency. When PRLS is developed around RLS, as shown in table 2, the steps 1 to step 5 can be done concurrently for each sub-filter. The time required for these steps is simply the time required by the longest or highest order sub-filter for steps 1 to 5 + time required for global broadcast of $e(n)$ + the time required by the EP to access $y_i(n)$ + the time required for global broadcast of $e(n)$ to N processor. Authors in [14] mentioned that the expression for time remains unchanged except for the first term when PRLS is developed around any FLS algorithm. The time for first term is replaced by the time required by the longest sub-filter for the computation of its gain $k_i(n)$, output $y_i(n)$ and $W_i(n)$ updated. Hence the smaller value of the longest sub-filter length, the greater will be the savings in computational time compared with the time requires by even FLS algorithm with one processor, especially if N is large. General expression for the computational complexity is not rewritten in [14] because they depend on the chosen configuration and the version of conventional or fast LS algorithm selected for the gain computation of the sub-filter.

Table 3 illustrates the concurrent implement of LAF (CLAF). It is notice that the steps 1 to step 4 can be done concurrently for each sub-filter. The time required for these steps is simply the time required by the longest sub-filter for steps 1 to step 4 + time required for global broadcast of $e(n)$ + the time required by the EP to access $y_i(n)$ + the time required for global broadcast of $e(n)$ to N processor. If we compared table 2 and table 3, less step is required for CLAF compared to PRLS. The time required for CLAF is less than that of PRLS. However, this 'less computational time' is not necessary applied to all concurrent implementation of fast versions of RLS. Therefore, CLAF has the potential of being used in real-time applications where computational time required per iteration is critical.

Step 1: Do for $i = 1, 2, \ldots N$	$y_i(n)=X_i^T(n)W_i(n)$
Step 2:	$e(n)=d(n)-\sum_{i=1}^{N} y_i(n)$
Step 3: Do for $i = 1, 2, \ldots N$	$W_i(n+1)= W_i(n)+ \tau X_i(n)\, e(n)$

Table 1: Concurrent Implementation of The LMS Algorithm [14]

Do steps 1 to 5 for $i = 1, 2, \ldots q$	Step 1	$Y_i(n)=\lambda^{-1}C_i(n-1)X_i(n)$
	Step 2	$k_i(n) = \dfrac{Y_i(n)}{1 + X_i^T(n)Y_i(n)}$
	Step 3	$C_i(n)=\lambda^{-1}C_i(n-1)- k_i(n)Y_i^T(n)$
	Step 4	$W_i(n)= W_i(n-1)+ k_i(n)\, e(n)$
	Step 5	$y_i(n)=X_i^T(n)W_i(n)$
	Step 6	$e(n)=d(n)-\sum_{i=1}^{q} y_i(n)$

Table 2: Concurrent Implementation of The RLS Algorithm (Develop around RLS) [14]

Do steps 1 to 4 for $i = 1, 2, \ldots q$	Step 1	$\alpha(n) = d(n) - \sum_{i=1}^{q} W_i(n-1) X_i(n)$
	Step 2	$K_i(n) = \dfrac{X_i(n)}{\lambda_1 + \lVert X_i(n) \rVert^2}\left(1 - \beta_i \dfrac{\lvert e(n-1) \rvert}{\lambda_2 + \lvert \alpha(n) \rvert}\right)$
	Step 3	$W_i(n) = W_i(n-1) + K_i(n)\alpha(n)$
	Step 4	$y_i(n) = X_i^T(n) W_i(n-1)$
	Step 5	$e(n) = d(n) - \sum_{i=1}^{q} y_i(n)$

Table 3: Concurrent Implementation of The LAF Algorithm

Stability, robustness to additive noise or large bounded input disturbance and independent of signal statistical properties : The proposed is a new approach in parallel implementation of adaptive filter. The new CLAF posses properties owned by LAF algorithm. Like LAF, the stability of the error dynamics between the desired response and super filter output is guaranteed even with the introduction of additive noise or large bounded input disturbances at the filter input. Unlike PLMS, the stability of the filter depends on the stability of the sub-filter. Proper selection of the *step-size* in LMS in each sub-filter is very important to assure the stability of the overall filter. Introduction of additive noise and large bounded input disturbances badly affect the stability of the PLMS filter. For RLS algorithm, it exhibits unstable behaviour as shown in [8]. Furthermore, unlike PLMS, CLAF is independent of signals' statistic properties.

Fast convergence - Convergence analysis of CLAF is similar to LAF [13]. The convergence rate of CLAF depends on the constant β in the expression (3.4). Obviously, smaller constant β gives faster error convergence. In addition, selection of β is simple, we can let β_i equal the same constant, as long as $0 \le \sum_{i=1}^{q} \beta_i < 1$ The convergence of PLMS is highly depends on the choice of the *step-size* in each sub-filter. A large value of *step-size* will lead to rapid convergence but the weight choice may then oscillate or become unstable, while low value imply slow convergence [1]-[3].

5 Simulation

The simulation examples are performed to demonstrate the performance of CLAF filter. The first example demonstrates CLAF's performance when the super filter input signal is corrupted by the additive random noise that is bounded. A super filter with 5 sub-filters, $q=5$ is considered. The adaptive gain is updated according to expression (3.5). In the first case, λ_1, λ_2 and β_i in (3.5) are chosen as follow:

$\lambda_1=\lambda_2=0.001$, and $\beta_1=\beta_2= ... =\beta_5=0.001$. The result illustrated in *Fig. 2a* that shows the comparison of $d(k)$ and $y(n)$. The square error. $e^2(n)$ is illustrated in *Fig. 2b*. The performance of the CLAF filter can be further improved by properly choosing smaller parameters λ_1, λ_2 and β_ι. It has been shown in [13], the smaller value of these parameters, the faster the error convergence rate and the smaller the error is.

Simulations of the same setup with PRLS and PLMS are also accomplished for comparison. The simulation of the same number of sub-filter with PRLS algorithm is first presented. The results in *Fig. 3a* and *Fig. 3b* (forgetting or weighting factor, $\rho= 0.2$) reveal the output signal of PRLS method has higher noise level compared to that of CLAF by observing the $e^2(n)$. Thus CLAF has fast convergence speed, good tracking property and is highly stable. Simulation results for PLMS are illustrated in *Fig. 4a* and *Fig. 4b*.

6 Conclusion

Implementation involving exploitation of parallelisms in the structure of the adaptive filter is addressed in this paper. The theoretical analysis and simulation results have indicated that the concurrent Lyapunov theory-based adaptive filtering (CLAF) algorithm is very powerful and stable. It is superior in various aspects such as stability, convergence and tracking ability compared to the gradient search based algorithms implemented concurrently. The CLAF will be particularly useful in the real-time implementation of large order filter when the computational time per iteration is critical. This scheme is independent of signals' stochastic properties. It has excellent convergence and high stability properties that are guaranteed by the Lyapunov stability theory. Hence the CLAF has provided a new and alternative approach to conventional parallel or concurrent algorithms and hopefully suggested a new research area of adaptive parallel signal processing

References

1. S. Haykin, Adaptive filter theory. Englewood Cliffs, NJ: Prentice-Hall (1985).
2. C.F.N. Cowan, P.M. Grant, Adaptive Filters: Prentice-Hall Signal Processing Series (1985).
3. Bernard Mulgrew, Colin F. N. Cowan, Adaptive filters and equalizers: Kluwer Academic Publishers (1984).
4. Dirk T. M. Slock, Thomas Kailath, "Numerical stable fast transversal filters for recursive least squares adaptive filtering", IEEE Trans. Signal Processing, **39** (1991).
5. J. M. Cioffi, T. Kailath, "Fast, recursive least squares transversal filters for adaptive filtering", IEEE Trans. Acoust., Speech, Signal Processing, vol. ASSP-32, **2** (1984) pp. 304-337.

6. Mariusz Zoltowski, "Why do optimal forgetting RLSs exhibit long term divergence and how can this be avoided?", Signal Processing **68** (1998) pp. 195-218.
7. J. M. Cioffi, T. Kailath, "Windowed fast transversal filters adaptive algorithms with normalization", IEEE Trans. Acoust., Speech, Signal Processing, vol. ASSP-33 **3** (1985) pp. 607-625.
8. M. Mueller, "Least-squares algorithms for adaptive equalizers", Bell Syst. Tech. J. **60** (1981) pp.1905-1925.
9. S. Ljung and L. Ljung, "Error propagation properties of least squares adaptation algorithms", Automatica **21** (1985) pp. 157-167.
10. D. Falconer and L. Ljung, "Application of fast Kalman estimation to adaptive equalization", IEEE Trans. Commum., vol. COMM-26 (1978) pp. 1439-1446.
11. M. Verhaegen, "Roundoff error propagation in four generally applicable, recursive least squares estimation schemes", Automatica 25 (1989) pp.437-444.
12. Mangesh M. Chansarkar and Uday B. Desai, "A robust least squares algorithm", IEEE Trans. on Signal Processing **45** (1997).
13. L. Ljung, "Analysis of recursive stochastic algorithms", IEEE Trans. Automat. Contr. **AC-22** (1977) pp. 551-575.
14. Man ZhiHong, H.R.Wu, W.Lai and Thong Nguyen, "Design of Adaptive Filters Using Lyapunov Stability Theory", The 6th IEEE International Workshop on Intelligent Signal Processing and Communication Systems **1** (1998) pp. 304-308.
15. Ajit Kumar Chaturvedi, Govind Sharma, "A new Family of Concurrent Algorithms for Adaptive Volterra and Linear Filters", IEEE Trans. on Signal Processing **47** (1999).
16. Slotine, J-J. E. and Li, W. Applied nonlinear control, Prentice-Hall, Englewood Cliffs, NJ (1991).

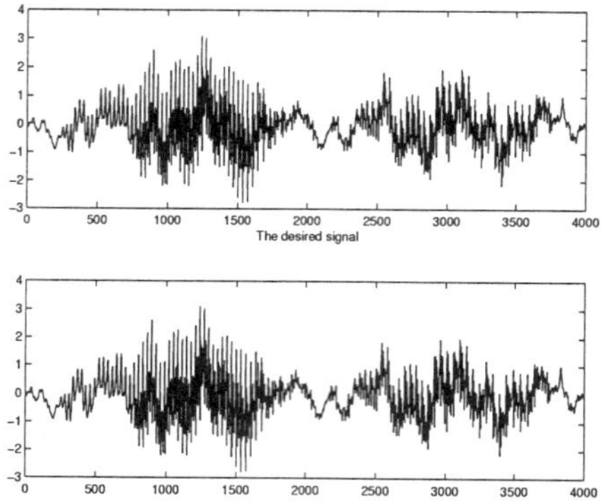

Fig. 2a: CLAF-Desired & filter outputs $d(n)$ & $y(n)$

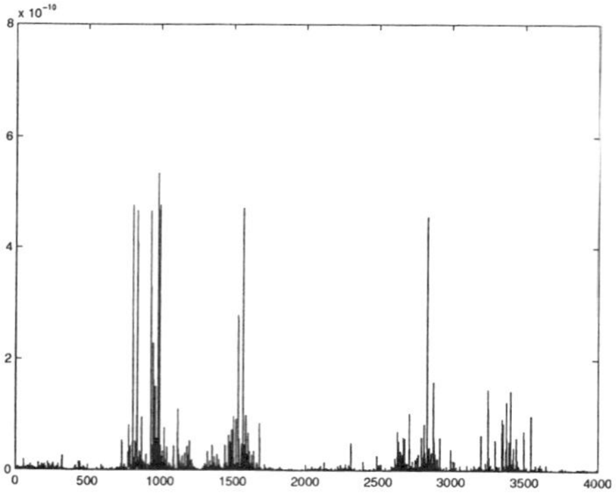

Fig. 2b: CLAF -The square error, $e^2(n)$

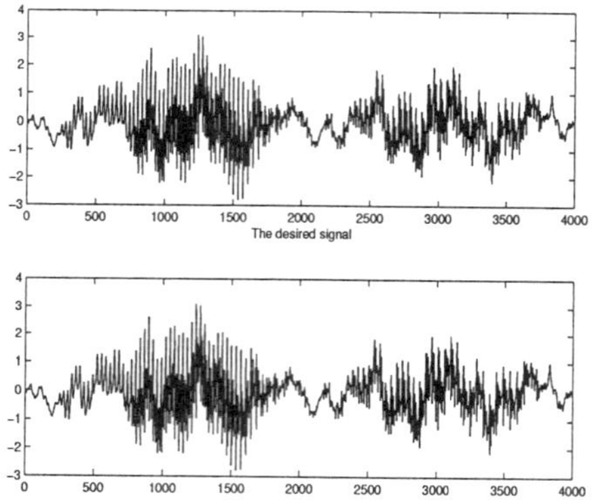

Fig. 3a: PRLS-Desired & filter outputs $d(n)$ & $y(n)$

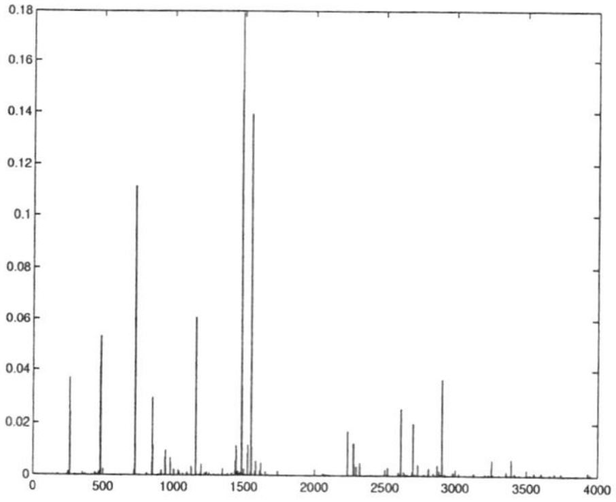

Fig. 3b: PRLS - The square error, $e^2(n)$

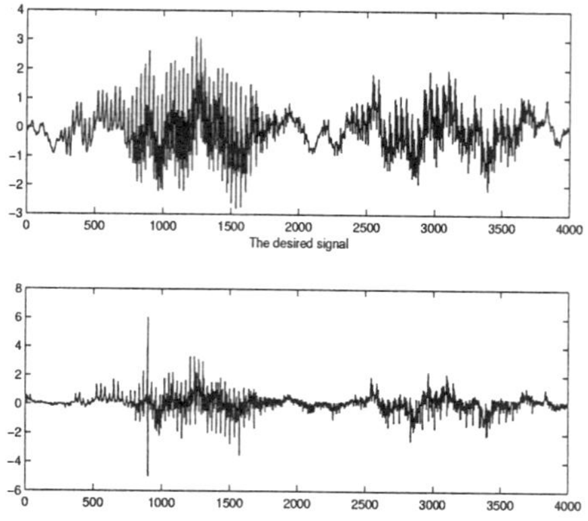

Fig. 4a: PLMS-Desired & filter outputs $d(n)$ & $y(n)$

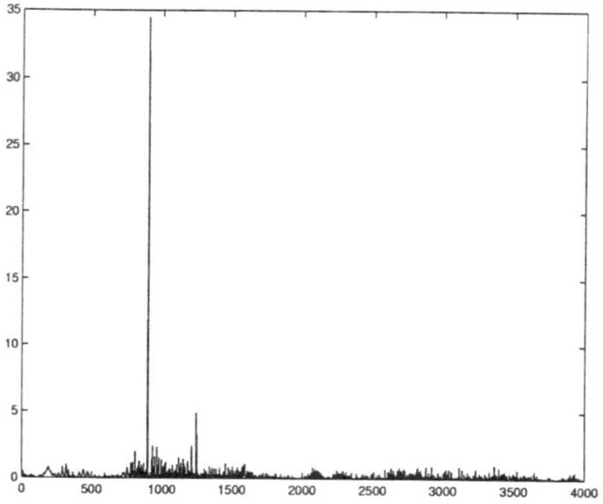

Fig. 4b: PLMS - The square error, $e^2(n)$

A PARALLEL IMAGE MATCHING ALGORITHM BASED ON ENTROPY FEATURE VECTOR

DONG KAIKUN, HU MINGZENG AND FANG BINXING

Computer Science and Engineering Dept., P.O. Box 320, Harbin Institute of Technology, Harbin 150001,P.R. China

E-mail: dkk@pact518.hit.edu.cn

Computer vision tasks require an enormous amount of computation, especially when the data is in image form, demanding high-performance computers for practical, real-time applications. Parallelism appears to be the only economical way to achieve the level of performance required for vision tasks. Based on the concept of entropy feature vector proposed in this paper, a parallel image matching algorithm suitable to SIMD computer is presented. Compared with the existed algorithms, the algorithm of this paper has the following advantages: (1) The spatial information of an image is appropriately introduced into the definition of image entropy. (2) A large number of division operations are eliminated, thus the algorithm is sped up and the complexity of implementation in hardware is greatly reduced. (3) The shortcoming of having to do global calculation in the first instance is overcome. Therefore the algorithm has very good locality and is suitable for parallel processing.

1 Introduction

Image matching is an important technique in computer vision and image processing. It has been widely used in aircraft navigation, target recognition and tracing, resource analysis, weather forecast, and medical diagnosis [1].

In aircraft navigation, the satellite or aerial photographs of the districts where the aircraft is going to fly over are taken and stored in the computer memory on the aircraft as datum image before the flight. While flying, the aircraft takes photographs of the districts where it arrives, namely real-time image, and matches it with the datum image stored in the memory to determine the position of the aircraft. Obviously, the image matching orientation technology is based on the assumption that the real-time image is accordant with the datum image. However, since the real-time image and the datum image are shot under different conditions (time, weather, angle, etc.) in practice, they do not satisfy strict consistency. In other words, it is a kind of matching of dissimilar images. There are three main disadvantage factors that affect the consistency between the real-time image and the datum image:

- respective interference noises in real-time image and datum image;
- geometric distortion between real-time image and datum image;
- gray difference between real-time image and datum image.

Many researches have been carried out about image matching technology for the past 30 years [1,2,3]. The algorithms presented can be classified into two kinds according to the consistency models they satisfied. One kind of algorithms are based on gray or color consistency. These methods match the real-time image with the datum image by a fixed size of window pixels according to a similarity criterion. Although these algorithms need a mountain of computation, they usually have good parallelism and are easy to be mapped onto special purpose architectures. The shortcoming of these algorithms is that all the disadvantage factors mentioned above have tangible effect on the matching result. The second kind of algorithms are based on feature consistency. In these methods, the features of real-time image and datum image are extracted and matched according to a criterion. Generally, these algorithms have good properties of resisting geometric distortion, gray difference and noise interference. However, most of the algorithms need to extract feature points or edge of the image, and the matching effect depends mainly on the quality of feature extraction. In fact, it is still a difficult work to segment or extract feature from the image of scenery in natural environment. In general, parallelism is not immediately evident in algorithms based on feature consistency.

In this paper, applying the concept of entropy feature vector, a parallel image matching algorithm based on feature consistency is presented, but it need not to extract feature points or edge of the image.

2 The Definition of Image Entropy Vector

Since the concept of entropy in physics was introduced into information theory by Shannon, it has been widely applied in signal and image processing [4,5,6].

Let $F=[f(x,y)]_{M\times N}$ be an image of size $M\times N$, where $f(x,y)$ is the gray value at (x,y); $f(x,y)\in G_L=\{0,1,\cdots,L-1\}$, the set of gray levels. In reference [1], the entropy of the image is defined as follows:

$$H_f=-\sum_{i=1}^{M}\sum_{j=1}^{N}p_{ij}\log p_{ij} \tag{1}$$

$$p_{ij}=f(i,j)\Big/\sum_{i=1}^{M}\sum_{j=1}^{N}f(i,j) \tag{2}$$

$p_{i,j}$ denotes the frequency of $f(x,y)$.

If $F=[f(x,y)]_{M\times N}$ is a subimage of an image, H_f is called local entropy.

From the definition above we can see that the entropy of an image gives additive property information of an image. The entropy is small when the change of the gray values is severe and large when the change of gray values is smooth. It has also been proved in reference [1] that the entropy has the property of resisting irradiation distortion, geometric distortion and noise interference. Then the entropy can be a kind of feature description used for image matching. But the definition has two important shortcomings:

First, for the reason of data dependence, the following computations must be performed in sequence.

- Calculation 1 $S=\sum_{i=1}^{M}\sum_{j=1}^{N} f(i,j)$
- Calculation 2 $p_{ij} = f(i,j)/S$
- Calculation 3 $H_f = -\sum_{i=1}^{M}\sum_{j=1}^{N} p_{ij}\log p_{ij}$

The computation of summing up all the pixel gray values in calculation1 is a global computation and can not be finished before all the pixels of the image have been scanned. At the same time, calculation2 brings a large numbers of divisions to calculate p_{ij}, so the complexity of implementation in hardware is greatly increased.

Another shortcoming of the definition is that no spatial information of the image has been introduced into the definition. Which means two images entirely different in structure may have the same entropy. So we define the entropy of an image as a two-dimensional vector. For image $F=[f(x,y)]_{M\times N}$, assume m, n are two positive integers that go into M, N respectively. Segment image F into $(M/m)\times(N/n)$ blocks, and the size of each block is $m\times n$. Define the entropy feature vector of image $F=[f(x,y)]_{M\times N}$ as

$$H_f = H_f(p,q) \tag{3}$$

Where $p=0,1,2,\cdots,M/m-1$, $q=0,1,2,\cdots,N/n-1$, $H_f(p,q)$ is the local entropy of the block (p,q) at row p and column q. To eliminate the data dependence and reduce the computation, we calculate local entropy via:

$$H_f(p,q) = -\frac{1}{S}\times\sum_{i=1}^{m}\sum_{j=1}^{n}(f(p\times m+i,q\times n+j)\times\log f(p\times m+i,q\times n+j))+\log S \tag{4}$$

$$S=\sum_{i=1}^{m}\sum_{j=1}^{n} f(p\times m+i,q\times n+j) \tag{5}$$

It is easy to prove that Equation (4) is identical with Equation (1).

Compared with the definition of image entropy in reference [1], the definition in this paper has the following advantages:

1. The spatial information of an image is appropriately introduced into the definition of image entropy.
2. A large number of division operations needed in calculating $p_{i,j}$ are eliminated.

   Suppose the size of the real-time image is M×N. To calculate the entropy of each candidate matching image of identical size, M×N division operations are needed using Equation (1). While in the method using Equation (4), only one division operation is needed. So, the complexity of implementation in hardware is greatly reduced. At the same time, the rounding and truncation errors corresponding to the division operations are eliminated. The cost is only one logarithm operation is added. As a result, the algorithm is sped up considerably.

3. Calculation of $p_{i,j}$ is not needed. The computation $\sum_{i=1}^{M}\sum_{j=1}^{N}(f(i,j)\times\log f(i,j))$ is executed directly and S is calculated at the same time. Finally, the local entropy H_f is obtained. So, the shortcoming of having to do global computation in the first instance is overcome. Instead, the global computation is executed along with local computations. Therefore the algorithm is suitable for parallel processing.

3 Parallel Image Matching Algorithm Based on Entropy Feature Vector

Based on the entropy feature vector defined above, a parallel image matching algorithm suitable to SIMD computer is put forward as follows, assuming the number of PEs is K and $(M/m)\times(N/n)$ can be divided by K.

Step1 Segment the real-time image into blocks of size $m\times n$. Allocate the image values of block (p,q) to the local memory of PE i, $i=(M/m)\times(N/n)\bmod K$, M, N is the number of rows and columns of the real-time image.

Step2 For $p=0,1,2,\cdots,M/m-1$, $q=0,1,2,\cdots,N/n-1$, calculate $H_f(p,q)$, the local entropy of block (p,q) via Equation (4) on PE i, where $i=(p\times m+q)\bmod K$.

Step3 Select a subimage of identical size with the real-time image from the datum image as candidate matching image. Segment the candidate matching image and allocate the image values in the same way as the real-time image in step1.

Step4 Calculate $H'_f=H_f'(p,q)$, the entropy feature vector of the candidate matching image in the same way as the real-time image in step2.

Step5 Calculate the absolute difference vector D_f between H_f and H'_f.

Step6 For $p=0,1,2,\cdots,M/m-1$, $q=0,1,2,\cdots,N/n-1$, judge if $D_f(p,q)$, the element of D_f is lower than an assumed threshold *T*. If the result is true, set the value of $D_f(p,q)$ with 0, otherwise set it with 1.

Step7 Calculate the sum of all the elements of D_f and take it as the counting matching result between the real-time image and the candidate matching image.

Step8 Select another candidate matching image that has not been matched and go to step3 until all the candidate matching images have been matched.

Step9 Take the candidate matching image which has smallest counting matching result as the ultimate matching image.

4 Discussion

1. Principles to determine the size of block while calculating the entropy feature vector. The block must be large enough to ensure that the irradiation distortions

will take place inside the blocks. On the other hand, the number of blocks must be sufficient to introduce enough spatial information into the definition of image entropy. So it is a tradeoff between the size of the block and the number of the blocks. The size of the block should be determined according to the application tasks.

2. The aim of using counting method in step6 is to limit the influence of the interference noises and gray difference in a local region. The contribution of a dismatch block to the matching result is the reciprocal of the number of the blocks in the real-time image. Computer simulations show that the algorithm is still effective when the real-time image has been influenced by local interference noises, gray difference and partly covering.
3. The threshold T used in step6 is determined beforehand by building the histogram of the values of the absolute difference vector between the entropy feature vector of the real-time image and that of the candidate matching images. Usually, the histogram has the characteristics of two humps, then the value at the valley point between the two humps can be selected as the threshold.
4. For the logarithm computation, Taylor formula is used to simplify the computation in reference [1]. But experiments show that the approximate calculation error may lead to wrong matching in some cases. To solve the problem, a logarithmic table is stored in the memory of the special purpose architecture. Since the gray levels of the image are limited, this method is practicable and easy to implement. By storing the logarithmic table, the algorithm is improved in both speed and accuracy.

5 Simulations and Results

Table 1. Simulation Results

Size of datum image	Size of real-time image	Correct matching ratio*	Correct matching ratio**	Runtime of sequential algorithm	Runtime*	Runtime**	Speed up*	Speed up**
300×300	64×64	81%	82%	1823054213	391281150	114924743	4.66	15.86
300×300	32×32	74%	77%	587580453	126996374	37991113	4.63	15.47
200×200	64×64	84%	86%	609199413	130752350	38403943	4.66	15.86
200×200	32×32	75%	79%	231924053	50126974	14995713	4.63	15.47

To evaluate the performance of the parallel image matching algorithm presented in this paper, A large number of computer simulation experiments were carried out under a parallel programming simulation environment developed by our lab. The experiment results are shown in Table 1. In the experiments, the datum image is satellite image, while the real-time image is cut from the aerial image of the same district. In every experiment group, the number of experiments is 400 and the number of PEs used is 16. The size of the block is 8×8 and the runtimes are expressed in clock cycles. The correct matching means that the distance between the matching point obtained in the experiment and the factual matching point is no more than one pixel. Correct matching ratio*, runtime* and speedup* denote the simulation results of the parallel algorithm based on the algorithm in reference [1], while correct matching ratio**, runtime** and speedup** denote the simulation results of the parallel algorithm presented in this paper.

We can see from Table 1 that the parallel algorithm of this paper is considerably sped up. The reason is that a large number of division operations are eliminated and the locality of the algorithm is improved. At the same time, by eliminating the rounding and truncation errors corresponding to the division operations, especially by storing a logarithmic table in the PE's memory of the computer, the calculation precision is improved and therefore the correct matching ratio is increased.

6 Conclusion

Image matching algorithms have two characteristics that make them suitable for parallel processing. An enormous amount of computation is required and intrinsic parallelism is usually contained in the algorithms.

In this paper, a parallel image matching algorithm based on entropy feature vector is put forward. Computer simulation experiments show that the algorithm is superior to the existed algorithms in both speed and accuracy.

References

1. Tian Jinwen, Su Kang, and Liu Jian, Image matching based on local entropy difference----algorithm and computer simulation. Journal of Astronautics, 20(1999) pp. 28–32.
2. Sing Bing Kang, Richard Szeliski, and Heung-Yeung Shum, NOTE a parallel feature tracker for extended image sequences, Computer Vision and Image Understanding 67(1997) pp. 296-310.
3. Clark F. Olson and Daniel P. Huttenlocher, Automatic target recognition by matching oriented edge pixels, IEEE transactions on Image Processing 6(1997) pp. 103–113.
4. Akira Shiozaki, Edge extraction using entropy operator. Computer Vision, Graphics, and Image Processing, 36(1986) pp. 1–9.
5. N. R. Pal, S. K. Pal, Object-background segmentation using new definitions of entropy. IEEE Proceedings. Pt. E, 136(1989) pp. 284–295.
6. Shung-Shing Lee, Shi-Jinn Horng, and Horng-Ren Tsai, Entropy thresholding and its parallel algorithm on the reconfigurable array of processors with wider bus networks, IEEE Transactions on Image Processing, 8(1999) pp. 1229-1242

Chapter 11
Parallel and Distributed Processing

OPTIMAL PLACEMENT OF WAVELENGTH CONVERTERS IN WDM NETWORKS FOR PARALLEL AND DISTRIBUTED COMPUTING SYSTEMS [a]

X.-H. JIA, D.-Z. DU[b], X.-D. HU[c], H.-J. HUANG[d], D.-Y. LI[e]
Department of Computer Science
City University of Hong Kong
Kowloon, Hong Kong
(e-mail: jia, dzd, xdhu, hejiao, dyli{@cs.cityu.edu.hk})

Using less wavelengths to serve more communication needs is one of the primary goals in the design of WDM networks. It is obvious that the number of wavelengths required in a WDM network is at least equal to the network load, which is defined to be the maximal number of channels in a link. By installing wavelength converters at some nodes in a network, the number of wavelengths needed can be made equal to the network load. In this paper we study the problem of placing the minimal number of converters in a special class of WDM networks for parallel and distributed computing systems, so that the number of wavelengths in use is equal to the network load. A suite of efficient algorithms are proposed to produce optimal solutions for this problem on the networks of special topologies including trees, rings, meshes, and hyper-cubes.

1 Introduction

Advances in electro-optic technologies have made optical networks a promising choice to meet the increasing demands for higher bandwidth and lower communication latency of high-performance computing and communication applications. *Wavelength division multiplexing* (WDM) [5, 13] is basically frequency division multiplexing in the optical frequency domain, where on a single optical fiber there are multiple communication channels at different wavelengths.

There are basically two types of architectures of WDM optical networks: single-hop systems and multihop systems. In *single-hop* systems [15], each pair of communication nodes has a logical channel configured and the same wavelength should be used through out the route of the channel. There is

[a]This work is supported in part by Research Grants of City Univ. of Hong Kong under grant No. 7000677, 7000927, 7001035, by CERG Research Grants of Hong Kong under grant No. 9040442, and by National 973 Information Technology and High-Performance Software Program of China under grant No. 1998030402.

[b]Permanent address: Dept. of Computer Science, Univ. of Minnesota, Minneapolis, MN 55455, USA. (dzd@cs.umn.edu)
[c]Permanent address: Inst. of Applied Math., Chinese Academy of Sciences, Beijing 100080, China. (xdhu@amath3.amt.ac.cn)
[d]Permanent address: Dept. of Math., Chaanxi Normal Univ., Xi'an 710062, China
[e]Permanent address: Dept. of Math., Central China Normal Univ., Hubei 430079, China.

no wavelength conversion in the intermediate nodes in the route of a channel. Although it is simple and has high speed in data transmission, single-hop architecture is not suitable to large sized systems due to the limited number of available wavelengths and the limited switching capacity of channels going through a node. As a result, multihop architecture becomes necessary for large sized networks. In *multihop* systems [12], the channel of a pair of nodes can consist of several path segments, each uses a wavelength. Wavelength conversion is thus needed at a node where the input and output fibers of the channel use different wavelengths. Wavelength conversion can be done either electronically or optically. In electronical method, optical signal is first converted into electronic signal and then switched (routed) electronically. Finally, the electronical signal is converted back to optical signal and transmitted optically. This *optical-electronical-optical* conversion is very time consuming compared with optical speed of data transmission. In all-optical method, hardware devices called optical wavelength converters are used for wavelength conversions. In either cases, the number of converters (the nodes which are capable of wavelength conversions) should be minimized in a system due to the delay of electronical conversions or the hardware cost of optical converters.

Wavelengths are a kind of scarce resource in WDM networks. The wavelength conflict law governing WDM networks states that wavelengths used in different channels over a fiber link must be mutually exclusive. That is, two channels sharing a physical fiber must use different wavelengths over the shared fiber. It is obvious that the number of wavelengths required is at least equal to the maximal number of channels over a fiber, because each channel over the fiber requires a different wavelength. However, it is not known about how many wavelengths are precisely sufficient, for a network whose load is given. We define the network load as the maximal number of channels over a fiber in the network. It has been pointed out [19] that by using wavelength converters in a network the number of wavelengths needed can be made equal to the network load, which is called *load-wavelength assignable.* A simple example is to make every network node capable of wavelength conversions, which is clearly a case of load-wavelength assignable. However, it is too expensive and also not necessary to place a wavelength converter at every network node.

In this paper we consider the problem of *optimal placement of converter* (OPC) in multihop WDM networks: Given a WDM network, place the minimal number of wavelength converters on the network so that the load-wavelength assignability can be achieved. Our work focuses on a class of network topologies for parallel and distributed computing system, which includes trees, rings, meshes, and hyper-cubes. A suite of efficient algorithms are proposed to produce optimal solutions to this problem on networks.

The study of OPC problem has great implications to network and system design. Firstly, by load-wavelength assignability, the number of wavelengths needed in a system is made minimal, because the low bound of the number of wavelengths is equal to the network load. Secondly, with load-wavelength assignability, the system maximally utilizes the network bandwidth without causing wavelength conflicts, so long as the network load is kept less or equal to the number of wavelengths employed. Thirdly, by using the minimal number of converters to achieve the load-wavelength assignability, it reduces the hardware cost of building a network, and it also makes the data communication faster because of less wavelength conversions.

2 Technical Preliminaries

2.1 Network Model

The WDM network under consideration is modeled as a connected graph $G(V, E)$, where V is the vertex-set representing the set of nodes in the network and E is the edge-set representing physical fiber links between nodes in the network. Each link carries two oppositely-directed fibers, for data transmissions in the two directions of the link.

In this paper we consider two types of communication channels: duplex (bidirectional) and unidirectional. In a duplex channel, data can be transmitted in both directions of the channel. The wavelength conflict rule for duplex channels is that channels over the same link must use different wavelengths on the link. In a unidirectional channel, data can be transmitted only in one direction from the source to the destination. The wavelength conflict rule for unidirectional channels is that channels over the same link and in the same direction must use different wavelengths. That is, two unidirectional channels over the same link but in opposite directions can use the same wavelength.

In this paper we assume *full conversion* at every converter. That is, each converter can provide conversions of all possible permutations of wavelengths. Our problem is to, for a given network, locate a minimal set of nodes so that the load-wavelength assignability can be achieved if this set of nodes are made capable of wavelength conversions. Formally, we define this set as following:

Definition. A set of nodes S, $S \subseteq V$, *is said to guarantee load-wavelength assignability if, by configuring each node in* S *a wavelength converter, the number of wavelengths needed to set up all channels in the system is equal to the network load.*

2.2 Related Work

In single-hop systems, minimizing the number of wavelengths in use can be done at two steps: routing and wavelength assignment. Since the number of wavelengths needed in a system is at least equal to the network load, an important method to reduce the number of wavelengths is to route channels in a load balancing fashion [1, 19], which aims to minimize the network load. This problem has been proved to be NP-hard even for some simple network topologies, such as ring [17]. A widely used approach [7] is to formalize the problem to a type of integer linear program and then find an approximate solution. After the routing is done (i.e., the network load is determined), assigning wavelengths properly to channels (by applying coloring algorithms) can also reduce the number wavelengths needed in a system. Some other research work is to study the minimal number of wavelengths needed when the network load is given [3, 6, 10, 14]. Due to the complexity of the problem, this kind of study is only limited to the networks of trees or rings. Some best results obtained in [3, 14, 19] are summarized at Table 1. By "αL wavelength being sufficient" we mean that any set of channels with network load L can be assigned by using at most αL wavelengths, and by "αL being necessary" we mean that assigning some set of channels with network load L requires at least αL wavelengths.

Network	Unidirectional channels	Duplex channels
Tree	$\frac{5}{3}L$ wavelengths are sufficient $\frac{5}{4}L$ wavelengths are necessary	$\frac{3}{2}L$ wavelengths are sufficient $\frac{3}{2}L$ wavelengths are necessary
Ring	$(2L-1)$wavelengths are sufficient $(2L-1)$wavelength are necessary	

Table 1. The number of wavelengths required for tree and ring networks.

In multihop systems, the major research topic is the study of configuring a physical network topology (where edges are fiber links) into a logical topology where edges are lightpaths [8, 13, 15]. A lightpath is a logical path in which only one wavelength is used, i.e., there is no wavelength conversion in the intermediate nodes of a lightpath. An important goal of the design of logical topology is to minimize the number of wavelengths in the system, which is similar to the design of single-hop systems (a lightpath is a single-hop channel). Then for a channel setup, it routes the channel through lightpaths. A channel consists of one or more lightpaths, with wavelength conversions at nodes where two lightpaths joint. Therefore, converters are required at the nodes where a lightpath originates or terminates.

Another major research area of multihop systems is the study of introducing wavelength converters and placing the converters to reduce the number of wavelengths needed [9, 16, 18, 19, 20]. In [20], a network with limited wavelength conversion is studied and the performance is analyzed. The work in [18] studies *sparse wavelength conversion*, where networks are comprised of a mix of nodes having full or no wavelength conversion. Some heuristics for wavelength assignment in the networks with wavelength conversions are proposed in [9, 18, 20], and their performance analysis are based upon probabilistic models and techniques (i.g., blocking probabilities of setting up channels). The recent work in [16] discusses how to improve traffic-carry capacity by providing limited wavelength conversion capability in a network. The discussion includes ring, star, tree and general topology networks.

Our work is to find the minimal number of converters and their placement in a network to achieve load-wavelength assignability. It is proved in [19] that to achieve load-wavelength assignment for unidirectional channels, no converter is needed in star networks and only one converter is required in ring networks.

Inspired by [19], we study this problem in a class of networks including trees, meshes, and hyper-cubes. We propose some efficient algorithms that can produce the optimal placements in these networks for unidirectional and duplex channels.

2.3 The Methodology

Since load-wavelength assignment in networks of stars and paths has been well studied [19], our approach is to decompose a general topology network into edge-disjoint simple subgraphs, such as paths or spiders. A *spider* is a tree which consists of several paths (called *legs*) with one end of each of these paths incident to a common node (called *body*). Paths and stars are two special cases of spiders.

The decomposition of a graph is done by a *splitting operation* described as follows. Given a graph $G(V, E)$ and a subset $S \subseteq V$, generate a new graph $G_S(V, E)$ by splitting each node $s \in S$ into $\delta(s)$ nodes, where $\delta(s)$ is the degree of s in $G(V, E)$. Each edge (s, t) in $G(V, E)$ becomes edge (s', t) in $G_S(V, E)$, where s' is a newly generated node from splitting s in $G(V, E)$.

By studying the reduced graph $G_S(V, E)$, we divide the OPC problem of general topology networks into the cases of special networks, such as paths and spiders. We will develop the necessary and sufficient conditions of OPC problem for duplex channels and unidirectional channels, respectively. Based on these conditions we can design efficient algorithms that can find the optimal solutions for the networks with special topologies including tree, mesh, and hyper-cube.

3 OPC Problem for Duplex Channels

3.1 The Basic Theory

The following two theorems give two sets of necessary and sufficient conditions for load-wavelength assignability.

Theorem 1 *Given graph $G(V, E)$, subset $S \subseteq V$ guarantees load-wavelength assignability if and only if every connected component of $G_S(V, E)$ is a path.*

Proof. "If": Given any set of routed channels with network load L in $G(V, E)$. Now consider them in $G_S(V, E)$. These channels which go through nodes in S are broken into several pieces. In each connected component, which is a path in $G_S(V, E)$, the channels which go through the entire or part of the path can be assigned by using L wavelengths without causing wavelength conflict. The wavelength assignment in each connected component of $G_S(V, E)$, can be done independently, and there will be no wavelength conflict between the channels in different components. This is because each node in S has full wavelength conversion capability.

"Only if": we can construct three channels such that each of them shares a link with the other two. Thus three wavelengths are needed even though the network load is two, contradicting the load-wavelength assignability. □

Theorem 2 *For graph $G(V, E)$, let S be the set of nodes whose degrees are greater than or equal to three. If S is not an empty set, then S is both sufficient and necessary for guaranteeing load-wavelength assignability.*

Proof. It follows from Theorem 1. □

3.2 OPC Problem on the Networks of Special Topologies

In this section, we discuss the OPC problem in the networks for parallel and distributed computing systems, which include trees, rings, meshes, and hypercubes.

Corollary 1 *To guarantee load-wavelength assignability on trees of n nodes, $\lfloor (n-2)/2 \rfloor$ converters are sufficient for all trees and necessary for some trees.*

Corollary 2 *To guarantee load-wavelength assignability on a ring, one converter is both sufficient and necessary.*

Corollary 3 *To guarantee load-wavelength assignability on meshes of n nodes, $(n-4)$ converters are both sufficient and necessary.*

Corollary 4 *To guarantee load-wavelength assignability on $(n \times n)$-torus or n-hypercube, for $n \geq 3$, n^2 or 2^n converters are both sufficient and necessary.*

4 OPC Problem for Unidirectional Channels

4.1 The Basic Theory

Different from duplex channels, the wavelength conflict rule for unidirectional channels requires that channels over the same link and in the same direction are assigned different wavelengths. The following two theorems give a set of necessary and sufficient conditions that a set guarantees load-wavelength assignability for unidirectional channels.

Theorem 3 *Given graph $G(V, E)$, subset $S \subseteq V$ guarantees load-wavelength assignability if and only if each connected component in $G_S(V, E)$ is a spider.*

Proof. "If": Given any set of routed channels with network load L in $G(V, E)$. Now consider them on $G_S(V, E)$. For a connected component in $G_S(V, E)$, which is a spider, channels intersecting with this spider are of the two cases: 1) crossing the spider body from one leg to another; 2) traversing within a leg. We consider wavelength assignment for two cases below.

Case 1. Channels go through from one leg to another. We introduce a bipartite multigraph $B(V_1 \cup V_2, E_{12})$ to represent these channels in the spider, where V_1 and V_2, $V_1 = V_2$, are the set of legs (i.e., each leg of the spider is represented as a node in V_1 and V_2). Each edge $e_{ij} \in E_{12}$ if there is a channel which goes through legs i and j for $i \neq j$. Assigning wavelengths to the channels without causing wavelength conflict becomes the problem of coloring the edges of graph $B(V_1 \cup V_2, E_{12})$ under the condition that two adjacent edges must be in different colors. Since there are at most L channels going from leg i to leg j for $i \neq j$, multigraph $B(V_1 \cup V_2, E_{12})$ has the maximum degree L. Thus, $B(V_1 \cup V_2, E_{12})$ can be colored by using at most L colors (refer to [2]).

Case 2. Channels traverse within a leg. Note that each channel belonging to Case 1 is cut into two parts, one in a leg heading the body and the other in another leg leaving the body. Now we can use the same argument as in the proof for Theorem 1 as follows: the channels heading the body of the spider are ordered from left to right by the spider body or their destinations, while the channels leaving the spider body are also ordered from left to right by the spider body or their sources. The channels which have been assigned wavelengths in the Case 1 retain the same wavelengths, and the rest of the channels in this leg will be assigned the wavelengths which are free. Thus, all channels (both in Case 1 and Case 2) can be assigned with at most L wavelengths.

"Only if": Assume that one of the connected components of $G_S(V, E)$ is not a spider. There are only two possibilities of the component: 1) there are two (or more) nodes having degree greater than two; or 2) it is a ring. For each of them, we can find an example that the network load is two, but three wavelengths are needed, that contradicts load-wavelength assignability. $\square$

Theorem 4 *If every node in $G(V,E)$ has degree greater than two, then $S \subseteq V$ guarantees load-wavelength assignability if and only if S is a vertex cover of $G(V,E)$.*

Proof. If follows from Theorem 3. □

Theorem 5 *If graph $G(V,E)$ has a node with degree greater than two, then there exists a minimal sized subset of V that guarantees load-wavelength assignability and every node in the set has degree greater than two in $G(V,E)$.*

Proof. Let $v \in V$ be the node with degree greater than two, and S be a minimal sized subset of V that guarantees load-wavelength assignability. By Theorem 3 each connected component of $G_S(V,E)$ is a spider. Now assume there is a node $s \in S$ with degree less than or equal to two. Let u be the closest node to s in a path between v and s, and u has degree greater than two.

Case 1. $u \in S$. Let $S' = S \setminus \{s\}$. It is obvious that each connected component of $G_{S'}(V,E)$ is still a spider, because s is a node of degree less than or equal to two.

Case 2. $u \notin S$. Let $S' = S \cup \{u\} \setminus \{s\}$. It is easy to see that each connected component of $G_{S'}(V,E)$ is still a spider, because substituting s with u only makes one component of $G_S(V,E)$ have a longer leg and another split into several paths.

In both cases, S' can guarantee load-wavelength assignability because of Theorem 3. In Case 1, S' is a proper subset of S, this contradicts to the minimal size of S. In Case 2, the substitution operation can be repeated until all nodes in S having degree less than or equal to two are replaced by the nodes with degree greater than two. The desired subset can thus be obtained. □

4.2 OPC Problem on Networks of Special Topologies

Again, in this section we consider our solutions for the networks of trees, meshes, torus, and hyper-cubes.

For tree networks, if no node has degree greater than two, then a tree becomes a path. According to Theorem 3 no converter is necessary for load-wavelength assignability. So we only consider the case that there exists at least one node with degree greater than two. Notice that Theorem 4 can not be applied for trees, as any trees have nodes of degree one. According to Theorem 5, we do not need to consider degree-one or degree-two nodes for placing converters. We use the following steps to find the minimal set that guarantees load-wavelength assignability.

1) remove every degree-two node by substituting two edges incident to the node with one edge incident to two endpoints (other than the degree-two node).

2) remove every degree-one node by condensing it to the node adjacent to it.

3) find the minimal vertex cover of the resultant tree.

Input A tree $G(V, E)$

Output A subset $C \subseteq V$ guaranteeing load-wavelength assignability

Step 1 Remove degree-two nodes from $G(V, E)$
$V' := V, \ E' := E.$
$V_2 := \{v \mid v \text{ is adjacent to exactly two nodes } v_1 \text{ and } v_2\},$
$V' := V' \setminus V_2.$
while $V_2 \neq \emptyset$ **do begin**
choose $v \in V_2$,
$E' := E' \cup \{(v_1, v_2)\} \setminus \{(v, v_1), (v, v_2)\},$
$V_2 := V_2 \setminus \{v\}.$
end-while

Step 2 Remove degree-one nodes from $G(V', E')$
$V_1 := \{u \mid u \text{ is adjacent to exactly one node } u_1\},$
$V' := V' \setminus V_1.$
while $V_1 \neq \emptyset$ **do begin**
choose $u \in V_1$,
$E' := E' \setminus \{(u, u_1)\},$
$V_1 := V_1 \setminus \{u\}.$
end-while

Step 3 Generate a minimal vertex cover of $G(V', E')$
$C := \emptyset$
$\overline{V} := V', \overline{E} := E'.$
while $\overline{E} \neq \emptyset$ **do begin** (Loop ends until all edges in E' are covered)
$V_1 := \{v \in \overline{V} \mid v \text{ has degree one in } G(\overline{V}, \overline{E})\},$
$C := C \cup \{u \in \overline{V} \setminus V_1 \mid u \text{ is adjacent to some } v \in V_1\},$
$\overline{V} := \overline{V} \setminus \{v \in \overline{V} \mid v \in C \text{ or } v \text{ is adjacent to some } u \in C\},$
$\overline{E} := \{(u, v) \in \overline{E} \mid u \text{ and } v \text{ are belong to } \overline{V}\}.$
end-while
return C.

Theorem 6 *The proposed algorithm can find the optimal solution of OPC problem in a network of tree in time of* $O(|E| + |V|)$.
Proof. Let $G(V', E')$ be the final graph obtained after Step 2 and C be the returned vertex cover of $G(V', E')$. According to Theorem 5, we know that there exists a solution of OPC problem in $G(V, E)$ that is a subset of V'.

In the following, we prove that a subset S of V' guarantees load-wavelength assignability in $G(V, E)$ if and only if it is a vertex cover of $G(V', E')$.

"If": We prove it by contradiction. Assume that $S \subset V'$ is a vertex cover of $G(V', E')$ but it does not guarantee load-wavelength assignability in $G(V, E)$. According to Theorem 3, there exists a connected component of $G_S(V, E)$ which is not a spider. This means that there exist two nodes x and y which are not in S and have degree greater than two in $G_S(V, E)$. Note there is a path in $G_S(V, E)$ between x and y and no node in the path is included in S. Moreover, nodes x and y are included in V', and removing degree-one and degree-two nodes from $G(V, E)$ does not destroy the connectivity between them. Thus x and y remain connected by the path in $G(V', E')$, which implies that all edges in the path are not covered by any node in S. This contradicts that S is a vertex cover of $G(V', E')$.
"Only if": We prove it again by contradiction. Assume that there exists a subset $S \subset V'$ that guarantees load-wavelength assignability in $G(V, E)$ but it is not a vertex cover. Then there are two nodes $x \in V'$ and $y \in V'$ such that $(x, y) \in E'$ but $x \notin S$ and $y \notin S$. Note x and y have degree greater than two in $G(V, E)$; otherwise they are removed away at Step 1 or Step 2. Hence the component of $G_S(V, E)$, which contains (x, y), is not a spider. This contradicts Theorem 4.

Now we prove that C, produced by our algorithm above, is the minimal vertex cover of $G(V', E')$. In the while-loop at Step 3, the nodes that are adjacent to degree-one nodes in current $\overline{V}$ are included in C. They can cover the edges incident to them. Thus these edges are removed from $\overline{E}$. In such way when $\overline{E}$ becomes empty, all edges in E' can be covered by some nodes in C. This means that C is a vertex cover of $G(V', E')$. Then, we prove C is the minimal. Assume C^* is a minimal vertex cover of $G(V', E')$. If C^* includes some degree-one nodes in $V_1 \subset \overline{V}$, then we can replace them with the nodes that are adjacent to them. It is obvious that such modified C^* remains a minimal vertex cover of $G(V', E')$. It is not difficult to see that the finally modified C^* is exactly the set of C, because this is the exact way how C is produced. Therefore C is minimal.

From above discussion we deduce that C is the optimal solution of OPC problem in $G(V, E)$.

Furthermore, the algorithm can finish in time of $O(|E| + |V|)$, this is because the key operation in all three steps is to check the degree of each node in the current graph and include or exclude the node and its incident edges in some sets. □

Corollary 5 *To guarantee load-wavelength assignability on trees of n nodes, $\lfloor (n-2)/4 \rfloor$ converters are sufficient for all trees and necessary for some trees.*
Corollary 6 *To guarantee load-wavelength assignability on $(n \times n)$-mesh, $2\lceil n/2 \rceil \lfloor n/2 \rfloor$ converters are both sufficient and necessary.*

Corollary 7 *To guarantee load-wavelength assignability on $(n \times n)$-torus, $n\lceil n/2 \rceil$ converters are both sufficient and necessary.*
Corollary 8 *To guarantee load-wavelength assignability on n-cube for $n \geq 3$, 2^{n-1} converters are both sufficient and necessary.*

5 Conclusions

We have found the necessary and sufficient conditions that a subset of nodes guarantees load-wavelength assignability on general WDM networks. From these conditions we obtained the optimal placement of converters on a class of WDM networks of special topologies including trees, rings, meshes, torus, and hyper-cubes. The proposed theorems and methodology can also be applied to other interconnecting networks for parallel computing networks, such as Banyan networks and Shuffle networks.

The results obtained from this paper are summarized in Table 2.

Networks	Unidirectional Channels	Duplex Channels
Star	1	0
tree of n nodes	$\lfloor (n-2)/4 \rfloor$	$\lfloor (n-2)/2 \rfloor$
ring of n nodes	1	1
$(n \times n)$-mesh	$2\lceil n/2 \rceil \lfloor n/2 \rfloor$	$n^2 - 4$
$(n \times n)$-torus	$n\lceil n/2 \rceil$	n^2
n-cube	2^{n-1}	2^n

Table 2. Number of converters needed for load-wavelength assignability.

References

1. D. Banerjee and B. Mukherjee, A practical approach for routing and wavelength assignment in large wavelength-routed optical networks, *IEEE J. Select. Areas Commun.*, 14 (5) (1996), pp. 903-908.
2. J. A. Bondy and U. S. R. Murty, Graph Theory with Applications, American Elsevier Publishing Co., Inc., New York, 1976.
3. T. Erlebach, K. Jansen, C. Kaklamanis, and P. Persiano, An optimal greedy algorithm in directed tree networks, *DIMACS Series in Discrete Mathematics and Theoretical Computer Science*, 40 (1998), pp. 117-129.
4. M. R. Garey and D. S. Johnson, Comuters and Intractability: A Guide to the Theory of NP-Completeness, W. H. Freeman, San Francisco, CA, 1979.
5. P. E. Green, Fiber-Optic Networks, Prentice-Hall, Cambridge, MA, 1992.
6. E. J. Harder and H. A. Choi, Gossiping in WDM all-optical square mesh networks, *DIMACS Series in Discrete Mathematics and Theoretical*

Computer Science, 48 (1998), pp. 75-84.
7. P. Klein, S. Plotkin, C. Stein, and É. Tardos, Faster approximation algorithms for the unit capacity concurrent flow problem with applications to routing and finding sparse cuts, *SIAM J. Computing*, 23 (3) (1994), pp. 466-487.
8. J. P. Labourdette and A. Acampora, Logically rearrangeable multihop lightwave networks, *IEEE Trans. Commun.*, 39 (8) (1991), pp. 1223-1230.
9. K.-C. Lee and V. O. K. Li, A wavelength-convertible optical network, *J. Lightwave Technology*, 11 (5) (1993), pp. 962-970.
10. M. Mihail, C. Kaklamanis, and S. Rao, Efficient access to optical bandwidth, *Proc. 36th Annual IEEE Symp. Foundations of Computer Science* (FOCS), 1995, pp. 548-557.
11. B. Mukherjee, WDM-Based local lightwave networks Part I: single-hop system, *IEEE Network*, 6 (3) (1992), pp. 12-26.
12. B. Mukherjee, WDM-based local lightwave networks Part II: multihop systems, *IEEE Network*, 6 (4) (1992), pp. 22-32.
13. B. Mukherjee, D. Banerjee, S. Ramamurthy, and A. Mukherjee, Some principles for designing a wide-area WDM optical network, *IEEE/ACM Trans. Networking*, 4 (5) (1996), pp. 684-695.
14. P. Raghavan and E. Upfal, Efficient routing in all-optical networks, *Proc. 26th Annual ACM Symp. Theory of Computing* (STOC), (1994), pp. 134-143.
15. R. Ramaswami and K. N. Sivarajan, Design of logical topologies for wavelength-routed optical networks, *IEEE J. Select. Areas Commun.*, 14 (5) (1996), pp. 840-851.
16. R. Ramaswami and G. Sasaki, Multiwavelength optical networks with limited wavelength conversion, *IEEE/ACM Trans. Networking*, 6 (6) (1998), pp. 744-754.
17. A. Schriver, P. Seymour, and P. Winkler, The ring loading problem, *SIAM J. Discrete Math.*, 11 (1) (1998), pp. 1-14.
18. S. Subramaniam, M. Azizoglu, and A. K. Somani, Connectivity and sparse wavelength conversion in wavelength-routing networks, *Proc. 1st IEEE Conf. Computer Commun.* (INFOCOM), (1996), pp. 148-155.
19. G. Wilfong and P. Winkler, Ring routing and wavelength translation, *Proc. 9th Annual ACM-SIAM Symp. Discrete Algorithms* (SODA), (1998), pp. 333-341.
20. J. Yates, J. Lacey, D. Everitt, and M. Summerfield, Limited-range wavelength translation in all-optical networks, *Proc. 1st IEEE Conf. Computer Commun.* (INFOCOM), (1996), pp. 954-961.

ON THE IMPACT OF CONTROL PROTOCOLS FOR OPTICAL NETWORKS ON EXECUTION TIME IN A PARALLEL ARCHITECTURE

JOÃO ANGELO MARTINI

Dep. de Informática – Universidade Estadual de Maringá – Maringá - PR
Brazil
E-mail: jangelo@din.uem.br

MARCOS ANTÔNIO CAVENAGHI

Dep. de Computação – Universidade Estadual Paulista – Bauru - SP
Brazil
E-mail: marcos@dco.bauru.unesp.br

ÁLVARO GARCIA NETO

Dep. de Física e Informática – Universidade de São Paulo – São Carlos - SP
Brazil

This work investigates the impact of control protocols for optical interconnection networks on execution time in a parallel architecture. Two single-hop Wavelength Division Multiplexing based networks were simulated. The first network uses a distributed control protocol based on TDM to manage communications. The second network uses a centralized control protocol. Both protocols avoid collisions. Simulations with different transmission rates were made in order to investigate execution times. Results show that the centralized control protocol is more appropriate to the studied architecture than the distributed control protocol. On both protocols, the control cycle length is a determinant factor that brings an upper boundary for the transmission rates.

1 Introduction

Interconnection networks are one of the main challenges in the design of any parallel architecture, being a determinant factor for performance, reliability and cost. The well known limitations of electronic interconnection networks, such as bandwidth and performance [1, 2, 3], led to the investigation of other technologies to support these requirements. These investigations brought to the light a promising technology: optical communication. This technology is intended to achieve the needs for bandwidth and performance required for a parallel architecture.

Interconnection networks based on this technology (optical interconnection networks) are widely studied. In this context, Wavelength Division Multiplexing (WDM) [4] can be used to implement such networks. WDM divides the fiber optics bandwidth in asynchronous channels, each one with a different wavelength and bit rate. This mechanism allows the use of high bandwidths in the order of Tbps.

Optical interconnection networks have advantages if compared to electronic interconnection networks [3]. Some of these advantages are: Bandwidth, Low Loss, Scalability, Modularity, Protocol Transparency, Multicasting.

2 The APO Architecture

Figure 1 shows the APO architecture [5]. This architecture is derived from the Wolf architecture [6] which was developed with two electronic interconnection networks.

2.1 Functional Description

The IO unit is responsible for the input of data packages and programs, and the output of the results. The MU is responsible for the matching of operands, e.g., on a two operand instruction, the first operand produced is stored in the MU and when the second operand is produced, the MU creates a package with both operands and sends the package to the IN. If the operand is part of a one operand instruction, the MU creates a package with this single operand and sends it to the IN. The IN is responsible for the communication strategies implemented in the architecture and the central point of this work, so it is discussed in Section 3.

The IN sends the package from the MU to the PE's using a round-robin policy. If all PE's are busy, the IN sends the package to the FIFO. The FIFO is a common buffer implemented in the architecture in order to avoid deadlocks due to the excess of existing packages. Each PE is made of one Instruction Memory (IM) and one Functional Unit (FU). The PE's are responsible for the execution of instructions: when a package arrives, it contains the operand(s) of an instruction; the IM uses control information stored in the incoming package to build an executable package. This executable package, besides the operands and control information, has the opcode (instruction) to be executed by the FU. The FU receives the executable package and executes it, producing data. These data are packed with control information and sent to the IN.

3 Interconnection Network (IN)

The existence of multiple channels in a WDM optical interconnection network demands the use of multi-access protocols in order to implement transmission. Two types of protocols are possible: the first type are the ones without any contention, allowing collisions in the network. These protocols have a mechanism to detect collisions and to threat them. The second type of protocols are the ones that avoid collisions. This type of protocol implements a policy to control the transmission in order to avoid collisions.

The choice of one type of protocol may bring advantages and disadvantages, depending on the characteristics of the communication system. Due to the intense traffic between the MU block and the PE block the probability of collisions is high, enforcing the choice on the second type of protocols: the ones that avoid collisions. Two categories of transmission control protocols are possible: distributed control protocols and centralized control protocols.

The APO interconnection network is based on the single-hop TT-FR (Tunable Transmitter - Fixed Receiver) WDM approach. In the context of a parallel architecture, single-hop is chosen due to the greater latencies imposed by the multi-hop approach. To send a data, a node has to tune its transmitter to the same frequency of the destination node's receiver. The control necessary to implement communication is done during the *control cycle*, while the transmission of the package is done during the *transmission cycle*.

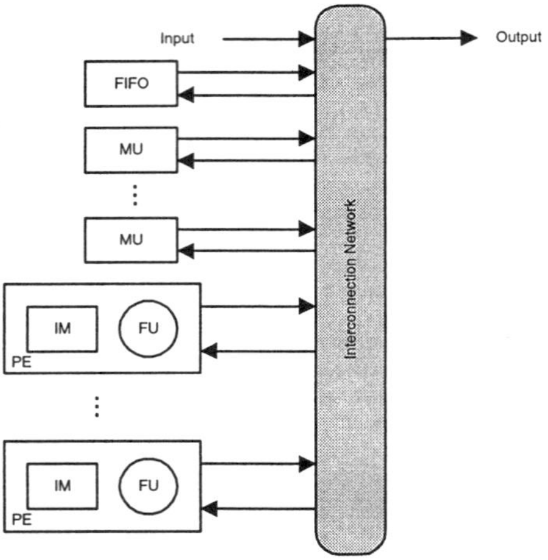

Figure 1: APO Architecture

3.1 Distributed Control Protocol

The Distributed Control Protocol (DCP) is based on the Time Division Multiplexing (TDM) policy: each node has a specific period of time allocated for its control cycle. Each node has a tunable transmitter responsible to send data to other nodes, a fixed receiver responsible to receive data from other nodes and a tunable receiver responsible to verify if the destination node is ready to receive data.

As an example: during the control cycle, node A tunes its verification receiver to the same frequency used by the destination node's receiver (say node B) to verify if this node is receiving data. If node B is not receiving data, node A tunes its transmitter to the frequency of node B's receiver and starts its transmission cycle. Otherwise, if node B is receiving data from another node, node A has to wait for its next control cycle, when it verifies again.

The distance between a transmitter and a receiver is a determinant factor in control cycle duration. To explain this point, consider two adjacent nodes (node A and node B) willing to transmit to the same destination (node C - it is assumed node C is not busy). After node A control cycle, it enters the transmission cycle and starts sending a package to node C. Node B's control cycle starts at the same time node A's transmission cycle. Therefore, node B's control cycle should be long enough in order to allow the package from node A starts reaching node C. If it is not so, node B could have the false impression that node C is not busy. It would certainly cause a collision.

3.2 Centralized Control Protocol

The Centralized Control Protocol (CCP) is based on a Centralized Controller (CC). If a node has data to be transmitted, it makes a request to the CC. All requests can be made in parallel during the control cycle to the CC. Inside a request package, there is the destination address. The CC uses its internal control table in order to verify if the destination address is not in use. This table stores information concerning the utilization of each node. If the table has no information about an address, it means the destination node is not in use, so the CC stores the destination address in its internal control table and gives a positive answer to the node that makes the request. CC uses a round-robin policy for management of requests.

During a control cycle, a node makes a request to the CC and waits for an answer. If this answer is negative, the node reenters its control cycle until its request is granted. If this answer is positive, the node starts its transmission cycle. When the node finishes to send the package, it sends a control package to the CC and enters another control cycle. The CC receives this control package and erases its table entry concerning the destination address used by the node.

The CC takes all requests and sends the answers in a round-robin fashion. The requests and answers have one byte of information. An answer with value 1 means the node is authorized to start its transmission cycle. An answer with value 0 means the node is not authorized to start its transmission cycle due to the presence of the requested address in the CC control table. An answer with value of 255 means the node is authorized to start its transmission cycle, but to the FIFO and not to the desired address (the desired address is busy).

4 Control Protocols Analyses

This section shows a comparative analyses of the two control protocols used to implement the APO architecture interconnection networks. Both protocols allow the implementation of fault tolerant mechanisms, broadcast and multicast.

DCP: A very important issue related to the TDM protocol is how the duration of the control cycle influences the high transmission rates on a WDM network: the control cycle has a fixed length, depending only on the tuning time of the verification receiver. Therefore, as the transmission rates increase transmission cycle lengths decrease and the time interval between two control cycles remains constant. This time interval limits system performance, when the control cycle length is next to the transmission cycle length.

CCP: The CCP is more complex than the DCP, but each node does not have to wait to enter its control cycle. This is an advantage, because the entire system can explore more parallelism than DCP. The control cycle is implemented using one Tx/Rx device inside the Centralized Controller for each node in the network. It implies a larger number of devices than the DCP. To decrease the numbers of Tx/Rx devices, the Centralized Controller could use a tunable Tx/Rx device. This approach would increase the control cycle length, degrading the performance of the entire system. The CCP is not as sensible as DCP to the control cycle length. An increase in the transmission rate causes a decrease in the transmission cycle length and control cycle length. As the devices in the Centralized Controller are not tunable, the control cycle length does not depend on the time to tune them.

5 Simulation Results and Analyses

This section shows simulation results obtained with a simulator for the APO architecture. This simulator is designed using the C++ language and implements the APO characteristics. The benchmarks used in this work are: Laplace, Matrix Multiplication, N-Queens, Quicksort. More information about these benchmarks can be found in [6]. It is used several transmission rates during the simulations. The transmission rates used are: Tx 1 for 2.5 Gbps, Tx 2 for 5.0 Gbps, Tx 4 for 10.0 Gbps, Tx 8 for 20 Gbps, Tx 16 for 40 Gbps, and Tx 160 for 400 Gbps to both protocols.

5.1 Comparative Analyses of Execution Times for DCP and CCP

Figure 2 shows execution times as a function of transmission rates (Tx). From Tx 1 to Tx 2, it is observed an improvement around 42% on execution time to all benchmarks used for DCP. It cannot be observed the same improvement for the other transmission rates. At these rates, the improvement on execution time diminish drastically, reaching 5% from Tx 16 to Tx 160 for almost all cases, but for N-Queens which execution time degrades.

An interesting point is that the improvement on execution time does not vary linearly with the increase on transmission rates for DCP. Two facts contribute to this behavior: the data package distribution policy (each node waits too much time for its control cycle, depending on the number of nodes, as seen in section 3.1) and the relationship between the length of the transmission cycle and the length of the control cycle (the control cycle has a fixed length, while the transmission cycle decreases as the transmission rate increases).

It is observed an improvement on execution time in a range from 40% to 49%, for all transmission rates and benchmarks used for CCP. This behavior is explained by the dynamic management of requests implemented by this protocol (section 3.2): the nodes can make requests in parallel.

One can see that from Tx 1 to Tx 2 the improvement in execution times is in the same range as from Tx 16 to Tx 160 (it halves execution times) for CCP. However, in the first case (Tx 1 to Tx 2), the increase in the transmission rate is doubled, while in the last case the transmission rate is multiplied by 10. This shows the influence of the control cycle length for high transmission rates for CCP. To quantify the differences between DCP and CCP, Table 1 shows the improvement (%) in execution time with CCP. The CCP has a better performance than DCP for all benchmarks and for all transmission rates. This improvement increases as the transmission rates increase: this behavior is caused by the influence of the DCP control cycle length as seen in section 3.1.

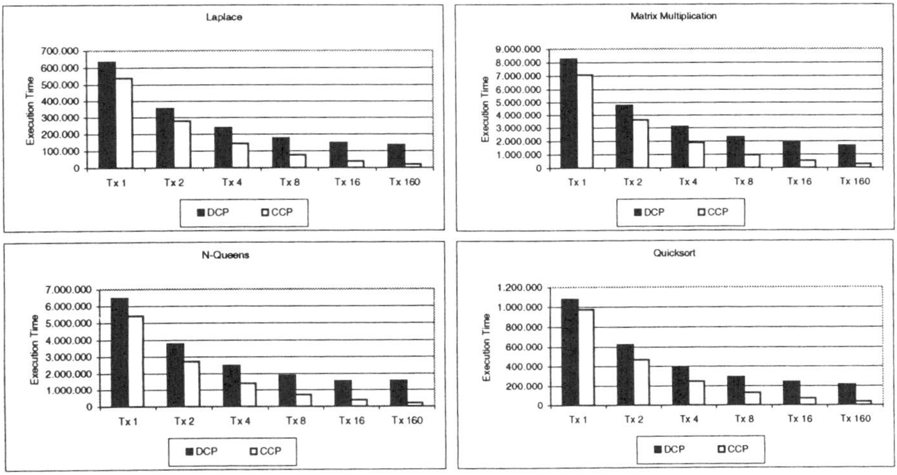

Figure 2: Simulation Results

Table 1: Improvement in Execution Time with CCP (%)

Benchmark	Tx 1	Tx 2	Tx 4	Tx 8	Tx 16	Tx 160
Laplace	14.9	21.6	40.1	56.1	73.7	84.6
Matrix Mult.	14.4	23.6	40.0	58.6	71.9	84.0
N-Queens	16.4	27.7	43.5	61.5	74.3	87.0
Quicksort	9.8	23.9	37.0	55.7	70.7	83.4

6 Conclusions

This work presented two control protocols for the APO architecture: Centralized Control Protocol (CCP) and Distributed Control Protocol (DCP). Execution times were investigated for several benchmarks and the results were analyzed as a function of transmission rates. The main conclusion is that CCP has better performance than DCP.

Results show that DCP performance is very sensible to the control cycle length for higher transmission rates, starting at Tx 4, degrading execution times. Considering transmission rates over Tx 16, CCP is also influenced negatively by the control cycle length. Therefore, for high speed networks the transmission rate is deeply influenced by the control cycle length, imposing an upper boundary around 40 Gbps (Tx 16).

In the near future, 40 Gbps may be an undesirable transmission rate boundary. New researches should be done in order to develop more efficient control protocols. These protocols should present a shorter control cycle, allowing higher transmission rates.

References

1. Stone, H. S. e Cocke, J. Computer Architecture in the 1990s. *IEEE Computer*, Vol. 24, N° 9, p. 30-38, September 1991.
2. Louri, A. e Sung, H. 3D Optical Interconnects for High-Speed Interchip and Interboard Communications. *IEEE Computer*, Vol. 27, N° 10, p. 27-37, October 1994.
3. Borella, M. et al. Optical Interconnects for Multiprocessor Architectures Using Wavelength-Division Multiplexing. In: Proceedings of the Twenty-Seventh Annual Hawaii International Conference on System Sciences, 1994, p. 499-508.
4. Borella, M. et al. Optical Components for WDM Lightwave Networks. *Proceedings of the IEEE*, Vol. 85, N° 8, p. 1274-1307, August 1997.
5. Martini, João A. et al. Proposal of a Dataflow Architecture with Optical Interconnection Network. In: Proceedings of High Performance Computing Symposium - HPC'99, 1999, San Diego, California. SCS Society for Computer Simulation International. p. 377-380.
6. Cavenaghi, M. A. et al. A Simple Mechanism to Deal with Sequential Code in Dataflow Architectures. In: Proceedings of International Conference on High Performance Computing (HiPC), Madras, India, 1998, p. 188-193.

QUEUEING MODELS OF PARALLEL SYSTEMS WITH SIMULTANEOUS RESOURCE POSSESSION

HENK JONKERS

Telematica Instituut, P.O. Box 589, 7500 AN Enschede, the Netherlands.
E-mail: jonkers@telin.nl

VICTOR F. NICOLA

Centre for Telematics and Information Technology, University of Twente, P.O. Box 217, 7500 AE Enschede, the Netherlands.
E-mail: nicola@cs.utwente.nl

Traditional queueing networks are still one of the most popular techniques for performance analysis of computer systems, because they combine efficient analysis with accurate performance predictions. However, they have some important limitations when applied to parallel and distributed systems. One of them is that solutions for simultaneous resource possession, which occurs in many parallel computing applications, are hard to find. In this paper we identify classes of scheduling disciplines for simultaneous resource possession, and derive an approximate analytical solution for one of them. We compare the scheduling disciplines with respect to their performance, and validate the accuracy of the approximation.

1 Introduction

On account of their conceptual simplicity and efficient analytical solutions, (separable) queueing models remain among the most popular techniques for performance analysis of computer and communication systems. However, queueing models have their limitations: due to their limited expressiveness, some important properties of systems cannot be studied.

One of the areas in which the limitations of queueing models are particularly apparent is performance evaluation of parallel and distributed computing systems. One of the problems to solve is how to study the combination of condition synchronisations and mutual exclusion. Another important problem, that has turned out to be particularly hard to solve, is *simultaneous resource possession* (SRP). In parallel processing, there can be several sources of SRP: several hardware resources that are needed simultaneously, two critical program sections that are entered simultaneously, or a combination of both.

In order to make queueing analysis also available for these types of applications, we are interested to find (approximate) solutions for queueing models with SRP. We propose practical solutions to extend the applicability of queueing analysis to some typical SRP patterns. For more complex situations, we will have to resort to other, less efficient, modelling and analysis techniques (e.g. stochastic Petri nets) or to quantitative simulation.

2 Related work

Few publications exist of analytical solutions for queueing networks with simultaneous resource possession. Although published already in 1982, Jacobson and Lazowska's *method of surrogates* [1] is still one of the most frequently cited works in this area. This method offers an iterative approximation for closed queueing networks with SRP. The *aggregate server method* of Agrawal and Buzen [2], specifically designed for the analysis of critical sections in programs, is an iterative method as well. Some solutions have been published for specific classes of closed queueing networks with SRP, e.g. by Kaufman [3], Courcoubetis [4], or some solutions based on decomposition and aggregation [5].

For open queueing networks, related literature is even more scarce. Under some circumstances, the approach of Ghodsi and Kant [6], based on the combination of task graphs and open queueing networks, can take into account the combination of mutual exclusion and hardware resource constraints. For a number of very specific types of open queueing networks, used to model production systems, (approximate) solutions are presented in [7]. We have not found solutions for a more general class of open queueing networks.

3 Example model

In this section we introduce a simple example that we use as an illustration throughout this paper. Consider a distributed-memory (DM) computer architecture with three processing nodes, as shown in Figure 1. The central node, P_0, is interconnected to node P_1 by a bidirectional interconnection link L_A and to node P_2 by link L_B.

We assume that all communications are *circuit-switched*: before a message is sent between two nodes, a connection is established in which the communication links on the path between the source and the destination node are claimed. The links in the circuit are not released until the message has been completely transmitted. Messages from P_1 to P_2 or vice versa can be transmitted directly by establishing a connection using both of the links L_A and L_B simultaneously; the central node P_0 is not involved. In this example, we will only consider the communication links as shared resources. We distinguish three classes of traffic: (1) messages from P_0 to P_1 or from P_1 to P_0 (needing L_A); (2) messages from P_0 to P_2 or from P_2 to P_0 (needing L_B); (3) messages from P_1 to P_2 or from P_2 to P_1 (needing L_A and L_B). In the case of class 3 messages simultaneous resource possession occurs, because the links L_A and L_B must both be claimed before a message of this class can be sent.

We assume that messages for the three traffic classes are generated at a rate of λ_1, λ_2 and λ_3, respectively. Messages vary in length and transmission time (the transmission time depends on the message length, but is independent of the distance between the nodes), with a mean transmission time $S = 1/\mu$.

Figure 2 shows a queueing model of this system. For each link there is a server in the model, and there is one queue for each traffic class. The two servers connected to the middle queue are both needed simultaneously to serve class 3 customers.

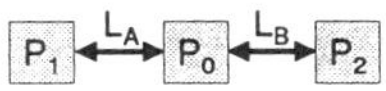

Figure 1. 3-Node DM architecture

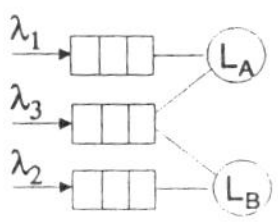

Figure 2. Queueing model of the architecture

4 Scheduling disciplines

In SRP situations, resource scheduling is more complex than in the single-resource case. Pure first-come first-serve (FCFS) scheduling is generally no longer possible, because the first job in line for one resource might also need other resources that are not yet available. Therefore, before we consider solutions for the SRP problem, we need to identify possible scheduling disciplines, and choose one discipline for further study.

First, we distinguish *non-priority* and *priority* disciplines. As a third class, we consider *processor sharing*. For each scheduling discipline, we give performance simulation results, with arrival rate λ for each of the three job classes in the example. We assume a service time of $S = 1$ time unit.

4.1 Non-priority scheduling

Non-priority scheduling disciplines for SRP provide the most straightforward generalisation of scheduling disciplines for single resource possession. The two main possibilities are *by reservation*, where a customer claims each of the needed resources as soon as they become available, and *simultaneously*, where the needed resources are claimed only when they are all available, as one atomic operation. The latter discipline is more efficient because, contrary to the former discipline, *blocking* is not possible here. Table 1 shows simulation results for these two scheduling disciplines using our example model from

Figure 2. $R_{1,2}$ denotes the mean response time for class 1 and class 2 jobs, and R_3 the mean response time for class 3 jobs.

4.2 Priority scheduling

As the simulation results show, the scheduling disciplines described in the previous subsection favour customers needing only one resource, especially for high workloads. In this section, we consider the possibility to give some sort of priority to customers needing more resources, in order to obtain more balanced response times. We can distinguish *non-preemptive* and *preemptive* priority. In the latter case, when a class 3 customer arrives, it claims both resources immediately (unless other class 3 customers are receiving service), and possibly interrupts the service of the low-priority (class 1 and 2) customers. Table 2 presents simulation results for the priority disciplines.

Table 1. Simulation of non-prio. disciplines

	reserv.		simult.	
λ	$R_{1,2}$	R_3	$R_{1,2}$	R_3
0.10	1.3	1.4	1.3	1.4
0.20	1.8	2.2	1.7	2.2
0.30	3.2	5.3	2.5	4.5

Table 2. Simulation of priority disciplines

	non-preempt.		preempt.	
λ	$R_{1,2}$	R_3	$R_{1,2}$	R_3
0.10	1.3	1.4	1.39	1.11
0.20	1.8	1.9	2.08	1.25
0.30	2.8	3.3	3.57	1.43

4.3 Processor sharing

In the single-resource possession case, processor sharing (PS) is a good approximation for a number of other scheduling disciplines. E.g., for a regular M/M/1 queue, the performance measures of PS scheduling are identical to those of FCFS. Although this will not be the case in the presence of SRP, PS might still offer a good approximation for other scheduling disciplines.

First we generalise the PS discipline to a SRP situation. The principle of PS is that the server capacity is equally shared between jobs in the queue. In the single resource possession case this means that, for a queue with n jobs, the effective service rate for a job is μ/n Considering our example model, with a total of n_1 jobs in queue 1, n_2 jobs in queue 2 and n_3 jobs in queue 3, server 1 is shared by $n_1 + n_3$ customers and server 2 by $n_2 + n_3$ customers. We make the additional assumption that *class 3 customers always require an equal capacity from both servers.* As a consequence, the capacity that remains for the other two classes is also equal, because of our assumption of equal server capacities. We identify two ways to achieve this.

In the first method, which we will call "maximum processor sharing", the *maximum* of the number of jobs in the class 1 and 2 queues determines the departure rate μ_3 for class 3 jobs, which (with a service time of S) results in:

$$\mu_3 = \frac{n_3}{S(n_3 + \max\{n_1, n_2\})} \tag{1}$$

The remaining capacity is available for the class 1 and class 2 jobs:

$$\mu_1 = \mu_2 = \frac{\max\{n_1, n_2\}}{S(n_3 + \max\{n_1, n_2\})} \tag{2}$$

In this method, class 1 and 2 jobs always get at least their share of the capacity, sometimes more (when there are more customers at the other resource): it can be considered as a kind of (weak) priority for these classes.

In the second method, "minimum processor sharing", the *minimum* number of jobs in the class 1 and 2 queues determines the departure rate μ_3. Again, the remaining capacity is available for class 1 and class 2 jobs:

$$\mu_3 = \frac{n_3}{S(n_3 + \min\{n_1, n_2\})} \quad \text{and} \quad \mu_1 = \mu_2 = \frac{\min\{n_1, n_2\}}{S(n_3 + \min\{n_1, n_2\})} \tag{3}$$

When $n_3 = 0$, all the capacity goes to the other jobs, i.e., $\mu_1 = \mu_2 = 1/S$. In this discipline, class 3 jobs have some sort of (weak) priority. Table 3 shows the simulation results for the two types of processor sharing scheduling.

5 Analytical solutions

For the preemptive priority discipline, an exact closed-form solution can be derived for the example model, using an approach similar to [8]. However, this solution cannot easily be generalised to allow for the analysis of more complex systems with SRP. In the remainder of this section, we derive an approximate solution for the maximum processor sharing case.

5.1 Approximate solution for maximum processor sharing

The approximate solution that we present in this section assumes *maximum* processor sharing, and is applicable to any open queueing network in which each job class needs at most two resources. We first consider the solution for the example model of Figure 2. The first approximation is that we assume that for the jobs that require only one resource (the class 1 and class 2 jobs in our example), the regular multiple-class M/M/1 expressions apply:

$$N_i \approx \frac{\rho_i}{1 - \rho_i - \rho_3} \quad \text{and} \quad R_i \approx \frac{S}{1 - \rho_i - \rho_3} \quad (\text{for } i = 1, 2) \tag{4}$$

Next, we observe that the service rate of class 3 jobs depends on the number of class 3 jobs, and the *maximum* of the number of class 1 jobs and the number of class 2 jobs in the queue. Let us denote this maximum by $N_{1,2}$. We now assume that $R_3 \approx (1 + N_{1,2} + N_3)S$. Combining this with Little's law, $N_3 = \lambda_3 R_3$, we can solve R_3:

$$R_3 \approx \frac{1 + N_{1,2}}{1 - \rho_3} S \tag{5}$$

Now the only thing we still need is an estimate for $N_{1,2}$. A lowerbound of $N_{1,2}$ can be derived when assuming that the number of jobs in queue 1 and queue 2 are independent, resulting following expression (we omit the derivation):

$$N_{1,2} \geq E(\max\{N_1, N_2\}) = \frac{\rho_1}{1 - (\rho_1 + \rho_3)} + \frac{\rho_2}{1 - (\rho_2 + \rho_3)} - \frac{\rho_1 \rho_2}{(1 - \rho_3)^2 - \rho_1 \rho_2} \tag{6}$$

We get a better approximation for $N_{1,2}$ when compensating for the dependency. Experiments show that the following approximation gives good results:

$$N_{1,2} \approx \frac{\rho_1}{1 - (\rho_1 + \rho_3)} + \frac{\rho_2}{1 - (\rho_2 + \rho_3)} - \frac{\rho_1 \rho_2}{(1 - \rho_3) - \rho_1 \rho_2} \tag{7}$$

Table 3. Simulation of PS disciplines

	maximum		minimum	
λ	$R_{1,2}$	R_3	$R_{1,2}$	R_3
0.10	1.25	1.39	1.37	1.13
0.20	1.69	2.02	1.95	1.38
0.30	2.63	3.36	3.14	1.92

Table 4. Analytical results of maximum PS

	Simulation		Analytical	
λ	$R_{1,2}$	R_3	$R_{1,2}$	R_3
0.10	1.25	1.39	1.25	1.38
0.20	1.69	2.02	1.67	2.02
0.30	2.63	3.36	2.50	3.36

5.2 *Generalised solution*

The above result can be generalised to any model in which every job requires at most 2 resources. Consider a job of class a requiring resources Q and R, denoting the utilisation of class a jobs on the resources by ρ_a. The total utilisation of other jobs using resource Q is denoted by ρ_b, and of other jobs using resource R by ρ_c; these can be jobs using only one resource, but they can also belong to other classes needing two resources. ρ_Q is the total utilisation of resource Q, i.e., $\rho_Q = \rho_a + \rho_b$; likewise, $\rho_R = \rho_a + \rho_c$. In a similar way as for our original example model, we use an approximation for N_{bc}, the expected value of the maximum of the number of non-class-a-customers:

$$N_{bc} \approx \frac{\rho_b}{1 - \rho_Q} + \frac{\rho_c}{1 - \rho_R} - \frac{\rho_b \rho_c}{1 - \rho_a - \rho_b \rho_c} \tag{8}$$

This finally results in the following expression for the response time:

$$R_a = \frac{1 + N_{bc}}{1 - \rho_a} S \tag{9}$$

Also in the general case, we use the regular M/M/1 solution as an approximation for job classes that need only one resource.

5.3 Validation

Table 4 compares our approximate solution to the simulation results from section 4.3. For this particular example, with a balanced workload, the approximation appears to be very accurate.

To validate the generalised solution, we consider an extension of the DM architecture from our original example with an extra node P_3, as shown in Figure 3. We assume that, unlike in the first example, the central node P_0 does not send or receive messages, so that all the communications require two links simultaneously. We again distinguish three traffic classes, with arrival rates λ_1, λ_2 and λ_3: (1) messages between P_1 and P_2 (using L_A and L_B); (2) messages between P_2 and P_3 (using L_B and L_C); (3) messages between P_1 and P_3 (using L_A and L_C). Figure 4 shows the queueing model for this situation.

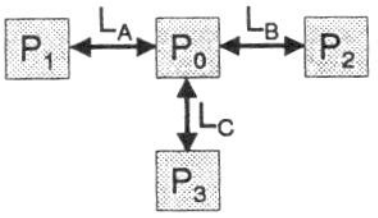

Figure 3. 4-Node DM architecture

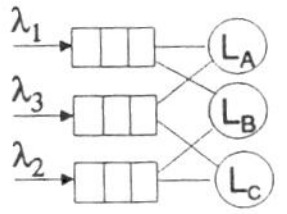

Figure 4. Queueing model of the architecture

Table 5 compares the analytical approximations to simulation results for this model, for several combinations of arrival rates. Although the errors are slightly higher for this model than for our standard example, the analytical predictions still remain within approximately 10% of the simulation results.

Table 5. Analytical results vs. simulation for a more general model

						Simulation			Analytical		
λ_1	λ_2	λ_3	ρ_A	ρ_B	ρ_C	R_1	R_2	R_3	R_1	R_2	R_3
0.1	0.2	0.3	0.3	0.4	0.5	2.00	2.18	2.22	1.91	2.13	2.20
0.2	0.2	0.2	0.4	0.4	0.4	2.07	2.07	2.07	2.02	2.02	2.02
0.2	0.3	0.5	0.5	0.7	0.8	4.23	5.75	6.17	3.80	5.33	6.06
0.3	0.4	0.5	0.7	0.8	0.9	7.10	11.14	11.83	6.33	11.11	12.37

6 Conclusions and future work

In this paper we considered simultaneous resource possession in the context of open queueing models for parallel processing systems. We identified three classes of scheduling disciplines for SRP and presented simulation results of their performance. For the maximum processor sharing discipline, we derived an analytical approximation, applicable to any open queueing network in which each job requires at most two resources simultaneously. Comparison with simulation results shows that the approximation errors are small.

Many practical and challenging SRP problems remain to be investigated. Some research issues directly related to the problem considered in this paper are to find (approximate) solutions for other disciplines, in particular minimum processor sharing, and a generalisation of the maximum processor sharing solution to allow for jobs requiring more than two resources.

Acknowledgement

This paper is based on research from the Testbed project [9], a collaboration of ABP, the Dutch Tax Department, ING Group, IBM and the Telematica Instituut, financially supported by the Dutch Ministry of Economic Affairs. The project develops a language, methods and tools for business process modelling and (re)design in the financial sector, and the results have been applied in several real-life business cases. We thank Piet Boekhoudt for his useful suggestions to improve this paper.

References

1. P.A. Jacobson and E.D. Lazowska. Analyzing queueing networks with simultaneous resource possession. *Comm. of the ACM*, 25:142–151, February 1982.
2. S.C. Agrawal and J.P. Buzen. The aggregate server method for analyzing serialization delays. *ACM Trans. on Computer Systems*, 1:116–143, May 1983.
3. J.S. Kaufman and W.S. Wong. Approximate analysis of a cyclic queueing network with applications to a simultaneous resource possession problem. *Performance Evaluation*, 11(3):187–200, 1990.
4. C.A. Courcoubetis and M.I. Reiman. Optimal control of queueing systems with simultaneous service requirements. *IEEE Trans. on Automatic Control*, 32(8):717–727, 1987.
5. D.J. Freund and J.N. Bexfield. A new aggregation approximation procedure for solving closed queueing networks with simultaneous resource possession. In *Proc. 1983 ACM SIGMETRICS Conference on Measuring and Modeling of Computer Systems*, pages 214–223, 1983.
6. M. Ghodsi and K. Kant. Performance modeling of concurrent systems under resource constraints. In D.J. Evans et al., editors, *Proc. Parallel Computing '89*, pages 589–594, Leiden, the Netherlands, August 1989.
7. J. Visschers, I. Adan, and J. Wessels. Product form solutions to production systems with simulaneous resource possession. Tech. rep. 99–15, Eindhoven University of Technology, Dept. of Mathematics and Computing Science, 1999.
8. V.F. Nicola. A single server queue with mixed types of interruptions. *Acta Informatica*, 23:465–486, 1986.
9. H. Franken and W. Janssen. Get a grip on changing business processes: Results from the Testbed project. *Knowledge & Process Management*, winter 1998.

PARALLEL PERFORMANCE RESEARCH OF SHORTEST PATH PROBLEM BASED ON PC CLUSTER

CHUNLI SUI GUOZHEN TAN JIZHEN NIU

Dept. of Computer Science and Engineering, Dalian Univ. of Tech., Dalian, Liaoning, P.R.China, 116024

E-mail: gztan@dlut.edu.cn, Tel:86-411-4707544

A shortest path parallel algorithm based on PC cluster is implemented. Two network models, the acyclic network model and the strongly connected random network model, are proposed. The experimental results on the models show high speedup and good parallel efficiency. Furthermore, the methods used to improve the parallel performance of PC cluster under different conditions are discussed.

1 Introduction

As the rapid development of computer network and other related technologies, innovative views are introduced to many existent computer theories and technologies. The essence of distributed computing is parallel, and parallel computing needs the integration of distributed control, therefore distributed computing becomes an important and strategic research field in many countries [1]. Nowadays network parallel computing system becomes a research hotspot [5], moreover, the great improvement of the performance of microcomputer and the rapid development of networking motivate its progress [1,3].

In communication network and transport network, shortest path problems hold a significant position. And high speed is essential in practical cases, the researches on the parallel computing make it possible to solve the large-scale problems fast.

In this paper data decomposition technique is used to implement shortest path parallel algorithm based on PC cluster. Two network models are proposed for simulation, and high speedup and good efficiency are gained on the models. Moreover, the methods to improve parallel performance on PC cluster are suggested and many factors that influence network parallel computing performance are discussed.

2 Parallelization of Dijkstra Algorithm

Data decomposition technique is used to implement the parallel Dijkstra algorithm in this paper. The number of data blocks depends on the number of hosts in the virtual environment. Each host performs the computing of one or several data blocks, and cooperates with others to accomplish the whole task.

The algorithm is described with the following notation:

(1)s denotes the source node

(2)dist[] denotes the temporary distance from the source node to other nodes

(3)w(i, j) denotes the weight of arc (i, j)
(4)u_i denotes the host which no. is i
Create the task group if it doesn't exist or join in the task group if the group exists
Get the member ID;
If member ID=0 then enable other hosts to execute the task End if
For each host par-do
For i =bn to en do dist(i) = w(s, i) End for
/*bn (en) is the start (end) node no. of the data domain */
End for
For k=1 to n-1 do
For each host par-do
    Search for the minimum value in the array dist[];
    If member ID doesn't equal to zero then
    Put the minimum value and the corresponding node no. into the buffer;
    Sending M_1 message to the host u_0;
    End if
End for
If member ID=0 then
    Upon receiving M_1 message from the host $u_1, u_2, \ldots u_k$ do:
    Get the data from the buffer;
    Search for the minimum value from the collection data of the p hosts;
    Put the minimum value and the corresponding node no. into the buffer;
    Broadcast M_2 message to the host $u_1, u_2, \ldots u_k$:
End if
For each host par-do
    If member ID doesn't equal to zero then
        Upon receiving M_2 message from u_0 do:
        Get the data from the buffer;
    End if
    Adjusting the value of the corresponding element of the array dist[];
End for
End for
If member ID =0 then output the results;

3 Methods to Improve Parallel Performance

3.1 Evaluation on Parallel Performance

The speedup S_p and the efficiency E_p are the general measurement of the parallel degree for an algorithm. Suppose that T_p denotes the parallel execution time in PC cluster containing p hosts and T_0 denotes the serial execution time to solve the same problem, then the speedup is defined as $S_p = T_0 / T_p$ and the efficiency is defined as $E_p = S_p / p$.

3.2 Methods to Improve Parallel Performance

1). Coarse Particle Size

Because of the great communication cost in PC cluster, decreasing the communication and synchronization between tasks is more important. Using coarse particle size is very appropriate. The following lemma is a widely used speedup model.

$$S_P = \frac{T1}{(\alpha 1 + \alpha 2/r + \alpha 3/p) * T1 + Td}$$

T_1: the serial execution time
T_d: the delay time caused by the communication and synchronization between tasks
α_1: the percentage of using one processor to complete the task
α_2: the percentage of using multiple processors (from 2 to p-1) to complete the task
α_3: the percentage of using p hosts to complete the task
r : the average number of hosts used during the corresponding time step.

The above model shows that the quantity of computation increases as the granularity increases, but the communication and synchronization decreases, thus the delay time decreases, which results in the improvement of performance.

2). Raw Message Passing Mode

Whether PC cluster is available or not depends on the network performance. In PC cluster environment the host type and the data type are identical, 'raw' coding mode can improve the efficiency markedly. And the tests indicate that in 10M/bps Ethernet the initialization time and transfer time of 'default' coding mode is almost the same as those of the 'raw' coding mode, but their packing time is quite different. Using 'raw' coding mode, the speed of packing is eight times as that of using 'default' coding mode [5,6].

4 Network Data Model

The experimental data are gained by creating the following two network models. The format used to represent the shortest path problems is gained by augmenting the First DIMACS Implementation Challenge file format.

- Acyclic Network Model

It is generated so that all nodes can be reached from the source node. To ensure this, one or more special connecting path is generated. It contains n-1 arcs: (1, 2), (2, 3), ... , (n-1, n). The other arcs are generated by choosing two distinct nodes independently at random and making the node with smaller ID the tail and the other node the head of the arc. The length of arc is chosen uniformly at random from the integer interval [L, U].

- Strongly Connected Random Network Model

Firstly a Hamilton cycle is generated to ensure the strongly connectivity, then other arcs are added randomly. The tail and the head of a random arc are chosen independently at random from the interval [1, n]. The length of arcs is chosen uniformly at random from the integer range [0,10000]. Random networks are widely used in testing optimization codes.

5 Results and Analyses

Four groups of experimental data are chosen from acyclic network model (Group A: 3000 nodes and 8000 arcs, Group B: 3000 nodes and 80000 arcs, Group C: 7000 nodes and 600000 arcs, Group D: 3000 nodes and 800000 arcs). The experimental results are illustrated in Figure 1 and Figure 2.

Number of hosts	Group A			Group C		
	Execution Time(s)	Speedup	Efficiency	Execution Time(s)	Speedup	Efficiency
1	3.88			181£ ®6		
2	3.81	1.02	0.51	172.61	1.05	0£ ®3
4	3.41	1.14	0.29	116.32	1.56	0£ ®9
6	4.45	0.87	0.15	79.42	2.28	0£ ®8
8	5.42	0.72	0.09	68.81	2.64	0£ ®3

Figure 1. Acyclic Network Model: Experimental results of group A and group C

Number of hosts	Group B			Group D		
	Execution Time(s)	Speedup	Efficiency	Execution Time(s)	Speedup	Efficiency
1	5.97			174.93		
2	5.35	1.12	0.56	199.00	0.88	0.44
4	4.80	1.24	0.31	104.23	1.68	0.42
6	5.17	1.15	0.19	80.23	2.18	0.36
8	6.10	0.98	0.12	68.81	2.54	0.32

Figure 2. Acyclic Network Model: Experimental results of group B and D

The corresponding speedup ratio curves and the efficiency curves are illustrated in Figure 3 and Figure 4.

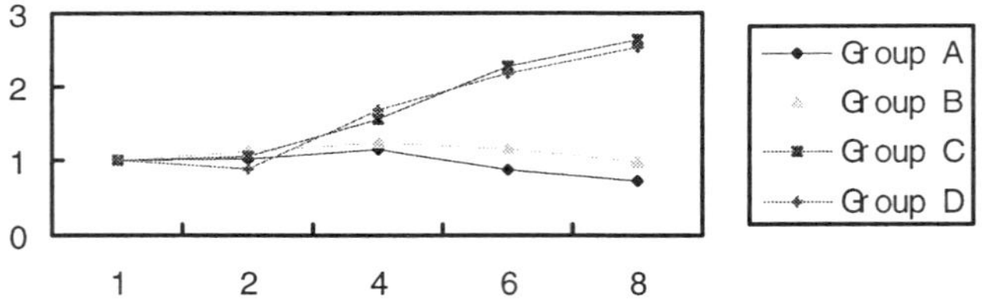

Figure 3. The Speedup Ratio Curve

It is indicated that speedup doesn't increase as the increasing of the number of the hosts. When the number of the hosts reaches to a value then the speedup for group A and group B descends unexpectedly. The major reason according to our analysis is as following:

1.The increase of hosts causes the increase of the communication and synchronism between them, which leads to the descending of the parallel performance.

2. The communication load is confined to the network loading and unloading capacity of LAN, if it is too large, the parallel performance descends dramatically.

It is shown in Figure 3 that if the quantity of the computation is great then the parallel performance is good and the speedup rises quickly; otherwise the parallel performance is bad and the speedup descends as the number of hosts reaches to some value.

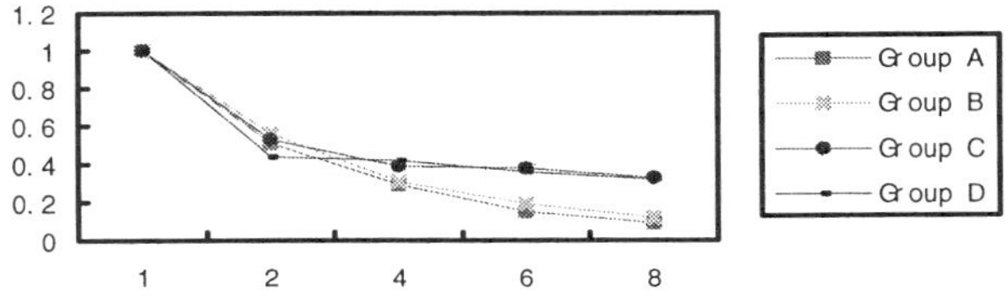

Figure 4 The Efficiency Curve

As is illustrated in Figure 4 the algorithm efficiency with experimental data group A and group B goes down dramatically as the increase of the hosts, which indicates that the algorithm's scalability is bad, and the hosts in cluster are not fully utilized; however to experimental data group C and D the efficiency curve drives to flat, and the parallel efficiency is always between 30% and 40%, each host is fully utilized, the scalability is good. It is because the influence of the communication decreases compared to the decrease of the propotion of the communication.

The experimental results of strongly connected random network are shown in Figure 5.

Number of Hosts	3000 nodes 8000 arcs			7000 nodes 600000 arcs		
	Execution Time(s)	Speedup	Efficiency	Execution Time(s)	Speedup	Efficiency
1	3.35			237.52		
2	3.10	1.08	0.54	111.80	2.12	1.06
3	2.98	1.12	0.37	79.88	2.97	0.99
4	3.08	1.09	0.27	75.38	3.15	0.79
5	3.83	0.87	0.17	62.58	3.80	0.76
6	4.17	0.80	0.13	54.20	4.38	0.73
7	4.98	0.67	0.10	46.97	5.06	0.72
8	5.60	0.60	0.07	45.58	5.21	0.65

Figure 5. Experimental results of strongly connected random network

As shown in Figure 5, when the quantity of computation is small the speedup even descend with the increase of host number. Otherwise, speedup rises quickly as the increase of the host number, and the parallel efficiency is very good as well. In the case of 8 hosts, the parallel efficiency is always above 50%, which indicates that the shortest path problems on strongly connected network are fit for parallel computing.

6 Strategies of Load Balancing

Load balancing plays an important role in improving the parallel efficiency. In this paper the static load balancing is used. The task distribution of the static load balancing is irrelevant to the state of the current host. User's task is distributed or redistributed according to the designer's experience or the collection of the system information. It is easily implemented and is effective for the underloaded network.

In parallel shortest path algorithm, data switching is needed after each host scans nodes of its own data block to implement synchronization. If the load is unbalanced, the hosts with too light load will wait for those with heavy load, which will affect the parallel performance.

The data are divided into several blocks and the task size for each host is assigned according to its current configuration before the task is started. By this way the waiting time between hosts is decreased as much as possible and the parallel performance is improved. Our experimental results proved this point.

However, this strategy doesn't consider the dynamic network bandwidth and the dynamic state of each host, this caused poor portability and bad efficiently. So our next work is to solve the task assignment problem on PC cluster.

7 Conclusion

We implemented the shortest path parallel algorithm on PC cluster and studied its performance on the acyclic network model and the strongly connected random network model. The experimental results indicate that for the same network model the speedup increases with the augment of the network scale. And on the strongly connected random network, the speedup increases rapidly with the increase of the hosts, and the parallel efficiency in this condition is very good. But for the small network the speedup will descend with the increase of hosts, the parallel execution time is even longer than the serial execution time.

References

1. Thomas E. Anderson, David E. Culler and David A. Patterson, A case for NOW(Network of Workstations), IEEE Micro. February 1995
2. Al Geist, et al. PVM: A User's Guide and Tutorial for Networked Parallel Computing. The MIT Press ,1994
3. Dhabaleswar K. Panda, et. Special Issue on Workstation Cluster and Network-Based Computing J. Parallel and Distributed Computing 1997 40,1-3
4. PVM:Parallel Virtual Machine http://www.epm.ornl.gov/pvm/pvmForeign.html
5. Sun Jiachang. Network Parallel Computing and Distributed Programming Environment. Science and Technology Publishing House 1996 (in Chinese)
6. Quan Huiyun. Introduction of Program Design on Parallel Computers. WUHAN University Publishing House 1998 (in Chinese)

COMMUNICATION IN THE LARPBS (OPTICAL BUS) MODEL: A CASE STUDY

BRIAN J. D'AURIOL

Department of Computer Science, The University of Texas at El Paso, El Paso, Texas, 79968-0518, USA

email: bdauriol@cs.utep.edu

A case-based analysis is presented of the Binary Prefix Sums computation primitive in the LARPBS optical bus model. A model of meta-data communication is developed for purposes of this analysis. The analysis reveals that the communication in the LARPBS model may be describable by such a meta-data model.

1 Introduction

Optical interconnection networks have received growing attention in the literature, in part, due to the widespread view in the research community that such optical-based networks can support teraflop or beyond high performance computing. Several different kinds of optical interconnection networks have been proposed. In particular, the linear optical bus interconnection network models provide for functional abstractions of communication and computation primitives (e.g. broadcasts and binary prefix sums). Further, it has been claimed [1] that such networks can be practically implemented.

Several linear optical bus-based models have appeared in the literature: *Array with Reconfigurable Optical Buses* (AROB) [2], *Linear Array with a Reconfigurable Pipelined Bus System* (LARPBS) [3], *Linear Pipelined Bus* (LPB) [4], and *Pipelined Optical Bus* (POB) [5]. A brief comparison of the four can be found in [1]. The focus in this paper is on the LARPBS model.

The LARPBS model is a parallel computational model that makes use of properties of light, unidirectional light pulse propagation and predictable propagation delay per unit length, to enable synchronized and concurrent access of the optical bus in a pipelined fashion [1]. Synchronized access is provided by the *coincident pulse technique* [6,3] where pulses along three distinct waveguides must be detected at particular synchronized points. In addition, the optical bus can be reconfigured by segmenting into multiple independent segments. The LARPBS model provides a set of communication (e.g. broadcast) and computation (e.g. binary prefix sums) primitives. These algorithms can be used as 'building blocks' to construct larger applications (see [7]).

One unique and perhaps controversial claim made of the LARPBS model is that many of the primitive operations have $O(1)$ *bus-cycle* complexity.

Hence, it is indicated that certain computations have a significant and moreover *fundamental* speedup over other comparable parallel implementations. However, little justification for this astonishing result has yet been published. In [7], a discussion is given concerning the validity of claiming a constant bus cycle in relation to fewer than approximately 1000 processor bus-based systems. Such justification is based on the relative optical communication speeds vs. processor cycle time and the consistent treatment in literature regarding how communication has been modeled. However, speedup in a parallel application depends on many factors, including how the application's communication pattern is harnessed. This paper focuses on the aspect of the application's communication requirements. Specifically, the Binary Prefix Sums primitive is analyzed as a case study. The analysis reveals that the communication in the LARPBS model may be describable by a meta-data model.

This paper is organized as follows. The LARPBS model is reviewed in Section 2. In Section 3, a meta-data model is developed as a tool for the case-based analysis. In Section 4 the meta-data model is applied to the Binary Prefix Sums computation on the LARPBS model. In Section 5, an algorithm is proposed to broadcast the conditional delay switch settings. Conclusions are presented in Section 6. The LARPBS model and the Binary Prefix Sums algorithm is presented in [1]. However, some of the notation is augmented and some minor notational errors have been corrected in this presentation.

2 LARPBS

A review of the LARPBS model as presented in [1] is conducted in this section.

The LARPBS model is illustrated in Figure 1. There are N processors $\mathcal{P} = (P_0, P_1, \ldots, P_{N-1})$ arranged in a linear topology that is connected by three waveguides, one for the data transmission of a message, one for the transmission of a *reference* pulse, and one for the transmission of the *select* pulse. The pulses are generated by appropriate optical devices shown in the figure as pulse injectors. The pulses can be detected by the pulse detectors. Due to the linear propagation of the pulse, pulses propagate from low numbered processors to higher number processors along the upper part of the waveguide (i.e., left to right in the figure). Hence, these pulses propagate along the bottom part of the waveguide from high numbered processors to lower number processors and are eventually detected by the pulse detectors. The waveguides have a defined length such that the first one half of the length (called the *transmission segment*) is reserved for the pulse injectors while the second one half of the length (called the *receiving segment*) is reserved for the pulse detectors.

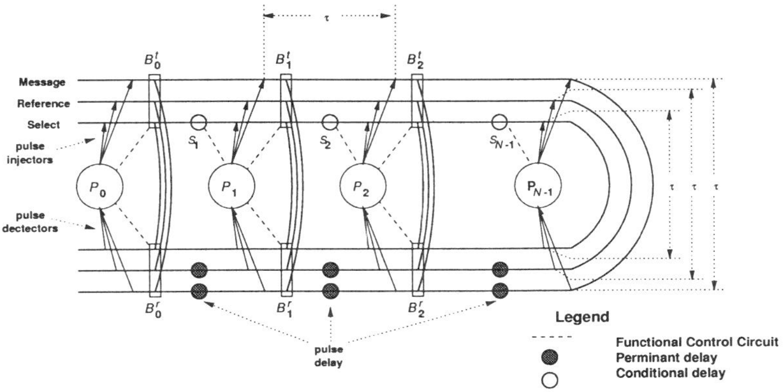

Figure 1. Overview of the LARPBS model

The reconfigurability of the optical bus is provided by the optical bus partition switches, B_i^t and B_i^r for $0 \leq i \leq N-2$ which directly connect the three waveguides from the transmission segment to the corresponding waveguides in the receiving segment, respectively, and at the same time, disconnects these waveguides as appropriate along the transmission and receiving segments. Thus, multiple independent optical buses can be configured. In this paper, $B_i^t = B_i^r = 1$ indicates a bus-split at P_i whereas $B_i^t = B_i^r = 0$ indicates that these switches do not partition the bus. For convenience, B_i will denote the combination of the two bus switches at P_i.

Let the propagation time of a pulse between any two processors be denoted by τ and let ω denote the duration of a pulse. In Figure 1, τ is illustrated as the constant ratio distance by the speed of light. For purposes of this study, the distance between the the pulse injector and the pulse detector for P_{N-1} is constant for all three waveguides and a pulse requires τ propagation time. In [1], for an optical signal of b bits, a collision-free requirement is that $\tau > b\omega$. To maximize the communication bandwidth, $b\omega$ should be as large as possible. A delay on the message and reference waveguides equal to ω is placed between every pair of detectors. In addition, *conditional* delay switches are placed between each pair of injectors on the select waveguide. Let $S_i, 1 \leq i \leq N-1$ denote a conditional switch. If $S_i = 1$ then a delay of ω is introduced and when $S_i = 0$, no delay is introduced. The set of all switches is denoted by $S = (S_1, S_2, \cdots, S_{N-1})$.

The *latency* L is defined as the sum of the propagation time of a pulse along a waveguide emitted by a source processor P_i and detected by a destination processor P_j. The latencies for the message, reference and select waveguides, denoted by L_m, L_r and L_s respectively are given by

$$L_m = L_r = (2N - 1 - i - j)\tau + (N - j - 1)\omega \tag{1}$$

$$L_s = (2N - 1 - i - j)\tau + \omega \sum_{k=i+1}^{N-1} S_k \tag{2}$$

The *bus cycle* is defined to be the optical signal propagation delay from P_0 to P_0, and in the literature (see for example [1]) has been stated to be $2N\tau$.

LARPBS uses a *coincident pulse* addressing scheme such that when P_j detects a pulse on both the select and reference waveguides, P_j then reads the b bit message from the message waveguide. A coincident pulse occurs in two situations,

- firstly, whenever

$$L_r = L_s, \qquad \text{that is,} \qquad j = N - \sum_{k=i+1}^{N-1} S_k - 1 \tag{3}$$

- secondly, whenever P_i delays the injection of the select pulse by whole units of ω.

Since communication is based on coincident pulses, communication based on these two situations is exploited in the LARPBS model. Clearly from Eq. (3), the switch settings affect addressability of the communication.

3 Meta-Data in the LARPBS Model

Two modes of communication are possible in the LARPBS model. In the first, a message pulse available on the message waveguide can be utilized to communicate specific information; this is referred to as *informational communication*. The second mode of communication is referred to as *meta-data communication* and is detailed subsequently.

In the case where the message content of a series of messages reflects a pattern of distribution of the input data, the message pulse may be ignored and instead, infer the message contents at the destination processor. For this to be possible, some state information regarding either or both of the LARPBS communication parameters must be globally known. For the moment, the delay switch configurations on the select waveguide are assumed globally known. Later on, the case that such information can be obtained in $O(1)$ time is presented.

Initially, let X denote the vector of input data: $X = (x_0, x_1, \ldots, x_{n-1})$ such that each $x_i \in X$ resides locally in processor P_i.

Let C denote a *meta-data configuration function* that provides for a partitioning of the switches according to the decision statement:

$$S_i = C(x_i) = \begin{cases} 1 & \text{if } C(x_i) \text{ is true,} \\ 0 & \text{if } C(x_i) \text{ is false.} \end{cases} \tag{4}$$

Thus, C will generate a particular distribution of switch settings.

C partitions $\mathcal{P}$ into two subsets when $P_i, 0 \le i \le N-1$ initiate simultaneous pulses (at the beginning of a bus cycle) on the select and reference waveguides. Hence, $t_{\text{ref}_i} = t_{\text{sel}_i}, 0 \le i \le N-1$. The two subsets of $\mathcal{P}$ are those which will detect a coincident pulse, denoted by $\mathcal{P}^p$, and those which do not, denoted by $\mathcal{P}^{np}$. This is evident from Eq. (3). Moreover, $(P_0, P_1, \ldots, P_j, P_{j+1}, \ldots P_{N-1})$ will be partitioned such that $\mathcal{P}^{np} = (P_k | 0 \le k \le j)$ and $\mathcal{P}^p = (P_k | j+1 \le k \le N-1)$. A grouping of the N coincident pulses therefore occurs at each $P_j \in \mathcal{P}^p$. For example, if all $S_i = 1, 1 \le i \le N-1$, then $\mathcal{P}^p = \mathcal{P}$ and $\mathcal{P}^{np} = \{\}$ with each $P_j \in \mathcal{P}^p$ detecting exactly one coincident pulse, whereas if all $S_i = 0, 1 \le i \le N-1$, then $\mathcal{P}^p = \{P_{N-1}\}$ and $\mathcal{P}^{np} = \mathcal{P} - \{P_{N-1}\}$ with P_{N-1} detecting N coincident pulses. The cardinality of $\mathcal{P}^p$ can be found by: $||\mathcal{P}^p|| = 1 + \sum_{i=1}^{N-1} S_i$.

For each $P_j \in \mathcal{P}^p$, a series of relations of the form $P_i \to P_j$ for some communication source $P_i \in \mathcal{P}$ describes the grouping of coincident pulses detected by P_j. This series of relations can be extended to all $P_j \in \mathcal{P}^p$. Consider a segment of switches $(S_s, S_{s+1}, \ldots, S_t, S_{t+1}), t \ge s$ such that $S_s = 1, S_{t+1} = 1$ and all $S_k = 0, s+1 \le k \le t$. Such a segment of switches is induced by C (ignoring the degenerate cases where $S_1 = 0$ or $S_{N-1} = 0$). All sources $P_s, P_{s+1}, \ldots, P_t$ will address the same destination processor over a corresponding unit of time. Hence, $P_s \to P_j, P_{s+1} \to P_j, \ldots, P_t \to P_j$.

Given the detection of a coincident pulse at P_j and the global state of the switches, P_i can be determined to be in the set of relations $P_i \to P_j$ for that P_j. Exactly, the meta-data communication from a source processor P_i to a particular destination processor P_j is described by

$$P_i \to P_{N-1-\Delta_j} \tag{5}$$

where Δ denotes a *time delay function* and is defined by:

$$\Delta_j = \sum_{k>j}^{N-1} S_k. \tag{6}$$

Essentially, Relation 5 is based on the addressing scheme of LARPBS where Eq. (6) determines the address of the recipient processor.

Every $P_j \in \mathcal{P}^p$ calculates Δ_j immediately following a switch reconfiguration (it is noted that Δ_j is computed by P_j). When P_j detects a coincident pulse, a table lookup is performed to determine P_i.

4 Case Study of the Meta-Data Communication in the Binary Prefix Sums Computation

The binary prefix sums calculation can be stated as follows. Given $X = (x_0, x_1, \cdots, x_{n-1})$ for $n \geq 1$ such that each $x_i \in \{0, 1\}$ for $0 \leq i \leq n-1$, compute a $Y = (y_0, y_1, \cdots, y_{n-1})$ such that $y_i = \sum_{j=0}^{j=i}(x_j)$ for $0 \leq i \leq n-1$. This calculation computes the number of '1's in a binary vector that occur previously to a given element in the binary vector, for example, if $X = (0, 1, 0, 1)$ then $Y = (0, 1, 1, 2)$. The sequential running time is $O(N)$. In [8] the parallel running time of prefix sums is given as of $\Theta(\log n)$. The LARPBS based algorithm is given in [1] and is $O(1)$ (bus-cycles).

As per the initial conditions, let X be the input binary vector such that $x_i \in X$ resides locally in processor P_i. The example shown in Table 1 and the associated LARPBS model shown in Figure 2 refers to $X = (1, 0, 1, 0, 1, 0, 1)$ and distributed as shown across the seven, P_0 through P_6, processors.

The decision statement for the first step of this algorithm is: "x_i equals 1.", hence, switch $S_i = 1$ if $x_i = 1$ and $S_i = 0, 1 \leq i \leq N-1$ otherwise. Table 1 illustrates the switch settings for this step in the row labeled Step 1; also, the switches that have had delays introduced are shown filled in Figure 2.

The first communication step of the algorithm has all $P_i, 0 \leq i \leq N-1$ initiate simultaneous pulses (at the beginning of a bus cycle) on the select and reference waveguides. Hence, $t_{\text{ref}_i} = t_{\text{sel}_i}, 0 \leq i \leq N-1$. Each processor, $P_j, N - ||\mathcal{P}^p|| \leq j \leq N-1$, computes the time delay function, Eq. (6), locally. The values computed for the example are shown in Table 1 in the row labeled Step 1. Each destination processor P_j determines the set of each source processors that initiated communication to it by Relation 5. For the example, Table 2 presents these calculations. For destination processor P_6, when it detects a coincident pulse, the set of possible source processors is $\{P_6\}$. However, when P_5 detects a coincident pulse, the set of possible source processors is $\{P_4, P_5\}$. In a similar way, all other processors can determine the source processor set corresponding to the detected coincident pulses. These sets are shown in the table entry labeled 'Time partition groups'. Lastly, the algorithm requires the source processor identification corresponding to the first coincident pulse. This will always be the highest number in the Time

Table 1. Binary prefix sums example ($B_i = 0$ unless otherwise noted).

Step	Description	Computation Results						
	Processors	P_0	P_1	P_2	P_3	P_4	P_5	P_6
	Distribution of X	1	0	1	0	1	0	1
1	Switch configuration		$S_1 = 0$	$S_2 = 1$	$S_3 = 0$	$S_4 = 1$	$S_5 = 0$	$S_6 = 1$
	Time delay function				2	1	1	0
	Time partition groups				$0, 1$	$2, 3$	$4, 5$	6
	Reconstructed message				1	3	5	6
2	Switch configuration		$S_1 = 0$	$S_2 = 0$	$S_3 = 0$	$S_4 = 0$	$S_5 = 0$	$S_6 = 0$
	Message Unicasts		3		4		5	6
3	Bus configuration		$B_1 = 1$		$B_3 = 1$		$B_5 = 1$	$B_6 = 1$
	Switch configuration		$S_1 = 0$	$S_2 = 0$	$S_3 = 0$	$S_4 = 0$	$S_5 = 0$	$S_6 = 0$
	Message Broadcasts	3	3	4	4	5	5	6
4	Computation Results	4						
5	Switch configuration		$S_1 = 0$	$S_2 = 0$	$S_3 = 0$	$S_4 = 0$	$S_5 = 0$	$S_6 = 0$
	Message Broadcast		4	4	4	4	4	4
6	Computation Results	1	1	2	2	3	3	4

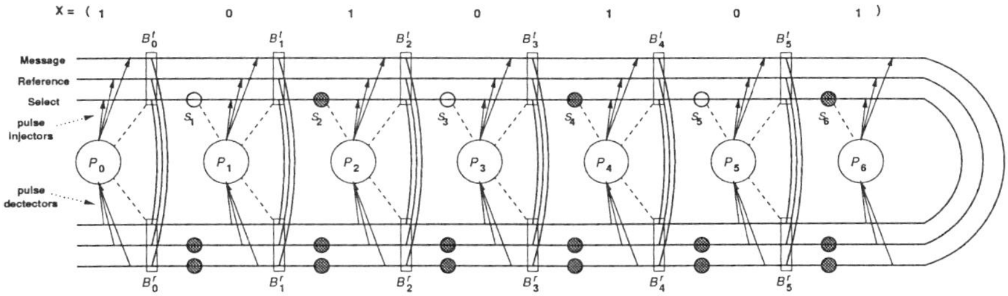

Figure 2. Binary prefix sums example: LARPBS model

partition group. Thus, the original information can now be reconstructed. In the example, this is shown in the table entry labeled 'Reconstructed message'.

Importantly, the major difference between the algorithm given here during this step and the original given in [1] is that the original requires an information message to be carried via the message waveguide. In the original algorithm, this information message merely carries the processor identification of the source processor. In the method given here, the message waveguide is not utilized, rather, only the detection of the select and reference pulses is

Table 2. Calculation of Relation 5 for Step 1 in the example given in Table 1.

i	Δ_i	Relation 5	i	Δ_i	Relation 5	i	Δ_i	Relation 5	i	Δ_i	Relation 5
0	3	$P_0 \to P_3$	2	2	$P_2 \to P_4$	4	1	$P_4 \to P_5$	6	0	$P_6 \to P_6$
1	3	$P_1 \to P_3$	3	2	$P_3 \to P_4$	5	1	$P_5 \to P_5$			

required.

In the next step, the processor address for those having received coincident pulses during the first step must be communicated to the originating source processors. In the original algorithm, the message waveguide is utilized to transmit the values obtained during Step 1. Since this reflects informational communication, this step does not exhibit meta-data communication.

The third step requires splitting the optical bus into sub-buses, where, in each sub-bus, a localized broadcast is performed. Since there is informational communication, this step also does not exhibit meta-data communication. Step 3 in Table 1 illustrates this step for the example.

The next step requires a single computation performed by P_0 where $y = x_0 + (N-1-j)$ for j the value received by P_0 in Step 3. Step 4 in Table 1 shows the result of this computation for the example.

Step 5 requires a broadcast of the value computed by P_0 to all processors; no meta-data communication is exhibited. The results from the broadcast for the example are shown in Step 5 of Table 1.

The last step of the algorithm requires a local computation for each $P_i, 1 \leq i \leq N-1$. This computation is $y = -(N-1-j)$ for j the value received by P_i from Step 5. The values distributed across the processors are the binary prefix sums for X. Table 1 displays the results for the example in Step 6.

In summary, the binary prefix sums algorithm on LARPBS exhibits both meta-data and informational data communication, where the meta-data communication occurs during the first step of the algorithm. Here, the meta-data configuration function was simply based on the binary value of the data input vector, X. Consequently, a pattern of switch settings was determined, thus impacting upon the latencies of subsequent communications. After the communications have completed, a set of receiving processors has obtained a series of coincident pulses. Assuming each recipient has knowledge of the global state of the switches, each recipient can calculate the originating processor identification for all coincident pulses. Such processor identification is used by the algorithm during subsequent processing. The version of the algorithm given here is also $O(1)$ bus-cycles.

5 Delay Switch Configuration

In the previous sections, it had been assumed that the switch configurations were globally known. This might be the case if, for example, the algorithm can be globally parameterized. The presentation of the binary prefix sums algorithm in Section 4 included qualitative descriptions of such global parameters for steps two through five: all switches set to 'off'. It is also possible that the switch control network be enhanced to provide for obtaining the switch settings by the processors. In general, however, the global state of the switch may not be known.

Consider Eq. (6) which describes the only parameter required to reconstruct the original message during meta-data communication. Eq. (6) essentially tallies the number of switches set to 'on' between P_j and P_{N-1} In fact, this is remarkably similar to the binary prefix sums algorithm presented earlier. Trivially, two further steps to the binary prefix sums algorithm may be added: a Step 7 where P_{N-1} broadcasts its computed value (4 in the example shown in Table 1) and a Step 8 where each processor subtracts the calculated prefix sum from the value broadcast in the previous step. Note that in fact the 'time delay function' (as in Table 1) can be computed from this procedure. Since the communication in Step 7 is $O(1)$, and if the original definition of the algorithm as given in [1] is used, then all necessary pre-information to complete a meta-data communication can be obtained by the processors in $O(1)$ bus-cycles. (optimizations may be considered in the algorithm to broadcast the switch states.)

6 Conclusions

Optical interconnection networks offer three advantages: high speed, high bandwidth and computational influence. The former two are well known advantages and essentially are the primary reasons for the evolutionary progress in this field. The latter advantage means that the nature of the communications has a positive performance effect on the computation beyond merely the high speed and bandwidth interconnect. This paper focused on the LARPBS optical bus model and specifically, on one computation primitive defined in that model. A case study based analysis was conducted of the Binary Prefix Sums computation primitive. The study was based on a notion of meta-data communication. The analysis reveals that the communication in the LARPBS model may be describable by such a meta-data model. On-going work includes the formalization of the meta-data model and its applicability in bus-based models.

Acknowledgements

The assistance of The Dept. of Math. & Comp. Sci. at the Univ. of Akron and the helpful suggestions from Dr. Abdullah Abonamah are acknowledged.

References

1. Yi Pan. Basic data movement operations on the LARPBS model. In K. Li, Y. Pan, and S.Q. Zheng, editors, *Parallel Computing Using Optical Interconnections*, pages 227–247. Kluwer Academic Publishers, 1998.
2. S. Pavel and S.G. Akl. On the power of arrays with optical pipelined buses. In H.R. Arabnia, editor, *Proc. of the International Conference on Parallel and Distributed Processing Techniques and Applications (PDPTA'96), Vol. III*, pages 1443–1453, Sunnyvale, California, USA, August 1996.
3. Y. Pan and K. Li. Linear array with a reconfigurable pipelined bus system — concepts and applications. In H.R. Arabnia, editor, *Proc. of the International Conference on Parallel and Distributed Processing Techniques and Applications (PDPTA'96), Vol. III*, pages 1431–1441, Sunnyvale, California, USA, August 1996.
4. J.L. Trahan, A.G. Bourgeois, Y. Pan, and Ramachandran Vaidyanathan. Optimally scaling permutation routing on reconfigurable linear arrays with optical buses. In *Second Merged Symposium IPPS/SPDP, 13th International Parallel Processing Symposium & 10th Symposium on Parallel and Distributed Processing*, San Juan, Puerto Roco, April 1999.
5. Y. Li, Y. Pan, and S.Q. Zheng. Pipelined time-division multiplexing optical bus with conditional delays. *Optical Engineering*, 36(9):2417–2424, September 1997.
6. S.P. Levitan, D.M. Chiarulli, and R.G. Melhem. Coincident pulse techniques for multiprocessor interconnection structures. *Applied Optics*, 29(4):2024–2033, 1990.
7. K. Li. Constant rime boolean matrix multiplication on a linear array with a reconfigurable pipelined bus system. *Journal of Supercomputing*, 11(4):391–403, 1997.
8. S.G. Akl. *The Design and Analysis of Parallel Algorithms.* Prentice Hall, 1989.

STRUCTURING DISTRIBUTED COMPUTATION AND VISUALIZATION USING FACET TREES

A.H.DAVIS, J. LU AND C. SUN
School of Computing and Information Technology
Griffith University,
Brisbane, Queensland 4111, Australia
E-mail: {horatio,jun,scz}@cit.gu.edu.au

Mathematical computing requires tools for collaborative work backed by the computational power of parallel processing, using existing applications. A framework for structuring distributed computation, based on a tree of shared objects, is presented; the components of this framework wrap around existing serial objects. An implementation, Concurrent Matlab, is presented and discussed.

1 Introduction and Motivation

This paper treats mathematical computation - simulation, modelling, and related tasks using high-performance compiled code steered by an interpreted language optimized for the task, running over a workspace of objects representing numbers and functions operating on those numbers. Matlab, Mathematica, Octave, and Maple are examples. Wood et al [13], Chen, Rine and Simon [3], and Saran et al [10] give good reasons for wishing to share these computations with other members of a research team distributed across a network. From different directions, they propose or describe solutions to the *collaborative visualization* problem: permitting several users to steer and visualize the results of a computation as it is run. To solve this problem, the simulation must run, information from it be abstracted and presented, and steering feedback obtained from users across a network, on a human (near-real) time scale.

The traditional approach is to distribute the computation explicitly. Matlab has the Parallel Toolbox[9] and the Cornell MultiTask Toolbox [15] which use wrappers around the Parallel Virtual Machine and the Message Passing Interface to provide explicit shared workspace objects, distributed computation and (by extension) distributed interaction. However, the programmer must concentrate more on the distribution than upon the mathematics, and collaborative interfaces must be hand-built.

Another approach is *conventional collaboration transparency.* One instance of the computation is run on a server and the interface is distributed to the interested parties by tools such as NetMeeting, SunForum, and TechTalk

[8]. The code need not be rebuilt to be collaboration-aware. This widens the applicability but wastes the multiple processors it runs on. Begole et al. [1] extend this to *flexible collaboration transparency* by replicating the code and state of an application on each node, and synchronizing their inputs. Useability and flexibility are enhanced by viewing an application as a set of objects, some of which are safely replaced by collaboration-aware equivalents.

The framework presented below extends this approach by viewing a computation as a tree of interacting objects. Leaves of the trees at different nodes can be identified as facets of the same conceptual object. These are transparently replaced by objects that are aware of the identity and act to maintain consistency and causality across nodes.

2 Framework and Nomenclature

A *simple object* is a mathematical object (variable, graphics primitive, or piece of code) that exists in one place at one time, where a *place* is a workspace of simple objects, executing independently of other places. Such objects have parents and children: a window has a graph in it, which has some axes, a line, and some labels. They thus structure naturally into trees. A *facet* is a simple object that cooperates with other peer facets to maintain a consistent distributed state, which it presents seamlessly to the objects in its' local workspace. A facet contrasts with an Orca object replica[4] by being identified with a node instead of cached, destroyed and recreated at need. It contrasts with the *chares* of Charm++ and the *data aggregates* of EPEE[7] by being a point of presence for the whole object, not a discrete fragment with explicit fragment interfaces.

Collections of facets that refer to the same conceptual object are aggregated into *mirrors*. Mirrors grow by merging; facets are initially single-facet mirrors, and seek other mirrors with the same identifier to merge. This poses the challenge of a distributed, deterministic identifying scheme for facets, mirrors and trees, and algorithms to efficiently search for identified facets.

A *rune* is a facet that encapsulates a value and an identifier, and additional metadata as property/value pairs. The nature of the primary value determines the use of the rune.

A mirror of runes which hold data implements a distributed data structure. The value held in that location must be consistent and fresh (all evaluations after a given assignment yield the same value as was assigned, irrespective of location). Algorithms to guarantee these properties must be implemented *within* the rune, but are a straightforward recasting of existing work[5].

Following the idea of a computation as a first-class value [6], the primary value may be a piece of serial code, which the facet insulates from communication and synchronization issues. A mirror of such runes represents a MIMD parallel computation.

A *glyph* is a rune which represents a component of a graphical interface, for example a line, isosurface, window, menu, or an input field. A mirror of glyphs represents a component of a collaborative interface, as each facet exists in front of a different user. A tree of glyphs expresses the hierarchy introduced above, branches of the tree being coherent subsets of the interface. Glyph values are the data they are displaying to or receiving from the user. Consistency maintenance of these values across a mirror is addressed by existing work[14] [11].

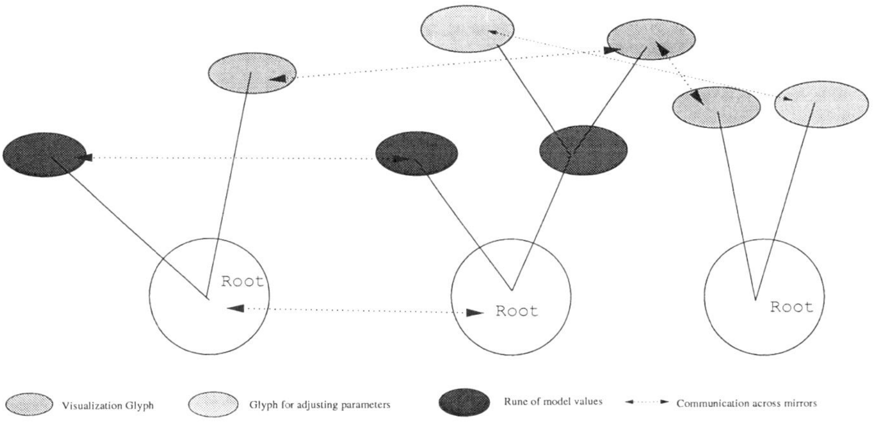

Figure 1. Three facet trees and three mirrors

The collection of facets at a place form a *facet tree*. Facet trees grow by *grafting*, where new leaves replace existing simple objects, or branches of other facet trees are cloned and attached. Growth begins from a facet named `Root`, which manages the place where the tree exists and provides a point of communication for other trees.

An *ensemble* is a forest of facet trees (and places) whose `Root` objects are facets of a single mirror. Ensembles may grow dynamically by seeding trees in new places. Communication across trees is done implicitly, by involving a local facet which then propagates the relevant information across the mirror.

In general, facets of a given mirror occupy different locations in different trees, and trees in an ensemble each have a different set of facets. The example in figure 1 has one computational mirror, shared across the left two trees, one GUI shared across all three, and a second GUI shared across the right two trees. Note also that the two GUIs are windows in their own right on the visualization tree, but are children of another window on the centre tree. This flexibility is characteristic.

3 Implementation - Concurrent Matlab

Concurrent Matlab is a toolbox that implements glyphs under Matlab. It provides the building blocks for collaborative interfaces to conventional computations. It is a set of C MEX-files for Matlab 5.2, running on an IBM SP2 and connected by the LAM[2] implementation of the Message Passing Interface. The ensemble is a set of daemons written in C, each controlling the standard input and output of a Matlab engine. The glyphs are wrappers around regular Matlab Handle Graphics objects, each rendered and manipulated by a specific daemon's engine. There is one daemon per user interface. One of these is distinguished as the root node, and presents a command prompt. This daemon's engine performs the computation.

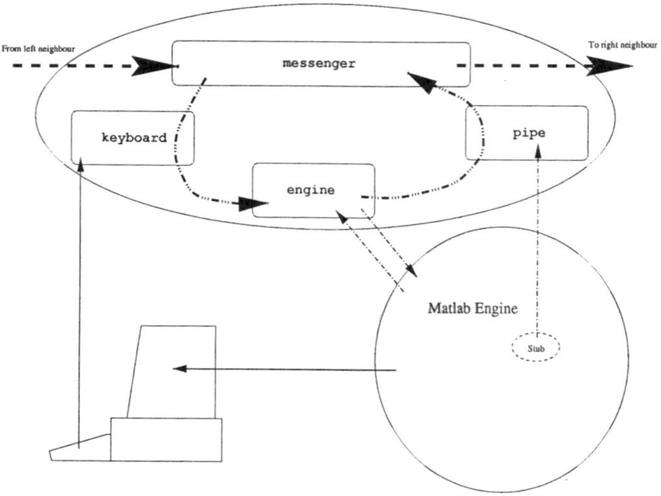

Figure 2. Implementation of a Concurrent Matlab node

Figure 2 shows the internal structure of a node. The daemon has four threads linked by two FIFO queues, inbound and outbound. The basic quantum of work is the `mxRequest`, which contains enough information to reproduce a single Matlab operation. The `messenger` thread takes `mxRequests` from the outbound queue and passes them via MPI to the next node in the ring. It also receives requests from the previous node and puts them on the inbound queue. The `keyboard` thread takes commands from the user and puts them on the inbound queue as `mxRequests`. The `engine` thread takes `mxRequests` from the inbound queue, uses the Matlab Engine API to reproduce them on the Matlab engine, and passes them to the outbound queue. The `tap` thread listens for requests raised in the local engine to create, delete, set a property or read a property of a HG object, or to execute a callback. The relevant primitives have been replaced with versions which also notify this thread, which places them on the outbound queue for other nodes to reproduce.

All daemons are members of a MPI intracommunicator, whose membership fixes the ensemble at startup. Each `mxRequest` passes from the outbound queue of one daemon to the inbound queue of its neighbour, and is absorbed after circling the ring. Consequently, requests raised at each node, or at different times on different nodes, remain causally ordered without a formal request history or timestamp scheme.

A small application was built with the toolbox for evaluation. Testing used two to four daemons, each running on a node of an IBM SP2, with LAM running in client-to-client mode over the high-performance switch. The goal was for communications latency to be small relative to Matlab computation and rendering times. This was in fact the case. The response time to graphical commands on the root node was excellent, but the round trip for callbacks from other nodes impacted responsiveness. Two limitations became evident. First, conflicting requests on the same mirror execute in inconsistent orders at different nodes. Adding timestamps and serialization is required. Second, there is no group awareness, which ensures that conflicting user requests will arise. Mirroring other users' cursors will supply it.

4 Conclusions and further work

This paper presents a framework that should help solve the collaborative visualization problem by distributing objects in the computation across a cluster of processors. The framework places the communication and synchronization logic within objects called *facets*. The executing serial code is not aware that the other modules it cooperates with are in other places, and the objects it acts on reflect that action elsewhere. The structure of these facets into trees enables flexible composition of a working set of data and code at each node. The visualization components of this framework have been implemented for Matlab, linked by MPI. The architecture and implementation limits of this system have been discussed, and solutions suggested. Future implementation efforts will focus on building the entire framework as a set of Java classes under Matlab, using appropriate algorithms from the REDUCE(REal-time Distributed Unconstrained Collaborative Editing) [12] and GRACE(GRAphic Collaborative Editing) [11] projects. The end result should be useable for production scientific coding.

Acknowledgments

This research was done using the facilities of the Queensland Parallel Supercomputing Foundation. Their help and support was invaluable. We would like to thank Andrew Lewis and an anonymous reviewer for their insightful comments and suggestions.

References

1. James Begole, Mary Beth Rosson, and Clifford Shaffer. "Flexible Collaboration Transparency: Supporting Worker Independence in Replicated Application-Sharing Systems." *ACM Transactions on Computer-Human Interaction*, 6, June 1999.
2. Gregory D. Burns, Raja B. Daoud, and James R. Vaigl. "LAM: An Open Cluster Environment for MPI." In *Proceedings of the 1994 Supercomputing Symposium*. SC94, June 1994.
3. Jim X. Chen, David Rine, and Horst D. Simon. "Advancing Interactive Visualization And Computational Steering." *IEEE Computational Science and Engineering*, December 1996.
4. Alan Fekete, M. Frans Kaashoek, and Nancy Lynch. "Implementing sequentially consistent shared objects using broadcast and point-to-point communication." *Journal of the ACM*, 45, January 1998.
5. Saniya Ben Hassen, Henri E. Bal, and Ceriel J. H. Jacobs. "A task- and data-parallel programming language based on shared objects." *ACM Transactions on Programming Language Systems*, 20, November 1998.
6. John Hughs. "Why Functional Programming Matters." *The Computer Journal*, 30, 1989.
7. J.Jezequel. "EPEE: An Eiffel environment to program distributed-memory parallel computers." *Journal of Object-Oriented Programming*, 6, 1993.
8. Y.N. Lakshman and Michael R. Miller. TechTalk: A Web Based System for Mathematical Collaboration. World Wide Web, http://penguin.mcs.drexel.edu/~techtalk/, 1998.
9. Pau'l Pauca, Kun Liu, Joel Hollingsworth, and Rudy Martinez. Parallel Toolbox for Matlab. World Wide Web, http://www.mthcsc.wfu.edu/pt/pt.html, 1995.
10. A. Saran, D. Agrawal, A. El Abbadi, T.R.Smith, and J.Su. "Scientific Modeling using Distributed Resources." In *Proceedings of the 1996 Conference on Geographical Information Systems*. Association for Computing Machinery, 1996.
11. C. Sun and D. Chen. "A multi-version approach to conflict resolution in distributed groupware systems." In *Proceedings of the 20th IEEE International Conference on Distributed Computing Systems*. IEEE, April 1999.
12. "C. Sun, et al. Achieving convergence, causality-preservation, and intention-preservation in real-time cooperative editing systems." *ACM Transactions on Computer-Human Interaction*. Vol.5, No.1, pp.63-108, March 1998.
13. Jason Wood, Helene Wright, and Ken Brodie. "Collaborative Visualization." Technical report, University of Leeds, 1996.
14. Y.Yang, C.Sun, Y. Zhang, and X. Jia. "Real-time Cooperative Editing on the Internet." *IEEE Internet Computing*, May/June 2000.
15. John A. Zollweg and Arun Verma. Cornell Multitask Toolbox for MATLAB. Cornell Theory Centre, 2000.

D & C METHOD FOR SOLVING LARGE PROBLEMS IN FIXED SIZE PROCESSOR ARRAY

YIN XINCHUN AND CHEN LING

State Key Laboratory for Novel Software Technology, Nanjing University, Nanjing 210093, P. R. China
Department of Computer Science and Engineering, Yangzhou University, Yangzhou 225009, P. R. China
E-mail:xcyin@dislab.nju.edu.cn

XIE LI

State Key Laboratory for Novel Software Technology, Nanjing University, Nanjing 210093, P. R. China
E-mail:xieli@nju.edu.cn

Solving large problems in a fixed size small processor array is more difficult mainly because the data arrays which pipeline through the processor array have to meet at the right place at the right time. Thus, partitioning and scheduling of data arrays for parallel computation in array processors are generally problem-oriented. In this paper we present a general partitioning and scheduling method for solving large problems in a small fixed size processor array. Given a processor array and its algorithm, a scheduling procedure which schedules the data and computations can be obtained by D&C technique. The method, which can be easily mechanized, is applicable to all the recurrence algorithms and processor arrays of various structures and shapes with or without local memory.

1 Introduction

A common problem encountered in array computation is the mismatch between the size of the processor array and the size of the data arrays. This problem is more critical in a systolic array because systolic arrays are usually small due to the limitations of bus width and chip pins. In a processor array, data scheduling is rather complex because data arrays which pipeline through the processor array have to meet at the right place at the right time. Generally, partitioning and scheduling affect the correctness as well as the efficiency of the computation. In a systolic array, an additional cause of inefficiency is the pipeline drain due to interrupted data flows.

A number of works on solving large problems in small processor array have been reported. Almost all of these are for solving one or more type of matrix problem by using a partitioning and scheduling method designed for the particular type of problem[1]. In order to find a general solution to the size mismatch problem in processor arrays. Moldovan *et al*[2] have extended their algorithm-array mapping method to fixed-size array. Chuang *et al*[3,4] have proposed methods for solving large problems in fixed-size processor array. However, not every processor array is suitable for these methods. These methods can be used only for the processor arrays with unique direction of data flow or for the algorithms which can be expressed by a loop program.

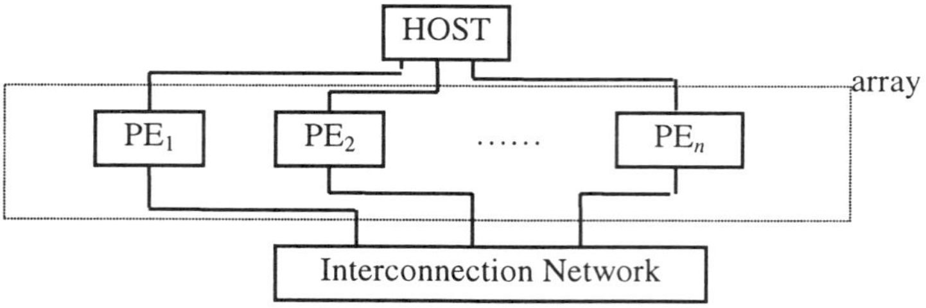

Figure.1

In this paper, we present a general partitioning and scheduling method for solving large problems in a small processor array. The method is based on the divide-and-conquer technique (D&C). The D&C technique is very useful in algorithm designing. It is suitable to a wide variety of problems. All the recurrence problems can be solved by this technique. D&C technique also provides a general method for partitioning large recurrence problem so as to solve them in fixed size processor arrays. Given a processor array and its algorithm, a scheduling procedure which schedules the data and computations on the fixed size processor array can be obtained by D&C technique. This method, which can be easily mechanized, is applicable to all the recurrence algorithms and processor arrays of various structures.

2 Architecture of the Array Processor

The SIMD array processor generally takes the structure shown in Figure 1. It employs a number of processor elements (PE). Each processor possibly has its own local memory. The input data can be fed into the array from a main memory or an external source. Data exchanges among the PEs are done via an inter-PE communication network, which performs all necessary data-routing and manipulation functions. This interconnection network is under the control of the host. The host computer is a general-purpose machine which serves as the "operating manager" of the entire system. The host computer supplies the array data and control signal. In our D&C method, an D&C procedure, which is a recurrence program, is generated and executed by the host so as to control the array to solve large problems. This D&C procedure, which is generated by compiling the user's program, indicates how the fixed size array solves a sequence of small subproblems in order to solve the large problem.

3 The Method

When solving a large size problem, a common technique is to decompose the problem into smaller parts, find solutions for the parts, and then combine the solutions for the parts into the solution for the whole. For general D&C technique, the subproblems can be formulated just like smaller versions of the original problem, thus the same processor array may be used repeatedly for different partitions of the problem. Therefore, D&C technique provides a general method to decompose large problems into smaller homogeneous subproblems.

The D&C method for solving large problem in fixed size processor array can be briefly stated as follows. Given a recurrently defined large problem $F(N)$ with size N and a smaller array $A(n)$ for the same kind of problem $F(n)$ of size n, here $n<N$, if we want to solve the large size problem $F(N)$ in $A(n)$, we can split the input data of $F(N)$ to form several subproblems $F(n_1)$, $F(n_2)$, ..., $F(n_r)$ which are all homogeneous to $F(N)$. If $n_i \bullet n$ for $i=1,2,\ldots,r$, we can solve $F(n_1)$, $F(n_2)$,..., $F(n_r)$ in $A(n)$ sequentially. Otherwise if there exists an $n_k>n$, we can further split the input data of $F(n_k)$ to form several subproblems. Repeat this procedure recurrencely until all the sizes of the subproblems are not greater than n, then solve these subproblens in $A(n)$ sequentially. After these subproblems are solved, their results are combined to form the final result of the large problem $F(N)$. The following D&C procedure, which is a recurrence program, explains this method:

Procedure F(I: input structure, O: output structure, N: integer of size);
  L_1, L_2, ..., L_r: input structure;
  M_1,M_2, ..., M_r: output structure;
  if N is not greater than n (the size of processor array $A(n)$)
    then solve F(I, O, N) in $A(n)$
    else
      split I into L_1, L_2, ..., L_r with size n_1, n_2,..., n_r, respectively;
      for j=1 to r do
        F(L_j, M_j, n_j)
      end for j;
      combine M_1, M_2,..., M_r into O
  end if
end procedure

This procedure indicates the schedule for the computations of $A(n)$. Based on this scheduling, the host controls the array and the data flow when this procedure is executed in the host. After the user feeds the input data I and program which describes his recurrence problem into the processor array, the host first compile the user's program to generate the D&C procedure. According to this procedure, the host then split the input data I into several parts. The host executes the D&C procedure recurrently to generate subproblems with small sizes which can fit the array. The host also arranges the order for solving these subproblems sequentially in the processor array and controls the data flow input into and output from the array. Once these subproblems are solved, the host combine their solutions into a solution for the original problem.

Based on the users program which describes the problem recurrently, the host can compile it into D&C procedure mechanically. Therefore, the method is generally applicable and can be easily implemented by a compiler. An efficient solution of large problem can be obtained a small array by this method.

4 Examples

4.1 Matrix multiplication

Suppose we have an array $A(n)$ which can perform multiplication of two matrices of size n If we want to solve $A*B=C$ in $A(n)$, here A, B, C are $N*N$ matrices and $N>n$. We denote this problem by MMUL(A, B, C, N). In our D&C method, we partition each matrix into four $(N/2)*(N/2)$ submatrices:

$$\begin{bmatrix} A_{11} & A_{12} \\ A_{21} & A_{22} \end{bmatrix} \cdot \begin{bmatrix} B_{11} & B_{12} \\ B_{21} & B_{22} \end{bmatrix} = \begin{bmatrix} C_{11} & C_{12} \\ C_{21} & C_{22} \end{bmatrix} \tag{1.1}$$

Here

$$\begin{aligned} C_{11} &= C_{11}^1 + C_{11}^2 = A_{11}B_{11} + A_{12}B_{21} \\ C_{12} &= C_{12}^1 + C_{12}^2 = A_{11}B_{12} + A_{12}B_{22} \\ C_{21} &= C_{21}^1 + C_{21}^2 = A_{21}B_{11} + A_{22}B_{21} \\ C_{22} &= C_{22}^1 + C_{22}^2 = A_{21}B_{12} + A_{22}B_{22} \end{aligned} \tag{1.2}$$

Thus, we partition large problem MMUL(A, B, C, N) of size N into 8 subproblems of size $N/2$. If $N/2 \bullet n$, we can use $A(n)$ 8 times to solve MMUL(A, B, C, N), otherwise, we partition each subproblem into 8 subproblems of size $N/4$. Repeat this partition recurrently until the sizes of the subproblems are not greater than n. Let $N=2^L$, $n=2^l$, $L-l=d$, repeating this partition d times, we can get 8^d subproblems of size n. Using $A(n)$ 8^d times, problem MMUL(A, B, C, N) can be solved.

The D&C procedure of MMUL(A, B, C, N) is as follow:

Procedure MMUL(A, B, C, N);
  if $N \bullet n$ then solve MMUL(A, B, C, N) in $A(n)$
    else
      split A, B according to (1.1);
      for i=1 to 2
        for j=1 to 2
          for k=1 to 2

MMUL (A_{ik}, B_{kj}, C_{ij}^{k}, $N/2$)

end for k

end for j

end for i;

combine C_{11}, C_{12}, C_{21}, C_{22} into C according to (1.2)

end if

end procedure

If Strassen's algorithm is used in each partition, we can obtain only 7 subproblems instead of 8:

$M_1=(A_{12}-A_{22})(B_{21}+B_{22})$
$M_2=(A_{11}+A_{22})(B_{11}+B_{22})$
$M_3=(A_{11}-A_{21})(B_{11}+B_{12})$
$M_4=(A_{11}+A_{12})\cdot B_{22}$
$M_5=A_{11}\cdot(B_{12}-B_{22})$
$M_6=A_{22}\cdot(B_{21}-B_{11})$
$M_7=(A_{21}+A_{22})\cdot B_{11}$

Here, $C_{11}=M_1+M_2-M_4+M_6$
$C_{12}=M_4+M_5$
$C_{21}=M_6+M_7$
$C_{22}=M_2-M_3+M_5-M_7$

After partitioning d times, only 7^d subproblems need to be solved.

4.2 *Fast Fourier Transform*

The output of discrete Fourier transform of sequence $S(k)$ (k= 0, 1,..., n-1), is defined to be the sequence $X(j)$ (j= 0, 1, ..., n-1), where

$$X(j)=\sum_{k=0}^{n-1} S(k)*W^{jk} \qquad j=0, 1,\dots, n\text{-}1$$

and $W=e^{\frac{2\pi i}{n}}, i=\sqrt{-1}$.

A processor array $A(n)$ with $n/2$ PEs can perform an n-point FFT of the sequence $S(k)$ of length n[5]. If we want to use $A(n)$ to solve large FFT problem of N points FFT(N), $N>n$, the D&C method also can be used.

Consider the fact that the FFT of N point sequence $S=\{S(k), k=0, 1, \dots, N\text{-}1\}$, can be computed in terms of the two $N/2$ points FFTs of the two sequences:

$$S_1=\{S(k)+S(N/2+k);\ k=0, 1,\dots, N/2\text{-}1\}$$
$$S_2=\{[S(k)-S(N/2+k)]\cdot W^k;\ k=0,1,\dots,N/2\text{-}1\} \qquad (2.1)$$

By executing the following D&C procedure, large problem FFT(N) can be solved in small array $A(n)$:

Procedure FFT(S, X, N);

if $N \bullet n$ then solve FFT(S, X, N) in $A(n)$

else split S into S_1 and S_2 according to (2.1);
FFT(S_1, X_1, $N/2$);
FFT(S_2, X_2, $N/2$);
combine X_1, X_2 into X
end if
end procedure

Let $N=2^L$, $n=2^l$,$d=L-l$, partitioning sequence S for d times, we can get 2^d sequences of length n whose FFT problem can be solved in $A(n)$. Using $A(n)$ for 2^d times, problem FFT(S, X, N) can be solved.

4.3 Batcher's odd-even merge

Suppose $A=\{a_1, a_2, \ldots, a_n\}$, $B=\{b_1, b_2, \ldots, b_n\}$ are two sorted sequences of length n, we want to merge them into a sorted sequence $C=\{c_1, c_2, \ldots, c_{2n}\}$ of length $2n$. In Batcher's algorithm, each of A, B is splited into two subsequences of length $n/2$:

$$A_1=\{a_1, a_3, \ldots, a_{n-1}\} \qquad A_2=\{a_2, a_4, \ldots, a_n\}$$
$$B_1=\{b_1, b_3, \ldots, b_{n-1}\} \qquad B_2=\{b_2, b_4, \ldots, b_n\} \qquad (3.1)$$

then merge A_1 and B_1 into $C_1=\{d_1, d_3, \ldots, d_{2n-1}\}$, merge A_2 and B_2 into $C_2=\{d_2, d_4, \ldots, d_{2n}\}$. In sequence $D=\{d_1, d_2, \ldots, d_{2n-1}, d_{2n}\}$, comparison-interchange operation is performed in each pair (d_{2i}, d_{2i+1}) to form sorted pair (c_{2i}, c_{2i+1}) for $i=1, 2, \ldots, n-1$. Let $c_1=d_1$, $c_{2n}=d_{2n}$, the result sequence $C=\{c_1, c_2, \ldots, c_{2n}\}$ is obtained.

It is obvious that the problem of merge two sorted sequences of length n can be partitioned into two merge problems of length $n/2$. Both in cube, shuffle-exchange or mesh connected SIMD machine Batcher's merge algorithm can be implemented[6]. Suppose we have such an array $A(n)$ which can only merge two sequences of length n, and we want to solve Merge(A, B, C, N), the problem of merging two sequences of length $N(N>n)$, in $A(n)$. We can use the following D&C procedure:

Procedure Merge(A, B, C, N);
if $N \bullet n$ then solve Merge(A, B, C, N) in $A(n)$
else split A into A_1 and A_2, B into B_1 and B_2 according to (3.1)
Merge (A_1, B_1, C_1, $N/2$);
Merge (A_2, B_2, C_2, $N/2$);
combine C_1 and C_2 into D and form C
end if
end procedure

If $N=2^L$, $n=2^l$, $d=L-l$, Merge(A, B, C, N) can be partitioned into 2^d merge problems of length n, and it can be solved by using $A(n)$ for 2^d times.

5 Conclusion

A general method of solving large problems in fixed size processor array is presented. The method is based on the D&C technique and is applicable to all recurrence problems. Since size limitation is a major disadvantage of processor array, the efficient solution of arbitrarily large problems is very important in high speed computation of array processor. Our method provides a mechanical way to partition computations and data of the large problem and to schedule the computations of fixed size processor array. It is a practical method to solve the size mismatch problem of processor array.

REFERENCE

1. Hwang K, Cheng Y H. Partitioned matrix algorithm for VLSI arithmetic systems, *IEEE Trans. on Computers*, Dec, 1982 C-31(12)pp. 549-558
2. Moldovan D I, Fortes J A B. Partitioning and mapping algorithms into fixed size systolic arrays, *IEEE Trans. on Computers*, Jan. 1986 C-35 (1)pp. 1-12
3. Chuang H Y H, He G. Design of problem-size independent systolic array systems, *Proc. of International Conf. on Computer Design*: VLSI in Computers, Oct. 1984
4. Chuang H Y H, Chen L. A general approach to solving arbitrarily large problems in a fixed size systolic array, *Proc. of 21st Hawaii International Conf. on System Science*, Jan. (1988)pp.195-204
5. Hwang K, Briggs F A. Computer architecture and parallel processing, McGraw-Hill Book Company, (1984)pp.367-373
6. Thompson C D, Kung H T. Sorting on a mesh-connected parallel computer, *Comm. of ACM*. 1997, 20(4):pp.263-271

Chapter 12
Fault-tolerant Computing

ROUTING IN HYPERCUBE NETWORKS WITH A CONSTANT FRACTION OF FAULTY NODES

JIANER CHEN, GUOJUN WANG, SONGQIAO CHEN
College of Information Engineering, Central-South University of Technology, ChangSha, Hunan 410083, P. R. China

We consider routing in hypercube networks with a very large number (i.e., up to a constant fraction) of faulty nodes. Simple and natural conditions are identified under which hypercube networks with a very large number of faulty nodes still remain connected. The conditions can be detected and maintained in a distributed manner based on localized management. Efficient routing algorithms on hypercube networks satisfying these conditions are developed. For a hypercube network that satisfies the conditions and may contain up to 37.5% faulty nodes, our algorithms run in linear time and for any two given non-faulty nodes find a routing path of length bounded by four times the Hamming distance between the two nodes. Moreover, our algorithms are distributed and local-information-based in the sense that each node in the network knows only its neighbors' status and no global information of the network is required by the algorithms.

1 Introduction

Routing has been a popular topic in the study of computer networks. With the continuous increasing in network size, routing in large size networks with faults has become unavoidable. In particular, it is important to know whether the non-faulty nodes in a given network with faults still remain connected. Let G be a network. The *fault tolerance* of G is the maximum integer k such that removing any k nodes in G does not disconnect the network [1]. Network fault tolerance has been another important issue in the study of computer networking [17]. In particular, routing in networks with faults has attracted considerable attention in the last decade [2,3,4,10,20].

Hypercube networks are among the earliest network models studied by researchers, and still remain as one of the most important and attractive network models. In particular, the high symmetry, the strong hierarchical structure, and the maximal fault tolerance are among the most attractive properties of the hypercube networks [1]. Several research and commercial hypercube machines have been built in recent years [5,11,12].

It is well-known [15] that the fault tolerance of the n-dimensional hypercube network H_n is $n-1$. Indeed, since H_n is n-regular (i.e., each node in H_n has

This work is supported by the China National Natural Science Foundation for Distinguished Young Scholars and by the Changjiang Scholar Reward Project.

exactly n neighbors), removing the n neighbors of any node u will obviously disconnect u from the other part of the network. In fact, this is the only way to remove n nodes to disconnect H_n [15]. Thus, the fault tolerance $n-1$ of H_n just characterizes this extreme case.

The shortcomings of using the above definition to measure hypercube networks' ability of toleranting faults have been observed. First of all, the probability that the n faulty nodes in H_n are exactly the n neighbors of a non-faulty node is very low. Therefore, the fault tolerance of H_n actually characterizes a very unlikely situation for the network H_n. Secondly, the ratio $(n-1)/2^n$ of the number of faulty nodes to the total number of nodes in H_n is too small to have a practical impact, in the following sense. Suppose each node in the network H_n has an equal probability ρ of failure, where $\rho > 0$ is a constant independent of the network size, then the expected number of faulty nodes in the n-dimensional hypercube network H_n is $\rho \cdot 2^n$. Thus, we can expect that in general there is always a constant fraction of faulty nodes in the network H_n. However, the ratio $(n-1)/2^n$ is in general much smaller than the constant ρ even if ρ is very small and n is moderate. For example, consider $n = 20$ and $\rho = 0.1\%$. Then the ratio $(n-1)/2^n < 0.002\%$, which is much smaller than ρ. On the other hand, previous research has given strong evidence that a hypercube network can tolerant a constant fraction of faulty nodes. For example, Najjar and Gaudiot [16] have demonstrated that for the 10-dimensional hypercube network with 1024 nodes, 33% of the nodes can fail and network can still remain connected with a probability of 99%. Thus, the definition above for the fault tolerance significantly underestimates the power of hypercube networks for toleranting network faults.

Much effort has been devoted that attempts to introduce more realistic definitions to measure networks' ability of toleranting faults. In particular, these studies try to allow the n-dimensional hypercube network to have more than $n-1$ faulty nodes. Several approaches, such as the concept of *forbidden set* [6,13,14] and *cluster fault tolerance model* [7,8], have been proposed for this purpose. In particular, based on the idea of the forbidden sets, the concept of *k-safe hypercube networks* has been introduced and studied by several researchers [6,9,14,18]. A hypercube network H_n is *k-safe* if each non-faulty node in H_n has at least k non-faulty neighbors.

It is not difficult to see that a k-safe n-dimensional hypercube network cannot tolerant more than $2^k(n-k)-1$ faulty nodes [14]. Moreover, only for 1-safe and 2-safe hypercube networks, efficient routing algorithms have been studied and developed [6,9,18]. Therefore, the study in this line of research still assumes that the number of faulty nodes in the n-dimensional hypercube network H_n is bounded by $O(n)$. To authors' knowledge, there has not been any development of efficient routing algorithms for a fault tolerance model that allows the number of faulty nodes to be larger than $O(n)$.

In the current paper, we introduce a new and natural definition for network fault tolerance. We show that under this new definition, the hypercube networks satisfying certain conditions can have a large fraction of faulty nodes while still keep the non-faulty nodes connected. The required conditions can be easily detected and maintained in a distributed manner based on localized management. Efficient routing algorithms on such hypercube networks are developed. Our routing algorithms are simple but powerful. First of all, our routing algorithms are applicable no matter whether the given hypercube network satisfies the required conditions: in case the network satisfies the required conditions, the algorithms successfully construct the routing path, while in case our algorithms fail in finding a routing path, they report correctly that the network does not satisfy the required conditions. Second, our algorithms are distributed and local-information-based, in the sense that each node in the network only knows its neighbors' status and no global information of the network is required by the algorithms. Finally, our algorithms are effective and efficient. For example, suppose that the given n-dimensional hypercube network H_n satisfies the required conditions. Then even in case that the network H_n has up to 37.5% faulty nodes, our algorithms will run in time $O(n)$ and for any two given non-faulty nodes successfully construct a routing path of length bounded by 4 times the Hamming distance between the two nodes.

2 The local subcube-connectivity

The *n-dimensional hypercube H_n* (or shortly the *n-cube*) consists of 2^n nodes, each is labeled by a distinguished binary string of length n. Two nodes in H_n are adjacent if the binary labels of them differ by exactly one bit. Each binary string $b_1 b_2 \cdots b_{n-k}$ of length $n-k$ corresponds to a *k-dimensional subcube H_k in H_n* (or shortly a *k-subcube*) of 2^k nodes whose labels are of the form $b_1 b_2 \cdots b_{n-k} x_{n-k+1} \cdots x_n$, where each x_j is either 0 or 1. The subcube H_k will also be written as $H_k = b_1 b_2 \cdots b_{n-k} * *$. It is easy to see that each k-subcube of H_n is isomorphic to the k-cube. Note that there are other subgraphs of H_n that are isomorphic to the k-cube. However, in this paper, we only consider "basic" k-subcubes of the form $b_1 b_2 \cdots b_{n-k} * *$.

Definition The n-cube network H_n is *locally k-subcube-connected* if in each k-dimensional subcube H_k of H_n, less than half of the nodes in H_k are faulty and the non-faulty nodes of H_k make a connected graph.

According to the definition, in a locally k-subcube-connected n-cube H_n, a k-subcube may have up to $2^{k-1} - 1$ faulty nodes. In consequence, the locally k-subcube-connected n-cube H_n may have totally up to $2^{n-k}(2^{k-1} - 1) = 2^{n-1} - 2^{n-k}$ faulty nodes. When k is large enough, this number can be arbitrarily close to one half of the total number of nodes in H_n.

We also point out that the conditions of the local k-subcube-connectivity of the n-cube H_n can be detected and maintained in a distributed manner based on localized management: for each k-subcube H_k in H_n, we can set up a managing program, executed on a processor in H_k, which manages and reports the status of the k-subcube H_k.

Lemma 2.1 *Let H_h be an h-subcube in a locally k-subcube-connected n-cube H_n, where $h \geq k$. Then the number of faulty nodes in H_h is less than half of the total number of nodes in H_h.*

Although a locally k-subcube-connected n-cube may contain a very large number of faulty nodes, the nice property of it is that it still keeps all the non-faulty nodes connected, as shown in the following theorem.

Theorem 2.2 *The non-faulty nodes in a locally k-subcube-connected n-dimensional hypercube H_n make a connected graph.*

PROOF. We prove by induction on all $h \geq k$ that the non-faulty nodes in any h-subcube H_h of H_n make a connected graph. This is true for $h = k$ by the definition of the local k-subcube-connectivity of the n-cube H_n.

Now suppose that $h > k$ and that H_h is an h-dimensional subcube of H_n. It suffices to show that for any two non-faulty nodes u and v in H_h, there is a path of non-faulty nodes in H_h that connects u and v. Let the h-subcube H_h be $H_h = b_1 b_2 \cdots b_{n-h} * *$, where $b_1 b_2 \cdots b_{n-h}$ is a fixed binary string of length $n - h$.

The h-subcube H_h can be decomposed into two $(h-1)$-dimensional subcubes H_{h-1}^0 and H_{h-1}^1, where $H_{h-1}^0 = b_1 \cdots b_{n-h} 0 * *$, and $H_{h-1}^1 = b_1 \cdots b_{n-h} 1 * *$. If the nodes u and v are both in H_{h-1}^0, or both in H_{h-1}^1, then by our inductive hypothesis, there is a path of non-faulty nodes in H_{h-1}^0, or in H_{h-1}^1, which connects u and v. In both cases, we will obtain a path of non-faulty nodes in H_h that connects the nodes u and v.

Now suppose that the node u is in H_{h-1}^0 and the node v is in H_{h-1}^1. Note that for each node $b_1 \cdots b_{n-h} 0 x_{n-h+2} \cdots x_n$ in H_{h-1}^0, there is exactly one adjacent node $b_1 \cdots b_{n-h} 1 x_{n-h+2} \cdots x_n$ in H_{h-1}^1. Thus, the 2^h nodes in H_h can be partitioned into 2^{h-1} pairs of adjacent nodes, each has one node in H_{h-1}^0 and the other node in H_{h-1}^1. By Lemma 2.1, the total number of faulty nodes in H_h is less than 2^{h-1}. Thus, there must be a pair of adjacent non-faulty nodes w_0 and w_1 such that w_0 is in H^0_{h-1} and w_1 is in H^1_{h-1}. By our inductive hypothesis, there is a path P_0 of non-faulty nodes in H^0_{h-1} that connects u and w_0, and there is also a path P_1 of non-faulty nodes in H^1_{h-1} that connects w_1 and v. Now the concatenation of the path P_0, the edge $[w_0, w_1]$, and the path P_1 gives a path of non-faulty nodes in H_h that connects u and v.

This proves, inductively, that for any two non-faulty nodes u and v in the locally k-subcube-connected n-cube H_n, there is a path of non-faulty nodes that connects u and v. In consequence, the non-faulty nodes of H_n make a connected graph. This completes the proof. □

Theorem 2.2 shows a nice property for the hypercube networks: local connectivity in a hypercube network implies global connectivity of the network. In many cases, the local connectivity of a hypercube network can be easily verified and Theorem 2.2 can be conveniently used to ensure the global connectivity of the hypercube network. The following corollary gives a simple example.

Corollary 2.3 *Let H_n be an n-dimensional hypercube in which each 3-dimensional subcube has at most two faulty nodes. Then the non-faulty nodes in H_n make a connected graph.*

PROOF. The connectivity of the 3-dimensional hypercube is 3 [15]. Thus, the non-faulty nodes of a 3-subcube with at most two faulty nodes make a connected graph. Therefore, the H_n given in the corollary is locally 3-subcube-connected. Now the corollary follows from Theorem 2.2. □

Combining Theorem 2.2 and Lemma 2.1 also gives us the corollary.

Corollary 2.4 *If the n-cube H_n is locally k-subcube-connected, then H_n is also locally h-subcube-connected for all $h \geq k$.*

PROOF. If the n-cube H_n is locally k-subcube-connected, then by the definition, for $h \geq k$ each of its h-subcube H_h is also locally k-subcube-connected. By Theorem 2.2, the non-faulty nodes of H_h make a connected graph. Moreover, by Lemma 2.1, the number of faulty nodes in H_h is less than half of the total number of nodes in H_h. Since H_h is an arbitrary h-subcube in H_n, this proves that the n-cube H_n is locally h-subcube-connected. □

The conditions in Theorem 2.2 require that k be fixed and that for *every* k-subcube, the number of faulty nodes be less than 2^{k-1} and the non-faulty nodes make a connected graph. Now we consider a more general situation, in which an entire k-subcube may become totally faulty. We will show that even in this situation where the faulty nodes are not distributed very uniformly, the n-cube can still remain connected.

Definition The n-dimensional hypercube network H_n is *locally subcube-connected* if for every k-subcube H_k of H_n, where $k \geq 1$, there is an h-subcube H_h containing H_k (thus $h \geq k$) such that H_h is locally h-subcube-connected.

The local k-subcube-connectivity obviously implies the local subcube-connectivity. On the other hand, the local subcube-connectivity provides more flexible conditions on the hypercube networks. To see this, let us compare the local subcube-connectivity with the local 3-subcube-connectivity. A locally subcube-connected n-cube H_n may have a 3-subcube H_3 such that H_3 contains more than half faulty nodes (in the worst case, even all 8 nodes in H_3 are faulty), or the non-faulty nodes in H_3 do not make a connected graph, as long as, say, the 5-subcube containing H_3 is locally 5-subcube-connected.

Theorem 2.5 *The non-faulty nodes in a locally subcube-connected n-dimensional hypercube H_n make a connected graph.*

PROOF. The theorem follows directly from the definition: since the n-cube H_n is locally subcube-connected and there is no other subcube in H_n that contains H_n, the n-cube H_n itself must be locally n-subcube-connected. Now by the definition of the local n-subcube-connectivity, the non-faulty nodes in H_n make a connected graph. □

From the proof of Theorem 2.5, we see that a locally subcube-connected n-cube H_n is actually locally n-subcube-connected. In fact, there must exist a smallest integer $k \geq 1$ such that the locally subcube-connected n-cube H_n is locally k-subcube-connected. However, such a k may not be given. This is another difference between local subcube-connectivity and local k-subcube-connectivity, which will affect the efficiency of our routing algorithms.

3 Routing in locally connected hypercube networks

Theorem 2.2 and Theorem 2.5 give conditions under which hypercube networks remain connected. Thus, under the conditions of the theorems, routing using only non-faulty nodes becomes possible. Unfortunately, the proofs of the theorems do not translate into efficient routing algorithms. In particular, to find a pair of adjacent non-faulty nodes, one in H^0_{n-1} and the other in H^1_{n-1}, would take time $O(2^{n-1})$ in the worst case. We are more interested in routing algorithms whose time is bounded by a low-degree polynomial of n.

We first present an efficient routing algorithm for locally k-subcube-connected hypercube networks. The algorithm is given in Figure 1.

Theorem 3.1 *If the input n-cube H_n is locally k-subcube-connected, then the algorithm* **Routing-I** *constructs a path of non-faulty nodes from u to v in time $O(n2^k)$.*

Algorithm. Routing-I

Input: an n-dimensional hypercube H_n with faults and two non-faulty nodes u and v in H_n

Output: a path of non-faulty nodes in H_n that connects u and v

1. let $u = u_1u_2 \cdots u_n$ and $v = v_1v_2 \cdots v_n$, where u_i and v_i are binary bits;
2. $w = w_1w_2 \cdots w_n$, where $w_j = u_j$ for all j;
3. initialize the path $P = [u]$;
4. **for** $i = 1$ **to** $n - k$ **do**

   {at this point, we have, inductively, a path P of non-faulty nodes from $u = u_1u_2 \cdots u_n$ to $w = w_1w_2 \cdots w_n$, where $w_j = v_j$ for $j = 1, 2, \ldots, i-1$.}

   if $w_i \neq v_i$ {so $v_i = \overline{w_i}$} **then**

   find two adjacent non-faulty nodes

   $w' = w_1 \cdots w_{i-1}w_iw_{i+1} \cdots w_{n-k}x_{n-k+1} \cdots x_n$ and

   $v' = w_1 \cdots w_{i-1}v_iw_{i+1} \cdots w_{n-k}x_{n-k+1} \cdots x_n$;

   extend the path P from w to w' in the k-subcube $w_1w_2 \cdots w_{n-k}**$, then to v';

   let $w = v'$;
5. {at this point, we have $w_j = v_j$ for all $j = 1, 2, \ldots, n-k$}

   extend the path P from w to v in the k-subcube $v_1v_2 \cdots v_{n-k} **$.

{**Remark.** if at any point the algorithm could not proceed, then **stop:** the n-cube H_n is not locally k-subcube-connected. }

Figure 1. Routing in a locally k-subcube-connected n-cube

PROOF. The constructed path P starts with a single node u. Inductively, assume that before the ith execution of the loop in Step 4, the path P of non-faulty nodes is from the source node u to a node w such that the first $i-1$ bits of w match the first $i-1$ bits of the destination node v. In the ith execution of the loop in Step 4, the algorithm "converts" the ith bit w_i of w into v_i. Consider the two k-subcubes $H_k^0 = w_1 \cdots w_{i-1}w_iw_{i+1} \cdots w_{n-k} **$ and $H_k^1 = w_1 \cdots w_{i-1}v_iw_{i+1} \cdots w_{n-k} **$ (note $v_i = \overline{w_i}$). Since each of H_k^0 and H_k^1 has less than half nodes that are faulty, we must be able to find two adjacent non-faulty nodes, $w' = w_1 \cdots w_{i-1}w_iw_{i+1} \cdots w_{n-k}x_{n-k+1} \cdots x_n$ and $v' = w_1 \cdots w_{i-1}v_iw_{i+1} \cdots w_{n-k}x_{n-k+1} \cdots x_n$, in H_k^0 and H_k^1, respectively. Finding the nodes w' and v' takes time $O(2^k)$. Now since the n-cube H_n is locally k-subcube-connected, the non-faulty nodes in the k-subcube H_k^0 are connected. Thus, we can find a path of non-faulty nodes, in time $O(2^k)$, from w to w' in the k-subcube H_k^0. Now since the nodes w' and v' are adjacent, the path P can be further extended from w' to v'. We then let $w = v'$. Note that now the node w has its first i bits identical to that of the destination node v.

Each execution of the loop in Step 4 takes time $O(2^k)$ to extend the path P. After the $n-k$ executions of the loop, the node w has its first $n-k$ bits identical to that of v. Thus, the nodes w and v now are in the same k-subcube H_k of H_n. Since the non-faulty nodes in H_k make a connected graph, we can spend another $O(2^k)$ time to further extend the path P from w to v in the k-subcube H_k, and complete a path of non-faulty nodes in H_n from u to v.

In conclusion, if the input n-cube H_n is locally k-subcube-connected, then the algorithm **Routing-I** constructs a path of non-faulty nodes from u to v. The running time of the algorithm, as discussed above, is bounded by $O((n-k)2^k) = O(n2^k)$. □

Remark 1. In case k is small, for example $k = 3$, the routing algorithm **Routing-I** runs in linear time. On the other hand, suppose k is large and H_n is locally k-subcube-connected. Then for each large k-subcube H_k, we may put no constraints on the structure of H_k. The only thing we can assume is that the subgraph consisting of the non-faulty nodes in H_k is connected and contains more than half of the nodes in H_k. Note that the subcube H_k may contain very structurally complicated subgraphs since the Subgraph Problem on Hypercubes is NP-hard [19]. Therefore, using a linear time $O(2^k)$ algorithm (e.g., a DFS procedure) to search for the non-faulty nodes in H_k seems unavoidable.

Remark 2. The algorithm **Routing-I** is distributed and local-information-based, in the following sense. No global information about the network H_n is required by the algorithm. The only thing we assume is that from each non-faulty node y, our algorithm can request the status of the neighbors of y. Step 4 of the algorithm may need some explanation. When we look for a non-faulty pair $\{w', v'\}$ in Step 4, we actually only search for non-faulty nodes in the k-subcube $w_1 \cdots w_{i-1} w_i w_{i+1} \cdots w_{n-k} **$, based only on the neighbors' status. For each non-faulty node y we find in the k-subcube $w_1 \cdots w_{i-1} w_i w_{i+1} \cdots w_{n-k} **$, we immediately check its neighbor y' in the k-subcube $w_1 \cdots w_{i-1} v_i w_{i+1} \cdots w_{n-k} **$. Therefore, the non-faulty pair $\{w', v'\}$ in the algorithm can be found using only local information.

Remark 3. The length of the path P constructed by the algorithm **Routing-I** is bounded by $(n-k+1)2^k - 1$, because in each execution of the loop in Step 4, the length of the path P is increased by at most 2^k, and Step 5 increases the path length by at most another $2^k - 1$. If k is small, the length of the path P is of order $O(n)$. Even when k is large, in many cases, the path length can be significantly reduced. For example, in each execution of the loop in Step 4, we may use BFS procedure to find the non-faulty nodes w' and v' such that w' is the closest such a node to w in the k-subcube $w_1 \cdots w_{i-1} w_i w_{i+1} \cdots w_{n-k} **$. In most cases, the distance from w to w' in the k-subcube $w_1 \cdots w_{i-1}w_iw_{i+1} \cdots w_{n-k} * *$ is much smaller than 2^k.

In particular, for locally 3-subcube-connected n-cube H_n, we have the following corollary. Note that a locally 3-subcube-connected n-cube H_n may contain up to $(3/8) \cdot 2^n$ faulty nodes, which is 37.5% of the total number of nodes in H_n.

Corollary 3.2 *For a locally 3-subcube-connected hypercube network H_n, the algorithm* **Routing-I** *runs in linear time and constructs a routing path from u to v of length bounded by 4 times the Hamming distance between u and v.*

PROOF. That the algorithm **Routing-I** runs in linear time was explained in Remark 1. Before the ith execution in the loop of Step 4, it is easy to see that we have $w_j = v_j$ for $1 \leq j \leq i-1$, and $w_j = u_j$ for $i \leq j \leq n-3$ (note we have $k = 3$ here). Therefore, only for the bit positions at which u and v differ, the path P needs to be extended. Since each of the 3-subcubes $w_1 \cdots w_{i-1}w_iw_{i+1} \cdots w_{n-3} * *$ and $w_1 \cdots w_{i-1}v_iw_{i+1} \cdots w_{n-3} * *$ contains at most three faulty nodes, the distance from w to the node w' in the 3-subcube $w_1 \cdots w_{i-1}w_iw_{i+1} \cdots w_{n-3} * *$ is at most 3. Therefore, the distance from w to the node v' is at most 4. In conclusion, for each bit position at which u and v differ, the path P increases its length by at most 4. This completes the proof of the corollary. □

Now we consider routing in a locally subcube-connected hypercube network. Consider the algorithm **Routing-II** given in Figure 2

Suppose that H_n is a locally subcube-connected n-cube given in the algorithm **Routing-II**, and let $k_{\min}$ be the smallest integer such that the n-cube H_n is locally $k_{\min}$-subcube-connected. Thus, in every $k_{\min}$-subcube, the number of faulty nodes is less than $2^{k_{\min}}/2$ and the non-faulty nodes make a connected graph. We show that the algorithm **Routing-II** constructs in time $O(n2^{k_{\min}})$ a path of non-faulty nodes from u to v in H_n. If the value $k_{\min}$ is known, then we can apply the algorithm **Routing-I** to construct the path. However, here we assume that the algorithm **Routing-II** does not know the value $k_{\min}$. Note that finding the value $k_{\min}$ directly in the n-cube H_n can be very time consuming.

Theorem 3.3 *Suppose that H_n is a locally subcube-connected n-cube in the algorithm* **Routing-II**, *and let $k_{\min}$ be the smallest integer such that the n-cube H_n is locally $k_{\min}$-subcube-connected. Then the algorithm* **Routing-II** *constructs a path of non-faulty nodes in H_n from u to v in time $O(n2^{k_{\min}})$.*

PROOF. Before the ith execution of the loop in Step 5 of the algorithm **Routing-II**, we assume inductively that we have constructed a path P of non-faulty nodes from u to $w = w_1w_2 \cdots w_n$ with $w_j = v_j$ for all $j = 1, 2, \ldots, i-1$. By the definition of the value $k_{\min}$, there must be an integer $k \leq k_{\min}$ such that both k-subcubes $H_k^0 = w_1 \cdots w_{i-1}w_iw_{i+1} \cdots w_{n-k} * *$ and

Algorithm. Routing-II

Input: an n-dimensional hypercube H_n with faults and two non-faulty nodes u and v in H_n

Output: a path of non-faulty nodes in H_n that connects u and v

1. let $u = u_1 u_2 \cdots u_n$ and $v = v_1 v_2 \cdots v_n$, where u_i and v_i are binary bits;
2. $w = w_1 w_2 \cdots w_n$, where $w_j = u_j$ for all j;
3. initialize the path $P = [u]$;
4. $i = 1$;
5. **while** $(i \leq n)$ **do**

   {at this point, we assume that we have a path P of non-faulty nodes from $u = u_1 u_2 \cdots u_n$ to $w = w_1 w_2 \cdots w_n$, where $w_j = v_j$ for $j = 1, 2, \ldots, i-1$.}

   if $w_i \neq v_i$ {so $v_i = \overline{w_i}$}
   then
   done = false;
   $k = 1$;
   while (not done) AND $(k \leq n - i)$ **do**
   if in the k-subcube $w_1 w_2 \cdots w_{n-k} * *$, there is a path of non-faulty nodes from w to a node $w' = w_1 \cdots w_{i-1} w_i w_{i+1} \cdots w_{n-k} x_{n-k+1} \cdots x_n$, and node $v' = w_1 \cdots w_{i-1} v_i w_{i+1} \cdots w_{n-k} x_{n-k+1} \cdots x_n$ is non-faulty
   then extend the path P from w to w' in the subcube $w_1 w_2 \cdots w_{n-k} * *$;
   extend the path P further from w' to v';
   $w = v'$;
   done = true;
   else $k = k + 1$;
   if $k > n - i$
   then
   while in the k-subcube $w_1 w_2 \cdots w_{n-k} * *$, there is no path of non-faulty nodes from the node w to the node v **do**
   $k = k + 1$;
   extend the path P from w to v in $w_1 w_2 \cdots w_{n-k} * *$;
   stop: The path constructed.
   else $i = i + 1$
   else $i = i + 1$;

{**Remark.** if at any point the algorithm could not proceed, then **stop:** the n-cube H_n is not locally subcube-connected.}

Figure 2. Routing in a locally subcube-connected n-cube

$H_k^1 = w_1 \cdots w_{i-1} v_i w_{i+1} \cdots w_{n-k} * *$ are locally k-subcube-connected. Now since both H_k^0 and H_k^1 have more than half non-faulty nodes, we must be able to find a non-faulty node $w' = w_1 \cdots w_{i-1} w_i w_{i+1} \cdots w_{n-i} x_{n-i+1} \cdots x_n$ in H_k^0 and a non-faulty node $v' = w_1 \cdots w_{i-1} v_i w_{i+1} \cdots w_{n-i} x_{n-i+1} \cdots x_n$ in H_k^1. Since all non-faulty nodes in H_k^0 are connected, the path P now can be extended in H_k^0 from w to w', then to v'. This completes the conversion of the ith bit of w from w_i to v_i. Note the difference from the algorithm **Routing-I** is that here we do not know the value $k_{\min}$. Thus, we try all possible values $k = 1, 2, \ldots$. Also noted is that in many cases, we may be able to find the nodes w' and v' in the subcubes H_k^0 and H_k^1, where k is much smaller than $k_{\min}$ (and maybe even the subcubes H_k^0 and H_k^1 are not locally k-subcube-connected). The point is that in the worst case when we have $k = k_{\min}$, the nodes w' and v' must exist in the subcubes H_k^0 and H_k^1.

For each value k, we need to check whether the non-faulty nodes w' and v' exist in the k-subcubes H_k^0 and H_k^1, respectively, such that w' is connected to w in H_k^0 and v' is adjacent to w'. All these can be done in time $O(2^k)$ for each value k using any standard searching procedure such as Depth First Search. Since such non-faulty nodes w' and v' must exist when we eventually reach $k = k_{\min}$, the total amount of time spent on each execution of the loop in Step 5 of the algorithm **Routing-II** is bounded by

$$O(2^1) + O(2^2) + \cdots O(2^{k_{\min}}) = O(2^{k_{\min}})$$

Therefore, the total time complexity of Step 5 of the algorithm **Routing-II** is $O(n2^{k_{\min}})$.

We should also explain the situation when k is increased in Step 5 and reaches $k > n-i$. Thus, no non-faulty nodes w' and v' are found in the $(n-i)$-subcubes H_{n-i}^0 and H_{n-i}^1. This gives us directly $k_{\min} > n-i$. Moreover, since the first $i-1$ bits of w and v are identical, the nodes w and v are now actually in the same $k_{\min}$-subcube. Thus, we try to find the smallest k such that w and v are connected in the same k-subcube, starting from $k = n-i+1$. Similar to the above analysis, this can be done in time $O(2^{k_{\min}})$.

Thus, in time $O(n2^{k_{\min}})$, the algorithm **Routing-II** constructs a path from u to v in the locally subcube-connected n-cube H_n. □

Again, we should point out that in general, the actual computation time of the algorithm **Routing-II** can be much better than $O(n2^{k_{\min}})$. This is particularly true when the n-cube H_n has relatively fewer faulty nodes so that most small subcubes in H_n are subcube-connected. In this case, converting each bit of w into the corresponding bit of v in general can be done in k-subcubes with k much smaller than $k_{\min}$.

References

1. S. B. Akers and B. Krishnamurthy, A group-theoretic model for symmetric interconnection networks, *IEEE Trans. Comput. 38*, (1989), pp. 555-565.
2. M.-S. Chen and K. G. Shin, Depth-first search approach for fault-tolerant routing in hypercube multicomputers, *IEEE Trans. Parallel Distrib. Syst. 1*, (1990), pp. 152-159.
3. T. C. Lee and P. Hayes, A fault-tolerant communication scheme for hypercube computers, *IEEE Trans. on Comput. 41*, (1992), pp. 1242-1256.
4. G.-M. Chiu and S.-P. Wu, A fault-tolerant routing strategy in hypercube computers, *IEEE Trans. Comput. 45*, (1996), pp. 143-154.
5. A. L. DeCegama, *The Technology of Parallel Processing – Parallel Processing Architectures and VLSI Hardware*, Prentice Hall, 1989.
6. A. H. Esfahanian, Generalized measures of fault tolerance with application to n-cube networks, *IEEE Trans. Comput. 38*, (1989), pp. 1586-1591.
7. Q.-P. Gu and S. Peng, Optimal algorithms for node-to-node fault tolerant routing in hypercubes, *The Computer Journal 39*, (1996), pp. 626-629.
8. Q.-P. Gu and S. Peng, k-pairwise cluster fault tolerant routing in hypercubes, *IEEE Trans. Comput. 46*, (1997), pp. 1042-1049.
9. Q.-P. Gu and S. Peng, Unicast in hypercubes with large number of faulty nodes, *IEEE Trans. Parallel Distrib. Syst. 10*, (1999), pp. 964-975.
10. Q.-P. Gu and S. Peng, An efficient algorithm for the k-pairwise disjoint paths problem in hypercubes, *Journal of Parallel and Distributed Computing 60*, (2000), pp. 764-774.
11. Intel Corp., *Intel iPSC System Overview*, Jan. 1986.
12. NCUBE Corp., *NCUBE/ten: An Overview*, Beaverton, OR, Nov. 1985.
13. S. Latifi, Combinatorial analysis of the fault diameter of the n-cube, *IEEE Trans. Comput. 42*, (1993), pp. 27-33.
14. S. Latifi, M. Hedge, and M. Naraghi-Pour, Conditional connectivity measures for large multiprocessor systems, *IEEE Trans. Comput. 43*, (1994), pp. 218-222.
15. F. T. Leighton, *Introduction to Parallel Algorithms and Architectures: Arrays, Trees, Hypercubes* , Morgan Kaufmann, San Mateo, CA, 1992.
16. W. Najjar and J. L. Gaudiot, Network resilience: a measure of network fault tolerance, *IEEE Trans. Comput. 39*, (1990), pp. 174-181.
17. M. O. Rabin, Efficient dispersal of information for security, load balancing, and fault tolerance, *Journal of ACM 36*, (1989), pp. 335-348.
18. S. B. Tien and C. S. Raghavendra, Algorithms and bounds for shortest paths and diameter in faulty hypercubes, *IEEE Trans. Parallel Distrib. Syst. 4*, (1993), pp. 713-718.
19. A. Wagner and D. Corneil, Embedding trees in a hypercube is NP-complete, *SIAM Journal on Computing 19*, (1990), pp. 570-590.
20. J. Wu, Reliable unicasting in faulty hypercubes using safety levels, *IEEE Trans. Comput. 46*, (1997), pp. 241-247.

Reliable Unicasting in Faulty Hypercube Multicomputers Based on Local Safety Information

Dong Xiang
Inst. of Microelectronics
Tsinghua University
Beijing, 100084, P. R. China
xd@dns.ime.tsinghua.edu.cn

Jie Wu
Dept. of Comp. Sci. and Eng.
Florida Atlantic University
Boca Raton, FL 33431, USA
jie@cse.fau.edu

Abstract

This paper studies fault-tolerant routing for injured hypercubes using local safety information. It is shown that a minimum feasible path is always available if the spanning subcube that contains both source and destination nodes is safe, even though the hypercube is fully unsafe. The safety information outside the spanning subcube is applied only when derouting is needed. A routing scheme based on local safety information is proposed and the extra cost to obtain local safety information is comparable to the one based on global safety information. The proposed algorithm guarantees to find a minimum feasible path if the spanning subcube is contained in a maximal safe subcube and the source is locally safe in the maximal safe subcube. Simulation results are provided to demonstrate the effectiveness of the method.

1 Introduction

The hypercube architecture has drawn considerable attention and was used by recent commercial machines, such as SGI Origin 2000 [5]. Recent studies show that the hypercube structure is quite suitable for distributed shared memory systems [3] and multicomputer systems [7] when the size of the system is not too large. Hypercube multicomputers can handle a reasonable amount of message traffic, and also provide some degree of fault-tolerance.

Fault-tolerant communication in direct networks has been studied extensively in [1,2,4,8-12]. Peercy and Banerjee [8] introduced a fault-tolerant routing mechanism that is based on routing tables. A distributed table-filing algorithm was presented to construct routing tables. Lee and Hayes [4] proposed the concept of safe node for the first time. Safety information is used to avoid faulty nodes and unsafe nodes which could cause communication difficulty. A fault-free node is called unsafe if it has two faulty or unsafe neighbors; otherwise, it is called safe. A safe node always has a minimum feasible path (i.e., a shortest fault-free path) to any destination in the cube. The proposed routing algorithm can route a message via a path of length no greater tahn two plus the Hamming distance between the source and dstination as long as the hypercube is not fully unsafe. Wu and Fernandez [9] and Chiu and Wu [2] refined the safe node concept by expanding the safe node set. Basically, a fault-free node is unsafe if it has at least two faulty neighbors or it has at least three unsafe and faulty neighbors; otherwise, it is safe. A feasible path of length no more than the Hamming distance between the source and the destination plus four can be established as long as the hypercube is not fully unsafe.

Wu [11] further enhanced the safe node concept by introducing the concept of safety level to assist fault-tolerant routing. The algorithm proposed by Wu guarantees to find a minimum feasible path if the safety level of the source is at least k when the Hamming distance between the source and destination nodes is k. Safety vector [10] and routing capability [1] are enhancements of safety level. Directed routing capability was also introduced in [1] to handle fault-tolerant routing in hypercubes by slightly relaxing the safety condition of routing capability.

In this paper, a new concept called *local safety* is introduced to facilitate fault-tolerant routing. This study is motivated by the fact that many fault-free nodes can still communicate through a minimum or near-minimum path even though they are unsafe under the refined safe node model [9]. Such cases occur when the spanning subcube that contains both nodes is safe. The status of subcubes are captured by local safety information. Local safety information of maximal safe subcubes is utilized by the fault-tolerant routing algorithm. A minimum feasible path exists if the spanning subcube is contained in a maximal safe subcube and the source is locally safe in the maximal safe subcube.

2 Preliminaries

An $n-$dimensional hypercube has 2^n processors (or nodes). Each processor u can be represented by a sequence of n binary bits $(u_n u_{n-1} \ldots u_2 u_1)$, where $u_i \in \{0, 1\}$. Two processors are connected by a bidirectional link if and only if the binary representations of the two processors differ in exactly one bit. The Hamming distance between two nodes s and d, denoted by $H(s, d)$, is the number of bits in which the labels of s and d differ. The spanning subcube $SC(s, d)$ between s and d represents the smallest subcube that contains s and d. We only consider message-passing between fault-free nodes. We consider node failure only. A path is feasible if there is no faulty node in the path. A path is called a *minimum feasible path* if length of the path is equal to the Hamming distance from the source to the destination.

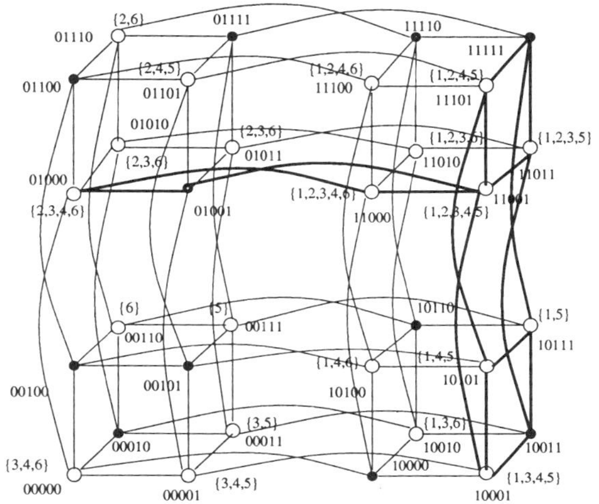

Figure 1: A Fully Unsafe 5−Cube with 11 Faulty Nodes

The safe node concept was introduced for the first time by Lee and Hayes [4], which was refined by Wu and Fernandez [9] and Chiu and Wu [2]. We consider only node failure in this paper. The method can also be extended to the mixed fault model with both node and link failures.

Definition 1 *(Wu and Fernandez [9] and Chiu and Wu [2]): A fault-free node in an $n-$dimensional hypercube is unsafe if it has at least two faulty neighbors, or it has at least three unsafe and faulty neighbors in total. A faulty cube is called fully unsafe if it contains no safe node; otherwise, it is safe.*

Definition 2 *(Chiu and Wu [2]) Unsafe nodes are classified according to degree of unsafeness: A node is ordinarily unsafe if it has at least one safe neighbor; otherwise, it is a strongly unsafe node.*

Definition 3 *A node in an $n-$cube is locally unsafe with respect to a subcube SC if it has at least two faulty neighbors, or at least three locally unsafe or faulty neighbors inside SC; otherwise, it is locally safe with respect to SC. A subcube is fully unsafe if it contains no locally safe node; otherwise, it is a safe subcube.*

Definition 4 *Locally unsafe nodes corresponding to a subcube SC is classified on the basis of local unsafeness degree: a locally unsafe node with respect to SC is called locally ordinarily unsafe if it has at least one locally safe neighbor; otherwise, it is a locally strongly unsafe node.*

The 5−cube as shown in Fig. 1, which contains 11 faulty nodes, is fully unsafe. Node 11011 is strongly unsafe in the 5−cube, but it is locally safe in the subcubes **0**, *1***, and locally ordinarily unsafe in ****1, where * indicates that bit can be assigned both 0 and 1. Consider message routing between 01110 and 10001. The nodes 01110 and 10001 are both strongly unsafe nodes in the 5-cube because the 5−cube is fully unsafe. It is hard to handle message routing between any two fault-free nodes inside the faulty 5−cube according to the safe node concepts [7,13,3]. The source 01110 has a fault-free neighbor 01010, which is locally safe in the maximal safe subcube **0**. It is quite easy to find a minimum feasible path from 01010 and 10001.

We shall show how local safety information increases the size of the safe node set, and enhances degree of fault-tolerance.

Lemma 1 *If a node is locally unsafe in a* $k-$*dimensional subcube* SC_1*, it is still locally unsafe in an* $m-$*dimensional* $(m > k)$ *subcube* SC_2 *if* SC_2 *contains* SC_1.

Proof: Assume s is locally unsafe corresponding to SC_1, s has k neighbors inside SC_1. Among the k neighbors, there are at least 2 faulty neighbors or at least 3 locally unsafe or faulty neighbors. The source s has $m-k$ extra neighbors in the $m-$dimensional subcube SC_2 and SC_2 contains SC_1. It is impossible for s to become locally safe in SC_2. ∎

Lemma 2 *Suppose a node* s *is locally safe in an* $m-$*dimensional subcube* SC_2*, it is still locally safe in a* $k-$*dimensional subcube* SC_1 $(k < m)$ *if* SC_2 *contains* SC_1.

Proof: The source s has m neighbors in the $m-$dimensional subcube SC_2. Among the m neighbors, s has at most one faulty neighbor and at most 2 locally unsafe or faulty neighbors in SC_2 according to Definition 4 because s is locally safe in SC_2. In the $k-$dimensional subcube SC_1, s has only k of the m neighbors in SC_2. Certainly, among the k neighbors, s has fewer than 2 faulty neighbors and fewer than 3 locally unsafe or faulty neighbors corresponding to SC_2. Therefore, the source s should still be locally safe in SC_1. ∎

Theorem 1 *Local safety information never decreases the size of the safe node set inside a subcube compared with that obtained by using global safety information.*

Definition 5 *We define an* $m-$*dimensional subcube as a maximal safe subcube if it is safe, and any* $k-$*dimensional* $(k \geq m+1)$ *subcube contains it is fully unsafe.*

The reason why we need maximal safe subcubes is to reduce calculation and storage of local safety information. A faulty hypercube has a unique set of maximal safe subcubes. The scheme to calculate local safety information is not introduced for simplicity, which can be found from [12].

The fully unsafe 5−cube as shown in Fig. 1 contains six 4−dimensional maximal safe subcubes. The six 4−dimensional maximal safe subcubes are 1****, *1***, **0**, ***0*, ****1, and ****0, which are represented by labels 1, 2, 3, 4, 5, and 6, respectively. Each fault-free node has a label to represent the subset of maximal safe subcubes that contain the node. Node 00000 has a label $\{3, 4, 6\}$ as shown in Fig. 1, which indicates that the maximal safe subcubes **0**, ***0*, and ****0 contains 00000.

3 Minimum Feasible Path Problem

The safety status of the spanning subcube $SC(s, d)$, the minimum subcube that contains the source s and the destination d, has important effects on message routing between s and d. The size of the safe node set in $SC(s, d)$ can be increased when considering local safety of the spanning subcube $SC(s, d)$, rather than based on the entire hypercube.

Theorem 2 *Assume the spanning subcube $SC(s, d)$ between a source s and a destination d is an $H(s, d)-$dimensional subcube ($H(s, d) < n$) in the faulty $n-$cube. There always exists a minimum feasible path from s to d if either s or d is locally safe in $SC(s, d)$ even though the faulty hypercube is fully unsafe.*

Proof: We only consider the case when the source s is locally safe. The case, when the destination is locally safe, is similar. We would like to prove the theorem by induction. When $H(s, d) = 1$, messages from s can be routed to d directly. There exists at least one fault-free neighbor s' in $SC(s, d)$ when $H(s, d) = 2$ because the source s is locally safe corresponding to $SC(s, d)$. Messages in s can be transmitted to the destination d via s'. When $H(s, d) = 3$, the source s has at least one neighbor s' in one of the minimum feasible paths between s and d where s' is locally safe corresponding to $SC(s, d)$. It is easy to find a path of length 2 from s' to d as stated above. Therefore, there exists at least one minimum feasible path from s to d when $H(s, d) = 3$.

Assume the theorem follows when $H(s, d) = k$. We would like to prove the theorem also holds when $H(s, d) = k + 1$ ($k > 3$). The source s has $k + 1$ neighbors in $k + 1$ distinct minimum feasible paths between s and d. Among the $k + 1$ neighbors, there exists at least one locally safe neighbor s' of s inside $SC(s, d)$ according to Definition 3. Node s' is also locally safe in $SC(s, d)$ according to Lemma 2, therefore, $SC(s', d)$ is also safe. There exists one minimum feasible path of length k between s' and d according to the premise because $H(s', d) = k$. It is clear that the theorem also holds when $H(s, d) = k + 1$. ∎

Corollary 1 *There exists a minimum feasible path from a source s to a destination d if both s and d are contained in a safe subcube SC and either s or d is locally safe in SC even if the hypercube is fully unsafe.*

In Theorem 3, we show it is easy to find a minimum feasible path when either the source s or the destination d is locally ordinarily unsafe, and the spanning subcube $SC(s, d)$ is a safe subcube.

Theorem 3 *Suppose $SC(s, d)$ is safe, both of s and d are locally unsafe in $SC(s, d)$. There always exists a minimum feasible path between s and d if either s or d is locally ordinarily unsafe even if the faulty hypercube is fully unsafe.*

Proof: There are two cases, (1) the source is locally ordinarily unsafe corresponding to $SC(s, d)$, (2) the destination is locally ordinarily unsafe inside $SC(s, d)$. We consider only case (1), proof of case (2) is similar.

Assume the source s is a locally ordinarily unsafe node, it has a locally safe neighbor s' inside $SC(s, d)$ according to Definition 4. Node s' is in one of the minimum feasible paths from s to d according to the premise, which should still be a locally safe node inside $SC(s', d)$ according to Lemma 2. The spanning subcube $SC(s', d)$ is thus safe according to Definition 3 because it contains at least one locally safe node s'. It is easy to find a minimum path from s' to d according to Theorem 2. ∎

Corollary 2 *There exists a feasible path of length no greater than $H(s, d) + 2$ from a source s to a destination d if the spanning subcube $SC(s, d)$ of s and d is contained in a safe subcube SC and either s or d is locally ordinarily unsafe in SC even if the hypercube and $SC(s, d)$ are fully unsafe.*

Chiu and Wu [2] proved that a strongly unsafe node always has an ordinarily unsafe node in a safe hypercube. We can extend the result to the following lemma.

Lemma 3 *Suppose the subcube SC is an $m-$dimensional safe subcube in a faulty $n-$cube ($n \geq m$). A locally strongly unsafe node in SC always has a locally ordinarily unsafe neighbor inside SC even though the faulty $n-$cube is fully unsafe.*

Theorem 4 *Let the spanning subcube $SC(s, d)$ be a safe subcube ($H(s, d) \leq n$) in a faulty $n-$cube, inside which both of the source s and the destination d are locally strongly unsafe. There always exists a minimum feasible path from s to d even if the hypercube is fully unsafe.*

Proof: The source s is a locally strongly unsafe node inside $SC(s, d)$ according to the premise. The source s has at least one locally ordinarily unsafe neighbor s' inside $SC(s, d)$ according to Lemma 3 because $SC(s, d)$ is a safe subcube.

All of s's $H(s,d)$ neighbors inside $SC(s,d)$ are in one of the minimum paths from s to d. Certainly, s' is in one of the minimum feasible paths from s to d. The node s' has at least one locally safe neighbor s'' corresponding to $SC(s,d)$ according to Definition 4. Among the $H(s,d)$ neighbors of s', one is s, and the other $H(s,d)-1$ are all in $H(s,d)-1$ distinct minimum paths from s' to d. Certainly, the node s'' is in one of the minimum paths of length $H(s,d)-2$ from s' to d. It is clear that s'' is also a locally safe node in the spanning subcube $SC(s'',d)$ according to Lemma 2 because $SC(s,d)$ contains $SC(s'',d)$. There always exists a minimum feasible path from a locally safe node s'' inside $SC(s'',d)$ to the destination d according to Theorem 2 because $SC(s'',d)$ is a safe subcube. ■

Corollary 3 *There exists a feasible path of length no greater than $H(s,d)+4$ from a source s to a destination d if $SC(s,d)$ is contained in a safe subcube SC_1 and both of s and d are locally strongly unsafe in SC_1 even if the hypercube and the spanning subcube $SC(s,d)$ are fully unsafe.*

Corollary 4 *There always exists a minimum feasible path from a source s to a destination d if the spanning subcube $SC(s,d)$ is safe even though the faulty hypercube is fully unsafe.*

Corollary 4 can be obtained easily from Theorems $2 \sim 4$.

In the rest of this section, we would like to illustrate the existence of a minimum feasible path from a source s to a destination d in a fully unsafe hypercube if the spanning subcube $SC(s,d)$ is also fully unsafe. In the following theorem, we show under certain conditions there still exists a minimum feasible path from s to d if there is a fault-free node s' in one of the minimum feasible paths from s to d and the subcube $SC(s',d)$ is safe even though the spanning subcube $SC(s,d)$ is fully unsafe.

Lemma 4 *Let s' be a fault-free neighbor of s and be in one of the minimum feasible paths from the source s to the destination d in a faulty $n-$cube. There always exists a minimum feasible path from s to d if the spanning subcube $SC(s',d)$ is safe even if the subcube $SC(s,d)$ is fully unsafe and the $n-$cube is fully unsafe.*

Proof: There exists a minimum feasible path from s' to d according to Theorem 4 because the $H(s',d)-$dimensional spanning subcube $SC(s',d)$ is a safe subcube and s' is fault-free. The node s' is in one of the minimum feasible paths from s to d according to the premise. The minimum feasible path from s to d has been found. This follows the theorem. ■

The above lemma can be generalized into the following theorem.

Theorem 5 *There exists a minimum feasible path from the source s to the destination d if there exists a node v along a minimum feasible path from s to d such that both $SC(s,v)$ and $SC(v,d)$ are safe.*

Theorem 5 can be generalized into the following theorem. Let $\{D_1, D_2, \ldots, D_k\}$ be a partition of $D(s,d)$, and $H(s,d)$ be the size of the set $D(s,d)$. Subcubes $SC(s,v_1)$, $SC(v_1,v_2)$, ..., $SC(v_{k-1},d)$ $(k \leq H(s,d))$ can be established based on the partition. Assume $SC(s,v_1)$ and $SC(v_1,v_2)$, $SC(v_1,v_2)$ and $SC(v_2,v_3)$, ..., $SC(v_{k-2},v_{k-1})$ and $SC(v_{k-1},d)$ have a common node $v_1, v_2, \ldots, v_{k-1}$, respectively.

Theorem 6 *There always exists a minimum feasible path from a source s to a destination d if* $SC(s,v_1)$, $SC(v_1,v_2)$, ..., $SC(v_{k-1},d)$ $(k \leq H(s,d))$ *are safe subcubes, and* $v_1, v_2, \ldots, v_{k-1}$ *are fault-free.*

4 Fault-Tolerant Routing Algorithm

A fault-tolerant routing algorithm is presented based on local safety information. Assume information about maximal safe subcubes of the hypercube is available at each node (like the one shown in Fig. 1). When the spanning subcube of a source and a destination is found to be contained in a maximal safe subcube, the following algorithm can always pass the message from the source to the destination. When a maximal safe subcube containing the spanning subcube is not available, route the message to a fault-free neighbor s', taking the preference to the one in a minimum feasible path from the source to the destination. Check whether the subcube $SC(s',d)$ is contained in a maximal safe subcube or not. If the subcube $SC(s',d)$ is contained in a maximal safe subcube, a feasible path has been found. The procedure *message-pass*(v,d,S) passes the message from v to d when it is certain that the message can be routed successfully inside the subcube S that contains the spanning subcube $SC(v,d)$. When the distance between the current node to the destination is equal to one, route the message via the dimensions they differ. If the distance between the current node and the destination is equal to 2, route the message to a fault-free neighbor along one of the minimum feasible paths from v to d. When the distance is greater than or equal to 3, pass the message as follows,

1. When the current node v is locally strongly unsafe inside the subcube S, route the message to one of its locally ordinarily unsafe neighbors in a minimum feasible path from v to d if possible; otherwise, route the message to a locally strongly unsafe neighbor of v in a minimum path from v to d if possible. When both of the above cases fail, route the message to a locally ordinarily unsafe neighbor in a non-minimum path from v to d, which is always available.
2. When v is locally ordinarily unsafe, route the message to a locally safe neighbor in a minimum feasible path from v to d if possible; otherwise, route the message to a locally ordinarily unsafe neighbor of v in a minimum feasible path from v to d if possible. When both cases do not meet, route the message to a locally safe neighbor of v in a non-minimum path from v to d.
3. When v is locally safe in S, route the message to a locally safe neighbor of v, which is in a minimum feasible path from v to d.

message-pass(v,d,S) /* v: current node; d: destination; S contains SC(v,d). */

1. If H(v,d) = 0, deliver the message to the local node. If H(v,d) = 1, then route the message to d via the only dimension v and d differ, exit.
2. If H(v,d) = 2, route the message to a fault-free neighbor of v along a minimum feasible path from v to d; exit.
3. If H(v,d) is greater than or equal to 3, do
   (a) if v is locally safe in S, route the message to a locally safe neighbor inside S along a minimum feasible path from v to d; exit.
   (b) assume v is locally ordinarily unsafe in S, route the message to a locally safe neighbor along a minimum feasible path from v to d if possible; otherwise, route the message to a locally ordinarily unsafe neighbor in a minimum feasible path from v to d; if both cases fail, route the message to a locally safe neighbor along a non-minimum path from v to d; exit.
   (c) assume v is locally strongly unsafe in the subcube S, route the message to a locally ordinarily unsafe neighbor in a minimum feasible path from v to d if possible; otherwise, route the message to a locally strongly unsafe neighbor in a minimum feasible path from v to d if possible; if both cases fail, route the message to a locally ordinarily unsafe neighbor in a non-minimum path from v to d; exit.

The fault-tolerant routing algorithm can be described as follows:

route(s,d) (fault-tolerant routing with local safety information)

1. If the spanning subcube SC(s,d) is contained in a maximal safe subcube msc, then call message-pass(s,d,msc); exit.
2. Select a neighbor s′ along a minimum feasible path from s to d where SC(s′,d) is contained in a maximal safe subcube msc, the order of preference for s′ is: locally safe, locally ordinarily unsafe, locally strongly unsafe, pass the message to s′; call message-pass(s′,d,msc) a t s′; exit.
3. Select a neighbor s′ along a non-minimum feasible path from s to d, where SC(s′,d) is contained in a maximal safe subcube msc. The preference order to select s′ is: locally safe, locally ordinarily unsafe, locally strongly unsafe, pass the message to s′; call message-pass(s′,d,msc) at s′; exit.
4. For all other cases, fail and exit at s.

Consider message passing from 11101 to 11010 in the hypercube presented in Fig. 1. The spanning subcube is 11*** which is contained in 1****. Node 11101 is locally safe in subcube 1****. There exists a minimum feasible path from 11101 to 11010. Consider message passing from 00110 to 11001. The message can be passed to 01110 or 00111 firstly because both $SC(00111, 11001)$ and $SC(00111, 11001)$ are maximal safe subcubes although the 5-cube is fully unsafe. A minimum feasible path from 00110 to 11001 can always be found using the algorithm route() based on local safety information.

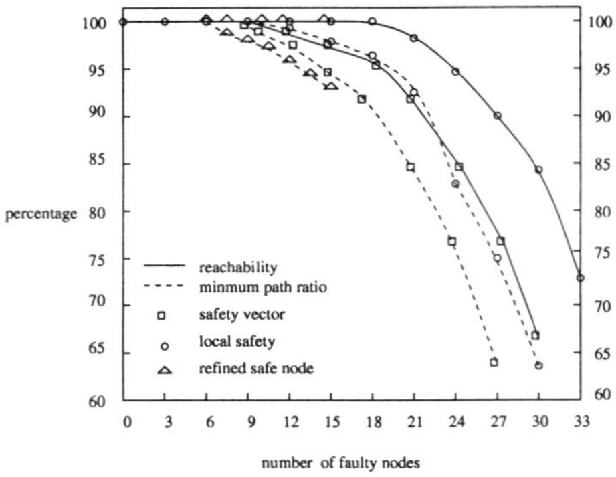

Figure 2: Performance evaluation for a 6−cube

Theorem 7 *Let s and d be a source and a destination, respectively. The algorithm route() can always route a message along a minimum feasible path if the spanning subcube $SC(s,d)$ is a maximal safe subcube.*

Theorem 8 *Let s and d be a source and a destination, respectively. The algorithm route() can always get a minimum feasible path if spanning subcube $SC(s,d)$ is contained in a maximal safe subcube, in which either the source or the destination is locally safe.*

The algorithm route() can still find a minimum feasible path even though the conditions given in Theorems 7 and 8 are not met in many cases.

Theorem 9 *Let s and d be the source and destination, respectively. The algorithm route() can always route a message along a feasible path of length no greater than $H(s,d)+4$ if the spanning subcube $SC(s,d)$ is contained in a maximal safe subcube.*

Theorem 10 *The algorithm route() can always find a feasible path of length no more than $k+2$ if the source s and destination d are contained in a maximal safe subcube.*

Theorem 11 *Let s and d be the source and destination, respectively. The algorithm route() can always find a feasible path of length no more than $H(s,d)+6$ if s has a fault-free neighbor s', where $SC(s',d)$ is contained in a maximal safe subcube msc.*

5 Simulation Results

We have implemented the proposed algorithm. Faulty nodes are injected into the hypercubes randomly. We present the average results of 50 trials. *reachability*

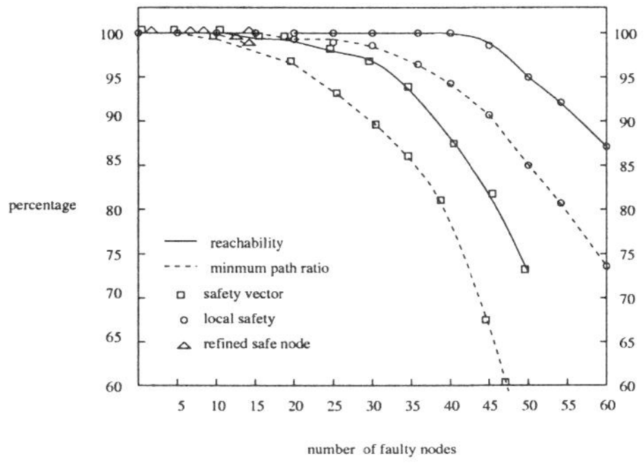

Figure 3: Performance evaluation for a 7−cube

indicates the percentage of successful message delivery, and *minimum path ratio* represents the ratio of message routing along a minimum feasible path. We do not include message routing between two neighboring nodes in the simulation experiments. We compare simulation results with ones based on refined safe node (Wu and Fernandez [9], Chiu and Wu [2]) and the safety vector [10] by Wu (also called routing capability [1] by Chiu and Chen). Simulation results show that local safety consistently works better than the refined safe node and safety vector.

As for the refined safe node, we record the simulation results when the probability for the hypercube to be safe is greater than a threshould. Simulation results present the case when the 6−cube contains as many as 14 faulty nodes. When the hypercube contains 14 faulty nodes, the router based on the refined safe node obtains about 92% minimum path ratio and 100% reachability, and safety vector obtains about 94% minimum path ratio and local safety gets more than 97% minimum path ratio. When the 6−cube contains more than 14 faulty nodes, the refined safe node does not apply. Simulation results show that the router based on the refined safe node gets more than 99% minimum path ratio and 100% reachability when the 7−cube contains 15 faulty nodes. When the 7−cube contains 45 faulty nodes, safety vector obtains more than 65% minimum path ratio and more than 80% reachability, and local safety gets about 90% minimum path ratio and 97% reachability.

6 Conclusions

A new concept called local safety was proposed to assist fault-tolerant message routing in hypercube multicomputers. It is found a minimum feasible path is always available if the spanning subcube is safe. A fully unsafe hypercube can be split into a unique set of maximal safe subcubes. In this way, many globally unsafe nodes become safe locally. The proposed algorithm guarantees to find a minimum feasible path if the spanning subcube is contained in a maximal safe subcube in which the source is locally safe. A feasible path of lenght no greater than the Hamming distance plus four exists if both the source and destination are contained in a maximal safe subcube. The algorithm guarantees to find a minimum feasible path from s to d of length no more than $H(s,d)+6$ if s has a fault-free neighbor s', where $SC(s',d)$ is contained in a maximal safe subcube. Simulation results were presented to demonstrate the effectiveness of the method comparing with the previous methods.

References

[1] G. M. Chiu and K. S. Chen, "Use of Routing Capability for Fault-Tolerant Routing in Hypercube Multicomputers," *IEEE Trans. Computers*, Vol. 46, No. 8, pp. 953-958, 1997.

[2] G. M. Chiu and P. S. Wu, "A Fault-Tolerant Routing Strategy in Hypercube Multicomputers," *IEEE Trans. Computers*, Vol. 45, No. 2, pp. 143-155, 1996.

[3] J. Duato and M. P. Malumbres, "Optimal Topology for Distributed Shared-Memory Multiprocessors: Hypercubes Again ?" Proc. 2-th *Int. Euro-Par Conf.*, pp. 205-212, 1996.

[4] T. C. Lee and J. P. Hayes, "A Fault-Tolerant Communication Scheme for Hypercube Computers," *IEEE Trans. Computers*, Vol. 41, No. 10, pp. 1242-1256, 1992.

[5] J. Laudon and D. Lenoski, "The SGI Origin: A ccNUMA Highly Scalable Server," Proc. of *Int. Symp. Comput. Architecture*, pp. 241-251, 1997.

[6] L. M. Ni and P. K. McKinley, "A Survey of Wormhole Routing Techniques in Direct Networks," *IEEE Computer*, Vo. 26, No. 2, pp. 62-76, 1993.

[7] M. Ould-Khaoua, "On Optimal Network for Multicomputers: Torus or Hypercube ?" Proc. of *4-th Int. Euro-Par Conf.*, pp. 989-992, 1998.

[8] M. Peercy and P. Banerjee, "Distributed Algorithms for Shortest Path, Deadlock-free Routing and Broadcasting in Arbitrarily Faulty Hypercubes," Proc. of *IEEE Fault-Tolerant Computing Symposium*, pp. 218-225, 1990.

[9] J. Wu and E. B. Fernandez, "Reliable Broadcasting in Faulty Hypercube Computers," *Microprocessing and Microprogramming*, Vol. 46, pp. 241-247, 1993.

[10] J. Wu, "Fault-Tolerant Distributed Unicasting Scheme for Cube-based Multicomputers," *Proc. of the 16th Int. Conf. on Distributed Computing Systems*, May 1996, 166-174.

[11] J. Wu, "Reliable Unicasting in Faulty Hypercubes Using Safety Levels," *IEEE Trans. Computers*, Vol. 46, pp. 241-247, 1997.

[12] D. Xiang and J. Wu, "Fault-Tolerant Multicasting in Hypercube Multicomputers Using Local Safety Information," Proc. of 13-th *Int. Conf. Parallel and Distributed Computing Systems,* pp. 529-534, Aug., 2000.

A RELIABLE ASYNCHRONOUS RPC ARCHITECTURE FOR WIRELESS NETWORKS

LEE MAN KEI AND JIA XIAOHUA

Computer Science Department, City University of Hong Kong
Hong Kong
E-mail: {mklee, jia}@cs.cityu.edu.hk

Asynchronous Remote Procedure Call (ARPC) is an RPC where the client will not be blocked waiting for the result. ARPC is very suitable for mobile environment due to its asynchronous nature. ARPC, however, cannot become a reliable and efficient communication method unless the problems, such as handoff and disconnection, are solved. This paper proposes an ARPC architecture, which is enhanced by several features that aim at avoiding packet lose during handoff, supporting for disconnection and minimizing communication overheads.

1 Introduction

The most common RPC protocol is synchronous RPC, in which the client will block itself after submitting an RPC request until it receives the result from the server, even though it is not essential as the result may not be required at once.

Asynchronous RPC (ARPC) is an RPC where clients can proceed without waiting for the results [3]. It is suitable for mobile environment. One reason is that as the communication delay becomes longer, the blocking time for mobile client is getting severe. Efficient usage of such blocking time thus becomes a key factor in improving mobile client application performance [4]. Another reason is that a client is often disconnected from the system to save power [1]. ARPC allows the client to be disconnected from the network and resumes connection later to collect the result, which is impossible for synchronous RPC. Although the semantic of ARPC seems well suited to mobile environment, several problems in wireless networks still have to be solved, such as the shortage of wireless bandwidth, handoff and disconnection of mobile hosts.

In this paper, we propose an ARPC architecture that facilitates ARPCs over wireless networks. To focus on the problems of wireless networks, we assume that components of wired networks are error free and have sufficient processing and storage capabilities. We also assume that clients are mobile and servers are fixed.

The structure of this paper is as follow: the background Mobile IP and ARPC mechanisms will be described in Session 2. The proposed ARPC architecture and its features will be discussed in Session 3. Our implementation experience will be briefly discussed in Session 4. Then, a performance analysis will be presented in Session 5. Finally, a conclusion will be given in Session 6.

2 Background

2.1 Mobile IP

In this paper, the addressing scheme of mobile hosts is based on **Mobile IP**, which is a standard [2] proposed by Internet Engineering Task Force (IETF). Each mobile host registers with a home agent (HA) and obtains its permanent IP address when it first connects to network. When it moves away from its HA, it registers with a foreign agent (FA) and is assigned a care-of-address (COA). The FA reports the COA of the mobile host to the HA. A binding table is used to match the mobile host IP with its current COA. The HA terminates the old connection with the old FA and tunnels messages to new FA after updating the binding table. When the mobile client sends a message to a fixed host, the mobile host IP is used as the return address and the message is sent directly to the fixed host from current FA. The fixed host replies the mobile host with the IP address of the mobile host. The message would be routed to its HA. The HA looks up the current COA of the mobile host from the binding table and sends the message to the current FA with the COA. The FA then relays the message to the mobile host.

2.2 Problems of Asynchronous RPC (ARPC) in Mobile Environment

When a client makes an ARPC, it creates a child thread to handle the ARPC and waits for the result. The parent thread keeps on proceeding with its own work [4]. In wireless network, regardless the server processing time, the time required for an ARPC can be quite long as the latency in wireless channel is long. During this long processing time, the mobile client may handoff and even disconnect from the network, which are the challenges for implementing ARPC in mobile environment.

Firstly, in Mobile IP addressing scheme, the handoff is not reliable enough. Consider a case where messages are sent to a mobile host. As described earlier, the HA intercepts all messages and tunnels them to the current FA. When the mobile host initiates a handoff, the HA tunnels packets to the new FA instead of the old one and tears down the old route. If there is any packet congested at the old route, it will be dropped by the old FA. It degrades the system performance as error recovery routine is triggered [2]. For an RPC, the result message may be dropped. It normally requires the client to retransmit the request. However, it creates problems for non-idempotent operations, not to mention the costs of wasted time and bandwidth.

Secondly, there is no support for disconnection of the mobile clients. If a mobile client disconnects for some reasons, such as for power saving, the result will be dropped [1]. The RPC fails even the mobile client resumes its connection later.

Thirdly, the wireless communication between client and server suffers limited available bandwidth while the valuable bandwidth has been spent on messages headers and connection setup. Though these overheads seem to be essential for each connection, it is desirable to reduce them for improving the system throughput.

3 Proposed Architecture for ARPC Agent in Wireless Networks

The existing RPC scheme suffers from poor efficiency and reliability in mobile environment since the scheme is not supposed to cater for frequent handoffs or even disconnections of mobile clients. To improve the performance of RPCs in wireless networks, we propose a new ARPC architecture as shown in Fig 1. The main feature is the introduction of an ARPC Agent. ARPC Agent is a process that cooperating with and running at the same site with the HA.

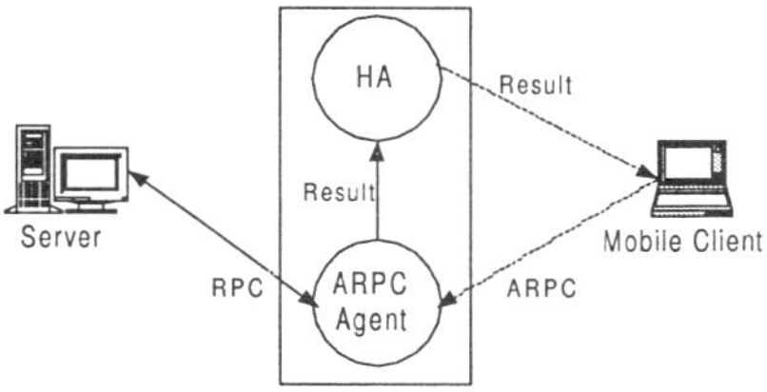

Figure 1. ARPC Agent Model

When a mobile client issues an ARPC request, the request is sent to the ARPC Agent. The Agent caches the request at its buffer and creates a thread that issues the RPC request to the server and waits for the result. When the result comes back, the Agent stores a copy of the result and forwards it to the mobile client by using its IP address. The Agent is required to cache the mobile client IP address, server IP address, the ARPC request and the ARPC result for each ARPC.

Mobile clients are required to return an acknowledgement back to the Agent whenever they receive the results. As the acknowledgement is returned, the Agent removes the buffered ARPC. When the Agent times out for the acknowledgement, it resends the result message periodically until an acknowledgement is received or the FA reports that the mobile client is disconnected from the network. For such case, the Agent keeps the result in its buffer until the client resumes communication later.

3.1 Handling of Handoff Operations

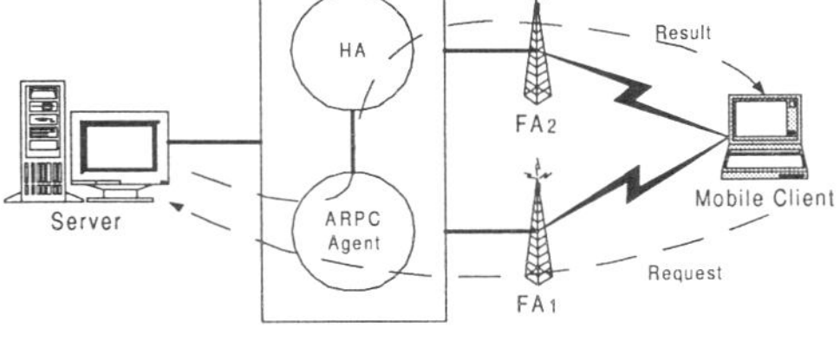

Figure 2. ARPC Messages flow during Handoff

When a mobile client issues an ARPC request and moves into another cell, we need to guarantee the delivery of results to the client correctly. If the mobile client moves away while the result is congested at the old FA and is finally dropped, the Agent times out. It resends the result periodically until the acknowledgement is received. As the handoff of mobile client is processed by the HA, the binding table of HA is updated during the handoff. The ARPC result will eventually be tunneled to the new FA. The mobile client thus can receive the result, as illustrated in above Fig. 2.

3.2 Support of Disconnections

Disconnection from the networks is a frequent operation in mobile environment to save power of mobile hosts. With the ARPC Agent, even if the mobile client disconnects from the network after issuing the request, the corresponding result can be retransmitted to the mobile client as the result is buffered at the Agent. The buffer is maintained in a permanent storage. It prevents the memory of the Agent being used up by accumulated RPCs and thus prevents the overflow of buffered messages as it is assumed that the host of the Agent has sufficient storage capacity.

When the mobile client resumes its connection at a FA, it registers its new COA with the HA. The HA is required to report this update to the ARPC Agent. The Agent then looks its buffer for any unacknowledged results buffered. If so, the Agent resends the results to the mobile client by Mobile IP as illustrated in Fig. 3. In this way, the mobile clients can collect all the results after resuming the disconnection without retransmitting processed requests.

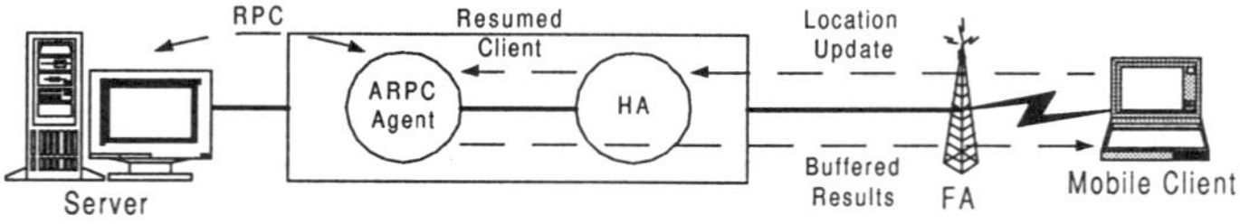

Figure 3. Retransmission upon Resume of Disconnection

The HA is enhanced with ARPC Agent to pick up the tasks since it is maintaining the binding table under Mobile IP scheme. When mobile hosts register their binding information to HA during each handoff and resumption of communication, the HA updated the COA of its mobile hosts. The HA thus becomes the only party that possesses accurate location of the mobile client upon resuming communication. It is the most suitable location for the ARPC Agent to process the ARPC requests for mobile clients and to trigger retransmissions.

3.3 Batch Processing of ARPC

In real world applications, RPC results are usually not required at once and the requests can be identified in earlier stages. Client applications can thus be optimized to issue the requests before they actually demand the results. In this case, the delay of RPCs is not critically important in the system, while the save of bandwidth on wireless channel can improve the system performance significantly. Hence, we group the ARPC requests together and send them as batches in earlier stages to reduce the overheads. As the requests are packed as a single request before sending out, the recipient of the single request must unpack it into separate requests and process them accordingly. Upon receiving a batched request, the Agent unpacks the requests and stores them as individual requests. Then the Agent issues the requests to corresponding servers and processes them accordingly as described earlier.

The batching is done by queuing all packed requests in FIFO order at client side. When the batch meets certain threshold, the whole queue is sent out. It is crucial to store the ARPC requests in FIFO order to maintain the client application semantics, serializability and consistency of remote information. The threshold is determined as the remaining waiting time of ARPCs. The waiting time is specified by the client. For real time ARPC, the waiting time can be specified as zero while others will be determined as positive number. As an APRC request is queued, a count down timer of duration specified by the waiting time is created. If any timer expires, the whole batch is sent out. It guarantees there is no starvation of requests, even the arrival rate of requests is low and the ARPCs are time critical.

4 Implementation Experience

A prototype of the proposed architecture has been implemented. The testbed consists of a laptop equipping a RadioLAN 10 Radionet Interface, a RadioLAN BackconeLINK base stations that connected to a 10BaseT Ethernet. The bandwidth of the RadioLAN is approximately 10Mbit/s. The laptop is programmed as client while the server is running on a Sun Workstations located at the ethernet segment. The prototype is built on top of Java RMI package that provides synchronous TCP/IP communication between client and server. The socket based RMI cannot support disconnection since disconnection implies terminating the TCP/IP channel and the disconnected channel cannot be resumed. This can be solved by using the connectionless UDP as long as the client resumes with the same IP address.

Disconnection is simulated by terminating the RadioLAN interface service at the laptop. The laptop would release the wireless channel and its MAC address and completely disconnects from the network while other processes is not interfered. The laptop resumes communication by restarting the interface service. The laptop regains the same IP address as the IP is explicitly specified by the laptop.

5 Performance Analysis

Since RPCs are processed asynchronously, the waiting time is no longer a dominant factor of the quality of RPCs. Instead, the processing time of each RPC and the number of RPCs issued contribute the major part of improvement. Following variables are introduced to justify the performance improved:

- T = mean transmission time between server and client
- S = mean service time of an RPC
- W = mean arrival time between RPCs, where $0 < W <= T + S$

- N = number of RPCs issued by client

Fig. 4 shows a comparison of RPCs which are processed synchronously and asynchronously where N = 3. The processing time of N RPCs processed synchronously and asynchronously can be generalized by the formulas:

$$T_{syn} = N\,(2T + S) + (N - 1)\,W$$
$$T_{asyn} = 2T + S + (N - 1)\,W$$

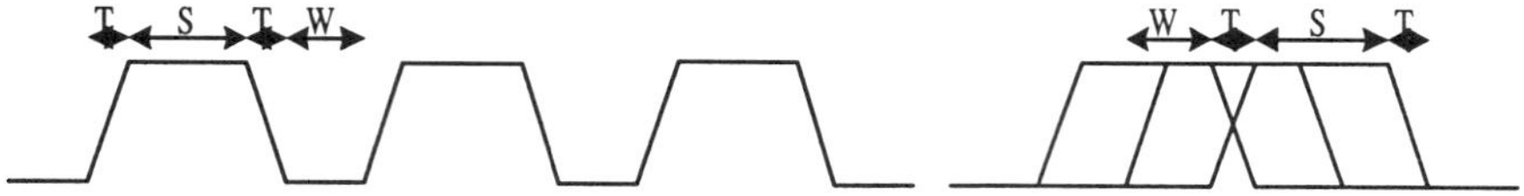

Figure 4. Synchronous vs. Asynchronous RPCs

Obviously, the asynchronously model saves time of (N – 1)(2T + S) over the synchronous model. That means no matter how many ARPCs are issued, the processing time is reduced to only one RPC processing time plus the message round strip time and the total waiting time for subsequent RPCs. Time saved is proportional to the mean RPC processing time and the number of RPCs issued.

6 Conclusion

Though synchronous RPC is popularly used in nowadays-distributed system, its blocking nature is not suitable for the mobile environment. It does not allow disconnection of mobile clients and cannot make effective use of the computing power during the long communication delay. In this paper, we proposed an asynchronous RPC architecture for wireless networks. The proposed architecture improves not only the reliability of the system but also the system performance. It avoids retransmission of non-idempotent requests and provides support to disconnected clients. We believe that our architecture can be acted as a basis for future development of wireless client-server based systems.

7 Reference

1. Bora A. Akyol & Donald C. Cox, "**Handling Mobility in a Wireless ATM Network**", IEEE Infocom, 1996, p. 1405 – 1413, Vol. 3
2. Charles E. Perkins, "**Mobile Networking Through Mobile IP**", IEEE Internet Computing, Jan – Feb, 1998, p. 58 - 69
3. Thomas Hopfner, Franz Fischer & Georg Färber, "**No Wait-RPC: Extending ONC RPC to a fully compatible Message Passing System**", IEEE IPPS/SPDP '98, Proceedings, p. 250 – 254
4. Liskov, B. & Shrira, L., "**Promises: Linguistic Support for Efficient Asynchronous Procedure Calls in Distributed System**", Proc. SIGPLAN '88

Fault-Tolerant Multicast Wormhole Routing in 2D Meshes

Jipeng Zhou & Francis C.M. Lau
Department of Computer Science and Information System
The University of Hong Kong, Hong Kong
E-mail:{jpzhou,fcmlau}@csis.hku.hk

Abstract

We present a deterministic and an adaptive fault-tolerant multicast wormhole routing algorithm for 2D meshes in this paper. The proposed algorithms are different from those in [2] [4], which are based on finding a Hamiltonian or Eulerian path in the network and cannot guarantee that each consecutive destination pair follows a shortest path in the multicast path when there is no faulty processor. The path-based multicast routing models in [3] and [1] are used to develop the fault-tolerant multicast wormhole routing algorithms here. The deadlock freedom of the proposed algorithms is dependent upon the order of the destination sets and the selection of the misrouting channels around the faulty PE. The proposed algorithms can tolerate faults in the one-fault model in 2D meshes. To the best of our knowledge, these algorithms are the first path-based fault-tolerant multicast algorithms using wormhole routing in the literature.

The given network with two virtual channels is decomposed into two mesh networks, VM_1 and VM_2, where each pair of adjacent processors is connected by a bidirectional virtual channel as shown in Figure 1; the dashed line denotes the virtual network VM_1, and the dotted line denotes VM_2. Each PE in VM_i, $i = 1, 2$, has four sets of ports that are connected to its four nearest neighbors, as shown in Figure 1, where $\{N_{i1}, E_{i1}, W_{i1}, S_{i1}\}$ and $\{N_{i2}, E_{i2}, W_{i2}, S_{i2}\}$ stand for the sets of input and output ports from/to the north, east, west and south neighbors in $VM_i, i = 1, 2$, respectively. Within a PE, any combination of the input ports can be connected to any combination of the output ports by the PE's routing software. This feature allows multiple messages to pass through a particular PE. Each node u is assigned a label $l(u)$. Figure 1 shows such a labeling in a 4×6 mesh, in which each node is represented by its integer coordinate (x, y). The label assignment function l for an $m \times n$ mesh can be expressed in terms of the $x-$ and $y-$coordinates of the nodes as following:

$$l(x,y) = \begin{cases} y * n + x & \text{if } y \text{ is even,} \\ y * n + n - x - 1 & \text{if } y \text{ is odd.} \end{cases}$$

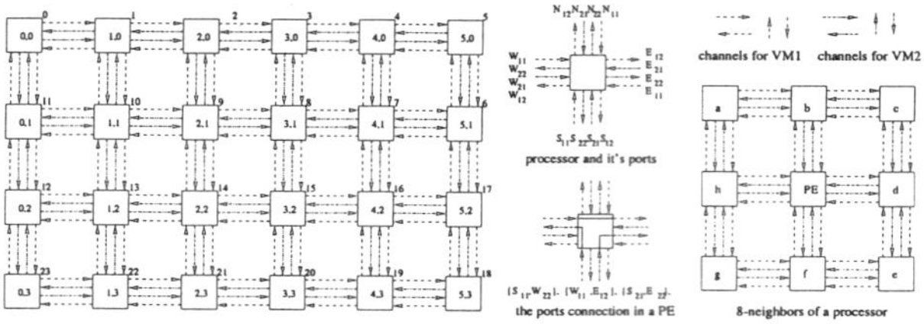

Figure 1: A 4 × 6 mesh with two virtual channels per physical channel.

This paper focuses on the development of routing protocols that can respond favorably to the presence of faulty components. There are two different types of faults, either the entire PE and its associated router would fail or just a physical link may fail. When a physical link fails, all virtual channels on that particular physical link are marked as faulty. When an entire PE fails, all physical links incident on the failed PE are also marked as faulty. Only faulty PEs are considered a basic faulty element for simplicity, and the one-fault model is used in this paper. We assume that each PE should know the states (faulty or safe) of its surrounding PEs after running a diagnostic program. Two PEs (x_0, y_0) and (x_1, y_1) are called 4-neighbors if $|x_0 - x_1| + |y_0 - y_1| = 1$, 8-neighbors if $max\{|x_0 - x_1|, |y_0 - y_1|\} \leq 1$. The one-fault model in this paper means that no two faulty PEs are 8-neighbors in 2D meshes.

1 Deterministic Routing

1.1 Deterministic Multicast Routing

Lin *et al.* [3] have developed *path-based* routing in which consecutive channels start from the source node and traverse each destination in the set. The algorithms described by Lin *et al.* in [3] have two parts: message preparation and routing. The first part splits the destination set for a message into two or more subsets, and then it sorts each subset. This part is called the split-and-sort function in [1]. The labeling effectively divides the network into two subnetworks. The *high-channel subnetwork* contains all of the channels whose direction is from lower-labeled nodes to higher-labeled nodes; an example is shown in (b) of Figure 2. The *low-channel network* contains all of the channels whose direction is from higher-labeled nodes to lower-labeled nodes; an example is shown in (c) of Figure 2. If the label of the destination node is greater than the label of the source node, the routing always takes place in the high-channel network; otherwise, it will take the low-channel network. The destination set D for a message generated at node n_s is divided into two subsets, D_H and D_L, such that D_H contains all the destination nodes with l value higher than $l(n_s)$ and D_L the nodes with l value lower than $l(n_s)$. The destination nodes in D_H are sorted in ascending order using l as the key. The same is done for D_L, but

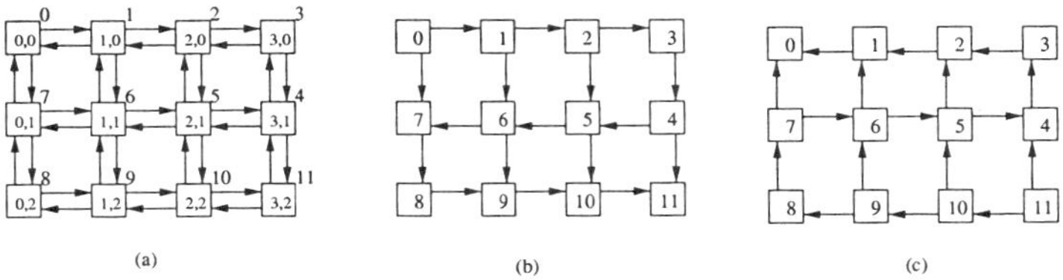

Figure 2: The high-channel and low-channel subnetwork in 3×4 mesh.

in descending order. The second part determines the path followed by the message until all the destination nodes are reached. It is determined by the routing function for deterministic routing or by the routing function and selection function for adaptive routing. Two deterministic algorithms have been described in [3]—dual-path and multi-path. They only differ in the message preparation part, splitting the destination set either into two subsets (dual-path) or into several subsets (multi-path). As we will only modify the routing function, we will focus on the dual-path algorithm in this paper.

Let V be the node set of the 2D mesh. The first step in finding a deadlock-free multicast algorithm for the 2D mesh is to define a routing function $R_1 : V \times V \rightarrow V$ that uses the two subnetworks in such a way as to avoid channel cycles. Here two nodes (i_0, j_0) and (i_1, j_1) are neighbors, which are 4-neighbors—*i.e.*, $|i_0 - i_1| + |j_0 - j_1| = 1$. One such routing function, for a source node u and destination node v, is defined as $R_1(u, v) = w$, such that w is a neighboring node of u, and, if $l(u) < l(v)$, then we have the following equation:

$$l(w) = max\{l(z) : l(z) \leq l(v) \text{ and z is a neighboring node of u}\},$$

or if $l(u) > l(v)$, then we have the following equation:

$$l(w) = min\{l(z) : l(z) \geq l(v) \text{ and z is a neighboring node of u}\}.$$

The routing algorithm defines a deterministic path for D_H in the high-channel network, and for D_L in low-channel network. As proved in [3], this routing function is deadlock-free and it forwards messages along a minimal path between successive destinations.

1.2 Deterministic Fault-Tolerant Multicast Routing

In order to present our deadlock-free fault-tolerant multicast routing algorithms in 2D meshes, the normal routing for D_H only uses the channel in the high-channel subnetwork of the virtual network VM_1, and the normal routing for D_L only uses the channel in the low-channel subnetwork of the virtual network VM_2; and one more virtual channel in the $y = 1$ and $y = m - 2$ rows is used to tolerate the faulty boundary PEs in the top edge and down edge of networks—these are virtual channels in VM_3, where each PE in these two rows has one more input and output port in the west direction, $\{W_{31}, W_{32}\}$, and in the east

Misrouting channel for D_L		Misrouting channel for D_H	
$\{W_{22}\} = h\bar{a}b$	$\{E_{22}\} = d\bar{e}f$	$\{N_{12}\} = h\bar{a}b$	$\{S_{12}\} = d\bar{e}f$
$\{W_{22}\} = h\bar{b}d$	$\{E_{22}\} = d\bar{f}h$	$\{E_{12}\} = h\bar{b}d$	$\{W_{12}\} = d\bar{f}h$
$\{N_{22}\} = b\bar{c}d$	$\{S_{22}\} = f\bar{g}h$	$\{E_{12}\} = b\bar{c}d$	$\{W_{12}\} = f\bar{g}h$
$\{N_{22}\} = b\bar{d}f$	$\{S_{22}\} = f\bar{h}b$	$\{S_{12}\} = b\bar{d}f$	$\{N_{12}\} = f\bar{h}b$

Table 1: Misrouting channel for faulty non-boundary PEs.

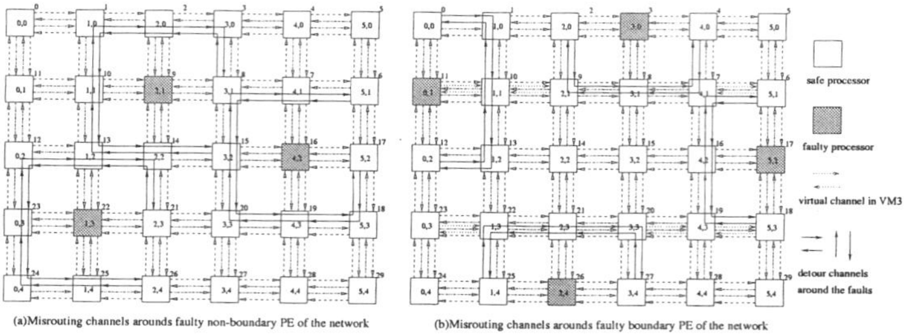

(a)Misrouting channels arounds faulty non-boundary PE of the network (b)Misrouting channels arounds faulty boundary PE of the network

Figure 3: Misrouting channels around the faulty PE.

direction, $\{E_{31}, E_{32}\}$, respectively. When a normal multicast routing is blocked by a faulty PE, the normal routing needs to detour around the faulty PE, which is called *misrouting*. The misrouting direction around the faulty PE for the corresponding normal routing is determined by the position and neighbors of the faulty PE. Here two nodes (i_0, j_0) and (i_1, j_1) are neighbors, which are 8-neighbors—*i.e.*, $max\{|i_0 - i_1|, |j_0 - j_1|\} \leq 1$. Each PE except the boundary PE of the mesh has eight neighbors, which are represented by the eight Boolean variables *a,b,c,d,e,f,g,h* and are shown in Figure 1. Each variable has a value 1 if the corresponding neighbor is a safe PE, has a value 0 if the corresponding neighbor is a faulty PE. For the boundary PE of the mesh, some neighbors do not exist, and the two dots over the corresponding variable denote that the neighbor does not exist and its value is equal to 1; for example $\ddot{h}$ denotes that the h neighbor of the PE does not exist and $\ddot{h} = 1$.

In multicast wormhole routing, the header flit contains the addresses of all destination PEs. The routing header starts from the source PE, transits through all destinations, comes to the last destination in the routing order where the message is consumed. According to the given routing function R_1 in the Section 1.1, the normal routings use function R_1, when the normal routing from the current PE u to the destination v is blocked by a faulty PE, i.e., $R_1(u, v) = w$, where w is a faulty PE; when w is not the boundary PE of the network, if $l(u) < l(v)$, the message is detoured around the faulty PE w along the channels in VM_1 according to misrouting for D_H in Table 1 until there is a PE w' such that $l(w) < l(w') \leq l(v)$; at this point, misrouting becomes normal routing from w'; if $l(u) > l(v)$, the message is detoured around the faulty PE w along the

/* Current PE $u = (u_x, u_y)$, current destination $v = (v_x, v_y)$ */

Faulty PE	Misrouting for D_L	Misrouting for D_H
left side	$\{N_{12}\} = b\bar{h}f$	$\{S_{22}\} = bhf$
	$\{N_{12}\} = h\bar{a}b$	$\{W_{12}\} = h\bar{a}b$
	$\{W_{22}\} = h\bar{g}f$	$\{S_{22}\} = h\bar{g}f$
	$\{E_{22}\} = \ddot{h}\bar{b}d$	$\{E_{12}\} = \ddot{h}\bar{f}d$
right side	$\{N_{22}\} = b\bar{d}f$	$\{S_{12}\} = bdf$
	$\{N_{22}\} = b\bar{c}d$	$\{E_{12}\} = b\bar{c}d$
	$\{E_{22}\} = d\bar{e}f$	$\{S_{12}\} = d\bar{e}f$
	$\{W_{22}\} = \ddot{d}\bar{b}h$	$\{W_{12}\} = \ddot{d}\bar{f}h$
top side	$\{W_{32}\} = h\bar{b}d$	$\{E_{32}\} = hbd$
	$\{N_{22}\} = b\bar{c}d$	$\{E_{32}\} = b\bar{c}d$
	$\{W_{32}\} = b\bar{a}h$	$\{N_{12}\} = b\bar{a}h$
	$\{S_{22}\} = \ddot{b}\bar{h}f$	$\{S_{12}\} = \ddot{b}\bar{d}f$
down side	$\{E_{32}\} = hfd$ & $u_x < v_x$	$\{W_{32}\} = hfd$ & $u_x < v_x$
	$\{W_{32}\} = hfd$ & $u_x > v_x$	$\{E_{32}\} = hfd$ & $u_x > v_x$
	$\{E_{32}\} = d\bar{e}f$ & $u_x < v_x$	$\{E_{32}\} = d\bar{e}f$ & $u_x < v_x$
	$\{S_{22}\} = d\bar{e}f$ & $u_x \geq v_x$	$\{S_{12}\} = d\bar{e}f$ & $u_x \geq v_x$
	$\{W_{32}\} = h\bar{g}f$ & $u_x > v_x$	$\{W_{32}\} = h\bar{g}f$ & $u_x > v_x$
	$\{S_{22}\} = h\bar{g}f$ & $u_x \leq v_x$	$\{S_{12}\} = h\bar{g}f$ & $u_x \leq v_x$
	$\{N_{22}\} = \ddot{f}\bar{d}b$ & $u_x < v_x$	$\{N_{12}\} = \ddot{f}\bar{d}b$ & $u_x < v_x$
	$\{N_{22}\} = \ddot{f}\bar{h}b$ & $u_x > v_x$	$\{N_{12}\} = \ddot{f}\bar{h}b$ & $u_x > v_x$

Table 2: Misrouting around the faulty boundary PE.

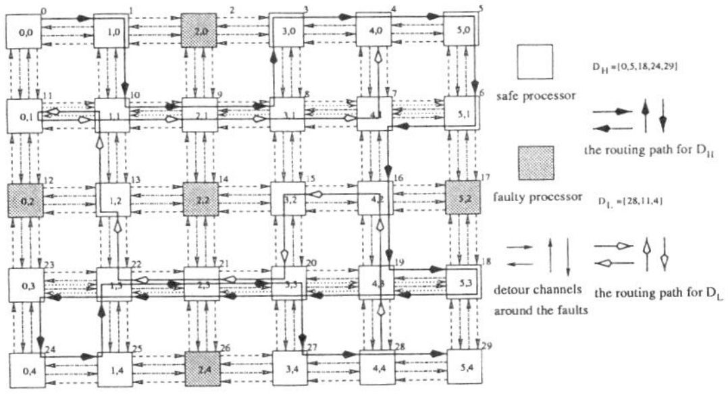

Figure 4: The fault-tolerant multicast routing paths for a D_H and a D_L.

channels in VM_2 according to misrouting for D_L in Table 1 until there is a PE w' such that $l(w) > l(w') \geq l(v)$ and misrouting becomes normal routing from w'. In Table 1, only the output port of the current PE is given, which is used to forward the message. The misroutings for D_H and D_L use the different virtual channels in VM_1 and VM_2 respectively, and all misrouting channels cannot form a waiting cycle around a faulty PE; some examples are shown in (a) of Figure 3. When w is a faulty boundary PE of the network, the message is detoured around the faulty PE w according to Table 2. The misrouting around the faulty boundary PE of the network may use the channels in VM_1, VM_2 or VM_3, and the message is detoured around the faulty PE w according to Table 2 until there is a PE w' such that $l(w) < l(w') \leq l(v)$ for D_H or $l(w) > l(w') \geq l(v)$ for D_L and then misrouting becomes normal routing from w'; the misroutings for D_H and D_L use different virtual channels respectively too, and all misrouting channels cannot form a waiting cycle around a faulty PE. Some examples are shown in (b) of Figure 3. In Figure 3, there are two chains (solid lines) around each faulty PE, which consist of misrouting channels; one chain is misrouting channels for D_H, another is for D_L, and all chains are disjointed, which can be proved by enumerating all misrouting channels in Table 1 and Table 2. In deterministic fault-tolerant multicast wormhole routing, the routings (normal and misrouting) for D_H and D_L use the different routing channels, which make the routing paths for D_H and D_L disjoint. An example is shown in Figure 4. The algorithm is deadlock free (proof omitted because of space constraint).

2 Adaptive Routing

In this section, we extend the adaptive multicast routing algorithm proposed by Duato in [1] to do fault-tolerant routing. The routing function R_1 in Section 1.1 defines minimal routing, where each physical channel is split into a set of additional virtual channels. Let C_1 be the set of original channels used by routing function R_1 and let C be the set of all the virtual channels in the network. Let C_{1H} be the set of channels belonging to C_1 that connect lower-label nodes to higher-label nodes and C_{1L} be the set of channels belonging to C_1 that connect higher-label nodes to lower-label nodes. Let C_{xyH} be the set of output channels from node x such that each channel belongs to a minimal path from x to y (where $l(x) < l(y)$) and the label of its destination node is not higher than the label of y. Let C_{xyL} be the set of output channels from node x such that each channel belongs to a minimal path from x to y (where $l(x) > l(y)$) and

$$\forall x, y \in N, R(x,y) = \begin{cases} R_1(x,y) \cup (C_{xyH} \cap (C - C_1)) & \text{if } l(x) < l(y), \\ R_1(x,y) \cup (C_{xyL} \cap (C - C_1)) & \text{if } l(x) > l(y). \end{cases}$$

Algorithm: Adaptive fault-tolerant multicast routing (AFTMR)
Input: A message with sorted destination address list $D_M = (d_1, d_2, \ldots, d_k)$,
  a local address $u = (u_x, u_y)$, node label assignment l and
  F the set of misrouting channels around faulty PEs
Procedure:
1. If $u = d_1$, then $D'_M = D_M - \{d_1\}$ and a copy of the message is
   forwarded to the local node; otherwise, $D'_M = D_M$.
2. If $D'_M = \phi$, then terminate the message transmission.
3. Let $v = d_i$ be the first address in D'_M.
4. If an outgoing channel from u in $R(u,v) - F$ or $R_1(u,v) \cap F$ is available
   forward the message along it
5. Else If there exist safe outgoing channels from u in $R(u,v) - F$ or $R_1(u,v) \cap F$
6.   wait for one of them
7. Else If $l(u) < l(v)$ and let $w \in R_1(u,v)$
8.   If w is a non-boundary faulty PE of the network
9.   the message is misrouted according to Table 1,
10.   If w is a boundary faulty PE of the network
11.   the message is misrouted around the faulty PE according to Table 2;
12.   until there is a PE w' such that $l(u) < l(w') \leq l(v)$
13. Else If $l(u) > l(v)$ and let $w \in R_1(u,v)$
14.   If w is a non-boundary faulty PE of the network
15.   the message is misrouted according to Table 1
16.   If w is a boundary faulty PE of the network
17.   the message is misrouted around the faulty PE according to Table 2;
18.   until there is a PE w' such that $l(u) > l(w') \geq l(v)$

The new routing function can use any of the new channels belonging to a minimal path between successive destinations, except when a node with a label higher (for $l(x) < l(y)$) or lower (for $l(x) > l(y)$) than the label of the destination node is reached, where $R_1(x,y)$ denotes the deterministic routing channel from x. When there is no faulty PE in the network, the adaptive multicast routing algorithm R is deadlock-free, which is proved by Duato [1]. Here the routing function R does not use all the minimal paths between successive destinations to satisfy the compatibility between the split-and-sort function and the routing function; some examples are given in [1]. In this section, we extend the adaptive multicast wormhole algorithm to become a fault-tolerant algorithm for 2D meshes. The adaptive fault-tolerant multicast wormhole routing algorithm needs the same virtual channels as the deterministic fault-tolerant multicast wormhole routing. The normal routing uses adaptive routing paths except misrouting channels around faulty PEs; the routings (normal and misrouting) along the misrouting channels around the faulty PEs only use deterministic paths according to algorithm AFTMR; an example is shown in Figure 5, where the normal routing from $(1,0)$ to $(4,2)$ can use the deterministic fault-tolerant routing path $1 \to 10 \to 13 \to 14 \to 15 \to 16$, which belongs to $R_1(w, d_i) \cap F$ or adaptive routing path $1 \to 2 \to 3 \to 4 \to 7 \to 16$, which belongs to $R(w, d_i) - F$. This

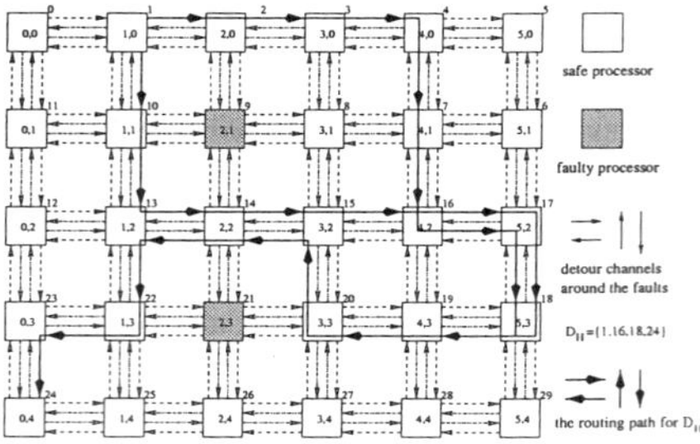

Figure 5: Adaptive fault-tolerant multicast wormhole routing paths for a D_H.

algorithm is deadlock-free (proof omitted).

3 Conclusion

A deterministic fault-tolerant multicast wormhole routing algorithm as well as an adaptive algorithm have been presented in this paper. The proposed algorithms are based on the multicast wormhole routing algorithms presented by Lin *et al.* [3] and Duato [1] respectively, and are valid for both unicast and multicast routing. This last property is very important for real machines, which can drastically simplify the implementation of the router. The deadlock freedom of the proposed algorithms is dependent on the order of the destination set and misrouting channels around faulty PEs. The disadvantage of the proposed algorithms is that they can only tolerate faults in the one-fault model, and the adaptive multicast algorithm sometimes does not allow all the minimal paths between successive destination nodes to be used.

References

[1] J. Duato, "A theory of deadlock-free adaptive multicast routing in wormhole networks", *IEEE Trans. Parallel and Distributed Systems*, Vol. 6, No. 9, pp. 976-987, Sept. 1995.

[2] R.L. Hadas, K. Watkins, and T. Hehre, "Fault-tolerant multicast routing in the mesh with no virtuals," *Proc. Second International Symposium on High Performance Computer architecture, Feb. 1996, San Jose, USA.*

[3] X. Lin, P.K. Mckinley, and L.M. Ni, "Deadlock-free multicast wormhole routing in 2D mesh multicomputers," *IEEE Trans. Parallel and Distributed Systems,* Vol. 5, No. 8, pp. 793-804, Aug. 1994.

[4] T.Y. Juang, Y.C. Tseng and M.H. Yang, "An Euler-path-based multicasting model for wormhole-routed networks:its application to damaged 2D tori and meshes", *1997 International Performance, Computing and Communications Conference,* Phoenix, USA, pp. 444-450, Feb. 1997.

SEPARABILITY OF SYMMETRIC DEGREE-FOUR CHORDAL RING NETWORKS

R.F.BROWNE

Institute of Information Sciences and Technology, Massey University, Palmerston North, New Zealand

E-mail: r.f.browne@massey.ac.nz

The separation of graphs into two or more components through the removal of a limited number of nodes or edges is an important problem in determining the fault tolerance of multi-computer systems. This paper considers the case of node loss in a symmetric degree four chordal ring network. The separated components may consist of individual nodes (*single separation*) or of clusters of nodes (*multiple separation*). Depending upon the exact specification of the network multiple separation can occur on the failure of four or five nodes. Multiple separation can occur in any chordal ring network on the failure of six nodes.

1 Introduction

Owing to its relevance to multi-computer systems and to communications networks the fault-tolerance of networks has received extensive attention. The distributed nature of networks represents both a strength and a weakness:

- The relatively large number of components involved means that component failure has a relatively high probability. For instance, a multi-computer system, based on microprocessors, will typically have many times the number of discrete ICs contained in a single-processor computer of equivalent power.
- If they are physically widely distributed and if they have a suitably high level of interconnectivity networks can be very resilient to the loss of individual components. The internet and telephone networks are both good examples.

Ideally a multi-computer system will exhibit 'graceful degradation' of processing power in the presence of failed components. In many cases a failed component would be replaced within a short time of the failure occurring ('short' compared to the mean time between failure), so that the system would have no more than one failed component at any one time. However there are cases in which this does not apply, including:

- Multi-computer networks in inaccessible locations such as a space vehicle ([1]). In most cases repair is impractical, and the vehicle may be able to operate in some limited capacity provided network connectivity is not lost.
- In particularly hostile environments (such as military applications) multiple failures may occur via a single event or within a short period. The ability of the system to continue to operate, at least for a short time, could be vital.

The subject can be approached from two equivalent perspectives: the reliability of a network (with reference to the physical components), or as the separability of a graph. In this paper graph terminology will be adopted.

Hu and Hwang [4] investigated the reliabilities of degree three chordal ring networks. Hu, Hwang, and Li [5] considered isolated and non-isolated cutsets in determining the survival reliability of double-loop networks. van Doorn [8] has derived an explicit expression for the connectivity of circulant graphs. Hwang [6] has obtained explicit (closed form) solutions for consecutive-k-out-of-n systems. Hwang and Wright [7] include directed degree three chordal rings in an analysis of network reliability. Statistical independence in node failures is assumed in the present paper, but this assumption has been questioned by Harms et.al. [3].

The degree four chordal ring network considered in this paper has been analysed by Browne and Hodgson [2] and is defined as follows. Consider a ring of N nodes, referred to as nodes 0, 1, ... (N-1). Each node is connected to its two nearest neighbours, so that node i is connected to nodes $(i\pm1)\%N$. ('%' stands for modulo). In addition each node has two chordal connections to nodes $(i\pm d)\%N$, where d is the chordal displacement of the network. These chords are referred to as the *forward* and *reverse* chords respectively. The pair (N,d) thus fully describes a chordal ring network.

Some of the concepts and definitions used in this paper are as follows. A *cutset* of a connected graph G is a set S of nodes such that removal of all nodes in S disconnects G and removal of some but not all nodes in S does not disconnect G. An *ordered cutset* is a cutset $\{c_i\}$ such that $c_i < c_{i+1}$. The *connectivity* of a connected graph G is the smallest number of nodes whose removal disconnects G (that is, the size of the smallest cutset of G). The *separability* or *vulnerability* of a graph is the extent to which the connectivity is subject to disruption when links or nodes are removed. The separation of individual nodes is referred to as *single separation*, while the separation of clusters of nodes is referred to as *multiple separation*.

In many applications the actual links are more likely to fail than the nodes, but in static multi-computer interconnection networks the links are typically short lengths of wire, and this paper will examine the effects of the loss of network nodes. This paper is organized as follows. In section 2 both single and multiple separability are described, and the implications of multiple separation are examined. Single and multiple separation of chordal ring networks are summarised in sections 4 and 5 respectively. A more detailed version of this paper is available at [9].

2. Separability

A random distribution of failed nodes may or may not lead to separation of the network. For a network with N nodes, suppose x of those nodes fail. If $S(x)$ and

$M(x)$ of all possible combinations lead to single and multiple separations respectively then the separability is defined by the probabilities

$$p_s = \frac{S(x)}{{}^{N-1}C_{x-1}} \text{ and } p_m = \frac{M(x)}{{}^{N-1}C_{x-1}}$$

In a multi-computer system single separation leads to the isolation of a functional processing unit. Ideally, suitable software would enable both the system and the isolated processor to either continue or to shut down in some predictable manner. In contrast, multiple separation has two potentially serious consequences:

- It creates multiple functional units with no communication between them.
- There is a sudden change in the accessible processing power.

In most cases, although single separation could have undesirable consequences, multiple separation presents a much more serious problem.

The remainder of this section examines the implications of multiple separation on multi-computer systems. That system could, for instance, be the interconnected control components of an aircraft or autonomous vehicle. In the presence of multiple separation in multi-computer systems neither component has direct means of determining whether the other component is still functioning. If there is a single supervisory computer, software could be employed to close down any components that cannot contact the supervisor, but this may not be the best strategy. In the absence of central supervision the best strategy is even less obvious, as the two components could continue to function, possibly in conflict with each other.

Another consequence of multiple separation is the sudden loss of accessible processing power. Suppose processing units are lost at a steady rate. The ideal relationship between (accessible) processing power and the number of failed nodes will show no substantial discontinuities. However, in the case of multiple separation the objective of 'graceful degradation' in performance is clearly not achievable, and the ability of the system to continue functioning at all would depend on a sophisticated level of software.

3 Terminology

The derivation of the results reported in this paper is based on cutsets. In particular, without loss of generality the first element of the cutset, c_0, will always be zero (since the graph is symmetric).

4 Single Separation

Designate by $p_s(j)$ the probability that the failure of j nodes at random will lead to single node separation. If p is the probability that any one node will fail within a given period of time (which could be in some specified hazardous action) then the probability of single separation is $\sum_j p_s(j)\left(1-(1-p)^j\right)$. If $p << 1$ the first one or two non-zero terms in the sequence of p_s values will provide a sufficiently good estimate of the probability of single node separation. A special case is that of $N = 2d$ which leads to the isolation of a node on the failure of three nodes, but this case is of little practical interest.

4.1 Separation on failure of four nodes

In any symmetric degree four chordal ring network, if node zero is a member of the cutset then, given that four edges contact node zero, there are four possible nodes that can be isolated, namely 1, N-1, d, N-d.

Thus, provided that the corresponding cutsets are distinct, there are four choices, giving a probability that the loss of four nodes chosen at random will lead to the separation of a single node of $\frac{4}{{}^{N-1}C_3}$. If $N = 2d+2$ there are only two distinct cutsets, so that the probability of the failure of four nodes leading to an isolated node becomes $\frac{2}{{}^{N-1}C_3}$.

4.2 Separation on failure of five nodes

The results for this case are quoted. In general the probability of single separation resulting from the loss of five nodes is $\frac{5(N-5)}{{}^{N-1}C_4}$.

In the particular case of two isolated nodes the probability of single separation becomes $\frac{5(N-6)}{{}^{N-1}C_4}$. This occurs when $d = 3$, and when $d = N\text{-}2n\text{-}1$, n any integer.

5 Multiple Separation

Sections 5.1, 5.2, 5.3 deal with the cases of four, five, and six nodes respectively. Separation based on more than six node failures is not explored in this paper since all degree four chordal ring networks can separate from six node failures. Designate by $p_m(j)$ the probability that the failure of j nodes at random will lead to multiple separation. As in Section 4, if the probability that any one node will fail within a given period of time is p then the probability of multiple separation is $\sum_j p_m(j)\left(1-(1-p)^j\right)$. If $p << 1$ it is sufficient to take the first non-zero term in the sequence of p_m values.

5.1 Separation on the failure of four nodes

There are three ways in which multiple separation can occur on the failure of four nodes (d = 2, d = ⌊N/2⌋, and d = N/2-1 for even N). In such cases the probability of multiple separation is

$$p_m = \frac{N/2 - 5}{{}^{N-1}C_3} = \frac{3(N-10)}{(N-1)(N-2)(N-3)}$$

It is worth noting that network designs that are liable to multiple separation after four failures are relatively inefficient from the point of view of the mean internode distance of the network, and hence are not a preferred interconnection topology.

5.2 Separation on five failed nodes

This occurs when N is a multiple of 3 and $d = N/3$. With this combination, no multiple separations arise from the removal of four nodes. However the set $\{j, j+d\}$

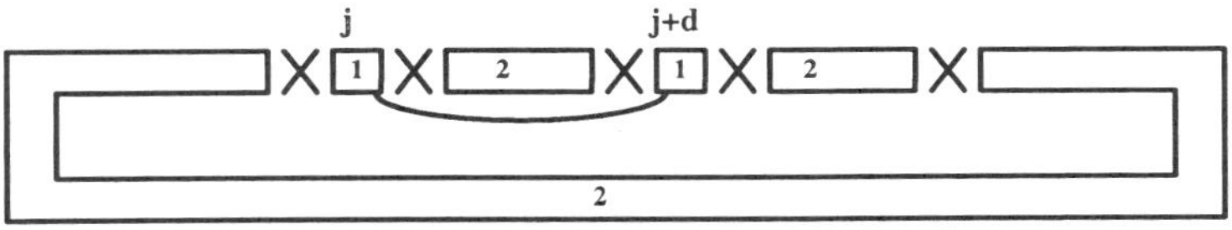

Figure 1. Separation on five failed nodes

is isolated on removal of the set of five nodes $\{j\pm1, j+d\pm1, j+2d\}$ (Figure 1). If one of the nodes removed is node zero then there are five cutsets that will result in multiple separation. Thus

$$p_m = \frac{5}{{}^{N-1}C_4} = \frac{120}{(N-1)(N-2)(N-3)(N-4)}$$

Such networks are relatively efficient as measured by mean internode distance, and hence could be encountered.

5.3 Separation on six failed nodes

The probabilities of multiple separation from the failure of six nodes in any network are fully enumerated in [9]. In the general case there are 12 possible combinations, but certain (N,D) pairs will lead to significantly higher values. For instance, if $N = n$, $d = 2n$, then the number of combinations is 12N-126, and the probability of multiple separation is given by dividing this figure by ${}^{N-1}C_5$. The probability of six node failures resulting in multiple separation is seen to become very small for graphs of more than 100 nodes. For example, the graph $N = 1000$, $d = 333$, (an example of $N = 6n+4$, $d = 2n+1$ with $n = 166$) results in $p_m = 1.45\text{E-}9$. It is in the region of small N that the probability of multiple separation becomes more significant. For instance, $N = 19$, $d = 6$ results in $p_m = 0.012$, and $N = 22$, $d = 7$ results in $p_m = 0.0068$. These are comparable to the probability that the failure of four nodes results in multiple separation (for example, $N = 21$ and $d = 10$ results in $p_m = 0.025$). However, as noted in Section 5.1 network designs that are liable to multiple separation after four failures have a comparatively poor communications efficiency and hence are unlikely to be encountered. Networks based on $N = 3n$, $d = n$ would have better performance, and exhibit a significant probability of multiple separation (for example, $N = 21$ and $d = 7$ results in $p_m = 0.00103$).

6 Conclusions

Separation of a graph into disconnected units represents a potentially-serious failure mode for networks described by the graph. In particular the ideal of 'graceful' degradation in the performance of a multi-computer system in the presence of component failures may not be valid. The analysis presented in this paper, for the degree four chordal ring network, is the subject of on-going research for other interconnection networks.

References

1. Bares J, Hebert M, Kanade T, Krotkov E, Mitchell T, Simmons R, Whittaker W, "Ambler: an autonomous rover for planetary exploration", IEEE Computer, **22** (1989), 18-26.
2. Browne R F, Hodgson R M, "Symmetric degree-four chordal ring networks", IEE Proc. E, **137** (1990), 310-318.
3. Harms D D, Kraetzl M, Colbourn C J, Devitt J S, "Network reliability: experiments with a symbolic algebra environment", CRC Press, (1995).
4. Hu X D and Hwang F K, "Reliabilities of chordal rings", Networks, **22** (1992), 487-501.
5. Hu X D, Hwang F K, and Li W-C W, "Most reliable double-loop networks in survival reliability", Networks, **23** (1993), 401-410.
6. Hwang F K, "Simplified reliabilities for consecutive-k-out-of-n systems", SIAM J. Algebraic and Discrete Methods, **7** (1986), 258-264.
7. Hwang F K and Wright P E, "Survival reliability of some double-loop networks and chordal rings", IEEE Trans Comp, **44** (1995), 1468-1471.
8. van Doorn E A, "Connectivity of circulant graphs", J. Graph Theory, **10** (1986), 9-14.
9. \\www-ist\rbrowne\myweb\ICA3PP\ICA3PP2000.htm

Chapter 13
High-Performance Data Management

Preliminary Development of a Genetically Enhanced High Performance KDD System for a Biologically Inspired Application

Reginald L. Walker
Computer Science Department
University of California at Los Angeles
Los Angeles, California 90095-1596, USA
E-mail: rwalker@cs.ucla.edu

A study is being conducted to develop enhancements for the methodologies that exist with current information retrieval (IR) systems that are valuable components of search engine technology. The IR system for a search engine prototype, the Tocorime Apicu Project, incorporates components of biological modeling, knowledge discovery in databases (KDD), evolutionary computations, and scientific computing. The goal of this project is to combine the diverse methodologies to create a genetically enhanced high-performance KDD model for this experimental search engine's indexer mechanisms. The simulator results were generated using message passing interface (MPI) on a network of SUN workstations.

1 Introduction

A bioinformatic approach is being used to design an experimental search engine prototype using the methodologies of evolutionary computations, biological modeling, and high-performance knowledge discovery in databases (KDD). This approach incorporates the methodologies of genetic algorithms (GA) and genetic programming (GP) in order to emulate unique aspects of the social structure of a biological model that resides in colonies. The methodologies of GA/GP used in the prototype differ from the traditional usage of these methodologies which generate populations of programs. This paper discusses the use of the evolutionary methodologies to generate populations of chromosome structures to solve the problem of knowledge discovery in a set of selected Web pages. The knowledge discovery system of a search engine is a component of its information retrieval (IR) system.

The benefit of incorporating the methodologies of the KDD model are: 1) long-term vision, 2) mechanisms for updating documents on distributed computers, 3) mechanisms for connecting Web pages, and 4) mechanisms for interpreting the relations between a diverse collection of Web pages. This approach, however, derives queries from the resulting data warehouses built by the search engines; and the IR system component, in turn, organizes the warehouse and presents the user with useful information. Thus, the incorporated structure and search methodologies of KDD systems do not require an in-depth knowledge by its end-users. The KDD IR system does require an intelligent tool[1,2] coupled with the methodology to eliminate repeated queries.

2 Related Work on Search Engine Technology and High-Performance Data Mining

A high-performance parallel text retrieval algorithm that supports multiple text queries[16] was studied to mimic the heavy query load associated with a highly accessed search engine over the Internet. The goal of this algorithm was to reduce the total communication time needed for processing a set of X concurrently arriving text queries in a set of N (equal to the number of processors) queries each time. The text retrieval system was implemented using the vector space model (VSM) which required that each processor collect each set of relevant documents associated with a query from the other $N-1$ nodes. The query set attempts to reduce the query collection time and reduce the number of transmitted messages. The VSM model represents each page as a query-term vector consisting of weights ranging between "0" and "1."

A data mining methodology for the parallel formulation of classification decision-tree learning[23] was based on induction and the frontier approach. This approach focused on removing several problems that limit the applicability of parallel decision-tree classification algorithms. One major limitation results from load imbalance which causes a performance degradation in the frontier approach. Other problems stem from the use of full hash tables of the whole classification system[17] residing on each node. This hash table usage limits the scalability of these types of algorithms with respect to runtime, memory, and communication requirements which reflect the data movement costs. The goal of parallel classification algorithms is to efficiently classify the training set in order to add/classify new data during the KDD process.

A high-performance data mining application was developed for a neural network environment[9] that can be expanded using genetic algorithms as the classification procedure. The authors applied the methodology of steepest descent via the back-propagation algorithm in order to show that the derivative of the error measure, with respect to each weight connection, is proportional to a weight change with negative constant of proportionality. This approach has the disadvantage of premature convergence; this can be alleviated via the methodologies of evolutionary computations.

A GA feature selector[5] incorporated the concept of multiple correlation into the design of a classifier/indexer. The multiple correlation model is used to represent a multi-objective fitness function[8] needed by the GA to automate the classification system. The applicability of a multi-objective fitness function stems from its usage to measure classification performance as well as

Table 1: Comparing the KDD Model and the Biological Model.

Phases of KDD Model	**Biological Model**	**KDD Model**
1	Information reception within the colony	Data selection
2	1) Cell cleaning 2) Garbage collection	Data cleaning 1) De-duplication of record 2) Lack of domain consistency (removal of pollutants) 3) Application of pattern recognition algorithms
3	Information reception within colony	Enrichment
4	Removal of debris	Coding
5	1) Speciation 2) Pattern recognition techniques	Data mining 1) clustering techniques 2) segmentation 3) visualization techniques
6	Protecting contents	Report

the domain relations among two or more independent factors and a single (the feature related) criteria.

Reference [19] evaluated the merits of a similarity metric for distributed association mining. This metric compares the resulting partitions of the global dataset in order to compute the correlation of each subset. The computed correlation measure is used to compare the partitions in terms of how they are correlated based on an adapted probe set (set of the most common attributes) of the global dataset. The metric can be used to cluster similar datasets in order to perform meaningful distributed data mining.

3 Model of the Genetically Enhanced KDD System

The goals of the KDD model [2] are to obtain an ever-increasing and better understanding of an ever-changing environment in order to find various types of *hidden* knowledge based on the complexity of the implemented model. The types of hidden knowledge are:

1. Shallow knowledge - results retrieved via a query tool

2. Multidimensional knowledge - results from the use of online analytical processing tools

3. Hidden knowledge - results of a search algorithm

4. Deep knowledge - information that can only be located if we have a clue that tells us where to look

Table 1 presents a comparison of the components associated with the KDD model and the requirements of this bioinformatic approach. The system requirements for the classification mechanisms of this evolutionary model place numerous demands on each node. Each word within each Web page may be compared with millions of other words extracted from Web pages that may eventually reside on a node over a period of generations following the application of the genetic operators. The application of the GP operators, as well as the intermediate application of the fitness measures, are used to recalculate the normalized fitness of each node. System requirements can be reduced in multiple ways, such as: 1) the removal of noise in each Web page which, without losing pertinent information, reduces the signal-to-noise ratio [21], as opposed to using the raw Web page, and 2) reducing the computational complexity [23] associated with applying the query techniques of KDD. The removal of noise in this context refers to the KDD process of data cleaning and represents a crucial component of data preparation [9]. This process incorporates the removal of duplicate Web pages as well as comments, stop words, non-stop words, non-contributory tags and their attributes, non-contributory attributes, and possibly corrects typographical errors such as commonly misspelled words.

The resulting fragments of Web pages that are generated during the transcription process eliminate irrelevant and/or redundant features that reduce execution time during the classification process. This transcription process can be classified as keyword indexing [5] which results in a more efficient representation of only the relevant information. The approach reduces the possibility of misclassification of Web pages. The goal of generating an *adaptive set* of search strings associated with randomly selected subsets of Web pages cannot be a result of any *a priori* knowledge of the final set of documents unless these documents also comprise the training set [4]. This is a major limitation of some clustering methodologies such as the K-means algorithm [3]. Adaptive probe sets [19] have been used with high-performance KDD application that incorporates the most commonly occurring information items using the technique that determines the *influential attributes* of a given data set. Adaptive techniques are required in order to adequately classify the contents of selected Web documents across the $n-1$ nodes in a high-performance implementation. The set of search strings associated with an application can have as many as 500,000 keywords [7]. This classification process also assists in that evolutionary process of forming species via the fitness measures [26]. The stochastic nature of the evolutionary operators and the KDD model associated with this GA/GP application [20,2] requires the repeated application of operators over a period of generations in order to obtain reliable results in order to generate solutions that are neat as well compact [10].

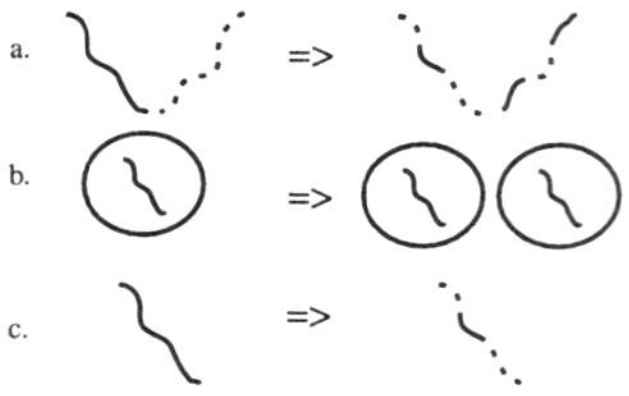

Figure 1: Genetic programming operators a) crossover, b) reproduction, and c) mutation.

4 Methodologies of Evolutionary Computations

Genetic programming (GP) is an evolutionary methodology [1,6,13,28] that extends and expands upon the techniques associated with genetic algorithms (GA) which are used to generate populations of computer programs. The evolutionary force of these methodologies reflects a population's fitness, which results from fitness evaluations [18,20] based on the application of genetic operators to individual members of a chosen population of programs. The operators furnished by these evolutionary methodologies are individual (or subgroup) migration, reproduction, crossover, and mutation. The outcome from applying the genetic operations to this string of information (chromosome or tree-structure representation) corresponds to computing a globally optimum (or near-optimum) point in the original search space of the problem.

The improvement of the solutions generated in the GP applications [20] is due to their evolution over a series of generations. Each successive generation is derived from an application of some combination of the primary genetic operators: *reproduction* and *crossover* (See Figure 1). The application of the GP crossover operator results in the sexual and asexual application of the reproduction operator [10,12]. And while the application of the former results in copying an individual into a new generation and/or subpopulation, the use of the latter results in a random selection of distinct points from two selected parents. It is suggested that the amount of genetic material transmitted be-

Table 2: Sequential and Parallel (3 nodes only) Timing Results for 1024 Web Pages. (Note: The user and sys timing results are generated by Node 0.)

	UNIX System Times (secs)	Run 1	Run 2	Run 3
	real	4:14:36.5	4:04:16.7	4:01:50.6
Sequential	user	43:58.8	42:42.8	42:54.3
Version	sys	29:55.6	28:15.4	28:35.4
	real	6:14:00.1	6:55:29.0	6:14:38.0
Parallel	user	6:16.9	6:31.0	6:24.6
Version	sys	4:07.8	4:11.8	4:17.3

tween generations via the crossover operator be restricted to small amounts in order to maintain diversity and slow convergence of the global population. Based on the values indicated by the fitness measure for two offspring—two potential members of a new generation—certain individuals of the population are stochastically selected as parents. Thus, the resulting children replace their parents in the existing population of solutions associated with a specific GA/GP application.

5 Methodologies of the Biological Model

The basic characteristics exhibited by the inhabitants of a honeybee colony[11,24,15] are the same as those used to adequately search the Web for valuable information. These basic characteristics have been translated so as to develop a model of an integrated search engine using the evolutionary methodologies of GA/GP. The evolutionary processes exhibited by the bee colony thus provide a biological model, not only for the storage, processing, and retrieval of valuable information, but also for Web crawlers, as well as for an advanced communication system.

Since the queen is the centralized control and coordination mechanism in the colony, queen simulators have been developed to control and coordinate all the process interactions within the simulated hives (Web sites). For mating purposes, drone simulators will also be introduced into the model. Some of the functionalities of the workers are integrated as components of a traditional operating system. Workers perform various tasks, such as: 1) cell cleaning/garbage collection, 2) comb building, 3) information reception within the colony, 4) parsing and distributing information to other members of the colony, 5) removal of debris, and 6) protecting information (see Table 1). Also, they perform routine inspections and provide access to a host of cell (memory) locations which can range from one to thousands of visits. The ability of the colony's workers to convert of natural elements into valuable resources have been simulated, thus providing a model for the indexing mechanisms that are essential in the organization of various sets of existing Web documents. The current indexer associated with this project, capable of organizing limited subsets of Web documents, provides a foundation for individual member simulators.

6 Simulation Studies for Testing the Transmission of Cultural Information

6.1 Application of Genetic Programming Fitness Measures

The crossover operator associated with this project randomly uses either a *one point crossover* or a *two point crossover* approach [22]. The number of genetic components involved in these transfers is also random since the chromosome structure that exists in each generation may have resulted from a previous application of the crossover operator. This approach is adequate when there are multiple chromosome structures. The sequential simulation required that a pseudo-chromosome be created in order to avoid the effects of panmictic selection [14] which may result premature convergence. The canonical fitness measures [12,26] incorporated a *raw fitness*, a*standardized fitness*, and an *adjusted fitness*. Two versions of the indexer software will be studied using cultural evolution. The current version does not restrict the transmission of genetic information between nodes chosen as parents for the crossover operator. The second version will restrict this transmission. Each approach will be measured using 200 generations with fitness computations associated with 16 randomly chosen search strings. The choice of 16 search strings reflects a reduced computation complexity for this study since complexity increases with the number of searches and incorporates the approach of adaptive probe sets [19].

The current implementation associated with cultural evolution reuses information associated with the initial transcription of each individual Web page. The original Web page undergoes a transcription process and the transcribed information is reused in all of the following generations. This approach reduces the overhead associated with re-transcribing each individual page. However, this approach does requires that each node re-compute its corresponding fitness measure associated with each generation even when it is not a candidate for the crossover operator. This issue will be resolved by computing normalized fitness measures associated with the generation of species resulting from the use of multiple sets of search strings.

The training set for these studies consisted of 1024 selected Web pages.

The ideal load balancing model [23] would result in $\frac{1024}{nprocs-1}$ residing on each node, where *nprocs* represents the number of processors (nodes). The overall goal of this research on indexers views each node as a Web server (ISP). Each ISP attempts to achieve the optimal distribution of the 1024 Web pages that will minimize the effort needed to efficiently recall any component of its content through the emulation of aspects of the biological model. $Node_0$ was used as a dedicated server node with the other nodes treated as its clients when the number of nodes was greater than one. The client nodes sent requests to the server node for Web pages and for access to the output channel. See Walker [25] for implementation issues. The number of pages that reside on each node varies based on the initial distribution coupled with the node's selection as a parent associated with the crossover operator. Currently, there is no fitness-proportionate probability [12] being used to select the crossover parents, only random selection. The first parent is randomly chosen, and the second parent is chosen by incrementing the node ID of the first parent by mimicking the ring communication pattern based on the MPI rank in order to determine adjacent nodes. The sequential simulation was conducted by creating a pseudo-chromosome structure in order to avoid the effects of panmictic selection [14] coupled with premature convergence.

6.2 Experimental Results

Timing results are shown in Table 2. The timing results are being generated by the UNIX system command—*/usr/bin/time*—which provides elapsed time, user time, and system time in seconds. The execution time required in these simulations created problems for the MPI timing routine, $MPI\_Wtime()$, due to the length of each simulation. The current fitness results reflect only the sequential and 3 node (parallel) results of this indexer mechanism on the set of 1024 Web pages that comprise the training set. The diversity among the fitness measures and corresponding page counts for this sequential test show the contents of the chromosome structures used to represent Web pages associated with $Node_0$ (shown in Figure 2).

Figures 2 and 3 shows the diversity associated with the fitness measures for 200 generations based on three test runs. The final representation of this information will reflect the worst fitness, average fitness, and best fitness based on a set of ten sequential executions. The numerical values associated with this final representation will be used to compute the complexity measures [27] for this evolutionary process. Scalability issues will also be addressed in the presentation of parallel results that are the main focus of the research effort.

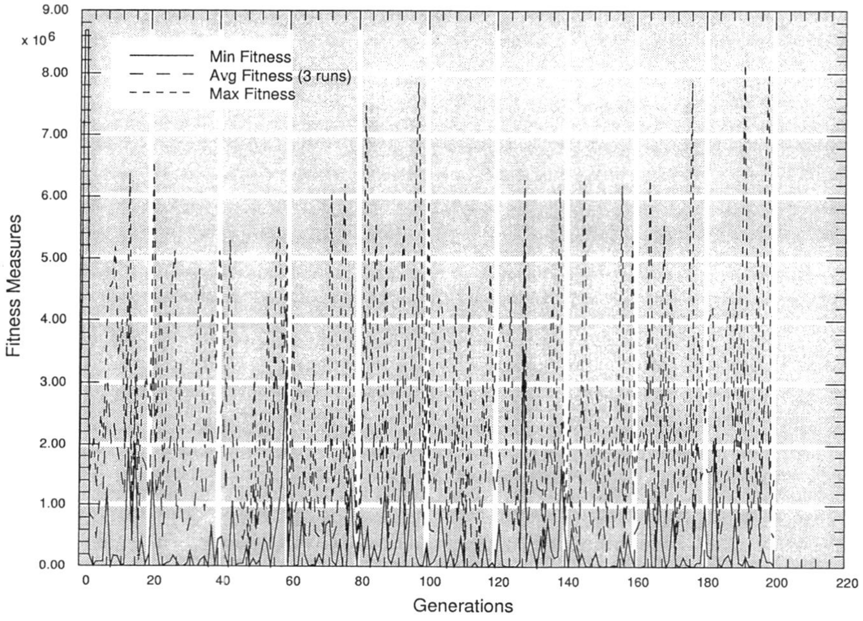

Figure 2: Fitness Measure vs. Generations for Sequential Version.

7 Conclusion

The methodologies of high-performance KDD provide a valuable extension to the preliminary implementation of this bioinformatic approach to this experimental search engine indexer. These methodologies are necessary for improving the IR systems associated with new and current engines which must acquire and incorporate an enormous amount of new/old information. The necessary mechanisms need advanced approaches in order to reduce acquired/redundant information into neat, compact formats. This project extends the basic approach of high-performance KDD to a model that exhibits the evolutionary qualities of the biological model by shrinking/expanding its data set over finite periods of time. The evolutionary qualities result in the continuous refinement of derived results coupled with a continuous incorporation of new (raw) information.

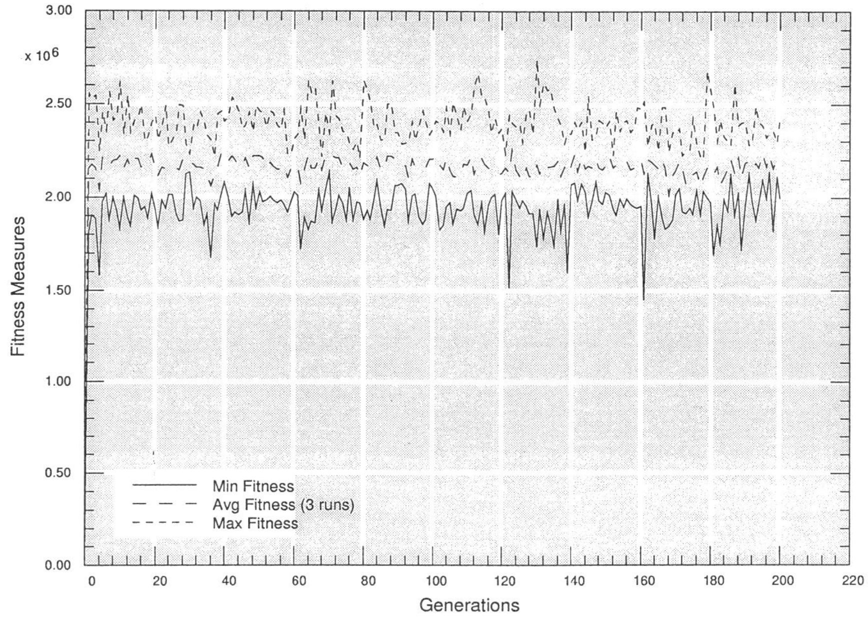

Figure 3: Fitness Measure vs. Generations for Parallel Version (2 Nodes Only).

Acknowledgements

The author wishes to thank Walter Karplus and Zhen-Su She for their direction and suggestions. The author acknowledges Elias Houstis, Ahmed K. Elmagarmid, Apostolos Hadjidimos, and Ann Catlin for their support, encouragement, and access to the computer systems at Purdue University. Special thanks to the Martha Lovette for their assistance with the GP figure in this paper. Plots were generated using *PSplot* written by Paul Dulaney (Raytheon Corporation).

Support for this work came from the Raytheon Fellowship Program, Honeybee Technologies, and Tapicu. The implementation results associated with the network of workstations originated on computers located in the Department of Computer Sciences, Purdue University, West Lafayette, IN.

References

1. P.J. Angeline in *Proc. of 3rd Conf. on Evolutionary Programming*, ed. A.V. Sebald and L.J. Fogel (World Scientific Press, Singapore, 1994).
2. P. Adriaans and D. Zantinge, *Data Mining* (Addison-Wesley, Harlow, England, 1996).
3. R. Baraglia *et al.*, in *IPDPS 2000 Workshops, LNCS 1800*, ed. J. Rolim et al. (Springer-Verlag, Berlin Heidelberg, 2000).
4. M.W. Berry and M. Browne *Understanding Search Engines: Mathematical Modeling and Text Retrieval*, (SIAM Press, Philadelphia, PA, 1999).
5. N. Chaikla and Y. Qi, *Knowledge and Information Systems* **1(3)**, 377 (1999).
6. C.D. Chapman and M.J. Jakiela, *J. of Mech. Design* **118**, 89 (1996).
7. Z. Chen *et al.*, *Knowledge and Information Systems* **1(3)**, 369 (1999).
8. C.A.C. Coello, *Knowledge and Information Systems* **1(3)**, 269 (1999).
9. M.C.A. Costa and N.F.F. Ebecken, in *Applications of High-Performance Computers in Engineering VI*, ed. M. Ingber et al. (WIT Press, Ashurst, Southampton, UK, 2000).
10. D.C. Dracopoulos and S. Kent, *Neural Computing & Applications* **6(4)**, 214 (1997).
11. J.B. Free, *The Social Organization of Honeybees* (Studies in Biology no. 81) (The Camelot Press Ltd, Southampton, 1970).
12. H. Juillè and J.B. Pollack in *Advances in Genetic Programming II*, ed. P. Angeline and K.E. Kinnear Jr. (MIT Press, Cambridge, MA, 1996).
13. J.R. Koza, in *Proc. of WESCON '95*, (IEEE Press, New York, 1995).
14. J.R. Koza and D. Andre, Technical Report STAN-CS-TR-95-1542 (Stanford University, Department of Computer Science, Palo Alto 1995).
15. M. Lindauer *Communication Among Social Bees* (Harvard University Press, Cambridge, Massachusetts, 1961).
16. B. Mamalis *et al.*, *Theory of Computing Systems* **32(6)**, 591 (1999).
17. W.A. Maniatty and M.J. Zaki, in *IPDPS 2000 Workshops, LNCS 1800*, ed. J. Rolim et al. (Springer-Verlag, Berlin Heidelberg, 2000).
18. M. Oussaidène *et al.* in *Proc. of the 1st Genetic Programming Conf.*, ed. J.R. Koza et al.
19. S. Parthasarathy and M. Ogihara in *IPDPS 2000 Workshops, LNCS 1800*, ed. J. Rolim et al. (Springer-Verlag, Berlin Heidelberg, 2000).
20. J. Sherrah *et al.* in *Proc. of the 1996 Australian New Zealand Conf. on Intelligent Information Systems*, ed. V.L. Narasimhan and L.C. Jain (IEEE Press, New York, 1996).
21. G.S.C. Slater in *Guide to Human Genome Computing (2nd edition)*, ed.

M.J. Bishop (Academic Press, San Diego, California, 1998).
22. W.M. Spears and V. Anand in *Proc. of the ISMIS '91*, ed. Z.W. Ras and M. Zemankova (Springer-Verlag, Berlin Heidelberg, 1999).
23. A. Srivastava *et al.*, *Data Mining and Knowledge Discovery* **3(3)**, 237 (1999).
24. K. von Frisch, *Bees: Their Vision, Chemical Senses, and Languages* (Cornell University Press, Ithaca, New York, 1964).
25. R.L. Walker, in *Applications of High-Performance Computers in Engineering VI*, ed. M. Ingber et al. (WIT Press, Ashurst, Southampton, UK, 2000).
26. R.L. Walker, in *Proc. of ASTC 2000*, ed. A. Tentner (SCS Press, San Diego, CA, 2000.
27. R.L. Walker in *IPDPS 2000 Workshops, LNCS 1800*, ed. J. Rolim et al. (Springer-Verlag, Berlin Heidelberg, 2000).
28. M.J. Willis *et al.* in *Proc. of Genetic Algorithms in Engineering Systems*, (IEE Press, London, UK, 1997).

PARALLEL AND DISTRIBUTED KNOWLEDGE DISCOVERY ON THE GRID: A REFERENCE ARCHITECTURE

M. CANNATARO AND D. TALIA
ISI-CNR, Via P. Bucci, cubo 41-c, 87036 RENDE (CS)
ITALY
E-mail:{cannataro, talia}@deis.unical.it

In an increasing number of scientific and commercial areas, tools and systems for the analysis of large data sets are emerging as important resources. In particular, when large data sets are coupled with geographic distribution of data, users and systems, it is necessary to combine different technologies for implementing high-performance distributed knowledge discovery systems. The discipline that study and use those tools is named Parallel and Distributed Knowledge Discovery (PDKD). In this paper we introduce a reference software architecture for PDKD systems that is built on top of computational grids that provide dependable, consistent, and pervasive access to high-end computational resources. The proposed architecture uses the grid services and defines a set of additional layers to implement the services of distributed knowledge discovery process on distributed computers where each node can be a sequential or a parallel machine.

1 Introduction

The information stored today in computers is very large and it is growing very rapidly. Whereas until some years ago the main problem was the lack of information, today and in the future the main problem is that we have too much information to deal with and it is hard to understand what in it is important. Just to give some examples, Wal-Mart handles about 20 million of transactions each day using a database of more that 4 terabytes, the NASA satellites system for earth observation generates 50 gigabytes of images each our, finally the Human Genoma project collected several terabytes of data on human genetic code that must be analyzed.

To solve these problems, computer scientists are working on software tools that can analyze data to find useful patterns in them. This operation is called *data mining* or *knowledge discovery in databases* (*KDD*). More properly, data mining is the basic component of the KDD process for the semi-automatic discovery of patterns, associations, changes, anomalies, and semantically significant structures and events in data. Typical examples of data mining tasks are data classification and clustering, event and values prediction, association rules discovery, and episodes detection [3].

Attempts to automate the process of knowledge extraction date from at least the early 1980s, with the work on statistical expert systems. But today new techniques, mainly in the artificial intelligence field, such as rule induction, neural networks, bayesian networks and genetic algorithms are used. The size of data sources mean that we cannot do it unaided, but must use fast computers, applying sophisticated software tools from statistics to artificial intelligence. Today data mining is used in commerce, scientific data analysis, banking, medicine and economics with very interesting, and sometime surprising, outcomes. Industries, finance companies, public administrations, scientific laboratories and Web-based enterprises are benefiting from this technology and they are gaining positions over competitors by discovering knowledge in their own databases.

Recently several KDD systems have been implemented on parallel computing platforms to achieve high performance in the analysis of large data sets that are stored in a single site. However, KDD systems that must be able to handle and analyze multi-site data repositories. The combination of large data set size, geographic distribution of data, users and resources, and computationally intensive analysis demand for a parallel and distributed data management and analysis infrastructure for *parallel and distributed knowledge discovery* (PDKD).

This paper discusses and proposes a reference architecture for geographically distributed PDKD systems called *Knowledge Grid*. The proposed architecture is built on top of a computational grid that provide dependable, consistent, and pervasive access to high-end computational resources. The proposed architecture uses the grid services and defines a set of additional layers to implement the services of distributed knowledge discovery process on world wide connected computers where each node can be a sequential or a parallel machine. The Knowledge Grid enables the collaboration of scientists that must mine data that are stored in different research centers as well as executive managers that must use a knowledge management system that operates on several data warehouses located in the different company establishments.

Some recent papers propose PDKD systems that address these issues, but there is no work in designing an integrating PDKD architecture that makes of use of the *grid computing* resources for data-mining petabyte-scale applications that both address high-performance and wide area operations.

This paper represents a first step in the design and implementation of a PDKD architecture that integrate data mining techniques and computational grid resources. Section 2 describes the existing approaches in the implementation of PDKD systems. Section 3 discusses the requirements of parallel and distributed data mining on grids and what basic services the grid offers as basic support for PDKD. Section 4 describes the Knowledge Grid architecture and define the features and services of each layer of the proposed architecture.

2 Existing Approaches for PDKD

In the literature are described some PDKD systems that support high-performance distributed data mining. Those systems operate on clusters of computers or over the Internet, but, none of those we know make use of the computational grid infrastructure for the implementation of the basic services of authentication, data access, communication and security.

Papyrus [7] is a distributed data mining system developed for clusters and super-clusters of workstations as composed four software layers: data management, data mining, predictive modeling, and agent or Bast. The data management layer is implemented as a global data warehouse that allows to move data from node to node. The Bast layer selects strategies and resources and move predictive models among the cluster nodes. Thus this system has the ability to combine data and models movement. For this Papyrus is based on mobile agents implemented using Java aglets.

Another interesting distributed data mining suite based on Java is PaDDMAS [11], a component-based tool set that integrates pre-developed or custom packages (that can be sequential or parallel) using a dataflow approach. PaDDMAS provides three types of components: data managemnt components, data analysis components and data visualization components. Each component is wrapped as a Java or CORBA object with its interface specified in XML. Components can be located at distributed nodes and connectivity to databases is provided thorough JDBC bridges.

Kensington Enterprise data mining [1] is a PDKD system based on a three-tier client/server architecture in which the three tiers include: client, application server and third-tier servers (RDBMS and parallel data mining service). The data models (knowledge) built on a remote server are moved, under the control of the application server, to the client node for evaluation. The Kensington system has been implemented in Java and uses the Enterprise JavaBeans component architecture. Via a CORBA interface C+MPI data mining packages can be integrated in the Java framework and databases located on the Internet can be accessed via a JDBC connection.

JAM [12] is an agent-based distributed data mining system that has been developed to mine data stored in different sites for building so called meta-models as a combination of several models learned at the different sites where data are stored. JAM uses Java applets to move data mining agents to remote sites. In this way, the knowledge discovery is speeded up by executing in parallel a number of data mining processes on different data subsets and then combining the results through meta-learning. A sort of meta-learning, called *collective data mining*, is implemented also in the BODHI system [8]. BODHI is another agent-based distributed data mining system implemented in Java as a hierarchy of four main components: the individual agents, the agent stations on each processing node, the facilitator for coordination of agent stations and the user interface for system configuration and control. Like JAM and the Kensington system, BODHI support the migration of mining agents over the nodes where data are stored and collect the produced models on a central node where models are combined and analyzed.

Besides the systems we discussed here, other distributed data mining systems that have recently been developed or are in development are WoRLD, MASSON [9], PADMA and DMA.

Concurrently with these research work on distributed data mining, several research groups are working in the computational grid area developing algorithms, components, and services that can be exploited in the implementation of distributed data mining systems. Thus, this work could be useful integrated with work on parallel and distributed data mining to obtain world-wide grid based PDKD systems for the analysis of large data collections in scientific and commercial areas.

3 Parallel and Distributed Data Mining on Grids

Traditional sequential KDD typically requires local (central) storage of data, which may not always be stored in a single repository. Their collection in some cases is not feasible because of their large size, limited network bandwidth, security concerns, scalability problems, or just because they are have different owners or are geographically distributed. PDKD is the application of the KDD techniques to distributed, large, possibly heterogeneous, volumes of data that are residing over computing nodes distributed on a geographic area. Several parallel algorithms for single data mining tasks such as classification, clustering and association have been designed in the past years. However, it lacks a proposal for integrated environments that use novel computing platforms to PDKD environments that integrate different sources, models, and tools. Parallel and distributed knowledge discovery is based on the use of high-bandwidth communication networks and high-performance parallel computers for the mining of data in a distributed and parallel fashion. This technology is particularly useful for large organizations, environments and enterprises that manage and analyze data that are geographically distributed in different data repositories or warehouses [5].

The Grid has emerged recently as an integrated infrastructure for high-performance distributed computation. Grid applications often involve large amounts of data and/or computing, and are not easily handled by today's Internet and Web infrastructures. Grid middleware targets technical challenges in such areas as communication, scheduling, security, information, data access, and fault detection [10]. However, till today no efforts are devoted to the development of PDKD tools and services on the computational grid. Because of the importance of data mining and grid technologies, it is very useful to develop data mining environments on grid platforms by deploying grid services for the extraction of knowledge from large distributed data repositories. The only effort that has been done in the direction of data intensive applications on the grid is the *Data Grid* project that aims to implement a data management architecture based on two main services: storage system and metadata management [2]. This project is not concerned with data mining issues, but its basic services could be used to implement higher-level grid services such as the ones we intend to develop.

Motivated by these considerations, we are working in the definition of a reference software architecture, which we call the *Knowledge Grid*, for the implementation of PDKD systems on top of grid toolkits such as Globus, Legion, and NASA IPG. We attempt to overcome the difficulties of wide area, multi-site operation by exploiting the underlying grid infrastructure that provides basic services such as communication, authentication, resource management, and information. To this end, we organize the knowledge grid architecture so that more specialized data mining tools are compatible with lower-level Grid mechanisms and also with the Data Grid services. This approach benefits from "standard" grid services that are more and more utilized and offers an open PDKD architecture that can be configured on top of grid middleware in a simple way.

3.1 Requirements

Here we identify the basic principles that motivate the architecture design of the grid-aware PDKD system we propose.

Data heterogeneity and large data size. The system must be able to cope with very large and high dimensional data sets that are geographically distributed and stored in different types of repositories as structured data in DBMS, text in files or semi-structured data in Web sites.

Algorithm integration and independence. The architecture must allow the integration of different data mining algorithms and suites and must be as independent as possible from the data mining algorithms used for knowledge extraction. A data interface orthogonal to the data mining tools so that data access will be uniform is to be defined.

Compatibility with grid infrastructure and grid awareness. The higher levels of the architecture use the basic grid services for implementing wide area communication, cooperation and resource management of a PDKD system. Thus the data mining services are interfaced with the lower levels of the grid infrastructure. The interface is aware of the grid services and accesses them for supporting the data mining components in the distributed execution of knowledge discovery tasks.

Openness. The system architecture must be open to be integrated with new data mining tools and knowledge discovery packages. Sequential and parallel analysis models will be added to extend the knowledge discovery services without affecting the lower levels of the Knowledge Grid architecture.

Scalability. The architecture must be scalable both in terms of number of nodes used for performing the distributed knowledge discovery tasks and in terms of performance achieved by using parallel computers to speed up the mining task.

Security and data privacy. Security and privacy issues are vital features in wide area distributed systems. The grid services offer a valid support to the PDKD system to cope with user authentication, security and privacy of data. Basic grid functionality (e.g., Globus security infrastructure - GSI) are able to support secure client-server interactions without impacting on the usability of the grid infrastructure and services.

3.2 *What the Grid offers*

As mentioned before, grid infrastructure tools, such as Globus [4] and Legion [6], provide basic services that can be effectively used in the development of the knowledge grid handling distributed, heterogeneous computing resources as a single virtual parallel computer. Just to outline the type of services, in tables 1 and 2 we list the core Globus services [4] and the Data Grid services [10]. These services address several PDKD requirements discussed before and need to be included in the Knowledge Grid architecture.

Table 1. Basic Globus Services.

Name	Description
GRAM	Resource allocation and process management
Nexus	Unicast and multicast communication services
GSI	Authentication and related security services
MDS (GIS)	Distributed access to structure and state information
HBM	Monitoring of status of system components
GASS	Remote access to data via seq. and parallel interfaces
GEM	Construction, caching, and location of executables
GARA	Advanced resource reservation and allocation

Table 2. Data Grid Services.

Name	Description
RSDF	Replica selection and data filtering services
RM	Replica management services
MS	Metadata information management services
SS	Storage system and data access services

For each of the listed services, C and/or Java application programming interface (API) is defined for use by developers, thus the higher-level components of a PDKD system will use these services by calling the corresponding APIs.

4 A Reference Architecture

The Knowledge Grid architecture is defined on top of grid toolkits and services, i.e. it uses basic grid services to build specific Knowledge Grid services. Following the Integrated Grid Architecture approach, these services can be developed in different ways using the available grid toolkits and services, such as Globus, Legion, SNIPE, etc. However, in this paper an architecture based on the Globus toolkits will be discussed.

As in Globus, the Knowledge Grid offers some global services based on the cooperation and combination of local services. For example, on each node of Globus the MDS (recently named GIS) service provides information about system components available on that node (local service), and it is implemented by a LDAP server. So the Global MDS services are obtained on the basis of the local services through the cooperation of those LDAP servers. In the Knowledge Grid, the discovery of data or algorithms is based on a Knowledge Directory Service (KDS), developed on and extending the basic Globus MDS service.

The Knowledge Grid, shown in figure 1, is composed by two main components:

- a set of knowledge grid-enabled (K-grid) nodes declaring their availability to participate to some PDKD computation, that are connected by,
- a grid infrastructure, offering basic grid-services (authentication, data location, service level negotiation, etc.) and implementing the Knowledge Grid services.

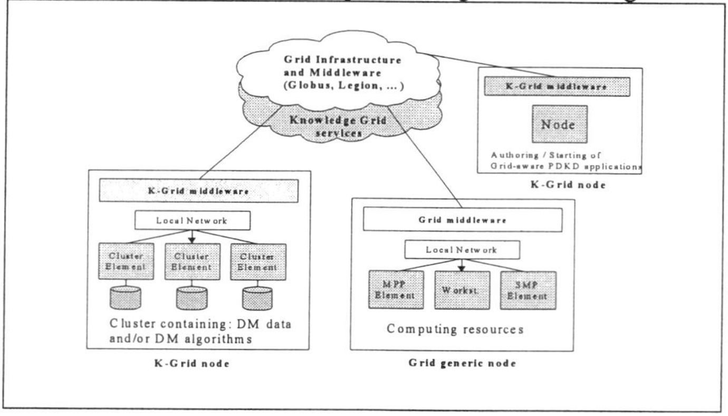

Figure 1. Knowledge Grid components interconnection with generic nodes and K-grid nodes.

Because of the grid infrastructure continues to serve pre-existing grid applications, generic grid nodes could not participate in the Knowledge grid. A K-grid node can start a PDKD application, or it just provide data for distributed data mining, or it can execute data mining packages. The users of the Knowledge Grid can be:

- Domain users, i.e. scientists that are mainly interested in executing available PDKD applications, analyzing and comparing their results with the knowledge available on the grid or that can develop their own PDKD applications composing existing DM tools and algorithms, using the Knowledge Grid services.
- Domain developers, that own or develop DM components, and allow their use to third party users by publishing them using the Knowledge Grid services.

- Data managers, that owns or produce data sources useful to conduct PDKD computations and allow their use to third party users by publishing them using the Knowledge Grid services.

The publishing of data sources availability requires the specification of a security access policy, based on the security services offered both by the core grid and by the Knowledge grid (e.g., access is allowed to some Globus users, but the data are to be aggregated or filtered before moving to the users). In the rest of the section the basic Knowledge Grid services will be presented.

4.1 Knowledge Grid services

The Knowledge Grid services (layers) are organized in two hierarchic levels: *core K-grid layer* and *high level K-grid layer*. The former refers to services directly implemented on the top of generic grid services, the latter are used to describe, develop and execute PDKD computations over the Knowledge Grid. The Knowledge Grid layers are depicted in figure 2. The figure shows layers as implemented on the top of Globus services, moreover, the knowledge grid data and metadata repositories are also shown.

4.1.1 Core K-grid layer

The core K-grid layer has to support the definition, composition and execution of a PDKD computation over the grid. Its main goals are the management of all metadata describing characteristics of data sources, third party data mining tools, data management, and data visualization tools and algorithms. Moreover, this layer has to coordinate the PDKD computation executions, attempting to match the application requirements and the available grid resources. This layer comprises the following basic services:

Knowledge Directory Service (KDS). This service extending the basic Globus MDS service, is responsible for maintaining a description of all the data and tools used in the Knowledge Grid. The metadata managed by the KDS regard the following kind of objects:

- data source providing the data to be mined, such as databases, plain files, XML documents and other structured or unstructured data. Usually data to be mined are extracted from their sources only when needed;
- tools and algorithms used to extract, filter and manipulate data (data management tools);
- tools and algorithms used to analyze (mine) data (data analysis tools);
- tools and algorithms used to visualize, store and manipulate PDKD computations results (data visualization tools);
- PDKD execution plans, they are graphs describing the interaction and data flow between data sources, DM tools, visualization tools, and result storing. An execution plan is an abstract description of a PDKD grid application;

- PDKD results, i.e. the "knowledge" discovered after a PDKD computation.

The metadata information are represented by XML (eXtensible Markup Language) documents and are stored in a *Knowledge Metadata Repository (KMR)*. For example, they describe the different sources of data that can be mined, as location, format, availability, available views and level of aggregation of data.

Whereas it could be infeasible to maintain the data to be mined in an ad hoc repository, it could be useful to maintain a repository of the "knowledge" discovered after a PDKD computation. These information (see below) are stored in a *Knowledge Base Repository (KBR)*, but the metadata describing them are managed by the KDS. The KDS is so used not only to search and access raw data, but also to find pre-discovered knowledge that can be used to compare the output of a given PDKD computation when varying data, or to apply data mining tools in an incremental way.

Because of the data management, analysis and visualization tools are usually pre-existent to the Knowledge Grid they should not be stored in any specialized repository (i.e. they resides over file systems or code libraries). However, to make them available to PDKD computations relevant metadata have to be stored in the KMR. In a similar way metadata are to be stored to allow the use of data sources. Another important repository is the *Knowledge Execution Plan (KEP)* storing the execution plans over the grid of PDKD computations.

Resource allocation and execution management. These services are used to find a mapping between an execution plan and available resources, with the goal of satisfying requirements (computing power, storage, memory, database, network bandwidth and latency) and constraints. The mapping has to be effectively obtained (co)- allocating resources. After the execution plan has been started, this layer had to manage and coordinate the application execution. Other than using the KDS and the MDS services, this layer is directly based on the GRAM services. Resource requests of single data mining programs are expressed using the Resource Specification Language (RSL). The analysis and processing of the execution plan will generate global resource requests that in turn are translated into local RSL requests for local GRAMs and communication requirements for Nexus or other high level communication services.

4.1.2 High level K-grid layer

The high-level K-grid layer comprises the services used to compose, to validate, and to execute a PDKD computation. Moreover, the layer offers services to store and analyze the knowledge discovered by PDKD computations. Main services are:

Data Access. The Data Access services are responsible for the search, selection (*Data search services*), extraction, transformation and delivery (*Data extraction services*) of data to be mined. The search and selection services are based on the core *KDS* service. On the basis of the user requirements and constraints, the Data access service automates (or assists the user in) the searching and finding of data sources to be analyzed by the DM tools.

The extraction, transformation and delivery of data to be mined (*Data extraction*) are based on the GASS services and use the KDS. After useful data have been found, the data mining tools can require some transformation, whereas the user requirements or security constraints can require some data filtering before extraction. These operations can usually be done after the DM tools are chosen. The extraction functions can be embedded in the data mining programs or, more usefully, can be coded and stored in a utility repository, accessible by the KDS.

Tools and algorithms access. This layer is responsible for the search, selection, downloading of data mining tools and algorithms. As before, the metadata regarding their availability, location, configuration, etc., are stored in the KMR and managed by the KDS, whereas the tools and algorithms are stored in the local storage facility of each K-grid node. A node wishing to "export" data mining tools to other users has to "publish" them using the KDS services, which store the metadata in the local portion of the KMR. Some relevant metadata are parameters, format of input/output data, kind of data m,ining algorithm implemented, resource requirements and constraints, and so on.

Execution plan management. An execution plan is an abstract description of a PDKD grid application. It is a graph describing the interaction and data flows between data sources, extraction tools, DM tools, visualization tools, storing of knowledge results in the KBR. In simplest cases the user can directly describe the execution plan, using a visual composition tool where the programs are connected to the data sources. However, due to the variety of results produced by the Data access and Tool access layers, different execution plans can be produced, in terms of data and tools location, strategies to move or stage intermediate results and so on. Thus, the Execution Plan management is a semi-automatic tool that takes the data and programs selected by the user, and generates a set of different, possible execution plans that satisfy user, data an algorithms requirements and constraints.

Execution plans are stored in a *Knowledge Execution Plan (KEP)* repository to allow the implementation of iterative knowledge discovery processes, e.g. periodical analysis of the same data sources that vary during time. More simply, the same execution plan can be used to analyze different set of data. Moreover, different execution plans can be used to analyze in parallel the same set of data, and to compare the results using different point of views (e.g. performance, accuracy).

Results presentation. This layer specifies how to generate, present and visualize the PDKD results (rules, associations, models, classification, etc.). Moreover, it offers the API to store in different formats these results in the Knowledge Base Repository. The result metadata, are stored in the KMR to be managed by the KDS. The KDS is so used not only to search and access raw data, but also to find pre-discovered knowledge that can be used to compare the output of a given PDKD computation when varying data, or to apply data mining tools in an incremental way.

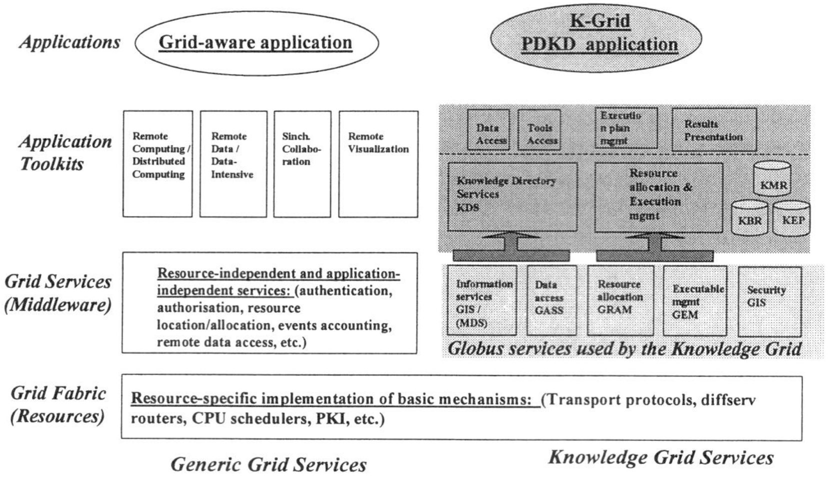

Figure 2. Knowledge Grid architecture layers.

Results presentation. This layer specifies how to generate, present and visualize the PDKD results (rules, associations, models, classification, etc.). Moreover, it offers the API to store in different formats these results in the Knowledge Base Repository. The result metadata, are stored in the KMR to be managed by the KDS.

5 Conclusion

Parallel and distributed data mining suites and computational grid technology are two critical elements of future high-performance computing environments that will enable entirely new classes of advanced applications. Their integration is a challenge whose achievements could produce many benefits in several strategic application areas. Combining the results and models emerging in these apparently far areas, it could empower PDKD and allow a new class of applications to be developed. Each of these areas could leverage on the counterpart efforts reducing costs, and domain scientists could be free to concentrate over specific problems, benefiting by this architectural independence. Furthermore, PDKD could benefits from the research efforts that are in progress in the computational grid area. This work represents the first steps in the process of studying the unification of PDKD and computational grid technologies and defining an integrating architecture for distributed data mining and knowledge discovery based on grid services. We hope that the definition of such an architecture will accelerate progress on very large-scale geographically distributed data mining by enabling the integration of currently disjoint approaches and revealing technology gaps that require further research and development. Finally, we plan to construct a first implementation for this architecture so as to enable large-scale experimentation.

References

1. Chattratichat J., Darlington J., Guo Y., Hedvall S., Köler M. and Syed J., An architecture for distributed enterprise data mining. *HPCN Europe 1999*, *Lecture Notes in Computer Science,* **1593** (*Springer*, 1999) pp. 573-582.
2. Chervenak A., Foster I., Kesselman C., Salisbury C. and Tuecke S., The Data Grid: towards an architecture for the distributed management and analysis of large scientific datasets. *Journal of Network and Computer Appls* (2000).
3. Fayyad U.M. and Uthurusamy R. (eds.), Data mining and knowledge discovery in databases. *Communications of the ACM* **39** (1997).
4. Foster I. and Kesselman C., Globus : a metacomputing infrastructure toolkit. *International Journal of Supercomputing Applications* **11** (1997) pp. 115-128.
5. Freitas A.A. and Lavington S.H., *Mining Very Large Databases with Parallel Processing* (Kluwer Academic Publishers, 1998).
6. Grimshaw A.S., Ferrari A., Knabe F., and Humphrey M., Wide-area computing: resource sharing on a large scale. *Computer* **32** (1999) pp. 29-37.
7. Grossman R., Bailey S., Kasif S., Mon D., Ramu A. and Malhi B., The preliminary design of papyrus: a system for high performance, distributed data mining over clusters, meta-clusters and super-clusters. *International KDD'98 Conference* (1998) pp. 37-43.
8. Kargupta H., Park B., Hershberger, D. and Johnson, E., Collective data mining: a new perspective toward distributed data mining. In HILLOL KARGUPTA AND PHILIP CHAN (eds.) *Advances in Distributed and Parallel Knowledge Discovery* (AAAI Press 1999).
9. Kimm H. and Ryu T.-W., A framework for distributed knowledge discovery system over heterogeneous networks using CORBA. *KDD2000 Workshop on Distributed and Parallel Knowledge Discovery* (2000).
10. Moore R., Baru C., Marciano R., Rajasekar A. and Wan M., Data-intensive computing. In I. FOSTER AND C. KESSELMAN (eds.) *The Grid: Blueprint for a Future Computing Inf.* (Morgan Kaufmann Publishers, 1999) pp. 105-129.
11. Rana O.F., Walker D.W., Li M., Lynden S. and Ward M., PaDDMAS: parallel and distributed data mining application suite. *Proc. International Parallel and Distributed Processing Symposium (IPDPS/SPDP)*, (IEEE Computer Society Press, 2000) pp. 387-392.
12. Stolfo S.J., Prodromidis A.L., Tselepis S., Lee W., Fan D.W., Chan P.K., JAM: Java agents for meta-learning over distributed databases. *International KDD'97 Conference* (1997) pp. 74-81.

A GRID DENSITY-BASED CLUSTERING ALGORITHM FOR LARGE DATABASES

Ning Chen[1],
Mathematics Institute, Chinese Academy of Sciences, Beijing, 100080, P. R. China
1, Department of Computer Science, City University of HongKong, Tat Chee Avenue, Kowloon, HongKong, P. R. China
E-mail: anchen1@yahoo.com

An Chen[2]
** Economics and Management School, Beijing Univ. of Aeronautics & Astronautics, 100083,*
2, Department of Management Sciences, City University of HongKong, Tat Chee Avenue, Kowloon, HongKong, P. R. China
E-mail: msanchen@cityu.edu.hk

Longxiang Zhou
Mathematics Institute, Chinese Academy of Sciences, Beijing, 100080, P. R. China
E-mail: lxzhou@math20.math.ac.cn

Clustering is an attractive task of data mining [FPS 96] which partitions data into a group of classes maximizing the intra-class similarity and minimizing the interclass similarity. Although many algorithms have been proposed for clustering, seldom was focused on clustering for high-dimensional database or incremental clustering. In this paper, we introduce a grid density-based clustering algorithm-GDCA which discover clusters in large spatial database firstly, then the computing complexity of the algorithm are discussed, some computing results such as the efficiency and the relative performance are given lastly.

1 Introduction

Clustering is a descriptive task that seeks to identify homogeneous groups of objects based on the values of their attributes (dimensions) [JD 88]. Clustering groups a set of data (without a predefined class attribute), based on the conceptual clustering principle: maximizing the intra-class similarity and minimizing the interclass similarity. Clustering techniques have been discussed extensively in the database literature as a tool for similarity search, customer segmentation, pattern recognition, trend analysis and classification. Recently, clustering has been recognized as a primary data mining method for knowledge discovery in spatial databases.

Many databases are very large and consist of millions of data objects with several tens to a few hundreds of dimensions, for example, image, CAD, geographic, and molecular biology data is usually transformed into high-dimensional feature vectors and stored in database. Automated clustering in high-dimensional databases is an important problem. Unfortunately, there are little clustering algorithms applicable to high-dimensional database. [AGGR 98] and [AP 99] discover clusters in subspace using multi scans of database.

Single scan clustering algorithms discover clusters with arbitrary shape in one scan of database. In contrast to hierarchical clustering and partition clustering, a predetermined cluster number is unnecessary which is usually very difficult to be determined especially in high-dimensional database. Furthermore, they can separate noise which is formal in real database from clusters. Since they depend on spatial data structure such as R*-tree to support the near or nearest neighborhood queries, they do not work efficiently due to the performance degeneration of R*-tree based index structures in high-dimensional data space. For example, DBSCAN [EKSX 96] has an almost quadratic time complexity for high-dimensional data. Due to the sparsity property of high-dimensional data space, noise becomes more ubiquitous than in low-dimensional space. It is feasible to improve the efficiency of DBSCAN by only searching the queries of core points. In this paper, we present a grid density-based clustering algorithm-GDCA. We first partition the data space into a number of units of same volume, and then deal with every unit in stead of every point. Only those units with the density no less than a given minimum density threshold are useful in extending clusters. It meets the following requirements for clustering algorithms: discovery of clusters with arbitrary shape, the ability of handling noise and good efficiency on large database.

The rest of the paper is organized as follows: We first discuss related work on clustering algorithms in section 2, some widely used algorithms such as DBSCAN, Generalized DBSCAN, DBCLASD, and FDC are given. In section 3, we present our notions of clustering. We develop a grid density-based clustering algorithm-GDCA which discover clusters in large spatial database in section 4. Experiments are performed on synthetic and real databases to evaluate the effectiveness and efficiency of our algorithms in Section 5. In section 6, we conclude the paper.

2 Related Work

Clustering has been studied in statistics, machine learning, spatial database, and data mining areas with different emphases. Clustering algorithms can be categorized into four main groups: hierarchical algorithms [GRK 98] [GRS 99] [ZRL 96], partition algorithms [NH 94] [EKX 95], density-based algorithms [EKSX 96] [EKSX 97] and grid-based algorithms [SCH 96] [WYM 97].

The application of clustering algorithms to large spatial databases raises the following requirements: (1) minimal number of input parameters, (2) discovery of clusters with arbitrary shape and (3) efficiency on large databases. Single scan clustering algorithms are presented to fulfil these requirements. The basic idea of a single scan algorithm is to group neighboring objects of the database into clusters based on a local cluster condition thus performing only one scan through the database. The result is, like in the case of partitioning algorithms, a single level clustering.

Density-based clustering methods group neighboring objects of the database into clusters based on a local cluster condition thus performing only one scan through the database. There are some related algorithms as follow.

DBSCAN (Density Based Spatial Clustering of Applications with Noise) finds dense regions that are separated by low density regions and clusters together the objects in the same dense region. A density-based cluster is defined as a maximal set of density-connected points that for each point of a cluster its Eps-neighborhood has to contain at least Minpts of points. DBSCAN requires the user to specify two parameters that are used to define minimum density for clustering –the radius Eps of the neighborhood of a point and the minimum number of points Minpts in the neighborhood. Clusters are then found by starting from an arbitrary point and if its neighborhood satisfies the minimum density, including the points in its neighborhood into the cluster. Those points whose Eps-neighborhood contains less than Minpts of points are marked noise. The noise points can be clustered if they belong to the Eps-neighborhood of a core point of a cluster in later process. The process is then repeated until there is no point which has not been clustered or marked noise. Since the region queries can be supported efficiently by spatial access method such as R*-tree[BKSS 90], the average rum time complexity of DBSCAN is O(N logN), where n is the number of data points in database. But overlap in directory of R*-tree is increasing very rapidly with growing dimensionality of the data, which leads to go through many paths for region queries. So, R*-tree can only adequately support an effective indexing of moderate values of dimensions. Even if a special indexing techniques [BSK 96] [BBK 98] for high-dimensional data is used, many points don't have sufficient information about the density of the data in high-dimensional space. [WSB 98] shows that all partitioning and clustering techniques for similarity search exhibit linear complexity at high dimensionality, and that existing methods are outperformed on average by a simple sequential scan if the number of dimensions exceeds around 10.

GDBSCAN (Generalized DBSCAN) [EKSX 97] generalized DBSCAN from two ways. First, any notion of a neighborhood can be used instead of an Ept-neighborhood, allowing a natural definition in the case of spatially extended objects if the definition of the neighborhood is based on a binary predicate which is symmetric and reflexive. Second, instead of simply counting the objects in neighborhood of an object, the definition of cardinality for a set of neighboring objects may take into account the non-spatial attributes of the objects as a means of assigning application specific weighs.

DBCLASD (Distribution Based Clustering of LArge Spatial Database) [XEKS98] discovers clusters of arbitrary density without requiring any input parameters. It assumes that the points inside of a cluster are uniformly distributed. The notion of a cluster is based on the distance of the points of a cluster to their nearest neighbors and the algorithm analyzes expected distribution of these distances for a cluster. DBCLASD incrementally augments an initial cluster by its neighboring points as long as the nearest neighbor distance set of the resulting cluster still fits the expected distribution. The retrieval of neighboring points is based on region queries, which are efficiently supported by spatial access methods. Its efficiency is between DBSCAN and CLARANS, close to DBSCAN.

For many real-data sets, there does not even exist a global parameter setting for which the result of the clustering algorithm describes the intrinsic clustering structure accurately. OPTICS [ABKS 99] computes an augmented clustering ordering the database objects. Users do not limit themselves to one global parameter setting. Instead, the augmented cluster ordering contains information which is equivalent to the density-based clustering corresponding to a broad range of parameter setting and thus is a versatile basis for both automatic and interactive cluster analysis.

FDC (Fast Density-based Clustering)[ZC 99] defines clusters by an equivalence relation on the objects in the database. It first stores all the data points in a k-d tree to partition the whole data space into a set of rectangular subspaces, each represented by a leaf node on the tree. Then it divides each subspace into equal sized cells whose length is Ept. Therefore, it only need to check the 3^d cells in order to find out all neighboring points for any point in the subspace. The runtime complexity of computing the Ept- neighborhood for all points is $O(N*3^d)$, where d is the dimensionality of the database. When d is a small integer, the time complexity of FDC is linear to the size of the database, which is much faster than that of DBSCAN. However, it's obvious that the runtime of FDC exponentially increases with the dimension number d. When d is large, for example d= 30, 3^d is around $2*10^{14}$, then the time complexity $O(N3^d) \neq O(N)$. Another drawback of FDC is that it need two passes of database. In the first scan, it assigns a new Cluster to a core point and its Eps-neighbor points and marks the equivalent clusters which intersect at same points. In the second scan, it re-labels all points in equivalent clusters with unique cluster.

3 Concepts and Definitions

Let $A=\{A_1,A_2,\ldots,A_d\}$ be a set of numerical attributes (dimensions) of the database, each dimension A_i having a bounded, totally ordered domain. $S = A_1\times A_2\times\ldots\times A_d$ is the minimum bounding hyper-rectangle of the database, constructing a d-dimensional numerical space. The input data $D = \{p_1, p_2, \ldots, p_N\}$ is the set of d-dimensional points, where $p_i = \{v_{i1}, v_{i2}, \ldots, v_{id}\}$, $v_{ij} \in A_j$, for $1 \le j \le d$, $1 \le i \le N$.

The first step is to partition the data space S into non-overlapping rectangle units, with the ith dimension being divided into m_i intervals of equal length. Assuming m is equal to m_i for all dimensions, S is divided into 2^m units. Let s_i is the length of the interval in dimension i. A d-dimensional point $p = \{v_1, v_2, \ldots, v_d\}$ is mapped into unit $c=\{r_1, r_2, \ldots, r_d\}$, $1 \le r_i \le m_i$, if $(r_i - 1)s_i \le v_i < r_i \times s_i$, $1 \le i \le d$, and $\{r_1, r_2, \ldots, r_d\}$ is called the position of c.

Definition 1: The density of unit c is defined as the number of data points contained in c, denoted by N(c). A unit is called a non-empty unit if at least one point contained in it. A unit is called a dense unit if its density is no less than δ, where density threshold δ is an input parameter. $C_{ne} = \{c|\ N(c) \ge 0\}$ is the set of non-empty units, and $C_d = \{\ c|\ N(c) \ge \delta\}$ is the set of dense units.

The number of non-empty units $|C_{ne}|$ can range from 1 to $\min(2^m, n)$ depending on the parameter m, the number of data points n and the distribution of the points. In high-dimensional data space, the overwhelming majority of the units are empty. For example, $N = 10^6$, d=100, there are around 10^{30} units even for m = 2, while $|C_{ne}|$ is at most 10^6 when the distribution of points is uniform. In low dimensional space, the number of non-empty units is exponential to d. As the dimensionality increases, it becomes linear to N. In general, the number of dense units $|C_d|$ is much less than the number of non-empty units due to the non-uniform distribution.

Definition 2: The distance between two units c_1 and c_2 is defined as $d(c_1, c_2) = dist(mean(c_1), mean(c_2))$, where the mean of a unit c $mean(c) = \sum_{x \in c} x / |c|$, $|c|$ is the number of points in c. The distance function can be Euclidean distance L_2 :$d_{ij} = \sqrt{\sum_{k=1}^{d} (v_{ik} - v_{jk})^2}$, where d_{ij} is the distance between two points p_i and p_j, and v_{ik} is the value of the kth attribute for p_i, or Manhatta distance L_1 : $d_{ij} = \sum_{k=1}^{d} | v_{ik} - v_{jk} |$.

Definition 3: The neighborhood of a unit c is defined as $near(c) = \{c'|c' \in C_{ne}, d(c',c) \le \tau\}$, where τ is another input parameter, representing the maximum distance of neighborhood.

Definition 4: (directly density-reachable) A unit c' is directly density-reachable from a unit c wrt. τ and δ if

(1) $c' \in near(c)$ and

(2) $c \in C_d$ (c is a dense unit)

Definition 5: (density-reachable) A unit c' is density-reachable from a unit c wrt. τ and δ if there is a chain of units $c_1, c_2, \ldots, c_k$, $c_1 = c$, $c_k = c'$, such that c_{i+1} is directly density-reachable from c_i.

Definition 6: (density-connected) A unit c' is density-connected to a unit c wrt. τ and δ if there is a unit c'' such that both c and c' is density-reachable from c''.

Definition 7: (cluster) Let D be a database of points and C_{ne} be the non-empty units mapped from D. A cluster C wrt τ and δ is a non-empty subset of C_{ne} with all points contained in them being assigned to C satisfying the following conditions:

(1) $\forall c, c'$: if $c \in C$ and c' is density-reachable from c wrt. τ and δ, then $c' \in C$.

(2) $\forall c, c' \in C$: c is density-connected to c' wrt. τ and δ.

Definition 8: (noise) Let $C_1, C_2, \ldots, C_k$, be the clusters of database C_{ne} wrt. τ and δ. We defined the noise units C_n as the set of units not belonging to any cluster C_i, i.e. $C_n = \{c \mid c \notin C_i, i=1,2,\ldots,k\}$. All points contained in C_n is assigned to noise, i.e., noise $= \{p \mid p \in C_n\}$.

Definition 9 (clustering) A clustering of database D is to partition D into a set of clusters $C_1, C_2, \ldots, C_k$ and C_n, $C_1 \cup C_2 \cup \ldots \cup C_k \cup C_n = D$ and $\forall i,j \in \{1,2,\ldots,k, n\}$, $C_i \cap C_j = \varnothing$.

Theorem 1: Let c be a dense unit. The set $C = \{c' \mid c' \in C_{ne}$ and c' is density-reachable from c wrt. τ and $\delta\}$ is a cluster wrt. τ and δ.

Theorem 2: Let C be a cluster wrt. τ and δ and c is an arbitrary dense unit in C. Then $C = \{c' \mid c' \in C_{ne}$ and c' is density-reachable from c wrt. τ and $\delta\}$.

Theorem 2 implies that a cluster can be determined by any dense unit contained in it. Starting from an arbitrary dense unit, a cluster is created by extending to its neighbor units. This procedure is applied to the new retrieved dense units until all density-reachable units from the start unit are retrieved. Then another unclustered dense unit is selected to discover a new cluster.

4 Grid-based Density Clustering Algorithm (GDCA)

4.1 The Algorithm

First, we describe the main steps of GDCA:

(1) Preprocess (partition the database space S into units):

Let m be the number of intervals divided for every dimension, δ be the minimum density of dense units. The preprocess step scans the database D, mapping each point into the unit in which it is contained and stores the non-empty units in a k-d tree [Ben 75]. For each non-empty unit $c \in C_{ne}$, in addition to its position, the number of points in c, the sum of the points and pointers to those points are stored.

(2) Clustering C_{ne}:

It is an essential step of GDCA which finds the cluster of units based on density-reachable and density-connected. To find a cluster, GDCA starts with an arbitrary dense unit c and retrieves all units density-reachable from c wrt.τ and δ. This procedure yields a cluster wrt.τ and δ according to lemma 1. Consequently, the procedure repeats by starting with an unclustered dense unit until there is no unclustered dense unit. The detail is described in procedure clustering().

(3) Map each point in D to the clusters:

For each point p in D, we assign p to the cluster C_i, if $p \in c$, and $c \in C_i$. If $p \in c$, $c \notin C_i$, for i=1,2,...,k, then p is assigned to noise.

Procedure clustering (C_{ne}, C_d, τ)

Input: C_{ne}: non-empty units of S, C_d: dense units of S, τ: the maximum distance from a dense unit to its neighborhood.

Output: a set of clusters of units: $C_1, C_2, \ldots, C_k$.

```
{ClusterId:= NextID(NOISE);
For i:=1 to | Cd | do
{startc = Cd.get(i);
 if startc.Clid = UNCLUSTERD then
 ExpandCluster(Cne, Cd, startc,ClusterId, τ)
 ClusterId := NextId (ClusterId);
 }
}
```

ExpandCluster finds a cluster starting from starts as the only unit in seeds. C_{ne}.regionQuery (CurrentC, τ) returns the neighbor units of CurrectC with the maximum distance τ by searching the k-d tree. For each unclustered unit in the query result, if it belongs to C_d, then we put the unit into seeds. When seeds is equal to empty, there is no density-reachable unit in the cluster, so the procedure is over.

```
ExpandCluster(Cne, Cd, startc,ClusterId, τ)
{
 ChangeClid(stratc, ClusterId);
 Seeds.append(startc);
 While seeds<> Empty do
 {CurrentC := seeds.first();
  result := Cne.regionQuery(CurrentC, τ);
  For i from 1 to results.size do
  { resultC := result.get(i);
   If resultC.Clid = UNCLUSTERD then
   { ChangeClid (resultC, ClusterId);
    If resultC ∈ Cd then seeds.append(resultC);
   }
```

```
  }
 seeds.delete (CurrentC);
 }
 }
```

4.2 Time Complexity of GDCA

For every point, no matter whether it is a core point or a boundary point, DBSCAN or FDC computes its Eps-neighbor points. In fact, the number of core points is much less than that of all points. It is unnecessary to search the neighborhood of the boundary points since no points can be density-reachable from them. But we don not know whether a point is a core point or a boundary point without searching its neighborhood. In GDCA, we deal with every unit in stead of every point. If the unit is small enough, all points in a unit are close enough to be considered as a subcluster. Then we can compute the dense units (similar to core points) in the pre-process. In the clustering step, we only extend these dense units in stead of all units. So, the time complexity of GDCA is $O(N+|C_d| \log |C_{ne}|)$.

GDCA has the following properties:

(1) GDCA only stores the non-empty units in k-d tree, the number of which is linear to N as the dimensionality increases. So, GDCA is applicable for high dimensionality.

(2) GDCA only searches the neighbor units of dense units, the number of which is much less than that of the non-empty units, especially in high-dimensional data space.

(3) The third step of GDCA can be merged with the second step. Then GDCA only scans the database once.

(4) A prune step is possible to prune the units which can't be density-reachable from any dense units. It first computes the nearest dense unit for every non-empty unit, if the distance is more than τ, then it prunes the unit from k-d tree. The pruned k-d tree is much smaller than the origin tree improving the efficiency of queries. Considering the incremental clustering, we store all non-empty units in k-d tree.

(5) Assuming the interval length of every dimension is equal to s, the distance between units is defined as Manhatta distance and the mean of a unit is the gravity center of the unit, Grid-based clustering become a special case of GDCA with $\tau = s$.

5 Performance Studies

In this section, we give the experiment results performed on a Sun workstation

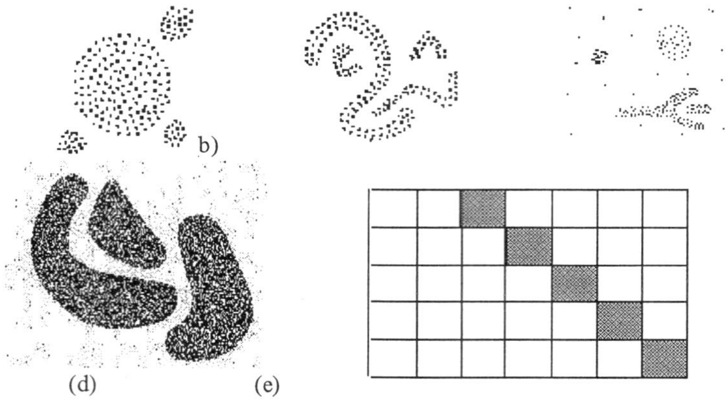

Figure 1: Examples of databases

running Solaris 2.6. We use both synthetic data and real data to evaluate the effectiveness and efficiency of our algorithm and study its scale-up properties.

5.1 Effectiveness

To evaluate the effectivity, we compare GDHD with DBSCAN and Grid clustering because they belong to the most well-known algorithms in clustering area. Figure 1 depicts 5 synthetic databases used in the experiments, (a)-(c) have been used in [EKSX 96], (e) is used to explain the improvement of GDHD over Grid clustering. In Example (e), the shadowed units represent dense units, forming one cluster. GDHD identifies all clusters with shapes and noise correctly from (a)-(d) as DBSCAN does if suitable values for parameters are set. Because grid clustering identifies cluster by extending a dense cell as seed along the orientation of dimensions, it is unable to discover the cluster from (e) by splitting the cluster into 5 small clusters, each consists of a single dense unit. While GDHD can merge the 5 units into one cluster.

5.2 Relative Performance

We perform GDCA on real data-SEQUOIA 2000 benchmark database to test its efficiency in contrast to DBSCAN. We extract a series of subsets from the original database having the different sizes from 10% to 50% of the original size. The relative performance of GDCA and DBSCAN is shown in Figure 2. Because GDCA deals with units in stead of points and the clustering process is independent of the database after preprocess, GDCA is much faster than DBSCAN especially for large number of

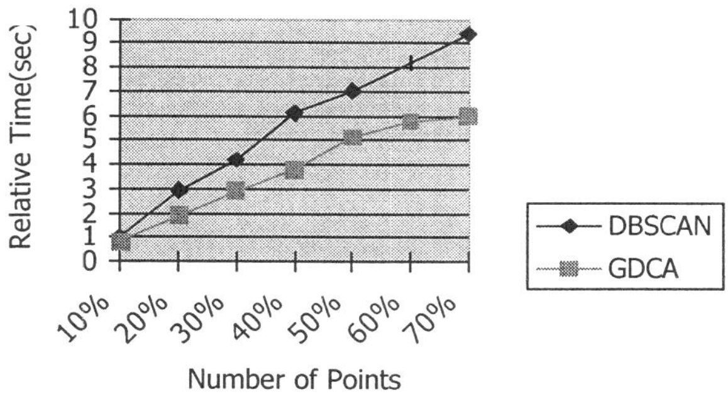

Figure 2: Execution Times

data.

6 Conclusion and Future Work

In this paper, we introduce a grid density-based clustering algorithm - GDCA which discover clusters in large spatial database. Experiments demonstrate that GDCA is superior to DBSCAN especially as the data volume is very large. The contributions of this paper includes:

(1) It gives the definition of unit density-reachable which is the basic of grid density-based clustering.

(2) It proposes a grid density-based clustering algorithm- GDCA, which improves the efficiency of DBSCAN.

Future work will consider the following issues. Clustering of GDCA depends on several parameters. An approach of determining these parameters is useful to users. In addition, using parallel processing we can speed up the efficiency especially when the number of units m or the number of dimensions d is high.

The potentially useful patterns discovered from large database may become old after a series of updates of the databases, which may lead to mistake in decision support. For example, consider a market basket database containing one transaction per customer, each transaction containing the set of items purchased by the customer. The transaction data can be used to cluster the customers such that customers with similar buying patterns are in a single cluster. But the transaction database is updated frequently everyday. While new transactions are being appended to the database, the old clustering is no longer applicable. So, it is important to keep the patterns up to data. Unfortunately, most clustering algorithms are applied to a static database at present. They have to be called from the beginning in order to represent the updated data. Due to the large size of the databases and the high time complexity of clustering algorithms, it is highly desirable to perform these updates incrementally. In the future, we plan to present the incremental algorithm of GDCA.

7 Acknowledgment

We thank Martin Ester for providing the code of DBSCAN algorithm.

Reference

[ABKS 99] M. Ankerst, M. Breunig, H. Kriegel, J. Sander: "OPTICS: Ordering Points to Identify the Clustering structure ", Proc. ACM SIGMOD Int. Conf. On Management of Data, Philadelphia, PA, 1999, pp49-60

[AGGR 98] R. Agrawal, J. Gehrke, D. Gunopolos, P. Raghavan: "Automatic Subspace Clustering of High Dimensional Data for Data Mining Application", Proc. ACM SIGMOD Int. Conf. On Management of Data,1998

[AP 99] C. Aggarwal, C. Procopiuc: " Fast Algorithms for Projected Clustering", Proc. ACM SIGMOD Int. Conf. On Management of Data, 1999, pp61-72

[BBK 98] S. Berchtold, C. BOhm, H. Kriegel: "The Pyramid-Technique: Towards Breaking the Curse of Dimensionality", Proc. ACM SIGMOD Int. Conf. 1998, pp142-153

[Ben 75] Bentley, J. L.: " Multidimensional binary search trees used for associative searching", Comm. ACM, Vol 18, No. 9,1975,pp509-517

[BKSS 90] Beckmann N., Kriegel H-P., Schneider R., Seeger B., " the R*-tree: An Efficient and Robust Access Method for Points and Rectangles", Proc. ACM SIGMOD Int. Conf. On Management of Data, Atlantic City, NJ, ACM Press, 1990, pp322-331

[BSK 96] Berchtold S., Keim D. A., Kriegel H.-P.: " The X-tree: An Index Structure foe High-Dimensional Data ",Proc.22th Int. Conf. On Very Large Databases, Bombay, India, Morgan Kaufmann, 1996, pp28-39

[EKSMX 98] Ester M. Kriegel H.-P , Sander J.,M. Wimmer, Xiaowei Xu: "Incremental Clustering for Mining in a Data Warehousing Environment", Proc. 24th VLDB Int. Conf. New York city, Aug. 1998,pp323-333

[EKSX 96] Ester M. Kriegel H.-P., Sander J., Xu X.:" A Density-Based Algorithm for Discovering Clusters in Large Spatial Databases with Noise" Proc. 2nd Int. Conf. On Knowledge Discovery and Data Mining, Portland, Oregon, AAAI Press, 1996

[EKSX 97] Ester M. Kriegel H.-P., Sander J., Xu X.: " Density-Connected Sets and their Application for Trend Detection in Spatial Databases " Proc. 3rd Int. Conf. On Knowledge Discovery and Data Mining, Newport Beach, Ca, AAAI Press, 1997

[EKX 95] Ester M. Kriegel H.-P., Xu X.: "Knowledge Discovery in Large Discovery in Large Spatial Databases: Focusing Techniques for Efficient Class Identification", Proc. 4th Int. Symp. On Large Spatial Databases, Portland, ME, 1995, in: Lecture Notes in Computer Science, Vol. 951, Springer, 1995, pp67-82

[FPS 96] Fayyad U.M., J. Piatetsky-Shapiro, G. Smyth: " From Data Mining to Knowledge Discovery: An overview" in: Advances in Knowledge Discovery and Data Mining, AAAI Press,1996,pp1-34

[GRK 98] S. Guha, R. Rastogi, K. Shim: " CURE: An Efficient Clustering Algorithm for Large database", ACM Multimedia 1995,pp361-362

[GRS 99] S. Guhu, R. Rastogi, K. Shim: "ROCK: A Robust Clustering Algorithm for Categorical Attributes"

[HK 98] Hinneburg A., Keim D.A.: "An efficient Approach to Clustering in Large Multimedia Databases with Noise", Proc. 4rd Int. Conf. On Knowledge Discovery and Data Mining, AAAI Press, 1998

[HK 99] Hinneburg A., Keim D.A.: " Optimal Grid-Clustering: Towards Breaking the curse of Dimensionality in High-dimensional Clustering", Proc. 25th Int. Conf. On VLDB, Edinburgh, Scotland, 1999

[JD 88] A. K. Jain, R. C. Dubes: " Algorithms for Clustering Data", Prentice Hall, 1988

[NH 94] R. Ng, Han J.: " Efficient and Effective Clustering Methods for Spatial Data Mining", Proc. 20th Int. Conf. On Very Large Databases, Santiago, Chile, Morgan Kaufmann, 1994, pp144-155

[SCH 96] Schikuta E.nn: "Grid clustering: An Efficient Hierarchical Clustering Method for Very Large Data Sets", Proc. 13th Conf. On Pattern Recognition, Vol. 2,IEEE Computer Society Press,pp101-105

[WSB 98] Roger Weber, Hans-J. Schek, Stephen Blott: " A Quantitative analysis and Performance Study for Similarity-search Methods in High-Dimensional Spaces", Proc. 24th Int. Conf. On VLDB, New York, USA, 1998, pp194-205

[WYM 97] Wang W., Yang J., Muntz R.: " STING: A Statistical Information Grid Approach to Spatial Data Mining ", Proc. 23rd Int. Conf. On VLDB, Morgan Kaufmann, 1997

[XEKS 98] Xu,X., Ester, M.,Kriegel, H.-P.,and Sander J.: "A Distribution-Based Clustering Algorithm for Mining in Large Spatial Databases", Proc. 4th Int. Conf. On Data Engineering, Orlando, Florida, 1998, IEEE Computer Society Press, pp324-331

[ZC 99] Bo Zhou, D. Cheung, B.Kao: "A Fast Algorithm for Density-Based Clustering", Prof .3rd,Int. Conf. PAKDD-99 Beijing, China, April, 1999, pp338-349

[ZRL 96] Zhang T., Ramakrishnan R., Linvy M.: "BIRCH: An efficient Data Clustering Method for Very Large Databases". Proc. ACM SIGMOD Int. Conf. On Management of Data, ACM Press, 1996, pp103-114

LOIS: THE "LIGHTS OUT" INTEGRITY SUBSYSTEM FOR ASSISTING DATA QUALITY ADMINISTRATORS

NICHOLAS J. CAINE

Department of Computer Science, Cardiff University,
P.O. Box 916, Cardiff, Wales, U.K. CF24 3XF
E-Mail: {N.J.Caine}@cs.cf.ac.uk

The continued increase in the use of database systems in commercial environments, particularly in mission-critical systems, means that the data stored by these systems are key assets of an organisation. The stored data, however, often contains many errors, which devalues their worth to the organisation.

Traditionally, database management systems contained no integrity checking sub-systems, which meant that all the integrity constraints had to be hard coded into the application program. Commercial database systems have emerged containing integrity checking sub-systems but even these support only limited integrity constraints (e.g. referential integrity). This still leaves corporate database designers with the problem of having to hard code the more complex integrity constraints either into the application logic or implementing them as triggers. In addition this means that the integrity sub-systems only check data entered via the standard input mechanism. It has been shown that there are other ways in which errors can get into the database, such as problems or flaws in the data acquisition process, disk related problems, unauthorised modification of the database by gaining access directly via the operating system, problems with the data update process, 'duplicate' and inconsistent data produced by different programs or departments within the same organisation. The Light's Out Integrity Sub-system (LOIS) is designed as a complementary integrity checking system for mission-critical systems. We are proposing an alternative way of checking the complex business rules against a database, which, using traditional integrity checking mechanisms would prove too expensive to be of practical use in high performance data management environments. For high performance data management, particularly in a distributed environment, the LOIS engine can be run on one processor accessing databases via the distributed capabilities of the RDBMS on other machines possibly in different countries.

1 Introduction

Organisations place great emphasis on their stored data as a key asset. Coupled with the increasing need for higher performance from their information systems and the integration of aging legacy systems, the task of maintaining good levels of data quality then becomes increasingly difficult for the database administrators. There are a number of root causes for poor data quality, for example, in [1] the authors identify poor process design, poor data migration, and poor data generation procedures as some of the ways in which poor quality data can creep into the database. Some errors may be introduced accidentally, as in the case of disk or network failure, or even poor design, while other errors may be the result of deliberate acts to alter the data by unauthorised means. Whatever the reason for the existence of these errors within the data, it remains a fact that the poor quality data is of little use to the organisation that owns the database. A further problem of maintaining good data quality is the processing overhead associated with checking integrity constraints at update or transaction commit time.

Traditionally, database management systems contained no integrity checking sub-systems, which meant that all the integrity constraints had to be hard coded into the application program. Recently commercial database systems have emerged containing integrity checking sub-systems but even these sub-systems support only very basic integrity constraints (e.g. referential integrity). This still leaves corporate database designers with the problem of having to hard code the more complex integrity constraints into the application program. This means that the integrity sub-systems only check data entered via the standard input mechanism. It has been shown that there are other ways in which errors can get into the database. Some examples are [2]: problems or flaws in the data acquisition process, disk related problems, unauthorised modification of the database by gaining access directly via the operating system, problems with the data update process, 'duplicate' and inconsistent data produced by different programs or departments within the organisation, etc. Some errors may also be introduced accidentally, as in the case of disk or network failure, or even poor design, while other errors may be the result of deliberate acts to alter the data by unauthorised means.

The root of poor quality data for most commercial organisations is the existence of legacy systems, and the need to migrate this data to new systems or to integrate into a data warehouse for later use with data mining techniques. The effects of poor data quality on an organisation can be quite devastating. For example, in [3] the author identifies a number of impacts of poor data quality on the organisation at both the operational and strategic levels. Operational level impacts include customer dissatisfaction, increased costs, less effective decision making and lower employee morale. At the strategic level the impact of poor data quality is far more severe, executives often make corporate strategic decisions based on reports compiled from data stored in the database. If the data is incorrect then the report is incorrect!. There have been numerous studies[4,5,6] on the damaging consequences of having poor quality data in the corporate information system, with typical error rates for the data being cited between 0.5% and 30% [5]. Where an organisation also has a data warehouse which is then data mined, poor quality data can have an impact on the organisations decision making capabilities based on the data warehouse, particularly when the data coming from production databases for the data warehouse needs to be cleaned up before any analysis can take place [7].

The Light's Out Integrity Sub-system (LOIS) is designed as a complementary integrity checking system for mission-critical systems. We are proposing an alternative way of checking complex business rules against a database, which using traditional integrity checking mechanisms would prove too expensive to be of practical use in high performance data management environments. Simpler constraints could still be applied using the database management system's integrity subsystem, for example a range check that an employee's age must be between 18 and 65 could be applied using the SQL check constraint available in the major database vendors.

2 LOIS Architecture

The architecture of LOIS (shown in Figure 2) comprises two main components:

- the System Utilisation Monitor (SUM): this component waits for periods of low system activity, and initiates or terminates constraint checking when such a period begins or ends. The LOIS architecture makes provision for two methods of activating the Constraint Checker; First the User-defined System time-table as shown in Figure 1, second the Dynamic Load Monitor, which samples the operating system load variable and compares the value with a user-defined threshold value.
- the Constraint Checker: when activated by the SUM, this component selects a constraint to check, extracts the query which implements the constraint from the constraint metadata, executes it and records details of any violations found. This process then repeats until the Constraint Selector is closed down by the SUM.

These components are supported by three sets of metadata:

- the Constraint Metadata: this stores details of the current set of constraints that are to be checked against the database, as defined by the following table:

  constraint(ConstraintID, SQLQueryString, Estimate)

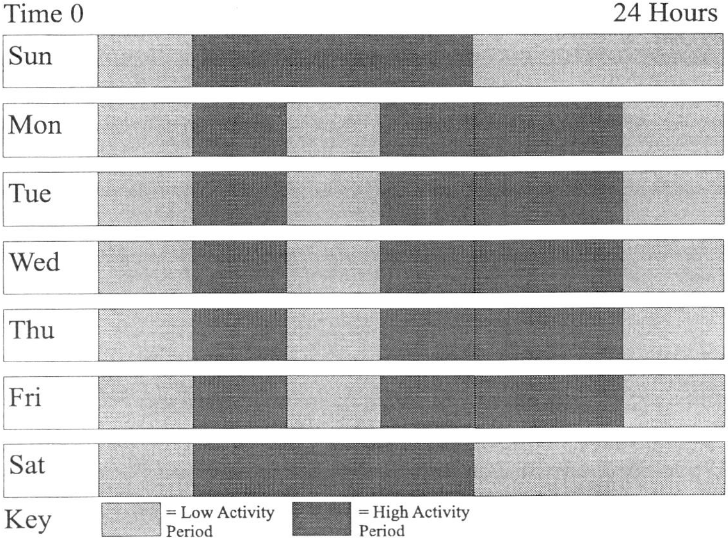

Figure 1. Example Timetable for Controlling LOIS

For each constraint, a unique identifier, an SQL query that can be used to detect violations of the constraint[a], and an estimate of the time required to execute the query are stored. In our current implementation, we have utilised the Oracle database *Explain Plan* functionality to describe the query plan it will use to execute a query in order to facilitate estimating the execution time of a constraint query [8]. This allows LOIS to take account of any optimisations performed by the DBMS within its estimates of query running times.

The constraint metadata may also contain some additional information about the constraints that are required for a particular constraint selection algorithm. Details are given alongside the description of the relevant algorithm in Section 3.

- the Constraint Violation Log: violations detected during the constraint checking process are stored in a constraint violation log table, for subse-

[a]In our current implementation, we require that the SQL constraint queries be defined by hand. However, as can be seen in Fig 2 the LOIS architecture makes provision for a constraint administration tool to assist the database administrator.

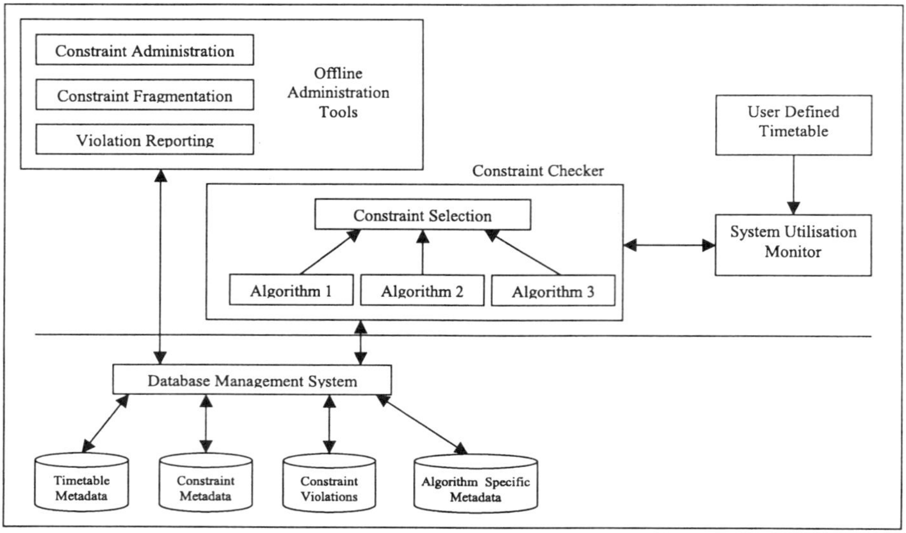

Figure 2. Overview of the LOIS Architecture

quent browsing or analysis by the database administrator. The violation log table has the following structure:

violation(ViolationId, ConstraintId, TableName, TableNameRowId, TimeDetected)

- the Timetable Metadata: the start and end times of the expected periods of low activity are stored within the following table:

  timetable(PeriodId, StartTime, EndTime, TimetableLength)

  A timetable may be of arbitrary length (although, a week or month are typical lengths) and may contain an arbitrary number of low and high periods of activity. The timetable metadata contains one tuple for each period of low activity, with the start and end times of the period stored as relative times (in minutes) from the start of the timetable cycle. The timetable length (also in minutes) is also stored with each period for convenience. At present, we assume that only one timetable is ever present in the system at any one time.

The LOIS architecture is designed such that the underlying relational database management system (RDBMS) can be easily changed. This enables LOIS to work with all the leading commercial database vendors, such as Oracle, Informix or IBM DB2. The only requirements placed on a RDBMS to work with LOIS, is the existence of an API and a query optimizer with the facility to generate query plans. The complete LOIS architecture makes provision for a number of off-line administration tools, which support such tasks as the configuration of LOIS, maintenance of the constraint metadata, maintenance of the system utilisation monitor and browsing of the violation log. These tools add only to the convenience of using LOIS, and will not be further described in this paper. Further description of the LOIS architecture and the constraint selection algorithms presented below, are discussed in a complementary technical report[9].

3 The Constraint Selection Algorithms

The LOIS architecture allows a range of different algorithms for the selection of constraints for checking, achieved by slotting a different algorithm into the Constraint Selector module. This feature has allowed us to compare the behaviours of three different constraint selection algorithms within our simulated legacy database system. Each algorithm makes use of different kinds of user-supplied information about the integrity constraints:

- *Trivial Constraint Selection:* constraints are selected for checking based on the order in which they are stored in the constraint metadata.
- *Prioritised Constraint Selection:* constraints are selected for checking based on a user-supplied partial ordering.
- *Cyclic Constraint Selection:* constraints are selected for checking based on user-supplied information about the maximum amount of time that may elapse between checks for each constraint.

Each algorithm attempts to make the best use of the available time, based on the pre-computed estimates of how long each one takes to check. For example, the Prioritised Constraint Selection algorithm will select a lower priority constraint for checking if there is not enough time in which to check a higher priority one. The basic algorithm used by the LOIS constraint checker is as follows:

load selected constraint metadata into in-memory structures
loop

determine amount of time left in low activity period
select a constraint that can be checked in the remaining time
if no such constraint can be found then
exit
else
evaluate the constraint query
log any violations found
update constraint metadata if appropriate
end if
end loop

This algorithm is invoked every time the constraint checker receives a signal indicating that a period of low activity has begun, and continues to execute until interrupted by a signal that the period has ended[b]. In general, the algorithm can be interrupted at any point, including during evaluation of the constraint checking query. However, certain parts of the algorithm are protected against interruption so that, once a constraint query has been evaluated completely, the updates to the violation log and the constraint metadata are guaranteed to be made in full.

4 Conclusion

Despite developments in integrity checking in commercial database systems, many organisations still face potentially very significant difficulties in achieving data quality necessary to ensure their effective operation and development. LOIS provides an efficent tool which can be used in conjunction with existing integrity checking mechanisms, whilst crucially not compromising the day to day use of the system. The use of data mining and data visualisation software on the violation log, can assist the administrator in identifying the possible source of the poor quality data. Even if the identified sources are external to the organisation, the data quality administrator now has the information necessary to implement a process to clean up the external data before it gets into the database.

[b]The only exception to this behaviour is when there are no more constraints that can be checked in the remaining time — in this case, the checker simply exits, rather than going into what is effectively a busy-wait loop for the remainder of the period.

Acknowledgements

This research is supported by a grant from the EPSRC and TenFold UK Ltd. The original idea for checking integrity constraints during periods of low activity was suggested by Jeff Walker of TenFold, Inc., and further input on the industrial context for data integrity within legacy systems was provided by Steve Clark and Mike Bermeister, of TenFold Solutions Ltd. We are also grateful to Professor Alex Gray and Dr Suzanne Embury for their advice and comments on this work.

References

1. Robert W. Pautke Errol C. Caby and Thomas C. Redman. Strategies for Improving Data Quality. *Data Quality Journal*, 1(1):4–12, 1995.
2. B. Patterson. The need for data quality. In *Proceedings of the 19th international Conference on Very Large Data Bases, Dublin, Ireland*, page 709, October 1993.
3. T.C. Redman. The Impact of Poor Data Quality on the Typical Enterprise. *Communications of the ACM*, 41(2):79–82, February 1998.
4. Chris Firth. Data quality in practice: Experience from the front line. In *Conference on Information Quality*, pages 65–71, October 1996.
5. T.C. Redman. *Data Quality for the Information Age.* Artech House, Inc., 1996.
6. William M. Bulkeley. Databases are Plagued by Reign of Error. *The Wall Street Journal*, (26), May 1992.
7. J.M. Artz. How Good Is That Data In The Warehouse. *Database For Advances in Information Systems*, 28(3):21–31, 1997.
8. Nicholas J. Caine. Generating Estimates for Evaluation of SQL Queries in Oracle. Technical report, Cardiff University, 1999.
9. Nicholas J. Caine and Suzanne M. Embury. LOIS: the "Lights Out" Integrity Sub-system. Technical report, Cardiff University, 2000.

Chapter 14
Posters

EVALUATING EFFECT OF OPTIMIZATION LEVEL ON VALUE PREDICTABILITY [a]

Kiichi Sugitani, Akihiko Hamano, Toshinori Sato and Itsujiro Arita
Department of Artificial Intelligence, Kyushu Institute of Technology
E-mail:{kiichi,akihiko,tsato,arita}@mickey.ai.kyutech.ac.jp

The practice of speculation in resolving data dependences based on value prediction has been studied as a means of extracting more instruction level parallelism. There are many studies on value prediction mechanisms with high predictabilities. However, to the best of our knowledge, the relationship between compiler optimization level and value predictability has not been investigated. In this paper we evaluate value predictability of several binaries which are compiled with different optimization levels. Detailed simulations reveal that value prediction is still effective for highly optimized binaries.

1 Introduction

In order to improve performance, modern microprocessors rely on exploiting instruction level parallelism (ILP). Recently, the practice of speculation in resolving data dependences has been studied as a means of extracting more ILP. An outcome of an instruction is predicted by value predictors [1, 2]. The instruction and its dependent ones can be executed simultaneously, thereby exploiting ILP aggressively. There are many studies on value prediction mechanisms with high predictabilities and on reducing their hardware cost. However, to the best of our knowledge, the relationship between compiler optimization level and value predictability has not been investigated. Someone might expect that sophisticated optimizations obviate value prediction. Therefore, in this paper we evaluate value predictability of several binaries which are compiled with different optimization levels.

2 Evaluation Methodology

We use a functional simulator for evaluating value predictability. We implemented the simulator using the SimpleScalar tool set (ver.2.0) [3]. The SimpleScalar/PISA instruction set architecture (ISA) is based on MIPS ISA. In this paper, we investigate last-value predictor [1] and hybrid predictor [2]. The former represents simple predictors and the latter does complex ones. The configuration of the hybrid predictor is based on [2].

Seven programs from eight SPEC95 CINT benchmarks are used for this study. The input files are modified so that evaluation time is practical. Each program is executed to completion. The binaries evaluated in this study are

[a]This work is supported in part by the grants from Japan Society for the Promotion of Science and from Fukuoka Industry, Science & Technology Foundation.

distributed by University of Michigan. They were compiled by GNU GCC (version 2.7.2.3) and MIRV [4]. For each compiler, three optimization levels, `-O0`, `-O1`, and `-O2`, were performed. In general, MIRV `-O0` executes considerably less instructions than GCC `-O0`, because MIRV has graph coloring allocation and copy propagation in `-O0` while GCC has no register allocation in `-O0` [4]. For the remaining optimization levels, the two compilers have almost equal abilities.

3 Simulation Results

In this section, we present simulation results. We use predictability, prediction coverage, and prediction accuracy as metrics for evaluation. We define the predictability as the number of instructions that are (correctly and incorrectly) predicted by a value predictor over that of all register-writing instructions. The prediction coverage is defined as the number of instructions correctly predicted over that of all register-writing instructions. The prediction accuracy is the percentage of instructions correctly predicted over all predicted instructions.

Figure 1 shows simulation results, when the last-value predictor is utilized to GCC binaries. The horizontal and vertical axes denote the optimization levels and the percentage respectively. Each bar, divided into two parts, indicates the predictability and the prediction coverage. The lower part (black) indicates the percentage of the instruction whose data value is correctly predicted. The upper part (gray) indicates the percentage that is mispredicted. That is, the lower part is the prediction coverage and the sum of the two parts is the predictability. For each group, bars from left to right indicate the results when the value predictor has 1024-, 2048-, 4096-, and 8192-entry tables, respectively. We can find the followings. First, in the case of `129.compress`, both the predictability and the prediction coverage are considerably reduced when the optimization level changes from `-O0` to `-O1`. This might mean that relatively high optimizations obviate the value prediction. Second, different from the previous observation, both the predictability and the prediction coverage are slightly improved as the optimization level becomes higher in the cases of the remaining programs. This denies the first investigation. Third, the efficiency of the value prediction changes little when the optimization level changes. Therefore, we can confirm that the conservative last-value predictor is still effective for highly optimized binaries.

Figure 2 shows simulation results, when the hybrid predictor is utilized to GCC binaries. The characteristics similar to the last-value predictor case is observed. However, two programs should be mentioned. In the case of `129.compress`, the difference in the predictability and the prediction coverage between `-O0` and `-O1` is considerably smaller than the last-value predictor case. In the case of `134.perl`, both the predictability and the prediction coverage

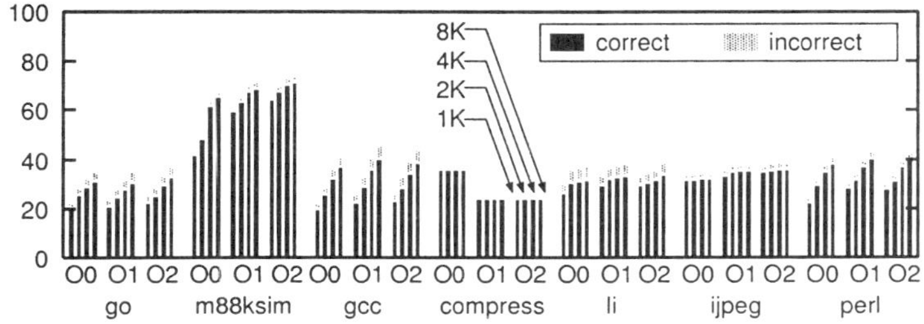

Figure 1: Influence of optimization in GCC on last-value predictors

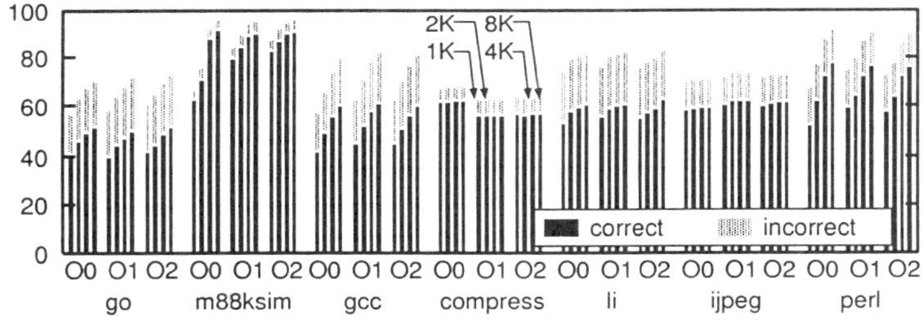

Figure 2: Influence of optimization in GCC on hybrid predictors

are slightly reduced as the optimization level becomes higher. However, these observations does not require the different conclusions from the last-value predictor case. In general, both the predictability and the prediction coverage hardly changes when different optimization levels are considered. And thus, the aggressive hybrid predictor is also effective for highly optimized binaries.

Figure 3 shows simulation results, when the last-value predictor is utilized to MIRV binaries. The different characteristics from GCC binaries can be observed. First, we can find that in general both the predictability and the prediction coverage are greater in the case of MIRV than in the case of GCC. This can be observed throughout programs and optimization levels. Second, it is generally found that both the predictability and the prediction coverage decrease slightly as the optimization level becomes higher. This difference from the GCC case can be found especially in the case of `099.go`. However, the decrease is not as large as that can be found in GCC `129.compress`. Thus, we can conclude that the conservative last-value predictor is still effective for MIRV binaries.

Figure 4 shows simulation results, when the hybrid predictor is utilized to MIRV binaries. The characteristics similar to the last-value predictor case is observed, while `099.go` shows considerably different behavior. Both the predictability and the prediction coverage, which are greater than in the GCC

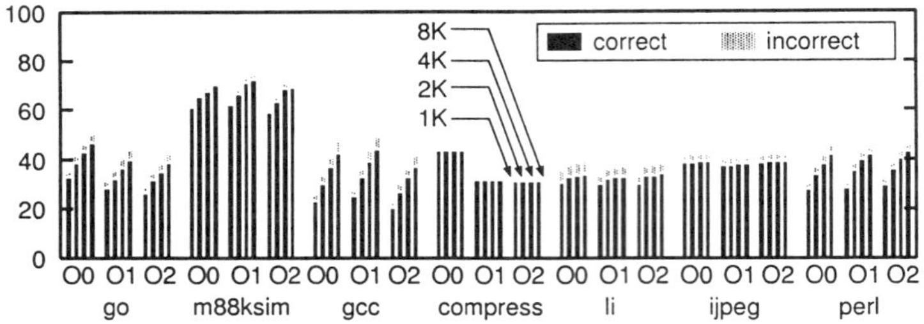

Figure 3: Influence of optimization in MIRV on last-value predictors

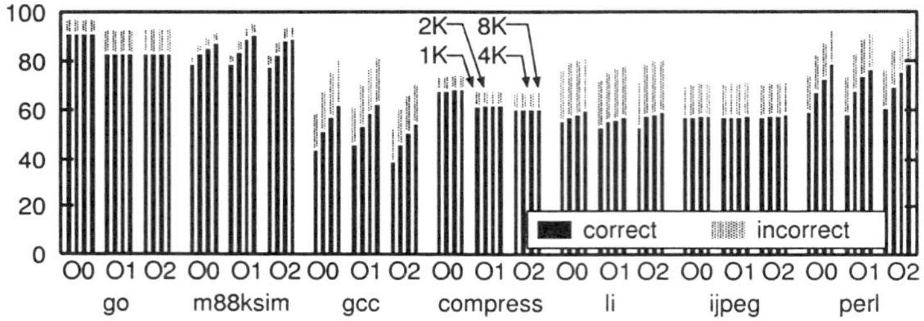

Figure 4: Influence of optimization in MIRV on hybrid predictors

case, are reduced slightly when higher optimization levels are applied. In addition, for `099.go` both the predictability and the prediction coverage are considerably reduced when the optimization level changes from `-O0` to `-O1`. However, we can conclude that the aggressive hybrid predictor is also effective for highly optimized binaries.

4 Conclusion

This paper evaluated value predictability of GCC and MIRV binaries which are compiled with different optimization levels. From detailed simulation results, we have found that both for GCC and MIRV the value prediction is still effective for binaries compiled with every optimization level.

References

1. M.H.Lipasti, J.P.Shen, "Exceeding the dataflow limit via value prediction", *29th Int'l Symp. on Microarchitecture*, 1996.
2. K.Wang, M.Franklin, "Highly accurate data value prediction using hybrid predictors", *30th Int'l Symp. on Microarchitecture*, 1997.
3. D.Burger, T.M.Austin, "The SimpleScalar tool set, version 2.0", *ACM SIGARCH Computer Architecture News*, vol.25, no.3, 1997.
4. M. Postiff, et al., "The MIRV SimpleScalar/PISA compiler", *Technical Report CSE-TR-421-00*, University of Michigan, 2000.

A NEW PARALLEL ALGORITHM OF IMAGE MOSAIC*

XINGHUA AN, XIAOGE WANG, ZHIHUI DU AND SAIHONG SONG
Department of Computer Science and Technology, Tsinghua University, Beijing China
E-mail:anxinghua@263.net, wang@tirc.cs.tsinghua.edu.cn

This paper presents a new fine-grain parallel algorithm for image mosaic. Together with an modified image merging algorithm, which can merge images with irregular boundaries, the application of this algorithm in the remote-sensing images mosaic shows that it has much better visual effect than traditional ones and obtains a good speedup on a cluster of PCs.
Keywords Mosaic, Fine-grain, Cluster

1 Introduction

Remote-sensing images taken at different times and areas are needed to be composed to a large one, called "image mosaic". Some sequential algorithms of image mosaic are discussed in [1, 2]. Because remote-sensing image usually consists of large amount of data, parallel processing becomes necessary. On the cluster of PCs, the communication case overhead is relatively high so the coarse-grain parallel algorithm usually over performs the fine-grain counterpart. But in image mosaic, generally a large portion of the image is not used in the process. Therefore, coarse-grain parallel method may not be a better choice. Another problem is how to minimize the gray level difference of original images to make the final mosaic image smooth and seamless [3].

In this paper, a new algorithm is proposed to address these technical problems.

2 The Description of the New Algorithm

The algorithm is designed in master-slave model. First, the master processor splits the final image by a grid. This grid is use in splitting all original images as well. Each piece of final image consists of one or more, if there is overlapping, pieces of original image. A "task", which is to construct one or more pieces of the final image, is sent to a slave processor to process. During the entire processing, tasks are sent out to the slaves and the results are collected dynamically.

There are two techniques to improve the efficiency of the algorithm:

1. The master processor dispatches the tasks with relatively more layers to run on remote slave processors while leaving the tasks with fewer layers for itself. It also doesn't need to send out a task that contains no overlapped layers. In this way, the cluster can use its resources more efficiently.

*Supported by 9th 5-year-plan. No: 96-B02-04-03

2. Because the processing time of a task can be estimated in advance, a greedy method can be used to reduce the time of master processor waiting for a free slave to dispatch a task by optimizing the task order to meet the needs of approximately the lowest processing time.

The image-merging formula is listed below, in which $\lambda i(0 \le \lambda i \le 1)$ is in proportion to the distance between pixel P and the top, bottom, left or right boundary of its original image. P1,P2 are the gray level of the overlapped pixels of two images to be merged respectively and P is the pixel's gray level of the merged image:

$\lambda = \min\{\lambda 1, \lambda 2, \lambda 3, \lambda 4\}$ $\qquad$ $P = \lambda * P1 + (1-\lambda) * P2$

3 Performance Examples

Table 1 shows an example of merging 10 images(300*300) into one(1000*1000). As another example, 8 TM remote-sensing images(7600*6600) are merged in 120 seconds using 8 processors. The final image, which looks smooth and seamless, is shown in Figure 1.

Table 1. processing time of 10 images(300*300) mosaic
T1 means using technique 1 in the algorithm.
T2 means using technique 1&2 in the algorithm.

Processors	2	4	6	8
T1 (s)	214	98	85	75
T2 (s)	206	92	78	70

Figure 1. 8 TM images mosaic

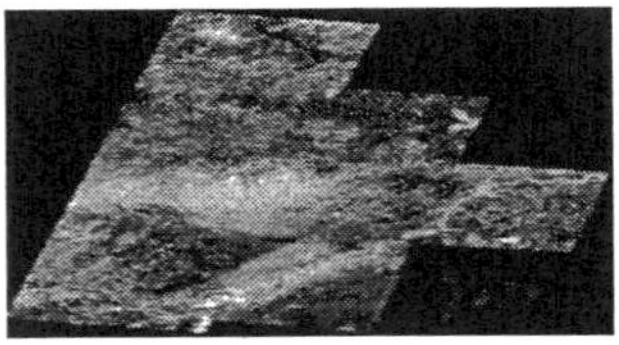

4 Conclusions and Future Work

This algorithm obtains a good speedup on a cluster of PCs. Based on fine grain, load-balancing is well-kept and data transmission is greatly reduced. Furthermore, its high efficiency and good visual effect make it more technical and practical.

An alternative grid-based splitting algorithm, which may enormously reduce unnecessary data transmission, is currently under investigation.

Reference

1. Jinwen Tian and Kang Su, Automatic seamless mosaic of aerial image, Journal of Huazhong University of Science and Technology(1998.11) pp. 10-13.
2. Afek Yehuda and Brand Ariel, Mosaicking of orthorectified aerial images, Photogrammetric Engineering and Remote Sensing (1998.2) pp. 115-125
3. Zhongkui Feng and Jianbo Liu, Analysis of geometry precision of TM digital image mosaic and discussion of mosaic method, Environment Remote Sensing. 1996.11(4) pp. 295-301.

FEEDBACK DRIVEN ONLINE SCHEDULING OF PROCESSES WITH IMPRECISE COMPUTATION

YONG WANG AND YAOXUE ZHANG

Department of Computer Science and Technology, Tsinghua University, Beijing100084, People's Republic of China

E-mail: wyong@acm.org, zyx@sun475.cs.tsinghua.edu.cn

In this paper, we propose an online feedback-driven scheme to schedule processes with imprecise computation. The scheme utilizes a PID controller to control the activity of admission control and scheduler. The aim of our scheme is to bind the deadline-missing ratio to a set point under different system workload level, which yields a balanced tradeoff between the precision of computation and CPU utilization.

1 Introduction

Problem of imprecise computation has been proposed by [1] as a model of flexible application, such as the compression and transformation of multimedia stream, heuristic search engine and search algorithm used by large-scale DBMS. It aims to make real-time system both easier to develop and more robust in the face of conditions such as transient overload. The imprecise computation is classified into 3 categories: monotonic, sieve and multiple versions [2]. Only monotonic processes are considered in this paper.

Most early work concentrated on scheduling periodic tasks with imprecise computation on single and multiple processors [3][4][5][6][7]. In general, the goal of these algorithms is to minimize the weighted sum of execution time of the unexecuted portions of all tasks in the system.

For real-time imprecise computation, the system deadline-missing ratio is affected by CPU utilization, which decided by the QoS to be provided. In applications such as multimedia server and database server, most tasks run as sporadic processes so that scheduler can hardly decide the future system workload. Applying feedback control theory such as PID control to process schedule in the area of RTOS is first proposed by J. A. Stankovic in [8]. In this paper, we try to enable the scheduler to predicate the coming system workload by the recent CPU utilization so that a trade-off can be made between the deadline-missing ratio and the QOS of the imprecise computation.

2 Feedback-driven scheduling for imprecise computation

2.1 Process model

We are given a set of independent and monotonic imprecise tasks **T={T₁, T₂, ... , Tₙ}** in which each task $\mathbf{T_i}$ is characterized by:

$$T_i = (r_i, d_i, M_i, O_i) i \in [1, n]$$

Where:

- Ready time $\mathbf{r_i}$ at which $\mathbf{T_i}$ becomes ready for execution. $\mathbf{r_i}$ of independent process is equal to the time when it's released.
- Deadline $\mathbf{d_i}$ by which $\mathbf{T_i}$ must be completed
- Mandatory part of compute time $\mathbf{M_i}$ that must be completed before deadline.
- Maximum optional part $\mathbf{O_i}$.

We define $\mathbf{O'_i/O_i}$ as Optional Ratio ($\mathbf{OR_i}$) where $\mathbf{O'_i(O'_i \square [0, O_i])}$ is executed optional part. We say the result of $\mathbf{T_i}$ is precise if $\mathbf{OR_i}$ equals to 1. The total execute time of $\mathbf{T_i}$ is: $\mathbf{M_i + O'_i}$.

2.2 System model

The whole system consists three main components: PID controller, scheduler and admission control. The system model is shown in figure 1.

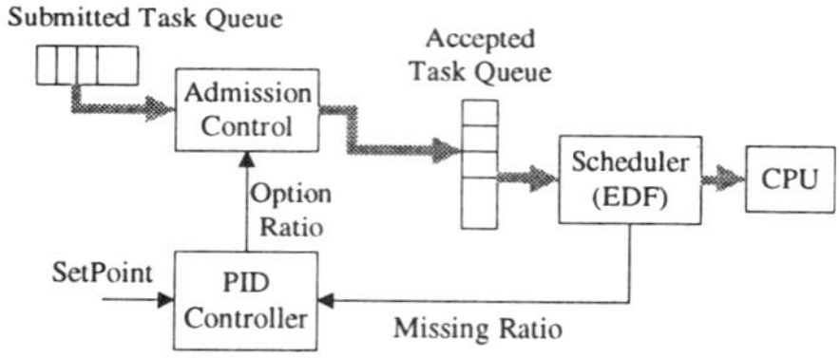

Figure 1. System Model

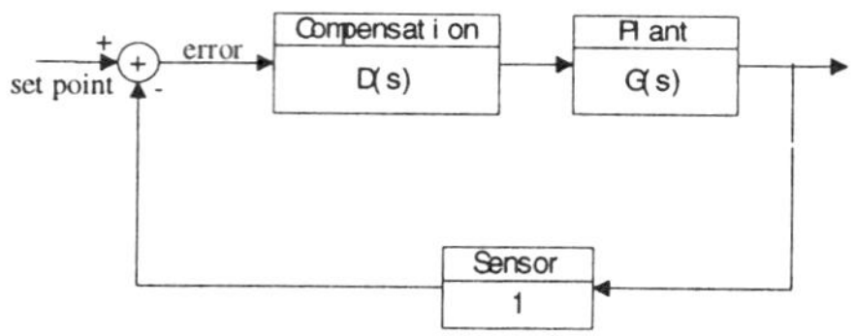

Figure2. Block Diagram of PID Controller

The admission control, which acts as plant of the PID controller, checks every task in Submitted Task Queue to decide if it satisfies the deadline and calculate the execute time: $\mathbf{M_i + O'_i}$ by the output of the PID controller with regard to recent system workload. Tasks passed the admission control are sent to Accepted Task Queue and ready for running.

2.3 PID controller

The PID controller is the core in our scheme. It takes deadline-missing ratio as input and then calculates for each process how long the optional part should be executed. The reason we choose PID is that it's difficult to build a precise model for dynamic system and self-adapting PID controller works well in this situation.

The key to build a stable PID controller with high performance is to choose right parameters. By control theory, the PID controller is represented by these variables:

Controlled variable: the quantity of the output that is measured and controlled. We choose the deadline-missing ratio as controlled variable. System deadline missing ratio is defined as the percentage of tasks that miss their deadline during recent period.

Set point: the expected value of controlled variable. It's the target of the whole control system. Missing ratio of zero maybe perfect for real-time systems, but the CPU utilization has to be sacrificed.

Error: the difference between the controlled variable and the set point.

Manipulated variable: the variable that verified by PID controller to affect the value of controlled variable. Optional ratio is our choice because it decides the system workload.

After identifying these variables, the block diagram of the PID controller is shown in Figure 2. **D(s)** and **G(s)** are transfer functions of the PID controller and the plant, respectively. In regard to control theory, $\mathbf{D(s)} = \mathbf{K_P} + \mathbf{K_I/s} + \mathbf{K_D s}$ and **G(s)** will be provided in next section. The PID controller used in our scheme is a digital variant with the following control formula:

$$c(n) = K_P e(n) + K_I \sum_{j=0}^{n} e(j) + K_D [e(n) - e(n-1)]$$

Where **c(n)** is the output to be used by admission control. **e(n)** is the error by the time of *n*-th sample. $\mathbf{K_P}$, $\mathbf{K_I}$ and $\mathbf{K_D}$ are tunable parameter of the PID controller.

2.4 *Scheduler and admission control*

Acting as the plant controlled by the PID controller, the admission control takes the output of the PID as its input and calculates the percentage of the optional part to be admitted. When a new process $\mathbf{T_i}$ ($\mathbf{r_i}$, $\mathbf{d_i}$, $\mathbf{M_i}$, $\mathbf{O_i}$) comes, what the admission control has to do is listed below:

1. Calculate the value of $\mathbf{O'_i}$ and check if $\mathbf{r_i} + \mathbf{M_i} + \mathbf{O'_i} > \mathbf{d_i}$.
2. If yes, $\mathbf{T_i}$ should be added to Accepted Task Queue and ready to be executed.
3. If no, $\mathbf{T_i}$ should be refused by admission control.
4. Recalculate the deadline-missing ratio and feed it back to PID controller.

The scheduling algorithm we choose is EDF (Earliest Deadline First) because it's a well-known scheduling algorithm for both static and dynamic scheduler. Other online schedule algorithms are also considerable for our scheme.

3 Experiment and result

3.1 *Simulation model*

A uni-processor simulator, which model is shown in figure 4, is developed to study our scheme.

Process Generator generates processes at specified intervals to simulate different system workload. All accepted and refused processes are recorded in Process Queue (PQ) and Missing Queue (MQ) respectively. PQ and MQ are periodically refreshed so that only recent processes are contained. By this model, the simulator can be characterized by: **Sim**($\mathbf{W_m}$, $\mathbf{W_p}$, **SP**, **SetPoint**, $\mathbf{K_P}$, $\mathbf{K_I}$, $\mathbf{K_D}$). $\mathbf{W_m}$ and $\mathbf{W_p}$ are the maximum time for a process to be hold in MQ and PQ. **SP** is the sample period. $\mathbf{K_P}$, $\mathbf{K_I}$ and $\mathbf{K_D}$ are the tunable parameters of the PID controller.

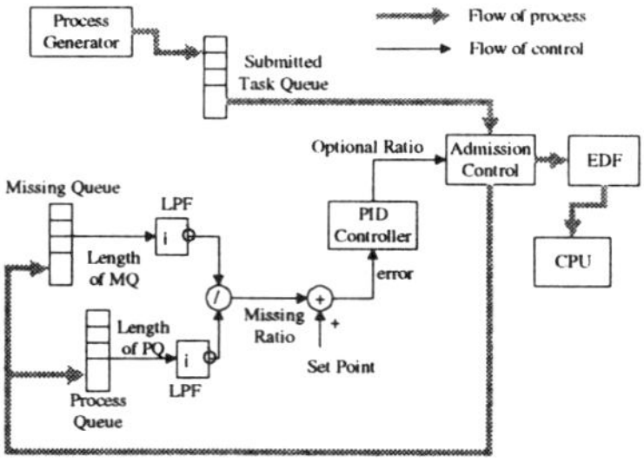

Figure 4. Simulation model

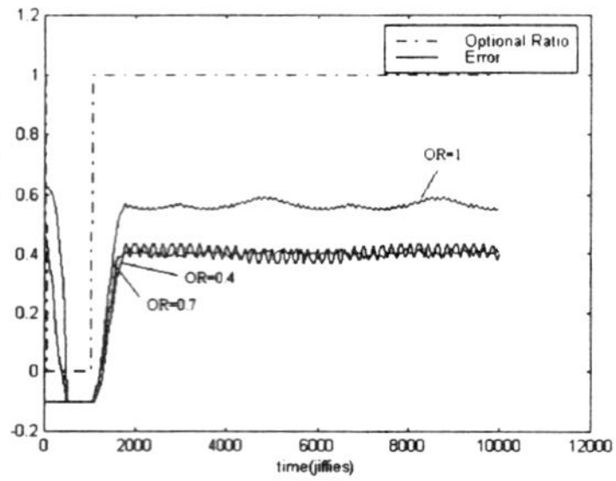

Figure 5. Step response of the plant

After new process is generated, it is sent to the PQ or MQ by the admission control. All processes contained in these two queues would be hold for up to a fixed period. The deadline-missing ratio at time **t** is then calculated by: **MR(t)=Length(MQ(t))/Length(PQ(t))**. Obviously, the PQ and MQ also function as two LPFs (Low Pass Filter) to remove the high-frequency oscillation of **MR(t)**.

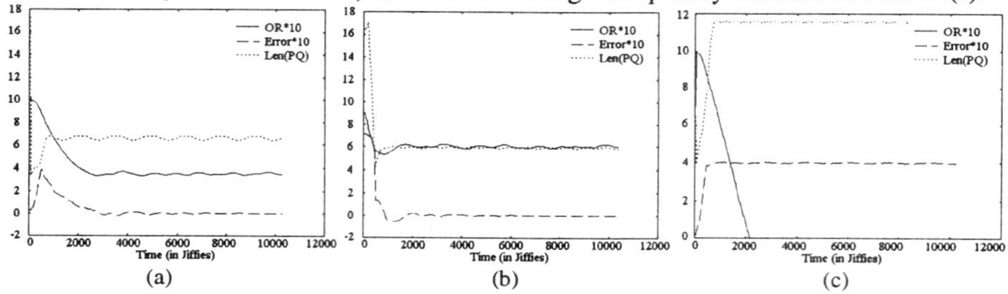

Figure 6. (a) Step response of **Sim**(300, 300, 30, 0.1, 0.04, 0.1) to $\mathbf{T_I}$(0, 10, 40, 20) Processes are generated at interval of 45 jiffies (b) Step response of **Sim**(300, 300, 30, 0.1, 0.04, 0.1) to $\mathbf{T_I}$(0,10,40.20) Processes are generated at interval of 55 jiffies (c) Step response of **Sim**(300, 300, 30, 0.1, 0.04, 0.1) to $\mathbf{T_I}$(0,10,40.5) Processes are generated at interval of 45 jiffies

This simulator is also used to figure out the transfer function of the plant by the way of studying the plant's step response with different Optional Ratio, which is shown in Figure 6(c).

3.2 Result and discussion

Figure 6(a)(b) illustrates the step response of **Sim**(300, 300, 30, 0.1, 0.4, 0.1, 0.1) under different system workload. The values of $\mathbf{K_P}$, $\mathbf{K_I}$ and $\mathbf{K_D}$ have been tuned to satisfy the stability condition. In this figure, the system starts with zero system workload. Then, the system workload and the missing ratio start to increase as well as the Process Generator continuously generates processes. At this time, the PID controller starts to adjust the system workload by the way of adjusting the value of Optional Ratio until the system reaches stabilization.

The performance of the PID controller is also affected by $\mathbf{O_i}$. Figure 6(c) illustrates the step response of **Sim**(300, 300, 30, 0.1, 0.4, 0.1, 0.1) to the system run processes with small $\mathbf{O_i}$ and we find that the system steady state error is about 0.4 while the Optional Ratio has already reached 0. That means the small length of the optional part cannot provide system with enough potentiality of adjusting the system workload.

4 Conclusion

In this paper, we propose a new PID control scheme for online scheduler of processes with imprecise computing. The scheme uses a PID controller to determine the percentage of optional part to be accepted by the admission control. We have implemented a simulator to study the performance of this scheme. The results of the experiments show that the system deadline-missing ratio is bound to the set point in varying system workload.

Reference

1. Jane W. S. Liu, Wei-Kuan Shih, Kwei-Jay Lin, Riccardo Bettati, and Jen-Yao Chung. Imprecise computations. *Proceedings of the IEEE*, **82**(1994).
2. Jane W. S. Liu, Kwei-Jay Lin and Wei-Kuan Shih. Algorithms for scheduling imprecise computations. *IEEE Computer*, **24**(1991) pp. 58-68.
3. Wei-Kuan Shih and Jane W. S. Liu. On-line scheduling of imprecise computations to minimize error. In *Proceedings, Real-Time Systems Symposium* (IEEE, 1992).
4. Jayanta K. Dey, James Kurose, and Don Towsley. On-line scheduling policies for a class of IRIS (increasing reward with increasing service) real-time tasks. *IEEE Transactions on Computers*, **45**(1996) pp. 802-813
5. J. Y. Chung, J. W. S. Liu, and K. J. Lin. Scheduling periodic jobs that allow imprecise results. *IEEE Transactions on Computers*, **39**(1990).
6. Ashok Khemka, K. V. Subrahmanyam, and R. K. Shyamasundar. Multi-processors scheduling for imprecise computations in a hard real-time environment. In *Proceedings of Seventh International Parallel Processing Symposium*, (IEEE, 1993) pp. 374-378.
7. J. Lee, and A. Tiao. A fuzzy rule-based approach to real-time scheduling. *Proceedings of 4th IEEE International Conference on Fuzzy Systems*, (IEEE,1995).
8. J. A. Stankovic, C. Lu, S. H. Son, and G. Tao. The Case for Feedback Control Real-Time Scheduling. *EuroMicro Conference on Real-Time Systems*(1999).

THE OPTIMAL MAXIMAL PREFIX ENCODING SCHEMES

Dongyang Long and Weijia Jia
Department of Computer Science, City University of Hong Kong
83 Tat Chee Avenue, Kowloon, Hong Kong, China
Email: {dylong, wjia} @cs.cityu.edu.hk

Data (information) encryption has three major objectives: (1) Security (or called Confidentiality for data): unauthorized persons cannot read/modify the data. (2) Error detection and correction for the data and (3) Efficiency: in order to save the transmission time and data storage, data should be compressed as much as possible. As the objectives may conflict with each other, existing crypt-algorithms such as DES (Data Encryption Standard) that did not achieve significant success in attaining the three objectives at the same time. It is widely recognized that encoding for error detection and correction is only concerned with block codes. If both efficient encryption and error detection and correction are sought in a particular encrypting algorithm, efficient encryption is usually taken as the primary objective over error detection and correction. In fact, efficiency is even crucial for encryption of information in a telecommunication environment. Additionally, encryption can be used to achieve integrity because data that cannot be read generally also cannot be changed in a meaningful manner. Furthermore, encryption is the basis of some protocols, which are a series steps, involving two or more parties, designed to accomplish a task. Some protocols ensure availability of sources. Thus, encryption is at the heart of methods for ensuring all goals of information security. Currently, encryption used in the protection of programs, database, networks, and electronic commerce are highly desirable.

Our motivation in conducting this research is to design a secure encoding scheme with high efficiency. We propose a novel encoding scheme based on maximal prefix codes. After introduced some basic concepts and notations of prefix codes, we give an algorithm of generating a maximal prefix code efficiently. We discuss relationships between Huffman encoding schemes and maximal prefix schemes and show that all Huffman encoding schemes are maximal prefix encoding schemes and have the shortest average code word length among all maximal prefix encoding schemes. In particular, we show that, for any maximal prefix code C over a finite alphabet Σ, there exists a suitable information source $I = (\Sigma_1, P)$ such that C is a Huffman code for $I = (\Sigma_1, P)$. Where $\Sigma_1 = \{s_1, s_2, \ldots, s_q\}$ is a source alphabet and P is a probability law that assigns to each element $s_i \in \Sigma_1$ a probability $P(s_i)$. Consequently, In some sense, Huffman codes is coincident with the class of maximal prefix codes. *Main results are as follows:*

♦ *Let Σ be a finite alphabet and n be any positive integer. It is shown that there is an algorithm such that generate a prefix code C containing n code words in polynomial time of n (i.e. $O(n^3)$).*

♦ *Let Σ be a finite alphabet and n be any positive integer. Then there is an efficient algorithm of generating a maximal prefix code.*

♦ *All Huffman encoding schemes are maximal prefix (or instantaneous) and have the shortest average code word length among all maximal prefix encoding schemes.*

♦ *If $C \subseteq \Sigma^+$ is a maximal prefix code. Then there must exist a suitable information source $I = (\Sigma_1, P)$ such that C is a Huffman code for $I = (\Sigma_1, P)$.*

We easily follow that $C = \{010, 011, 0^3 10^3, 0^3 1010, 0^3 1^3 0, 0^3 1^2 0^2, 0^3 10^2 1, 0^3 101^2, 0^3 1^4, 0^3 1^2 01, 0^5 10^5, 0^5 1010^3\}$ is a prefix code. We immediately construct a maximal prefix code $M = C \cup (\{0,1\}^{11} - C\{0,1\}^*)$. However, the maximal prefix code M contains $2^{11} - 2\times 2^8 - 8\times 2^3 = 2048 - 512 - 64 = 1472$ code words. According to the above fourth statement, we can easily design and implement a more secure encoding scheme with high efficiency by the maximal prefix code M.

CHARM: A CHECKPOINT-BASED ROLLBACK RECOVERY AND PROCESS MIGRATION SYSTEM FOR CLUSTER OF WORKSTATIONS *

DONGSHENG WANG [A,B], XIAOTIE DENG [B], WEIMIN ZHENG [A]

[A] *Department of Computer Science, Tsinghua University, Beijing 100084, China*
[B] *Department of Computer Science, City University of Hong Kong*
Tat Chee Avenue Kowloon, Hong Kong

In this paper, we present a Checkpoint-based Rollback recovery and process Migration (ChaRM) system for cluster of workstations. ChaRM offers functions for on-line maintenance of software and hardware, fault detection, checkpointing and rollback recovery, process migration and system reconfiguration, etc. By employing novel techniques and algorithms, ChaRM is distinguished from other similar systems in the following features: First, ChaRM realizes upgrade and degradation auto-reconfiguration by quasi-asynchronous process migration and checkpoint mirroring. New node can be added to join a computation on-line, and the computation can survives as long as one node still lives. Second, it can support open systems using write operation buffering. The worst-case overhead of file checkpointing is lower than other known methods. Third, it can recover any fault occurred during checkpointing or rollback recovery.

1 Checkpointing in ChaRM system

Numbers of checkpointing and rollback recovery (CRR) techniques have been proposed in the literature for parallel/distributed systems. Rollback propagation and the associated domino effect have been the primary concerns of those techniques. ChaRM uses a low-overhead coordinated checkpointing protocol, whose in-transit messages are cleaned through comparing message sequence number. No additional control messages are needed between pairs of application processes during synchronization process. Other systems such as MPVM and CoCheck etc. incur a large overhead because of $O(N^2)$ control messages used to flush in-transit messages, where N is the number of application processes.

2 Libcsm-- a Checkpoint Library supporting file checkpointing

Libcsm is a checkpoint library for ChaRM, it is implemented based on Libckpt. The novel feature of Libcsm is that it can supports file I/O operation. Libcsm uses Modification Operation Buffering (MOB) technique to optimize the performance. The main idea of MOB is to make all the modifications between two checkpoints atomic as a whole. That is, either all the modifications are executed (if the process

*Supported by National "863 High-tech Program(863-306-ZD01-02-01)"

runs correctly to the next checkpoint), or all the modifications are aborted (if not). While volatile checkpointing saves volatile state to stable storage, checkpoint of user files is achieved in MOB by buffering all modification operations (including the writing, deleting operation, etc.) after a checkpoint. At the time of the next checkpoint, the buffered operations are flushed from the buffer to the corresponding user files and then the buffer is cleared.

3 Quasi-asynchronous process migration

A novel migration protocol implemented in ChaRM is quasi-asynchronous migration. Non-migration processes (NMP) are allowed to execute during most time of the migration. Message flushing and message delaying techniques are used to guarantee that the migration is correct. In comparison with other migration methods, our method has some advantages. The overhead of NMPs is much lower than synchronous migration: NMPs' overhead in quasi-asynchronous migration is much less than the migration processes because NMPs only do some coordination at the beginning and the end of the migration. However, NMPs' overhead in synchronous migration is almost the same as the migration processes. Quasi-asynchronous migration also has some advantages over asynchronous migration. Although in asynchronous migration there is no explicit participation of NMPs, a message that cannot find its receiver after migration has to be forwarded. As a result, a message sequencing mechanism has to be used in order to guarantee correct delivery of messages. This incurs extra communication overhead for asynchronous migration approach. Therefore, there is no significant difference between quasi-asynchronous and asynchronous migration in the measure of NMPs' overhead. However, it is much easier to implement quasi-asynchronous migration than to implement asynchronous migration.

4 Checkpoint mirroring and system configuration

In ChaRM system, application processes in one node save their checkpoints information and in-transit messages to local disk instead of network file system, this can avoid producing burst network traffic and reduce the checkpointing time. Checkpointing to local disk can recover any number of node transient or intermission faults. ChaRM uses checkpoint mirroring to tolerate one or more node permanent faults. When a node fails, the recovery information of application processes running on the node will be available on the other nodes. Three levels of reconfigurations are realized in ChaRM system. They are reconfiguration in same level, in degradation level and in upgrade level. New node can be added to join a computation on-line, and the computation can survives as long as one node still lives.

The Design and Implementation of a Distributed Knowledge Based System: DKBS-1

HaiYi Zhang
Department of computer Science, Harbin Institute of Technology, HeilongJiang, 150001, China
MingJun Lan
Lanzhou Institute of Physics, Gansu, 730000, China

Abstract

In this paper, we propose a new knowledge model, and based on the model, we present the design and implementation of a distributed knowledge based system, called DKBS-1. The paper describes the logical structure of DKBS-1, and the knowledge representation, storage, and management for DKBS-1. Finally, the paper describes the design and implementation of the inference mechanism for DKBS-1.

Keywords: Distributed Knowledge Base, AI, Expert Systems, Database (DB).

1 Introduction

Advanced technologies for intelligent information processing systems have been developing at high speed, and are applied to all kinds of applications. Currently many of research results are concerned about individual application background. There are different views on the meaning of distribution in DKBS ([4],[7]) and in this paper we believe that the meaning of distribution of DKBS includes not only physical distribution but also logical distribution. It includes physical distribution of components in the system, physical and logical distribution for the knowledge, distribution of functionality and parallel processing of various processing mechanisms.

2. Basic Concepts and Related Knowledge

2.1 The Logical Base and Knowledge Distribution Model

Because the knowledge base is distributed and accessed by multiple users, the consistency of the knowledge base is a key issue in a DKBS [5]. Each knowledge base must guarantee the consistency. However, the consideration of consistency in a DKBS should be done in various layers [2]. So we can see that there are many inconsistencies in real life and it is very hard to build a unified knowledge base. But these inconsistencies reflect the different aspects for human beings to know the real world. So it is necessary for us to initiate these inconsistencies, to preserve them and to deal with them.

Nowadays most systems based on knowledge do not differentiate between knowledge and belief. Such systems cannot deal with inconsistencies caused by knowledge relativity. To solve the problem, we need to modify the knowledge model of the system. Here, the logical foundation of DKBS is no longer the first order logic. So we propose a distributed knowledge model (DKM).

2.2 Logical Structure Design of the DKBS–1

DKBS–1 is an experimental distributed knowledge based system and was first applied to agriculture. The system adopts a star structure. The logical structure of the central node is showed in Figure 1

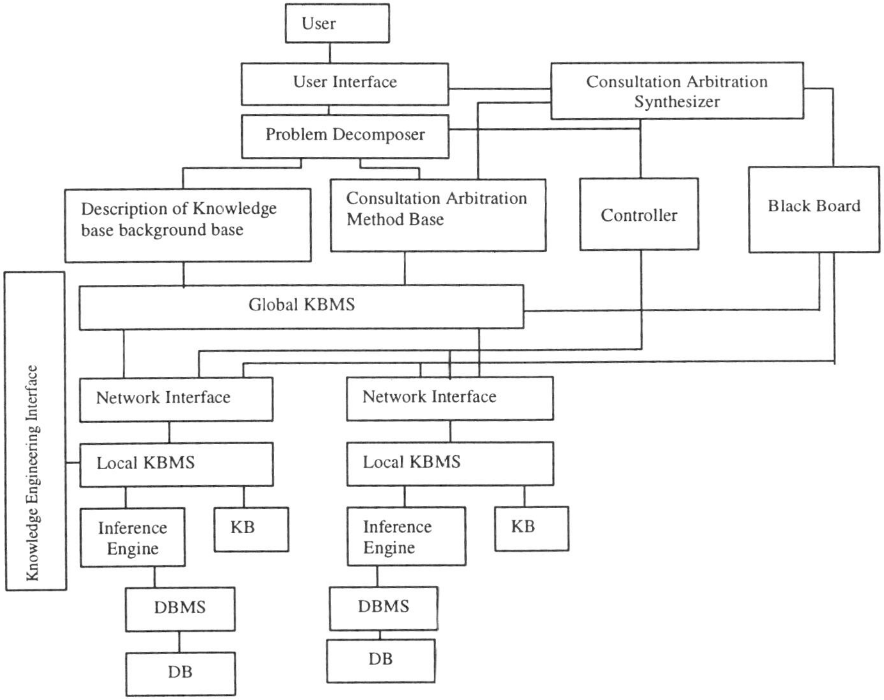

Figure 1 Logical structure of the central node

In this structure, the user interface presents the task assigned by a user to a problem decomposer for processing. The problem decomposer decomposes the task according to the task content and knowledge source description base, and fills in the problem description area in the blackboard. After decomposing completely, the problem decomposer returns the mark to the controller. The controller individually starts local KBMS and network interface following the description of each sub-task in the blackboard problem area [3], and then allocates the sub-task to corresponding local KBMS, which maybe on the current node or a remote node. After completing the sub-task, each knowledge base fills in the conclusion to individual conclusion area in the blackboard.

The controller starts a consultation arbitration synthesizer according to the global KBMS and returns a completion mark of the network interface. According to the contents of individual conclusion area, the consultation arbitration synthesizer forms a conclusion and explanation and fills them into the blackboard conclusion area, or forms a consult scheme according to individual conclusion of inconsistency (using the consultation arbitration method base), and resubmits the scheme to the controller. Again the controller starts the global KBMS and the cycle restarts. Every related KB will deal with the conclusion following the consultation scheme and submits the consultation conclusion to the controller. Once again the controller starts the consultation arbitration synthesizer to deal with the consultation conclusion, forms the final conclusion and explanation or submits all inconsistent conclusions to the user.

3 Knowledge Representation, Storage and Management in DKBS–1

In order to process distributed knowledge efficiently, the system is required not only to have a powerful ability to deduce results and to solve problems but also is required reasonably to represent, to organize, to access, to search and to maintain large scale knowledge ([1],[8]).

3.1 Knowledge Representation and Access

We have the following considerations:1 Each knowledge base may be different, 2. Support for the commonly used knowledge representations, 3.The conversion for knowledge representations. We used relational databases to access the knowledge base.

3.2 The Knowledge Base

The knowledge base has the following components: a commonly used database, the knowledge sources background description base, domain knowledge base, consultation method base, fact base, function base. All these bases above are stored using Microsoft SQL server or Access databases, managed by DBMS and accessed through ODBC access interfaces [6].

4 Knowledge Base Maintaining Tools

The knowledge base maintaining tools include a knowledge editor. The knowledge editor enters acquired knowledge with visual methods. It has a function of syntax checking. The editor points out the location and type of error and helps the user to correct the error. Also the knowledge editor has the function of consistency checking for the knowledge base. After the editor checks the syntax, it performs consistency checking. After the knowledge base is created, we need to make a knowledge base precision. Making the knowledge base precision is to complete precision and to complete all targets for the knowledge base. The purpose is to enhance the quality of the system. The result of making the knowledge base precision is submitted to an evaluating system (or experts). The evaluation result is used to guide further precision.

The DKBS–1 supports two knowledge base management tools that are based on production rule knowledge representation: interactive knowledge base management tool and editing knowledge base management tool. Each tool is implemented by independent EXE components, and are integrated in the DKBS–1 environment and shared by users. Their functions include Support friendly user interfaces, allow user to operate the knowledge base. Support automatic checking mechanisms for the rule base, Define a knowledge base description script language and allow users to maintain knowledge, Describe all rules for users entering.

5 Inference Mechanisms in DKBS-1

REASON is the inference engine in DKBS–1. REASON is designed as an independent inference engine. Because a KB is implemented by using the relational database, the design of REASON includes two aspects: One is a design for the DB interface, the other is a design for the interface mechanism.

5.1 Compiling for Rules and searching the Database

The inference engine REASON relies on the sub-problem that the system appoints. After the problem proposed by an end user is decomposed, the system determines the rules related to inference according to the main hypothesis inference goal for sub-problems. The rule compiler selects those rules from the rule base, loads them into the memory and creates an AND/OR net. The AND/OR net describes a structure of the problem space that is given according to logic connection between rules in the rule base. Finally, the rules are submitted to inference to complete the solution of the problem.

The searching of the database is based on the AND/OR Net. In DKBS–1, the knowledge base and the bottom layer of the database are connected. According to every rule's front component of the rule set (node set) in AND/OR Net, the system can obtain all data that are possibly related in reasoning by searching and store them into the fact base. By this strategy we can greatly reduce exchanging time from memory to storage.

5.2 Inference mechanism

There are two reasoning cases in the system:

1. Sub-problem solving. The rule set that the inference engine directly uses contains the rules that are expressed with an AND/OR Net. The procedure of reasoning in the AND/OR Net is the procedure of solving identification. The inference engine uses the inference method that is a mixture of forward and backward. The searching for a solution space uses the depth-first strategy.
2. Solving after consulting the consultation is a key features in a DKBS. When solving the same sub-problem many KBs give inconsistent conclusions, therefore the consulting process is needed. After consulting the conclusion for the problem is obtained.

The algorithm for the inference engine is as follow:

1. Starting the inference engine,
2. Reading the inference task from the blackboard,
3. Rule base compiling,
4. Database searching,
5. Reasoning,
6. Consulting, obtaining conclusion,
7. Writing the conclusion on the black board,
8. End.

The inference engine REASON possesses three features: A. Efficient; the inference procedure is a depth-first searching procedure for the AND/OR Net, therefore the inference path is limited; B. Flexible; the inference engine is not only used for whole examining and commenting procedure but also sub-tasks of examining and commenting, C. General utilization; the inference engine unifies processes for calculating rules and judging rules.

The DKBS–1 currently runs in a local network under the Windows NT environment.

6. Summary

The main achievements of this research can be listed below:

1. Presented a new structure of distributed knowledge bases: The system is different from the traditional structure. It provides a distributed knowledge base structure that is composed of rule base, fact base, problem base, argument base, goal base and dictionary base. Among them, problem base, argument base and goal base are useful to check the syntax of rules, morphology and consistency. The dictionary base also allows the system to interpret function of multimedia.

2. Designed the rule base's organization structure and rule's syntax structure: We designed the rule base's two-level structure: storage module and user module.
3. Implemented the checking rule morphology and syntax and the generation of the inference tree. According to the rule syntax structure and the referencing problem base, argument base and goal base, the system checks for rule morphology and syntax. Based on the rule base the system dynamically generates the inference tree.

In addition to the above achievements, we also implemented the capabilities for checking the loops in the rule base, checking the consistency of the rule base, and the checking of redundant rules, conflict rules and appurtenant rules. We are currently experimenting the system to obtain further performance data.

References

1. R. Davis, H. Shrobe, and P. Szolovits, What Is a Knowledge Representation? *AI Magazine*, 1993, Vol.14, No.1:17-33.
2. B. Hayes-Roth, An architecture for adaptive intelligent systems. *Artificial Intelligence*, 72:329-365,1995.
3. H. P. Nii. Blackboard systems. In A. Barr, P.R. Cohen, and E. A. Feigenbaum, editors, *The handbook of Artificial Intelligence*, Volume 4. Chapter 16. Addison-Wesley, 1989.
4. E. Oliveira, and R. Camacho, A Shell for cooperating expert systems. *Expert System*. May 1991, Vol.8, No.2:75-84.
5. J. R. Quinlan, Internal Consistency Implausible Reasoning Systems, *New Generation Computing*, Vol. 3 1985 pp157-180.
6. E. A. Rundensteiner, The Role of AI in Databases versus the Role of Database Theory in AI: An Opinion, *Artificial Intelligence in databases and Information Systems*, Elsevien Science Publisher B. V, North-Holland IFIP, 1990.
7. S. Vadera and S. Nechab, The MD Shell and its use to develop Dust-Expert. *Expert System*. August 1995,Vol.12,No.3:231-237.
8. H. J. Watson and R. I. Mann, Expert System: Past, Present, and Future. *Journal of International System management*. 1998, Vol. 5, No. 4:39-46.

EFFICIENT INTELLIGENT SEARCH SYSTEM FOR WEB INFORMATION MINING (EIS)

SANDING LUO

City University of Hong Kong, Tat Chee Avenue, Kowloon, Hong Kong
R P CHINA
E-mail: sdluo@cs.cityu.edu.hk

This paper presents a novel search mechanism using adjustable multi-priority and dynamical rules to guide abstract target information from the web page.

1 Introduction

Surfing the Internet can be a frustrating experience when searching for a particular piece of information. The Internet is so vast that identifying and locating a specific document is difficult with existing browser software. There is a great deal of studies about search process control on navigation. In this paper we introduce a simple method guiding navigation and information mining. The aim is to focus on an algorithm for searching mechanism and target information mining.

2 The searching strategy

To implement search automatically, we concern some issues that are "Interesting" URLs, Features of target URL, Distinct anchors and Search guide. To find perfect target messages, description of search path and control rule must be established so as to navigate to the information users required. We aim at improving speed and the extent of information mining via accepting or rejecting some links under corrective rules of judgment and advancement.

1. Set group of base URLs initial priority, and then put them into new URL buffer which is a multiple stack. It pops a URL from the highest priority level to the Internet collection module to obtain HTML text from the Internet every time.
2. More URLs and their corresponding anchors are found out. The description of them are clues to achieve "interesting" web page.
3. To guarantee search convergence, we should bring forward any necessary restrictive conditions. The URLs checked must be avoided. The reason is to change the network architecture to tree structure, and disconnect loop.
4. To achieve compendious result, we have to discover interesting target information from each web page, so we must establish a module of target information and define an extraction method for it.

5. To continually obtain information in the search process, in order to improve search efficiency, it is necessary to regulate, modify and modulate the knowledge rules or parameters of rule-base according to the current status.

3 Search path evaluation and control

There are some certain routes and hotspot glossaries when people search for information on the Internet by experience. We need such thought that simulates manual search process, seeks for one or multiple key links, and closes up to web pages with a great deal of information from base URL address. $W = \{w_1, w_2, w_3, \ldots w_n\}$ describe possible keywords of the key link. They may be selected from the concept word base of the system or achieved from the user interface.

In a general situation, we set up a glossary collection of several different judgments. The keyword set W is extended into three parts: $WS=\{Wp, Wm, Wr\}$. The algorithm (rule) of decision for anchors (A) is shown as follow:

if $Wr(A) \cap A \neq$. then P←0 ; for Refused keyword set *Wr;*
else { if $Wp(A) \cap A \neq$. then P←P+1; for Plus keyword set Wp;
else P←P-1; } for Minus keyword set Wm

Because URL buffer is based on priority, and it is a first-in-last-out (FILO) stack, so, when a new search address is popped out, we adopt the depth priority search way insides same priority, which helps to find the target quickly.

But, static $WS=\{Wp, Wm, Wr\}$ sometimes can not converge very well. We change static WS to series set WS_1, WS_2, … , WS_M as dynamic WS based on current state of search change WS_k to WS_{k+1} by dynamic regulate rules.

4 Instance and Experiments

We use logical model, descriptive model, and a demonstrative model to describe target information. Using the search and decision mechanism to search some special information, e.g. web-published Email addresses of all staff in a certain university.

The initial priority can be set to 2. The maximum priority is often set to 3. For *Wp*, we considered anchor and link at same time. For *Wr* we used non-domain name. For dynamic *WS*, we added ~(userID) to *Wr* when some user's mail address is found. For target information module, we used pattern *@*.*[.*][.*]. The experiment contrast shows that it is more efficient than other existing method and is very simple for implement on web server. The initial priority can provide enough search space, and the maximum priority can avoid too many useless pages to be retrieved. The Email report mined is satisfactory results under almost all cases.

A POLYNOMIAL ALGORITHM FOR CYCLIC EDGE CONNECTIVITY OF CUBIC GRAPHS

DINGJUN LOU LIHUA TENG XIANGJUN WU

Department of Computer Science, Zhongshan University, Guangzhou 510275, P R China

1 Introduction

For a connected graph G, a **cyclic edge cutset,** C-e-c for short, is an edge cutset whose deletion disconnects the graph, such that two of the components created each must contain at least one cycle. The **cyclic edge connectivity** $c\lambda(G)$ is the minimum cardinality of all the C-e-c's of G. If no C-e-c exists, we set $c\lambda(G)=0$. The concept of cyclic edge connectivity was introduced by Tait[7] and studied, in particular, for planar graphs by Plummer[6].

In a paper of Peroche[5], several sorts of connectivity, including cyclic edge connectivity, and their relations are studied. In the references [1], [2] and [4], the relation of cyclic edge connectivity and n-extendability of graphs is studied.

How to compute cyclic edge connectivity of an arbitrary graph has not been studied by any literatures as far as we know. Even for cubic graphs, the distribution of C-e-c's in them is not known up to recent. If there are polynomial such cutsets in a cubic graph, is it possible to find them out in polynomial time is a problem that follows. This paper presents a recursive algorithm to find out all the C-e-c's of an input cubic graph, the time complexity is bounded by $O(n^3\log_2 n)$. This concludes positive answers to the last two questions.

2 A Rough Description of the Recursive Algorithm

Let G be a 3-connected graph and e be an edge of G. We consider the following operation of removing e from G, denoted by $G\Theta e$:

(1)Delete e from G to get G-e;

(2)If some endvertices of e have degree two in G-e, then suppress them;

(3)If multipul edges occur after (2), then replace them by single edges to make the graph simple.

What is the relation between the minimum C-e-c's of $G\Theta e$ and those of G. We discuss this in three cases, which are illustrated below. Let S be a C-e-c of G, e=xy be the removed edge in the algorihtm, and S' be a C-e-c of $G\Theta e$.

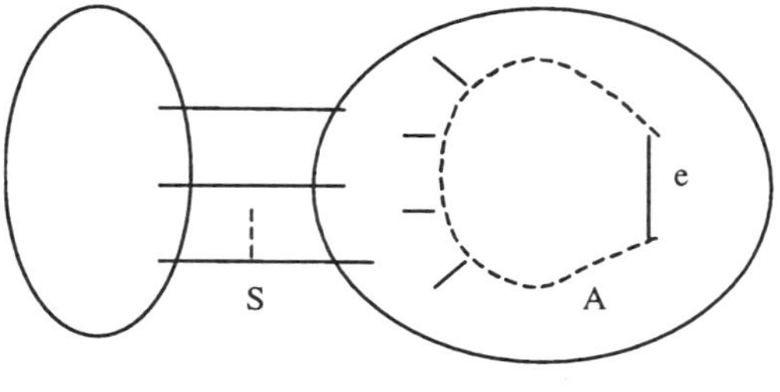

Case 1: e is contained in the only cycle of component A, S cannot be found in $G\Theta e$.

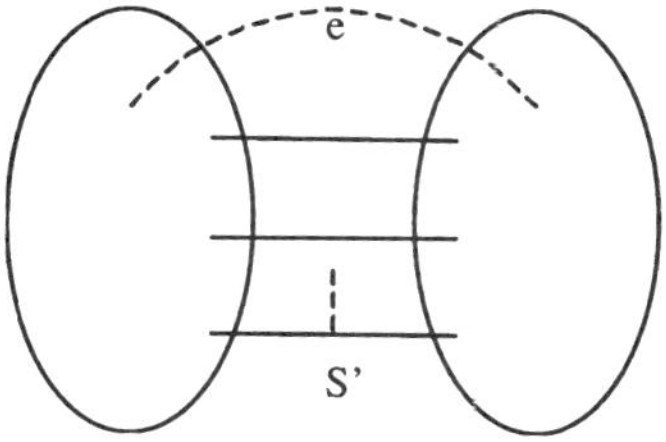

Case 2: the cyclic edge connectivity of G may be larger than that of GΘe by 1

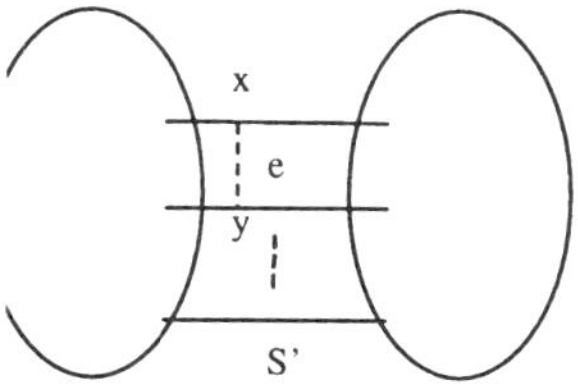

Case 3: S' in GΘe is divided into two C-e-c's in G.

3 The Flowchat of the Algorithm

Cyclic_connectivity(G):
0) if G=K_4 then return null;
1) if κ(G)=1 or κ(G)=2 then
2) if G has a C-e-c then
3) return C-e-c's through finding out all the minimum vertex cutsets
4) else return null
5) choose an edge e=xy of G; let G':=GΘe;
6) S:=Cyclic_connectivity(G') {recursively call the algorithm}
7) Compare each C-e-c in S with that of G, this includes three cases discussed above, and then return those minimun C-e-c's of G. End of the algorithm.

References

1. Holton D. A., Lou D. J. and Plummer M. D., On the 2-extendability of Planar Graphs, Discrete Math., North-Holland, **96**(1991), 81-99.
2. Holton D. A. and Plummer M. D., Matching Extension and Connectivity in graphs □, Proc. Sixth International Conference on the Theory and Applications of Graphs (Kalamazoo, 1988), John Wiley & Sons, New York, 1988, 651-665.
3. Hopcroft J. E. and Tarjan R. E., Dividing a graph into triconnected components, SIAM J. Computing 2:3 (1973).
4. Lou D. J. and Holton D. A., Lower Bound of Cyclic Edge Connectivity for n-extendability of Regular Graphs, Discrete Math., North-Holland, **112**(1993),139-150.
5. Peroche B., On Several Sorts of Connectivity, Discrete Math., North-Holland, **46**(1983) 267-277.
6. Plummer M. D., On the cyclic connectivity of planar graphs, in: Y. Alavi, D. R. Lick and A. T. White, eds., Graph Theory and Applications (Springer-Verlag, Berlin, 1972) 235-242.
7. Tait P. G., Remarks on the colouring of maps, Proc. Roy. Soc. Edingburg **10** (1880) 501-503.

THE PARALLEL GENETIC ALGORITHM EMBEDDED WITH DOWNHILL

MENG DING, ZHIHUI DU, SANLI LI, QUNSHENG MA
Dept of Computer Sci&Tech, Tsinghua Univ, 100084 Beijing, China
Contact Author: Zhihui Du,Meng Ding
Phone: 86-10-62783820 Fax:86-10-62771138
duzh@bitfoot.com,dingmeng@263.net

This paper introduces and analyzes the algorithm of Parallel Genetic Algorithm (PGA) embedded with Downhill which is applied to the optimization of continuous functions with the support to MPI environment. Selection of genetic factors is discussed and comparison with traditional GA is made to illustrate the effectiveness of the algorithm.

1 Introduction

Genetic Algorithm (GA) is a part of evolutionary computing. GAs are inherently parallel optimization procedures utilizing a "survival of the fittest" approach. A basic GA employs selection, crossover and mutation operators. Generally speaking, GA is a global optimization algorithm but Downhill is a local optimization algorithm. In this paper, the fast convergence of Downhill and the ability to find global optima of GA are combined in one new algorithm.We also introduce the parallel genetic algorithm[1]. Parallel search greatly overcomes the problems in population diversity. Furthermore, with best local minimas broadcasted to every node at certain frequency, convergence time is remarkably reduced.

2 Algorithm Description and Parameter Discussion

A closer study of the algorithm is made as follows:

1. Encoding. The chromosome should always contain information about solution which it represents.Here we use binary encoding.

2. Selection and Elitism. We tried both the Roulette wheel selection and the rank selection. When creating new population by crossover and mutation, we are very likely to lose the best chromosome. This brings us down to Elitism. The method first copies the best chromosome or a few best chromosomes,the rest part is done in traditional way. Elitism can rapidly increase the performance of the GA.

3. Downhill. Two different downhill methods (Depth first and Breadth first) are implemented. Depth first downhill first steps down the hill following one decreasing direction , then repeats the process in another direction, step by step

until it can not go down any more. Breadth first downhill goes down one step towards one direction each time, then repeats the process in all directions.

4. Communication.We use the coarse grained model.Subpopulations are mapped onto different processors. The PGA allows the independent evolution of the subpopulation for a certain time.Migration takes place at fixed generation.Only the best individuals migrate and they are the start solution of the next loop.

3 Performance Evaluation

The algorithm has been implemented on a cluster system with 8 computing nodes. Each node is SMP architecture that contains dual Pentium III 500Mhz CPU. The nodes are interconnected by 100Mbps Ethernet.The Operating System is Linux and the parallel supporting system is mpich-1.1.1. Evaluation of probabilistic search algorithms is not a easy task.First, Typical functions are tested many times using the PGA and the global optima of all the functions are found.PGA converges within less time than simple GA and SA*[2].Then, the PGA is used for a large scale QCBED(Quantitative analysis of Convergence Beam Electron Diffraction) problem with 9 optimization parameters. At first, Downhill is not included and the parallel GA achieves higher performance than simple GA and SA. When downhill is taken into account, the convergence speed improves 5-10 times. For example, it will take the serial method 20 hours to find a satisfactory approximate solution for the 9-dimentional QCBED problem, while the Parallel Genetic Algorithm embedded with Downhill needs only about 2 hours.

Algorithm	Platform	OptimizingTime(hours)	Optimizing Result
Serial	SGIWork-station	40	0.09
SPMD SA+Downhill	THNPSC-1	0.25	0.05
		3	0.025
SPMD GA+Downhill	THNPSC-1	0.10	0.05
		2.5	0.03

Table 1 Comparison of Different Algorithms for QCBED Problems, SA:Simulated Annealing

4 Reference

1. H.Muhlenbein , M.Schomisch , J.Born : *The parallel genetic algorithm as a function optimizer* , Parallel Computing 17 (1991) 619-632.
2. Zhihui Du, Sanli Li, *Massively Parallel Simulated Annealing Embedded with Downhil* ,IEEE Computer Society. Dec2-3,1999:297:302, Melbourne, Austria.

Appendix A1. Program Committee

Conference Co-Chairs

Horace Ip, City U of Hong Kong, China
Andrzej Goscinski, Deakin U, Australia

Program Committee Co-Chairs

Weijia Jia, City U of Hong Kong, China
Wanlei Zhou, Deakin U, Australia

Committee Members

D Abramson, Monash U, Australia
A Ananda, National U. of Singapore, Singapore
M Baker, Portsmouth U, UK
A Barak, Hebrew U of Jerusalem, Israel
F Berman, U of California, San Diego, USA
A Bode, Technical U of Munich, Germany
R Brent, Oxford U, UK
M Bubak, U of Mining & Metallurgy, Poland
R Buyya, Monash U, Australia
J Cao, HK Polytechnic U, Hong Kong, China
S Chanson, HK U of Sci & Tech, Hong Kong, China
J Chen, Texas A&M U, USA
X Chen, U of Tsukuba, Japan
T Y Cheung, City U of Hong Kong, China
F Y L Chin, U of Hong Kong, China
T Cortes, U of Politecnica de Catalunya, Spain
X Deng, City U of Hong Kong, China
B J d'Auriol, U of Texas at El Paso, USA
J Dongarra, U of Tennessee, USA
D Z Du, U of Minnesota, USA
W Gao, Institute Comput Tech, USA
A Geist, Oak Ridge National Labs, USA
A Goscinski, Deakin U, Australia
S Hariri, Syracuse U, USA
L Hertzberger, U of Amsterdam, The Netherlands
M Hobbs, Hewlett-Packard Labs, USA
S J Horng, National Taiwan U of Sci & Tech, Taiwan
D Frank Hsu, Fordham U, USA
A Hurson, Pennsylvania State U, USA
K Hwang, U of Southern California, USA
W Jia, City U of Hong Kong, China
X Jia, City U of Hong Kong, China
P Kacsuk, MTA SZTAKI Research Inst, Hungary
J Kaiser, U of Ulm, Germany

K Kavi, U of Alabama, Huntsville, USA
Z Kedem, New York U, USA
T Kikuno, Osaka U, Japan
C T King, National Tsing Hua U, Taiwan
C Kitowski, U of Mining and Metallurgy, Poland
T L Kunii, HOSEI U, Japan
D Laforenza, CNUCE Institute of the Italian National Research Council, Italy
C H Lee, City U of Hong Kong, China
K Li, SUNY at New Paltz, USA
J Liu, U of Illinois at Urbana-Champaign, USA
Z Liu, National Natural Sci Foundation, China
T Ludwig, Technische U, Germany
C McDonald, U of Western Aust, Australia
E Nett, Otto-von-Guericke U, Germany
Y Pan, U of Dayton, USA
M Paprzycki, U of Southern Mississippi, USA
C K Poon, City U of Hong Kong, China
K Qiu, Acadia U, Canada
R Raje, Purdue U, USA
M Raynal, IRISA, France
E H M Sha, U of Notre Dame, USA
H Sandhu, York U, Canada
H Shen, Griffith U, Australia
B Shirazi, U of Texas at Arlington, USA
J Silcock, Deakin U, Australia
M Singhal, Ohio State U, USA
S Srinivas, Dalhousie U, Canada
T Sterling, California Inst of Tech, USA
C Sun, Griffith U, Australia
B Szymanski, Rensselear Polytechnic Inst, USA
P Tang, U of Southern Queensland, Australia
Y M Teo, National U of Singapore, Singapore
J Walpole, OGI of Sci & Tech USA
P Wan, Illinois Institute of Technology, USA
J Wu, Florida Atlantic U, USA
J Xue, U of New South Wales, Australia
C Yuen, National U of Singapore, Singapore
A Zomaya, U of Western Australia, Australia
W Zhao, Texas A&M U, USA
S Zheng, U of Texas Dallas, USA
W Zheng, Tsinghua U, China
W Zhou, Deakin U, Australia

Publicity Coordinators:

Xiaohua Jia, City U of Hong Kong, China
Jiannong Cao, Hong Kong Polytechnic U, China

Treasurer:

Qing Li, City U of Hong Kong, China

Local Arrangements Coordinators:

Binhai Zhu, City U of Hong Kong, China
C K Poon, City U of Hong Kong, China
Rynson Lau, City U of Hong Kong, China
M. Campbell, Deakin U, Australia
C. Chen, Deakin U, Australia
M. Lan, Deakin U, Australia

Appendix A2. Organisers and Major Sponsors

Organised by:

City University of Hong Kong, Hong Kong
Deakin University, Australia

Sponsored by:

City University of Hong Kong, Hong Kong
Deakin University, Australia
The Croucher Foundation

In cooperation with:

IEEE (Hong Kong Section) Computer Chapter

Appendix A3. List of Technical Reviewers

David Abramson, Monash U., Australia
A.L. Ananda, National U. of Singapore, Singapore
Mark Baker, Portsmouth U, UK
Amnon Barak, Hebrew U of Jerusalem, Israel
Francine Berman, U of California, San Diego, USA
R.F. Browne, Massey U., New Zealand
Marian Bubak, U of Mining & Metallurgy, Poland
Rajkumar Buyya, Monash U, Australia
Jiannong Cao, HK Polytechnic U, Hong Kong, China
Henri Casanova, U of California, San Diego, USA
Samuel Chanson, HK U of Sci & Tech, Hong Kong, China
Changgui Chen, Deakin U., Australia
Jianer Chen, Texas A&M U, USA
Xing Chen, U of Tsukuba, Japan
To-yat Cheung, City U of Hong Kong, China
Francis Chin, U of Hong Kong, China
Morshed Chowdhury, Deakin U., Australia
Tay- Seng Chuan, National U. of Singapore, Singapore
Toni Cortes, U of Politecnica de Catalunya, Spain
Ovidiu Daescu, U of Texas Dallas, USA
A.H. Davis, Griffith U, Australia
Brian J. d'Auriol, U of Texas at El Paso, USA
Xiaotie Deng, City U of Hong Kong, China
D.Z. Du, U of Minnesota, USA
A Geist, Oak Ridge National Labs, USA
Andrzej Goscinski, Deakin U., Australia
Ananth Grama, Purdue U., USA
Salim Hariri, Syracuse U, USA
Diana Hecht, U of Alabama, Huntsville, USA
L. Hertzberger, U of Amsterdam, The Netherlands
Jose Ignacio Hidalgo, CNUCE Inst. of the Italian National Research Council, Italy
Michael Hobbs, Hewlett-Packard Labs, USA
Shi-Jinn Horng, National Taiwan U of Sci & Tech, Taiwan
A.R. Hurson, Pennsylvania State U, USA
Kenji Ishida, HiroshimaU, Japan
Xiaohua Jia, City U of Hong Kong, China
Weijia Jia, City U of Hong Kong, China
Emil Jovanov, U of Alabama, Huntsville, USA
Peter Kacsuk, MTA SZTAKI Research Inst, Hungary
Joerg Kaiser, U of Ulm, Germany
Yoshiaki Kakuda, HiroshimaU, Japan

Krishna Kavi, U of Alabama, Huntsville, USA
Zvi Kedem, New York U, USA
Tohru Kikuno, Osaka U, Japan
Chung-Ta King, National Tsing Hua U, Taiwan
Hiroyuki Kitajima, Tohoku U., Japan
Jacek Kitowski, U of Mining and Metallurgy, Poland
Derrick Kondo, U of California, San Diego, USA
Domenico Laforenza, CNUCE Inst. of the Italian National Research Council, Italy
Keqin Li, SUNY at New Paltz, USA
J. Lim, Pennsylvania State U, USA
Markus Lindermeier, Technical U of Munich, Germany
Zhiyong Liu, National Natural Sci Foundation, China
Thomas Ludwig, Technische U, Germany
Kzia Meirman, Hebrew U of Jerusalem, Israel
Snehasis Mukhopadhyay, Purdue U, USA
Yi Pan, U of Dayton, USA
Marcin Paprzycki, U of Southern Mississippi, USA
Chung Keung Poon, City U of Hong Kong, China
Xiao Qin, Griffith U, Australia
Guenther Rackl, Technical U of Munich, Germany
Kentaro Sano, Tohoku U., Japan
M. Schulz, Technical U of Munich, Germany
Edwin Sha, U of Texas Dallas, USA
Behrooz Shirazi, U of Texas at Arlington, USA
Greg Shunk, U of Alabama, Huntsville, USA
Jackie Silcock, Deakin U, Australia
Mukesh Singhal, Ohio State U, USA
Michelle Strout, U of California, San Diego, USA
Boleslaw Szymanski, Rensselear Polytechnic Inst, USA
Peiyi Tang, U of Southern Queensland, Australia
Kai-Ming Ting, Deakin U, Australia
Jonathan Walpole, OGI of Sci & Tech USA
J. Weidendoerfer, Technical U of Munich, Germany
John Weir, U of Alabama, Huntsville, USA
Earl Wells, U of Alabama, Huntsville, USA
Jie Wu, Florida Atlantic U, USA
Jingling Xue, U of New South Wales, Australia
C.K. Yuen, National U. of Singapore, Singapore
S.Q. Zheng, U of Texas Dallas, USA
Weimin Zheng, Tsinghua U, China
Wanlei Zhou, Deakin U, Australia
Albert Zomaya, U of Western Australia, Australia

Appendix A4. Author Index